WEBSTE
UNIVERSAL
ENGLISH
THESAURUS

WEBSTER'S UNIVERSAL ENGLISH THESAURUS

**GEDDES&
GROSSET**

Contents

Thesaurus   7

Appendices

   Appendix I: Abbreviations   417

   Appendix II: Phrases and Quotations from Latin, Greek and Modern

      Foreign Languages   436

   Appendix III: Words Listed by Suffix   453

   Appendix IV: Classified Word-lists   468

abandon v. abdicate, back-pedal, cede, chuck, desert, desist, discontinue, ditch, drop, evacuate, forgo, forsake, give up, jilt, leave, leave behind, leave in the lurch, quit, relinquish, renounce, repudiate, resign, scrap, sink, surrender, vacate, waive, withdraw from, yield.
antonyms continue, persist, support.
n. dash, recklessness, unrestraint, wantonness, wildness.
antonym restraint.

abandoned adj. cast aside, cast away, cast out, corrupt, debauched, depraved, derelict, deserted, desolate, discarded, dissipated, dissolute, dropped, forlorn, forsaken, jilted, left, neglected, outcast, profligate, rejected, relinquished, reprobate, scorned, sinful, unoccupied, vacant, wanton, wicked.
antonyms cherished, restrained.

abase v. belittle, cast down, debase, degrade, demean, discredit, disgrace, dishonor, downgrade, humble, humiliate, lower, malign, mortify, reduce, vitiate.
antonyms elevate, honor.

abashed adj. affronted, ashamed, astounded, bewildered, chagrined, confounded, confused, cowed, discomfited, discomposed, disconcerted, discountenanced, discouraged, dismayed, dum(b)founded, embarrassed, floored, humbled, humiliated, mortified, nonplused, perturbed, shamefaced, taken aback.
antonyms at ease, audacious, composed.

abate v. alleviate, appease, attenuate, bate, decline, decrease, deduct, diminish, discount, dull, dwindle, ease, ebb, fade, fall off, lessen, let up, mitigate, moderate, mollify, pacify, quell, rebate, reduce, relieve, remit, sink, slacken, slake, slow, subside, subtract, taper off, wane, weaken.
antonyms increase, strengthen.

abbreviate v. abridge, abstract, clip, compress, condense, contract, curtail, cut, digest, epitomize, lessen, précis, reduce, shorten, shrink, summarize, trim, truncate.
antonyms amplify, extend.

abbreviation n. abridgment, abstract, abstraction, clipping, compendium, compression, condensation, conspectus, contraction, curtailment, digest, epitome, précis, reduction, résumé, shortening, summarization, summary, summation, synopsis, trimming, truncation.
antonyms expansion, extension.

abdicate v. abandon, abjure, abnegate, cede, demit, forgo, give up, quit, relinquish, renounce, repudiate, resign, retire, surrender, vacate, yield.

abduct v. abduce, appropriate, carry off, kidnap, lay hold of, make off with, rape, run away with, run off with, seduce, seize, snatch, spirit away.

abduction n. appropriation, enlevement, kidnap, rape, seduction, seizure, theft.

aberrant adj. abnormal, anomalous, atypical, corrupt, corrupted, defective, degenerate, depraved, deviant, different, divergent, eccentric, egregious, erroneous, incongruous, irregular, odd, peculiar, perverse, perverted, queer, quirky, rambling, roving, straying, untypical, wandering, wrong.
antonyms normal, straight.

aberration n. aberrancy, abnormality, anomaly, defect, delusion, deviation, divergence, eccentricity, freak, hallucination, illusion, irregularity, lapse, nonconformity, oddity, peculiarity, quirk, rambling, rogue, straying, vagary, wandering.
antonym conformity.

abet v. aid, assist, back, condone, connive, egg on, encourage, goad, help, incite, promote, prompt, sanction, second, spur, succor, support, sustain, uphold, urge.
antonym discourage.

abeyance n. adjournment, deferral, discontinuation, inactivity, intermission, lull, postponement, recess, remission, reservation, suspension, waiting.
antonyms activity, continuation.

abhor v. abominate, despise, detest, execrate, hate, loathe, recoil from, shrink from, shudder at, spurn.
antonyms adore, love.

abhorrent adj. abominable, absonant, despiteful, detestable, disgusting, distasteful, execrable, hated, hateful, heinous, horrible, horrid, loathsome, nauseating, obnoxious, odious, offensive, repellent, repugnant, repulsive, revolting.
antonym attractive.

abide v. accept, bear, brook, continue, endure, last, outlive, persist, put up with, remain, stand, stay, stomach, submit to, suffer, survive, tarry, tolerate.
antonyms dispute, quit.

ability n. adeptness, adroitness, aptitude, capability, capacity, competence, competency, deftness, dexterity, endowment, energy, expertise, expertness, facility, faculty, flair, forte, genius, gift, knack, know-how, long suit, nous, potentiality, power, proficiency, qualification, savoir-faire, savvy, skill, strength, talent, touch.
antonyms inability, incompetence.

abject adj. base, contemptible, cringing, debased, degenerate, degraded, deplorable, despicable, dishonorable, execrable, fawning, forlorn, groveling, hopeless, humiliating, ignoble, ignominious, low, mean, miserable, outcast, pathetic, pitiable, servile, slavish, sordid, submissive, vile, worthless, wretched.
antonym exalted.

able *adj.* accomplished, adept, adequate, adroit, capable, clever, competent, deft, dexterous, effective, efficient, experienced, expert, fit, fitted, gifted, ingenious, masterful, masterly, powerful, practiced, proficient, qualified, skilful, skilled, strong, talented.
antonyms incapable, incompetent.

able-bodied *adj.* firm, fit, hale, hardy, healthy, hearty, lusty, powerful, robust, sound, stalwart, staunch, stout, strapping, strong, sturdy, tough, vigorous.
antonyms delicate, infirm.

abnegation *n.* abandonment, abjuration, abstinence, acquiescence, continence, disallowance, eschewal, forbearance, giving up, refusal, rejection, relinquishment, renunciation, sacrifice, self-denial, submission, surrender, temperance.
antonyms acceptance, support.

abnormal *adj.* aberrant, anomalous, atypical, curious, deviant, different, divergent, eccentric, erratic, exceptional, extraordinary, irregular, monstrous, odd, paranormal, peculiar, queer, singular, strange, uncanny, uncommon, unexpected, unnatural, untypical, unusual, wayward, weird.
antonyms normal, straight.

abode *n.* domicile, dwelling, dwelling-place, habitat, habitation, home, house, lodging, pad, place, quarters, residence.

abolish *v.* abrogate, annihilate, annul, blot out, cancel, destroy, do away with, eliminate, end, eradicate, expunge, exterminate, extinguish, extirpate, get rid of, invalidate, kibosh, nullify, obliterate, overthrow, overturn, put an end to, put the kibosh on, quash, repeal, repudiate, rescind, revoke, sink, stamp out, subvert, suppress, terminate, vitiate, void, wipe out.
antonyms continue, retain.

abolition *n.* abolishment, abrogation, annihilation, annulment, cancellation, destruction, dissolution, elimination, end, ending, eradication, expunction, extermination, extinction, extirpation, invalidation, nullification, obliteration, overthrow, overturning, quashing, repeal, repudiation, rescission, revocation, subversion, suppression, termination, vitiation, voiding, withdrawal.
antonyms continuance, retention.

abominable *adj.* abhorrent, accursed, appalling, atrocious, base, beastly, contemptible, despicable, detestable, disgusting, execrable, foul, hateful, heinous, hellish, horrible, horrid, loathsome, nauseating, nauseous, nefast, obnoxious, odious, repellent, reprehensible, repugnant, repulsive, revolting, terrible, vile, villainous, wretched.
antonyms delightful, desirable.

abomination *n.* abhorrence, anathema, animosity, animus, antipathy, aversion, bête noire, bugbear, curse, detestation, disgrace, disgust, distaste, evil, execration, hate, hatred, horror, hostility, loathing, odium, offence, plague, repugnance, revulsion, torment. *antonyms* adoration, delight.

abort *v.* arrest, call off, check, end, fail, frustrate, halt, miscarry, nullify, stop, terminate, thwart.
antonym continue.

abortion *n.* aborticide, disappointment, failure, feticide, fiasco, freak, frustration, misadventure, misbirth, miscarriage, monster, monstrosity, termination, thwarting.
antonyms continuation, success.

abortive *adj.* barren, bootless, failed, failing, fruitless, futile, idle, ineffective, ineffectual, misborn, miscarried, sterile, unavailing, unproductive, unsuccessful, useless, vain.
antonym successful.

abound *v.* be plentiful, brim over, crowd, exuberate, flourish, increase, infest, luxuriate, overflow, proliferate, run riot, superabound, swarm, swell, teem, thrive.
antonym be in short supply.

about *prep.* adjacent to, all over, anent, around, as regards, beside, busy with, circa, close to, concerned with, concerning, connected with, encircling, encompassing, engaged on, in respect to, in the matter of, near, nearby, on, over, re, referring to, regarding, relating to, relative to, respecting, round, surrounding, through, throughout, touching, with reference to, with regard to, with respect to.
adv. active, almost, approaching, approximately, around, astir, close to, from place to place, here and there, hither and thither, in motion, in the region of, more or less, nearing, nearly, present, roughly, stirring, to and fro.

about-turn *n.* about-face, apostasy, backtrack, enantiodromia, reversal, right-about (face), switch, turnabout, turn(a-)round, U-turn, volte-face.

above *prep.* atop, before, beyond, exceeding, higher than, in excess of, on top of, over, prior to, superior to, surpassing, upon.
antonyms below, under.
adv. aloft, atop, earlier, heavenwards, in heaven, on high, overhead, supra.
antonym below.
adj. above-mentioned, above-stated, aforementioned, aforesaid, earlier, foregoing, preceding, previous, prior.

above-board *adj.* candid, fair, fair and square, forthright, frank, guileless, honest, honorable, legitimate, on the level, open, overt, reputable, square, straight, straightforward, true, trustworthy, truthful, upright, veracious.
antonyms shady, underhand.

abrasion *n.* abrading, chafe, chafing, erosion, friction, grating, graze, grinding, levigation, rubbing, scouring, scrape, scraping, scratch, scratching, scuff, scuffing, trituration, wearing away, wearing down.

abrasive *adj.* abradant, annoying, attritional, biting, caustic, chafing, erodent, erosive, frictional, galling, grating, hurtful, irritating, nasty, rough, scraping, scratching, scratchy, scuffing, sharp, unpleasant.
antonyms pleasant, smooth.

abreast *adj.* acquainted, au courant, au fait, conversant,

familiar, in the picture, in touch, informed, knowledgeable, on the ball, up to date.
antonyms out of touch, unaware.

abridge *v.* abbreviate, abstract, circumscribe, clip, compress, concentrate, condense, contract, curtail, cut, cut down, decrease, digest, diminish, dock, epitomize, lessen, lop, précis, prune, reduce, shorten, summarize, synopsize, trim, truncate.
antonyms amplify, pad.

abridgment *n.* abbreviation, abrégé, abstract, compendium, compression, concentration, condensation, conspectus, contraction, curtailment, cutting, decrease, digest, diminishing, diminution, epitome, lessening, limitation, outline, précis, pruning, reduction, restriction, résumé, shortening, summary, synopsis, truncation.
antonyms expansion, padding.

abroad *adv.* about, at large, away, circulating, current, elsewhere, extensively, far, far and wide, forth, in circulation, in foreign parts, out, out of the country, out-of-doors, outside, overseas, publicly, widely.

abrupt *adj.* blunt, brief, brisk, broken, brusque, curt, direct, disconnected, discontinuous, discourteous, gruff, hasty, headlong, hurried, impolite, irregular, jerky, precipitate, precipitous, prerupt, quick, rapid, rough, rude, sharp, sheer, short, snappy, steep, sudden, surprising, swift, terse, unannounced, unceremonious, uncivil, uneven, unexpected, unforeseen, ungracious.
antonyms ceremonious, expansive, leisurely.

abscond *v.* absquatulate, beat it, bolt, clear out, decamp, disappear, do a bunk, escape, flee, flit, fly, hightail it, make off, quit, run off, scram, skedaddle, skip, take French leave, vamoose.

absence *n.* absenteeism, absent-mindedness, abstraction, dearth, default, defect, deficiency, distraction, inattention, lack, need, non-appearance, non-attendance, non-existence, omission, paucity, preoccupation, privation, reverie, scarcity, truancy, unavailability, vacancy, vacuity, want.
antonyms existence, presence.

absent *adj.* absent-minded, absorbed, abstracted, away, bemused, blank, day-dreaming, distracted, distrait(e), dreamy, elsewhere, empty, faraway, gone, heedless, inattentive, lacking, missing, musing, non-existent, not present, oblivious, out, preoccupied, truant, unavailable, unaware, unconscious, unheeding, unthinking, vacant, vague, wanting, withdrawn, wool-gathering.
antonyms aware, present.

absent-minded *adj.* absent, absorbed, abstracted, bemused, distracted, distrait(e), dreaming, dreamy, engrossed, faraway, forgetful, heedless, impractical, inattentive, musing, oblivious, otherwordly, pensive, preoccupied, scatterbrained, unaware, unconscious, unheeding, unthinking, withdrawn, wool-gathering.
antonyms matter-of-fact, attentive, practical.

absolute *adj.* absolutist, actual, almighty, arbitrary, autarchical, autocratic, autonomous, categorical, certain, complete, conclusive, consummate, decided, decisive, definite, definitive, despotic, dictatorial, downright, entire, exact, exhaustive, final, flawless, free, full, genuine, independent, indubitable, infallible, omnipotent, out-and-out, outright, peremptory, perfect, positive, precise, pure, sheer, sovereign, supreme, sure, terminative, thorough, total, totalitarian, tyrannical, unadulterated, unalloyed, unambiguous, unbounded, unconditional, uncontrolled, undivided, unequivocal, unlimited, unmitigated, unmixed, unqualified, unquestionable, unrestrained, unrestricted, utter.
antonyms conditional, partial.

absolutely *adv.* actually, arbitrarily, autocratically, autonomously, bang, categorically, certainly, completely, conclusively, consummately, dead, decidedly, decisively, definitely, despotically, diametrically, dictatorially, entirely, exactly, exhaustively, finally, fully, genuinely, indubitably, infallibly, peremptorily, perfectly, positively, precisely, purely, sovereignly, supremely, surely, thoroughly, totally, truly, tyrannically, unambiguously, unconditionally, unequivocally, unmitigatedly, unquestionably, unrestrainedly, utterly, wholly.

absolution *n.* acquittal, acquittance, amnesty, compurgation, deliverance, discharge, dispensation, emancipation, exculpation, exemption, exoneration, forgiveness, forgiving, freeing, indulgence, liberation, mercy, pardon, purgation, redemption, release, remission, shriving, vindication.
antonym condemnation.

absolve *v.* acquit, clear, deliver, discharge, emancipate, exculpate, excuse, exempt, exonerate, forgive, free, justify, let off, liberate, loose, pardon, ransom, redeem, release, remit, set free, shrive, vindicate.
antonym charge.

absorb *v.* apprehend, assimilate, captivate, consume, coopt, devour, digest, drink in, engage, engross, engulf, enthral(l), enwrap, exhaust, fascinate, fill (up), fix, grip, hold, imbibe, immerse, incorporate, ingest, involve, monopolize, occupy, osmose, preoccupy, receive, retain, rivet, soak up, sorb, submerge, suck up, take in, understand, utilize.
antonyms dissipate, exude.

absorbing *adj.* amusing, arresting, captivating, compulsive, diverting, engrossing, entertaining, enthralling, fascinating, gripping, interesting, intriguing, preoccupying, riveting, spellbinding, unputdownable.
antonyms boring, off-putting.

abstain *v.* avoid, cease, decline, deny, desist, eschew, forbear, forgo, give up, keep from, refrain, refuse, reject, renounce, resist, shun, stop, swear off, withhold.
antonym indulge.

abstemious *adj.* abstinent, ascetic, austere, continent, disciplined, frugal, moderate, restrained, self-denying, self-disciplined, sober, sparing, temperate.
antonyms gluttonous, intemperate, luxurious.

abstinence *n.* abstemiousness, abstinency, asceticism, avoidance, continence, forbearance, frugality, moderation, nephalism, non-indulgence, refraining, self-denial, self-discipline, self-restraint, soberness, sobriety, teetotalism, temperance.
antonym self-indulgence.

abstract *adj.* abstruse, academic, arcane, complex, conceptual, deep, discrete, general, generalized, hypothetical, indefinite, intellectual, metaphysical, non-concrete, occult, philosophical, profound, recondite, separate, subtle, theoretic, theoretical, unpractical, unrealistic.
antonym concrete.
n. abbreviation, abridgment, abstractive, compendium, compression, condensation, conspectus, digest, epitome, essence, outline, précis, recapitulation, résumé, summary, synopsis.
v. abbreviate, abridge, compress, condense, detach, digest, dissociate, epitomize, extract, isolate, outline, précis, purloin, remove, separate, shorten, steal, summarize, withdraw.
antonyms expand, insert.

abstraction *n.* absence, absent-mindedness, absorption, bemusedness, concept, conception, dissociation, distraction, dream, dreaminess, formula, generalization, generality, hypothesis, idea, inattention, notion, pensiveness, preoccupation, remoteness, separation, theorem, theory, thought, withdrawal, wool-gathering.

abstruse *adj.* abstract, arcane, complex, cryptic, dark, deep, devious, difficult, enigmatic, esoteric, hermetic, hidden, incomprehensible, mysterious, mystical, obscure, occult, perplexing, profound, puzzling, recondite, subtle, tortuous, unfathomable, unobvious, vague.
antonyms concrete, obvious.

absurd *adj.* anomalous, comical, crazy, daft, derisory, fantastic, farcical, foolish, funny, humorous, idiotic, illogical, implausible, incongruous, irrational, laughable, ludicrous, meaningless, nonsensical, paradoxical, preposterous, ridiculous, risible, senseless, silly, stupid, unreasonable, untenable.
antonyms logical, rational, sensible.

absurdity *n.* comicality, craziness, daftness, farce, farcicality, farcicalness, fatuity, fatuousness, folly, foolery, foolishness, idiocy, illogicality, illogicalness, incongruity, irrationality, joke, ludicrousness, meaninglessness, nonsense, nonsensicality, preposterousness, ridiculousness, senselessness, silliness, stupidity, unreasonableness.

abundance *n.* affluence, ampleness, amplitude, bonanza, bounty, copiousness, exuberance, fortune, fullness, glut, heap, lavishness, luxuriance, luxuriancy, milk and honey, munificence, oodles, opulence, plenitude, plenteousness, plenty, pleroma, plethora, prodigality, profusion, riches, richness, scads, uberty, wealth.
antonyms dearth, scarcity.

abundant *adj.* ample, bounteous, bountiful, copious, exuberant, filled, full, generous, in plenty, lavish, luxuriant, overflowing, plenteous, plentiful, prodigal, profuse, rank, rich, superabundant, teeming, uberous, unstinted, well-provided, well-supplied.
antonyms scarce, sparse.

abuse *v.* batter, calumniate, castigate, curse, damage, deceive, defame, denigrate, disparage, exploit, harm, hurt, ill-treat, impose on, injure, insult, inveigh against, libel, malign, maltreat, manhandle, mar, misapply, miscall, misemploy, misuse, molest, objurgate, oppress, oppugn, revile, scold, slander, slate, smear, spoil, swear at, take advantage of, traduce, upbraid, vilify, violate, vituperate, wrong.
antonyms cherish, compliment, praise.
n. affront, blame, calumniation, calumny, castigation, censure, contumely, curses, cursing, damage, defamation, denigration, derision, diatribe, disparagement, execration, exploitation, flyting, harm, hurt, ill-treatment, imposition, injury, insults, invective, libel, malediction, maltreatment, manhandling, misapplication, misconduct, misdeed, misuse, obloquy, offence, oppression, opprobrium, reproach, revilement, scolding, sin, slander, spoiling, swearing, tirade, traducement, upbraiding, vilification, violation, vitriol, vituperation, wrong, wrong-doing.
antonyms attention, care.

abusive *adj.* brutal, calumniating, calumnious, castigating, censorious, contumelious, cruel, defamatory, denigrating, derisive, derogatory, destructive, disparaging, harmful, hurtful, injurious, insulting, invective, libelous, maligning, objurgatory, offensive, opprobrious, pejorative, reproachful, reviling, rough, rude, scathing, scolding, slanderous, traducing, upbraiding, vilifying, vituperative.
antonym complimentary.

abysmal *adj.* abyssal, bottomless, boundless, complete, deep, endless, extreme, immeasurable, incalculable, infinite, profound, thorough, unending, unfathomable, vast, yawning.

academic *adj.* abstract, bookish, collegiate, conjectural, donnish, educational, erudite, highbrow, hypothetical, impractical, instructional, learned, lettered, literary, notional, pedagogical, scholarly, scholastic, speculative, studious, theoretical, well-read.
n. academe, academician, don, fellow, lecturer, man of letters, master, pedant, professor, pundit, savant, scholar, scholastic, schoolman, student, tutor.

accede *v.* accept, acquiesce, admit, agree, assent, assume, attain, capitulate, comply, concede, concur, consent, defer, endorse, grant, inherit, submit, succeed (to), yield.
antonyms demur, object.

accelerate *v.* advance, antedate, dispatch, expedite, facilitate, festinate, forward, further, hasten, hurry, pick up speed, precipitate, promote, quicken, speed, speed up, spur, step on the gas, step on the juice, step up, stimulate.
antonyms delay, slow down.

accent *n.* accentuation, arsis, articulation, beat, cadence,

emphasis, enunciation, force, ictus, inflection, intensity, intonation, modulation, pitch, pronunciation, pulsation, pulse, rhythm, stress, thesis, timbre, tonality, tone.
v. accentuate, emphasize, stress, underline, underscore.

accept *v.* abide by, accede, acknowledge, acquiesce, acquire, admit, adopt, affirm, agree to, approve, assume, avow, bear, believe, bow to, brook, concur with, consent to, co-operate with, defer to, gain, get, have, jump at, obtain, put up with, receive, recognize, secure, stand, stomach, submit to, suffer, swallow, take, take on, tolerate, undertake, wear, yield to.
antonyms demur, reject.

acceptable *adj.* adequate, admissible, agreeable, all right, conventional, correct, delightful, desirable, done, grateful, gratifying, moderate, passable, pleasant, pleasing, satisfactory, standard, suitable, tolerable, unexceptionable, unobjectionable, welcome.
antonyms unsatisfactory, unwelcome.

access *n.* adit, admission, admittance, approach, avenue, course, door, entering, entrance, entrée, entry, gateway, increase, ingress, key, onset, passage, passageway, path, road, upsurge, upsurgence.
antonyms egress, outlet.

accessible *adj.* achievable, affable, approachable, at hand, attainable, available, come-at-able, conversable, cordial, exposed, friendly, get-at-able, handy, informal, liable, near, nearby, obtainable, on hand, open, possible, procurable, reachable, ready, sociable, subject, susceptible, vulnerable, wide-open.
antonym inaccessible.

accessory *n.* abettor, accompaniment, accomplice, addition, adjunct, adjuvant, adornment, aid, appendage, assistant, associate, attachment, colleague, component, confederate, conniver, convenience, decoration, embellishment, extension, extra, frill, help, helper, particeps criminis, partner, supplement, trim, trimming.
adj. abetting, additional, adjuvant, adventitious, aiding, ancillary, assisting, auxiliary, contributory, extra, incidental, secondary, subordinate, subsidiary, supplemental, supplementary.

accident *n.* blow, calamity, casualty, chance, collision, contingency, contretemps, crash, disaster, fate, fluke, fortuity, fortune, happenstance, hazard, luck, misadventure, miscarriage, mischance, misfortune, mishap, pile-up, prang, serendipity, shunt.

accidental *adj.* adventitious, adventive, casual, chance, contingent, fluky, fortuitous, haphazard, inadvertent, incidental, random, serendipitous, unanticipated, uncalculated, uncertain, unexpected, unforeseen, unintended, unintentional, unlooked-for, unplanned, unpremeditated, unwitting.
antonyms intentional, premeditated.

acclaim *v.* announce, applaud, approve, celebrate, cheer, clap, commend, crown, declare, eulogize, exalt, extol, hail, honor, laud, praise, salute, welcome.
antonym demean.

n. acclamation, applause, approbation, approval, celebration, cheering, clapping, commendation, eulogizing, eulogy, exaltation, honor, laudation, ovation, plaudits, praise, welcome.
antonyms brickbats, criticism, vituperation.

accommodate *v.* acclimatize, accustom, adapt, adjust, afford, aid, assist, attune, billet, board, cater for, comply, compose, conform, domicile, entertain, fit, furnish, harbor, harmonize, help, house, lodge, modify, oblige, provide, put up, quarter, reconcile, serve, settle, shelter, supply.

accommodating *adj.* complaisant, considerate, co-operative, friendly, helpful, hospitable, indulgent, kind, obliging, polite, sympathetic, unselfish, willing.
antonym disobliging.

accommodation[1] *n.* adaptation, adjustment, assistance, compliance, composition, compromise, conformity, fitting, harmonization, harmony, help, modification, reconciliation, settlement.

accommodation[2] *n.* bed and breakfast, billet, board, digs, domicile, dwelling, harboring, house, housing, lodgings, quartering, quarters, residence, shelter, sheltering.

accompany *v.* attend, belong to, chaperon, co-exist, coincide, complement, conduct, consort, convoy, escort, follow, go with, occur with, squire, supplement, usher.

accomplice *n.* abettor, accessory, ally, assistant, associate, coadjutor, collaborator, colleague, confederate, conspirator, helper, helpmate, henchman, mate, particeps criminis, participator, partner, practisant.

accomplish *v.* achieve, attain, bring about, bring off, carry out, compass, complete, conclude, consummate, discharge, do, effect, effectuate, engineer, execute, finish, fulfil, manage, obtain, perform, produce, realize.

accomplished *adj.* adept, adroit, consummate, cultivated, expert, facile, gifted, masterly, polished, practiced, professional, proficient, skilful, skilled, talented.
antonym inexpert.

accomplishment *n.* ability, achievement, act, aptitude, art, attainment, capability, carrying out, completion, conclusion, consummation, coup, deed, discharge, doing, effecting, execution, exploit, faculty, feat, finishing, forte, fruition, fulfilment, futurition, gift, management, perfection, performance, production, proficiency, realization, skill, stroke, talent, triumph.

accord *v.* agree, allow, assent, bestow, concede, concur, confer, conform, correspond, endow, fit, give, grant, harmonize, jibe, match, present, render, suit, tally, tender, vouchsafe.
antonym disagree.
n. accordance, agreement, assent, concert, concurrence, conformity, congruence, congruity, consort, correspondence, harmony, rapport, symmetry, sympathy, unanimity, unity.
antonym discord.

accordingly *adv.* appropriately, as a result, as requested, consequently, correspondingly, ergo, fitly, hence, in accord with, in accordance, in consequence, properly, so, suitably, therefore, thus.

according to after, after the manner of, agreeably to, commensurate with, consistent with, in accordance with, in compliance with, in conformity with, in keeping with, in line with, in obedience to, in proportion, in relation, in the light of, in the manner of, obedient to.

account[1] *n.* advantage, basis, benefit, cause, chronicle, communiqué, concern, consequence, consideration, description, detail, distinction, esteem, estimation, explanation, ground, grounds, history, honor, import, importance, interest, memoir, merit, motive, narration, narrative, note, performance, portrayal, presentation, profit, rank, reason, recital, reckoning, record, regard, relation, report, reputation, repute, sake, score, significance, sketch, standing, statement, story, tale, use, value, version, worth, write-up.
v. adjudge, appraise, assess, believe, consider, count, deem, esteem, estimate, explain, gauge, hold, judge, rate, reckon, regard, think, value, weigh.

account for answer for, clarify, clear up, destroy, elucidate, explain, illuminate, incapacitate, justify, kill, put paid to, rationalize, vindicate.

account[2] *n.* balance, bill, book, books, charge, check, computation, inventory, invoice, journal, ledger, reckoning, register, score, statement, tab, tally, tick.

accountable *adj.* amenable, answerable, blamable, bound, charged with, liable, obligated, obliged, responsible.

accredit *v.* appoint, approve, ascribe, assign, attribute, authorize, certificate, certify, commission, credit, depute, empower, enable, endorse, entrust, guarantee, license, okay, qualify, recognize, sanction, vouch for.

accrue *v.* accumulate, amass, arise, be added, build up, collect, emanate, enlarge, ensue, fall due, flow, follow, gather, grow, increase, issue, proceed, redound, result, spring up.

accumulate *v.* accrue, agglomerate, aggregate, amass, assemble, build up, collect, cumulate, gather, grow, hoard, increase, multiply, pile up, stash, stockpile, store.
antonyms diffuse, disseminate.

accumulation *n.* accretion, aggregation, assemblage, augmentation, backlog, build-up, collection, conglomeration, gathering, growth, heap, hoard, increase, mass, pile, reserve, stack, stock, stockpile, store.

accurate *adj.* authentic, careful, close, correct, exact, factual, faithful, faultless, just, letter-perfect, mathematical, meticulous, minute, nice, perfect, precise, proper, regular, right, rigorous, scrupulous, sound, spot-on, strict, true, truthful, unerring, veracious, veridical, well-aimed, well-directed, well-judged, word-perfect.
antonyms inaccurate, wrong.

accursed *adj.* abominable, anathematized, bedeviled, bewitched, blighted, condemned, cursed, damned, despicable, detestable, doomed, execrable, foredoomed, hateful, hellish, hopeless, horrible, ill-fated, ill-omened, jinxed, luckless, ruined, star-crossed, undone, unfortunate, unholy, unlucky, wretched.
antonym blessed.

accusation *n.* accusal, allegation, arraignment, attribution, charge, citation, complaint, crimination, delation, denunciation, gravamen, impeachment, imputation, incrimination, indictment, plaint, recrimination.

accuse *v.* allege, arraign, attaint, attribute, blame, censure, charge, cite, criminate, delate, denounce, impeach, impugn, impute, incriminate, indict, inform against, recriminate, tax.

accustom *v.* acclimatize, acculturate, acquaint, adapt, adjust, discipline, exercise, familiarize, habituate, harden, inure, season, train.

ache *v.* agonize, covet, crave, desire, grieve, hanker, hunger, hurt, itch, long, mourn, need, pain, pine, pound, rack, smart, sorrow, suffer, throb, twinge, yearn.
n. anguish, craving, desire, grief, hankering, hunger, hurt, itch, longing, misery, mourning, need, pain, pang, pining, pounding, smart, smarting, soreness, sorrow, suffering, throb, throbbing, yearning.

achieve *v.* accomplish, acquire, attain, bring about, carry out, compass, complete, consummate, do, earn, effect, effectuate, execute, finish, fulfil, gain, get, manage, obtain, perform, procure, produce, reach, realize, score, strike, succeed, win.
antonyms fail, miss.

achievement *n.* accomplishment, acquirement, act, attainment, completion, deed, effort, execution, exploit, feat, fruition, fulfilment, magnum opus, performance, production, qualification, realization, stroke, success.

acid *adj.* acerbic, acidulous, acrid, astringent, biting, bitter, caustic, corrosive, cutting, harsh, hurtful, ill-natured, incisive, mordant, morose, pungent, sharp, sour, stinging, tart, trenchant, vinegarish, vinegary, vitriolic.

acid test crucial test, touchstone, verification.

acknowledge *v.* accede, accept, acquiesce, address, admit, affirm, agree to, allow, answer, attest, avouch, concede, confess, confirm, declare, endorse, grant, greet, hail, notice, own, profess, react to, recognize, reply to, respond to, return, salute, vouch for, witness, yield.

acme *n.* apex, apogee, climax, crest, crown, culmination, height, high point, maximum, optimum, peak, pinnacle, sublimation, sublimity, summit, top, vertex, zenith.
antonym nadir.

acquaint *v.* accustom, advise, announce, apprize, brief, disclose, divulge, enlighten, familiarize, inform, notify, reveal, tell.

acquaintance *n.* associate, association, awareness, chum, cognizance, colleague, companionship, confrère, consociate, contact, conversance, conversancy, experience, familiarity, fellowship, intimacy, knowledge, relationship, understanding.

acquiesce *v.* accede, accept, agree, allow, approve,

assent, comply, concur, conform, consent, defer, give in, submit, yield.

antonyms disagree, object.

acquire *v.* achieve, amass, appropriate, attain, buy, collect, cop, earn, gain, gather, get, net, obtain, pick up, procure, realize, receive, secure, win.

antonyms forfeit, forgo, relinquish.

acquirements *n.* accomplishments, achievements, acquisitions, attainments, attributes, culture, erudition, knowledge, learning, mastery, qualifications, skills.

acquisition *n.* accession, achievement, acquest, acquirement, appropriation, attainment, buy, gain, gaining, learning, obtainment, possession, prize, procurement, property, purchase, pursuit, securing, take-over.

acquisitive *adj.* avaricious, avid, covetous, grabbing, grasping, greedy, insatiable, mercenary, possessive, predatory, rapacious, voracious.

antonym generous.

acquit *v.* absolve, bear, behave, clear, comport, conduct, deliver, discharge, dismiss, exculpate, excuse, exonerate, free, fulfil, liberate, pay, pay off, perform, release, relieve, repay, reprieve, satisfy, settle, vindicate.

antonym convict.

acrid *adj.* acerbic, acid, acrimonious, astringent, biting, bitter, burning, caustic, cutting, harsh, incisive, irritating, malicious, mordant, nasty, pungent, sarcastic, sardonic, sharp, stinging, tart, trenchant, venomous, virulent, vitriolic.

acrimonious *adj.* abusive, acerbic, astringent, atrabilious, biting, bitter, caustic, censorious, churlish, crabbed, cutting, ill-tempered, irascible, mordant, peevish, petulant, pungent, rancorous, sarcastic, severe, sharp, spiteful, splenetic, tart, testy, trenchant, virulent, waspish.

antonyms irenic, kindly, peaccable.

acrobat *n.* aerialist, balancer, contortionist, equilibrist, funambulist, gymnast, somersaulter, stunt-girl, stuntman, tumbler, voltigeur.

act *n.* accomplishment, achievement, action, affectation, attitude, bill, blow, counterfeit, decree, deed, dissimulation, doing, edict, enactment, enterprise, execution, exertion, exploit, fake, feat, feigning, front, gest, gig, law, make-believe, maneuver, measure, move, operation, ordinance, performance, pose, posture, pretense, proceeding, resolution, routine, sham, show, sketch, spiel, stance, statute, step, stroke, transaction, turn, undertaking. *v.* acquit, act out, affect, assume, bear, behave, carry, carry out, characterize, comport, conduct, counterfeit, dissimulate, do, enact, execute, exert, feign, function, go about, imitate, impersonate, make, mime, mimic, move, operate, perform, personate, personify, play, portray, pose, posture, pretend, put on, react, represent, seem, serve, sham, simulate, strike, take effect, undertake, work.

act up carry on, cause trouble, give bother, give trouble, horse around, make waves, malfunction, mess about, misbehave, muck about, play up, rock the boat.

act (up)on affect, alter, carry out, change, comply with, conform to, execute, follow, fulfil, heed, influence, modify, obey, sway, transform, yield to.

acting *adj.* interim, pro tem, provisional, reserve, stand-by, stop-gap, substitute, supply, surrogate, temporary. *n.* affectation, assuming, bluff, characterization, counterfeiting, dissimulation, dramatics, enacting, feigning, histrionicism, histrionics, histrionism, imitating, imitation, impersonation, imposture, melodrama, performance, performing, play-acting, playing, portrayal, portraying, posing, posturing, pretense, pretending, putting on, seeming, shamming, stagecraft, theatre, theatricals.

action *n.* accomplishment, achievement, act, activity, affray, agency, battle, case, cause, clash, combat, conflict, contest, deed, effect, effort, encounter, endeavor, energy, engagement, enterprise, exercise, exertion, exploit, feat, fight, fighting, force, fray, functioning, influence, lawsuit, litigation, liveliness, mechanism, motion, move, movement, operation, performance, power, proceeding, process, prosecution, skirmish, sortie, spirit, stop, stroke, suit, undertaking, vigor, vim, vitality, warfare, work, working, works.

actions *n.* address, air, bearing, behavior, comportment, conduct, demeanor, deportment, manners, mien, port, ways.

activate *v.* actuate, animate, arouse, bestir, energize, excite, fire, galvanize, impel, initiate, mobilize, motivate, move, prompt, propel, rouse, set in motion, set off, start, stimulate, stir, switch on, trigger.

antonyms arrest, deactivate, stop.

active *adj.* acting, activist, aggressive, agile, alert, ambitious, animated, assertive, assiduous, astir, bustling, busy, committed, deedy, devoted, diligent, doing, effectual, energetic, engaged, enterprising, enthusiastic, forceful, forward, full, functioning, hard-working, in force, in operation, industrious, involved, light-footed, live, lively, militant, moving, nimble, occupied, on the go, on the move, operate, quick, running, sedulous, spirited, sprightly, spry, stirabout, stirring, strenuous, through-going, vibrant, vigorous, vital, vivacious, working, zealous.

antonyms dormant, inactive, inert, passive.

activity *n.* act, action, activeness, animation, avocation, bustle, commotion, deed, endeavor, enterprise, exercise, exertion, hobby, hurly-burly, hustle, industry, interest, job, kerfuffle, labor, life, liveliness, motion, movement, occupation, pastime, project, pursuit, scheme, stir, task, undertaking, venture, work.

actor *n.* actress, agent, artist, comedian, doer, executor, factor, functionary, guiser, ham, hamfatter, histrio, histrion, impersonator, masquerader, mime, mummer, operative, operator, participant, participator, performer, perpetrator, personator, play-actor, player, practitioner, Roscius, Thespian, tragedian, trouper, worker.

actual *adj.* absolute, authentic, bona fide, categorical, certain, concrete, confirmed, corporeal, current, de facto, definite, existent, extant, factual, genuine, indisputable, indubitable, legitimate, live, living, material, physical, positive, present, present-day, prevailing, real, realistic, substantial, tangible, thingy, true, truthful, unquestionable, verified, veritable.
antonyms apparent, imaginary, theoretical.

actuality *n.* corporeality, fact, factuality, historicity, materiality, reality, realness, substance, substantiality, truth, verity.

acute[1] *adj.* astute, canny, clever, critical, crucial, cutting, dangerous, decisive, discerning, discriminating, distressing, essential, excruciating, exquisite, extreme, fierce, grave, important, incisive, ingenious, insightful, intense, intuitive, judicious, keen, lancinating, observant, overpowering, overwhelming, penetrating, perceptive, percipient, perspicacious, piercing, poignant, pointed, powerful, racking, sagacious, sapient, sensitive, serious, severe, sharp, shooting, shrewd, shrill, smart, stabbing, subtle, sudden, urgent, violent, vital.
antonyms chronic, mild, obtuse.

acute[2] *adj.* acicular, apiculate, cuspate, cuspidate, needle-shaped, peaked, pointed, sharp, sharpened.
antonym obtuse.

adamant *adj.* adamantine, determined, firm, fixed, flinty, hard, immovable, impenetrable, indestructible, inexorable, inflexible, infrangible, insistent, intransigent, obdurate, resolute, rigid, rock-like, rocky, set, steely, stiff, stony, stubborn, tough, unbending, unbreakable, uncompromising, unrelenting, unshakable, unyielding.
antonyms flexible, pliant, yielding.

adapt *v.* acclimatize, accommodate, adjust, alter, apply, attemper, change, comply, conform, contemper, convert, customize, familiarize, fashion, fit, habituate, harmonize, match, metamorphose, modify, prepare, proportion, qualify, refashion, remodel, shape, suit, tailor.

add *v.* adjoin, affix, amplify, annex, append, attach, augment, combine, compute, count, include, join, reckon, subjoin, sum up, superimpose, supplement, tack on, tot up, total.
antonym subtract.

add up add, amount, be consistent, be plausible, be reasonable, come to, compute, count, count up, hang together, hold water, imply, indicate, make sense, mean, reckon, reveal, ring true, signify, stand to reason, sum up, tally, tot up, total.

addict *n.* acid-head, adherent, buff, devotee, dope-fiend, enthusiast, fan, fiend, follower, freak, head, hop-head, junkie, mainliner, nut, pot-head, tripper, user.

address[1] *n.* abode, department, direction, domicile, dwelling, home, house, inscription, location, lodging, place, residence, situation, superscription, whereabouts.

address[2] *n.* adroitness, air, allocution, application, art, bearing, declamation, deftness, dexterity, discourse, discretion, dispatch, disquisition, dissertation, expedition, expertise, expertness, facility, harangue, ingenuity, lecture, manner, oration, sermon, skilfulness, skill, speech, tact, talk.
v. accost, address (oneself) to, apostrophize, apply (oneself) to, approach, attend to, bespeak, buttonhole, concentrate on, devote (oneself) to, discourse, engage in, focus on, greet, hail, harangue, invoke, lecture, orate, salute, sermonize, speak, speak to, take care of, talk, talk to, turn to, undertake.

adept *adj.* able, accomplished, ace, adroit, deft, dexterous, experienced, expert, masterful, masterly, nimble, polished, practiced, proficient, skilful, skilled, versed.
antonyms bungling, incompetent, inept.
n. ace, dab hand, dabster, deacon, don, expert, genius, maestro, mahatma, master, old hand, pastmaster, wizard.
antonyms bungler, incompetent.

adequate *adj.* able, acceptable, capable, commensurate, competent, condign, efficacious, enough, fair, fit, passable, presentable, requisite, respectable, satisfactory, serviceable, sufficient, suitable, tolerable.
antonyms inadequate, insufficient.

adhere *v.* abide by, accrete, agree, attach, cement, cleave, cleave to, cling, coalesce, cohere, combine, comply with, fasten, fix, follow, fulfil, glue, heed, hold, hold fast, join, keep, link, maintain, mind, obey, observe, paste, respect, stand by, stick, stick fast, support, unite.

adherent *n.* admirer, advocate, aficionado, devotee, disciple, enthusiast, fan, follower, freak, hanger-on, henchman, nut, partisan, satellite, sectary, supporter, upholder, votary.

adhesive *adj.* adherent, adhering, attaching, clinging, cohesive, emplastic, gluey, glutinous, gummy, holding, mucilaginous, sticking, sticky, tacky, tenacious.
n. cement, glue, gum, mountant, mucilage, paste, tape.

adjacent *adj.* abutting, adjoining, alongside, beside, bordering, close, conterminant, conterminate, conterminous, contiguous, juxtaposed, near, neighboring, next, proximate, touching, vicinal.

adjoin *v.* abut, add, affix, annex, append, approximate, attach, border, combine, communicate with, connect, couple, impinge, interconnect, join, juxtapose, link, meet, neighbor, touch, unite, verge.

adjourn *v.* continue, defer, delay, discontinue, interrupt, postpone, prorogue, put off, recess, stay, suspend.
antonym convene.

adjust *v.* acclimatize, accommodate, accustom, adapt, alter, arrange, balance, change, coapt, compose, concert, conform, convert, dispose, fine-tune, fit, fix, harmonize, jiggle, measure, modify, order, proportion, reconcile, rectify, redress, refashion, regulate, remodel, reshape, set, settle, shape, square, suit, temper, tune.
antonyms derange, disarrange, upset.

administer *v.* adhibit, apply, assign, conduct, contribute, control, direct, disburse, dispense, dispose, distribute, dole out, execute, give, govern, head, impose, lead, manage, measure out, mete out, officiate, organize, oversee, perform, preside over, provide, regulate, rule, run, superintend, supervise, supply.

administration *n.* adhibition, administering, application, conduct, control, direction, directorship, disbursement, dispensation, disposal, distribution, execution, executive, governing, governing body, government, leadership, management, ministry, organization, overseeing, performance, provision, regime, regulation, rule, ruling, running, settlement, superintendence, supervision, supply, term of office.

admirable *adj.* choice, commendable, creditable, deserving, estimable, excellent, exquisite, fine, laudable, meritorious, praiseworthy, rare, respected, superior, valuable, wonderful, worthy.
antonym despicable.

admiration *n.* adoration, affection, amazement, appreciation, approbation, approval, astonishment, awe, delight, esteem, fureur, idolism, pleasure, praise, regard, respect, reverence, surprise, veneration, wonder, wonderment, worship.
antonym contempt.

admire *v.* adore, applaud, appreciate, approve, esteem, iconize, idolize, laud, praise, prize, respect, revere, value, venerate, worship.
antonym despise.

admissible *adj.* acceptable, allowable, allowed, equitable, justifiable, lawful, legitimate, licit, passable, permissible, permitted, tolerable, tolerated.
antonyms illegitimate, inadmissible.

admission *n.* acceptance, access, acknowledgment, adhibition, admittance, admitting, affirmation, allowance, avowal, concession, confession, declaration, disclosure, divulgence, entrance, entrée, entry, exposé, granting, inclusion, ingress, initiation, introduction, owning, profession, revelation.
antonyms denial, exclusion.

admit *v.* accept, acknowledge, adhibit, affirm, agree, allow, allow to enter, avow, concede, confess, declare, disclose, divulge, give access, grant, initiate, introduce, intromit, let, let in, permit, profess, receive, recognize, reveal, take in.
antonyms exclude, gainsay.

admittance *n.* acceptance, access, admitting, allowing, entrance, entrée, entry, ingress, letting in, passage, reception.

admonish *v.* advise, berate, caution, censure, check, chide, counsel, enjoin, exhort, forewarn, rebuke, reprehend, reprimand, reproach, reprove, scold, upbraid, warn.

admonition *n.* advice, berating, caution, censure, counsel, pi-jaw, rebuke, reprehension, reprimand, reproach, reproof, scolding, warning.

ado *n.* agitation, bother, business, bustle, ceremony,

commotion, confusion, delay, disturbance, excitement, ferment, flurry, fuss, hassle, hurly-burly, kerfuffle, labor, pother, stir, to-do, trouble, tumult, turmoil.
antonyms calm, tranquility.

adolescence *n.* boyhood, boyishness, childishness, development, girlhood, girlishness, immaturity, juvenescence, juvenility, minority, puberty, puerility, teens, transition, youth, youthfulness.
antonym senescence.

adopt *v.* accept, affect, appropriate, approve, assume, back, choose, embrace, endorse, espouse, follow, foster, maintain, ratify, sanction, select, support, take in, take on, take up.
antonyms disown, repudiate.

adoration *n.* admiration, esteem, estimation, exaltation, glorification, honor, idolatry, idolization, love, magnification, reverence, veneration, worship.
antonyms abhorrence, detestation.

adore *v.* admire, cherish, dote on, esteem, exalt, glorify, honor, idolatrize, idolize, love, magnify, revere, reverence, venerate, worship.
antonyms abhor, hate.

adorn *v.* adonize, apparel, array, beautify, bedeck, bedight, bedizen, begem, bejewel, bestick, crown, deck, decorate, dight, doll up, embellish, emblazon, enhance, enrich, furbish, garnish, gild, grace, impearl, miniate, ornament, tart up, trick out, trim.

adrift *adj.* aimless, amiss, anchorless, astray, at sea, directionless, goalless, insecure, off course, purposeless, rootless, rudderless, unsettled, wrong.
antonyms anchored, stable.

adroit *adj.* able, adept, apt, artful, clever, cunning, deft, dexterous, expert, habile, ingenious, masterful, neat, nimble, proficient, quick, resourceful, skilful, skilled, slick.
antonyms clumsy, inept, maladroit.

adult *adj.* developed, full-grown, fully grown, grown-up, mature, of age, ripe, ripened.
antonym immature.

advance *v.* accelerate, adduce, allege, ameliorate, assist, benefit, bring forward, cite, elevate, expedite, facilitate, foster, furnish, further, go ahead, go forward, grow, hasten, improve, increase, lend, move on, multiply, offer, pay beforehand, present, press on, proceed, proffer, profit, progress, promote, prosper, provide, raise, send forward, speed, submit, suggest, supply, thrive, upgrade.
antonyms impede, retard, retreat.
n. advancement, amelioration, betterment, breakthrough, credit, deposit, development, down payment, furtherance, gain, growth, headway, improvement, increase, loan, preferment, prepayment, profit, progress, promotion, retainer, rise, step.
antonym recession.
adj. beforehand, early, foremost, forward, in front, leading, preliminary, prior.

advantage *n.* account, aid, ascendancy, asset, assistances, avail, benefit, blessing, boon, boot, convenience, dominance, edge, expediency, fruit, gain, good, help, hold, interest, lead, leverage, precedence, pre-eminence, profit, purchase, service, start, superiority, sway, upper hand, use, usefulness, utility, welfare.
antonyms disadvantage, hindrance.

adventure *n.* chance, contingency, enterprise, experience, exploit, gest, hazard, incident, occurrence, risk, speculation, undertaking, venture.

adventurous *adj.* adventuresome, audacious, bold, dangerous, daredevil, daring, dauntless, doughty, enterprising, foolhardy, game, hazardous, headstrong, impetuous, intrepid, perilous, plucky, rash, reckless, risky, spunky, swashbuckling, temerarious, venturesome.
antonyms cautious, chary, prudent.

adversary *n.* antagonist, assailant, attacker, competitor, contestant, enemy, foe, foeman, opponent, opposer, rival.
antonyms ally, supporter.

adverse *adj.* antagonistic, conflicting, contrary, counter, counter-productive, detrimental, disadvantageous, hostile, hurtful, inauspicious, inexpedient, inimical, injurious, inopportune, negative, noxious, opposing, opposite, reluctant, repugnant, uncongenial, unfavorable, unfortunate, unfriendly, unlucky, unpropitious, untoward, unwilling.
antonyms advantageous, propitious.

adversity *n.* affliction, bad luck, blight, calamity, catastrophe, contretemps, disaster, distress, hard times, hardship, ill-fortune, ill-luck, mischance, misery, misfortune, mishap, reverse, sorrow, suffering, trial, tribulation, trouble, woe, wretchedness.
antonym prosperity.

advertise *v.* advise, announce, apprize, blazon, broadcast, bruit, declare, display, flaunt, herald, inform, make known, notify, plug, praise, proclaim, promote, promulgate, publicize, publish, puff, push, tout, trumpet.

advertisement *n.* ad, advert, announcement, bill, blurb, circular, commercial, display, handbill, handout, hype, leaflet, notice, placard, plug, poster, promotion, propaganda, propagation, publicity, puff, puffery.

advice *n.* admonition, caution, communication, conseil, counsel, direction, do's and don'ts, guidance, help, information, injunction, instruction, intelligence, memorandum, notice, notification, opinion, recommendation, rede, suggestion, view, warning, wisdom, word.

advisable *adj.* advantageous, appropriate, apt, beneficial, correct, desirable, expedient, fit, fitting, judicious, meet, politic, profitable, proper, prudent, recommended, seemly, sensible, sound, suggested, suitable, wise.
antonyms inadvisable, injudicious.

advise *v.* acquaint, apprize, bethink, caution, commend, counsel, enjoin, forewarn, guide, inform, instruct, make known, notify, recommend, report, suggest, teach, tell, tutor, urge, warn.

adviser *n.* admonitor, aide, authority, coach, confidant, consultant, counsel, counselor, éminence grise, guide, helper, instructor, lawyer, mentor, monitor, preceptor, righthand man, solicitor, teacher, therapist, tutor.

advocate *v.* adopt, advise, argue for, campaign for, champion, countenance, defend, encourage, endorse, espouse, favor, justify, patronize, plead for, press for, promote, propose, recommend, subscribe to, support, uphold, urge.
antonyms deprecate, disparage, impugn.
n. apologist, apostle, attorney, backer, barrister, campaigner, champion, counsel, counselor, defender, interceder, intercessor, lawyer, mediator, paraclete, patron, pleader, promoter, proponent, proposer, solicitor, speaker, spokesman, supporter, upholder, vindicator.
antonyms critic, opponent.

affable *adj.* agreeable, amiable, amicable, approachable, benevolent, benign, civil, congenial, cordial, courteous, expansive, free, friendly, genial, good-humored, good-natured, gracious, kindly, mild, obliging, open, pleasant, sociable, suave, urbane, warm.
antonyms cool, reserved, reticent, unfriendly.

affair *n.* activity, adventure, amour, amourette, business, circumstance, concern, connection, episode, event, happening, incident, interest, intrigue, liaison, matter, occurrence, operation, organization, party, proceeding, project, question, reception, relationship, responsibility, romance, subject, topic, transaction, undertaking.

affect[1] *v.* act on, agitate, alter, apply to, attack, bear upon, change, concern, disturb, grieve, grip, impinge upon, impress, influence, interest, involve, melt, modify, move, overcome, penetrate, pertain to, perturb, prevail over, regard, relate to, seize, soften, stir, strike, sway, touch, transform, trouble, upset.

affect[2] *v.* adopt, aspire to, assume, contrive, counterfeit, fake, feign, imitate, pretend, profess, put on, sham, simulate.

affected[1] *adj.* afflicted, agitated, altered, changed, concerned, damaged, distressed, gripped, hurt, impaired, impressed, influenced, injured, melted, moved, perturbed, smitten, stimulated, stirred, swayed, touched, troubled, upset.

affected[2] *adj.* alembicated, artificial, assumed, bogus, chichi, conceited, contrived, counterfeit, debby, euphuistic, fake, feigned, fussy, greenery-yallery, hyperaesthesic, hyperaesthetic, insincere, lah-di-dah, literose, mannered, mincing, minikin, namby-pamby, niminy-piminy, phoney, pompous, precious, pretended, pretentious, put-on, sham, simulated, spurious, stiff, studied, unnatural.
antonyms genuine, natural.

affection *n.* amity, attachment, care, desire, devotion,

favor, feeling, fondness, friendliness, good will, inclination, kindness, liking, love, partiality, passion, penchant, predilection, predisposition, proclivity, propensity, regard, tenderness, warmth.
antonyms antipathy, dislike.

affectionate *adj.* amiable, amorous, attached, caring, cordial, devoted, doting, fond, friendly, kind, loving, passionate, responsive, solicitous, tender, warm, warm-hearted.
antonyms cold, undemonstrative.

affirm *v.* assert, asseverate, attest, aver, avouch, avow, certify, confirm, corroborate, declare, depose, endorse, maintain, pronounce, ratify, state, swear, testify, witness.

afflict *v.* beset, burden, distress, grieve, harass, harm, harrow, hurt, oppress, pain, plague, rack, smite, strike, torment, torture, trouble, try, visit, wound, wring.
antonyms comfort, solace.

affliction *n.* adversity, calamity, cross, curse, depression, disaster, disease, distress, grief, hardship, illness, misery, misfortune, ordeal, pain, plague, scourge, sickness, sorrow, suffering, torment, trial, tribulation, trouble, visitation, woe, wretchedness.
antonyms comfort, consolation, solace.

affluent *adj.* comfortable, flourishing, flush, loaded, moneyed, opulent, pecunious, prosperous, rich, wealthy, well-heeled, well-off, well-to-do.
antonyms impecunious, impoverished, poor.

afford *v.* bear, bestow, cope with, engender, furnish, generate, give, grant, impart, manage, offer, produce, provide, render, spare, stand, supply, sustain, yield.

affront *v.* abuse, anger, annoy, displease, gall, incense, insult, irritate, nettle, offend, outrage, pique, provoke, slight, snub, vex.
antonyms appease, compliment.
n. abuse, discourtesy, disrespect, facer, indignity, injury, insult, offense, outrage, provocation, rudeness, slap in the face, slight, slur, snub, vexation, wrong.
antonym compliment.

afraid *adj.* aghast, alarmed, anxious, apprehensive, cowardly, diffident, distrustful, faint-hearted, fearful, frightened, intimidated, nervous, regretful, reluctant, scared, sorry, suspicious, timid, timorous, tremulous, unhappy.
antonyms confident, unafraid.

after *prep.* afterwards, as a result of, behind, below, following, in consequence of, later, post, subsequent to, subsequently, succeeding, thereafter.
antonym before.

again *adv.* afresh, also, anew, another time, au contraire, besides, bis, conversely, da capo, de integro, de novo, ditto, encore, furthermore, in addition, moreover, on the contrary, on the other hand, once more.

against *prep.* abutting, across, adjacent to, athwart, close up to, confronting, contra, counter to, facing, fronting, hostile to, in contact with, in contrast to, in defiance

of, in exchange for, in opposition to, in the face of, on, opposed to, opposing, opposite to, resisting, touching, versus.
antonyms for, pro.

age *n.* aeon, agedness, anility, caducity, date, day, days, decline, decrepitude, dotage, duration, elderliness, epoch, era, generation, lifetime, majority, maturity, old age, period, senescence, senility, seniority, span, the sere and yellow, time, years.
antonyms salad days, youth.
v. decline, degenerate, deteriorate, grow old, mature, mellow, obsolesce, ripen, season.

aged *adj.* advanced, age-old, ancient, antiquated, antique, decrepit, elderly, geriatric, gray, hoary, old, patriarchal, senescent, sere, superannuated, time-worn, venerable, worn-out.
antonyms young, youthful.

agency *n.* action, activity, bureau, business, department, effect, effectuation, efficiency, finger, force, handling, influence, instrumentality, intercession, intervention, means, mechanism, mediation, medium, office, offices, operation, organization, power, work, workings.

agent *n.* actor, agency, author, cause, channel, delegate, deputy, doer, emissary, envoy, executor, factor, force, functionary, go-between, instrument, intermediary, legate, means, middleman, mover, negotiator, operative, operator, organ, performer, power, practisant, rep, representative, substitute, surrogate, vehicle, vicar, worker.

aggravate *v.* annoy, exacerbate, exaggerate, exasperate, harass, hassle, heighten, incense, increase, inflame, intensify, irk, irritate, magnify, needle, nettle, peeve, pester, provoke, tease, vex, worsen.
antonyms alleviate, appease, mollify.

aggregate *n.* accumulation, agglomeration, aggregation, amount, assemblage, body, bulk, collection, combination, entirety, generality, heap, herd, lump, mass, mixture, pile, sum, throng, total, totality, whole.
adj. accumulated, added, assembled, collected, collective, combined, complete, composite, corporate, cumulative, mixed, total, united.
antonyms individual, particular.
v. accumulate, add up, agglomerate, amass, amount to, assemble, cluster, collect, combine, conglomerate, heap, mix, pile, total.

aggression *n.* aggressiveness, antagonism, assault, attack, bellicosity, belligerence, combativeness, destructiveness, encroachment, hostility, impingement, incursion, injury, intrusion, invasion, jingoism, militancy, offence, offensive, onslaught, provocation, pugnacity, raid.

aggressive *adj.* argumentative, assertive, bellicose, belligerent, bold, butch, combative, contentious, destructive, disputatious, dynamic, energetic, enterprising, forceful, go-ahead, hostile, intrusive, invasive, jingoistic, militant, offensive, provocative, pugnacious, pushful, pushing, pushy, quarrelsome, scrappy, vigorous, zealous.

antonyms peaceable, submissive.

aghast *adj.* afraid, amazed, appalled, astonished, astounded, awestruck, confounded, dismayed, frightened, horrified, horror-struck, shocked, startled, stunned, stupefied, terrified, thunder-struck.

agile *adj.* active, acute, adroit, alert, brisk, clever, fleet, flexible, limber, lissome, lithe, lively, mobile, nimble, prompt, quick, quick-witted, sharp, smart, sprightly, spry, supple, swift.

antonyms clumsy, stiff, torpid.

agility *n.* activity, acuteness, adroitness, alertness, briskness, cleverness, flexibility, lissomeness, litheness, liveliness, mobility, nimbleness, promptitude, promptness, quickness, quick-wittedness, sharpness, sprightliness, spryness, suppleness, swiftness.

antonyms sluggishness, stiffness, torpidity.

agitate *v.* alarm, arouse, beat, churn, confuse, convulse, discompose, disconcert, disquiet, distract, disturb, excite, ferment, flurry, fluster, incite, inflame, perturb, rattle, rock, rouse, ruffle, shake, stimulate, stir, toss, trouble, unnerve, unsettle, upset, work up, worry.

antonyms calm, tranquilize.

agitated *adj.* anxious, discomposed, distracted, feverish, flurried, flustered, in a lather, insecure, jumpy, nervous, perturbed, restive, restless, ruffled, tumultuous, twitchy, uneasy, unnerved, unsettled, upset, wrought-up.

antonyms calm, composed.

agony *n.* affliction, anguish, distress, misery, pain, pangs, paroxysm, spasm, suffering, throes, torment, torture, tribulation, woe, wretchedness.

agree *v.* accede, accord, acquiesce, admit, allow, answer, assent, chime, coincide, comply, concede, concord, concur, conform, consent, consort, contract, correspond, cotton, covenant, engage, fadge, fit, fix, get on, grant, harmonize, homologate, jibe, match, permit, promise, see eye to eye, settle, side with, square, suit, tally, yield.

antonyms conflict, disagree.

agreeable *adj.* acceptable, acquiescent, amenable, amicable, appropriate, approving, attractive, befitting, compatible, complying, concurring, conformable, congenial, consenting, consistent, d'accord, delectable, delightful, enjoyable, fitting, gemütlich, gratifying, in accord, likable, palatable, pleasant, pleasing, pleasurable, proper, responsive, satisfying, suitable, sympathetic, well-disposed, willing.

antonyms disagreeable, distasteful, incompatible, nasty.

agreement[1] *n.* acceptance, accord, accordance, adherence, affinity, analogy, closing, compact, compatibility, complaisance, compliance, concert, concord, concordat, concurrence, conformity, congruence, congruity, consentience, consistency, consonance, consort,

convention, correspondence, harmony, modus vivendi, preconcert, resemblance, respondence, similarity, suitableness, sympathy, unanimity, union, unison.

antonym disagreement.

agreement[2] *n.* arrangement, bargain, compact, concordat, contract, covenant, deal, pact, settlement, treaty, understanding.

agriculture *n.* agribusiness, agronomics, agronomy, cultivation, culture, farming, geoponics, husbandry, tillage.

ahead *adj., adv.* advanced, along, at an advantage, at the head, before, earlier on, forwards, in advance, in front, in the forefront, in the lead, in the vanguard, leading, onwards, superior, to the fore, winning.

aid *v.* abet, accommodate, adminiculate, assist, befriend, boost, ease, encourage, expedite, facilitate, favor, help, oblige, promote, prop, rally round, relieve, second, serve, subsidize, succor, support, sustain.

antonyms impede, obstruct.

n. a leg up, adminicle, aidance, assistance, assistant, benefit, contribution, donation, encouragement, favor, help, helper, patronage, prop, relief, service, sponsorship, subsidy, subvention, succor, support, supporter.

antonyms impediment, obstruction.

ail *v.* afflict, annoy, be indisposed, bother, decline, distress, droop, fail, irritate, languish, pain, pine, sicken, trouble, upset, weaken, worry.

antonyms comfort, flourish.

ailing *adj.* debilitated, diseased, feeble, frail, ill, indisposed, infirm, invalid, languishing, off-color, out of sorts, peaky, poorly, sick, sickly, suffering, under the weather, unsound, unwell, weak, weakly.

antonyms flourishing, healthy.

ailment *n.* affliction, complaint, disability, disease, disorder, illness, indisposition, infection, infirmity, malady, sickness, weakness.

aim *v.* address, aspire, attempt, beam, design, direct, draw a bead, endeavor, essay, head for, intend, level, mean, plan, point, propose, purpose, resolve, seek, set one's sights on, sight, strive, take aim, target, train, try, want, wish, zero in on.

n. ambition, aspiration, course, desideratum, design, desire, direction, dream, end, goal, hope, intent, intention, mark, motive, object, objective, plan, purpose, scheme, target, telos, wish.

aimless *adj.* chance, desultory, directionless, erratic, feckless, frivolous, goalless, haphazard, irresolute, pointless, purposeless, rambling, random, stray, undirected, unguided, unmotivated, unpredictable, vagrant, wayward.

antonyms determined, positive, purposeful.

air *n.* ambience, ambient, appearance, aria, atmosphere, aura, bearing, blast, breath, breeze, character, demeanor, draught, effect, ether, feeling, flavor, heavens, impression, lay, look, manner, melody, mood, motif, oxygen, puff, quality, sky, song, strain, style, theme, tone, tune, waft, whiff, wind, zephyr.

v. aerate, broadcast, circulate, communicate, declare, disclose, display, disseminate, divulge, exhibit, expose, express, freshen, give vent to, make known, make public, parade, proclaim, publicize, publish, reveal, tell, utter, vaunt, ventilate, voice.

airy *adj.* aerial, blithe, blowy, bodiless, breezy, buoyant, cheerful, cheery, debonair, delicate, disembodied, drafty, ethereal, fanciful, flimsy, fresh, frolicsome, gay, graceful, gusty, happy, high-spirited, illusory, imaginary, immaterial, incorporeal, insouciant, insubstantial, jaunty, light, light-hearted, lively, lofty, merry, nimble, nonchalant, off-hand, open, roomy, spacious, spectral, sportive, sprightly, trifling, uncluttered, unreal, unsubstantial, vaporous, visionary, weightless, well-ventilated, windy.
antonyms close, heavy, oppressive, stuffy.

aisle *n.* alleyway, ambulatory, corridor, deambulatory, division, gangway, lane, passage, passageway, path, walkway.

akin *adj.* affiliated, agnate, alike, allied, analogous, cognate, comparable, congenial, connected, consanguineous, consonant, corresponding, kin, kindred, like, parallel, related, similar.
antonym alien.

alarm *v.* affright, agitate, daunt, dismay, distress, frighten, give (someone) a turn, panic, put the wind up (someone), scare, startle, terrify, terrorize, unnerve.
antonyms calm, reassure, soothe.
n. alarm-bell, alert, anxiety, apprehension, bell, consternation, danger signal, dismay, distress, distress signal, fear, fright, horror, larum, larum-bell, nervousness, panic, scare, siren, terror, tocsin, trepidation, unease, uneasiness, warning.
antonym composure.

alarming *adj.* daunting, direful, dismaying, distressing, disturbing, dreadful, frightening, ominous, scaring, shocking, startling, terrifying, threatening, unnerving.
antonym reassuring.

alcoholic *adj.* ardent, brewed, distilled, fermented, hard, inebriant, inebriating, intoxicating, spirituous, strong, vinous.
n. bibber, boozer, dipso, dipsomaniac, drunk, drunkard, hard drinker, inebriate, lush, piss artist, soak, sot, sponge, tippler, toper, tosspot, wino.

alert *adj.* active, agile, attentive, brisk, careful, circumspect, heedful, lively, nimble, observant, on the ball, on the lookout, on the qui vive, perceptive, prepared, quick, ready, sharp-eyed, sharp-witted, spirited, sprightly, vigilant, wary, watchful, wide-awake.
antonyms listless, slow.
n. alarm, signal, siren, tocsin, warning.
v. alarm, forewarn, inform, notify, signal, tip off, warn.

alias *n.* allonym, anonym, assumed name, false name, nick-name, nom de guerre, nom de plume, pen name, pseudonym, soubriquet, stage name.

adv. alias dictus, also, also called, also known as, formerly, otherwise, otherwise called.

alibi *n.* cover-up, defence, excuse, explanation, justification, plea, pretext, reason, story.

alien *adj.* adverse, antagonistic, conflicting, contrary, estranged, exotic, extraneous, foreign, inappropriate, incompatible, incongruous, inimical, opposed, outlandish, remote, repugnant, separated, strange, unfamiliar.
antonym akin.
n. emigrant, foreigner, immigrant, metic, newcomer, outlander, outsider, stranger.
antonym native.

alight[1] *v.* come down, come to rest, debark, descend, detrain, disembark, disentrain, dismount, get down, get off, land, light, perch, settle, touch down.
antonyms ascend, board, rise.

alight[2] *adj.* ablaze, afire, aflame, blazing, bright, brilliant, burning, fiery, flaming, flaring, ignited, illuminated, illumined, lighted, lit, lit up, on fire, radiant, shining.
antonym dark.

alive *adj.* active, alert, animate, animated, awake, breathing, brisk, cheerful, eager, energetic, existent, existing, extant, functioning, having life, in existence, in force, life-like, live, lively, living, operative, quick, real, spirited, sprightly, spry, subsisting, vibrant, vigorous, vital, vivacious, zestful.
antonyms dead, lifeless.

alive with abounding in, bristling with, bustling with, buzzing with, crawling with, crowded with, infested with, lousy with, overflowing with, overrun by, stiff with, swarming with, teeming with, thronged with.

allay *v.* allege, alleviate, appease, assuage, blunt, calm, check, compose, diminish, dull, ease, lessen, lull, mitigate, moderate, mollify, pacify, quell, quiet, reduce, relieve, slake, smooth, soften, soothe, subdue, tranquilize.
antonyms exacerbate, intensify.

allege *v.* adduce, advance, affirm, assert, asseverate, attest, aver, avow, charge, claim, contend, declare, depose, hold, insist, maintain, plead, profess, put forward, state.

allegiance *n.* adherence, constancy, devotion, duty, faithfulness, fealty, fidelity, friendship, homage, loyalty, obedience, obligation, support.
antonyms disloyalty, enmity.

allegory *n.* analogy, apologue, comparison, emblem, fable, metaphor, myth, parable, story, symbol, symbolism, tale.

alleviate *v.* abate, allay, assuage, blunt, check, cushion, deaden, diminish, dull, ease, lessen, lighten, mitigate, moderate, modify, mollify, palliate, quell, quench, quiet, reduce, relieve, slacken, slake, smooth, soften, soothe, subdue, temper.
antonym aggravate.

alley *n.* alleyway, back street, close, entry, gate, lane, mall, passage, passageway, pathway, walk.

alliance *n.* affiliation, affinity, agreement, association, bloc, bond, cartel, coalition, combination, compact, concordat, confederacy, confederation, conglomerate, connection, consociation, consortium, faction, federation, guild, league, marriage, pact, partnership, syndicate, treaty, union.

antonyms divorce, enmity, estrangement, hostility.

allot *v.* allocate, apportion, appropriate, assign, budget, designate, dispense, distribute, earmark, grant, mete, render, set aside, share out.

allow *v.* accord, acknowledge, acquiesce, admeasure, admit, allocate, allot, apportion, approve, assign, authorize, bear, brook, concede, confess, deduct, endure, give, give leave, grant, let, own, permit, provide, put up with, remit, sanction, spare, stand, suffer, tolerate.

antonyms deny, forbid.

allow for arrange for, bear in mind, consider, foresee, include, keep in mind, keep in view, make allowances for, make concessions for, make provision for, plan for, provide for, take into account.

antonym discount.

allowance *n.* admission, allocation, allotment, amount, annuity, apportionment, concession, deduction, discount, emolument, grant, lot, measure, pension, portion, quota, ration, rebate, reduction, remittance, sanction, share, stint, stipend, subsidy, sufferance, tolerance, weighting, X-factor.

allude *v.* adumbrate, advert, cite, glance, hint, imply, infer, insinuate, intimate, mention, refer, remark, speak of, suggest, touch upon.

allure *v.* attract, beguile, cajole, captivate, charm, coax, decoy, disarm, enchant, enrapture, entice, entrance, fascinate, interest, inveigle, lead on, lure, persuade, seduce, tempt, win over.

antonym repel.

n. appeal, attraction, captivation, charm, enchantment, enticement, fascination, glamor, lure, magnetism, persuasion, seductiveness, temptation.

ally *n.* abettor, accessory, accomplice, associate, coadjutor, collaborator, colleague, confederate, confrere, consort, coworker, friend, helper, helpmate, leaguer, partner, sidekick.

antonyms antagonist, enemy.

v. affiliate, amalgamate, associate, band together, collaborate, combine, confederate, conjoin, connect, fraternize, join, join forces, league, marry, team up, unify, unite.

antonym estrange.

almighty *adj.* absolute, all-powerful, awful, desperate, enormous, excessive, great, intense, invincible, loud, omnipotent, overpowering, overwhelming, plenipotent, severe, supreme, terrible, unlimited.

antonyms impotent, insignificant, weak.

almost *adv.* about, all but, approaching, approximately, as good as, close to, just about, nearing, nearly, not far from, not quite, practically, towards, virtually, well-nigh.

alms *n.* benefaction, beneficence, bounty, charity, donation, gift, largess(e), offerings, relief.

alone *adj., adv.* abandoned, apart, by itself, by oneself, deserted, desolate, detached, discrete, forlorn, forsaken, incomparable, isolated, just, lonely, lonesome, matchless, mere, nonpareil, on one's own, only, peerless, separate, simply, single, single-handed, singular, sole, solitary, unaccompanied, unaided, unassisted, unattended, uncombined, unconnected, unequaled, unescorted, unique, unparalleled, unsurpassed.

aloof *adj.* chilly, cold, cool, detached, distant, forbidding, formal, haughty, inaccessible, indifferent, offish, remote, reserved, reticent, stand-offish, supercilious, unapproachable, uncompanionable, unforthcoming, unfriendly, uninterested, unresponsive, unsociable, unsympathetic.

antonyms concerned, sociable.

also *adv.* additionally, along with, and, as well, as well as, besides, ditto, further, furthermore, in addition, including, moreover, plus, therewithal, to boot, too.

alter *v.* adapt, adjust, amend, bushel, castrate, change, convert, diversify, emend, metamorphose, modify, qualify, recast, reform, remodel, reshape, revise, shift, take liberties with, transform, transmute, transpose, turn, vary.

antonym fix.

alteration *n.* adaptation, adjustment, amendment, castration, change, conversion, difference, diversification, emendation, interchanging, metamorphosis, modification, reciprocation, reformation, remodeling, reshaping, revision, rotation, shift, transfiguration, transformation, transmutation, transposition, variance, variation, vicissitude.

antonym fixity.

altercation *n.* argument, bickering, clash, contention, controversy, debate, disagreement, discord, dispute, dissension, fracas, logomachy, quarrel, row, sparring, squabble, wrangle.

alternate *v.* alter, change, fluctuate, follow one another, interchange, intersperse, oscillate, reciprocate, rotate, substitute, take turns, transpose, vary.

adj. alternating, alternative, another, different, every other, every second, interchanging, reciprocal, reciprocating, reciprocative, rotating, second, substitute.

alternative *n.* back-up, choice, option, other, preference, recourse, selection, substitute.

adj. alternate, another, different, fall-back, fringe, other, second, substitute, unconventional, unorthodox.

although *conj.* admitting that, albeit, conceding that, even if, even supposing, even though, granted that, howbeit, notwithstanding, though, while.

altitude *n.* elevation, height, loftiness, stature, tallness.

antonym depth.

altogether *adv.* absolutely, all in all, all told, as a whole, collectively, completely, entirely, fully, generally, holusbolus, in all, in general, in sum, in toto, on the whole, perfectly, quite, thoroughly, totally, utterly, wholesale, wholly.

altruism *n.* considerateness, disinterestedness, generosity, humanity, philanthropy, public spirit, self-abnegation, self-sacrifice, social conscience, unself, unselfishness.
antonym selfishness.

always *adv.* aye, consistently, constantly, continually, endlessly, eternally, ever, everlastingly, evermore, every time, forever, in perpetuum, invariably, perpetually, regularly, repeatedly, sempiternally, unceasingly, unfailingly, without exception.
antonym never.

amalgamate *v.* alloy, ally, blend, coalesce, coalize, combine, commingle, compound, fuse, homogenize, incorporate, integrate, intermix, merge, mingle, synthesize, unify, unite.
antonym separate.

amass *v.* accumulate, agglomerate, agglutinate, aggregate, assemble, collect, compile, foregather, garner, gather, heap up, hoard, pile up, rake up, scrape together.

amateur *n.* buff, dabbler, dilettante, do-it-yourselfer, fancier, ham, layman, non-professional.
antonym professional.

amaze *v.* alarm, astonish, astound, bewilder, confound, daze, disconcert, dismay, dumbfound, electrify, flabbergast, floor, shock, stagger, startle, stun, stupefy, surprise, wow.

ambiguous *adj.* ambivalent, amphibolic, amphibological, amphibolous, confused, confusing, cryptic, Delphic, double-barrelled, double-meaning, doubtful, dubious, enigmatic, enigmatical, equivocal, inconclusive, indefinite, indeterminate, louche, multivocal, obscure, oracular, puzzling, uncertain, unclear, vague, woolly.
antonyms clear.

ambition *n.* aim, aspiration, avidity, craving, design, desire, dream, drive, eagerness, end, enterprise, goal, hankering, hope, hunger, ideal, intent, longing, object, objective, purpose, push, striving, target, wish, yearning, zeal.
antonyms apathy, diffidence.

ambitious *adj.* arduous, aspiring, assertive, avid, bold, challenging, demanding, desirous, difficult, driving, eager, elaborate, energetic, enterprising, enthusiastic, exacting, fervid, formidable, go-ahead, grandiose, hard, hopeful, impressive, industrious, intent, keen, pretentious, purposeful, pushy, severe, strenuous, striving, zealous.
antonym unassuming.

amble *v.* dawdle, drift, meander, mosey, perambulate, promenade, ramble, saunter, stroll, toddle, walk, wander.
antonyms march, stride.

ambush *n.* ambuscade, concealment, cover, emboscata, hiding, hiding-place, retreat, shelter, snare, trap, waylaying.
v. ambuscade, bushwhack, ensnare, entrap, surprise, trap, waylay.

amend *v.* adjust, alter, ameliorate, better, change, correct, emend, emendate, enhance, fix, improve, mend, modify, qualify, rectify, redress, reform, remedy, repair, revise.
antonyms impair, worsen.

amends *n.* atonement, compensation, expiation, indemnification, indemnity, mitigation, quittance, recompense, redress, reparation, requital, restitution, restoration, satisfaction.

amiable *adj.* accessible, affable, agreeable, approachable, attractive, benign, biddable, charming, cheerful, companionable, complaisant, congenial, conversable, delightful, engaging, friendly, gemütlich, genial, good-humored, good-natured, good-tempered, kind, kindly, likable, lovable, obliging, pleasant, pleasing, sociable, sweet, winning, winsome.
antonyms hostile, unfriendly.

amid *conj.* amidst, among, amongst, in the middle of, in the midst of, in the thick of, surrounded by.

amiss *adj.* awry, defective, erroneous, fallacious, false, faulty, improper, inaccurate, inappropriate, incorrect, out of order, unsuitable, untoward, wonky, wrong.
adv. ill, imperfect, imprecise, out of kilter.
antonyms right, well.

among *prep.* amid, amidst, amongst, between, in the middle of, in the midst of, in the thick of, midst, mongst, surrounded by, together with, with.

amorous *adj.* affectionate, amatory, ardent, attached, doting, enamored, erotic, fond, impassioned, in love, lovesick, loving, lustful, passionate, randy, tender, uxorious.
antonyms cold, indifferent.

amount *n.* addition, aggregate, bulk, entirety, expanse, extent, lot, magnitude, mass, measure, number, quantity, quantum, quota, sum, sum total, supply, total, volume, whole.

amount to add up to, aggregate, approximate to, be equivalent to, be tantamount to, become, come to, equal, grow, mean, purport, run to, total.

ample *adj.* abundant, big, bountiful, broad, capacious, commodious, considerable, copious, expansive, extensive, full, generous, goodly, great, handsome, large, lavish, liberal, munificent, plenteous, plentiful, plenty, profuse, rich, roomy, spacious, substantial, sufficient, unrestricted, voluminous, wide. *antonyms* insufficient, meager.

amplify *v.* add to, augment, boost, broaden, bulk out, deepen, develop, dilate, elaborate, enhance, enlarge, expand, expatiate, extend, fill out, heighten, increase, intensify, lengthen, magnify, raise, strengthen, supplement, widen.
antonym reduce.

amuse *v.* absorb, beguile, charm, cheer, cheer up, delight, disport, divert, engross, enliven, entertain, enthral, gladden, interest, occupy, please, popjoy, recreate, regale, relax, slay, tickle.
antonym bore.

amusement *n.* beguilement, delight, disportment, distraction, diversion, enjoyment, entertainment, fun, game, gladdening, hilarity, hobby, interest, joke, lark, laughter, merriment, mirth, pastime, pleasure, prank, recreation, regalement, sport.
antonyms bore, boredom.

amusing *adj.* amusive, charming, cheerful, cheering, comical, delightful, diverting, droll, enjoyable, entertaining, facetious, funny, gladdening, hilarious, humorous, interesting, jocular, jolly, killing, laughable, lively, ludicrous, merry, pleasant, pleasing, risible, sportive, witty.
antonym boring.

analogous *adj.* agreeing, akin, alike, comparable, correlative, corresponding, equivalent, homologous, like, matching, parallel, reciprocal, related, resembling, similar.
antonym disparate.

analysis *n.* anatomization, anatomy, assay, breakdown, dissection, dissolution, division, enquiry, estimation, evaluation, examination, exegesis, explanation, explication, exposition, interpretation, investigation, judgment, opinion, reasoning, reduction, resolution, review, scrutiny, separation, sifting, study, test.

analyze *v.* anatomize, assay, break down, consider, dissect, dissolve, divide, estimate, evaluate, examine, interpret, investigate, judge, reduce, resolve, review, scrutinize, separate, sift, study, test.

ancestral *adj.* atavistic, avital, familial, genealogical, genetic, hereditary, lineal, parental.

ancestry *n.* ancestors, antecedents, antecessors, blood, derivation, descent, extraction, family, forebears, forefathers, genealogy, heredity, heritage, house, line, lineage, origin, parentage, pedigree, progenitors, race, roots, stirps, stock.

anchor *n.* grapnel, kedge, killick, mainstay, mud-hook, pillar of strength, prop, security, staff, support.
v. affix, attach, fasten, fix, make fast, moor.

ancient *adj.* aged, age-old, antediluvian, antiquated, antique, archaic, bygone, démodé, early, fossilized, hoary, immemorial, obsolete, old, olden, old-fashioned, original, outmoded, out-of-date, preadamic, prehistoric, primeval, primordial, pristine, superannuated, timeworn, venerable, world-old.
antonym modern.

anecdote *n.* exemplum, fable, reminiscence, sketch, story, tale, yarn.

anemic *adj.* ashen, bloodless, chalky, characterless, colorless, dull, enervated, exsanguine, exsanguin(e)ous, feeble, frail, ineffectual, infirm, insipid, pale, pallid, pasty, sallow, sickly, spiritless, toneless, wan, weak, whey-faced.
antonyms full-blooded, ruddy, sanguine.

anesthetic *n.* analgesic, anodyne, narcotic, opiate, painkiller, palliative, sedative, soporific, stupefacient, stupefactive.

anesthetize *v.* benumb, deaden, desensitize, dope, dull, etherize, lull, mull, numb, stupefy.

angel *n.* archangel, backer, benefactor, cherub, darling, divine messenger, fairy godmother, guardian spirit, ideal, paragon, principality, saint, seraph, supporter, treasure.
antonyms devil, fiend.

angelic *adj.* adorable, beatific, beautiful, celestial, cherubic, divine, entrancing, ethereal, exemplary, heavenly, holy, innocent, lovely, pious, pure, saintly, seraphic, unworldly, virtuous. *antonyms* devilish, fiendish.

anger *n.* annoyance, antagonism, bad blood, bile, bitterness, choler, dander, displeasure, dudgeon, exasperation, fury, gall, indignation, ire, irritability, irritation, monkey, outrage, passion, pique, rage, rancor, resentment, spleen, temper, vexation, wrath.
antonym forbearance.
v. affront, aggravate, annoy, antagonize, bother, bug, displease, enrage, exasperate, fret, frustrate, gall, incense, infuriate, irk, irritate, madden, miff, needle, nettle, offend, outrage, pique, provoke, rile, ruffle, vex.
antonyms appease, calm, please.

angry *adj.* aggravated, annoyed, antagonized, bitter, burned up, choked, choleric, chuffed, disgruntled, displeased, enraged, exasperated, furious, heated, hot, incensed, indignant, infuriated, irascible, irate, ireful, irked, irritable, irritated, mad, miffed, needled, nettled, outraged, passionate, piqued, provoked, raging, rancorous, ratty, red-headed, resentful, riled, shirty, splenetic, stomachful, tumultuous, uptight, waxy, wrathful, wroth.
antonyms calm, content.

anguish *n.* agony, angst, anxiety, desolation, distress, dole, dolor, grief, heartache, heartbreak, misery, pain, pang, rack, sorrow, suffering, torment, torture, tribulation, woe, wretchedness.
antonyms happiness, solace.

animal *n.* barbarian, beast, brute, creature, critter, cur, hound, mammal, monster, pig, savage, swine.
adj. bestial, bodily, brutish, carnal, faunal, feral, ferine, fleshly, gross, inhuman, instinctive, physical, piggish, savage, sensual, wild, zoic.

animate *v.* activate, arouse, embolden, encourage, energize, enliven, excite, fire, galvanize, goad, impel, incite, inspire, inspirit, instigate, invest, invigorate, irradiate, kindle, move, quicken, reactivate, revive, revivify, rouse, spark, spur, stimulate, stir, suffuse, urge, vitalize, vivify.
antonyms dull, inhibit.
adj. alive, breathing, conscious, live, living, sentient.
antonyms dull, spiritless.

animated *adj.* active, airy, alive, ardent, brisk, buoyant,

eager, ebullient, energetic, enthusiastic, excited, fervent, gay, glowing, impassioned, lively, passionate, quick, radiant, spirited, sprightly, vehement, vibrant, vigorous, vital, vivacious, vivid, zestful.
antonyms inert, sluggish.

animosity *n.* acrimony, animus, antagonism, antipathy, bad blood, bitterness, enmity, feud, feuding, hate, hatred, hostility, ill-will, loathing, malevolence, malice, malignity, odium, rancor, resentment, spite.
antonym goodwill.

annex *v.* acquire, add, adjoin, affix, append, appropriate, arrogate, attach, connect, conquer, expropriate, fasten, incorporate, join, occupy, purloin, seize, subjoin, tack, take over, unite, usurp.
n. addendum, additament, addition, adjunct, appendix, attachment, supplement.

annihilate *v.* abolish, assassinate, destroy, eliminate, eradicate, erase, exterminate, extinguish, extirpate, liquidate, murder, nullify, obliterate, raze, rub out, thrash, trounce, wipe out.

announce *v.* advertise, blazon, broadcast, declare, disclose, divulge, intimate, leak, make known, notify, preconize, proclaim, promulgate, propound, publicize, publish, report, reveal, state.
antonym suppress.

announcement *n.* advertisement, broadcast, bulletin, communiqué, declaration, disclosure, dispatch, divulgation, divulgence, intimation, notification, proclamation, promulgation, publication, report, revelation, statement.

annoy *v.* aggravate, anger, badger, bore, bother, bug, chagrin, contrary, displease, disturb, exasperate, fash, gall, get, give the pigs, harass, harm, harry, hip, hump, incommode, irk, irritate, madden, molest, needle, nettle, peeve, pester, pique, plague, provoke, rile, ruffle, tease, trouble, vex. *antonyms* gratify, please.

annulment *n.* abolition, abrogation, cancellation, cassation, countermanding, disannulment, invalidation, negation, nullification, quashing, recall, repeal, rescindment, rescission, retraction, reversal, revocation, suspension, voiding.
antonyms enactment, restoration.

anoint *v.* anele, bless, consecrate, daub, dedicate, embrocate, grease, hallow, lard, lubricate, oil, rub, sanctify, smear.

answer *n.* acknowledgment, apology, comeback, counter-buff, countercharge, defence, explanation, outcome, plea, reaction, rebuttal, reciprocation, refutation, rejoinder, reply, report, resolution, response, retaliation, retort, return, riposte, solution, vindication.
v. acknowledge, agree, balance, conform, correlate, correspond, do, echo, explain, fill, fit, fulfil, match up to, meet, pass, qualify, react, reciprocate, refute, rejoin, reply, resolve, respond, retaliate, retort, return, satisfy, serve, solve, succeed, suffice, suit, work.

antagonism *n.* animosity, animus, antipathy, competition, conflict, contention, discord, dissension, friction, hostility, ill-feeling, ill-will, opposition, rivalry.
antonyms rapport, sympathy.

antagonist *n.* adversary, competitor, contender, contestant, disputant, enemy, foe, opponent, opposer, rival.
antonyms ally, supporter.

anthology *n.* analects, choice, collection, compendium, compilation, digest, divan, florilegium, garland, miscellany, selection, spicilegium, treasury.

anticipate *v.* antedate, apprehend, await, bank on, beat to it, count upon, earlierize, expect, forecast, foredate, foresee, forestall, foretaste, foretell, forethink, hope for, intercept, look for, look forward to, predict, preempt, prevent.

anticipation *n.* apprehension, awaiting, expectancy, expectation, foresight, foretaste, forethought, forewarning, hope, preconception, premonition, prescience, presentiment, prodrome, prolepsis.

antics *n.* buffoonery, capers, clownery, clowning, didoes, doings, escapades, foolery, foolishness, frolics, larks, mischief, monkey tricks, playfulness, pranks, silliness, skylarking, stunts, tomfoolery, tricks, zanyism.

antipathy *n.* abhorrence, allergy, animosity, animus, antagonism, aversion, bad blood, contrariety, disgust, dislike, distaste, enmity, hate, hatred, hostility, ill-will, incompatibility, loathing, odium, opposition, rancor, repugnance, repulsion, resentment.
antonyms rapport, sympathy.

antiquated *adj.* anachronistic, ancient, antediluvian, antique, archaic, dated, démodé, elderly, fogeyish, fossilized, obsolete, old, old hat, old-fashioned, old-fogeyish, outdated, outmoded, out-of-date, outworn, passé, quaint, superannuated, unfashionable.
antonyms forward-looking, modern.

antique *adj.* aged, ancient, antiquarian, archaic, elderly, obsolete, old, old-fashioned, outdated, quaint, superannuated, vintage.
n. antiquity, bibelot, bygone, curio, curiosity, heirloom, knick-knack, museum-piece, object of virtu, period piece, rarity, relic.

anxiety *n.* angst, anxiousness, apprehension, care, concern, craving, desire, disquiet, disquietude, distress, dread, dysthymia, eagerness, foreboding, fretfulness, impatience, keenness, misgiving, nervousness, presentiment, restlessness, solicitude, suspense, tension, torment, torture, unease, uneasiness, watchfulness, willingness, worriment, worry.
antonym composure.

anxious *adj.* afraid, angst-ridden, apprehensive, avid, careful, concerned, desirous, disquieted, distressed, disturbed, eager, expectant, fearful, fretful, impatient, in suspense, intent, itching, keen, nervous, on tenterhooks, overwrought, restless, solicitous, taut, tense, tormented, tortured, troubled, uneasy, unquiet, watchful, worried, yearning.
antonym composed.

apartment *n.* accommodation, chambers, compartment, condominium, flat, living quarters, lodgings, maisonette, pad, penthouse, quarters, room, rooms, suite, tenement.

apathy *n.* accidie, acedia, coldness, coolness, emotionlessness, impassibility, impassivity, incuriousness, indifference, inertia, insensibility, lethargy, listlessness, passiveness, passivity, phlegm, sluggishness, torpor, unconcern, unfeelingness, uninterestedness, unresponsiveness.
antonyms concern, warmth.

aperture *n.* breach, chink, cleft, crack, eye, eyelet, fissure, foramen, gap, hole, interstice, opening, orifice, passage, perforation, rent, rift, slit, slot, space, vent.

apex *n.* acme, apogee, climax, consummation, crest, crown, crowning point, culmination, fastigium, height, high point, peak, pinnacle, point, summit, tip, top, vertex, zenith.
antonym nadir.

apologetic *adj.* compunctious, conscience-stricken, contrite, excusatory, penitent, regretful, remorseful, repentant, rueful, sorry.
antonym defiant.

apology *n.* acknowledgment, apologia, confession, defence, excuse, explanation, extenuation, justification, palliation, plea, semblance, substitute, travesty, vindication.
antonym defiance.

apostate *n.* defector, deserter, heretic, recidivist, recreant, renegade, renegado, runagate, tergiversator, traitor, turncoat.
antonyms adherent, convert, loyalist.
adj. disloyal, faithless, false, heretical, perfidious, recreant, renegate, traitorous, treacherous, unfaithful, unorthodox, untrue.
antonym faithful.

apostle *n.* advocate, champion, crusader, evangelist, exponent, herald, messenger, missionary, pioneer, preacher, promoter, propagandist, propagator, proponent, proselytizer.

appal *v.* alarm, astound, daunt, disconcert, disgust, dishearten, dismay, frighten, harrow, horrify, intimidate, outrage, petrify, scare, shock, terrify, unnerve.
antonyms encourage, reassure.

appalling *adj.* alarming, astounding, awful, daunting, dire, disheartening, dismaying, dreadful, fearful, frightening, frightful, ghastly, grim, harrowing, hideous, horrible, horrid, horrific, horrifying, intimidating, loathsome, petrifying, scaring, shocking, startling, terrible, terrifying, unnerving, wretched.
antonym reassuring.

apparatus *n.* appliance, bureaucracy, contraption, device, equipment, framework, gadget, gear, gismo, hierarchy, implements, machine, machinery, materials, means, mechanism, network, organization, outfit, setup, structure, system, tackle, tools, utensils.

apparel *n.* accouterments, array, attire, clothes, clothing, costume, dress, equipment, garb, garments, garniture, gear, guise, habiliments, habit, outfit, raiment, rig-out, robes, suit, trappings, vestiture, vestments, wardrobe, weeds.

apparent *adj.* clear, conspicuous, declared, discernible, distinct, evident, indubitable, manifest, marked, noticeable, obvious, on paper, open, ostensible, outward, overt, patent, perceptible, plain, seeming, specious, superficial, unmistakable, visible.
antonyms obscure, real.

apparition *n.* chimera, eidolon, ghost, manifestation, materialization, phantasm, phantom, presence, revenant, shade, specter, spirit, spook, umbra, vision, visitant, visitation, wraith.

appeal[1] *n.* adjuration, application, entreaty, imploration, invocation, orison, petition, plea, prayer, request, solicitation, suit, supplication.
v. address, adjure, apply, ask, beg, beseech, call, call upon, entreat, implore, invoke, petition, plead, pray, refer, request, resort to, solicit, sue, supplicate.

appeal[2] *n.* allure, attraction, attractiveness, beauty, charisma, charm, enchantment, fascination, interest, magnetism, winsomeness.
v. allure, attract, charm, draw, engage, entice, fascinate, interest, invite, lure, please, tempt.

appear *v.* act, arise, arrive, attend, be published, bob up, come into sight, come into view, come out, come to light, crop up, develop, emerge, enter, issue, leak out, look, loom, materialize, occur, perform, play, rise, seem, show, show up, surface, take part, transpire, turn out, turn up.
antonym disappear.

appearance *n.* advent, air, appearing, arrival, aspect, bearing, brow, cast, character, coming, début, demeanor, emergence, expression, face, facies, favor, figure, form, front, guise, illusion, image, impression, introduction, look, looks, manner, mien, physiognomy, presence, pretense, seeming, semblance, show, the cut of one's jib.
antonyms disappearance, reality.

appease *v.* allay, assuage, blunt, calm, compose, conciliate, diminish, ease, give a sop to, humor, lessen, lull, mitigate, mollify, pacify, placate, propitiate, quell, quench, quiet, reconcile, satisfy, soften, soothe, subdue, tranquilize.
antonym aggravate.

append *v.* add, adjoin, affix, annex, attach, conjoin, fasten, join, subjoin, tack on.

appendage *n.* accessory, addendum, addition, adjunct, affix, ancillary, annexe, appendix, appurtenance, attachment, auxiliary, excrescence, extremity, limb, member, projection, prosthesis, protuberance, supplement, tab, tag.

appertaining *adj.* applicable, applying, belonging, characteristic, connected, germane, pertinent, related, relevant.

appetite *n.* appetence, appetency, craving, demand, desire, eagerness, hankering, hunger, inclination, keenness, liking, limosis, longing, orexis, passion, predilection, proclivity, propensity, relish, stomach, taste, willingness, yearning, zeal, zest.
antonym distaste.

appetizer *n.* antipasto, apéritif, bonne bouche, canapé, cocktail, foretaste, hors d'oeuvre, preview, sample, taste, taster, tidbit, whet.

applaud *v.* acclaim, approve, cheer, clap, commend, compliment, congratulate, encourage, eulogize, extol, laud, ovate, praise.
antonyms censure, disparage.

appliance *n.* apparatus, contraption, contrivance, device, gadget, gismo, implement, instrument, machine, mechanism, tool.

applicable *adj.* apposite, appropriate, apropos, apt, befitting, fit, fitting, germane, legitimate, pertinent, proper, related, relevant, suitable, suited, useful, valid.
antonym inapplicable.

apply[1] *v.* adhibit, administer, appose, assign, bring into play, bring to bear, direct, employ, engage, execute, exercise, implement, ply, practice, resort to, set, use, utilize, wield.

apply[2] *v.* appertain, be relevant, fit, have force, pertain, refer, relate, suit.

apply[3] *v.* anoint, cover with, lay on, paint, place, put on, rub, smear, spread on, use.

apply[4] *v.* appeal, ask for, claim, indent for, inquire, petition, put in, request, requisition, solicit, sue.

apply[5] *v.* address, bend, buckle down, commit, concentrate, dedicate, devote, direct, give, persevere, settle down, study, throw.

appoint *v.* allot, arrange, assign, charge, choose, command, commission, constitute, co-opt, decide, decree, delegate, designate, destine, detail, determine, devote, direct, elect, engage, enjoin, equip, establish, fit out, fix, furnish, install, name, nominate, ordain, outfit, plenish, provide, select, set, settle, supply.
antonyms dismiss, reject.

appointment *n.* allotment, arrangement, assignation, assignment, choice, choosing, commissioning, consultation, date, delegation, election, engagement, installation, interview, job, meeting, naming, nomination, office, place, position, post, rendezvous, selection, session, situation, station, tryst.

appraise *v.* assay, assess, estimate, evaluate, examine, gauge, inspect, judge, price, rate, review, size up, survey, valuate, value.

appreciate[1] *v.* acknowledge, admire, be sensible of, be sensitive to, cherish, comprehend, dig, do justice to, enjoy, esteem, estimate, know, like, perceive, prize, realize, recognize, regard, relish, respect, savor, sympathize with, take kindly to, treasure, understand, value.
antonyms despise, overlook.

appreciate[2] *v.* enhance, gain, grow, improve, increase, inflate, mount, rise, strengthen.
antonym depreciate.

apprehend[1] *v.* arrest, bust, capture, catch, collar, detain, get, grab, nab, nick, pinch, run in, seize, take.

apprehend[2] *v.* appreciate, believe, comprehend, conceive, consider, discern, grasp, imagine, know, perceive, realize, recognize, see, twig, understand.

apprehension[1] *n.* arrest, capture, catching, seizure, taking.

apprehension[2] *n.* alarm, anxiety, apprehensiveness, awareness, belief, comprehension, concept, conception, concern, conjecture, discernment, disquiet, doubt, dread, fear, fore-boding, grasp, idea, impression, intellect, intellection, intelligence, ken, knowledge, misgiving, mistrust, nervousness, notion, opinion, perception, premonition, presentiment, qualm, sentiment, suspicion, thought, understanding, unease, uneasiness, uptake, view, worry.

apprehensive *adj.* afraid, alarmed, anxious, concerned, disquieted, distrustful, disturbed, doubtful, fearful, mistrustful, nervous, solicitous, suspicious, uneasy, worried.
antonym confident.

apprentice *n.* beginner, cub, learner, neophyte, newcomer, novice, probationer, pupil, recruit, starter, student, trainee, tyro.
antonym expert.

approach *v.* advance, anear, appeal to, apply to, approximate, be like, begin, broach, catch up, come close, come near to, commence, compare with, draw near, embark on, gain on, introduce, make advances, make overtures, meet, mention, near, reach, resemble, set about, sound out, undertake.
n. access, advance, advent, appeal, application, approximation, arrival, attitude, avenue, course, doorway, entrance, gesture, invitation, landfall, likeness, manner, means, method, mode, modus operandi, motion, nearing, offer, overture, passage, procedure, proposal, proposition, resemblance, road, semblance, style, system, technique, threshold, way.

appropriate *adj.* applicable, apposite, appurtenant, apropos, apt, becoming, befitting, belonging, condign, congruous, correct, felicitous, fit, fitting, germane, meet, merited, opportune, pertinent, proper, relevant, right, seasonable, seemly, spot-on, suitable, timely, to the point, well-chosen, well-suited, well-timed.
antonym inappropriate.
v. allocate, allot, annex, apportion, arrogate, assign, assume, commandeer, confiscate, devote, earmark, embezzle, expropriate, filch, impound, impropriate, misappropriate, pilfer, pocket, possess oneself of, pre-empt, purloin, seize, set apart, steal, take, usurp.

approval *n.* acclaim, acclamation, acquiescence, admiration, adoption, agreement, applause, appreciation, approbation, approof, assent, authorization, blessing, certification, commendation, compliance, concurrence, confirmation, consent, countenance, endorsement, esteem, favor, go-ahead, good opinion, green light, honor, imprimatur, leave, licence, liking, mandate, OK, permission, plaudits, praise, ratification, recommendation, regard, respect, sanction, support, validation. *antonym* disapproval.

approve *v.* accede to, accept, acclaim, admire, adopt, advocate, agree to, allow, applaud, appreciate, assent to, authorize, back, bless, commend, comply with, concur in, confirm, consent to, countenance, dig, endorse, esteem, favor, homologate, like, mandate, OK, pass, permit, praise, ratify, recommend, regard, respect, rubber-stamp, sanction, second, support, take kindly to, uphold, validate. *antonym* disapprove.

approximate *adj.* close, comparable, conjectural, estimated, extrapolated, guessed, inexact, like, loose, near, relative, rough, similar, verging on. *antonym* exact. *v.* approach, be tantamount to, border on, resemble, verge on.

apt *adj.* accurate, adept, applicable, apposite, appropriate, apropos, astute, befitting, bright, clever, condign, correct, disposed, expert, fair, fit, fitting, germane, gifted, given, inclined, ingenious, intelligent, liable, likely, meet, pertinent, prompt, prone, proper, quick, ready, relevant, seasonable, seemly, sharp, skilful, smart, spot-on, suitable, talented, teachable, tending, timely. *antonym* inapt.

aptitude *n.* ability, aptness, bent, capability, capacity, cleverness, disposition, facility, faculty, flair, gift, inclination, intelligence, knack, leaning, penchant, predilection, proclivity, proficiency, proneness, propensity, quickness, talent, tendency. *antonym* inaptitude.

aptness *n.* ability, accuracy, applicability, appositeness, appropriateness, aptitude, becomingness, bent, capability, capacity, cleverness, condignness, congruousness, correctness, disposition, facility, faculty, felicitousness, felicity, fitness, fittingness, flair, germaneness, gift, inclination, intelligence, knack, leaning, liability, likelihood, likeliness, opportuneness, pertinence, predilection, proclivity, proficiency, proneness, propensity, properness, quickness, readiness, relevance, rightness, seemliness, suitability, talent, tendency, timeliness.

arbitrary *adj.* absolute, autocratic, capricious, chance, despotic, dictatorial, discretionary, dogmatic, domineering, erratic, fanciful, high-handed, imperious, inconsistent, instinctive, magisterial, optional, overbearing, peremptory, personal, random, subjective, summary, tyrannical, tyrannous, unreasonable, unreasoned, unsupported, whimsical, wilful. *antonyms* circumspect, rational, reasoned.

architecture *n.* architectonics, arrangement, building, composition, construction, design, framework, make-up, planning, structure, style.

ardent *adj.* amorous, avid, devoted, eager, enthusiastic, fervent, fervid, fierce, fiery, hot, hot-blooded, impassioned, intense, keen, lusty, passionate, perfervid, spirited, vehement, warm, zealous. *antonym* dispassionate.

ardor *n.* animation, avidity, devotion, eagerness, earnestness, empressement, enthusiasm, feeling, fervor, fire, heat, intensity, keenness, lust, passion, spirit, vehemence, warmth, zeal, zest. *antonyms* coolness, indifference.

arduous *adj.* backbreaking, burdensome, daunting, difficult, exhausting, fatiguing, formidable, grueling, hard, harsh, herculean, laborious, onerous, punishing, rigorous, severe, strenuous, taxing, tiring, toilsome, tough, troublesome, trying, uphill, wearisome. *antonym* easy.

area *n.* arena, bailiwick, ball-park, breadth, canvas, compass, department, district, domain, environs, expanse, extent, field, locality, neighborhood, part, patch, portion, province, range, realm, region, scope, section, sector, size, sphere, stretch, terrain, territory, tract, width, zone.

argue *v.* altercate, argufy, assert, bicker, chop logic, claim, contend, convince, debate, demonstrate, denote, disagree, discuss, display, dispute, evidence, evince, exhibit, expostulate, fall out, fence, feud, fight, haggle, hold, imply, indicate, join issue, logicize, maintain, manifest, moot, persuade, plead, prevail upon, prove, quarrel, question, reason, remonstrate, show, squabble, suggest, talk into, wrangle.

argument *n.* abstract, altercation, argumentation, assertion, barney, beef, bickering, case, claim, clash, contention, controversy, debate, defence, demonstration, dialectic, difference, disagreement, discussion, dispute, exposition, expostulation, feud, fight, gist, ground, lemma, logic, logomachy, outline, plea, pleading, plot, polemic, quarrel, questioning, quodlibet, reason, reasoning, remonstrance, remonstration, row, set-to, shouting-match, squabble, story, story line, subject, summary, synopsis, theme, thesis, wrangle.

arid *adj.* baked, barren, boring, colorless, desert, desiccated, dreary, droughty, dry, dull, empty, flat, infertile, jejune, lifeless, moistureless, monotonous, parched, spiritless, sterile, tedious, torrid, torrefied, uninspired, uninteresting, unproductive, vapid, waste, waterless. *antonyms* fertile, lively.

arise *v.* appear, ascend, begin, climb, come to light, commence, crop up, derive, emanate, emerge, ensue, flow, follow, get up, go up, grow, happen, issue, lift, mount, occur, originate, proceed, result, rise, set in, soar, spring, stand up, start, stem, tower, wake up.

aristocrat *n.* eupatrid, grand seigneur, grande dame, grandee, lady, lord, lordling, nob, noble, nobleman, noblewoman, optimate, patrician, peer, peeress, swell, toff.

antonym commoner.

arm[1] *n.* appendage, authority, bough, brachium, branch, channel, department, detachment, division, estuary, extension, firth, inlet, limb, offshoot, projection, section, sector, sound, strait, sway, tributary, upper limb.

arm[2] *v.* accouter, ammunition, array, brace, empanoply, equip, forearm, fortify, furnish, gird, issue with, munition, outfit, prepare, prime, protect, provide, reinforce, rig, steel, strengthen, supply.

army *n.* armed force, array, arrière-ban, cohorts, gang, horde, host, land forces, legions, military, militia, mob, multitude, pack, soldiers, soldiery, swarm, the junior service, throng, troops.

aroma *n.* bouquet, fragrance, fumet(te), odor, perfume, redolence, savor, scent, smell.

arouse *v.* agitate, animate, awaken, bestir, call forth, disentrance, enliven, evoke, excite, foment, foster, galvanize, goad, incite, inflame, instigate, kindle, move, prompt, provoke, quicken, rouse, sharpen, spark, spur, startle, stimulate, stir up, summon up, wake up, waken, warm, whet, whip up.

antonyms calm, lull, quieten.

arraign *v.* accuse, attack, call to account, charge, denounce, impeach, impugn, incriminate, indict, prosecute.

arrange[1] *v.* adjust, align, array, categorize, class, classify, collocate, concert, construct, contrive, co-ordinate, design, determine, devise, dispose, distribute, fettle, file, fix, form, group, lay out, marshal, methodize, order, organise, plan, position, prepare, project, range, rank, regulate, schedule, set out, settle, sift, sort, sort out, stage-manage, style, swing, systematize, tidy, trim.

arrange[2] *v.* adapt, harmonize, instrument, orchestrate, score, set.

arrangement[1] *n.* adjustment, agreement, alignment, array, Ausgleich, battery, classification, compact, compromise, construction, deal, design, display, disposition, form, grouping, layout, line-up, marshaling, method, modus vivendi, order, ordering, organization, plan, planning, preconcert, preparation, provision, ranging, rank, schedule, scheme, settlement, set-up, spacing, structure, system, tabulation, taxis, terms.

arrangement[2] *n.* adaptation, harmonization, instrumentation, interpretation, orchestration, score, setting, version.

array *n.* apparel, arrangement, assemblage, attire, battery, clothes, collection, display, disposition, dress, equipage, exhibition, exposition, finery, formation, garb, garments, line-up, marshaling, muster, order, parade, raiment, regalia, robes, show, supply.

v. accouter, adorn, align, apparel, arrange, assemble, attire, bedeck, bedizen, caparison, clothe, deck, decorate, display, dispose, draw up, dress, equip, exhibit, form up, garb, group, habilitate, line up, marshal, muster, order, outfit, parade, range, rig out, robe, show, supply, trick out, wrap.

arrest *v.* absorb, apprehend, block, bust, capture, catch, check, collar, delay, detain, divert, end, engage, engross, fascinate, grip, halt, hinder, hold, impede, inhibit, interrupt, intrigue, lay, nab, nick, nip, obstruct, occupy, pinch, prevent, restrain, retard, run in, seize, slow, stall, stanch, stay, stem, stop, suppress.

n. apprehension, blockage, bust, caption, capture, cessation, check, cop, delay, detention, end, halt, hindrance, inhibition, interruption, obstruction, prevention, restraint, seizure, stalling, stay, stoppage, suppression, suspension.

arrival *n.* accession, advent, appearance, approach, caller, comer, coming, débutant(e), entrance, entrant, happening, incomer, landfall, newcomer, occurrence, visitant, visitor.

antonym departure.

arrive *v.* alight, appear, attain, befall, come, enter, fetch, get to the top, happen, land, make it, materialize, occur, reach, show, show up, succeed, turn up.

antonyms depart.

arrogance *n.* airs, conceit, conceitedness, condescension, contempt, contemptuousness, contumely, disdain, disdainfulness, haughtiness, hauteur, high-handedness, hubris, imperiousness, insolence, loftiness, lordliness, morgue, presumption, presumptuousness, pretension, pretentiousness, pride, scorn, scornfulness, superciliousness, superiority, uppishness.

antonym humility.

arrogant *adj.* assuming, conceited, condescending, contemptuous, contumelious, disdainful, fastuous, haughty, high and mighty, high-handed, hubristic, imperious, insolent, lordly, on the high ropes, overbearing, overweening, presumptuous, proud, scornful, supercilious, superior, uppish.

antonym humble.

art *n.* address, adroitness, aptitude, artfulness, artifice, artistry, artwork, astuteness, contrivance, craft, craftiness, craftsmanship, cunning, deceit, dexterity, draughtsmanship, drawing, expertise, facility, finesse, guile, ingenuity, knack, knowledge, mastery, method, métier, painting, profession, sculpture, skill, slyness, subtlety, trade, trick, trickery, virtu, virtuosity, visuals, wiliness.

artful *adj.* adept, adroit, canny, clever, crafty, cunning, deceitful, designing, devious, dexterous, fly, foxy, ingenious, masterly, politic, resourceful, rusé, scheming, sharp, shrewd, skilful, sly, smart, subtle, tricksy, tricky, vulpine, wily.

antonyms artless, ingenuous, naïve.

article *n.* account, bit, clause, commodity, composition, constituent, count, detail, discourse, division, element, essay, feature, head, heading, item, matter, object, paper, paragraph, part, particular, piece, point, portion, report, review, section, story, thing, unit.

artifice *n.* adroitness, artfulness, chicanery, cleverness, contrivance, cozenage, craft, craftiness, cunning, deception, deftness, device, dodge, duplicity, expedient, facility, finesse, fraud, guile, hoax, invention, machination, maneuver, manipulation, ruse, scheme, shift, skill, slyness, stratagem, strategy, subterfuge, subtlety, tactic, trick, trickery, wile.

artificial *adj.* affected, assumed, bogus, contrived, counterfeit, ersatz, factitious, fake, false, feigned, forced, hyped up, imitation, insincere, made-up, man-made, mannered, manufactured, meretricious, mock, nonnatural, phony, plastic, pretended, pseudo, sham, simulated, specious, spurious, stagey, synthetic, unnatural. *antonyms* genuine, natural.

artisan *n.* artificer, craftsman, expert, handicraftsman, journeyman, mechanic, operative, technician, workman.

artist *n.* colorist, craftsman, draughtsman, expert, maestro, master, painter, portraitist, portrait-painter, sculptor, water-colorist.

artless *adj.* candid, childlike, direct, frank, genuine, guileless, honest, humble, ingenuous, innocent, naïf, naïve, naked, natural, open, plain, primitive, pure, simple, sincere, straightforward, true, trustful, trusting, unadorned, unaffected, uncontrived, undesigning, unpretentious, unsophisticated, unwary, unworldly. *antonym* artful.

ascend *v.* climb, float up, fly up, go up, lift off, mount, move up, rise, scale, slope upwards, soar, take off, tower. *antonym* descend.

ascertain *v.* confirm, detect, determine, discover, establish, find out, fix, identify, learn, locate, make certain, settle, verify.

ascribe *v.* accredit, arrogate, assign, attribute, chalk up to, charge, credit, impute, put down.

ashamed *adj.* abashed, apologetic, bashful, blushing, chagrined, confused, conscience-stricken, crestfallen, discomfited, comfited, discomposed, distressed, embarrassed, guilty, hesitant, humbled, humiliated, modest, mortified, prudish, red in the face, redfaced, reluctant, remorseful, self-conscious, shamefaced, sheepish, shy, sorry, unwilling, verecund. *antonyms* defiant, shameless.

ask *v.* appeal, apply, beg, beseech, bid, catechize, claim, clamor, crave, demand, enquire, entreat, implore, importune, indent, interrogate, invite, order, petition, plead, pray, press, query, question, quiz, request, require, seek, solicit, sue, summon, supplicate.

askance *adv.* contemptuously, disapprovingly, disdainfully, distrustfully, doubtfully, dubiously, indirectly, mistrustfully, obliquely, sceptically, scornfully, sideways, suspiciously.

askew *adv., adj.* aglee, agley, aslant, asymmetric, awry, cock-eyed, crooked, crookedly, lopsided, oblique, offcenter, out of line, skew, skew-whiff, squint.

asleep *adj.* benumbed, comatose, dead to the world, dormant, dormient, dozing, fast asleep, inactive, inert, napping, numb, reposing, sleeping, slumbering, snoozing, sound asleep, unconscious.

aspect *n.* air, angle, appearance, attitude, bearing, condition, countenance, demeanor, direction, elevation, exposure, expression, face, facet, feature, look, manner, mien, outlook, physiognomy, point of view, position, prospect, scene, side, situation, standpoint, view, visage.

aspersion *n.* abuse, animadversion, calumny, censure, criticism, defamation, denigration, derogation, detraction, disparagement, mud-slinging, obloquy, reproach, slander, slur, smear, traducement, vilification, vituperation. *antonyms* commendation, compliment.

asphyxiate *v.* burke, choke, garrotte, smother, stifle, strangle, strangulate, suffocate, throttle.

aspirant *n.* applicant, aspirer, candidate, competitor, contestant, hopeful, postulant, seeker, striver, suitor.

aspire *v.* aim, crave, desire, dream, ettle, hanker, hope, intend, long, purpose, pursue, seek, wish, yearn.

aspiring *adj.* ambitious, aspirant, eager, endeavoring, enterprising, hopeful, keen, longing, optimistic, striving, wishful, would-be.

ass[1] *n.* blockhead, bonehead, cretin, dolt, dope, dunce, fool, half-wit, idiot, moron, nincompoop, ninny, nitwit, numskull, schmuck, simpleton, twerp, twit.

ass[2] *n.* burro, cardophagus, cuddy, donkey, hinny, jackass, jenny, Jerusalem pony, moke, mule.

assail *v.* abuse, assault, attack, belabor, berate, beset, bombard, charge, criticize, encounter, fall upon, impugn, invade, lay into, malign, maltreat, pelt, revile, set about, set upon, strike, vilify.

assassinate *v.* dispatch, eliminate, hit, kill, liquidate, murder, rub out, slay.

assault *n.* aggression, attack, blitz, charge, incursion, invasion, offensive, onset, onslaught, raid, storm, storming, strike.
v. assail, attack, beset, charge, fall on, hit, invade, lay violent hands on, set upon, storm, strike.

assemble *v.* accumulate, amass, build, collect, compose, congregate, construct, convene, convocate, convoke, erect, fabricate, flock, forgather, gather, group, join up, levy, make, manufacture, marshal, meet, mobilize, muster, muster (up), piece, rally, round up, set up, summon, together. *antonym* disperse.

assembly *n.* agora, assemblage, ball, body, building, caucus, collection, company, conclave, concourse, conference, congregation, congress, consistory, construction, convention, convocation, council, crowd, diet, divan, ecclesia, erection, fabrication, fitting, flock, gathering, group, indaba, joining, levy, manufacture, mass, meeting, moot, multitude, panegyry, rally, reception, setting up, soirée, synod, throng.

assent *v.* accede, accept, acquiesce, agree, allow, approve, comply, concede, concur, consent, grant, permit, sanction, submit, subscribe, yield.
antonym disagree. *n.* acceptance, accession, accord, acquiescence, agreement, approval, capitulation, compliance, concession, concurrence, consent, permission, sanction, submission.

assert *v.* advance, affirm, allege, asseverate, attest, aver, avouch, avow, claim, constate, contend, declare, defend, dogmatize, insist, lay down, maintain, predicate, press, profess, promote, pronounce, protest, state, stress, swear, testify to, thrust forward, uphold, vindicate.
antonym deny.

assertion *n.* affirmance, affirmation, allegation, asseveration, attestation, averment, avowal, claim, constatation, contention, declaration, dictum, gratis dictum, ipse dixit, predication, profession, pronouncement, statement, vindication, vouch, word.
antonym denial.

assess *v.* appraise, compute, consider, demand, determine, estimate, evaluate, fix, gauge, impose, investigate, judge, levy, rate, reckon, review, size up, tax, value, weigh.

asset *n.* advantage, aid, benefit, blessing, help, plus, resource, service, strength, virtue.
antonym liability.

assign *v.* accredit, adjudge, allocate, allot, apart, appoint, apportion, arrogate, ascribe, attribute, choose, consign, delegate, designate, determine, dispense, distribute, fix, give, grant, name, nominate, put down, select, set, specify, stipulate.

assignment *n.* allocation, allotment, appointment, apportionment, ascription, attribution, charge, commission, consignment, delegation, designation, determination, dispensation, distribution, duty, errand, giving, grant, imposition, job, mission, nomination, position, post, responsibility, selection, specification, task.

assimilate *v.* absorb, accept, acclimatize, accommodate, acculturate, accustom, adapt, adjust, blend, conform, digest, fit, homogenize, imbibe, incorporate, ingest, intermix, learn, merge, mingle, take in, tolerate.
antonym reject.

assist *v.* abet, accommodate, aid, back, benefit, bestead, boost, collaborate, co-operate, enable, expedite, facilitate, further, help, rally round, reinforce, relieve, second, serve, succor, support, sustain.
antonym thwart.

assistance *n.* a leg up, abetment, accommodation, adjutancy, aid, backing, benefit, boost, collaboration, comfort, co-operation, furtherance, help, reinforcement, relief, succor, support, sustainment.
antonym hindrance.

assistant *n.* abettor, accessory, accomplice, adjutant, aide, ally, ancillary, associate, auxiliary, backer, coadjutor, collaborator, colleague, confederate, co-operator, Girl Friday, helper, helpmate, henchman, Man Friday, partner, Person Friday, right-hand man, second, subordinate, subsidiary, supporter.

associate *v.* accompany, affiliate, ally, amalgamate, combine, company, confederate, conjoin, connect, consort, correlate, couple, fraternize, hang around, hobnob, identify, join, league, link, mingle, mix, pair, relate, socialize, unite, yoke.
n. affiliate, ally, assistant, bedfellow, coadjutor, collaborator, colleague, companion, compeer, comrade, confederate, confrère, co-worker, fellow, follower, friend, leaguer, mate, partner, peer, side-kick.

association *n.* affiliation, alliance, analogy, band, blend, bloc, bond, cartel, clique, club, coalition, combination, combine, companionship, company, compound, comradeship, concomitance, confederacy, confederation, connection, consociation, consortium, conspiracy, co-operative, corporation, correlation, familiarity, federation, fellowship, fraternization, fraternity, friendship, Gesellschaft, group, intimacy, joining, juxtaposition, league, linkage, mixture, organization, pairing, partnership, relation, relations, relationship, resemblance, society, syndicate, syndication, tie, trust, union, Verein.

assortment *n.* arrangement, array, assemblage, categorization, choice, classification, collection, disposition, distribution, diversity, farrago, grading, grouping, hotchpotch, jumble, medley, mélange, miscellany, mishmash, mixture, olio, olla-podrida, pot-pourri, ranging, salad, salmagundi, selection, sift, sifting, sorting, variety.

assuage *v.* allay, alleviate, appease, calm, dull, ease, lessen, lighten, lower, lull, mitigate, moderate, mollify, pacify, palliate, quench, quieten, reduce, relieve, satisfy, slake, soften, soothe, still, temper, tranquilize.
antonym exacerbate.

assume *v.* accept, acquire, adopt, affect, appropriate, arrogate, believe, commandeer, counterfeit, deduce, don, embrace, expect, expropriate, fancy, feign, guess, imagine, infer, opine, postulate, pre-empt, premise, presume, presuppose, pretend to, put on, seize, sham, shoulder, simulate, strike, suppose, surmise, suspect, take, take for granted, take on, take over, take up, think, understand, undertake, usurp.

assumption *n.* acceptance, acquisition, adoption, appropriation, arrogance, arrogation, audacity, belief, bumptiousness, conceit, conjecture, expectation, expropriation, fancy, guess, guesswork, hypothesis, impudence, inference, postulate, postulation, pre-emption, premise, premiss, presumption, presumptuousness, presupposition, pride, seizure, self-importance, supposition, surmise, suspicion, theory, understanding, undertaking, usurpation.

assurance *n.* affirmation, aplomb, assertion, asseveration, assuredness, audacity, boldness, certainty, certitude, chutzpah, confidence, conviction, coolness, courage, declaration, firmness, gall, guarantee, nerve, oath, pledge, plerophory, poise, positiveness, profession, promise, protestation, security, self-confidence, self-reliance, sureness, vow, word.

antonym uncertainty.

assure *v.* affirm, attest, boost, certify, clinch, comfort, confirm, convince, embolden, encourage, ensure, guarantee, hearten, persuade, pledge, promise, reassure, seal, secure, soothe, strengthen, swear, tell, vow, warrant.

astonish *v.* amaze, astound, baffle, bewilder, confound, daze, dumbfound, electrify, flabbergast, floor, nonplus, shock, stagger, startle, stun, stupefy, surprise, wow.

astound *v.* abash, amaze, astonish, baffle, bewilder, confound, daze, dumbfound, electrify, flabbergast, overwhelm, shake, shock, stagger, stun, stupefy, surprise, wow.

astute *adj.* acute, adroit, artful, astucious, calculating, canny, clever, crafty, cunning, discerning, fly, foxy, intelligent, keen, knowing, penetrating, perceptive, percipient, perspicacious, politic, prudent, sagacious, sharp, shrewd, sly, subtle, wily, wise.

antonym stupid.

asunder *adv.* apart, in half, in pieces, in twain, in two, into pieces, to bits, to pieces.

asylum *n.* bedlam, bughouse, cover, funny farm, harbor, haven, hospital, institution, loony-bin, madhouse, mental hospital, nuthouse, preserve, refuge, reserve, retreat, safety, sanctuary, shelter.

athletic *adj.* active, brawny, energetic, fit, husky, muscular, powerful, robust, sinewy, strapping, strong, sturdy, thewy, vigorous, well-knit, well-proportioned, wiry.

antonym puny.

atone *v.* aby(e), compensate, expiate, make amends, make up for, offset, pay for, propitiate, recompense, reconcile, redeem, redress, remedy.

atrocious *adj.* abominable, barbaric, brutal, cruel, diabolical, execrable, fell, fiendish, flagitious, ghastly, grievous, heinous, hideous, horrible, horrifying, infamous, infernal, inhuman, monstrous, piacular, ruthless, savage, shocking, terrible, vicious, vile, villainous, wicked.

attach *v.* add, adhere, adhibit, affix, annex, append, articulate, ascribe, assign, associate, attract, attribute, belong, bind, captivate, combine, connect, couple, fasten, fix, impute, join, link, place, put, relate to, secure, stick, tie, unite, weld.

antonyms detach, unfasten.

attachment *n.* accessory, accouterment, adapter, addition, adhesion, adhibition, adjunct, affection, affinity, appendage, appurtenance, attraction, bond, codicil, cohesion, confiscation, connection, connector, coupling, devotion, esteem, extension, extra, fastener, fastening, fidelity, fitting, fixture, fondness, friendship, joint, junction, liking, link, love, loyalty, partiality, predilection, regard, seizure, supplement, tenderness, tie.

attack *n.* abuse, access, aggression, assailment, assault, battery, blitz, bombardment, bout, broadside, censure, charge, convulsion, criticism, fit, foray, impugnment, incursion, inroad, invasion, invective, kamikaze, offensive, onset, onslaught, paroxysm, raid, rush, seizure, spasm, spell, strike, stroke.

v. abuse, assail, assault, belabor, berate, blame, censure, charge, chastise, criticize, denounce, do over, fake, fall on, flay, have one's knife in, impugn, invade, inveigh against, lash, lay into, light into, make at, malign, mob, put the boot in, raid, rate, revile, rush, set about, set on, snipe, storm, strafe, strike, vilify, visit, wade into.

attain *v.* accomplish, achieve, acquire, arrive at, bag, compass, complete, earn, effect, fulfil, gain, get, grasp, net, obtain, procure, reach, realize, reap, secure, touch, win.

attainment *n.* ability, accomplishment, achievement, acquirement, acquisition, aptitude, art, capability, competence, completion, consummation, facility, feat, fulfilment, gift, mastery, procurement, proficiency, reaching, realization, skill, success, talent.

attempt *n.* assault, assay, attack, bash, bid, coup d'essai, crack, effort, endeavor, essay, experiment, go, move, push, shot, shy, stab, struggle, trial, try, undertaking, venture. *v.* aspire, endeavor, essay, experiment, have a bash, have a crack, have a go, have a shot, seek, strive, tackle, try, try one's hand at, try one's luck at, undertake, venture.

attend *v.* accompany, appear, arise from, assist, be all ears, be present, care for, chaperon, companion, convoy, escort, follow, frequent, give ear, guard, hear, hearken, heed, help, lend an ear, listen, look after, mark, mind, minister to, note, notice, nurse, observe, pay attention, pay heed, pin back one's ears, regard, result from, serve, squire, succor, take care of, tend, usher, visit, wait upon, watch.

attendant *n.* accompanier, acolyte, aide, assistant, auxiliary, batman, bed captain, chaperon, companion, custodian, equerry, escort, famulus, flunkey, follower, ghillie, guard, guide, helper, jäger, lackey, lady-help, lady-in-waiting, lady's-maid, livery-servant, marshal, menial, page, poursuivant, retainer, servant, steward, underling, usher, waiter.

adj. accessory, accompanying, associated, attached, concomitant, consequent, incidental, related, resultant, subsequent.

attention *n.* advertence, advertency, alertness, attentiveness, awareness, care, civility, concentration, concern, consciousness, consideration, contemplation, courtesy, deference, ear, gallantry, heed, heedfulness, intentness, mindfulness, ministration, notice, observation, politeness, recognition, regard, respect, service, thought, thoughtfulness, treatment, vigilance.

antonyms disregard, inattention.

attentive *adj.* accommodating, advertent, alert, awake, careful, civil, concentrating, conscientious, considerate, courteous, deferential, devoted, gallant, gracious, heedful, intent, kind, mindful, obliging, observant, polite, regardant, studious, thoughtful, vigilant, watchful.

antonyms heedless, inattentive, inconsiderate.

attest *v.* adjure, affirm, assert, authenticate, aver, certify, confirm, corroborate, declare, demonstrate, depose, display, endorse, evidence, evince, exhibit, manifest, prove, ratify, seal, show, substantiate, swear, testify, verify, vouch, warrant, witness.

attire *n.* accouterments, apparel, array, clothes, clothing, costume, dress, finery, garb, garments, gear, get-up, habiliments, habit, outfit, raiment, rig-out, robes, togs, uniform, vestment, wear, weeds.

v. accouter, adorn, apparel, array, caparison, clothe, costume, deck out, dress, equip, garb, habilitate, outfit, prepare, rig out, robe, turn out.

attitude *n.* affectation, air, Anschauung, approach, aspect, bearing, carriage, condition, demeanor, disposition, feeling, manner, mien, mood, opinion, outlook, perspective, point of view, pose, position, posture, stance, view, Weltanschauung.

attractive *adj.* agreeable, alluring, appealing, appetible, beautiful, beddable, captivating, catching, catchy, charming, comely, enchanting, engaging, enticing, epigamous, fair, fascinating, fetching, glamorous, good-looking, gorgeous, handsome, interesting, inviting, jolie laide, lovely, magnetic, nubile, personable, pleasant, pleasing, prepossessing, pretty, seductive, snazzy, stunning, taky, tempting, toothsome, voluptuous, winning, winsome.

antonyms repellent, unattractive.

attribute *v.* accredit, apply, arrogate, ascribe, assign, blame, charge, credit, impute, put down, refer.

n. affection, aspect, character, characteristic, facet, feature, idiosyncrasy, mark, note, peculiarity, point, property, quality, quirk, sign, symbol, trait, virtue.

auction *n.* cant, roup, sale, vendue.

audacious *adj.* adventurous, assuming, assured, bold, brave, brazen, cheeky, courageous, dare-devil, daring, dauntless, death-defying, der-doing, disrespectful, enterprising, fearless, forward, impertinent, impudent, insolent, intrepid, pert, plucky, presumptuous, rash, reckless, risky, rude, shameless, unabashed, valiant, venturesome.

antonyms cautious, reserved, timid.

audacity *n.* adventurousness, assurance, audaciousness, boldness, brass neck, bravery, brazenness, cheek, chutzpah, courage, daring, dauntlessness, defiance, derring-do, disrespectfulness, effrontery, enterprise, fearlessness, foolhardiness, forwardness, gall, guts, impertinence, impudence, insolence, intrepidity, nerve, pertness, presumption, rashness, recklessness, rudeness, shamelessness, valor, venturesomeness.

antonyms caution, reserve, timidity.

audible *adj.* appreciable, clear, detectable, discernible, distinct, hearable, perceptible, recognizable.

antonym inaudible.

augment *v.* add to, amplify, boost, dilate, eke out, enhance, enlarge, expand, extend, grow, heighten, increase, inflate, intensify, magnify, multiply, raise, reinforce, strengthen, supplement, swell.

antonym decrease.

auspicious *adj.* bright, cheerful, encouraging, favorable, felicitous, fortunate, happy, hopeful, lucky, opportune, optimistic, promising, propitious, prosperous, rosy, white.

antonyms inauspicious, ominous.

austere *adj.* abstemious, abstinent, ascetic, astringent, bitter, bleak, chaste, cold, conservative, continent, Dantean, Dantesque, economical, exacting, forbidding, formal, grave, grim, hard, harsh, plain, puritanical, restrained, rigid, rigorous, self-denying, self-disciplined, serious, severe, simple, sober, solemn, sour, spare, Spartan, stark, stern, strict, stringent, unadorned, unembellished, unornamented, unrelenting.

antonyms elaborate, extravagant, genial.

authentic *adj.* accurate, actual, authoritative, bona fide, certain, dependable, dinkum, factual, faithful, genuine, honest, kosher, legitimate, original, pure, real, reliable, simon-pure, true, true-to-life, trustworthy, valid, veracious, veritable.

antonyms counterfeit, inauthentic, spurious.

authenticate *v.* accredit, attest, authorize, avouch, certify, confirm, corroborate, endorse, guarantee, validate, verify, vouch for, warrant.

author *n.* architect, begetter, composer, creator, designer, fabricator, fashioner, father, forger, founder, framer, initiator, inventor, maker, mover, originator, paperstainer, parent, pen, penman, penwoman, planner, prime mover, producer, volumist, writer.

authoritative *adj.* accepted, accurate, approved, assured, authentic, authorized, cathedratic, commanding, confident, convincing, decisive, definitive, dependable, factual, faithful, learned, legitimate, magisterial, magistrial, masterly, official, reliable, sanctioned, scholarly, sound, sovereign, true, trustworthy, truthful, valid, veritable.

antonym unreliable.

authority[1] *n.* administration, ascendancy, attestation, authorization, avowal, charge, command, control, declaration, domination, dominion, evidence, force, government, imperium, influence, jurisdiction, justification, licence, management, might, officialdom, permission, permit, power, prerogative, profession, right, rule, sanction, sovereignty, statement, strength, supremacy, sway, testimony, textbook, warrant, weight, word.

authority[2] *n.* arbiter, bible, connoisseur, expert, judge, master, professional, pundit, sage, scholar, specialist.

autocrat *n.* absolutist, authoritarian, Caesar, cham, despot, dictator, fascist, Hitler, panjandrum, totalitarian, tyrant.

automatic *adj.* automated, certain, habitual, inescapable, inevitable, instinctive, involuntary, mechanical, mechanized, natural, necessary, perfunctory, push-button, reflex, robot, robot-like, routine, self-acting, self-activating, self-moving, self-propelling, self-regulating, spontaneous, unavoidable, unbidden, unconscious, unthinking, unwilled, vegetative.

automobile *n.* armored car, convertible, coupe, fastback, gocart, hot rod, jeep, land-rover, limousine, racing car, roadster, sedan, sports car, station wagon.

auxiliary *adj.* accessory, adjuvant, adminicular, aiding, ancillary, assistant, assisting, back-up, emergency, helping, reserve, secondary, subsidiary, substitute, supplementary, supporting, supportive.
n. accessory, accomplice, adminicle, ally, ancillary, assistant, associate, companion, confederate, foederatus, helper, partner, reserve, subordinate, supporter.

avail *v.* advance, advantage, aid, assist, benefit, boot, dow, exploit, help, make the most of, profit, serve, work.
n. advantage, aid, assistance, benefit, boot, good, help, profit, purpose, service, use, value.

available *adj.* accessible, at hand, attainable, convenient, disengaged, free, handy, obtainable, on hand, on tap, procurable, ready, to hand, vacant, within reach.
antonym unavailable.

avarice *n.* acquisitiveness, cheese-paring, covetousness, cupidity, greed, greediness, meanness, miserliness, niggardliness, parsimoniousness, parsimony, penny-pinching, penuriousness, predatoriness, rapacity, stinginess, tight-fistedness.
antonym generosity.

average *n.* mean, mediocrity, medium, midpoint, norm, par, rule, run, standard.
antonyms exception, extreme.
adj. common, commonplace, everyday, fair, general, indifferent, intermediate, mean, medial, median, mediocre, medium, middle, middling, moderate, normal, ordinary, passable, regular, run-of-the-mill, satisfactory, so-so, standard, tolerable, typical, undistinguished, unexceptional, unremarkable, usual.
antonyms exceptional, extreme.

averse *adj.* antagonistic, antipathetic, disapproving, disinclined, hostile, ill-disposed, inimical, loath, opposed, reluctant, unfavorable, unwilling.
antonyms sympathetic, willing.

aversion *n.* abhorrence, abomination, anathema, animosity, antagonism, antipathy, detestation, disapproval, disgust, disinclination, dislike, distaste, hate, hatred, horror, hostility, loathing, odium, opposition, phobia, phobism, reluctance, repugnance, repulsion, revulsion, unwillingness.
antonyms liking, sympathy.

avert *v.* avoid, deflect, evade, fend off, forestall, frustrate, obviate, parry, preclude, prevent, stave off, turn, turn aside, turn away, ward off.

avid *adj.* acquisitive, ardent, avaricious, covetous, dedicated, devoted, eager, earnest, enthusiastic, fanatical, fervent, grasping, greedy, hungry, insatiable, intense, keen, passionate, rapacious, ravenous, thirsty, voracious, zealous.
antonym indifferent.

avocation *n.* business, calling, distraction, diversion, employment, hobby, interest, job, occupation, pastime, profession, pursuit, recreation, relaxation, sideline, trade, vocation, work.

avoid *v.* abstain from, avert, balk, bypass, circumvent, dodge, duck, elude, escape, eschew, evade, evite, funk, get out of, obviate, prevent, refrain from, shirk, shun, side-step, steer clear of.

award *v.* accord, adjudge, allot, allow, apportion, assign, bestow, confer, determine, dispense, distribute, endow, gift, give, grant, present.
n. adjudication, allotment, allowance, bestowal, conferment, conferral, decision, decoration, dispensation, endowment, gift, grant, judgment, order, presentation, prize, trophy.

aware *adj.* acquainted, alive to, appreciative, apprized, attentive, au courant, cognizant, conscient, conscious, conversant, enlightened, familiar, heedful, hep, hip, informed, knowing, knowledgeable, mindful, observant, on the ball, on the qui vive, sensible, sensitive, sentient, sharp, shrewd.
antonyms insensitive, unaware.

awe *n.* admiration, amazement, apprehension, astonishment, dread, fear, respect, reverence, terror, veneration, wonder, wonderment.
antonym contempt.
v. amaze, astonish, cow, daunt, frighten, horrify, impress, intimidate, overwhelm, stun, terrify.

awful *adj.* abysmal, alarming, amazing, atrocious, august, awe-inspiring, awesome, blood-curdling, dire, dread, dreadful, eldritch, fearful, fearsome, frightful, ghastly, gruesome, harrowing, hideous, horrendous, horrible, horrific, horrifying, majestic, nasty, portentous, shocking, solemn, spine-chilling, terrible, tremendous, ugly, unpleasant.

awkward *adj.* annoying, bloody-minded, blundering, bungling, chancy, clownish, clumsy, coarse, compromising, cubbish, cumbersome, delicate, difficult, disobliging, embarrassed, embarrassing, exasperating, farouche, fiddly, gauche, gawky, graceless, ham-fisted, ham-handed, hazardous, ill at ease, inconvenient, inelegant, inept, inexpedient, inexpert, inopportune, intractable, intransigent, irritable, left-handed, maladroit, obstinate, painful, perplexing, perverse, prickly, risky, rude, spastic, sticky, stubborn, thorny, ticklish, touchy, troublesome, trying, uncomfortable, unco-operative, unco-ordinated, uncouth, ungainly, ungraceful, unhandy, unhelpful, unmanageable, unpleasant, unrefined, unskilful, untimely, untoward, unwieldy, vexatious, vexing.

antonyms amenable, convenient, elegant, graceful, straightforward.

awry *adv., adj.* aglee, amiss, askew, asymmetrical, cock-eyed, crooked, misaligned, oblique, off-center, out of kilter, skew-whiff, twisted, uneven, unevenly, wonky, wrong.

antonyms straight, symmetrical.

axiom *n.* adage, aphorism, apophthegm, byword, dictum, fundamental, gnome, maxim, postulate, precept, principle, truism, truth.

B

babble *v.* blab, burble, cackle, chatter, gabble, gibber, gurgle, jabber, mumble, murmur, mutter, prate, prattle, purl, twattle.

n. burble, clamor, drivel, gabble, gibberish, lallation, lalling, murmur, purl, purling, twattle.

baby *n.* babe, bairn, child, infant, nursling, papoose, suckling, tiny, toddler, wean, weanling, youngling.

adj. diminutive, dwarf, Lilliputian, little, midget, mini, miniature, minute, pygmy, small, small-scale, tiny, toy, wee.

v. cocker, coddle, cosset, humor, indulge, mollycoddle, overindulge, pamper, pander to, pet, spoil, spoonfeed.

babyish *adj.* baby, childish, foolish, immature, infantile, jejune, juvenile, naïve, namby-pamby, puerile, silly, sissy, soft, spoilt.

antonyms mature, precocious.

back¹ *v.* advocate, assist, boost, buttress, champion, countenance, countersign, encourage, endorse, favor, finance, sanction, second, side with, sponsor, subsidize, support, sustain, underwrite.

antonym discourage.

back up aid, assist, bolster, champion, confirm, corroborate, endorse, reinforce, second, substantiate, support.

antonym let down.

back² *n.* backside, end, hind part, hindquarters, posterior, rear, reverse, stern, tail, tail end, tergum, verso.

adj. end, hind, hindmost, posterior, rear, reverse, tail.

back³ *v.* backtrack, recede, recoil, regress, retire, retreat, reverse, withdraw.

back⁴ *adj.* delayed, earlier, elapsed, former, outdated, overdue, past, previous, prior, superseded.

backbiting *n.* abuse, aspersion, bitchiness, calumniation, calumny, cattiness, criticism, defamation, denigration, detraction, disparagement, gossip, malice, revilement, scandalmongering, slagging, slander, spite, spitefulness, vilification, vituperation.

antonym praise.

backbone *n.* basis, bottle, character, core, courage, determination, firmness, foundation, grit, hardihood, mainstay, mettle, nerve, pluck, power, resolution, resolve, spine, stamina, staunchness, steadfastness, strength, support, tenacity, toughness, vertebral column, will.

antonyms spinelessness, weakness.

backbreaking *adj.* arduous, crushing, exhausting, grueling, hard, heavy, killing, laborious, punishing, strenuous, tiring, toilsome, wearing, wearisome.

antonym easy.

backer *n.* advocate, benefactor, bottle-holder, champion, patron, promoter, second, seconder, sponsor, subscriber, supporter, underwriter, well-wisher.

backfire *v.* boomerang, come home to roost, fail, flop, miscarry, rebound, recoil, ricochet.

background *n.* breeding, circumstances, credentials, culture, dossier, education, environment, experience, fond, grounding, history, milieu, preparation, record, surroundings, tradition, upbringing.

backing *n.* accompaniment, advocacy, aid, assistance, championing, championship, encouragement, endorsement, favor, funds, grant, helpers, moral support, patronage, sanction, seconding, sponsorship, subsidy, support.

backlash *n.* backfire, boomerang, counterblast, kickback, reaction, recoil, repercussion, reprisal, resentment, response, retaliation.

backlog *n.* accumulation, excess, hoard, leeway, mountain, reserve, reserves, resources, stock, supply.

backslide *v.* apostatize, default, defect, fall from grace, lapse, regress, relapse, renegue, retrogress, revert, sin, slip, stray, weaken.

antonym persevere.

backward *adj.* bashful, behind, behindhand, diffident, dull, hesitant, hesitating, immature, late, reluctant, retarded, shy, slow, sluggish, stupid, subnormal, tardy, underdeveloped, unwilling, wavering.

antonyms forward, precocious.

bad *adj.* adverse, ailing, base, blameworthy, consciencestricken, contrite, corrupt, criminal, damaging, dangerous, decayed, defective, deficient, deleterious, delinquent, despondent, detrimental, disastrous, discouraged, discouraging, diseased, disobedient, distressed, distressing, evil, fallacious, faulty, gloomy, grave, grim, grotty, guilty, harmful, harsh, ill, illaudable, immoral, imperfect, inadequate, incorrect, inferior, injurious, mean, melancholy, mischievous, mouldy, naughty, noxious, off, offensive, onkus, painful, piacular, poor, putrid, rancid, regretful, remorseful, ropy, rotten, rueful, ruinous, sad, serious, severe, shoddy, sick, sinful, somber, sorry, sour, spoilt, stormy, substandard, terrible, troubled, unfortunate, unhealthy, unpleasant, unruly, unsatisfactory, unwell, upset, vile, wicked, wrong.

badger *v.* bait, bully, bullyrag, chivvy, goad, harass, harry, hassle, hound, importune, nag, pester, plague, torment.

baffle *v.* amaze, astound, balk, bamboozle, bemuse, bewilder, check, confound, confuse, daze, defeat, disconcert, dumbfound, flabbergast, floor, flummox, foil, frustrate, hinder, mystify, nonplus, perplex, puzzle, stump, stun, stymie, thwart, upset. *antonyms* enlighten, help.

bag *v.* acquire, appropriate, capture, catch, commandeer, corner, gain, get, grab, kill, land, obtain, reserve, shoot, take, trap.

n. carrier, container, dorlach, Dorothy bag, dressing-case, Gladstone bag, grab-bag, grip, gripsack, hand-bag, haversack, hold-all, holder, pack, poke, reticule, rucksack, sack, satchel, satchet, scrip, shoulder-bag, tote-bag, valise.

bail *n.* bond, guarantee, guaranty, pledge, security, surety, warranty.

bait *n.* allurement, attraction, bribe, carrot, decoy, enticement, inducement, lure, temptation.

antonym disincentive.

v. annoy, gall, goad, harass, hound, irk, irritate, needle, persecute, provoke, tease, torment.

balance *v.* adjust, assess, calculate, compare, compute, consider, counteract, counterbalance, counterpoise, deliberate, equalize, equate, equilibrate, equipoise, equiponderate, estimate, evaluate, level, librate, match, neutralize, offset, parallel, poise, settle, square, stabilize, steady, tally, total, weigh.

antonyms overbalance, unbalance.

n. composure, correspondence, difference, equality, equanimity, equilibrium, equipoise, equity, equivalence, evenness, parity, poise, remainder, residue, rest, self-possession, stability, stasis, steadiness, surplus, symmetry.

antonyms imbalance, instability.

bald *adj.* bald-headed, baldpated, bare, barren, bleak, depilated, direct, downright, exposed, forthright, glabrate, glabrous, hairless, naked, outright, peeled, plain, severe, simple, stark, straight, straightforward, treeless, unadorned, uncompromising, uncovered, undisguised, unvarnished.

antonyms adorned, hirsute.

baleful *adj.* deadly, destructive, evil, fell, harmful, hurtful, injurious, malevolent, malignant, menacing, mournful, noxious, ominous, pernicious, ruinous, sad, sinister, venomous, woeful.

antonyms auspicious, favorable.

balk, baulk *v.* baffle, bar, boggle, check, counteract, defeat, demur, disconcert, dodge, evade, flinch, foil, forestall, frustrate, hesitate, hinder, jib, make difficulties, obstruct, prevent, recoil, refuse, resist, shirk, shrink, stall, thwart.

ball[1] *n.* bauble, bobble, bullet, clew, conglomeration, drop, globe, globule, orb, pellet, pill, shot, slug, sphere, spheroid.

ball[2] *n.* assembly, carnival, dance, dinner-dance, fandango, hop, masquerade, party, ridotto, rout, soirée.

ballad *n.* carol, composition, ditty, folk-song, lay, poem, pop-song, shanty, song.

ballet *n.* ballet-dancing, dancing, leg-business.

balloon *v.* bag, belly, billow, blow up, bulge, dilate, distend, enlarge, expand, inflate, puff out, swell.

ballot *n.* election, plebiscite, poll, polling, referendum, vote, voting.

balmy[1] *adj.* clement, gentle, mild, pleasant, soft, summery, temperate.

antonym inclement.

balmy[2] *adj.* barmy, crazy, daft, dippy, dotty, foolish, idiotic, insane, loony, mad, nuts, nutty, odd, round the bend, silly, stupid.

antonyms rational, sane, sensible.

ban *v.* anathematize, banish, bar, debar, disallow, exclude, forbid, interdict, ostracize, outlaw, prohibit, proscribe, restrict, suppress.

antonym permit.

n. anathematization, boycott, censorship, condemnation, curse, denunciation, embargo, interdiction, outlawry, prohibition, proscription, restriction, stoppage, suppression, taboo.

antonyms dispensation, permission.

banal *adj.* boring, clichéd, cliché-ridden, commonplace, corny, empty, everyday, hackneyed, humdrum, jejune, old hat, ordinary, pedestrian, platitudinous, stale, stereotyped, stock, threadbare, tired, trite, unimaginative, unoriginal, vapid.

antonym original.

band[1] *n.* bandage, bandeau, belt, binding, bond, chain, cincture, cord, fascia, fetter, fillet, ligature, manacle, ribbon, shackle, strap, strip, swath, tape, tie, vitta.

band[2] *n.* association, body, clique, club, combo, company, coterie, crew, ensemble, flock, gang, group, herd, horde, orchestra, party, range, society, troop, waits.

v. affiliate, ally, amalgamate, collaborate, consolidate, federate, gather, group, join, merge, unite.

antonyms disband, disperse.

bandit *n.* brigand, buccaneer, cowboy, dacoit, desperado, footpad, freebooter, gangster, gunman, highwayman, hijacker, marauder, outlaw, pirate, racketeer, robber, ruffian, thief.

bang *n.* blow, boom, box, bump, clang, clap, clash, collision, crash, cuff, detonation, explosion, hit, knock, noise, peal, pop, punch, report, shot, slam, smack, stroke, thud, thump, wallop, whack.

v. bash, boom, bump, burst, clang, clatter, crash, detonate, drum, echo, explode, hammer, knock, peal, pound, pummel, rap, resound, slam, stamp, strike, thump, thunder.

adv. directly, hard, headlong, noisily, plumb, precisely, right, slap, smack, straight, suddenly.

banish *v.* ban, bar, blacklist, debar, deport, discard, dislodge, dismiss, dispel, eject, eliminate, eradicate, evict, exclude, excommunicate, exile, expatriate, expel, get rid of, ostracize, oust, outlaw, remove, shut out, transport.

antonyms recall, welcome.

bank[1] *n.* accumulation, cache, depository, fund, hoard, pool, repository, reserve, reservoir, savings, stock, stockpile, store, storehouse, treasury.

v. accumulate, deposit, keep, save, stockpile, store.
antonym spend.

bank[2] *n.* acclivity, banking, brink, bund, earthwork, edge, embankment, fail-dike, heap, margin, mass, mound, pile, rampart, ridge, rivage, shallow, shoal, shore, side, slope, tilt.
v. accumulate, aggrade, amass, camber, cant, drift, heap, incline, mass, mound, pile, pitch, slant, slope, stack, tilt, tip.

bank[3] *n.* array, bench, echelon, file, group, line, rank, row, sequence, series, succession, tier, train.

banner *n.* banderol(e), bannerol, burgee, colors, ensign, fanion, flag, gonfalon, labarum, oriflamme, pennant, pennon, standard, streamer, vexillum.

banquet *n.* binge, dinner, feast, meal, repast, revel, treat, wayzgoose.

banter *n.* badinage, chaff, chaffing, cross-talk, derision, dicacity, jesting, joking, kidding, mockery, persiflage, pleasantry, quiz, raillery, repartee, ribbing, ridicule, word play.

bar[1] *n.* barricade, barrier, batten, check, cross-piece, deterrent, deterrment, hindrance, impediment, obstacle, obstruction, overslaugh, paling, pole, preventive, rail, railing, rod, shaft, stake, stanchion, stick, stop.
v. ban, barricade, blackball, bolt, debar, exclude, fasten, forbid, hinder, latch, lock, obstruct, preclude, prevent, prohibit, restrain, secure.

bar[2] *n.* bierkeller, boozer, canteen, counter, dive, doggery, dram-shop, estaminet, exchange, gin-palace, ginshop, groggery, grogshop, honky-tonk, howff, inn, joint, lounge, nineteenth hole, pub, public house, saloon, tavern, vaults, watering-hole.

bar[3] *n.* advocates, attorneys, barristers, bench, counsel, court, courtroom, dock, law court, tribunal.

bar[4] *n.* block, chunk, ingot, lump, nugget, slab, wedge.

barbarian *n.* ape, boor, brute, clod, hooligan, hottentot, hun, ignoramus, illiterate, lout, lowbrow, oaf, philistine, ruffian, savage, tramontane, vandal, vulgarian, yahoo. *adj.* boorish, brutish, coarse, crude, lowbrow, philistine, rough, tramontane, uncivilized, uncouth, uncultivated, uncultured, unsophisticated, vulgar.

barbarous *adj.* barbarian, barbaric, brutal, brutish, coarse, crude, cruel, ferocious, heartless, heathenish, ignorant, inhuman, monstrous, philistine, primitive, rough, rude, ruthless, savage, uncivilized, uncouth, uncultured, unlettered, unrefined, vicious, vulgar, wild.
antonyms civilized, cultured, educated.

bare *adj.* austere, bald, barren, basic, blank, defoliate, defoliated, denudated, denuded, disfurnished, empty, essential, explicit, exposed, hard, lacking, literal, mean, naked, napless, nude, open, peeled, plain, poor, scanty, scarce, severe, sheer, shorn, simple, spare, stark, stripped, unadorned, unarmed, unclad, unclothed, uncovered, undisguised, undressed, unembellished, unforested, unfurnished, unprovided, unsheathed,
untimbered, unvarnished, unwooded, vacant, void, wanting, woodless.

barefaced *adj.* arrant, audacious, bald, blatant, bold, brash, brazen, flagrant, glaring, impudent, insolent, manifest, naked, obvious, open, palpable, patent, shameless, transparent, unabashed, unconcealed.

barely[1] *adv.* almost, hardly, just, scarcely, sparingly, sparsely.

barely[2] *adv.* explicitly, nakedly, openly, plainly.

bargain *n.* agreement, arrangement, compact, contract, discount, giveaway, negotiation, pact, pledge, promise, reduction, snip, steal, stipulation, transaction, treaty, understanding.
v. agree, barter, broke, buy, chaffer, contract, covenant, deal, dicker, haggle, higgle, negotiate, promise, sell, stipulate, trade, traffic, transact.

bargain for anticipate, consider, contemplate, expect, foresee, imagine, include, look for, plan for, reckon on.

baroque *adj.* bizarre, bold, convoluted, elaborate, extravagant, exuberant, fanciful, fantastic, flamboyant, florid, grotesque, ornate, overdecorated, overwrought, rococo, vigorous, whimsical.
antonym plain.

barren *adj.* arid, boring, childless, desert, desolate dry, dull, empty, flat, fruitless, infecund, infertile, jejune, lackluster, pointless, profitless, stale, sterile, unbearing, unfruitful, uninformative, uninspiring, uninstructive, uninteresting, unproductive, unprolific, unrewarding, useless, vapid, waste.
antonyms fertile, productive, useful.

barricade *n.* barrier, blockade, bulwark, fence, obstruction, palisade, protection, rampart, screen, stockade.
v. bar, block, blockade, defend, fortify, obstruct, palisade, protect, screen.

barrier *n.* bail, bar, barricade, blockade, boom, boundary, bulkhead, check, difficulty, ditch, drawback, fence, fortification, handicap, hindrance, hurdle, impediment, limitation, obstacle, obstruction, railing, rampart, restriction, stop, stumbling-block, transverse, wall.

barter *v.* bargain, chaffer, deal, dicker, exchange, haggle, higgle, negotiate, sell, swap, switch, trade, traffic, truck.

base[1] *n.* basis, bed, bottom, camp, center, core, essence, essential, foot, foundation, fundamental, groundwork, headquarters, heart, home, key, origin, pedestal, plinth, post, principal, rest, root, settlement, socle, source, stand, standard, starting-point, station, substrate, substructure, support, underpinning, understructure.
v. build, construct, depend, derive, establish, found, ground, hinge, locate, station.

base[2] *adj.* abject, contemptible, corrupt, counterfeit, depraved, disgraceful, disreputable, dog, evil, groveling, humble, ignoble, ignominious, immoral, infamous, low, lowly, low-minded, low-thoughted, mean, menial, miserable, paltry, pitiful, poor, scandalous, servile, shameful, slavish, sordid, sorry, valueless, vile, villainous, vulgar, wicked, worthless, wretched.

base[3] *adj.* adulterated, alloyed, artificial, bastard, counterfeit, debased, fake, forged, fraudulent, impure, inferior, pinchbeck, spurious.

bashful *adj.* abashed, backward, blushing, confused, coy, diffident, embarrassed, hesitant, inhibited, modest, nervous, reserved, reticent, retiring, self-conscious, self-effacing, shamefaced, sheepish, shrinking, shy, timid, timorous, unforthcoming, verecund.
antonym confident.

basic *adj.* central, elementary, essential, fundamental, important, indispensable, inherent, intrinsic, key, necessary, primary, radical, root, underlying, vital.
antonyms inessential, peripheral.

basis *n.* approach, base, bottom, core, essential, fond, footing, foundation, fundamental, ground, groundwork, heart, keynote, pedestal, premise, principle, support, thrust.

bask *v.* apricate, delight in, enjoy, laze, lie, lounge, luxuriate, relax, relish, revel, savor, sunbathe, wallow.

bastion *n.* bulwark, citadel, defence, fastness, fortress, mainstay, pillar, prop, redoubt, rock, stronghold, support, tower of strength.

batch *n.* amount, assemblage, assortment, bunch, collection, consignment, contingent, group, lot, pack, parcel, quantity, set.

bath *n.* ablution, bathtub, cleaning, douche, douse, hamman, Jacuzzi®., scrubbing, shower, soak, tub, wash.
v. bathe, clean, douse, lave, shower, soak, tub, wash.

bathe *v.* cleanse, cover, dook, dunk, encompass, flood, immerse, moisten, rinse, soak, steep, stew, suffuse, swim, wash, wet.
n. dip, dook, rinse, soak, swim, wash.

bathos *n.* anticlimax, comedown, let-down.

battalion *n.* army, brigade, company, contingent, division, force, herd, horde, host, legion, mass, multitude, phalanx, platoon, regiment, squadron, throng.

batten *v.* barricade, board up, clamp down, fasten, fix, nail down, secure, tighten.

batter *v.* abuse, assault, bash, beat, belabor, bruise, buffet, crush, dash, deface, demolish, destroy, disfigure, distress, hurt, injure, lash, maltreat, mangle, manhandle, mar, maul, pelt, pound, pummel, ruin, shatter, smash, thrash, wallop.

battery *n.* artillery, assault, attack, barrage, beating, cannon, cannonry, emplacements, guns, mayhem, onslaught, progression, sequence, series, set, thrashing, violence.

battle *n.* action, affray, attack, campaign, clash, combat, conflict, contest, controversy, crusade, debate, disagreement, dispute, encounter, engagement, fight, fray, hostilities, row, skirmish, strife, struggle, war, warfare.
v. agitate, argue, campaign, clamor, combat, contend, contest, crusade, dispute, feud, fight, strive, struggle, war.

bauble *n.* bagatelle, flamfew, gewgaw, gimcrack, kickshaw, knick-knack, plaything, tinsel, toy, trifle, trinket.

bawd *n.* brothel-keeper, madam, panderess, pimp, procuress.

bawdy *adj.* blue, coarse, dirty, erotic, gross, improper, indecent, indecorous, indelicate, lascivious, lecherous, lewd, libidinous, licentious, lustful, obscene, pornographic, prurient, ribald, risqué, rude, salacious, smutty, suggestive, vulgar.
antonyms chaste, clean.

bawl *v.* bellow, blubber, call, caterwaul, clamor, cry, halloo, howl, roar, shout, sob, squall, vociferate, wail, waul, weep, yell.

bay[1] *n.* arm, bight, cove, embayment, fjord, gulf, inlet, reach.

bay[2] *n.* alcove, booth, carrel, compartment, cubicle, embrasure, niche, nook, opening, recess, stall.

bay[3] *v.* bark, bawl, bell, bellow, cry, holler, howl, roar.

bazaar *n.* agora, alcaicería, alcázar, bring-and-buy, exchange, fair, fête, market, market-place, mart, sale.

beach *n.* coast, foreshore, lido, littoral, margin, plage, riviera, sand, sands, seaboard, seashore, seaside, shingle, shore, strand, water's edge.

beachcomber *n.* Autolycus, forager, loafer, loiterer, scavenger, scrounger, wayfarer. **beacon** *n.* beam, bonfire, fanal, flare, lighthouse, pharos, rocket, sign, signal, watch-fire.

bead *n.* blob, bubble, dot, drop, droplet, glob, globule, pearl, pellet, pill, spherule.

beak *n.* bill, bow, mandibles, neb, nib, nose, nozzle, proboscis, projection, prow, ram, rostrum, snout, stem.

beam *n.* arbor, bar, boom, girder, gleam, glimmer, glint, glow, joist, plank, radiation, rafter, ray, shaft, spar, stanchion, stream, support, timber.
v. broadcast, effulge, emit, fulgurate, glare, glimmer, glitter, glow, grin, laugh, radiate, shine, smile, transmit.

beaming *adj.* beautiful, bright, brilliant, cheerful, effulgent, flashing, gleaming, glistening, glittering, glowing, grinning, happy, joyful, lambent, radiant, refulgent, scintillating, shining, smiling, sparkling, sunny.
antonyms lowering, sullen.

bear[1] *v.* abide, admit, allow, beget, bring, brook, carry, cherish, convey, endure, entertain, exhibit, hack, harbor, have, hold, maintain, move, permit, possess, put up with, shoulder, stomach, suffer, support, sustain, take, tolerate, tote, transport, undergo, uphold, weather, weigh upon.

bear[2] *v.* breed, bring forth, develop, drop, engender, generate, give birth to, give up, produce, propagate, yield.

bearable *adj.* acceptable, endurable, livable(-with), manageable, sufferable, supportable, sustainable, tolerable.

bearing *n.* air, application, aspect, attitude, behavior, carriage, comportment, connection, course, demeanor, deportment, direction, import, manner, mien, pertinence, poise, posture, presence, reference, relation, relevance, significance.

bearings *n.* aim, course, direction, inclination, location, orientation, position, situation, tack, track, way, whereabouts.

beast *n.* animal, ape, barbarian, brute, creature, devil, fiend, monster, pig, sadist, savage, swine.

beastly *adj.* barbarous, bestial, brutal, brutish, coarse, cruel, depraved, disagreeable, foul, inhuman, mean, monstrous, nasty, repulsive, rotten, sadistic, savage, sensual, swinish, terrible, unpleasant, vile.

beat[1] *v.* bang, bash, baste, bastinade, bastinado, batter, belabor, bethump, bethwack, bless, bludgeon, bruise, buffet, cane, contuse, cudgel, curry, ding, drub, dunt, fashion, flog, forge, form, fustigate, hammer, hit, impinge, knobble, knock, knout, knubble, lam, lash, lay into, malleate, maul, mill, model, nubble, pelt, pound, punch, shape, slat, strap, strike, swipe, tan, thrash, thwack, trounce, vapulate, verberate, warm, welt, whale, wham, whip, work.

n. blow, hit, lash, punch, shake, slap, strike, swing, thump.

adj. exhausted, fatigued, jiggered, tired, wearied, worn out, zonked.

beat[2] *v.* best, conquer, defeat, excel, hammer, outdo, outrun, outstrip, overcome, overwhelm, slaughter, subdue, surpass, trounce, vanquish.

beat[3] *v.* flutter, palpitate, patter, pound, pulsate, pulse, quake, quiver, race, shake, throb, thump, tremble, vibrate.

n. accent, cadence, flutter, measure, meter, palpitation, pulsation, pulse, rhyme, rhythm, stress, throb, time.

beat[4] *n.* circuit, course, journey, path, round, rounds, route, territory, way.

beaten[1] *adj.* baffled, cowed, defeated, disappointed, disheartened, frustrated, overcome, ruined, surpassed, thwarted, vanquished, worsted.

beaten[2] *adj.* fashioned, forged, formed, hammered, malleated, shaped, stamped, worked.

beaten[3] *adj.* blended, foamy, frothy, mixed, pounded, stirred, tenderized, whipped, whisked.

beating *n.* belting, caning, chastisement, conquest, corporal punishment, defeat, downfall, dressing, drubbing, flogging, lamming, overthrow, rout, ruin, slapping, smacking, thrashing, vapulation, verberation, warming, whaling, whipping.

adj. pounding, pulsatile, pulsating, pulsative, pulsatory, pulsing, racing, throbbing, thumping.

beau *n.* admirer, Adonis, boyfriend, cavalier, coxcomb, dandy, escort, fancy man, fiancé, fop, gallant, Jack-a-dandy, ladies' man, lover, popinjay, suitor, swain, sweetheart, swell.

beautiful *adj.* alluring, appealing, attractive, beau, beauteous, belle, charming, comely, delightful, exquisite, fair, fine, good-looking, gorgeous, graceful, handsome, lovely, pleasing, pulchritudinous, radiant, ravishing, stunning.

antonyms plain, ugly.

beauty[1] *n.* allure, attractiveness, bloom, charm, comeliness, elegance, excellence, exquisitness, fairness, glamor, grace, handsomeness, loveliness, pleasure, pulchritude, seemliness, symmetry.

antonym ugliness.

beauty[2] *n.* belle, charmer, corker, cracker, femme fatale, goddess, good-looker, knockout, lovely, siren, stunner, Venus.

antonym frump.

becalmed *adj.* at a standstill, idle, motionless, still, stranded, stuck.

because *conj.* as, by reason of, for, forasmuch, forwhy, in that, inasmuch as, on account of, owing to, since, thanks to.

beckon *v.* allure, attract, bid, call, coax, decoy, draw, entice, gesticulate, gesture, invite, lure, motion, nod, pull, signal, summon, tempt, waft.

become *v.* befit, behove, embellish, enhance, fit, flatter, grace, harmonize, ornament, set off, suit.

becoming *adj.* appropriate, attractive, befitting, charming, comely, comme il faut, compatible, congruous, decent, decorous, enhancing, fit, fitting, flattering, graceful, maidenly, meet, neat, pretty, proper, seemly, suitable, tasteful, worthy.

antonym unbecoming.

bed[1] *n.* bedstead, berth, bunk, cot, couch, divan, kip, mattress, pallet, palliasse, sack, the downy.

bed[2] *n.* base, border, bottom, channel, foundation, garden, groundwork, layer, matrix, patch, plot, row, stratus, strip, substratum, wadi, watercourse.

v. base, embed, establish, fix, found, ground, implant, insert, plant, settle.

bedeck *v.* adorn, array, beautify, bedight, bedizen, decorate, embellish, festoon, garnish, ornament, trick out, trim.

antonym strip.

bedevil *v.* afflict, annoy, besiege, confound, distress, fret, frustrate, harass, irk, irritate, pester, plague, tease, torment, torture, trouble, vex, worry.

bedlam *n.* anarchy, babel, chaos, clamor, commotion, confusion, furore, hubbub, hullabaloo, madhouse, noise, pandemonium, tumult, turmoil, uproar.

antonym calm.

bedraggled *adj.* dirty, disheveled, disordered, messy, muddied, muddy, scruffy, slovenly, sodden, soiled, stained, sullied, unkempt, untidy.

antonym tidy.

beef[1] *n.* beefiness, brawn, bulk, flesh, fleshiness, heftiness, muscle, robustness, sinew, strength.

beef[2] *n.* complaint, criticism, dispute, dissatisfaction, grievance, gripe, grouse, grumble, objection, protest.

v. complain, criticize, gripe, grumble, moan, object.

antonym approve.

beefy *adj.* brawny, bulky, burly, corpulent, fat, fleshy, heavy, hefty, hulking, muscular, plump, podgy, pudgy, rotund, stalwart, stocky, strapping, sturdy.
antonym slight.

befall *v.* arrive, betide, chance, ensue, fall, follow, happen, materialize, occur, supervene, take place.

before *adv.* ahead, earlier, formerly, in advance, in front, previously, sooner.
antonyms after, later.
prep. ahead of, earlier than, in advance of, in anticipation of, in front of, in preparation for, previous to, prior to, sooner than.
conj. in case, rather than.

befriend *v.* aid, assist, back, benefit, comfort, encourage, favor, help, patronize, stand by, succor, support, sustain, take a liking to, take under one's wing, uphold, welcome.
antonym neglect.

befuddled *adj.* baffled, bewildered, confused, dazed, fuddled, groggy, hazy, inebriated, intoxicated, muddled, woozy.
antonym lucid.

beg *v.* beseech, cadge, crave, desire, entreat, fleech, implore, importune, petition, plead, pray, prog, request, require, schnorr, scrounge, shool, skelder, solicit, sponge on, supplicate, touch.

beget *v.* breed, bring, cause, create, effect, engender, father, gender, generate, get, give rise to, occasion, procreate, produce, propagate, result in, sire, spawn.

beggar[1] *n.* Abraham-man, bankrupt, beadsman, besognio, bluegown, cadger, canter, derelict, down-and-out, hobo, lazzarone, mendicant, pauper, schnorrer, scrounger, sponger, starveling, supplicant, toe-rag, toe-ragger, tramp, vagrant.

beggar[2] *v.* baffle, challenge, defy, exceed, surpass, transcend.

begin *v.* activate, actuate, appear, arise, commence, crop up, dawn, emerge, happen, inaugurate, initiate, instigate, institute, introduce, originate, prepare, set about, set in, spring, start.
antonyms end, finish.

beginner *n.* abecedarian, alphabetarian, amateur, apprentice, cheechako, cub, fledgling, freshman, greenhorn, initiate, Johnny-raw, learner, neophyte, novice, recruit, rookie, rooky, starter, student, tenderfoot, tiro, trainee.
antonyms expert, old hand, veteran.

beginning *n.* birth, commencement, embryo, establishment, fons et origo, fountainhead, germ, inauguration, inception, inchoation, initiation, introduction, onset, opening, origin, outset, preface, prelude, prime, rise, root, rudiments, seed, source, start, starting point.
antonyms end, finish.
adj. early, elementary, inaugural, inauguratory, inceptive, inchoative, incipient, initial, introductory, nascent, primal, primary, primeval.

begrudge *v.* covet, envy, grudge, mind, resent, stint.
antonym allow.

beguiling *adj.* alluring, appealing, attractive, bewitching, captivating, charming, diverting, enchanting, entertaining, enticing, interesting, intriguing.
antonyms offensive, repulsive.

behalf *n.* account, advantage, authority, benefit, defense, good, interest, name, part, profit, sake, side, support.

behave *v.* acquit, act, bear, comport, conduct, demean, deport, function, operate, perform, react, respond, run, work.

behavior *n.* action, actions, bearing, carriage, comportment, conduct, dealings, demeanor, deportment, doings, functioning, habits, manner, manners, operation, performance, reaction, response, ways.

behead *v.* decapitate, decollate, execute, guillotine, unhead.

behest *n.* authority, bidding, charge, command, commandment, decree, dictate, direction, fiat, injunction, instruction, mandate, order, ordinance, precept, wish.

behind *prep.* after, backing, causing, following, for, initiating, instigating, later than, responsible for, supporting.
adv. after, afterwards, behindhand, en arrière, following, in arrears, in debt, in the wake of, next, overdue, subsequently.
n. ass, backside, bottom, butt, buttocks, derrière, fanny, posterior, prat, rear, rump, seat, sit-upon, tail, tush.

behold *v.* consider, contemplate, descry, discern, espy, eye, look at, note, observe, perceive, regard, scan, survey, view, watch, witness.
interj. ecce, lo, look, mark, observe, see, voici, voilà, watch.

being[1] *n.* actuality, animation, entity, essence, existence, haecceity, life, living, nature, quiddity, reality, soul, spirit, substance.

being[2] *n.* animal, beast, body, creature, human being, individual, mortal, sentient, thing.

belabor *v.* attack, bash, batter, beat, belt, berate, castigate, censure, chastise, criticize, flay, flog, lambast, lay into, thrash, whip.

belated *adj.* behind-hand, delayed, late, overdue, retarded, tardy, unpunctual.
antonyms punctual, timely.

belch *v.* burp, discharge, disgorge, emit, eruct, eructate, erupt, gush, hiccup, spew, vent.
n. burp, eructation, eruption, hiccup.

beleaguered *adj.* badgered, beset, besieged, bothered, harassed, hedged about, hedged in, persecuted, plagued, surrounded, vexed, worried.

belie *v.* conceal, confute, contradict, deceive, deny, disguise, disprove, falsify, gainsay, mislead, misrepresent, negate, refute, repudiate, run counter to, understate.
antonym attest.

belief *n.* assurance, confidence, conviction, credence, credit, credo, creed, doctrine, dogma, expectation, faith, feeling, ideology, impression, intuition, ism, judgment, notion, opinion, persuasion, presumption, principle, principles, reliance, sureness, surety, tenet, theory, trust, view.

antonym disbelief.

believe *v.* accept, assume, be under the impression, conjecture, consider, count on, credit, deem, depend on, gather, guess, hold, imagine, judge, maintain, postulate, presume, reckon, rely on, speculate, suppose, swallow, swear by, think, trust, wear.

antonym disbelieve.

believer *n.* adherent, catechumen, convert, devotee, disciple, follower, proselyte, supporter, upholder, votary, zealot.

antonyms apostate, sceptic, unbeliever.

belittle *v.* decry, deprecate, depreciate, deride, derogate, detract, diminish, dismiss, disparage, downgrade, lessen, minimize, ridicule, run down, scorn, underestimate, underrate, undervalue, vilipend.

antonym exaggerate.

belligerent *adj.* aggressive, antagonistic, argumentative, bellicose, bullying, combative, contentious, forceful, militant, pugnacious, quarrelsome, violent, warlike, warring.

antonym peaceable.

bellow *v.* bell, call, clamor, cry, howl, roar, scream, shout, shriek, troat, yell.

belly *n.* abdomen, bowels, bread-basket, corporation, gut, guts, insides, paunch, pot, sound-board, stomach, tummy, uterus, venter, vitals, womb.

v. bag, balloon, billow, blow up, bulge, dilate, distend, expand, fill out, inflate, swell.

antonyms deflate, shrink.

belonging *n.* acceptance, affinity, association, attachment, closeness, compatibility, fellow-feeling, fellowship, inclusion, kinship, link, linkage, loyalty, rapport, relationship.

antonym antipathy.

belongings *n.* accouterments, chattels, effects, gear, goods, impedimenta, paraphernalia, possessions, stuff, things, traps.

beloved *adj.* admired, adored, cherished, darling, dear, dearest, favorite, loved, pet, precious, prized, revered, sweet, treasured.

n. adored, darling, dear, dearest, favorite, inamorata, inamorato, lover, pet, precious, sweet, sweetheart.

below *adv.* beneath, down, infra, lower, lower down, under, underneath.

prep. inferior to, lesser than, 'neath, subject to, subordinate to, under, underneath, unworthy of.

belt[1] *n.* area, band, ceinture, cincture, cingulum, cummerbund, district, girdle, girth, layer, region, sash, strait, stretch, strip, swathe, tract, waistband, zone, zonule, zonulet.

v. circle, encircle, girdle, ring, surround.

belt[2] *v.* bolt, career, charge, dash, hurry, race, rush, speed.

bemoan *v.* bewail, deplore, grieve for, lament, mourn, regret, rue, sigh for, sorrow over, weep for.

antonym gloat.

bend *v.* aim, bow, brace, buckle, compel, constrain, contort, couch, crankle, crimp, crouch, curve, deflect, direct, dispose, diverge, embow, fasten, flex, incline, incurvate, incurve, influence, lean, mold, nerve, persuade, shape, stoop, string, subdue, submit, sway, swerve, turn, twist, veer, warp, yield.

n. angle, arc, bight, bought, bow, corner, crank, crook, curvature, curve, elbow, flexure, genu, hook, incurvation, incurvature, incurve, inflexure, loop, turn, twist, zigzag.

beneath *adv.* below, lower, lower down, under, underneath.

prep. below, inferior to, infra dig(nitatem), lower than, 'neath, subject to, subordinate to, unbefitting, under, underneath, unworthy of.

benediction *n.* beatitude, Benedictus, benison, blessing, consecration, favor, grace, invocation, orison, prayer, thanksgiving.

antonyms anathema, curse, execration.

beneficial *adj.* advantageous, benign, benignant, edifying, favorable, gainful, healthful, helpful, improving, nourishing, nutritious, profitable, restorative, rewarding, salubrious, salutary, serviceable, useful, valuable, wholesome.

antonym harmful.

benefit *n.* advantage, aid, asset, assistance, avail, betterment, blessing, boon, favor, gain, good, help, interest, profit, service, use, weal, welfare.

antonym harm.

v. advance, advantage, aid, ameliorate, amend, assist, avail, better, enhance, further, improve, profit, promote, serve.

antonyms harm, hinder, undermine.

benevolence *n.* altruism, benignity, bounty, charity, compassion, fellow-feeling, generosity, goodness, goodwill, humanity, kind-heartedness, kindliness, kindness, munificence, sympathy.

antonym meanness.

benevolent *adj.* altruistic, beneficent, benign, bounteous, bountiful, caring, charitable, compassionate, considerate, generous, good-will, humane, humanitarian, kind, kind-hearted, kindly, liberal, loving, philanthropic, solicitous, well-disposed.

antonym mean.

bent *adj.* angled, arched, bowed, coudé, criminal, crooked, curved, dishonest, doubled, falcate, folded, homosexual, hunched, inbent, inflexed, retorted, retroverted, stolen, stooped, twisted, untrustworthy.

antonym straight.

n. ability, aptitude, capacity, facility, faculty, flair, forte, gift, inclination, knack, leaning, penchant, preference, proclivity, propensity, talent, tendency.

berate *v.* castigate, censure, chastise, chide, criticize, flyte, jump down the throat of, rail at, rate, rebuke, reprimand, reproach, reprove, revile, scold, tell off, upbraid, vituperate.

antonym praise.

beseech *v.* adjure, ask, beg, call on, conjure, crave, desire, entreat, implore, importune, obsecrate, petition, plead, pray, solicit, sue, supplicate.

beset *v.* assail, attack, badger, bamboozle, bedevil, besiege, embarrass, encircle, enclose, encompass, entangle, environ, faze, harass, hassle, hem in, perplex, pester, plague, surround.

beside *prep.* abreast of, abutting on, adjacent, bordering on, close to, near, neighboring, next door to, next to, overlooking, upsides with.

besides *adv.* additionally, also, as well, extra, further, furthermore, in addition, into the bargain, moreover, otherwise, to boot, too, withal.

prep. apart from, in addition to, other than, over and above.

besiege *v.* assail, badger, belay, beleaguer, beset, blockade, bother, confine, dun, encircle, encompass, environ, harass, harry, hound, importune, nag, pester, plague, surround, trouble.

bespeak *v.* attest, betoken, demonstrate, denote, display, evidence, evince, exhibit, forebode, foretell, imply, indicate, predict, proclaim, reveal, show, signify, suggest, testify to.

best *adj.* advantageous, apt, correct, excellent, finest, first, first-class, first-rate, foremost, greatest, highest, incomparable, largest, leading, makeless, matchless, nonpareil, optimal, optimum, outstanding, perfect, preeminent, preferable, principal, right, superlative, supreme, transcendent, unequaled, unsurpassed.

antonym worst.

adv. excellently, exceptionally, extremely, greatly, superlatively, surpassingly.

antonym worst.

n. choice, cream, crème de la crème, élite, favorite, finest, first, flower, hardest, nonpareil, pick, prime, the tops, top, utmost.

antonym worst.

v. beat, conquer, defeat, get the better of, have the laugh of, lick, outclass, outdo, outwit, surpass, thrash, trounce, vanquish, worst.

bestial *adj.* animal, barbaric, barbarous, beastly, brutal, brutish, carnal, degraded, depraved, feral, gross, inhuman, savage, sensual, sordid, subhuman, swinish, vile.

antonyms civilized, humane.

bestow *v.* accord, allot, apportion, award, bequeath, commit, confer, donate, dower, endow, entrust, give, grant, impart, lavish, lend, present, transmit, wreak.

antonym deprive.

bet *n.* accumulator, ante, bid, flutter, gamble, hazard, pledge, risk, speculation, stake, venture, wager.

v. ante, bid, chance, gamble, hazard, lay, pledge, punt, risk, speculate, stake, venture, wager.

betray *v.* abandon, beguile, corrupt, deceive, delude, desert, disclose, discover, divulge, dob in, double-cross, dupe, ensnare, entrap, evince, expose, forsake, give away, grass, inform on, jilt, manifest, mislead, reveal, seduce, sell, sell down the river, sell out, shop, show, tell, testify against, turn state's evidence, undo.

antonyms defend, fulfil, protect.

betrothal *n.* engagement, espousal, fiançailles, handfast, plight, promise, troth, vow.

better *adj.* bigger, cured, finer, fitter, greater, healthier, improving, larger, longer, on the mend, preferable, progressing, recovered, recovering, restored, stronger, superior, surpassing, worthier.

antonym worse.

v. advance, ameliorate, amend, beat, cap, correct, enhance, exceed, excel, forward, further, go one further than, improve, improve on, increase, meliorate, mend, outdo, outstrip, overtake, overtop, promote, raise, rectify, redress, reform, strengthen, surpass, top, transcend.

antonyms deteriorate, worsen.

between *prep.* amidst, among, amongst, betwixt, inter-, mid.

beware *v.* avoid, give a wide berth to, guard against, heed, look out, mind, shun, steer clear of, take heed, watch out.

antonyms brave, dare.

bewilder *v.* baffle, bamboozle, befuddle, bemuse, buffalo, confound, confuse, daze, disconcert, disorient, fuddle, maze, muddle, mystify, perplex, puzzle, stupefy, tie in knots.

bewitch *v.* allure, attract, beguile, captivate, charm, elfshoot, enchant, enrapture, ensorcell, entrance, fascinate, forspeak, hex, hoodoo, hypnotize, jinx, obsess, possess, spellbind, voodoo, witch.

beyond *prep.* above, across, apart from, away from, before, further than, out of range, out of reach of, over, past, remote from, superior to, yonder.

bias *n.* angle, bent, bigotry, distortion, editorialization, favoritism, inclination, intolerance, leaning, onesidedness, parti pris, partiality, penchant, predilection, predisposition, prejudice, proclivity, proneness, propensity, slant, tendency, tendentiousness, turn, unfairness, viewiness.

antonyms fairness, impartiality.

v. angle, distort, earwig, editorialize, influence, jaundice, load, load the dice, predispose, prejudice, slant, sway, twist, warp, weight.

bibulous *adj.* alcoholic, crapulous, dipsomaniac, drunken, inebriate, intemperate, sottish, thirsty, tipsy.

antonyms sober, temperate.

bicker *v.* altercate, argue, clash, disagree, dispute, feud, fight, quarrel, row, scrap, spar, squabble, wrangle.

antonym agree.

bid *v.* ask, call, charge, command, desire, direct, enjoin, greet, instruct, invite, offer, proclaim, propose, request, require, say, solicit, summon, tell, wish.

n. advance, amount, ante, attempt, crack, effort,

endeavor, go, offer, price, proposal, proposition, submission, sum, tender, try, venture.

bidding *n.* behest, call, charge, command, demand, dictate, direction, injunction, instruction, invitation, order, request, requirement, summons.

big *adj.* adult, altruistic, beefy, benevolent, boastful, bombastic, bulky, burly, buxom, colossal, considerable, corpulent, elder, elephantine, eminent, enormous, extensive, gargantuan, generous, gigantic, gracious, great, grown, grown-up, heroic, huge, hulking, immense, important, influential, large, leading, lofty, magnanimous, main, mammoth, man-sized, massive, mature, mighty, momentous, noble, paramount, plonking, ponderous, powerful, prime, principal, prodigious, prominent, serious, significant, sizable, spacious, stout, substantial, titanic, tolerant, unselfish, valuable, vast, voluminous, weighty.
antonyms little, small.

bigot *n.* chauvinist, dogmatist, fanatic, racist, religionist, sectarian, sexist, verkrampte, zealot.
antonyms humanitarian, liberal.

bigoted *adj.* biased, blinkered, chauvinist, closed, dogmatic, illiberal, intolerant, narrow, narrow-minded, obstinate, opinionated, prejudiced, sectarian, twisted, verkrampte, warped.
antonyms broad-minded, enlightened, liberal.

bilious *adj.* choleric, crabby, cross, crotchety, grouchy, grumpy, irritable, liverish, nauseated, out of sorts, peevish, queasy, sick, sickly, testy.

bilk *v.* balk, bamboozle, cheat, con, cozen, deceive, defraud, do, do out of, fleece, foil, rook, sting, swindle, thwart, trick.

bill[1] *n.* account, advertisement, battels, broadsheet, broadside, bulletin, card, catalog, charges, check, chit, circular, greenback, handbill, hand-out, inventory, invoice, leaflet, legislation, list, listing, measure, note, notice, placard, playbill, poster, program, proposal, reckoning, roster, schedule, score, sheet, statement, syllabus, tab, tally.
v. advertise, announce, charge, debit, invoice, list, post, reckon, record.

bill[2] *n.* beak, mandible, neb, nib, rostrum.

billow *v.* balloon, belly, expand, fill out, heave, puff out, roll, seethe, spread, surge, swell, undulate.

bind *v.* astrict, astringe, attach, bandage, border, cinch, clamp, colligate, compel, complain, confine, constipate, constrain, cover, detain, dress, edge, encase, engage, fasten, finish, force, glue, hamper, harden, hinder, hitch, indenture, lash, necessitate, obligate, oblige, prescribe, require, restrain, restrict, rope, seal, secure, stick, strap, swathe, thirl, tie, trim, truss, wrap.
n. bore, difficulty, dilemma, embarrassment, hole, impasse, nuisance, predicament, quandary.

binding *adj.* compulsory, conclusive, imperative, indissoluble, irrevocable, mandatory, necessary, obligatory, permanent, requisite, strict, unalterable, unbreakable.

n. bandage, border, covering, deligation, edging, stricture, syndesis, tape, trimming, wrapping.

birth *n.* ancestry, background, beginning, birthright, blood, breeding, childbirth, delivery, derivation, descent, emergence, extraction, family, fell, genealogy, genesis, geniture, line, lineage, nativity, nobility, origin, parentage, parturition, pedigree, race, rise, source, stirps, stock, strain.

biscuit *n.* cake, cookie, cracker, hardtack, rusk, wafer.

bit *n.* atom, chip, crumb, fragment, grain, instant, iota, jiffy, jot, mammock, minute, mite, moment, morsel, part, period, piece, scrap, second, segment, sippet, slice, snippet, speck, spell, tick, time, tittle, while, whit.

bite *v.* burn, champ, chew, clamp, corrode, crunch, crush, cut, gnaw, knap, masticate, nibble, nip, pierce, pinch, rend, seize, smart, snap, sting, tear, tingle, wound.
n. edge, food, grip, kick, morsel, morsure, mouthful, nip, piece, pinch, piquancy, prick, punch, pungency, refreshment, smarting, snack, spice, sting, taste, wound.

biting *adj.* astringent, bitter, blighting, caustic, cold, cutting, cynical, freezing, harsh, hurtful, incisive, mordant, nipping, penetrating, piercing, raw, sarcastic, scathing, severe, sharp, stinging, tart, trenchant, withering.
antonyms bland, mild.

bitter *adj.* acerb, acerbic, acid, acrid, acrimonious, astringent, begrudging, biting, calamitous, crabbed, cruel, cynical, dire, distressing, embittered, fierce, freezing, galling, grievous, harsh, hateful, heartbreaking, hostile, intense, ironic, jaundiced, merciless, morose, odious, painful, poignant, rancorous, raw, resentful, ruthless, sarcastic, savage, severe, sharp, sore, sour, stinging, sullen, tart, unsweetened, vexatious, vinegary, waspish.
antonyms contented, genial, sweet.

bizarre *adj.* abnormal, comical, curious, deviant, eccentric, extraordinary, extravagant, fantastic, freakish, grotesque, ludicrous, odd, off-beat, outlandish, outré, peculiar, quaint, queer, ridiculous, strange, unusual, way-out, weird.
antonym normal.

black *adj.* angry, atrocious, bad, begrimed, coal-black, coaly, dark, darksome, depressing, dingy, dirty, dismal, doleful, dusky, ebony, evil, filthy, funereal, furious, gloomy, grim, grimy, grubby, hopeless, horrible, hostile, inky, jet, jet-black, jetty, lugubrious, menacing, moonless, morel, mournful, murky, nefarious, ominous, overcast, pitchy, raven, resentful, sable, sad, sloe, soiled, somber, sooty, stained, starless, Stygian, sullen, swarthy, threatening, thunderous, villainous, wicked.
v. ban, bar, blacklist, boycott, taboo.

blackball *v.* ban, bar, blacklist, debar, exclude, expel, ostracize, oust, pip, reject, repudiate, snub, veto.

blacken *v.* befoul, begrime, besmirch, calumniate, cloud, darken, decry, defame, defile, denigrate, detract, dishonor, malign, revile, slander, smear, smirch, smudge, soil, stain, sully, taint, tarnish, traduce, vilify. *antonyms* enhance, praise.

blackmail *n.* blood-sucking, chantage, exaction, extortion, hush money, intimidation, milking, pay-off, protection, ransom.
v. bleed, bribe, coerce, compel, demand, force, hold to ransom, lean on, milk, put the black on, squeeze, threaten.

blackout *n.* censorship, coma, concealment, cover-up, faint, oblivion, power cut, secrecy, suppression, swoon, syncope, unconsciousness.

bladder *n.* aveole, bag, bursa, cecum, capsule, cell, cyst, pocket, pouch, receptacle, sac, theca, utricle, vesica, vesicle, vesicula.

blade *n.* dagger, edge, knife, rapier, scalpel, sword, vane.

blame *n.* accountability, accusation, animadversion, castigation, censure, charge, complaint, condemnation, criticism, culpability, discommendation, fault, guilt, incrimination, liability, obloquy, onus, rap, recrimination, reprimand, reproach, reproof, responsibility, stick, stricture.
v. accuse, admonish, censure, charge, chide, condemn, criticize, disapprove, discommend, dispraise, find fault with, rebuke, reprehend, reprimand, reproach, reprove, tax, upbraid.
antonym exonerate.

blameless *adj.* above reproach, clean, clear, faultless, guiltless, immaculate, impeccable, inculpable, innocent, irreprehensible, irreproachable, irreprovable, perfect, sinless, stainless, unblamable, unblemished, unimpeachable, unspotted, unsullied, untarnished, upright, virtuous.
antonym guilty.

blanch *v.* bleach, blench, drain, etiolate, fade, pale, wan, whiten.
antonyms blush, color, redden.

bland *adv.* affable, amiable, balmy, boring, calm, characterless, congenial, courteous, demulcent, dull, fair-spoken, flat, friendly, gentle, gracious, humdrum, hypoallergenic, impassive, inscrutable, insipid, mild, mollifying, monotonous, nondescript, non-irritant, smooth, soft, soothing, suave, tasteless, tedious, temperate, unexciting, uninspiring, uninteresting, urbane, vapid, weak.
antonyms piquant, sharp.

blandishments *n.* blarney, cajolery, coaxing, compliments, enticements, fawning, flattery, inducements, ingratiation, inveiglement, lip-salve, persuasiveness, soft soap, sweet talk, sycophancy, wheedling.

blank *adj.* apathetic, bare, bewildered, clean, clear, confounded, confused, deadpan, disconcerted, dull, dumbfounded, empty, expressionless, featureless, glazed, hollow, immobile, impassive, inane, inscrutable, lifeless, muddled, nonplused, plain, poker-faced, sheer, spotless, staring, uncomprehending, unfilled, unmarked, unrhymed, vacant, vacuous, vague, void, white.
n. break, emptiness, gap, nothingness, space, tabula rasa, vacancy, vacuity, vacuum, void.

blanket *n.* carpet, cloak, coat, coating, cover, covering, coverlet, envelope, film, housing, layer, mackinaw, manta, mantle, rug, sheet, wrapper, wrapping.
adj. across-the-board, all-embracing, all-inclusive, comprehensive, inclusive, overall, sweeping, wide-ranging.
v. cloak, cloud, coat, conceal, cover, deaden, eclipse, hide, mask, muffle, obscure, surround.

blare *v.* blast, boom, clamor, clang, honk, hoot, peal, resound, ring, roar, scream, shriek, toot, trumpet.

blasphemous *adj.* execrative, godless, hubristic, impious, imprecatory, irreligious, irreverent, profane, sacrilegious, ungodly.

blasphemy *n.* curse, cursing, defilement, desecration, execration, expletive, hubris, impiety, impiousness, imprecation, irreverence, outrage, profanation, profaneness, profanity, sacrilege, swearing, violation.

blast[1] *n.* blare, blow, boom, honk, hoot, peal, roar, scream, shriek, sound, wail.

blast[2] *n.* bang, bluster, burst, clap, crack, crash, detonation, discharge, draught, eruption, explosion, flatus, gale, gust, hail, outburst, salvo, squall, storm, tempest, volley.
v. assail, attack, blight, blow up, burst, castigate, demolish, destroy, explode, flay, kill, lash, ruin, shatter, shrivel, storm at, wither.

blasted *adj.* blighted, desolated, destroyed, devastated, ravaged, ruined, scorched, shattered, wasted, withered.

blatant *adj.* arrant, bald, barefaced, brazen, clamorous, conspicuous, egregious, flagrant, flaunting, glaring, harsh, loud, naked, noisy, obtrusive, obvious, ostentatious, outright, overt, prominent, pronounced, sheer, unmitigated.

blather *n.* blether, chatter, chatterbox, chatterer, chitchat, claptrap, drivel, gibberish, gibble-gabble, gobbledegook, jabbering, loquacity, moonshine, nonsense, prattle, prattler, twaddle.
v. blabber, chatter, gab, gabble, haver, jabber, prattle.

bleach *v.* blanch, decolorise, etiolate, fade, lighten, pale, peroxide, whiten.

bleak *adj.* bare, barren, blae, blasted, cheerless, chilly, cold, colorless, comfortless, delightless, depressing, desolate, discouraging, disheartening, dismal, dreary, empty, exposed, gaunt, gloomy, grim, hopeless, joyless, leaden, loveless, open, raw, somber, unsheltered, weather-beaten, windswept, windy.
antonyms cheerful, congenial.

bleary *adj.* blurred, blurry, cloudy, dim, fogged, foggy, fuzzy, hazy, indistinct, misty, muddy, murky, obscured, rheumy, watery.

bleed *v.* blackmail, deplete, drain, exhaust, exploit, extort, extract, extravasate, exude, fleece, flow, gush, hemorrhage, leech, milk, ooze, reduce, run, sap, seep, spurt, squeeze, suck dry, trickle, weep.

blemish *n.* birthmark, blot, blotch, blur, botch, defect, deformity, disfigurement, disgrace, dishonor, fault, flaw, imperfection, mackle, macula, maculation, mark, naevus, smudge, speck, spot, stain, taint.

v. besmirch, blot, blotch, blur, damage, deface, disfigure, flaw, impair, injure, maculate, mar, mark, smirch, smudge, spoil, spot, stain, sully, taint, tarnish.

blend *v.* amalgamate, coalesce, combine, complement, compound, contemper, fit, fuse, harmonize, intermix, meld, merge, mingle, mix, synthesize, unite.
antonym separate.
n. alloy, amalgam, amalgamation, combination, composite, compound, concoction, fusion, interunion, meld, mix, mixture, synthesis, union.

bless *v.* anoint, approve, bestow, consecrate, countenance, dedicate, endow, exalt, extol, favor, glorify, grace, hallow, magnify, ordain, praise, provide, sanctify, thank.
antonyms condemn, curse.

blessed *adj.* adored, beatified, blissful, contented, divine, endowed, favored, fortunate, glad, hallowed, happy, holy, joyful, joyous, lucky, prosperous, revered, sacred, sanctified.
antonym cursed.

blessing *n.* advantage, approbation, approval, authority, backing, benedicite, benediction, benefit, benison, boon, bounty, commendation, concurrence, consecration, consent, countenance, dedication, favor, fortune, gain, gift, godsend, grace, help, invocation, kindness, leave, permission, profit, sanction, service, support, thanksgiving, windfall.
antonyms blight, condemnation, curse.

blight *n.* affliction, bane, cancer, canker, check, contamination, corruption, curse, decay, depression, disease, evil, fungus, infestation, mildew, pest, pestilence, plague, pollution, rot, scourge, set-back, woe.
antonyms blessing, boon.
v. annihilate, blast, crush, dash, destroy, disappoint, frustrate, injure, mar, ruin, shatter, shrivel, spoil, undermine, wither, wreck.
antonym bless.

blind *adj.* amaurotic, beetle-eyed, blinkered, careless, closed, concealed, dark, dim, eyeless, hasty, heedless, hidden, ignorant, impetuous, inattentive, inconsiderate, indifferent, indiscriminate, injudicious, insensate, insensitive, irrational, mindless, neglectful, oblivious, obscured, obstructed, prejudiced, purblind, rash, reckless, sand-blind, senseless, sightless, stone-blind, thoughtless, unaware, uncontrollable, uncritical, undiscerning, unobservant, unobserving, unreasoning, unseeing, unsighted, unthinking, violent, visionless, wild.
antonyms aware, clear, sighted.

n. camouflage, cloak, cover, cover-up, distraction, façade, feint, front, mask, masquerade, screen, smoke-screen.

blink *v.* bat, condone, connive at, disregard, flash, flicker, flutter, gleam, glimmer, glimpse, ignore, nictate, nictitate, overlook, peer, pink, scintillate, shine, sparkle, squint, twinkle, wink.

bliss *n.* beatitude, blessedness, blissfulness, ecstasy, euphoria, felicity, gladness, happiness, heaven, joy, nirvana, paradise, rapture.
antonyms damnation, misery.

blister *n.* abscess, bleb, boil, bubble, bulla, canker, carbuncle, cyst, furuncle, papilla, papula, papule, pimple, pompholyx, pustule, sore, swelling, ulcer, vesicle, vesicula, welt, wen.

blithe *adj.* animated, buoyant, carefree, careless, casual, cheerful, cheery, debonair, gay, gladsome, happy, heedless, jaunty, light-hearted, lightsome, lively, merry, mirthful, nonchalant, sprightly, sunny, thoughtless, unconcerned, untroubled, vivacious.
antonym morose.

bloated *adj.* blown up, bombastic, dilated, distended, dropsical, edematous, enlarged, expanded, inflated, sated, swollen, tumescent, tumid, turgid.
antonyms shriveled, shrunken, thin.

blob *n.* ball, bead, bobble, bubble, dab, dew-drop, drop, droplet, glob, globule, gob, lump, mass, pearl, pellet, pill, spot.

block *n.* bar, barrier, blockage, brick, cake, chunk, cube, delay, hang-up, hindrance, hunk, impediment, ingot, jam, let, lump, mass, obstacle, obstruction, piece, resistance, square, stoppage, tranche.
v. arrest, bar, check, choke, clog, close, dam up, deter, halt, hinder, impede, obstruct, obturate, oppilate, plug, scotch, stonewall, stop, stop up, thwart, trig.

blockade *n.* barricade, barrier, beleaguerment, closure, encirclement, obstruction, restriction, siege, stoppage.

blockhead *n.* bonehead, boodle, chump, dolt, dullard, dunce, fool, idiot, ignoramus, jobernowl, klutz, leatherhead, loggerhead, log-head, noodle, numskull, pigsconce, pinhead, pot-head, thickhead, thick-skull.
antonyms brain, genius.

blood *n.* ancestry, anger, birth, bloodshed, consanguinity, descendants, descent, extraction, family, kindred, kinship, lineage, murder, relations, relationship, temper, temperament.

bloodcurdling *adj.* appalling, chilling, dreadful, eldritch, fearful, frightening, hair-raising, horrendous, horrible, horrid, horrifying, scaring, spine-chilling, terrifying, weird.

bloodshed *n.* bloodletting, butchery, carnage, gore, killing, massacre, murder, slaughter, slaying.

bloodthirsty *adj.* barbaric, barbarous, brutal, cruel, ferocious, inhuman, murderous, ruthless, sanguinary, savage, slaughterous, vicious, warlike.

bloody *adj.* bleeding, bloodstained, blooming, brutal, cruel, ferocious, fierce, gaping, murderous, raw, sanguinary, sanguine, sanguineous, sanguinolent, savage.

bloom *n.* beauty, blossom, blossoming, blow, blush, bud, efflorescence, florescence, flourishing, flower, flush, freshness, glaucescence, glow, health, heyday, luster, perfection, prime, radiance, rosiness, vigor.
v. blossom, blow, bud, burgeon, develop, flourish, grow, open, prosper, sprout, succeed, thrive, wax.
antonym wither.

blooming *adj.* blossoming, bonny, florescent, flowering, healthful, healthy, rosy, ruddy.
antonym ailing.

blossom *n.* bloom, bud, floret, flower, flowers.
v. bloom, blow, burgeon, develop, effloresce, flourish, flower, grow, mature, progress, prosper, thrive.
antonym wither.

blot *n.* blemish, blotch, defect, disgrace, fault, flaw, mackle, macula, mark, patch, smear, smudge, speck, splodge, spot, stain, taint.
v. bespatter, blur, disfigure, disgrace, maculate, mar, mark, smudge, spoil, spot, stain, sully, taint, tarnish.

blow[1] *v.* bear, blare, blast, breathe, buffet, drive, exhale, fan, fling, flow, flutter, mouth, pant, pipe, play, puff, rush, sound, stream, sweep, toot, trumpet, vibrate, waft, whirl, whisk, wind.
n. blast, draft, flurry, gale, gust, puff, squall, tempest, wind.

blow[2] *n.* affliction, bang, bash, bat, belt, biff, bombshell, bop, box, buff, buffet, calamity, catastrophe, clap, clip, clout, clump, comedown, concussion, counterbluff, crack, disappointment, disaster, douse, haymaker, hit, jab, jolt, knock, knuckle sandwich, misfortune, oner, poke, punch, rap, reverse, setback, shock, siscrary, slap, slat, slosh, smack, sock, sockdologer, souse, stroke, swash, swat, swipe, thump, upset, wallop, wap, welt, whack, whang, winder.

blue[1] *adj.* aquamarine, azure, cerulean, cobalt, cyan, indigo, navy, sapphire, turquoise, ultramarine, watchet.

blue[2] *adj.* black, bleak, dejected, depressed, despondent, dismal, dispirited, doleful, down in the dumps, downcast, down-hearted, fed up, gloomy, glum, low, melancholy, miserable, morose, sad, unhappy.
antonym cheerful.

blue[3] *adv.* bawdy, coarse, dirty, improper, indecent, lewd, naughty, near the bone, near the knuckle, obscene, offensive, pornographic, risqué, smutty, vulgar.
antonym decent.

blueprint *n.* archetype, design, draft, guide, model, outline, pattern, pilot, plan, project, prototype, sketch.

blues *n.* blue devils, dejection, depression, despondency, doldrums, dumps, gloom, gloominess, glumness, melancholy, miseries, moodiness.
antonym euphoria.

bluff[1] *n.* bank, brow, cliff, crag, escarp, escarpment, foreland, headland, height, knoll, peak, precipice, promontory, ridge, scarp, slope.

adj. affable, blunt, candid, direct, downright, frank, genial, good-natured, hearty, open, outspoken, plainspoken, straightforward.
antonyms diplomatic, refined.

bluff[2] *v.* bamboozle, blind, deceive, defraud, delude, fake, feign, grift, hoodwink, humbug, lie, mislead, pretend, sham.
n. bluster, boast, braggadocio, bravado, deceit, deception, fake, fanfaronade, feint, fraud, grift, humbug, idle boast, lie, pretence, sham, show, subterfuge, trick.

blunder *n.* bêtise, bevue, bloomer, boner, boob, booboo, bungle, clanger, clinker, error, fault, faux pas, floater, fluff, gaffe, gaucherie, goof, howler, impropriety, inaccuracy, indiscretion, mistake, oversight, pratfall, slip, slip-up, solecism.
v. blow it, botch, bumble, bungle, err, flounder, flub, fluff, fumble, goof, miscalculate, misjudge, mismanage, muff it, slip up, stumble.

blunt *adj.* abrupt, bluff, brusque, candid, curt, direct, discourteous, downright, dull, dulled, edgeless, explicit, forthright, frank, honest, impolite, insensitive, obtuse, outspoken, plain-spoken, pointless, retuse, rounded, rude, straightforward, stubbed, stumpy, tactless, thick, trenchant, unceremonious, uncivil, unpolished, unsharpened.
antonyms sharp, tactful.
v. abate, allay, alleviate, anesthetize, bate, dampen, deaden, disedge, dull, hebetate, numb, obtund, palliate, rebate, retund, soften, stupefy, unedge, weaken.
antonyms intensify, sharpen.

blur *v.* becloud, befog, blear, blemish, blot, blotch, cloud, darken, dim, fog, mask, obfuscate, obscure, scumble, smear, smutch, soften, spot, stain.
n. blear, blot, blotch, cloudiness, confusion, dimness, fog, fuzziness, haze, indistinctness, muddle, obscurity, smear, smudge, spot, stain.

blush *v.* color, crimson, flush, glow, mantle, redden.
antonym blanch.
n. color, erubescence, flush, glow, reddening, rosiness, ruddiness, suffusion.

board[1] *n.* beam, clapboard, deal, lath, panel, plank, sheet, slab, slat, timber, two-by-four.

board[2] commons, food, grub, meals, provisions, rations, repasts, table, victuals.
v. accommodate, bed, billet, feed, house, lodge, put up, quarter, room, table.

board[3] *n.* advisers, chamber, commission, committee, conclave, council, directorate, directors, jury, panel, trustees.

board[4] *v.* catch, embark, embus, emplane, enter, entrain, mount.

boast *v.* be all mouth, blazon, blow, bluster, bounce, brag, claim, crow, exaggerate, exhibit, gasconade, possess, puff, rodomontade, show off, strut, swagger, talk big, trumpet, vaunt.
antonym deprecate.

n. avowal, brag, claim, fanfaronade, gasconade, gem, joy, pride, rodomontade, swank, treasure, vaunt.

body[1] *n.* being, bod, build, bulk, cadaver, carcass, consistency, corpse, corpus, creature, density, essence, figure, firmness, form, frame, human, individual, mass, material, matter, mortal, opacity, person, physique, relics, remains, richness, shape, solidity, stiff, substance, substantiality, tabernacle, torso, trunk.

body[2] *n.* association, band, bevy, bloc, cartel, collection, company, confederation, congress, corporation, crowd, group, horde, majority, mass, mob, multitude, society, syndicate, throng.

bogus *adj.* artificial, counterfeit, dummy, ersatz, fake, false, forged, fraudulent, imitation, phony, pinchbeck, pseudo, sham, spoof, spurious, unauthentic.
antonym genuine.

boil[1] *v.* agitate, brew, bubble, churn, decoct, effervesce, erupt, explode, fizz, foam, froth, fulminate, fume, gurgle, mantle, parboil, rage, rave, seethe, simmer, sizzle, spume, steam, stew, storm, wallop.

boil down abridge, abstract, concentrate, condense, decrease, digest, distil, epitomize, reduce, summarize, synopsize.

boil[2] *n.* abscess, anthrax, bleb, blister, carbuncle, furuncle, gathering, gumboil, inflammation, papule, parulis, pimple, pock, pustule, tumor, ulcer, whelk.

boisterous *adj.* blusterous, blustery, bouncy, clamorous, disorderly, exuberant, gusty, impetuous, loud, noisy, obstreperous, rackety, raging, rambunctious, riotous, roisting, rollicking, rough, rowdy, rumbustious, squally, tempestuous, termagant, tumultous, turbulent, unrestrained, unruly, uproarious, vociferous, wild.
antonyms calm, quiet, restrained.

bold *adj.* adventurous, audacious, brash, brave, brazen, bright, cheeky, colorful, confident, conspicuous, courageous, daring, dauntless, enterprising, extrovert, eye-catching, fearless, flamboyant, flashy, forceful, forward, fresh, gallant, heroic, impudent, insolent, intrepid, jazzy, lively, loud, malapert, outgoing, pert, plucky, prominent, pronounced, saucy, shameless, showy, spirited, striking, strong, unabashed, unashamed, unbashful, valiant, valorous, venturesome, vivid.
antonyms diffident, restrained.

bolt *n.* arrow, bar, bound, catch, dart, dash, elopement, escape, fastener, flight, flit, latch, lock, missile, peg, pin, projectile, rivet, rod, rush, shaft, sneck, sprint, thunderbolt.
v. abscond, bar, bound, cram, dart, dash, devour, discharge, elope, escape, expel, fasten, fetter, flee, fly, gobble, gorge, gulp, guzzle, hurtle, jump, latch, leap, lock, run, rush, secure, spring, sprint, stuff, wolf.

bomb *n.* A-bomb, bombshell, charge, egg, explosive, grenade, mine, missile, mortar-bomb, petrol bomb, projectile, rocket, shell, torpedo.

v. attack, blow up, bombard, collapse, come a cropper, come to grief, destroy, fail, flop, misfire, shell, strafe, torpedo.

bond *n.* affiliation, affinity, agreement, attachment, band, binding, chain, compact, connection, contract, copula, cord, covenant, fastening, fetter, ligament, ligature, link, manacle, obligation, pledge, promise, relation, shackle, tie, union, vinculum, word.
v. bind, connect, fasten, fuse, glue, gum, paste, seal, unite.

bondage *n.* captivity, confinement, durance, duress, enslavement, enthralment, imprisonment, incarceration, restraint, serfdom, servitude, slavery, subjection, subjugation, subservience, thraldom, vassalage, yoke.
antonyms freedom, independence.

book *n.* album booklet, codex, companion, diary, hornbook, incunable, incunabulum, jotter, lectionary, manual, manuscript, notebook, pad, paperback, publication, roll, scroll, textbook, tome, tract, volume, work.
v. arrange, arrest, bag, charter, engage, enter, insert, list, log, note, organize, post, procure, program, record, register, reserve, schedule.
antonym cancel.

boom[1] *v.* bang, blare, blast, crash, explode, resound, reverberate, roar, roll, rumble, sound, thunder.
n. bang, blast, burst, clang, clap, crash, explosion, reverberation, roar, rumble, thunder.

boom[2] *v.* develop, escalate, expand, explode, flourish, gain, go from strength to strength, grow, increase, intensify, prosper, spurt, strengthen, succeed, swell, thrive.
antonyms collapse, fail.
n. advance, boost, development, escalation, expansion, explosion, gain, growth, improvement, increase, jump, spurt, upsurge, upturn.
antonyms collapse, failure.

boon *n.* advantage, benefaction, benefit, blessing, donation, favor, gift, godsend, grant, gratification, gratuity, kindness, petition, present, windfall.
antonyms blight, disadvantage.

boor *n.* barbarian, brute, bumpkin, churl, clodhopper, goop, Goth, hayseed, hedgehog, hick, hog, lout, oaf, peasant, philistine, rube, rustic, vulgarian, yokel.
antonyms aesthete, charmer.

boorish *adj.* awkward, barbaric, bearish, churlish, clodhopping, clownish, coarse, crude, gross, gruff, ill-bred, inconsiderate, loutish, lubberly, lumpen, oafish, rude, ruffianly, rustic, slobbish, uncivilized, uncouth, uneducated, unrefined, vulgar.
antonyms cultured, polite, refined.

boost *n.* addition, advancement, ego-trip, encouragement, enhancement, expansion, fillip, heave, help, hoist, hype, improvement, increase, increment, jump, lift, praise, promotion, push, rise, supplement, thrust.
antonyms blow, setback.

v. advance, advertise, aid, amplify, assist, augment, bolster, develop, elevate, encourage, enhance, enlarge, expand, foster, further, heave, heighten, hoist, improve, increase, inspire, jack up, lift, plug, praise, promote, push, raise, supplement, support, sustain, thrust.
antonyms hinder, undermine.

boot[1] *n.* bootee, galosh, gumshoe, jackboot, loafer, moccasin, mule, overshoe, platform, pump, riding-boot, rubber, sneaker, top-boot, wader, wellington.
v. bounce, dismiss, eject, expel, fire, give the bum's rush, give the heave, kick, kick out, knock, oust, punt, sack, shove.

boot[2] *v.* advantage, aid, avail, benefit, help, profit, serve.

bootless *adj.* barren, fruitless, futile, ineffective, on a hiding to nothing, pointless, profitless, sterile, unavailing, unproductive, unsuccessful, useless, vain, worthless.
antonyms profitable, useful.

bootlicking *n.* ass-licking, back-scratching, crawling, cringing, deference, faggery, fagging, fawning, flattery, groveling, heepishness, ingratiation, lackeying, obsequiousness, servility, sycophancy, toadying.

booty *n.* boodle, bunce, gains, haul, loot, pickings, pillage, plunder, spoil, spoils, swag, takings, winnings.

border *n.* borderline, bound, boundary, bounds, brim, brink, circumference, confine, confines, demarcation, edge, fringe, frontier, hem, limit, limits, lip, list, march, margin, perimeter, periphery, rand, rim, screed, selvage, skirt, surround, trimming, valance, verge.
adj. boundary, circumscriptive, dividing, frontier, limitary, limitrophe, marginal, perimeter, separating, side.

borderline *adj.* ambivalent, doubtful, iffy, indecisive, indefinite, indeterminate, marginal, problematic, uncertain.
antonyms certain, definite.

bore[1] *v.* burrow, countermine, drill, gouge, mine, penetrate, perforate, pierce, sap, sink, thrill, tunnel, undermine.

bore[2] *v.* annoy, bother, bug, fatigue, irk, irritate, jade, pester, tire, trouble, vex, weary, worry.
antonyms charm, interest.
n. annoyance, bind, bother, drag, dullard, headache, nuisance, pain, pain in the neck, pest, schmo, terebrant, trial, vexation, vieux jeu, yawn.
antonym pleasure.

boredom *n.* acedia, apathy, doldrums, dullness, ennui, flatness, irksomeness, listlessness, monotony, sameness, tediousness, tedium, vapors, weariness, wearisomeness, world-weariness.
antonym interest.

boring *adj.* commonplace, dead, dreary, dry, dull, ennuying, flat, ho-hum, humdrum, insipid, irksome, monotonous, repetitious, routine, stale, stupid, tedious, tiresome, tiring, trite, unamusing, undiverting, unedifying, uneventful, unexciting, unfunny, unimagi-

native, uninspired, uninteresting, unvaried, unwitty, vapid, wearisome.
antonyms interesting, original.

borrow *v.* adopt, ape, appropriate, cadge, copy, crib, derive, draw, echo, filch, imitate, list, mimic, obtain, pilfer, pirate, plagiarize, scrounge, sponge, steal, take, use, usurp.

bosom *n.* breast, bust, center, chest, circle, core, heart, midst, protection, sanctuary, shelter.
adj. boon, cherished, close, confidential, dear, favorite, inseparable, intimate.

boss[1] *n.* administrator, baron, captain, chief, director, employer, executive, foreman, gaffer, governor, head, leader, manager, master, overseer, owner, superintendent, supervisor, supremo.
v. administrate, command, control, direct, employ, manage, oversee, run, superintend, supervise.

boss[2] *n.* knob, knub, knubble, nub, nubble, omphalos, point, protuberance, stud, tip, umbo.

bossy *adj.* arrogant, authoritarian, autocratic, demanding, despotic, dictatorial, domineering, exacting, hectoring, high-handed, imperious, insistent, lordly, oppressive, overbearing, tyrannical.
antonyms unassertive.

botch *v.* blunder, bungle, butcher, cobble, corpse, do carelessly, flub, fudge, fumble, goof, louse up, mar, mend, mess, mismanage, muff, patch, ruin, screw up, spoil.
antonyms accomplish, succeed. *n.* balls-up, blunder, bungle, cock-up, failure, farce, hash, mess, miscarriage, muddle, shambles.
antonyms success.

bother *v.* alarm, annoy, bore, chivvy, concern, dismay, distress, disturb, dog, harass, harry, hassle, inconvenience, irk, irritate, molest, nag, pester, plague, pother, pudder, trouble, upset, vex, worry.
n. aggravation, annoyance, bustle, consternation, difficulty, flurry, fuss, hassle, inconvenience, irritation, kerfuffle, molestation, nuisance, palaver, perplexity, pest, pother, problem, pudder, strain, trouble, vexation, worry.

bothersome *adj.* aggravating, annoying, boring, distressing, exasperating, inconvenient, infuriating, irksome, irritating, laborious, tedious, tiresome, troublesome, vexatious, vexing, wearisome.

bottom *n.* ass, backside, base, basis, behind, bum, butt, buttocks, core, depths, derrière, essence, floor, foot, foundation, fundament, fundus, ground, groundwork, heart, nadir, origin, pedestal, plinth, posterior, principle, rear, rear end, root, rump, seat, sit-upon, socle, sole, source, substance, substratum, substructure, support, tail, underneath, underside, understratum.

bounce *v.* bob, bound, bump, dap, dismiss, eject, expel, jounce, jump, kick out, leap, oust, rebound, recoil, resile, ricochet, spring, throw out.
n. animation, bound, dap, dynamism, ebullience, elasticity, energy, exuberance, give, go, life, liveliness, pep,

rebound, recoil, resilience, spring, springiness, vigor, vitality, vivacity, zip.

bound[1] *adj.* bandaged, beholden, cased, certain, chained, committed, compelled, constrained, destined, doomed, duty-bound, fastened, fated, fixed, forced, held, liable, manacled, obligated, obliged, pinioned, pledged, required, restricted, secured, sure, tied, tied up.

bound[2] *v.* bob, bounce, caper, frisk, gallumph, gambol, hurdle, jump, leap, lope, loup, lunge, pounce, prance, skip, spring, vault.
n. bob, bounce, caper, dance, frisk, gambado, gambol, jump, leap, lope, loup, lunge, pounce, prance, scamper, skip, spring, vault.

boundary *n.* abuttal, barrier, border, borderline, bounds, bourne, brink, confines, demarcation, edge, extremity, fringe, frontier, junction, limes, limits, line, march, margin, mete, perimeter, termination, verge.
adj. border, demarcation, frontier, limitary, limitrophe, perimeter.

boundless *adj.* countless, endless, illimitable, immeasurable, immense, incalculable, indefatigable, inexhaustible, infinite, interminable, interminate, limitless, measureless, prodigious, unbounded, unconfined, unending, unflagging, unlimited, untold, vast.
antonym limited.

bounty *n.* allowance, almsgiving, annuity, assistance, beneficence, benevolence, bonus, charity, donation, generosity, gift, grace, grant, gratuity, kindness, largesse, liberality, philanthropy, premium, present, recompense, reward.

bourgeois *adj.* Biedermeier, circumscribed, commonplace, conformist, conservative, conventional, dull, hide-bound, humdrum, kitsch, materialistic, middle-class, pedestrian, tawdry, traditional, trite, trivial, unadventurous, unimaginative, uninspired, unoriginal, vulgar.
antonyms bohemian, original, unconventional.
n. conformist, petit bourgeois, philistine, plebeian, stick-in-the-mud.
antonyms bohemian, nonconformist.

bout *n.* battle, competition, contest, course, encounter, engagement, fight, fit, go, heat, match, period, round, run, session, set-to, spell, spree, stint, stretch, struggle, term, time, turn, venue.

bow[1] *v.* accept, acquiesce, bend, bob, capitulate, comply, concede, conquer, consent, crush, curtsey, defer, depress, droop, genuflect, give in, incline, kowtow, nod, overpower, stoop, subdue, subjugate, submit, surrender, vanquish, yield.
n. acknowledgment, bending, bob, curtsey, genuflexion, inclination, kowtow, nod, obeisance, salaam, salutation.

bow out abandon, back out, bunk off, chicken out, defect, desert, give up, opt out, pull out, quit, resign, retire, stand down, step down, withdraw.

bow[2] *n.* beak, head, prow, rostrum, stem.

bowels *n.* belly, center, core, depths, entrails, guts, heart, hold, innards, inside, insides, interior, intestines, middle, viscera, vitals.

bowl[1] *n.* basin, container, cruse, dish, pan, porringer, receptacle, sink, tureen, vessel.

bowl[2] *n.* jack, wood.
v. fling, hurl, pitch, revolve, roll, rotate, spin, throw, trundle, whirl.

bowl over amaze, astonish, astound, dumbfound, fell, flabbergast, floor, stagger, startle, stun, surprise, topple, unbalance.

bowl[3] *n.* amphitheater, arena, auditorium, coliseum, field, ground, hall, hippodrome, stadium.

box[1] *n.* bijou, carton, case, casket, chest, coffer, coffin, coffret, consignment, container, coop, fund, pack, package, portmanteau, present, pyx, pyxis, receptacle, trunk.
v. case, embox, encase, pack, package, wrap.

box[2] *v.* buffet, butt, clout, cuff, fight, hit, punch, slap, sock, spar, strike, thwack, wallop, whack, wham, whang.
n. blow, buffet, clout, cuff, punch, slap, stroke, thump, wallop, wham, whang.

boy *n.* callant, cub, dandiprat, fellow, gamin, gossoon, halfling, imp, junior, kid, lad, loon, loonie, man-child, nipper, puppy, schoolboy, spalpeen, stripling, urchin, whippersnapper, youngster, youth.

boycott *v.* ban, bar, black, blackball, blacklist, cold-shoulder, disallow, embargo, exclude, ignore, ostracize, outlaw, prohibit, proscribe, refuse, reject, spurn.
antonyms encourage, support.

boyfriend *n.* admirer, beau, date, fancy man, fellow, inamorato, lover, man, steady, suitor, swain, sweetheart, young man.

brace[1] *n.* binder, bracer, bracket, buttress, cleat, corset, nogging, prop, reinforcement, shoring, stanchion, stay, strap, strut, support, truss. *v.* bandage, bind, bolster, buttress, fasten, fortify, prop, reinforce, shore (up), steady, strap, strengthen, support, tie, tighten.

brace[2] *n.* couple, doubleton, duo, pair, twosome.

bracing *adj.* brisk, crisp, energetic, energizing, enlivening, exhilarating, fortifying, fresh, invigorating, refreshing, restorative, reviving, rousing, stimulating, strengthening, tonic, vigorous.
antonym debilitating.

brag *v.* bluster, boast, crow, fanfaronade, rodomontade, swagger, talk big, trumpet, vapor, vaunt.
antonym deprecate.

braid *v.* entwine, interlace, intertwine, interweave, lace, plait, ravel, twine, twist, weave, wind.
antonyms undo, untwist.

brain[1] *n.* boffin, egghead, expert, genius, highbrow, intellect, intellectual, mastermind, prodigy, pundit, sage, savant, scholar, wizard.
antonym simpleton.

brain[2] *n.* cerebrum, gray matter, intellect, mind, sensorium, sensory.

brake *n.* check, constraint, control, curb, drag, rein, restraint, restriction, retardment.

v. check, decelerate, drag, halt, moderate, pull up, retard, slacken, slow, stop.

antonym accelerate.

branch *n.* arm, bough, chapter, department, division, grain, limb, lodge, office, offshoot, part, prong, ramification, ramus, section, shoot, sprig, subdivision, subsection, whip, wing, witty.

branch out bifurcate, broaden out, develop, divaricate, diversify, enlarge, expand, extend, increase, move on, multiply, proliferate, ramify, vary.

brand *n.* brand-name, class, emblem, grade, hallmark, kind, label, line, logo, make, mark, marker, marque, quality, sign, sort, species, stamp, symbol, trademark, type, variety.

v. burn, censure, denounce, discredit, disgrace, label, mark, scar, stain, stamp, stigmatize, taint, type.

brave *adj.* audacious, bold, courageous, daring, dauntless, doughty, fearless, fine, gallant, game, glorious, hardy, heroic, indomitable, intrepid, plucky, resolute, resplendent, splendid, stalwart, stoic, stoical, stouthearted, unafraid, undaunted, unflinching, valiant, valorous.

antonyms cowardly, timid.

v. accost, bear, beard, challenge, confront, dare, defy, encounter, endure, face, face up to, stand up to, suffer, withstand.

antonyms capitulate, crumple.

brawl *n.* affray, altercation, argument, bagarre, battle, broil, bust-up, clash, disorder, dispute, dog-fight, Donnybrook, dust-up, fight, fracas, fray, free-for-all, mêlée, punch-up, quarrel, row, ruckus, rumpus, scrap, scuffle, squabble, tumult, uproar, wrangle.

v. altercate, argue, battle, come to blows, dispute, fight, flyte, quarrel, row, scrap, scuffle, squabble, tussle, wrangle, wrestle.

brawn *n.* beef, beefiness, brawniness, bulk, bulkiness, flesh, meat, might, muscle, muscles, muscularity, power, robustness, sinews, strength, thews.

brazen *adj.* assured, audacious, barefaced, blatant, bold, brash, brassy, defiant, flagrant, forward, immodest, impudent, insolent, malapert, pert, saucy, shameless, unabashed, unashamed.

antonym shamefaced.

breach *n.* alienation, aperture, break, break-up, chasm, cleft, contravention, crack, crevice, difference, disaffection, disagreement, discontinuity, disobedience, disruption, dissension, dissociation, division, estrangement, fissure, gap, hole, infraction, infringement, lapse, offence, opening, parting, quarrel, rent, rift, rupture, schism, scission, scissure, secession, separation, severance, split, transgression, trespass, variance, violation.

break *v.* abandon, absorb, announce, appear, bankrupt, batter, beat, better, breach, burst, bust, contravene, cow, crack, crash, cripple, cushion, cut, dash, defeat, degrade, demolish, demoralize, destroy, diminish, discharge, disclose, discontinue, disintegrate, disobey, dispirit, disregard, divide, divulge, emerge, enervate, enfeeble, erupt, escape, exceed, excel, explode, flee, flout, fly, fract, fracture, fragment, go phut, happen, humiliate, impair, impart, incapacitate, inform, infract, infringe, interrupt, jigger, knacker, knap, lessen, moderate, modify, occur, outdo, outstrip, part, pause, proclaim, reduce, rend, rest, retard, reveal, ruin, separate, sever, shatter, shiver, smash, snap, soften, splinter, split, stave, stop, subdue, surpass, suspend, tame, tear, tell, transgress, undermine, undo, violate, weaken, worst.

n. abruption, advantage, alienation, breach, breather, chance, cleft, crack, crevice, disaffection, discontinuity, dispute, disruption, divergence, division, estrangement, fissure, fortune, fracture, gap, gash, halt, hiatus, hole, interlude, intermission, interruption, interval, lapse, letup, lull, opening, opportunity, pause, quarrel, recess, rent, respite, rest, rift, rupture, schism, separation, split, suspension, tear, time-out.

breed *v.* arouse, bear, beget, bring forth, bring up, cause, create, cultivate, develop, discipline, educate, engender, foster, generate, hatch, induce, instruct, make, multiply, nourish, nurture, occasion, originate, procreate, produce, propagate, raise, rear, reproduce, train.

n. family, ilk, kind, line, lineage, pedigree, progeny, race, sort, species, stamp, stock, strain, type, variety.

breeze *n.* air, breath, cat's-paw, draft, flurry, gale, gust, waft, whiff, wind, zephyr.

v. flit, glide, hurry, sail, sally, sweep, trip, wander.

breezy *adj.* airy, animated, blithe, blowing, blowy, blustery, bright, buoyant, carefree, careless, casual, cheerful, debonair, easy-going, exhilarating, fresh, gusty, informal, insouciant, jaunty, light, light-hearted, lively, nonchalant, sprightly, squally, sunny, untroubled, vivacious, windy.

antonyms calm, staid.

brevity *n.* abruptness, briefness, brusqueness, conciseness, concision, crispness, curtness, economy, ephemerality, evanescence, fugacity, impermanence, incisiveness, laconicism, laconism, pithiness, shortness, succinctness, summariness, terseness, transience, transitoriness.

antonyms longevity, permanence, verbosity.

brew *v.* boil, build up, concoct, contrive, cook, decoct, develop, devise, excite, ferment, foment, gather, hatch, infuse, mix, plan, plot, prepare, project, scheme, seethe, soak, steep, stew.

n. beverage, blend, bouillon, brewage, broth, concoction, distillation, drink, fermentation, gruel, infusion, liquor, mixture, potion, preparation, stew.

bribe *n.* allurement, back-hander, baksheesh, boodle, dash, enticement, graft, grease, hush money, incentive, inducement, kickback, pay-off, payola, protection money, refresher, slush fund, sweetener.

v. buy off, buy over, corrupt, reward, square, suborn.

bridle *v.* check, contain, control, curb, govern, master, moderate, rein in, repress, restrain, subdue.

brief *adj.* abrupt, aphoristic, blunt, brusque, capsular, compendious, compressed, concise, crisp, cursory, curt, ephemeral, fast, fleeting, fugacious, fugitive, hasty, laconic, limited, momentary, passing, pithy, quick, sharp, short, short-lived, succinct, surly, swift, temporary, terse, thumbnail, transient, transitory. *antonyms* long, long-lived, verbose.

n. advice, argument, briefing, case, contention, data, defense, demonstration, directions, directive, dossier, instructions, mandate, orders, outline, précis, remit, summary.

v. advise, direct, explain, fill in, gen up, guide, inform, instruct, prepare, prime.

brigand *n.* bandit, cateran, dacoit, desperado, footpad, freebooter, gangster, haiduk, heister, highwayman, klepht, marauder, outlaw, plunderer, robber, ruffian.

bright *adj.* ablaze, acute, astute, auspicious, beaming, blazing, brainy, breezy, brilliant, burnished, cheerful, clear, clear-headed, clever, cloudless, dazzling, effulgent, encouraging, excellent, favorable, flashing, fulgent, gay, genial, glad, glaring, gleaming, glistening, glittering, glorious, glowing, golden, happy, hopeful, illuminated, illustrious, ingenious, intelligent, intense, inventive, jolly, joyful, joyous, keen, lambent, lamping, light-hearted, limpid, lively, lucent, lucid, luculent, luminous, lustrous, magnificent, merry, observant, optimistic, pellucid, perceptive, percipient, perspicacious, polished, prefulgent, promising, propitious, prosperous, quick, quick-witted, radiant, resplendent, rosy, scintillating, sharp, sheeny, shimmering, shining, smart, sparkling, splendid, sunny, translucent, transparent, twinkling, unclouded, undulled, untarnished, vivacious, vivid, wide-awake.

antonyms depressing, dull, stupid.

brilliant *adj.* ablaze, accomplished, adroit, animated, astute, blazing, brainy, bright, celebrated, clever, coruscating, dazzling, effulgent, eminent, exceptional, expert, famous, gemmy, gifted, glaring, glittering, glorious, glossy, illustrious, ingenious, intellectual, intelligent, intense, inventive, lambent, luminous, magnificent, masterly, outstanding, quick, refulgent, scintillating, shining, showy, skilful, sparkling, splendid, star, star-like, superb, talented, vivacious, vivid, witty.

antonyms dull, restrained, stupid, undistinguished.

brim *n.* border, brink, circumference, edge, lip, marge, margin, perimeter, periphery, rim, skirt, verge.

bring *v.* accompany, accustom, add, attract, bear, carry, cause, command, conduct, convey, convince, create, deliver, dispose, draw, earn, effect, engender, escort, fetch, force, gather, generate, get, gross, guide, induce, inflict, influence, introduce, lead, make, move, net,

occasion, persuade, produce, prompt, return, sway, take, transfer, transport, usher, wreak, yield.

brink *n.* bank, border, boundary, brim, edge, extremity, fringe, limit, lip, marge, margin, point, rim, skirt, threshold, verge, waterside.

brisk *adj.* active, agile, alert, allegro, bracing, bright, brushy, bustling, busy, crank, crisp, effervescing, energetic, exhilarating, expeditious, fresh, galliard, invigorating, keen, lively, nimble, nippy, no-nonsense, prompt, quick, refreshing, sharp, snappy, speedy, spirited, sprightly, spry, stimulating, vigorous.

antonym sluggish.

briskly *adv.* abruptly, actively, allegro, brightly, decisively, efficiently, energetically, expeditiously, incisively, nimbly, promptly, quickly, rapidly, readily, smartly, vigorously.

antonym sluggishly.

bristle *n.* barb, hair, prickle, spine, stubble, thorn, vibrissa, whisker.

v. bridle, draw oneself up, horripilate, prickle, react, rise, seethe, spit.

brittle *adj.* anxious, breakable, crackly, crisp, crumbling, crumbly, curt, delicate, edgy, fragile, frail, frangible, friable, frush, irritable, nervous, nervy, shattery, shivery, short, tense.

antonyms durable, resilient, sturdy.

broach *v.* crack open, introduce, launch into, mention, pierce, propose, puncture, raise, start, suggest, tap, uncork, utter.

broad *adj.* all-embracing, ample, beamy, blue, capacious, catholic, coarse, comprehensive, eclectic, encyclopedic, enlightened, expansive, extensive, far-reaching, general, generous, gross, improper, inclusive, indecent, indelicate, large, latitudinous, roomy, spacious, square, sweeping, tolerant, universal, unlimited, unrefined, vast, voluminous, vulgar, wide, wide-ranging, widespread.

antonym narrow.

broadcast *v.* advertise, air, announce, beam, cable, circulate, disseminate, proclaim, promulgate, publicize, publish, radio, relay, report, show, spread, televise, transmit.

n. program, relay, show, telecast, transmission.

broaden *v.* augment, branch out, develop, diversify, enlarge, enlighten, expand, extend, increase, open up, spread, stretch, supplement, swell, thicken, widen.

broad-minded *adj.* catholic, cosmopolitan, dispassionate, enlightened, flexible, free-thinking, indulgent, liberal, open-minded, permissive, receptive, tolerant, unbiased, unprejudiced, verligte.

brochure *n.* advertisement, booklet, broadsheet, broadside, circular, folder, handbill, hand-out, leaflet, pamphlet.

broil *n.* affray, altercation, argument, brawl, brouhaha, dispute, disturbance, fracas, fray, imbroglio, quarrel, scrimmage, scrum, stramash, strife, tumult, wrangle.

broken *adj.* bankrupt, beaten, betrayed, browbeaten, burst, crippled, crushed, defeated, defective, demolished, demoralized, destroyed, disconnected, discontinuous, dishonored, disjointed, dismantled, dispersed, disregarded, disturbed, down, dud, duff, erratic, exhausted, faulty, feeble, forgotten, fracted, fractured, fragmentary, fragmented, halting, hesitating, humbled, ignored, imperfect, incoherent, incomplete, infirm, infringed, intermittent, interrupted, isolated, jiggered, kaput, knackered, oppressed, out of order, overpowered, prerupt, rent, retracted, routed, ruined, run-down, ruptured, separated, severed, shattered, shivered, spasmodic, spent, stammering, subdued, tamed, traduced, transgressed, uncertain, vanquished, variegated, weak.

broken-hearted *adj.* crestfallen, dejected, desolate, despairing, despondent, devastated, disappointed, disconsolate, grief-stricken, hard-hit, heartbroken, heartsick, heartsore, inconsolable, miserable, mournful, prostrated, sorrowful, unhappy, wretched.

bromide *n.* anodyne, banality, cliché, commonplace, platitude, stereotype, truism.

brooch *n.* badge, breastpin, clasp, clip, pin, prop.

brood *v.* agonize, cover, dwell on, fret, go over, hatch, incubate, meditate, mope, mull over, muse, ponder, rehearse, repine, ruminate.
n. birth, chicks, children, clutch, family, hatch, issue, litter, nide, offspring, progeny, spawn, young.

brook[1] *n.* beck, burn, channel, freshet, gill, inlet, mill, rill, rivulet, runnel, stream, streamlet, watercourse.

brook[2] *v.* abide, accept, allow, bear, countenance, endure, permit, stand, stomach, submit to, suffer, support, swallow, thole, tolerate, withstand.

brother *n.* associate, blood-brother, brer, chum, colleague, companion, compeer, comrade, confrère, cousin, fellow, fellow-creature, friar, friend, kin, kinsman, mate, monk, pal, partner, relation, relative, religieux, religious, sibling.

brotherhood *n.* affiliation, alliance, association, clan, clique, community, confederacy, confederation, confraternity, confrérie, coterie, fraternity, guild, league, society, union.

brotherly *adj.* affectionate, amicable, benevolent, caring, concerned, cordial, fraternal, friendly, kind, loving, neighborly, philanthropic, supervisory, sympathetic.
antonyms callous, unbrotherly.

brow *n.* appearance, aspect, bearing, brink, cliff, countenance, crown, edge, eyebrow, face, forehead, front, mien, peak, ridge, rim, summit, temples, tip, top, verge, visage.

browbeat *v.* awe, batter, bludgeon, bulldoze, bully, coerce, cow, domineer, dragoon, hector, hound, intimidate, oppress, overbear, threaten, tyrannize.
antonym coax.

brown *adj.* auburn, bay, brick, bronze, bronzed, browned, brunette, chestnut, chocolate, coffee, dark, donkey, dun, dusky, fuscous, ginger, hazel, mahogany, russet, rust, rusty, sunburnt, tan, tanned, tawny, titian, toasted, umber, vandyke brown.

brown study absence, absent-mindedness, absorption, abstraction, contemplation, meditation, musing, pensiveness, preoccupation, reflection, reverie, rumination.

browse *v.* crop, dip into, eat, feed, flick through, graze, leaf through, nibble, pasture, peruse, scan, skim, survey.

bruise *v.* blacken, blemish, contund, contuse, crush, discolor, grieve, hurt, injure, insult, mar, mark, offend, pound, pulverize, stain, wound.
n. blemish, contusion, discoloration, injury, mark, rainbow, shiner, swelling.

brunt *n.* burden, force, impact, impetus, pressure, shock, strain, stress, thrust, violence, weight.

brush[1] *n.* besom, broom, sweeper.
v. buff, burnish, caress, clean, contact, flick, glance, graze, kiss, paint, polish, rub, scrape, shine, stroke, sweep, touch, wash.

brush[2] *n.* brushwood, bushes, frith, ground cover, scrub, shrubs, thicket, undergrowth, underwood.

brush[3] *n.* clash, conflict, confrontation, dust-up, encounter, fight, fracas, incident, run-in, scrap, set-to, skirmish, tussle.

brush-off *n.* cold shoulder, discouragement, dismissal, go-by, rebuff, refusal, rejection, repudiation, repulse, slight, snub.
antonym encouragement.

brusque *adj.* abrupt, blunt, curt, discourteous, gruff, hasty, impolite, sharp, short, surly, tactless, tart, terse, uncivil, undiplomatic.
antonyms courteous, tactful.

brutal *adj.* animal, barbarous, bearish, beastly, bestial, bloodthirsty, boarish, brute, brutish, callous, carnal, coarse, crude, cruel, doggish, ferocious, gruff, harsh, heartless, impolite, inhuman, inhumane, insensitive, merciless, pitiless, remorseless, rough, rude, ruthless, savage, sensual, severe, uncivil, uncivilized, unfeeling, unmannerly, unsympathetic, vicious.
antonyms humane, kindly.

brute *n.* animal, barbarian, beast, bête, boor, creature, devil, fiend, lout, monster, ogre, sadist, savage, swine.
antonym gentleman.
adj. bestial, bodily, carnal, coarse, depraved, fleshly, gross, instinctive, mindless, physical, senseless, sensual, unthinking.
antonym refined.

bubble[1] *n.* ball, bead, bladder, blister, blob, drop, droplet, globule, vesicle.
v. babble, boil, burble, effervesce, fizz, foam, froth, gurgle, murmur, percolate, purl, ripple, seethe, sparkle, trickle, trill, wallop.

bubble[2] *n.* bagatelle, delusion, fantasy, fraud, illusion, sting, toy, trifle, vanity.

buccaneer *n.* corsair, filibuster, freebooter, pirate, privateer, sea-robber, sea-rover, sea-wolf.

buck[1] *n.* beau, blade, blood, coxcomb, dandy, fop, gallant, playboy, popinjay, spark, swell.

buck[2] *v.* bound, cheer, dislodge, encourage, gladden, gratify, hearten, inspirit, jerk, jump, leap, please, prance, spring, start, throw, unseat, vault.

bucket *n.* bail, barrel, basin, can, cask, kibble, pail, pan, pitcher, vessel.

buckle *n.* bend, bulge, catch, clasp, clip, contortion, distortion, fastener, hasp, kink, twist, warp.
v. bend, bulge, catch, cave in, clasp, close, collapse, connect, contort, crumple, distort, fasten, fold, hitch, hook, secure, twist, warp, wrinkle.

bud *n.* embryo, germ, knosp, shoot, sprig, sprout.
v. burgeon, develop, grow, pullulate, shoot, sprout.
antonyms waste away, wither.

budge *v.* bend, change, convince, dislodge, give (way), inch, influence, move, persuade, propel, push, remove, roll, shift, slide, stir, sway, yield.

budget *n.* allocation, allotment, allowance, cost, estimate, finances, fonds, funds, means, resources.
v. allocate, apportion, cost, estimate, plan, ration.

buff[1] *adj.* fawn, fulvid, fulvous, khaki, sandy, straw, tan, yellowish, yellowish-brown.
v. brush, burnish, polish, polish up, rub, shine, smooth.

buff[2] *n.* addict, admirer, aficionado, bug, cognoscente, connoisseur, devotee, enthusiast, expert, fan, fiend, freak.

buffet[1] *n.* café, cafeteria, counter, snack-bar, snack-counter.

buffet[2] *v.* bang, batter, beat, box, bump, clobber, clout, cuff, flail, hit, jar, knock, pound, pummel, push, rap, shove, slap, strike, thump, wallop.
n. bang, blow, box, bump, clout, cuff, jar, jolt, knock, push, rap, shove, slap, smack, thump, wallop.

buffoon *n.* clown, comedian, comic, droll, fool, goliard, harlequin, jester, joker, merry-andrew, mountebank, scaramouch, schmuck, tomfool, vice, wag, zany.

bug *n.* addict, admirer, bacterium, blemish, buff, catch, craze, defect, disease, enthusiast, error, fad, failing, fan, fault, fiend, flaw, freak, germ, gremlin, imperfection, infection, mania, micro-organism, obsession, rage, snarl-up, virus.
v. annoy, badger, bother, disturb, get, harass, irk, irritate, needle, nettle, pester, plague, vex.

bugbear *n.* anathema, bane, b&eced;te noire, bloodybones, bogey, bugaboo, devil, dread, fiend, horror, Mumbo-jumbo, nightmare, pet hate, poker, rawhead.

build *v.* assemble, augment, base, begin, big, constitute, construct, develop, edify, enlarge, erect, escalate, establish, extend, fabricate, form, formulate, found, improve, inaugurate, increase, initiate, institute, intensify, knock together, make, originate, raise, strengthen.
antonyms destroy, knock down, lessen, weaken.

n. body, figure, form, frame, physique, shape, size, structure.

building *n.* architecture, construction, domicile, dwelling, edifice, erection, fabric, fabrication, house, pile, structure.
antonym destruction.

build-up *n.* accretion, accumulation, ballyhoo, development, enlargement, escalation, expansion, gain, growth, heap, hype, increase, load, mass, plug, promotion, publicity, puff, stack, stockpile, store.
antonyms decrease, reduction.

bulge *n.* belly, boost, bump, distension, hump, increase, intensification, lump, projection, protrusion, protuberance, rise, surge, swelling, upsurge.
v. bag, belly, bulb, dilate, distend, enlarge, expand, hump, project, protrude, sag, strout, swell.

bulk *n.* amplitude, bigness, body, dimensions, extensity, extent, generality, immensity, largeness, magnitude, majority, mass, most, plurality, preponderance, size, substance, volume, weight.

bulky *adj.* big, colossal, cumbersome, enormous, heavy, hefty, huge, hulking, immense, large, lumping, mammoth, massive, massy, ponderous, substantial, unmanageable, unwieldy, volumed, voluminous, weighty.
antonyms handy, insubstantial, small.

bulldoze *v.* browbeat, buffalo, bully, clear, coerce, cow, demolish, drive, flatten, force, hector, intimidate, knock down, level, propel, push, push through, raze, shove, thrust.

bulletin *n.* announcement, communication, communiqué, dispatch, dope, message, newsflash, notification, report, sitrep, statement.

bully *n.* bouncer, browbeater, bucko, bully-boy, bully-rook, coercionist, harasser, intimidator, killcrow, oppressor, persecutor, rowdy, ruffian, termagant, tormentor, tough, tyrant.
v. bluster, browbeat, bulldoze, bullyrag, coerce, cow, domineer, haze, hector, intimidate, oppress, overbear, persecute, push around, swagger, terrorize, tyrannize.
antonyms coax, persuade.

bulwark *n.* bastion, buffer, buttress, defense, embankment, fortification, guard, mainstay, outwork, partition, rampart, redoubt, safeguard, security, support.

bumbling *adj.* awkward, blundering, botching, bungling, clumsy, footling, foozling, incompetent, inefficient, inept, lumbering, maladroit, muddled, stumbling.
antonyms competent, efficient.

bump *v.* bang, bounce, budge, collide (with), crash, dislodge, displace, hit, jar, jerk, jolt, jostle, jounce, knock, move, rattle, remove, shake, shift, slam, strike.
n. bang, blow, bulge, collision, contusion, crash, hit, hump, impact, jar, jolt, knob, knock, knot, lump, node, nodule, protuberance, rap, shock, smash, swelling, thud, thump.

bumptious *adj.* arrogant, boastful, brash, cocky, conceited, egotistic, forward, full of oneself, impudent,

overbearing, over-confident, pompous, presumptuous, pushy, self-assertive, self-important, showy, swaggering, vainglorious, vaunting.
antonyms humble, modest.

bumpy *adj.* bouncy, choppy, irregular, jarring, jerky, jolting, jolty, knobbly, knobby, lumpy, rough, rutted, uneven.
antonym smooth.

bunch *n.* assortment, band, batch, bouquet, bundle, clump, cluster, collection, crew, crowd, fascicle, fascicule, flock, gang, gathering, group-knot, heap, lot, mass, mob, multitude, number, parcel, party, pile, quantity, sheaf, spray, stack, swarm, team, troop, tuft.
v. assemble, bundle, cluster, collect, congregate, crowd, flock, group, herd, huddle, mass, pack.
antonyms scatter, spread out.

bundle *n.* accumulation, assortment, bag, bale, batch, box, bunch, carton, collection, consignment, crate, drum, fascicle, fascicule, group, heap, mass, Matilda, pack, package, packet, pallet, parcel, pile, quantity, roll, shock, shook, stack, stook, swag, truss.
v. bale, bind, fasten, pack, palletize, tie, truss, wrap.

bungle *v.* blunder, bodge, boob, botch, bumble, cock up, duff, flub, footle, foozle, foul up, fudge, goof, louse up, mar, mess up, miscalculate, mismanage, muff, mull, ruin, screw up, spoil.
n. blunder, boob, boo-boo, botch-up, cock-up, foul-up, mull.

buoyant *adj.* afloat, animated, blithe, bouncy, breezy, bright, bullish, carefree, cheerful, debonair, floatable, floating, happy, jaunty, joyful, light, light-hearted, lively, peppy, rising, sprightly, sunny, weightless.
antonym depressed.

burden *n.* affliction, anxiety, bear, care, cargo, clog, dead weight, encumbrance, grievance, load, millstone, obligation, obstruction, onus, responsibility, sorrow, strain, stress, trial, trouble, weight, worry.
v. bother, encumber, handicap, lade, lie hard on, lie heavy on, load, oppress, overload, overwhelm, strain, tax, worry.
antonyms disburden, lighten, relieve.

burdensome *adj.* crushing, difficult, distressing, exacting, heavy, irksome, onerous, oppressive, taxing, troublesome, trying, wearisome, weighty.
antonyms easy, light.

bureau *n.* agency, branch, counter, department, desk, division, office, service.

bureaucrat *n.* administrator, apparatchik, bureaucratist, chinovnik, civil servant, functionary, mandarin, minister, office-holder, officer, official.

burglar *n.* cat-burglar, cracksman, house-breaker, picklock, pilferer, robber, thief, yegg.

burial *n.* burying, entombment, exequies, funeral, inhumation, interment, obsequies, sepulcher, sepulture.

burly *adj.* athletic, beefy, big, brawny, bulky, heavy, hefty, hulking, husky, muscular, powerful, stocky, stout, strapping, strong, sturdy, thickset, well-built.
antonyms puny, slim, small, thin.

burn *v.* bite, blaze, brand, calcine, cauterize, char, combust, conflagrate, consume, corrode, deflagrate, desire, expend, flame, flare, flash, flicker, fume, glow, hurt, ignite, incinerate, kindle, light, oxidize, pain, parch, scorch, seethe, shrivel, simmer, singe, smart, smoke, smolder, sting, tingle, toast, use, wither, yearn.

burnish *v.* brighten, buff, furbish, glaze, polish, polish up, rub, shine.
antonym tarnish.
n. gloss, luster, patina, polish, sheen, shine.

burrow *n.* den, earth, hole, lair, retreat, set(t), shelter, tunnel, warren.
v. delve, dig, earth, excavate, mine, tunnel, undermine.

burst *v.* barge, blow up, break, crack, dehisce, disintegrate, erupt, explode, fragment, gush, puncture, run, rupture, rush, shatter, shiver, split, spout, tear.
n. bang, blast, blasting, blow-out, blow-up, breach, break, crack, discharge, eruption, explosion, fit, gallop, gush, gust, outbreak, outburst, outpouring, rupture, rush, spate, split, spurt, surge, torrent.
adj. broken, flat, kaput, punctured, rent, ruptured, split, torn.

bury *v.* absorb, conceal, cover, embed, enclose, engage, engross, engulf, enshroud, entomb, hide, immerse, implant, inearth, inhume, inter, interest, lay to rest, occupy, secrete, sepulcher, shroud, sink, submerge.
antonyms disinter, uncover.

business *n.* affair, assignment, bargaining, calling, career, commerce, company, concern, corporation, craft, dealings, duty, employment, enterprise, establishment, firm, function, industry, issue, job, line, line of country, manufacturing, matter, merchandising, métier, occupation, organization, palaver, point, problem, profession, pursuit, question, responsibility, selling, subject, task, topic, trade, trading, transaction(s), venture, vocation, work.

bustle *v.* dash, flutter, fuss, hasten, hurry, rush, scamper, scramble, scurry, scuttle, stir, tear.
n. activity, ado, agitation, commotion, excitement, flurry, fuss, haste, hurly-burly, hurry, palaver, pother, stir, to-do, toing and froing, tumult.

bustling *adj.* active, astir, busy, buzzing, crowded, energetic, eventful, full, humming, lively, restless, rushing, stirring, swarming, teeming, thronged.
antonym quiet.

busy *adj.* active, assiduous, brisk, diligent, eident, employed, energetic, engaged, engrossed, exacting, full, fussy, hectic, industrious, inquisitive, interfering, lively, meddlesome, meddling, nosy, occupied, officious, persevering, prying, restless, slaving, stirabout, stirring, strenuous, tireless, tiring, troublesome, unleisured, versant, working.
antonyms idle, quiet.

v. absorb, bother, concern, employ, engage, engross, immerse, interest, occupy.

busybody *n.* eavesdropper, gossip, intriguer, intruder, meddler, nosey parker, pantopragmatic, pry, scandal-monger, snoop, snooper, troublemaker.

butcher *n.* destroyer, killcow, killer, murderer, slaughterer, slayer.

v. assassinate, botch, carve, clean, cut, destroy, dress, exterminate, joint, kill, liquidate, massacre, mutilate, prepare, ruin, slaughter, slay, spoil, wreck.

butt[1] *n.* base, end, foot, haft, handle, hilt, shaft, shank, stock, stub, tail, tip.

butt[2] *n.* dupe, laughing-stock, mark, object, point, subject, target, victim.

butt[3] *v., n.* buck, buffet, bump, bunt, hit, jab, knock, poke, prod, punch, push, ram, shove, thrust.

buttocks *n.* ass, backside, beam end, behind, bottom, breach, bum, cheeks, derrière, fanny, haunches, hinderend, hinderlin(g)s, hindquarters, natch, nates, posterior, prat, rear, rump, seat, tush.

buttress *n.* abutment, brace, mainstay, pier, prop, reinforcement, shore, stanchion, stay, strut, support.

v. bolster up, brace, hold up, prop up, reinforce, shore up, strengthen, support, sustain, uphold.

antonyms weaken.

buxom *adj.* ample, bosomy, busty, chesty, comely, debonair, hearty, jocund, jolly, lively, lusty, merry, plump, robust, voluptuous, well-rounded, winsome.

antonyms petite, slim, small.

buy *v.* acquire, bribe, corrupt, fix, get, obtain, procure, purchase, square, suborn.

antonym sell.

n. acquisition, bargain, deal, purchase.

buzz *n.* bombilation, bombination, buzzing, drone, gossip, hearsay, hiss, hum, murmur, news, purr, report, ring, ringing, rumor, scandal, susurration, susurrus, whir(r), whisper, whizz.

v. bombilate, bombinate, drone, hum, murmur, reverberate, ring, susurrate, whir(r), whisper, whizz.

by *prep.* along, beside, near, next to, over, past, through, via.

adv. aside, at hand, away, beyond, close, handy, near, past.

bygone *adj.* ancient, antiquated, departed, erstwhile, forepast, forgotten, former, lost, olden, past, previous.

antonyms modern, recent.

n. antique, grievance, oldie.

bypass *v.* avoid, circumvent, ignore, neglect, outflank.

n. detour, ring road.

by-product *n.* after-effect, consequence, epiphenomenon, fall-out, repercussion, result, side-effect.

bystander *n.* eye-witness, looker-on, observer, onlooker, passer-by, spectator, watcher, witness.

C

cab *n.* hack, minicab, taxi, taxicab, vettura.

cabin *n.* berth, bothy, chalet, compartment, cot, cot-house, cottage, crib, deck-house, hovel, hut, lodge, quarters, room, shack, shanty, shed.

cabinet *n.* almirah, case, chiffonier, closet, commode, cupboard, dresser, escritoire, locker.

cable *n.* chain, cord, hawser, line, mooring, rope.

cache *n.* accumulation, fund, garner, hoard, repository, reserve, stockpile, store, storehouse, supply, treasure-store.

v. bury, conceal, hide, secrete, stash, store, stow.

cad *n.* blackguard, bounder, caitiff, churl, cur, dastard, heel, knave, oik, poltroon, rat, rotter, skunk, swine, worm.

antonym gentleman.

café *n.* cafeteria, coffee bar, coffee shop, estaminet, greasy spoon, restaurant, snack bar, tea-room.

cag(e)y *adj.* careful, chary, circumspect, discreet, guarded, non-committal, secretive, shrewd, wary, wily.

antonyms frank, indiscreet, open.

calamity *n.* adversity, affliction, cataclysm, catastrophe, desolation, disaster, distress, downfall, misadventure, mischance, misfortune, mishap, reverse, ruin, scourge, tragedy, trial, tribulation, woe, wretchedness.

antonyms blessing, godsend.

calculate *v.* aim, cipher, compute, consider, count, determine, enumerate, estimate, figure, gauge, intend, judge, plan, rate, reckon, value, weigh, work out.

calculating *adj.* canny, cautious, contriving, crafty, cunning, designing, devious, Machiavellian, manipulative, politic, scheming, sharp, shrewd, sly.

antonyms artless, naïve, open.

calculation *n.* answer, caution, ciphering, circumspection, computation, deliberation, estimate, estimation, figuring, forecast, foresight, forethought, judgment, planning, precaution, reckoning, result.

call *v.* announce, appoint, arouse, assemble, awaken, bid, christen, collect, consider, contact, convene, convoke, cry, declare, decree, denominate, designate, dub, elect, entitle, estimate, gather, hail, halloo, invite, judge, label, muster, name, ordain, order, phone, proclaim, rally, regard, rouse, shout, style, summon, telephone, term, think, waken, yell. *n.* announcement, appeal, cause, claim, command, cry, demand, excuse, grounds, hail, invitation, justification, need, notice, occasion, order, plea, reason, request, right, ring, scream, shout, signal, summons, supplication, urge, visit, whoop, yell.

calling *n.* business, career, employment, field, job, line, line of country, métier, mission, occupation, profession, province, pursuit, trade, vocation, work.

callous *adj.* case-hardened, cold, hard-bitten, hard-boiled, hardened, hard-hearted, heartless, indifferent, indurated, insensate, insensible, insensitive, inured, obdurate, soulless, thick-skinned, uncaring, unfeeling, unresponsive, unsouled, unsusceptible, unsympathetic.

antonyms kind, sensitive, sympathetic.

calm *adj.* balmy, collected, composed, cool, dispassionate, equable, halcyon, impassive, imperturbable, laid back, mild, pacific, passionless, peaceful, placid, quiet, relaxed, restful, sedate, self-collected, self-possessed, serene, smooth, still, stilly, tranquil, unapprehensive, unclouded, undisturbed, unemotional, uneventful, unexcitable, unexcited, unflappable, unflustered, unmoved, unperturbed, unruffled, untroubled, windless.

antonyms excitable, rough, stormy, wild, worried.

v. compose, hush, mollify, pacify, placate, quieten, relax, soothe.

antonyms excite, irritate, worry.

n. calmness, dispassion, hush, peace, peacefulness, quiet, repose, serenity, stillness.

antonyms restlessness, storminess.

campaign *n.* attack, crusade, drive, excursion, expedition, jihad, movement, offensive, operation, promotion, push.

v. advocate, attack, crusade, fight, promote, push.

can *n.* canister, cannikin, container, jar, jerrycan, pail, receptacle, tin.

canal *n.* waterway, zanja.

cancel *v.* abolish, abort, abrogate, adeem, annul, compensate, counterbalance, countermand, delete, efface, eliminate, erase, expunge, neutralize, nullify, obliterate, offset, quash, redeem, repeal, repudiate, rescind, revoke, scrub, strike.

candid *adj.* blunt, clear, fair, forthright, frank, free, guileless, ingenuous, just, open, outspoken, plain, shining, sincere, straightforward, truthful, unbiased, uncontrived, unequivocal, unposed, unprejudiced.

antonyms cagey, devious, evasive.

candidate *n.* applicant, aspirant, claimant, competitor, contender, contestant, doctorand, entrant, nominee, possibility, pretendant, pretender, runner, solicitant, suitor.

candor *n.* artlessness, directness, fairness, forthrightness, franchise, frankness, guilelessness, honesty, ingenuousness, naïvety, openness, outspokenness, plain-dealing, simplicity, sincerity, straightforwardness, truthfulness, unequivocalness.

antonyms cageyness, deviousness, evasiveness.

canny *adj.* acute, artful, astute, careful, cautious,

circumspect, clever, comfortable, gentle, harmless, innocent, judicious, knowing, lucky, perspicacious, prudent, sagacious, sharp, shrewd, skilful, sly, subtle, wise, worldly-wise.
antonyms foolish, imprudent.

canopy *n.* awning, baldachin, covering, dais, shade, sunshade, tabernacle, tester, umbrella.

cant[1] *n.* argot, humbug, hypocrisy, insincerity, jargon, lingo, pretentiousness, sanctimoniousness, slang, thieves' Latin, vernacular.

cant[2] *n.* angle, bevel, incline, jerk, rise, slant, slope, tilt, toss.

cantankerous *adj.* bad-tempered, captious, carnaptious, choleric, contrary, crabbed, crabby, cranky, crotchety, crusty, difficult, disagreeable, feisty, grouchy, grumpy, ill-humored, ill-natured, irascible, irritable, peevish, perverse, piggish, quarrelsome, testy.
antonyms good-natured, pleasant.

canyon *n.* box-canyon, cañon, coulée, gorge, gulch, gully, ravine.

cap *v.* beat, better, complete, cover, crown, eclipse, exceed, excel, finish, outdo, outstrip, surpass, top, transcend.
n. beret, bonnet, chapka, cowl, fez, glengarry, hat, shako, skullcap, yarmulka.

capability *n.* ability, capacity, competence, facility, faculty, means, potential, potentiality, power, proficiency, qualification, skill, talent.

capable *adj.* able, accomplished, adept, adequate, apt, clever, competent, disposed, efficient, experienced, fitted, gifted, intelligent, liable, masterly, predisposed, proficient, qualified, skilful, suited, susceptible, talented.
antonyms incapable, incompetent, useless.

capacity *n.* ability, amplitude, appointment, aptitude, aptness, brains, caliber, capability, cleverness, compass, competence, competency, dimensions, efficiency, extent, facility, faculty, forte, function, genius, gift, intelligence, magnitude, office, position, post, power, province, range, readiness, role, room, scope, service, size, space, sphere, strength, volume. **cape**[1] *n.* foreland, head, headland, ness, peninsula, point, promontory, tongue.

cape[2] *n.* cloak, coat, cope, mantle, pelerine, pelisse, poncho, robe, shawl, wrap.

caper *v.* bounce, bound, capriole, cavort, dance, frisk, frolic, gambol, hop, jump, leap, romp, skip, spring.
n. affair, antic, business, capriole, dido, escapade, gambado, gambol, high jinks, hop, jape, jest, jump, lark, leap, mischief, prank, revel, sport, stunt.

capital[1] *adj.* cardinal, central, chief, controlling, essential, excellent, fine, first, first-rate, foremost, great, important, leading, main, major, overruling, paramount, pre-eminent, primary, prime, principal, splendid, superb, upper-case.
antonyms minor, sad, unfortunate.

capital[2] *n.* assets, cash, finance, finances, financing, fonds, funds, investment(s), means, money, principal, property, resources, stock, wealth, wherewithal.

capricious *adj.* changeable, crotchety, erratic, fanciful, fickle, fitful, freakish, humorous, impulsive, inconstant, mercurial, odd, queer, quirky, uncertain, unpredictable, variable, wayward, whimsical.
antonyms sensible, steady.

captain *n.* boss, chief, chieftain, commander, head, leader, master, officer, patron, pilot, skip, skipper.

captivate *v.* allure, attract, beguile, besot, bewitch, charm, dazzle, enamor, enchain, enchant, enrapture, enslave, ensnare, enthrall, entrance, fascinate, hypnotize, infatuate, lure, mesmerize, seduce, win.
antonyms appal, repel.

captive *n.* convict, detainee, hostage, internee, prisoner, slave.
adj. caged, confined, enchained, enslaved, ensnared, imprisoned, incarcerated, restricted, secure, subjugated.
antonym free.

captivity *n.* bondage, confinement, custody, detention, durance, duress, enchainment, enthralment, imprisonment, incarceration, internment, restraint, servitude, slavery, thraldom, vassalage.
antonym freedom.

capture *v.* apprehend, arrest, bag, catch, collar, cop, feel someone's collar, lift, nab, secure, seize, snaffle, take.
n. apprehension, arrest, catch, imprisonment, seizure, taking, trapping.

car *n.* auto, automobile, caboose, diner, freight car, handcar, Pullman, sleeper, smoker, streetcar.

carcass *n.* body, cadaver, corpse, framework, hulk, relics, remains, shell, skeleton, stiff.

cardinal *adj.* capital, central, chief, essential, first, foremost, fundamental, greatest, highest, important, key, leading, main, paramount, pre-eminent, primary, prime, principal.

care *n.* affliction, anxiety, attention, burden, carefulness, caution, charge, circumspection, concern, consideration, control, custody, direction, disquiet, forethought, guardianship, hardship, heed, interest, keeping, leading-strings, management, meticulousness, ministration, pains, perplexity, pressure, protection, prudence, regard, responsibility, solicitude, stress, supervision, tribulation, trouble, vexation, vigilance, ward, watchfulness, woe, worry.
antonyms carelessness, inattention, thoughtlessness.

career *n.* calling, course, employment, job, life-work, livelihood, occupation, passage, path, procedure, progress, pursuit, race, vocation, walk.
v. bolt, dash, gallop, hurtle, race, run, rush, shoot, speed, tear.

carefree *adj.* airy, blithe, breezy, buoyant, careless, cheerful, cheery, easy-going, happy, happy-go-lucky, insouciant, jaunty, laid-back, light-hearted, lightsome, radiant, sunny, untroubled, unworried.
antonyms anxious, worried.

careful *adj.* accurate, alert, attentive, cautious, chary, circumspect, concerned, conscientious, discreet, fastidious, heedful, judicious, meticulous, mindful, painstaking, particular, precise, protective, prudent, punctilious, scrupulous, softly-softly, solicitous, thoughtful, thrifty, vigilant, wary, watchful.
antonyms careless, inattentive, thoughtless.

careless *adj.* absent-minded, casual, cursory, derelict, forgetful, heedless, hit-or-miss, inaccurate, incautious, inconsiderate, indiscreet, irresponsible, lackadaisical, messy, neglectful, negligent, nonchalant, offhand, perfunctory, regardless, remiss, slap-dash, slipshod, sloppy, thoughtless, uncaring, unconcerned, unguarded, unmindful, unstudied, untenty, unthinking.
antonyms accurate, careful, meticulous, thoughtful.

caress *v.* canoodle, cuddle, embrace, fondle, hug, kiss, lallygag (lollygag), nuzzle, paw, pet, rub, stroke, touch.
n. cuddle, embrace, fondle, hug, kiss, pat, stroke.

cargo *n.* baggage, consignment, contents, freight, goods, haul, lading, load, merchandise, pay-load, shipment, tonnage, ware.

caricature *n.* burlesque, cartoon, distortion, farce, lampoon, mimicry, parody, Pasquil, Pasquin, pasquinade, representation, satire, send-up, take-off, travesty.
v. burlesque, distort, lampoon, mimic, mock, parody, pasquinade, ridicule, satirize, send up, take off.

carnage *n.* blood-bath, bloodshed, butchery, havoc, holocaust, massacre, murder, shambles, slaughter.

carnal *adj.* animal, bodily, corporeal, earthly, erotic, fleshly, human, impure, lascivious, lecherous, lewd, libidinous, licentious, lustful, mundane, natural, physical, profane, prurient, salacious, secular, sensual, sensuous, sexual, sublunary, temporal, unchaste, unregenerate, unspiritual, voluptuous, wanton, worldly.
antonyms chaste, pure, spiritual.

carnival *n.* celebration, fair, Fasching, festival, fête, fiesta, gala, holiday, jamboree, jubilee, Mardi Gras, merrymaking, revelry, wassail, wassail-bout, wassailry.

carol *n.* canticle, canzonet, chorus, ditty, hymn, lay, noel, song, strain, wassail.

carp *v.* cavil, censure, complain, criticize, hypercriticize, knock, nag, quibble, reproach, ultracrepidate.
antonym praise.

carpet *n.* Axminster, kali, mat, Navaho, Persian, rug, Wilton.

carping *adj.* biting, bitter, captious, caviling, critical, fault-finding, grouchy, hypercritical, nagging, nit-picking, picky, reproachful, Zoilean.
n. censure, complaints, criticism, disparagement, knocking, reproofs, Zoilism.
antonyms compliments, praise.

carriage *n.* air, bearing, behavior, cab, carrying, chaise, coach, comportment, conduct, conveyance, conveying, delivery, demeanor, deportment, four-wheeler, freight, gait, manner, mien, posture, presence, transport, transportation, vehicle, vettura, voiture, wagon, wagonette.

carry *v.* accomplish, bear, bring, broadcast, capture, chair, communicate, conduct, convey, display, disseminate, drive, effect, fetch, gain, give, haul, hip, impel, influence, lift, lug, maintain, motivate, move, offer, publish, relay, release, secure, shoulder, spur, stand, stock, suffer, support, sustain, take, tote, transfer, transmit, transport, underpin, uphold, urge, win.

carve *v.* chip, chisel, cut, divide, engrave, etch, fashion, form, grave, hack, hew, incise, indent, make, mold, sculp(t), sculpture, slash, slice, tool, whittle.

case[1] *n.* box, cabinet, canister, capsule, carton, cartridge, casing, casket, chest, compact, container, cover, covering, crate, envelope, étui, folder, holder, integument, jacket, receptacle, sheath, shell, showcase, suit-case, tray, trunk, wrapper, wrapping.
v. encase, enclose, skin.

case[2] *n.* argument, circumstances, condition, context, contingency, dilemma, event, example, illustration, instance, occasion, occurrence, plight, point, position, predicament, situation, specimen, state, thesis.
v. investigate, reconnoiter.

case[3] *n.* action, argument, cause, dispute, lawsuit, proceedings, process, suit, trial.

cash *n.* bank-notes, bread, bucks, bullion, change, coin, coinage, currency, dough, funds, hard currency, hard money, money, notes, payment, readies, ready, ready money, resources, specie, wherewithal.
v. encash, liquidate, realize.

casserole *n.* pot-au-feu, stew-pan.

cast[1] *v.* abandon, add, allot, appoint, assign, bestow, calculate, categorize, choose, chuck, compute, deposit, diffuse, distribute, drive, drop, emit, figure, fling, forecast, form, found, give, hurl, impel, launch, lob, model, mold, name, pick, pitch, project, radiate, reckon, reject, scatter, select, set, shape, shed, shy, sling, spread, throw, thrust, toss, total.
n. air, appearance, complexion, demeanor, fling, form, lob, look, manner, mien, quality, semblance, shade, stamp, style, throw, thrust, tinge, tone, toss, turn.

cast[2] *n.* actors, artistes, characters, company, dramatis personae, entertainers, performers, players, troupe.

caste *n.* class, degree, estate, grade, lineage, order, position, race, rank, species, station, status, stratum.

castle *n.* casbah (kasba, kasbah), château, citadel, donjon, fastness, fortress, keep, mansion, motte and bailey, palace, peel, schloss, stronghold, tower.

casual *adj.* accidental, apathetic, blasé, chance, contingent, cursory, fortuitous, incidental, indifferent, informal, insouciant, irregular, lackadaisical, negligent, nonchalant, occasional, offhand, perfunctory, random, relaxed, serendipitous, stray, unceremonious, uncertain, unconcerned, unexpected, unforeseen, unintentional, unpremeditated.
antonyms deliberate, painstaking, planned.

casualty *n.* death, injured, injury, loss, sufferer, victim, wounded.

catalog *n.* directory, gazetteer, index, inventory, list, litany, record, register, roll, roster, schedule, table.
v. accession, alphabetize, classify, codify, file, index, inventory, list, record, register.

catastrophe *n.* adversity, affliction, blow, calamity, cataclysm, conclusion, culmination, curtain, debacle (débâcle), dénouement, devastation, disaster, end, failure, fiasco, finale, ill, mischance, misfortune, mishap, reverse, ruin, termination, tragedy, trial, trouble, upheaval, upshot, winding-up.

catch *v.* apprehend, arrest, benet, bewitch, captivate, capture, charm, clutch, contract, cop, delight, detect, develop, discern, discover, enchant, enrapture, ensnare, entangle, entrap, expose, fascinate, feel, follow, grab, grasp, grip, hear, incur, nab, nail, perceive, recognize, seize, sense, snare, snatch, surprise, take, twig, unmask.
antonyms drop, free, miss.
n. bolt, clasp, clip, detent, disadvantage, drawback, fastener, hasp, hitch, hook, latch, obstacle, parti, snag, sneck, snib, trap, trick.

catching *adj.* attractive, captivating, charming, communicable, contagious, enchanting, fascinating, fetching, infectious, infective, taking, transferable, transmissible, transmittable, winning, winsome.
antonyms boring, ugly, unattractive.

catchy *adj.* attractive, captivating, confusing, deceptive, haunting, memorable, popular.
antonyms boring, dull.

category *n.* chapter, class, classification, department, division, grade, grouping, head, heading, list, order, rank, section, sort, type.

cater *v.* furnish, humor, indulge, outfit, pander, provide, provision, purvey, supply, victual.

cause *n.* account, agency, agent, aim, attempt, basis, beginning, belief, causation, consideration, conviction, creator, end, enterprise, genesis, grounds, ideal, impulse, incentive, inducement, mainspring, maker, motivation, motive, movement, object, origin, originator, producer, purpose, reason, root, source, spring, stimulus, undertaking.
antonyms effect, result.
v. begin, compel, create, effect, engender, generate, give rise to, incite, induce, motivate, occasion, precipitate, produce, provoke, result in.

caustic *adj.* acidulous, acrid, acrimonious, astringent, biting, bitter, burning, corroding, corrosive, cutting, escharotic, keen, mordant, pungent, sarcastic, scathing, severe, stinging, trenchant, virulent, waspish.
antonyms mild, soothing.

caution *n.* admonition, advice, alertness, care, carefulness, circumspection, counsel, deliberation, discretion, forethought, heed, heedfulness, injunction, prudence, via trita, via tuta, vigilance, wariness, warning, watchfulness.
v. admonish, advise, urge, warn.

cautious *adj.* alert, cagey, careful, chary, circumspect, discreet, guarded, heedful, judicious, politic, prudent, scrupulous, softly-softly, tentative, unadventurous, vigilant, wary, watchful.
antonyms heedless, imprudent, incautious.

cavalcade *n.* array, march-past, parade, procession, retinue, spectacle, train, troop.

cavalier *n.* attendant, beau, blade, chevalier, equestrian, escort, gallant, gentleman, horseman, knight, partner, royalist.
adj. arrogant, cavalierish, condescending, curt, disdainful, free-and-easy, gay, haughty, insolent, lofty, lordly, misproud, off-hand, scornful, supercilious, swaggering.

cave *n.* antre, cavern, cavity, den, grotto, hole, hollow, mattamore, pothole.

cavity *n.* antrum, belly, caries, crater, dent, gap, hole, hollow, pit, pot-hole, sinus, vacuole, ventricle, well, womb.

cavort *v.* caper, caracole, dance, frisk, frolic, gambol, hop, prance, romp, skip, sport.

cease *v.* call a halt, call it a day, conclude, culminate, desist, die, discontinue, end, fail, finish, halt, pack in, poop out, refrain, stay, stop, terminate.
antonyms begin, start.

cede *v.* abandon, abdicate, allow, concede, convey, give up, grant, relinquish, renounce, resign, surrender, transfer, yield.

celebrate *v.* bless, commemorate, commend, emblazon, eulogize, exalt, extol, glorify, honor, keep, laud, live it up, observe, perform, praise, proclaim, publicize, rejoice, reverence, solemnize, toast, wassail, whoop it up.

celebrated *adj.* acclaimed, big, distingué, distinguished, eminent, exalted, famed, famous, glorious, illustrious, lionized, notable, outstanding, popular, pre-eminent, prominent, renowned, revered, well-known.
antonyms obscure, unknown.

celebrity *n.* big name, big shot, bigwig, dignitary, distinction, éclat, eminence, fame, glory, honor, lion, luminary, name, notability, personage, personality, popularity, pre-eminence, prestige, prominence, renown, reputation, repute, star, stardom, superstar, VIP.
antonyms nobody, obscurity.

celestial *adj.* angelic, astral, divine, elysian, empyrean, eternal, ethereal, godlike, heavenly, immortal, paradisaic(al), seraphic, spiritual, starry, sublime, supernatural, transcendental.
antonyms earthly, mundane.

cement *v.* attach, bind, bond, cohere, combine, fix together, glue, gum, join, plaster, seal, solder, stick, unite, weld.
n. adhesive, concrete, glue, gum, mortar, paste, plaster, sealant.

censure *n.* admonishment, admonition, blame, castigation, condemnation, criticism, disapproval, obloquy,

rebuke, remonstrance, reprehension, reprimand, reproach, reprobation, reproof, stricture, telling-off, vituperation.
antonyms approval, compliments, praise.
v. abuse, admonish, animadvert, berate, blame, castigate, chide, condemn, criticize, decry, denounce, jump on, rebuke, reprehend, reprimand, reproach, reprobate, reprove, scold, slam, tell off, upbraid.
antonyms approve, compliment, praise.
center *n.* bull's-eye, core, crux, focus, heart, hub, Mecca, mid, middle, mid-point, nave, nucleus, omphalos, pivot.
antonyms edge, outskirts, periphery.
v. cluster, concentrate, converge, focus, gravitate, hinge, pivot, revolve.
central *adj.* chief, essential, focal, fundamental, important, inner, interior, key, main, mean, median, mid, middle, pivotal, primary, principal, vital.
antonyms minor, peripheral.
ceremonious *adj.* civil, courteous, courtly, deferential, dignified, exact, formal, grand, polite, pompous, precise, punctilious, ritual, solemn, starchy, stately, stiff.
antonyms informal, relaxed, unceremonious.
ceremony *n.* celebration, ceremonial, commemoration, decorum, etiquette, event, form, formality, function, niceties, observance, parade, pomp, propriety, protocol, rite, ritual, service, show, solemnities.
certain *adj.* ascertained, assured, bound, conclusive, confident, constant, convinced, convincing, decided, definite, dependable, destined, determinate, established, express, fated, fixed, incontrovertible, individual, indubitable, ineluctable, inescapable, inevitable, inexorable, irrefutable, known, one, particular, plain, positive, precise, regular, reliable, resolved, satisfied, settled, some, special, specific, stable, steady, sure, true, trustworthy, undeniable, undoubted, unequivocal, unfailing, unmistakable, unquestionable, valid.
antonyms doubtful, hesitant, uncertain, unsure.
certainly *adv.* doubtlessly, naturally, of course, questionless.
certainty *n.* assurance, authoritativeness, certitude, confidence, conviction, fact, faith, indubitableness, inevitability, nap, plerophoria, plerophory, positiveness, reality, sure thing, sureness, surety, trust, truth, validity.
antonyms doubt, hesitation, uncertainty.
certificate *n.* attestation, authorization, award, credentials, diploma, document, endorsement, guarantee, license, pass, qualification, testimonial, validation, voucher, warrant.
certify *v.* ascertain, assure, attest, authenticate, authorize, aver, avow, confirm, corroborate, declare, endorse, evidence, guarantee, notify, show, testify, validate, verify, vouch, witness.
certitude *n.* assurance, certainty, confidence, conviction, plerophoria, plerophory.
antonym doubt.

cessation *n.* abeyance, arrest, arresting, break, ceasing, desistance, discontinuance, discontinuation, discontinuing, end, ending, halt, halting, hiatus, intermission, interruption, interval, let-up, pause, recess, remission, respite, rest, standstill, stay, stoppage, stopping, suspension, termination.
antonym commencement.
chafe *v.* abrade, anger, annoy, enrage, exasperate, fret, fume, gall, get, grate, heat, incense, inflame, irritate, offend, provoke, rage, rasp, rub, scrape, scratch, vex, wear, worry.
chagrin *n.* annoyance, discomfiture, discomposure, displeasure, disquiet, dissatisfaction, embarrassment, exasperation, fretfulness, humiliation, indignation, irritation, mortification, peevishness, spleen, vexation.
antonyms delight, pleasure.
v. annoy, displease, disquiet, dissatisfy, embarrass, exasperate, humiliate, irk, irritate, mortify, peeve, vex.
chain *n.* bond, catena, concatenation, coupling, fetter, fob, link, manacle, progression, restraint, sequence, series, set, shackle, string, succession, train, union, vinculum.
v. bind, confine, enslave, fasten, fetter, gyve, handcuff, manacle, restrain, secure, shackle, tether, trammel.
antonyms free, release.
chairman *n.* chair, chairperson, chairwoman, convenor, director, master of ceremonies, MC, president, presider, speaker, spokesman, toastmaster.
challenge *v.* accost, beard, brave, confront, dare, defy, demand, dispute, impugn, provoke, query, question, stimulate, summon, tax, test, throw down the gauntlet, try.
n. confrontation, dare, defiance, gauntlet, hurdle, interrogation, obstacle, poser, provocation, question, test, trial, ultimatum.
chamber *n.* apartment, assembly, bed-chamber, bedroom, boudoir, camera, cavity, closet, compartment, council, cubicle, enclosure, hall, legislature, parliament, room, vault.
chance *n.* accident, act of God, coincidence, contingency, destiny, fate, fortuity, fortune, gamble, happenstance, hazard, jeopardy, liability, likelihood, luck, misfortune, occasion, odds, opening, opportunity, peril, possibility, probability, prospect, providence, risk, speculation, time, uncertainty, venture.
antonyms certainty, law, necessity.
v. befall, gamble, happen, hazard, occur, risk, stake, transpire, try, venture, wager.
adj. accidental, casual, contingent, fortuitous, inadvertent, incidental, random, serendipitous, unforeseeable, unforeseen, unintended, unintentional, unlooked-for.
antonyms certain, deliberate, intentional.
change *v.* alter, alternate, barter, convert, denature, displace, diversify, exchange, fluctuate, interchange, metamorphose, moderate, modify, mutate, reform, remodel,

remove, reorganize, replace, restyle, shift, substitute, swap, take liberties with, trade, transfigure, transform, transmit, transmute, transpose, vacillate, vary, veer. *n.* alteration, break, chop, conversion, difference, diversion, exchange, innovation, interchange, metamorphosis, metanoia, modification, mutation, novelty, permutation, revolution, satisfaction, sea-change, shift, substitution, trade, transformation, transition, transmutation, transposition, upheaval, variation, variety, vicissitude.

changeable *adj.* capricious, chameleonic, changeful, erratic, fickle, fitful, fluid, inconstant, irregular, kaleidoscopic, labile, mercurial, mobile, mutable, protean, shifting, uncertain, unpredictable, unreliable, unsettled, unstable, unsteady, vacillating, variable, vicissitudinous, volatile, wavering, windy.
antonyms constant, reliable, unchangeable.

chaos *n.* anarchy, bedlam, confusion, disorder, disorganization, entropy, lawlessness, pandemonium, snafu, tohu bohu, tumult, unreason.
antonym order.

chaotic *adj.* anarchic, confused, deranged, disordered, disorganized, lawless, purposeless, rampageous, riotous, shambolic, snafu, topsy-turvy, tumultous, tumultuary, uncontrolled.
antonyms organized, purposive.

character[1] *n.* attributes, bent, caliber, cast, complexion, constitution, disposition, feature, honor, individuality, integrity, kidney, make-up, nature, peculiarity, personality, physiognomy, position, quality, rank, rectitude, reputation, stamp, status, strength, temper, temperament, type, uprightness.

character[2] *n.* card, customer, eccentric, fellow, guy, individual, joker, oddball, oddity, original, part, person, persona, portrayal, role, sort, type.

character[3] *n.* cipher, device, emblem, figure, hieroglyph, ideogram, ideograph, letter, logo, mark, rune, sign, symbol, type.

characteristic *adj.* discriminative, distinctive, distinguishing, idiosyncratic, individual, peculiar, representative, singular, special, specific, symbolic, symptomatic, typical, vintage.
antonyms uncharacteristic, untypical.
n. attribute, faculty, feature, hallmark, idiosyncrasy, lineament, mannerism, mark, peculiarity, property, quality, symptom, thing, trait.

charitable *adj.* accommodating, beneficent, benevolent, benign, benignant, bountiful, broad-minded, clement, compassionate, considerate, eleemosynary, favorable, forgiving, generous, gracious, humane, indulgent, kind, kindly, lavish, lenient, liberal, magnanimous, mild, philanthropic, sympathetic, tolerant, understanding.
antonyms uncharitable, unforgiving.

charity *n.* affection, agape, alms-giving, altruism, assistance, benefaction, beneficence, benevolence, benignity, benignness, bountifulness, bounty, clemency, compassion, endowment, fund, generosity, gift, goodness, hand-out, humanity, indulgence, love, philanthropy, relief, tender-heartedness.

charm *v.* allure, attract, becharm, beguile, bewitch, cajole, captivate, delight, enamor, enchant, enrapture, entrance, fascinate, mesmerize, please, win.
n. abraxas, allure, allurement, amulet, appeal, attraction, attractiveness, desirability, enchantment, fascination, fetish, grisgris, idol, ju-ju, magic, magnetism, medicine, obeah, obi, phylactery, porte-bonheur, sorcery, spell, talisman, trinket, weird.

charming *adj.* appealing, attractive, bewitching, captivating, delectable, delightful, engaging, eye-catching, fetching, honeyed, irresistible, lovely, pleasant, pleasing, seductive, sweet, winning, winsome.
antonyms ugly, unattractive.

chart *n.* abac, alignment chart, blueprint, diagram, graph, map, nomograph, plan, table, tabulation.
v. delineate, draft, draw, graph, map out, mark, outline, place, plot, shape, sketch.

charter *n.* accreditation, authorization, bond, concession, contract, deed, document, franchise, indenture, license, permit, prerogative, privilege, right.
v. authorize, commission, employ, engage, hire, lease, rent, sanction.

chase *v.* course, drive, expel, follow, hunt, hurry, pursue, rush, track.
n. coursing, hunt, hunting, pursuit, race, run, rush, venery.

chasm *n.* abysm, abyss, breach, canyon, cavity, cleft, crater, crevasse, fissure, gap, gorge, gulf, hiatus, hollow, opening, ravine, rent, rift, split, void.

chaste *adj.* austere, decent, decorous, elegant, immaculate, incorrupt, innocent, maidenly, modest, moral, neat, pure, refined, restrained, simple, unaffected, undefiled, unsullied, unvulgar, vestal, virginal, virginly, virtuous, wholesome.
antonyms indecorous, lewd.

chasten *v.* admonish, afflict, castigate, chastise, correct, cow, curb, discipline, humble, humiliate, repress, reprove, soften, subdue, tame.

chastise *v.* beat, berate, castigate, censure, correct, discipline, flog, flyte, lash, punish, reprove, scold, scourge, smack, spank, upbraid, whip.

chat *n.* chatter, chinwag, confab, coze, crack, gossip, heart-to-heart, natter, rap, talk, tête-à-tête, visit.
v. chatter, chew the fat, crack, gossip, jaw, natter, rabbit (on), talk, visit, yackety-yak.

chatter *n.* babble, blather, blether, chat, gab, gabfest, gossip, jabber, prate, prattle, prattlement, tattle, tonguework, twaddle.
v. babble, blab, blather, blether, chat, clack, clatter, gab, gossip, jabber, prate, prattle, prittle-prattle, talk like a pengun, tattle, twaddle, yackety-yak.

cheap *adj.* à bon marché, bargain, base, budget, common, contemptible, cut-price, despicable, dirt-cheap, dog-cheap, economical, economy, inexpensive, inferior, jitney, keen, knock-down, low, low-cost, low-priced, mean, paltry, poor, reasonable, reduced, sale, scurvy, second-rate, shoddy, sordid, tatty, tawdry, uncostly, vulgar, worthless.

antonyms costly, excellent, noble, superior.

cheat *v.* baffle, bam, bamboozle, beguile, bilk, check, chisel, chouse, cog, con, cozen, deceive, defeat, defraud, deprive, diddle, do, double-cross, dupe, finagle, fleece, fob, foil, fool, frustrate, fudge, grift, gudgeon, gull, gyp, hand (someone) a lemon, hoax, hocus, hoodwink, mislead, prevent, queer, rip off, screw, short-change, skin, smouch, swindle, thwart, touch, trick, trim, victimize.

n. artifice, bilker, charlatan, cheater, chouse, cogger, con man, cozener, deceit, deceiver, deception, dodger, double-crosser, extortioner, fraud, grifter, impostor, imposture, knave, picaroon, rip-off, rogue, shark, sharp, sharper, short-changer, snap, swindle, swindler, trickery, trickster, welsher.

check[1] *v.* compare, confirm, examine, give the once-over, inspect, investigate, monitor, note, probe, research, scrutinize, study, test, verify.

n. audit, examination, inspection, investigation, research, scrutiny, tab, test.

check[2] *v.* arrest, bar, blame, bridle, chide, control, curb, damp, delay, halt, hinder, impede, inhibit, limit, obstruct, pause, rebuke, repress, reprimand, reprove, restrain, retard, scold, stop, thwart.

n. blow, constraint, control, curb, damp, damper, disappointment, frustration, hindrance, impediment, inhibition, limitation, obstruction, rejection, restraint, reverse, setback, stoppage.

check[3] *n.* bill, counterfoil, token.

cheek[1] *n.* audacity, brass, brass neck, brazenness, brazenry, disrespect, effrontery, face, gall, impertinence, impudence, insolence, nerve, sauce, temerity.

cheek[2] *n.* buttock, face, gena, jowl.

cheer *v.* acclaim, animate, applaud, brighten, clap, comfort, console, elate, elevate, encheer, encourage, enhearten, enliven, exhilarate, gladden, hail, hearten, hurrah, incite, inspirit, solace, uplift, warm.

antonyms boo, dishearten, jeer.

n. acclamation, animation, applause, bravo, buoyancy, cheerfulness, comfort, gaiety, gladness, glee, hoorah, hopefulness, hurrah, joy, liveliness, merriment, merrymaking, mirth, optimism, ovation, plaudits, solace.

cheerful *adj.* animated, blithe, bobbish, bright, bucked, buoyant, canty, cheery, chipper, chirpy, chirrupy, contented, enlivening, enthusiastic, eupeptic, gay, gaysome, genial, glad, gladsome, happy, hearty, jaunty, jolly, jovial, joyful, joyous, light-hearted, lightsome, light-spirited, merry, optimistic, perky, pleasant, sparkling, sprightly, sunny, upbeat, winsome.

antonym sad.

cherish *v.* comfort, cosset, encourage, entertain, foster,

harbor, make much of, nourish, nurse, nurture, prize, shelter, support, sustain, tender, treasure, value.

chest *n.* ark, box, case, casket, coffer, crate, kist, strongbox, trunk.

chew *v.* champ, crunch, gnaw, grind, manducate, masticate, munch.

chic *adj.* à la mode, chichi, elegant, fashionable, modish, smart, stylish, trendy.

antonyms out-moded, unfashionable.

chide *v.* admonish, berate, blame, censure, check, criticize, lecture, objurgate, rate, rebuke, reprehend, reprimand, reproach, reprove, scold, tell off, upbraid.

antonym praise.

chief *adj.* capital, cardinal, central, especial, essential, foremost, grand, highest, key, leading, main, outstanding, paramount, predominant, pre-eminent, premier, prevailing, primal, primary, prime, principal, superior, supreme, uppermost, vital.

antonyms junior, minor, unimportant.

n. boss, captain, chieftain, cock of the loft, commander, coryphaeus, director, duke, governor, head, kaid, kingpin, leader, lord, manager, master, paramount, paramount chief, principal, ringleader, ruler, superintendent, superior, supremo, suzerain.

chiefly *adv.* especially, essentially, for the most part, generally, mainly, mostly, predominantly, primarily, principally, usually.

childish *adj.* boyish, foolish, frivolous, girlish, hypocoristic, hypocoristical, immature, infantile, juvenile, puerile, silly, simple, trifling, weak, young.

antonyms adult, sensible.

chill *adj.* aloof, biting, bleak, chilly, cold, cool, depressing, distant, freezing, frigid, hostile, parky, raw, sharp, stony, unfriendly, unresponsive, unwelcoming, wintry.

antonyms friendly, warm.

v. congeal, cool, dampen, depress, discourage, dishearten, dismay, freeze, frighten, refrigerate, terrify.

n. bite, cold, coldness, coolness, coolth, crispness, frigidity, nip, rawness, sharpness.

chilly *adj.* aloof, blowy, breezy, brisk, cold, cool, crisp, draughty, fresh, frigid, hostile, nippy, parky, penetrating, sharp, stony, unfriendly, unresponsive, unsympathetic, unwelcoming.

antonyms friendly, warm.

chirp *v., n.* cheep, chirrup, peep, pipe, tweet, twitter, warble, whistle.

chivalrous *adj.* bold, brave, chivalric, courageous, courteous, courtly, gallant, gentlemanly, Grandisonian, heroic, honorable, knightly, polite, true, valiant.

antonyms cowardly, ungallant.

chivalry *n.* boldness, bravery, courage, courtesy, courtliness, gallantry, gentlemanliness, knight-errantry, knighthood, politeness.

choice *n.* alternative, choosing, decision, dilemma, discrimination, election, espousal, opting, option, pick, preference, say, selection, variety.

adj. best, dainty, elect, élite, excellent, exclusive, exquisite, hand-picked, nice, plum, precious, prime, prize, rare, select, special, superior, uncommon, unusual, valuable.
antonym inferior.

choke *v.* asphyxiate, bar, block, clog, close, congest, constrict, dam, gag, obstruct, occlude, overpower, reach, retch, smother, stifle, stop, strangle, suffocate, suppress, throttle.

choose *v.* adopt, cull, designate, desire, elect, espouse, fix on, opt for, pick, plump for, predestine, prefer, see fit, select, settle on, single out, take, vote for, wish.

chop *v.* cleave, cut, divide, fell, hack, hew, lop, sever, shear, slash, slice, truncate.

chore *n.* burden, duty, errand, fag, job, stint, task, trouble.

chronic *adj.* appalling, atrocious, awful, confirmed, deep-rooted, deep-seated, dreadful, habitual, incessant, incurable, ineradicable, ingrained, inveterate, persistent, terrible.
antonym temporary.

chronicle *n.* account, annals, chanson de geste, diary, epic, gest(e), history, journal, narrative, record, register, saga, story.
v. enter, list, narrate, record, recount, register, relate, report, tell, write down.

chuckle *v.* chortle, crow, exult, giggle, laugh, snigger, snort, titter.

chummy *adj.* affectionate, close, friendly, intimate, matey, pally, sociable, thick.

chunk *n.* block, chuck, dod, dollop, hunk, lump, mass, piece, portion, slab, wad, wodge.

chunky *adj.* beefy, brawny, dumpy, fat, square, stocky, stubby, thick, thickset.
antonym slim.

cinema *n.* big screen, filmhouse, flicks, movies, picturehouse, picture-palace.

circle *n.* area, assembly, band, bounds, circuit, circumference, class, clique, club, coil, company, compass, cordon, coterie, crowd, cycle, disc, domain, enclosure, fellowship, field, fraternity, globe, group, gyre, lap, loop, orb, orbit, perimeter, periphery, province, range, realm, region, revolution, ring, round, roundance, roundel, roundlet, rundle, scene, school, set, society, sphere, turn.
v. belt, circumambulate, circumnavigate, circumscribe, coil, compass, curl, curve, encircle, enclose, encompass, envelop, gird, girdle, hem in, loop, pivot, revolve, ring, rotate, surround, tour, whirl.

circuit *n.* ambit, area, boundary, bounds, circumference, compass, course, district, eyre, journey, limit, orbit, perambulation, range, region, revolution, round, route, tour, track, tract.

circuitous *adj.* ambagious, anfractuous, cagey, devious, indirect, labyrinthine, meandering, oblique, periphrastic, rambling, roundabout, tortuous, winding.
antonyms direct, straight.

circular *adj.* annular, discoid(al), disc-shaped, hoop-shaped, ring-shaped, round.
n. advert, announcement, handbill, leaflet, letter, notice, pamphlet.

circumference *n.* border, boundary, bounds, circuit, edge, extremity, fringe, limits, margin, outline, perimeter, periphery, rim, verge.

circumspection *n.* canniness, care, caution, chariness, deliberation, discretion, guardedness, prudence, wariness.

circumstance *n.* accident, condition, contingency, detail, element, event, fact, factor, happening, happenstance, incident, item, occurrence, particular, position, respect, situation.

circumstances *n.* conditions, galère, lifestyle, means, position, resources, situation, state, state of affairs, station, status, times.

cite *v.* accite, adduce, advance, call, enumerate, evidence, extract, mention, name, quote, specify, subpoena, summon.

citizen *n.* burgess, burgher, city-dweller, denizen, dweller, freeman, inhabitant, oppidan, ratepayer, resident, subject, townsman, urbanite.

city *n.* conurbation, megalopolis, metropolis, municipality, town.

civil *adj.* accommodating, affable, civic, civilized, complaisant, courteous, courtly, domestic, home, interior, internal, internecine, lay, municipal, obliging, polished, polite, political, refined, secular, temporal, urbane, well-bred, well-mannered.
antonym uncivil.

civilization *n.* advancement, cultivation, culture, development, education, enlightenment, kultur, progress, refinement, sophistication, urbanity.
antonyms barbarity, primitiveness.

civilize *v.* ameliorate, cultivate, educate, enlighten, humanize, improve, meliorate, perfect, polish, refine, sophisticate, tame.

claim *v.* affirm, allege, arrogate, ask, assert, challenge, collect, demand, exact, hold, insist, maintain, need, profess, request, require, state, take, uphold.
n. affirmation, allegation, application, assertion, call, demand, insistence, petition, pretension, privilege, protestation, request, requirement, right, title.

clamor *n.* agitation, babel, blare, brouhaha, commotion, complaint, din, exclamation, hubbub, hue, hullabaloo, katzenjammer, noise, outcry, racket, shout, shouting, uproar, vociferation.
antonym silence.

clan *n.* band, brotherhood, clique, confraternity, coterie, faction, family, fraternity, gens, group, house, phratry, race, sect, sept, set, society, sodality, tribe.

clandestine *adj.* backroom, behind-door, cloak-and-dagger, closet, concealed, covert, fraudulent, furtive, hidden, private, secret, sly, sneaky, stealthy, surreptitious, surreptitious, underground, underhand, under-the-counter.
antonym open.

clarify *v.* cleanse, define, elucidate, explain, gloss, illuminate, purify, refine, resolve, shed/throw light on, simplify.
antonym obscure.

clash *v.* bang, clang, clank, clatter, conflict, crash, disagree, feud, fight, grapple, jangle, jar, quarrel, rattle, war, wrangle.
n. brush, clank, clatter, collision, conflict, confrontation, disagreement, fight, jangle, jar, noise, show-down.

clasp *n.* agraffe, brooch, buckle, catch, clip, embrace, fastener, fastening, grasp, grip, hasp, hold, hook, hug, pin, snap, tach(e).
v. attach, clutch, concatenate, connect, embrace, enclasp, enfold, fasten, grapple, grasp, grip, hold, hug, press, seize, squeeze.

class[1] *n.* caliber, caste, category, classification, collection, denomination, department, description, division, genre, genus, grade, group, grouping, ilk, kidney, kind, kingdom, league, order, phylum, quality, rank, section, set, sort, species, sphere, status, style, taxon, type, value.
v. assort, brand, categorize, classify, codify, designate, grade, group, rank, rate.

class[2] *n.* course, lecture, seminar, teach-in, tutorial.

classic *adj.* abiding, ageless, archetypal, Augustan, best, characteristic, chaste, consummate, deathless, definitive, enduring, established, excellent, exemplary, finest, first-rate, ideal, immortal, lasting, master, masterly, model, paradigmatic, quintessential, refined, regular, restrained, standard, time-honored, traditional, typical, undying, usual.
antonym second-rate.
n. chef d'oeuvre, exemplar, masterpiece, masterwork, model, paradigm, pièce de résistance, prototype, standard.

classification *n.* analysis, arrangement, cataloging, categorization, codification, digestion, grading, pigeonholing, sorting, taxis, taxonomy.

classify *v.* arrange, assort, catalog, categorize, codify, digest, dispose, distribute, file, grade, pigeon-hole, rank, sort, systematize, tabulate.

clause *n.* article, chapter, condition, demand, heading, item, paragraph, part, passage, point, provision, proviso, section, specification, stipulation, subsection.

claw *n.* griff(e), gripper, nail, nipper, pincer, pounce, talon, tentacle, unguis.
v. dig, graze, lacerate, mangle, maul, rip, scrabble, scrape, scratch, tear.

clean *adj.* antiseptic, chaste, clarified, complete, conclusive, decent, decisive, decontaminated, delicate, elegant, entire, exemplary, faultless, final, flawless, fresh, good, graceful, guiltless, honest, honorable, hygienic, immaculate, innocent, laundered, moral, natural, neat, perfect, pure, purified, respectable, sanitary, simple, spotless, sterile, sterilized, thorough, tidy, total, trim, unblemished, unadulterated, uncluttered, uncontaminated, undefiled, unimpaired, unpolluted, unsoiled, unspotted, unstained, unsullied, upright, virtuous, washed, whole.
antonyms dirty, indecent, polluted, unsterile.
v. bath, cleanse, deodorize, deterge, disinfect, dust, launder, lave, mop, purge, purify, rinse, sanitize, scour, scrub, sponge, swab, sweep, vacuum, wash.
antonyms defile, dirty.

clean up sanitize, tidy, wash.

cleanse *v.* absolve, absterge, catharize, clean, clear, deterge, detoxicate, detoxify, lustrate, purge, purify, rinse, scavenge, scour, scrub, wash.
antonyms defile, dirty.

clear *adj.* apparent, audible, bright, certain, clean, cloudless, coherent, comprehensible, conspicuous, convinced, crystalline, decided, definite, diaphanous, disengaged, distinct, eidetic, empty, evident, explicit, express, fair, fine, free, glassy, guiltless, halcyon, hyaline, immaculate, incontrovertible, innocent, intelligible, light, limpid, lucid, luculent, luminous, manifest, obvious, open, palpable, patent, pellucid, perceptible, perspicuous, plain, positive, pronounced, pure, recognizable, resolved, satisfied, see-through, serene, sharp, shining, smooth, stainless, sunny, sure, translucent, transparent, unambiguous, unblemished, unclouded, undefiled, undimmed, undulled, unequivocal, unhampered, unhindered, unimpeded, unlimited, unmistakable, unobstructed, unquestionable, untarnished, untroubled, well-defined.
antonyms cloudy, fuzzy, guilty, vague.
v. absolve, acquire, acquit, brighten, clarify, clean, cleanse, decode, decongest, deoppilate, disengage, disentangle, earn, emancipate, erase, excuse, exonerate, extricate, fix, free, gain, jump, justify, leap, liberate, lighten, loosen, make, miss, open, pass over, purify, reap, refine, rid, secure, strip, tidy, unblock, unclog, uncloud, unload, unpack, unscramble, vault, vindicate, wipe.
antonyms block, condemn, defile, dirty.

clearly *adv.* distinctly, evidently, incontestably, incontrovertibly, manifestly, markedly, obviously, openly, plainly, undeniably, undoubtedly.
antonyms indistinctly, vaguely.

clemency *n.* compassion, forebearance, forgiveness, generosity, humanity, indulgence, kindness, lenience, leniency, lenity, magnanimity, mercifulness, mercy, mildness, moderation, soft-heartedness, tenderness.
antonyms harshness, ruthlessness.

clerical *adj.* ecclesiastical, pastoral, priestly, sacerdotal.

clerk *n.* account-keeper, assistant, copyist, official, pen-driver, pen-pusher, protocolist, quill-driver, quillman, receptionist, shop-assistant, writer.

clever *adj.* able, adroit, apt, astute, brainy, bright, canny, capable, cunning, deep, dexterous, discerning, elegant, expert, gifted, gleg, good-natured, habile, ingenious, intelligent, inventive, keen, knowing, knowledgeable,

quick, quick-witted, rational, resourceful, sagacious, sensible, shrewd, skilful, smart, talented, witty.
antonyms foolish, naïve, senseless.

clever dick smart alec, smart-ass, smartypants, wiseling, witling, wit-monger.

cleverness *n.* ability, adroitness, astuteness, brains, brightness, canniness, cunning, dexterity, flair, gift, gumption, ingenuity, intelligence, nous, quickness, resourcefulness, sagacity, sense, sharpness, shrewdness, smartness, talent, wit.
antonyms foolishness, naïvety, senselessness.

client *n.* applicant, buyer, consumer, customer, dependant, habitué, patient, patron, protégé, shopper.

cliff *n.* bluff, crag, escarpment, face, overhang, precipice, rock-face, scar, scarp.

climate *n.* ambience, atmosphere, clime, country, disposition, feeling, milieu, mood, region, setting, temper, temperature, tendency, trend, weather.

climax *n.* acme, apogee, culmination, head, height, high point, highlight, orgasm, peak, summit, top, zenith.
antonyms bathos, low point, nadir.

climb *v.* ascend, clamber, mount, rise, scale, shin up, soar, swarm (up), top.

clip[1] *v.* crop, curtail, cut, dock, pare, poll, pollard, prune, shear, shorten, snip, trim.

clip[2] *v.* box, clobber, clout, cuff, hit, knock, punch, skelp, slap, smack, sock, thump, wallop, whack.
n. blow, box, clout, cuff, hit, knock, punch, skelp, slap, smack, sock, thump, wallop, whack.

clip[3] *n.* gallop, lick, rate, speed.

clip[4] *v.* attach, fasten, fix, hold, pin, staple.

cloak *n.* blind, cape, coat, cover, front, mantle, mask, pretext, shield, wrap.
v. camouflage, conceal, cover, disguise, hide, mask, obscure, screen, veil.

clog *v.* ball, block, burden, congest, dam up, gaum, hamper, hinder, impede, jam, obstruct, occlude, shackle, stop up, stuff.
antonym unblock.
n. burden, dead-weight, drag, encumbrance, hindrance, impediment, obstruction.

cloistered *adj.* cloistral, confined, enclosed, hermitic, insulated, protected, reclusive, restricted, secluded, sequestered, sheltered, shielded, withdrawn.
antonyms open, urbane.

close[1] *v.* bar, block, cease, choke, clog, cloture, complete, conclude, confine, connect, cork, couple, culminate, discontinue, end, fill, finish, fuse, grapple, join, lock, mothball, obstruct, plug, seal, secure, shut, stop, terminate, unite, wind up.
n. cadence, cessation, completion, conclusion, culmination, denouement, end, ending, finale, finish, junction, pause, stop, termination, wind-up.

close[2] *adj.* accurate, adjacent, adjoining, airless, alert, approaching, approximative, assiduous, at hand, attached, attentive, careful, compact, concentrated, confidential, confined, congested, conscientious, cramped, cropped, crowded, dear, dense, detailed, devoted, dogged, earnest, exact, faithful, familiar, fixed, frowsty, fuggy, handy, hard by, heavy, hidden, humid, illiberal, imminent, impending, impenetrable, inseparable, intense, intent, intimate, jam-packed, keen, literal, loving, mean, mingy, minute, miserly, muggy, narrow, near, near-by, neighboring, niggardly, nigh, oppressive, packed, painstaking, parsimonious, penurious, precise, private, reserved, reticent, retired, rigorous, searching, secluded, secret, secretive, short, solid, stale, stifling, stingy, strict, stuffy, suffocating, sweltering, taciturn, thick, thorough, tight, tight-fisted, uncommunicative, unforthcoming, ungenerous, unventilated.
antonyms careless, cool, far, unfriendly.

cloth *n.* dish-cloth, duster, fabric, face-cloth, material, rag, stuff, textiles, tissue, towel.

clothe *v.* accouter, apparel, array, attire, bedizen, caparison, cover, deck, drape, enclothe, endow, enwrap, equip, garb, habilitate, habit, invest, outfit, rig, robe, swathe, vest.
antonyms unclothe, undress.

clothes *n.* apparel, attire, clobber, clothing, costume, dress, duds, ensemble, garb, garments, garmenture, gear, getup, habiliments, habit(s), outfit, raiment, rig-out, threads, toggery, togs, vestiture, vestments, vesture, wardrobe, wear, weeds.

cloud *n.* billow, crowd, darkness, flock, fog, gloom, haze, horde, host, mist, multitude, murk, nebula, nebulosity, obscurity, shower, swarm, throng, vapor, waterdog, weft, woolpack.
v. becloud, confuse, darken, defame, dim, disorient, distort, dull, eclipse, impair, muddle, obfuscate, obscure, overcast, overshadow, shade, shadow, stain, veil.
antonym clear.

cloudy *adj.* blurred, blurry, confused, dark, dim, dismal, dull, emulsified, hazy, indistinct, leaden, lightless, lowering, muddy, murky, nebulous, nubilous, obscure, opaque, overcast, somber, sullen, sunless.
antonyms clear, sunny.

club[1] *n.* bat, bludgeon, cosh, cudgel, mace, mere, stick, truncheon, waddy.
v. bash, baste, batter, beat, bludgeon, clobber, clout, cosh, hammer, hit, pummel, strike.

club[2] *n.* association, bunch, circle, clique, combination, company, fraternity, group, guild, lodge, order, set, society, sodality, union.

clue *n.* clavis, evidence, hint, idea, indication, inkling, intimation, lead, notion, pointer, sign, suggestion, suspicion, tip, tip-off, trace.

clumsy *adj.* awkward, blundering, bumbling, bungling, cack-handed, chuckle, clumping, crude, gauche, gawky, ham-fisted, ham-handed, heavy, hulking, ill-made, inept, inexpert, lubber, lubberly, lumbering, maladroit, ponderous, rough, shapeless, squab, unco-ordinated,

uncouth, ungainly, ungraceful, unhandy, unskilful, unwieldy.
antonym graceful.

cluster *n.* assemblage, batch, bunch, clump, collection, gathering, glomeration, group, knot, mass.
v. assemble, bunch, collect, flock, gather, group.

clutch *v.* catch, clasp, embrace, fasten, grab, grapple, grasp, grip, hang on to, seize, snatch.

coalition *n.* affiliation, alliance, amalgam, amalgamation, association, bloc, coadunation, combination, compact, confederacy, confederation, conjunction, federation, fusion, integration, league, merger, union.

coarse *adj.* bawdy, blowzy, boorish, brutish, coarse-grained, crude, earthly, foul-mouthed, homespun, immodest, impolite, improper, impure, indelicate, inelegant, loutish, mean, offensive, Rabelaisian, ribald, rough, rude, smutty, Sotadic, uncivil, unfinished, unpolished, unprocessed, unpurified, unrefined, vulgar.
antonyms fine, polite, refined, sophisticated.

coast *n.* coastline, littoral, seaboard, seaside, shore.
v. cruise, drift, free-wheel, glide, sail.

coax *v.* allure, beguile, cajole, decoy, entice, flatter, inveigle, persuade, soft-soap, sweet-talk, wheedle, whilly, whilly-wha(w), wile.
antonym force.

coddle *v.* baby, cocker, cosset, humor, indulge, mollycoddle, nurse, pamper, pet, spoil.

code *n.* canon, cipher, convention, cryptograph, custom, ethics, etiquette, manners, maxim, regulations, rules, system.
v. encipher, encode.

coerce *v.* bludgeon, browbeat, bulldoze, bully, compel, constrain, dragoon, drive, drum, force, intimidate, pressgang, pressurize.
antonyms coax, persuade.

coercion *n.* browbeating, bullying, compulsion, constraint, direct action, duress, force, intimidation, pressure, threats.
antonym persuasion.

cognizance *n.* acknowledgment, apprehension, cognition, knowledge, notice, perception, percipience, recognition, regard.
antonym unawareness.

cognizant *adj.* acquainted, aware, conscious, conversant, familiar, informed, knowledgeable, versed, witting.
antonym unaware.

coherent *adj.* articulate, comprehensible, consistent, intelligible, logical, lucid, meaningful, orderly, organized, rational, reasoned, sensible, systematic.

coincide *v.* accord, agree, co-exist, concur, correspond, harmonize, match, square, tally.

coincidence *n.* accident, chance, concomitance, concurrence, conjunction, correlation, correspondence, eventuality, fluke, fortuity, luck, synchronism.

coincidental *adj.* accident, casual, chance, coincident, concomitant, concurrent, fluky, fortuitous, lucky, simultaneous, synchronous, unintentional, unplanned.
antonyms deliberate, planned.

cold *adj.* agued, algid, aloof, apathetic, arctic, benumbed, biting, bitter, bleak, brumal, chill, chilled, chilly, cold-blooded, cool, dead, distant, freezing, frigid, frosty, frozen, gelid, glacial, icy, inclement, indifferent, inhospitable, lukewarm, numbed, parky, passionless, phlegmatic, raw, reserved, shivery, spiritless, stand-offish, stony, undemonstrative, unfeeling, unfriendly, unheated, unmoved, unresponsive, unsympathetic, wintry.
antonyms friendly, warm.
n. catarrh, chill, chilliness, coldness, frigidity, frostiness, hypothermia, iciness, inclemency.
antonyms friendliness, warmth.

cold fish iceberg.

collapse *v.* crumple, fail, faint, fall, fold, founder, peg out, sink, subside.
n. breakdown, cave-in, crash, debacle (débâcle), detumescence, disintegration, downfall, exhaustion, failure, faint, flop, subsidence.

colleague *n.* aide, aider, ally, assistant, associate, auxiliary, bedfellow, coadjutor, collaborator, companion, comrade, confederate, confrère, helper, partner, teammate, workmate.

collect *v.* accumulate, acquire, aggregate, amass, assemble, cluster, congregate, convene, converge, forgather, gather, gather together, heap, hoard, muster, obtain, raise, rally, save, secure, stockpile, uplift.

collected *adj.* assembled, calm, composed, confident, cool, efficient, gathered, imperturbable, placid, poised, self-possessed, serene, together, unperturbed, unruffled.
antonyms disorganized, dithery, worried.

collection *n.* accumulation, anthology, assemblage, assembly, assortment, caboodle, cluster, company, compilation, congeries, conglomerate, conglomeration, congregation, convocation, crowd, festschrift, gathering, group, harvesting, heap, hoard, ingathering, inning, jingbang, job-lot, mass, pile, set, spicilege, stockpile, store, whip-round.

collective *adj.* aggregate, combined, common, composite, concerted, congregated, co-operative, corporate, cumulative, joint, shared, unified, united.
n. aggregate, assemblage, corporation, gathering, group.

collision *n.* accident, bump, clash, clashing, conflict, confrontation, crash, encounter, impact, opposition, pile-up, prang, rencounter, skirmish, smash.

collusion *n.* artifice, cahoots, coactivity, complicity, connivance, conspiracy, craft, deceit, fraudulent, intrigue.

color[1] *n.* animation, appearance, bloom, blush, brilliance, chroma, colorant, coloration, complexion, disguise, dye, façade, flush, glow, guise, hue, liveliness, paint, pigment, pigmentation, plausibility, pretense, pretext, race, reason, rosiness, ruddiness, semblance, shade, timbre, tincture, tinge, tint, variety, vividness, wash, water-color.

v. blush, burn, colorwash, disguise, distort, dye, embroider, encolor, exaggerate, falsify, flush, misrepresent, paint, pervert, prejudice, redden, slant, stain, strain, taint, tinge, tint.

color² *n.* colors, ensign, flag, standard.

color-blind *adj.* dichromatic.

colorful *adj.* bright, brilliant, distinctive, graphic, intense, interesting, jazzy, kaleidoscopic, lively, motley, multicolored, parti-colored, picturesque, psychedelic, rich, stimulating, unusual, variegated, vibrant, vivid. *antonyms* colorless, drab, plain.

coma *n.* catalepsy, drowsiness, hypnosis, insensibility, lethargy, oblivion, somnolence, sopor, stupor, torpor, trance, unconsciousness.

combat *n.* action, battle, bout, clash, conflict, contest, duel, encounter, engagement, fight, hostilities, j(i)u-jitsu, judo, karate, kendo, kung fu, skirmish, struggle, war, warfare.

v. battle, contend, contest, defy, engage, fight, oppose, resist, strive, struggle, withstand.

combination *n.* alliance, amalgam, amalgamation, association, blend, cabal, cartel, coalescence, coalition, combine, composite, composition, compound, confederacy, confederation, conjunction, connection, consortium, conspiracy, federation, meld, merger, mix, mixture, syndicate, unification, union.

combine *v.* amalgamate, associate, bind, blend, bond, coadunate, compound, conjoin, connect, cooperate, fuse, incorporate, integrate, join, link, marry, meld, merge, mix, peace, pool, sythesize, unify, unite. *antonym* separate.

come *v.* advance, appear, approach, arrive, attain, become, draw near, ejaculate, enter, happen, materialize, move, near, occur, originate, reach. *antonyms* depart, go, leave.

comedian *n.* card, clown, comic, droll, funny man, gagster, humorist, jester, joker, jokesmith, laugh, wag, wit.

comely *adj.* attractive, beautiful, becoming, blooming, bonny, buxom, callipygian, callipygous, decent, decorous, fair, fit, fitting, gainly, good-looking, graceful, handsome, lovely, pleasing, pretty, proper, pulchritudinous, seemly, suitable, wholesome, winsome.

come-uppance *n.* chastening, deserts, dues, merit, punishment, rebuke, recompense, requital, retribution.

comfort *v.* alleviate, assuage, cheer, console, ease, encheer, encourage, enliven, gladden, hearten, inspirit, invigorate, reassure, refresh, relieve, solace, soothe, strengthen.

n. aid, alleviation, cheer, compensation, consolation, cosiness, ease, easy street, encouragement, enjoyment, help, luxury, opulence, relief, satisfaction, snugness, succor, support, well-being. *antonyms* distress, torment.

comfortable *adj.* adequate, affluent, agreeable, ample, canny, commodious, contented, convenient, cosy, delightful, easy, enjoyable, gemütlich, gratified, happy, homely, loose, loose-fitting, pleasant, prosperous, relaxed, relaxing, restful, roomy, serene, snug, well-off, well-to-do. *antonyms* poor, uncomfortable.

comical *adj.* absurd, amusing, comic, diverting, droll, entertaining, farcical, funny, hilarious, humorous, laughable, ludicrous, priceless, ridiculous, risible, side-splitting, silly, whimsical. *antonyms* sad, unamusing.

command *v.* bid, charge, compel, control, demand, direct, dominate, enjoin, govern, head, lead, manage, order, reign over, require, rule, supervise, sway.

n. authority, behest, bidding, charge, commandment, control, decree, dictation, diktat, direction, directive, domination, dominion, edict, fiat, government, grasp, injunction, instruction, management, mandate, mastery, order, power, precept, requirement, rule, supervision, sway, ukase, ultimatum.

commandeer *v.* appropriate, confiscate, expropriate, hijack, requisition, seize, sequester, sequestrate, usurp.

commanding *adj.* advantageous, assertive, authoritative, autocratic, compelling, controlling, decisive, dominant, dominating, forceful, imposing, impressive, peremptory, superior.

commando *n.* fedayee, Green Beret, soldier.

commence *v.* begin, embark on, inaugurate, initiate, open, originate, start. *antonyms* cease, finish.

commend *v.* acclaim, applaud, approve, commit, compliment, confide, consign, deliver, entrust, eulogize, extol, praise, recommend, yield. *antonym* criticize.

commendable *adj.* admirable, creditable, deserving, estimable, excellent, exemplary, laudable, meritorious, noble, praiseworthy, worthy. *antonyms* blameworthy, poor.

commendation *n.* acclaim, acclamation, accolade, applause, approbation, approval, credit, encomium, encouragement, panegyric, praise, recommendation. *antonyms* blame, criticism.

commensurate *adj.* acceptable, adequate, appropriate, coextensive, comparable, compatible, consistent, corresponding, due, equivalent, fitting, just, meet, proportionate, sufficient. *antonym* inappropriate.

comment *v.* animadvert, annotate, criticize, descant, elucidate, explain, gloss, interpose, interpret, mention, note, observe, opine, remark, say.

n. animadversion, annotation, commentary, criticism, elucidation, explanation, exposition, footnote, illustration, marginal note, marginalia, note, observation, remark, statement.

commerce *n.* business, communication, dealing(s), exchange, intercourse, merchandising, relations, trade, traffic.

commission *n.* allowance, appointment, authority, board, brokerage, brok(er)age, charge, committee, compensation, cut, delegation, deputation, duty, employment, errand, fee, function, mandate, mission, percentage, rake-off, representative, task, trust, warrant.
v. appoint, ask for, authorize, contract, delegate, depute, empower, engage, nominate, order, request, select, send.

commit *v.* align, bind, commend, compromise, confide, confine, consign, deliver, deposit, do, enact, endanger, engage, entrust, execute, give, imprison, involve, obligate, perform, perpetrate, pledge.

commitment *n.* adherence, assurance, dedication, devotion, duty, engagement, guarantee, involvement, liability, loyalty, obligation, pledge, promise, responsibility, tie, undertaking, vow, word.

committee *n.* advisory group, board, cabinet, commission, council, jury, panel, table, task force, think-tank, working party.

commodious *adj.* ample, capacious, comfortable, expansive, extensive, large, loose, roomy, spacious.
antonym cramped.

commodities *n.* goods, merchandise, output, produce, products, stock, things, wares.

common *adj.* accepted, average, coarse, collective, commonplace, communal, conventional, customary, daily, everyday, familiar, flat, frequent, general, habitual, hackneyed, humdrum, inferior, low, mutual, obscure, ordinary, pedestrian, plain, plebby, plebeian, popular, prevailing, prevalent, public, regular, routine, run-of-the-mill, simple, social, stale, standard, stock, trite, tritical, undistinguished, unexceptional, universal, usual, vulgar, widespread, workaday.
antonyms noteworthy, uncommon.

commonplace *adj.* common, customary, everyday, humdrum, obvious, ordinary, pedestrian, quotidian, stale, threadbare, trite, uninteresting, widespread, worn out.
antonyms exceptional, rare.
n. banality, cliché, platitude, truism.

common-sense *adj.* astute, common-sensical, down-to-earth, hard-headed, judicious, level-headed, matter-of-fact, practical, pragmatical, realistic, reasonable, sane, sensible, shrewd, sound.
antonym foolish.

commotion *n.* ado, agitation, ballyhoo, bobbery, brouhaha, burst-up, bustle, bust-up, carfuffle, disorder, disturbance, excitement, ferment, fracas, furore, fuss, hubbub, hullabaloo, hurly-burly, perturbation, pother, pudder, racket, riot, rumpus, to-do, toss, tumult, turmoil, uproar.

communicable *adj.* catching, contagious, conveyable, impartible, infectious, infective, spreadable, transferable, transmittable.

communicate *v.* acquaint, announce, bestow, connect, contact, convey, correspond, declare, diffuse, disclose, disseminate, divulge, impart, inform, intimate, notify, proclaim, promulgate, publish, report, reveal, signify, spread, transmit, unfold.

communication *n.* announcement, bulletin, communiqué, connection, contact, conversation, converse, correspondence, disclosure, dispatch, dissemination, information, intelligence, intercourse, intimation, message, news, promulgation, report, statement, transmission, word.

communicative *adj.* candid, chatty, conversable, conversational, expansive, extrovert, forthcoming, frank, free, friendly, informative, loquacious, open, outgoing, sociable, talkative, unreserved, voluble.
antonym reticent.

communion *n.* accord, affinity, agreement, closeness, communing, concord, converse, empathy, Eucharist, fellow-feeling, fellowship, harmony, Holy Communion, housel, intercourse, Lord's Supper, Mass, participation, rapport, Sacrament, sympathy, togetherness, unity.

community *n.* affinity, agreement, association, body politic, brotherhood, coincidence, colony, commonness, commonwealth, company, concurrence, confraternity, confrèrie, correspondence, district, fellowship, fraternity, identity, kibbutz, kindredness, likeness, locality, nest, people, populace, population, public, residents, sameness, similarity, society, state.

compact[1] *adj.* brief, close, compendious, compressed, concise, condensed, dense, firm, impenetrable, solid, stocky, succinct, thick, well-knit.
antonyms diffuse, rambling, rangy.
v. compress, condense, consolidate, cram, flatten, ram, squeeze, tamp.

compact[2] *n.* agreement, alliance, arrangement, bargain, bond, concordat, contract, covenant, deal, entente, pact, settlement, treaty, understanding.

companion *n.* accomplice, aide, ally, assistant, associate, attendant, attender, buddy, chaperon, cohort, colleague, compeer, complement, comrade, confederate, confidant, confidante, consort, counterpart, crony, duenna, escort, fellow, follower, friend, intimate, mate, partner, satellite, shadow, squire, twin.

companionship *n.* camaraderie, companionhood, company, comradeship, confraternity, consociation, conviviality, esprit de corps, fellowship, fraternity, friendship, rapport, support, sympathy, togetherness.

company[1] *n.* assemblage, assembly, association, band, body, business, cartel, circle, collection, community, concern, concourse, consociation, consortium, convention, corporation, coterie, crew, crowd, ensemble, establishment, firm, fraternity, gathering, group, house, league, line, partnership, party, set, set-out, syndicate, throng, troop, troupe.

company[2] *n.* attendance, callers, companionhood,

companionship, fellowship, guests, party, presence, society, support, visitors.

comparable *adj.* akin, alike, analogous, cognate, commensurate, correspondent, corresponding, equal, equivalent, kindred, parallel, proportionate, related, similar, tantamount.
antonym unlike.

compare *v.* balance, collate, confront, contrast, correlate, emulate, equal, equate, juxtapose, liken, match, parallel, resemble, similize, vie, weigh.

comparison *n.* analogy, collation, comparability, contrast, correlation, distinction, juxtaposition, likeness, parallel, parallelism, resemblance, similarity, similitude.

compartment *n.* alcove, area, bay, berth, booth, box, carrel, carriage, category, cell, chamber, cubby-hole, cubicle, department, division, locker, niche, pigeon-hole, section, stall, subdivision.

compassion *n.* charity, clemency, commiseration, concern, condolence, fellow-feeling, heart, humanity, kindness, loving-kindness, mercy, pity, ruth, sorrow, sympathy, tenderness, understanding, weltschmerz, yearning.
antonym indifference.

compassionate *adj.* benevolent, caring, charitable, clement, humane, humanitarian, indulgent, kind-hearted, kindly, lenient, merciful, piteous, pitying, supportive, sympathetic, tender, tender-hearted, understanding, warm-hearted.
antonym indifferent.

compatibility *n.* accord, affinity, agreement, amity, concord, congeniality, consistency, consonance, correspondence, empathy, fellowship, harmony, like-mindedness, rapport, reconcilability, sympathy, understanding, unity.
antonyms antagonism, antipathy, incompatibility.

compatible *adj.* accordant, adaptable, agreeable, conformable, congenial, congruent, congruous, consistent, consonant, harmonious, kindred, like-minded, reconcilable, suitable, sympathetic.
antonyms antagonistic, antipathetic, incompatible.

compel *v.* browbeat, bulldoze, bully, coact, coerce, constrain, dragoon, drive, enforce, exact, force, hustle, impel, make, necessitate, obligate, oblige, press-gang, pressurize, strongarm, urge.

compensate *v.* atone, balance, cancel, counteract, counterbalance, countervail, expiate, guerdon, indemnify, offset, recompense, recover, recuperate, redeem, redress, refund, reimburse, remunerate, repay, requite, restore, reward, satisfy.

compensation *n.* amends, atonement, comfort, consolation, damages, guerdon, indemnification, indemnity, payment, quittance, recompense, redress, refund, reimbursement, remuneration, reparation, repayment, requital, restitution, restoration, return, reward, satisfaction, solatium.

compete *v.* battle, challenge, contend, contest, duel, emulate, fight, oppose, rival, strive, struggle, tussle, vie.

competence *n.* ability, adequacy, appropriateness, aptitude, capability, capacity, competency, experience, expertise, facility, fitness, proficiency, skill, suitability, technique.
antonym incompetence.

competent *adj.* able, adapted, adequate, appropriate, belonging, capable, clever, efficient, endowed, equal, fit, legitimate, masterly, pertinent, proficient, qualified, satisfactory, strong, sufficient, suitable, trained, well-qualified.
antonym incompetent.

competition *n.* challenge, challengers, championship, combativeness, competitiveness, competitors, contention, contest, corrivalry, cup, emulation, event, field, match, opposition, quiz, race, rivalry, rivals, series, strife, struggle, tournament, tourney, trial.

competitor *n.* adversary, agonist, antagonist, challenger, competition, contender, contestant, corrival, emulator, entrant, opponent, opposition, rival.

complain *v.* beef, belly-ache, bemoan, bewail, bind, bitch, bleat, carp, deplore, fuss, girn, grieve, gripe, groan, grouse, growl, grumble, kvetch, lament, moan, squeal, whine, whinge.

complaint[1] *n.* accusation, annoyance, beef, belly-ache, bitch, bleat, censure, charge, criticism, dissatisfaction, fault-finding, girn, gravamen, grievance, gripe, grouse, grumble, lament, moan, nit-picking, plaint, querimony, remonstrance, squawk, stricture, wail, whinge, winge.

complaint[2] *n.* affliction, ailment, disease, disorder, illness, indisposition, malady, malaise, sickness, trouble, upset.

complement *n.* aggregate, capacity, companion, completion, consummation, counterpart, entirety, fellow, quota, sum, supplement, total, totality, wholeness.

complete *adj.* absolute, accomplished, achieved, all, concluded, consummate, ended, entire, equipped, faultless, finished, full, intact, integral, integrate, out-and-out, perfect, plenary, root-and-branch, self-contained, thorough, thoroughgoing, thorough-paced, total, unabbreviated, unabridged, unbroken, uncut, undivided, unedited, unexpurgated, unimpaired, utter, whole, whole-hog.
antonyms imperfect, incomplete.
v. accomplish, achieve, cap, clinch, close, conclude, consummate, crown, discharge, do, effect, end, execute, finalize, finish, fulfil, perfect, perform, realize, settle, terminate, wind up.

completion *n.* accomplishment, achievement, attainment, close, conclusion, consummation, crowning, culmination, discharge, end, expiration, finalization, finish, fruition, fulfilment, perfection, plenitude, realization, settlement, telos, termination.

complex *adj.* ambagious, Byzantine, circuitous, complicated, composite, compound, compounded, convoluted, Daedalian, devious, diverse, elaborate, heterogeneous, intricate, involved, knotty, labyrinthine, manifold, mingled, mixed, multifarious, multipartite, multiple, plexiform, polymerous, ramified, tangled, tortuous. *antonym* simple.

n. aggregate, composite, establishment, fixation, hang-up, idée fixe, institute, network, obsession, organization, phobia, preoccupation, scheme, structure, syndrome, synthesis, system.

complexion *n.* appearance, aspect, cast, character, color, coloring, composition, countenance, disposition, guise, hue, kind, light, look, make-up, nature, pigmentation, rud, skin, stamp, temperament, type.

compliant *adj.* accommodating, acquiescent, agreeable, amenable, biddable, complaisant, conformable, deferential, docile, obedient, obliging, passive, submissive, tractable, yielding.

antonyms disobedient, intractable.

complicated *adj.* ambivalent, baroque, Byzantine, complex, convoluted, devious, difficult, elaborate, entangled, intricate, involved, labyrinthine, perplexing, problematic, puzzling, rigmarole, tangled, tortuous, troublesome.

antonyms easy, simple.

compliment *n.* accolade, admiration, bouquet, commendation, congratulations, courtesy, douceur, encomium, eulogy, favor, felicitation, flattery, honor, plaudit, praise, tribute.

antonyms criticism, insult.

v. admire, applaud, commend, congratulate, eulogize, extol, felicitate, flatter, laud, praise, salute.

antonyms condemn, insult.

complimentary *adj.* admiring, appreciative, approving, commendatory, congratulatory, courtesy, encomiastic, eulogistic, favorable, flattering, free, gratis, honorary, laudatory, panegyrical.

antonyms critical, insulting, unflattering.

comply *v.* accede, accommodate, accord, acquiesce, agree, assent, conform, consent, defer, discharge, fall in, follow, fulfil, obey, oblige, observe, perform, respect, satisfy, submit, yield.

antonyms disobey, resist.

component *n.* bit, constituent, element, factor, ingredient, item, part, piece, spare part, unit.

comport *v.* acquit, act, bear, behave, carry, conduct, demean, deport, perform.

compose *v.* adjust, arrange, build, calm, collect, compound, comprise, constitute, construct, contrive, control, create, devise, fashion, form, frame, govern, imagine, indite, invent, make, meditate the muse, pacify, produce, quell, quiet, recollect, reconcile, regulate, resolve, settle, soothe, still, structure, tranquilize, write.

composed *adj.* calm, collected, complacent, confident, cool, imperturbable, level-headed, placid, poised, relaxed, self-possessed, serene, together, tranquil, unflappable, unruffled, unworried.

antonym agitated.

composer *n.* arranger, author, bard, creator, maker, originator, poet, songsmith, songwriter, tunesmith, writer.

composition *n.* arrangement, balance, combination, compilation, compromise, concord, confection, configuration, congruity, consonance, constitution, creation, design, essay, exaration, exercise, form, formation, formulation, harmony, invention, lay-out, lucubration, make-up, making, mixture, opus, organization, piece, placing, production, proportion, structure, study, symmetry, work, writing.

composure *n.* aplomb, assurance, calm, calmness, confidence, cool, coolness, dignity, dispassion, ease, equanimity, impassivity, imperturbability, placidity, poise, sang-froid, savoir-faire, sedateness, self-assurance, self-possession, serenity, tranquility.

antonym discomposure.

compound *v.* aggravate, alloy, amalgamate, augment, blend, coalesce, combine, complicate, compose, concoct, exacerbate, fuse, heighten, increase, intensify, intermingle, magnify, mingle, mix, synthesize, unite, worsen.

n. alloy, amalgam, amalgamation, blend, combination, composite, composition, confection, conglomerate, conglomeration, fusion, medley, mixture, synthesis.

adj. complex, complicated, composite, conglomerate, intricate, mixed, multiple.

comprehend *v.* appreciate, apprehend, assimilate, compass, comprise, conceive, cover, discern, embrace, encompass, fathom, grasp, include, know, penetrate, perceive, see, see daylight, tumble to, twig, understand.

antonym misunderstand.

comprehension *n.* appreciation, apprehension, capacity, conception, discernment, grasp, intellection, intelligence, intension, judgment, knowledge, perception, realization, sense, understanding.

antonym incomprehension.

comprehensive *adj.* across-the-board, all-embracing, all-inclusive, blanket, broad, catholic, compendious, complete, encyclopedic, exhaustive, extensive, full, general, inclusive, omnibus, sweeping, thorough, wide.

antonyms incomplete, selective.

compress *v.* abbreviate, astrict, astringe, compact, concentrate, condense, constrict, contract, cram, crowd, crush, flatten, impact, jam, précis, press, shorten, squash, squeeze, stuff, summarize, synopsize, telescope, wedge.

antonyms diffuse, expand, separate.

comprise *v.* comprehend, consist of, contain, cover, embody, embrace, encompass, include, incorporate, involve, subsume.

compromise[1] *v.* adapt, adjust, agree, arbitrate, bargain, concede, make concessions, negotiate, retire, retreat, settle.

antonyms differ, quarrel.

n. accommodation, accord, adjustment, agreement,

bargain, concession, co-operation, settlement, trade-off, via media.

antonyms disagreement, intransigence.

compulsion *n.* coercion, constraint, demand, distress, drive, duress, exigency, force, impulse, necessity, need, obligation, obsession, preoccupation, pressure, urge, urgency.

antonyms freedom, liberty.

compulsory *adj.* binding, de rigueur, forced, imperative, mandatory, obligatory, required, requisite, stipulated, stipulatory.

antonyms optional, voluntary.

compute *v.* assess, calculate, count, enumerate, estimate, evaluate, figure, measure, rate, reckon, sum, tally, total.

computer *n.* adding machine, analog computer, calculator, data processor, digital computer, mainframe, processor, word processor.

comrade *n.* Achates, ally, associate, brother, buddy, bully-rook, butty, china, cobber, colleague, companion, compatriot, compeer, confederate, co-worker, crony, fellow, frater, friend, mate, pal, partner, side-kick.

con *v.* bamboozle, beguile, bilk, bluff, bunko, cheat, cozen, deceive, defraud, double-cross, dupe, fiddle, grift, gull, hoax, hoodwink, humbug, inveigle, mislead, racket, rip off, rook, swindle, trick.

n. bluff, deception, fraud, grift, kidology, scam, swindle, trick.

conceal *v.* bury, camouflage, cloak, cover, disguise, dissemble, hide, keep dark, mask, obscure, screen, secrete, shelter, sink, smother, submerge, suppress, veil.

antonym reveal.

concede *v.* accept, acknowledge, admit, allow, cede, confess, forfeit, grant, own, recognize, relinquish, sacrifice, surrender, yield.

antonyms deny, dispute.

conceit[1] *n.* arrogance, assumption, cockiness, complacency, conceitedness, egotism, narcissism, pride, self-assumption, self-conceit, self-importance, self-love, self-pride, self-satisfaction, swagger, vainglory, vainness, vanity.

antonyms diffidence, modesty.

conceit[2] *n.* belief, caprice, concetto, fancy, fantasy, freak, humor, idea, image, imagination, impulse, jeu d'esprit, judgment, notion, opinion, quip, quirk, thought, vagary, whim, whimsy, wit.

conceited *adj.* arrogant, assuming, bigheaded, cocky, complacent, egotistical, highty-tighty, hoity-toity, immodest, narcissistic, overweening, self-important, self-satisfied, stuck-up, swell-headed, swollen-headed, toffee-nose(d), uppist, uppity, vain, vainglorious, windy.

antonyms diffident, modest.

conceive *v.* appreciate, apprehend, believe, comprehend, contrive, create, design, develop, devise, envisage, fancy, form, formulate, germinate, grasp, ideate, imagine,

invent, originate, produce, project, purpose, realize, suppose, think, understand, visualize.

concentrate *v.* absorb, accumulate, attend, attract, center, cluster, collect, condense, congregate, converge, crowd, draw, engross, focus, foregather, gather, huddle, intensify.

antonyms disperse, distract, separate.

n. apozem, decoction, decocture, distillate, distillation, elixir, essence, extract, juice, quintessence.

concentrated *adj.* all-out, compact, condensed, deep, dense, evaporated, hard, intense, intensive, reduced, rich, thickened, undiluted.

antonyms desultory, diffuse, diluted.

concept *n.* abstraction, conception, conceptualization, construct, hyphothesis, idea, image, impression, invention, notion, pattern, picture, plan, theory, type, view, visualization.

conception *n.* appreciation, apprehension, beginning, birth, clue, comprehension, concept, design, envisagement, fertilization, formation, germination, idea, image, impregnation, impression, inauguration, inception, initiation, inkling, insemination, invention, knowledge, launching, notion, origin, outset, perception, picture, plan, understanding, visualization.

concern *v.* affect, bother, disquiet, distress, disturb, interest, involve, pertain to, perturb, refer to, regard, relate to, touch, trouble, upset, worry.

n. affair, anxiety, apprehension, attention, bearing, burden, business, care, charge, company, consideration, corporation, disquiet, disquietude, distress, enterprise, establishment, field, firm, heed, house, importance, interest, involvement, job, matter, mission, occupation, organization, perturbation, reference, relation, relevance, responsibility, solicitude, stake, task, transaction, unease, uneasiness, worry.

antonym unconcern.

concerning *prep.* about, anent, apropos of, as regards, germane to, in regard to, in the matter of, re, regarding, relating to, relevant to, respecting, touching, with reference to, with regard to.

concerted *adj.* collaborative, collective, combined, co-ordinated, joint, organized, planned, prearranged, shared, united.

antonyms disorganized, separate, unco-ordinated.

concession *n.* acknowledgment, adjustment, admission, allowance, assent, boon, compromise, exception, favor, grant, indulgence, permit, privilege, relaxation, sacrifice, surrender, yielding.

concise *adj.* abbreviated, abridged, aphoristic, brief, compact, compendious, compressed, condensed, epigrammatic, gnomic, laconic, pithy, short, succinct, summary, synoptic, terse, thumbnail.

antonyms diffuse, expansive.

conclude *v.* accomplish, assume, cease, clinch, close, complete, consummate, culminate, decide, deduce, determine, effect, end, establish, finish, fix, gather, infer, judge, opine, reckon, resolve, settle, suppose, surmise, terminate.

concluding *adj.* closing, epilogic, epilogistic, final, last, perorating, terminal, ultimate.
antonym introductory.

conclusion *n.* answer, assumption, clincher, close, come-off, completion, consequence, consummation, conviction, culmination, decision, deduction, end, explicit, finale, fine, finis, finish, illation, inference, issue, judgment, opinion, outcome, resolution, result, settlement, solution, termination, upshot, verdict.

conclusive *adj.* clear, clinching, convincing, decisive, definite, definitive, final, incontrovertible, irrefragable, irrefutable, manifest, ultimate, unanswerable, unappealable, unarguable, undeniable.
antonym inconclusive.

concord *n.* accord, agreement, amicability, amity, brotherliness, compact, concert, concordat, consensus, consonance, convention, diapason, entente, friendship, harmony, peace, protocol, rapport, treaty, unanimity, unison.
antonym discord.

concrete *adj.* actual, calcified, compact, compressed, conglomerated, consolidated, definite, explicit, factual, firm, material, perceptible, petrified, physical, real, seeable, sensible, solid, solidified, specific, substantial, tactile, tangible, touchable, visible.
antonym abstract.

concur *v.* accede, accord, acquiesce, agree, approve, assent, coincide, combine, comply, consent, co-operate, harmonize, join, meet, unite.
antonym disagree.

condemn *v.* ban, blame, castigate, censure, convict, damn, decry, denounce, disapprove, disparage, doom, pan, proscribe, reprehend, reproach, reprobate, reprove, revile, sentence, slam, slate, upbraid.
antonyms approve, praise.

condense *v.* abbreviate, abridge, capsulize, coagulate, compact, compress, concentrate, contract, crystallize, curtail, decoct, distil, encapsulate, epitomize, evaporate, inspissate, precipitate, précis, reduce, shorten, solidify, summarize, synopsize, thicken.
antonyms dilute, expand.

condition *n.* ailment, arrangement, article, case, caste, circumstances, class, complaint, defect, demand, diathesis, disease, disorder, estate, fettle, fitness, grade, health, infirmity, kilter, level, liability, limitation, malady, modification, nick, obligation, order, plight, position, predicament, prerequisite, problem, provision, proviso, qualification, rank, requirement, requisite, restriction, rule, shape, situation, state, status, stipulation, stratum, terms, trim, understanding, weakness.
v. accustom, adapt, adjust, attune, determine, educate, equip, groom, habituate, hone, indoctrinate, inure, limit, prepare, prime, ready, restrict, season, temper, train, tune.

conditional *adj.* contingent, dependent, limited, provisional, qualified, relative, restricted, tied.
antonym unconditional.

condolence *n.* commiseration, compassion, condolences, consolation, pity, support, sympathy.
antonym congratulation.

conduct *n.* actions, administration, attitude, bearing, behavior, carriage, comportment, control, co-ordination, demeanor, deportment, direction, discharge, escort, guidance, guide, leadership, management, manners, mien, orchestration, organization, running, supervision, ways.
v. accompany, acquit, act, administer, attend, bear, behave, carry, chair, comport, control, convey, demean, deport, direct, escort, govern, guide, handle, lead, manage, orchestrate, organize, pilot, regulate, run, solicit, steer, supervise, transact, usher.

confederate *adj.* allied, associated, combined, federal, federated.
n. abettor, accessory, accomplice, ally, assistant, associate, collaborator, colleague, conspirator, friend, leaguer, partner, practisant, supporter.
v. ally, amalgamate, associate, bind, combine, federate, join, merge, unite, weld.

confer *v.* accord, award, bestow, consult, converse, deliberate, discourse, discuss, give, grant, impart, lay heads together, lend, parley, powwow, present, talk, vouchsafe.

confess *v.* acknowledge, admit, affirm, agnize, allow, assert, attest, aver, betray, concede, confide, confirm, declare, disclose, divulge, evince, expose, grant, manifest, own, own up, profess, prove, recognize, reveal, show.
antonyms conceal, deny.

confession *n.* acknowledgment, admission, affirmation, assertion, attestation, averment, avowal, confidences, confiteor, declaration, disclosure, divulgence, exposé, exposure, profession, revelation, unbosoming, unburdening, verbal.
antonyms concealment, denial.

confidence *n.* aplomb, assurance, belief, boldness, calmness, communication, composure, confession, coolness, courage, credence, dependence, disclosure, divulgence, faith, firmness, nerve, reliance, savoir-faire, secret, self-assurance, self-confidence, self-possession, self-reliance, trust.
antonyms diffidence, distrust.

confident *adj.* assured, bold, certain, composed, convinced, cool, dauntless, fearless, persuaded, positive, sanguine, satisfied, secure, self-assured, self-confident, self-possessed, self-reliant, sure, unabashed, unbashful, unselfconscious.
antonyms diffident, sceptical.

confidential *adj.* classified, close, closed, faithful, familiar, hush-hush, in camera, intimate, private, privy, secret, tête-à-tête, trusted, trustworthy, trusty.
antonyms common, public.

confine *v.* bind, bound, cage, chamber, circumscribe, constrain, cramp, crib, emmew, enclose, immew, immure, imprison, incarcerate, inhibit, intern, keep, keep prisoner, limit, mew, repress, restrain, restrict, shackle, shut up, thirl, trammel.
antonym free.

confirm *v.* approve, assure, attest, authenticate, back, buttress, clinch, corroborate, endorse, establish, evidence, fix, fortify, homologate, prove, ratify, reinforce, sanction, settle, strengthen, substantiate, support, validate, verify, witness to.
antonym deny.

confirmation *n.* acceptance, agreement, approval, assent, attestation, authentication, backing, clincher, corroboration, endorsement, evidence, proof, ratification, sanction, substantiation, support, testimony, validation, verification, witness.
antonym denial.

confirmed *adj.* authenticated, chronic, committed, corroborated, deep-dyed, dyed-in-the-wool, entrenched, established, habitual, hardened, incorrigible, incurable, ingrained, inured, inveterate, irredeemable, long-established, long-standing, proved, proven, rooted, seasoned, substantiated, unredeemed.
antonyms uncommitted, unconfirmed.

conflict *n.* agony, ambivalence, antagonism, antipathy, Armageddon, battle, brawl, clash, collision, combat, confrontation, contention, contest, difference, disagreement, discord, dissension, encounter, engagement, feud, fight, fracas, friction, hostility, interference, opposition, quarrel, set-to, skirmish, strife, turmoil, unrest, variance, war, warfare.
antonyms agreement, concord.
v. battle, clash, collide, combat, contend, contest, contradict, differ, disagree, fight, interfere, oppose, strive, struggle, war, wrangle.
antonym agree.

conform *v.* accommodate, accord, adapt, adjust, agree, assimilate, comply, correspond, follow, harmonize, match, obey, quadrate, square, suit, tally, yield.
antonym differ.

conformity *n.* affinity, agreement, allegiance, Babbitry, compliance, congruity, consonance, conventionalism, conventionality, correspondence, Gleichschaltung, harmony, likeness, observance, orthodoxy, resemblance, similarity, traditionalism.
antonyms difference, nonconformity.

comfound *v.* abash, amaze, astonish, astound, baffle, bamboozle, bewilder, confuse, contradict, demolish, destroy, discombobulate, dismay, dumbfound, flabbergast, mystify, nonplus, overthrow, overwhelm, perplex, ruin, startle, stupefy, surprise, thwart, unshape, upset.

confront *v.* accost, address, appose, beard, brave, challenge, defy, encounter, face, front, oppose.
antonym evade.

confuse *v.* abash, addle, baffle, befuddle, bemuse, bewilder, buffalo, burble, confound, darken, demoralize, disarrange, discomfit, discompose, disconcert, discountenance, disorder, disorient, disorientate, embarrass, embrangle, flummox, fluster, intermingle, involve, jumble, maze, mingle, mistake, mix up, mortify, muddle, mystify, nonplus, obscure, perplex, puzzle, rattle, shame, tangle, tie in knots.
antonyms clarify, enlighten, reassure.

confused *adj.* addle-brained, addle(d), addle-headed, addlepated, baffled, bewildered, bushed, chaotic, dazed, désorienté, disarranged, discombobulated, disordered, disorderly, disorganized, disorientated, distracted, embarrassed, flummoxed, fuddled, higgledy-piggledy, jumbled, maffled, mistaken, misunderstood, muddled, muddle-headed, muzzy, nonplused, perplexed, puzzled, puzzle-headed, streaked, topsy-turvy, tosticated, untidy, upset.
antonym clear.

confusion *n.* abashment, Babel, befuddlement, bemusement, bewilderment, bustle, chagrin, chaos, clutter, combustion, commotion, demoralization, disarrangement, discomfiture, disorder, disorganization, disorientation, distraction, égarement, embarrassment, embroglio, embroilment, fluster, foul-up, hotchpotch, hubble-bubble, hugger-mugger, imbroglio, jumble, mess, mix-up, muddle, mystification, overthrow, palaver, perdition, perplexity, perturbation, pie, puzzlement, screw-up, shambles, shame, tangle, tizz(y), topsyturviness, topsyturvy, topsyturvydom, toss, turmoil, untidiness, upheaval, welter.
antonyms clarity, composure, order.

congratulate *v.* compliment, felicitate, gratulate.
antonym commiserate.

congregate *v.* accumulate, assemble, bunch, clump, cluster, collect, concentrate, conglomerate, convene, converge, convoke, crowd, flock, foregather, gather, mass, meet, muster, rally, rendezvous, throng.
antonyms dismiss, disperse.

congress *n.* assembly, conclave, conference, convention, convocation, council, diet, forum, legislature, meeting, parliament, synod.

congruity *n.* agreement, coincidence, compatibility, concinnity, concurrence, conformity, congruence, congruousness, consistency, correspondence, harmony, identity, match, parallelism.
antonym incongruity.

conjecture *v.* assume, estimate, extrapolate, fancy, guess, hypothesize, imagine, infer, opine, reckon, speculate, suppose, surmise, suspect, theorize.
n. assumption, conclusion, estimate, extrapolation, fancy, guess, guesstimate, guesswork, hypothesis, inference, notion, opinion, presumption, projection, speculation, supposition, surmise, theorizing, theory.

conjunction *n.* amalgamation, association, coincidence, combination, concurrence, juxtaposition, syzygy, unification, union, unition.

connect *v.* affix, ally, associate, cohere, combine, compaginate, concatenate, couple, enlink, fasten, join, link, relate, unite.
antonym disconnect.

connection *n.* acquaintance, affinity, alliance, ally, arthrosis, associate, association, attachment, bond, catenation, coherence, commerce, communication, compagination, conjunction, contact, context, correlation, correspondence, coupling, fastening, friend, hook-up, intercourse, interrelation, intimacy, junction, kin, kindred, kinsman, kith, link, marriage, reference, relation, relationship, relative, relevance, sponsor, tie, tie-in, union.
antonym disconnection.

conquer *v.* acquire, annex, beat, best, checkmate, crush, defeat, discomfit, get the better of, humble, master, obtain, occupy, overcome, overpower, overrun, overthrow, prevail, quell, rout, seize, subdue, subjugate, succeed, surmount, triumph, vanquish, win, worst.
antonyms surrender, yield.

conquest *n.* acquisition, annexation, appropriation, captivation, coup, defeat, discomfiture, enchantment, enthralment, enticement, invasion, inveiglement, mastery, occupation, overthrow, rout, seduction, subjection, subjugation, takeover, triumph, vanquishment, victory.

conscientious *adj.* careful, diligent, exact, faithful, hardworking, high-minded, high-principled, honest, honorable, incorruptible, just, meticulous, moral, painstaking, particular, punctilious, responsible, scrupulous, solicitous, straightforward, strict, through, upright.
antonyms careless, irresponsible.

conscious *adj.* alert, alive, awake, aware, calculated, cognizant, deliberate, heedful, intentional, knowing, mindful, percipient, premeditated, rational, reasoning, reflective, regardful, responsible, responsive, self-conscious, sensible, sentient, studied, wilful, witting.
antonym unconscious.

consecrate *v.* beatify, dedicate, devote, exalt, hallow, ordain, revere, sanctify, venerate.

consecutive *adj.* chronological, continuous, following, running, sequential, seriatim, succeeding, successive, unbroken, uninterrupted.
antonym discontinuous.

consent *v.* accede, acquiesce, admit, agree, allow, approve, assent, comply, concede, concur, grant, homologate, permit, yield.
antonyms oppose, refuse.
n. accordance, acquiescence, agreement, approval, assent, compliance, concession, concurrence, consentience, go-ahead, green light, permission, sanction.
antonyms opposition, refusal.

consequence *n.* account, concern, distinction, effect, eminence, end, event, fall-out, import, importance, interest, issue, moment, notability, note, outcome, portent, rank, repercussion, repute, result, side effect, significance, standing, status, upshot, value, weight.
antonym cause.

consequential *adj.* arrogant, bumptious, conceited, consequent, eventful, far-reaching, grave, important, impressive, indirect, inflated, momentous, noteworthy, pompous, pretentious, resultant, self-important, serious, significant, supercilious, vainglorious, weighty.
antonyms inconsequential, unimportant.

consequently *adv.* accordingly, consequentially, ergo, hence, inferentially, necessarily, subsequently, therefore, thus.

conservative *adj.* cautious, conventional, die-hard, establishmentarian, guarded, hidebound, middle-of-the-road, moderate, quiet, reactionary, right-wing, sober, Tory, traditional, unexaggerated, unprogressive, verkrampte.
antonyms left-wing, radical.
n. diehard, moderate, moss-back, reactionary, right-winger, stick-in-the-mud, Tory, traditionalist.
antonyms left-winger, radical.

conserve *v.* guard, hoard, husband, keep, maintain, nurse, preserve, protect, save.
antonyms squander, use, waste.

consider *v.* believe, bethink, cogitate, consult, contemplate, count, deem, deliberate, discuss, examine, judge, meditate, mull over, muse, perpend, ponder, rate, reflect, regard, remember, respect, revolve, ruminate, study, think, weigh.
antonym ignore.

considerable *adj.* abundant, ample, appreciable, big, comfortable, distinguished, goodly, great, important, influential, large, lavish, marked, much, noteworthy, noticeable, plentiful, reasonable, renowned, significant, sizable, substantial, tidy, tolerable, venerable.
antonyms insignificant, slight.

considerate *adj.* attentive, charitable, circumspect, concerned, discreet, forbearing, gracious, kind, kindly, mindful, obliging, patient, solicitous, tactful, thoughtful, unselfish.
antonyms selfish, thoughtless.

consideration *n.* analysis, attention, cogitation, concern, considerateness, contemplation, deliberation, discussion, examination, factor, fee, friendliness, issue, kindliness, kindness, meditation, payment, perquisite, point, recompense, reflection, regard, remuneration, respect, review, reward, rumination, scrutiny, solicitude, study, tact, thought, thoughtfulness, tip.
antonyms disdain, disregard.

consistent *adj.* accordant, agreeing, coherent, compatible, congruous, consonant, constant, dependable, harmonious, logical, of a piece, persistent, regular, steady, unchanging, undeviating, unfailing, uniform.
antonyms erratic, inconsistent.

consolation *n.* aid, alleviation, assuagement, cheer, comfort, ease, easement, encouragement, help, relief, solace, succor, support.
antonym discouragement.

console *v.* assuage, calm, cheer, comfort, encourage, hearten, solace, soothe.
antonyms agitate, upset.

consolidate *v.* affiliate, amalgamate, cement, combine, compact, condense, confederate, conjoin, federate, fortify, fuse, harden, join, reinforce, secure, solidify, stabilize, strengthen, thicken, unify, unite.

consort *n.* associate, companion, fellow, helpmate, helpmeet, husband, partner, spouse, wife.
v. accord, agree, associate, correspond, fraternize, harmonize, jibe, mingle, mix, square, tally.

conspicuous *adj.* apparent, blatant, clear, discernible, evident, flagrant, flashy, garish, glaring, kenspeck(le), manifest, noticeable, obvious, patent, perceptible, remarked, showy, visible.
antonym inconspicuous.

conspiracy *n.* cabal, collusion, complot, confederacy, fix, frame-up, intrigue, league, machination, plot, scheme, treason.

conspire *v.* cabal, collude, combine, complot, concur, conduce, confederate, contribute, contrive, co-operate, devise, hatch, intrigue, machinate, maneuver, plot, scheme, tend, treason.

constancy *n.* determination, devotion, faithfulness, fidelity, firmness, fixedness, loyalty, permanence, perseverance, regularity, resolution, stability, steadfastness, steadiness, tenacity, uniformity.
antonyms inconstancy, irregularity.

constant *adj.* attached, ceaseless, changeless, continual, continuous, dependable, determined, devoted, dogged, endless, eternal, even, everlasting, faithful, firm, fixed, habitual, immutable, incessant, interminable, invariable, loyal, never-ending, non-stop, permanent, perpetual, persevering, persistent, regular, relentless, resolute, stable, staunch, steadfast, steady, sustained, tried-and-true, true, trustworthy, trusty, unalterable, unbroken, unchangeable, unfailing, unflagging, uniform, uninterrupted, unrelenting, unremitting, unshaken, unvarying, unwavering.
antonyms fickle, fitful, irregular, occasional, variable.

constantly *adv.* always, continually, continuously, endlessly, everlastingly, incessantly, interminably, invariably, non-stop, perpetually, relentlessly, steadfastly, uniformly.
antonym occasionally.

consternation *n.* alarm, amazement, anxiety, awe, bewilderment, confusion, dismay, disquietude, distress, dread, fear, fright, horror, panic, perturbation, shock, terror, trepidation.
antonym composure.

constitute *v.* appoint, authorize, commission, compose, comprise, create, delegate, depute, empower, enact, establish, fix, form, found, inaugurate, make, name, nominate, ordain.

constitution *n.* build, character, composition, configuration, construction, disposition, establishment, form, formation, habit, health, make-up, nature, organization, physique, structure, temper, temperament.

constrain *v.* bind, bulldoze, chain, check, coerce, compel, confine, constrict, curb, drive, force, impel, necessitate, oblige, pressure, pressurize, railroad, restrain, urge.

construct *v.* assemble, build, compose, create, design, elevate, engineer, erect, establish, fabricate, fashion, form, formulate, found, frame, knock together, make, manufacture, model, organize, raise, shape.
antonyms demolish, destroy.

construction *n.* assembly, building, composition, constitution, creation, edifice, erection, fabric, fabrication, figure, form, formation, model, organization, shape, structure.
antonym destruction.

constructive *adj.* advantageous, beneficial, helpful, positive, practical, productive, useful, valuable.
antonyms destructive, negative, unhelpful.

construe *v.* analyze, decipher, deduce, explain, expound, infer, interpret, parse, read, render, take, translate.

consult *v.* ask, commune, confer, consider, debate, deliberate, interrogate, parley, powwow, question, regard, respect.

consume *v.* absorb, annihilate, decay, demolish, deplete, destroy, devastate, devour, discuss, dissipate, drain, eat, employ, engulf, envelop, exhaust, expend, gobble, guzzle, lessen, ravage, spend, squander, swallow, use (up), utilize, vanish, waste, wear out.

consumer *n.* buyer, customer, end-user, purchaser, shopper, user.

consummate *v.* accomplish, achieve, cap, compass, complete, conclude, crown, effectuate, end, finish, fulfil, perfect, perform, terminate.
adj. absolute, accomplished, complete, conspicuous, distinguished, finished, matchless, perfect, polished, practised, skilled, superb, superior, supreme, total, transcendent, ultimate, unqualified, utter.
antonym imperfect.

consummation *n.* achievement, actualization, completion, culmination, end, fulfilment, perfection, realization, termination.

contact *n.* acquaintance, approximation, association, communication, connection, contiguity, contingence, impact, junction, juxtaposition, meeting, tangency, touch, union.
v. approach, call, get hold of, notify, phone, reach, ring.

contagious *adj.* catching, communicable, epidemic, epizootic, infectious, pestiferous, pestilential, spreading, transmissible, zymotic.

contain *v.* accommodate, check, comprehend, comprise,

control, curb, embody, embrace, enclose, entomb, hold, include, incorporate, involve, limit, repress, restrain, seat, stifle.
antonym exclude.

contaminate *v.* adulterate, befoul, besmirch, corrupt, debase, defile, deprave, infect, pollute, soil, stain, sully, taint, tarnish, vitiate.
antonym purify.

contemplate *v.* behold, cerebrate, consider, deliberate, design, envisage, examine, expect, eye, foresee, inspect, intend, mean, meditate, mull over, observe, plan, ponder, propose, reflect on, regard, ruminate, scrutinize, study, survey, view.

contemplative *adj.* cerebral, intent, introspective, meditative, musing, pensive, rapt, reflective, ruminative, thoughtful.
antonyms impulsive, thoughtless.

contemporary *adj.* à la mode, coetaneous, coeval, co-existent, co-existing, concurrent, contemporaneous, conterminous, coterminous, current, latest, modern, newfangled, present, present-day, recent, synchronous, ultra-modern, up-to-date, up-to-the-minute, with it.
antonyms preceding, succeeding.

contempt *n.* condescension, contemptuousness, contumely, derision, despite, detestation, disdain, disgrace, dishonor, disregard, disrespect, humiliation, loathing, mockery, neglect, scorn, shame, slight.
antonyms admiration, regard.

contemptible *adj.* abject, base, cheap, degenerate, despicable, detestable, ignominious, loathsome, low, lowdown, mean, paltry, pitiful, scurvy, shabby, shameful, vile, worthless, wretched.
antonyms admirable, honorable.

contemptuous *adj.* arrogant, cavalier, condescending, contumacious, contumelious, cynical, derisive, disdainful, haughty, high and mighty, insolent, insulting, scornful, sneering, supercilious, tossy, withering.
antonyms humble, polite, respectful.

contend *v.* affirm, allege, argue, assert, aver, avow, clash, compete, contest, cope, debate, declare, dispute, emulate, grapple, hold, jostle, litigate, maintain, skirmish, strive, struggle, vie, wrestle.

content[1] *v.* appease, delight, gladden, gratify, humor, indulge, mollify, pacify, placate, please, reconcile, satisfy, suffice.
antonym displease.
n. comfort, contentment, delight, ease, gratification, happiness, peace, pleasure, satisfaction.
antonym discontent.
adj. agreeable, comfortable, contented, fulfilled, pleased, satisfied, untroubled.
antonym dissatisfied.

content[2] *n.* burden, capacity, essence, gist, ideas, load, matter, meaning, measure, significance, size, subject matter, substance, text, thoughts, volume.

contented *adj.* cheerful, comfortable, complacent, content, glad, gratified, happy, placid, pleased, relaxed, satisfied, serene, thankful.
antonym discontented.

contention *n.* affirmation, allegation, argument, assertion, asseveration, belief, claim, competition, contest, controversy, debate, declaration, discord, dispute, dissension, enmity, feuding, ground, hostility, idea, opinion, position, profession, rivalry, stand, strife, struggle, thesis, view, wrangling.

contentment *n.* comfort, complacency, content, contentedness, ease, equanimity, fulfilment, gladness, gratification, happiness, peace, peacefulness, placidity, pleasure, repletion, satisfaction, serenity.
antonym dissatisfaction.

contest *n.* affray, altercation, battle, combat, competition, concours, conflict, controversy, debate, discord, dispute, encounter, fight, game, match, olympiad, set-to, shock, struggle, tournament, trial.
v. argue against, challenge, compete, contend, debate, deny, dispute, doubt, fight, litigate, oppose, question, refute, strive, vie.

continence *n.* abstemiousness, abstinence, asceticism, celibacy, chastity, moderation, self-control, self-restraint, sobriety, temperance.
antonym incontinence.

contingency *n.* accident, arbitrariness, chance, emergency, event, eventuality, fortuity, happening, incident, juncture, possibility, randomness, uncertainty.

contingent *n.* batch, body, bunch, company, complement, deputation, detachment, group, mission, quota, section, set.

continual *adj.* ceaseless, constant, continuous, endless, eternal, everlasting, frequent, incessant, interminable, oft-repeated, perpetual, recurrent, regular, repeated, repetitive, unbroken, unceasing, uninterrupted, unremitting.
antonyms intermittent, occasional, temporary.

continue *v.* abide, aby(e), adjourn, carry on, endure, extend, go on, last, lengthen, maintain, persevere, persist, proceed, project, prolong, pursue, reach, recommence, remain, rest, resume, stay, stick at, survive, sustain.
antonyms discontinue, stop.

continuous *adj.* connected, consecutive, constant, continued, extended, non-stop, prolonged, unbroken, unceasing, undivided, uninterrupted.
antonyms discontinuous, intermittent, sporadic.

contract *v.* abbreviate, abridge, acquire, agree, arrange, bargain, catch, clinch, close, compress, condense, confine, constrict, constringe, covenant, curtail, develop, dwindle, engage, epitomize, incur, lessen, narrow, negotiate, pledge, purse, reduce, shrink, shrivel, stipulate, tighten, wither, wrinkle.
antonyms enlarge, expand, lengthen.
n. agreement, arrangement, bargain, bond, commission,

commitment, compact, concordat, convention, covenant, deal, engagement, handfast, instrument, pact, settlement, stipulation, transaction, treaty, understanding.

contraction *n.* abbreviation, astringency, compression, constriction, diminution, elision, narrowing, reduction, retrenchment, shortening, shrinkage, shriveling, tensing, tightening.

antonyms expansion, growth.

contradict *v.* belie, challenge, contravene, controvert, counter, counteract, deny, disaffirm, dispute, gainsay, impugn, negate, oppose.

antonyms agree, confirm, corroborate.

contradictory *adj.* antagonistic, antithetical, conflicting, contrary, discrepant, dissident, double-mouthed, incompatible, inconsistent, irreconcilable, opposed, opposite, paradoxical, repugnant, unreconciled.

antonym consistent.

contrary *adj.* adverse, antagonistic, arsy-versy, awkward, balky, cantankerous, clashing, contradictory, counter, cross-grained, cussed, difficult, discordant, disobliging, froward, hostile, inconsistent, inimical, intractable, intractible, obstinate, opposed, opposite, paradoxical, perverse, stroppy, thrawn, unaccommodating, wayward, wilful.

antonyms like, obliging, similar.

n. antithesis, converse, opposite, reverse.

contrast *n.* comparison, contraposition, contrariety, counter-view, difference, differentiation, disparity, dissimilarity, distinction, divergence, foil, opposition, set-off.

antonym similarity.

v. compare, differ, differentiate, discriminate, distinguish, oppose, set off.

contribute *v.* add, afford, bestow, conduce, dob in, donate, furnish, give, help, kick in, lead, provide, subscribe, supply, tend.

antonyms subtract, withhold.

contribution *n.* addition, bestowal, donation, gift, grant, gratuity, handout, input, offering, subscription.

contrive *v.* arrange, compass, concoct, construct, create, design, devise, effect, engineer, excogitate, fabricate, frame, improvise, invent, manage, maneuver, plan, plot, scheme, wangle.

control *v.* boss, bridle, check, command, conduct, confine, constrain, contain, curb, determine, direct, dominate, govern, lead, limit, manage, manipulate, master, monitor, oversee, pilot, regiment, regulate, repress, restrain, rule, run, stage-manage, steer, subdue, superintend, supervise, suppress, verify.

n. authority, brake, charge, check, clutches, command, curb, direction, dirigism(e), discipline, governance, government, guidance, jurisdiction, leading-strings, leash, limitation, management, mastery, oversight, regulation, rule, superintendence, supervision, supremacy.

controversy *n.* altercation, argument, contention, debate,

disagreement, discussion, dispute, dissension, polemic, quarrel, squabble, strife, war of words, wrangle, wrangling.

antonyms accord, agreement.

convenience *n.* accessibility, accommodation, advantage, amenity, appliance, appropriateness, availability, benefit, chance, comfort, ease, enjoyment, facility, fitness, handiness, help, leisure, opportuneness, opportunity, satisfaction, service, serviceability, suitability, timeliness, use, usefulness, utility.

convenient *adj.* accessible, adapted, advantageous, appropriate, at hand, available, beneficial, commodious, fit, fitted, handy, helpful, labor-saving, nearby, opportune, seasonable, serviceable, suitable, suited, timely, useful, utile, well-timed.

antonyms awkward, inconvenient.

convention *n.* agreement, assembly, bargain, code, compact, conclave, concordat, conference, congress, contract, convocation, council, custom, delegates, etiquette, formality, matter of form, meeting, pact, practice, propriety, protocol, representatives, stipulation, synod, tradition, treaty, understanding, usage.

conventional *adj.* accepted, arbitrary, bourgeois, common, commonplace, copybook, correct, customary, decorous, expected, formal, habitual, hackneyed, hidebound, iconic, nomic, normal, ordinary, orthodox, pedestrian, prevailing, prevalent, proper, prosaic, regular, ritual, routine, run-of-the-mill, standard, stereotyped, straight, stylized, traditional, unoriginal, uptight, usual, wonted.

antonyms exotic, unconventional, unusual.

conversant with acquainted with, apprised of, au fait with, experienced in, familiar with, informed about, knowledgeable about, practiced in, proficient in, skilled in, versant with, versed in.

antonym ignorant of.

conversation *n.* chat, chinwag, chitchat, colloquy, communication, communion, confab, confabulation, conference, converse, dialogue, discourse, discussion, exchange, gossip, intercourse, interlocution, powwow, talk, tête-à-tête.

converse[1] *v.* chat, colloquize, commune, confabulate, confer, discourse, talk.

converse[2] *n.* antithesis, contrary, counterpart, obverse, opposite, reverse.

adj. antipodal, antipodean, contrary, counter, opposite, reverse, reversed, transposed.

conversion *n.* adaptation, alteration, change, metamorphosis, metanoia, modification, permutation, proselytization, rebirth, reconstruction, reformation, regeneration, remodeling, reorganization, transfiguration, transformation, transmogrification, transmutation.

convert *v.* adapt, alter, apply, appropriate, baptize, change, convince, interchange, metamorphose, modify, permute, proselytize, reform, regenerate, remodel, reorganize, restyle, revise, save, transform, transmogrify, transmute, transpose, turn.

n. catechumen, disciple, neophyte, proselyte, vert.

convey *v.* bear, bequeath, bring, carry, cede, communicate, conduct, deliver, demise, devolve, disclose, fetch, forward, grant, guide, impart, lease, move, relate, reveal, send, steal, support, tell, transfer, transmit, transport, waft, will.

conveyance *n.* carriage, movement, shipment, transfer, transference, transmission, transport, transportation, tran(s)shipment, vehicle, wagonage.

convict *v.* attaint, condemn, imprison, sentence.

n. con, criminal, culprit, felon, forçat, jail-bird, lag, malefactor, prisoner.

conviction *n.* assurance, belief, certainty, certitude, confidence, convincement, creed, earnestness, faith, fervor, firmness, opinion, persuasion, plerophory, principle, reliance, tenet, view.

convince *v.* assure, confirm, persuade, reassure, satisfy, sway, win over.

convivial *adj.* back-slapping, cheerful, festive, friendly, fun-loving, gay, genial, hearty, hilarious, jolly, jovial, lively, merry, mirthful, sociable.

antonym taciturn.

convoy *n.* attendance, attendant, escort, fleet, guard, protection, train.

cool *adj.* aloof, apathetic, audacious, bold, brazen, calm, cheeky, chilled, chilling, chilly, coldish, collected, composed, cosmopolitan, dégagé, deliberate, dispassionate, distant, down-beat, elegant, frigid, impertinent, imperturbable, impudent, incurious, indifferent, laid-back, level-headed, lukewarm, nippy, offhand, placid, pleasant, presumptuous, quiet, refreshing, relaxed, reserved, satisfying, self-controlled, self-possessed, serene, shameless, sophisticated, stand-offish, together, uncommunicative, unconcerned, unemotional, unenthusiastic, unexcited, unfriendly, unheated, uninterested, unresponsive, unruffled, unwelcoming, urbane.

antonyms excited, friendly, hot, warm.

v. abate, allay, assuage, calm, chill, dampen, defuse, fan, freeze, lessen, moderate, quiet, refrigerate, temper.

antonyms excite, heat, warm. *n.* calmness, collectedness, composure, control, poise, sangfroid, self-control, self-discipline, self-possession, temper.

co-operate *v.* abet, aid, assist, collaborate, combine, concur, conduce, conspire, contribute, co-ordinate, help, play along, play ball.

co-ordinate *v.* codify, correlate, grade, graduate, harmonize, integrate, match, mesh, organize, relate, synchronize, systematize, tabulate.

adj. coequal, correlative, correspondent, equal, equipotent, equivalent, parallel, reciprocal.

copious *adj.* abundant, ample, bounteous, bountiful, extensive, exuberant, full, generous, great, huge, inexhaustible, lavish, liberal, luxuriant, overflowing, plenteous, plentiful, profuse, rich, superabundant.

antonyms meager, scarce.

copy *n.* apograph, archetype, autotype, borrowing, calque, carbon copy, counterfeit, crib, duplicate, ectype, engrossment, exemplar, facsimile, flimsy, forgery, image, imitation, likeness, loan translation, loan-word, model, Ozalid®;, pattern, photocopy, Photostat®;, plagiarization, print, replica, replication, representation, reproduction, tracing, transcript, transcription, Xerox®;.

antonym original.

v. ape, borrow, counterfeit, crib, duplicate, echo, emulate, engross, exemplify, extract, facsimile, follow, imitate, mimic, mirror, parrot, personate, photocopy, Photostat®;, plagiarize, repeat, replicate, reproduce, simulate, transcribe, Xerox®;.

cordial *adj.* affable, affectionate, agreeable, cheerful, earnest, friendly, genial, heartfelt, hearty, invigorating, pleasant, restorative, sociable, stimulating, warm, warm-hearted, welcoming, whole-hearted.

antonyms aloof, cool, hostile.

core *n.* center, crux, essence, germ, gist, heart, kernel, nitty-gritty, nub, nucleus, pith.

antonyms exterior, perimeter, surface.

corporation[1] *n.* association, authorities, body, combine, conglomerate, council, society.

corporation[2] *n.* beer belly, paunch, pod, pot, pot-belly, spare tire.

corpse *n.* body, cadaver, carcass, deader, remains, skeleton, stiff.

corpulent *adj.* adipose, beefy, bulky, burly, fat, fattish, fleshy, large, lusty, obese, overweight, plump, poddy, podgy, portly, pot-bellied, pudgy, roly-poly, rotund, stout, tubby, well-padded.

antonym thin.

correct *v.* adjust, admonish, amend, blue-pencil, chasten, chastise, chide, counterbalance, cure, debug, discipline, emend, emendate, improve, punish, rectify, redress, reform, regulate, remedy, reprimand, reprove, right.

adj. acceptable, accurate, appropriate, comme il faut, diplomatic, equitable, exact, faultless, fitting, flawless, jake, just, OK, precise, proper, regular, right, seemly, standard, strict, true, well-formed, word-perfect.

antonyms inaccurate, incorrect, wrong.

correction *n.* adjustment, admonition, alteration, amendment, castigation, chastisement, discipline, emendation, improvement, modification, punishment, rectification, reformation, reproof, righting.

correlation *n.* alternation, correspondence, equivalence, interaction, interchange, interdependence, interrelationship, link, reciprocity, relationship.

correspond *v.* accord, agree, answer, coincide, communicate, complement, concur, conform, correlate, dovetail, fit, harmonize, match, square, tally, write.

correspondent *n.* contributor, journalist, penpal, reporter, writer.

adj. analogous, comparable, equivalent, like, matching, parallel, reciprocal, similar.

corridor *n.* aisle, ambulatory, foyer, hallway, lobby, passage, passageway, vestibule.

corrode *v.* canker, consume, corrupt, crumble, deteriorate, disintegrate, eat away, erode, fret, impair, oxidize, rust, waste, wear away.

corrupt *adj.* abandoned, adulterate(d), altered, bent, bribed, contaminated, crooked, debased, decayed, defiled, degenerate, demoralized, depraved, dishonest, dishonored, dissolute, distorted, doctored, falsified, fraudulent, infected, polluted, profligate, putrescent, putrid, rotten, shady, tainted, unethical, unprincipled, unscrupulous, venal, vicious.

antonyms honest, trustworthy, upright.

v. adulterate, barbarize, bribe, canker, contaminate, debase, debauch, defile, demoralize, deprave, doctor, empoison, entice, fix, infect, lure, pervert, putrefy, seduce, spoil, square, suborn, subvert, taint, vitiate.

antonym purify.

corruption *n.* adulteration, baseness, bribery, bribing, crookedness, debasement, decadence, decay, defilement, degeneration, degradation, demoralization, depravity, dishonesty, distortion, doctoring, evil, extortion, falsification, fiddling, foulness, fraud, fraudulence, fraudulency, graft, immorality, impurity, infection, iniquity, jobbery, leprosy, malversation, perversion, pollution, profiteering, profligacy, putrefaction, putrescence, rot, rottenness, shadiness, sinfulness, turpitude, ulcer, unscrupulousness, venality, vice, viciousness, virus, wickedness.

antonyms honesty, purification.

cost *n.* amount, charge, damage, deprivation, detriment, disbursement, expenditure, expense, figure, harm, hurt, injury, loss, outlay, payment, penalty, price, rate, sacrifice, worth.

costly *adj.* catastrophic, damaging, dear, deleterious, disastrous, excessive, exorbitant, expensive, extortionate, gorgeous, harmful, highly-priced, lavish, loss-making, luxurious, opulent, precious, priceless, pricy, rich, ruinous, sacrificial, splendid, steep, sumptuous, valuable.

antonyms cheap, inexpensive.

costume *n.* apparel, attire, clothing, dress, ensemble, garb, get-up, livery, outfit, raiment, robes, uniform, vestment.

cough *n.* bark, hack, tussis.

v. bark, hack, harrumph, hawk, hem, hoast.

council *n.* assembly, board, cabinet, chamber, committee, conclave, conference, congress, consistory, consult, convention, convocation, diet, divan, ministry, panchayat, panel, parliament, soviet, syndicate, synod, volost.

counsel *n.* admonition, advice, advocate, attorney, barrister, caution, consideration, consultation, deliberation, direction, forethought, guidance, information,

lawyer, plan, purpose, recommendation, solicitor, suggestion, warning. *v.* admonish, advise, advocate, caution, direct, exhort, guide, instruct, recommend, suggest, urge, warn.

count *v.* add, ascribe, calculate, check, compute, consider, deem, enumerate, esteem, estimate, hold, impute, include, judge, list, matter, number, rate, reckon, regard, score, signify, tally, tell, think, tot up, total, weigh.

n. addition, calculation, computation, enumeration, numbering, poll, reckoning, sum, tally, total.

countenance *n.* acquiescence, aid, air, appearance, approval, aspect, assistance, backing, demeanor, endorsement, expression, face, favor, features, help, look, mien, physiognomy, sanction, support, visage.

v. abet, acquiesce, agree to, aid, approve, back, brook, champion, condone, encourage, endorse, endure, help, sanction, support, tolerate.

counteract *v.* act against, annul, check, contravene, counterbalance, countervail, cross, defeat, foil, frustrate, hinder, invalidate, negate, neutralize, offset, oppose, resist, thwart, undo.

antonyms assist, support.

counterfeit *v.* copy, fabricate, fake, feign, forge, imitate, impersonate, phony, pretend, sham, simulate.

adj. bogus, copied, ersatz, faked, false, feigned, forged, fraudulent, imitation, phony, postiche, pretend(ed), pseud, pseudo, sham, simular, simulated, simulate(d), spurious, supposititious.

antonym genuine.

n. copy, fake, forgery, fraud, imitant, imitation, phantasm(a), phony, reproduction, sham.

country *n.* backwoods, boondocks, citizenry, citizens, clime, commonwealth, community, countryside, electors, farmland, fatherland, green belt, homeland, inhabitants, kingdom, land, motherland, nation, nationality, outback, outdoors, part, people, populace, provinces, public, realm, region, society, sovereign state, state, sticks, terrain, territory, voters.

adj. agrarian, agrestic, arcadian, bucolic, georgic, landed, pastoral, provincial, rude, rural, rustic.

antonyms oppidan, urban.

couple *n.* brace, Darby and Joan, duo, dyad, pair, span, team, twain, twosome, yoke.

v. accompany, buckle, clasp, conjoin, connect, copulate, fornicate, hitch, join, link, marry, pair, unite, wed, yoke.

courage *n.* boldness, bottle, bravery, daring, dauntlessness, fearlessness, firmness, fortitude, gallantry, grit, guts, hardihood, heroism, mettle, nerve, pluck, resolution, spirit, spunk, stomach, valor.

antonym cowardice.

courageous *adj.* audacious, bold, brave, daring, dauntless, dreadless, fearless, gallant, gutsy, hardy, heroic, high-hearted, indomitable, intrepid, lion-hearted, plucky, resolute, stout-hearted, valiant, valorous.

antonym cowardly.

course *n.* advance, advancement, channel, circuit, circus, classes, continuity, current, curriculum, development, diadrom, direction, duration, flight-path, flow, furtherance, hippodrome, lap, lapse, lectures, line, march, method, mode, movement, orbit, order, passage, passing, path, piste, plan, policy, procedure, program, progress, progression, race, race-course, race-track, raik, regimen, road, round, route, schedule, sequence, series, studies, succession, sweep, syllabus, tack, term, time, track, trail, trajectory, unfolding, vector, voyage, way, wheel.

v. chase, dash, flow, follow, gush, hunt, move, pour, pursue, race, run, scud, scurry, speed, stream, surge, tumble.

courteous *adj.* affable, attentive, ceremonious, civil, considerate, courtly, debonair, elegant, gallant, gracious, mannerly, obliging, polished, polite, refined, respectful, urbane, well-bred, well-mannered.

antonyms discourteous, rude.

courtesy *n.* affability, attention, benevolence, breeding, civility, comity, consent, consideration, courteousness, courtliness, elegance, favor, gallantness, gallantry, generosity, gentilesse, graciousness, indulgence, kindness, manners, polish, politeness, urbanity.

antonyms discourtesy, rudeness.

covenant *n.* arrangement, bargain, bond, commitment, compact, concordat, contract, convention, deed, engagement, pact, pledge, promise, stipulation, treaty, trust, undertaking.

v. agree, bargain, contract, engage, pledge, promise, stipulate, undertake.

cover *v.* balance, camouflage, canopy, clad, cloak, clothe, coat, compensate, comprehend, comprise, conceal, consider, contain, counterbalance, curtain, daub, defend, describe, detail, disguise, dress, eclipse, embody, embrace, encase, encompass, enshroud, envelop, examine, guard, hide, hood, house, include, incorporate, insure, invest, investigate, involve, layer, mantle, mask, narrate, obscure, offset, overlay, overspread, protect, recount, reinforce, relate, report, screen, secrete, shade, sheathe, shelter, shield, shroud, suffuse, survey, veil.

n. bedspread, binding, camouflage, canopy, cap, case, cloak, clothing, coating, compensation, concealment, confederate, covering, cover-up, defence, disguise, dress, envelope, façade, front, guard, indemnity, insurance, jacket, lid, mask, payment, pretense, pretext, protection, refuge, reimbursement, sanctuary, screen, sheath, shelter, shield, smoke, spread, top, undergrowth, veil, woods, wrapper.

covert *adj.* clandestine, concealed, disguised, dissembled, hidden, private, secret, sneaky, stealthy, subreptitious, surreptitious, ulterior, under the table, underhand, unsuspected, veiled.

antonym open.

covetous *adj.* acquisitive, avaricious, close-fisted, envious, grasping, greedy, insatiable, jealous, mercenary, rapacious, thirsting, yearning. *antonyms* generous, temperate.

coward *n.* caitiff, chicken, craven, dastard, faint-heart, funk, hilding, nithing, poltroon, recreant, renegade, scaredy-cat, skulker, sneak, yellow-belly, yellow-dog. *antonym* hero.

cowardice *n.* faint-heartedness, fear, funk, gutlessness, pusillanimity, spinelessness.

antonyms courage, valor.

cowardly *adj.* base, caitiff, chicken, chicken-hearted, chicken-livered, craven, dastard(ly), faint-hearted, fearful, gutless, hilding, lily-livered, nesh, nithing, pusillanimous, recreant, scared, shrinking, soft, spineless, timorous, unheroic, weak, weak-kneed, white-livered, yellow, yellow-bellied.

antonym courageous.

cower *v.* cringe, crouch, flinch, grovel, quail, ruck, shake, shiver, shrink, skulk, tremble.

coy *adj.* arch, backward, bashful, coquettish, demure, diffident, evasive, flirtatious, kittenish, maidenly, modest, prudish, reserved, retiring, self-effacing, shrinking, shy, skittish, timid, virginal.

antonyms forward, impudent, sober.

crack *v.* break, buffet, burst, chap, chip, chop, cleave, clip, clout, collapse, crackle, crash, craze, cuff, decipher, detonate, explode, fathom, fracture, pop, ring, rive, slap, snap, solve, splinter, split, succumb, thump, wallop, whack, yield.

n. attempt, blow, breach, break, buffet, burst, chap, chink, chip, clap, cleft, clip, clout, cranny, crash, craze, crevasse, crevice, cuff, dig, expert, explosion, fent, fissure, flaw, fracture, gag, gap, go, insult, interstice, jibe, joke, moment, opportunity, pop, quip, report, rift, slap, smack, snap, stab, thump, try, wallop, whack, wisecrack, witticism.

adj. ace, choice, élite, excellent, first-class, first-rate, hand-picked, superior, top-notch.

craft *n.* ability, aircraft, aptitude, art, artfulness, artifice, artistry, barque, boat, business, calling, cleverness, contrivance, craftiness, cunning, deceit, dexterity, duplicity, employment, expertise, expertness, guile, handicraft, handiwork, ingenuity, knack, know-how, line, occupation, plane, pursuit, ruse, scheme, ship, shrewdness, skill, spacecraft, spaceship, stratagem, subterfuge, subtlety, technique, trade, trickery, vessel, vocation, wiles, work, workmanship.

antonyms naïvety, openness.

craftiness *n.* artfulness, astuteness, canniness, cunning, deceit, deviousness, double-dealing, duplicity, foxiness, guile, shrewdness, slyness, subtlety, trickiness, underhandedness, vulpinism, wiliness.

antonyms naïvety, openness.

crafty *adj.* artful, astute, calculating, canny, cunning, deceitful, designing, devious, duplicitous, foxy, fraudulent, guileful, insidious, knowing, machiavellian, scheming, sharp, shrewd, sly, subtle, tricksy, tricky, versute, vulpine, wily.

antonyms naïve, open.

craggy *adj.* broken, brusque, cragged, jagged, jaggy, precipitous, rocky, rough, rugged, stony, surly, uneven.
antonyms pleasant, smooth.

crank *n.* eccentric, loony, madman, nutter.

cranky *adj.* bizarre, capricious, crabbed, cross, crotchety, dotty, eccentric, erratic, freakish, freaky, funny, idiosyncratic, irritable, odd, peculiar, prickly, queer, quirky, strange, surly, viewy, wacky.
antonyms normal, placid, sensible.

crash *n.* accident, bang, bankruptcy, boom, bump, clang, clash, clatter, clattering, collapse, collision, debacle (débâcle), depression, din, downfall, failure, fragor, jar, jolt, pile-up, prang, racket, ruin, smash, smashing, smash-up, thud, thump, thunder, wreck.
v. bang, break, bump, collapse, collide, dash, disintegrate, fail, fall, fold (up), fracture, fragment, go bust, go under, hurtle, lurch, overbalance, pitch, plunge, prang, shatter, shiver, smash, splinter, sprawl, topple.
adj. concentrated, emergency, immediate, intensive, round-the-clock, telescoped, urgent.

crave *v.* ask, beg, beseech, desire, entreat, fancy, hanker after, hunger after, implore, long for, need, petition, pine for, require, seek, solicit, supplicate, thirst for, want, yearn for, yen for.
antonyms dislike, spurn.

craving *n.* appetence, appetency, appetite, cacoethes, desire, hankering, hunger, longing, lust, thirst, urge, yearning, yen.
antonyms dislike, distaste.

crazy *adj.* absurd, ardent, bananas, barmy, bats, batty, berserk, bird-brained, bizarre, bonkers, cockeyed, cracked, crazed, cuckoo, daffy, daft, delirious, demented, deranged, derisory, devoted, dippy, eager, eccentric, enamored, enthusiastic, fanatical, fantastic, fatuous, foolhardy, foolish, fruity, half-baked, hysterical, idiotic, ill-conceived, impracticable, imprudent, inane, inappropriate, infatuated, insane, irresponsible, ludicrous, lunatic, mad, maniacal, mental, nonsensical, nuts, nutty, odd, off one's rocker, outrageous, passionate, peculiar, pixil(l)ated, potty, preposterous, puerile, quixotic, ridiculous, scatty, senseless, short-sighted, silly, smitten, strange, touched, unbalanced, unhinged, unrealistic, unwise, unworkable, up the pole, wacky, weird, wild, zany, zealous.
antonyms sane, sensible.

creak *v.* grate, grind, groan, rasp, scrape, scratch, screak, screech, squeak, squeal.

create *v.* appoint, beget, cause, coin, compose, concoct, constitute, design, develop, devise, engender, establish, form, formulate, found, generate, hatch, initiate, install, institute, invent, invest, make, occasion, originate, produce, set up, sire, spawn.
antonym destroy.

creative *adj.* adept, artistic, clever, fertile, gifted, imaginative, ingenious, inspired, inventive, original, productive, resourceful, stimulating, talented, visionary.
antonym unimaginative.

credence *n.* belief, confidence, credit, dependence, faith, reliance, support, trust.
antonym distrust.

credible *adj.* believable, conceivable, convincing, dependable, honest, imaginable, likely, persuasive, plausible, possible, probable, reasonable, reliable, sincere, supposable, tenable, thinkable, trustworthy, trusty.
antonyms implausible, unreliable.

credit *n.* acclaim, acknowledgment, approval, belief, character, clout, commendation, confidence, credence, distinction, esteem, estimation, faith, fame, glory, honor, influence, kudos, merit, position, praise, prestige, recognition, regard, reliance, reputation, repute, standing, status, thanks, tribute, trust.
antonym discredit.
v. accept, believe, buy, subscribe to, swallow, trust.
antonym disbelieve.

creditable *adj.* admirable, commendable, deserving, estimable, excellent, exemplary, good, honorable, laudable, meritorious, praiseworthy, reputable, respectable, sterling, worthy.
antonyms blameworthy, shameful.

credulous *adj.* dupable, green, gullible, naïve, trusting, uncritical, unsuspecting, unsuspicious, wide-eyed.
antonym skeptical.

creed *n.* articles, belief, canon, catechism, confession, credo, doctrine, dogma, faith, persuasion, principles, tenets.

creek *n.* bay, bight, brook, cove, fiord, firth, frith, inlet, rivulet, stream, streamlet, tributary, voe, watercourse.

creepy *adj.* awful, direful, disturbing, eerie, frightening, ghoulish, gruesome, hair-raising, horrible, macabre, menacing, nightmarish, ominous, scary, sinister, spookish, spooky, terrifying, threatening, unearthly, unpleasant, weird.
antonyms normal, pleasant.

crime *n.* atrocity, corruption, delinquency, fault, felony, flagitiousness, guilt, illegality, iniquity, law-breaking, malefaction, malfeasance, misconduct, misdeed, misdemeanor, offense, outrage, sin, transgression, trespass, unrighteousness, vice, villainy, violation, wickedness, wrong, wrongdoing.

criminal *n.* con, convict, crook, culprit, delinquent, evildoer, felon, infractor, jail-bird, law-breaker, malefactor, offender, sinner, transgressor.
adj. bent, corrupt, crooked, culpable, deplorable, felonious, flagitious, foolish, illegal, immoral, indictable, iniquitous, lawless, malfeasant, nefarious, peccant, preposterous, ridiculous, scandalous, senseless, unlawful, unrighteous, vicious, villainous, wicked, wrong.
antonyms honest, upright.

cripple *v.* cramp, damage, debilitate, destroy, disable, enfeeble, halt, hamstring, impair, incapacitate, lame, maim, mutilate, paralyze, ruin, sabotage, spoil, vitiate, weaken.

crippled *adj.* deformed, disabled, enfeebled, handicapped, incapacitated, invalid, lame, paralyzed.

crisis *n.* calamity, catastrophe, climacteric, climax, confrontation, conjuncture, crunch, crux, culmination, difficulty, dilemma, disaster, emergency, exigency, extremity, height, impasse, mess, pinch, plight, predicament, quandary, strait, trouble.

crisp *adj.* bracing, brief, brisk, brittle, brusque, clear, crispy, crumbly, crunchy, decisive, firm, forthright, fresh, incisive, invigorating, neat, orderly, pithy, refreshing, short, smart, snappy, spruce, succinct, tart, terse, tidy, vigorous.

antonyms flabby, limp, vague.

criterion *n.* bench-mark, canon, gauge, measure, norm, precedent, principle, proof, rule, shibboleth, standard, test, touchstone, yardstick.

critic *n.* analyst, animadverter, arbiter, Aristarch, attacker, authority, carper, caviler, censor, censurer, commentator, connoisseur, detractor, expert, expositor, fault-finder, feuilletonist, judge, knocker, Momus, pundit, reviewer, reviler, vilifier, Zoilist.

critical *adj.* accurate, all-important, analytical, captious, carping, caviling, censorious, climacteric, crucial, dangerous, deciding, decisive, derogatory, diagnostic, disapproving, discerning, discriminating, disparaging, fastidious, fault-finding, grave, hairy, high-priority, judicious, momentous, nagging, niggling, nit-picking, penetrating, perceptive, perilous, pivotal, precarious, precise, pressing, psychological, risky, serious, sharp-tongued, uncomplimentary, urgent, vital, Zoilean.

antonyms uncritical, unimportant.

criticize *v.* analyze, animadvert, appraise, assess, badmouth, blame, carp, censure, condemn, crab, decry, disparage, evaluate, excoriate, judge, knock, pan, review, roast, scarify, slag, slam, slash, slate, snipe.

antonym praise.

critique *n.* analysis, appraisal, assessment, commentary, essay, evaluation, examination, review.

crony *n.* accomplice, ally, associate, buddy, china, chum, colleague, companion, comrade, follower, friend, henchman, mate, pal, sidekick.

crooked[1] *adj.* bent, corrupt, crafty, criminal, deceitful, discreditable, dishonest, dishonorable, dubious, fraudulent, illegal, knavish, nefarious, questionable, shady, shifty, treacherous, underhand, unethical, unlawful, unprincipled, unscrupulous.

antonym honest.

crooked[2] *adj.* anfractuous, angled, askew, asymmetric, awry, bent, bowed, crank, cranky, crippled, crump, curved, deformed, deviating, disfigured, distorted, hooked, irregular, lopsided, meandering, misshapen, off-center, skew-whiff, slanted, slanting, squint, tilted, tortuous, twisted, twisting, uneven, warped, winding, zigzag.

antonym straight.

crop[1] *n.* fruits, gathering, growth, harvest, ingathering, produce, vintage, yield.

v. browse, clip, collect, curtail, cut, garner, gather, graze, harvest, lop, mow, nibble, pare, pick, prune, reap, reduce, shear, shingle, shorten, snip, top, trim, yield.

crop[2] *n.* craw, gizzard, gullet, maw, oesophagus, throat.

cross *adj.* adverse, angry, annoyed, cantankerous, captious, churlish, contrary, cranky, crosswise, crotchety, crusty, disagreeable, displeased, fractious, fretful, grouchy, grumpy, hybrid, ill-humored, ill-tempered, impatient, interchanged, intersecting, irascible, irritable, oblique, opposed, opposing, opposite, peeved, peevish, pettish, petulant, querulous, reciprocal, shirty, short, snappish, snappy, splenetic, sullen, surly, testy, transverse, unfavorable, vexed, waspish.

antonyms calm, placid, pleasant.

v. annoy, bestride, blend, block, bridge, cancel, crisscross, crossbreed, cross-fertilize, cross-pollinate, decussate, deny, foil, ford, frustrate, hinder, hybridize, impede, interbreed, intercross, interfere, intersect, intertwine, lace, meet, mix, mongrelize, obstruct, oppose, resist, span, thwart, traverse, zigzag.

n. affliction, amalgam, blend, burden, combination, cross-breed, crossing, crossroads, crucifix, cur, grief, holy-rood, hybrid, hybridization, intersection, load, misery, misfortune, mixture, mongrel, rood, trial, tribulation, trouble, woe, worry.

crouch *v.* bend, bow, cower, cringe, duck, hunch, kneel, ruck, squat, stoop.

crow *v.* bluster, boast, brag, exult, flourish, gloat, prate, rejoice, triumph, vaunt.

crowd *n.* army, assembly, attendance, audience, boodle, bunch, caboodle, circle, clique, company, concourse, flock, gate, group, herd, hoi polloi, horde, host, house, lot, many-headed beast/monster, mass, masses, mob, multitude, pack, people, populace, press, proletariat, public, rabble, riff-raff, set, spectators, squash, swarm, the many, throng, troupe.

v. bundle, cluster, compress, congest, congregate, cram, elbow, flock, for(e)gather, gather, huddle, jostle, mass, muster, pack, pile, press, push, shove, squeeze, stream, surge, swarm, throng.

crown *n.* acme, apex, bays, chaplet, circlet, coronal, coronet, crest, diadem, distinction, forehead, garland, head, honor, kudos, laurel wreath, laurels, monarch, monarchy, pate, perfection, pinnacle, prize, royalty, ruler, skull, sovereign, sovereignty, summit, tiara, tip, top, trophy, ultimate, zenith.

v. adorn, biff, box, cap, clout, complete, consummate, cuff, dignify, festoon, finish, fulfil, honor, instal, perfect, punch, reward, surmount, terminate, top.

crude *adj.* amateurish, blue, boorish, clumsy, coarse, crass, dirty, earthy, gross, half-baked, immature, inartistic, indecent, lewd, makeshift, natural, obscene, outline, primitive, raw, rough, rough-hewn, rude, rudimentary, sketchy, smutty, tactless, tasteless, uncouth, undeveloped, undigested, unfinished, unformed, unpolished, unprepared, unprocessed, unrefined, unsubtle, vulgar. *antonyms* finished, polite, refined, tasteful.

cruel *adj.* atrocious, barbarous, bitter, bloodthirsty, brutal, brutish, butcherly, callous, cold-blooded, cutting, depraved, excruciating, fell, ferocious, fierce, flinty, grim, hard, hard-hearted, harsh, heartless, heathenish, hellish, immane, implacable, inclement, inexorable, inhuman, inhumane, malevolent, marble-breasted, merciless, murderous, painful, pitiless, poignant, ravening, raw, relentless, remorseless, ruthless, sadistic, sanguinary, savage, severe, spiteful, stony-hearted, unfeeling, ungentle, unkind, unmerciful, unnatural, unrelenting, vengeful, vicious. *antonyms* compassionate, kind, merciful.

cruelty *n.* barbarity, bestiality, bloodthirstiness, brutality, brutishness, callousness, depravity, ferocity, fiendishness, hard-heartedness, harshness, heartlessness, immanity, inhumanity, mercilessness, murderousness, ruthlessness, sadism, savagery, severity, spite, spitefulness, tyranny, ungentleness, venom, viciousness. *antonyms* compassion, kindness, mercy.

crumb *n.* atom, bit, grain, iota, jot, mite, morsel, particle, scrap, shred, sliver, snippet, soupçon, speck.

crunch *v.* champ, chomp, grind, masticate, munch, scranch.
n. crisis, crux, emergency, pinch, test.

crush *v.* abash, break, browbeat, bruise, chagrin, champ, comminute, compress, conquer, contuse, crease, crumble, crumple, crunch, embrace, enfold, extinguish, hug, humiliate, mash, mortify, overcome, overpower, overwhelm, pound, press, pulverize, quash, quell, rumple, shame, smash, squabash, squeeze, squelch, steamroller, subdue, vanquish, wrinkle.
n. check, crowd, huddle, jam.

cry *v.* advertise, announce, bark, bawl, beg, bellow, beseech, bewail, blubber, boo-hoo, broadcast, bruit, call, caterwaul, clamor, ejaculate, entreat, exclaim, greet, hail, halloo, hawk, holler, howl, implore, keen, lament, mewl, miaow, miaul, noise, plead, pray, proclaim, promulgate, pule, roar, scream, screech, shout, shriek, snivel, sob, squall, squeal, trumpet, vociferate, wail, weep, whimper, whine, whinge, whoop, yell, yowl.
n. announcement, appeal, battle-cry, bawl(ing), bellow, blubber(ing), call, caterwaul, caterwaul(ing), ejaculation, entreaty, exclamation, greet, holler, hoot, howl, keening, lament, lamentation, miaow, miaul, outcry, petition, plaint, plea, prayer, proclamation, report, roar, rumor, scream, screech, shriek, slogan, snivel(ing), sob(bing), sorrowing, squall, squawk, squeal, supplication, utterance, wail(ing), watch-word, weep(ing), whoop, yell, yelp, yoo-hoo.

cryptic *adj.* abstruse, ambiguous, aprocryphal, arcane, bizarre, cabbalistic, dark, Delphic, enigmatic, equivocal, esoteric, hidden, mysterious, obscure, occult, oracular, perplexing, puzzling, recondite, secret, strange, vague, veiled. *antonyms* clear, obvious, straightforward.

cuddly *adj.* buxom, cosy, cuddlesome, curvaceous, huggable, lovable, plump, soft, warm.

cull *v.* amass, choose, collect, decimate, destroy, gather, glean, kill, pick, pick out, pluck, select, sift, thin, winnow.

culpable *adj.* answerable, blamable, blameworthy, censurable, guilty, liable, offending, peccant, reprehensible, sinful, to blame, wrong. *antonyms* blameless, innocent.

culprit *n.* criminal, delinquent, evil-doer, felon, guilty party, law-breaker, malefactor, miscreant, offender, rascal, sinner, transgressor, wrong-doer.

cultivate *v.* aid, ameliorate, better, cherish, civilize, court, develop, discipline, elevate, encourage, enrich, farm, fertilize, forward, foster, further, harvest, help, improve, patronize, plant, plow, polish, prepare, promote, pursue, refine, school, support, tend, till, train, work. *antonym* neglect.

cultivation *n.* advancement, advocacy, agronomy, breeding, civilization, civility, culture, development, discernment, discrimination, education, encouragement, enhancement, enlightenment, farming, fostering, furtherance, gardening, gentility, help, husbandry, learning, letters, manners, nurture, patronage, planting, plowing, polish, promotion, pursuit, refinement, schooling, study, support, taste, tillage, tilling, tilth, working.

cultural *adj.* aesthetic, artistic, arty, broadening, civilizing, developmental, edifying, educational, educative, elevating, enlightening, enriching, humane, humanizing, liberal.

culture *n.* accomplishment, aestheticism, agriculture, agronomy, art, breeding, civilization, cultivation, customs, education, elevation, enlightenment, erudition, farming, gentility, husbandry, improvement, Kultur, lifestyle, mores, polish, politeness, refinement, society, taste, the arts, urbanity.

cultured *adj.* accomplished, advanced, aesthetic, arty, civilized, educated, enlightened, erudite, genteel, highbrow, knowledgeable, polished, refined, scholarly, urbane, versed, well-bred, well-informed, well-read. *antonyms* ignorant, uncultured.

cumbersome *adj.* awkward, bulky, burdensome, clumsy, cumbrous, embarrassing, heavy, hefty, incommodious, inconvenient, onerous, oppressive, ponderous, unmanageable, unwieldy, weighty. *antonyms* convenient, manageable.

cunning *adj.* adroit, arch, artful, astute, canny, crafty, deep, deft, devious, dexterous, foxy, guileful, imaginative, ingenious, knowing, leery, Machiavellian, rusé, sharp, shifty, shrewd, skilful, sneaky, subtle, tricky, vulpine, wily. *antonyms* gullible, naïve.

n. ability, adroitness, art, artfulness, artifice, astuteness, cleverness, craftiness, deceitfulness, deftness, deviousness, dexterity, finesse, foxiness, guile, ingenuity, policy, shrewdness, skill, slyness, subtlety, trickery, vulpinism, wiliness.

antonyms openness, simplicity.

curb *v.* bit, bridle, check, constrain, contain, control, hamper, hinder, hobble, impede, inhibit, moderate, muzzle, repress, restrain, restrict, retard, subdue, suppress. *antonyms* encourage, foster, goad.

n. brake, bridle, check, control, deterrent, hamper, hobble, limitation, rein, restraint.

cure[1] *v.* alleviate, correct, ease, heal, help, mend, rehabilitate, relieve, remedy, restore.

n. alleviation, antidote, corrective, detoxicant, febrifuge, healing, medicine, panacea, panpharmacon, recovery, remedy, restorative, specific, treatment, vulnerary.

cure[2] *v.* brine, dry, kipper, pickle, preserve, salt, smoke.

curiosity *n.* bibelot, bygone, celebrity, curio, freak, inquisitiveness, interest, knick-knack, marvel, nosiness, novelty, object of virtu, objet d'art, objet de vertu, oddity, phenomenon, prying, rarity, sight, snooping, spectacle, trinket, wonder.

curious *adj.* bizarre, enquiring, exotic, extraordinary, funny, inquisitive, interested, marvelous, meddling, mysterious, nosy, novel, odd, peculiar, peeping, peering, prying, puzzled, puzzling, quaint, queer, questioning, rare, searching, singular, snoopy, strange, unconventional, unexpected, unique, unorthodox, unusual, wonderful.

antonyms incurious, indifferent, normal, ordinary, uninterested.

current *adj.* accepted, circulating, common, contemporary, customary, extant, fashionable, general, on-going, popular, present, present-day, prevailing, prevalent, reigning, rife, trendy, up-to-date, up-to-the-minute, widespread.

antonyms antiquated, old-fashioned.

n. atmosphere, course, draft, drift, feeling, flow, inclination, jet, juice, mood, progression, river, stream, tendency, thermal, tide, trend, undercurrent.

curse *n.* affliction, anathema, ban, bane, blasphemy, burden, calamity, cross, damn, denunciation, disaster, evil, excommunication, execration, expletive, imprecation, jinx, malediction, malison, misfortune, oath, obscenity, ordeal, plague, scourge, swearing, swear-word, torment, tribulation, trouble, vexation, woe.

antonyms advantage, blessing.

v. accurse, afflict, anathematize, blaspheme, blight, blind, blow, burden, cuss, damn, destroy, doom, excommunicate, execrate, fulminate, imprecate, plague, scourge, swear, torment, trouble, vex.

antonym bless.

cursory *adj.* brief, careless, casual, desultory, fleeting, hasty, hurried, offhand, passing, perfunctory, quick, rapid, slap-dash, slight, summary, superficial.

antonyms painstaking, thorough.

curt *adj.* abrupt, blunt, brief, brusque, concise, gruff, laconic, offhand, pithy, rude, sharp, short, short-spoken, snappish, succinct, summary, tart, terse, unceremonious, uncivil, ungracious.

antonym voluble.

curtail *v.* abbreviate, abridge, circumscribe, contract, cut, decrease, dock, lessen, lop, pare, prune, reduce, restrict, retrench, shorten, trim, truncate.

antonyms extend, lengthen, prolong.

curtain *v.* conceal, drape, hide, screen, shield, shroud, shutter, veil.

n. arras, backdrop, drapery, hanging, portière, tab, tapestry, vitrage.

curve *v.* arc, arch, bend, bow, coil, hook, incurvate, incurve, inflect, spiral, swerve, turn, twist, wind.

n. arc, bend, camber, curvature, half-moon, incurvation, incurvature, inflexure, loop, trajectory, turn.

cushion *n.* bean-bag, bolster, buffer, hassock, headrest, pad, pillion, pillow, shock absorber, squab. *v.* allay, bolster, buttress, cradle, dampen, deaden, lessen, mitigate, muffle, pillow, protect, soften, stifle, support, suppress.

custodian *n.* caretaker, castellan, chatelaine, claviger, conservator, curator, guardian, keeper, overseer, protector, superintendent, warden, warder, watch-dog, watchman.

custody *n.* aegis, arrest, auspices, care, charge, confinement, custodianship, detention, durance, duress, guardianship, holding, imprisonment, incarceration, keeping, observation, possession, preservation, protection, retention, safe-keeping, supervision, trusteeship, tutelage, ward, wardship, watch.

custom *n.* consuetude, convention, customers, etiquette, fashion, form, formality, habit, habitude, manner, mode, observance, observation, patronage, policy, practice, praxis, procedure, ritual, routine, rule, style, thew, trade, tradition, usage, use, way, wont.

customary *adj.* accepted, accustomed, acknowledged, common, confirmed, conventional, established, everyday, familiar, fashionable, favorite, general, habitual, nomic, normal, ordinary, popular, prevailing, regular, routine, traditional, usual, wonted.

antonyms occasional, rare, unusual.

customer *n.* buyer, client, consumer, habitué, patron, prospect, punter, purchaser, regular, shopper, vendee.

cut *v.* abbreviate, abridge, avoid, bisect, carve, castrate, chip, chisel, chop, cleave, clip, cold-shoulder, condense, contract, cross, curtail, decrease, delete, dissect, divide, dock, edit, engrave, excise, fashion, fell, form, gash, gather, gride, grieve, hack, harvest, hew, hurt, ignore, incise, insult, interrupt, intersect, lacerate, lop, lower, mow, nick, notch, pain, pare, part, penetrate, pierce, précis, prune, rationalize, reap, reduce, saw, scissor, score, sculpt, sculpture, segment, sever, shape, share, shave, shorten, slash, slice, slight, slim, slit, sned, snub, split, spurn, sting, sunder, trim, truncate, whittle, wound.

n. abscission, blow, chop, configuration, cutback, decrease, decrement, diminution, division, economy, fall, fashion, form, gash, graze, groove, incision, incisure, insection, kickback, laceration, look, lowering, mode, nick, percentage, piece, portion, race, rake-off, reduction, rent, rip, saving, section, shape, share, slash, slice, slit, snick, stroke, style, wound.

cut back check, crop, curb, decrease, economize, lessen, lop, lower, prune, reduce, retrench, slash, trim.

cut in interjaculate, interject, interpose, interrupt, intervene, intrude.

cut off abscind, block, disconnect, discontinue, disinherit, disown, end, excide, excise, exscind, halt, intercept, interclude, interrupt, intersect, isolate, obstruct, prescind, renounce, separate, sever, stop, suspend.

cut short abbreviate, abort, arrest, check, crop, curtail,

dock, halt, interrupt, postpone, prune, reduce, stop, terminate.

antonym prolong.

cut-throat *n.* assassin, bravo, butcher, executioner, hatchet man, hit-man, homicide, killer, liquidator, murderer, slayer, thug.

adj. barbarous, bloodthirsty, bloody, brutal, competitive, cruel, dog-eat-dog, ferine, ferocious, fierce, homicidal, murderous, relentless, ruthless, savage, thuggish, unprincipled, vicious, violent.

cutting *adj.* acid, acrimonious, barbed, biting, bitter, caustic, chill, hurtful, incisive, keen, malicious, mordant, numbing, penetrating, piercing, pointed, raw, sarcastic, sardonic, scathing, severe, sharp, stinging, trenchant, wounding.

n. bit, cleavage, clipping, piece, scion, scission, slice.

cynical *adj.* contemptuous, derisive, distrustful, ironic, mephistophelian, mephistophilic, misanthropic(al), mocking, mordant, pessimistic, sarcastic, sardonic, sceptical, scoffing, scornful, sharp-tongued, sneering.

dab[1] *v.* blot, daub, pat, stipple, swab, tap, touch, wipe. *n.* bit, dollop, drop, fingerprint, fleck, flick, pat, peck, smear, smidgen, smudge, speck, spot, stroke, tap, touch, trace.

dab[2] ace, adept, dab hand, dabster, expert, pastmaster, wizard.

dabble *v.* dally, dip, fiddle, guddle, moisten, paddle, potter, spatter, splash, sprinkle, tinker, toy, trifle, wet.

daft *adj.* absurd, asinine, berserk, besotted, crackers, crazy, daffy, delirious, demented, deranged, dop(e)y, doting, dotty, foolish, giddy, hysterical, idiotic, inane, infatuated, insane, lunatic, mad, mental, nuts, nutty, potty, scatty, screwy, silly, simple, stupid, touched, unhinged, witless.
antonyms bright, sane.

daily *adj.* circadian, common, commonplace, customary, day-to-day, diurnal, everyday, normal, ordinary, quotidian, regular, routine.

dainty *adj.* charming, choice, choos(e)y, delectable, delicate, delicious, dinky, elegant, exquisite, fastidious, fine, finical, finicking, finicky, friand(e), fussy, genty, graceful, lickerish, liquorish, meticulous, mignon(ne), mincing, minikin, neat, nice, palatable, particular, petite, pretty, refined, savory, scrupulous, tasty, tender, toothsome.
antonyms clumsy, gross.
n. bonbon, bonne-bouche, delicacy, fancy, sweetmeat, tidbit.

dally *v.* canoodle, dawdle, delay, dilly-dally, fiddle-faddle, flirt, frivol, linger, loiter, play, procrastinate, sport, tamper, tarry, toy, trifle.
antonyms hasten, hurry.

dam *n.* an(n)icut, barrage, barrier, blockage, embankment, hindrance, obstruction, wall.
v. barricade, block, check, choke, confine, obstruct, restrict, stanch, staunch, stem.

damage *n.* destruction, detriment, devastation, disprofit, harm, hurt, impairment, injury, loss, mischief, mutilation, scathe, suffering.
antonym repair.
v. deface, harm, hurt, impair, incapacitate, injure, mar, mutilate, play havoc with, play hell with, ruin, spoil, tamper with, weaken, wreck.
antonyms fix, repair.

dame *n.* baroness, broad, dowager, female, lady, matron, noblewoman, peeress, woman.

damn *v.* abuse, anathematize, blaspheme, blast, castigate, censure, condemn, criticize, curse, dang, darn, dash, denounce, denunciate, doom, excoriate, execrate,

imprecate, pan, revile, sentence, slam, slate, swear.
antonym bless.
n. brass farthing, darn, dash, hoot, iota, jot, monkey's, tinker's cuss, two hoots, whit.

damnable *adj.* abominable, accursed, atrocious, culpable, cursed, despicable, detestable, execrable, hateful, horrible, iniquitous, offensive, sinful, wicked.
antonyms admirable, praiseworthy.

damp *n.* clamminess, dampness, dankness, dew, drizzle, fog, humidity, mist, moisture, muzziness, vapor, wet.
antonym dryness.
adj. clammy, dank, dewy, dripping, drizzly, humid, misty, moist, muggish, muggy, sodden, soggy, sopping, vaporous, vaporish, vapory, wet.
antonyms arid, dry.
v. allay, bedew, check, chill, cool, curb, dampen, dash, deaden, deject, depress, diminish, discourage, dispirit, dull, inhibit, moderate, moisten, restrain, stifle, wet.
antonym dry.

dampen *v.* bedew, besprinkle, check, dash, deaden, decrease, depress, deter, diminish, dishearten, dismay, dull, lessen, moderate, moisten, muffle, reduce, restrain, smother, spray, stifle, wet.
antonyms dry, encourage.

dance *v.* caper, frolic, gambol, hoof it, hop, jig, juke, kantikoy, prance, rock, skip, spin, stomp, sway, swing, tread a measure, whirl.
n. bal masqué, bal paré, ball, hop, kantikoy, kick-up, knees-up, prom, shindig, social.

danger *n.* endangerment, hazard, insecurity, jeopardy, liability, menace, peril, precariousness, risk, threat, trouble, venture, vulnerability.
antonyms safety, security.

dangerous *adj.* alarming, breakneck, chancy, critical, daring, exposed, grave, hairy, harmful, hazardous, insecure, menacing, nasty, parlous, perilous, precarious, reckless, risky, serious, severe, threatening, tickly, treacherous, ugly, unsafe, vulnerable.
antonyms harmless, safe, secure.

dangle *v.* droop, flap, flaunt, flourish, hang, lure, sway, swing, tantalize, tempt, trail, wave.

dank *adj.* chilly, clammy, damp, dewy, dripping, moist, rheumy, slimy, soggy.
antonym dry.

dapper *adj.* active, brisk, chic, dainty, natty, neat, nimble, smart, spiffy, spruce, spry, stylish, trig, trim, well-dressed, well-groomed.
antonyms disheveled, dowdy, scruffy, shabby, sloppy.

dappled *adj.* bespeckled, brindled, checkered, dotted,

flecked, freckled, mottled, piebald, pied, speckled, spotted, stippled, variegated.

dare *v.* adventure, brave, challenge, defy, endanger, gamble, goad, have the gall, hazard, presume, provoke, risk, stake, taunt, venture.

n. challenge, gauntlet, provocation, taunt.

daredevil *n.* adventurer, desperado, exhibitionist, Hotspur, madcap, stuntman.

antonym coward.

adj. adventurous, audacious, bold, daring, death-defying, fearless, madcap, rash, reckless.

antonyms cautious, prudent, timid.

daring *adj.* adventurous, audacious, bold, brave, brazen, dauntless, fearless, game, impulsive, intrepid, plucky, rash, reckless, valiant, venturesome.

antonyms afraid, timid.

n. audacity, boldness, bottle, bravery, bravura, courage, defiance, derring-do, fearlessness, gall, grit, guts, intrepidity, nerve, pluck, prowess, rashness, spirit, spunk, temerity.

antonyms cowardice, timidity.

dark *adj.* abstruse, angry, aphotic, arcane, atrocious, benighted, black, bleak, brunette, caliginous, cheerless, cloudy, concealed, cryptic, damnable, darkling, dark-skinned, darksome, deep, dim, dingy, dismal, doleful, dour, drab, dusky, ebony, enigmatic, evil, forbidding, foul, frowning, gloomy, glowering, glum, grim, hellish, hidden, horrible, ignorant, indistinct, infamous, infernal, joyless, lightless, melanic, melanous, midnight, mirk, mirky, morbid, morose, mournful, murk, murky, mysterious, mystic, nefarious, obscure, occult, ominous, overcast, pitch-black, pitchy, puzzling, recondite, sable, satanic, scowling, secret, shadowy, shady, sinful, sinister, somber, sulky, sullen, sunless, swarthy, tenebr(i)ous, threatening, uncultivated, unenlightened, unillumed, unilluminated, unlettered, unlit, vile, wicked.

antonyms bright, happy, light, lucid.

n. concealment, darkness, dimness, dusk, evening, gloom, ignorance, mirk, mirkiness, murk, murkiness, night, nightfall, night-time, obscurity, secrecy, twilight, yin.

antonyms brightness, light.

darling *n.* acushla, apple of one's eye, asthore, beloved, blue-eyed boy, dear, dearest, fair-haired boy, favorite, jo(e), lady-love, love, lovey, machree, mavourneen, minikin, pet, poppet, sweetheart, true-love.

adj. adored, beloved, cherished, dear, precious, treasured, white-headed.

dart *v.* bound, cast, dartle, dash, flash, fling, flit, fly, hurl, launch, propel, race, run, rush, scoot, send, shoot, sling, spring, sprint, start, tear, throw, whistle, whizz.

n. arrow, barb, bolt, flight, shaft.

dash[1] *v.* abash, blight, break, cast, chagrin, confound, crash, dampen, destroy, ding, disappoint, discomfort, discourage, fling, foil, frustrate, hurl, ruin, shatter, shiver, slam, sling, smash, splinter, spoil, throw, thwart.

n. bit, bravura, brio, da(u)d, drop, élan, flair, flavor, flourish, hint, little, panache, pinch, smack, soupçon, spirit, sprinkling, style, suggestion, tinge, touch, verve, vigor, vivacity.

dash[2] *v.* be off like a shot, bolt, bound, dart, dartle, fly, haste(n), hurry, race, run, rush, speed, spring, sprint, tear.

n. bolt, dart, race, run, rush, sprint, spurt.

dashing *adj.* bold, dapper, daring, dazzling, debonair, doggy, elegant, exuberant, flamboyant, gallant, impressive, jaunty, lively, plucky, showy, smart, spirited, sporty, stylish, swashbuckling, swish.

antonym drab.

dastardly *adj.* base, caitiff, contemptible, cowardly, craven, despicable, faint-hearted, lily-livered, low, mean, niddering, pusillanimous, recreant, sneaking, sneaky, spiritless, timorous, underhand, vile.

antonyms heroic, noble.

data *n.* details, documents, dope, facts, figures, info, information, input, materials, statistics.

date[1] *n.* age, epoch, era, period, point, point in time, stage, time.

date[2] *n.* appointment, assignation, engagement, escort, friend, meeting, partner, rendezvous, steady, tryst.

dated *adj.* antiquated, archaic, démodé, obsolescent, obsolete, old hat, old-fashioned, out, outdated, outmoded, out-of-date, passé, superseded, unfashionable.

antonyms fashionable, up-to-the-minute.

daub *v.* begrime, besmear, blur, coat, cover, dedaub, deface, dirty, gaum, grime, paint, plaster, smear, smirch, smudge, spatter, splatter, stain, sully.

n. blot, blotch, smear, splash, splodge, splotch, spot, stain.

daunt *v.* alarm, appal, cow, deter, discourage, dishearten, dismay, dispirit, frighten, intimidate, overawe, put off, scare, shake, subdue, terrify, unnerve.

antonyms encourage, hearten.

dauntless *adj.* bold, brave, courageous, daring, doughty, fearless, gallant, game, heroic, indomitable, intrepid, lion-hearted, plucky, resolute, stout-hearted, undaunted, unflinching, valiant, valorous.

antonyms discouraged, disheartened.

dawn *n.* advent, aurora, beginning, birth, cock-crow(ing), dawning, daybreak, daylight, day-peep, dayspring, emergence, genesis, inception, morning, onset, origin, outset, peep of day, rise, start, sunrise, sun-up.

antonyms dusk, sundown, sunset.

v. appear, begin, break, brighten, develop, emerge, gleam, glimmer, hit, initiate, lighten, occur, open, originate, register, rise, strike, unfold.

daydream *n.* castles in Spain, castles in the air, dream, dwa(l)m, fantasy, figment, fond hope, imagining, musing, phantasm, pipe dream, reverie, star-gazing, vision, wish, wool-gathering.

v. dream, fancy, fantasize, hallucinate, imagine, muse, stargaze.

daze *v.* amaze, astonish, astound, befog, benumb, bewilder, blind, confuse, dazzle, dumbfound, flabbergast, numb, paralyze, perplex, shock, stagger, startle, stun, stupefy, surprise.
n. bewilderment, confusion, distraction, dwa(l)m, shock, stupor, trance.

dazzle *v.* amaze, astonish, awe, bedazzle, blind, blur, confuse, daze, fascinate, hypnotize, impress, overawe, overpower, overwhelm, scintillate, sparkle, stupefy.

dead[1] *adj.* ad patres, apathetic, barren, boring, breathless, callous, cold, dead-and-alive, dead-beat, deceased, defunct, departed, dull, exhausted, extinct, flat, frigid, glassy, glazed, gone, inactive, inanimate, indifferent, inert, inoperative, insipid, late, lifeless, lukewarm, napoo, numb, obsolete, paralyzed, perished, spent, spiritless, stagnant, stale, sterile, stiff, still, tasteless, tired, torpid, unemployed, uninteresting, unprofitable, unresponsive, useless, vapid, wooden, worn out.
antonyms active, alive, animated.

dead[2] *adj.* absolute, complete, downright, entire, outright, perfect, thorough, total, unqualified, utter.
adv. absolutely, completely, entirely, exactly, perfectly, quite, totally.

deaden *v.* abate, allay, alleviate, anesthetize, benumb, blunt, check, cushion, damp, dampen, desensitize, diminish, dull, hush, impair, lessen, muffle, mute, numb, obtund, paralyze, quieten, reduce, smother, stifle, suppress, weaken.
antonym enliven.

deadlock *n.* halt, impasse, stalemate, standstill.

deadly *adj.* accurate, ashen, baleful, baneful, boring, cruel, dangerous, death-dealing, deathful, deathlike, deathly, destructive, devastating, dull, effective, exact, fatal, feral, funest, ghastly, ghostly, grim, implacable, lethal, malignant, monotonous, mortal, noxious, pallid, pernicious, pestilent, poisonous, precise, ruthless, savage, sure, tedious, thanatoid, true, unerring, unfailing, uninteresting, unrelenting, venomous, wearisome, white.
antonyms harmless, healthy.

deaf *adj.* hard of hearing, heedless, indifferent, oblivious, stone-deaf, unconcerned, unmindful, unmoved.
antonyms aware, conscious.

deafening *adj.* booming, dinning, ear-piercing, ear-splitting, fortissimo, piercing, resounding, ringing, roaring, thunderous.
antonyms pianissimo, quiet.

deal *v.* allot, apportion, assign, bargain, bestow, dispense, distribute, divide, dole out, give, mete out, negotiate, reward, sell, share, stock, trade, traffic, treat.
n. agreement, amount, arrangement, bargain, buy, contract, degree, distribution, extent, hand, pact, portion, quantity, round, share, transaction, understanding.

dear *adj.* beloved, cherished, close, costly, darling, esteemed, expensive, familiar, favorite, high-priced, intimate, loved, overpriced, precious, pric(e)y, prized, respected, treasured, valued.
antonyms cheap, hateful.
n. angel, beloved, darling, dearie, deary, loved one, precious, treasure.

dearth *n.* absence, barrenness, deficiency, exiguousness, famine, inadequacy, insufficiency, lack, need, paucity, poverty, scantiness, scarcity, shortage, sparseness, sparsity, want.
antonyms abundance, excess.

death *n.* annihilation, bane, bereavement, cessation, curtains, decease, demise, departure, destruction, dissolution, dormition, downfall, dying, end, eradication, exit, expiration, extermination, extinction, fatality, finish, grave, loss, obliteration, passing, quietus, release, ruin, ruination, undoing.
antonyms birth, life.

debase *v.* abase, adulterate, allay, bastardize, cheapen, contaminate, corrupt, defile, degrade, demean, depreciate, devalue, diminish, disgrace, dishonor, embase, humble, humiliate, impair, lower, pollute, reduce, shame, taint, vitiate.
antonyms elevate, upgrade.

debate *v.* argue, cogitate, consider, contend, contest, controvert, deliberate, discuss, dispute, logicize, meditate on, mull over, ponder, question, reflect, revolve, ruminate, weigh, wrangle.
antonym agree.
n. altercation, argument, cogitation, consideration, contention, controversy, deliberation, discussion, disputation, dispute, meditation, polemic, quodlibet, reflection.
antonym agreement.

debauched *adj.* abandoned, corrupt, corrupted, debased, degenerate, degraded, depraved, dissipated, dissolute, immoral, intemperate, lewd, licentious, perverted, profligate, raddled, rakehell, rakehelly, wanton.
antonyms decent, pure, virtuous.

debonair *adj.* affable, breezy, buoyant, charming, cheerful, courteous, dashing, elegant, gay, jaunty, lighthearted, refined, smooth, sprightly, suave, urbane, wellbred.

debris *n.* bits, brash, detritus, drift, dross, duff, eluvium, exuviae, fragments, litter, moraine, pieces, remains, rubbish, rubble, ruins, sweepings, trash, waste, wreck, wreckage.

debt *n.* arrears, bill, claim, commitment, debit, due, duty, indebtedness, liability, obligation, score, sin.
antonyms asset, credit.

decay *v.* atrophy, canker, corrode, crumble, decline, decompose, decompound, degenerate, deteriorate, disintegrate, dissolve, dote, dwindle, mortify, molder, perish, putrefy, rot, shrivel, sink, spoil, wane, waste away, wear away, wither.
antonyms flourish, grow, ripen.
n. atrophy, caries, collapse, consenescence, decadence,

decline, decomposition, decrepitness, decrepitude, degeneracy, degeneration, deterioration, disintegration, dying, fading, failing, gangrene, labefactation, labefaction, mortification, perishing, putrefaction, putrescence, putridity, putridness, rot, rotting, wasting, withering.

deceased *adj.* dead, defunct, departed, expired, extinct, finished, former, gone, late, lifeless, lost.

n. dead, decedent, departed.

deceit *n.* abuse, artifice, blind, cheat, cheating, chicanery, con, cozenage, craftiness, cunning, deceitfulness, deception, dissimulation, double-dealing, duplicity, fake, feint, fraud, fraudulence, guile, hypocrisy, imposition, imposture, misrepresentation, pretense, ruse, sham, shift, slyness, stratagem, subterfuge, swindle, treachery, trick, trickery, underhandedness, wile.

antonyms honesty, openness.

deceitful *adj.* collusive, counterfeit, crafty, deceiving, deceptive, designing, dishonest, disingenuous, double-dealing, duplicitous, elusory, fallacious, false, fraudulent, guileful, hypocritical, illusory, insincere, knavish, prestigious, Punic, rusé, sneaky, treacherous, tricky, two-faced, underhand, untrustworthy.

antonyms honest, open, trustworthy.

deceive *v.* abuse, bamboozle, befool, beguile, betray, camouflage, cheat, cog, con, cozen, delude, diddle, disappoint, dissemble, dissimulate, double-cross, dupe, ensnare, entrap, flam, fool, gag, gammon, gull, have on, hoax, hood-wink, impose upon, lead on, mislead, outwit, seel, swindle, take for a ride, take in, trick, two-time.

antonym enlighten.

decency *n.* appropriateness, civility, correctness, courtesy, decorum, etiquette, fitness, good form, good manners, helpfulness, modesty, propriety, respectability, seemliness, thoughtfulness.

antonyms discourtesy, indecency.

decent *adj.* acceptable, accommodating, adequate, ample, appropriate, average, becoming, befitting, chaste, comely, comme il faut, competent, courteous, decorous, delicate, fair, fit, fitting, friendly, generous, gracious, gradely, helpful, kind, modest, nice, obliging, passable, polite, presentable, proper, pure, reasonable, respectable, satisfactory, seemly, sufficient, suitable, thoughtful, tolerable.

antonyms disobliging, indecent, poor.

deception *n.* artifice, bluff, cheat, conning, craftiness, cunning, deceitfulness, deceit, deceptiveness, decoy, defraudation, defraudment, dissembling, dissimulation, duplicity, false-pretences, feint, flim-flam, fraud, fraudulence, guile, gullery, hoax, hype, hypocrisy, illusion, imposition, imposture, insincerity, legerdemain, leg-pull, lie, ruse, sell, sham, snare, stratagem, subterfuge, take-in, treachery, trick, trickery, wile.

antonyms artlessness, openness.

deceptive *adj.* ambiguous, catchy, delusive, delusory,

dishonest, elusory, fake, fallacious, false, fraudulent, illusive, illusory, misleading, mock, specious, spurious, unreliable.

antonyms artless, genuine, open.

decide *v.* adjudge, adjudicate, choose, conclude, decree, determine, dijudicate, elect, end, fix, judge, opt, purpose, reach a decision, resolve, settle.

decipher *v.* construe, crack, decode, decrypt, deduce, explain, figure out, interpret, make out, read, solve, transliterate, uncipher, understand, unfold, unravel, unscramble.

antonym encode.

decision *n.* arbitrament, arbitration, arrêt, conclusion, decisiveness, determination, fetwa, finding, firmness, judgment, outcome, parti, purpose, purposefulness, resoluteness, resolution, resolve, result, ruling, settlement, verdict.

decisive *adj.* absolute, conclusive, critical, crucial, crunch, decided, definite, definitive, determinate, determined, fateful, final, firm, forceful, forthright, incisive, influential, momentous, positive, resolute, significant, strong-minded, supreme, trenchant.

antonyms indecisive, insignificant.

declaration *n.* acknowledgment, affirmation, announcement, assertion, asseveration, attestation, averment, avouchment, avowal, deposition, disclosure, edict, manifesto, notification, proclamation, profession, promulgation, pronouncement, pronunciamento, protestation, revelation, statement, testimony.

declare *v.* affirm, announce, assert, attest, aver, avouch, avow, certify, claim, confess, confirm, convey, disclose, maintain, manifest, nuncupate, proclaim, profess, pronounce, reveal, show, state, swear, testify, validate, witness.

decline[1] *v.* avoid, balk, decay, decrease, degenerate, deny, deteriorate, deviate, diminish, droop, dwindle, ebb, fade, fail, fall, fall off, flag, forgo, languish, lessen, pine, refuse, reject, shrink, sink, turn down, wane, weaken, worsen.

n. abatement, consumption, decay, declension, decrepitude, degeneration, deterioration, deviation, diminution, downturn, dwindling, enfeeblement, failing, falling-off, lessening, paracme, phthisis, recession, senility, slump, tuberculosis, weakening, worsening.

decline[2] *v.* descend, dip, sink, slant, slope.

n. brae, declination, declivity, descent, deviation, dip, divergence, hill, incline, obliqueness, obliquity, slope.

decompose *v.* analyze, atomize, break down, break up, crumble, decay, decompound, degrade, disintegrate, dissolve, distil, fall apart, fester, fractionate, putrefy, rot, separate, spoil.

antonyms combine, unite.

decorate[1] *v.* adorn, beautify, bedeck, color, deck, do up, embellish, enrich, furbish, grace, impearl, miniate, ornament, paint, paper, prettify, renovate, tart up, trick out, trim, wallpaper.

decorate[2] *v.* bemedal, cite, crown, garland, honor.

decoration[1] *n.* adornment, arabesque, bauble, beautification, curlicue, elaboration, embellishment, enrichment, falderal, flounce, flourish, frill, frou-frou, furbelow, garnish, ornament, ornamentation, pass(e)ment, passementerie, scroll, spangle, trimming, trinket.

decoration[2] *n.* award, badge, colors, crown, emblem, garland, garter, laurel, laurel-wreath, medal, order, ribbon, star.

decoy *n.* attraction, bait, ensnarement, enticement, inducement, lure, pretence, roper(-in), trap.
v. allure, attract, bait, beguile, deceive, draw, ensnare, entice, entrap, inveigle, lead, lure, seduce, tempt.

decrease *v.* abate, ablate, contract, curtail, cut down, decline, diminish, drop, dwindle, ease, fall off, lessen, lower, peter out, reduce, shrink, slacken, slim, subside, taper, wane.
antonym increase.
n. abatement, ablation, contraction, cutback, decline, decrement, degression, diminution, downturn, dwindling, ebb, falling-off, lessening, loss, reduction, shrinkage, step-down, subsidence.
antonym increase.

decree *n.* act, command, decretal, dictum, edict, enactment, firman, hatti-sherif, indiction, interlocution, interlocutor, law, mandate, order, ordinance, precept, proclamation, regulation, ruling, statute, ukase.
v. command, decide, determine, dictate, enact, lay down, ordain, order, prescribe, proclaim, pronounce, rescript, rule.

decrepit *adj.* aged, antiquated, battered, broken-backed, broken-down, crippled, debilitated, deteriorated, dilapidated, doddering, doddery, feeble, frail, incapacitated, infirm, ramshackle, rickety, run-down, superannuated, tumble-down, warby, wasted, weak, worn-out.
antonyms fit, well-cared-for, youthful.

decry *v.* abuse, belittle, blame, censure, condemn, criticize, cry down, declaim against, denounce, depreciate, derogate, detract, devalue, discredit, disparage, inveigh against, rail against, run down, traduce, underestimate, underrate, undervalue.
antonyms praise, value.

dedicate *v.* address, assign, bless, commit, consecrate, devote, give over to, hallow, inscribe, offer, pledge, present, sacrifice, sanctify, set apart, surrender.

dedicated *adj.* committed, devoted, enthusiastic, given over to, purposeful, single-hearted, single-minded, sworn, whole-hearted, zealous.
antonyms apathetic, uncommitted.

deduct *v.* decrease by, knock off, reduce by, remove, subduct, subtract, take away, withdraw.
antonym add.

deed[1] *n.* achievement, act, action, exploit, fact, factum, feat, gest(e), performance, reality, truth.

deed[2] *n.* contract, document, indenture, instrument, record, title, transaction.

deem *v.* account, adjudge, believe, conceive, consider, esteem, estimate, hold, imagine, judge, reckon, regard, suppose, think.

deep *adj.* absorbed, abstract, abstruse, abyssal, acute, arcane, artful, astute, bass, booming, bottomless, broad, canny, cryptic, cunning, dark, designing, devious, discerning, engrossed, esoteric, extreme, far, fathomless, full-toned, grave, great, hidden, immersed, insidious, intense, knowing, learned, lost, low, low-pitched, mysterious, obscure, penetrating, preoccupied, profound, rapt, recondite, resonant, rich, sagacious, scheming, secret, shrewd, sonorous, strong, unfathomable, unfathomed, unplumbed, unsoundable, unsounded, vivid, wide, wise, yawning.
antonyms open, shallow.
n. briny, drink, high seas, main, ocean, sea.

deface *v.* blemish, damage, deform, destroy, disfeature, disfigure, impair, injure, mar, mutilate, obliterate, spoil, sully, tarnish, vandalize.
antonym repair.

defamation *n.* aspersion, calumny, denigration, derogation, disparagement, innuendo, libel, mud-slinging, obloquy, opprobrium, scandal, slander, slur, smear, traducement, vilification.
antonym praise.

default *n.* absence, defalcation, defect, deficiency, dereliction, failure, fault, lack, lapse, neglect, non-payment, omission, want.
v. backslide, bilk, defraud, dodge, evade, fail, levant, neglect, rat, swindle, welsh.

defeat *v.* baffle, balk, beat, best, checkmate, clobber, confound, conquer, counteract, crush, disappoint, discomfit, down, foil, frustrate, get the better of, outbargain, overpower, overthrow, overwhelm, psych out, quell, repulse, rout, ruin, stump, subdue, subjugate, tank, thump, thwart, trounce, vanquish, vote down, whop.
n. beating, conquest, débâcle, disappointment, discomfiture, failure, frustration, overthrow, rebuff, repulse, reverse, rout, setback, thwarting, trouncing, vanquishment, Waterloo.

defect *n.* absence, blemish, bug, default, deficiency, error, failing, fault, flaw, frailty, hamartia, imperfection, inadequacy, lack, mistake, shortcoming, spot, taint, want, weakness.
v. apostatize, break faith, desert, rebel, renegue, revolt, tergiversate.

defective *adj.* abnormal, broken, deficient, faulty, flawed, imperfect, inadequate, incomplete, insufficient, kaput, out of order, retarded, scant, short, subnormal.
antonyms normal, operative.

defend *n.* assert, bulwark, champion, contest, cover, endorse, espouse, fortify, guard, justify, maintain, plead, preserve, protect, safeguard, screen, secure, shelter, shield, speak up for, stand by, stand up for, support, sustain, uphold, vindicate, watch over.
antonym attack.

defensive *adj.* apologetic, aposematic, averting, cautious, defending, opposing, protective, safeguarding, self-justifying, wary, watchful, withstanding. *antonym* bold.

defer[1] *v.* adjourn, delay, hold over, postpone, procrastinate, prorogue, protract, put off, put on ice, shelve, suspend, waive.

defer[2] *v.* accede, bow, capitulate, comply, give way, kowtow, respect, submit, yield.

deference *n.* acquiescence, attention, capitulation, civility, complaisance, compliance, consideration, courtesy, esteem, homage, honor, morigeration, obedience, obeisance, obsequiousness, politeness, regard, respect, reverence, submission, submissiveness, thoughtfulness, veneration, yielding.

defiant *adj.* aggressive, audacious, bold, challenging, contumacious, daring, disobedient, insolent, insubordinate, intransigent, mutinous, obstinate, provocative, rebellious, recalcitrant, refractory, truculent, uncooperative. *antonyms* acquiescent, submissive.

deficient *adj.* defectible, defective, exiguous, faulty, flawed, impaired, imperfect, inadequate, incomplete, inferior, insufficient, lacking, meager, scanty, scarce, short, skimpy, unsatisfactory, wanting, weak. *antonyms* excessive, superfluous.

defile[1] *v.* abuse, befoul, besmirch, contaminate, corrupt, debase, deflower, defoul, degrade, desecrate, dirty, disgrace, dishonor, inquinate, make foul, molest, pollute, profane, rape, ravish, seduce, smear, soil, stain, sully, taint, tarnish, violate, vitiate. *antonym* cleanse.

defile[2] *n.* gorge, gulch, gully, pass, passage, ravine.

define *v.* bound, characterize, circumscribe, delimit, delimitate, delineate, demarcate, describe, designate, detail, determine, explain, expound, interpret, limit, mark out, outline, specify, spell out.

definite *adj.* assured, certain, clear, clear-cut, decided, determined, exact, explicit, express, fixed, guaranteed, marked, obvious, particular, positive, precise, settled, specific, substantive, sure. *antonyms* indefinite, vague.

definitely *adv.* absolutely, beyond doubt, categorically, certainly, clearly, decidedly, doubtless, doubtlessly, easily, finally, indeed, indubitably, obviously, plainly, positively, surely, undeniably, unequivocally, unmistakably, unquestionably, without doubt, without fail.

definition[1] *n.* clarification, delimitation, delineation, demarcation, description, determination, elucidation, explanation, exposition, interpretation, outlining, settling.

definition[2] *n.* clarity, clearness, contrast, distinctness, focus, precision, sharpness.

deft *adj.* able, adept, adroit, agile, clever, dexterous, expert, feat, habile, handy, neat, nifty, nimble, proficient, skilful. *antonym* clumsy.

defunct *adj.* dead, deceased, departed, expired, extinct, gone, inoperative, invalid, kaput, non-existent, obsolete, passé. *antonyms* alive, live, operative.

defy *v.* baffle, beard, beat, brave, challenge, confront, contemn, dare, defeat, despise, disregard, elude, face, flout, foil, frustrate, outdare, provoke, repel, repulse, resist, scorn, slight, spurn, thwart, withstand. *antonyms* flinch, quail, yield.

degenerate *adj.* base, corrupt, debased, debauched, decadent, degenerated, degraded, depraved, deteriorated, dissolute, effete, fallen, immoral, low, mean, perverted. *antonyms* upright, virtuous.
v. age, decay, decline, decrease, deteriorate, fall off, lapse, regress, retrogress, rot, sink, slip, worsen. *antonym* improve.

degrade *v.* abase, adulterate, break, brutalize, cashier, cheapen, corrupt, debase, declass, demean, demote, depose, deprive, deteriorate, discredit, disennoble, disgrace, disgrade, dishonor, disrank, disrate, downgrade, embase, humble, humiliate, impair, injure, lower, pervert, shame, unfrock, ungown, vitiate, weaken.
antonyms enhance, improve.

degree *n.* caliber, class, division, doctorate, extent, gradation, grade, intensity, interval, level, limit, mark, masterate, measure, notch, order, point, position, proportion, quality, quantity, range, rank, rate, ratio, run, scale, scope, severity, stage, standard, standing, station, status, step, unit.

deign *v.* condescend, consent, demean oneself, lower oneself, stoop, vouchsafe.

dejected *adj.* abattu, alamort, blue, cast down, crestfallen, depressed, despondent, disconsolate, disheartened, dismal, doleful, down, downcast, downhearted, gloomy, glum, jaw-fallen, low, low-spirited, melancholy, miserable, morose, sad, spiritless, woebegone, wretched.
antonyms bright, happy, high-spirited.

delectable *adj.* adorable, agreeable, ambrosial, ambrosian, appetizing, charming, dainty, delicious, delightful, enjoyable, enticing, flavorsome, gratifying, inviting, luscious, lush, palatable, pleasant, pleasurable, satisfying, scrumptious, tasty, toothsome, yummy.
antonyms horrid, unpleasant.

delegate *n.* agent, ambassador, commissioner, deputy, envoy, legate, messenger, nuncio, representative.
v. accredit, appoint, assign, authorize, charge, commission, consign, depute, designate, devolve, empower, entrust, give, hand over, mandate, name, nominate, pass on, relegate, transfer.

delete *v.* blot out, blue-pencil, cancel, cross out, dele, edit, edit out, efface, erase, expunge, obliterate, remove, rub out, strike, strike out. *antonym* add in.

deleterious *adj.* bad, damaging, destructive, detrimental,

harmful, hurtful, injurious, noxious, pernicious, prejudicial, ruinous.

antonyms enhancing, helpful.

deliberate *v.* cogitate, consider, consult, debate, discuss,
meditate, mull over, ponder, reflect, ruminate, think, weigh.
adj. advised, calculated, careful, cautious, circumspect,
conscious, considered, designed, heedful, intentional,
measured, methodical, planned, ponderous, prearranged, premeditated, prudent, purposeful, slow, studied, thoughtful, unhurried, volitive, voulu, wary, wilful, willed, witting.

antonyms chance, unintentional.

delicate *adj.* accurate, ailing, careful, choice, considerate, critical, dainty, debilitated, deft, delicious, detailed,
diaphanous, difficult, diplomatic, discreet, discriminating, eggshell, elegant, elfin, exquisite, faint, fastidious, fine, flimsy, fragile, frail, friand(e), gauzy, graceful, hazardous, kid-glove, minikin, minute, muted, pastel, precarious, precise, prudish, pure, refined, risky,
savory, scrupulous, sensible, sensitive, sickly, skilled,
slender, slight, soft, softly-softly, squeamish, sticky,
subdued, subtle, tactful, tender, ticklish, touchy, weak.

antonyms harsh, imprecise, strong.

delicious *adj.* agreeable, ambrosial, ambrosian, appetizing, charming, choice, dainty, delectable, delightful,
enjoyable, entertaining, exquisite, flavorsome,
goluptious, luscious, mouthwatering, nectareous, palatable, pleasant, pleasing, savory, scrummy, scrumptious, tasty, toothsome, yummy.

antonym unpleasant.

delight *n.* bliss, ecstasy, enjoyment, felicity, gladness,
gratification, happiness, heaven, joy, jubilation, pleasure, rapture, transport.

antonyms dismay, displeasure.

v. amuse, charm, cheer, divert, enchant, gladden, gratify,
please, ravish, rejoice, satisfy, thrill, tickle.

antonyms dismay, displease.

delightful *adj.* agreeable, amusing, captivating, charming, congenial, delectable, delightsome, enchanting, engaging, enjoyable, entertaining, fascinating, fetching,
gratifying, heavenly, pleasant, pleasing, pleasurable,
rapturous, ravishing, scrummy, scrumptious, sweet,
thrilling, wizard.

antonym horrible.

delirious *adj.* bacchic, beside oneself, corybantic, crazy,
demented, deranged, ecstatic, excited, frantic, frenzied,
hysterical, incoherent, insane, light-headed, mad,
maenadic, raving, unhinged, wild.

antonym sane.

deliver *v.* acquit, administer, aim, announce, bear, bring,
carry, cart, cede, commit, convey, deal, declare, direct, discharge, dispense, distribute, emancipate, feed,
free, give, give forth, give up, grant, hand over, inflict, launch, liberate, loose, make over, pass, present,
proclaim, pronounce, publish, ransom, read, redeem,
release, relinquish, rescue, resign, save, strike,

supply, surrender, throw, transfer, transport, turn
over, utter, yield.

deluge *n.* avalanche, barrage, cataclysm, downpour,
flood, hail, inundation, rush, spate, torrent.

v. bury, douse, drench, drown, engulf, flood, inundate,
overload, overrun, overwhelm, soak, submerge, swamp.

delusion *n.* deception, error, fallacy, fancy, fata Morgana,
hallucination, illusion, mirage, misapprehension,
misbelief, misconception, mistake, phantasm.

demand *v.* ask, call for, challenge, claim, exact, expect,
inquire, insist on, interrogate, involve, necessitate, need,
order, question, request, require, take, want.

antonyms cede, supply.

n. bidding, call, charge, claim, desire, inquiry, interrogation, necessity, need, order, question, request, requirement, requisition, want.

antonym supply.

demean *v.* abase, condescend, debase, degrade, deign,
descend, humble, lower, stoop.

antonym enhance.

demeanor *n.* air, bearing, behavior, carriage, comportment, conduct, deportment, manner, mien, port.

demented *adj.* crazed, crazy, deranged, distracted, distraught, dotty, foolish, frenzied, idiotic, insane, lunatic, mad, maenadic, maniacal, manic, non compos mentis, nutty, unbalanced, unhinged.

antonym sane.

demolish *v.* annihilate, bulldoze, consume, defeat, destroy, devour, dilapidate, dismantle, down, eat, flatten, gobble, gulp, guzzle, knock down, level, overthrow, overturn, pull down, pulverize, raze, ruin, tear
down, unbuild, undo, wreck.

antonym build up.

demolition *n.* bulldozing, destruction, dismantling,
leveling, razing, wrecking.

demon[1] *n.* afrit, daemon, daimon, devil, evil spirit, fallen
angel, fiend, genius, goblin, guardian spirit, incubus,
monster, numen, rakshas, rakshasa, succubus, villain,
warlock.

demon[2] *n.* ace, addict, dab hand, fanatic, fiend, master,
pastmaster, wizard.

demonstrate[1] *v.* describe, display, establish, evidence,
evince, exhibit, explain, expound, illustrate, indicate,
manifest, prove, show, substantiate, teach, testify to.

demonstrate[2] *v.* march, parade, picket, protest, rally,
sit in.

demonstration[1] *n.* affirmation, confirmation, deixis,
description, display, evidence, exhibition, explanation,
exposition, expression, illustration, manifestation,
presentation, proof, substantiation, test, testimony,
trial, validation.

demonstration[2] *v.* demo, march, parade, picket, protest, rally, sit-in, work-in.

demur *v.* balk, cavil, disagree, dispute, dissent, doubt,
hesitate, object, pause, protest, refuse, take exception, waver.

n. arrière pensée, compunction, demurral, demurrer, dissent, hesitation, misgiving, objection, protest, qualm, reservation, scruple.

demure *adj.* coy, decorous, diffident, grave, maidenly, modest, priggish, prim, prissy, prudish, reserved, reticent, retiring, sedate, shy, sober, staid, strait-laced.
antonym forward.

den *n.* cave, cavern, cloister, cubby-hole, earth, haunt, hide-away, hide-out, hole, lair, retreat, sanctuary, sanctum, set(t), shelter, study.

denial *n.* abjuration, abnegation, contradiction, denegation, disaffirmance, disaffirmation, disavowal, disclaimer, dismissal, dissent, gainsay, negation, prohibition, rebuff, refusal, rejection, renunciation, repudiation, repulse, retraction, veto.

denounce *v.* accuse, anathematize, arraign, assail, attack, brand, castigate, censure, condemn, declaim, against, decry, denunciate, fulminate, hereticate, impugn, inveigh against, proscribe, revile, stigmatize, vilify, vilipend.
antonym praise.

dense *adj.* blockish, close, close-knit, compact, compressed, condensed, crass, crowded, dull, heavy, impenetrable, jam-packed, obtuse, opaque, packed, slow, slow-witted, solid, stolid, stupid, substantial, thick, thickset, thick-witted.
antonyms clever, sparse.

dent *n.* bang, chip, concavity, crater, depression, dimple, dint, dip, dunt, hollow, impression, indentation, pit.
v. depress, dint, gouge, indent, push in.

deny *v.* abjure, begrudge, contradict, decline, disaffirm, disagree with, disallow, disavow, discard, disclaim, disown, disprove, forbid, gainsay, negative, oppose, rebuff, recant, refuse, refute, reject, renounce, repudiate, revoke, traverse, turn down, veto, withhold.
antonyms admit, allow.

depart *v.* absent oneself, decamp, deviate, differ, digress, disappear, diverge, escape, exit, go, leave, levant, make off, migrate, mizzle, quit, remove, retire, retreat, set forth, stray, swerve, take one's leave, toddle, vanish, vary, veer, withdraw.
antonyms arrive, keep to.

departure *n.* abandonment, branching, branching, out, change, decession, deviation, difference, digression, divergence, exit, exodus, going, innovation, leave-taking, leaving, lucky, novelty, removal, retirement, shift, variation, veering, withdrawal.
antonym arrival.

depend on anticipate, bank on, build upon, calculate on, count on, expect, hang on, hinge on, lean on, reckon on, rely upon, rest on, revolve around, trust in, turn to.

dependable *adj.* certain, conscientious, faithful, gilt-edged, honest, reliable, responsible, steady, sure, trustworthy, trusty, unfailing.
antonyms undependable, unreliable.

dependent *adj.* adjective, conditional, contingent, defenceless, depending, determined by, feudal, helpless, immature, liable to, relative, reliant, relying on, subject, subject to, subordinate, tributary, vulnerable, weak.
antonym independent.

depict *v.* caricature, characterize, delineate, describe, detail, draw, illustrate, limn, narrate, outline, paint, picture, portray, render, reproduce, sculpt, sketch, trace.

deplore *v.* abhor, bemoan, bewail, censure, condemn, denounce, deprecate, grieve for, lament, mourn, regret, repent of, rue.
antonym praise.

deport[1] *v.* banish, exile, expatriate, expel, extradite, ostracize, oust.

deport[2] *v.* acquit, act, bear, behave, carry, comport, conduct, hold, manage.

deportment *n.* air, appearance, aspect, bearing, behavior, carriage, cast, comportment, conduct, demeanor, etiquette, manner, mien, pose, posture, stance.

deposit[1] *v.* drop, dump, lay, locate, park, place, precipitate, put, settle, sit.
n. accumulation, alluvium, deposition, dregs, hypostasis, lees, precipitate, sediment, silt.

deposit[2] *v.* amass, bank, consign, depone, entrust, file, hoard, lodge, reposit, save, store.
n. bailment, down payment, instalment, money, part payment, pledge, retainer, security, stake, warranty.

depreciate *v.* belittle, decrease, decry, deflate, denigrate, deride, derogate, detract, devaluate, devalue, disparage, downgrade, drop, fall, lessen, lower, minimize, misprize, reduce, ridicule, scorn, slump, traduce, underestimate, underrate, undervalue.
antonyms appreciate, overrate, praise.

depress *v.* burden, cheapen, chill, damp, daunt, debilitate, deject, depreciate, devaluate, devalue, devitalize, diminish, discourage, dishearten, dispirit, downgrade, drain, enervate, engloom, exhaust, flatten, hip, impair, lessen, level, lower, oppress, overburden, press, reduce, sadden, sap, squash, tire, undermine, upset, weaken, weary.
antonym cheer.

depression[1] *n.* blues, cafard, decline, dejection, demission, despair, despondency, doldrums, dolefulness, downheartedness, dullness, dumps, exanimation, gloominess, glumness, hard times, heart-heaviness, hopelessness, inactivity, low spirits, lowness, mal du siècle, megrims, melancholia, melancholy, panophobia, recession, sadness, slump, stagnation, vapors.
antonyms cheerfulness, prosperity.

depression[2] *n.* basin, bowl, cavity, concavity, dent, dimple, dint, dip, dish, excavation, fossa, fossula, fovea, foveola, hollow, hollowness, impression, indentation, pit, sag, sink, umbilicus, valley.
antonyms convexity, prominence, protuberance.

deprive *v.* amerce, bereave, denude, deny, despoil,

dispossess, divest, expropriate, mulct, rob, starve, strip.

antonyms bestow.

deputation *n.* appointment, assignment, commission, delegates, delegation, deputies, deputing, designation, embassy, legation, mission, nomination, representatives.

derelict *adj.* abandoned, deserted, desolate, dilapidated, discarded, forlorn, forsaken, neglected, ruined.
n. dosser, down-and-out, drifter, hobo, outcast, toerag, tramp, vagrant, wastrel.

dereliction *n.* abandonment, abdication, apostasy, betrayal, delinquency, desertion, evasion, failure, faithlessness, fault, forsaking, neglect, negligence, relinquishment, remissness, renegation, renunciation.
antonyms devotion, faithfulness, fulfilment.

derision *n.* contempt, contumely, dicacity, disdain, disparagement, disrespect, insult, irrision, laughter, mockery, raillery, ridicule, satire, scoffing, scorn, sneering.
antonym praise.

derivation *n.* acquisition, ancestry, basis, beginning, deduction, descent, etymology, extraction, foundation, genealogy, inference, origin, root, source.

derive *v.* acquire, arise, borrow, collect, crib, deduce, descend, develop, draw, elicit, emanate, extract, flow, follow, gain, gather, get, glean, grow, infer, issue, lift, obtain, originate, proceed, procure, receive, spring, stem, trace.

descend *v.* alight, arrive, assail, assault, attack, condescend, degenerate, dégringoler, deign, derive, deteriorate, develop, dip, dismount, drop, fall, gravitate, incline, invade, issue, leap, originate, plummet, plunge, pounce, proceed, raid, sink, slant, slope, spring, stem, stoop, subside, swoop, tumble.

descendants *n.* children, epigones, epigoni, epigons, family, issue, line, lineage, offspring, posterity, progeny, race, scions, seed, sons, and daughters, successors.

describe *v.* characterize, define, delineate, depict, detail, draw, enlarge on, explain, express, illustrate, mark out, narrate, outline, portray, present, recount, relate, report, sketch, specify, tell, trace.

description *n.* account, brand, breed, category, characterization, class, delineation, depiction, detail, explanation, exposition, genre, genus, hypotyposis, ilk, kidney, kind, narration, narrative, order, outline, portrayal, presentation, report, representation, sketch, sort, species, specification, type, variety, word-painting, word-picture.

desecration *n.* blasphemy, debasement, defilement, dishonoring, impiety, insult, invasion, pollution, profanation, sacrilege, violation.

desert[1] *n.* solitude, vacuum, vast, void, waste, wasteland, wilderness, wilds.
adj. arid, bare, barren, desolate, droughty, dry, eremic, infertile, lonely, solitary, sterile, uncultivated, uninhabited, unproductive, untilled, waste, waterless, wild.

desert[2] *v.* abandon, abscond, apostatize, backslide, betray, decamp, deceive, defect, forsake, give up, jilt, leave, leave in the lurch, maroon, quit, rat on, relinquish, renegue, renounce, resign, strand, tergiversate, vacate.

desert[3] *n.* come-uppance, demerit, deserts, due, guerdon, meed, merit, payment, recompense, remuneration, requital, retribution, return, reward, right, virtue, worth.

deserter *n.* absconder, apostate, backslider, betrayer, defector, delinquent, escapee, fugitive, rat, renegade, runaway, traitor, truant.

deserve *v.* ask for, earn, gain, incur, justify, merit, procure, rate, warrant, win.

design *n.* aim, arrangement, blueprint, composition, configuration, conformation, conspiracy, construction, contrivance, delineation, draft, drawing, end, enterprise, exemplar, figure, form, goal, guide, intent, intention, intrigue, machination, maneuver, meaning, model, motif, object, objective, organization, outline, pattern, plan, plot, project, prototype, purpose, schema, schema, shape, sketch, structure, style, target, undertaking.
v. aim, conceive, construct, contrive, create, delineate, describe, destine, develop, devise, draft, draw, draw up, fabricate, fashion, form, intend, invent, make, mean, model, originate, outline, plan, project, propose, purpose, scheme, shape, sketch, structure, tailor, trace.

designate *v.* allot, appoint, assign, bill, call, characterize, choose, christen, code-name, deem, define, delegate, denominate, denote, depute, describe, docket, dub, earmark, entitle, indicate, label, name, nickname, nominate, select, show, specify, stipulate, style, term, ticket, title.

desirable *adj.* adorable, advantageous, advisable, agreeable, alluring, appetible, appropriate, attractive, beneficial, captivating, covetable, eligible, enviable, expedient, fascinating, fetching, good, nubile, pleasing, plummy, preferable, profitable, seductive, sensible, sexy, tempting, worthwhile. *antonyms* undesirable.

desire *v.* ask, aspire to, beg, covet, crave, desiderate, entreat, fancy, hanker after, hunger for, importune, lack, long for, need, petition, request, solicit, want, wish for, yearn for.
n. appeal, appetence, appetency, appetite, ardor, aspiration, besoin, concupiscence, covetousness, craving, cupidity, desideration, entreaty, greed, hankering, hot pants, importunity, kama, kamadeva, lasciviousness, lechery, libido, longing, lust, lustfulness, month's mind, need, passion, petition, request, solicitation, supplication, velleity, want, wish, yearning, yen.

desist *v.* abstain, break off, cease, come to a halt, discontinue, end, forbear, give over, give up, halt, leave off, pause, peter out, refrain, remit, stop, suspend.
antonyms continue, resume.

desolate *adj.* abandoned, arid, bare, barren, benighted, bereft, bleak, cheerless, comfortless, companionless,

dejected, depopulated, depressed, depressing, desert, desolated, despondent, disconsolate, disheartened, dismal, dismayed, distressed, downcast, dreary, forlorn, forsaken, gloomy, god-forsaken, grieved, inconsolable, lonely, melancholy, miserable, ravaged, ruined, solitary, unfrequented, uninhabited, unpopulous, unsolaced, waste, wild, wretched.
antonym cheerful.

v. denude, depopulate, despoil, destroy, devastate, lay waste, pillage, plunder, ravage, ruin, spoil, waste, wreck.

despair *v.* capitulate, collapse, crumple, despond, give in, give up, lose heart, lose hope, quit, surrender.
antonym hope.

n. anguish, dejection, depression, desperation, despond, despondency, emptiness, gloom, hopelessness, inconsolableness, melancholy, misery, ordeal, pain, resourcelessness, sorrow, trial, tribulation, wretchedness.
antonyms cheerfulness, resilience.

desperado *n.* bandit, brigand, cateran, criminal, cutthroat, dacoit, gangster, gunman, heavy, hood, hoodlum, lawbreaker, mugger, outlaw, ruffian, thug.

desperate *adj.* grave, abandoned, acute, audacious, critical, dangerous, daring, despairing, despondent, determined, dire, do-or-die, drastic, extreme, foolhardy, forlorn, frantic, frenzied, furious, great, hasty, hazardous, headlong, headstrong, hopeless, impetuous, inconsolable, irremediable, irretrievable, madcap, precipitate, rash, reckless, risky, serious, severe, temerarious, urgent, violent, wild, wretched.

despicable *adj.* abhorrent, abject, base, cheap, contemptible, degrading, detestable, disgraceful, disgusting, disreputable, hateful, ignoble, ignominious, infamous, low, mean, reprehensible, reprobate, scurvy, shameful, sordid, unprincipled, vile, worthless, wretched.
antonyms laudable, noble.

despise *v.* abhor, condemn, deplore, deride, detest, disdain, dislike, disregard, ignore, loathe, misprize, revile, scorn, slight, spurn, undervalue, vilipend.
antonyms appreciate, prize.

despite *prep.* against, defying, heedless of, in spite of, in the face of, in the teeth of, notwithstanding, regardless of, undeterred by.

despoil *v.* bereave, denude, depredate, deprive, destroy, devastate, disgarnish, dispossess, divest, loot, maraud, pillage, plunder, ransack, ravage, rifle, rob, spoliate, strip, vandalize, wreck.
antonyms adorn, enrich.

despondent *adj.* blue, broken-hearted, dejected, depressed, despairing, disconsolate, discouraged, disheartened, dispirited, doleful, down, downcast, downhearted, gloomy, glum, hopeless, inconsolable, low, low-spirited, melancholy, miserable, morose, mournful, overwhelmed, sad, sorrowful, woebegone, wretched.
antonyms cheerful, hopeful.

despot *n.* absolutist, autocrat, boss, dictator, monocrat, oppressor, tyrant.
antonyms democrat, egalitarian, liberal.

despotic *adj.* absolute, absolutist, arbitrary, arrogant, authoritarian, autocratic, bossy, dictatorial, domineering, imperious, monocratic, oppressive, overbearing, peremptory, tyrannical.
antonyms democratic, egalitarian, liberal, tolerant.

destiny *n.* cup, doom, fate, fortune, joss, karma, kismet, lot, Moira, portion, predestiny, weird.

destitute *adj.* bankrupt, beggared, bereft, deficient, depleted, deprived, devoid of, distressed, down and out, impecunious, impoverished, indigent, innocent of, insolvent, lacking, necessitous, needy, penniless, penurious, poor, poverty-stricken, skint, strapped, wanting.
antonyms prosperous, wealthy.

destroy *v.* annihilate, banjax, break, canker, crush, demolish, destruct, devastate, dismantle, dispatch, eliminate, eradicate, extinguish, extirpate, gut, kill, level, nullify, overthrow, ravage, raze, ruin, sabotage, scuttle, shatter, slay, slight, smash, stonker, thwart, torpedo, undermine, undo, unshape, vaporize, waste, wreck, zap.
antonym create.

destruction *n.* annihilation, bane, confutation, crushing, defeat, demolition, depopulation, desolation, devastation, downfall, elimination, end, eradication, estrepement, extermination, extinction, extirpation, havoc, liquidation, massacre, nullification, overthrow, ravagement, ruin, ruination, shattering, slaughter, undoing, wastage, wrack, wreckage.
antonym creation.

destructive *adj.* adverse, antagonistic, baleful, baneful, calamitous, cataclysmic, catastrophic, contrary, damaging, deadly, deathful, deleterious, derogatory, detrimental, devastating, disastrous, discouraging, disparaging, disruptive, fatal, harmful, hostile, hurtful, injurious, invalidating, lethal, malignant, mischievous, negative, noxious, nullifying, pernicious, pestful, pestiferous, pestilent, pestilential, ruinous, slaughterous, subversive, undermining, vexatious, vicious.
antonyms creative, positive, productive.

detach *v.* abstract, alienate, cut off, deglutinate, disconnect, disengage, disentangle, disjoin, dissociate, disunite, divide, estrange, free, isolate, loosen, remove, segregate, separate, sever, uncouple, undo, unfasten, unfix, unhitch.
antonym attach.

detail *n.* aspect, attribute, complexity, complication, component, count, elaborateness, elaboration, element, fact, factor, feature, ingredient, intricacy, item, meticulousness, nicety, particular, particularity, point, refinement, respect, specific, specificity, technicality, thoroughness, triviality.

v. allocate, appoint, assign, catalog, charge, commission, delegate, delineate, depict, depute, describe, detach, enarrate, enumerate, individualize, itemize, list, narrate, overname, particularize, portray, recount, rehearse, relate, send, specify.

detain v. arrest, buttonhole, check, confine, delay, hinder, hold, hold up, impede, intern, keep, prevent, restrain, retard, slow, stay, stop.
antonym release.

detect v. ascertain, catch, descry, discern, disclose, discover, distinguish, espy, expose, find, identify, note, notice, observe, perceive, recognize, reveal, scent, sight, spot, spy, track down, uncover, unmask.

deterioration n. atrophy, corrosion, debasement, decline, degeneration, degradation, dégringolade, depreciation, descent, dilapidation, disintegration, downturn, drop, failing, fall, falling-off, lapse, pejoration, retrogression, slump, tabes, tabescence, vitiation, wastage, worsening.
antonym improvement.

determination n. backbone, conclusion, constancy, conviction, decision, dedication, doggedness, drive, firmness, fortitude, indomitability, insistence, intention, judgment, obstinacy, perseverance, persistence, pertinacity, purpose, resoluteness, resolution, resolve, result, settlement, single-mindedness, solution, steadfastness, stubbornness, tenacity, verdict, will, willpower.
antonym irresolution.

determine v. affect, arbitrate, ascertain, certify, check, choose, conclude, control, decide, detect, dictate, direct, discover, elect, end, establish, finish, fix, govern, guide, identify, impel, impose, incline, induce, influence, intend, lead, learn, modify, ordain, point, purpose, regulate, resolve, rule, settle, shape, terminate, undertake, verify.

detest v. abhor, abominate, deplore, despise, dislike, execrate, hate, loathe, recoil from.
antonym adore.

detour n. bypass, bypath, byroad, byway, circumbendibus, deviation, digression, diversion, excursus.

detriment n. damage, disadvantage, disservice, evil, harm, hurt, ill, impairment, injury, loss, mischief, prejudice.
antonym advantage.

detrimental adj. adverse, baleful, damaging, deleterious, destructive, disadvantageous, harmful, hurtful, inimical, injurious, mischievous, noxious, pernicious, prejudicial, unfavorable, untoward.
antonym advantageous.

develop v. acquire, advance, amplify, augment, begin, bloom, blossom, branch out, breed, broaden, commence, contract, cultivate, dilate, diversify, elaborate, engender, enlarge, ensue, establish, evolve, expand, flourish, follow, form, foster, generate, grow, happen, invent, make headway, mature, move on, originate, pick up, progress, promote, prosper, result, ripen, sprout, start, unfold.

development n. advance, advancement, blooming, blossoming, change, circumstance, detail, elaboration, event, evolution, expansion, extension, furtherance, growth, happening, improvement, incident, increase, issue, maturation, maturity, occurrence, outcome, phenomenon, phylogenesis, phylogeny, progress, progression, promotion, refinement, result, ripening, situation, spread, unfolding, unraveling, upbuilding, upshot.

deviate v. aberrate, depart, differ, digress, divagate, diverge, drift, err, go astray, go off the rails, part, stray, swerve, turn, turn aside, vary, veer, wander, yaw.

device n. apparatus, appliance, artifice, badge, blazon, colophon, contraption, contrivance, crest, design, dodge, emblem, episemon, expedient, figure, gadget, gambit, gimmick, gismo, implement, improvisation, insignia, instrument, invention, logo, machination, maneuver, motif, motto, plan, plot, ploy, project, ruse, scheme, shield, shift, stratagem, strategy, stunt, symbol, tactic, token, tool, trick, utensil, wile.

devilish adj. accursed, black-hearted, damnable, demoniac, demoniacal, diabolic, diabolical, execrable, fiendish, hellish, impious, infernal, iniquitous, mischievous, monstrous, nefarious, satanic, wicked.

devious adj. calculating, circuitous, confusing, crooked, cunning, deceitful, deviating, dishonest, disingenuous, double-dealing, erratic, evasive, excursive, indirect, insidious, insincere, misleading, rambling, roundabout, scheming, slippery, sly, subtle, surreptitious, tortuous, treacherous, tricky, underhand, wandering, wily, winding.
antonyms artless, candid, straightforward.

devise v. arrange, compass, compose, conceive, concoct, construct, contrive, design, excogitate, forge, form, formulate, frame, imagine, invent, plan, plot, prepare, project, scheme, shape.

devote v. allocate, allot, apply, appropriate, assign, commit, consecrate, dedicate, enshrine, give, oneself, pledge, reserve, sacrifice, set apart, set aside, surrender.

devoted adj. ardent, attentive, caring, committed, concerned, constant, dedicated, devout, faithful, fond, loving, loyal, staunch, steadfast, tireless, true, unremitting, unswerving.
antonyms inconstant, indifferent, negligent.

devotion n. adherence, adoration, affection, allegiance, ardor, assiduity, attachment, commitment, consecration, constancy, dedication, devoutness, earnestness, faith, faithfulness, fervor, fidelity, fondness, godliness, holiness, indefatigability, love, loyalty, partiality, passion, piety, prayer, regard, religiousness, reverence, sanctity, sedulousness, spirituality, steadfastness, support, worship, zeal.
antonyms inconstancy, negligence.

devour v. absorb, annihilate, bolt, consume, cram,

destroy, dispatch, down, eat, engulf, feast on, feast one's eyes on, gluttonize, gobble, gorge, gormandize, gulp, guzzle, polish off, ravage, relish, revel in, spend, stuff, swallow, waste, wolf.

devout *adj.* ardent, constant, deep, devoted, earnest, faithful, fervent, genuine, godly, heartfelt, holy, intense, orthodox, passionate, pious, prayerful, profound, pure, religious, reverent, saintly, serious, sincere, staunch, steadfast, unswerving, whole-hearted, zealous.
antonyms insincere, uncommitted.

dexterity *n.* ability, address, adroitness, agility, aptitude, art, artistry, cleverness, cunning, deftness, effortlessness, expertise, expertness, facility, finesse, handiness, ingenuity, knack, legerdemain, mastery, neatness, nimbleness, proficiency, readiness, skilfulness, skill, smoothness, tact, touch.
antonyms clumsiness, ineptitude.

dexterous *adj.* able, active, acute, adept, adroit, agile, apt, clever, cunning, deft, expert, facile, feat, habile, handy, ingenious, light-handed, masterly, neat, neathanded, nifty, nimble, nimble-fingered, nippy, proficient, prompt, quick, skilful.
antonyms clumsy, inept.

dialect *n.* accent, diction, Doric, idiom, jargon, language, lingo, localism, patois, pronunciation, provincialism, regionalism, speech, tongue, vernacular.

dialogue *n.* causerie, colloquy, communication, confabulation, conference, conversation, converse, debate, discourse, discussion, duologue, exchange, interchange, interlocution, lines, script, stichomythia, table talk, talk.

diary *n.* appointment book, chronicle, commonplace book, day-book, diurnal, engagement book, journal, journal intime, logbook, year-book.

diatribe *n.* abuse, attack, castigation, criticism, denunciation, flyting, harangue, insult, invective, onslaught, philippic, reviling, stricture, tirade, upbraiding, vituperation.
antonyms bouquet, encomium, praise.

dictate *v.* announce, command, decree, direct, enjoin, impose, instruct, ordain, order, prescribe, pronounce, rule, say, speak, transmit, utter.
n. behest, bidding, code, command, decree, dictation, dictum, direction, edict, fiat, injunction, law, mandate, order, ordinance, precept, principle, requirement, ruling, statute, ultimatum, word.

dictator *n.* autarch, autocrat, Big Brother, boss, despot, supremo, tyrant.

die *v.* breathe one's last, croak, decay, decease, decline, depart, desire, disappear, dwindle, ebb, end, expire, fade, finish, fizzle out, gangrene, go over to the majority, go to one's (long) account, hunger, kick in, kick it, kick the bucket, languish, lapse, long for, pass, pass away, pass over, peg out, perish, peter out, pine for, pop off, run down, sink, slip the cable, snuff it, starve,

stop, subside, succumb, suffer, vanish, wane, wilt, wither, yearn.

difference *n.* alteration, argument, balance, change, clash, conflict, contention, contrariety, contrast, contretemps, controversy, debate, deviation, differentia, differentiation, difformity, disagreement, discordance, discrepancy, discreteness, disparateness, disparity, dispute, dissimilarity, distinction, distinctness, divergence, diversity, exception, idiosyncrasy, jizz, particularity, peculiarity, quarrel, remainder, rest, set-to, singularity, strife, tiff, unlikeness, variation, variety, wrangle.
antonyms agreement, conformity, uniformity.

different *adj.* altered, anomalous, assorted, at odds, at variance, atypical, bizarre, changed, clashing, contrasting, deviating, discrepant, discrete, disparate, dissimilar, distinct, distinctive, divergent, divers, diverse, eccentric, extraordinary, inconsistent, individual, manifold, many, miscellaneous, multifarious, numerous, opposed, original, other, peculiar, rare, separate, several, singular, special, strange, sundry, unalike, uncommon, unconventional, unique, unlike, unusual, varied, various.
antonyms conventional, normal, same, similar, uniform.

differentiate *v.* adapt, alter, change, contrast, convert, demarcate, discern, discriminate, distinguish, individualize, mark off, modify, particularize, separate, tell apart, transform.
antonyms assimilate, associate, confuse, link.

difficult *adj.* abstract, abstruse, arduous, Augean, baffling, burdensome, captious, complex, complicated, dark, delicate, demanding, difficile, disruptive, enigmatical, fastidious, formidable, fractious, fussy, Gordian, grim, hard, herculean, iffy, intractable, intricate, involved, knotty, laborious, obscure, obstinate, obstreperous, onerous, painful, perplexing, perverse, problematic, problematical, recalcitrant, refractory, rigid, steep, sticky, stiff, straitened, strenuous, stubborn, thorny, ticklish, tiresome, toilsome, tough, troublesome, trying, unamenable, unco-operative, unmanageable, uphill, wearisome.
antonyms easy, straightforward.

difficulty *n.* a bad patch, arduousness, awkwardness, block, complication, dilemma, distress, embarrassment, fix, hang-up, hardship, hiccup, hindrance, hole, hurdle, impediment, jam, labor, laboriousness, mess, nineholes, objection, obstacle, opposition, pain, painfulness, perplexity, pickle, pinch, pitfall, plight, predicament, problem, protest, quandary, scruple, spot, strain, strait, straits, strenuousness, stumbling-block, trial, tribulation, trouble, vexata quaestio, vexed question.
antonyms advantage, ease.

diffidence *n.* abashment, backwardness, bashfulness, constraint, doubt, fear, hesitancy, hesitation, humility, inhibition, insecurity, meekness, modesty, reluctance, reserve, self-consciousness, self-distrust, self-doubt,

self-effacement, shamefacedness, shamefast, sheep-
ishness, shyness, tentativeness, timidity, timidness,
timorousness, unassertiveness.
antonym confidence.

diffuse *adj.* ambagious, circuitous, circumlocutory, copious, diffused, digressive, disconnected, discursive,
dispersed, long-winded, loose, maundering, meandering, prolix, rambling, scattered, unconcentrated, unco-
ordinated, vague, verbose, waffling, wordy.
antonyms concentrated, succinct.
v. circulate, dispense, disperse, disseminate, dissipate,
distribute, propagate, scatter, spread, winnow.
antonyms concentrate, suppress.

dig[1] *v.* burrow, delve, drive, excavate, go into, gouge,
graft, grub, hoe, howk, investigate, jab, mine, penetrate, pierce, poke, probe, prod, punch, quarry, research, scoop, search, spit, thrust, till, tunnel.
n. aspersion, barb, crack, cut, gibe, insinuation, insult,
jab, jeer, poke, prod, punch, quip, sneer, taunt, thrust,
wisecrack.
antonym compliment.

dig[2] *v.* adore, appreciate, be into, enjoy, fancy, follow,
get a kick out of, get off on, go a bundle on, go for, go
overboard about, groove, have the hots for, like, love,
understand, warm to.
antonym hate.

digest *v.* abridge, absorb, arrange, assimilate, classify,
codify, compress, condense, consider, contemplate,
dispose, dissolve, grasp, incorporate, ingest, macerate, master, meditate, methodize, ponder, process, reduce, shorten, stomach, study, summarize, systematize, tabulate, take in, understand.
n. abbreviation, abridgment, abstract, compendium,
compression, condensation, epitome, précis, reduction, résumé, summary, synopsis.

dignified *adj.* august, decorous, distinguished, exalted,
formal, grave, honorable, imposing, impressive, lofty,
lordly, majestic, noble, oro(ro)tund, reserved, solemn,
stately, upright.
antonym undignified.

dignify *v.* adorn, advance, aggrandize, apotheosize, distinguish, elevate, ennoble, exalt, glorify, honor, promote, raise.
antonyms degrade, demean.

dignity *n.* amour-propre, courtliness, decorum, elevation, eminence, excellence, glory, grandeur, gravitas,
gravity, greatness, hauteur, honor, importance, loftiness, majesty, nobility, nobleness, pride, propriety,
rank, respectability, self-esteem, self-importance, self-
possession, self-regard, self-respect, solemnity, standing, stateliness, station, status.

digress *v.* depart, deviate, divagate, diverge, drift,
excurse, expatiate, go off at a tangent, ramble, stray,
wander.

dilate *v.* amplify, broaden, descant, detail, develop, distend, dwell on, elaborate, enlarge, expand, expatiate,
expound, extend, increase, puff out, spin out, stretch,
swell, widen.
antonyms abbreviate, constrict, curtail.

dilemma *n.* bind, corner, difficulty, embarrassment, fix,
jam, mess, perplexity, pickle, pinch, plight, predicament, problem, puzzle, quandary, spot, strait.

diligent *adj.* active, assiduous, attentive, busy, careful,
conscientious, constant, dogged, earnest, hard-working, indefatigable, industrious, laborious, painstaking,
persevering, persistent, pertinacious, sedulous, studious, tireless.
antonyms dilatory, lazy.

dim *adj.* bleary, blurred, caliginous, cloudy, confused,
dark, darkish, dense, depressing, dingy, discouraging,
dull, dumb, dusky, faint, feeble, foggy, fuzzy, gloomy,
gray, hazy, ill-defined, imperfect, indistinct, intangible, lackluster, misty, muted, obscure, obscured, obtuse, opaque, overcast, pale, remote, shadowy, slow,
somber, stupid, sullied, tarnished, tenebrious, thick,
unclear, unfavorable, unilluminated, unpromising,
vague, weak.
antonyms bright, distinct.
v. becloud, bedim, blear, blur, cloud, darken, dull, fade,
lower, obscure, tarnish.
antonyms brighten, illuminate.

dimension(s) *n.* amplitude, bulk, capacity, extent, greatness, importance, largeness, magnitude, measure, range,
scale, scope, size.

diminish *v.* abate, bate, belittle, cheapen, contract, curtail, cut, deactivate, decline, decrease, demean, depreciate, devalue, dwindle, ebb, fade, lessen, lower, minify,
peter out, recede, reduce, retrench, shrink, shrivel, sink,
slacken, subside, taper off, wane, weaken.
antonyms enhance, enlarge, increase.

diminutive *adj.* bantam, dinky, Lilliputian, little, midget,
mini, miniature, minute, petite, pint-size(d), pocket(-
sized), pygmy, small, tiny, undersized, wee.
antonyms big, great, huge, large.
n. hypocorisma, pet-name.

din *n.* babble, chirm, clamor, clangor, clash, clatter, commotion, crash, hubbub, hullabaloo, noise, outcry, pandemonium, racket, randan, row, shout, uproar.
antonyms calm, quiet.

dine *v.* banquet, break bread, eat, feast, feed, lunch, sup.

dingy *adj.* bedimmed, colorless, dark, dim, dirty,
discolored, drab, dreary, dull, dusky, faded, fuscous,
gloomy, grimy, murky, obscure, run-down, seedy,
shabby, soiled, somber, tacky, worn.
antonyms bright, clean.

dip *v.* bathe, decline, descend, disappear, dook, dop, douse,
droop, drop, duck, dunk, fade, fall, immerse, ladle, lower,
plunge, rinse, sag, scoop, set, sink, slope, slump, souse,
spoon, subside, tilt.
n. basin, bathe, concavity, concoction, decline, depression, dilution, dive, dook, douche, drenching, ducking,
fall, hole, hollow, immersion, incline, infusion, lowering,

mixture, plunge, preparation, sag, slip, slope, slump, soaking, solution, suspension, swim.

diplomacy *n.* artfulness, craft, delicacy, discretion, finesse, maneuvering, savoir-faire, skill, statecraft, statesmanship, subtlety, tact, tactfulness.

diplomatic *adj.* discreet, judicious, polite, politic, prudent, sagacious, sensitive, subtle, tactful.

antonyms rude, tactless, thoughtless.

dire *adj.* alarming, appalling, awful, calamitous, cataclysmic, catastrophic, critical, crucial, cruel, crying, desperate, disastrous, dismal, distressing, drastic, dreadful, exigent, extreme, fearful, gloomy, grave, grim, horrible, horrid, ominous, portentous, pressing, ruinous, terrible, urgent, woeful.

direct[1] *v.* address, administer, advise, aim, bid, case, charge, command, conduct, control, dictate, dispose, enjoin, fix, focus, govern, guide, handle, indicate, instruct, intend, label, lead, level, mail, manage, mastermind, mean, order, oversee, point, regulate, route, rule, run, send, show, stage-manage, superintend, superscribe, supervise, train, turn.

direct[2] *adj.* absolute, blunt, candid, categorical, downright, explicit, express, face-to-face, first-hand, frank, head-on, honest, immediate, man-to-man, matter-of-fact, non-stop, open, outright, outspoken, personal, plain, plain-spoken, point-blank, shortest, sincere, straight, straightforward, through, unambiguous, unbroken, undeviating, unequivocal, uninterrupted.

antonyms crooked, devious, indirect.

direction *n.* address, administration, aim, approach, bearing, bent, bias, charge, command, control, course, current, drift, end, government, guidance, label, leadership, line, management, mark, order, orientation, oversight, path, proclivity, purpose, road, route, superintendence, superscription, supervision, tack, tendency, tenor, track, trend, way.

directions *n.* briefing, guidance, guidelines, indication, instructions, orders, plan, recipe, recommendations, regulations.

directly *adv.* bluntly, candidly, dead, due, exactly, face-to-face, forthwith, frankly, honestly, immediately, instantaneously, instantly, openly, personally, plainly, point-blank, precisely, presently, promptly, pronto, quickly, right away, soon, speedily, straight, straightaway, straight-forwardly, truthfully, unequivocally, unerringly, unswervingly.

antonym indirectly.

dirt *n.* clay, crud, dust, earth, excrement, filth, grime, impurity, indecency, loam, mire, muck, mud, obscenity, ordure, pornography, slime, smudge, smut, smutch, soil, sordor, stain, tarnish, vomit, yuck.

antonyms cleanliness, cleanness.

dirty *adj.* angry, base, beggarly, begrimed, bitter, blue, clouded, contemptible, corrupt, cowardly, crooked, cruddy, dark, despicable, dishonest, dull, filthy, foul, fraudulent, grimy, grubby, ignominious, illegal, indecent, low, low-down, maculate, manky, mean, messy, miry, mucky, muddy, nasty, obscene, off-color, piggish, polluted, pornographic, risqué, salacious, scruffy, scurvy, shabby, sluttish, smutty, soiled, sordid, squalid, sullied, treacherous, unclean, unfair, unscrupulous, unsporting, unsterile, unswept, vile, vulgar, yucky.

antonyms clean, spotless.

v. bedaub, begrime, besmear, besmirch, besmut, bespatter, blacken, defile, foul, mess up, muddy, pollute, smear, smirch, smudge, soil, soss, spoil, stain, sully.

antonyms clean, cleanse.

disability *n.* affliction, ailment, complaint, crippledom, defect, disablement, disorder, disqualification, handicap, impairment, impotency, inability, incapacitation, incapacity, incompetency, infirmity, malady, unfitness, weakness.

disable *v.* cripple, damage, debilitate, disenable, disqualify, enfeeble, hamstring, handicap, immobilize, impair, incapacitate, invalidate, lame, paralyze, prostrate, unfit, unman, weaken.

disabled *adj.* bedridden, crippled, handicapped, hors de combat, immobilized, incapacitated, infirm, lame, maimed, mangled, mutilated, paralyzed, weak, weakened, wrecked.

antonyms able, able-bodied.

disadvantage *n.* burden, damage, debit, detriment, disservice, drawback, flaw, fly in the ointment, handicap, hardship, harm, hindrance, hurt, impediment, inconvenience, injury, liability, loss, minus, nuisance, prejudice, privation, snag, trouble, unfavorableness, weakness.

antonyms advantage, benefit.

v. hamper, handicap, hinder, inconvenience, wrongfoot.

antonyms aid, help.

disagree *v.* altercate, argue, bicker, bother, clash, conflict, contend, contest, contradict, counter, depart, deviate, differ, discomfort, dissent, distress, diverge, fall out, hurt, nauseate, object, oppose, quarrel, run counter to, sicken, spat, squabble, take issue with, tiff, trouble, upset, vary, wrangle.

antonym agree.

disagreement *n.* altercation, argument, clash, conflict, debate, difference, discord, discrepancy, disparity, dispute, dissent, dissimilarity, dissimilitude, divergence, diversity, division, falling-out, incompatibility, incongruity, misunderstanding, quarrel, squabble, strife, tiff, unlikeness, variance, wrangle.

antonym agreement.

disappear *v.* cease, dematerialize, depart, dissolve, ebb, end, escape, evanesce, evaporate, expire, fade, flee, fly, go, pass, perish, recede, retire, scarper, vamoose, vanish, wane, withdraw.

antonym appear.

disappoint *v.* baffle, balk, chagrin, dash, deceive, defeat, delude, disconcert, disenchant, disgruntle, dishearten, disillusion, dismay, dissatisfy, fail, foil, frustrate, hamper, hinder, let down, miff, sadden, thwart, vex.
antonyms delight, please, satisfy.

disappointment[1] *n.* bafflement, chagrin, discontent, discouragement, disenchantment, disillusionment, displeasure, dissatisfaction, distress, failure, frustration, mortification, regret.
antonyms delight, pleasure, satisfaction.

disappointment[2] *n.* blow, calamity, comedown, disaster, drop, failure, fiasco, frost, lemon, let-down, misfortune, setback, swiz, swizzle.
antonyms boost, success.

disapprove of blame, censure, condemn, denounce, deplore, deprecate, disallow, discountenance, dislike, disparage, object to, reject, spurn, take exception to.
antonym approve of.

disarm[1] *v.* deactivate, demilitarize, demobilize, disable, disband, unarm, unweapon. *antonym* arm.

disarm[2] appease, conciliate, modify, persuade, win over.

disaster *n.* accident, act of God, blow, calamity, cataclysm, catastrophe, curtains, debacle, misadventure, mischance, misfortune, mishap, reverse, ruin, ruination, stroke, tragedy, trouble.
antonyms success, triumph.

disband *v.* break up, demobilize, dismiss, disperse, dissolve, part company, retire, scatter, separate.
antonyms assemble, band, combine.

disbelief *n.* distrust, doubt, dubiety, incredulity, mistrust, rejection, scepticism, suspicion, unbelief.
antonym belief.

discard *v.* abandon, cashier, cast aside, dispense with, dispose of, ditch, drop, dump, jettison, leave off, reject, relinquish, remove, repudiate, scrap, shed.
antonyms adopt, embrace, espouse.

discern *v.* ascertain, behold, descry, detect, determine, differentiate, discover, discriminate, distinguish, espy, judge, make out, notice, observe, perceive, recognize, see, wot.

discernment *n.* acumen, acuteness, ascertainment, astuteness, awareness, clear-sightedness, cleverness, discrimination, ingenuity, insight, intelligence, judgment, keenness, penetration, perception, perceptiveness, percipience, perspicacity, sagacity, sharpness, understanding, wisdom.

discharge *v.* absolve, accomplish, acquit, carry out, cashier, clear, detonate, disburden, discard, disembogue, dismiss, dispense, drum out, effectuate, egest, eject, emit, empty, excrete, execute, exonerate, expel, explode, exude, fire, free, fulfil, give off, gush, honor, leak, let off, liberate, meet, offload, ooze, oust, pardon, pay, perform, release, relieve, remove, sack, satisfy, set off, settle, shoot, unburden, unload, vent, void, volley.
antonyms employ, engage, hire.
n. accomplishment, achievement, acquittal, acquittance,

blast, burst, clearance, congé, defluxion, demobilization, detonation, disburdening, discharging, dismissal, effluent, ejecta, ejectamenta, ejection, emission, emptying, excretion, execution, exoneration, explosion, firing, flight, flow, flux, fluxion, fulfilment, fusillade, gleet, glit, liberation, mittimus, observance, ooze, pardon, payment, performance, pus, quietus, quittance, release, remittance, report, salvo, satisfaction, secretion, seepage, settlement, shot, suppuration, the boot, the sack, unburdening, unloading, vent, voidance, voiding, volley, whiff.

disciple *n.* acolyte, adherent, apostle, believer, catechumen, chela, convert, devotee, follower, learner, partisan, proselyte, pupil, student, supporter, votary.

discipline *n.* castigation, chastisement, conduct, control, correction, course, curriculum, drill, exercise, martinetism, method, orderliness, practice, punishment, regimen, regulation, restraint, self-control, specialty, strictness, subject, training.
antonyms carelessness, negligence.
v. break in, castigate, chasten, chastise, check, control, correct, drill, educate, exercise, form, govern, habituate, instruct, inure, penalize, prepare, punish, regulate, reprimand, reprove, restrain, toughen, train.

disclaim *v.* abandon, abjure, abnegate, decline, deny, disacknowledge, disaffirm, disallow, disavow, disown, forswear, reject, renounce, repudiate.
antonyms accept, acknowledge, claim.

disclose *v.* broadcast, communicate, confess, discover, divulge, exhibit, expose, impart, lay, lay bare, leak, let slip, propale, publish, relate, reveal, show, tell, unbare, unbosom, unburden, uncover, unfold, unveil, utter.
antonyms conceal, hide.

discomfit *v.* abash, baffle, balk, beat, checkmate, confound, confuse, defeat, demoralize, discompose, disconcert, embarrass, faze, flurry, fluster, foil, frustrate, humble, humiliate, outwit, overcome, perplex, perturb, rattle, ruffle, thwart, trump, unsettle, vanquish, worry, worst.

discomfort *n.* ache, annoyance, disquiet, distress, hardship, hurt, inquietude, irritant, irritation, malaise, trouble, uneasiness, unpleasantness, unpleasantry, vexation.
antonyms comfort, ease.

disconcerted *adj.* annoyed, bewildered, confused, discombobulated, discomfited, distracted, disturbed, embarrassed, fazed, flurried, flustered, mixed-up, nonplused, perturbed, rattled, ruffled, taken aback, thrown, troubled, unsettled, upset.

disconnect *v.* cut off, detach, disengage, divide, part, separate, sever, uncouple, ungear, unhitch, unhook, unlink, unplug, unyoke.
antonyms attach, connect, engage.

disconsolate *adj.* crushed, dejected, desolate, despairing, dispirited, forlorn, gloomy, grief-stricken, heartbroken, heavy-hearted, hopeless, inconsolable, melancholy, miserable, sad, unhappy, unsolaced, woeful, wretched.

antonyms cheerful, cheery.

discontent *n.* discontentment, displeasure, disquiet, dissatisfaction, envy, fretfulness, impatience, regret, restlessness, uneasiness, unhappiness, unrest, vexation.

antonym content.

discontinue *v.* abandon, break off, cancel, cease, drop, end, finish, halt, interrupt, pause, quit, stop, suspend, terminate.

antonym continue.

discord *n.* cacophony, clashing, conflict, contention, difference, din, disagreement, discordance, disharmony, dispute, dissension, dissonance, disunity, division, friction, harshness, incompatibility, jangle, jarring, opposition, racket, rupture, split, strife, tumult, variance, wrangling.

antonyms agreement, concord, harmony.

discourage *v.* abash, awe, check, chill, cow, curb, damp, dampen, dash, daunt, deject, demoralize, deprecate, depress, deter, discountenance, disfavor, dishearten, dismay, dispirit, dissuade, frighten, hinder, inhibit, intimidate, overawe, prevent, put off, restrain, scare, unman, unnerve.

antonyms encourage, favor, hearten, inspire.

discourteous *adj.* abrupt, bad-mannered, boorish, brusque, curt, disrespectful, ill-bred, ill-mannered, impolite, insolent, offhand, rude, slighting, unceremonious, uncivil, uncourteous, ungracious, unmannerly.

antonyms courteous, polite, respectful.

discover *v.* ascertain, conceive, contrive, descry, design, detect, determine, devise, dig up, discern, disclose, espy, find, invent, learn, light on, locate, notice, originate, perceive, pioneer, realize, recognize, reveal, see, spot, suss out, uncover, unearth.

antonyms conceal, hide.

discredit *v.* blame, censure, challenge, defame, degrade, deny, disbelieve, discount, disgrace, dishonor, disparage, dispute, distrust, doubt, explode, mistrust, question, reproach, slander, slur, smear, vilify.

antonyms believe, credit.

n. aspersion, blame, censure, disgrace, dishonor, disrepute, distrust, doubt, ignominy, ill-repute, imputation, mistrust, odium, opprobrium, question, reproach, scandal, shame, skepticism, slur, smear, stigma, suspicion.

antonym credit.

discreet *adj.* careful, cautious, circumspect, considerate, delicate, diplomatic, discerning, guarded, judicious, politic, prudent, reserved, sagacious, sensible, softly-softly, tactful, wary.

antonyms careless, indiscreet, tactless.

discrepancy *n.* conflict, contrariety, difference, disagreement, discordance, disparity, dissimilarity, dissonance, divergence, imparity, incongruity, inconsistency, inequality, variance, variation.

discretion *n.* acumen, care, carefulness, caution, choice, circumspection, consideration, diplomacy, discernment, disposition, heedfulness, inclination, judgment, judiciousness, liking, maturity, mind, option, pleasure, predilection, preference, prudence, responsibility, sagacity, tact, volition, wariness, will, wisdom, wish.

antonym indiscretion.

discriminating *adj.* acute, astute, critical, cultivated, discerning, discriminant, fastidious, nasute, particular, perceptive, selective, sensitive, tasteful.

discrimination[1] *n.* bias, bigotry, favoritism, inequity, intolerance, Jim Crow, prejudice, unfairness.

discrimination[2] *n.* acumen, acuteness, discernment, insight, judgment, keenness, penetration, perception, percipience, refinement, sagacity, subtlety, taste.

discuss *v.* argue, confer, consider, consult, converse, debate, deliberate, examine, lay heads together, rap.

discussion *n.* analysis, argument, colloquium, colloquy, confabulation, conference, consideration, consultation, conversation, debate, deliberation, dialogue, discourse, examination, exchange, gabfest, moot, quodlibet, rap, review, scrutiny, seminar, symposium, talkfest.

disdain *v.* belittle, contemn, deride, despise, disavow, disregard, misprize, pooh-pooh, rebuff, reject, scorn, slight, sneer at, spurn, undervalue.

antonyms admire, respect.

n. arrogance, contempt, contumely, deprecation, derision, dislike, haughtiness, hauteur, imperiousness, indifference, scorn, sneering, snobbishness, superciliousness.

antonyms admiration, respect.

disdainful *adj.* aloof, arrogant, contemptuous, derisive, haughty, hoity-toity, imperious, insolent, proud, scornful, sneering, supercilious, superior, uppish.

antonyms admiring, respectful.

disease *n.* affection, affliction, ailment, blight, cancer, canker, complaint, condition, contagion, contamination, disorder, distemper, epidemic, epizootic, idiopathy, ill-health, illness, indisposition, infection, infirmity, malady, malaise, murrain, pest, plague, sickness, upset.

antonym health.

disentangle *v.* clarify, debarrass, detach, disconnect, disembarrass, disengage, disentwine, disinvolve, extricate, free, loose, ravel out, resolve, separate, sever, simplify, unfold, unravel, unsnarl, untangle, untwine, untwist.

antonym entangle.

disfigured *adj.* damaged, defaced, deformed, flawed, ruined, scarred, spoilt, ugly.

antonym adorned.

disgrace *n.* aspersion, attaint, baseness, blemish, blot, contempt, defamation, degradation, discredit, disesteem, disfavor, dishonor, disrepute, dog-house, ignominy, infamy, obloquy, odium, opprobrium, reproach, scandal, shame, slur, stain, stigma.

antonyms esteem, honor, respect.

v. abase, attaint, defame, degrade, discredit, disfavor, dishonor, disparage, humiliate, reproach, scandalize, shame, slur, stain, stigmatize, sully, taint.

antonyms honor, respect.

disgraceful *adj.* appalling, blameworthy, contemptible, degrading, detestable, discreditable, dishonorable, disreputable, dreadful, ignominious, infamous, low, mean, opprobrious, scandalous, shameful, shocking, unworthy.

antonyms honorable, respectable.

disguise *v.* camouflage, cloak, conceal, cover, deceive, dissemble, dissimulate, dress up, explain away, fake, falsify, fudge, hide, mask, misrepresent, screen, secrete, shroud, veil.

antonyms expose, reveal, uncover.

n. camouflage, cloak, concealment, costume, cover, coverture, deception, dissimulation, façade, front, get-up, mask, masquerade, pretence, screen, semblance, travesty, trickery, veil, veneer, visor.

disgust *v.* displease, nauseate, offend, outrage, put off, repel, revolt, scandalize, scunner, sicken.

antonyms delight, gratify, tempt.

n. abhorrence, abomination, antipathy, aversion, detestation, dislike, disrelish, distaste, hatefulness, hatred, loathing, nausea, odium, repugnance, repulsion, revulsion.

antonyms admiration, liking.

disgusting *adj.* abominable, detestable, distasteful, foul, gross, hateful, loathsome, nasty, nauseating, nauseous, objectionable, obnoxious, obscene, odious, offensive, repellent, repugnant, revolting, shameless, sickening, sickmaking, stinking, ugsome, unappetizing, vile, vulgar. *antonyms* attractive, delightful, pleasant.

dish[1] *n.* bowl, fare, food, plate, platter, porringer, ramekin, recipe, salver, trencher.

dish[2] *v.* finish, ruin, spoil, torpedo, wreck.

dishearten *v.* cast down, crush, damp, dampen, dash, daunt, deject, depress, deter, discourage, dismay, dispirit, frighten, weary.

disheartened *adj.* crestfallen, crushed, daunted, dejected, depressed, disappointed, discouraged, dismayed, dispirited, downcast, downhearted, frightened, weary.

antonyms encouraged, heartened.

disheveled *adj.* bedraggled, blowsy, disarranged, disordered, frowsy, messy, mussy, ruffled, rumpled, slovenly, tousled, uncombed, unkempt, untidy.

antonyms neat, spruce, tidy.

dishonest *adj.* bent, cheating, corrupt, crafty, crooked, deceitful, deceiving, deceptive, designing, disreputable, double-dealing, false, fraudulent, guileful, immoral, knavish, lying, mendacious, perfidious, shady, snide, swindling, treacherous, unethical, unfair, unprincipled, unscrupulous, untrustworthy, untruthful, wrongful.

antonym fair, honest, scrupulous, trustworthy.

dishonor *v.* abase, blacken, corrupt, debase, debauch, defame, defile, deflower, degrade, demean, discredit, disgrace, disparage, pollute, rape, ravish, seduce, shame, sully.

antonym honor.

n. abasement, abuse, affront, aspersion, degradation, discourtesy, discredit, disfavor, disgrace, disrepute, ignominy, imputation, indignity, infamy, insult, obloquy, odium, offence, opprobrium, outrage, reproach, scandal, shame, slight, slur.

antonym honor.

disinclined *adj.* antipathetic, averse, hesitant, indisposed, loath, opposed, reluctant, resistant, undisposed, unenthusiastic, unwilling.

antonyms inclined, willing.

disingenuous *adj.* artful, cunning, deceitful, designing, devious, dishonest, duplicitous, guileful, insidious, insincere, shifty, two-faced, uncandid, wily.

antonyms artless, frank, ingenuous, naive.

disintegrate *v.* break up, crumble, decompose, disunite, fall apart, molder, rot, separate, shatter, splinter.

antonyms combine, merge, unite.

disinterested *adj.* candid, detached, dispassionate, equitable, even-handed, impartial, impersonal, neutral, openminded, unbiased, uninvolved, unprejudiced, unselfish.

antonyms biased, concerned, interested, prejudiced.

dislike *n.* animosity, animus, antagonism, antipathy, aversion, detestation, disapprobation, disapproval, disgust, disinclination, displeasure, disrelish, distaste, dyspathy, enmity, hatred, hostility, loathing, repugnance.

antonyms attachment, liking, predilection.

v. abhor, abominate, despise, detest, disapprove, disfavor, disrelish, hate, keck, loathe, scorn, shun.

antonyms favor, like, prefer.

disloyal *adj.* apostate, disaffected, faithless, false, perfidious, seditious, subversive, traitorous, treacherous, treasonable, two-faced, unfaithful, unleal, unpatriotic, untrustworthy, unwifely.

antonym loyal.

dismal *adj.* black, bleak, burdan, cheerless, dark, depressing, despondent, discouraging, doleful, dolorous, dowie, dreary, dreich, forlorn, funereal, ghostful, gloomy, gruesome, hopeless, incompetent, inept, lac(h)rymose, lonesome, long-faced, long-visaged, lowering, low-spirited, lugubrious, melancholy, poor, sad, sepulchral, somber, sorrowful, stupid, thick, useless.

antonyms bright, cheerful.

dismantle *v.* demolish, demount, disassemble, dismount, raze, strike, strip, unrig.

antonym assemble.

dismay *v.* affright, alarm, appal, consternate, daunt, depress, disappoint, disconcert, discourage, dishearten, disillusion, dispirit, distress, frighten, horrify, paralyze, put off, scare, terrify, unnerve, unsettle.

antonym encourage.

n. agitation, alarm, anxiety, apprehension, consternation,

disappointment, distress, dread, fear, fright, funk, horror, panic, terror, trepidation, upset.
antonyms boldness, encouragement.

dismiss *v.* ax, banish, bounce, bowler-hat, cashier, chassé, chuck, disband, discharge, discount, dispel, disperse, disregard, dissolve, drop, fire, free, give (someone) the push, lay off, let go, oust, pooh-pooh, reject, release, relegate, remove, repudiate, sack, send packing, set aside, shelve, spurn.
antonyms accept, appoint.

disobedient *adj.* contrary, contumacious, defiant, disorderly, froward, insubordinate, intractable, mischievous, naughty, obstreperous, refractory, unruly, wayward, wilful.
antonym obedient.

disobey *v.* contravene, defy, disregard, flout, ignore, infringe, overstep, rebel, resist, transgress, violate.
antonym obey.

disorder *n.* affliction, ailment, brawl, chaos, clamor, clutter, commotion, complaint, confusion, derangement, disarray, disease, disorderliness, disorganization, disturbance, fight, fracas, hubbub, hullabaloo, illness, indisposition, irregularity, jumble, malady, mess, misarrangement, misarray, misorder, misrule, muddle, muss(e), mussiness, quarrel, riot, rumpus, shambles, sickness, tumult, untidiness, uproar.
antonym order.

v. clutter, confound, confuse, derange, disarrange, discompose, disorganize, disrank, disturb, jumble, mess up, misorder, mix up, muddle, scatter, unsettle, upset.
antonyms arrange, organize.

disorganization *n.* chaos, confusion, derangement, disarray, disjointedness, dislocation, disorder, disruption, incoherence, unconnectedness.
antonyms order, tidiness.

disorganized *adj.* chaotic, confused, disordered, haphazard, jumbled, muddled, shambolic, shuffled, topsyturvy, unmethodical, unorganized, unregulated, unsifted, unsorted, unstructured, unsystematic, unsystematized.
antonyms organized, tidy.

disown *v.* abandon, abnegate, cast off, deny, disacknowledge, disallow, disavow, disclaim, reject, renounce, repudiate, unget.
antonym accept.

disparage *v.* belittle, criticize, decry, defame, degrade, denigrate, deprecate, depreciate, deride, derogate, detract from, discredit, disdain, dishonor, dismiss, disvalue, malign, minimize, ridicule, run down, scorn, slander, traduce, underestimate, underrate, undervalue, vilify, vilipend.
antonym praise.

disparagement *n.* aspersion, belittlement, condemnation, contempt, contumely, criticism, debasement, decrial, decrying, degradation, denunciation, deprecation, depreciation, derision, derogation, detraction,

discredit, disdain, ridicule, scorn, slander, underestimation, vilification.
antonym praise.

dispassionate *adj.* calm, candid, collected, composed, cool, detached, disinterested, fair, impartial, impersonal, imperturbable, indifferent, moderate, neutral, objective, quiet, serene, sober, temperate, unbiased, unemotional, unexcitable, unexcited, uninvolved, unmoved, unprejudiced, unruffled.
antonyms biased, emotional.

dispatch[1], **despatch** *v.* accelerate, conclude, discharge, dismiss, dispose of, expedite, finish, hasten, hurry, perform, quicken, settle.
antonym impede.

n. alacrity, celerity, dépêche, expedition, haste, precipitateness, promptitude, promptness, quickness, rapidity, speed, swiftness.
antonym slowness.

dispatch[2], **despatch** *v.* consign, express, forward, remit, send, transmit.
n. account, bulletin, communication, communiqué, document, instruction, item, letter, message, missive, news, piece, report, story.

dispatch[3], **despatch** *v.* assassinate, bump off, execute, kill, murder, rub out, slaughter, slay, waste.

dispel *v.* allay, banish, discuss, dismiss, disperse, dissipate, drive off, eliminate, expel, melt away, resolve, rout, scatter.
antonym give rise to.

dispense *v.* administer, allocate, allot, apply, apportion, assign, deal out, direct, disburse, discharge, distribute, dole out, enforce, except, excuse, execute, exempt, exonerate, implement, let off, measure, mete out, mix, operate, prepare, release, relieve, reprieve, share, supply, undertake.

disperse *v.* broadcast, circulate, diffuse, disappear, disband, dismiss, dispel, disseminate, dissipate, dissolve, distribute, drive off, evanesce, melt away, rout, scatter, separate, spread, strew, vanish.
antonym gather.

dispirited *adj.* brassed off, browned off, cast down, crestfallen, dejected, depressed, despondent, discouraged, disheartened, down, downcast, fed up, gloomy, glum, low, morose, sad.
antonym encouraged.

displace *v.* cashier, crowd out, depose, derange, disarrange, discard, discharge, dislocate, dislodge, dismiss, dispossess, disturb, eject, evict, fire, luxate, misplace, move, oust, remove, replace, sack, shift, succeed, supersede, supplant, transpose, unsettle.

display *v.* betray, blazon, boast, demonstrate, disclose, evidence, evince, exhibit, expand, expose, extend, flash, flaunt, flourish, manifest, model, parade, present, reveal, show, show off, showcase, splash, sport, unfold, unfurl, unveil, vaunt, wear.
antonym hide.

n. array, demonstration, étalage, exhibition, exposition, exposure, flourish, manifestation, ostentation, pageant, parade, pomp, presentation, revelation, show, spectacle, splurge.

displeasure *n.* anger, annoyance, disapprobation, disapproval, discontent, disfavor, disgruntlement, dudgeon, huff, indignation, irritation, offense, pique, resentment, vexation, wrath.
antonyms gratification, pleasure.

disposal *n.* arrangement, array, assignment, authority, bequest, bestowal, clearance, conduct, consignment, control, conveyance, determination, direction, discarding, discretion, dispensation, disposition, distribution, dumping, ejection, gift, government, jettisoning, management, ordering, position, regulation, relinquishment, removal, responsibility, riddance, scrapping, settlement, transfer.
antonym provision.

dispose *v.* actuate, adapt, adjust, align, arrange, array, bias, condition, determine, dispone, distribute, fix, group, incline, induce, influence, lay, lead, marshal, motivate, move, order, place, position, predispose, prompt, put, range, rank, regulate, set, settle, situate, stand, tempt.

disposition *n.* adjustment, arrangement, bent, bias, character, classification, constitution, control, direction, disposal, distribution, grain, grouping, habit, inclination, kidney, leaning, make-up, management, nature, ordering, organization, placement, predisposition, proclivity, proneness, propensity, readiness, regulation, spirit, temper, temperament, tendency, velleity.

dispossess *v.* deprive, dislodge, disseize, divest, eject, evict, expel, oust, rob, strip, unhouse.
antonyms give, provide.

disprove *v.* answer, confute, contradict, controvert, discredit, explode, expose, invalidate, negate, rebut, refute.
antonym prove.

dispute *v.* altercate, argue, brawl, challenge, clash, contend, contest, contradict, controvert, debate, deny, discuss, doubt, gainsay, impugn, litigate, moot, oppugn, quarrel, question, spar, squabble, traverse, wrangle.
antonym agree.
n. altercation, argument, brawl, conflict, contention, controversy, debate, disagreement, discord, discussion, dissension, disturbance, feud, friction, quarrel, spar, squabble, strife, wrangle.
antonym agreement.

disqualify *v.* debar, disable, disauthorize, disentitle, dishabilitate, disprivilege, incapacitate, invalidate, preclude, prohibit, rule out, unfit.
antonyms accept, allow.

disregard *v.* brush aside, cold-shoulder, contemn, despise, discount, disdain, disobey, disparage, ignore, laugh off, make light of, neglect, overlook, pass over, pooh-pooh, slight, snub, turn a blind eye to.
antonyms note, pay attention to.

n. brush-off, contempt, disdain, disesteem, disrespect, heedlessness, ignoring, inattention, indifference, neglect, negligence, oversight, slight.
antonym attention.

disrepair *n.* collapse, decay, deterioration, dilapidation, ruin, ruination, shabbiness, unrepair.
antonyms good repair, restoration.

disreputable *adj.* base, contemptible, derogatory, discreditable, disgraceful, dishonorable, disorderly, disrespectable, ignominious, infamous, louche, low, mean, notorious, opprobrious, scandalous, seedy, shady, shameful, shocking, unprincipled.
antonyms decent, honorable.

disrespectful *adj.* bad-tempered, cheeky, contemptuous, discourteous, impertinent, impolite, impudent, insolent, insulting, irreverent, rude, uncivil, unmannerly.
antonym respectful.

dissect *v.* analyze, anatomize, break down, dismember, examine, explore, inspect, investigate, pore over, scrutinize, study.

disseminate *v.* broadcast, circulate, diffuse, disperse, dissipate, distribute, evangelize, proclaim, promulgate, propagate, publicize, publish, scatter, sow, spread.

dissent *v.* decline, differ, disagree, disconsent, object, protest, quibble, refuse.
antonyms agree, consent.
n. difference, disagreement, discord, dissension, dissidence, nonconformity, objection, opposition, quibble, refusal, resistance.
antonym agreement.

dissertation *n.* critique, discourse, disquisition, essay, exposition, monograph, paper, prolegomena, propaedeutic, thesis, treatise.

dissident *adj.* differing, disagreeing, discordant, dissentient, dissenting, heterodox, nonconformist, recusant, schismatic.
antonyms acquiescent, agreeing.
n. agitator, dissenter, protestor, rebel, recusant, refus(e)nik, schismatic.
antonym assenter.

dissimilar *adj.* different, disparate, divergent, diverse, heterogeneous, incompatible, mismatched, unlike, unrelated, various.
antonyms compatible, similar.

dissimulation *n.* act, affectation, concealment, deceit, deception, dissembling, double-dealing, duplicity, feigning, hypocrisy, play-acting, pretence, sham, wile.
antonym openness.

dissipate *v.* burn up, consume, deplete, disappear, dispel, disperse, dissolve, evaporate, expend, fritter away, lavish, rig, scatter, spend, squander, vanish, wanton, waste.
antonym accumulate.

dissolute *adj.* abandoned, corrupt, debauched, degenerate, depraved, dissipated, immoral, lax, lewd, libertine, licentious, loose, profligate, rakehell, rakehelly, rakish, unrestrained, vicious, wanton, wide, wild. *antonym* virtuous.

dissolve *v.* break up, crumble, decompose, deliquesce, destroy, diffuse, disappear, discontinue, disintegrate, dismiss, disorganize, disperse, dissipate, disunite, divorce, dwindle, end, evanesce, evaporate, fade, flux, fuse, liquefy, loose, melt, overthrow, perish, ruin, separate, sever, soften, suspend, terminate, thaw, vanish, wind up.

dissuade *v.* dehort, deter, discourage, disincline, divert, expostulate, put off, remonstrate, warn. *antonym* persuade.

distant *adj.* abroad, afar, aloof, apart, ceremonious, cold, cool, disparate, dispersed, distinct, faint, far, faraway, far-flung, far-off, formal, haughty, indirect, indistinct, isolated, obscure, outlying, out-of-the-way, remote, removed, reserved, restrained, reticent, scattered, separate, slight, stand-offish, stiff, unapproachable, uncertain, unfriendly, withdrawn. *antonyms* close, friendly.

distasteful *adj.* abhorrent, aversive, disagreeable, displeasing, dissatisfying, loathsome, nasty, nauseous, objectionable, obnoxious, offensive, repugnant, repulsive, undesirable, uninviting, unpalatable, unpleasant, unsavory. *antonym* pleasing.

distend *v.* balloon, bloat, bulge, dilate, enlarge, expand, fill out, increase, inflate, intumesce, puff, stretch, swell, widen. *antonym* deflate.

distinct *adj.* apparent, clear, clear-cut, decided, definite, detached, different, discrete, dissimilar, evident, individual, lucid, manifest, marked, noticeable, obvious, palpable, patent, plain, recognizable, separate, several, sharp, unambiguous, unconnected, unmistakable, well-defined. *antonyms* fuzzy, hazy, indistinct.

distinction[1] *n.* characteristic, contradistinction, contrast, difference, differential, differentiation, diorism, discernment, discrimination, dissimilarity, distinctiveness, division, feature, individuality, mark, nuance, particularity, peculiarity, penetration, perception, quality, separation.

distinction[2] *n.* account, celebrity, consequence, credit, eminence, excellence, fame, glory, greatness, honor, importance, merit, name, note, prestige, prominence, quality, rank, renown, reputation, repute, significance, superiority, worth. *antonym* insignificance.

distinctive *adj.* characteristic, different, discriminative, discriminatory, distinguishing, extraordinary, idiosyncratic, individual, inimitable, original, peculiar, singular, special, typical, uncommon, unique. *antonym* common.

distinguish *v.* ascertain, categorize, celebrate, characterize, classify, decide, determine, differentiate, dignify, discern, discriminate, honor, immortalize, individualize, judge, know, make out, mark, perceive, pick out, recognize, see, separate, signalize, tell, tell apart.

distinguished *adj.* acclaimed, celebrated, conspicuous, distingué, eminent, eximious, extraordinary, famed, famous, illustrious, marked, nameworthy, notable, noted, outstanding, renowned, signal, striking, well-known. *antonyms* insignificant, ordinary.

distort *v.* bend, bias, buckle, color, contort, deform, disfigure, falsify, garble, miscolor, misrepresent, misshape, pervert, skew, slant, torture, twist, warp, wrench, wrest, wring.

distract *v.* agitate, amuse, beguile, bewilder, confound, confuse, derange, discompose, disconcert, disturb, divert, engross, entertain, faze, harass, madden, occupy, perplex, puzzle, sidetrack, torment, trouble.

distracted *adj.* agitated, bemused, bewildered, confounded, confused, crazy, deranged, distraught, éperdu(e), flustered, frantic, frenzied, grief-stricken, harassed, hassled, insane, mad, maddened, overwrought, perplexed, puzzled, raving, troubled, wild, worked up, wrought up. *antonyms* calm, untroubled.

distraction *n.* aberration, abstraction, agitation, alienation, amusement, beguilement, bewilderment, commotion, confusion, delirium, derangement, desperation, discord, disorder, disturbance, diversion, divertissement, entertainment, frenzy, hallucination, harassment, incoherence, insanity, interference, interruption, mania, pastime, recreation.

distress *n.* adversity, affliction, agony, anguish, anxiety, calamity, depravation, desolation, destitution, difficulties, discomfort, grief, hardship, heartache, indigence, katzenjammer, misery, misfortune, need, pain, pauperism, poverty, privation, sadness, sorrow, strait(s), suffering, torment, torture, trial, trouble, woe, worry, wretchedness. *antonyms* comfort, ease, security. *v.* afflict, agonize, bother, constrain, cut up, disturb, grieve, harass, harrow, pain, perplex, sadden, straiten, torment, trouble, upset, worry, wound. *antonyms* assist, comfort.

distribute *v.* administer, allocate, allot, apportion, arrange, assign, assort, bestow, carve up, categorize, circulate, class, classify, convey, deal, deliver, diffuse, dish out, dispense, disperse, dispose, disseminate, divide, dole, file, give, group, hand out, mete, scatter, share, spread, strew. *antonyms* collect, gather in.

district *n.* area, canton, cantred, cantret, community, gau, hundred, locale, locality, neighborhood, parish, precinct, quarter, region, sector, vicinity, ward.

distrust *v.* disbelieve, discredit, doubt, misbelieve, miscredit, misdeem, mistrust, question, suspect. *antonym* trust.

n. disbelief, doubt, misfaith, misgiving, mistrust, qualm, question, skepticism, suspicion, untrust, wariness.
antonym trust.

disturb *v.* affray, agitate, alarm, annoy, bother, concuss, confound, confuse, derange, disarrange, discompose, disorder, order, disorganize, disrupt, distract, distress, excite, fluster, harass, interrupt, muddle, perturb, pester, rouse, ruffle, shake, startle, trouble, unsettle, upset, worry.
antonyms calm, quiet, reassure.

disturbance *n.* agitation, annoyance, bother, brawl, breeze, broil, burst-up, bust-up, commotion, confusion, derangement, disorder, distraction, fracas, fray, hindrance, hubbub, interruption, intrusion, katzenjammer, kick-up, misarrangement, molestation, muss(e), perturbation, riot, ruckus, ruction, shake-up, stour, stramash, tumult, turmoil, unrest, upheaval, uproar, upset, upturn.
antonyms peace, quiet.

disturbed *adj.* agitated, anxious, apprehensive, bothered, concerned, confused, discomposed, disordered, disquieted, flustered, maladjusted, neurotic, troubled, unbalanced, uneasy, unrestful, upset, worried.
antonyms calm, sane.

disuse *n.* abandonment, decay, desuetude, discontinuance, disusage, idleness, neglect.
antonym use.

diverge *v.* bifurcate, branch, conflict, depart, deviate, differ, digress, disagree, dissent, divaricate, divide, fork, part, radiate, separate, split, spread, stray, vary, wander.
antonyms agree, come together, join.

diverse *adj.* assorted, different, differing, discrete, disparate, dissimilar, distinct, divergent, diversified, heterogeneous, manifold, many, miscellaneous, multifarious, multiform, numerous, separate, several, some, sundry, unlike, varied, various, varying.
antonym identical.

diversify *v.* alter, assort, branch out, change, expand, mix, spread out, variegate, vary.

diversion *n.* alteration, amusement, beguilement, change, deflection, delight, departure, detour, deviation, digression, disportment, distraction, divertissement, enjoyment, entertainment, game, gratification, pastime, play, pleasure, recreation, relaxation, sport, variation.

divert *v.* amuse, avert, beguile, deflect, delight, detract, distract, entertain, gratify, hive off, recreate, redirect, regale, side-track, switch, tickle.
antonyms direct, irritate.

divide *v.* alienate, allocate, allot, apportion, arrange, bisect, break up, categorize, classify, cleave, cut, deal out, detach, disconnect, dispense, distribute, disunite, divvy, estrange, grade, group, part, partition, portion, segment, segregate, separate, sever, share, shear, sort, split, subdivide, sunder.
antonyms collect, gather, join.

divide out allocate, allot, apportion, dole out, measure out, morsel, parcel out, share, share out.

divine *adj.* angelic, beatific, beautiful, blissful, celestial, consecrated, exalted, excellent, glorious, godlike, heavenly, holy, marvelous, mystical, perfect, rapturous, religious, sacred, sanctified, spiritual, splendid, superhuman, superlative, supernatural, supreme, transcendent, transcendental, transmundane, wonderful.
n. churchman, clergyman, cleric, ecclesiastic, minister, parson, pastor, prelate, priest, reverend.
v. apprehend, conjecture, deduce, foretell, guess, hariolate, haruspicate, infer, intuit, perceive, prognosticate, suppose, surmise, suspect, understand.

division *n.* allotment, apportionment, bisection, border, boundary, branch, breach, category, class, compartment, cutting, demarcation, department, detaching, dichotomy, disagreement, discord, distribution, disunion, divide, divider, dividing, estrangement, feud, group, head, part, partition, portion, rupture, schism, scission, section, sector, segment, separation, sept, sharing, side, split, splitting, stream, variance, wapentake, ward, watershed, wing.
antonyms agreement, multiplication, unification.

divorce *n.* annulment, breach, break, break-up, decree nisi, diffarreation, dissolution, disunion, rupture, separation, severance, split-up.
v. annul, cancel, disconnect, dissever, dissociate, dissolve, disunite, divide, part, separate, sever, split up, sunder.
antonyms marry, unify.

divulge *v.* betray, broadcast, communicate, confess, declare, disclose, evulgate, exhibit, expose, impart, leak, let slip, proclaim, promulgate, publish, reveal, spill, tell, uncover.

dizzy *adj.* befuddled, bemused, bewildered, capricious, confused, dazed, dazzled, faint, fickle, flighty, foolish, frivolous, giddy, light-headed, lofty, muddled, reeling, scatterbrained, shaky, staggering, steep, swimming, vertiginous, wobbly, woozy.

do *v.* accomplish, achieve, act, adapt, answer, arrange, behave, carry out, cause, cheat, complete, con, conclude, cover, cozen, create, deceive, decipher, decode, defraud, discharge, dupe, effect, end, execute, explore, fare, fix, fleece, give, hoax, implement, make, manage, organize, pass muster, perform, prepare, present, proceed, produce, put on, render, resolve, satisfy, serve, solve, suffice, suit, swindle, tour, transact, translate, transpose, travel, trick, undertake, visit, work, work out.
n. affair, event, function, gathering, occasion, party.

docile *adj.* amenable, biddable, complaisant, compliant, ductile, manageable, obedient, obliging, pliable, pliant, submissive, teachable, tractable, unmurmuring, unprotesting, unquestioning.
antonyms truculent, unco-operative.

dock[1] *n.* boat-yard, harbor, marina, pier, quay, waterfront, wharf.

v. anchor, berth, drop anchor, join up, land, link up, moor, put in, rendezvous, tie up, unite.

dock[2] *v.* clip, crop, curtail, cut, decaudate, decrease, deduct, diminish, lessen, reduce, shorten, subtract, truncate, withhold.

doctor *n.* clinician, doctoress, doctress, general practitioner, GP, hakim, internist, leech, medic, medical officer, medical practitioner, medicaster, medico, physician, pill(s).

v. adulterate, alter, botch, change, cobble, cook, cut, dilute, disguise, falsify, fix, fudge, hocus, load, medicate, mend, misrepresent, patch, pervert, repair, spike, tamper with, treat.

doctrine *n.* belief, canon, concept, conviction, creed, dogma, ism, opinion, precept, principle, teaching, tenet.

document *n.* certificate, chirograph, deed, form, instrument, paper, parchment, record, report.

v. authenticate, back, certify, cite, corroborate, detail, enumerate, instance, list, particularize, prove, substantiate, support, validate, verify.

dodge *v.* avoid, dart, deceive, duck, elude, equivocate, evade, fend off, fudge, hedge, parry, shift, shirk, shuffle, side-step, skive, swerve, swing the lead, trick.

n. chicane, contrivance, device, feint, machination, maneuver, ploy, ruse, scheme, stratagem, subterfuge, trick, wheeze, wile.

dogged *adj.* determined, firm, indefatigable, indomitable, obstinate, persevering, persistent, pertinacious, relentless, resolute, single-minded, staunch, steadfast, steady, stubborn, tenacious, unflagging, unshakable, unyielding.

antonym irresolute.

dogma *n.* article, article of faith, belief, conviction, credendum, credo, creed, doctrine, opinion, precept, principle, teaching, tenet.

dogmatic *adj.* affirmative, arbitrary, assertive, authoritative, canonical, categorical, dictatorial, didactic, doctrinaire, doctrinal, downright, emphatic, ex cathedra, high-dried, imperious, magisterial, obdurate, opinionated, oracular, overbearing, peremptory, pontific(al), positive.

doings *n.* actions, activities, acts, adventures, affairs, concerns, dealings, deeds, events, exploits, goings-on, handiwork, happenings, proceedings, transactions.

dole *n.* allocation, allotment, allowance, alms, apportionment, benefit, dispensation, dispersal, distribution, division, donation, gift, grant, gratuity, issuance, modicum, parcel, pittance, portion, quota, share.

doleful *adj.* blue, cheerless, depressing, dismal, distressing, dolorous, dreary, forlorn, funereal, gloomy, lugubrious, melancholy, mournful, painful, pathetic, pitiful, rueful, sad, somber, sorrowful, woebegone, woeful, wretched.

antonym cheerful.

dolt *n.* ass, beetlebrain, beetlehead, besom-head, blockhead, bonehead, booby, boodle, bufflehead, bull-calf, calf, chump, clod, clodhopper, clodpate, clodpoll, clot, clunk, dimwit, dope, dullard, dunce, fool, galoot, half-wit, idiot, ignoramus, leather-head, loggerhead, loghead, lurdan(e), lurden, mutt, mutton-head, nitwit, nutcase, palooka, sheep's-head, simpleton, turnip.

domain *n.* area, authority, bailiwick, business, concern, demesne, department, discipline, dominion, empire, estate, field, jurisdiction, kingdom, lands, orbit, pidgin, policies, power, province, realm, region, scope, specialty, sphere, sway, territory.

domestic *adj.* autochthonic, domal, domesticated, domiciliary, family, home, home-bred, home-loving, homely, house, household, house-trained, housewifely, indigenous, internal, native, pet, private, stay-at-home, tame, trained.

n. au pair, char, charwoman, daily, daily help, help, maid, scullery maid, servant, slavey, woman.

domesticate *v.* acclimatize, accustom, break, domesticize, familiarize, habituate, house-train, naturalize, tame, train.

domicile *n.* abode, dwelling, habitation, home, house, lodging(s), mansion, quarters, residence, residency, settlement.

dominate *v.* bestride, control, direct, domineer, dwarf, eclipse, govern, have the whip hand, keep under one's thumb, lead, master, monopolize, outshine, overbear, overgang, overlook, overrule, overshadow, predominate, prevail, rule, tyrannize.

domination *n.* ascendancy, authority, command, control, despotism, dictatorship, hegemony, influence, leadership, mastery, oppression, power, repression, rule, subjection, subordination, superiority, suppression, supremacy, sway, tyranny.

domineering *adj.* arrogant, authoritarian, autocratic, bossy, coercive, despotic, dictatorial, harsh, high-handed, imperious, iron-handed, magisterial, masterful, oppressive, overbearing, severe, tyrannical.

antonyms meek, obsequious, servile.

don *v.* affect, assume, clothe oneself in, dress in, get into, put on.

antonym doff.

donate *v.* bequeath, bestow, chip in, confer, contribute, cough up, fork out, gift, give, impart, present, proffer, subscribe.

donation *n.* alms, benefaction, boon, conferment, contribution, gift, grant, gratuity, largess(e), offering, present, presentation, subscription.

done *adj.* acceptable, accomplished, advised, agreed, completed, concluded, consummated, conventional, cooked, cooked to a turn, de rigueur, depleted, drained, ended, executed, exhausted, fatigued, finished, OK, over, perfected, proper, ready, realized, settled, spent, terminated, through, used up.

doom *n.* Armageddon, catastrophe, condemnation, death, death-knell, decision, decree, destiny, destruction, Doomsday, downfall, fate, fortune, judgment,

Judgment Day, karma, kismet, lot, portion, ruin, sentence, the Last Judgment, the last trump, verdict.
v. condemn, consign, damn, decree, destine, foredoom, foreordain, judge, predestine, preordain, sentence, threaten.

doomed *adj.* accursed, bedeviled, bewitched, condemned, cursed, fated, fey, hopeless, ill-fated, ill-omened, ill-starred, luckless, star-crossed.

dormant *adj.* asleep, comatose, fallow, hibernating, inactive, inert, inoperative, latent, latescent, quiescent, sleeping, sluggish, slumbering, suspended, torpid, undeveloped, unrealized.
antonyms active.

dose *n.* dosage, draught, drench, hit, measure, portion, potion, prescription, quantity, shot, slug.
v. administer, dispense, drench, medicate, treat.

doting *adj.* adoring, devoted, fond, foolish, indulgent, lovesick, soft.

double *adj.* bifarious, bifold, binate, coupled, diploid, doubled, dual, duple, duplex, duplicate, paired, twice, twin, twofold.
v. duplicate, enlarge, fold, geminate, grow, increase, magnify, multiply, repeat.
n. clone, copy, counterpart, dead ringer, dead spit, Doppelgänger, duplicate, fellow, image, impersonator, lookalike, mate, replica, ringer, spitting image, twin.

double-cross *v.* betray, cheat, con, cozen, defraud, hoodwink, mislead, swindle, trick, two-time.

double-dealer *n.* betrayer, cheat, con man, cozener, deceiver, dissembler, double-crosser, fraud, hypocrite, Machiavellian, rogue, swindler, traitor, two-timer.

doubt *v.* be dubious, be uncertain, demur, discredit, distrust, dubitate, fear, fluctuate, hesitate, misgive, mistrust, query, question, scruple, suspect, vacillate, waver.
antonyms believe, trust.
n. ambiguity, apprehension, arrière pensée, confusion, difficulty, dilemma, disquiet, distrust, dubiety, fear, hesitancy, hesitation, incredulity, indecision, irresolution, misgiving, mistrust, perplexity, problem, qualm, quandary, reservation, skepticism, suspense, suspicion, uncertainty, vacillation.
antonyms belief, certainty, confidence, trust.

doubtful *adj.* ambiguous, debatable, disreputable, distrustful, dubious, dubitable, equivocal, hazardous, hesitant, hesitating, inconclusive, indefinite, indeterminate, irresolute, litigious, obscure, perplexed, precarious, problematic, problematical, questionable, sceptical, shady, suspect, suspicious, tentative, uncertain, unclear, unconfirmed, unconvinced, undecided, unresolved, unsettled, unsure, vacillating, vague, wavering.
antonyms certain, definite.

doubtless *adv.* apparently, assuredly, certainly, clearly, indisputably, most likely, of course, ostensibly, out of question, precisely, presumably, probably, questionless,

seemingly, supposedly, surely, truly, undoubtedly, unquestionably, without doubt.

doughty *adj.* able, bold, brave, courageous, daring, dauntless, fearless, gallant, game, hardy, heroic, intrepid, redoubtable, resolute, stout-hearted, strong, valiant, valorous.
antonyms cowardly, weak.

douse, dowse *v.* blow out, dip, drench, duck, dunk, extinguish, immerge, immerse, plunge, put out, saturate, smother, snuff, soak, souse, steep, submerge.

dowdy *adj.* dingy, drab, frowzy, frumpish, frumpy, ill-dressed, old-fashioned, scrubby, shabby, slovenly, tacky, tatty, unfashionable, unmodish, unsmart.
antonyms dressy, smart, spruce.

downcast *adj.* cheerless, chopfallen, crestfallen, daunted, dejected, depressed, despondent, disappointed, disconsolate, discouraged, disheartened, dismayed, dispirited, down, miserable, sad, unhappy. *antonyms* cheerful, elated, happy.

downfall *n.* breakdown, cloudburst, collapse, comedown, come-uppance, debacle, deluge, descent, destruction, disgrace, downpour, failure, fall, humiliation, overthrow, rainstorm, ruin, undoing, Waterloo.

downgrade *v.* belittle, decry, degrade, demote, denigrate, detract from, disparage, humble, lower, reduce in rank, run down.
antonyms improve, upgrade.

downhearted *adj.* blue, chopfallen, crestfallen, dejected, depressed, despondent, discouraged, disheartened, dismayed, dispirited, downcast, gloomy, glum, jaw-fallen, low-spirited, sad, sorrowful, unhappy.
antonyms cheerful, enthusiastic, happy.

downpour *n.* cloudburst, deluge, downcome, flood, inundation, rainstorm, torrent, water-spout.

downright *adj.* absolute, blatant, blunt, candid, categorical, clear, complete, explicit, forthright, frank, honest, open, out-and-out, outright, outspoken, plain, positive, simple, sincere, straightforward, thoroughgoing, total, undisguised, unequivocal, unqualified, utter, wholesale.

dowry *n.* dot, dower, endowment, faculty, gift, inheritance, legacy, portion, provision, share, talent, wedding-dower.

drab *adj.* cheerless, colorless, dingy, dismal, dreary, dull, dun-colored, flat, gloomy, gray, lackluster, mousy, shabby, somber, uninspired, vapid.
antonym bright.

draft[1] *v.* compose, delineate, design, draw, draw up, formulate, outline, plan, sketch.
n. abstract, delineation, ébauche, outline, plan, protocol, rough, sketch, version.

draft[2] *n.* bill, check, order, postal order.

draft[3] *n.* cup, current, dose, dragging, drawing, drench, drink, flow, haulage, influx, movement, portion, potation, puff, pulling, quantity, traction.

drag *v.* crawl, creep, dawdle, draggle, draw, hale, harl, haul, inch, lag, linger, loiter, lug, pull, schlep, shamble, shuffle, straggle, sweep, tow, trail, tug, yank.

n. annoyance, bore, bother, brake, drogue, nuisance, pain, pest, pill.

drain *v.* bleed, consume, deplete, discharge, dissipate, down, draw off, drink up, dry, effuse, empty, emulge, evacuate, exhaust, exude, finish, flow out, lade, leak, milk, ooze, quaff, remove, sap, seep, strain, swallow, tap, tax, trickle, use up, weary, withdraw.

antonym fill.

n. channel, conduit, culvert, depletion, ditch, drag, duct, exhaustion, expenditure, grip, outlet, pipe, reduction, sap, sewer, sink, sough, stank, strain, trench, water-course, withdrawal.

drama *n.* acting, crisis, dramatics, dramatization, dramaturgy, excitement, histrionics, kabuki, kathakali, melodrama, play, scene, show, spectacle, stage-craft, theater, theatricals, Thespian art, turmoil.

dramatist *n.* comedian, dramaturge, dramaturgist, playwright, play-writer, screen-writer, scriptwriter, tragedian.

drape *v.* adorn, array, cloak, cover, dangle, droop, drop, enrap, fold, hang, suspend, swathe, vest, wrap.

drastic *adj.* desperate, dire, draconian, extreme, far-reaching, forceful, harsh, heroic, radical, severe, strong.

antonym mild.

draw[1] *v.* allure, attenuate, attract, borrow, breathe in, bring forth, choose, deduce, delineate, depict, derive, design, drag, drain, elicit, elongate, engage, entice, entrain, evoke, extend, extort, extract, get, haul, induce, infer, influence, inhale, inspire, invite, lengthen, make, map out, mark out, outline, paint, pencil, persuade, pick, portray, puff, pull, respire, select, sketch, stretch, suck, take, tow, trace, tug, unsheathe.

antonyms propel, push.

n. appeal, attraction, bait, enticement, interest, lure, pull.

draw[2] *v.* be equal, be even, be neck and neck, dead-heat, tie. *n.* dead-heat, deadlock, impasse, stalemate, tie.

drawback *n.* block, defect, deficiency, désagrément, detriment, difficulty, disability, disadvantage, fault, flaw, fly in the ointment, handicap, hindrance, hitch, impediment, imperfection, nuisance, obstacle, pull-back, snag, stumbling, trouble.

antonym advantage.

drawing *n.* cartoon, delineation, depiction, graphic, illustration, outline, picture, portrait, portrayal, representation, sketch, study.

drawn *adj.* fatigued, fraught, haggard, harassed, harrowed, hassled, pinched, sapped, strained, stressed, taut, tense, tired, worn.

dread *v.* cringe at, fear, flinch, quail, shrink from, shudder, shy, tremble.

n. alarm, apprehension, aversion, awe, dismay, disquiet, fear, fright, funk, heebie-jeebies, horror, misgiving, terror, trepidation, worry.

antonyms confidence, security.

adj. alarming, awe-inspiring, awful, dire, dreaded, dreadful, frightening, frightful, ghastly, grisly, gruesome, horrible, terrible, terrifying.

dreadful *adj.* alarming, appalling, awful, dire, distressing, fearful, formidable, frightful, ghastly, grievous, grisly, gruesome, harrowing, hideous, horrendous, horrible, monstrous, shocking, terrible, tragic, tremendous.

antonym comforting.

dream *n.* ambition, aspiration, beauty, castle in Spain, castle in the air, daydream, delight, delusion, design, desire, fantasy, goal, hallucination, hope, illusion, imagination, joy, marvel, notion, phantasm, pipe-dream, pleasure, reverie, speculation, trance, treasure, vagary, vision, wish.

v. conjure, daydream, envisage, fancy, fantasize, hallucinate, imagine, muse, star-gaze, think, visualize.

dreamer *n.* daydreamer, Don Quixote, fantasist, fantasizer, fantast, idealist, John o'dreams, Johnny-head-in-the-air, romancer, star-gazer, theorizer, utopian, visionary, Walter Mitty, wool-gatherer.

antonyms pragmatist, realist.

dreary *adj.* bleak, boring, cheerless, colorless, comfortless, commonplace, depressing, dismal, doleful, downcast, drab, drear, dreich, dull, forlorn, gloomy, glum, humdrum, joyless, lifeless, lonely, lonesome, melancholy, monotonous, mournful, routine, sad, solitary, somber, sorrowful, tedious, trite, uneventful, uninteresting, wearisome, wretched.

antonyms bright, interesting.

dregs *n.* canaille, deposit, draff, dross, excrement, faeces, fag-end, fecula, grounds, lags, lees, left-overs, mother, outcasts, rabble, residue, residuum, riff-raff, scourings, scum, sediment, tailings, trash, waste.

drench *v.* douse, drouk, drown, duck, flood, imbrue, imbue, immerse, inundate, saturate, soak, souse, steep, wet.

dress *n.* apparel, attire, caparison, clothes, clothing, costume, ensemble, frock, garb, garment, garments, gear, getup, gown, guise, habiliments, habit, outfit, raiment, rigout, robe, suit, togs, vestment.

v. accouter, adjust, adorn, align, apparel, arrange, array, attire, bandage, bedeck, bedizen, betrim, bind up, boun, busk, caparison, change, clothe, deck, decorate, dispose, don, drape, embellish, fit, furbish, garb, garnish, groom, habilitate, habit, ornament, plaster, prepare, put on, rig, robe, set, straighten, tend, treat, trim.

antonyms disrobe, strip, undress.

dressing *n.* bandage, compress, emplastron, emplastrum, ligature, pad, plaster, pledget, poultice, spica, tourniquet.

dressy *adj.* classy, elaborate, elegant, formal, natty, ornate, ritzy, smart, stylish, swanky, swish.

antonyms dowdy, scruffy.

dribble *v.* drip, drivel, drool, drop, leak, ooze, run, saliva, seep, slaver, slobber, sprinkle, trickle.

n. drip, droplet, gobbet, leak, seepage, sprinkling, trickle.

drift *v.* accumulate, amass, coast, drive, float, freewheel, gather, meander, pile up, stray, waft, wander.

n. accumulation, aim, bank, course, current, design, direction, dune, flow, gist, heap, implication, import, impulse, intention, mass, meaning, mound, movement, object, pile, purport, ridge, rush, scope, significance, sweep, tendency, tenor, thrust, trend.

drifter *n.* beachcomber, hobo, intinerant, rolling stone, rover, swagman, tramp, vagabond, vagrant, wanderer.

drill[1] *v.* coach, discipline, exercise, instruct, practice, rehearse, teach, train, tutor.

n. coaching, discipline, exercise, instruction, practice, preparation, repetition, training, tuition.

drill[2] *v.* bore, penetrate, perforate, pierce, puncture, transpierce.

n. awl, bit, borer, gimlet.

drink *v.* absorb, bib, booze, carouse, down, drain, dram, gulp, guzzle, hit the bottle, imbibe, indulge, knock back, liquefy, liquor up, partake of, quaff, revel, sip, suck, sup, swallow, swig, swill, tank up, tipple, tope, toss off, wassail, water.

n. alcohol, ambrosia, beverage, bev(v)y, booze, deochandoris, dose, dram, draught, glass, gulp, hooch, liquid, liquor, noggin, plonk, potion, refreshment, sensation, sip, slug, snifter, snort, spirits, stiffener, suck, swallow, swig, swizzle, taste, the bottle, tickler, tiff, tipple, toss, tot.

drip *v.* dribble, drizzle, drop, exude, filter, plop, splash, sprinkle, trickle, weep.

n. dribble, dripping, drop, leak, milk-sop, ninny, softy, stillicide, trickle, weakling, weed, wet.

drive *v.* actuate, bear, coerce, compel, constrain, dash, dig, direct, force, goad, guide, hammer, handle, harass, herd, hurl, impel, manage, motivate, motor, oblige, operate, overburden, overwork, plunge, press, prod, propel, push, ram, ride, rush, send, sink, spur, stab, steer, task, tax, thrust, travel, urge.

n. action, advance, ambition, appeal, campaign, crusade, determination, effort, energy, enterprise, excursion, get-up-and-go, hurl, initiative, jaunt, journey, motivation, outing, pressure, push, ride, run, spin, surge, trip, turn, vigor, vim, zip.

drivel *n.* blathering, bunkum, eyewash, gibberish, gobbledegook, guff, gush, jive, mumbo-jumbo, nonsense, slush, stultiloquy, twaddle, waffle.

driver *n.* cabbie, cabman, charioteer, chauffeur, coachman, Jehu, motorist, trucker, vetturino, voiturier, wagoner.

droll *adj.* amusing, clownish, comic, comical, diverting, eccentric, entertaining, farcical, funny, humorous, jocular, laughable, ludicrous, pawky, quaint, ridiculous, risible, waggish, whimsical, witty.

drone *v.* bombilate, bombinate, buzz, chant, drawl, hum, intone, purr, thrum, vibrate, whirr.

n. buzz, chant, hum, murmuring, purr, thrum, vibration, whirr, whirring.

drool *v.* dote, dribble, drivel, enthuse, fondle, gloat, gush, rave, salivate, slaver, slobber, water at the mouth.

droop *v.* bend, dangle, decline, despond, diminish, drop, fade, faint, fall down, falter, flag, hang (down) sag, languish, lose heart, sink, slouch, slump, stoop, wilt, wither.

antonyms rise, straighten.

drop *n.* abyss, bead, bubble, chasm, cut, dab, dash, decline, declivity, decrease, descent, deterioration, downturn, drib, driblet, drip, droplet, fall, falling-off, glob, globule, globulet, goutte, gutta, lowering, mouthful, nip, pearl, pinch, plunge, precipice, reduction, shot, sip, slope, slump, spot, taste, tear, tot, trace, trickle.

v. abandon, cease, chuck, decline, depress, descend, desert, diminish, discontinue, disown, dive, dribble, drip, droop, fall, forsake, give up, jilt, kick, leave, lower, plummet, plunge, quit, reject, relinquish, remit, renounce, repudiate, sink, stop, terminate, throw over, trickle, tumble.

antonyms mount, rise.

drop-out *n.* Bohemian, deviant, dissenter, dissentient, hippie, loner, malcontent, non-conformist, rebel, renegade.

droppings *n.* dung, egesta, excrement, excreta, faeces, fumet, guano, manure, ordure, spraint, stools.

dross *n.* crust, debris, dregs, impurity, lees, recrement, refuse, remains, rubbish, scoria, scum, trash, waste.

drove *n.* collection, company, crowd, drift, flock, gathering, herd, horde, mob, multitude, press, swarm, throng.

drown *v.* deaden, deluge, drench, engulf, extinguish, flood, go under, immerse, inundate, muffle, obliterate, overcome, overpower, overwhelm, silence, sink, stifle, submerge, swallow up, swamp, wipe out.

drowsiness *n.* dopeyness, doziness, grogginess, lethargy, narcosis, oscitancy, sleepiness, sluggishness, somnolence, torpor.

drowsy *adj.* comatose, dazed, dopey, dozy, dreamy, drugged, heavy, lethargic, lulling, nodding, restful, sleepy, somniculous, somnolent, soothing, soporific, tired, torpid.

antonyms alert, awake.

drubbing *n.* beating, clobbering, defeat, flogging, hammering, licking, pounding, pummeling, thrashing, trouncing, walloping, whipping, whitewash.

drudge *n.* afterguard, devil, dogsbody, factotum, galleyslave, hack, jackal, lackey, maid-of-all-work, man-of-all-work, menial, scullion, servant, skivvy, slave, toiler, worker.

v. beaver, droil, grind, labor, moil, plod, plug away, slave, toil, work.

antonyms idle, laze.

drudgery *n.* chore, collar-work, donkey-work, drudgism, fag, faggery, grind, hack-work, labor, labor improbus, skivvying, slavery, slog, sweat, sweated labor, toil.

drug *n.* depressant, dope, kef, medicament, medication, medicine, Mickey, Mickey Finn, narcotic, opiate, physic, poison, potion, remedy, stimulant.

v. anesthetize, deaden, dope, dose, drench, knock out, load, medicate, numb, poison, stupefy, treat.

drug-addict *n.* acid head, dope-fiend, head, hop-head, hype, junkie, tripper.

drugged *adj.* comatose, doped, dopey, high, looped, spaced out, stoned, stupefied, tripping, turned on, zonked.

druggist *n.* apothecary, chemist, pharmacologist.

drunk *adj.* a peg too low, a sheet (three sheets) in the wind, bevvied, blind, blotto, bonkers, bottled, canned, cockeyed, corked, corny, drunken, fou, fuddled, half-seas-over, in liquor, inebriate, inebriated, intoxicated, legless, liquored, lit up, loaded, lushy, maggoty, maudlin, merry, moony, moppy, mops and brooms, mortal, muddled, nappy, obfuscated, paralytic, pickled, pie-eyed, pissed, pixilated, plastered, shickered, sloshed, soaked, sottish, soused, sowdrunk, sozzled, stewed, stoned, stotious, tanked up, temulent, tiddly, tight, tipsy, up the pole, well-oiled, wet.
antonym sober.

n. boozer, drunkard, inebriate, lush, soak, sot, toper, wino.

drunkard *n.* alcoholic, bacchant, carouser, dipsomaniac, drinker, drunk, lush, soak, sot, souse, sponge, tippler, toper, tosspot, wino.

dry *adj.* arid, barren, boring, cutting, cynical, deadpan, dehydrated, desiccated, dreary, dried up, droll, droughty, drouthy, dull, juiceless, keen, low-key, moistureless, monotonous, parched, pawky, plain, sapless, sarcastic, sec, secco, sharp, sly, tedious, thirsty, tiresome, torrid, uninteresting, waterless, withered, xeric.
antonyms interesting, sweet, wet.

v. dehumidify, dehydrate, desiccate, drain, exsiccate, harden, mummify, parch, sear, shrivel, welt, wilt, wither, wizen.
antonyms soak, wet.

dub *v.* bestow, call, christen, confer, denominate, designate, entitle, knight, label, name, nickname, style, tag, term.

dubious *adj.* ambiguous, debatable, doubtful, equivocal, fishy, hesitant, iffy, indefinite, indeterminate, obscure, problematical, questionable, shady, skeptical, speculative, suspect, suspicious, uncertain, unclear, unconvinced, undecided, undependable, unreliable, unsettled, unsure, untrustworthy, wavering.
antonyms certain, reliable, trustworthy.

duck[1] *v.* avoid, bend, bob, bow, crouch, dodge, drop, escape, evade, lower, shirk, shun, sidestep, squat, stoop.

duck[2] *v.* dip, dive, dook, douse, dunk, immerse, plunge, souse, submerge, wet.

duct *n.* blood, canal, channel, conduit, fistula, funnel, passage, pipe, tube, vas, vessel.

due *adj.* adequate, ample, appropriate, becoming, bounden, deserved, enough, expected, fit, fitting, in arrears, just, justified, mature, merited, obligatory, outstanding, owed, owing, payable, plenty of, proper, requisite, returnable, right, rightful, scheduled, sufficient, suitable, unpaid, well-earned.

n. birthright, come-uppance, deserts, merits, prerogative, privilege, right(s).

adv. dead, direct, directly, exactly, precisely, straight.

duel *n.* affair of honor, clash, competition, contest, duello, encounter, engagement, fight, monomachia, monomachy, rivalry, single combat, struggle.

v. battle, clash, compete, contend, contest, fight, rival, struggle, vie.

dues *n.* charge(s), contribution, fee, levy, subscription.

duffer *n.* blunderer, bonehead, booby, bungler, clod, clot, dolt, galoot, lubber, lummox, muff, oaf.

dull *adj.* apathetic, blank, blockish, blunt, blunted, Boeotian, boring, bovine, callous, cloudy, commonplace, corny, dead, dead-and-alive, dense, depressed, dim, dimwitted, dismal, doltish, drab, dreary, dry, dulled, edgeless, empty, faded, featureless, feeble, flat, gloomy, heavy, humdrum, inactive, indifferent, indistinct, insensible, insensitive, insipid, lackluster, leaden, lifeless, listless, monotonous, mopish, muffled, mumpish, murky, muted, opaque, overcast, passionless, pedestrian, plain, prosaic, run-of-the-mill, slack, sleepy, slow, sluggish, somber, stodgy, stolid, stultifying, stupid, subdued, subfusc, sullen, sunless, tame, tedious, thick, tiresome, toneless, torpid, turbid, uneventful, unexciting, unfunny, ungifted, unidea'd, unimaginative, unintelligent, uninteresting, unlively, unresponsive, unsharpened, unsunny, unsympathetic, untalented, vacuous, vapid.
antonyms alert, bright, clear, exciting, sharp.

v. allay, alleviate, assuage, blunt, cloud, dampen, darken, deject, depress, dim, discourage, disedge, dishearten, dispirit, fade, hebetate, lessen, mitigate, moderate, muffle, obscure, obtund, opiate, palliate, paralyze, rebate, relieve, sadden, soften, stain, stupefy, subdue, sully, tarnish.
antonyms brighten, sharpen, stimulate.

dullard *n.* blockhead, bonehead, chump, clod, clot, dimwit, dolt, dope, dummy, dunce, dunderhead, flat tire, idiot, ignoramus, imbecile, moron, nitwit, noodle, numskull, oaf, simpleton, vegetable.
antonym brain.

dumb *adj.* aphonic, aphonous, dense, dimwitted, dull, foolish, inarticulate, mum, mute, silent, soundless, speechless, stupid, thick, tongue-tied, unintelligent, voiceless, wordless.
antonym intelligent.

dum(b)founded *adj.* amazed, astonished, astounded, bewildered, bowled over, breathless, confounded, confused, dumb, flabbergasted, floored, knocked sideways, nonplused, overcome, overwhelmed, paralyzed, speechless, staggered, startled, stunned, taken aback, thrown, thunderstruck.

dump *v.* deposit, discharge, dispose of, ditch, drop, empty out, get rid of, jettison, let fall, offload, park, scrap, throw away, throw down, tip, unload.

n. coup, hole, hovel, joint, junk-yard, landhill, mess, midden, pigsty, rubbish-heap, rubbish-tip, shack, shanty, slum, tip.

dunce *n.* ass, blockhead, bonehead, dimwit, dolt, donkey, duffer, dullard, dunderhead, goose, half-wit, ignoramus, loggerhead, log-head, loon, moron, nincompoop, numskull, simpleton.

antonyms brain, intellectual.

dungeon *n.* cage, cell, donjon, lock-up, oubliette, pit, prison, vault.

dupe *n.* cat's-paw, fall guy, flat, geck, gull, instrument, mug, pawn, pigeon, puppet, push-over, sap, simpleton, sitter, soft mark, stooge, sucker, tool, victim.

v. bamboozle, beguile, cheat, con, cozen, deceive, defraud, delude, gammon, grift, gudgeon, gull, hoax, hoodwink, humbug, outwit, overreach, pigeon, rip off, swindle, trick.

duplicate *adj.* corresponding, geminate, identical, matched, matching, twin, twofold.

n. carbon copy, copy, facsimile, match, photocopy, Photostat®;, replica, reproduction, Xerox®;.

v. clone, copy, ditto, double, echo, geminate, photocopy, Photostat®;, repeat, replicate, reproduce, Xerox®;.

duplicity *n.* artifice, chicanery, deceit, deception, dishonesty, dissimulation, double-dealing, falsehood, fraud, guile, hypocrisy, mendacity, perfidy, treachery.

durability *n.* constancy, durableness, endurance, imperishability, lastingness, longevity, permanence, persistence, stability, strength.

antonyms fragility, impermanence, weakness.

durable *adj.* abiding, constant, dependable, enduring, fast, firm, fixed, hard-wearing, lasting, long-lasting, perdurable, permanent, persistent, reliable, resistant, sound, stable, strong, sturdy, substantial, tough, unfading.

antonyms fragile, impermanent, perishable, weak.

duration *n.* continuance, continuation, extent, fullness, length, period, perpetuation, prolongation, span, spell, stretch, term-time.

antonym shortening.

duress *n.* bullying, captivity, coaction, coercion, compulsion, confinement, constraint, force, hardship, imprisonment, incarceration, pressure, restraint, threat.

dusky *adj.* caliginous, cloudy, crepuscular, dark, dark-hued, darkish, dim, fuliginous, gloomy, murky, obscure, overcast, sable, shadowy, shady, sooty, subfusc, swarthy, tenebr(i)ous, twilight, twilit, umbrose, veiled.

antonyms bright, light, white.

dusty *adj.* chalky, crumbly, dirty, filthy, friable, granular, grubby, powdery, pulverous, sandy, sooty, unswept.

antonyms clean, hard, polished, solid.

dutiful *adj.* acquiescent, complaisant, compliant, conscientious, deferential, devoted, docile, duteous, filial, obedient, punctilious, regardful, respectful, reverential, submissive.

duty *n.* allegiance, assignment, business, calling, charge, chore, customs, debt, deference, devoir, due, engagement, excise, function, impost, job, levy, loyalty, mission, obedience, obligation, office, onus, province, respect, responsibility, reverence, role, service, tariff, task, tax, toll, work.

dwarf *n.* droich, durgan, elf, gnome, goblin, homuncle, homuncule, homunculus, hop-o'-my-thumb, Lilliputian, manikin, midget, pygmy, Tom Thumb.

adj. baby, bonsai, diminutive, dwarfed, dwarfish, Lilliputian, mini, miniature, petite, pint-size(d), pocket, small, tiny, undersized.

antonym large.

v. check, dim, diminish, dominate, lower, minimize, overshadow, retard, stunt.

dwell *v.* abide, bide, hang out, inhabit, live, lodge, people, populate, quarter, remain, reside, rest, settle, sojourn, stay, stop, tenant.

dwelling *n.* abode, domicile, dwelling-house, establishment, habitation, home, house, lodge, lodging, quarters, residence, tent, tepee.

dwindle *v.* abate, contract, decay, decline, decrease, die, die out, diminish, disappear, ebb, fade, fall, lessen, peter out, pine, shrink, shrivel, sink, subside, tail off, taper off, vanish, wane, waste away, weaken, wither.

antonym increase.

dying *adj.* at death's door, declining, disappearing, ebbing, expiring, fading, failing, final, going, in articulo mortis, in extremis, moribund, mortal, not long for this world, obsolescent, passing, perishing, sinking, vanishing.

antonyms coming, reviving.

dynamic *adj.* active, driving, electric, energetic, forceful, go-ahead, go-getting, high-powered, lively, powerful, self-starting, spirited, vigorous, vital, zippy.

antonyms apathetic, inactive, slow.

E

eager *adj.* agog, anxious, ardent, athirst, avid, desirous, earnest, empressé, enthusiastic, fervent, fervid, fervorous, freck, greedy, gung-ho, hot, hungry, impatient, intent, keen, longing, perfervid, raring, unshrinking, vehement, yearning, zealous.
antonyms apathetic, unenthusiastic.

early *adj.* advanced, forward, matutinal, matutine, prehistoric, premature, primeval, primitive, primordial, undeveloped, untimely, young.
adv. ahead of time, beforehand, betimes, in advance, in good time, prematurely, too soon.
antonym late.

earmark *v.* allocate, designate, keep back, label, put aside, reserve, set aside, tag.

earn *v.* acquire, attain, bring in, collect, deserve, draw, gain, get, gross, make, merit, net, obtain, procure, rate, realize, reap, receive, warrant, win.
antonyms lose, spend.

earnest *adj.* ardent, close, constant, determined, devoted, eager, enthusiastic, fervent, fervid, firm, fixed, grave, heartfelt, impassioned, intent, keen, passionate, purposeful, resolute, resolved, serious, sincere, solemn, stable, staid, steady, thoughtful, urgent, vehement, warm, zealous.
antonyms apathetic, flippant, unenthusiastic.
n. assurance, deposit, determination, down payment, guarantee, pledge, promise, resolution, security, seriousness, sincerity, token, truth.

earnings *n.* emoluments, gain, income, pay, proceeds, profits, receipts, remuneration, return, revenue, reward, salary, stipend, takings, wages.
antonyms expenses, outgoings.

earth[1] *n.* geosphere, globe, middle-earth, middle-world, Midgard, orb, planet, sphere, world.

earth[2] *n.* clay, clod, dirt, ground, humus, land, loam, mold, sod, soil, topsoil.

earthly *adj.* base, carnal, conceivable, earthern, feasible, fleshly, gross, human, imaginable, likely, low, material, materialistic, mortal, mundane, physical, possible, practical, profane, secular, sensual, slight, slightest, sordid, sublunar, sublunary, tellurian, telluric, temporal, terrene, terrestrial, vile, worldly.
antonyms heavenly, spiritual.

earthy *adj.* bawdy, blue, coarse, crude, down-to-earth, homely, indecorous, lusty, natural, raunchy, ribald, robust, rough, simple, uninhibited, unrefined, unsophisticated, vulgar.
antonyms cultured, refined.

ease *n.* affluence, aplomb, calmness, comfort, composure, content, contentment, deftness, dexterity, easiness, effortlessness, enjoyment, facileness, facility, flexibility, freedom, happiness, informality, insouciance, leisure, liberty, naturalness, nonchalance, peace, peace of mind, poise, quiet, quietude, readiness, relaxation, repose, rest, restfulness, serenity, simplicity, solace, tranquility, unaffectedness, unconstraint, unreservedness.
antonyms difficulty, discomfort.
v. abate, aid, allay, alleviate, appease, assist, assuage, calm, comfort, disburden, edge, expedite, facilitate, forward, further, guide, inch, lessen, lighten, maneuver, mitigate, moderate, mollify, pacify, palliate, quiet, relax, relent, relieve, simplify, slacken, slide, slip, smooth, solace, soothe, speed up, squeeze, steer, still, tranquilize.
antonyms hinder, retard, torment.

easily[1] *adv.* comfortably, effortlessly, facilely, readily, simply, smoothly, standing on one's head, with one arm tied behind one's back.
antonym laboriously.

easily[2] *adv.* absolutely, by far, certainly, clearly, definitely, doubtlessly, far and away, indisputably, indubitably, plainly, probably, simply, surely, undeniably, undoubtedly, unequivocally, unquestionably, well.

easy *adj.* a doddle, a piece of cake, a pushover, accommodating, affable, amenable, biddable, calm, carefree, casual, child's play, clear, comfortable, compliant, contented, cushy, docile, easeful, easy-going, effortless, facile, flexible, friendly, gentle, graceful, gracious, gullible, idiot-proof, indulgent, informal, leisurely, lenient, liberal, light, manageable, mild, moderate, natural, no bother, open, painless, peaceful, permissive, pleasant, pliant, quiet, relaxed, satisfied, serene, simple, smooth, soft, straightforward, submissive, suggestible, susceptible, temperate, tolerant, tractable, tranquil, trusting, unaffected, unburdensome, unceremonious, uncomplicated, unconstrained, undemanding, undisturbed, unexacting, unforced, unhurried, unlabored, unoppressive, unpretentious, untroubled, unworried, well-to-do, yielding.
antonyms demanding, difficult, fast, impossible, intolerant.

easy-going *adj.* amenable, calm, carefree, casual, complacent, easy, easy-osy, even-tempered, flexible, happy-go-lucky, indulgent, insouciant, laid-back, lenient, liberal, mild, moderate, nonchalant, permissive, placid, relaxed, serene, tolerant, unconcerned, uncritical, undemanding, unhurried, unworried.
antonyms fussy, intolerant.

eat *v.* banquet, break bread, chew, chop, consume,

corrode, crumble, decay, devour, dine, dissolve, erode, feed, grub, ingest, knock back, manducate, munch, pig, rot, scoff, swallow, wear away.

eavesdrop *v.* bug, earwig, listen in, monitor, overhear, snoop, spy, tap.

eavesdropper *n.* listener, monitor, snoop, snooper, spy.

ebb *v.* abate, decay, decline, decrease, degenerate, deteriorate, diminish, drop, dwindle, fade away, fall away, fall back, flag, flow back, go out, lessen, peter out, recede, reflow, retire, retreat, retrocede, shrink, sink, slacken, subside, wane, weaken, withdraw.
antonyms increase, rise.
n. decay, decline, decrease, degeneration, deterioration, diminution, drop, dwindling, ebb tide, flagging, lessening, low tide, low water, reflow, refluence, reflux, regression, retreat, retrocession, shrinkage, sinking, slackening, subsidence, wane, waning, weakening, withdrawal.
antonyms flow, increase, rising.

ebullient *adj.* boiling, breezy, bright, bubbling, buoyant, chirpy, effervescent, effusive, elated, enthusiastic, excited, exhilarated, exuberant, foaming, frothing, frothy, gushing, irrepressible, seething, vivacious, zestful.
antonyms apathetic, dull, lifeless.

eccentric *adj.* aberrant, abnormal, anomalous, bizarre, capricious, dotty, erratic, fey, freakish, fruity, idiosyncratic, irregular, nuts, nutty, odd, offbeat, outlandish, peculiar, queer, quirky, screwball, screwy, singular, spac(e)y, strange, uncommon, unconventional, way-out, weird, whimsical.
antonyms normal, sane.
n. case, character, crank, freak, fruit-cake, nonconformist, nut, nutter, oddball, oddity, queer fish, screwball, weirdie, weirdo.

eccentricity *n.* aberration, abnormality, anomaly, bizarreness, bizarrerie, caprice, capriciousness, foible, freakishness, idiosyncrasy, irregularity, nonconformity, oddity, outlandishness, peculiarity, queerness, quirk, singularity, strangeness, unconventionality, waywardness, weirdness, whimsicality.
antonyms normalcy, normality, ordinariness.

ecclesiastic(al) *adj.* church, churchly, churchy, clerical, divine, holy, pastoral, priestly, religious, spiritual, templar.

echelon *n.* degree, grade, level, place, position, rank, status, step, tier.

echo *v.* ape, copy, echoize, imitate, mimic, mirror, parallel, parrot, recall, reflect, reiterate, repeat, reproduce, resemble, resound, reverberate, ring, second.
n. allusion, answer, copy, evocation, hint, image, imitation, intimation, memory, mirror image, parallel, reflection, reiteration, reminder, repetition, reproduction, reverberation, suggestion, sympathy, trace.

eclectic *adj.* all-embracing, broad, catholic, comprehensive,

dilettantish, diverse, diversified, general, heterogeneous, liberal, many-sided, multifarious, selective, varied, wide-ranging.
antonyms narrow, one-sided.

eclipse *v.* blot out, cloud, darken, dim, dwarf, exceed, excel, extinguish, obscure, outdo, outshine, overshadow, shroud, surpass, transcend, veil.
n. darkening, decline, deliquium, diminution, dimming, extinction, failure, fall, loss, obscuration, occultation, overshadowing, shading.

economical *adj.* careful, cheap, cost-effective, economic, economizing, efficient, fair, frugal, inexpensive, labor-saving, low, low-priced, modest, prudent, reasonable, saving, scrimping, sparing, thrifty, time-saving.
antonyms expensive, uneconomical.

economize *v.* cut back, cut corners, husband, retrench, save, scrimp, tighten one's belt.
antonym squander.

economy *n.* frugality, frugalness, husbandry, parsimony, providence, prudence, restraint, retrenchment, saving, scrimping, sparingness, thrift, thriftiness.
antonym improvidence.

ecstasy *n.* bliss, delight, ecstasis, elation, enthusiasm, euphoria, exaltation, fervor, frenzy, joy, rapture, ravishment, rhapsody, seventh heaven, sublimation, trance, transport.
antonym torment.

ecstatic *adj.* blissful, delirious, elated, enraptured, enthusiastic, entranced, euphoric, exultant, fervent, frenzied, joyful, joyous, on cloud nine, over the moon, overjoyed, rapturous, rhapsodic, transported.
antonym downcast.

edge *n.* acuteness, advantage, animation, arris, ascendancy, bezel, bite, border, bound, boundary, brim, brink, cantle, contour, dominance, effectiveness, force, fringe, incisiveness, interest, keenness, lead, limit, line, lip, margin, outline, perimeter, periphery, point, pungency, rim, sharpness, side, sting, superiority, threshold, upper hand, urgency, verge, zest.
v. bind, border, creep, drib, ease, fringe, gravitate, hem, hone, inch, rim, shape, sharpen, sidle, steal, strop, trim, verge, whet, work, worm.

edgy *adj.* anxious, ill at ease, irascible, irritable, keyed-up, nervous, on edge, prickly, restive, tense, testy, touchy.
antonym calm.

edict *n.* act, command, decree, dictate, dictum, enactment, fiat, injunction, law, mandate, manifesto, order, ordinance, proclamation, pronouncement, pronunciamento, regulation, rescript, ruling, statute, ukase.

edifice *n.* building, construction, erection, structure.

edit *v.* adapt, annotate, assemble, blue-pencil, bowdlerize, censor, check, compose, condense, correct, emend, polish, rearrange, redact, reorder, rephrase, revise, rewrite, select.

educate *v.* catechize, civilize, coach, cultivate, develop, discipline, drill, edify, exercise, improve, indoctrinate, inform, instruct, learn, mature, rear, school, teach, train, tutor.

education *n.* breeding, civilization, coaching, cultivation, culture, development, discipline, drilling, edification, enlightenment, erudition, guidance, improvement, indoctrination, instruction, knowledge, nurture, scholarship, schooling, teaching, training, tuition, tutelage, tutoring.

eerie *adj.* awesome, chilling, creepy, eldritch, fearful, frightening, ghastly, ghostly, mysterious, scary, spectral, spine-chilling, spooky, strange, uncanny, unearthly, unnatural, weird.
antonyms natural, ordinary.

efface *v.* annihilate, blank out, blot out, blue-pencil, cancel, cross out, delete, destroy, dim, eliminate, eradicate, erase, excise, expunge, extirpate, humble, lower, obliterate, raze, remove, rub out, wipe out, withdraw.

effect *n.* action, aftermath, clout, conclusion, consequence, drift, éclat, effectiveness, efficacy, efficiency, enforcement, essence, event, execution, fact, force, fruit, impact, implementation, import, impression, influence, issue, meaning, operation, outcome, power, purport, purpose, reality, result, sense, significance, strength, tenor, upshot, use, validity, vigor, weight, work. *v.* accomplish, achieve, actuate, cause, complete, consummate, create, effectuate, execute, fulfil, initiate, make, perform, produce, wreak.

effective *adj.* able, active, adequate, capable, cogent, compelling, competent, convincing, current, effectual, efficacious, efficient, emphatic, energetic, forceful, forcible, implemental, impressive, moving, operative, perficient, persuasive, potent, powerful, productive, real, serviceable, striking, telling, useful.
antonyms ineffective, useless.

efficiency *n.* ability, adeptness, capability, competence, competency, economy, effectiveness, efficacy, mastery, power, productivity, proficiency, readiness, skilfulness, skill.
antonym inefficiency.

efficient *adj.* able, adept, businesslike, capable, competent, economic, effective, effectual, powerful, productive, proficient, ready, skilful, streamlined, well-conducted, well-ordered, well-organized, well-regulated, workmanlike.
antonym inefficient.

effort *n.* accomplishment, achievement, application, attempt, conatus, creation, deed, endeavor, energy, essay, exertion, feat, force, go, job, labor, molimen, nisus, pains, power, product, production, shot, stab, strain, stress, stretch, striving, struggle, toil, travail, trouble, try, work.

effortless *adj.* easy, facile, painless, simple, smooth, uncomplicated, undemanding, unlabored.
antonym difficult.

egg on coax, encourage, exhort, goad, incite, prick, prod, prompt, push, spur, stimulate, urge, wheedle.
antonym discourage.

egghead *n.* brain, Einstein, genius, headpiece, intellect, intellectual, scholar.

egoism *n.* amour-propre, egocentricity, egomania, egotism, narcissism, self-absorption, self-centeredness, self-importance, self-interest, selfishness, self-love, self-regard, self-seeking.
antonym altruism.

eject *v.* banish, belch, boot out, bounce, deport, discharge, disgorge, dislodge, dismiss, dispossess, drive out, emit, evacuate, evict, exile, expel, fire, kick out, oust, remove, sack, spew, spout, throw out, turn out, unhouse, vomit.

elaborate *adj.* careful, complex, complicated, daedal(ic), decorated, dedal(ian), detailed, exact, extravagant, fancy, fussy, intricate, involved, labored, minute, ornamental, ornate, ostentatious, painstaking, perfected, precise, showy, skilful, studied, thorough.
antonyms plain, simple.
v. amplify, complicate, decorate, detail, develop, devise, embellish, enhance, enlarge, expand, expatiate, explain, flesh out, garnish, improve, ornament, polish, refine.
antonyms précis, simplify.

elapse *v.* go by, lapse, pass, slip away.

elastic *adj.* accommodating, adaptable, adjustable, bouncy, buoyant, complaisant, compliant, distensible, ductile, flexible, irrepressible, plastic, pliable, pliant, resilient, rubbery, springy, stretchable, stretchy, supple, tolerant, variable, yielding.
antonym rigid.

elated *adj.* animated, blissful, cheered, delighted, ecstatic, euphoric, excited, exhilarated, exultant, gleeful, joyful, joyous, jubilant, on the high ropes, over the moon, overjoyed, pleased, proud, roused.
antonym downcast.

elder *adj.* aîné(e), ancient, eigne, first-born, older, senior.
antonym younger.
n. deacon, presbyter, senior.

elderly *adj.* aged, aging, badgerly, hoary, old, senile.
antonyms young, youthful.

elect *v.* adopt, appoint, choose, designate, determine, opt for, pick, prefer, select, vote.
adj. choice, chosen, designate, designated, elite, hand-picked, picked, preferred, presumptive, prospective, select, selected, to be.

electrify *v.* amaze, animate, astonish, astound, excite, fire, galvanize, invigorate, jolt, rouse, shock, stagger, startle, stimulate, stir, stun, thrill.
antonym bore.

elegant *adj.* à la mode, appropriate, apt, artistic, beautiful, chic, choice, clever, comely, concinnous, courtly, cultivated, debonair, delicate, effective, exquisite, fashionable, fine, genteel, graceful, handsome, ingenious,

luxurious, modish, neat, nice, polished, refined, simple, smooth, stylish, sumptuous, tasteful.
antonym inelegant.

elementary *adj.* basic, clear, easy, elemental, facile, fundamental, initial, introductory, original, plain, primary, principial, rudimentary, simple, straightforward, uncomplicated.
antonyms advanced, complex.

elevate *v.* advance, aggrandize, animate, augment, boost, brighten, buoy up, cheer, elate, exalt, excite, exhilarate, hearten, heighten, hoist, increase, intensify, lift, magnify, prefer, promote, raise, rouse, sublimate, swell, upgrade, uplift, upraise.
antonyms lessen, lower.

elfin *adj.* arch, charming, delicate, elfish, elflike, elvish, frolicsome, impish, mischievous, petite, playful, puckish, small, sprightly.

elicit *v.* cause, derive, draw out, educe, evoke, evolve, exact, extort, extract, fish, mole out, obtain, wrest, wring.

eligible *adj.* acceptable, appropriate, available, desirable, fit, proper, qualified, suitable, suited, worthy.
antonym ineligible.

eliminate *v.* annihilate, bump off, cut out, delete, dispense with, dispose of, disregard, do away with, drop, eject, eradicate, exclude, expel, expunge, exterminate, extinguish, get rid of, ignore, kill, knock out, liquidate, murder, omit, reject, remove, rub out, slay, stamp out, take out, terminate, waste.
antonym accept.

elite *n.* aristocracy, best, cream, crème de la crème, elect, establishment, flower, gentry, high society, meritocracy, nobility, pick.
adj. aristocratic, best, choice, crack, exclusive, first-class, noble, pick, selected, top, top-class, upper-class.
antonyms ordinary, run-of-the-mill.

elongated *adj.* extended, lengthened, long, prolonged, protracted, stretched.

elope *v.* abscond, bolt, decamp, disappear, do a bunk, escape, leave, run away, run off, slip away, steal away.

eloquent *adj.* articulate, Demosthenic, expressive, fluent, forceful, graceful, honeyed, meaningful, moving, persuasive, plausible, pregnant, revealing, silver-tongued, stirring, suggestive, telling, vivid, vocal, voluble, well-expressed.
antonyms inarticulate, tongue-tied.

elude *v.* avoid, baffle, beat, circumvent, confound, dodge, duck, escape, evade, flee, foil, frustrate, outrun, puzzle, shirk, shun, stump, thwart.

emaciated *adj.* atrophied, attenuate, attenuated, cadaverous, gaunt, haggard, lank, lean, meager, pinched, scrawny, skeletal, tabefied, tabescent, thin, wasted.
antonyms plump, well-fed.

emancipate *v.* deliver, discharge, disencumber, disenthral, enfranchise, free, liberate, manumit, release, set free, unbind, unchain, unfetter, unshackle.
antonym enslave.

embankment *n.* bund, causeway, causey, defenses, earthwork, levee, rampart.

embargo *n.* ban, bar, barrier, blockage, check, hindrance, impediment, interdict, interdiction, prohibition, proscription, restraint, restriction, seizure, stoppage.
v. ban, bar, block, check, embar, impede, interdict, prohibit, proscribe, restrict, seize, stop.
antonym allow.

embark *v.* board ship, emplane, entrain, take ship.
antonym disembark.

embarrass *v.* abash, chagrin, confuse, discomfit, discomfort, discompose, disconcert, discountenance, distress, fluster, mortify, shame, show up.

embassy *n.* consulate, delegation, deputation, embassade, embassage, legation, mission.

embed *v.* fix, imbed, implant, insert, plant, root, set, sink.

embellish *v.* adorn, beautify, bedeck, deck, decorate, dress up, elaborate, embroider, enhance, enrich, exaggerate, festoon, garnish, gild, grace, ornament, trim, varnish.
antonyms denude, simplify.

embezzle *v.* abstract, appropriate, defalcate, filch, misapply, misappropriate, misuse, peculate, pilfer, pinch, purloin, steal, sting.

embitter *v.* acerbate, aggravate, alienate, anger, disaffect, disillusion, empoison, envenom, exacerbate, exasperate, poison, sour, worsen.
antonym pacify.

emblem *n.* badge, crest, device, figure, ichthys, image, insignia, mark, representation, sigil, sign, symbol, token, type.

embody *v.* codify, collect, combine, comprehend, comprise, concentrate, concretize, consolidate, contain, encarnalize, exemplify, express, incarnate, include, incorporate, integrate, manifest, organize, personify, realize, reify, represent, stand for, symbolize, systematize, typify.

embrace *v.* accept, canoodle, clasp, complect, comprehend, comprise, contain, cover, cuddle, dally, embody, embosom, encircle, enclose, encompass, enfold, enlace, espouse, grab, grasp, halse, hold, hug, inarm, include, incorporate, involve, neck, receive, seize, snog, squeeze, subsume, take up, welcome.
n. accolade, clasp, clinch, cuddle, hug, squeeze.

embroidery *n.* fancywork, needle-point, needlework, sewing, tapestry, tatting.

embroil *v.* confound, confuse, distract, disturb, encumber, enmesh, ensnare, entangle, implicate, incriminate, involve, mire, mix up, muddle, perplex, trouble.

emerge *v.* appear, arise, crop up, debouch, develop, eclose, emanate, issue, materialize, proceed, rise, surface, transpire, turn up.
antonyms disappear, fade.

emergency *n.* crisis, crunch, danger, difficulty, exigency, extremity, necessity, pass, pinch, plight, predicament, quandary, scrape, strait.

adj. alternative, back-up, extra, fall-back, reserve, spare, substitute.

eminent *adj.* august, celebrated, conspicuous, distinguished, elevated, esteemed, exalted, famous, grand, great, high, high-ranking, illustrious, important, notable, noted, noteworthy, outstanding, paramount, pre-eminent, prestigious, prominent, renowned, reputable, respected, revered, signal, superior, well-known. *antonyms* unimportant, unknown.

emissary *n.* agent, ambassador, courier, delegate, deputy, envoy, herald, legate, messenger, nuncio, plenipotentiary, representative, scout, spy.

emit *v.* diffuse, discharge, eject, emanate, exhale, exude, give off, give out, issue, radiate, shed, vent. *antonym* absorb.

emotion *n.* affect, agitation, ardor, excitement, feeling, fervor, passion, perturbation, reaction, sensation, sentiment, vehemence, warmth.

emotional *adj.* affecting, ardent, demonstrative, emotive, enthusiastic, excitable, exciting, feeling, fervent, fervid, fiery, heart-warming, heated, hot-blooded, impassioned, moved, moving, overcharged, passionate, pathetic, poignant, responsive, roused, sensitive, sentimental, stirred, stirring, susceptible, tear-jerking, temperamental, tempestuous, tender, thrilling, touching, volcanic, warm, zealous. *antonyms* calm, cold, detached, emotionless, unemotional.

emphasis *n.* accent, accentuation, attention, force, import, importance, impressiveness, insistence, intensity, mark, moment, positiveness, power, pre-eminence, priority, prominence, significance, strength, stress, underscoring, urgency, weight.

emphatic *adj.* absolute, categorical, certain, decided, definite, direct, distinct, earnest, energetic, forceful, forcible, graphic, important, impressive, insistent, marked, momentous, positive, powerful, pronounced, punctuated, resounding, significant, striking, strong, telling, trenchant, unequivocal, unmistakable, vigorous, vivid. *antonyms* quiet, understated, unemphatic.

employ *v.* apply, apprentice, bring to bear, commission, engage, enlist, exercise, exert, fill, hire, indent(ure), occupy, ply, retain, spend, take on, take up, use, utilize. *n.* employment, hire, pay, service.

employee *n.* hand, job-holder, member of staff, staffer, wage-earner, worker, workman.

employer *n.* boss, business, company, establishment, firm, gaffer, organization, outfit, owner, padrone, patron, proprietor, taskmaster, workmaster, workmistress.

employment *n.* application, avocation, business, calling, craft, employ, engagement, enlistment, errand, exercise, exercitation, exertion, hire, job, line, métier, occupation, profession, pursuit, service, trade, use, utilization, vocation, work. *antonym* unemployment.

empower *v.* accredit, allow, authorize, commission, delegate, enable, enfranchise, entitle, license, permit, qualify, sanction, warrant.

empty *adj.* absent, aimless, banal, bare, blank, bootless, cheap, clear, deserted, desolate, destitute, expressionless, famished, frivolous, fruitless, futile, hollow, hungry, idle, inane, ineffective, insincere, insubstantial, meaningless, purposeless, ravenous, senseless, silly, starving, superficial, trivial, unfed, unfilled, unfrequented, unfurnished, uninhabited, unintelligent, unoccupied, unreal, unsatisfactory, unsubstantial, untenanted, vacant, vacuous, vain, valueless, viduous, void, waste, worthless. *antonyms* filled, full, replete. *v.* clear, consume, deplete, discharge, drain, dump, evacuate, exhaust, gut, lade, pour out, unburden, unload, vacate, void. *antonym* fill.

emulate *v.* challenge, compete with, contend with, copy, echo, follow, imitate, match, mimic, rival, vie with.

enable *v.* accredit, allow, authorize, capacitate, commission, empower, endue, equip, facilitate, fit, license, permit, prepare, qualify, sanction, warrant. *antonyms* inhibit, prevent.

enact *v.* act (out), authorize, command, decree, depict, establish, impersonate, legislate, ordain, order, pass, perform, personate, play, portray, proclaim, ratify, represent, sanction. *antonym* repeal.

enchant *v.* becharm, beguile, bewitch, captivate, charm, delight, enamor, enrapture, enravish, ensorcell, enthral, fascinate, hypnotize, mesmerize, spellbind. *antonyms* bore, disenchant.

encircle *v.* begird, circle, circumscribe, compass, enclose, encompass, enfold, engird, engirdle, enlace, enring, envelop, environ, enwreathe, gird, girdle, hem in, ring, surround.

enclose *v.* bound, circumscribe, compass, comprehend, confine, contain, cover, embale, embosom, embrace, encase, encircle, encompass, enlock, environ, fence, hedge, hem in, hold, inclose, include, incorporate, insert, pen, shut in, wall in, wrap.

encompass *v.* admit, begird, bring about, cause, circle, circumscribe, comprehend, comprise, contain, contrive, cover, devise, effect, embody, embrace, encircle, enclose, envelop, environ, girdle, hem in, hold, include, incorporate, involve, manage, ring, subsume, surround.

encounter *v.* chance upon, clash with, combat, come upon, confront, contend, cross swords with, engage, experience, face, fight, grapple with, happen on, meet, rencontre, rencounter, run across, run into, strive, struggle. *n.* action, battle, brush, clash, collision, combat, conflict, confrontation, contest, dispute, engagement, fight, meeting, rencontre, rencounter, run-in, set-to, skirmish.

encourage *v.* abet, advance, advocate, aid, animate, boost, buoy up, cheer, comfort, console, egg on, embolden, embrave, favor, forward, foster, further, hearten, help, incite, inspire, inspirit, promote, rally, reassure, rouse, second, spirit, spur, stimulate, strengthen, succor, support, urge.

antonyms depress, discourage, dissuade.

encroach *v.* appropriate, arrogate, impinge, infringe, intrude, invade, make inroads, muscle in, obtrude, overstep, trench, trespass, usurp.

encumber *v.* burden, clog, cramp, cumber, embarrass, hamper, handicap, hinder, impede, incommode, inconvenience, lumber, obstruct, oppress, overload, retard, saddle, slow down, trammel, weigh down.

end *n.* aim, annihilation, aspiration, attainment, bit, bound, boundary, butt, cessation, close, closure, completion, conclusion, consequence, consummation, culmination, curtain, death, demise, dénouement, design, destruction, dissolution, doom, downfall, drift, edge, ending, expiration, expiry, extent, extermination, extinction, extreme, extremity, finale, fine, finis, finish, fragment, goal, intent, intention, issue, left-over, limit, object, objective, outcome, part, pay-off, piece, point, portion, purpose, reason, remainder, remnant, resolution, responsibility, result, ruin, ruination, scrap, share, side, stop, stub, telos, termination, terminus, tip, upshot, wind-up.

antonyms beginning, opening, start.

v. abate, abolish, annihilate, cease, close, complete, conclude, culminate, destroy, dissolve, expire, exterminate, extinguish, fetch up, finish, resolve, ruin, sopite, stop, terminate, wind up.

antonyms begin, start.

endanger *v.* compromise, expose, hazard, imperil, jeopardize, risk, threaten.

antonyms protect, shelter, shield.

endearing *adj.* adorable, attractive, captivating, charming, delightful, enchanting, engaging, lovable, sweet, winning, winsome.

endeavor *n.* aim, attempt, conatus, crack, effort, enterprise, essay, go, nisus, shot, stab, trial, try, undertaking, venture.

v. aim, aspire, attempt, essay, labor, strive, struggle, take pains, try, undertake, venture.

endless *adj.* boundless, ceaseless, constant, continual, continuous, eternal, everlasting, immortal, incessant, infinite, interminable, interminate, limitless, measureless, monotonous, overlong, perpetual, Sisyphean, termless, unbounded, unbroken, undivided, undying, unending, uninterrupted, unlimited, whole.

endorse *v.* adopt, advocate, affirm, approve, authorize, back, champion, confirm, countenance, countersign, favor, indorse, ratify, recommend, sanction, sign, subscribe to, superscribe, support, sustain, undersign, vouch for, warrant.

antonyms denounce, disapprove.

endow *v.* award, bequeath, bestow, confer, donate, dower, endue, enrich, favor, finance, fund, furnish, give, grant, invest, leave, make over, present, provide, settle on, supply, will.

antonym divest.

endowment *n.* ability, aptitude, attribute, award, benefaction, bequest, bestowal, boon, capability, capacity, donation, dotation, dowry, faculty, flair, fund, genius, gift, grant, income, largesse, legacy, power, presentation, property, provision, qualification, quality, revenue, talent.

endure *v.* abear, abide, aby(e), allow, bear, brave, brook, continue, cope with, countenance, digest, experience, go through, hold, last, live, perdure, permit, persist, prevail, put up with, remain, stand, stay, stick, stomach, submit to, suffer, support, survive, sustain, swallow, thole, tolerate, undergo, weather, withstand.

antonyms cease, end.

enemy *n.* adversary, antagonist, competitor, foe, foeman, opponent, opposer, Philistine, rival, the opposition.

antonyms ally, friend.

energy *n.* activity, animation, ardor, brio, drive, efficiency, élan, exertion, fire, force, forcefulness, get-up-and-go, intensity, inworking, jism, juice, life, liveliness, pluck, power, spirit, stamina, steam, strength, strenuousness, verve, vigor, vim, vitality, vivacity, vroom, zeal, zest, zip.

antonyms inertia, lethargy, weakness.

enervate *v.* debilitate, deplete, devitalize, enfeeble, exhaust, fatigue, incapacitate, paralyze, prostrate, sap, tire, unman, unnerve, weaken, wear out.

antonyms activate, energize.

enfold *v.* clasp, embrace, encircle, enclose, encompass, envelop, enwrap, fold, hold, hug, shroud, swathe, wimple, wrap (up).

enforce *v.* administer, apply, carry out, coact, coerce, compel, constrain, discharge, exact, execute, implement, impose, insist on, oblige, prosecute, reinforce, require, urge.

engage *v.* absorb, activate, affiance, agree, allure, apply, appoint, arrest, assail, attach, attack, attract, bespeak, betroth, bind, book, busy, captivate, catch, charm, charter, combat, commission, commit, contract, covenant, draw, embark, employ, enamor, enchant, encounter, energize, engross, enlist, enrol, enter, fascinate, fit, fix, gain, grip, guarantee, hire, interact, interconnect, interlock, involve, join, lease, meet, mesh, obligate, oblige, occupy, operate, partake, participate, pledge, practice, prearrange, preoccupy, promise, rent, reserve, retain, secure, take on, tie up, undertake, vouch, vow, win.

antonyms discharge, disengage, dismiss.

engaged *adj.* absorbed, affianced, betrothed, busy, committed, employed, engrossed, immersed, involved, occupied, pledged, preoccupied, promised, spoken for, tied up, unavailable.

engaging *adj.* agreeable, appealing, attractive, beguiling,

captivating, charming, enchanting, fascinating, fetching, likable, lovable, pleasant, pleasing, prepossessing, winning, winsome.
antonyms boring, loathsome.

engender *v.* beget, breed, bring about, cause, create, encourage, excite, father, foment, generate, give rise to, hatch, incite, induce, instigate, lead to, make, nurture, occasion, precipitate, procreate, produce, propagate, provoke, sire, spawn.

engineer *n.* architect, contriver, designer, deviser, driver, inventor, operator, originator, planner.
v. cause, concoct, contrive, control, create, devise, effect, encompass, finagle, machinate, manage, maneuver, manipulate, mastermind, originate, plan, plot, scheme, wangle.

engrave *v.* blaze, carve, chase, chisel, cut, embed, enchase, etch, fix, grave, impress, imprint, infix, ingrain, inscribe, lodge, mark, print.

engross *v.* absorb, arrest, corner, engage, engulf, fixate, hold, immerse, involve, monopolize, occupy, preoccupy, rivet.

engulf *v.* absorb, bury, consume, deluge, drown, encompass, engross, envelop, flood, immerse, ingulf, inundate, overrun, overwhelm, plunge, submerge, swallow up, swamp.

enhance *v.* amplify, augment, boost, complement, elevate, embellish, escalate, exalt, heighten, improve, increase, intensify, lift, magnify, raise, reinforce, strengthen, swell.
antonyms decrease, minimize.

enigma *n.* brain-teaser, conundrum, mystery, poser, problem, puzzle, riddle.

enigmatic *adj.* ambiguous, cryptic, Delphic, doubtful, enigmatical, equivocal, impenetrable, incomprehensible, indecipherable, inexplicable, inscrutable, mysterious, obscure, perplexing, puzzling, recondite, riddling, strange, uncertain, unfathomable, unintelligible.
antonyms simple, straightforward.

enjoy *v.* appreciate, delight in, dig, experience, have, like, make a meal of, own, possess, rejoice in, relish, revel in, savor, take pleasure in, use.
antonyms abhor, detest.

enjoyment *n.* advantage, amusement, benefit, comfort, delectation, delight, diversion, ease, entertainment, exercise, fun, gaiety, gladness, gratification, gusto, happiness, indulgence, jollity, joy, ownership, pleasure, possession, recreation, relish, satisfaction, use, zest.
antonyms displeasure, dissatisfaction.

enlarge *v.* add to, amplify, augment, blow up, broaden, descant, develop, diffuse, dilate, distend, elaborate, elongate, expand, expatiate, extend, greaten, grow, heighten, increase, inflate, intumesce, jumboize, lengthen, magnify, multiply, stretch, swell, wax, widen.
antonyms decrease, diminish, shrink.

enlighten *v.* advise, apprise, civilize, counsel, edify,

educate, illuminate, indoctrinate, inform, instruct, teach, undeceive.
antonyms confuse, puzzle.

enlist *v.* conscript, employ, engage, enrol, enter, gather, join (up), muster, obtain, procure, recruit, register, secure, sign up, volunteer.

enliven *v.* animate, brighten, buoy up, cheer (up), excite, exhilarate, fire, gladden, hearten, inspire, inspirit, invigorate, kindle, liven (up), pep up, perk up, quicken, rouse, spark, stimulate, vitalize, vivify, wake up.
antonyms subdue.

enmity *n.* acrimony, animosity, animus, antagonism, antipathy, aversion, bad blood, bitterness, feud, hate, hatred, hostility, ill-will, invidiousness, malevolence, malice, malignity, rancor, spite, venom.
antonyms amity, friendship.

enormity *n.* abomination, atrociousness, atrocity, crime, depravity, disgrace, evil, evilness, flagitiousness, heinousness, horror, iniquity, monstrosity, monstrousness, nefariousness, outrage, outrageousness, turpitude, viciousness, vileness, villainy, wickedness.
antonyms triviality, unimportance.

enormous *adj.* abominable, astronomic(al), atrocious, Brobdingnagian, colossal, cyclopean, depraved, disgraceful, evil, excessive, gargantuan, gigantic, gross, heinous, herculean, huge, hulking, immense, jumbo, leviathan, mammoth, massive, monstrous, mountainous, nefarious, odious, outrageous, prodigious, titanic, tremendous, vast, vasty, vicious, vile, villainous, wicked.
antonyms small, tiny.

enough *adj.* abundant, adequate, ample, enow, plenty, sufficient.
n. abundance, adequacy, plenitude, plenty, repletion, sufficiency.
adv. abundantly, adequately, amply, aplenty, enow, fairly, moderately, passably, reasonably, satisfactorily, sufficiently, tolerably.

enquiry, inquiry *n.* examination, exploration, inquest, inspection, investigation, probe, query, quest, question, research, scrutiny, search, study, survey.

enrage *v.* acerbate, aggravate, anger, exasperate, incense, incite, inflame, infuriate, irritate, madden, make someone's hackles rise, provoke.
antonyms calm, placate, soothe.

enrich *v.* adorn, aggrandize, ameliorate, augment, cultivate, decorate, develop, embellish, endow, enhance, fortify, grace, improve, ornament, prosper, refine, supplement.
antonym impoverish.

enrol(l) *v.* accept, admit, chronicle, empanel, engage, enlist, enregister, inscribe, join up, list, matriculate, note, record, recruit, register, sign on, sign up, take on.
antonyms leave, reject.

enshrine *v.* apotheosize, cherish, consecrate, dedicate, embalm, exalt, hallow, idolize, preserve, revere, sanctify, treasure.

ensign *n.* badge, banner, colors, flag, gonfalon, jack, oriflamme, pennant, pennon, standard, streamer.

enslave *v.* bind, conquer, dominate, enchain, enthrall, overcome, subject, subjugate, yoke.
antonyms emancipate, free.

ensue *v.* arise, attend, befall, derive, eventuate, flow, follow, happen, issue, proceed, result, stem, succeed, supervene, turn out, turn up.
antonym precede.

ensure *v.* certify, clinch, confirm, effect, guarantee, guard, insure, protect, safeguard, secure, warrant.

entangle *v.* ball, bewilder, catch, complicate, compromise, confuse, embroil, enlace, enmesh, ensnare, entoil, entrap, foul, implicate, involve, jumble, knot, mat, mix up, muddle, perplex, puzzle, ravel, snag, snare, snarl, tangle, trammel, trap, twist.
antonym disentangle.

entanglement *n.* complication, confusion, difficulty, embarrassment, ensnarement, entoilment, entrapment, imbroglio, involvement, jumble, knot, liaison, mesh, mess, mix-up, muddle, predicament, snare, snarl-up, tangle, tie, toils, trap.
antonym disentanglement.

enter *v.* arrive, begin, board, commence, embark upon, enlist, enrol, inscribe, insert, introduce, join, list, log, note, offer, participate, participate in, penetrate, pierce, present, proffer, record, register, set about, set down, sign up, start, submit, take down, take up, tender.
antonyms delete, issue, leave.

enterprise *n.* activity, adventure, adventurousness, alertness, audacity, boldness, business, company, concern, daring, dash, drive, eagerness, effort, emprise, endeavor, energy, enthusiasm, essay, establishment, firm, get-up-and-go, gumption, imagination, initiative, operation, plan, program, project, push, readiness, resource, resourcefulness, spirit, undertaking, venture, vigor, zeal.
antonyms apathy, inertia.

enterprising *adj.* active, adventurous, alert, ambitious, aspiring, audacious, bold, daring, dashing, eager, energetic, enthusiastic, go-ahead, imaginative, intrepid, keen, pushful, ready, resourceful, self-reliant, spirited, stirring, up-and-coming, venturesome, vigorous, zealous.
antonyms lethargic, unadventurous.

entertain *v.* accommodate, accourt, amuse, charm, cheer, cherish, conceive, consider, contemplate, countenance, delight, divert, fête, foster, harbor, hold, imagine, lodge, maintain, occupy, please, ponder, put up, recreate, regale, support, treat.
antonyms bore, reject.

enthral(l) *v.* beguile, captivate, charm, enchant, enrapture, enravish, entrance, fascinate, grip, hypnotize, intrigue, mesmerize, rivet, spellbind, thrill.
antonyms bore, weary.

enthusiasm *n.* ardor, avidity, craze, devotion, eagerness, earnestness, empressement, entraînement, estro, excitement, fad, fervor, frenzy, hobby, hobby-horse, interest, keenness, mania, oomph, passion, rage, relish, spirit, vehemence, warmth, zeal, zest.
antonym apathy.

enthusiastic *adj.* ardent, avid, devoted, eager, earnest, ebullient, empressé, excited, exuberant, fervent, fervid, forceful, gung-ho, hearty, keen, keen as mustard, lively, passionate, spirited, unstinting, vehement, vigorous, warm, whole-hearted, zealous.
antonyms apathetic, reluctant, unenthusiastic.

entice *v.* allure, attract, beguile, blandish, cajole, coax, decoy, draw, induce, inveigle, lead on, lure, persuade, prevail on, seduce, sweet-talk, tempt, wheedle.

entire *adj.* absolute, all-in, complete, continuous, full, intact, integrated, outright, perfect, sound, thorough, total, unabridged, unbroken, uncut, undamaged, undiminished, undivided, unified, unmarked, unmarred, unmitigated, unreserved, unrestricted, whole.
antonyms impaired, incomplete, partial.

entirely *adv.* absolutely, altogether, completely, every inch, exclusively, fully, hook line and sinker, in toto, lock stock and barrel, only, perfectly, solely, thoroughly, totally, unreservedly, utterly, wholly, without exception, without reservation.
antonym partially.

entitle *v.* accredit, allow, authorize, call, christen, denominate, designate, dub, empower, enable, enfranchise, label, license, name, permit, style, term, title, warrant.

entourage *n.* associates, attendants, claque, companions, company, cortège, coterie, court, escort, followers, following, retainers, retinue, staff, suite, train.

entrance[1] *n.* access, admission, admittance, appearance, arrival, atrium, avenue, beginning, commencement, debut, door, doorway, entrée, entry, gate, ingress, initiation, inlet, introduction, opening, outset, passage, portal, start.
antonyms departure, exit.

entrance[2] *v.* bewitch, captivate, charm, delight, enchant, enrapture, enravish, enthrall, fascinate, gladden, hypnotize, magnetize, mesmerize, ravish, spellbind, transport.
antonyms bore, repel.

entreat *v.* appeal to, ask, beg, beseech, conjure, crave, enjoin, exhort, flagitate, implore, importune, invoke, petition, plead with, pray, request, sue, supplicate.

entreaty *n.* appeal, entreatment, exhortation, importunity, invocation, petition, plea, prayer, request, solicitation, suing, suit, supplication.

entrust *v.* assign, authorize, charge, commend, commit, confide, consign, delegate, deliver, depute, invest, trust, turn over.

enumerate *v.* calculate, cite, count, detail, itemize, list, mention, name, number, quote, recapitulate, recite, reckon, recount, rehearse, relate, specify, spell out, tell.

enunciate *v.* articulate, broadcast, declare, enounce, proclaim, promulgate, pronounce, propound, publish, say, sound, speak, state, utter, vocalize, voice.

envelop *v.* blanket, cloak, conceal, cover, embrace, encase, encircle, enclose, encompass, enfold, engulf, enshroud, enwrap, enwreathe, hide, obscure, sheathe, shroud, surround, swaddle, swathe, veil, wrap.

environment *n.* ambience, atmosphere, background, conditions, context, domain, element, entourage, habitat, locale, medium, milieu, scene, setting, situation, surroundings, territory.

envisage *v.* anticipate, conceive of, conceptualize, contemplate, envision, fancy, foresee, ideate, image, imagine, picture, preconceive, predict, see, visualize.

envoy *n.* agent, ambassador, courier, delegate, deputy, diplomat, elchi, emissary, intermediary, legate, messenger, minister, nuncio, plenipotentiary, representative.

envy *n.* covetousness, cupidity, dissatisfaction, enviousness, grudge, hatred, ill-will, jealousy, malice, malignity, resentfulness, resentment, spite.

v. begrudge, covet, crave, grudge, resent.

epicure *n.* arbiter elegantiae, bon vivant, bon viveur, connoisseur, epicurean, gastronome, glutton, gourmand, gourmet, hedonist, sensualist, sybarite, voluptuary.

epidemic *adj.* epizootic, general, pandemic, prevailing, prevalent, rampant, rife, sweeping, wide-ranging, widespread.

n. growth, outbreak, pandemic, plague, rash, spread, upsurge, wave.

episode *n.* adventure, affaire, business, chapter, circumstance, event, experience, happening, incident, instalment, matter, occasion, occurrence, part, passage, scene, section.

epitomize *v.* abbreviate, abridge, abstract, compress, condense, contract, curtail, cut, embody, encapsulate, exemplify, illustrate, incarnate, personify, précis, reduce, represent, shorten, summarize, symbolize, typify.

antonyms elaborate, expand.

epoch *n.* age, date, epocha, era, period, time.

equal *adj.* able, adequate, alike, balanced, capable, commensurate, competent, corresponding, egalitarian, equable, equivalent, even, even-handed, evenly-balanced, evenly-matched, evenly-proportioned, fair, fifty-fifty, fit, identical, impartial, just, level-pegging, like, matched, proportionate, ready, regular, sufficient, suitable, symmetrical, tantamount, the same, unbiased, uniform, unvarying, up to.

antonyms different, inequitable, unequal.

n. brother, coequal, compeer, counterpart, equivalent, fellow, match, mate, parallel, peer, rival, twin.

v. balance, commeasure, correspond to, equalize, equate, even, level, match, parallel, rival, square with, tally with.

equanimity *n.* aplomb, calm, calmness, composure, coolness, equability, equableness, imperturbability, levelheadedness, peace, phlegm, placidity, poise, presence of mind, sang-froid, self-possession, serenity, steadiness, tranquility.

antonyms alarm, anxiety, discomposure.

equilibrium *n.* balance, calm, calmness, collectedness, composure, cool, coolness, counterpoise, equanimity, equipoise, equiponderance, evenness, poise, rest, self-possession, serenity, stability, steadiness, symmetry.

antonym imbalance.

equip *v.* accouter, arm, array, attire, bedight, deck out, dight, dress, endow, fit out, fit up, furnish, habilitate, kit out, outfit, prepare, provide, rig, stock, supply.

equipment *n.* accessories, accouterments, apparatus, appurtenances, baggage, equipage, furnishings, furniture, gear, graith, impedimenta, implements, material, matériel, muniments, outfit, paraphernalia, rig-out, stuff, supplies, tackle, things, tools, traps.

equitable *adj.* disinterested, dispassionate, due, ethical, even-handed, fair, fair-and-square, honest, impartial, just, legitimate, objective, proper, proportionate, reasonable, right, rightful, square, unbiased, unprejudiced.

antonyms inequitable, unfair.

equity *n.* disinterestedness, equality, equitableness, even-handedness, fair play, fair-mindedness, fairness, honesty, impartiality, integrity, justice, justness, objectivity, reasonableness, rectitude, righteousness, uprightness.

antonym inequity.

equivalent *adj.* alike, commensurate, comparable, convertible, correlative, correspondent, corresponding, equal, equipollent, equipotent, even, homologous, homotypal, homotypic, interchangeable, same, similar, substitutable, synonymous, tantamount, twin.

antonyms dissimilar, unlike.

n. correlative, correspondent, counterpart, equal, homologue, homotype, match, opposite number, parallel, peer, twin.

equivocal *adj.* ambiguous, ambivalent, casuistical, confusing, Delphic, doubtful, dubious, evasive, indefinite, indeterminate, misleading, oblique, obscure, oracular, questionable, suspicious, uncertain, vague.

antonyms clear, unequivocal.

equivocate *v.* dodge, evade, fence, fudge, hedge, mislead, palter, parry, prevaricate, pussyfoot, quibble, shift, shuffle, sidestep, tergiversate, weasel.

era *n.* age, century, cycle, date, day, days, eon, epoch, generation, period, stage, time.

eradicate *v.* abolish, annihilate, deracinate, destroy, efface, eliminate, erase, expunge, exterminate, extinguish, extirpate, get rid of, obliterate, raze, remove, root out, stamp out, suppress, unroot, uproot, weed out.

erase *v.* blot out, cancel, cleanse, delete, efface, eliminate, eradicate, expunge, get rid of, obliterate, remove, rub out.

erect *adj.* elevated, engorged, firm, hard, perpendicular, pricked, raised, rigid, standing, stiff, straight, taut, tense, tumescent, upright, upstanding, vertical.

antonyms limp, relaxed.

v. assemble, build, constitute, construct, create, elevate, establish, fabricate, form, found, initiate, institute, lift, mount, organize, pitch, put up, raise, rear, set up.

erection *n.* assembly, building, construction, creation, edifice, elevation, establishment, fabrication, manufacture, pile, raising, rigidity, stiffness, structure, tumescence.

erode *v.* abrade, consume, corrade, corrode, denude, destroy, deteriorate, disintegrate, eat away, grind down, spoil, wear away, wear down.

erotic *adj.* amatorial, amatorious, amatory, amorous, aphrodisiac, carnal, concupiscent, erogenic, erogenous, erotogenic, erotogenous, libidinous, lustful, rousing, seductive, sensual, sexy, stimulating, suggestive, titillating, venereal, voluptuous.

err *v.* blunder, deviate, fail, go astray, lapse, misapprehend, misbehave, miscalculate, misjudge, mistake, misunderstand, offend, sin, slip up, stray, stumble, transgress, trespass, trip up, wander.

errand *n.* assignment, charge, commission, duty, job, message, mission, task.

errant *adj.* aberrant, deviant, erring, itinerant, journeying, loose, nomadic, offending, peccant, peripatetic, rambling, roaming, roving, sinful, sinning, stray, straying, vagrant, wandering, wayward, wrong.

erratic *adj.* aberrant, abnormal, capricious, changeable, desultory, directionless, eccentric, fitful, fluctuating, inconsistent, inconstant, irregular, meandering, planetary, shifting, unpredictable, unreliable, unstable, variable, wandering, wayward.

antonyms consistent, reliable, stable, straight.

erroneous *adj.* amiss, fallacious, false, faulty, flawed, illogical, inaccurate, incorrect, inexact, invalid, mistaken, specious, spurious, unfounded, unsound, untrue, wrong.

antonym correct.

error *n.* barbarism, bêtise, bish, bloomer, blunder, boner, boob, corrigendum, delinquency, delusion, deviation, erratum, fallacy, fault, faux pas, flaw, gaucherie, howler, ignorance, ignoratio elenchi, illusion, inaccuracy, inexactitude, lapse, lapsus calami, lapsus linguae, lapsus memoriae, literal, malapropism, misapprehension, miscalculation, misconception, miscopy, miscorrection, misdeed, misprint, mistake, misunderstanding, mumpsimus, offence, omission, oversight, overslip, sin, slip, slip-up, solecism, transgression, trespass, wrong, wrongdoing.

erudite *adj.* academic, cultivated, cultured, educated, highbrow, knowledgeable, learned, lettered, literate,

profound, recondite, scholarly, scholastic, well-educated, well-read, wise.

antonym unlettered.

erupt *v.* belch, break, break out, burst, discharge, eruct, eructate, explode, flare, gush, rift, spew, spout, vent, vomit.

escalate *v.* accelerate, amplify, ascend, climb, enlarge, expand, extend, grow, heighten, increase, intensify, magnify, mount, raise, rise, spiral, step up.

antonym diminish.

antonym inevitable.

escapade *n.* adventure, antic, caper, doing, escapado, exploit, fling, fredaine, gest, lark, prank, romp, scrape, spree, stunt, trick.

escape *v.* abscond, avoid, baffle, bolt, break free, break loose, break off, break out, circumvent, decamp, discharge, do a bunk, dodge, drain, duck, elude, emanate, evade, flee, flit, flow, fly, foil, get away, gush, issue, leak, ooze, pass, pour forth, scape, scarper, seep, shake off, shun, skedaddle, skip, slip, slip away, spurt, take it on the run, take to one's heels, trickle, vamoose.

n. abscondence, avoidance, bolt, break, break-out, circumvention, decampment, discharge, distraction, diversion, drain, effluence, effluent, efflux, effluxion, elusion, emanation, emission, escapism, evasion, flight, flit, getaway, gush, jail-break, leak, leakage, meuse, out, outflow, outlet, outpour, pastime, recreation, relaxation, relief, safetyvalve, seepage, spurt, vent.

escort *n.* aide, attendant, beau, bodyguard, chaperon, cicisbeo, companion, company, convoy, cortège, entourage, gigolo, guard, guardian, guide, partner, pilot, procession, protection, protector, retinue, safeguard, squire, suite, train.

v. accompany, chaperon, chum, company, conduct, convoy, guard, guide, lead, partner, protect, shepherd, squire, usher.

especially *adv.* chiefly, conspicuously, eminently, exceedingly, exceptionally, exclusively, expressly, extraordinarily, mainly, markedly, notably, noticeably, outstandingly, particularly, passing, peculiarly, pre-eminently, principally, remarkably, signally, singularly, specially, specifically, strikingly, supremely, uncommonly, uniquely, unusually, very.

espousal *n.* adoption, advocacy, affiance, alliance, backing, betrothal, betrothing, bridal, championing, championship, defence, embracing, engagement, espousing, maintenance, marriage, matrimony, nuptials, plighting, spousal, support, wedding.

essay[1] *n.* article, assignment, commentary, composition, critique, discourse, disquisition, dissertation, essayette, leader, paper, piece, review, thesis, tract, treatise.

essay[2] *n.* attempt, bash, bid, crack, effort, endeavor, exertion, experiment, go, shot, stab, struggle, test, trial, try, undertaking, venture, whack, whirl.

v. attempt, endeavor, go for, have a bash, have a crack,

have a go, have a stab, strain, strive, struggle, tackle, take on, test, try, undertake.

essence *n.* alma, attar, attributes, being, center, character, characteristics, concentrate, core, crux, decoction, decocture, distillate, elixir, ens, entity, esse, extract, fragrance, haecceity, heart, hypostasis, inscape, kernel, life, lifeblood, marrow, meaning, nature, perfume, pith, principle, properties, qualities, quality, quiddit, quiddity, quintessence, scent, significance, soul, spirit, spirits, substance, tincture, virtuality, whatness.

essential[1] *adj.* absolute, basic, cardinal, characteristic, complete, constituent, constitutional, constitutive, crucial, definitive, elemental, elementary, formal, fundamental, ideal, important, indispensable, inherent, innate, intrinsic, key, main, necessary, needed, perfect, principal, quintessential, required, requisite, typical, vital.
antonym inessential.
n. basic, fundamental, must, necessary, necessity, prerequisite, principle, qualification, quality, requirement, requisite, rudiment, sine qua non.
antonym inessential.

essential[2] *adj.* concentrated, decocted, distilled, ethereal, extracted, pure, purified, rectified, refined, volatile.

establish *v.* affirm, attest to, authenticate, authorize, base, certify, confirm, constitute, corroborate, create, decree, demonstrate, enact, ensconce, entrench, fix, form, found, ground, implant, inaugurate, install, institute, introduce, invent, lodge, ordain, organize, plant, prove, radicate, ratify, root, sanction, seat, secure, set up, settle, show, start, station, substantiate, validate, verify.

esteem *v.* account, adjudge, admire, believe, calculate, cherish, consider, count, deem, estimate, hold, honor, include, judge, like, love, prize, rate, reckon, regard, regard highly, respect, revere, reverence, think, treasure, value, venerate, view.
n. account, admiration, consideration, count, credit, estimation, good opinion, honor, judgment, love, reckoning, regard, respect, reverence, veneration.

estimate *v.* appraise, approximate, assess, believe, calculate, compute, conjecture, consider, count, evaluate, gauge, guess, judge, number, opine, rank, rate, reckon, surmise, think, value.
n. appraisal, appraisement, approximation, assessment, belief, computation, conceit, conception, conjecture, estimation, evaluation, guess, guesstimate, judgment, opinion, reckoning, surmise, valuation.

estimation *n.* account, admiration, appraisal, appreciation, assessment, belief, calculation, computation, conception, consideration, credit, esteem, estimate, evaluation, good opinion, honor, judgment, opinion, rating, reckoning, regard, respect, reverence, veneration, view.

etch *v.* bite, burn, carve, corrode, cut, dig, engrave, furrow, grave, groove, hatch, impress, imprint, incise, ingrain, inscribe, stamp.

eternal *adj.* abiding, ceaseless, changeless, constant, deathless, durable, endless, enduring, eonian, eterne, everlasting, eviternal, illimitable, immortal, immutable, imperishable, incessant, indestructible, infinite, interminable, lasting, limitless, never-ending, perennial, permanent, perpetual, sempiternal, timeless, unbegotten, unceasing, unchanging, undying, unending, unextinguishable, unremitting.
antonyms changeable, ephemeral, temporary.

ethical *adj.* commendable, conscientious, correct, decent, fair, fitting, good, honest, honorable, just, meet, moral, noble, principled, proper, right, righteous, seemly, upright, virtuous.
antonym unethical.

etiquette *n.* ceremony, civility, code, convention, conventionalities, correctness, courtesy, customs, decency, decorum, formalities, manners, politeness, politesse, propriety, protocol, rules, seemliness, usage, use.

eulogy *n.* acclaim, acclamation, accolade, applause, commendation, compliment, encomium, exaltation, glorification, laud, laudation, laudatory, paean, panegyric, plaudit, praise, tribute.
antonym condemnation.

euphemism *n.* evasion, fig-leaf, genteelism, hypocorism, hypocorisma, polite term, politeness, substitution, under-statement.

euphoria *n.* bliss, buoyancy, cheerfulness, cloud nine, ecstasy, elation, enthusiasm, euphory, exaltation, exhilaration, exultation, glee, high, high spirits, intoxication, joy, joyousness, jubilation, rapture, transport.
antonym depression.

evacuate[1] *v.* abandon, clear, clear out, decamp, depart, desert, forsake, leave, quit, relinquish, remove, retire from, vacate, withdraw.

evacuate[2] *v.* defecate, discharge, eject, eliminate, empty, excrete, expel, purge, void.

evade *v.* avert, avoid, balk, blink, chicken out of, circumvent, cop out, decline, dodge, duck, elude, equivocate, escape, fence, fend off, fudge, hedge, parry, prevaricate, quibble, scrimshank, shirk, shun, sidestep, skive, steer clear of, temporize.
antonym face.

evaluate *v.* appraise, assay, assess, calculate, compute, estimate, gauge, judge, rank, rate, reckon, size up, value, weigh.

evaporate *v.* condense, dehydrate, dematerialize, desiccate, disappear, dispel, disperse, dissipate, dissolve, distil, dry, evanesce, exhale, fade, melt (away), vanish, vaporize, vapor.

evasive *adj.* ambiguous, cag(e)y, casuistic, casuistical, cunning, deceitful, deceptive, devious, disingenuous, dissembling, elusive, elusory, equivocating, indirect, misleading, oblique, prevaricating, secretive, shifty, shuffling, slippery, sophistical, tricky, unforthcoming, vacillating.
antonyms direct, frank.

even *adj.* abreast, alongside, balanced, calm, coequal, commensurate, comparable, complanate, composed, constant, cool, disinterested, dispassionate, drawn, equable, equal, equalized, equanimous, equitable, even-tempered, fair, fair and square, fifty-fifty, flat, fluent, flush, horizontal, identical, impartial, impassive, imperturbable, just, level, level-pegging, like, matching, metrical, monotonous, neck and neck, on a par, parallel, peaceful, placid, plane, plumb, proportionate, quits, regular, rhythmical, serene, side by side, similar, smooth, square, stable, steady, straight, symmetrical, tied, tranquil, true, unbiased, unbroken, undisturbed, unexcitable, unexcited, uniform, uninterrupted, unprejudiced, unruffled, unvarying, unwavering, well-balanced.
antonyms unequal, uneven.
adv. all the more, also, although, as well, at all, directly, exactly, hardly, including, just, much, scarcely, so much as, still, yet.
v. align, balance, equal, equalize, flatten, flush, level, match, regularize, regulate, smooth, square, stabilize, steady, straighten.

evening *n.* crepuscule, dusk, eve, even, eventide, forenight, gloaming, Hesper, Hesperus, nightfall, sundown, sunset, twilight, vesper.
adj. crepuscular, twilight, vesperal, vespertinal, vespertine.

event *n.* adventure, affair, bout, business, case, circumstance, competition, conclusion, consequence, contest, effect, end, engagement, episode, eventuality, experience, fact, game, happening, incident, issue, match, matter, milestone, occasion, occurrence, outcome, possibility, result, termination, tournament, upshot.

even-tempered *adj.* calm, composed, cool, cool-headed, equable, equanimous, impassive, imperturbable, level-headed, peaceable, peaceful, placid, serene, stable, steady, tranquil, unexcitable, unfussed, unruffled.
antonym excitable.

eventual *adj.* concluding, consequent, ensuing, final, future, impending, last, later, overall, planned, projected, prospective, resulting, subsequent, ultimate.

eventually *adv.* after all, at last, at length, finally, in one's own good time, sooner or later, subsequently, ultimately.

ever *adv.* always, at all, at all times, at any time, ceaselessly, constantly, continually, endlessly, eternally, everlastingly, evermore, for ever, in any case, in any circumstances, incessantly, on any account, perpetually, unceasingly, unendingly.

everlasting *adj.* abiding, boring, ceaseless, changeless, constant, continual, continuous, deathless, durable, endless, enduring, eternal, immarcescible, immortal, imperishable, incessant, indestructible, infinite, interminable, lasting, monotonous, never-ending, perdurable, permanent, perpetual, relentless, tedious, timeless, unceasing, unchanging, undying, unfading, uninterrupted, unremitting.
antonyms temporary, transient.

evermore *adv.* always, eternally, ever, ever after, for aye, for ever, for ever and a day, for ever and ever, henceforth, hereafter, in perpetuum, in saecula saeculorum, till doomsday, to the end of time, unceasingly.

everyday *adj.* accustomed, banal, boring, circadian, common, common-or-garden, commonplace, conventional, customary, daily, diurnal, dull, familiar, frequent, habitual, informal, monotonous, mundane, normal, ordinary, plain, prosaic, quotidian, regular, routine, run-of-the-mill, simple, stock, unexceptional, unimaginative, usual, wonted, workaday.
antonyms exceptional, special.

evict *v.* boot out, cast out, chuck out, defenestrate, dislodge, dispossess, disseize, eject, expel, expropriate, give the bum's rush, kick out, oust, put out, remove, show the door, turf out.

evidence *n.* affirmation, attestation, betrayal, confirmation, corroboration, data, declaration, demonstration, deposition, documentation, grounds, hint, indication, manifestation, mark, pledge, proof, sign, substantiation, suggestion, testimony, token, voucher, witness.
v. affirm, attest, betray, confirm, demonstrate, denote, display, establish, evince, exhibit, indicate, manifest, prove, reveal, show, signify, testify to, witness.

evident *adj.* apparent, clear, clear-cut, confessed, conspicuous, detectable, discernible, distinct, incontestable, incontrovertible, indisputable, manifest, noticeable, obvious, ostensible, palpable, patent, perceptible, plain, tangible, undeniable, unmistakable, visible.
antonym uncertain.

evil *adj.* adverse, bad, baleful, baneful, base, blackguardly, black-hearted, calamitous, catastrophic, corrupt, cruel, deadly, deleterious, depraved, destructive, detrimental, devilish, dire, disastrous, facinorous, flagitious, foul, ghastly, grim, harmful, heinous, hurtful, immoral, inauspicious, inimical, iniquitous, injurious, knavish, malefactory, malefic, maleficent, malevolent, malicious, malignant, mephitic, mischievous, miscreant, nefarious, nefast, nocuous, noisome, noxious, offensive, painful, perfidious, pernicious, pestiferous, pestilential, poisonous, putrid, reprobate, ruinous, sinful, sorrowful, ugly, unfortunate, unlucky, unpleasant, unspeakable, vicious, vile, villainous, wicked, woeful, wrong.
n. adversity, affliction, amiss, badness, bane, baseness, blow, calamity, catastrophe, corruption, curse, demonry, depravity, disaster, distress, facinorousness, flagitiousness, foulness, harm, heinousness, hurt, hydra, ill, immorality, impiety, improbity, iniquity, injury, knavery, maleficence, malignity, mischief, misery, misfortune, pain, perfidy, ruin, sin, sinfulness, sorrow, suffering, turpitude, ulcer, vice, viciousness, villainy, wickedness, woe, wrong, wrong-doing.

evoke *v.* activate, actuate, arouse, awaken, call, call forth, call up, conjure up, educe, elicit, excite, induce, invoke, produce, provoke, raise, recall, rekindle, stimulate, stir, summon, summon up.
antonyms quell, suppress.

evolve *v.* derive, descend, develop, disclose, elaborate, emerge, enlarge, expand, grow, increase, mature, progress, result, unravel.

exact *adj.* accurate, blow-by-blow, careful, close, correct, definite, detailed, explicit, express, factual, faithful, faultless, finical, finicky, flawless, identical, letter-perfect, literal, methodical, meticulous, nice, orderly, painstaking, particular, perfectionist, perjink, precise, punctilious, right, rigorous, scrupulous, severe, specific, square, strict, true, unambiguous, unequivocal, unerring, veracious, very, word-perfect.
antonym inexact.

v. bleed, claim, command, compel, demand, extort, extract, force, impose, insist on, milk, require, requisition, squeeze, wrest, wring.

exactly *adv.* absolutely, accurately, bang, carefully, correctly, dead, definitely, explicitly, expressly, faithfully, faultlessly, just, literally, literatim, methodically, particularly, plumb, precisely, punctiliously, quite, rigorously, scrupulously, severely, specifically, strictly, to the letter, truly, truthfully, unambiguously, unequivocally, unerringly, veraciously, verbatim.
interj. absolutely, agreed, certainly, indeed, just so, of course, precisely, quite, right, true.

exaggerate *v.* amplify, bounce, caricature, distend, embellish, embroider, emphasize, enlarge, exalt, hyperbolize, inflate, magnify, overdo, overdraw, overemphasize, overestimate, oversell, overstate, pile it on.
antonyms belittle, understate.

exalt *v.* acclaim, advance, aggrandize, animate, apotheosize, applaud, arouse, bless, crown, deify, delight, dignify, elate, electrify, elevate, enliven, ennoble, enthrone, excite, exhilarate, extol, fire, glorify, heighten, honor, idolize, inspire, inspirit, laud, magnify, praise, promote, raise, revere, reverence, stimulate, sublimize, thrill, upgrade, uplift, venerate, worship.
antonym debase.

examination *n.* analysis, appraisal, assay, audit, catechism, check, check-up, critique, cross-examination, cross-questioning, docimasy, exam, exploration, inquiry, inquisition, inspection, interrogation, investigation, observation, once-over, perusal, probe, questioning, quiz, research, review, scan, scrutinization, scrutiny, search, sift, study, survey, test, trial, visitation, viva.

examine *v.* analyze, appraise, assay, audit, case, catechize, check (out), consider, cross-examine, cross-question, explore, grill, inquire, inspect, interrogate, investigate, jerque, peruse, ponder, pore over, probe, question, quiz, review, scan, scrutinize, sift, study, survey, sus out, test, vet, visit, weigh.

example *n.* admonition, archetype, case, case in point, caution, citation, ensample, exemplar, exemplification, exemplum, ideal, illustration, instance, lesson, mirror, model, occurrence, paradigm, paragon, parallel, pattern, praxis, precedent, prototype, sample, specimen, standard, type, warning.

exasperate *v.* aggravate, anger, annoy, bug, enrage, exacerbate, excite, exulcerate, gall, get, get in someone's hair, get on someone's nerves, get on someone's wick, get to, goad, incense, inflame, infuriate, irk, irritate, madden, needle, nettle, peeve, pique, plague, provoke, rankle, rile, rouse, vex.
antonyms calm, soothe.

excavate *v.* burrow, cut, delve, dig, dig out, dig up, disinter, drive, exhume, gouge, hollow, mine, quarry, sap, scoop, stope, trench, tunnel, uncover, undermine, unearth.

exceed *v.* beat, better, cap, contravene, eclipse, excel, out-distance, outdo, outreach, outrival, outrun, outshine, outstrip, overdo, overstep, overtake, pass, surmount, surpass, take liberties with, top, transcend, transgress.

exceedingly *adv.* amazingly, astonishingly, enormously, especially, exceeding, exceptionally, excessively, extraordinarily, extremely, greatly, highly, hugely, inordinately, passing, superlatively, surpassingly, unprecedentedly, unusually, vastly, very.

excel *v.* beat, better, cap, eclipse, exceed, outclass, outdo, outperform, outrank, outrival, outshine, outstrip, overshadow, pass, predominate, shine, stand out, surmount, surpass, top, transcend, trump.

excellence *n.* distinction, eminence, fineness, goodness, greatness, merit, perfection, pre-eminence, purity, quality, superiority, supremacy, transcendence, virtue, water, worth.
antonym inferiority.

excellent *adj.* A1, admirable, beaut, bosker, boss, brave, bully, capital, champion, choice, commendable, copacetic, corking, crack, cracking, distinguished, estimable, exemplary, eximious, exquisite, fine, first-class, first-rate, good, great, hot stuff, laudable, meritorious, nonpareil, notable, noted, noteworthy, outstanding, peerless, prime, remarkable, ripping, select, splendid, sterling, stunning, superb, supereminent, superior, superlative, surpassing, tipping, tiptop, top-flight, top-notch, topping, unequaled, unexceptionable, up to dick, way-out, wonderful, worthy.
antonym inferior.

except *prep.* apart from, bar, barring, besides, but, except for, excepting, excluding, exclusive of, leaving out, less, minus, not counting, omitting, other than, save, saving.

v. ban, bar, debar, disallow, eliminate, exclude, leave out, omit, pass over, reject, rule out.

exception *n.* abnormality, anomaly, curiosity, debarment, departure, deviation, disallowment, eccentricity, excepting, exclusion, exemption, freak, inconsistency, irregularity, oddity, omission, peculiarity, prodigy, quirk, rarity, rejection, special case.

exceptional *adj.* aberrant, abnormal, anomalous, atypical, curious, deviant, eccentric, excellent, extraordinary, freakish, inconsistent, irregular, marvelous, notable, noteworthy, odd, outstanding, peculiar, phenomenal, prodigious, quirky, rare, remarkable, singular, special, strange, superior, superlative, uncommon, unconventional, unequaled, unexpected, unusual.
antonyms mediocre, unexceptional.

excerpt *n.* citation, extract, fragment, gobbet, part, passage, pericope, portion, quotation, quote, scrap, section, selection.
v. borrow, cite, crib, cull, extract, lift, mine, quarry, quote, select.

excess *n.* debauchery, diarrhoea, dissipation, dissoluteness, excesses, exorbitance, extravagance, glut, gluttony, immoderateness, immoderation, intemperance, left-over, libertinism, licentiousness, overabundance, overdose, overflow, overflush, overindulgence, overkill, overload, plethora, prodigality, remainder, superabundance, superfluity, surfeit, surplus, unrestraint.
antonym dearth.
adj. additional, extra, left-over, redundant, remaining, residual, spare, superfluous, supernumerary, surplus.

exchange *v.* bandy, bargain, barter, change, commute, convert, interchange, reciprocate, replace, substitute, swap, switch, toss about, trade, truck.
n. bargain, barter, bourse, brush, chat, commerce, conversation, converse, conversation, dealing, interchange, intercourse, market, quid pro quo, reciprocity, replacement, substitution, swap, switch, tit for tat, trade, traffic, truck.

excite *v.* activate, actuate, acrate, affect, agitate, animate, arouse, awaken, discompose, disturb, elate, electrify, elicit, engender, evoke, fire, foment, galvanize, generate, ignite, impress, incite, induce, inflame, initiate, inspire, instigate, kindle, motivate, move, provoke, quicken, rouse, stimulate, stir up, suscitate, sway, thrill, titillate, touch, turn on, upset, waken, warm, whet.
antonyms bore, quell.

excitement *n.* action, activity, ado, adventure, agitation, animation, brouhaha, clamor, commotion, deliriousness, delirium, discomposure, eagerness, elation, enthusiasm, excitation, ferment, fever, flurry, furore, fuss, heat, hubbub, hue and cry, hurly-burly, kerfuffle, kicks, passion, perturbation, restlessness, stimulation, stimulus, tew, thrill, titillation, tumult, unrest, urge.
antonyms apathy, calm.

exclaim *v.* blurt, call, cry, declare, ejaculate, interject, proclaim, shout, utter, vociferate.

exclamation *n.* call, cry, ecphonesis, ejaculation, expletive, interjection, outcry, shout, utterance, vociferation.

exclude *v.* anathematize, ban, bar, blackball, blacklist, bounce, boycott, debar, disallow, eject, eliminate, embargo, evict, except, excommunicate, expel, forbid, ignore, include out, interclude, interdict, keep out, leave out, omit, ostracize, oust, preclude, prohibit, proscribe, refuse, reject, remove, repudiate, rule out, shut out, veto.
antonyms admit, allow, include.

exclusion *n.* ban, bar, boycott, debarment, disfellowship, ejection, elimination, embargo, eviction, exception, expulsion, forbiddal, forbiddance, interdict, non-admission, omission, ostracization, preclusion, prohibition, proscription, refusal, rejection, removal, repudiation, veto.
antonyms admittance, allowance, inclusion.

exclusive *adj.* absolute, arrogant, chic, choice, clannish, classy, cliquey, cliquish, closed, complete, confined, discriminative, elegant, entire, esoteric, exclusory, fashionable, full, limited, luxurious, monopolistic, narrow, only, peculiar, posh, private, restricted, restrictive, select, selective, selfish, single, snobbish, sole, total, undivided, unique, unshared, whole.

excruciating *adj.* acute, agonizing, atrocious, bitter, burning, exquisite, extreme, harrowing, insufferable, intense, intolerable, painful, piercing, racking, savage, searing, severe, sharp, tormenting, torturing, torturous, unbearable, unendurable.

excursion *n.* airing, breather, day trip, detour, deviation, digression, divagation, ecbole, episode, excursus, expedition, jaunt, journey, outing, ramble, ride, sashay, tour, trip, walk, wandering, wayzgoose.

excuse *v.* absolve, acquit, apologize for, condone, defend, discharge, exculpate, exempt, exonerate, explain, extenuate, forgive, free, ignore, indulge, justify, let off, liberate, mitigate, overlook, palliate, pardon, release, relieve, sanction, spare, tolerate, vindicate, warrant, wink at.
n. alibi, apology, cop-out, defence, disguise, evasion, exculpation, exoneration, expedient, explanation, extenuation, grounds, justification, makeshift, mitigation, mockery, palliation, parody, plea, pretense, pretext, put-off, reason, semblance, shift, substitute, subterfuge, travesty, vindication.

execrate *v.* abhor, abominate, anathematize, blast, condemn, curse, damn, denounce, denunciate, deplore, despise, detest, excoriate, fulminate, hate, imprecate, inveigh against, loathe, revile, vilify.
antonyms commend, praise.

execute[1] *v.* behead, burn, crucify, decapitate, decollate, electrocute, guillotine, hang, kill, liquidate, put to death, shoot.

execute[2] *v.* accomplish, achieve, administer, complete, consummate, deliver, discharge, dispatch, do, effect, effectuate, enact, enforce, expedite, finish, fulfil, implement, perform, prosecute, realize, render, seal, serve, sign, validate.

executive *n.* administration, administrator, controller, director, directorate, directors, government, hierarchy, leadership, management, manager, official, organizer. *adj.* administrative, controlling, decision-making, directing, directorial, governing, gubernatorial, guiding, leading, managerial, organizational, organizing, regulating, supervisory.

exemplify *v.* demonstrate, depict, display, embody, ensample, epitomize, evidence, example, exhibit, illustrate, instance, manifest, represent, show, typify.

exempt *v.* absolve, discharge, dismiss, except, excuse, exonerate, free, let off, liberate, make an exception of, release, relieve, spare.
adj. absolved, clear, discharged, excepted, excluded, excused, favored, free, immune, liberated, released, spared.
antonym liable.

exercise *v.* afflict, agitate, annoy, apply, burden, discharge, discipline, distress, disturb, drill, employ, enjoy, exert, habituate, inure, occupy, operate, pain, perturb, practice, preoccupy, train, trouble, try, upset, use, utilize, vex, wield, work out, worry.
n. accomplishment, action, activity, aerobics, application, assignment, daily dozen, discharge, discipline, drill, drilling, effort, employment, enjoyment, exercitation, exertion, fulfilment, implementation, krieg(s)spiel, labor, lesson, operation, physical jerks, practice, problem, schooling, school-work, task, toil, training, use, utilization, war-game, work, work-out.

exertion *n.* action, application, assiduity, attempt, diligence, effort, employment, endeavor, exercise, industry, labor, operation, pains, perseverance, sedulousness, strain, stretch, struggle, toil, travail, trial, use, utilization, work.
antonyms idleness, rest.

exhale *v.* breathe (out), discharge, eject, emanate, emit, evaporate, expel, expire, give off, issue, respire, steam.
antonym inhale.

exhaust *v.* bankrupt, beggar, consume, cripple, debilitate, deplete, disable, dissipate, drain, dry, empty, enervate, enfeeble, expend, fatigue, finish, impoverish, overtax, overtire, overwork, prostrate, run through, sap, spend, squander, strain, tax, tire (out), use up, void, waste, weaken, wear out, weary.
antonym refresh.
n. discharge, education, effluvium, emanation, emission, exhalation, fumes.

exhaustive *adj.* all-embracing, all-inclusive, all-out, complete, comprehensive, definitive, detailed, encyclopedic, expansive, extensive, far-reaching, full, full-scale, in-depth, intensive, sweeping, thorough, thoroughgoing, total.
antonym incomplete.

exhibit *v.* air, demonstrate, disclose, display, evidence, evince, expose, express, flaunt, indicate, manifest, offer, parade, present, reveal, show, showcase, sport.
antonym hide.

n. display, exhibition, illustration, model, show.

exhilarate *v.* animate, cheer, delight, elate, energize, enhearten, enliven, exalt, excite, gladden, hearten, inspirit, invigorate, lift, stimulate, thrill, vitalize.
antonyms bore, discourage.

exhort *v.* admonish, advise, beseech, bid, call upon, caution, counsel, encourage, enjoin, entreat, goad, implore, incite, inflame, inspire, instigate, persuade, press, spur, urge, warn.

exigent *adj.* acute, arduous, constraining, critical, crucial, demanding, difficult, exacting, exhausting, hard, harsh, imperative, importunate, insistent, necessary, needful, pressing, rigorous, severe, stiff, strict, stringent, taxing, tough, urgent.
antonym mild.

exile *n.* banishment, deportation, deportee, émigré, exilement, expatriate, expatriation, expulsion, galut(h), ostracism, outcast, proscription, refugee, separation.
v. banish, deport, drive out, expatriate, expel, ostracize, oust, proscribe.

exist *v.* abide, be, be available, be extant, breathe, continue, endure, happen, have one's being, last, live, obtain, occur, prevail, remain, stand, subsist, survive.

exit *n.* adieu, aperture, congé, departure, door, doorway, egress, evacuation, exodus, farewell, gate, going, leave-taking, outlet, retirement, retreat, vent, way out, withdrawal.
antonym entrance.
v. arrive, depart, enter, issue, leave, retire, retreat, take one's leave, withdraw.

exodus *n.* departure, evacuation, exit, flight, hegira, leaving, long march, migration, retirement, retreat, withdrawal.

exonerate *v.* absolve, acquit, clear, discharge, disculpate, dismiss, except, exculpate, excuse, exempt, free, justify, let off, liberate, pardon, release, relieve, vindicate.
antonym incriminate.

exorbitant *adj.* enormous, excessive, extortionate, extravagant, extreme, immoderate, inordinate, monstrous, out-rageous, preposterous, unconscionable, undue, unreasonable, unwarranted.
antonyms fair, reasonable.

exorcism *n.* adjuration, deliverance, expulsion, exsufflation, purification.

exotic *adj.* alien, bizarre, colorful, curious, different, external, extraneous, extraordinary, extrinsic, fascinating, foreign, foreign-looking, glamorous, imported, introduced, mysterious, naturalized, outlandish, outré, peculiar, recherché, strange, striking, unfamiliar, unusual.
antonym ordinary.

expand *v.* amplify, augment, bloat, blow up, branch out, broaden, develop, diffuse, dilate, dispread, distend, diversify, elaborate, embellish, enlarge, expatiate, expound, extend, fatten, fill out, flesh out, grow, heighten,

increase, inflate, lengthen, magnify, multiply, open, outspread, prolong, protract, snowball, spread, stretch, swell, thicken, unfold, unfurl, unravel, unroll, wax, widen.
antonyms contract, précis.

expansive *adj.* affable, all-embracing, broad, communicative, comprehensive, dilating, distending, easy, effusive, elastic, expanding, expatiative, expatiatory, extendable, extensive, far-reaching, free, friendly, garrulous, genial, inclusive, loquacious, open, outgoing, sociable, stretching, stretchy, swelling, talkative, thorough, unreserved, voluminous, warm, wide, wide-ranging, widespread.
antonyms cold, reserved.

expect *v.* anticipate, assume, await, bank on, bargain for, believe, calculate, conjecture, contemplate, count on, demand, envisage, forecast, foresee, hope for, imagine, insist on, look for, look forward to, predict, presume, project, reckon, rely on, require, suppose, surmise, think, trust, want, wish.

expectant *adj.* agog, anticipating, anxious, apprehensive, awaiting, curious, eager, enceinte, expecting, gravid, hopeful, in suspense, pregnant, ready, watchful.

expecting *adj.* enceinte, expectant, gravid, in the club, in the family way, pregnant, with child.

expedient *adj.* advantageous, advisable, appropriate, beneficial, convenient, desirable, effective, fit, helpful, judicious, meet, opportune, politic, practical, pragmatic, profitable, proper, prudent, serviceable, suitable, useful, utilitarian, worthwhile.
antonym inexpedient.
n. contrivance, device, dodge, makeshift, maneuver, means, measure, method, resort, resource, ruse, scheme, shift, stop-gap, stratagem, substitute.

expedition[1] *n.* company, crusade, enterprise, excursion, exploration, explorers, hike, journey, mission, pilgrimage, quest, raid, ramble, safari, sail, team, tour, travelers, trek, trip, undertaking, voyage, voyagers.

expedition[2] *n.* alacrity, briskness, celerity, dispatch, expeditiousness, haste, hurry, immediacy, promptness, quickness, rapidity, readiness, speed, swiftness.
antonym delay.

expel *v.* ban, banish, bar, belch, blackball, cast out, disbar, discharge, dislodge, dismiss, drive out, drum out, egest, eject, evict, exclude, exile, expatriate, hoof out, oust, proscribe, remove, send packing, spew, throw out, turf out.
antonym admit.

expend *v.* consume, disburse, dissipate, employ, exhaust, fork out, pay, shell out, spend, use, use up.
antonym save.

expense *n.* charge, consumption, cost, damage, disbursement, expenditure, loss, outlay, output, payment, sacrifice, spending, toll, use.

expensive *adj.* costly, dear, excessive, exorbitant, extortionate, extravagant, high-priced, inordinate, lavish, overpriced, rich, steep, stiff.
antonyms cheap, inexpensive.

experience *n.* adventure, affair, assay, contact, doing, encounter, episode, event, evidence, exposure, familiarity, happening, incident, involvement, know-how, knowledge, observation, occurrence, ordeal, participation, practice, proof, taste, test, training, trial, understanding.
antonym inexperience.
v. apprehend, behold, empathize, encounter, endure, face, feel, have, know, meet, observe, perceive, sample, sense, suffer, sustain, taste, try, undergo.

experienced *adj.* accomplished, adept, capable, competent, expert, familiar, knowing, knowledgeable, master, mature, practiced, professional, qualified, schooled, seasoned, skilful, sophisticated, tested, trained, travailed, traveled, tried, veteran, well-versed, wise, worldly, worldly-wise.
antonym inexperienced.

experiment *n.* assay, attempt, ballon d'essai, examination, experimentation, heurism, investigation, procedure, proof, research, test, trial, trial and error, trial run, venture.
v. assay, examine, investigate, research, sample, test, try, verify.

expert *n.* ace, adept, authority, boffin, connoisseur, dab hand, dabster, deacon, dean, maestro, master, pastmaster, pro, professional, specialist, virtuoso, wizard.
adj. able, adept, adroit, apt, clever, crack, deft, dexterous, experienced, facile, handy, knowledgeable, master, masterly, practiced, professional, proficient, qualified, skilful, skilled, trained, virtuoso.
antonym novice.

expire *v.* cease, close, conclude, decease, depart, die, discontinue, emit, end, exhale, finish, lapse, perish, run out, stop, terminate.
antonyms begin, continue.

explain *v.* account for, clarify, clear up, construe, decipher, decode, define, demonstrate, describe, disclose, elucidate, enucleate, excuse, explicate, expound, gloss, gloze, illustrate, interpret, justify, resolve, simplify, solve, spell out, teach, translate, unfold, unravel, untangle.
antonyms obfuscate, obscure.

explanation *n.* account, answer, cause, clarification, definition, demonstration, description, éclaircissement, elucidation, enucleation, excuse, exegesis, explication, exposition, gloss, illustration, interpretation, justification, legend, meaning, mitigation, motive, reason, resolution, sense, significance, solution, vindication, voice-over.

explicit *adj.* absolute, accurate, categorical, certain, clear, declared, definite, detailed, direct, distinct, exact, express, frank, open, outspoken, patent, plain, positive,

precise, specific, stated, straightforward, unambiguous, unequivocal, unqualified, unreserved.
antonyms inexplicit, vague.

exploit *n.* accomplishment, achievement, adventure, attainment, deed, feat, gest(e), stunt.
v. abuse, bleed, capitalize on, cash in on, fleece, impose on, make capital out of, manipulate, milk, misuse, profit by, rip off, skin, soak, take advantage of, turn to account, use, utilize.

explore *v.* analyze, case, examine, inspect, investigate, probe, prospect, reconnoiter, research, scout, scrutinize, search, survey, tour, travel, traverse.

explosion *n.* bang, blast, burst, clap, crack, debunking, detonation, discharge, discrediting, eruption, fit, outbreak, outburst, paroxysm, refutation, report.

explosive *adj.* charged, dangerous, fiery, hazardous, overwrought, perilous, stormy, tense, touchy, ugly, unstable, vehement, violent, volatile, volcanic.
antonym calm.
n. cordite, dynamite, gelignite, gun-powder, jelly, lyddite, melinite, nitroglycerine, TNT.

exponent *n.* advocate, backer, champion, commentator, defender, demonstrator, elucidator, example, executant, exegetist, exemplar, expositor, expounder, illustration, illustrator, indication, interpreter, model, performer, player, presenter, promoter, propagandist, proponent, representative, sample, specimen, spokesman, spokeswoman, supporter, type, upholder.

expose *v.* air, betray, bring to light, denounce, detect, disclose, display, divulge, endanger, exhibit, hazard, imperil, jeopardize, manifest, present, reveal, risk, show, uncover, unearth, unmask, unveil, wash one's dirty linen in public.
antonym cover.

exposition *n.* account, commentary, critique, demonstration, description, discourse, display, elucidation, exegesis, exhibition, explanation, explication, expo, fair, illustration, interpretation, monograph, paper, presentation, show, study, thesis.

expound *v.* describe, elucidate, explain, explicate, illustrate, interpet, preach, sermonize, set forth, spell out, unfold.

express *v.* articulate, assert, asseverate, bespeak, communicate, conceive, convey, couch, declare, denote, depict, designate, disclose, divulge, embody, enunciate, evince, exhibit, extract, force out, formulate, formulize, indicate, intimate, manifest, phrase, pronounce, put, put across, represent, reveal, say, show, signify, speak, stand for, state, symbolize, tell, testify, utter, verbalize, voice, word.
adj. accurate, categorical, certain, clear, clear-cut, definite, direct, distinct, especial, exact, explicit, fast, high-speed, manifest, non-stop, outright, particular, plain, pointed, precise, quick, rapid, singular, special, speedy, stated, swift, unambiguous, unqualified.
antonym vague.

expression *n.* air, announcement, appearance, aspect, assertion, asseveration, communication, countenance, declaration, delivery, demonstration, diction, embodiment, emphasis, enunciation, execution, exhibition, face, idiom, indication, intonation, language, locution, look, manifestation, mention, mien, phrase, phraseology, phrasing, pronouncement, reflex, remark, representation, set phrase, show, sign, speaking, speech, statement, style, symbol, term, token, turn of phrase, utterance, verbalism, verbalization, voicing, word, wording.

expressive *adj.* allusive, demonstrative, eloquent, emphatic, energetic, forcible, indicative, informative, lively, meaningful, mobile, moving, poignant, pointed, pregnant, representative, revealing, significant, striking, strong, suggestive, sympathetic, telling, thoughtful, vivid.
antonyms expressionless, poker-faced.

expressly *adv.* absolutely, categorically, clearly, decidedly, definitely, distinctly, especially, exactly, explicitly, intentionally, manifestly, on purpose, outright, particularly, plainly, pointedly, positively, precisely, purposely, specially, specifically, unambiguously, unequivocally.

expulsion *n.* banishment, debarment, disbarment, discharge, dislodgment, dislodging, dismissal, ejection, ejectment, eviction, exclusion, exile, expatriation, extrusion, proscription, removal.

expunge *v.* abolish, annihilate, annul, blot out, cancel, delete, destroy, efface, eradicate, erase, exterminate, extinguish, extirpate, obliterate, raze, remove, uncreate, unmake, wipe out.

expurgate *v.* blue-pencil, bowdlerize, censor, clean up, cut, emend, purge, purify, sanitize.

exquisite *adj.* acute, admirable, alembicated, appreciative, attractive, beautiful, charming, choice, comely, consummate, cultivated, dainty, delicate, delicious, discerning, discriminating, elegant, excellent, excruciating, fastidious, fine, flawless, impeccable, incomparable, intense, keen, lovely, matchless, meticulous, outstanding, peerless, perfect, piercing, pleasing, poignant, polished, precious, rare, refined, select, selective, sensitive, sharp, splendid, striking, superb, superlative, too-too.
antonyms flawed, imperfect, poor, ugly.

extant *adj.* alive, existent, existing, in existence, living, remaining, subsistent, subsisting, surviving.
antonyms dead, extinct, non-existent.

extemporary *adj.* ad-lib, expedient, extemporaneous, extempore, free, impromptu, improvisatory, improvised, jazz, made-up, makeshift, offhand, off-the-cuff, on-the-spot, spontaneous, temporary, unplanned, unpremeditated, unprepared, unrehearsed.
antonym planned.

extemporize *v.* ad-lib, autoschediaze, improvise, make up, play by ear.

extend *v.* advance, amplify, attain, augment, bestow, broaden, confer, continue, develop, dilate, drag out, draw out, elongate, enhance, enlarge, expand, give, grant, hold out, impart, increase, last, lengthen, offer, present, proffer, prolong, protract, pull out, reach, spin out, spread, stretch, supplement, take, uncoil, unfold, unfurl, unroll, widen, yield.
antonym shorten.

extension *n.* accretion, addendum, addition, adjunct, amplification, annexe, appendage, appendix, augmentation, branch, broadening, continuation, delay, development, dilatation, distension, el, elongation, enhancement, enlargement, expansion, extent, increase, lengthening, postponement, prolongation, protraction, spread, stretching, supplement, widening, wing.

extensive *adj.* all-inclusive, broad, capacious, commodious, comprehensive, expanded, expansive, extended, far-flung, far-reaching, general, great, huge, large, large-scale, lengthy, long, pervasive, prevalent, protracted, roomy, spacious, sweeping, thorough, thoroughgoing, universal, unrestricted, vast, voluminous, wholesale, wide, wide-spread.
antonyms narrow, restricted.

extent *n.* amount, amplitude, area, bounds, breadth, bulk, compass, degree, dimension(s), duration, expanse, expansion, length, magnitude, measure, play, proportions, quantity, range, reach, scope, size, sphere, spread, stretch, sweep, term, time, volume, width.

extenuating *adj.* exculpatory, extenuative, extenuatory, justifying, mitigating, moderating, palliative, qualifying.

exterior *n.* appearance, aspect, coating, covering, externals, façade, face, finish, outside, shell, skin, superficies, surface.
antonym interior.
adj. alien, exotic, external, extraneous, extrinsic, foreign, outer, outermost, outside, outward, peripheral, superficial, surface, surrounding.
antonym interior.

exterminate *v.* abolish, annihilate, deracinate, destroy, eliminate, eradicate, extirpate, massacre, wipe out.

external *adj.* alien, apparent, exoteric, exotic, exterior, extern, externe, extramural, extraneous, extrinsic, foreign, independent, outer, outermost, outside, outward, superficial, surface, visible.
antonym internal.

extinct *adj.* abolished, dead, defunct, doused, ended, exterminated, extinguished, gone, inactive, lost, obsolete, out, quenched, terminated, vanished, void.
antonyms extant, living.

extinction *n.* abolition, annihilation, death, destruction, eradication, excision, extermination, extinguishment, extirpation, obliteration, oblivion, quietus.

extinguish *v.* abolish, annihilate, destroy, douse, dout, eliminate, end, eradicate, erase, expunge, exterminate, extirpate, kill, obscure, put out, quench, remove, slake, smother, snuff out, stifle, suppress.

extol *v.* acclaim, applaud, celebrate, commend, cry up, eulogize, exalt, glorify, laud, magnify, panegyrize, praise, puff.
antonyms blame, denigrate.

extort *v.* blackmail, bleed, bully, coerce, exact, extract, force, milk, squeeze, wrest, wring.

extra *adj.* accessory, added, additional, ancillary, auxiliary, excess, extraneous, for good measure, fresh, further, gash, inessential, leftover, more, needless, new, other, redundant, reserve, spare, supererogatory, superfluous, super-numerary, supplemental, supplementary, surplus, unnecessary, unneeded, unused.
antonym integral.
n. accessory, addendum, addition, adjunct, affix, appendage, appurtenance, attachment, bonus, complement, extension, lagniappe, plus(s)age, supernumerary, supplement.
adv. especially, exceptionally, extraordinarily, extremely, particularly, remarkably, uncommonly, unusually.

extract *v.* abstract, choose, cite, cull, decoct, deduce, derive, develop, distil, draw, draw out, educe, elicit, enucleate, evoke, evolve, evulse, exact, express, extirpate, gather, get, glean, obtain, quote, reap, remove, select, uproot, withdraw, wrest, wring.
antonym insert.
n. abstract, apozem, citation, clip, clipping, concentrate, cutting, decoction, decocture, distillate, distillation, essence, excerpt, juice, passage, quotation, selection.

extraordinary *adj.* amazing, bizarre, curious, exceptional, fantastic, marvelous, notable, noteworthy, odd, outstanding, particular, peculiar, phenomenal, rare, remarkable, significant, singular, special, strange, striking, surprising, uncommon, uncontemplated, unfamiliar, unheard-of, unimaginable, unique, unprecedented, unusual, unwonted, weird, wonderful.
antonyms commonplace, ordinary.

extravagant *adj.* absurd, costly, exaggerated, excessive, exorbitant, expensive, extortionate, fanciful, fancy, fantastic, flamboyant, flashy, foolish, garish, gaudy, grandiose, hyperbolic, hyperbolical, immoderate, improvident, imprudent, inordinate, lavish, ornate, ostentatious, outrageous, outré, overpriced, preposterous, pretentious, prodigal, profligate, reckless, showy, spendthrift, steep, thriftless, unreasonable, unrestrained, unthrifty, wasteful, wild.
antonyms moderate, thrifty.

extreme *adj.* acute, deep-dyed, dire, double-dyed, downright, Draconian, drastic, egregious, exaggerated, exceptional, excessive, exquisite, extraordinary, extravagant, fanatical, faraway, far-off, farthest, final, great, greatest, harsh, high, highest, immoderate, inordinate, intemperate, intense, last, maximum, out-and-out, outermost, outrageous, radical, red-hot, remarkable, remotest, rigid, severe, sheer, stern, strict, supreme,

terminal, ultimate, ultra, unbending, uncommon, un-compromising, unconventional, unreasonable, unusual, utmost, utter, uttermost, worst, zealous.
antonyms mild, moderate.
n. acme, apex, apogee, boundary, climax, consummation, depth, edge, end, excess, extremity, height, limit, maximum, minimum, nadir, peak, pinnacle, pole, termination, top, ultimate, utmost, zenith.

extremism *n.* fanaticism, radicalism, terrorism, ultraism, zeal, zealotism, zealotry.
antonym moderation.

extricate *v.* clear, deliver, disembarrass, disembrangle, disembroil, disengage, disentangle, disintricate, free, liberate, release, relieve, remove, rescue, withdraw.
antonym involve.

exuberant *adj.* abundant, animated, baroque, buoyant, cheerful, copious, eager, ebullient, effervescent, effusive, elated, energetic, enthusiastic, exaggerated, excessive, excited, exhilarated, fulsome, high-spirited, lavish, lively, lush, luxuriant, overdone, overflowing, plenteous, plentiful, prodigal, profuse, rambunctious, rank, rich, sparkling, spirited, sprightly, superabundant, superfluous, teeming, vigorous, vivacious, zestful.
antonyms apathetic, lifeless, scant.

exult *v.* boast, brag, celebrate, crow, delight, gloat, glory, jubilate, rejoice, relish, revel, taunt, triumph.

eye *n.* appreciation, belief, discernment, discrimination, eyeball, glim, judgment, keeker, mind, opinion, optic, orb, peeper, perception, recognition, taste, viewpoint.
v. contemplate, examine, eye up, gaze at, glance at, inspect, leer at, look at, make eyes at, observe, ogle, peruse, regard, scan, scrutinize, stare at, study, survey, view, watch.

F

fable *n.* allegory, apologue, fabliau, fabrication, fairy story, falsehood, fantasy, fib, fiction, figment, invention, legend, lie, Märchen, myth, narrative, old wives' tale, parable, romance, saga, story, tale, tall story, untruth, yarn.

fabled *adj.* fabulous, famed, famous, feigned, fictional, legendary, mythical, renowned, storied.
antonym unknown.

fabric *n.* cloth, constitution, construction, foundations, framework, infrastructure, make-up, material, organization, structure, stuff, textile, texture, web.

fabricate *v.* assemble, build, coin, concoct, construct, create, devise, erect, fake, falsify, fashion, feign, forge, form, frame, invent, make, manufacture, shape, trump up.

fabrication *n.* assemblage, assembly, building, cock-and-bull story, concoction, construction, erection, fable, fairy story, fake, falsehood, fiction, figment, forgery, frame-up, invention, lie, manufacture, myth, production, story, untruth.
antonym truth.

fabulous *adj.* amazing, apocryphal, astounding, breathtaking, fabled, false, fantastic, feigned, fictitious, imaginary, immense, inconceivable, incredible, invented, legendary, marvelous, mythical, phenomenal, renowned, spectacular, superb, unbelievable, unreal, wonderful.
antonyms moderate, real, small.

façade *n.* appearance, cloak, cover, disguise, exterior, face, front, frontage, guise, mask, pretense, semblance, show, veil, veneer.

face *n.* air, appearance, aspect, assurance, audacity, authority, boatrace, boldness, brass neck, cheek, confidence, countenance, cover, dial, dignity, disguise, display, effrontery, expression, exterior, façade, facet, favor, features, front, frown, gall, grimace, honor, image, impudence, kisser, lineaments, look, mask, metope, moue, mug, nerve, outside, phiz, phizog, physiognomy, pout, prestige, presumption, pretence, reputation, sauce, scowl, self-respect, semblance, show, side, smirk, snoot, standing, status, surface, visage.
v. clad, coat, confront, cope with, cover, deal with, defy, dress, encounter, experience, finish, front, give on to, level, line, meet, oppose, overlay, overlook, sheathe, surface, tackle, veneer.

facet *n.* angle, aspect, characteristic, face, feature, part, phase, plane, point, side, slant, surface.

facetious *adj.* amusing, comical, droll, facete, flippant, frivolous, funny, humorous, jesting, jocose, jocular, merry, playful, pleasant, tongue-in-cheek, unserious, waggish, witty.
antonym serious.

facile *adj.* adept, adroit, complaisant, cursory, dexterous, easy, effortless, fluent, glib, hasty, light, plausible, proficient, quick, ready, shallow, simple, skilful, slick, smooth, superficial, uncomplicated, yielding.
antonyms clumsy, implausible, profound.

facilitate *v.* assist, ease, expedite, forward, further, grease, help, promote, speed up.

facilities *n.* amenity, appliance, convenience, equipment, means, mod cons, opportunity, prerequisites, resource.

facility *n.* ability, adeptness, adroitness, bent, dexterity, ease, efficiency, effortlessness, expertness, fluency, gift, knack, proficiency, quickness, readiness, skilfulness, skill, smoothness, talent, turn.

facsimile *n.* carbon, carbon copy, copy, duplicate, image, mimeograph, photocopy, Photostat®;, print, replica, repro, reproduction, transcript, Xerox®;.

fact *n.* act, actuality, certainty, circumstance, datum, deed, detail, event, fait accompli, feature, gospel, happening, incident, item, occurrence, particular, point, reality, specific, truth.

faction[1] *n.* band, bloc, cabal, cadre, camp, caucus, clique, coalition, combination, confederacy, contingent, coterie, crowd, division, gang, ginger group, group, junta, lobby, minority, party, pressure group, ring, section, sector, set, splinter group, splinter party, troop.

faction[2] *n.* conflict, disagreement, discord, disharmony, dissension, disunity, division, divisiveness, fighting, friction, infighting, quarreling, rebellion, sedition, strife, tumult, turbulence.
antonyms agreement, peace.

factitious *adj.* affected, artificial, assumed, contrived, counterfeit, engineered, fabricated, fake, false, imitation, insincere, made-up, manufactured, mock, phony, pinchbeck, pretended, put-on, sham, simulated, spurious, supposititious, synthetic, unnatural, unreal.
antonym genuine.

factor *n.* agent, aspect, cause, circumstance, component, consideration, deputy, determinant, element, estate manager, influence, item, joker, middleman, parameter, part, point, reeve, steward, thing, unknown quantity.

factory *n.* hacienda, manufactory, mill, plant, shop, shop-floor, works.

factual *adj.* accurate, authentic, circumstantial, close, correct, credible, detailed, exact, faithful, genuine, literal, objective, precise, real, straight, sure, true, unadorned, unbiased, veritable.
antonym false.

faculty[1] *n.* academics, department, discipline, lecturers, profession, school, staff.

faculty[2] *n.* ability, adroitness, aptitude, bent, brain-power, capability, capacity, cleverness, dexterity, facility, gift, knack, power, propensity, readiness, skill, talent, turn.

faculty[3] *n.* authorization, authority, license, prerogative, privilege, right.

fad *n.* affectation, craze, crotchet, fancy, fashion, mania, mode, rage, trend, vogue, whim.

fade *v.* blanch, bleach, blench, decline, die, dim, diminish, disappear, discolor, disperse, dissolve, droop, dull, dwindle, ebb, etiolate, evanesce, fail, fall, flag, languish, pale, perish, shrivel, vanish, wane, wilt, wither, yellow.

fagged *adj.* all in, beat, exhausted, fatigued, jaded, jiggered, knackered, on one's last legs, wasted, weary, worn out, zonked.
antonym refreshed.

fail *v.* abandon, cease, come to grief, conk out, crack up, crash, cut out, decline, desert, die, disappoint, droop, dwindle, fade, fall, flop, flub, flunk, fold, forget, forsake, founder, fudge, give out, give up, go bankrupt, go bust, go to the wall, go under, gutter, languish, lay an egg, let down, miscarry, misfire, miss, miss one's trip, neglect, omit, peter out, plow, sink, smash, underachieve, underperform, wane, weaken.
antonyms gain, improve, prosper, succeed.

failing *n.* blemish, blind spot, decay, decline, defect, deficiency, deterioration, drawback, error, failure, fault, flaw, foible, frailty, hamartia, imperfection, lapse, miscarriage, misfortune, peccadillo, shortcoming, weakness.
antonyms advantage, strength.
adj. collapsing, decaying, declining, deteriorating, drooping, dwindling, dying, flagging, languishing, moribund, waning, weak, weakening.
antonyms thriving, vigorous.
prep. in default of, in the absence of, lacking, wanting, without.

failure *n.* abortion, also-ran, bankruptcy, breakdown, bummer, collapse, crash, cropper, damp squib, dead duck, decay, decline, default, defeat, deficiency, dereliction, deterioration, disappointment, downfall, dud, failing, fiasco, flivver, flop, folding, frost, frustration, goner, incompetent, insolvency, loser, loss, miscarriage, neglect, negligence, no-hoper, non-performance, omission, remissness, ruin, shortcoming, slip-up, stoppage, turkey, unsuccess, wash-out, wreck.
antonym success.

faint *adj.* bleached, delicate, dim, distant, dizzy, drooping, dull, enervated, exhausted, faded, faltering, fatigued, feeble, feint, giddy, hazy, hushed, ill-defined, indistinct, languid, lethargic, light, light-headed, low, muffled, muted, muzzy, remote, slight, soft, subdued, thin, unenthusiastic, vague, vertiginous, weak, whispered, woozy.
antonyms clear, strong.

v. black out, collapse, droop, drop, flag, flake out, keel over, pass out, swoon.
n. blackout, collapse, deliquium, swoon, syncope, unconsciousness.

fair[1] *adj.* adequate, all right, average, beauteous, beautiful, bonny, bright, clean, clear, clement, cloudless, comely, decent, disinterested, dispassionate, dry, equal, equitable, even-handed, favorable, fine, handsome, honest, honorable, impartial, just, lawful, legitimate, lovely, mediocre, middling, moderate, not bad, objective, OK, on the level, passable, pretty, proper, reasonable, respectable, satisfactory, so-so, square, sunny, sunshiny, tolerable, trustworthy, unbiased, unclouded, unprejudiced, upright, well-favored.
antonyms cloudy, inclement, poor, unfair.

fair[2] *adj.* blond(e), fair-haired, fair-headed, flaxen, light, tow-headed.
antonym dark.

fair[3] *n.* bang, bazaar, carnival, expo, exposition, festival, fête, gaff, gala, kermis, market, show.

fairly *adv.* absolutely, adequately, deservedly, equitably, ex aequo, fully, honestly, impartially, justly, moderately, objectively, plainly, positively, pretty, properly, quite, rather, really, reasonably, somewhat, tolerably, unbiasedly, veritably.
antonym unfairly.

fairness *n.* decency, disinterestedness, equitableness, equity, impartiality, justice, legitimacy, legitimateness, rightfulness, rightness, unbiasedness, uprightness.
antonym unfairness.

fairy *n.* brownie, buggane, elf, fay, fée, hob, hobgoblin, leprechaun, Mab, peri, pisky, pixie, Robin Goodfellow, rusalka, sprite.

faith *n.* allegiance, assurance, belief, church, communion, confidence, constancy, conviction, credence, credit, creed, denomination, dependence, dogma, faithfulness, fealty, fidelity, honesty, honor, loyalty, persuasion, pledge, promise, reliance, religion, sincerity, trust, truth, truthfulness, uberrima fides, vow, word, word of honor.
antonyms mistrust, treachery, unfaithfulness.

faithful *adj.* accurate, attached, card-carrying, close, constant, convinced, dependable, devoted, exact, just, leal, loyal, precise, reliable, soothfast, soothful, staunch, steadfast, strict, true, true-blue, true-hearted, trusty, truthful, unswerving, unwavering.
antonyms disloyal, inaccurate, treacherous.
n. adherents, believers, brethren, communicants, congregation, followers, supporters.

faithless *adj.* adulterous, delusive, disloyal, doubting, false, false-hearted, fickle, inconstant, perfidious, punic, recreant, traitorous, treacherous, unbelieving, unfaithful, unreliable, untrue, untrustworthy, untruthful.
antonyms believing, faithful.

fake *v.* affect, assume, copy, counterfeit, fabricate, feign, forge, phony, pretend, put on, sham, simulate.

n. charlatan, copy, forgery, fraud, hoax, imitant, imitation, impostor, mountebank, phony, reproduction, sham, simulation.

adj. affected, artificial, assumed, bastard, bogus, counterfeit, ersatz, false, forged, hyped up, imitation, mock, phony, pinchbeck, pretended, pseudo, reproduction, sham, simulated, spurious.

antonym genuine.

fall *v.* abate, backslide, become, befall, capitulate, cascade, chance, collapse, come about, come to pass, crash, decline, decrease, depreciate, descend, die, diminish, dive, drop, drop down, dwindle, ebb, err, fall away, fall off, fall out, flag, give in, give up, give way, go a purler, go astray, go down, happen, incline, keel over, lapse, lessen, measure one's length, meet one's end, nose-dive, occur, offend, perish, pitch, plummet, plunge, push, resign, settle, sin, sink, slope, slump, souse, stumble, subside, succumb, surrender, take place, topple, transgress, trespass, trip, trip over, tumble, yield, yield to temptation.

antonym rise.

n. capitulation, collapse, cropper, cut, death, decline, declivity, decrease, defeat, degradation, descent, destruction, diminution, dip, dive, downfall, downgrade, drop, dwindling, failure, incline, lapse, lessening, lowering, nose-dive, overthrow, plummet, plunge, pusher, reduction, resignation, ruin, sin, slant, slip, slope, slump, souse, spill, surrender, transgression, tumble, voluntary.

antonym rise.

fallacious *adj.* casuistical, deceptive, delusive, delusory, erroneous, false, fictitious, illogical, illusory, incorrect, misleading, mistaken, sophistic, sophistical, spurious, untrue, wrong.

antonyms correct, true.

fallacy *n.* casuistry, deceit, deception, deceptiveness, delusion, error, falsehood, faultiness, flaw, illusion, inconsistency, misapprehension, misconception, mistake, sophism, sophistry, untruth.

antonym truth.

fallow *adj.* dormant, idle, inactive, inert, resting, uncultivated, undeveloped, unplanted, unsown, untilled, unused.

false *adj.* artificial, bastard, bogus, concocted, counterfeit, deceitful, deceiving, deceptive, delusive, dishonest, dishonorable, disloyal, double-dealing, double-faced, duplicitous, erroneous, ersatz, faithless, fake, fallacious, false-hearted, faulty, feigned, fictitious, forged, fraudulent, hypocritical, illusive, imitation, improper, inaccurate, incorrect, inexact, invalid, lying, mendacious, misleading, mistaken, mock, perfidious, postiche, pretended, pseud, pseudo, sham, simulated, spurious, synthetic, treacherous, treasonable, trumped-up, truthless, two-faced, unfaithful, unfounded, unreal, unreliable, unsound, untrue, untrustworthy, untruthful, wrong.

antonyms honest, reliable, true.

falsehood *n.* deceit, deception, dishonesty, dissimulation, fable, fabrication, fib, fiction, inexactitude, inveracity, lie, mendacity, misstatement, perjury, prevarication, pseudery, story, unfact, untruth, untruthfulness.

antonyms truth, truthfulness.

falsify *v.* adulterate, alter, belie, cook, counterfeit, distort, doctor, fake, forge, garble, misrepresent, misstate, pervert, sophisticate, take liberties with, tamper with.

falter *v.* break, fail, flag, flinch, halt, hem and haw, hesitate, shake, stammer, stumble, stutter, totter, tremble, vacillate, waver.

fame *n.* celebrity, credit, eminence, esteem, glory, honor, illustriousness, kudos, name, prominence, renown, reputation, repute, stardom.

famed *adj.* acclaimed, celebrated, famous, noted, recognized, renowned, well-known, widely-known.

antonym unknown.

familiar *adj.* abreast, accustomed, acquainted, amicable, au courant, au fait, aware, bold, chummy, close, common, common-or-garden, confidential, conscious, conventional, conversant, cordial, customary, disrespectful, domestic, easy, everyday, forward, free, free-and-easy, frequent, friendly, household, impudent, informal, intimate, intrusive, knowledgeable, mundane, near, open, ordinary, overfree, presuming, presumptuous, private, recognizable, relaxed, repeated, routine, stock, unceremonious, unconstrained, unreserved, versed, well-known.

antonyms formal, reserved, unfamiliar, unversed.

familiarity *n.* acquaintance, acquaintanceship, awareness, boldness, check, closeness, conversance, disrespect, ease, experience, fellowship, forwardness, freedom, friendliness, grasp, impertinence, impudence, informality, intimacy, liberties, liberty, license, naturalness, openness, presumption, sociability, unceremoniousness, understanding.

antonyms formality, reservation, unfamiliarity.

familiarize *v.* acclimatize, accustom, brief, coach, habituate, instruct, inure, prime, school, season, train.

family *n.* ancestors, ancestry, birth, blood, brood, children, clan, class, classification, descendants, descent, dynasty, extraction, folk, forebears, forefathers, genealogy, genre, group, house, household, issue, kin, kind, kindred, kinsmen, kith and kin, line, lineage, ménage, network, offspring, parentage, pedigree, people, progeny, quiverful, race, relations, relatives, sept, stemma, stirps, strain, subdivision, system, tribe.

family tree ancestry, extraction, genealogy, line, lineage, pedigree, stemma, stirps.

famine *n.* dearth, destitution, hunger, scarcity, starvation, want.

antonym plenty.

famous *adj.* acclaimed, celebrated, conspicuous, distinguished, eminent, excellent, famed, far-famed, glorious, great, honored, illustrious, legendary, lionized, notable, noted, prominent, remarkable, renowned, signal, well-known.

antonym unknown.

fan[1] *v.* aggravate, agitate, air-condition, air-cool, arouse, blow, cool, enkindle, excite, impassion, increase, provoke, refresh, rouse, stimulate, stir up, ventilate, whip up, winnow, work up.

n. air-conditioner, blower, extractor fan, flabellum, propeller, punkah, vane, ventilator.

fan[2] *n.* adherent, admirer, aficionado, buff, devotee, enthusiast, fiend, follower, freak, groupie, lover, rooter, supporter, zealot.

fanatic *n.* activist, addict, bigot, demoniac, devotee, energumen, enthusiast, extremist, fiend, freak, militant, visionary, zealot.

fancy *v.* be attracted to, believe, conceive, conjecture, crave, desire, dream of, favor, go for, guess, hanker after, have an eye for, imagine, infer, like, long for, lust after, picture, prefer, reckon, relish, suppose, surmise, take a liking to, take to, think, think likely, whim, wish for, yearn for, yen for.

antonym dislike.

n. caprice, chim(a)era, conception, daydream, delusion, desire, dream, fantasy, fondness, hankering, humor, idea, image, imagination, impression, impulse, inclination, liking, nightmare, notion, partiality, penchant, phantasm, predilection, preference, relish, thought, urge, vapor, velleity, vision, whim.

antonyms dislike, fact, reality.

adj. baroque, capricious, chimerical, decorated, decorative, delusive, elaborate, elegant, embellished, extravagant, fanciful, fantastic, far-fetched, illusory, ornamented, ornate, rococo, whimsical.

antonym plain.

fantastic *adj.* absurd, ambitious, capricious, chimerical, comical, eccentric, enormous, excellent, exotic, extravagant, extreme, fanciful, fantasque, far-fetched, first-rate, freakish, grandiose, great, grotesque, illusory, imaginative, implausible, incredible, irrational, ludicrous, mad, marvelous, odd, out of this world, outlandish, outré, overwhelming, peculiar, phantasmagorical, preposterous, quaint, queer, ridiculous, rococo, sensational, severe, strange, superb, tremendous, unlikely, unreal, unrealistic, visionary, weird, whimsical, wild, wonderful.

antonyms ordinary, plain, poor.

fantasy *n.* apparition, caprice, creativity, daydream, delusion, dream, dreamery, fancy, fantasia, fantasque, flight of fancy, hallucination, illusion, imagination, invention, mirage, nightmare, originality, phantasy, pipedream, reverie, vision, whimsy.

antonym reality.

far *adv.* a good way, a long way, afar, considerably, decidedly, deep, extremely, greatly, incomparably, miles, much.

antonym near.

adj. distal, distant, faraway, far-flung, far-off, far-removed, further, god-forsaken, long, opposite, other, outlying, out-of-the-way, remote, removed.

antonyms close, nearby.

fare[1] *n.* charge, cost, fee, passage, passenger, pick-up, price, traveler.

fare[2] *n.* board, commons, diet, eatables, food, meals, menu, provisions, rations, sustenance, table, victuals.

fare[3] *v.* be, do, get along, get on, go, go on, happen, make out, manage, proceed, prosper, turn out.

farewell *n.* adieu, departure, good-bye, leave-taking, parting, send-off, valediction.

antonym hello.

adj. final, parting, valedictory.

interj. aloha, bye-bye, cheers, ciao, good-bye.

farm *n.* acreage, acres, bowery, croft, farmstead, grange, holding, homestead, kolkhoz, land, mains, plantation, ranch, smallholding, station.

v. cultivate, operate, plant, till, work the land.

fascinate *v.* absorb, allure, beguile, bewitch, captivate, charm, delight, enchant, engross, enrapture, enravish, enthrall, entrance, hypnotize, infatuate, intrigue, mesmerize, rivet, spellbind, transfix.

antonym bore.

fashion *n.* appearance, attitude, beau monde, configuration, convention, craze, custom, cut, demeanor, dernier cri, description, fad, figure, form, guise, haut ton, haute couture, high society, jet set, kind, latest, line, look, make, manner, method, mode, model, mold, pattern, rage, shape, sort, style, trend, type, usage, vogue, way.

v. accommodate, adapt, adjust, alter, construct, contrive, create, design, fit, forge, form, make, manufacture, mold, shape, suit, tailor, work.

fashionable *adj.* à la mode, alamode, all the rage, chic, chichi, contemporary, current, customary, funky, genteel, in, in vogue, latest, modern, modish, popular, prevailing, smart, snazzy, stylish, swagger, tippy, tony, tonish, trend-setting, trendy, up-to-date, up-to-the-minute, usual, with it.

antonym unfashionable.

fast[1] *adj.* accelerated, brisk, fleet, flying, hasty, hurried, mercurial, nippy, quick, rapid, spanking, speedy, swift, winged.

antonym slow.

adv. apace, hastily, hell for leather, hurriedly, like a flash, like a shot, posthaste, presto, quickly, rapidly, speedily, swiftly, ventre à terre.

antonym slowly.

fast[2] *adj.* close, constant, fastened, firm, fixed, fortified, immovable, impregnable, lasting, loyal, permanent, secure, sound, staunch, steadfast, tight, unflinching, unwavering.

antonyms impermanent, loose.

adv. close, deeply, firmly, fixedly, near, rigidly, securely, soundly, sound(ly), tightly, unflinchingly.

antonym loosely.

fast³ *adj.* dissipated, dissolute, extravagant, immoral, intemperate, licentious, loose, profligate, promiscuous, rakehell, rakehelly, rakish, reckless, self-indulgent, wanton, whorish, wild.
antonyms chaste, moral.

fast⁴ *v.* abstain, bant, diet, go hungry, starve.
n. abstinence, diet, fasting, starvation, xerophagy.
antonyms gluttony, self-indulgence.

fasten *v.* affix, aim, anchor, attach, belay, bend, bind, bolt, chain, clamp, concentrate, connect, direct, fix, focus, grip, infibulate, join, lace, link, lock, nail, rivet, seal, secure, spar, tie, unite.
antonym unfasten.

fastidious *adj.* choosy, critical, dainty, difficult, discriminating, finical, finicky, fussy, hypercritical, meticulous, overnice, particular, pernickety, picky, precise, punctilious, squeamish.
antonym undemanding.

fat *adj.* abdominous, adipose, affluent, beefy, blowzy, corpulent, cushy, elephantine, fatling, fatty, fertile, fleshed, fleshy, flourishing, fozy, fruitful, greasy, gross, heavy, jammy, lucrative, lush, obese, oily, oleaginous, overweight, paunchy, pinguid, plump, poddy, podgy, portly, pot-bellied, productive, profitable, prosperous, pudgy, remunerative, rich, roly-poly, rotund, round, solid, squab, stout, suety, thriving, tubbish, tubby, well-upholstered.
antonyms thin, unproductive.
n. adipose tissue, blubber, brown fat, cellulite, corpulence, degras, embonpoint, fatness, flab, obesity, overweight, paunch, pot (belly), speck.

fatal *adj.* baleful, baneful, calamitous, catastrophic, deadly, destructive, disastrous, final, incurable, killing, lethal, malignant, mortal, mortiferous, mortific, pernicious, ruinous, terminal, vital.
antonym harmless.

fatality *n.* casualty, deadliness, death, disaster, lethalness, loss, mortality, unavoidability.

fate *n.* chance, cup, death, destiny, destruction, divine will, doom, downfall, end, fortune, future, horoscope, issue, joss, karma, kismet, lot, Moira, nemesis, outcome, portion, predestination, predestiny, providence, ruin, stars, upshot, weird.

father *n.* abbé, ancestor, architect, author, begetter, confessor, creator, curé, dad, daddy, elder, forebear, forefather, founder, generant, genitor, governor, inventor, leader, maker, old boy, old man, originator, pa, padre, papa, pappy, parent, pastor, pater, paterfamilias, patriarch, patron, pop, poppa, pops, predecessor, priest, prime mover, procreator, progenitor, senator, sire.
v. beget, conceive, create, dream up, engender, establish, found, get, institute, invent, originate, procreate, produce, sire.

fatherland *n.* home, homeland, mother-country, motherland, native land, old country.

fatherly *adj.* affectionate, avuncular, benevolent, benign, forbearing, indulgent, kind, kindly, paternal, patriarchal, protective, supportive, tender.
antonyms cold, harsh, unkind.

fathom *v.* comprehend, deduce, divine, estimate, gauge, get to the bottom of, grasp, interpret, measure, penetrate, plumb, plummet, probe, see, sound, understand, work out.

fatigue *v.* do in, drain, exhaust, fag, jade, knacker, overtire, shatter, tire, weaken, wear out, weary, whack.
antonym refresh.
n. debility, decay, degeneration, ennui, failure, heaviness, languor, lethargy, listlessness, overtiredness, tiredness.
antonyms energy, freshness.

fault *n.* accountability, blemish, blunder, boner, boob, booboo, culpability, defect, deficiency, delict, delinquency, demerit, dislocation, drawback, error, failing, flaw, frailty, goof, hamartia, imperfection, inaccuracy, indiscretion, infirmity, lack, lapse, liability, misconduct, misdeed, misdemeanor, mistake, negligence, offense, omission, oversight, peccadillo, responsibility, shortcoming, sin, slip, slip-up, snag, solecism, transgression, trespass, weakness, wrong.
antonyms advantage, strength.
v. blame, call to account, censure, criticize, find fault with, impugn, pick a hole in someone's coat, pick at, pick holes in.
antonym praise.

faulty *adj.* bad, blemished, broken, casuistic, damaged, defective, erroneous, fallacious, flawed, illogical, impaired, imperfect, imprecise, inaccurate, incorrect, invalid, malfunctioning, out of order, specious, unsound, weak, wrong.

favor *n.* acceptance, approbation, approval, backing, badge, benefit, bias, boon, championship, courtesy, decoration, esteem, favoritism, friendliness, gift, good turn, goodwill, grace indulgence, keepsake, kindness, knot, love-token, memento, obligement, partiality, patronage, present, regard, rosette, service, smile, souvenir, support, token.
antonym disfavor.
v. abet, accommodate, advance, advocate, aid, approve, assist, back, befriend, champion, choose, commend, countenance, ease, encourage, esteem, extenuate, facilitate, fancy, have in one's good books, help, indulge, like, oblige, opt for, pamper, patronize, prefer, promote, resemble, spare, spoil, succor, support, take after, take kindly to, value.
antonyms disfavor, hinder, thwart.

favorite *adj.* best-loved, choice, dearest, esteemed, favored, pet, preferred.
antonyms hated, unfavorite.
n. beloved, blue-eyed boy, choice, darling, dear, form horse, idol, pet, pick, preference, teacher's pet, the apple of one's eye, whitehead, whiteheaded boy.
antonym pet hate.

favoritism *n.* bias, biasedness, injustice, jobs for the boys, nepotism, old school tie, one-sidedness, partiality, partisanship, preference, preferential treatment. *antonym* impartiality.

fear *n.* agitation, alarm, anxiety, apprehension, apprehensiveness, awe, bogey, bugbear, concern, consternation, cravenness, danger, dismay, disquietude, distress, doubt, dread, foreboding(s), fright, funk, heart-quake, horror, likelihood, misgiving(s), nightmare, panic, phobia, phobism, qualms, reverence, risk, solicitude, specter, suspicion, terror, timidity, tremors, trepidation, unease, uneasiness, veneration, wonder, worry. *antonyms* courage, fortitude.

v. anticipate, apprehend, dread, expect, foresee, respect, reverence, shudder at, suspect, take fright, tremble, venerate, worry.

fearless *adj.* aweless, bold, brave, confident, courageous, daring, dauntless, doughty, gallant, game, gutsy, heroic, impavid, indomitable, intrepid, lion-hearted, plucky, unabashed, unafraid, unapprehensive, unblenching, unblinking, undaunted, unflinching, valiant, valorous.

antonyms afraid, timid.

feast *n.* banquet, barbecue, beanfeast, beano, binge, blowout, carousal, carouse, celebration, delight, dinner, enjoyment, entertainment, epulation, festival, fête, gala day, gaudy, gratification, holiday, holy day, jollification, junket, pig, pleasure, repast, revels, saint's day, spread, treat.

v. delight, eat one's fill, entertain, gladden, gorge, gormandize, gratify, indulge, overindulge, regale, rejoice, stuff, stuff one's face, thrill, treat, wine and dine.

feat *n.* accomplishment, achievement, act, attainment, deed, exploit, gest(e), performance.

feature *n.* article, aspect, attraction, attribute, character, characteristic, column, comment, draw, facet, factor, hallmark, highlight, innovation, item, lineament, mark, peculiarity, piece, point, property, quality, report, special, specialty, story, trait.

v. accentuate, emphasize, headline, highlight, play up, present, promote, push, recommend, show, spotlight, star.

fee *n.* account, bill, charge, compensation, emolument, hire, honorarium, pay, payment, recompense, remuneration, retainer, terms, toll.

feeble *adj.* debilitated, delicate, doddering, effete, enervated, enfeebled, exhausted, failing, faint, flat, flimsy, forceless, frail, fushionless, inadequate, incompetent, indecisive, ineffective, ineffectual, inefficient, inform, insignificant, insufficient, lame, languid, paltry, poor, powerless, puny, shilpit, sickly, silly, slight, tame, thin, unconvincing, vacillating, weak, weakened, weakly.

antonyms strong, worthy.

feed *v.* augment, bolster, cater for, dine, eat, encourage, fare, foster, fuel, graze, grub, nourish, nurture, pasture, provide for, provision, strengthen, subsist, supply, sustain, victual.

n. banquet, feast, fodder, food, forage, meal, nosh, pasturage, pasture, provender, repast, silage, spread, tuck-in, victuals.

feed in inject, input, key in, supply.

feed on consume, devour, eat, exist on, live on, partake of.

feel *v.* appear, believe, caress, consider, deem, empathize, endure, enjoy, experience, explore, finger, fondle, fumble, go through, grope, handle, have, have a hunch, hold, intuit, judge, know, manipulate, maul, notice, observe, paw, perceive, reckon, resemble, seem, sense, sound, stroke, suffer, take to heart, test, think, touch, try, undergo.

n. bent, feeling, finish, gift, impression, knack, quality, sense, surface, texture, touch, vibes.

feeling *n.* (a)esthesia, (a)esthesis, affection, air, ambience, appreciation, apprehension, ardor, atmosphere, aura, compassion, concern, consciousness, emotion, empathy, Empfindung, feel, fervor, fondness, heat, hunch, idea, impression, inclination, inkling, instinct, intensity, mood, notion, opinion, passion, perception, pity, point of view, presentiment, quality, sensation, sense, sensibility, sensitivity, sentiment, sentimentality, suspicion, sympathy, touch, understanding, vibes, vibrations, view, warmth.

fellowship *n.* amity, association, brotherhood, camaraderie, club, communion, companionability, companionableness, companionship, endowment, familiarity, fraternization, fraternity, guild, intercourse, intimacy, kindliness, league, order, sisterhood, sociability, society, sodality.

feminine *adj.* delicate, effeminate, effete, gentle, girlish, graceful, ladylike, modest, petticoat, sissy, soft, tender, unmanly, unmasculine, weak, womanish, womanly.

antonym masculine.

ferocious *adj.* barbaric, barbarous, bloodthirsty, bloody, brutal, brutish, catamountain, cruel, fearsome, feral, fiendish, fierce, homicidal, inhuman, merciless, murderous, pitiless, predatory, rapacious, ravening, relentless, ruthless, sadistic, sanguinary, savage, truculent, vicious, violent, wild.

antonyms gentle, mild.

fertile *adj.* abundant, fat, fecund, feracious, flowering, fructiferous, fructuous, frugiferous, fruit-bearing, fruitful, generative, lush, luxuriant, plenteous, plentiful, potent, productive, prolific, rich, teeming, uberous, virile, yielding.

antonyms arid, barren.

festival *n.* anniversary, carnival, celebration, commemoration, eisteddfod, entertainment, feast, festa, festivities, fête, field day, fiesta, gala, holiday, holy day, jubilee, junketing, merry-make, merrymaking, merrynight, mod, puja, saint's day, treat.

festive *adj.* carnival, celebratory, cheery, Christmassy, convivial, cordial, en fête, festal, festivous, gala, gay, gleeful, happy, hearty, holiday, jolly, jovial, joyful, joyous, jubilant, merry, mirthful, rollicking, sportive, uproarious.
antonyms gloomy, sober, somber.

fetch *v.* be good for, bring, bring in, carry, conduct, convey, deliver, draw, earn, elicit, escort, evoke, get, go for, lead, make, obtain, produce, realize, retrieve, sell for, transport, uplift, utter, yield.

fetching *adj.* alluring, attractive, beguiling, captivating, charming, cute, disarming, enchanting, enticing, fascinating, pretty, sweet, taking, winning, winsome.
antonym repellent.

feud *n.* animosity, antagonism, argument, bad blood, bickering, bitterness, conflict, contention, disagreement, discord, dispute, dissension, enmity, estrangement, faction, feuding, grudge, hostility, ill will, quarrel, rivalry, row, strife, variance, vendetta.
antonyms agreement, peace.
v. altercate, argue, be at odds, bicker, brawl, clash, contend, dispute, duel, fight, quarrel, row, squabble, war, wrangle.
antonym agree.

fever *n.* agitation, calenture, delirium, ecstasy, excitement, febricity, febricula, febricule, ferment, fervor, feverishness, flush, frenzy, heat, intensity, passion, pyrexia, restlessness, temperature, turmoil, unrest.

fiber *n.* backbone, bast, caliber, character, courage, determination, essence, fibril, filament, filasse, funicle, grit, guts, nature, nerve, pile, pluck, quality, resolution, sinew, spirit, stamina, staple, strand, strength, substance, temperament, tenacity, tendril, texture, thread, toughness.

fickle *adj.* capricious, changeable, disloyal, dizzy, erratic, faithless, fitful, flighty, fluctuating, inconstant, irresolute, mercurial, mutable, quicksilver, treacherous, unfaithful, unpredictable, unreliable, unstable, unsteady, vacillating, variable, volage, volageous, volatile, wind-changing.
antonym constant.

fiction *n.* canard, cock-and-bull story, concoction, fable, fabrication, falsehood, fancy, fantasy, feuilleton, fib, figment, imagination, improvisation, invention, legend, lie, myth, novel, parable, romance, story, story-telling, tale, tall story, untruth, whopper, yarn.
antonym truth.

fictitious *adj.* aprocryphal, artificial, assumed, bogus, counterfeit, fabricated, false, fanciful, feigned, fictive, fraudulent, imaginary, imagined, improvised, invented, made-up, make-believe, mythical, non-existent, spurious, supposed, suppositional, supposititious, unreal, untrue.
antonyms genuine, real.

fidelity *n.* accuracy, adherence, allegiance, authenticity, closeness, constancy, correspondence, dedication, de pendability, devotedness, devotion, dutifulness, exactitude, exactness, faith, faithfulness, fealty, incorruptibility, integrity, lealty, loyalty, preciseness, precision, reliability, scrupulousness, staunchness, steadfastness, true-heartedness, trustworthiness.
antonyms inaccuracy, inconstancy, treachery.

fidget *v.* bustle, chafe, fiddle, fidge, fike, fret, jerk, jiggle, jitter, jump, mess about, play around, squirm, toy, twitch, worry.
n. agitation, anxiety, creeps, discomposure, edginess, fidgetiness, fidgets, heebie-jeebies, jimjams, jitteriness, jitters, jumpiness, nerves, nerviness, nervousness, restlessness, shakes, twitchiness, unease, uneasiness, willies.

fierce *adj.* baleful, barbarous, blustery, boisterous, brutal, cruel, cut-throat, dangerous, fearsome, fell, feral, ferocious, fiery, frightening, furious, grim, howling, intense, keen, menacing, merciless, murderous, passionate, powerful, raging, relentless, savage, stern, stormy, strong, tempestuous, threatening, truculent, tumultuous, uncontrollable, unrelenting, untamed, vicious, violent, wild.
antonyms calm, gentle, kind.

fiercely *adv.* ardently, bitterly, fanatically, ferociously, furiously, implacably, intensely, keenly, menacingly, mercilessly, murderously, passionately, relentlessly, savagely, sternly, tempestuously, tigerishly, tooth and nail, viciously, violently, wildly, zealously.
antonyms gently, kindly.

fight *v.* altercate, argue, assault, battle, bear arms against, bicker, box, brawl, clash, close, combat, conduct, conflict, contend, contest, cross swords, defy, dispute, do battle, engage, exchange, blows, fence, feud, grapple, joust, lock horns, measure strength, measure swords, mell, mix it, oppose, prosecute, quarrel, resist, scrap, scuffle, skirmish, spar, squabble, stand up to, strive, struggle, take the field, tilt, tussle, wage, wage war, war, withstand, wrangle, wrestle.
n. action, affray, altercation, argument, barney, battle, belligerence, bicker, bout, brawl, brush, clash, combat, conflict, contest, courage, dispute, dissension, dogfight, duel, encounter, engagement, fisticuffs, fracas, fray, free-for-all, gameness, hostilities, joust, luctation, mêlée, mettle, militancy, monomachy, passage of arms, pluck, pugnacity, quarrel, rammy, resilience, resistance, riot, row, ruck, rumble, scrap, scuffle, set-to, skirmish, spirit, strength, struggle, tenacity, tussle, war.

fighter *n.* adventurer, antagonist, battler, belligerent, boxer, brave, bruiser, champion, combatant, contender, contestant, disputant, fighting man, filibuster, free lance, gladiator, man-at-arms, mercenary, militant, prize-fighter, pugilist, soldier, soldier of fortune, swordsman, trouper, warrior, wrestler.

figment *n.* concoction, creation, deception, delusion, fable, fabrication, falsehood, fancy, fiction, illusion,

figure 138 **fine**

improvisation, invention, mare's nest, production, work.

figure *n.* amount, body, build, celebrity, character, chassis, cipher, configuration, conformation, cost, depiction, design, device, diagram, digit, dignitary, drawing, embellishment, emblem, form, frame, illustration, image, leader, motif, notability, notable, number, numeral, outline, pattern, personage, personality, physique, presence, price, proportions, representation, shadow, shape, sign, silhouette, sketch, somebody, sum, symbol, torso, total, trope, value.

v. act, add, appear, believe, calculate, compute, count, estimate, feature, guess, judge, opine, reckon, sum, surmise, tally, think, tot up, work out.

file[1] *v.* abrade, burnish, furbish, grate, hone, pare, plane, polish, rasp, refine, rub (down), sand, scour, scrape, shape, shave, smooth, trim, whet.

file[2] *n.* binder, cabinet, case, date, documents, dossier, folder, information, portfolio, record.

v. capture, document, enter, memorize, pigeonhole, process, record, register, slot in, store.

file[3] *n.* column, cortège, line, list, procession, queue, row, stream, string, trail, train.

v. defile, march, parade, stream, trail, troop.

fill *v.* assign, block, bung, charge, clog, close, congest, cork, cram, crowd, discharge, drench, engage, englut, engorge, execute, fulfil, furnish, glut, gorge, hold, imbue, impregnate, inflate, load, occupy, officiate, overspread, pack, perform, permeate, pervade, plug, replenish, sate, satiate, satisfy, saturate, seal, soak, stock, stop, stuff, suffuse, supply, surfeit, swell, take up. *antonyms* clear, empty.

n. abundance, ample, enough, plenty, sufficiency, sufficient.

fillip *n.* boost, flick, goad, impetus, incentive, prod, push, shove, spice, spur, stimulus, zest. *antonym* damper.

filter *v.* clarify, dribble, escape, exude, filtrate, leach, leak, ooze, penetrate, percolate, purify, refine, screen, seep, sieve, sift, strain, transpire, transude, trickle, well. *n.* colander, gauze, membrane, mesh, riddle, sieve, sifter, strainer.

filth *n.* bilge, carrion, coarseness, colluvies, contamination, coprolalia, coprophilia, corruption, crud, defilement, dirt, dirty-mindedness, dung, excrement, excreta, faex, feces, filthiness, foulness, garbage, grime, grossness, gunge, impurity, indecency, muck, nastiness, obscenity, ordure, pollution, pornography, putrefaction, putrescence, refuse, scatology, sewage, slime, sludge, smut, smuttiness, soil, sordes, sordidness, squalor, sullage, uncleanness, vileness, vulgarity.

antonyms cleanliness, decency, purity.

filthy *adj.* Augean, base, bawdy, begrimed, black, blackened, blue, coarse, contemptible, coprolaliac, coprophilous, corrupt, depraved, despicable, dirty, dirty-minded, fecal, feculent, foul, foul-mouthed, grimy, gross, grubby, impure, indecent, lavatorial, lewd, licentious, low, mean, miry, mucky, muddy, nasty, nasty-minded, obscene, offensive, polluted, pornographic, putrid, scatological, scurrilous, slimy, smoky, smutty, sooty, sordid, squalid, suggestive, swinish, unclean, unwashed, vicious, vile, vulgar.

antonyms clean, decent, inoffensive, pure.

final *adj.* absolute, clinching, closing, concluding, conclusive, conclusory, decided, decisive, definite, definitive, desinent, desinential, determinate, dying, eleventh-hour, end, eventual, finished, incontrovertible, irrefragable, irrefutable, irrevocable, last, last-minute, latest, settled, terminal, terminating, ultimate, undeniable.

finalize *v.* agree, clinch, complete, conclude, decide, dispose of, finish, get signed and sealed, get taped, resolve, round off, seal, settle, sew up, tie up, work out, wrap up.

finally *adv.* absolutely, at last, at length, completely, conclusively, convincingly, decisively, definitely, eventually, for ever, for good, for good and all, in conclusion, in the end, inescapably, inexorably, irreversibly, irrevocably, lastly, once and for all, permanently, ultimately.

find *v.* achieve, acquire, ascertain, attain, bring, catch, chance on, come across, consider, contribute, cough up, descry, detect, discover, earn, encounter, espy, experience, expose, ferret out, furnish, gain, get, hit on, judge, learn, light on, locate, meet, note, notice, observe, obtain, perceive, procure, provide, reach, realize, recognize, recover, rediscover, regain, remark, repossess, retrieve, spot, stumble on, supply, think, track down, turn up, uncover, unearth, win.

n. acquisition, asset, bargain, catch, coup, discovery, good buy, unconsidered trifle.

fine[1] *adj.* abstruse, acceptable, acute, admirable, agreeable, all right, attractive, balmy, beau, beaut, beautiful, bonny, brave, braw, bright, brilliant, choice, clear, clement, cloudless, convenient, critical, cutting, dainty, dandy, delicate, diaphanous, discriminating, dry, elegant, elusive, excellent, exceptional, expensive, exquisite, fair, fastidious, fine-drawn, first-class, first-rate, flimsy, four-square, fragile, gauzy, good, good-looking, goodly, gorgeous, gossamer, great, hair-splitting, handsome, honed, hunky-dory, impressive, intelligent, jake, keen, light, lovely, magnificent, masterly, minute, nice, OK, ornate, outstanding, pleasant, polished, powdery, precise, pure, quick, rare, refined, robust, satisfactory, select, sensitive, sharp, sheer, showy, skilful, skilled, slender, small, smart, solid, splendid, sterling, strong, sturdy, stylish, sublime, subtle, suitable, sunny, superior, supreme, tasteful, tenuous, thin, tickety-boo, unalloyed, virtuoso, well-favored, wiredrawn.

fine[2] *v.* amerce, mulct, penalize, punish, sting.

n. amercement, amerciament, damages, forfeit, forfeiture, mulct, penalty, punishment.

finesse *n.* address, adeptness, adroitness, artfulness, artifice, cleverness, craft, deftness, delicacy, diplomacy, discretion, elegance, expertise, gracefulness, know-how, neatness, polish, quickness, refinement, savoir-faire, skill, sophistication, subtlety, tact.

v. bluff, evade, manipulate, maneuver, trick.

finicky *adj.* choosy, critical, dainty, delicate, difficult, fastidious, finical, finicking, fussy, hypercritical, meticulous, nice, nit-picking, overnice, particular, pernickety, scrupulous, squeamish, tricky.

antonyms easy, easy-going.

finish *v.* accomplish, achieve, annihilate, best, buff, burnish, cease, close, coat, complete, conclude, consume, consummate, culminate, deal with, defeat, destroy, devour, discharge, dispatch, dispose of, do, drain, drink, eat, elaborate, empty, encompass, end, execute, exhaust, expend, exterminate, face, finalize, fulfil, get rid of, gild, hone, kill, lacquer, overcome, overpower, overthrow, perfect, polish, put an end to, put the last hand to, refine, round off, rout, ruin, settle, smooth, smooth off, sophisticate, spend, stain, stop, terminate, texture, use (up), veneer, wax, wind up, worst, zap.

n. annihilation, appearance, bankruptcy, burnish, cessation, close, closing, completion, conclusion, coup de grâce, culmination, cultivation, culture, curtain, curtains, death, defeat, dénouement, elaboration, end, end of the road, ending, finale, gloss, grain, liquidation, luster, patina, perfection, polish, refinement, ruin, shine, smoothness, sophistication, surface, termination, texture, wind-up.

fire *n.* animation, ardor, bale-fire, barrage, blaze, bombardment, bonfire, brio, broadside, burning, cannonade, combustion, conflagration, dash, eagerness, earnestness, élan, enthusiasm, excitement, feeling, fervency, fervidity, fervidness, fervor, feu de joie, fierceness, flak, flames, force, fusillade, heat, impetuosity, inferno, intensity, life, light, luster, passion, radiance, salvo, scintillation, shelling, sniping, sparkle, spirit, splendor, verve, vigor, virtuosity, vivacity, volley, warmth, zeal.

v. activate, animate, arouse, boot out, cashier, depose, detonate, discharge, dismiss, eject, electrify, enkindle, enliven, excite, explode, galvanize, give marching orders, give the bum's rush, hurl, ignite, impassion, incite, inflame, inspire, inspirit, kindle, launch, let off, light, loose, put a match to, quicken, rouse, sack, send off, set alight, set fire to, set off, set on fire, shell, shoot, show the door, stimulate, stir, touch off, trigger off, whet.

firm[1] *adj.* abiding, adamant, anchored, balanced, braced, cast-iron, cemented, changeless, committed, compact, compressed, concentrated, congealed, constant, convinced, crisp, definite, dense, dependable, determined, dogged, durable, embedded, enduring, established, fast,

fastened, fixed, grounded, hard, hardened, immovable, impregnable, indurate, inelastic, inflexible, iron-hearted, jelled, jellified, motionless, obdurate, reliable, resolute, resolved, rigid, robust, secure, secured, set, settled, solid, solidified, stable, stationary, staunch, steadfast, steady, stiff, strict, strong, sturdy, substantial, sure, taut, tight, true, unalterable, unassailable, unbending, unchanging, undeviating, unfaltering, unflinching, unmoved, unmoving, unshakable, unshakeable, unshaken, unshifting, unswerving, unwavering, unyielding, well-knit.

antonyms infirm, soft, unsound.

firm[2] *n.* association, business, company, concern, conglomerate, corporation, enterprise, establishment, house, institution, organization, outfit, partnership, set-up, syndicate.

first *adj.* basic, cardinal, chief, earliest, eldest, elementary, embryonic, foremost, fundamental, head, highest, initial, introductory, key, leading, maiden, main, oldest, opening, original, paramount, predominant, preeminent, premier, primal, primary, prime, primeval, primitive, primordial, principal, prior, pristine, rudimentary, ruling, senior, sovereign, uppermost.

adv. at the outset, before all else, beforehand, early on, firstly, in preference, in the beginning, initially, originally, primarily, rather, sooner, to begin with, to start with.

fishy *adj.* doubtful, dubious, fish-like, funny, glassy, implausible, improbable, irregular, odd, piscatorial, piscatory, pisciform, piscine, queer, questionable, rummy, shady, suspect, suspicious, unlikely, vacant.

antonyms honest, legitimate.

fissile *adj.* cleavable, divisible, easily split, fissionable, fissive, flaky, scissile, separable, severable.

fission *n.* breaking, cleavage, division, parting, rending, rupture, schism, scission, severance, splitting.

fit[1] *adj.* able, able-bodied, adapted, adequate, apposite, appropriate, apt, becoming, blooming, capable, commensurate, competent, condign, convenient, correct, deserving, due, eligible, equipped, expedient, fit as a fiddle, fitted, fitting, hale, hale and hearty, healthy, in fine fettle, in good form, in good nick, in good shape, in good trim, in the pink, meet, prepared, proper, qualified, ready, right, robust, satisfactory, seemly, sound, strapping, strong, sturdy, suitable, suited, trained, trim, well, well-suited, worthy.

antonym unfit.

v. accommodate, accord, adapt, adjust, agree, alter, arrange, assimilate, belong, change, concur, conform, correspond, dispose, dovetail, fashion, fay, figure, follow, gee, go, harmonize, interlock, join, match, meet, modify, place, position, reconcile, shape, suit, tally.

fit[2] *n.* access, attack, bout, burst, caprice, convulsion, eruption, exies, explosion, fancy, humor, mood, outbreak, outburst, paroxysm, seizure, spasm, spell, storm, surge, whim.

fitful *adj.* broken, desultory, disturbed, erratic, fluctuating, haphazard, intermittent, irregular, occasional, spasmodic, sporadic, uneven, unstable, unsteady, variable. *antonyms* regular, steady.

fitting *adj.* apposite, appropriate, apt, becoming, comme il faut, condign, correct, decent, decorous, deserved, desirable, harmonious, meet, merited, proper, right, seasonable, seemly, suitable. *antonym* unsuitable.
n. accessory, attachment, component, connection, fitment, fixture, part, piece, unit.

fix[1] *v.* adjust, agree on, anchor, appoint, arrange, arrive at, attach, bind, cement, conclude, confirm, congeal, connect, consolidate, correct, couple, decide, define, determine, direct, embed, establish, fasten, fiddle, finalize, firm, focus, freeze, glue, harden, implant, inculcate, influence, install, irradicate, limit, link, locate, make, manipulate, maneuver, mend, nail, name, ordain, pin, place, plant, point, position, prearrange, preordain, produce, regulate, repair, resolve, restore, rigidify, rigidize, rivet, root, seal, seat, secure, see to, set, settle, solidify, sort, sort out, specify, stabilize, stick, stiffen, straighten, swing, thicken, tidy, tie.
n. corner, difficulty, dilemma, embarrassment, hole, jam, mess, muddle, nineholes, pickle, plight, predicament, quagmire, quandary, scrape, spot.

fix[2] *n.* dose, hit, injection, jag, score, shot, slug.

fixation *n.* complex, compulsion, fetish, hang-up, idée fixe, infatuation, mania, monomania, obsession, preoccupation, thing.

flabbergasted *adj.* amazed, astonished, astounded, bowled over, confounded, dazed, disconcerted, dumbfounded, nonplused, overcome, overwhelmed, speechless, staggered, stunned, stupefied.

flagrant *adj.* arrant, atrocious, audacious, barefaced, blatant, bold, brazen, conspicuous, crying, egregious, enormous, flagitious, flaunting, glaring, heinous, immodest, infamous, notorious, open, ostentatious, outrageous, overt, rank, scandalous, shameless, unashamed, undisguised.
antonyms covert, secret.

flair *n.* ability, accomplishment, acumen, aptitude, chic, dash, discernment, elegance, facility, faculty, feel, genius, gift, knack, mastery, nose, panache, skill, style, stylishness, talent, taste.
antonym ineptitude.

flamboyant *adj.* baroque, brilliant, colorful, dashing, dazzling, elaborate, exciting, extravagant, flashy, florid, gaudy, glamorous, jaunty, ornate, ostentatious, rich, showy, striking, stylish, swashbuckling, theatrical.
antonyms modest, restrained.

flame *v.* beam, blaze, burn, flare, flash, glare, glow, radiate, shine.
n. affection, ardor, beau, blaze, brightness, enthusiasm, fervency, fervor, fire, flake, flammule, heart-throb, intensity, keenness, light, lover, passion, radiance, sweetheart, warmth, zeal.

flash *v.* blaze, bolt, brandish, coruscate, dart, dash, display, exhibit, expose, flare, flaunt, flicker, flourish, fly, fulgurate, fulminate, glare, gleam, glint, glisten, glitter, light, race, scintillate, shimmer, shoot, show, sparkle, speed, sprint, streak, sweep, twinkle, whistle.
n. blaze, bluette, burst, coruscation, dazzle, demonstration, display, flare, flaught, flicker, fulguration, gleam, hint, instant, jiff, jiffy, manifestation, moment, outburst, ray, scintillation, second, shaft, shake, shimmer, show, sign, spark, sparkle, split second, streak, touch, trice, twinkle, twinkling.

flashy *adj.* bold, brassy, cheap, flamboyant, flash, garish, gaudy, glamorous, glittery, glitzy, jazzy, loud, meretricious, obtrusive, ostentatious, raffish, rakish, ritzy, showy, snazzy, tacky, tasteless, tawdry, tig(e)rish, tinselly, vulgar.
antonyms plain, simple, tasteful.

flat[1] *adj.* even, horizontal, lamellar, lamelliform, level, leveled, low, outstretched, planar, plane, prone, prostrate, reclining, recumbent, smooth, spread-eagled, supine, unbroken, uniform.
n. lowland, marsh, morass, moss, mud flat, plain, shallow, shoal, strand, swamp.

flat[2] *adj.* bored, boring, burst, collapsed, dead, deflated, depressed, dull, empty, flavorless, insipid, jejune, lackluster, lifeless, monotonous, pointless, prosaic, punctured, spiritless, stale, tedious, uninteresting, unpalatable, vapid, watery, weak.

flat[3] *adj.* absolute, categorical, direct, downright, explicit, final, fixed, out-and-out, peremptory, plain, pointblank, positive, straight, total, uncompromising, unconditional, unequivocal, unqualified.
antonym equivocal.
adv. absolutely, categorically, completely, entirely, exactly, point-blank, precisely, totally, utterly.

flat[4] *n.* apartment, bed-sit, bed-sitter, maison(n)ette, pad, penthouse, pied-à-terre, rooms, tenement.

flatly *adv.* absolutely, categorically, completely, peremptorily, point-blank, positively, uncompromisingly, unconditionally, unhesitatingly.

flattery *n.* adulation, backscratching, blandishment, blarney, bootlicking, butter, cajolement, cajolery, eulogy, fawning, flannel, flapdoodle, fleechment, fulsomeness, ingratiation, obsequiousness, servility, soap, soft sawder, soft soap, sugar, sweet talk, sycophancy, sycophantism, taffy, toadyism, unctuousness.
antonym criticism.

flaunt *v.* air, boast, brandish, dangle, display, disport, exhibit, flash, flourish, parade, show off, sport, vaunt, wield.

flavor *n.* aroma, aspect, character, essence, extract, feel, feeling, flavoring, hint, odor, piquancy, property, quality, relish, sapidity, savor, savoriness, seasoning, smack, soupçon, stamp, style, suggestion, tang, taste, tastiness, tinge, tone, touch, zest, zing.

v. contaminate, ginger up, imbue, infuse, lace, leaven, season, spice, taint.

flaw *n.* blemish, breach, break, cleft, crack, craze, crevice, defect, disfigurement, failing, fallacy, fault, fissure, fracture, hamartia, imperfection, lapse, macula, mark, mistake, rent, rift, shortcoming, slip, speck, split, spot, tear, weakness, wreath.

flee *v.* abscond, avoid, beat a hasty retreat, bolt, bunk (off), cut and run, decamp, depart, escape, fly, get away, leave, make off, make oneself scarce, scarper, scram, shun, skedaddle, split, take flight, take it on the lam, take off, take to one's heels, vamoose, vanish, withdraw.

antonyms stand, stay.

fleece *v.* bilk, bleed, cheat, clip, con, defraud, diddle, mulct, overcharge, plunder, rifle, rip off, rob, rook, shear, skin, soak, squeeze, steal, sting, swindle.

fleet[1] *n.* argosy, armada, escadrille, flota, flotilla, navy, squadron, task force.

fleet[2] *adj.* expeditious, fast, flying, light-footed, mercurial, meteoric, nimble, quick, rapid, speedy, swift, velocipede, winged.

antonym slow.

fleeting *adj.* brief, disappearing, ephemeral, evanescent, flitting, flying, fugacious, fugitive, impermanent, momentary, passing, short, short-lived, temporary, transient, transitory, vanishing.

antonym lasting.

fleshy *adj.* ample, beefy, brawny, carneous, carnose, chubby, chunky, corpulent, fat, flabby, hefty, meaty, obese, overweight, paunchy, plump, podgy, portly, rotund, stout, tubby, well-padded.

antonym thin.

flexible *adj.* accommodating, adaptable, adjustable, agreeable, amenable, bendable, biddable, complaisant, complaint, discretionary, docile, double-jointed, ductile, elastic, flexile, gentle, limber, lissome, lithe, loose-limbed, manageable, mobile, moldable, open, plastic, pliable, pliant, responsive, springy, stretchy, supple, tensile, tractable, variable, whippy, willowy, withy, yielding.

antonym inflexible.

flighty *adj.* bird-brained, bird-witted, capricious, changeable, dizzy, fickle, frivolous, giddy, hare-brained, impetuous, impulsive, inconstant, irresponsible, light-headed, mercurial, rattle-brained, rattle-headed, rattle-pated, scatterbrained, silly, skittish, thoughtless, unbalanced, unstable, unsteady, volage, volageous, volatile, whisky-frisky, wild.

antonym steady.

flimsy *adj.* cardboard, chiffon, cobwebby, delicate, diaphanous, ethereal, feeble, fragile, frail, frivolous, gauzy, gimcrack, gossamer, implausible, inadequate, insubstantial, light, makeshift, meager, poor, rickety,

shaky, shallow, sheer, slight, superficial, thin, transparent, trivial, unconvincing, unsatisfactory, unsubstantial, vaporous, weak.

antonym sturdy.

fling *v.* bung, cant, cast, catapult, chuck, heave, hurl, jerk, let fly, lob, pitch, precipitate, propel, send, shoot, shy, sling, slug, souse, throw, toss.

n. attempt, bash, binge, cast, crack, gamble, go, heave, indulgence, lob, pitch, shot, spree, stab, throw, toss, trial, try, turn, venture, whirl.

flippant *adj.* brash, cheeky, cocky, disrespectful, flip, frivolous, glib, impertinent, impudent, irreverent, malapert, nonchalant, offhand, pert, pococurante, rude, saucy, superficial, unserious.

antonym earnest.

flit *v.* beat, bob, dance, dart, elapse, flash, fleet, flutter, fly, pass, skim, slip, speed, volitate, whisk, wing.

flock *v.* bunch, cluster, collect, congregate, converge, crowd, gather, gravitate, group, herd, huddle, mass, swarm, throng, troop.

n. assembly, bevy, collection, colony, company, congregation, convoy, crowd, drove, flight, gaggle, gathering, group, herd, horde, host, mass, multitude, pack, shoal, skein, swarm, throng.

flog *v.* beat, birch, breech, chastise, drive, drub, flagellate, flay, hide, knout, k(o)urbash, larrup, lash, overexert, overtax, overwork, punish, push, scourge, strain, swish, tat, tax, thrash, trounce, vapulate, verberate, welt, whack, whale, whang, whip, whop.

flood *v.* bog down, brim, choke, deluge, drench, drown, engulf, fill, flow, glut, gush, immerse, inundate, overflow, oversupply, overwhelm, pour, rush, saturate, soak, submerge, surge, swamp, swarm, sweep.

n. abundance, alluvion, bore, cataclysm, debacle, deluge, diluvion, diluvium, downpour, eagre, flash flood, flow, freshet, glut, inundation, multitude, outpouring, overflow, plethora, profusion, rush, spate, stream, superfluity, tide, torrent.

antonyms dearth, drought, trickle.

florid *adj.* baroque, blowzy, bombastic, busy, coloratura, elaborate, embellished, euphuistic, figurative, flamboyant, flourishy, flowery, flushed, fussy, grandiloquent, high-colored, high-falutin(g), high-flown, melismatic, ornate, over-elaborate, purple, raddled, red, rococo, rubicund, ruddy. *antonyms* pale, plain.

flourish[1] *v.* advance, bloom, blossom, boom, burgeon, develop, do well, flower, get on, grow, increase, mushroom, progress, prosper, succeed, thrive, wax.

antonyms fail, languish.

flourish[2] *v.* brandish, display, flaunt, flutter, parade, shake, sweep, swing, swish, twirl, vaunt, wag, wave, wield.

n. arabesque, brandishing, ceremony, curlicue, dash, decoration, display, élan, embellishment, fanfare, ornament, ornamentation, panache, parade, paraph, pizzazz, plume, shaking, show, sweep, twirling, wave.

flout *v.* affront, contemn, defy, deride, disregard, insult, jeer at, mock, outrage, reject, ridicule, scoff at, scorn, scout, spurn, taunt.

antonym respect.

flow *v.* arise, bubble, cascade, circulate, course, deluge, derive, distil, drift, emanate, emerge, flood, glide, gush, inundate, issue, move, originate, overflow, pour, proceed, purl, result, ripple, roll, run, rush, slide, slip, spew, spill, spring, spurt, squirt, stream, surge, sweep, swirl, teem, well, whirl.

n. abundance, cascade, course, current, deluge, drift, effluence, efflux, effusion, emanation, flood, flowage, flux, fluxion, gush, outflow, outpouring, plenty, plethora, spate, spurt, stream, succession, tide, train, wash.

fluctuate *v.* alter, alternate, change, ebb and flow, float, hesitate, oscillate, pendulate, rise and fall, seesaw, shift, shuffle, sway, swing, undulate, vacillate, vary, veer, waver.

fluent *adj.* articulate, easy, effortless, eloquent, facile, flowing, fluid, glib, mellifluous, natural, ready, smooth, smooth-talking, voluble, well-versed.

antonym tongue-tied.

fluff *n.* down, dust, dustball, floccus, flosh, floss, flue, fug, fuzz, lint, nap, oose, pile.

v. balls up, botch, bungle, cock up, fumble, mess up, muddle, muff, screw up, spoil.

antonym bring off.

fluid *adj.* adaptable, adjustable, aqueous, changeable, diffluent, easy, elegant, feline, flexible, floating, flowing, fluctuating, fluent, fluidal, fluidic, graceful, inconstant, indefinite, liquefied, liquid, melted, mercurial, mobile, molten, mutable, protean, running, runny, shifting, sinuous, smooth, unstable, watery.

antonyms solid, stable.

n. humor, juice, liquid, liquor, sanies, sap, solution.

fluke *n.* accident, blessing, break, chance, coincidence, fortuity, freak, lucky break, quirk, serendipity, stroke, windfall.

flummoxed *adj.* at a loss, at sea, baffled, befuddled, bewildered, confounded, confused, foxed, mystified, nonplused, perplexed, puzzled, stumped, stymied.

flush[1] *v.* blush, burn, color, crimson, flame, glow, go red, mantle, redden, rouge, suffuse.

antonym pale.

n. bloom, blush, color, freshness, glow, redness, rosiness, rud, vigor.

flush[2] *v.* cleanse, douche, drench, eject, empty, evacuate, expel, hose, rinse, swab, syringe, wash.

adj. abundant, affluent, full, generous, in funds, lavish, liberal, moneyed, overflowing, prodigal, prosperous, rich, rolling, wealthy, well-heeled, well-off, well-supplied, well-to-do.

flush[3] *adj.* even, flat, level, plane, smooth, square, true.

flush[4] *v.* discover, disturb, drive out, force out, rouse, run to earth, start, uncover.

fluster *v.* abash, agitate, bother, bustle, confound, confuse, discombobulate, disconcert, discountenance, disturb, embarrass, excite, faze, flurry, hassle, heat, hurry, perturb, pother, pudder, rattle, ruffle, unnerve, unsettle, upset.

antonym calm.

n. agitation, bustle, commotion, discomposure, distraction, disturbance, dither, embarrassment, faze, flap, flurry, flutter, furore, kerfuffle, perturbation, ruffle, state, tizzy, turmoil.

antonym calm.

fly[1] *v.* abscond, aviate, avoid, bolt, career, clear out, dart, dash, decamp, disappear, display, elapse, escape, flap, flee, flit, float, flutter, get away, glide, hare, hasten, hasten away, hedge-hop, hightail it, hoist, hover, hurry, light out, mount, operate, pass, pilot, race, raise, retreat, roll by, run, run for it, rush, sail, scamper, scarper, scoot, shoot, show, shun, skim, soar, speed, sprint, take flight, take off, take to one's heels, take wing, tear, vamoose, volitate, wave, whisk, whiz, wing, zoom.

fly[2] *adj.* alert, artful, astute, canny, careful, cunning, knowing, nobody's fool, on the ball, prudent, sagacious, sharp, shrewd, smart, wide-awake.

foam *n.* barm, bubbles, effervescence, foaminess, froth, frothiness, head, lather, scum, spume, spumescence, suds.

v. boil, bubble, effervesce, fizz, froth, lather, spume.

foe *n.* adversary, antagonist, enemy, foeman, ill-wisher, opponent, rival.

antonym friend.

fog *n.* bewilderment, blanket, blindness, brume, confusion, daze, gloom, haze, London particular, miasma, mist, muddle, murk, murkiness, obscurity, pea-souper, perplexity, puzzlement, smog, stupor, trance, vagueness.

v. becloud, bedim, befuddle, bewilder, blanket, blind, cloud, confuse, darken, daze, dim, dull, mist, muddle, obfuscate, obscure, perplex, shroud, steam up, stupefy.

foible *n.* crotchet, defect, eccentricity, failing, fault, habit, idiosyncrasy, imperfection, infirmity, oddity, oddness, peculiarity, quirk, shortcoming, strangeness, weakness.

foist *v.* fob off, force, get rid of, impose, insert, insinuate, interpolate, introduce, palm off, pass off, thrust, unload, wish on.

fold *v.* bend, clasp, close, collapse, crash, crease, crimp, crumple, dog-ear, double, embrace, enclose, enfold, entwine, envelop, fail, fake, gather, go bust, hug, intertwine, overlap, pleat, ply, shut down, tuck, wrap, wrap up.

n. bend, corrugation, crease, crimp, duplicature, furrow, knife-edge, layer, overlap, pleat, ply, turn, wimple, wrinkle.

follow *v.* accompany, accord, act according to, appreciate, arise, attend, catch, catch on, chase, come after,

come next, comply, comprehend, conform, cultivate, dangle, develop, dog, emanate, ensue, escort, fathom, get, get the picture, grasp, haunt, heed, hound, hunt, imitate, keep abreast of, live up to, mind, note, obey, observe, pursue, realize, regard, result, second, see, shadow, stag, stalk, succeed, supersede, supervene, supplant, support, tag along, tail, track, trail, twig, understand, watch.
antonyms desert, precede.

follower *n.* acolyte, adherent, admirer, Anthony, apostle, attendant, backer, believer, buff, cohort, companion, convert, devotee, disciple, emulator, fan, fancier, freak, galloglass, habitué, hanger-on, heeler, helper, henchman, imitator, lackey, minion, partisan, poodle-dog, poursuivant, pupil, representative, retainer, running dog, servitor, sidekick, supporter, tantony, votary, worshipper.
antonyms leader, opponent.

following *adj.* coming, consecutive, consequent, consequential, ensuing, later, next, resulting, sequent, subsequent, succeeding, successive.
n. audience, backing, circle, claque, clientèle, coterie, entourage, fans, followers, patronage, public, retinue, suite, support, supporters, train.

folly[1] *n.* absurdity, craziness, daftness, fatuity, foolishness, idiocy, illogicality, imbecility, imprudence, indiscretion, insanity, irrationality, irresponsibility, lunacy, madness, moonraking, moria, nonsense, preposterousness, rashness, recklessness, senselessness, silliness, stupidity, unreason, unwisdom.
antonym prudence.

folly[2] *n.* belvedere, gazebo, monument, tower, whim.
fond *adj.* absurd, adoring, affectionate, amorous, caring, credulous, deluded, devoted, doting, empty, foolish, indiscreet, indulgent, loving, naive, over-optimistic, sanguine, tender, uxorious, vain, warm.
antonyms hostile, realistic.

fondness *n.* affection, attachment, devotion, engouement, enthusiasm, fancy, inclination, kindness, leaning, liking, love, partiality, penchant, predilection, preference, soft spot, susceptibility, taste, tenderness, weakness.
antonym aversion.

food *n.* aliment, ambrosia, board, bread, cheer, chow, comestibles, commons, cooking, cuisine, diet, eatables, eats, edibles, fare, feed, fodder, foodstuffs, forage, grub, larder, meat, menu, nosh, nourishment, nouriture, nutriment, nutrition, pabulum, pap, prog, provand, provend, provender, proviant, provisions, rations, refreshment, scoff, scran, stores, subsistence, sustenance, table, tack, tommy, tuck, tucker, viands, victuals, vittles, vivers.

fool *n.* ass, bécasse, berk, besom-head, bête, bird-brain, blockhead, bonehead, boodle, buffethead, buffoon, burk, butt, capocchia, Charlie, chump, clodpate, clot, clown, cluck, comic, coxcomb, cuckoo, daftie, daw, dawcock, dimwit, dizzard, Dogberry, dolt, dope, dottle, droll, drongo, dumb-bell, dumb-cluck, dumbo, dunce, dunderhead, dunderpate, dupe, easy mark, fall guy, fathead, fon, galah, gaupus, git, goon, goop, goose, greenhorn, gudgeon, gull, halfwit, harlequin, idiot, ignoramus, illiterate, imbecile, jackass, Jack-fool, jerk, jester, jobernowl, josh, joskin, leather-head, loggerhead, log-head, loon, madhaun, merryandrew, mooncalf, moron, motley, mug, nig-nog, nincompoop, ninny, nit, nitwit, nong, noodle, numskull, pierrot, pot-head, prat, prick, punchinello, sap, saphead, sawney, schmo, schmuck, silly, silly-billy, simpleton, soft, softhead, softie, softy, stooge, stupe, stupid, sucker, tomfool, Tom-noddy, turnip, twerp, twit, wally, want-wit, wimp, witling, wooden-head, yap, zany, zombie.
v. act dido, act the fool, act up, bamboozle, be silly, beguile, bluff, cavort, cheat, clown, con, cozen, cut capers, daff, deceive, delude, diddle, dupe, feign, fiddle, fon, frolic, gull, have on, hoax, hoodwink, horse around, jest, joke, kid, lark, meddle, mess, mess about, mislead, monkey, play, play the fool, play the goat, play up, pretend, put one over on, string, string along, swindle, take in, tamper, tease, toy, trick, trifle.

foolish *adj.* absurd, brainless, cockle-brained, crazy, daft, desipient, doited, doltish, dotish, dottled, dunder-headed, étourdi(e), fatuous, glaikit, gudgeon, half-baked, half-witted, hare-brained, idiotic, idle-headed, ill-advised, illaudable, ill-considered, ill-judged, imbecile, imbecilic, imprudent, incautious, indiscreet, inept, injudicious, insipient, lean-witted, ludicrous, mad, moronic, nonsensical, potty, ridiculous, senseless, short-sighted, silly, simple, simple-minded, sottish, stupid, tomfool, unintelligent, unreasonable, unwise, weak, wet, witless.
antonym wise.

footing *n.* base, basis, condition, conditions, establishment, foot-hold, foundation, grade, ground, groundwork, installation, position, purchase, rank, relations, relationship, settlement, standing, state, status, terms.

footnotes *n.* annotations, apparatus criticus, commentary, marginalia, notes, scholia.

footprint *n.* footmark, spoor, trace, track, trail, vestige.

footstep *n.* footfall, plod, step, tramp, tread, trudge.

fop *n.* beau, coxcomb, dandy, dude, exquisite, Jack-a-dandy, Jessie, macaroni, muscadin, musk-cat, pansy, peacock, petit maître, popinjay, spark, swell.

forbearance *n.* abstinence, avoidance, clemency, endurance, indulgence, leniency, lenity, longanimity, long-suffering, mildness, moderation, patience, refraining, resignation, restraint, self-control, sufferance, temperance, tolerance, toleration.
antonym intolerance.

forbid *v.* ban, block, contraindicate, debar, deny, disallow, exclude, hinder, inhibit, interdict, outlaw, preclude, prevent, prohibit, proscribe, refuse, rule out, veto. *antonym* allow.

forbidding *adj.* abhorrent, awesome, daunting, formidable, frightening, gaunt, grim, hostile, inhospitable, menacing, off-putting, ominous, repellent, repulsive, sinister, threatening, unapproachable, unfriendly.
antonyms approachable, congenial.

force[1] *n.* aggression, arm-twisting, beef, big stick, bite, coercion, cogency, compulsion, constraint, drive, duress, dynamism, effect, effectiveness, efficacy, emphasis, energy, enforcement, fierceness, foison, forcefulness, fushion, impact, impetus, impulse, incentive, influence, intensity, jism, life, mailed fist, might, momentum, motivation, muscle, persistence, persuasiveness, potency, power, pressure, punch, shock, steam, stimulus, strength, stress, validity, vehemence, vigor, violence, vis, vitality, weight.
v. bulldoze, coerce, compel, constrain, drag, drive, exact, extort, impel, impose, lean on, make, necessitate, obligate, oblige, press, press-gang, pressure, pressurize, prize, propel, push, strong-arm, thrust, urge, wrench, wrest, wring.

force[2] *n.* army, battalion, body, corps, detachment, detail, division, effective, enomoty, host, legion, patrol, phalanx, regiment, squad, squadron, troop, unit, Wehrmacht.

forceful *adj.* cogent, compelling, convincing, domineering, drastic, dynamic, effective, emphatic, energetic, persuasive, pithy, potent, powerful, strong, telling, urgent, vigorous, weighty.
antonym feeble.

forcible *adj.* active, aggressive, coercive, cogent, compelling, compulsory, drastic, effective, efficient, energetic, forceful, impressive, mighty, pithy, potent, powerful, strong, telling, urgent, vehement, violent, weighty.
antonym feeble.

forebear *n.* ancestor, antecedent, antecessor, father, forefather, forerunner, predecessor, primogenitor, progenitor.
antonym descendant.

foreboding *n.* anticipation, anxiety, apprehension, apprehensiveness, augury, boding, chill, dread, fear, foreshadowing, foretoken, hoodoo, intuition, misgiving, omen, portent, prediction, prefigurement, premonition, presage, presentiment, prodrome, prodromus, prognostication, sign, token, warning, worry.

forecast *v.* augur, bode, calculate, conjecture, divine, estimate, expect, foresee, foretell, plan, predict, prognosticate, prophesy.
n. augury, conjecture, foresight, forethought, guess, guesstimate, outlook, planning, prediction, prognosis, prognostication, projection, prophecy.

foregoing *adj.* above, aforementioned, antecedent, anterior, earlier, former, preceding, previous, prior, prodromal, prodromic.

foreign *adj.* adventitious, adventive, alien, borrowed, distant, exotic, external, extraneous, extrinsic, fremd, imported, incongruous, irrelevant, outlandish, outside,

overseas, remote, strange, tramontane, unassimilable, uncharacteristic, unfamiliar, unknown, unnative, unrelated.
antonym native.

foreigner *n.* alien, Ausländer, barbarian, dago, étranger, étrangère, immigrant, incomer, metic, newcomer, outlander, stranger, uitlander, wog, wop.
antonym native.

foreman *n.* charge-hand, charge-man, gaffer, ganger, gangsman, overman, overseer, oversman, steward, straw boss, supervisor.

foremost *adj.* cardinal, central, chief, first, front, headmost, highest, inaugural, initial, leading, main, paramount, preeminent, primary, prime, principal, salient, supreme, uppermost.

forerunner *n.* ancestor, announcer, antecedent, antecessor, envoy, forebear, foregoer, foretoken, harbinger, herald, indication, omen, portent, precursor, predecessor, premonition, prodrome, prodromus, progenitor, prognostic, prototype, sign, token, vaunt-courier.
antonyms aftermath, result.

foreshadow *v.* adumbrate, anticipate, augur, betoken, bode, forebode, forepoint, foreshow, foresignify, foretoken, imply, import, indicate, omen, portend, predict, prefigure, presage, promise, prophesy, signal.

foresight *n.* anticipation, care, caution, circumspection, farsightedness, forethought, perspicacity, precaution, preparedness, prescience, prevision, providence, provision, prudence, readiness, vision.
antonym improvidence.

forestall *v.* anticipate, avert, balk, circumvent, frustrate, head off, hinder, intercept, obstruct, obviate, parry, preclude, pre-empt, prevent, thwart, ward off.
antonyms encourage, facilitate.

foretell *v.* adumbrate, augur, bode, forebode, forecast, foresay, foreshadow, foreshow, forespeak, forewarn, portend, predict, presage, presignify, prognosticate, prophesy, signify, soothsay, vaticinate.

forever *adv.* always, ceaselessly, constantly, continually, endlessly, eternally, everlastingly, evermore, for all time, for good and all, for keeps, in perpetuity, in saecula saeculorum, incessantly, interminably, permanently, perpetually, persistently, till the cows come home, till the end of time, unremittingly, world without end.

forewarn *v.* admonish, advise, alert, apprize, caution, dissuade, previse, tip off.

forfeit *n.* amercement, damages, escheat, fine, forfeiture, loss, mulct, penalization, penalty, surrender.
v. abandon, forgo, give up, lose, relinquish, renounce, sacrifice, surrender.

forge[1] *v.* beat out, cast, coin, construct, contrive, copy, counterfeit, create, devise, fabricate, fake, falsify, fashion, feign, form, frame, hammer out, imitate, invent, make, mold, shape, simulate, work.

forge[2] *v.* advance, gain ground, improve, make great strides, make headway, press on, proceed, progress, push on.

forget *v.* consign to oblivion, discount, dismiss, disregard, fail, ignore, lose sight of, misremember, neglect, omit, overlook, think no more of, unlearn.
antonym remember.

forgetful *adj.* absent-minded, amnesiac, amnesic, careless, dreamy, heedless, inattentive, lax, neglectful, negligent, oblivious, unmindful, unretentive.
antonyms attentive, heedful.

forgive *v.* absolve, acquit, condone, exculpate, excuse, exonerate, let off, overlook, pardon, remit, shrive.
antonym censure.

forgiving *adj.* clement, compassionate, forbearing, humane, indulgent, lenient, magnanimous, merciful, mild, remissive, soft-hearted, sparing, tolerant.
antonym censorious.

forgo, forego *v.* abandon, abjure, abstain from, cede, do without, eschew, forfeit, give up, pass up, refrain from, relinquish, renounce, resign, sacrifice, surrender, waive, yield.
antonyms claim, indulge in, insist on.

forgotten *adj.* blotted out, buried, bygone, disregarded, ignored, irrecoverable, irretrievable, lost, neglected, obliterated, omitted, out of mind, overlooked, past, past recall, past recollection, unrecalled, unremembered, unretrieved.
antonym remembered.

forlorn *adj.* abandoned, abject, bereft, cheerless, comfortless, deserted, desolate, desperate, destitute, disconsolate, forgotten, forsaken, friendless, helpless, homeless, hopeless, lonely, lost, miserable, pathetic, piteous, pitiable, pitiful, unhappy, woebegone, woeful, wretched.
antonym hopeful.

form *v.* accumulate, acquire, appear, arrange, assemble, bring up, build, combine, compose, comprise, concoct, constitute, construct, contract, contrive, create, crystallize, cultivate, design, develop, devise, discipline, dispose, draw up, educate, establish, evolve, fabricate, fashion, forge, formulate, found, frame, group, grow, hatch, instruct, invent, make, make up, manufacture, materialize, model, mold, organize, pattern, plan, produce, put together, rear, rise, school, serve as, settle, shape, take shape, teach, train. *n.* anatomy, appearance, application, arrangement, behavior, being, body, build, cast, ceremony, character, class, condition, conduct, configuration, construction, convention, custom, cut, description, design, document, etiquette, fashion, fettle, figure, fitness, formality, format, formation, frame, framework, genre, Gestalt, grade, guise, harmony, health, kind, manifestation, manner, manners, matrix, method, mode, model, mold, nature, nick, order, orderliness, organization, outline, paper, pattern, person, physique, plan, practice,

procedure, proportion, protocol, questionnaire, rank, ritual, rule, schedule, semblance, shape, sheet, silhouette, sort, species, spirits, stamp, structure, style, symmetry, system, trim, type, variety, way.

formal *adj.* academic, aloof, approved, ceremonial, ceremonious, conventional, correct, exact, explicit, express, fixed, full-dress, impersonal, lawful, legal, methodical, nominal, official, perfunctory, precise, prescribed, prim, punctilious, recognized, regular, reserved, rigid, ritualistic, set, solemn, starch, starched, starchy, stiff, stiff-necked, stilted, strict, unbending.
antonym informal.

formality *n.* ceremoniousness, ceremony, convenance, convention, conventionality, correctness, custom, decorum, etiquette, form, formalism, gesture, matter of form, politeness, politesse, procedure, propriety, protocol, punctilio, red tape, rite, ritual.
antonym informality.

former *adj.* above, aforementioned, aforesaid, ancient, antecedent, anterior, bygone, departed, earlier, erstwhile, ex-, first mentioned, foregoing, late, long ago, of yore, old, old-time, one-time, past, preceding, pre-existent, previous, prior, pristine, quondam, sometime, umwhile, whilom.
antonyms current, future, later, present, prospective, subsequent.

formidable *adj.* alarming, appalling, arduous, awesome, challenging, colossal, dangerous, daunting, difficult, dismaying, dreadful, enormous, fearful, frightening, frightful, great, horrible, huge, impressive, indomitable, intimidating, leviathan, mammoth, menacing, mighty, onerous, overwhelming, powerful, puissant, redoubtable, shocking, staggering, terrific, terrifying, threatening, toilsome, tremendous.
antonyms easy, genial.

forsake *v.* abandon, abdicate, cast off, desert, discard, disown, forgo, forswear, give up, jettison, jilt, leave, leave in the lurch, quit, reject, relinquish, renounce, repudiate, surrender, throw over, turn one's back on, vacate, yield.
antonyms resume, revert to.

forte *n.* aptitude, bent, gift, long suit, métier, skill, specialty, strength, strong point, talent.
antonyms inadequacy, weak point.

forthcoming[1] *adj.* accessible, approaching, at hand, available, coming, expected, future, imminent, impending, obtainable, projected, prospective, ready.

forthcoming[2] *adj.* chatty, communicative, conversational, expansive, frank, free, informative, loquacious, open, sociable, talkative, unreserved.
antonyms bygone, distant, lacking, reserved.

forthright *adj.* above-board, blunt, bold, candid, direct, four-square, frank, open, outspoken, plain-speaking, plain-spoken, straightforward, straight-from-the-shoulder, trenchant, unequivocal.
antonyms devious, tactful.

forthwith *adv.* at once, directly, eftsoons, immediately, incontinent, instanter, instantly, posthaste, pronto, quickly, right away, straightaway, tout de suite, without delay.

fortify *v.* boost, brace, bulwark, buttress, cheer, confirm, embattle, embolden, encourage, entrench, garrison, hearten, invigorate, lace, load, mix, munify, protect, reassure, reinforce, secure, shore up, spike, steel, stiffen, strengthen, support, sustain.
antonyms dilute, weaken.

fortuitous *adj.* accidental, adventitious, arbitrary, casual, chance, coincidental, contingent, felicitous, fluky, fortunate, happy, incidental, lucky, providential, random, serendipitous, unexpected, unforeseen, unintentional, unplanned.
antonym intentional.

fortunate *adj.* advantageous, auspicious, blessed, bright, convenient, encouraging, favorable, favored, felicitous, fortuitous, golden, happy, helpful, lucky, opportune, profitable, promising, propitious, prosperous, providential, rosy, serendipitous, successful, timely, well-off, well-timed.
antonym unfortunate.

fortune[1] *n.* affluence, assets, bomb, bundle, estate, income, king's ransom, means, mint, opulence, packet, pile, possessions, property, prosperity, riches, treasure, wealth.

fortune[2] *n.* accident, adventures, chance, circumstances, contingency, cup, destiny, doom, expectation, experience, fate, fortuity, hap, happenstance, hazard, history, kismet, life, lot, luck, portion, providence, star, success, weird.

fortune-telling *n.* augury, chiromancy, crystal-gazing, divination, dukkeripen, palmistry, prediction, prognostication, prophecy, second sight.

forward[1] *adj.* advance, advanced, early, enterprising, first, fore, foremost, forward-looking, front, go-ahead, head, leading, onward, precocious, premature, progressive, well-advanced, well-developed.
antonym retrograde.
adv. ahead, en avant, forth, forwards, into view, on, onward, out, outward, to light, to the fore, to the surface.
antonym backward.
v. accelerate, advance, aid, assist, back, dispatch, encourage, expedite, facilitate, favor, foster, freight, further, hasten, help, hurry, post, promote, route, send, send on, ship, speed, support, transmit.
antonyms impede, obstruct.

forward[2] *adj.* assertive, assuming, audacious, bare-faced, bold, brash, brass-necked, brazen, brazen-faced, cheeky, confident, familiar, fresh, impertinent, impudent, malapert, officious, overweening, pert, presuming, presumptuous, pushy.
antonym diffident.

fossilized *adj.* anachronistic, antediluvian, antiquated, archaic, archaistic, dead, démodé, extinct, exuvial, inflexible, obsolete, old-fashioned, old-fog(e)yish, ossified, out of date, outmoded, passé, petrified, prehistoric, stony, superannuated.
antonym up-to-date.

foul *adj.* abhorrent, abominable, abusive, bad, base, blasphemous, blue, blustery, choked, coarse, contaminated, crooked, despicable, detestable, dirty, disagreeable, disfigured, disgraceful, disgusting, dishonest, dishonorable, entangled, fetid, filthy, foggy, foul-mouthed, fraudulent, gross, hateful, heinous, impure, indecent, inequitable, infamous, iniquitous, lewd, loathsome, low, malodorous, mephitic, murky, nasty, nauseating, nefarious, noisome, notorious, obscene, offensive, polluted, profane, putrid, rainy, rank, repulsive, revolting, rotten, rough, scandalous, scatological, scurrilous, shady, shameful, smutty, squalid, stinking, stormy, sullied, tainted, unclean, underhand, unfair, unfavorable, unjust, unsportsmanlike, untidy, vicious, vile, virose, vulgar, wet, wicked, wild.
antonyms clean, fair, pure, worthy.
v. befoul, begrime, besmear, besmirch, block, catch, choke, clog, contaminate, defile, dirty, ensnare, entangle, foul up, jam, pollute, smear, snarl, soil, stain, sully, taint, twist.
antonyms clean, clear, disentangle.

found *v.* base, bottom, build, constitute, construct, create, endow, erect, establish, fix, ground, inaugurate, initiate, institute, organize, originate, plant, raise, rest, root, set up, settle, start, sustain.

foundation *n.* base, basis, bedrock, bottom, endowment, establishment, fond, footing, ground, groundwork, inauguration, institution, organization, setting up, settlement, substance, substratum, substructure, underpinning.

foxy *adj.* artful, astute, canny, crafty, cunning, devious, fly, guileful, knowing, sharp, shrewd, sly, tricky, vulpine, wily.
antonyms naïve, open.

fractious *adj.* awkward, captious, choleric, crabbed, crabby, cross, crotchety, fretful, froward, grouchy, irritable, peevish, pettish, petulant, quarrelsome, querulous, recalcitrant, refractory, testy, touchy, unruly.
antonyms complaisant, placid.

fracture *n.* breach, break, cleft, crack, fissure, gap, opening, rent, rift, rupture, schism, scission, split.
v. break, crack, rupture, splinter, split.
antonym join.

fragile *adj.* breakable, brittle, dainty, delicate, feeble, fine, flimsy, frail, frangible, infirm, insubstantial, shattery, slight, weak.
antonyms durable, robust, tough.

fragment *n.* bit, cantlet, chip, flinder, fraction, frazzle, fritter, morceau, morsel, ort, part, particle, piece, portion, remnant, scrap, shard, shatter, sheave, shiver, shred, sliver.

v. break, break up, come apart, come to pieces, crumble, disintegrate, disunite, divide, fractionalize, fritter, shatter, shiver, splinter, split, split up.

antonyms hold together, join.

fragrance *n.* aroma, balm, balminess, bouquet, fragrancy, odor, perfume, redolence, scent, smell.

fragrant *adj.* aromatic, balmy, balsamy, odoriferous, odorous, perfumed, redolent, suaveolent, sweet, sweet-scented, sweet-smelling.

antonyms smelly, unscented.

frail *adj.* breakable, brittle, decrepit, delicate, feeble, flimsy, fragile, frangible, infirm, insubstantial, puny, slight, tender, unchaste, unsound, vulnerable, weak.

antonyms firm, robust, strong, tough.

frame *v.* assemble, block out, build, case, compose, conceive, concoct, constitute, construct, contrive, cook up, devise, draft, draw up, enclose, enframe, fabricate, fashion, forge, form, formulate, hatch, institute, invent, make, manufacture, map out, model, mold, mount, plan, put together, redact, set up, shape, sketch, surround, trap, victimize.

n. anatomy, body, bodyshell, bodywork, build, carcass, casing, chassis, construction, fabric, flake, form, framework, monture, morphology, mount, mounting, physique, scaffolding, scheme, setting, shell, skeleton, structure, system.

frank *adj.* artless, blunt, candid, direct, downright, forthright, four-square, free, honest, ingenuous, open, outright, outspoken, plain, plain-spoken, simple-hearted, sincere, straight, straightforward, transparent, truthful, unconcealed, undisguised, unreserved, unrestricted.

frantic *adj.* berserk, beside oneself, desperate, distracted, distraught, fraught, frenetic, frenzied, furious, hairless, hectic, mad, overwrought, raging, raving, wild.

antonym calm.

fraternize *v.* affiliate, associate, concur, consort, cooperate, forgather, hobnob, mingle, mix, socialize, sympathize, unite.

antonyms ignore, shun.

fraud[1] *n.* artifice, cheat, chicane, chicanery, craft, deceit, deception, double-dealing, duplicity, fake, forgery, guile, hoax, humbug, imposture, sham, sharp practice, spuriousness, swindling, swiz, swizzle, take-in, treachery, trickery.

fraud[2] *n.* bluffer, charlatan, cheat, counterfeit, double-dealer, hoaxer, impostor, malingerer, mountebank, phony, pretender, pseud, quack, swindler.

fraudulent *adj.* bogus, counterfeit, crafty, criminal, crooked, deceitful, deceptive, dishonest, double-dealing, duplicitous, false, knavish, phony, sham, specious, spurious, swindling, treacherous.

antonyms genuine, honest.

fray *n.* affray, bagarre, barney, battle, brawl, broil, clash, combat, conflict, disturbance, Donnybrook, dust-up, fight, free-for-all, mêlée, quarrel, rammy, riot, row, ruckus, ruction, rumble, rumpus, scuffle, set-to, shindy.

freak[1] *n.* aberration, abnormality, abortion, anomaly, caprice, crotchet, fad, fancy, folly, grotesque, humor, irregularity, lusus naturae, malformation, misgrowth, monster, monstrosity, mutant, oddity, queer fish, quirk, rara avis, sport, teratism, turn, twist, vagary, weirdie, weirdo, whim, whimsy. *adj.* aberrant, abnormal, atypical, bizarre, capricious, erratic, exceptional, fluky, fortuitous, odd, queer, surprise, unaccountable, unexpected, unforeseen, unparalleled, unpredictable, unpredicted, unusual.

antonyms common, expected.

freak[2] *n.* addict, aficionado, buff, devotee, enthusiast, fan, fanatic, fiend, monomaniac, nut, votary.

freckle *n.* fernitickle, heatspot, lentigo.

free *adj.* able, allowed, at large, at leisure, at liberty, autarchic, autonomous, available, bounteous, bountiful, buckshee, casual, charitable, clear, complimentary, cost-free, dégagé, democratic, disengaged, eager, easy, emancipated, empty, extra, familiar, footloose, forward, frank, free and easy, free of charge, generous, gratis, hospitable, idle, independent, informal, laidback, lavish, lax, leisured, liberal, liberated, loose, munificent, natural, off the hook, on the house, on the loose, open, open-handed, permitted, prodigal, relaxed, self-governing, self-ruling, solute, sovereign, spare, spontaneous, unattached, unbidden, unbowed, unceremonious, uncommitted, unconstrained, unemployed, unencumbered, unengaged, unfettered, unforced, unhampered, unhindered, unimpeded, uninhabited, uninhibited, unobstructed, unoccupied, unpaid, unpent, unpreoccupied, unregimented, unregulated, unrestrained, unrestricted, unsparing, unstinting, untrammeled, unused, vacant, willing, without charge.

antonyms attached, confined, costly, formal, mean, niggardly, restricted, tied.

adv. abundantly, copiously, for free, for love, for nothing, freely, gratis, idly, loosely, without charge.

antonym meanly.

v. absolve, affranchise, clear, debarrass, declassify, decolonize, decontrol, deliver, disburden, discage, discharge, disembarrass, disembrangle, disenchain, disengage, disenslave, disentangle, disenthral, disimprison, disprison, emancipate, exempt, extricate, let go, liberate, loose, manumit, ransom, release, relieve, rescue, rid, set free, turn loose, unbind, unburden, uncage, unchain, undo, unfetter, unhand, unleash, unlock, unloose, unmanacle, unmew, unpen, unshackle, unstick, untether, untie, unyoke.

antonyms confine, enslave, imprison.

freedom *n.* abandon, ability, affranchisement, autonomy, boldness, brazenness, candor, carte-blanche, deliverance, directness, discretion, disrespect, ease, elbowroom, emancipation, exemption, facility, familiarity, flexibility, forwardness, frankness, free rein, home rule, immunity, impertinence, impunity, independence, informality, ingenuousness, lack of restraint or reserve, latitude, laxity, leeway, liberty, Liberty Hall, license, manumission, openness, opportunity, overfamiliarity, play, power, presumption, privilege, range, release, scope, self-government, uhuru, unconstraint. *antonyms* confinement, reserve, restriction.

freely *adv.* abundantly, amply, bountifully, candidly, cleanly, copiously, easily, extravagantly, frankly, generously, lavishly, liberally, loosely, of one's own accord, open-handedly, openly, plainly, readily, smoothly, spontaneously, sponte sua, unchallenged, unreservedly, unstintingly, voluntarily, willingly. *antonyms* evasively, meanly, roughly, under duress.

freight *n.* bulk, burden, cargo, carriage, charge, consignment, contents, conveyance, fee, goods, haul, lading, load, merchandise, pay-load, shipment, tonnage, transportation.

frenzy *n.* aberration, agitation, bout, burst, convulsion, delirium, derangement, distraction, estrus, fit, fury, hysteria, insanity, lunacy, madness, mania, must, outburst, paroxysm, passion, rage, seizure, spasm, transport, turmoil. *antonyms* calm, placidness.

frequent[1] *adj.* common, commonplace, constant, continual, customary, everyday, familiar, habitual, incessant, numerous, persistent, recurrent, recurring, regular, reiterated, repeated, usual. *antonym* infrequent.

frequent[2] *v.* associate with, attend, crowd, hang about, hang out at, haunt, haunt about, patronize, resort, visit.

fresh *adj.* added, additional, alert, artless, auxiliary, blooming, bold, bouncing, bracing, brazen, bright, brisk, callow, cheeky, chipper, clean, clear, cool, crisp, crude, dewy, different, disrespectful, energetic, extra, fair, familiar, flip, florid, forward, further, glowing, green, hardy, healthy, impudent, inexperienced, innovative, insolent, inventive, invigorated, invigorating, keen, latest, lively, malapert, modern, modernistic, more, natural, new, new-fangled, novel, original, other, pert, presumptuous, pure, raw, recent, refreshed, refreshing, renewed, rested, restored, revived, rosy, ruddy, saucy, span, spanking, sparkling, spick, sprightly, spry, stiff, supplementary, sweet, unblown, unconventional, uncultivated, undimmed, unhackneyed, unjaded, unjaundiced, unpolluted, unsoured, unspoilt, untrained, untried, unusual, unwarped, unwearied, up-to-date, verdant, vernal, vigorous, virescent, vital, vivid, warm, wholesome, young, youthful. *antonyms* experienced, faded, old hat, polite, stale, tired.

fret *v.* abrade, agitate, agonize, annoy, bother, brood, chafe, chagrin, corrode, distress, disturb, eat into, erode, fray, gall, goad, grieve, harass, irk, irritate, nag, nettle, peeve, pique, provoke, rankle, repine, rile, ripple, rub, ruffle, torment, trouble, vex, wear, wear away, worry. *antonym* calm.

fretful *adj.* cantankerous, captious, complaining, cross, crotchety, edgy, fractious, irritable, peevish, petulant, querulous, short-tempered, snappish, snappy, splenetic, testy, thrawn, touchy, uneasy. *antonym* calm.

friction *n.* abrasion, animosity, antagonism, attrition, bad blood, bad feeling, bickering, chafing, conflict, contention, disagreement, discontent, discord, disharmony, dispute, dissension, erosion, fretting, grating, hostility, ill-feeling, incompatibility, irritation, limation, opposition, quarreling, rasping, resentment, resistance, rivalry, rubbing, scraping, wearing away, wrangling, xerotripsis.

friend *n.* Achates, adherent, advocate, ally, alter ego, associate, backer, benefactor, boon companion, bosom friend, buddy, china, chum, cobber, companion, comrade, confidant, crony, familiar, gossip, intimate, mate, paisano, pal, partisan, partner, patron, playmate, sidekick, soul mate, supporter, well-wisher. *antonym* enemy.

friendly *adj.* affable, affectionate, amiable, amicable, approachable, attached, attentive, auspicious, beneficial, benevolent, benign, chummy, close, clubby, companionable, comradely, conciliatory, confiding, convivial, cordial, familiar, Favonian, fond, fraternal, gemütlich, genial, good, helpful, intimate, kind, kindly, maty, neighborly, outgoing, palsy-walsy, peaceable, propitious, receptive, sociable, sympathetic, thick, welcoming, well-disposed. *antonyms* cold, unsociable.

friendship *n.* affection, affinity, alliance, amity, attachment, benevolence, closeness, concord, familiarity, fellowship, fondness, friendliness, goodwill, harmony, intimacy, love, neighborliness, rapport, regard. *antonym* enmity.

fright *n.* alarm, apprehension, consternation, dismay, dread, eyesore, fear, fleg, funk, horror, mess, monstrosity, panic, quaking, scare, scarecrow, shock, sight, spectacle, sweat, terror, the shivers, trepidation.

frighten *v.* affray, affright, affrighten, alarm, appal, cow, daunt, dismay, fleg, intimidate, petrify, scare, scare stiff, shock, spook, startle, terrify, terrorize, unman, unnerve. *antonyms* calm, reassure.

frigid *adj.* aloof, arctic, austere, brumous, chill, chilly, cold, cold-hearted, cool, forbidding, formal, frore, frostbound, frosty, frozen, gelid, glacial, icy, lifeless, passionless, passive, repellent, rigid, stand-offish, stiff, unanimated, unapproachable, unbending, unfeeling, unloving, unresponsive, wintry. *antonyms* responsive, warm.

fringe *n.* borderline, edge, fimbriation, frisette, limits, march, marches, margin, outskirts, perimeter, periphery. *adj.* alternative, unconventional, unofficial, unorthodox. *v.* border, edge, enclose, fimbriate, skirt, surround, trim.

frisky *adj.* bouncy, buckish, coltish, frolicsome, gamesome, high-spirited, kittenish, lively, playful,

rollicking, romping, skittish, spirited, sportive.
antonym quiet.

frolic *v.* caper, cavort, cut capers, frisk, gambol, gammock, lark, make merry, play, rollick, romp, skylark, sport, wanton.

n. amusement, antic, drollery, escapade, fun, gaiety, gambado, gambol, game, gammock, gilravage, high jinks, lark, merriment, prank, razzle-dazzle, revel, rig, romp, skylarking, sport, spree.

front *n.* air, anterior, appearance, aspect, bearing, beginning, blind, countenance, cover, cover-up, demeanor, disguise, expression, exterior, façade, face, facing, fore, forefront, foreground, forepart, front line, frontage, head, lead, manner, mask, metope, mien, obverse, pretence, pretext, show, top, van, vanguard.
antonym back.

adj. anterior, anticous, first, fore, foremost, head, lead, leading.
antonyms back, last, least, posterior.

v. confront, face, look over, meet, oppose, overlook.

frontier *n.* borderland, borderline, bound, boundary, bourn(e), confines, edge, limit, march, marches, perimeter, verge.
adj. backwoods, limitrophe, outlying, pioneering.

frown *v.* glare, glower, grimace, lower, scowl.
n. dirty look, glare, glower, grimace, moue, scowl.

frugal *adj.* abstemious, careful, cheese-paring, economical, meager, niggardly, parsimonious, penny-wise, provident, prudent, saving, sparing, Spartan, thrifty, ungenerous.
antonym wasteful.

fruitful *adj.* abundant, advantageous, beneficial, copious, effective, fecund, feracious, fertile, flush, fructiferous, fructuous, gainful, plenteous, plentiful, productive, profitable, profuse, prolific, rewarding, rich, spawning, successful, teeming, uberous, useful, well-spent, worthwhile.
antonyms barren, fruitless.

fruitfulness *n.* fecundity, feracity, fertility, productiveness, profitability, uberty, usefulness.
antonym fruitlessness.

fruitless *adj.* abortive, barren, bootless, futile, hopeless, idle, ineffectual, pointless, profitless, unavailing, unfruitful, unproductive, unprofitable, unsuccessful, useless, vain.
antonyms fruitful, successful.

frustrate *v.* baffle, balk, block, bugger, check, circumvent, confront, counter, countermine, crab, defeat, depress, disappoint, discourage, dishearten, foil, forestall, inhibit, neutralize, nullify, scotch, spike, stymie, thwart.
antonyms fulfil, further, promote.

fuddled *adj.* bemused, confused, drunk, groggy, hazy, inebriated, intoxicated, muddled, mused, muzzy, sozzled, stupefied, tipsy, woozy.
antonyms clear, sober.

fuel *n.* ammunition, eilding, encouragement, fodder, food, incitement, material, means, nourishment, provocation.

v. charge, encourage, fan, feed, fire, incite, inflame, nourish, stoke up, sustain.
antonyms damp down, discourage.

fugitive *n.* deserter, escapee, refugee, runagate, runaway.
adj. brief, elusive, ephemeral, evanescent, fleeing, fleeting, flitting, flying, fugacious, intangible, momentary, passing, short, short-lived, temporary, transient, transitory, unstable.
antonym permanent.

fulfill *v.* accomplish, achieve, answer, carry out, complete, comply with, conclude, conform to, consummate, discharge, effect, effectuate, execute, fill, finish, implement, keep, meet, obey, observe, perfect, perform, realize, satisfy.
antonyms break, defect, fail, frustrate.

full *adj.* abundant, adequate, all-inclusive, ample, baggy, brimful, brimming, broad, buxom, capacious, chock-a-block, chock-full, clear, complete, comprehensive, copious, crammed, crowded, curvaceous, deep, detailed, distinct, entire, exhaustive, extensive, filled, generous, gorged, intact, jammed, large, loaded, loud, maximum, occupied, orotund, packed, plenary, plenteous, plentiful, plump, replete, resonant, rich, rounded, sated, satiated, satisfied, saturated, stocked, sufficient, taken, thorough, unabbreviated, unabridged, uncut, unedited, unexpurgated, voluminous, voluptuous.
antonyms empty, incomplete.

full-blooded *adj.* gusty, hearty, lusty, mettlesome, red-blooded, thoroughbred, vigorous, virile, whole-hearted.

full-grown *adj.* adult, developed, full-aged, full-blown, full-scale, grown-up, marriageable, mature, nubile, of age, ripe.
antonyms undeveloped, young.

fullness *n.* abundance, adequateness, ampleness, broadness, clearness, completeness, comprehensiveness, copiousness, curvaceousness, dilation, distension, enlargement, entirety, extensiveness, fill, glut, loudness, orotundity, plenitude, plenty, pleroma, profusion, repletion, resonance, richness, roundness, satiety, saturation, strength, sufficiency, swelling, totality, tumescence, vastness, voluptuousness, wealth, wholeness.
antonyms emptiness, incompleteness.

full-scale *adj.* all-encompassing, all-out, comprehensive, exhaustive, extensive, full-dress, in-depth, intensive, major, proper, sweeping, thorough, thoroughgoing, wide-ranging.
antonym partial.

fulminate *v.* animadvert, criticize, curse, denounce, detonate, fume, inveigh, protest, rage, rail, thunder, vilipend, vituperate.
antonym praise.

fulsome *adj.* adulatory, cloying, effusive, excessive, extravagant, fawning, gross, immoderate, ingratiating, inordinate, insincere, nauseating, nauseous, offensive, overdone, rank, saccharine, sickening, smarmy, sycophantic, unctuous.
antonym sincere.

fume v. boil, chafe, fizz, get steamed up, give off, rage, rant, rave, reek, seethe, smoke, smolder, storm.

fun n. amusement, buffoonery, cheer, clowning, distraction, diversion, enjoyment, entertainment, foolery, frolic, gaiety, game, gammock, high jinks, horseplay, jesting, jocularity, joking, jollification, jollity, joy, junketing, merriment, merrymaking, mirth, nonsense, play, playfulness, pleasure, recreation, romp, skylarking, sport, teasing, tomfoolery, treat, waggery, whoopee.

function[1] n. activity, business, capacity, charge, concern, duty, employment, exercise, faculty, job, mission, occupation, office, operation, part, post, province, purpose, raison d'être, responsibility, role, situation, task.

v. act, be in running order, behave, do duty, functionate, go, officiate, operate, perform, run, serve, work.

function[2] n. affair, dinner, do, gathering, junket, luncheon, party, reception, shindig.

fundamental adj. axiomatic, basal, basic, basilar, cardinal, central, constitutional, crucial, elementary, essential, first, important, indispensable, integral, intrinsic, key, keynote, necessary, organic, primal, primary, prime, principal, rudimentary, underlying, vital.
antonym advanced.

n. axiom, basic, cornerstone, essential, first principle, law, principle, rudiment, rule, sine qua non.

funereal adj. dark, deathlike, depressing, dirgelike, dismal, dreary, exequial, feral, funebral, funebrial, gloomy, grave, lamenting, lugubrious, mournful, sad, sepulchral, solemn, somber, woeful.
antonyms happy, lively.

funny adj. a card, a caution, a scream, absurd, amusing, comic, comical, curious, diverting, droll, dubious, entertaining, facetious, farcical, funny ha-ha, funny peculiar, hilarious, humorous, jocose, jocular, jolly, killing, laughable, ludicrous, mirth-provoking, mysterious, odd, peculiar, perplexing, puzzling, queer, remarkable, rich, ridiculous, riotous, risible, side-splitting, silly, slapstick, strange, suspicious, unusual, waggish, weird, witty.
antonyms sad, solemn, unamusing, unfunny.

furious adj. acharné, agitated, angry, boiling, boisterous, enraged, fierce, fizzing, frantic, frenzied, fuming, furibund, impetuous, incensed, infuriated, intense, livid, mad, maddened, maenadic, raging, savage, stormy, tempestuous, tumultuous, turbulent, up in arms, vehement, violent, waxy, wild, wrathful, wroth.
antonyms calm, pleased.

furnish v. afford, appoint, bedight, bestow, decorate, endow, equip, fit out, fit up, give, grant, offer, outfit, present, provide, provision, reveal, rig, stake, stock, store, suit, supply.
antonym divest.

furore n. commotion, craze, disturbance, enthusiasm,

excitement, flap, frenzy, fury, fuss, hullabaloo, mania, outburst, outcry, rage, stir, to-do, tumult, uproar.
antonym calm.

furtherance n. advancement, advancing, advocacy, backing, boosting, carrying-out, championship, promoting, promotion, prosecution, pursuit.

furthermore adv. additionally, also, as well, besides, further, in addition, into the bargain, likewise, moreover, not to mention, to boot, too, what's more.

furtive adj. back-door, backstairs, clandestine, cloaked, conspiratorial, covert, hidden, secret, secretive, skulking, slinking, sly, sneaking, sneaky, stealthy, surreptitious, underhand.
antonym open.

fury[1] n. anger, desperation, ferocity, fierceness, force, frenzy, impetuosity, intensity, ire, madness, passion, power, rage, savagery, severity, tempestuousness, turbulence, vehemence, violence, wax, wrath.
antonym calm.

fury[2] n. bacchante, hag, harridan, hell-cat, shrew, spitfire, termagant, virago, vixen.

fuss n. ado, agitation, bother, brouhaha, bustle, coil, commotion, confusion, difficulty, display, doodah, excitement, fantigue, fash, fidget, fikery, flap, flurry, fluster, flutter, furore, hassle, hoo-ha, hurry, kerfuffle, objection, palaver, pother, pudder, row, squabble, stew, stir, to-do, trouble, unrest, upset, worry.
antonym calm.

v. bustle, chafe, complain, emote, fash, fidget, flap, fret, fume, niggle, pother, pudder, take pains, worry.

futile adj. abortive, barren, bootless, empty, forlorn, fruitless, hollow, idle, ineffectual, nugatory, otiose, pointless, profitless, Sisyphean, sterile, trifling, trivial, unavailing, unimportant, unproductive, unprofitable, unsuccessful, useless, vain, valueless, worthless.
antonyms fruitful, profitable.

futility n. aimlessness, bootlessness, emptiness, fruitlessness, hollowness, idleness, ineffectiveness, otioseness, pointlessness, triviality, unimportance, uselessness, vanity.
antonyms fruitfulness, profitability.

future n. expectation, futurition, futurity, hereafter, outlook, prospects.
antonym past.

adj. approaching, coming, designate, destined, eventual, expected, fated, forthcoming, impending, in the offing, later, prospective, rising, subsequent, to be, to come, ultimate, unborn.
antonym past.

fuzzy adj. bleary, blurred, blurry, distanceless, distorted, downy, faint, fluffy, frizzy, hazy, ill-defined, indistinct, linty, muffled, napped, shadowy, unclear, unfocused, vague, woolly.
antonyms base, distinct.

gab *v.* babble, blabber, blather, blether, buzz, chatter, drivel, gossip, jabber, jaw, prattle, talk, tattle, yabber, yak, yatter. *n.* blab, blarney, blethering, blethers, chat, chatter, chitchat, conversation, drivel, gossip, loquacity, palaver, prattle, prattling, small talk, tête-à-tête, tittle-tattle, tongue-wagging, yabber, yackety-yak, yak, yatter.

gabble *v.* babble, blab, blabber, blether, cackle, chatter, gaggle, gibber, gush, jabber, prattle, rattle, splutter, spout, sputter, yabber, yatter.
n. babble, blabber, blethering, cackling, chatter, drivel, gibberish, jargon, nonsense, prattle, twaddle, waffle, yabber, yatter.

gad about dot about, gallivant, ramble, range, roam, rove, run around, stray, traipse, wander.

gadabout *n.* gallivanter, pleasure-seeker, rambler, rover, runabout, stravaiger, wanderer.

gadget *n.* appliance, contraption, contrivance, device, doodad, gimmick, gismo, gizmo, invention, jiggumbob, jigjam, jigmaree, novelty, thing, thingumajig, tool, widget.

gaffer *n.* boss, foreman, ganger, manager, overman, overseer, superintendent, supervisor.

gag[1] *v.* choke, choke up, curb, disgorge, gasp, heave, muffle, muzzle, puke, quiet, retch, silence, spew, stifle, still, stop up, suppress, throttle, throw up, vomit.

gag[2] *n.* funny, hoax, jest, joke, one-liner, pun, quip, wisecrack, witticism.

gaiety *n.* animation, blitheness, blithesomeness, brightness, brilliance, celebration, cheerfulness, color, colorfulness, conviviality, effervescence, elation, exhilaration, festivity, fun, galliardize, gaudiness, glee, glitter, good humor, high spirits, hilarity, joie de vivre, jollification, jollity, joviality, joyousness, light-heartedness, liveliness, merriment, merrymaking, mirth, revelry, revels, show, showiness, sparkle, sprightliness, vivacity.
antonyms drabness, dreariness, sadness.

gain *v.* achieve, acquire, advance, arrive at, attain, avail, bag, bring in, capture, clear, collect, come to, earn, enlist, gather, get, get to, glean, harvest, impetrate, improve, increase, make, net, obtain, pick up, procure, produce, profit, progress, reach, realize, reap, secure, win, win over, yield.
antonym lose.
n. accretion, achievement, acquisition, advance, advancement, advantage, attainment, benefit, bunce, dividend, earnings, emolument, growth, headway, improvement, income, increase, increment, lucre, proceeds, produce, profit, progress, pudding, return, rise, winnings, yield.
antonyms loss, losses.

gainful *adj.* advantageous, beneficial, feracious, fructuous, fruitful, lucrative, moneymaking, paying, productive, profitable, remunerative, rewarding, useful, worthwhile.
antonym useless.

gainsay *v.* contradict, contravene, controvert, deny, disaffirm, disagree with, dispute, nay-say.
antonym agree.

gait *n.* bearing, carriage, manner, pace, step, stride, tread, walk.

gala *n.* carnival, celebration, festival, festivity, fête, glorification, jamboree, jubilee, Mardi Gras, pageant, party, procession.

gale *n.* blast, burst, cyclone, eruption, explosion, fit, howl, hurricane, outbreak, outburst, peal, ripsnorter, shout, shriek, squall, storm, tempest, tornado, typhoon.

gall[1] *n.* acrimony, animosity, animus, antipathy, assurance, bad blood, bile, bitterness, brass, brass neck, brazenness, cheek, effrontery, enmity, hostility, impertinence, impudence, insolence, malevolence, malice, malignity, neck, nerve, presumption, presumptuousness, rancor, sauciness, sourness, spite, spleen, venom, virulence.
antonyms friendliness, modesty, reserve.

gall[2] *v.* abrade, aggravate, annoy, bark, bother, chafe, exasperate, excoriate, fret, get, get to, graze, harass, hurt, irk, irritate, nag, nettle, peeve, pester, plague, provoke, rankle, rile, rub raw, ruffle, scrape, skin, vex.

gallant *adj.* attentive, august, bold, brave, chivalrous, courageous, courteous, courtly, daring, dashing, dauntless, dignified, doughty, elegant, fearless, game, gentlemanly, glorious, gracious, grand, heroic, high-spirited, honorable, imposing, indomitable, intrepid, lion-hearted, lofty, magnanimous, magnificent, manful, manly, mettlesome, noble, plucky, polite, splendid, stately, valiant, valorous.
antonyms cowardly, craven, ungentlemanly.
n. admirer, adventurer, beau, blade, boyfriend, buck, cavalier, champion, cicisbeo, dandy, daredevil, escort, fop, hero, knight, ladies' man, lady-killer, lover, paramour, suitor, wooer.

gallantry *n.* attention, attentiveness, audacity, boldness, bravery, chivalry, courage, courageousness, courteousness, courtesy, courtliness, daring, dauntlessness, derring-do, elegance, fearlessness, gentlemanliness, graciousness, heroism, intrepidity, manliness, mettle, nerve, nobility, pluck, politeness, politesse, prowess, spirit, valiance, valor.

antonyms cowardice, ungentlemanliness.

gallery *n.* arcade, art-gallery, balcony, circle, gods, grandstand, loggia, museum, passage, pawn, spectators, walk.

galling *adj.* aggravating, annoying, bitter, bothersome, exasperating, harassing, humiliating, infuriating, irksome, irritating, nettling, plaguing, provoking, rankling, vexatious, vexing.

antonym pleasing.

galore *adv.* aplenty, everywhere, heaps of, in abundance, in numbers, in profusion, lots of, millions of, stacks of, to spare, tons of.

antonym scarce.

gamble *v.* back, bet, chance, gaff, game, have a flutter, hazard, play, punt, risk, speculate, stake, stick one's neck out, take a chance, try one's luck, venture, wager. *n.* bet, chance, flutter, leap in the dark, lottery, punt, risk, speculation, uncertainty, venture, wager.

gambol *v.* bounce, bound, caper, cavort, curvet, cut a caper, frisk, frolic, hop, jump, prance, rollick, skip. *n.* antic, bound, caper, frisk, frolic, gambado, hop, jump, prance, skip, spring.

game[1] *n.* adventure, amusement, business, competition, contest, design, device, distraction, diversion, enterprise, entertainment, event, frolic, fun, jest, joke, lark, line, main, match, meeting, merriment, merry-making, occupation, pastime, plan, play, plot, ploy, proceeding, recreation, romp, round, scheme, sport, stratagem, strategy, tactic, tournament, trick, undertaking.

game[2] *n.* animals, bag, flesh, game-birds, meat, prey, quarry, spoils.

game[3] *adj.* bold, brave, courageous, dauntless, desirous, disposed, dogged, eager, fearless, gallant, gamy, heroic, inclined, interested, intrepid, persevering, persistent, plucky, prepared, ready, resolute, spirited, spunky, unflinching, valiant, valorous, willing.

antonyms cowardly, unwilling.

game[4] *adj.* bad, crippled, deformed, disabled, gammy, gouty, hobbling, incapacitated, injured, lame, maimed.

gamut *n.* area, catalog, compass, field, range, scale, scope, series, spectrum, sweep.

gang *n.* band, circle, clique, club, coffle, company, core, coterie, crew, crowd, group, herd, horde, lot, mob, pack, party, ring, set, shift, squad, team, troupe.

gangling *adj.* angular, awkward, bony, gangly, gauche, gawky, lanky, loose-jointed, rangy, raw-boned, skinny, spindly, tall, ungainly.

gangster *n.* bandit, brigand, crook, desperado, heavy, hood, hoodlum, mobster, racketeer, robber, rough, ruffian, thug, tough.

gap *n.* blank, breach, break, chink, cleft, crack, cranny, crevice, diastema, difference, disagreement, discontinuity, disparateness, disparity, divergence, divide, hiatus, hole, inconsistency, interlude, intermission,

interruption, interspace, interstice, interval, lacuna, lull, opening, pause, recess, rent, rift, space, vacuity, void.

gape *v.* crack, dehisce, gawk, gawp, goggle, open, split, stare, wonder, yawn.

garb *n.* accouterments, apparel, appearance, array, aspect, attire, clothes, clothing, costume, covering, cut, dress, fashion, garment, gear, guise, habiliment, habit, look, mode, outfit, raiment, robes, style, uniform, vestments, wear. *v.* apparel, array, attire, clothe, cover, dress, habilitate, rig out, robe.

garbage *n.* bits and pieces, debris, detritus, dross, filth, gash, junk, litter, muck, odds and ends, offal, refuse, rubbish, scourings, scraps, slops, sweepings, swill, trash, waste.

garble *v.* confuse, corrupt, distort, doctor, edit, falsify, jumble, misinterpret, misquote, misreport, misrepresent, misstate, mistranslate, mix up, muddle, mutilate, pervert, slant, tamper with, twist.

antonym decipher.

gargantuan *adj.* big, Brobdingnag(ian), colossal, elephantine, enormous, giant, gigantic, huge, immense, large, leviathan, mammoth, massive, monstrous, monumental, mountainous, prodigious, titanic, towering, tremendous, vast.

antonym small.

garments *n.* apparel, array, attire, clothes, clothing, costume, dress, duds, garb, gear, get-up, habiliment, habit, outfit, raiment, robes, togs, uniform, vestments, wear.

garnish *v.* adorn, beautify, bedeck, deck, decorate, embellish, enhance, furnish, grace, ornament, set off, trim.

antonym divest.

n. adornment, decoration, embellishment, enhancement, garnishment, garnishry, garniture, ornament, ornamentation, relish, trim, trimming.

garrulous *adj.* babbling, chattering, chatty, diffuse, effusive, gabby, gassy, glib, gossiping, gushing, long-winded, loquacious, mouthy, prating, prattling, prolix, prosy, talkative, verbose, voluble, windy, wordy, yabbering.

antonyms taciturn, terse.

gash *v.* cleave, cut, gouge, incise, lacerate, nick, notch, rend, score, slash, slit, split, tear, wound. *n.* cleft, cut, gouge, incision, laceration, nick, notch, rent, score, slash, slit, split, tear, wound.

gasp *v.* blow, breathe, choke, ejaculate, gulp, pant, puff, utter. *n.* blow, breath, ejaculation, exclamation, gulp, pant, puff.

gather *v.* accumulate, amass, assemble, assume, build, clasp, collect, conclude, congregate, convene, crop, cull, deduce, deepen, draw, embrace, enfold, enlarge, expand, flock, fold, foregather, garner, glean, group, grow, harvest, heap, hear, heighten, hoard, hold, hug, increase, infer, intensify, learn, make, marshal, mass, muster,

pick, pile up, pleat, pluck, pucker, rake up, reap, rise, round up, ruche, ruffle, select, shirr, stockpile, surmise, swell, thicken, tuck, understand, wax.
antonyms dissipate, scatter.

gathering *n.* accumulation, acquisition, aggregate, assemblage, assembly, collection, company, concentration, conclave, concourse, congregation, congress, convention, convocation, crowd, fest, flock, gain, galère, get-together, group, heap, hoard, jamboree, kgotla, knot, mass, meeting, moot, muster, omnium-gatherum, party, pile, procurement, rally, round-up, rout, stock, stockpile, throng, turn-out.
antonym scattering.

gaudy *adj.* bright, brilliant, chintzy, flash, flashy, florid, garish, gay, glaring, glitzy, loud, meretricious, ostentatious, raffish, showy, tasteless, tawdry, tinsel(ly), vulgar.
antonyms drab, plain, quiet.

gaunt *adj.* angular, attenuated, bare, bleak, bony, cadaverous, desolate, dismal, dreary, emaciated, forbidding, forlorn, grim, haggard, hagged, harsh, hollow-eyed, lank, lean, meager, pinched, rawboned, scraggy, scrawny, skeletal, skinny, spare, thin, wasted.
antonyms hale, plump.

gay[1] *adj.* animated, blithe, boon, bright, brilliant, carefree, cavalier, cheerful, colorful, convivial, debonair, festive, flamboyant, flashy, fresh, frivolous, frolicsome, fun-loving, gamesome, garish, gaudy, glad, gleeful, happy, hilarious, insouciant, jolly, jovial, joyful, joyous, lifesome, lighthearted, lightsome, lively, merry, playful, pleasure-seeking, rakish, riant, rich, rollicking, rorty, showy, sparkish, sparkling, sportive, sunny, tit(t)upy, vivacious, vivid, waggish.
antonyms gloomy, sad.

gay[2] *adj.* bent, dikey, homosexual, lesbian, queer.
antonyms heterosexual, straight.
n. dike, homo, homosexual, lesbian, poof, queer, sapphist.
antonym heterosexual.

gaze *v.* contemplate, gape, gaup, gawp, look, ogle, regard, stare, view, watch.
n. gaup, gawp, look, stare.

gear *n.* accessories, accouterments, affair, apparatus, apparel, armor, array, attire, baggage, belongings, business, clothes, clothing, cog, costume, doings, dress, effects, equipment, garb, garments, gearing, get-up, habit, harness, instruments, kit, luggage, machinery, matter, mechanism, outfit, paraphernalia, possessions, rigging, rig-out, stuff, supplies, tackle, things, togs, tools, trappings, traps, wear, works.
v. adapt, adjust, equip, fit, harness, rig, suit, tailor.

gel *v.* coagulate, congeal, crystallize, finalize, form, gee, gel, gelatinate, gelatinize, harden, jelly, materialize, set, solidify, take form, take shape, thicken.
antonym disintegrate.

gem *n.* angel, bijou, brick, flower, honey, jewel, masterpiece,

pearl, pick, pièce de résistance, precious stone, prize, stone, treasure.

general *adj.* accepted, accustomed, across-the-board, all-inclusive, approximate, blanket, broad, catholic, collective, common, comprehensive, conventional, customary, ecumenic, ecumenical, encyclopedic, everyday, extensive, generic, habitual, ill-defined, imprecise, inaccurate, indefinite, indiscriminate, inexact, loose, miscellaneous, normal, ordinary, panoramic, popular, prevailing, prevalent, public, regular, sweeping, total, typical, universal, unspecific, usual, vague, widespread.
antonyms limited, novel, particular.
n. chief, c-in-c, commander, commander in chief, generalissimo, hetman, leader, marshal, officer.

generally *adv.* approximately, as a rule, broadly, by and large, characteristically, chiefly, commonly, conventionally, customarily, extensively, for the most part, habitually, in the main, largely, mainly, mostly, normally, on average, on the whole, ordinarily, popularly, predominantly, principally, publicly, regularly, typically, universally, usually, widely.
antonym rarely.

generate *v.* beget, breed, bring about, cause, create, engender, father, form, gender, give rise to, initiate, make, originate, procreate, produce, propagate, spawn, whip up.
antonym prevent.

generation *n.* age, age group, begetting, breed, breeding, creation, crop, day, days, engendering, engenderment, engend(r)ure, epoch, era, formation, generating, genesis, geniture, origination, period, procreation, production, progeniture, propagation, reproduction, time, times.

generosity *n.* beneficence, benevolence, big-heartedness, bounteousness, bounty, charity, goodness, highmindedness, kindness, large-heartedness, liberality, magnanimity, munificence, nobleness, openhandedness, soft-heartedness, unselfishness, unsparingness.
antonyms meanness, selfishness.

generous *adj.* abundant, ample, beneficent, benevolent, big-hearted, bounteous, bountiful, charitable, copious, disinterested, free, full, good, high-minded, hospitable, kind, large-hearted, large-minded, lavish, liberal, lofty, magnanimous, munificent, noble, open-handed, overflowing, plentiful, princely, rich, soft-boiled, softhearted, ungrudging, unreproachful, unresentful, unselfish, unsparing, unstinted, unstinting.
antonyms mean, selfish.

genesis *n.* beginning, birth, commencement, creation, dawn, engendering, formation, foundation, founding, generation, inception, initiation, origin, outset, propagation, root, source, start.
antonym end.

genius[1] *n.* adept, brain, expert, intellect, maestro, master, master-hand, mastermind, pastmaster, virtuoso.

genius[2] *n.* ability, aptitude, bent, brightness, brilliance, capacity, endowment, faculty, flair, gift, inclination, intellect, knack, propensity, talent, turn.

genius[3] *n.* daemon, double, genie, ka, spirit.

genre *n.* brand, category, character, class, fashion, genus, group, kind, race, school, sort, species, strain, style, type, variety.

genteel *adj.* aristocratic, civil, courteous, courtly, cultivated, cultured, elegant, fashionable, formal, gentlemanly, graceful, ladylike, mannerly, polished, polite, refined, respectable, stylish, urbane, well-bred, well-mannered.

antonyms crude, rough, unpolished.

gentle *adj.* amiable, aristocratic, balmy, benign, biddable, bland, broken, calm, canny, clement, compassionate, courteous, cultured, docile, easy, elegant, genteel, gentleman-like, gentlemanly, gradual, high-born, humane, imperceptible, kind, kindly, ladylike, lamb-like, lenient, light, low, maidenly, manageable, meek, merciful, mild, moderate, muted, noble, pacific, peaceful, placid, polished, polite, quiet, refined, serene, slight, slow, smooth, soft, soothing, sweet, sweet-tempered, tame, temperate, tender, tractable, tranquil, untroubled, upper-class, well-born, well-bred.

antonyms crude, rough, unkind, unpolished.

genuine *adj.* actual, artless, authentic, bona fide, candid, earnest, frank, heartfelt, honest, kosher, legitimate, natural, original, pukka, pure, real, simon-pure, sincere, sound, sterling, sure-enough, true, unadulterate(d), unaffected, unalloyed, unfeigned, unsophisticated, veritable.

antonyms artificial, insincere.

genus *n.* breed, category, class, division, genre, group, kind, order, race, set, sort, species, taxon, type.

germ *n.* bacterium, beginning, bud, bug, cause, egg, embryo, microbe, micro-organism, nucleus, origin, ovule, ovum, root, rudiment, seed, source, spark, spore, sprout, virus, zyme.

germinate *v.* bud, develop, generate, grow, originate, pullulate, root, shoot, sprout, swell, vegetate.

gesture *n.* act, action, gesticulation, indication, motion, sign, signal, wave.

v. gesticulate, indicate, motion, point, sign, signal, wave.

get *v.* achieve, acquire, affect, annoy, arouse, arrange, arrest, arrive, attain, baffle, bag, become, bother, bring, bug, capture, catch, coax, collar, come, come by, come down with, communicate with, comprehend, confound, contact, contract, contrive, convince, earn, excite, fathom, fetch, fix, follow, gain, glean, grab, grow, hear, impetrate, impress, induce, influence, inherit, irk, irritate, make, make it, manage, move, mystify, net, nonplus, notice, obtain, perceive, perplex, persuade, pick up, pique, prevail upon, procure, puzzle, reach, realize, reap, receive, secure, see, seize, stimulate, stir, stump, succeed, sway, take, touch, trap, turn, twig, understand, upset, vex, wangle, wax, wheedle, win.

antonyms lose, misunderstand, pacify.

ghastly *adj.* ashen, cadaverous, deathlike, deathly, dreadful, frightful, ghostly, grim, grisly, gruesome, hideous, horrendous, horrible, horrid, livid, loathsome, lurid, pale, pallid, repellent, shocking, spectral, terrible, terrifying, wan.

antonym delightful.

ghost *n.* apparition, astral body, duppy, eidolon, fetch, glimmer, gytrash, hint, jumby, larva, lemur, manes, phantasm, phantom, possibility, revenant, semblance, shade, shadow, simulacrum, soul, specter, spirit, spook, suggestion, trace, umbra, visitant, white-lady.

ghoulish *adj.* grisly, gruesome, macabre, morbid, revolting, sick, unhealthy, unwholesome.

giant *n.* behemoth, colossus, Goliath, Hercules, jotun, leviathan, monster, Patagonian, titan.

adj. Atlantean, Babylonian, Brobdingnag(ian), colossal, cyclopean, elephantine, enormous, gargantuan, gigantean, gigantesque, gigantic, huge, immense, jumble, king-size, large, leviathan, mammoth, monstrous, Patagonian, prodigious, rounceval, titanic, vast.

giddy *adj.* capricious, careless, changeable, changeful, dizzy, dizzying, erratic, faint, fickle, flighty, frivolous, heedless, impulsive, inconstant, irresolute, irresponsible, lightheaded, reckless, reeling, scatterbrained, scatty, silly, thoughtless, unbalanced, unstable, unsteady, vacillating, vertiginous, volage, volageous, volatile, wild.

antonyms sensible, sober.

gift *n.* ability, aptitude, attribute, benefaction, benificence, bent, bequest, bonus, boon, bounty, cadeau, capability, capacity, contribution, cumshaw, deodate, dolly, donary, donation, donative, douceur, earnest, endowment, faculty, flair, foy, freebie, genius, grant, gratuity, knack, largess(e), legacy, manna, offering, power, present, sop, talent, turn, xenium.

gigantic *adj.* Atlantean, Babylonian, Brobdingnag(ian), colossal, cyclopean, elephantine, enormous, gargantuan, giant, herculean, huge, immense, leviathan, mammoth, monstrous, Patagonian, prodigious, rounceval, stupendous, titanic, tremendous, vast.

antonym small.

giggle *v.* chortle, chuckle, laugh, snigger, tee-hee, titter. *n.* chortle, chuckle, fou rire, laugh, snigger, tee-hee, titter.

gild *v.* adorn, array, beautify, bedeck, brighten, coat, deck, dress up, embellish, embroider, enhance, enrich, festoon, garnish, grace, ornament, paint, trim.

gingerly *adv.* carefully, cautiously, charily, circumspectly, daintily, delicately, fastidiously, gently, hesitantly, reluctantly, squeamishly, suspiciously, timidly, warily.

antonyms carelessly, roughly.

gird *v.* belt, bind, blockade, brace, encircle, enclose, encompass, enfold, engird, environ, enzone, fortify, girdle, hem in, pen, prepare, ready, ring, steel, surround.

girdle *n.* band, belt, ceinture, cestus, cincture, cingulum, corset, cummerbund, fillet, sash, waistband, zona, zone, zonule.

v. bind, bound, encircle, enclose, encompass, engird, environ, enzone, gird, gird round, go round, hem, ring, surround.

girl *n.* backfisch, bird, chick, chicken, chit, colleen, damsel, daughter, demoiselle, filly, fizgig, flapper, flibbertigibbet, floosie, fluff, fräulein, gal, giglet, girl-friend, gouge, grisette, judy, lass, lassie, maid, maiden, miss, moppet, peach, piece, popsy(-wopsy), quean, quine, sheila, sweetheart, wench.

girth *n.* band, belly-band, bulk, circumference, measure, saddle-band, size, strap.

gist *n.* core, direction, drift, essence, force, idea, import, marrow, matter, meaning, nub, pith, point, quintessence, sense, significance, substance.

give *v.* accord, administer, admit, allow, announce, award, bend, bestow, break, cause, cede, collapse, commit, communicate, concede, confer, consign, contribute, deliver, demonstrate, devote, display, do, donate, emit, engender, entrust, evidence, fall, furnish, grant, hand, hand over, impart, indicate, issue, lead, lend, make, make over, manifest, notify, occasion, offer, pay, perform, permit, present, produce, proffer, pronounce, provide, publish, recede, relinquish, render, retire, set forth, show, sink, state, supply, surrender, transmit, utter, vouchsafe, yield.

antonyms hold out, take, withstand.

given *adj.* addicted, admitted, agreed, apt, bestowed, disposed, granted, inclined, liable, likely, prone, specified.

glacial *adj.* antagonistic, arctic, biting, bitter, brumous, chill, chilly, cold, freezing, frigid, frore, frosty, frozen, gelid, hostile, icy, inimical, piercing, polar, raw, Siberian, stiff, unfriendly, wintry.

antonym warm.

glad *adj.* animated, blithe, blithesome, bright, cheerful, cheering, cheery, chuffed, contented, delighted, delightful, felicitous, gay, gleeful, gratified, gratifying, happy, jocund, jovial, joyful, joyous, merry, over the moon, overjoyed, pleasant, pleased, pleasing, willing.

antonym sad.

gladness *n.* animation, blitheness, blithesomeness, brightness, cheerfulness, delight, felicity, gaiety, glee, happiness, high spirits, hilarity, jollity, joy, joyousness, mirth, pleasure.

antonym sadness.

glamor *n.* allure, appeal, attraction, beauty, bewitchment, charm, enchantment, fascination, magic, magnetism, prestige, ravishment, witchery.

glamorous *adj.* alluring, attractive, beautiful, bewitching, captivating, charming, classy, dazzling, elegant, enchanting, entrancing, exciting, fascinating, glittering, glossy, gorgeous, lovely, prestigious, smart.

antonyms boring, drab, plain.

glance[1] *v.* browse, dip, flip, gaze, glimpse, leaf, look, peek, peep, riffle, scan, skim, thumb, touch on, view.

n. allusion, coup d'oeil, dekko, gander, glimpse, look, mention, once over, peek, peep, reference, squint, view.

glance[2] *v.* bounce, brush, cannon, carom, coruscate, flash, gleam, glimmer, glint, glisten, glister, glitter, graze, rebound, reflect, ricochet, shimmer, shine, skim, twinkle.

glare *v.* blaze, coruscate, dazzle, flame, flare, frown, glower, look daggers, lower, scowl, shine.

n. black look, blaze, brilliance, dazzle, dirty look, flame, flare, flashiness, floridness, frown, gaudiness, glow, glower, light, look, loudness, lower, scowl, showiness, stare, tawdriness.

glaring *adj.* audacious, blatant, blazing, bright, conspicuous, dazzling, dreadful, egregious, flagrant, flashy, florid, garish, glowing, gross, horrendous, loud, manifest, obvious, open, outrageous, outstanding, overt, patent, rank, terrible, unconcealed, visible.

antonyms dull, hidden, minor.

glass *n.* beaker, crystal, goblet, lens, looking-glass, magnifying glass, pane, pocket-lens, roemer, rummer, schooner, tumbler, vitrics, window.

glassy *adj.* blank, clear, cold, dazed, dull, empty, expressionless, fixed, glasslike, glazed, glazy, glossy, hyaline, icy, lifeless, shiny, slick, slippery, smooth, transparent, vacant, vitreous, vitriform.

glaze *v.* burnish, coat, crystallize, enamel, furbish, gloss, lacquer, polish, varnish.

n. coat, enamel, finish, gloss, lacquer, luster, patina, polish, shine, varnish.

gleam *n.* beam, brightness, brilliance, coruscation, flash, flicker, glimmer, glint, gloss, glow, hint, inkling, luster, ray, sheen, shimmer, sparkle, splendor, suggestion, trace.

v. coruscate, flare, flash, glance, glimmer, glint, glisten, glister, glitter, glow, scintillate, shimmer, shine, sparkle.

glean *v.* accumulate, amass, collect, cull, find out, garner, gather, harvest, learn, pick (up), reap, select.

glee *n.* cheerfulness, delight, elation, exhilaration, exuberance, exultation, fun, gaiety, gladness, gratification, hilarity, jocularity, jollity, joviality, joy, joyfulness, joyousness, liveliness, merriment, mirth, pleasure, sprightliness, triumph, verve.

gleeful *adj.* beside oneself, cheerful, cock-a-hoop, delighted, elated, exuberant, exultant, gay, gleesome, gratified, happy, jovial, joyful, joyous, jubilant, merry, mirthful, over the moon, overjoyed, pleased, triumphant.

antonym sad.

glib *adj.* artful, easy, facile, fast-talking, fluent, garrulous, insincere, logodaedalic, plausible, quick, ready, slick, slippery, smooth, smooth-spoken, smooth-tongued, suave, talkative, voluble.

antonyms implausible, tongue-tied.

glide v. coast, drift, float, flow, fly, glissade, roll, run, sail, skate, skim, slide, slip, soar, volplane.

glimmer v. blink, flicker, gleam, glint, glisten, glitter, glow, shimmer, shine, sparkle, twinkle.

n. blink, flicker, gleam, glimmering, glint, glow, grain, hint, inkling, ray, shimmer, sparkle, suggestion, trace, twinkle.

glimpse n. glance, gliff, glim, glisk, look, peek, peep, sight, sighting, squint.

v. descry, espy, sight, spot, spy, view.

glint v. flash, gleam, glimmer, glitter, reflect, shine, sparkle, twinkle.

n. flash, gleam, glimmer, glimmering, glitter, shine, sparkle, twinkle, twinkling.

glisten v. coruscate, flash, glance, glare, gleam, glimmer, glint, glister, glitter, scintillate, shimmer, shine, sparkle, twinkle.

glitter v. coruscate, flare, flash, glare, gleam, glimmer, glint, glisten, scintillate, shimmer, shine, spangle, sparkle, twinkle.

n. beam, brightness, brilliance, clinquant, display, flash, gaudiness, glamor, glare, gleam, luster, pageantry, radiance, scintillation, sheen, shimmer, shine, show, showiness, sparkle, splendor, tinsel.

gloat v. crow, exult, eye, glory, ogle, rejoice, relish, revel in, rub it in, triumph, vaunt.

global adj. all-encompassing, all-inclusive, all-out, comprehensive, encyclopedic, exhaustive, general, globular, international, pandemic, planetary, spherical, thorough, total, unbounded, universal, unlimited, world, world-wide.

antonyms limited, parochial.

globe n. ball, earth, orb, planet, round, roundure, sphere, world.

gloom n. blackness, blues, cloud, cloudiness, damp, dark, darkness, dejection, depression, desolation, despair, despondency, dimness, downheartedness, dullness, dusk, duskiness, gloominess, glumness, low spirits, melancholy, misery, murk, murkiness, obscurity, sadness, shade, shadow, sorrow, twilight, unhappiness, woe.

antonym brightness.

gloomy adj. bad, black, blue, chapfallen, cheerless, comfortless, crepuscular, crestfallen, dark, darksome, dejected, delightless, depressing, despondent, dim, disheartening, dismal, dispirited, dispiriting, down, down in the dumps, down in the mouth, down-beat, downcast, downhearted, dreary, dreich, dull, dusky, gloomful, glum, joyless, long-faced, long-visaged, low-spirited, melancholy, mirk(y), miserable, moody, morose, murk(y), obscure, overcast, pessimistic, sad, saddening, saturnine, sepulchral, shadowy, somber, Stygian, sullen, tenebrous.

antonym bright.

glorify v. adore, adorn, aggrandize, apoetheosize, augment, beatify, bless, canonize, celebrate, deify, dignify, elevate, enhance, ennoble, enshrine, eulogize, exalt, extol, honor, hymn, idolize, illuminate, immortalize, laud, lift up, magnify, panegyrize, praise, raise, revere, sanctify, venerate, worship.

antonyms denounce, vilify.

glorious adj. beautiful, bright, brilliant, celebrated, dazzling, delightful, distinguished, divine, drunk, effulgent, elated, elevated, eminent, enjoyable, excellent, famed, famous, fine, gorgeous, grand, great, heavenly, honored, illustrious, intoxicated, magnificent, majestic, marvelous, noble, noted, pleasurable, radiant, renowned, resplendent, shining, splendid, sublime, superb, tipsy, triumphant, wonderful.

antonyms dreadful, inglorious, plain, unknown.

glory n. adoration, beauty, benediction, blessing, brightness, brilliance, celebrity, dignity, distinction, effulgence, eminence, exaltation, fame, gloire, gloria, gorgeousness, grandeur, gratitude, greatness, heaven, homage, honor, illustriousness, immortality, kudos, laudation, luster, magnificence, majesty, nobility, pageantry, pomp, praise, prestige, radiance, renown, resplendence, richness, splendor, sublimity, thanksgiving, triumph, veneration, worship.

antonyms blame, restraint.

v. boast, crow, delight, exult, gloat, pride oneself, rejoice, relish, revel, triumph.

gloss[1] n. appearance, brightness, brilliance, burnish, façade, front, gleam, luster, mask, polish, semblance, sheen, shine, show, surface, varnish, veneer, windowdressing.

gloss[2] n. annotation, comment, commentary, elucidation, explanation, footnote, interpretation, note, postillation, scholion, scholium, translation.

v. annotate, comment, construe, elucidate, explain, interpret, postil, postillate, translate.

glossary n. dictionary, idioticon, lexicon, phrase-book, vocabulary, word-book, word-list.

glossy adj. bright, brilliant, burnished, enameled, glacé, glassy, glazed, lustrous, polished, sheeny, shining, shiny, silken, silky, sleek, smooth.

antonym mat(t).

glow n. ardor, bloom, blush, brightness, brilliance, burning, earnestness, effulgence, enthusiasm, excitement, fervor, flush, gleam, glimmer, gusto, impetuosity, incandescence, intensity, lambency, light, luminosity, passion, phosphorescence, radiance, reddening, redness, rosiness, splendor, vehemence, vividness, warmth.

v. blush, brighten, burn, color, fill, flush, gleam, glimmer, glowing, radiate, redden, shine, smolder, thrill, tingle.

glower v. frown, glare, look daggers, lower, scowl.

n. black look, dirty look, frown, glare, look, lower, scowl, stare.

glowing adj. adulatory, aglow, beaming, bright, complimentary, ecstatic, enthusiastic, eulogistic, flaming, florid, flushed, gleamy, lambent, laudatory, luminous, panegyrical, rave, red, rhapsodic, rich, ruddy, suffused, vibrant, vivid, warm.

antonyms dull, restrained.

glue *n.* adhesive, cement, fish-glue, gum, isinglass, mucilage, paste, size.

v. affix, agglutinate, cement, fix, gum, paste, seal, stick.

glum *adj.* chapfallen, churlish, crabbed, crestfallen, dejected, doleful, down, gloomy, glumpish, glumpy, gruff, grumpy, ill-humored, low, moody, morose, pessimistic, saturnine, sour, sulky, sullen, surly.

antonyms ecstatic, happy.

glut *n.* excess, overabundance, oversupply, pleroma, saturation, superabundance, superfluity, surfeit, surplus.

antonyms lack, scarcity.

v. choke, clog, cram, deluge, englut, fill, flesh, flood, gorge, inundate, overfeed, overload, oversupply, sate, satiate, saturate, stuff.

glutton *n.* cormorant, free-liver, gannet, gobbler, gorger, gormandizer, gourmand, guzzler, hog, omnivore, pig, trencherman, whale.

antonym ascetic.

gluttony *n.* edacity, esurience, gormandize, gormandizing, gormandism, greed, greediness, gulosity, insatiability, omnivorousness, piggishness, rapaciousness, rapacity, voraciousness, voracity.

antonyms abstinence, asceticism.

gnarled *adj.* contorted, distorted, gnarly, gnarred, knarred, knotted, knotty, knurled, leathery, rough, rugged, twisted, weather-beaten, wrinkled.

gnaw *v.* bite, chew, consume, devour, distress, eat, erode, fret, harry, haunt, munch, nag, nibble, niggle, plague, prey, trouble, wear, worry.

go *v.* accord, advance, agree, avail, beat it, blend, chime, complement, concur, conduce, connect, contribute, correspond, decamp, decease, depart, develop, die, disappear, elapse, eventuate, expire, extend, fare, fit, flow, function, gee, happen, harmonize, incline, jib, journey, lapse, lead, lead to, leave, levant, make for, match, mosey, move, naff off, nip, operate, pass, pass away, perform, perish, proceed, progress, rate, reach, repair, result, retreat, roll, run, sally, scram, serve, shift, shove off, slip, span, spread, stretch, suit, take one's leave, tend, travel, trot, vanish, wag, walk, wend, withdraw, work.

n. animation, attempt, bid, crack, drive, dynamism, effort, energy, essay, force, get-up-and-go, life, oomph, pep, shot, spirit, stab, try, turn, verve, vigor, vim, vitality, vivacity, whack, whirl, zest.

goad *n.* fillip, impetus, incentive, incitement, irritation, jab, motivation, poke, pressure, prod, push, spur, stimulation, stimulus, thrust, urge.

v. annoy, arouse, badger, bullyrag, chivvy, drive, egg on, exasperate, exhort, harass, hassle, hector, hound, impel, incite, infuriate, instigate, irritate, lash, madden,

nag, needle, persecute, prick, prod, prompt, propel, push, spur, stimulate, sting, urge, vex, worry.

go-ahead *n.* agreement, assent, authorization, clearance, consent, fiat, green light, leave, OK, permission, sanction.

antonyms ban, embargo, moratorium, veto.

adj. ambitious, avant-garde, enterprising, goey, go-getting, pioneering, progressive, up-and-coming.

antonyms sluggish, unenterprising.

goal *n.* aim, ambition, aspiration, bourn(e), design, destination, destiny, end, grail, intention, limit, mark, object, objective, purpose, target.

gobble *v.* bolt, consume, cram, devour, gorge, gulp, guttle, guzzle, hog, put away, shovel, slabber, stuff, swallow, wire into, wolf.

go-between *n.* agent, broker, contact, dealer, factor, informer, intermediary, internuncio, liaison, mediator, medium, messenger, middleman, ombudsman, pander, pimp, procuress.

goblet *n.* balloon glass, brandy-glass, chalice, drinking-cup, hanap, Paris, goblet, quaich, rummer, tass, wineglass.

goblin *n.* barghest, bogey, bogle, brownie, bugbear, demon, esprit follet, fiend, gremlin, hobgoblin, imp, kelpie, kobold, lubber fiend, nis, nix, nixie, red-cap, redcowl, spirit, sprite.

God, god *n.* Allah, avatar, Brahma, deity, divinity, genius, Godhead, Holy One, idol, Jah, Jehovah, joss, Jove, kami, lar, Lord, Lord God, monad, Mumbo-jumbo, numen, penates, power, Providence, spirit, the Almighty, the Creator, tutelar, tutelary, Yahweh, Zeus.

godlike *adj.* celestial, deiform, divine, exalted, heavenly, saintly, sublime, superhuman, theomorphic, transcendent.

godly *adj.* blameless, devout, god-fearing, good, holy, innocent, pious, pure, religious, righteous, saintly, virtuous.

antonyms godless, impious.

golden *adj.* advantageous, aureate, auric, auspicious, best, blissful, blond(e), bright, brilliant, delightful, excellent, fair, favorable, favored, flaxen, flourishing, glorious, happy, inaurate, invaluable, joyful, lustrous, opportune, precious, priceless, promising, propitious, prosperous, resplendent, rich, rosy, shining, successful, timely, valuable, xanthous, yellow.

gone *adj.* absent, astray, away, broken, bygone, closed, concluded, consumed, dead, deceased, defunct, departed, disappeared, done, elapsed, ended, extinct, finished, kaput, lacking, lost, missed, missing, over, over and done with, past, pregnant, spent, used, vanished, wanting.

good *adj.* able, acceptable, accomplished, adept, adequate, admirable, adroit, advantageous, agreeable, altruistic, amiable, ample, appropriate, approved, approving, auspicious, authentic, balmy, beneficent, beneficial, benevolent, benign, bona fide, bonzer, boshta, bosker,

bright, brotherly, budgeree, buoyant, calm, capable, capital, charitable, cheerful, choice, clear, clever, cloudless, commendable, competent, complete, congenial, considerate, convenient, convivial, correct, decorous, dependable, deserving, dexterous, dutiful, eatable, efficient, enjoyable, entire, estimable, ethical, excellent, exemplary, expert, extensive, fair, favorable, fine, first-class, first-rate, fit, fitting, friendly, full, genuine, gracious, gratifying, great, happy, healthy, helpful, honest, honorable, humane, kind, kindly, large, legitimate, long, loyal, mannerly, merciful, meritorious, mild, moral, nice, noble, nourishing, nutritious, obedient, obliging, opportune, orderly, pious, pleasant, pleasing, pleasurable, polite, positive, praiseworthy, precious, presentable, professional, proficient, profitable, proper, propitious, rattling, real, reliable, right, righteous, safe, salubrious, salutary, satisfactory, satisfying, seemly, serviceable, sizeable, skilful, skilled, solid, sound, special, splendid, substantial, sufficient, suitable, sunny, super, superior, sustaining, talented, tested, thorough, tranquil, true, trustworthy, uncorrupted, untainted, upright, useful, valid, valuable, virtuous, well-behaved, well-disposed, well-mannered, whole, wholesome, worthwhile, worthy.
n. advantage, avail, behalf, behoof, benefit, boon, convenience, excellence, gain, goodness, interest, merit, morality, probity, profit, rectitude, right, righteousness, service, uprightness, use, usefulness, virtue, weal, welfare, well-being, worth, worthiness.

good-bye *n., interj.* adieu, adiós, arrivederci, au revoir, auf Wiedersehen, chin-chin, ciao, farewell, leave-taking, parting, valediction, valedictory.

good-humored *adj.* affable, amiable, approachable, blithe, cheerful, congenial, expansive, genial, good-tempered, happy, jocund, jovial, pleasant.
antonym ill-humored.

good-looking *adj.* attractive, beautiful, bonny, comely, easy on the eye, fair, handsome, personable, presentable, pretty, well-favored, well-looking, well-proportioned, well-set-up.
antonyms ill-favored, plain, ugly.

good-natured *adj.* agreeable, amenable, approachable, benevolent, broad-minded, friendly, gentle, good-hearted, helpful, kind, kind-hearted, kindly, neighborly, open-minded, sympathetic, tolerant, warm-hearted.
antonym ill-natured.

goodness *n.* advantage, altruism, beneficence, benefit, benevolence, condescension, excellence, fairness, friendliness, generosity, goodwill, graciousness, honesty, honor, humaneness, humanity, integrity, justness, kindliness, kindness, mercy, merit, morality, nourishment, nutrition, piety, probity, quality, rectitude, righteousness, salubriousness, superiority, unselfishness, uprightness, value, virtue, wholesomeness, worth.
antonyms badness, inferiority, wickedness.

goods *n.* appurtenances, bags and baggage, belongings, chattels, commodities, effects, furnishings, furniture, gear, merchandise, movables, paraphernalia, plenishing, possessions, property, stock, stuff, traps, vendibles, wares.

goodwill *n.* altruism, amity, benevolence, compassion, earnestness, favor, friendliness, friendship, generosity, heartiness, kindliness, loving-kindness, sincerity, sympathy, zeal.
antonym ill-will.

gooseflesh *n.* creeps, duck bumps, formication, goose bumps, goose-pimples, grue, heebie-jeebies, horripilation, horrors, shivers, shudders.

gore[1] *n.* blood, bloodiness, bloodshed, butchery, carnage, cruor, grume, slaughter.

gore[2] *v.* impale, penetrate, pierce, rend, spear, spit, stab, stick, transfix, wound.
n. flare, gair, godet, gusset.

gorge[1] *n.* abyss, barranca, canyon, chasm, cleft, clough, defile, fissure, gap, gulch, gully, pass, ravine.

gorge[2] *v.* bolt, cram, devour, feed, fill, fill one's face, glut, gluttonize, gobble, gormandize, gulp, guzzle, hog, make a pig of oneself, overeat, sate, satiate, stuff, surfeit, swallow, wolf.
antonym abstain.

gorgeous *adj.* attractive, beautiful, bright, brilliant, dazzling, delightful, elegant, enjoyable, exquisite, fine, flamboyant, glamorous, glittering, glorious, good, good-looking, grand, lovely, luxuriant, luxurious, magnificent, opulent, pleasing, ravishing, resplendent, rich, showy, splendid, splendiferous, stunning, sumptuous, superb.
antonyms dull, plain, seedy.

gory *adj.* blood-soaked, bloodstained, bloodthirsty, bloody, brutal, ensanguined, murderous, sanguinary, sanguineous, sanguinolent, savage.

gossamer *adj.* airy, cobwebby, delicate, diaphanous, fine, flimsy, gauzy, insubstantial, light, sheer, shimmering, silky, thin, translucent, transparent.
antonyms heavy, opaque, thick.

gossip[1] *n.* blether, bush telegraph, causerie, chinwag, chitchat, clash, clish-clash, clishmaclaver, gup, hearsay, idle talk, jaw, newsmongering, prattle, report, rumor, scandal, schmooze, small talk, tittle-tattle, yackety-yak.

gossip[2] *n.* babbler, blatherskite, blether, bletherskate, busybody, chatterbox, chatterer, gossip-monger, newsmonger, nosy parker, prattler, quidnunc, rumorer, scandalmonger, tabby, talebearer, tattler, telltale, whisperer.
v. blather, blether, bruit, chat, clash, gabble, jaw, prattle, rumor, tattle, tell tales, whisper.

gouge *v.* chisel, claw, cut, dig, extract, force, gash, grave, groove, hack, hollow, incise, scoop, score, scratch, slash.
n. cut, furrow, gash, groove, hack, hollow, incision, notch, scoop, score, scratch, slash, trench.

gourmand *n.* cormorant, free-liver, gannet, glutton,

gorger, gormandizer, guzzler, hog, omnivore, pig, trencherman, whale.

antonym ascetic.

gourmet *n.* arbiter elegantiae, arbiter elegantiarum, bon vivant, bon viveur, connoisseur, dainty eater, epicure, epicurean, gastronome, gastronomer, gastrosoph, gastrosopher.

antonym omnivore.

govern *v.* administer, allay, bridle, check, command, conduct, contain, control, curb, decide, determine, direct, discipline, guide, influence, inhibit, lead, manage, master, order, oversee, pilot, preside, quell, regulate, reign, restrain, rule, steer, subdue, superintend, supervise, sway, tame, underlie.

government *n.* administration, authority, charge, command, conduct, control, direction, domination, dominion, Establishment, executive, governance, guidance, kingcraft, law, management, ministry, polity, powers-that-be, raj, régime, regimen, regulation, restraint, rule, sovereignty, state, statecraft, superintendence, supervision, surveillance, sway.

governor *n.* adelantado, administrator, alcalde, alderman, boss, chief, commander, commissioner, comptroller, controller, corrector, director, executive, gubernator, hakim, head, leader, manager, naik, overseer, ruler, superintendent, supervisor, vali.

gown *n.* costume, creation, dress, dressing-gown, frock, garb, garment, habit, kirtle, négligé, robe.

grab *v.* affect, annex, appropriate, bag, capture, catch, catch hold of, clutch, collar, commandeer, grasp, grip, impress, latch on to, nab, pluck, ramp, rap, seize, snap up, snatch, strike, usurp.

grace[1] *n.* attractiveness, beauty, benefaction, beneficence, benevolence, benignity, benison, breeding, charity, charm, clemency, comeliness, compassion, compassionateness, consideration, courtesy, cultivation, decency, decorum, deftness, ease, elegance, eloquence, etiquette, favor, finesse, fluency, forgiveness, generosity, goodness, goodwill, gracefulness, graciousness, indulgence, kindliness, kindness, leniency, lenity, love, loveliness, mannerliness, manners, mercifulness, mercy, merit, pardon, pleasantness, poise, polish, propriety, quarter, refinement, reprieve, shapeliness, tact, tastefulness, unction, virtue.

v. adorn, beautify, bedeck, deck, decorate, dignify, distinguish, dress, elevate, embellish, enhance, enrich, favor, garnish, glorify, honor, ornament, prettify, set off, trim.

antonyms deface, detract from, spoil.

grace[2] *n.* benediction, benedictus, blessing, consecration, prayer, thanks, thanksgiving.

graceful *adj.* agile, balletic, beautiful, becoming, charming, comely, deft, easy, elegant, facile, feat, feline, fine, flowing, fluid, gainly, genty, gracile, lightsome, natural, pleasing, pliant, slender, smooth, suave, supple, tasteful, willowish, willowy.

antonym graceless.

gracious *adj.* accommodating, affable, affluent, amenable, amiable, beneficent, benevolent, benign, benignant, charitable, chivalrous, civil, compassionate, complaisant, condescending, considerate, cordial, courteous, courtly, elegant, friendly, grand, hospitable, indulgent, kind, kindly, lenient, loving, luxurious, merciful, mild, obliging, pleasant, pleasing, polite, refined, sweet, well-mannered.

antonym ungracious.

grade *n.* acclivity, bank, brand, category, class, condition, dan, declivity, degree, downgrade, echelon, gradation, gradient, group, hill, incline, level, mark, notch, order, place, position, quality, rank, rise, rung, size, slope, stage, station, step, upgrade.

v. arrange, blend, brand, categorize, class, classify, docket, evaluate, group, label, mark, order, pigeon-hole, range, rank, rate, shade, size, sort, type, value.

gradual *adj.* cautious, continuous, deliberate, even, gentle, graduated, leisurely, measured, moderate, piecemeal, progressive, regular, slow, steady, step-by-step, successive, unhurried.

antonyms precipitate, sudden.

graduate[1] *v.* arrange, calibrate, classify, grade, group, make the grade, mark off, measure out, order, pass, proportion, qualify, range, rank, regulate, sort.

graduate[2] *n.* alumna, alumnus, bachelor, diplomate, diplômé, diplômée, doctor, fellow, graduand, licentiate, literate, master, member.

graft *n.* bud, engraft, engraftation, engraftment, heteroplasty, imp, implant, implantation, insert, scion, shoot, splice, sprout, transplant.

v. engraft, implant, insert, join, splice, transplant.

grain *n.* atom, bit, cereals, corn, crumb, doit, fiber, fragment, granule, grist, grits, iota, jot, kernel, marking, mite, modicum, molecule, morsel, mote, nap, ounce, panic, particle, pattern, piece, scintilla, scrap, scruple, seed, smidgeon, spark, speck, surface, suspicion, texture, trace, weave, whit.

grand *adj.* A1, admirable, affluent, ambitious, august, chief, condescending, dignified, elevated, eminent, exalted, excellent, fine, first-class, first-rate, glorious, gracious, grandiose, great, haughty, head, highest, illustrious, imperious, imposing, impressive, large, leading, lofty, lordly, luxurious, magnificent, main, majestic, marvelous, monumental, noble, opulent, ostentatious, outstanding, palatial, patronizing, pompous, pre-eminent, pretentious, princely, principal, regal, senior, smashing, splendid, stately, striking, sublime, sumptuous, super, superb, supreme, wonderful.

grandeur *n.* augustness, dignity, graciousness, gravitas, greatness, hauteur, imperiousness, importance, loftiness, magnificence, majesty, morgue, nobility, pomp, splendor, state, stateliness, sublimity.

antonyms humbleness, lowliness, simplicity.

grandiose *adj.* affected, ambitious, bombastic, euphuistic, extravagant, flamboyant, grand, high-flown,

imposing, impressive, lofty, magnificent, majestic, monumental, ostentatious, pompous, ponderous, pretentious, showy, stately, Wagnerian, weighty.
antonym unpretentious.

grant *v.* accede to, accord, acknowledge, admit, agree to, allocate, allot, allow, apportion, assign, award, bestow, cede, concede, confer, consent to, convey, deign, dispense, donate, give, impart, permit, present, provide, transfer, transmit, vouchsafe, yield.
antonyms deny, refuse.
n. accord, admission, allocation, allotment, allowance, annuity, award, benefaction, bequest, boon, bounty, bursary, concession, donation, endowment, gift, honorarium, present, scholarship, subsidy, subvention.

granular *adj.* crumbly, grainy, granulase, granulated, granulous, gravelly, gritty, murly, rough, sabulose, sabulous, sandy.

graphic *adj.* blow-by-blow, clear, cogent, delineated, delineative, descriptive, detailed, diagrammatic, drawn, explicit, expressive, forcible, illustrative, lively, lucid, pictorial, picturesque, representational, seen, specific, striking, telling, visible, visual, vivid.
antonyms impressionistic, vague.

grapple *v.* attack, battle, catch, clash, clasp, clinch, close, clutch, combat, come to grips, confront, contend, cope, deal with, encounter, engage, face, fasten, fight, grab, grasp, grip, gripe, hold, hug, lay hold, make fast, seize, snatch, struggle, tackle, tussle, wrestle.
antonyms avoid, evade.

grasping *adj.* acquisitive, avaricious, close-fisted, covetous, greedy, mean, mercenary, miserly, niggardly, parsimonious, penny-pinching, rapacious, selfish, stingy, tight-fisted, usurious.
antonym generous.

grass[2] *n.* ganja, hash, hay, hemp, joint, marijuana, pot, reefer.

grate *v.* aggravate, annoy, chafe, comminute, creak, exasperate, fret, gall, get on one's nerves, granulate, gride, grind, irk, irritate, jar, mince, nettle, peeve, pulverize, rankle, rasp, rub, scrape, scratch, set one's teeth on edge, shred, triturate, vex.

grateful *adj.* appreciative, aware, beholden, indebted, mindful, obligated, obliged, sensible, thankful.
antonym ungrateful.

gratify *v.* appease, cater to, content, delight, favor, fulfil, gladden, humor, indulge, pander to, please, pleasure, recompense, requite, satisfy, thrill.
antonyms frustrate, thwart.

grating[1] *adj.* annoying, cacophonous, disagreeable, discordant, displeasing, grinding, harsh, horrisonant, irksome, irritating, jarring, rasping, raucous, scraping, squeaky, strident, unharmonious, unmelodious, unpleasant, vexatious.
antonyms harmonious, pleasing.

grating[2] *n.* grid, grill, grille, hack, heck, lattice, latticework, treillage, treille, trellis, trelliswork.

gratitude *n.* acknowledgment, appreciation, awareness, gratefulness, indebtedness, mindfulness, obligation, recognition, thankfulness, thanks.
antonym ingratitude.

gratuity *n.* baksheesh, beer-money, benefaction, bonus, boon, bounty, dash, donation, donative, douceur, drink-money, gift, lagniappe, largess, perquisite, pourboire, present, recompense, reward, tip, Trinkgeld.

grave[1] *n.* barrow, burial-place, burying-place, cairn, cist, crypt, long home, mausoleum, pit, sepulcher, tomb, vault.

grave[2] *adj.* acute, Catonian, critical, crucial, dangerous, depressing, dignified, disquieting, dour, dull, earnest, exigent, gloomy, grim, grim-faced, hazardous, heavy, important, leaden, long-faced, momentous, muted, perilous, ponderous, preoccupied, pressing, quiet, reserved, restrained, sad, sage, saturnine, sedate, serious, severe, significant, sober, solemn, somber, staid, subdued, thoughtful, threatening, unsmiling, urgent, vital, weighty.
antonyms cheerful, light, slight, trivial.

gravel *n.* chesil, grail, hogging, shingle.

gravitate *v.* descend, drop, fall, head for, incline, lean, move, precipitate, settle, sink, tend.

gravity *n.* acuteness, consequence, demureness, dignity, earnestness, exigency, gloom, gravitas, grimness, hazardousness, importance, magnitude, moment, momentousness, perilousness, ponderousness, reserve, restraint, sedateness, seriousness, severity, significance, sobriety, solemnity, somberness, thoughtfulness, urgency, weightiness.
antonyms gaiety, levity, triviality.

gray *adj.* aged, ancient, anonymous, ashen, bloodless, characterless, cheerless, cloudy, colorless, dark, depressing, dim, dismal, drab, dreary, dull, elderly, experienced, glaucous, gloomy, grège, greige, griseous, grizzle, grizzled, hoar, hoary, indistinct, leaden, liard, livid, mature, murksome, murky, neutral, old, overcast, pale, pallid, sunless, uncertain, unclear, unidentifiable, venerable, wan.

graze[1] *v.* batten, browse, crop, feed, fodder, pasture.

graze[2] *v.* abrade, bark, brush, chafe, gride, rub, scart, score, scotch, scrape, scratch, shave, skim, skin, touch.
n. abrasion, score, scrape, scratch.

grease *n.* dope, dripping, fat, gunge, lard, oil, ointment, sebum, tallow, unction, unguent, wax.

greasy *adj.* fatty, fawning, glib, groveling, ingratiating, lardy, oily, oleaginous, sebaceous, slick, slimy, slippery, smarmy, smeary, smooth, sycophantic, tallowy, toadying, unctuous, waxy.

great *adj.* able, ace, active, adept, admirable, adroit, august, big, bulky, capital, celebrated, chief, colossal, consequential, considerable, crack, critical, crucial, decided, devoted, dignified, distinguished, eminent, enormous, enthusiastic, exalted, excellent, excessive, expert, extended, extensive, extravagant, extreme, fab,

fabulous, famed, famous, fantastic, fine, finished, first-rate, generous, gigantic, glorious, good, grand, grave, great-hearted, grievous, heavy, heroic, high, high-minded, huge, idealistic, illustrious, immense, important, impressive, inordinate, invaluable, jake, keen, large, leading, lengthy, lofty, long, magnanimous, main, major, mammoth, manifold, marked, marvelous, massive, masterly, momentous, multitudinous, munificent, noble, nonpareil, notable, noteworthy, noticeable, outstanding, paramount, ponderous, precious, pre-eminent, priceless, primary, princely, principal, prodigious, proficient, prolific, prolonged, prominent, pronounced, protracted, remarkable, renowned, senior, serious, significant, skilful, skilled, strong, stupendous, sublime, superb, superior, superlative, swingeing, talented, terrific, tremendous, valuable, vast, virtuoso, voluminous, weighty, wonderful, zealous.
antonyms insignificant, pusillanimous, small, unimportant.

greed *n.* acquisitiveness, anxiety, avidity, covetousness, craving, cupidity, desire, eagerness, edacity, esurience, esuriency, gluttony, gormandizing, gormandism, gourmandize, greediness, gulosity, hunger, insatiability, insatiableness, itchy palm, land-hunger, longing, plutolatry, rapacity, ravenousness, selfishness, voraciousness, voracity.
antonym abstemiousness.

greedy *adj.* acquisitive, anxious, avaricious, avid, covetous, craving, curious, desirous, eager, edacious, esurient, gare, gluttonish, gluttonous, gormandizing, grasping, gripple, gutsy, hoggery, hoggish, hungry, impatient, insatiable, itchy-palmed, land-grabbing, piggish, rapacious, ravenous, selfish, ventripotent, voracious.
antonym abstemious.

green *adj.* blooming, budding, callow, covetous, credulous, emerald, envious, flourishing, fresh, glaucous, grassy, grudging, gullible, ignorant, ill, immature, inexperienced, inexpert, ingenuous, innocent, jealous, leafy, naive, nauseous, new, pale, pliable, raw, recent, resentful, sick, starry-eyed, supple, tender, unhealthy, unpracticed, unripe, unseasoned, unsophisticated, untrained, untried, unversed, verdant, verdurous, vert, virescent, virid, viridescent, vitreous, wan, wet behind the ears, young.
n. common, grass, greensward, lawn, sward, turf.

greenhorn *n.* apprentice, beginner, catechumen, fledgling, ignoramus, ingénué, initiate, Johnnie raw, learner, naïf, neophyte, newcomer, novice, novitiate, recruit, rookie, simpleton, tenderfoot, tyro.
antonyms old hand, veteran.

greenhouse *n.* conservatory, glasshouse, hothouse, nursery, pavilion, vinery.

greet *v.* accost, acknowledge, address, compliment, hail, hallo, halloo, meet, receive, salute, wave to, welcome.
antonym ignore.

gregarious *adj.* affable, chummy, companionable, convivial, cordial, extrovert, friendly, outgoing, pally, sociable, social, warm.
antonym unsociable.

grief *n.* ache, affliction, agony, anguish, bereavement, blow, burden, dejection, desiderium, desolation, distress, dole, grievance, heartache, heartbreak, lamentation, misery, mournfulness, mourning, pain, regret, remorse, sadness, sorrow, suffering, tragedy, trial, tribulation, trouble, woe.
antonym happiness.

grief-stricken *adj.* afflicted, agonized, broken, broken-hearted, crushed, desolate, despairing, devastated, disconsolate, distracted, grieving, heartbroken, inconsolable, mourning, overcome, overwhelmed, sad, sorrowful, sorrowing, stricken, unhappy, woebegone, wretched.
antonym overjoyed.

grievance *n.* affliction, beef, bitch, charge, complaint, damage, distress, gravamen, grief, gripe, grouse, hardship, injury, injustice, moan, peeve, resentment, sorrow, trial, tribulation, trouble, unhappiness, wrong.

grieve *v.* ache, afflict, agonize, bemoan, bewail, complain, crush, cut to the quick, deplore, distress, disturb, eat one's heart out, harrow, hurt, injure, lament, mourn, pain, regret, rue, sadden, sorrow, suffer, upset, wail, weep, wound.

grieved *adj.* abashed, affronted, ashamed, desolated, displeased, distressed, horrified, hurt, injured, offended, pained, sad, saddened, shocked, sorry, upset, wounded.

grievous *adj.* appalling, atrocious, burdensome, calamitous, damaging, deplorable, devastating, distressing, dreadful, flagrant, glaring, grave, harmful, heart-rending, heavy, heinous, hurtful, injurious, intolerable, lamentable, monstrous, mournful, offensive, oppressive, outrageous, overwhelming, painful, pitiful, plightful, severe, shameful, shocking, sorrowful, tragic, unbearable, wounding.

grim *adj.* adamant, cruel, doom-laden, dour, fearsome, ferocious, fierce, forbidding, formidable, frightening, frightful, ghastly, grisly, gruesome, harsh, hideous, horrible, horrid, implacable, merciless, morose, relentless, repellent, resolute, ruthless, severe, shocking, sinister, stern, sullen, surly, terrible, unpleasant, unrelenting, unwelcome, unyielding.
antonyms benign, congenial, pleasant.

grimace *n.* face, fit of the face, frown, moue, mouth, pout, scowl, smirk, sneer, wry face.
v. fleer, frown, girn, make a face, mop, mop and mow, mouth, mow, mug, pout, scowl, smirk, sneer.

grimy *adj.* begrimed, besmeared, besmirched, contaminated, dirty, filthy, foul, grubby, murky, reechy, smudgy, smutty, soiled, sooty, squalid.
antonyms clean, pure.

grind *v.* abrade, beaver, bray, comminute, crush, drudge, file, gnash, granulate, grate, grit, kibble, labor, levigate, lucubrate, mill, polish, pound, powder, pulverize, sand, scrape, sharpen, slave, smooth, sweat, swot, toil, triturate, whet.

n. chore, drudgery, exertion, grindstone, labor, round, routine, slavery, sweat, task, toil.

grip *n.* acquaintance, clasp, clutches, comprehension, control, domination, embrace, grasp, handclasp, hold, influence, keeping, mastery, perception, possession, power, purchase, sway, tenure, understanding.

v. absorb, catch, clasp, clutch, compel, divert, engross, enthrall, entrance, fascinate, grasp, hold, involve, latch on to, mesmerize, rivet, seize, spellbind, thrill, vice.

gripe *v.* beef, bellyache, bitch, carp, complain, groan, grouch, grouse, grumble, moan, nag, whine, whinge.

n. ache, aching, affliction, beef, bitch, colic, collywobbles, complaint, cramps, distress, grievance, griping, groan, grouch, grouse, grumble, moan, objection, pain, pang, pinching, spasm, stomach-ache, twinge.

grit[1] *n.* chesil, dust, grail, gravel, hogging, pebbles, sand, shingle, swarf.

v. clench, gnash, grate, grind, lock.

grit[2] backbone, bottle, bravery, courage, determination, doggedness, foison, fortitude, fushion, gameness, guts, hardihood, mettle, nerve, perseverance, pluck, resolution, spine, spirit, spunk, stamina, staying power, tenacity, toughness.

groan *n.* complaint, cry, moan, objection, outcry, protest, sigh, wail.

antonym cheer.

v. complain, cry, lament, moan, object, protest, sigh, wail.

antonym cheer.

groggy *adj.* befuddled, confused, dazed, dizzy, dopey, faint, fuddled, knocked-up, muzzy, punch-drunk, reeling, shaky, stunned, stupefied, unsteady, weak, wobbly, woozy.

antonym lucid.

groom *v.* brush, clean, coach, curry, dress, drill, educate, neaten, nurture, preen, prepare, prime, primp, prink, ready, school, smarten, spruce up, tart up, tend, tidy, titivate, train, turn out, tutor.

groove *n.* canal, cannelure, chamfer, channel, chase, cut, cutting, flute, furrow, gutter, hollow, indentation, kerf, rabbet, rebate, rigol, rut, score, scrobe, sulcus, trench, vallecula. *antonym* ridge.

grope *v.* cast about, feel, feel about, feel up, finger, fish, flounder, fumble, goose, grabble, probe, scrabble, search.

gross[1] *adj.* apparent, arrant, bawdy, bestial, big, blatant, blue, boorish, broad, brutish, bulky, callous, coarse, colossal, corpulent, crass, crude, cumbersome, dense, downright, dull, earthy, egregious, fat, flagrant, foul, glaring, great, grievous, heavy, heinous, huge, hulking, ignorant, immense, imperceptive, improper, impure, indecent, indelicate, insensitive, large, lewd, low,

lumpish, manifest, massive, obese, obscene, obtuse, obvious, offensive, outrageous, outright, overweight, plain, rank, ribald, rude, sensual, serious, shameful, shameless, sheer, shocking, slow, sluggish, smutty, tasteless, thick, uncivil, uncouth, uncultured, undiscriminating, undisguised, unfeeling, unmitigated, unseemly, unsophisticated, unwieldy, utter, vulgar.

antonyms delicate, fine, seemly, slight.

gross[2] *n.* aggregate, bulk, entirety, sum, total, totality, whole.

adj. aggregate, all-inclusive, complete, entire, inclusive, total, whole.

v. accumulate, aggregate, bring, earn, make, rake in, take, total.

grotesque *adj.* absurd, antic, bizarre, deformed, distorted, extravagant, fanciful, fantastic, freakish, gruesome, hideous, incongruous, laughable, ludicrous, macabre, malformed, misshapen, monstrous, odd, outlandish, preposterous, ridiculous, rococo, strange, ugly, unnatural, unsightly, weird.

n. bizarrerie, extravaganza, fantastic figure, gargoyle, gobbo, grotesquerie, manikin.

grotto *n.* catacomb, cave, cavern, chamber, dene-hole, grot, souterrain, subterranean (chamber), subterrene, underground chamber.

grouch *v.* beef, bellyache, bitch, carp, complain, find fault, gripe, grouse, grumble, moan, whine, whinge.

antonym acquiesce.

n. belly-acher, churl, complainer, complaint, crab, crosspatch, crotcheteer, curmudgeon, fault-finder, grievance, gripe, grouse, grouser, grumble, grumbler, malcontent, moan, moaner, murmer, murmurer, mutterer, objection, whiner, whinge, whinger.

grouchy *adj.* bad-tempered, cantankerous, captious, churlish, complaining, cross, crotchety, discontented, dissatisfied, grumbling, grumpy, ill-tempered, irascible, irritable, mutinous, peevish, petulant, querulous, sulky, surly, testy, truculent.

antonym contented.

ground *n.* arena, background, ball-park, bottom, clay, clod, deck, dirt, dry land, dust, earth, field, foundation, land, loam, mold, park, pitch, sod, soil, solum, stadium, surface, terra firma, terrain, turf.

v. acquaint with, base, build up, coach, drill, establish, familiarize with, fix, found, inform, initiate, instruct, introduce, prepare, set, settle, teach, train, tutor.

groundless *adj.* absurd, baseless, chimerical, empty, false, gratuitous, idle, illusory, imaginary, irrational, unauthorized, uncalled-for, unfounded, unjustified, unproven, unprovoked, unreasonable, unsubstantiated, unsupported, unwarranted.

antonyms justified, reasonable.

grounds[1] *n.* acres, area, country, district, domain, estate, fields, gardens, habitat, holding, land, park, property, realm, surroundings, terrain, territory, tract.

grounds[2] *n.* account, argument, base, basis, call, cause, excuse, factor, foundation, inducement, justification, motive, occasion, premise, pretext, principle, rationale, reason, score, vindication.

grounds[3] *n.* deposit, dregs, grouts, lees, precipitate, precipitation, sediment, settlings.

groundwork *n.* base, basis, cornerstone, essentials, footing, foundation, fundamentals, homework, preliminaries, preparation, research, spadework, underpinnings.

group *n.* accumulation, aggregation, assemblage, association, band, batch, bracket, bunch, category, caucus, circle, class, classification, classis, clique, clump, cluster, clutch, cohort, collection, collective, combination, company, conclave, conglomeration, congregation, constellation, core, coterie, covey, crowd, detachment, faction, formation, front, galère, gang, gathering, Gemeinschaft, genus, grouping, knot, lot, nexus, organization, pack, parti, party, pop-group, set, shower, species, squad, squadron, team, troop.

v. arrange, assemble, associate, assort, band, bracket, categorize, class, classify, cluster, collect, congregate, consort, deploy, dispose, fraternize, gather, get together, link, marshal, mass, order, organize, range, sort.

grouse *v.* beef, belly-ache, bitch, carp, complain, find fault, fret, fuss, gripe, grouch, grumble, moan, mutter, whine, whinge.

antonym acquiesce.

n. belly-ache, complaint, grievance, gripe, grouch, grumble, moan, murmur, mutter, objection, peeve, whine, whinge.

grovel *v.* abase oneself, backscratch, bootlick, cower, crawl, creep, cringe, crouch, defer, demean oneself, fawn, flatter, kowtow, sneak, sycophantize, toady.

groveling *adj.* backscratching, bootlicking, fawning, flattering, ingratiating, obsequious, sycophantic, wormy.

antonyms outspoken, straightforward.

grow *v.* advance, arise, augment, become, branch out, breed, broaden, burgeon, cultivate, develop, diversify, enlarge, evolve, expand, extend, farm, flourish, flower, germinate, get, heighten, improve, increase, issue, mature, multiply, nurture, originate, produce, progress, proliferate, propagate, prosper, raise, ripen, rise, shoot, spread, spring, sprout, stem, stretch, succeed, swell, thicken, thrive, turn, vegetate, wax, widen.

antonyms decrease, fail, halt.

grown-up *adj.* adult, full-grown, fully-fledged, fully-grown, mature, of age.

antonyms childish, immature.

n. adult, gentleman, lady, man, woman.

antonym child.

growth *n.* accrescence, accretion, advance, advancement, aggrandizement, augmentation, auxesis, broadening, change, crop, cultivation, development, diversification, enlargement, evolution, excrement, excrescence, expansion, extension, flowering, gall, germination, growing,

heightening, improvement, increase, intumescence, lump, maturation, multiplication, outgrowth, produce, production, progress, proliferation, prosperity, protuberance, ripening, rise, shooting, sprouting, stretching, success, swelling, thickening, transformation, tumor, vegetation, waxing, widening.

antonyms decrease, failure, stagnation, stoppage.

grub[1] *v.* burrow, delve, dig, explore, ferret, forage, grout, hunt, investigate, nose, probe, pull up, root, rootle, rummage, scour, uproot.

n. caterpillar, chrysalis, larva, maggot, nymph, pupa, worm.

grub[2] *n.* chow, commons, eats, edibles, fodder, food, nosh, provisions, rations, scoff, sustenance, victuals.

grubby *adj.* crummy, dirty, filthy, fly-blown, frowzy, grimy, manky, mean, messy, mucky, scruffy, seedy, shabby, slovenly, smutty, soiled, sordid, squalid, unkempt, untidy, unwashed.

antonyms clean, smart.

grudge *n.* animosity, animus, antagonism, antipathy, aversion, bitterness, dislike, enmity, envy, grievance, hard feelings, hate, ill-will, jealousy, malevolence, malice, pique, rancor, resentment, spite.

antonyms favor, regard.

v. begrudge, covet, dislike, envy, mind, niggard, object to, regret, repine, resent, stint, take exception to.

antonyms applaud, approve.

grueling *adj.* arduous, backbreaking, brutal, crushing, demanding, difficult, exhausting, fatiguing, fierce, grinding, hard, hard-going, harsh, laborious, punishing, severe, stern, stiff, strenuous, taxing, tiring, tough, trying, uphill, wearing, wearying.

antonym easy.

gruesome *adj.* abominable, awful, chilling, eldritch, fearful, fearsome, ghastly, grim, grisly, grooly, hideous, horrible, horrid, horrific, horrifying, loathsome, macabre, monstrous, repellent, repugnant, repulsive, shocking, sick, spine-chilling, terrible, weird.

antonyms charming, congenial.

gruff *adj.* abrupt, bad-tempered, bearish, blunt, brusque, churlish, crabbed, croaking, crusty, curt, discourteous, gravelly, grouchy, grumpy, guttural, harsh, hoarse, husky, ill-humored, ill-natured, impolite, low, rasping, rough, rude, sour, sullen, surly, throaty, uncivil, ungracious, unmannerly.

antonyms clear, courteous, sweet.

grumble *v.* beef, bellyache, bitch, bleat, carp, chunter, complain, croak, find fault, gripe, grouch, grouse, growl, gurgle, moan, murmur, mutter, nark, repine, roar, rumble, whine.

antonym acquiesce.

n. beef, bitch, bleat, complaint, grievance, gripe, grouch, grouse, growl, gurgle, moan, murmur, muttering, objection, roar, rumble, whinge.

grumpy *adj.* bad-tempered, cantankerous, churlish, crabbed, cross, crotchety, discontented, grouchy, grumbling, ill-tempered, irritable, mutinous, peevish, petulant, querulous, sulky, sullen, surly, testy, truculent.

antonyms civil, contented.

guarantee *n.* assurance, attestation, bond, certainty, collateral, covenant, earnest, endorsement, guaranty, insurance, oath, pledge, promise, security, surety, testimonial, undertaking, voucher, warranty, word, word of honor.

v. answer for, assure, avouch, certify, ensure, insure, maintain, make certain, make sure of, pledge, promise, protect, secure, swear, underwrite, vouch for, warrant.

guarantor *n.* angel, backer, bailsman, bondsman, covenanter, guarantee, referee, sponsor, supporter, surety, underwriter, voucher, warrantor.

guard *v.* be on the qui vive, be on the watch, beware, conserve, cover, defend, escort, keep, look out, mind, oversee, patrol, police, preserve, protect, safeguard, save, screen, secure, sentinel, shelter, shield, supervise, tend, ward, watch.

n. attention, backstop, barrier, buffer, bulwark, bumper, care, caution, convoy, custodian, defense, defender, escort, guarantee, heed, lookout, minder, pad, patrol, picket, precaution, protection, protector, rampart, safeguard, screen, security, sentinel, sentry, shield, vigilance, wall, warder, wariness, watch, watchfulness, watchman.

guarded *adj.* cagey, careful, cautious, circumspect, discreet, disingenuous, non-committal, prudent, reserved, restrained, reticent, secretive, suspicious, uncommunicative, unforthcoming, wary, watchful.

antonyms frank, whole-hearted.

guardian *n.* attendant, champion, conservator, curator, custodian, defender, depositary, depository, escort, fiduciary, guard, keeper, minder, preserver, protector, trustee, warden, warder.

guess *v.* assume, believe, conjecture, dare say, deem, divine, estimate, fancy, fathom, feel, guesstimate, hazard, hypothesize, imagine, intuit, judge, opine, penetrate, predict, reckon, solve, speculate, suppose, surmise, suspect, think, work out.

n. assumption, belief, conjecture, fancy, feeling, guesstimate, hypothesis, intuition, judgment, notion, opinion, prediction, reckoning, shot (in the dark), speculation, supposition, surmise, suspicion, theory.

guest *n.* boarder, caller, company, freeloader, habitué, lodger, parasite, regular, roomer, visitant, visitor.

guide *v.* accompany, advise, attend, command, conduct, control, convoy, counsel, direct, educate, escort, govern, handle, head, influence, instruct, lead, manage, maneuver, oversee, pilot, point, regulate, rule, shape, shepherd, steer, superintend, supervise, sway, teach, train, usher, vector.

n. ABC, adviser, attendant, beacon, catalog, chaperon, cicerone, clue, companion, conductor, controller, counselor, courier, criterion, director, directory, dragoman, escort, example, exemplar, guide-book, guideline, handbook, ideal, index, indication, informant, inspiration, instructions, key, landmark, leader, lodestar, manual, mark, marker, master, mentor, model, monitor, paradigm, pilot, pointer, praxis, sign, signal, signpost, standard, steersman, teacher, template, usher, vade-mecum.

guild *n.* association, brotherhood, chapel, club, company, corporation, fellowship, fraternity, incorporation, league, lodge, order, organization, society, union.

guile *n.* art, artfulness, artifice, cleverness, craft, craftiness, cunning, deceit, deception, deviousness, disingenuity, duplicity, gamesmanship, knavery, ruse, slyness, treachery, trickery, trickiness, wiliness.

antonyms artlessness, guilelessness.

guileless *adj.* artless, candid, direct, frank, genuine, honest, ingenuous, innocent, naïve, natural, open, simple, sincere, straightforward, transparent, trusting, truthful, unreserved, unsophisticated, unworldly.

antonyms artful, guileful.

guilt *n.* blamability, blame, blameworthiness, compunction, conscience, contrition, criminality, culpability, delinquency, disgrace, dishonor, guiltiness, guilty conscience, infamy, iniquity, mens rea, regret, remorse, responsibility, self-condemnation, self-reproach, self-reproof, shame, sinfulness, stigma, wickedness, wrong.

antonyms innocence, shamelessness.

guilty *adj.* ashamed, blamable, blameworthy, compunctious, conscience-stricken, contrite, convicted, criminal, culpable, delinquent, errant, erring, evil, felonious, guilt-ridden, hangdog, illicit, iniquitous, nefarious, nocent, offending, penitent, regretful, remorseful, repentant, reprehensible, responsible, rueful, shamefaced, sheepish, sinful, sorry, wicked, wrong.

antonyms guiltless, innocent.

guise *n.* air, appearance, aspect, behavior, custom, demeanor, disguise, dress, façade, face, fashion, features, form, front, likeness, manner, mask, mode, pretense, semblance, shape, show.

gulf *n.* abyss, basin, bay, bight, breach, chasm, cleft, gap, gorge, opening, rent, rift, separation, split, void, whirlpool.

gullible *adj.* born yesterday, credulous, foolish, glaikit, green, innocent, naïve, trusting, unsuspecting, verdant.

antonym astute.

gully *n.* channel, ditch, donga, geo, gio, gulch, gutter, ravine, watercourse.

gulp *v.* bolt, choke, devour, gasp, gobble, gollop, gormandize, guzzle, knock back, quaff, stifle, stuff, swallow, swig, swill, toss off, wolf.

antonyms nibble, sip.

n. draft, mouthful, slug, swallow, swig.

gun *n.* equalizer, gat, heater, peacemaker, persuader, piece, pistol, shooter, shooting-iron, tool.

gush *v.* babble, blather, burst, cascade, chatter, drivel, effuse, enthuse, flood, flow, jabber, jet, pour, run, rush, spout, spurt, stream, yatter.

n. babble, burst, cascade, chatter, ebullition, effusion, eruption, exuberance, flood, flow, jet, outburst, outflow, rush, spout, spurt, stream, tide, torrent.

gust *n.* blast, blow, breeze, burst, flaught, flaw, flurry, gale, puff, rush, squall, williwaw.

v. blast, blow, bluster, breeze, puff, squall.

gutter *n.* channel, conduit, ditch, drain, duct, grip, kennel, pipe, rigol(l), sluice, trench, trough, tube.

gypsy *n.* Bohemian, diddicoy, faw, gipsy, gitana, gitano, nomad, rambler, roamer, Romany, rover, tink, tinker, traveler, tsigane, tzigany, vagabond, vagrant, wanderer, Zigeuner, Zincalo, Zingaro.

H

habit[1] *n.* accustomedness, addiction, assuetude, bent, constitution, convention, custom, dependence, diathesis, disposition, fixation, frame of mind, habitude, inclination, make-up, manner, mannerism, mode, mores, nature, obsession, practice, proclivity, propensity, quirk, routine, rule, second nature, tendency, usage, vice, way, weakness, wont.

habit[2] *n.* apparel, attire, clothes, clothing, dress, garb, garment, habiliment.

habitation *n.* abode, cottage, domicile, dwelling, dwelling-place, home, house, hut, inhabitance, inhabitancy, inhabitation, living quarters, lodging, mansion, occupancy, occupation, quarters, residence, tenancy.

habitual *adj.* accustomed, chronic, common, confirmed, constant, customary, established, familiar, fixed, frequent, hardened, ingrained, inveterate, natural, normal, ordinary, persistent, recurrent, regular, routine, standard, traditional, usual, wonted.
antonym occasional.

habituate *v.* acclimatize, accustom, break in, condition, discipline, familiarize, harden, inure, school, season, tame, train.

hack[1] *v.* bark, chop, cough, cut, gash, haggle, hew, kick, lacerate, mangle, mutilate, notch, rasp, slash.
n. bark, chop, cough, cut, gash, notch, rasp, slash.

hack[2] *adj.* banal, hackneyed, mediocre, pedestrian, poor, stereotyped, tired, undistinguished, uninspired, unoriginal.
n. crock, drudge, horse, jade, journalist, nag, paper-stainer, penny-a-liner, scribbler, slave.

hackneyed *adj.* banal, clichéd, common, commonplace, corny, hack, hand-me-down, overworked, pedestrian, percoct, played-out, run-of-the-mill, second-hand, stale, stereotyped, stock, threadbare, time-worn, tired, trite, unoriginal, worn-out.
antonyms arresting, new.

hag *n.* battle-ax, beldame, crone, fury, harpy, harridan, ogress, shrew, termagant, virago, vixen, witch.

haggard *adj.* cadaverous, careworn, drawn, emaciated, gaunt, ghastly, hagged, hollow-eyed, pinched, shrunken, thin, wan, wasted, wrinkled.
antonym hale.

haggle *v.* bargain, barter, bicker, cavil, chaffer, dicker, dispute, higgle, palter, quarrel, squabble, wrangle.

hail[1] *n.* barrage, bombardment, rain, shower, storm, torrent, volley.
v. assail, barrage, batter, bombard, pelt, rain, shower, storm, volley.

hail[2] *v.* acclaim, accost, acknowledge, address, applaud, call, cheer, exalt, flag down, glorify, greet, halloo, honor, salute, shout, signal to, wave, welcome.
n. call, cry, halloo, holla, shout.

hair-do *n.* coiffure, cut, haircut, hairstyle, perm, set, style.

hairdresser *n.* barber, coiffeur, coiffeuse, friseur, hairstylist, stylist.

hairless *adj.* bald, bald-headed, beardless, clean-shaven, depilated, desperate, frantic, glabrate, glabrous, shorn, tonsured.
antonym hairy.

hair-raising *adj.* alarming, bloodcurdling, breathtaking, creepy, eerie, exciting, frightening, ghastly, ghostly, horrifying, petrifying, scary, shocking, spine-chilling, startling, terrifying, thrilling.
antonym calming.

hairy *adj.* bearded, bewhiskered, bushy, crinigerous, crinite, crinose, dangerous, dicey, difficult, fleecy, furry, hazardous, hirsute, hispid, lanuginose, lanuginous, perilous, pilose, pilous, risky, scaring, shaggy, stubbly, villose, villous, woolly.
antonyms bald, clean-shaven.

hale *adj.* able-bodied, athletic, blooming, fit, flourishing, healthy, hearty, in fine fettle, in the pink, robust, sound, strong, vigorous, well, youthful.
antonym ill.

half-baked *adj.* brainless, crazy, foolish, harebrained, illconceived, ill-judged, impractical, senseless, shortsighted, silly, stupid, unplanned.
antonym sensible.

half-hearted *adj.* apathetic, cool, indifferent, lackadaisical, lackluster, listless, lukewarm, neutral, passive, perfunctory, uninterested.
antonym enthusiastic.

half-wit *n.* cretin, dimwit, dolt, dullard, dunce, dunderhead, fool, gaupus, idiot, imbecile, moron, nitwit, nut, simpleton, underwit, witling.
antonym brain.

hall *n.* assembly-room, auditorium, aula, basilica, chamber, concert-hall, concourse, corridor, entrance-hall, entry, foyer, hallway, lobby, salon, saloon, vestibule.

hallowed *adj.* age-old, beatified, blessed, consecrated, dedicated, established, holy, honored, inviolable, revered, sacred, sacrosanct, sanctified.

hallucination *n.* aberration, apparition, delusion, dream, fantasy, figment, illusion, mirage, phantasmagoria, pink elephants, vision.

halt *v.* arrest, block, break off, call it a day, cease, check, curb, desist, draw up, end, impede, obstruct, pack it in, quit, rest, stem, stop, terminate, wait.
antonyms assist, continue, start.

n. arrest, break, close, end, étape, impasse, interruption, pause, stand, standstill, stop, stoppage, termination, way point.

antonyms continuation, start.

halting *adj.* awkward, broken, faltering, hesitant, imperfect, labored, stammering, stumbling, stuttering, uncertain.

antonym fluent.

hammer *v.* bang, beat, clobber, defeat, din, dolly, drive, drive home, drub, drum, form, grind, hit, impress upon, instruct, knock, make, malleate, pan, repeat, shape, slate, thrash, trounce, worst.

n. beetle, gavel, madge, mall, mallet, maul, monkey.

hamper *v.* bind, cramp, cumber, curb, curtail, distort, embarrass, encumber, entangle, fetter, frustrate, hamshackle, hamstring, handicap, hinder, hobble, hold up, impede, interfere with, obstruct, pinch, prevent, restrain, restrict, shackle, slow down, tangle, thwart, trammel.

antonyms aid, expedite.

hamstrung *adj.* balked, crippled, disabled, foiled, frustrated, handicapped, helpless, hors de combat, incapacitated, paralyzed, stymied.

hand[1] *n.* ability, agency, aid, applause, art, artistry, assistance, calligraphy, cheirography, clap, daddle, direction, fist, flipper, handwriting, help, influence, mitt, ovation, palm, part, participation, paw, penmanship, pud, puddy, script, share, skill, support.

v. aid, assist, conduct, convey, deliver, give, guide, help, lead, offer, pass, present, provide, transmit, yield.

hand[2] *n.* artificer, artisan, craftsman, employee, farmhand, hired man, hireling, laborer, operative, orra man, redneck, worker, workman.

handicap *n.* barrier, block, defect, disability, disadvantage, drawback, encumbrance, hindrance, impairment, impediment, impost, limitation, millstone, obstacle, odds, penalty, restriction, shortcoming, stumbling-block.

antonyms assistance, benefit.

v. burden, disadvantage, encumber, hamper, hamstring, hinder, impede, limit, restrict, retard.

antonyms assist, further.

handiness *n.* accessibility, adroitness, aptitude, availability, cleverness, closeness, convenience, deftness, dexterity, efficiency, expertise, knack, practicality, proficiency, proximity, skill, usefulness, workability.

antonym clumsiness.

handkerchief *n.* fogle, handkercher, hanky, monteith, mouchoir, nose-rag, romal, rumal, sudary, wipe.

handle *n.* ear, grip, haft, handfast, handgrip, heft, helve, hilt, knob, lug, stock, wythe.

v. administer, carry, conduct, control, cope with, deal in, deal with, direct, discourse, discuss, feel, finger, fondle, grasp, guide, hold, manage, manipulate, maneuver, market, maul, operate, paw, pick up, poke,

sell, steer, stock, supervise, touch, trade, traffic in, treat, use, wield.

hand-out[1] *n.* alms, charity, dole, freebie, issue, largess(e), share, share-out.

hand-out[2] *n.* bulletin, circular, free sample, leaflet, literature, press release, statement.

handsome *adj.* abundant, admirable, ample, attractive, beau, becoming, bountiful, braw, comely, considerable, elegant, feat(e)ous, featuous, featurely, fine, generous, good-looking, graceful, gracious, large, liberal, magnanimous, majestic, personable, plentiful, seemly, sizeable, stately, well-favored, well-looking, well-proportioned, well-set-up.

antonyms mean, stingy, ugly.

handy *adj.* accessible, adept, adroit, at hand, available, clever, close, convenient, deft, dexterous, expert, helpful, manageable, near, nearby, neat, nimble, practical, proficient, ready, serviceable, skilful, skilled, useful.

antonyms clumsy, inconvenient, unwieldy.

hang *v.* adhere, attach, bow, cling, cover, dangle, deck, decorate, depend, drape, drift, droop, drop, execute, fasten, fix, float, furnish, gibbet, hold, hover, incline, lean, loll, lower, remain, rest, sag, stick, string up, suspend, suspercollate, swing, trail, weep.

hanker for/after covet, crave, desire, hunger for, itch for, long for, lust after, pine for, thirst for, want, wish, yearn for, yen for.

antonym dislike.

haphazard *adj.* accidental, aimless, arbitrary, careless, casual, chance, disorderly, disorganized, flukey, hit-or-miss, indiscriminate, promiscuous, random, slapdash, slipshod, unmethodical, unsystematic.

antonyms deliberate, planned.

hapless *adj.* cursed, ill-fated, ill-starred, jinxed, luckless, miserable, star-crossed, unfortunate, unhappy, unlucky, wretched.

antonym lucky.

happen *v.* appear, arise, befall, chance, come about, crop up, develop, ensue, eventuate, fall out, follow, materialize, occur, result, supervene, take place, transpire, turn out.

happening *n.* accident, adventure, affair, case, chance, circumstance, episode, event, experience, incident, occasion, occurrence, phenomenon, proceeding, scene.

happiness *n.* beatitude, blessedness, bliss, cheer, cheerfulness, cheeriness, chirpiness, contentment, delight, ecstasy, elation, enjoyment, exuberance, felicity, gaiety, gladness, high spirits, joy, joyfulness, jubilation, light-heartedness, merriment, pleasure, satisfaction, well-being.

antonym unhappiness.

happy *adj.* advantageous, appropriate, apt, auspicious, befitting, blessed, blest, blissful, blithe, chance, cheerful, content, contented, convenient, delighted, ecstatic, elated, enviable, favorable, felicitous, fit, fitting, fortunate, glad, gratified, gruntled, idyllic, jolly, joyful,

joyous, jubilant, lucky, merry, opportune, over the moon, overjoyed, pleased, promising, propitious, satisfactory, Saturnian, seasonable, starry-eyed, successful, sunny, thrilled, timely, well-timed.
antonym unhappy.

happy-go-lucky *adj.* blithe, carefree, casual, cheerful, devil-may-care, easy-going, heedless, improvident, insouciant, irresponsible, light-hearted, nonchalant, reckless, unconcerned, untroubled, unworried.
antonyms anxious, wary.

harangue *n.* address, declamation, diatribe, discourse, exhortation, homily, lecture, oration, paternoster, peroration, philippic, sermon, speech, spiel, tirade.
v. address, declaim, descant, exhort, hold forth, lecture, monolog(u)ize, orate, perorate, preach, rant, rhetorize, sermonize, spout.

harass *v.* annoy, badger, bait, beleaguer, bother, chivvy, distress, disturb, exasperate, exhaust, fatigue, harry, hassle, hound, perplex, persecute, pester, plague, tease, tire, torment, trash, trouble, vex, wear out, weary, worry.
antonym assist.

harbinger *n.* avant-courier, forerunner, foretoken, herald, indication, messenger, omen, portent, precursor, presage, sign, warning.

harbor *n.* anchorage, asylum, covert, destination, haven, marina, port, refuge, roadstead, sanctuary, sanctum, security, shelter.
v. believe, cherish, cling to, conceal, entertain, foster, hide, hold, imagine, lodge, maintain, nurse, nurture, protect, retain, secrete, shelter, shield.

hard *adj.* acrimonious, actual, adamantine, alcoholic, angry, antagonistic, arduous, backbreaking, baffling, bare, bitter, burdensome, calamitous, callous, cast-iron, cold, compact, complex, complicated, cruel, crusty, dark, definite, dense, difficult, disagreeable, disastrous, distressing, driving, exacting, exhausting, fatiguing, fierce, firm, flinty, forceful, formidable, grievous, grim, habit-forming, hard-hearted, harsh, heavy, Herculean, hostile, impenetrable, implacable, indisputable, inflexible, intolerable, intricate, involved, irony, knotty, laborious, marbly, obdurate, painful, perplexing, pitiless, plain, powerful, puzzling, rancorous, resentful, rigid, rigorous, ruthless, sclerous, severe, shrewd, solid, stern, stiff, stony, strenuous, strict, strong, stubborn, tangled, thorny, toilsome, tough, undeniable, unfathomable, unfeeling, ungentle, unjust, unkind, unpleasant, unrelenting, unsparing, unsympathetic, unvarnished, unyielding, uphill, verified, violent, wearying.
antonyms harmless, kind, mild, non-alcoholic, pleasant, pleasing, soft, yielding.
adv. agonizingly, assiduously, badly, bitterly, close, completely, determinedly, diligently, distressingly, doggedly, earnestly, energetically, fiercely, forcefully, forcibly, fully, hardly, harshly, heavily, industriously, intensely, intently, keenly, laboriously, near, painfully,

persistently, powerfully, rancorously, reluctantly, resentfully, roughly, severely, sharply, slowly, sorely, steadily, strenuously, strongly, uneasily, untiringly, vigorously, violently, with difficulty.
antonyms gently, mildly, moderately, unenthusiastically.

harden *v.* accustom, anneal, bake, brace, brutalize, buttress, cake, case-harden, concrete, fortify, freeze, gird, habituate, indurate, inure, nerve, reinforce, sclerose, season, set, solidify, steel, stiffen, strengthen, toughen, train.
antonym soften.

hard-headed *adj.* astute, clear-thinking, cool, hard-boiled, level-headed, practical, pragmatic, realistic, sensible, shrewd, tough, unsentimental.
antonym unrealistic.

hard-hearted *adj.* callous, cold, cruel, hard, heartless, indifferent, inhuman, insensitive, intolerant, iron-hearted, marble-breasted, marble-hearted, merciless, pitiless, stony, uncaring, uncompassionate, unfeeling, unkind, unsympathetic.
antonyms kind, merciful.

hardly *adv.* barely, by no means, faintly, harshly, infrequently, just, no way, not at all, not quite, only, only just, roughly, scarcely, severely, with difficulty.
antonyms easily, very.

hardship *n.* adversity, affliction, austerity, burden, calamity, destitution, difficulty, fatigue, grievance, labor, misery, misfortune, need, oppression, persecution, privation, strait, suffering, toil, torment, trial, tribulation, trouble, want.
antonym ease.

hardy *adj.* audacious, bold, brave, brazen, courageous, daring, firm, fit, foolhardy, hale, headstrong, healthy, hearty, heroic, impudent, intrepid, lusty, manly, plucky, rash, reckless, resolute, robust, rugged, sound, Spartan, stalwart, stout, stout-hearted, strong, sturdy, tough, valiant, valorous, vigorous.
antonyms unhealthy, weak.

harm *n.* abuse, damage, detriment, disservice, evil, hurt, ill, immorality, impairment, iniquity, injury, loss, mischief, misfortune, scathe, sin, sinfulness, vice, wickedness, wrong.
antonyms benefit, service.
v. abuse, blemish, damage, hurt, ill-treat, ill-use, impair, injure, maltreat, mar, molest, ruin, scathe, spoil, wound.
antonyms benefit, improve.

harmful *adj.* baleful, baneful, damaging, deleterious, destructive, detrimental, disadvantageous, evil, hurtful, injurious, noxious, pernicious, pestful, pestiferous, pestilent, scatheful.
antonym harmless.

harmless *adj.* gentle, innocent, innocuous, innoxious, inoffensive, non-toxic, safe, scatheless, unharmed, uninjured, unobjectionable, unscathed.
antonym harmful.

harmonious *adj.* according, agreeable, amicable, compatible, concinnous, concordant, congenial, congruous, consonant, consonous, co-ordinated, cordial, correspondent, dulcet, euharmonic, euphonic, euphonious, eurhythmic, friendly, harmonic, harmonizing, matching, mellifluous, melodious, musical, sweet-sounding, sympathetic, symphonious, tuneful.
antonym inharmonious.

harmony *n.* accord, agreement, amicability, amity, balance, chime, compatibility, concinnity, concord, conformity, congruity, consensus, consistency, consonance, co-operation, co-ordination, correspondence, correspondency, diapason, euphony, eurhythmy, fitness, friendship, goodwill, like-mindedness, melodiousness, melody, parallelism, peace, rapport, suitability, symmetry, sympathy, tune, tunefulness, unanimity, understanding, unity.
antonym discord.

harness *n.* equipment, gear, reins, straps, tack, tackle, trappings.
v. apply, channel, control, couple, employ, exploit, make use of, mobilize, saddle, turn to account, use, utilize, yoke.

harry *v.* annoy, badger, bedevil, chivvy, depredate, despoil, devastate, disturb, fret, harass, hassle, maraud, molest, persecute, pester, pillage, plague, plunder, raid, ravage, rob, sack, tease, torment, trouble, vex, worry.
antonyms aid, calm.

harsh *adj.* abrasive, abusive, austere, bitter, bleak, brutal, coarse, comfortless, croaking, crude, cruel, discordant, dissonant, dour, Draconian, glaring, grating, grim, guttural, hard, jarring, pitiless, punitive, rasping, raucous, relentless, rough, ruthless, scabrous, severe, sharp, Spartan, stark, stern, strident, stringent, unfeeling, ungentle, unkind, unmelodious, unpleasant, unrelenting.
antonyms mild, smooth, soft.

harvest *n.* collection, consequence, crop, effect, fruition, harvesting, harvest-time, hockey, ingathering, inning, produce, product, reaping, result, return, vendage, yield.
v. accumulate, acquire, amass, collect, garner, gather, mow, pick, pluck, reap.

haste *n.* alacrity, briskness, bustle, celerity, dispatch, expedition, fleetness, hastiness, hurry, hustle, impetuosity, nimbleness, precipitance, precipitancy, precipitateness, precipitation, promptitude, quickness, rapidity, rapidness, rashness, recklessness, rush, speed, swiftness, urgency, velocity.
antonyms care, deliberation, slowness.

hasten *v.* accelerate, advance, bolt, dash, dispatch, expedite, fly, gallop, goad, haste, have it on one's toes, hightail it, hurry, make haste, precipitate, press, quicken, race, run, rush, scurry, scuttle, speed, speed up, sprint, step on it, step up, tear, trot, urge.
antonym dawdle.

hasty *adj.* brief, brisk, brusque, cursory, eager, excited, expeditious, fast, fiery, fleet, fleeting, foolhardy, headlong, heedless, hot-headed, hot-tempered, hurried, impatient, impetuous, impulsive, indiscreet, irascible, irritable, passing, passionate, perfunctory, precipitant, precipitate, prompt, quick-tempered, rapid, rash, reckless, rushed, short, snappy, speedy, subitaneous, superficial, swift, thoughtless, urgent.
antonyms careful, deliberate, placid, slow.

hat *n.* beret, biretta, boater, bonnet, bowler, cap, lid, night-cap, poke-bonnet, skull-cap, sombrero, sou'wester, top-hat, trilby, yarmulka.

hatch *v.* breed, brood, conceive, concoct, contrive, cook up, design, develop, devise, dream up, incubate, originate, plan, plot, project, scheme, think up.

hate *v.* abhor, abominate, despise, detest, dislike, execrate, loathe, spite.
antonym like.
n. abhorrence, abomination, animosity, animus, antagonism, antipathy, averseness, aversion, detestation, dislike, enmity, execration, hatred, hostility, loathing, odium, odium theologicum.
antonym like. **hateful** *adj.* abhorrent, abominable, damnable, despicable, detestable, disgusting, execrable, forbidding, foul, hate-worthy, heinous, horrible, loathsome, obnoxious, odious, offensive, repellent, repugnant, repulsive, revolting, vile.
antonym pleasing.

hatred *n.* abomination, animosity, animus, antagonism, antipathy, aversion, despite, detestation, dislike, enmity, execration, hate, ill-will, misandry, misanthropy, odium, repugnance, revulsion.
antonym like.

haughtiness *n.* airs, aloofness, arrogance, conceit, contempt, contemptuousness, disdain, hauteur, insolence, loftiness, pomposity, pride, snobbishness, snootiness, superciliousness.
antonyms friendliness, humility.

haughty *adj.* arrogant, assuming, cavalier, conceited, contemptuous, disdainful, fastuous, high, high and mighty, highty-tighty, hoity-toity, imperious, lofty, overweening, proud, scornful, snobbish, snooty, stiff-necked, stomachful, stuck-up, supercilious, superior, uppish.
antonyms friendly, humble.

haul *v.* bouse, carry, cart, convey, drag, draw, hale, heave, hump, lug, move, pull, tow, trail, transport, trice, tug.
n. booty, bunce, catch, drag, find, gain, harvest, heave, loot, pull, spoils, swag, takings, tug, yield.

have *v.* accept, acquire, allow, bear, beget, cheat, comprehend, comprise, consider, contain, deceive, deliver, dupe, embody, endure, enjoy, entertain, experience, feel, fool, gain, get, give birth to, hold, include, keep, obtain, occupy, outwit, own, permit, possess, procure, produce, put up with, receive, retain, secure, suffer, sustain, swindle, take, tolerate, trick, undergo.

havoc *n.* carnage, chaos, confusion, damage, depopulation, desolation, despoliation, destruction, devastation, disorder, disruption, mayhem, rack and ruin, ravages, ruin, shambles, slaughter, waste, wreck.

hazard *n.* accident, chance, coincidence, danger, deathtrap, endangerment, fluke, imperilment, jeopardy, luck, mischance, misfortune, mishap, peril, risk, threat.
antonym safety.
v. advance, attempt, chance, conjecture, dare, endanger, expose, gamble, imperil, jeopardize, offer, presume, proffer, risk, speculate, stake, submit, suggest, suppose, threaten, venture, volunteer.

hazardous *adj.* chancy, dangerous, dicey, difficult, fraught, hairy, haphazard, insecure, perilous, precarious, risky, thorny, ticklish, uncertain, unpredictable, unsafe.
antonyms safe, secure.

hazy *adj.* blurry, clouded, cloudy, dim, distanceless, dull, faint, foggy, fuzzy, ill-defined, indefinite, indistinct, loose, milky, misty, muddled, muzzy, nebulous, obscure, overcast, smoky, uncertain, unclear, vague, veiled.
antonyms clear, definite.

head *n.* ability, apex, aptitude, bean, beginning, bonce, boss, brain, brains, branch, capacity, cape, captain, caput, category, chief, chieftain, chump, class, climax, commander, commencement, conclusion, conk, cop, cranium, crest, crisis, crown, culmination, department, director, division, end, faculty, flair, fore, forefront, foreland, front, godfather, head teacher, heading, headland, headmaster, headmistress, height, intellect, intelligence, knowledge box, leader, manager, master, mastermind, mentality, mind, nab, napper, nob, noddle, nut, origin, pate, peak, pitch, point, principal, promontory, rise, sconce, section, skull, source, start, subject, summit, super, superintendent, supervisor, talent, tête, thought, tip, top, topic, top-knot, turning-point, understanding, upperworks, van, vanguard, vertex.
antonyms foot, subordinate, tail.
adj. arch, chief, dominant, first, foremost, front, highest, leading, main, pre-eminent, premier, prime, principal, supreme, top, topmost.
v. aim, cap, command, control, crown, direct, govern, guide, lead, make a beeline, make for, manage, oversee, point, precede, rule, run, steer, superintend, supervise, top, turn.

headstrong *adj.* bull-headed, contrary, foolhardy, fractious, froward, heedless, imprudent, impulsive, intractable, mulish, obstinate, perverse, pig-headed, rash, reckless, self-willed, stubborn, ungovernable, unruly, wilful.
antonyms biddable, docile, obedient.

headway *n.* advance, improvement, inroad(s), progress, progression, way.

heady *adj.* exciting, exhilarating, hasty, impetuous, impulsive, inconsiderate, inebriant, intoxicating, overpowering, potent, precipitate, rash, reckless, spirituous, stimulating, strong, thoughtless, thrilling.

heal *v.* alleviate, ameliorate, balsam, compose, conciliate, cure, harmonize, mend, patch up, physic, reconcile, regenerate, remedy, restore, salve, settle, soothe, treat.

healthy *adj.* active, beneficial, blooming, bracing, fine, fit, flourishing, good, hale (and hearty), hardy, healthful, health-giving, hearty, hygienic, in fine feather, in fine fettle, in fine form, in good condition, in good shape, in the pink, invigorating, nourishing, nutritious, physically fit, robust, salubrious, salutary, salutiferous, sound, strong, sturdy, vigorous, well, wholesome.
antonyms diseased, ill, infirm, sick, unhealthy.

heap *n.* accumulation, acervation, aggregation, bing, clamp, cock, collection, cumulus, hoard, lot, mass, mound, mountain, pile, ruck, stack, stockpile, store.
v. accumulate, amass, assign, augment, bank, bestow, build, burden, collect, confer, gather, hoard, increase, lavish, load, mound, pile, shower, stack, stockpile, store.

hear *v.* acknowledge, ascertain, attend, catch, discover, eavesdrop, examine, find, gather, hark, hearken, heed, investigate, judge, learn, listen, overhear, pick up, try, understand.

heart *n.* affection, benevolence, boldness, bravery, center, character, compassion, concern, core, courage, crux, disposition, emotion, essence, feeling, fortitude, guts, hub, humanity, inclination, kernel, love, marrow, mettle, middle, mind, nature, nerve, nerve center, nub, nucleus, pith, pity, pluck, purpose, quintessence, resolution, root, sentiment, soul, spirit, spunk, sympathy, temperament, tenderness, ticker, understanding, will.

heart and soul absolutely, completely, devotedly, eagerly, entirely, gladly, heartily, unreservedly, wholeheartedly.

heartache *n.* affliction, agony, anguish, bitterness, dejection, despair, despondency, distress, grief, heartbreak, heart-sickness, pain, remorse, sorrow, suffering, torment, torture.

heartbroken *adj.* broken-hearted, crestfallen, crushed, dejected, desolate, despondent, disappointed, disconsolate, disheartened, dispirited, down, downcast, grieved, heart-sick, miserable, woebegone.
antonyms delighted, elated.

hearten *v.* animate, assure, buck up, buoy up, cheer, comfort, console, embolden, encourage, gladden, incite, inspire, inspirit, pep up, reassure, revivify, rouse, stimulate.
antonym dishearten.

heartless *adj.* brutal, callous, cold, cold-blooded, cold-hearted, cruel, hard, hard-hearted, harsh, inhuman, merciless, pitiless, stern, uncaring, unfeeling, unkind.
antonyms considerate, kind, merciful, sympathetic.

heart-rending *adj.* affecting, distressing, harrowing, heart-breaking, moving, pathetic, piteous, pitiful, poignant, sad, tear-jerking, tragic.

hearty *adj.* active, affable, ample, ardent, cordial, doughty, eager, earnest, ebullient, effusive, energetic, enthusiastic, exuberant, filling, friendly, generous, genial, genuine, hale, hardy, healthy, heartfelt, honest, jovial, nourishing, real, robust, sincere, sizeable, solid, sound, square, stalwart, strong, substantial, true, unfeigned, unreserved, vigorous, warm, well, whole-hearted.
antonyms cold, emotionless.

heat *n.* agitation, ardor, calefaction, earnestness, excitement, fervor, fever, fieriness, fury, hotness, impetuosity, incandescence, intensity, passion, sizzle, sultriness, swelter, torridity, vehemence, violence, warmness, warmth, zeal.
antonyms cold(ness), coolness.
v. animate, calefy, chafe, excite, flush, glow, impassion, inflame, inspirit, reheat, rouse, stimulate, stir, toast, warm up.
antonyms chill, cool.

heated *adj.* acrimonious, angry, bitter, excited, fierce, fiery, frenzied, furious, impassioned, intense, passionate, perfervid, raging, stormy, tempestuous, vehement, violent.
antonym dispassionate.

heave *v.* billow, breathe, cast, chuck, dilate, drag, elevate, exhale, expand, fling, gag, groan, haul, heft, hitch, hoist, hurl, let fly, lever, lift, palpitate, pant, pitch, puff, pull, raise, retch, rise, send, sigh, sling, sob, spew, surge, suspire, swell, throb, throw, throw up, toss, tug, vomit, yomp.

heaven *n.* bliss, ecstasy, Elysian fields, Elysium, empyrean, enchantment, ether, felicity, fiddler's green, firmament, happiness, happy hunting-ground(s), hereafter, Land of the Leal, next world, nirvana, paradise, rapture, sky, Swarga, transport, utopia, Valhalla, welkin, Zion.
antonym hell.

heavenly *adj.* alluring, ambrosial, angelic, beatific, beautiful, blessed, blest, blissful, celestial, delightful, divine, empyrean, entrancing, exquisite, extra-terrestrial, glorious, godlike, holy, immortal, lovely, paradisaic(al), paradisal, paradisean, paradisial, paradisian, paradisic, rapturous, ravishing, seraphic, sublime, superhuman, supernal, supernatural, Uranian, wonderful.
antonym hellish.

heavy *adj.* abundant, apathetic, boisterous, bulky, burdened, burdensome, clumpy, complex, considerable, copious, crestfallen, deep, dejected, depressed, despondent, difficult, disconsolate, downcast, drowsy, dull, encumbered, excessive, gloomy, grave, grieving, grievous, hard, harsh, hefty, inactive, indolent, inert, intolerable, laborious, laden, large, leaden, listless, loaded, lumping, lumpish, massive, melancholy, onerous, oppressed, oppressive, ponderous, portly, pro-

found, profuse, rough, sad, serious, severe, slow, sluggish, solemn, sorrowful, squabbish, stodgy, stormy, stupid, tedious, tempestuous, torpid, turbulent, vexatious, violent, wearisome, weighted, weighty, wild, wooden.
antonyms airy, insignificant, light.

heckle *v.* bait, barrack, catcall, disrupt, gibe, interrupt, jeer, pester, shout down, taunt.

heed *n.* animadversion, attention, care, caution, consideration, ear, heedfulness, mind, note, notice, reck, regard, respect, thought, watchfulness.
antonyms inattention, indifference, unconcern.
v. animadvert, attend, consider, follow, listen, mark, mind, note, obey, observe, regard, take notice of.
antonyms disregard, ignore.

heedless *adj.* careless, étourdi(e), foolhardy, imprudent, inattentive, incautious, incurious, inobservant, neglectful, negligent, oblivious, precipitate, rash, reckless, thoughtless, uncaring, unconcerned, unheedful, unheedy, unmindful, unobservant, unthinking.
antonym heedful.

height *n.* acme, altitude, apex, apogee, ceiling, celsitude, climax, crest, crown, culmination, degree, dignity, elevation, eminence, exaltation, extremity, grandeur, highness, hill, limit, loftiness, maximum, mountain, ne plus ultra, peak, pinnacle, prominence, stature, summit, tallness, top, ultimate, utmost, uttermost, vertex, zenith.
antonym depth.

heighten *v.* add to, aggrandize, aggravate, amplify, augment, elevate, enhance, ennoble, exalt, greaten, improve, increase, intensify, magnify, raise, sharpen, strengthen, uplift.
antonyms decrease, diminish.

heinous *adj.* abhorrent, abominable, atrocious, awful, evil, execrable, facinorous, flagrant, grave, hateful, hideous, immitigable, infamous, iniquitous, monstrous, nefarious, odious, outrageous, revolting, shocking, unspeakable, vicious, villainous.

hello *interj.* chin-chin, ciao, hail, hi, hiya, how-do-you-do, howdy, salve, what cheer, wotcher.
antonym good-bye.

help[1] *v.* abet, abstain, aid, alleviate, ameliorate, assist, avoid, back, befriend, bestead, control, co-operate, cure, ease, eschew, facilitate, forbear, heal, hinder, improve, keep from, lend a hand, mitigate, prevent, promote, rally round, refrain from, relieve, remedy, resist, restore, save, second, serve, shun, stand by, succor, support, withstand.
antonym hinder.
n. adjuvant, advice, aid, aidance, assistance, avail, benefit, co-operation, guidance, leg up, service, support, use, utility.
antonym hindrance.

help[2] *n.* assistant, daily, employee, hand, helper, worker.

helper *n.* abettor, adjutant, aide, aider, ally, assistant, attendant, auxiliary, coadjutor, collaborator, colleague, deputy, girl Friday, helpmate, man Friday, mate, PA, partner, person Friday, right-hand man, Samaritan, second, subsidiary, supporter.

helpful *adj.* accommodating, adjuvant, advantageous, beneficent, beneficial, benevolent, caring, considerate, constructive, co-operative, favorable, fortunate, friendly, furthersome, kind, neighborly, practical, productive, profitable, serviceable, supportive, sympathetic, timely, useful.
antonyms futile, useless, worthless.

helpless *adj.* abandoned, adynamic, aidless, debilitated, defenceless, dependent, destitute, disabled, exposed, feeble, forlorn, friendless, impotent, incapable, incompetent, infirm, paralyzed, powerless, unfit, unprotected, vulnerable, weak.
antonyms competent, enterprising, independent, resourceful, strong.

helter-skelter *adv.* carelessly, confusedly, hastily, headlong, hurriedly, impulsively, pell-mell, rashly, recklessly, wildly.
adj. anyhow, confused, disordered, disorganized, haphazard, higgledy-piggledy, hit-or-miss, jumbled, muddled, random, topsy-turvy, unsystematic.

hem *n.* border, edge, fringe, margin, skirt, trimming.
v. beset, border, circumscribe, confine, edge, enclose, engird, environ, fimbriate, gird, hedge, restrict, skirt, surround.

hemerrhoids *n.* emerods, piles.

hence *adv.* accordingly, ergo, therefore, thus.

herald *n.* courier, crier, forerunner, harbinger, indication, messenger, omen, precursor, sign, signal, token, vaunt-courier.
v. advertise, announce, broadcast, forebode, foretoken, harbinger, indicate, pave the way, portend, precede, presage, proclaim, prognosticate, promise, publicize, publish, show, trumpet, usher in.

herculean *adj.* arduous, athletic, brawny, colossal, daunting, demanding, difficult, enormous, exacting, exhausting, formidable, gigantic, great, grueling, hard, heavy, huge, husky, laborious, large, mammoth, massive, mighty, muscular, onerous, powerful, prodigious, rugged, sinewy, stalwart, strapping, strenuous, strong, sturdy, titanic, toil-some, tough, tremendous.

herd *n.* assemblage, canaille, collection, cowherd, crowd, crush, drove, flock, herdboy, herdsman, horde, mass, mob, multitude, populace, press, rabble, riff-raff, shepherd, swarm, the hoi polloi, the masses, the plebs, throng, vulgus.
v. assemble, associate, collect, congregate, drive, flock, force, gather, goad, guard, guide, huddle, lead, muster, protect, rally, shepherd, spur, watch.

heretic *n.* apostate, dissenter, dissident, free-thinker, non-conformist, renegade, revisionist, schismatic, sectarian, separatist.
antonym conformist.

heritage *n.* bequest, birthright, deserts, due, endowment, estate, history, inheritance, legacy, lot, past, patrimony, portion, record, share, tradition.

hermit *n.* anchoret, anchorite, ascetic, eremite, monk, recluse, solitaire, solitarian, solitary, stylite.

hero *n.* celebrity, champion, conqueror, exemplar, goody, heart-throb, idol, male lead, paragon, protagonist, star, superstar, victor.

heroic *adj.* bold, brave, classic, classical, courageous, daring, dauntless, doughty, elevated, epic, exaggerated, extravagant, fearless, gallant, game, grand, grandiose, gritty, high-flown, Homeric, inflated, intrepid, legendary, lion-hearted, mythological, spunky, stouthearted, undaunted, valiant, valorous.
antonyms cowardly, pusillanimous, timid.

heroism *n.* boldness, bravery, courage, courageousness, daring, derring-do, fearlessness, fortitude, gallantry, gameness, grit, intrepidity, prowess, spirit, valor.
antonyms cowardice, pusillanimity, timidity.

hesitant *adj.* diffident, dilatory, doubtful, half-hearted, halting, hesitating, hesitative, hesitatory, irresolute, reluctant, sceptical, shy, swithering, timid, uncertain, unsure, vacillating, wavering.
antonyms resolute, staunch.

hesitate *v.* balk, be reluctant, be uncertain, be unwilling, boggle, delay, demur, dither, doubt, dubitate, falter, fumble, halt, haver, pause, scruple, shillyshally, shrink from, stammer, stumble, stutter, swither, think twice, vacillate, wait, waver.

hesitation *n.* delay, demurral, doubt, dubiety, faltering, fumbling, hesitancy, indecision, irresolution, misdoubt, misgiving(s), qualm(s), reluctance, scruple(s), second thought(s), stammering, stumbling, stuttering, swithering, uncertainty, unwillingness, vacillation.
antonyms alacrity, assurance, eagerness.

hidden *adj.* abstruse, cabbalistic(al), clandestine, close, concealed, covered, covert, cryptic, dark, de(a)rn, delitescent, doggo, hermetic, hermetical, latent, mysterious, mystic, mystical, obscure, occult, recondite, secret, shrouded, ulterior, unapparent, unseen, veiled.
antonyms open, showing.

hide[1] *v.* abscond, bury, cache, camouflage, cloak, conceal, cover, disguise, earth, eclipse, ensconce, feal, go to ground, go underground, hole up, keep dark, lie low, mask, obscure, occult, screen, secrete, shadow, shelter, shroud, stash, suppress, take cover, tappice, veil, withhold.
antonyms display, reveal, show.

hide[2] *n.* deacon, fell, flaught, nebris, pelt, skin.

hideous *adj.* abominable, appalling, awful, detestable, disgusting, dreadful, frightful, gash, gashful, gashly, ghastly, grim, grisly, grotesque, gruesome, horrendous, horrible, horrid, loathsome, macabre, monstrous, odious, repulsive, revolting, shocking, sickening, terrible, terrifying, ugly, ugsome, unsightly.
antonym beautiful.

high *adj.* acute, altissimo, alto, arch, arrogant, boastful, boisterous, bouncy, bragging, capital, cheerful, chief, consequential, costly, dear, delirious, despotic, distinguished, domineering, elated, elevated, eminent, euphoric, exalted, excessive, excited, exhilarated, exorbitant, expensive, extraordinary, extravagant, extreme, exuberant, freaked out, gamy, grand, grave, great, haughty, high-pitched, important, inebriated, influential, intensified, intoxicated, joyful, lavish, leading, light-hearted, lofty, lordly, luxurious, merry, mountain(s)-high, niffy, orthian, ostentatious, overbearing, penetrating, piercing, piping, pongy, powerful, prominent, proud, rich, ruling, serious, sharp, shrill, significant, soaring, soprano, spaced out, steep, stiff, stoned, strident, strong, superior, tainted, tall, towering, treble, tripping, tumultuous, turbulent, tyrannical, vainglorious, whiffy.
antonyms deep, low, lowly, short.
n. apex, apogee, delirium, ecstasy, euphoria, height, intoxication, level, peak, record, summit, top, trip, zenith.
antonyms low, nadir.

highbrow *n.* aesthete, boffin, Brahmin, brain, egghead, intellectual, long-hair, mandarin, mastermind, savant, scholar.
adj. bookish, brainy, cultivated, cultured, deep, intellectual, long-haired, serious, sophisticated.
antonym lowbrow.

highly *adv.* appreciatively, approvingly, considerably, decidedly, eminently, enthusiastically, exceptionally, extraordinarily, extremely, favorably, greatly, immensely, supremely, tremendously, vastly, very, warmly, well.

high-minded *adj.* elevated, ethical, fair, good, honorable, idealistic, lofty, magnanimous, moral, noble, principled, pure, righteous, scrupulous, upright, virtuous, worthy.
antonyms immoral, unscrupulous.

high-priced *adj.* costly, dear, excessive, exorbitant, expensive, extortionate, high, pricy, steep, stiff, unreasonable.
antonym cheap.

high-spirited *adj.* animated, boisterous, bold, bouncy, daring, dashing, ebullient, effervescent, energetic, exuberant, frolicsome, lively, mettlesome, peppy, sparkling, spirited, spunky, vibrant, vital, vivacious.
antonyms downcast, glum.

highwayman *n.* bandit, bandolero, footpad, knight of the road, land-pirate, rank-rider, robber.

hilarious *adj.* amusing, comical, convivial, entertaining, funny, gay, happy, humorous, hysterical, jolly, jovial, joyful, joyous, killing, merry, mirthful, noisy, rollicking, side-splitting, uproarious.
antonyms grave, serious.

hinder *v.* arrest, check, counteract, debar, delay, deter, embar, encumber, forelay, frustrate, hamper, hamstring, handicap, hold back, hold up, impede, interrupt, obstruct, oppose, prevent, retard, slow down, stop, stymie, thwart, trammel.
antonyms aid, assist, help.

hindrance *n.* bar, barrier, check, demurrage, deterrent, difficulty, drag, drawback, encumbrance, handicap, hitch, impediment, interruption, limitation, obstacle, obstruction, pull-back, remora, restraint, restriction, snag, stoppage, stumbling-block, trammel.
antonyms aid, assistance, help.

hinge *v.* be contingent, center, depend, hang, pivot, rest, revolve around, turn.
n. articulation, condition, foundation, garnet, joint, premise, principle.

hint *n.* advice, allusion, breath, clue, dash, help, implication, indication, inkling, innuendo, insinuation, intimation, mention, pointer, reminder, scintilla, sign, signal, soupçon, speck, subindication, suggestion, suspicion, taste, tinge, tip, tip-off, touch, trace, undertone, whiff, whisper, wrinkle.
v. allude, imply, indicate, inkle, innuendo, insinuate, intimate, mention, prompt, subindicate, suggest, tip off.

hire *v.* appoint, book, charter, commission, employ, engage, lease, let, rent, reserve, retain, sign up, take on.
antonyms dismiss, fire.
n. charge, cost, fare, fee, price, rent, rental, toll.

history *n.* account, annals, antecedents, antiquity, autobiography, biography, chronicle, chronology, days of old, days of yore, genealogy, memoirs, narration, narrative, olden days, recapitulation, recital, record, relation, saga, story, tale, the past.

hit *v.* accomplish, achieve, affect, arrive at, attain, bang, bash, batter, beat, belt, bump, clip, clobber, clock, clonk, clout, collide with, crown, cuff, damage, devastate, flog, frap, fustigate, gain, impinge on, influence, knock, lob, move, overwhelm, prop, punch, reach, secure, slap, slog, slosh, slug, smack, smash, smite, sock, strike, swat, thump, touch, volley, wallop, whack, wham, whap, w(h)op, wipe.
n. blow, bump, clash, clout, collision, cuff, impact, knock, rap, sell-out, sensation, shot, slap, slog, slosh, smack, smash, sock, stroke, success, swipe, triumph, venue, wallop, winner.

hitch *v.* attach, connect, couple, fasten, harness, heave, hike (up), hitch-hike, hoi(c)k, hoist, jerk, join, pull, tether, thumb a lift, tie, tug, unite, yank, yoke.
antonyms unfasten, unhitch.
n. catch, check, delay, difficulty, drawback, hiccup, hindrance, hold-up, impediment, mishap, problem, snag, stick, stoppage, trouble.

hoard *n.* accumulation, cache, fund, heap, mass, pile, profusion, reserve, reservoir, stockpile, store, supply, treasure-trove. *v.* accumulate, amass, cache, coffer, collect, deposit, garner, gather, hive, husband, lay up, put by, reposit, save, stash away, stockpile, store, treasure.
antonyms spend, squander, use.

hoarse *adj.* croaky, discordant, grating, gravelly, growling, gruff, guttural, harsh, husky, rasping, raspy, raucous, rough, throaty.
antonyms clear, smooth.

hoax *n.* bam, cheat, cod, con, deception, fast one, fraud, grift, hum, huntiegowk, hunt-the-gowk, imposture, joke, josh, leg-pull, practical joke, prank, put-on, quiz, ruse, spoof, string, swindle, trick.
v. bam, bamboozle, befool, bluff, cod, con, deceive, delude, dupe, fool, gammon, gull, have on, hoodwink, hornswoggle, hum, lead on, pull someone's leg, spoof, string, stuff, swindle, take for a ride, trick.

hobble *v.* clog, dodder, falter, fasten, fetter, halt, hamshackle, hamstring, hirple, limp, restrict, shackle, shamble, shuffle, stagger, stumble, tie, totter.

hobby *n.* avocation, diversion, pastime, pursuit, recreation, relaxation, sideline.

hoist *v.* elevate, erect, heave, jack up, lift, raise, rear, uplift, upraise.
n. crane, davit, elevator, jack, lift, tackle, winch.

hold *v.* accommodate, account, adhere, apply, arrest, assemble, assume, be in force, be the case, bear, believe, bond, brace, call, carry, carry on, celebrate, check, clasp, cleave, clinch, cling, clip, clutch, comprise, conduct, confine, consider, contain, continue, convene, cradle, curb, deem, delay, detain, embrace, endure, enfold, entertain, esteem, exist, grasp, grip, have, hold good, imprison, judge, keep, last, maintain, occupy, operate, own, persevere, persist, possess, preside over, presume, prop, reckon, regard, remain, remain true, remain valid, resist, restrain, retain, run, seat, shoulder, solemnize, stand up, stay, stick, stop, summon, support, suspend, sustain, take, think, view, wear.
n. anchorage, asendancy, authority, clasp, clout, clutch, control, dominance, dominion, foothold, footing, grasp, grip, holt, influence, leverage, mastery, prop, pull, purchase, stay, support, sway, vantage.

hold-up[1] *n.* bottle-neck, delay, difficulty, gridlock, hitch, obstruction, setback, snag, stoppage, (traffic) jam, trouble, wait.

hold-up[2] *n.* heist, robbery, stick-up.

hole *n.* aperture, breach, break, burrow, cave, cavern, cavity, chamber, covert, crack, defect, den, depression, dilemma, dimple, discrepancy, dive, dump, earth, error, excavation, eyelet, fallacy, fault, fissure, fix, flaw, foramen, fovea, gap, hollow, hovel, imbroglio, inconsistency, jam, joint, lair, loophole, mess, nest, opening, orifice, outlet, perforation, pit, pocket, pore, predicament, puncture, quandary, rent, retreat, scoop, scrape, shaft, shelter, slum, split, spot, tangle, tear, tight spot, vent, ventage.

hollow *adj.* artificial, cavernous, concave, coreless, cynical, deaf, deceitful, deceptive, deep, deep-set, depressed, dished, dull, empty, expressionless, faithless, false, famished, flat, fleeting, flimsy, fruitless, futile, gaunt, glenoid(al), hungry, hypocritical, indented, insincere, lanternjawed, low, meaningless, muffled, muted, pointless, Pyrrhic, ravenous, reverberant, rumbling, sepulchral, specious, starved, sunken, toneless, treacherous, unavailing, unfilled, unreal, unreliable, unsound, useless, vacant, vain, void, weak, worthless.
n. basin, bottom, bowl, cave, cavern, cavity, channel, concave, concavity, coomb, crater, cup, dale, dell, den, dent, depression, dimple, dingle, dint, dish, druse, excavation, fossa, fossula, fovea, foveola, foveole, geode, glen, groove, hole, hope, how(e), indentation, invagination, pit, trough, umbilicus, vacuity, valley, vlei, well, womb.
v. burrow, channel, dent, dig, dint, dish, excavate, furrow, gouge, groove, indent, pit, scoop.

holocaust *n.* annihilation, carnage, conflagration, destruction, devastation, extermination, extinction, flames, genocide, hecatomb, immolation, inferno, mass murder, massacre, pogrom, sacrifice, slaughter.

holy *adj.* blessed, consecrated, dedicated, devout, divine, evangelical, evangelistic, faithful, god-fearing, godly, good, hallowed, perfect, pietistic, pious, pure, religiose, religious, righteous, sacred, sacrosanct, saintly, sanctified, sanctimonious, spiritual, sublime, unctuous, venerable, venerated, virtuous.
antonyms impious, unsanctified, wicked.

homage *n.* acknowledgment, admiration, adoration, adulation, allegiance, awe, deference, devotion, duty, esteem, faithfulness, fealty, fidelity, honor, loyalty, obeisance, praise, recognition, regard, respect, reverence, service, tribute, veneration, worship.

home *n.* abode, almshouse, asylum, birthplace, blighty, clinic, domicile, dwelling, dwelling-place, element, environment, family, fireside, habitat, habitation, haunt, hearth, home ground, home town, homestead, hospice, hospital, house, household, institution, native heath, nest, nursing-home, old people's home, pad, pied-à-terre, range, residence, roof, sanatorium, stamping-ground, territory.
adj. candid, central, direct, domestic, domiciliary, familiar, family, household, incisive, inland, internal, intimate, local, national, native, penetrating, plain, pointed, unanswerable, uncomfortable, wounding.

homely *adj.* comfortable, comfy, congenial, cosy, domestic, easy, everyday, familiar, folksy, friendly, gemütlich, homelike, homespun, hom(e)y, informal, intimate, modest, natural, ordinary, plain, relaxed, simple, snug, unaffected, unassuming, unpretentious, unsophisticated, welcoming.
antonyms formal, unfamiliar.

homesickness *n.* Heimweh, mal du pays, nostalgia, nostomania.
antonym wanderlust.

homicide *n.* assassin, assassination, bloodshed, cutthroat, killer, killing, liquidator, manslaughter, murder, murderer, slayer, slaying.

homily *n.* address, discourse, harangue, heart-to-heart, lecture, postil, preachment, sermon, spiel, talk.

honest *adj.* above-board, authentic, bona fide, candid, chaste, conscientious, decent, direct, equitable, ethical, fair, fair and square, forthright, four-square, frank, genuine, high-minded, honorable, humble, impartial, ingenuous, jake, just, law-abiding, legitimate, modest, objective, on the level, open, outright, outspoken, plain, plain-hearted, proper, real, reliable, reputable, respectable, scrupulous, seemly, simple, sincere, soothfast, square, straight, straightforward, true, trustworthy, trusty, truthful, undisguised, unequivocal, unfeigned, unreserved, upright, veracious, virtuous, well-gotten, well-won, white.
antonyms covert, devious, dishonest, dishonorable.

honestly *adv.* by fair means, candidly, cleanly, conscientiously, directly, dispassionately, equitably, ethically, fairly, frankly, honorably, in all sincerity, in good faith, justly, lawfully, legally, legitimately, objectively, on the level, openly, outright, plainly, really, scrupulously, sincerely, straight, straight out, truly, truthfully, undisguisedly, unreservedly, uprightly, verily.
antonyms dishonestly, dishonorably.

honesty *n.* artlessness, bluntness, candor, equity, evenhandedness, explicitness, fairness, faithfulness, fidelity, frankness, genuineness, honor, incorruptibility, integrity, justness, morality, objectivity, openness, outspokenness, plain-heartedness, plainness, plainspeaking, probity, rectitude, reputability, scrupulousness, sincerity, sooth, squareness, straightforwardness, straightness, trustworthiness, truthfulness, unreserve, uprightness, veracity, verity, virtue.
antonyms deviousness, dishonesty.

honor *n.* acclaim, accolade, acknowledgment, admiration, adoration, chastity, commendation, compliment, credit, decency, deference, dignity, distinction, duty, elevation, esteem, fairness, favor, good name, goodness, homage, honesty, honorableness, honorificabilitudinity, innocence, integrity, kudos, laudation, laurels, loyalty, modesty, morality, pleasure, praise, principles, privilege, probity, purity, rank, recognition, rectitude, regard, renown, reputation, repute, respect, reverence, righteousness, self-respect, tribute, trust, trustworthiness, uprightness, veneration, virginity, virtue, worship. *antonyms* disgrace, dishonor, obloquy.
v. accept, acclaim, acknowledge, admire, adore, applaud, appreciate, carry out, cash, celebrate, clear, commemorate, commend, compliment, credit, crown, decorate, dignify, discharge, esteem, exalt, execute, fulfil, glorify, hallow, homage, keep, laud, laureate, lionize, observe, pass, pay, pay homage, perform, praise, prize, remember, respect, revere, reverence, take, value, venerate, worship.
antonyms betray, debase, disgrace, dishonor.

honorable *adj.* creditable, distinguished, eminent, equitable,

estimable, ethical, fair, great, high-minded, honest, illustrious, irreproachable, just, meritorious, moral, noble, prestigious, principled, proper, renowned, reputable, respectable, respected, right, righteous, sincere, straight, true, trustworthy, trusty, unexceptionable, upright, upstanding, venerable, virtuous, worthful, worthy.
antonyms dishonest, dishonorable, unworthy.

honorary *adj.* complimentary, ex officio, formal, honorific, honoris causa, in name only, nominal, titular, unofficial, unpaid, virtute officii.
antonyms gainful, paid, salaried, waged.

hop *v.* bound, caper, dance, fly, frisk, hitch, hobble, jump, leap, limp, nip, prance, skip, spring, vault.
n. ball, barn-dance, bounce, bound, crossing, dance, flight, jump, leap, skip, social, spring, step, trip, vault.

hope *n.* ambition, anticipation, aspiration, assumption, assurance, belief, confidence, conviction, desire, dream, expectancy, expectation, faith, hopefulness, longing, optimism, promise, prospect, wish.
antonyms apathy, despair, pessimism.
v. anticipate, aspire, assume, await, believe, contemplate, desire, expect, foresee, long, reckon on, rely, trust, wish.
antonym despair.

hopeful *adj.* assured, auspicious, bright, bullish, buoyant, cheerful, confident, encouraging, expectant, favorable, heartening, optimistic, promising, propitious, reassuring, rosy, sanguine.
antonyms despairing, discouraging, pessimistic.
n. great white hope, white hope, wunderkind.

hopeless *adj.* defeatist, dejected, demoralized, despairing, desperate, despondent, disconsolate, downhearted, foolish, forlorn, futile, helpless, impossible, impracticable, inadequate, incompetent, incorrigible, incurable, ineffectual, irredeemable, irremediable, irreparable, irreversible, lost, madcap, past cure, pessimistic, pointless, poor, reckless, unachievable, unattainable, useless, vain, woebegone, worthless, wretched.
antonyms curable, hopeful, optimistic.

horde *n.* band, bevy, concourse, crew, crowd, drove, flock, gang, herd, host, mob, multitude, pack, press, swarm, throng, troop.

horizon *n.* compass, ken, perspective, prospect, purview, range, realm, scope, skyline, sphere, stretch, verge, vista.

horrible *adj.* abhorrent, abominable, appalling, atrocious, awful, beastly, bloodcurdling, cruel, disagreeable, dreadful, fearful, fearsome, frightful, ghastly, grim, grisly, gruesome, heinous, hideous, horrid, horrific, loathsome, macabre, nasty, repulsive, revolting, shameful, shocking, terrible, terrifying, unkind, unpleasant, weird.
antonyms agreeable, pleasant.

horrid *adj.* abominable, alarming, appalling, awful, beastly, bloodcurdling, cruel, despicable, disagreeable, disgusting, dreadful, formidable, frightening, hair-raising,

harrowing, hateful, hideous, horrible, horrific, mean, nasty, odious, offensive, repulsive, revolting, shocking, terrible, terrifying, unkind, unpleasant.
antonyms agreeable, lovely, pleasant.

horror *n.* abhorrence, abomination, alarm, antipathy, apprehension, aversion, awe, awfulness, consternation, detestation, disgust, dismay, dread, fear, fright, frightfulness, ghastliness, gooseflesh, goose-pimples, grimness, hatred, hideousness, horripilation, loathing, outrage, panic, repugnance, revulsion, shock, terror.

horseplay *n.* buffoonery, capers, clowning, desipience, fooling, fooling around, fun and games, high jinks, pranks, romping, rough-and-tumble, rough-housing, rough-stuff, rumpus, skylarking.

hospitable *adj.* accessible, amenable, amicable, approachable, bountiful, congenial, convivial, cordial, couthie, friendly, gemütlich, generous, genial, gracious, kind, liberal, liv(e)able, open-minded, receptive, responsive, sociable, tolerant, welcoming.
antonyms hostile, inhospitable.

hospital *n.* clinic, lazaret, lazaretto, leprosarium, leproserie, leprosery, sanatorium.

hospitality *n.* cheer, congeniality, conviviality, cordiality, friendliness, generosity, graciousness, openhandedness, sociability, warmth, welcome.
antonyms hostility, inhospitality.

hostile *adj.* adverse, alien, antagonistic, anti, antipathetic, bellicose, belligerent, contrary, ill-disposed, inhospitable, inimical, malevolent, opposed, opposite, oppugnant, rancorous, unfriendly, ungenial, unkind, unpropitious, unsympathetic, unwelcoming, warlike.
antonyms friendly, sympathetic.

hostility *n.* abhorrence, animosity, animus, antagonism, antipathy, aversion, breach, detestation, disaffection, dislike, enmity, estrangement, hate, hatred, ill-will, malevolence, malice, opposition, resentment, unfriendliness.
antonyms friendliness, sympathy.

hot *adj.* acrid, animated, approved, ardent, biting, blistering, boiling, burning, candent, clever, close, dangerous, eager, excellent, excited, exciting, favored, febrile, fervent, fervid, fevered, feverish, fierce, fiery, flaming, fresh, heated, hotheaded, impetuous, impulsive, in demand, in vogue, incandescent, inflamed, intense, irascible, latest, lustful, near, new, passionate, peppery, perfervid, piping, piquant, popular, pungent, quick, raging, recent, risky, roasting, scalding, scorching, searing, sensual, sharp, sizzling, skilful, sought-after, spicy, steaming, stormy, strong, sultry, sweltering, torrid, touchy, tropical, vehement, violent, voluptuous, warm, zealous.
antonyms calm, cold, mild, moderate.

hotbed *n.* breeding-ground, cradle, den, forcing-house, hive, nest, nidus, nursery, school, seedbed.

hot-blooded *adj.* ardent, bold, eager, excitable, fervent, fiery, heated, high-spirited, homothermous, impetuous, impulsive, lustful, lusty, passionate, perfervid, precipitate, rash, sensual, spirited, temperamental, warm-blooded, wild.
antonyms cool, dispassionate.

hotel *n.* auberge, boarding-house, doss-house, flophouse, Gasthaus, Gasthof, guest-house, hostelry, hydro, hydropathic, inn, motel, pension, pub, public house, tavern.

hotheaded *adj.* daredevil, fiery, foolhardy, hasty, headstrong, hot-tempered, impetuous, impulsive, intemperate, madcap, over-eager, precipitate, quick-tempered, rash, reckless, unruly, volatile.
antonyms calm, cool.

hound *v.* badger, chase, chivvy, drive, dun, goad, harass, harry, hunt (down), impel, importune, persecute, pester, prod, provoke, pursue.

house *n.* abode, ancestry, biggin, blood, building, business, clan, company, concern, domicile, dwelling, dynasty, edifice, establishment, family, family tree, firm, gens, habitation, home, homestead, hostelry, hotel, household, inn, kindred, line, lineage, lodgings, maison, maison(n)ette, ménage, organization, outfit, parliament, partnership, pied-à-terre, public house, race, residence, roof, stem, tavern, tribe.
v. accommodate, bed, billet, board, contain, cover, domicile, domiciliate, harbor, hold, keep, lodge, place, protect, put up, quarter, sheathe, shelter, store, take in.

household *n.* establishment, family, family circle, home, house, ménage, set-up.
adj. common, domestic, domiciliary, established, everyday, familiar, family, home, ordinary, plain, well-known.

householder *n.* franklin, freeholder, goodman, head of the household, home-owner, house-father, landlord, occupant, occupier, owner, property owner, proprietor, resident, tenant.

housing *n.* accommodation, case, casing, container, cover, covering, dwellings, enclosure, habitation, holder, homes, houses, living quarters, matrix, protection, roof, sheath, shelter.

hovel *n.* bothy, but-and-ben, cabin, cot, croft, den, doghole, dump, hole, hut, hutch, shack, shanty, shed.

hover *v.* alternate, dally, dither, drift, falter, flap, float, fluctuate, flutter, fly, hang, hang about, hesitate, impend, linger, loom, menace, oscillate, pause, poise, seesaw, threaten, vacillate, waver.

however *conj.* anyhow, but, even so, howbeit, in spite of that, natheless, nevertheless, nonetheless, notwithstanding, still, though, yet.

howl *n.* bay, bellow, clamor, cry, groan, holler, hoot, outcry, roar, scream, shriek, ululation, wail, yell, yelp, yowl.
v. bellow, cry, holler, hoot, lament, quest, roar, scream, shout, shriek, ululate, wail, waul, weep, yawl, yell, yelp.

hub *n.* axis, center, core, focal point, focus, heart, linchpin, middle, nave, nerve center, pivot.

hubbub *n.* ado, agitation, babel, bedlam, brouhaha, chaos, clamor, coil, confusion, din, disorder, disturbance, hue and cry, hullabaloo, hurly-burly, kerfuffle, noise, palaver, pandemonium, racket, riot, rowdedow, rowdydow, ruckus, ruction, rumpus, tumult, turbulence, uproar, upset.
antonym calm.

huckster *n.* barker, chapman, dealer, haggler, hawker, packman, pedlar, pitcher, salesman, tinker, vendor.

huddle *n.* clump, clutch, conclave, confab, conference, confusion, crowd, discussion, disorder, heap, jumble, knot, mass, meeting, mess, muddle.
v. cluster, conglomerate, congregate, converge, crouch, crowd, cuddle, curl up, flock, gather, gravitate, hunch, nestle, press, ruck, snuggle, throng.
antonym disperse.

hue *n.* aspect, cast, character, color, complexion, dye, light, nuance, shade, tincture, tinge, tint, tone.

huffy *adj.* angry, crabbed, cross, crotchety, crusty, disgruntled, grumpy, hoity-toity, huffish, irritable, miffed, miffy, moody, moping, morose, offended, peevish, pettish, petulant, querulous, resentful, shirty, short, snappy, sulky, surly, testy, touchy, waspish.
antonyms cheery, happy.

hug *v.* cherish, clasp, cling to, cuddle, embrace, enclose, enfold, follow, grip, hold, lock, nurse, retain, skirt, squeeze.
n. clasp, clinch, cuddle, embrace, squeeze.

huge *adj.* Babylonian, Brobdingnagian, bulky, colossal, Cyclopean, enormous, extensive, gargantuan, giant, gigantean, gigantesque, gigantic, great, gross, immense, jumbo, large, leviathan, mammoth, massive, monumental, mountainous, Patagonian, prodigious, rounceval, stupendous, swingeing, thundering, titanic, tremendous, unwieldy, vast, walloping, whacking.
antonyms dainty, tiny.

hulking *adj.* awkward, bulky, cloddish, clodhopping, clumsy, cumbersome, galumphing, gross, hulky, loutish, lubberly, lumbering, lumpish, massive, oafish, overgrown, ponderous, ungainly, unwieldy.
antonyms delicate, small.

hullabaloo *n.* agitation, babel, bedlam, brouhaha, chaos, clamor, commotion, confusion, din, disturbance, furore, fuss, hubbub, hue and cry, hurly-burly, kerfuffle, noise, outcry, pandemonium, panic, racket, ruckus, ruction, rumpus, to-do, tumult, turmoil, uproar.

hum *v.* bombilate, bombinate, bum, bustle, buzz, croon, drone, lilt, move, mumble, murmur, pulsate, pulse, purr, sing, stir, susurrate, throb, thrum, vibrate, whirr, zoom.
n. bombilation, bombination, bustle, busyness, buzz, drone, mumble, murmur, noise, pulsation, pulse, purr, purring, singing, stir, susurration, susurrus, throb, thrum, vibration, whirr.

human *adj.* anthropoid, approachable, compassionate, considerate, fallible, fleshly, forgivable, hominoid, humane, kind, kindly, man-like, mortal, natural, reasonable, susceptible, understandable, understanding, vulnerable. *antonym* inhuman.
n. body, child, creature, hominid, homo sapiens, human being, individual, living soul, man, mortal, person, soul, wight, woman.

humane *adj.* beneficent, benevolent, benign, charitable, civilizing, clement, compassionate, forbearing, forgiving, gentle, good, good-natured, human, humanizing, kind, kind-hearted, kindly, lenient, loving, magnanimous, merciful, mild, sympathetic, tender, understanding.
antonym inhumane.

humanitarian *adj.* altruistic, beneficent, benevolent, charitable, compassionate, humane, philanthropic, philanthropical, public-spirited.
n. altruist, benefactor, do-gooder, Good Samaritan, philanthrope, philanthropist.
antonyms egoist, self-seeker.

humanitarianism *n.* beneficence, benevolence, charitableness, charity, compassionateness, do-goodery, generosity, goodwill, humanism, loving-kindness, philanthropy.
antonyms egoism, self-seeking.

humanity *n.* altruism, benevolence, benignity, brotherly love, charity, compassion, everyman, fellow-feeling, flesh, generosity, gentleness, goodwill, Homo sapiens, human nature, human race, humankind, humaneness, kind-heartedness, kindness, loving-kindness, man, mandom, mankind, men, mercy, mortality, people, philanthropy, sympathy, tenderness, tolerance, understanding.
antonym inhumanity.

humble *adj.* common, commonplace, courteous, deferential, demiss, docile, homespun, humdrum, insignificant, low, low-born, lowly, mean, meek, modest, obedient, obliging, obscure, obsequious, ordinary, plebeian, polite, poor, respectful, self-effacing, servile, simple, submissive, subservient, supplicatory, unassertive, unassuming, undistinguished, unimportant, unostentatious, unpretending, unpretentious.
antonyms assertive, important, pretentious, proud.
v. abase, abash, break, bring down, bring low, chagrin, chasten, confound, crush, debase, deflate, degrade, demean, discomfit, discredit, disgrace, humiliate, lower, mortify, reduce, shame, sink, subdue, take down a peg.
antonyms exalt, raise.

humbly *adv.* deferentially, diffidently, docilely, heepishly, meekly, modestly, obsequiously, respectfully, servilely, simply, submissively, subserviently, unassumingly, unpretentiously.
antonyms confidently, defiantly.

humbug *n.* baloney, blague, bluff, bounce, bullshit, bunk, bunkum, cant, charlatan, charlatanry, cheat, claptrap, con, con man, deceit, deception, dodge, eyewash, faker, feint, fraud, fudge, gaff, gammon, hoax, hollowness, hype, hypocrisy, imposition, impostor, imposture, mountebank, nonsense, phony, pretense, pseud, quack, quackery, rubbish, ruse, sham, shenanigans, swindle, swindler, trick, trickery, trickster, wile.

v. bamboozle, befool, beguile, cajole, cheat, cozen, deceive, delude, dupe, fool, gammon, gull, hoax, hoodwink, impose, mislead, swindle, trick.

humdrum *adj.* boring, commonplace, dreary, droning, dull, everyday, humble, monotonous, mundane, ordinary, prosy, repetitious, routine, tedious, tiresome, uneventful, uninteresting, unvaried, wearisome.
antonyms exceptional, unusual.

humid *adj.* clammy, damp, dank, moist, muggy, soggy, steamy, sticky, sultry, vaporous, watery, wet.
antonym dry.

humiliate *v.* abase, abash, bring low, chagrin, chasten, confound, crush, debase, deflate, degrade, discomfit, discredit, disgrace, embarrass, humble, mortify, shame, subdue, undignify.
antonyms boost, dignify, exalt, vindicate.

humiliation *n.* abasement, affront, chagrin, condescension, deflation, degradation, discomfiture, discrediting, disgrace, dishonor, embarrassment, humbling, ignominy, indignity, mortification, put-down, rebuff, resignation, shame, snub.
antonyms gratification, triumph.

humor *n.* amusement, badinage, banter, bent, bias, caprice, choler, comedy, conceit, disposition, drollery, facetiousness, fancy, farce, frame of mind, fun, funniness, gags, jesting, jests, jocoseness, jocosity, jocularity, jokes, joking, ludicrousness, melancholy, mood, phlegm, pleasantries, propensity, quirk, raillery, repartee, spirits, temper, temperament, vagary, vein, whim, wisecracks, wit, witticisms, wittiness.
v. accommodate, appease, coax, comply with, cosset, favor, flatter, go along with, gratify, indulge, mollify, pamper, spoil.
antonym thwart.

humorous *adj.* absurd, amusing, comic, comical, entertaining, facetious, farcical, funny, hilarious, humoristic, jocose, jocular, laughable, ludicrous, merry, playful, pleasant, Rabelaisian, satirical, side-splitting, waggish, whimsical, wisecracking, witty, zany.
antonym humorless.

hunger *n.* appetence, appetency, appetite, craving, desire, emptiness, esurience, esuriency, famine, greediness, hungriness, itch, lust, rapacity, ravenousness, starvation, voracity, yearning, yen, yird-hunger.
antonyms appeasement, satisfaction.
v. ache, crave, desire, hanker, itch, long, lust, pine, starve, thirst, want, wish, yearn.

hungry *adj.* aching, appetitive, athirst, avid, covetous, craving, desirous, eager, empty, esurient, famished, famishing, greedy, hollow, hungerful, keen, lean, longing, peckish, ravenous, sharp-set, starved, starving,

underfed, undernourished, voracious, yearning.
antonyms replete, satisfied.

hunt *v.* chase, chevy, course, dog, ferret, forage, gun for, hound, investigate, look for, pursue, rummage, scour, search, seek, stalk, track, trail.
n. battue, chase, chevy, hue and cry, hunting, investigation, pursuit, quest, search, venation.

hurl *v.* cast, catapult, chuck, dash, fire, fling, heave, launch, let fly, pitch, project, propel, send, shy, sling, throw, toss.

hurried *adj.* breakneck, brief, careless, cursory, hasty, headlong, hectic, passing, perfunctory, precipitate, quick, rushed, shallow, short, slapdash, speedy, superficial, swift, unthorough.
antonym leisurely.

hurry *v.* accelerate, belt, bustle, dash, dispatch, expedite, festinate, fly, get a move on, goad, hasten, hightail it, hump, hustle, jump to it, look lively, move, pike, quicken, rush, scoot, scurry, scutter, scuttle, shake a leg, shift, speed up, step on it, step on the gas, urge.
antonyms dally, delay.
n. bustle, celerity, commotion, dispatch, expedition, flurry, haste, precipitance, precipitancy, precipitation, promptitude, quickness, rush, scurry, speed, sweat, urgency.
antonyms calm, leisureliness.

hurt *v.* abuse, ache, afflict, aggrieve, annoy, bruise, burn, damage, disable, distress, grieve, harm, impair, injure, maim, maltreat, mar, pain, sadden, smart, spoil, sting, throb, tingle, torture, upset, wound.
n. abuse, bruise, damage, detriment, disadvantage, discomfort, distress, harm, injury, lesion, loss, mischief, pain, pang, scathe, sore, soreness, suffering, wound, wrong.
adj. aggrieved, annoyed, bruised, crushed, cut, damaged, displeased, grazed, harmed, huffed, injured, maimed, miffed, offended, pained, piqued, rueful, sad, saddened, scarred, scraped, scratched, wounded.

hurtful *adj.* catty, cruel, cutting, damaging, derogatory, destructive, detrimental, disadvantageous, distressing, harmful, humiliating, injurious, malefactory, malefic, maleficent, malicious, malificious, malignant, mean, mischievous, nasty, nocuous, pernicious, pestful, pestiferous, pestilent(ial), pointed, prejudicial, scathing, spiteful, unkind, upsetting, vicious, wounding.
antonyms helpful, kind.

hurtle *v.* bowl, charge, chase, crash, dash, fly, plunge, race, rattle, rush, scoot, scramble, shoot, speed, spin, spurt, tear.

husband[1] *v.* budget, conserve, economize, eke out, hoard, ration, save, save up, store, use sparingly.
antonyms squander, waste.

husband[2] *n.* Benedick, consort, goodman, hubby, man, married man, mate, old man, spouse.

hush *v.* calm, compose, mollify, mute, muzzle, quieten, settle, shush, silence, soothe, still.

antonyms disturb, rouse.

n. calm, calmness, peace, peacefulness, quiet, quietness, repose, serenity, silence, still, stillness, tranquility.

antonyms clamor, uproar.

interj. belt up, euphemeite, favete linguis, hold your tongue, leave it out, not another word, pipe down, quiet, say no more, shush, shut up, ssh, stow it, unberufen, wheesht, whisht.

husk *n.* bark, bract, bran, case, chaff, covering, glume, hull, pod, rind, shell, shuck, tegmen.

husky[1] *adj.* croaking, croaky, gruff, guttural, harsh, hoarse, low, rasping, raucous, rough, roupy, throaty.

husky[2] *adj.* beefy, brawny, burly, hefty, muscular, powerful, rugged, stocky, strapping, strong, sturdy, thickset, tough.

hustle *v.* bustle, crowd, elbow, force, frog-march, haste, hasten, hurry, impel, jog, jostle, pressgang, pressure, push, rush, shove, thrust.

hut *n.* booth, bothan, bothy, cabin, caboose, crib, den, hogan, hovel, kraal, lean-to, shack, shanty, shebang, shed, shelter, shiel, shieling, tilt.

hybrid *n.* amalgam, combination, composite, compound, conglomerate, cross, crossbreed, half-blood, half-breed, heterogeny, mixture, mongrel, mule, pastiche.

adj. bastard, combined, composite, compound, cross, heterogeneous, hybridous, hyphenated, mixed, mongrel, mule, patchwork.

antonyms pure, pure-bred.

hygiene *n.* asepsis, cleanliness, disinfection, hygienics, purity, salubriousness, salubrity, salutariness, sanitariness, sanitation, sterility, wholesomeness.

antonyms filth, insanitariness.

hygienic *adj.* aseptic, clean, cleanly, disinfected, germ-free, healthy, pure, salubrious, salutary, sanitary, sterile, wholesome.

antonym unhygenic.

hyperbole *n.* enlargement, exaggeration, excess, extravagance, magnification, overkill, overplay, overstatement.

antonyms meiosis, understatement.

hypercritical *adj.* captious, carping, caviling, censorious, exceptious, fault-finding, finicky, fussy, hair-splitting, niggling, nit-picking, over-particular, pedantic, pernickety, quibbling, strict, ultracrepidarian, Zoilean.

antonyms tolerant, uncritical.

hypnotic *adj.* compelling, dazzling, fascinating, irresistible, magnetic, mesmeric, mesmerizing, narcotic, opiate, sleep-inducing, somniferous, soothing, soporific, spellbinding.

hypnotize *v.* bewitch, captivate, dazzle, entrance, fascinate, magnetize, mesmerize, spellbind, stupefy.

hypocrisy *n.* cant, deceit, deceitfulness, deception, dissembling, double-talk, duplicity, falsity, imposture, insincerity, lip-service, pharisaicalness, pharisaism, phariseeism, phoneyness, pietism, pretense, quackery, sanctimoniousness, self-righteousness, speciousness, Tartuffism, two-facedness.

antonyms humility, sincerity.

hypocrite *n.* canter, charlatan, deceiver, dissembler, fraud, Holy Willie, impostor, mountebank, Pharisee, phony, pretender, pseud, pseudo, Tartuffe, whited sepulcher.

hypocritical *adj.* canting, deceitful, deceptive, dissembling, double-faced, duplicitous, false, fraudulent, hollow, insincere, Pecksniffian, pharisaic(al), phony, pietistic, sanctimonious, self-pious, self-righteous, specious, spurious, Tartuffian, Tartuffish, two-faced.

antonyms genuine, humble, sincere.

hypothesis *n.* assumption, conjecture, guess, postulate, postulatum, premise, premiss, presumption, proposition, starting-point, supposition, theory, thesis.

hypothetical *adj.* academic, assumed, conjectural, imaginary, postulated, proposed, putative, speculative, supposed, suppositional, theoretical.

antonyms actual, real.

I

idea *n.* abstraction, aim, approximation, archetype, belief, clue, conceit, concept, conception, conceptualization, conclusion, conjecture, construct, conviction, design, doctrine, end, essence, estimate, fancy, form, guess, guesstimate, hint, hypothesis, idée fixe, image, import, impression, inkling, intention, interpretation, intimation, judgment, meaning, monomania, notion, object, opinion, pattern, perception, plan, purpose, reason, recept, recommendation, scheme, sense, significance, solution, suggestion, surmise, suspicion, teaching, theory, thought, type, understanding, view, viewpoint, vision.

ideal *n.* archetype, criterion, dreamboat, epitome, example, exemplar, image, last word, model, ne plus ultra, nonpareil, paradigm, paragon, pattern, perfection, pink of perfection, principle, prototype, standard, type. *adj.* abstract, archetypal, best, classic, complete, conceptual, consummate, fanciful, highest, hypothetical, imaginary, impractical, model, optimal, optimum, perfect, quintessential, supreme, theoretical, transcendent, transcendental, unattainable, unreal, Utopian, visionary.

idealistic *adj.* impracticable, impractical, optimistic, perfectionist, quixotic, romantic, starry-eyed, unrealistic, utopian, visionary.
antonyms pragmatic, realistic.

identify *v.* catalog, classify, detect, diagnose, distinguish, finger, know, label, make out, name, pick out, pinpoint, place, recognize, single out, specify, spot, tag.

identity *n.* accord, coincidence, correspondence, empathy, existence, haecceity, individuality, oneness, particularity, personality, quiddity, rapport, sameness, self, selfhood, singularity, unanimity, uniqueness, unity.

ideology *n.* belief(s), convictions, creed, doctrine(s), dogma, ethic, faith, ideas, metaphysics, philosophy, principles, speculation, tenets, Weltanschauung, world view.

idiom *n.* colloquialism, expression, idiolect, idiotism, jargon, language, locution, parlance, phrase, regionalism, set phrase, style, talk, turn of phrase, usage, vernacular.

idiot *n.* ament, ass, blockhead, booby, cretin, cuckoo, dimwit, dolt, dumbbell, dummy, dunderhead, fat-head, featherbrain, fool, golem, half-wit, imbecile, mental defective, mooncalf, moron, natural, nidget, nig-nog, nincompoop, nitwit, noodle, saphead, schlep, schmo, schmuck, simpleton, thick, thickhead.

idiotic *adj.* asinine, crazy, cretinous, daft, dumb, fatheaded, fatuous, foolhardy, foolish, hair-brained, half-witted, harebrained, idiotical, imbecile, imbecilic, inane, insane, loony, lunatic, moronic, nutty, screwy, senseless, simple, stupid, tomfool, unintelligent.
antonyms sane, sensible.

idle *adj.* abortive, bootless, dead, dormant, dronish, empty, foolish, frivolous, fruitless, futile, good-for-nothing, groundless, inactive, indolent, ineffective, ineffectual, inoperative, jobless, lackadaisical, lazy, mothballed, nugatory, of no avail, otiose, pointless, purposeless, redundant, shiftless, slothful, sluggish, stationary, superficial, torpid, trivial, unavailing, unbusy, unemployed, unproductive, unsuccessful, unused, useless, vain, work-shy, worthless.
antonyms active, effective, purposeful.
v. coast, dally, dawdle, drift, fool, fritter, kill time, lally-gag, laze, lie up, loiter, lounge, potter, rest on one's laurels, shirk, skive, slack, take it easy, tick over, vegetate, waste, while.
antonyms act, work.

idol *n.* beloved, darling, deity, favorite, fetish, god, graven image, hero, icon, image, joss, ju-ju, Mumbo-jumbo, pet, pin-up, superstar.

idolize *v.* admire, adore, apotheosize, deify, dote on, exalt, glorify, hero-worship, iconize, lionize, love, revere, reverence, venerate, worship. *antonym* vilify.

ignoble *adj.* abject, base, base-born, caddish, common, contemptible, cowardly, craven, dastardly, degenerate, degraded, despicable, disgraceful, dishonorable, heinous, humble, infamous, low, low-born, lowly, mean, petty, plebeian, shabby, shameless, unworthy, vile, vulgar, worthless, wretched.
antonyms honorable, noble.

ignominious *adj.* abject, crushing, degrading, despicable, discreditable, disgraceful, dishonorable, disreputable, humiliating, indecorous, inglorious, mortifying, scandalous, shameful, sorry, undignified.
antonyms honorable, triumphant.

ignorant *adj.* as thick as two short planks, benighted, blind, bookless, clueless, crass, dense, green, gross, half-baked, idealess, ill-informed, illiterate, ill-versed, inexperienced, innocent, innumerate, insensitive, know-nothing, naïve, nescient, oblivious, pig-ignorant, stupid, thick, unacquainted, unaware, unconscious, uncultivated, uneducated, unenlightened, unidea'd, uninformed, uninitiated, uninstructed, unknowing, unlearned, unlettered, unread, unscholarly, unschooled, untaught, untrained, untutored, unwitting.
antonyms knowlegeable, wise.

ignore *v.* blink, cold-shoulder, cut, disregard, neglect, omit, overlook, pass over, pay no attention to,

pigeon-hole, reject, send to Coventry, set aside, shut one's eyes to, slight, take no notice of, turn a blind eye to, turn a deaf ear to, turn one's back on.
antonym note.

ill[1] *adj.* ailing, dicky, diseased, frail, funny, indisposed, infirm, laid up, not up to snuff, off-color, on the sick list, out of sorts, peelie-wally, poorly, queasy, queer, seedy, sick, under the weather, unhealthy, unwell, valetudinarian.
antonym well.
n. affliction, ailment, complaint, disease, disorder, illness, indisposition, infection, infirmity, malady, malaise, sickness.

ill[2] *adj.* acrimonious, adverse, antagonistic, bad, cantankerous, cross, damaging, deleterious, detrimental, difficult, disturbing, evil, foul, harmful, harsh, hateful, hostile, hurtful, inauspicious, incorrect, inimical, iniquitous, injurious, malevolent, malicious, ominous, reprehensible, ruinous, sinister, sullen, surly, threatening, unfavorable, unfortunate, unfriendly, unhealthy, unkind, unlucky, unpromising, unpropitious, unwholesome, vile, wicked, wrong.
antonyms beneficial, fortunate, good, kind.
n. abuse, affliction, badness, cruelty, damage, depravity, destruction, evil, harm, hurt, ill-usage, injury, malice, mischief, misery, misfortune, pain, sorrow, suffering, trial, tribulation, trouble, unpleasantness, wickedness, woe.
antonym benefit.
adv. amiss, badly, by no means, hard, hardly, inauspiciously, insufficiently, poorly, scantily, scarcely, unfavorably, unluckily, wrongfully.
antonym well.

ill-advised *adj.* daft, foolhardy, foolish, hasty, hazardous, ill-considered, ill-judged, impolitic, imprudent, inappropriate, incautious, indiscreet, injudicious, misguided, overhasty, rash, reckless, short-sighted, thoughtless, unseemly, unwise, wrong-headed.
antonym sensible.

ill-assorted *adj.* discordant, incompatible, incongruous, inharmonious, misallied, mismatched, uncongenial, unsuited.
antonym harmonious.

illegal *adj.* actionable, banned, black-market, contraband, criminal, felonious, forbidden, illicit, outlawed, pirate, prohibited, proscribed, unauthorized, unconstitutional, under-the-counter, unlawful, unlicensed, wrongful, wrongous.
antonym legal.

ill-fated *adj.* blighted, doomed, forlorn, hapless, ill-omened, ill-starred, infaust, luckless, star-crossed, unfortunate, unhappy, unlucky.
antonym lucky.

illiberal *adj.* bigoted, close-fisted, hidebound, intolerant, mean, miserly, narrow-minded, niggardly, parsimonious, petty, prejudiced, reactionary, small-minded, sordid, stingy, tight, tightfisted, uncharitable, ungenerous, verkrampte.
antonym liberal.

illicit *adj.* black, black-market, bootleg, clandestine, contraband, criminal, felonious, forbidden, furtive, guilty, illegal, illegitimate, ill-gotten, immoral, improper, inadmissible, prohibited, unauthorized, unlawful, unlicensed, unsanctioned, wrong.
antonyms legal, licit.

illiterate *adj.* analphabetic, benighted, ignorant, uncultured, uneducated, unlettered, untaught, untutored.
antonym literate.

ill-natured *adj.* bad-tempered, churlish, crabbed, cross, cross-grained, disagreeable, disobliging, malevolent, malicious, malignant, mean, nasty, perverse, petulant, spiteful, sulky, sullen, surly, unfriendly, unkind, unpleasant, vicious, vindictive.
antonym good-natured.

illness *n.* affliction, ailment, attack, complaint, disability, disease, disorder, distemper, dyscrasia, idiopathy, ill-being, ill-health, indisposition, infirmity, malady, malaise, sickness.
antonym health.

illogical *adj.* absurd, fallacious, faulty, illegitimate, inconclusive, inconsistent, incorrect, invalid, irrational, meaningless, senseless, sophistical, specious, spurious, unreasonable, unscientific, unsound.
antonym logical.

ill-tempered *adj.* bad-tempered, choleric, cross, curt, grumpy, ill-humored, ill-natured, impatient, irascible, irritable, sharp, spiteful, testy, tetchy, touchy, vicious, vixenish, vixenly.
antonym good-tempered.

ill-treatment *n.* abuse, damage, harm, ill-use, injury, maltreatment, manhandling, mishandling, mistreatment, misuse, neglect.
antonym care.

illuminate *v.* adorn, beacon, brighten, clarify, clear up, decorate, edify, elucidate, enlighten, explain, illumine, illustrate, instruct, irradiate, light, light up, limn, miniate, ornament.
antonyms darken, deface, divest.

illusion *n.* apparition, chimera, daydream, deception, delusion, error, fallacy, fancy, fantasy, figment, hallucination, ignis fatuus, maya, mirage, misapprehension, misconception, phantasm, semblance, will-o'-the-wisp.
antonym reality.

illusory *adj.* apparent, Barmecidal, beguiling, chimerical, deceitful, deceptive, deluding, delusive, fallacious, false, hallucinatory, illusive, misleading, mistaken, seeming, sham, unreal, unsubstantial, untrue, vain.
antonym real.

illustrate *v.* adorn, clarify, decorate, demonstrate, depict, draw, elucidate, emphasize, exemplify, exhibit, explain, illuminate, instance, interpret, miniate, ornament, picture, show, sketch.

illustration 182 **immensity**

illustration *n.* adornment, analogy, case, case in point, clarification, decoration, delineation, demonstration, drawing, elucidation, example, exemplification, explanation, figure, graphic, half-tone, instance, interpretation, photograph, picture, plate, representation, sketch, specimen.

illustrious *adj.* brilliant, celebrated, distinguished, eminent, exalted, excellent, famed, famous, glorious, great, magnificent, noble, notable, noted, outstanding, prominent, remarkable, renowned, resplendent, signal, splendid.
antonyms inglorious, shameful.

image *n.* appearance, conceit, concept, conception, counterpart, dead ringer, Doppelgänger, double, effigies, effigy, eidolon, eikon, facsimile, figure, icon, idea, idol, impression, likeness, perception, picture, portrait, reflection, replica, representation, semblance, similitude, simulacrum, spit, spitting image, statue, trope.

imaginary *adj.* assumed, Barmecidal, chimerical, dreamlike, fancied, fanciful, fictional, fictitious, hallucinatory, hypothetical, ideal, illusive, illusory, imagined, insubstantial, invented, legendary, made-up, mythological, non-existent, phantasmal, shadowy, supposed, unreal, unsubstantial, visionary.
antonym real.

imagination *n.* chimera, conception, creativity, enterprise, fancy, idea, ideality, illusion, image, imaginativeness, ingenuity, innovativeness, innovatoriness, insight, inspiration, invention, inventiveness, notion, originality, resourcefulness, supposition, unreality, vision, wit, wittiness.
antonyms reality, unimaginativeness.

imaginative *adj.* clever, creative, dreamy, enterprising, fanciful, fantastic, fertile, ingenious, innovative, inspired, inventive, original, poetical, resourceful, visionary, vivid.
antonym unimaginative.

imagine *v.* apprehend, assume, believe, conceive, conceptualize, conjecture, conjure up, create, deduce, deem, devise, dream up, envisage, envision, fancy, fantasize, frame, gather, guess, ideate, infer, invent, judge, picture, plan, project, realize, scheme, suppose, surmise, suspect, take it, think, think of, think up, visualize.

imbecile *n.* ament, blockhead, bungler, clown, cretin, dolt, dotard, fool, half-wit, idiot, moron, thickhead.
adj. anile, asinine, doltish, fatuous, feeble-minded, foolish, idiotic, imbecilic, inane, ludicrous, moronic, senile, simple, stupid, thick, witless.
antonyms intelligent, sensible.

imbibe *v.* absorb, acquire, assimilate, consume, drink, drink in, gain, gather, gulp, ingest, knock back, lap up, quaff, receive, sink, sip, soak in, soak up, swallow, swig, take in.

imitate *v.* affect, ape, burlesque, caricature, clone, copy, copy-cat, counterfeit, do, duplicate, echo, emulate, follow, follow suit, forge, impersonate, mimic, mirror, mock, monkey, parody, parrot, personate, repeat, reproduce, send up, simulate, spoof, take off, travesty.

imitation *n.* apery, aping, copy, counterfeit, counterfeiting, duplication, echoing, echopraxia, echopraxis, fake, forgery, impersonation, impression, likeness, mimesis, mimicry, mockery, parody, reflection, replica, reproduction, resemblance, sham, simulation, substitution, take-off, travesty.
adj. artificial, dummy, ersatz, man-made, mock, phony, pinchbeck, pseudo, repro, reproduction, sham, simulated, synthetic.
antonym genuine.

immaculate *adj.* blameless, clean, faultless, flawless, guiltless, impeccable, incorrupt, innocent, neat, perfect, pure, scrupulous, sinless, spick-and-span, spotless, spruce, stainless, trim, unblemished, uncontaminated, undefiled, unexceptionable, unpolluted, unsullied, untainted, untarnished, virtuous.
antonyms contaminated, spoiled.

immature *adj.* adolescent, babyish, callow, childish, crude, green, immatured, imperfect, inexperienced, infantile, jejune, juvenile, premature, puerile, raw, under-age, undeveloped, unfinished, unfledged, unformed, unripe, unseasonable, untimely, young.
antonym mature.

immeasurable *adj.* bottomless, boundless, endless, illimitable, immense, immensurable, incalculable, inestimable, inexhaustible, infinite, limitless, measureless, unbounded, unfathomable, unlimited, unmeasurable, vast.
antonym limited.

immediate *adj.* actual, adjacent, close, contiguous, current, direct, existing, extant, instant, instantaneous, near, nearest, neighboring, next, on hand, present, pressing, primary, prompt, proximate, recent, unhesitating, up-to-date, urgent.
antonym distant.

immediately *adv.* at once, closely, directly, forthwith, incontinent, instantly, lickety-split, nearly, now, off the top of one's head, on the instant, posthaste, promptly, pronto, right away, straight away, straight off, straight way, tout de suite, unhesitatingly, without delay.
antonyms eventually, never.

immense *adj.* Brobdingnag(ian), colossal, cyclopean, elephantine, enormous, extensive, giant, gigantic, great, herculean, huge, illimitable, immeasurable, infinite, interminable, jumbo, large, limitless, mammoth, massive, monstrous, monumental, prodigious, rounceval, stupendous, Titanesque, titanic, tremendous, vast.
antonym minute.

immensity *n.* bulk, enormousness, expanse, extent, greatness, hugeness, infinity, magnitude, massiveness, scope, size, sweep, vastness.
antonym minuteness.

immerse *v.* bathe, demerge, demerse, dip, douse, duck, dunk, plunge, sink, submerge, submerse.

immigrate *v.* come in, migrate, move in, remove, resettle, settle.
antonym emigrate.

imminent *adj.* afoot, approaching, at hand, brewing, close, coming, forthcoming, gathering, impending, in the air, in the offing, looming, menacing, near, nigh, overhanging, threatening.
antonym far-off.

immoderately *adv.* exaggeratedly, excessively, exorbitantly, extravagantly, extremely, inordinately, unduly, unjustifiably, unreasonably, unrestrainedly, wantonly, without measure.
antonym moderately.

immoral *adj.* abandoned, bad, corrupt, debauched, degenerate, depraved, dishonest, dissolute, evil, foul, impure, indecent, iniquitous, lecherous, lewd, licentious, nefarious, obscene, pornographic, profligate, reprobate, sinful, unchaste, unethical, unprincipled, unrighteous, unscrupulous, vicious, vile, wanton, wicked, wrong.
antonym moral.
antonym morality.

immortal *adj.* abiding, ambrosial, constant, deathless, endless, enduring, eternal, everlasting, imperishable, incorruptible, indestructible, lasting, perennial, perpetual, sempiternal, timeless, undying, unfading, unforgettable.
antonym mortal.
n. deity, divinity, genius, god, goddess, great, hero, Olympian.

immortalize *v.* apotheosize, celebrate, commemorate, deify, enshrine, eternalize, eternize, exalt, glorify, hallow, memorialize, perpetuate, solemnize.

immune *adj.* clear, exempt, free, insusceptible, insusceptive, invulnerable, proof, protected, resistant, safe, unaffected, unsusceptible.
antonym susceptible.

immutable *adj.* abiding, changeless, constant, enduring, fixed, inflexible, invariable, lasting, permanent, perpetual, sacrosanct, solid, stable, steadfast, unalterable, unchangeable.
antonym mutable.

impact *n.* aftermath, bang, blow, brunt, bump, burden, collision, concussion, consequences, contact, crash, effect, force, impression, influence, jolt, knock, knock-on effect, meaning, power, repercussions, shock, significance, smash, stroke, thrust, thump, weight.
v. clash, collide, crash, crush, fix, hit, press together, strike, wedge.

impair *v.* blunt, craze, damage, debilitate, decrease, deteriorate, devalue, diminish, enervate, enfeeble, harm, hinder, injure, lessen, mar, reduce, spoil, undermine, vitiate, weaken, worsen.
antonym enhance.

impart *v.* accord, afford, bestow, communicate, confer, contribute, convey, disclose, discover, divulge, give, grant, hand over, lend, make known, offer, pass on, relate, reveal, tell, yield.

impartial *adj.* detached, disinterested, dispassionate, equal, equitable, even-handed, fair, just, neutral, non-discriminating, non-partisan, objective, open-minded, uncommitted, unbiased, unprejudiced.
antonym biased.

impartiality *n.* detachment, disinterest, disinterestedness, dispassion, equality, equity, even-handedness, fairness, neutrality, non-partisanship, objectivity, open-mindedness, unbiasedness.
antonym bias.

impasse *n.* blind alley, cul-de-sac, dead end, deadlock, halt, nonplus, stalemate, stand-off, standstill.

impassioned *adj.* animated, ardent, blazing, enthusiastic, excited, fervent, fervid, fiery, furious, glowing, heated, inflamed, inspired, intense, passionate, rousing, spirited, stirring, vehement, vigorous, violent, vivid, warm.
antonyms apathetic, mild.

impassive *adj.* aloof, apathetic, blockish, callous, calm, composed, cool, dispassionate, emotionless, expressionless, immobile, impassible, imperturbable, indifferent, inscrutable, insensible, insusceptible, laid back, phlegmatic, poker-faced, reserved, serene, stoical, stolid, unconcerned, unemotional, unexcitable, unfeeling, unimpressible, unmoved, unruffled.
antonyms moved, responsive, warm.

impede *v.* bar, block, brake, check, clog, curb, delay, disrupt, hamper, hinder, hobble, hold up, let, obstruct, restrain, retard, slow, stop, thwart, trammel.
antonym aid.

impediment *n.* bar, barrier, block, burr, check, clog, curb, defect, difficulty, encumbrance, hindrance, let, log, obstacle, obstruction, snag, stammer, stumbling-block, stutter.
antonym aid.

impel *v.* actuate, chivvy, compel, constrain, drive, excite, force, goad, incite, induce, influence, inspire, instigate, motivate, move, oblige, poke, power, prod, prompt, propel, push, spur, stimulate, urge.
antonym dissuade.

impending *adj.* approaching, brewing, close, collecting, coming, forthcoming, gathering, hovering, imminent, in store, looming, menacing, near, nearing, threatening.
antonym remote.

impenetrable *adj.* arcane, baffling, cabbalistic, cryptic, dark, dense, enigmatic(al), fathomless, hermetic, hidden, impassable, impermeable, impervious, incomprehensible, indiscernible, inexplicable, inscrutable, inviolable, mysterious, obscure, solid, thick, unfathomable, unintelligible, unpiercable.
antonyms intelligible, penetrable.

imperative *adj.* authoritative, autocratic, bossy, commanding,

compulsory, crucial, dictatorial, domineering, essential, exigent, high-handed, imperious, indispensable, insistent, lordly, magisterial, obligatory, peremptory, pressing, tyrannical, tyrannous, urgent, vital.
antonyms humble, optional.

imperceptible *adj.* faint, fine, gradual, impalpable, inapparent, inappreciable, inaudible, inconsensequential, indiscernible, indistinguishable, infinitesimal, insensible, invisible, microscopic, minute, shadowy, slight, small, subtle, tiny, undetectable, unnoticeable.
antonym perceptible.

imperfection *n.* blemish, blot, blotch, crack, defect, deficiency, dent, failing, fallibility, fault, flaw, foible, frailty, glitch, inadequacy, incompleteness, insufficiency, peccadillo, shortcoming, stain, taint, weakness.
antonyms asset, perfection.

imperil *v.* compromise, endanger, expose, hazard, jeopardize, risk, threaten.

impersonal *adj.* aloof, bureaucratic, businesslike, cold, detached, dispassionate, faceless, formal, frosty, glassy, inhuman, neutral, official, remote, unfriendly, unsympathetic.
antonym friendly.

impersonate *v.* act, ape, caricature, do, imitate, masquerade as, mimic, mock, parody, personate, pose as, take off.

impertinence *n.* assurance, audacity, backchat, boldness, brass, brazenness, cheek, discourtesy, disrespect, effrontery, forwardness, impoliteness, impudence, incivility, insolence, malapertness, nerve, pertness, politeness, presumption, rudeness, sauce, sauciness.

impertinent *adj.* bold, brattish, brazen, bumptious, cheeky, discourteous, disrespectful, forward, fresh, ill-mannered, impolite, impudent, insolent, interfering, malapert, pert, presumptuous, rude, saucy, uncivil, unmannerly.
antonym polite.

impetuous *adj.* ardent, bull-headed, eager, furious, hasty, headlong, impassioned, impulsive, overhasty, passionate, precipitate, rash, spontaneous, tearaway, unplanned, unpremeditated, unreflecting, unrestrained, unthinking.
antonym circumspect.

implacable *adj.* cruel, immovable, inappeasable, inexorable, inflexible, intractable, intransigent, irreconcilable, merciless, pitiless, rancorous, relentless, remorseless, ruthless, unappeasable, unbending, uncompromising, unforgiving, unrelenting, unyielding.
antonym placable.

implausible *adj.* dubious, far-fetched, flimsy, improbable, incredible, suspect, thin, transparent, unbelievable, unconvincing, unlikely, unplausible, unreasonable, weak.
antonym plausible.

implicate *v.* associate, compromise, connect, embroil, entangle, include, incriminate, inculpate, involve, throw suspicion on.
antonyms absolve, exonerate.

implicit *adj.* absolute, constant, contained, entire, firm, fixed, full, implied, inherent, latent, presupposed, steadfast, tacit, total, undeclared, understood, unhesitating, unqualified, unquestioning, unreserved, unshakable, unshaken, unspoken, wholehearted.
antonym explicit.

implore *v.* ask, beg, beseech, crave, entreat, importune, plead, pray, solicit, supplicate, wheedle.

imply *v.* betoken, connote, denote, entail, evidence, hint, import, indicate, insinuate, intimate, involve, mean, point to, presuppose, require, signify, suggest.
antonym state.

impolite *adj.* abrupt, bad-mannered, boorish, churlish, clumsy, coarse, cross, discourteous, disrespectful, gauche, ill-bred, ill-mannered, indecorous, indelicate, inept, insolent, loutish, rough, rude, uncivil, uncourteous, ungallant, ungentlemanly, ungracious, unladylike, unmannerly, unrefined.
antonym polite.

import *n.* bearing, consequence, drift, essence, gist, implication, importance, intention, magnitude, meaning, message, moment, nub, purport, sense, significance, substance, thrust, weight.
v. betoken, bring in, imply, indicate, introduce, mean, purport, signify.

important *adj.* basic, eminent, essential, far-reaching, foremost, grave, heavy, high-level, high-ranking, influential, key, keynote, large, leading, material, meaningful, momentous, notable, noteworthy, on the map, outstanding, powerful, pre-eminent, primary, prominent, relevant, salient, seminal, serious, signal, significant, substantial, urgent, valuable, valued, weighty.
antonym unimportant.

impose[1] *v.* appoint, burden, charge (with), decree, dictate, encumber, enforce, enjoin, establish, exact, fix, impone, inflict, institute, introduce, lay, levy, ordain, place, prescribe, promulgate, put, saddle, set.

impose[2] *v.* butt in, encroach, foist, force oneself, gate crash, horn in, impone, interpose, intrude, obtrude, presume, take liberties, trespass.

imposing *adj.* august, commanding, dignified, distinguished, effective, grand, grandiose, impressive, majestic, ortund, pompous, stately, striking.
antonyms modest, unimposing.

imposition[1] *n.* application, decree, exaction, infliction, introduction, levying, promulgation.

imposition[2] *n.* burden, charge, cheek, constraint, deception, duty, encroachment, intrusion, levy, liberty, lines, presumption, punishment, task, tax.

impossible *adj.* absurd, hopeless, impracticable, inadmissible, inconceivable, insoluble, intolerable, ludicrous, outrageous, preposterous, unacceptable, unachievable, unattainable, ungovernable, unobtainable,

unreasonable, untenable, unthinkable, unviable, unworkable.
antonym possible.

impractical *adj.* academic, idealistic, impossible, impracticable, inoperable, ivory-tower, non-viable, romantic, starry-eyed, unbusinesslike, unrealistic, unserviceable, unworkable, visionary, wild. *antonym* practical.

impregnable *adj.* fast, fortified, immovable, impenetrable, impugnable, indestructible, invincible, invulnerable, secure, solid, strong, unassailable, unbeatable, unconquerable.
antonym vulnerable.

impress *v.* affect, emboss, emphasize, engrave, excite, fix, grab, imprint, inculcate, indent, influence, inspire, instil, make one's mark, mark, move, namedrop, print, slay, stamp, stand out, stir, strike, sway, touch, wow.

impression[1] *n.* awareness, belief, concept, consciousness, conviction, effect, fancy, feeling, hunch, idea, impact, influence, memory, notion, opinion, reaction, recollection, sense, suspicion, sway.

impression[2] *n.* dent, edition, engram, engramma, hollow, impress, imprint, imprinting, incuse, indentation, issue, mark, niello, outline, pressure, printing, stamp, stamping.

impression[3] *n.* apery, aping, burlesque, imitation, impersonation, parody, send-up, take-off.

impressive *adj.* affecting, effective, exciting, forcible, foudroyant, frappant, imposing, moving, powerful, stirring, striking, touching.
antonym unimpressive.

impromptu *adj.* ad-lib, autoschediastic, extemporaneous, extempore, extemporised, improvised, off the cuff, off-hand, offhand, spontaneous, unpremeditated, unprepared, unrehearsed, unscripted, unstudied.
antonyms planned, rehearsed.
adv. ad lib, extempore, off the cuff, off the top of one's head, on the spur of the moment, spontaneously.
n. autoschediasm, extemporisation, improvisation, voluntary.

improper *adj.* abnormal, erroneous, false, illegitimate, illtimed, impolite, inaccurate, inadmissible, inapplicable, inapposite, inappropriate, inapt, incongruous, incorrect, indecent, indecorous, indelicate, infelicitous, inopportune, irregular, malapropos, off-color, out of place, risqué, smutty, suggestive, unbecoming, uncalled-for, unfit, unfitting, unmaidenly, unparliamentary, unprintable, unquotable, unrepeatable, unseasonable, unseemly, unsuitable, unsuited, untoward, unwarranted, vulgar, wrong.
antonym proper.

improve *v.* advance, ameliorate, amend, augment, better, correct, culture, develop, embourgeoise, enhance, gentrify, help, increase, look up, meliorate, mend, mend one's ways, perk up, pick up, polish, progress, rally, recover, rectify, recuperate, reform, rise, touch up,

turn over a new leaf, turn the corner, up, upgrade.
antonyms decline, diminish.

improvement *n.* advance, advancement, amelioration, amendment, augmentation, bettering, betterment, correction, development, embourgeoisement, enhancement, furtherance, gain, gentrification, increase, melioration, progress, rally, recovery, rectification, reformation, rise, upswing.

improvident *adj.* careless, feckless, heedless, imprudent, Micawberish, negligent, prodigal, profligate, reckless, shiftless, spendthrift, thoughtless, thriftless, underprepared, uneconomical, unprepared, unthrifty, wasteful.
antonym thrifty.

improvisation *n.* ad-lib, ad-libbing, autoschediasm, expedient, extemporising, impromptu, invention, makeshift, spontaneity, vamp.

imprudent *adj.* careless, foolhardy, foolish, hasty, heedless, ill-advised, ill-considered, ill-judged, impolitic, improvident, incautious, inconsiderate, indiscreet, injudicious, irresponsible, overhasty, rash, reckless, short-sighted, temerarious, unthinking, unwise.
antonym prudent.

impudence *n.* assurance, audacity, backchat, boldness, brass neck, brazenness, cheek, chutzpah, effrontery, face, impertinence, impudicity, insolence, lip, malapertness, neck, nerve, pertness, presumption, presumptuousness, rudeness, sauciness, shamelessness.
antonym politeness.

impudent *adj.* audacious, bold, bold-faced, brazen, brazen-faced, cheeky, cocky, forward, fresh, immodest, impertinent, insolent, malapert, pert, presumptuous, rude, saucy, shameless.
antonym polite.

impulse *n.* caprice, catalyst, conatus, desire, drive, feeling, force, impetus, incitement, inclination, influence, instinct, momentum, motive, movement, notion, passion, pressure, push, resolve, stimulus, surge, thrust, urge, whim, wish.

impulsive *adj.* hasty, headlong, impetuous, instinctive, intuitive, passionate, precipitant, precipitate, quick, rash, reckless, spontaneous, unconsidered, unpredictable, unpremeditated.
antonym cautious.

impure *adj.* admixed, adulterated, alloyed, carnal, coarse, contaminated, corrupt, debased, defiled, dirty, feculent, filthy, foul, gross, immodest, immoral, indecent, indelicate, infected, lascivious, lewd, licentious, lustful, mixed, obscene, polluted, prurient, salacious, smutty, sullied, tainted, turbid, unchaste, unclean, unrefined, unwholesome, vicious, vitiated.
antonyms chaste, pure.

imputation *n.* accusation, arrogation, ascription, aspersion, attribution, blame, censure, charge, insinuation, reproach, slander, slur, suggestion.

in abeyance dormant, hanging fire, on ice, pending, shelved, suspended.

in camera behind closed doors, hugger-mugger, in private, in secret, privately, secretly, sub rosa, under the rose. *antonym* openly.

in confidence in private, privately, secretly, sub rosa, under the rose.

in depth comprehensively, exhaustively, extensively, in detail, intensively, thoroughly. *antonyms* broadly, superficially.

in effect actually, effectively, essentially, for practical purposes, in actuality, in fact, in reality, in the end, in truth, really, to all intents and purposes, virtually, when all is said and done.

in force binding, current, effective, gregatim, in crowds, in droves, in flocks, in hordes, in large numbers, in operation, in strength, on the statute, book, operative, valid, working. *antonym* inoperative.

in good part cheerfully, cordially, good-naturedly, laughingly, well. *antonyms* angrily, touchily.

in keeping appropriate, befitting, fit, fitting, harmonious, in harmony, of a piece, suitable. *antonym* inappropriate.

in motion afoot, functioning, going, in progress, moving, on the go, operational, running, sailing, traveling, under way. *antonym* stationary.

in order acceptable, all right, allowed, appropriate, arranged, called for, correct, done, fitting, in sequence, neat, OK, orderly, permitted, right, shipshape, suitable, tidy. *antonyms* disallowed, out of order.

in order to intending to, so that, to, with a view to, with the intention of, with the purpose of.

in part a little, in some measure, part way, partially, partly, slightly, somewhat, to a certain extent, to some degree. *antonym* wholly.

in passing accidentally, by the by(e), by the way, en passant, incidentally.

in person as large as life, bodily, in propria persona, personally.

in principle en principe, ideally, in essence, in theory, theoretically.

in spite of despite, notwithstanding.

in the light of bearing/keeping in mind, because of, considering, in view of, taking into account.

in the money affluent, flush, loaded, opulent, prosperous, rich, rolling in it, wealthy, well-heeled, well-off, well-to-do. *antonym* poor.

in the mood disposed, in the right frame of mind, inclined, interested, keen, minded, of a mind, willing.

in the offing at hand, close at hand, coming up, imminent, in sight, on the horizon, on the way. *antonym* far off.

in the red bankrupt, in arrears, in debt, insolvent, on the rocks, overdrawn. *antonym* in credit.

in two minds dithering, hesitant, hesitating, shilly-shallying, swithering, uncertain, undecided, unsure, vacillating, wavering. *antonym* certain.

in vain bootlessly, fruitlessly, ineffectually, to no avail, unsuccessfully, uselessly, vainly. *antonym* successfully.

inability *n.* disability, disqualification, handicap, impotence, inadequacy, incapability, incapacity, incompetence, ineptitude, ineptness, powerlessness, weakness. *antonym* ability.

inaccurate *adj.* careless, defective, discrepant, erroneous, faulty, imprecise, in error, incorrect, inexact, loose, mistaken, out, unfaithful, unreliable, unrepresentative, unsound, wide of the mark, wild, wrong. *antonym* accurate.

inactive *adj.* abeyant, dormant, dull, idle, immobile, indolent, inert, inoperative, jobless, kicking one's heels, latent, lazy, lethargic, low-key, mothballed, out of service, out of work, passive, quiet, sedentary, sleepy, slothful, slow, sluggish, somnolent, stagnant, stagnating, torpid, unemployed, unoccupied, unused. *antonym* active.

inactivity *n.* abeyance, abeyancy, dilatoriness, dolce far niente, dormancy, dullness, heaviness, hibernation, idleness, immobility, inaction, indolence, inertia, inertness, languor, lassitude, laziness, lethargy, passivity, quiescence, sloth, sluggishness, stagnation, stasis, torpor, unemployment, vegetation. *antonym* activeness.

inadequate *adj.* defective, deficient, faulty, imperfect, inapt, incapable, incommensurate, incompetent, incomplete, ineffective, ineffectual, inefficacious, inefficient, insubstantial, insufficient, leaving a little/a lot/much to be desired, meager, niggardly, scanty, short, sketchy, skimpy, sparse, unequal, unfitted, unqualified, wanting. *antonym* adequate.

inadvertent *adj.* accidental, careless, chance, heedless, inattentive, negligent, thoughtless, unguarded, unheeding, unintended, unintentional, unplanned, unpremeditated, unthinking, unwitting. *antonym* deliberate.

inane *adj.* asinine, daft, drippy, empty, fatuous, foolish, frivolous, futile, idiotic, imbecilic, mindless, nutty, puerile, senseless, silly, stupid, trifling, unintelligent, vacuous, vain, vapid, worthless. *antonym* sensible.

inanimate *adj.* abiotic, dead, defunct, dormant, dull, exanimate, extinct, heavy, inactive, inert, inorganic, insensate, insentient, leaden, lifeless, listless, slow, spiritless, stagnant, torpid. *antonyms* alive, animate, lively, living.

inappropriate *adj.* disproportionate, ill-fitted, ill-suited, ill-timed, improper, incongruous, infelicitous, malapropos, out of place, tactless, tasteless, unbecoming, unbefitting, unfit, unfitting, unseemly, unsuitable, untimely.
antonym appropriate.

inarticulate *adj.* blurred, dumb, dysarthric, dysphasic, dyspraxic, faltering, halting, hesitant, incoherent, incomprehensible, indistinct, muffled, mumbled, mute, silent, speechless, tongue-tied, unclear, unintelligible, unspoken, unuttered, unvoiced, voiceless, wordless.
antonym articulate.

inattentive *adj.* absent-minded, careless, deaf, distracted, distrait, dreaming, dreamy, heedless, inadvertent, neglectful, negligent, preoccupied, regardless, remiss, unheeding, unmindful, unobservant, vague.
antonym attentive.

inaugurate *v.* begin, christen, commence, commission, consecrate, dedicate, enthrone, han(d)sel, induct, initiate, install, instate, institute, introduce, invest, kick off, launch, open, ordain, originate, set up, start, start off, usher in.

incapable *adj.* disqualified, drunk, feeble, helpless, impotent, inadequate, incompetent, ineffective, ineffectual, inept, insufficient, powerless, tipsy, unable, unfit, unfitted, unqualified, weak.
antonyms capable, sober.

incarcerate *v.* cage, commit, confine, coop up, detain, encage, gaol, immure, impound, imprison, intern, jail, lock up, put away, restrain, restrict, send down, wall in.
antonym free.

incense[1] *n.* adulation, aroma, balm, bouquet, fragrance, homage, joss-stick, perfume, scent, worship.

incense[2] *v.* anger, enrage, exasperate, excite, inflame, infuriate, irritate, madden, make one see red, make one's blood boil, make one's hackles rise, provoke, raise one's hackles, rile.
antonym calm.

incentive *n.* bait, carrot, cause, consideration, encouragement, enticement, impetus, impulse, inducement, lure, motivation, motive, reason, reward, spur, stimulant, stimulus.
antonym disincentive.

inception *n.* beginning, birth, commencement, dawn, inauguration, initiation, installation, kick-off, origin, outset, rise, start.
antonym end.

incessant *adj.* ceaseless, constant, continual, continuous, endless, eternal, everlasting, interminable, never-ending, non-stop, perpetual, persistent, relentless, unbroken, unceasing, unending, unrelenting, unremitting, weariless.
antonym intermittent.

incident *n.* adventure, affair(e), brush, circumstance, clash, commotion, confrontation, contretemps, disturbance, episode, event, fight, happening, mishap, occasion, occurrence, scene, skirmish.

incidental *adj.* accidental, accompanying, ancillary, attendant, casual, chance, concomitant, contingent, contributory, fortuitous, incident, inconsequential, inessential, irrelevant, minor, non-essential, occasional, odd, random, related, secondary, subordinate, subsidiary.
antonym essential.

incidentally *adv.* accidentally, by chance, by the by(e), by the way, casually, digressively, en passant, fortuitously, in passing, parenthetically.

incinerate *v.* burn, char, cremate, reduce to ashes.

incisive *adj.* acid, acute, astucious, astute, biting, caustic, cutting, keen, mordant, penetrating, perceptive, perspicacious, piercing, sarcastic, sardonic, satirical, severe, sharp, tart, trenchant.
antonym woolly.

incite *v.* abet, animate, drive, egg on, encourage, excite, foment, goad, impel, inflame, instigate, prompt, provoke, put up to, rouse, set on, solicit, spur, stimulate, stir up, urge, whip up.
antonym restrain.

incitement *n.* abetment, agitation, encouragement, goad, hortation, impetus, impulse, inducement, instigation, motivation, motive, prompting, provocation, spur, stimulus.
antonyms check, discouragement.

inclination[1] *n.* affection, aptitude, bent, bias, clinamen, desire, disposition, fancy, fondness, ingenium, leaning, liking, month's mind, partiality, penchant, predilection, predisposition, prejudice, proclivity, proneness, propensity, stomach, taste, tendency, turn, turn of mind, velleity, wish.
antonym disinclination.

inclination[2] *n.* angle, bend, bending, bow, bowing, clinamen, deviation, gradient, incline, leaning, nod, pitch, slant, slope, tilt.

incline[1] *v.* affect, bias, dispose, influence, nod, persuade, predispose, prejudice, stoop, sway.

incline[2] *v.* bend, bevel, bow, cant, deviate, diverge, lean, slant, slope, tend, tilt, tip, veer.
n. acclivity, ascent, brae, declivity, descent, dip, grade, gradient, hill, ramp, rise, slope.

inclose *see* **enclose.**

include *v.* add, allow for, comprehend, comprise, connote, contain, cover, embody, embrace, enclose, encompass, incorporate, involve, number among, rope in, subsume, take in, take into account.
antonyms exclude, ignore.

incoherent *adj.* confused, disconnected, disjointed, dislocated, disordered, inarticulate, inconsequent, inconsistent, jumbled, loose, muddled, rambling, stammering, stuttering, unconnected, unco-ordinated, unintelligible, unjointed, wandering, wild.
antonym coherent.

income *n.* earnings, gains, interest, means, pay, proceeds, profits, receipts, returns, revenue, salary, takings, wages, yield.
antonym expenses.

incomparable *adj.* brilliant, inimitable, matchless, paramount, peerless, superb, superlative, supreme, transcendent, unequaled, unmatched, unparalleled, unrivaled.
antonyms poor, run-of-the-mill.

incompetence *n.* bungling, inability, inadequacy, incapability, incapacity, incompetency, ineffectiveness, ineffectuality, ineffectualness, inefficiency, ineptitude, ineptness, insufficiency, stupidity, unfitness, uselessness.
antonym competence.

incomprehensible *adj.* above one's head, all Greek, arcane, baffling, beyond one's comprehension, beyond one's grasp, double-Dutch, enigmatic, impenetrable, inapprehensible, inconceivable, inscrutable, mysterious, obscure, opaque, perplexing, puzzling, unfathomable, unimaginable, unintelligible, unthinkable.
antonym comprehensible.

inconceivable *adj.* implausible, incogitable, incredible, mind-boggling, out of the question, staggering, unbelievable, unheard-of, unimaginable, unknowable, unthinkable.
antonym conceivable.

incongruous *adj.* absurd, conflicting, contradictory, contrary, disconsonant, discordant, dissociable, extraneous, improper, inappropriate, inapt, incoherent, incompatible, inconcinnous, inconsistent, out of keeping, out of place, unbecoming, unsuitable, unsuited.
antonyms consistent, harmonious.

inconsiderate *adj.* careless, imprudent, indelicate, insensitive, intolerant, rash, rude, self-centered, selfish, tactless, thoughtless, unconcerned, ungracious, unkind, unthinking.
antonym considerate.

inconsistency *n.* changeableness, contrariety, disagreement, discrepancy, disparity, divergence, fickleness, incompatibility, incongruity, inconsonance, inconstancy, instability, paradox, unpredictability, unreliability, unsteadiness, variance.
antonym consistency.

inconsistent *adj.* at odds, at variance, capricious, changeable, conflicting, contradictory, contrary, discordant, discrepant, erratic, fickle, incoherent, incompatible, incongruous, inconstant, irreconcilable, irregular, unpredictable, unstable, unsteady, variable, varying.
antonym constant.

inconspicuous *adj.* camouflaged, hidden, insignificant, lowkey, modest, muted, ordinary, plain, quiet, retiring, unassuming, unnoticeable, unobtrusive, unostentatious.
antonym conspicuous.

inconstant *adj.* capricious, changeable, changeful, erratic, fickle, fluctuating, inconsistent, irresolute, mercurial, moonish, mutable, uncertain, undependable, unreliable, unsettled, unstable, unsteady, vacillating, variable, varying, volatile, wavering, wayward.
antonym constant.

inconvenient *adj.* annoying, awkward, bothersome, cumbersome, difficult, disadvantageous, disturbing, embarrassing, inopportune, tiresome, troublesome, unhandy, unmanageable, unseasonable, unsocial, unsuitable, untimely, untoward, unwieldy, vexatious.
antonym convenient.

incorrect *adj.* erroneous, false, faulty, flawed, illegitimate, imprecise, improper, inaccurate, inappropriate, inexact, mistaken, out, specious, ungrammatical, unidiomatic, unsuitable, untrue, wrong.
antonym correct.

incorruptible *adj.* everlasting, honest, honorable, imperishable, incorrupt, just, straight, trustworthy, unbribable, undecaying, upright.
antonym corruptible.

increase *v.* add to, advance, aggrandize, amplify, augment, boost, build up, develop, dilate, eke, eke out, enhance, enlarge, escalate, expand, extend, greaten, grow, heighten, inflate, intensify, magnify, mount, multiply, proliferate, prolong, pullulate, raise, snowball, soar, spread, step up, strengthen, swell, wax.
antonym decrease.

n. accrescence, addition, augment, augmentation, auxesis, boost, development, enlargement, escalation, expansion, extension, gain, growth, increment, intensification, proliferation, rise, step-up, surge, upsurge, upsurgence, upturn.
antonym decrease.

incredible *adj.* absurd, amazing, astonishing, astounding, extraordinary, fabulous, far-fetched, great, implausible, impossible, improbable, inconceivable, inspired, marvelous, preposterous, prodigious, superb, superhuman, unbelievable, unimaginable, unthinkable, wonderful.
antonyms believable, run-of-the-mill.

incriminate *v.* accuse, arraign, blame, charge, criminate, impeach, implicate, inculpate, indict, involve, point the finger at, recriminate, stigmatize.
antonym exonerate.

incurious *adj.* apathetic, careless, inattentive, indifferent, unconcerned, uncurious, unenquiring, uninquiring, uninquisitive, uninterested, unreflective.
antonym curious.

indebted *adj.* beholden, grateful, in debt, obligated, obliged, thankful.

indecency *n.* bawdiness, coarseness, crudity, foulness, grossness, immodesty, impropriety, impurity, indecorum, indelicacy, lewdness, licentiousness, obscenity, outrageousness, pornography, Rabelaisianism, smut, smuttiness, unseemliness, vileness, vulgarity.
antonyms decency, modesty.

indecent *adj.* blue, coarse, crude, dirty, filthy, foul, gross, immodest, improper, impure, indecorous, indelicate, lewd, licentious, near the knuckle, offensive, outrageous, pornographic, Rabelaisian, salacious, scatological, smutty, tasteless, unbecoming, uncomely, unseemly, vile, vulgar.
antonyms decent, modest.

indecisive *adj.* doubtful, faltering, hesitating, hung, in two minds, inconclusive, indefinite, indeterminate, irresolute, pussyfooting, swithering, tentative, uncertain, unclear, undecided, undetermined, unsure, vacillating, wavering.
antonym decisive.

indeed *adv.* actually, certainly, doubtlessly, forsooth, positively, really, strictly, to be sure, truly, undeniably, undoubtedly, verily, veritably.

indefinite *adj.* ambiguous, confused, doubtful, equivocal, evasive, general, ill-defined, imprecise, indeterminate, indistinct, inexact, loose, obscure, uncertain, unclear, undecided, undefined, undetermined, unfixed, unfocus(s)ed, unformed, unformulated, unknown, unlimited, unresolved, unsettled, vague.
antonyms clear, limited.

indelicate *adj.* blue, coarse, crude, embarrassing, gross, immodest, improper, indecent, indecorous, low, obscene, off-color, offensive, risqué, rude, suggestive, tasteless, unbecoming, unmaidenly, unseemly, untoward, vulgar, warm.
antonym delicate.

indemnity *n.* amnesty, compensation, excusal, exemption, guarantee, immunity, impunity, insurance, privilege, protection, redress, reimbursement, remuneration, reparation, requital, restitution, satisfaction, security.

independent *adj.* absolute, autarchical, autocephalous, autogenous, autonomous, bold, crossbench, decontrolled, free, individualistic, liberated, non-aligned, one's own man, self-contained, self-determining, self-governing, self-reliant, self-sufficient, self-supporting, separate, separated, sovereign, unaided, unbiased, unconnected, unconstrained, uncontrolled, unconventional, unrelated, upon one's legs.
antonyms conventional, dependent, timid.

indestructible *adj.* abiding, durable, enduring, eternal, everlasting, immortal, imperishable, incorruptible, indissoluble, infrangible, lasting, permanent, unbreakable, unfading.
antonyms breakable, mortal.

indicate *v.* add up to, bespeak, betoken, denote, designate, display, evince, express, imply, manifest, mark, point out, point to, read, record, register, reveal, show, signify, specify, suggest, telegraph, tip.

indication *n.* clue, endeixis, evidence, explanation, forewarning, hint, index, inkling, intimation, manifestation, mark, note, omen, portent, prognostic, sign, signal, signpost, suggestion, symptom, warning.

indict *v.* accuse, arraign, charge, criminate, impeach, incriminate, prosecute, recriminate, summon, summons, tax.
antonym exonerate.

indictment *n.* accusation, allegation, charge, crimination, impeachment, incrimination, prosecution, recrimination, summons.
antonym exoneration.

indifference *n.* aloofness, apathy, callousness, coldness, coolness, detachment, disinterestedness, dispassion, disregard, equity, heedlessness, impartiality, inattention, insignificance, irrelevance, latitudinarianism, negligence, neutrality, objectivity, pococurant(e)ism, stoicalness, unconcern, unimportance.
antonyms bias, interest.

indifferent *adj.* aloof, apathetic, average, callous, careless, cold, cool, detached, disinterested, dispassionate, distant, equitable, fair, heedless, immaterial, impartial, impervious, inattentive, incurious, insignificant, jack easy, mediocre, middling, moderate, neutral, non-aligned, objective, ordinary, passable, perfunctory, pococurante, regardless, so-so, unbiased, uncaring, unconcerned, undistinguished, unenquiring, unenthusiastic, unexcited, unimportant, unimpressed, uninspired, uninterested, uninvolved, unmoved, unprejudiced, unresponsive, unsympathetic.
antonyms biased, interested.

indigence *n.* deprivation, destitution, distress, necessity, need, penury, poverty, privation, want.
antonym affluence.

indigenous *adj.* aboriginal, autochthonous, home-grown, indigene, local, native, original.
antonym foreign.

indigent *adj.* destitute, impecunious, impoverished, in forma pauperis, in want, necessitous, needy, penniless, penurious, poor, poverty-stricken, straitened.
antonym affluent.

indignant *adj.* angry, annoyed, disgruntled, exasperated, fuming, furibund, furious, heated, huffy, in a paddy, in a wax, incensed, irate, livid, mad, marked, miffed, peeved, provoked, resentful, riled, scornful, sore, waxy, wrathful, wroth.
antonym pleased.

indignation *n.* anger, exasperation, fury, ire, pique, rage, resentment, scorn, umbrage, wax, wrath.
antonym pleasure.

indignity *n.* abuse, affront, contempt, contumely, disgrace, dishonor, disrespect, humiliation, incivility, injury, insult, obloquy, opprobrium, outrage, reproach, slight, snub.
antonym honor.

indirect *adj.* ancillary, backhanded, circuitous, circumlocutory, collateral, contingent, crooked, devious, incidental, meandering, mediate, oblique, periphrastic, rambling, roundabout, secondary, slanted, subsidiary, tortuous, unintended, wandering, winding, zigzag.
antonym direct.

indiscretion *n.* boob, brick, error, faux pas, folly, foolishness, gaffe, imprudence, mistake, rashness, recklessness, slip, slip of the tongue, tactlessness, temerarity.
antonym discretion.

indispensable *adj.* basic, crucial, essential, imperative, key, necessary, needed, needful, required, requisite, vital.
antonym unnecessary.

indistinct *adj.* ambiguous, bleary, blurred, confused, dim, distant, doubtful, faint, fuzzy, hazy, ill-defined, indefinite, indeterminate, indiscernible, indistinguishable, misty, muffled, mumbled, obscure, shadowy, slurred, unclear, undefined, unintelligible, vague.
antonym distinct.

indistinguishable *adj.* alike, identical, interchangeable, same, tantamount, twin.
antonyms distinguishable, unalike.

individual *n.* being, bloke, body, chap, character, creature, fellow, individuum, mortal, party, person, personage, punter, soul.
adj. characteristic, discrete, distinct, distinctive, exclusive, identical, idiosyncratic, own, particular, peculiar, personal, personalized, proper, respective, separate, several, single, singular, special, specific, unique.

individuality *n.* character, discreteness, distinction, distinctiveness, haecceity, originality, peculiarity, personality, separateness, singularity, unicity, uniqueness.
antonym sameness.

indolent *adj.* fainéant, idle, inactive, inert, lackadaisical, languid, lazy, lethargic, listless, lumpish, slack, slothful, slow, sluggard, sluggish, torpid.
antonyms active, enthusiastic, industrious.

indomitable *adj.* bold, intrepid, invincible, resolute, staunch, steadfast, unbeatable, unconquerable, undaunted, unflinching, untameable, unyielding.
antonyms compliant, timid.

induce *v.* actuate, bring about, cause, convince, draw, effect, encourage, engender, generate, get, give rise to, impel, incite, influence, instigate, lead to, move, occasion, persuade, press, prevail upon, produce, prompt, talk into.

inducement *n.* attraction, bait, carrot, cause, come-on, consideration, encouragement, impulse, incentive, incitement, influence, lure, motive, reason, reward, spur, stimulus.
antonym disincentive.

induct *v.* consecrate, enthrone, inaugurate, initiate, install, introduce, invest, ordain, swear in.

indulge *v.* baby, cocker, coddle, cosset, favor, foster, give in to, go along with, gratify, humor, mollycoddle, pamper, pander to, pet, regale, satiate, satisfy, spoil, treat (oneself), yield to.

indulge in give free rein to, give oneself up to, give way to, luxuriate in, revel in, wallow in.

indulgent *adj.* complaisant, compliant, easy-going, favorable, fond, forbearing, gentle, gratifying, intemperate, kind, kindly, lenient, liberal, mild, permissive, prodigal, self-indulgent, tender, tolerant, understanding.
antonyms moderate, strict.

industrious *adj.* active, assiduous, busy, conscientious, deedy, diligent, energetic, hard-working, laborious, persevering, persistent, productive, purposeful, sedulous, steady, tireless, zealous.
antonym indolent.

industriously *adv.* assiduously, conscientiously, diligently, doggedly, hard, perseveringly, sedulously, steadily, with one's nose to the grindstone.
antonym indolently.

inebriated *adj.* befuddled, blind drunk, blotto, drunk, glorious, half seas over, half-cut, half-drunk, in one's cups, incapable, inebriate, intoxicated, legless, merry, paralytic, pie-eyed, plastered, sloshed, smashed, sozzled, stoned, stotious, three sheets in the wind, tight, tipsy, tired and emotional, under the influence.
antonym sober.

ineffective, ineffectual *adj.* abortive, barren, bootless, emasculate, feeble, fruitless, futile, idle, impotent, inadequate, incompetent, ineffective, ineffectual, inefficacious, inefficient, inept, lame, powerless, unavailing, unproductive, useless, vain, void, weak, worthless.
antonyms effective, effectual.

inefficient *adj.* incompetent, inept, inexpert, money-wasting, negligent, slipshod, sloppy, time-wasting, unworkmanlike, wasteful.
antonym efficient.

ineligible *adj.* disqualified, improper, inappropriate, incompetent, objectionable, unacceptable, undesirable, unequipped, unfit, unfitted, unqualified, unsuitable, unworthy.
antonym eligible.

inept *adj.* absurd, awkward, bungling, cack-handed, clumsy, fatuous, futile, gauche, improper, inappropriate, inapt, incompetent, inexpert, infelicitous, irrelevant, maladroit, malapropos, meaningless, ridiculous, unfit, unhandy, unskilful, unworkmanlike.
antonyms adroit, apt.

inequity *n.* abuse, bias, discrimination, injustice, maltreatment, mistreatment, one-sidedness, partiality, prejudice, unfairness, unjustness.
antonym equity.

inert *adj.* apathetic, dead, dormant, dull, idle, immobile, inactive, inanimate, indolent, insensible, lazy, leaden, lifeless, motionless, nerveless, numb, passive, quiescent, senseless, slack, sleepy, slothful, sluggish, somnolent, static, still, torpid, unmoving, unreacting, unresponsive.
antonyms alive, animated.

inertia *n.* accedia, accidie, apathy, deadness, drowsiness, dullness, idleness, immobility, inactivity, indolence,

insensibility, languor, lassitude, laziness, lethargy, listlessness, nervelessness, numbness, passivity, sleepiness, sloth, sluggishness, somnolence, stillness, stupor, torpor, unresponsiveness.
antonyms activity, liveliness.

inevitable *adj.* assured, automatic, certain, compulsory, decreed, destined, fated, fixed, ineluctable, inescapable, inexorable, irrevocable, mandatory, necessary, obligatory, ordained, settled, sure, unalterable, unavertable, unavoidable, unpreventable, unshunnable.
antonyms alterable, avoidable, uncertain.

inexorable *adj.* adamant, cruel, hard, harsh, immovable, implacable, ineluctable, inescapable, inflexible, intransigent, irreconcilable, irresistible, irrevocable, merciless, obdurate, pitiless, relentless, remorseless, severe, unalterable, unappeasable, unavertable, unbending, uncompromising, unrelenting, unyielding.
antonyms flexible, lenient, yielding.

inexperienced *adj.* amateur, callow, fresh, green, immature, inexpert, innocent, nescient, new, raw, unaccustomed, unacquainted, unbearded, unfamiliar, unpractical, unpracticed, unschooled, unseasoned, unskilled, unsophisticated, untrained, untraveled, untried, unused, unversed, verdant.
antonym experienced.

inexplicable *adj.* baffling, enigmatic, impenetrable, incomprehensible, incredible, inscrutable, insoluble, intractable, miraculous, mysterious, mystifying, puzzling, strange, unaccountable, unexplainable, unfathomable, unintelligible, unsolvable.
antonym explicable.

infallibility *n.* accuracy, dependability, faultlessness, impeccability, inerrancy, inevitability, irrefutability, irreproachability, omniscience, perfection, reliability, safety, supremacy, sureness, trustworthiness, unerringness.
antonym fallibility.

infamous *adj.* abhorrent, abominable, atrocious, base, dastardly, despicable, detestable, discreditable, disgraceful, dishonorable, disreputable, egregious, execrable, facinorous, flagitious, hateful, heinous, ignoble, ignominious, illfamed, iniquitous, knavish, loathsome, monstrous, nefarious, notorious, odious, opprobrious, outrageous, scandalous, scurvy, shameful, shocking, vile, villainous, wicked.
antonym glorious.

infantile *adj.* adolescent, babyish, childish, immature, juvenile, puerile, tender, undeveloped, young, youthful.
antonyms adult, mature.

infatuation *n.* besottedness, crush, dotage, engouement, fascination, fixation, folly, fondness, intoxication, madness, mania, obsession, passion, possession.
antonyms disenchantment, indifference.

infect *v.* affect, blight, canker, contaminate, corrupt, defile, enthuse, influence, inject, inspire, pervert, poison, pollute, taint, touch, vitiate.

infection *n.* contagion, contamination, corruption, defilement, disease, epidemic, illness, inflammation, influence, miasma, pestilence, poison, pollution, sepsis, septicity, taint, virus.

infectious *adj.* catching, communicable, contagious, contaminating, corrupting, deadly, defiling, epidemic, infective, miasmic, miasmous, pestilential, poisoning, poisonous, polluting, spreading, transmissible, transmittable, venemous, virulent, vitiating.

infer *v.* assume, conclude, conjecture, construe, deduce, derive, extract, extrapolate, gather, presume, surmise, understand.

inference *n.* assumption, conclusion, conjecture, consequence, construction, corollary, deduction, extrapolation, illation, interpretation, presumption, reading, surmise.

inferior *adj.* bad, crummy, dog, grotty, humble, imperfect, indifferent, junior, lesser, low, lower, low-grade, mean, mediocre, menial, minor, one-horse, paravail, poor, poorer, provant, schlock, secondary, second-class, secondrate, shoddy, slipshod, slovenly, subordinate, subsidiary, substandard, under, underneath, undistinguished, unsatisfactory, unworthy, worse.
antonym superior.
n. junior, menial, minion, subordinate, underling, understrapper, vassal.
antonym superior.

inferiority *n.* badness, baseness, deficiency, humbleness, imperfection, inadequacy, insignificance, lowliness, meanness, mediocrity, shoddiness, slovenliness, subordination, subservience, unimportance, unworthiness, worthlessness.
antonym superiority.

infernal *adj.* accursed, Acherontic, chthonian, chthonic, damnable, damned, demonic, devilish, diabolical, fiendish, Hadean, hellish, malevolent, malicious, Mephistophelian, Plutonian, satanic, Stygian, Tartarean, underworld.
antonym heavenly.

infiltrator *n.* entr(y)ist, insinuator, intruder, penetrator, seditionary, spy, subversive, subverter.

infinite *adj.* absolute, bottomless, boundless, countless, enormous, eternal, everlasting, fathomless, illimitable, immeasurable, immense, incomputable, inestimable, inexhaustible, interminable, limitless, measureless, never-ending, numberless, perpetual, stupendous, total, unbounded, uncountable, uncounted, unfathomable, untold, vast, wide.
antonym finite.

infinitesimal *adj.* atomic, exiguous, imperceptible, inappreciable, inconsiderable, insignificant, microscopic, minuscule, minute, negligible, paltry, teeny, tiny, unnoticeable, wee.
antonyms significant, substantial.

infirm *adj.* ailing, crippled, debilitated, decrepit, dicky, doddering, doddery, enfeebled, failing, faltering, feeble,

fickle, frail, hesitant, indecisive, insecure, irresolute, lame, poorly, sickly, unreliable, wavering, weak, wobbly.
antonyms healthy, strong.

infirmity *n.* ailment, complaint, debility, decrepitude, defect, deficiency, dickiness, disease, disorder, failing, fault, feebleness, foible, frailty, ill health, illness, imperfection, instability, malady, sickliness, sickness, vulnerability, weakness.
antonyms health, strength.

inflame *v.* aggravate, agitate, anger, arouse, embitter, enkindle, enrage, exacerbate, exasperate, excite, fan, fire, foment, fuel, galvanize, heat, ignite, impassion, incense, increase, infatuate, infuriate, intensify, intoxicate, kindle, madden, provoke, ravish, rile, rouse, stimulate, worsen.
antonyms cool, quench.

inflammation *n.* abscess, burning, empyema, erythema, heat, infection, painfulness, rash, redness, sepsis, septicity, sore, soreness, tenderness.

inflammatory *adj.* anarchic, demagogic, explosive, fiery, incendiary, incitative, inflaming, instigative, insurgent, intemperate, provocative, rabble-rousing, rabid, riotous, seditious.
antonyms calming, pacific.

inflate *v.* aerate, aggrandize, amplify, balloon, bloat, blow out, blow up, bombast, boost, dilate, distend, enlarge, escalate, exaggerate, expand, increase, puff out, puff up, pump up, swell, tumefy.
antonym deflate.

inflexible *adj.* adamant, dyed-in-the-wool, entrenched, fast, firm, fixed, hard, hardened, immovable, immutable, implacable, inelastic, inexorable, intractable, intransigent, iron, non-flexible, obdurate, obstinate, relentless, resolute, rigid, rigorous, set, steadfast, steely, stiff, strict, stringent, stubborn, taut, unaccommodating, unadaptable, unbending, unchangeable, uncompromising, unpliable, unpliant, unsupple, unyielding.
antonym flexible.

inflict *v.* administer, afflict, apply, burden, deal, deliver, enforce, exact, force, impose, lay, levy, mete, perpetrate, visit, wreak.

influence *n.* agency, ascendancy, authority, bias, charisma, clout, connections, control, credit, direction, domination, drag, effect, éminence grise, good offices, guidance, hold, importance, leverage, magnetism, mastery, power, pressure, prestige, pull, reach, rule, scope, spell, standing, strength, string-pulling, sway, teaching, training, weight, wire-pulling.
v. affect, alter, arouse, bias, change, control, direct, dispose, dominate, edge, guide, head, impel, impress, incite, incline, induce, instigate, maneuver, manipulate, modify, motivate, move, persuade, point, predispose, prompt, pull, pull wires, rouse, strings, sway, teach, train, weigh with.

influential *adj.* ascendant, authoritative, charismatic, cogent, compelling, controlling, dominant, dominating, effective, efficacious, forcible, guiding, important, instrumental, leading, momentous, moving, persuasive, potent, powerful, significant, strong, telling, weighty, well-placed.
antonym ineffectual.

inform[1] *v.* acquaint, advise, apprize, brief, clue up, communicate, enlighten, fill in, illuminate, impart, instruct, intimate, leak, notify, teach, tell, tip off, wise up.

inform[2] *v.* animate, characterize, endue, fill, illuminate, imbue, inspire, invest, irradiate, light up, permeate, suffuse, typify.

informal *adj.* approachable, casual, colloquial, congenial, cosy, easy, familiar, free, homely, irregular, natural, relaxed, relaxing, simple, unbuttoned, unceremonious, unconstrained, unofficial, unorthodox, unpretentious, unsolemn.
antonym formal.

informality *n.* approachability, casualness, congeniality, cosiness, ease, familiarity, freedom, homeliness, irregularity, naturalness, relaxation, simplicity, unceremoniousness, unpretentiousness.
antonym formality.

information *n.* advices, blurb, briefing, bulletin, bumf, clues, communiqué, data, databank, database, dope, dossier, enlightenment, facts, gen, illumination, info, input, instruction, intelligence, knowledge, low-down, message, news, notice, report, tidings, word.

informative *adj.* chatty, communicative, constructive, edifying, educational, enlightening, forthcoming, gossipy, illuminating, informatory, instructive, newsy, revealing, revelatory, useful, valuable.
antonym uninformative.

informer *n.* betrayer, canary, denouncer, denunciator, fink, fiz(z)gig, grass, Judas, nark, singer, sneak, snitch(er), snout, squeak, squealer, stool pigeon, stoolie, supergrass.

infrequent *adj.* exceptional, intermittent, occasional, rare, scanty, sparse, spasmodic, sporadic, uncommon, unusual.
antonym frequent.

infringement *n.* breach, contravention, defiance, encroachment, evasion, infraction, intrusion, invasion, non-compliance, non-observance, transgression, trespass, violation.

ingenious *adj.* adroit, bright, brilliant, clever, crafty, creative, cunning, daedal, Daedalian, daedalic, dedalian, deft, dexterous, fertile, Gordian, imaginative, innovative, intricate, inventive, masterly, original, pretty, ready, resourceful, shrewd, skilful, sly, subtle.
antonyms clumsy, unimaginative.

ingenuity *n.* adroitness, cleverness, cunning, deftness, faculty, flair, genius, gift, ingeniousness, innovativeness, invention, inventiveness, knack, originality, resourcefulness, sharpness, shrewdness, skill, slyness, turn.
antonyms clumsiness, dullness.

ingenuous *adj.* artless, candid, childlike, frank, guileless, honest, innocent, naïf, naïve, open, plain, simple, sincere, trustful, trusting, unreserved, unsophisticated, unstudied.
antonyms artful, sly.

ingratiating *adj.* bland, bootlicking, crawling, fawning, flattering, obsequious, servile, smooth-tongued, suave, sycophantic, time-serving, toadying, unctuous, whilly, whillywha(w).

ingratitude *n.* thanklessness, unappreciativeness, ungraciousness, ungratefulness.
antonym gratitude.

ingredient *n.* component, constituent, element, factor, part.

inhabit *v.* abide, bide, dwell, habit, live, lodge, make one's home, occupy, people, populate, possess, reside, settle, settle in, stay, take up one's abode, tenant.

inhabitant *n.* aborigine, autochthon, burgher, citizen, denizen, dweller, habitant, indigene, indweller, inmate, lodger, native, occupant, occupier, resident, residentiary, resider, settler, tenant.

inherent *adj.* basic, characteristic, congenital, connate, essential, fundamental, hereditary, immanent, inborn, inbred, inbuilt, ingrained, inherited, innate, instinctive, intrinsic, inwrought, native, natural.

inheritance *n.* accession, bequest, birthright, descent, heredity, heritage, heritament, legacy, patrimony, succession.

inhibit *v.* arrest, bar, bridle, check, constrain, cramp, curb, debar, discourage, forbid, frustrate, hinder, hold, impede, interfere with, obstruct, prevent, prohibit, repress, restrain, stanch, stem, stop, suppress, thwart.

inhuman *adj.* animal, barbaric, barbarous, bestial, brutal, brutish, callous, cold-blooded, cruel, diabolical, fiendish, heartless, inhumane, insensate, merciless, pitiless, remorseless, ruthless, savage, sublime, unfeeling, vicious.
antonym human.

inimical *adj.* adverse, antagonistic, antipathetic, contrary, destructive, disaffected, harmful, hostile, hurtful, ill-disposed, inhospitable, injurious, intolerant, noxious, opposed, oppugnant, pernicious, repugnant, unfavorable, unfriendly, unwelcoming.
antonyms favorable, friendly, sympathetic.

inimitable *adj.* consummate, distinctive, exceptional, incomparable, matchless, nonpareil, peerless, sublime, superlative, supreme, unequaled, unexampled, unique, unmatched, unparalleled, unrivaled, unsurpassable, unsurpassed.

iniquitous *adj.* abominable, accursed, atrocious, awful, base, criminal, dreadful, evil, facinorous, flagitious, heinous, immoral, infamous, nefarious, nefast, reprehensible, reprobate, sinful, unjust, unrighteous, vicious, wicked.
antonym virtuous.

iniquity *n.* abomination, baseness, crime, enormity, evil, evil-doing, heinousness, impiety, infamy, injustice, misdeed, offence, sin, sinfulness, ungodliness, unrighteousness, vice, viciousness, wickedness, wrong, wrong-doing.
antonym virtue.

initial *adj.* beginning, commencing, early, embryonic, first, formative, inaugural, inauguratory, inceptive, inchoate, incipient, infant, introductory, opening, original, primary.
antonym final.

initiate *v.* activate, actuate, begin, cause, coach, commence, inaugurate, indoctrinate, induce, induct, instate, institute, instruct, introduce, invest, launch, open, originate, prompt, start, stimulate, teach, train.
n. authority, beginner, catechumen, cognoscente, connoisseur, convert, entrant, epopt, expert, insider, learner, member, newcomer, novice, novitiate, probationer, proselyte, recruit, sage, savant, tenderfoot, tiro.

initiative *n.* advantage, ambition, drive, dynamism, energy, enterprise, forcefulness, get-up-and-go, goeyness, innovativeness, inventiveness, lead, move, originality, prompting, push, recommendation, resource, resourcefulness, suggestion.

injure *v.* abuse, aggrieve, blemish, blight, break, cripple, damage, deface, disable, disfigure, disserve, harm, hurt, ill-treat, impair, maim, maltreat, mar, ruin, scathe, spoil, tarnish, undermine, vandalize, vitiate, weaken, wound, wrong.

injurious *adj.* adverse, bad, baneful, calumnious, corrupting, damaging, deleterious, destructive, detrimental, disadvantageous, harmful, hurtful, iniquitous, insulting, libelous, mischievous, noxious, pernicious, prejudicial, ruinous, slanderous, unconducive, unhealthy, unjust, wrongful.
antonyms beneficial, favorable.

injury *n.* abuse, annoyance, damage, damnification, detriment, disservice, evil, grievance, harm, hurt, ill, impairment, injustice, insult, lesion, loss, mischief, noyance, prejudice, ruin, scathe, trauma, vexation, wound, wrong.

injustice *n.* bias, discrimination, disparity, favoritism, imposition, inequality, inequitableness, inequity, iniquity, onesidedness, oppression, partiality, partisanship, prejudice, unevenness, unfairness, unjustness, unlawfulness, unreason, wrong.
antonym justice.

inn *n.* albergo, alehouse, auberge, caravanserai, hostelry, hotel, howff, khan, local, public, public house, roadhouse, saloon, serai, tavern.

innate *adj.* basic, congenital, connate, constitutional, essential, fundamental, immanent, inborn, inbred, ingenerate, ingrained, inherent, inherited, instinctive, intrinsic, intuitive, native, natural.

innocent *adj.* Arcadian, artless, benign, bereft of, blameless, canny, chaste, childlike, clear, credulous, dewy-eyed, faultless, frank, free of, fresh, green, guileless, guiltless, gullible, harmless, honest, immaculate,

impeccable, incorrupt, ingenuous, innocuous, inoffensive, intact, irreproachable, naïve, natural, nescient, open, pristine, pure, righteous, simple, sinless, spotless, stainless, trustful, trusting, unblemished, uncontaminated, unimpeachable, unobjectionable, unoffending, unsullied, unsuspicious, untainted, untouched, unworldly, verdant, virginal, well-intentioned, well-meaning, well-meant.
antonyms experienced, guilty, knowing.
n. babe, babe in arms, beginner, child, greenhorn, infant, ingénu, ingénue, neophyte, tenderfoot.
antonyms connoisseur, expert.

innocuous *adj.* bland, harmless, hypo-allergenic, innocent, innoxious, inoffensive, non-irritant, safe, unimpeachable, unobjectionable.
antonym harmful.

innovative *adj.* adventurous, bold, daring, enterprising, fresh, go-ahead, goey, imaginative, inventive, modernizing, new, on the move, original, progressive, reforming, resourceful, revolutionary.
antonyms conservative, unimaginative.

innuendo *n.* aspersion, hint, implication, imputation, insinuation, intimation, overtone, slant, slur, suggestion, whisper.

inoperative *adj.* broken, broken-down, defective, hors de combat, idle, ineffective, ineffectual, inefficacious, invalid, non-active, non-functioning, nugatory, out of action, out of commission, out of order, out of service, unserviceable, unused, unworkable, useless.
antonym operative.

inopportune *adj.* clumsy, ill-chosen, ill-timed, inappropriate, inauspicious, inconvenient, infelicitous, mal-apropos, mistimed, tactless, unfortunate, unpropitious, unseasonable, unsuitable, untimely, wrong-timed.
antonym opportune.

inquire *v.* ask, catechize, delve, enquire, examine, explore, inspect, interrogate, investigate, look into, probe, query, quest, question, reconnoiter, scout, scrutinize, search, speir.

inquiring *adj.* analytical, curious, doubtful, eager, inquisitive, interested, interrogatory, investigative, investigatory, nosy, outward-looking, probing, prying, questing, questioning, searching, skeptical, wondering, zetetic.
antonym incurious.

inquiry *n.* enquiry, examination, exploration, inquest, interrogation, investigation, perquisition, postmortem, probe, query, question, research, scrutiny, search, study, survey, witch-hunt, zetetic.

inquisitive *adj.* curious, eager, inquiring, intrusive, investigative, meddlesome, nosy, peeping, peering, probing, prying, questing, questioning, snooping, snoopy.
antonym incurious.

insane *adj.* barmy, batty, bizarre, bonkers, brainsick, cracked, crackers, crazed, cuckoo, daft, delirious,

demented, deranged, distracted, disturbed, fatuous, foolish, idiotic, impractical, irrational, irresponsible, loony, loopy, lunatic, mad, manic, mental, mentally ill, non compos mentis, nuts, nutty, preposterous, psychotic, queer, schizoid, schizophrenic, screwy, senseless, stupid, touched, unbalanced, unhinged.
antonym sane.

insanity *n.* aberration, alienation, amentia, brainsickness, brainstorm, craziness, delirium, dementia, derangement, folly, frenzy, infatuation, irresponsibility, lunacy, madness, mania, mental illness, neurosis, preposterousness, psychoneurosis, psychosis, senselessness, stupidity.
antonym sanity.

insatiable *adj.* esurient, gluttonous, greedy, immoderate, incontrollable, inordinate, insatiate, intemperate, persistent, quenchless, rapacious, ravenous, unappeasable, uncurbable, unquenchable, unsatisfiable, voracious.
antonym moderate.

inscrutable *adj.* baffling, blank, cryptic, dead-pan, deep, enigmatic, esoteric, expressionless, hidden, impassive, impenetrable, incomprehensible, inexplicable, mysterious, poker-faced, sphinx-like, undiscoverable, unexplainable, unfathomable, unintelligible, unknowable, unsearchable.
antonyms clear, comprehensible, expressive.

insecure *adj.* afraid, anxious, apprehensive, dangerous, defenseless, diffident, exposed, expugnable, flimsy, frail, hazardous, insubstantial, jerry-built, loose, nervous, perilous, precarious, pregnable, rickety, rocky, shaky, shoogly, uncertain, unconfident, uneasy, unguarded, unprotected, unsafe, unshielded, unsound, unstable, unsteady, unsure, vulnerable, weak, wobbly, worried.
antonyms confident, safe, secure.

insensible[1] *adj.* anesthetized, apathetic, blind, callous, cataleptic, cold, deaf, dull, hard-hearted, impassive, impercipient, impervious, indifferent, inert, insensate, marble, nerveless, numb, numbed, oblivious, senseless, stupid, torpid, unaffected, unaware, unconscious, unfeeling, unmindful, unmoved, unnoticing, unobservant, unresponsive, unsusceptible, untouched.
antonyms conscious, sensible.

insensible[2] *adj.* imperceivable, imperceptible, inappreciable, minuscule, minute, negligible, tiny, unnoticeable.
antonym appreciable.

insensitive *adj.* blunted, callous, crass, dead, hardened, immune, impenetrable, imperceptive, impercipient, impervious, indifferent, insusceptible, obtuse, pachydermatous, proof, resistant, tactless, thick-skinned, tough, unaffected, uncaring, unconcerned, unfeeling, unimpressionable, unmoved, unreactive, unresponsive, unsensitive, unsusceptible.
antonym sensitive.

insight *n.* acumen, acuteness, apprehension, awareness, comprehension, discernment, grasp, ingenuity, intelligence, intuition, intuitiveness, judgment, knowledge, observation, penetration, perception, percipience, perspicacity, sensitivity, shrewdness, understanding, vision, wisdom.

insignificant *adj.* dinky, flimsy, humble, immaterial, inappreciable, inconsequential, inconsiderable, insubstantial, irrelevant, meager, meaningless, Mickey Mouse, minor, negligible, nondescript, nonessential, nugatory, paltry, petty, piddling, scanty, scrub, tiny, trifling, trivial, unimportant, unsubstantial.
antonym significant.

insincere *adj.* artificial, canting, deceitful, deceptive, devious, dishonest, disingenuous, dissembling, dissimulating, double-dealing, duplicitous, evasive, faithless, false, hollow, hypocritical, lip-deep, lying, mendacious, perfidious, phony, pretended, synthetic, two-faced, unfaithful, ungenuine, untrue, untruthful.
antonym sincere.

insinuate *v.* allude, get at, hint, imply, indicate, innuendo, intimate, suggest.

insipid *adj.* anemic, banal, bland, characterless, colorless, dilute, drab, dry, dull, fade, flat, flavorless, insulse, jejune, lash, lifeless, limp, missish, missy, monotonous, pointless, prosaic, prosy, savorless, spiritless, stale, tame, tasteless, trite, unappetizing, unimaginative, uninteresting, unsavory, vapid, watery, weak, wearish, weedy, wishy-washy.
antonyms appetizing, piquant, punchy, tasty.

insist *v.* assert, asseverate, aver, claim, contend, demand, dwell on, emphasize, harp on, hold, maintain, persist, reiterate, repeat, request, require, stand firm, stress, swear, urge, vow.

insolence *n.* abuse, arrogance, assurance, audacity, backchat, boldness, cheek, cheekiness, chutzpah, contemptuousness, contumely, defiance, disrespect, effrontery, forwardness, gall, gum, hubris, impertinence, impudence, incivility, insubordination, lip, malapertness, offensiveness, pertness, presumption, presumptuousness, rudeness, sauce, sauciness.
antonyms politeness, respect.

insolent *adj.* abusive, arrogant, bold, brazen, cheeky, contemptuous, contumelious, defiant, disrespectful, forward, fresh, hubristic, impertinent, impudent, insubordinate, insulting, malapert, pert, presumptuous, rude, saucy, uncivil.
antonyms polite, respectful.

insoluble *adj.* baffling, impenetrable, indecipherable, inexplicable, inextricable, intractable, mysterious, mystifying, obscure, perplexing, unaccountable, unexplainable, unfathomable, unsolvable.
antonym explicable.

insolvent *adj.* bankrupt, broke, bust, defaulting, destitute, failed, flat broke, in queer street, on the rocks, ruined.
antonym solvent.

inspect *v.* audit, check, examine, give the once-over, investigate, look over, oversee, peruse, reconnoiter, scan, scrutinize, search, study, superintend, supervise, survey, vet, visit.

inspection *n.* audit, autopsy, check, check-up, examination, investigation, once-over, post-mortem, reconnaissance, review, scan, scrutiny, search, superintendence, supervision, surveillance, survey, vidimus, visitation.

inspiration *n.* afflation, afflatus, Aganippe, arousal, awakening, brainstorm, brain-wave, creativity, elevation, encouragement, enthusiasm, estro, exaltation, genius, Hippocrene, illumination, influence, insight, muse, Muse, revelation, spur, stimulation, stimulus, Svengali, taghairm.

inspire *v.* activate, animate, arouse, encourage, enkindle, enliven, enthuse, excite, fill, galvanize, hearten, imbue, influence, infuse, inhale, inspirit, instil, motivate, produce, quicken, spark off, spur, stimulate, stir, trigger.

inspiring *adj.* affecting, emboldening, encouraging, exciting, exhilarating, heartening, inspiriting, invigorating, moving, rousing, stimulating, stirring, uplifting.
antonyms dull, uninspiring.

instal(l) *v.* consecrate, ensconce, establish, fix, inaugurate, induct, instate, institute, introduce, invest, lay, locate, lodge, ordain, place, plant, position, put, set, set up, settle, site, situate, station.

installation *n.* base, consecration, equipment, establishment, fitting, inauguration, induction, instalment, instatement, investiture, location, machinery, ordination, placing, plant, positioning, post, siting, station, system.

instance[1] *n.* case, case in point, citation, example, illustration, occasion, occurrence, precedent, sample, situation, time.
v. adduce, cite, mention, name, point to, quote, refer to, specify.

instance[2] *n.* advice, application, behest, demand, entreaty, exhortation, importunity, impulse, incitement, initiative, insistence, instigation, pressure, prompting, request, solicitation, urging.

instant *n.* flash, jiffy, juncture, minute, mo, moment, occasion, point, second, shake, split second, tick, time, trice, twinkling, two shakes.
adj. convenience, direct, fast, immediate, instantaneous, on-the-spot, precooked, prompt, quick, rapid, ready-mixed, split-second, unhesitating, urgent.

instantaneous *adj.* direct, immediate, instant, on-the-spot, prompt, rapid, unhesitating.
antonym eventual.

instantly *adv.* at once, directly, forthwith, immediately, instantaneously, now, on the spot, pronto, quicksticks, right away, straight away, there and then, tout de suite, without delay.
antonym eventually.

instigate *v.* actuate, cause, encourage, excite, foment, generate, impel, incite, influence, initiate, inspire, kindle, move, persuade, prompt, provoke, rouse, set on, spur, start, stimulate, stir up, urge, whip up.

instinct *n.* ability, aptitude, faculty, feel, feeling, flair, gift, gut feeling, gut reaction, id, impulse, intuition, knack, nose, predisposition, proclivity, sixth sense, talent, tendency, urge.

instinctive *adj.* automatic, gut, immediate, impulsive, inborn, inherent, innate, instinctual, intuitional, intuitive, involuntary, mechanical, native, natural, reflex, spontaneous, unlearned, unpremeditated, unthinking, visceral.

antonyms conscious, deliberate, voluntary.

institute[1] *v.* appoint, begin, commence, constitute, create, enact, establish, fix, found, inaugurate, induct, initiate, install, introduce, invest, launch, open, ordain, organize, originate, pioneer, set up, settle, start.

antonyms abolish, cancel, discontinue.

institute[2] *n.* custom, decree, doctrine, dogma, edict, firman, indiction, irade, law, maxim, precedent, precept, principle, regulation, rescript, rule, tenet, ukase.

institute[3] *n.* academy, association, college, conservatory, foundation, guild, institution, organization, poly, polytechnic, school, seminary, society.

instruct *v.* acquaint, advise, apprize, bid, brief, catechize, charge, coach, command, counsel, direct, discipline, drill, educate, enjoin, enlighten, ground, guide, inform, mandate, notify, order, school, teach, tell, train, tutor.

instruction *n.* apprenticeship, briefing, catechesis, catechizing, coaching, command, direction, directive, discipline, drilling, education, enlightenment, grounding, guidance, information, injunction, lesson(s), mandate, order, preparation, ruling, schooling, teaching, training, tuition, tutelage.

instructions *n.* advice, book of words, commands, directions, guidance, handbook, information, key, legend, orders, recommendations, rules.

instrument *n.* agency, agent, apparatus, appliance, cat'spaw, channel, contraption, contrivance, device, doodad, dupe, factor, force, gadget, implement, means, mechanism, medium, organ, pawn, puppet, tool, utensil, vehicle, way, widget.

insubordinate *adj.* contumacious, defiant, disobedient, disorderly, fractious, impertinent, impudent, insurgent, mutinous, rebellious, recalcitrant, refractory, riotous, rude, seditious, turbulent, undisciplined, ungovernable, unruly.

antonyms docile, obedient.

insubstantial *adj.* chimerical, ephemeral, false, fanciful, feeble, flimsy, frail, idle, illusory, imaginary, immaterial, incorporeal, moonshine, poor, slight, tenuous, thin, unreal, vaporous, weak, windy, yeasty.

antonyms real, strong.

insufficient *adj.* deficient, inadequate, incapable, incommensurate, lacking, scanty, scarce, short, sparse, wanting.

antonyms excessive, sufficient.

insulation *n.* cushioning, deadening, deafening, padding, protection, stuffing.

insult *v.* abuse, affront, call names, fling/throw mud at, give offence to, injure, libel, miscall, offend, outrage, revile, slag, slander, slight, snub, vilify, vilipend.

antonyms compliment, honor.

n. abuse, affront, aspersion, contumely, indignity, insolence, libel, offence, outrage, rudeness, slander, slap in the face, slight, snub.

antonyms compliment, honor.

insulting *adj.* abusive, affronting, contemptuous, degrading, disparaging, insolent, libelous, offensive, rude, scurrilous, slanderous, slighting.

antonyms complimentary, respectful.

insurance *n.* assurance, cover, coverage, guarantee, indemnification, indemnity, policy, premium, protection, provision, safeguard, security, warranty.

insure *v.* assure, cover, guarantee, indemnify, protect, underwrite, warrant.

intact *adj.* all in one piece, complete, entire, inviolate, perfect, scatheless, sound, together, unbroken, undamaged, undefiled, unharmed, unhurt, unimpaired, uninjured, unscathed, untouched, unviolated, virgin, whole.

antonyms broken, damaged, harmed.

integrated *adj.* cohesive, concordant, connected, desegregated, harmonious, interrelated, part and parcel, unified, unsegregated, unseparated.

antonym unintegrated.

integration *n.* amalgamation, assimilation, blending, combining, commingling, desegregation, fusing, harmony, incorporation, mixing, unification.

antonym separation.

integrity *n.* candor, coherence, cohesion, completeness, entireness, goodness, honesty, honor, incorruptibility, principle, probity, purity, rectitude, righteousness, soundness, unity, uprightness, virtue, wholeness.

antonyms dishonesty, incompleteness, unreliability.

intellect *n.* brain, brain power, brains, egghead, genius, highbrow, intellectual, intelligence, judgment, mind, nous, reason, sense, thinker, understanding.

antonym dunce.

intellectual *adj.* bookish, cerebral, deep-browed, discursive, highbrow, intelligent, mental, noetic, rational, scholarly, studious, thoughtful.

antonym low-brow.

n. academic, egghead, headpiece, highbrow, mastermind, thinker.

antonym low-brow.

intelligence *n.* acuity, acumen, advice, alertness, aptitude, brain power, brains, brightness, capacity, cleverness, comprehension, data, discernment, disclosure, facts, findings, gen, gray matter, information, intellect, intellectuality, knowledge, low-down, mind, news, notice, notification, nous, penetration, perception,

quickness, reason, report, rumor, tidings, tip-off, understanding, word.
antonym foolishness.

intelligent *adj.* acute, alert, apt, brainy, bright, clever, deep-browed, discerning, enlightened, instructed, knowing, penetrating, perspicacious, quick, quick-witted, rational, razor-sharp, sharp, smart, thinking, well-informed.
antonyms foolish, unintelligent.

intend *v.* aim, consign, contemplate, design, destine, determine, earmark, have a mind, mark out, mean, meditate, plan, project, propose, purpose, scheme, set apart.

intense *adj.* acute, agonizing, ardent, burning, close, concentrated, consuming, eager, earnest, energetic, fanatical, fervent, fervid, fierce, forceful, forcible, great, harsh, heightened, impassioned, intensive, keen, passionate, powerful, profound, severe, strained, strong, vehement.
antonyms apathetic, mild.

intensify *v.* add to, aggravate, boost, concentrate, deepen, emphasize, enhance, escalate, exacerbate, fire, fuel, heighten, hot up, increase, magnify, quicken, redouble, reinforce, sharpen, step up, strengthen, whet, whip up.
antonyms damp down, die down.

intensity *n.* accent, ardor, concentration, depth, earnestness, emotion, energy, excess, extremity, fanaticism, fervency, fervor, fierceness, fire, force, intenseness, keenness, passion, potency, power, severity, strain, strength, tension, vehemence, vigor, voltage.

intent *adj.* absorbed, alert, attentive, bent, committed, concentrated, concentrating, determined, eager, earnest, engrossed, fixed, hell-bent, industrious, intense, mindful, occupied, piercing, preoccupied, rapt, resolute, resolved, set, steadfast, steady, watchful, wrapped up.
antonyms absent-minded, distracted.
n. aim, design, end, goal, intention, meaning, object, objective, plan, purpose.

intention *n.* aim, concept, design, end, end in view, goal, idea, intent, meaning, object, objective, plan, point, purpose, scope, target, view.

intentional *adj.* calculated, deliberate, designed, intended, meant, planned, prearranged, preconcerted, premeditated, purposed, studied, wilful.
antonym accidental.

intentionally *adv.* by design, deliberately, designedly, meaningly, on purpose, wilfully, with malice aforethought.
antonym accidentally.

intercept *v.* arrest, block, catch, check, cut off, deflect, delay, frustrate, head off, impede, interrupt, obstruct, retard, seize, stop, take, thwart.

intercourse[1] *n.* association, commerce, communication, communion, congress, connection, contact, conversation, converse, correspondence, dealings, intercommunication, traffic, truck.

intercourse[2] *n.* carnal knowledge, coition, coitus, copulation, embraces, intimacy, love-making, sex, sexual relations, venery.

interest *n.* activity, advantage, affair, affection, attention, attentiveness, attraction, authority, bag, benefit, business, care, claim, commitment, concern, consequence, curiosity, diversion, finger, gain, good, hobby, importance, influence, investment, involvement, line of country, matter, moment, note, notice, participation, pastime, portion, preoccupation, profit, pursuit, regard, relaxation, relevance, right, share, significance, stake, study, suspicion, sympathy, weight.
antonyms boredom, irrelevance.
v. affect, amuse, attract, concern, divert, engage, engross, fascinate, intrigue, involve, move, touch, warm.
antonym bore.

interested *adj.* affected, attentive, attracted, biased, concerned, curious, drawn, engrossed, fascinated, implicated, intent, involved, keen, partisan, predisposed, prejudiced, responsive, simulated.
antonyms apathetic, indifferent, unaffected.

interesting *adj.* absorbing, amusing, amusive, appealing, attractive, compelling, curious, engaging, engrossing, entertaining, gripping, intriguing, provocative, stimulating, thought-provoking, unusual, viewable, visitable.
antonym boring.

interfere *v.* block, butt in, clash, collide, conflict, cramp, frustrate, hamper, handicap, hinder, impede, inhibit, interlope, intermeddle, interpose, intervene, intrude, meddle, obstruct, poke one's nose in, stick one's oar in, tamper, trammel.
antonyms assist, forbear.

interference *n.* clashing, collision, conflict, do-goodery, do-goodism, impedance, intervention, intrusion, meddlesomeness, meddling, mush, obstruction, opposition, prying, statics, white noise.
antonyms assistance, forbearance.

interior *adj.* central, domestic, hidden, home, inland, inly, inner, inside, internal, intimate, inward, mental, pectoral, personal, private, remote, secret, spiritual, up-country.
antonyms exterior, external.
n. bowels, center, core, heart, heartland, hinterland, inside, up-country.

interject *v.* call, cry, exclaim, interjaculate, interpolate, interpose, interrupt, introduce, shout.

interlude *n.* break, breathing-space, breathing-time, breathing-while, delay, episode, halt, hiatus, intermission, interval, pause, respite, rest, spell, stop, stoppage, wait.

intermediate *adj.* halfway, in-between, intermediary, interposed, intervening, mean, medial, median, mid, middle, midway, transitional.
antonym extreme.

interminable *adj.* boundless, ceaseless, dragging, endless, everlasting, immeasurable, infinite, limitless, long, long-drawn-out, long-winded, never-ending, perpetual, prolix, protracted, unbounded, unlimited, wearisome. *antonym* limited.

intermittent *adj.* broken, discontinuous, fitful, irregular, occasional, periodic, periodical, punctuated, recurrent, recurring, remittent, spasmodic, sporadic, stop-go. *antonym* continuous.

internal *adj.* domestic, in-house, inner, inside, interior, intimate, inward, private, subjective. *antonym* external.

interpose *v.* come between, insert, intercede, interfere, interjaculate, interject, interrupt, intervene, introduce, intrude, mediate, offer, place between, step in, thrust in. *antonym* forbear.

interpret *v.* adapt, clarify, construe, decipher, decode, define, elucidate, explain, explicate, expound, paraphrase, read, render, solve, take, throw light on, translate, understand, unfold.

interpretation *n.* anagoge, anagogy, analysis, clarification, construction, diagnosis, elucidation, exegesis, explanation, explication, exposition, meaning, performance, portrayal, reading, rendering, rendition, sense, signification, translation, understanding, version.

interrogate *v.* ask, catechize, cross-examine, cross-question, debrief, enquire, examine, give (someone) the third degree, grill, inquire, investigate, pump, question, quiz.

interrupt *v.* barge in, break, break in, break off, butt in, check, cut, cut off, cut short, delay, disconnect, discontinue, disjoin, disturb, disunite, divide, heckle, hinder, hold up, interfere, interjaculate, interject, intrude, obstruct, punctuate, separate, sever, stay, stop, suspend. *antonym* forbear.

interruption *n.* break, cessation, disconnection, discontinuance, disruption, dissolution, disturbance, disuniting, division, halt, hiatus, hindrance, hitch, impediment, intrusion, obstacle, obstruction, pause, separation, severance, stop, stoppage, suspension.

interval *n.* break, delay, distance, entr'acte, gap, hiatus, inbetween, interim, interlude, intermission, interspace, interstice, meantime, meanwhile, opening, pause, period, playtime, rest, season, space, spell, term, time, wait.

intervene *v.* arbitrate, befall, ensue, happen, intercede, interfere, interpose oneself, interrupt, intrude, involve, mediate, occur, step in, succeed, supervene, take a hand.

interview *n.* audience, conference, consultation, dialogue, enquiry, evaluation, inquisition, meeting, oral, oral examination, press conference, talk, viva.
v. examine, interrogate, question, viva.

intimacy *n.* brotherliness, closeness, coition, coitus, confidence, confidentiality, copulating, copulation, familiarity, fornication, fraternization, friendship, intercourse, sexual intercourse, sisterliness, understanding.

intimate[1] *v.* allude, announce, communicate, declare, hint, impart, imply, indicate, insinuate, state, suggest, tell.

intimate[2] *adj.* as thick as thieves, bosom, cherished, close, confidential, cosy, dear, deep, deep-seated, detailed, exhaustive, friendly, gremial, informal, innermost, internal, near, palsy-walsy, penetrating, personal, private, privy, profound, secret, warm. *antonyms* cold, distant, unfriendly.
n. Achates, associate, bosom buddy, buddy, china, chum, comrade, confidant, confidante, crony, familiar, friend, mate, mucker, pal, repository. *antonym* stranger.

intimation *n.* allusion, announcement, communication, declaration, hint, indication, inkling, insinuation, notice, reminder, statement, suggestion, warning.

intimidate *v.* alarm, appal, browbeat, bulldoze, bully, coerce, cow, daunt, dishearten, dismay, dispirit, frighten, lean on, overawe, psych out, put the frighteners on, scare, subdue, terrify, terrorize, threaten. *antonym* persuade.

intolerant *adj.* bigoted, chauvinistic, dictatorial, dogmatic, fanatical, illiberal, impatient, narrow, narrow-minded, opinionated, opinionative, opinioned, persecuting, prejudiced, racialist, racist, small-minded, uncharitable. *antonym* tolerant.

intoxicated *adj.* blotto, canned, cut, disguised in liquor, dizzy, drunk, drunken, ebriate, ebriated, ebriose, elated, enraptured, euphoric, excited, exhilarated, fuddled, glorious, half seas over, high, in one's cups, incapable, inebriate, inebriated, infatuated, legless, lit up, looped, pickled, pissed, pixil(l)ated, plastered, sent, sloshed, smashed, sozzled, stewed, stiff, stimulated, stoned, stotious, three sheets in the wind, tight, tipsy, under the influence, up the pole, zonked. *antonym* sober.

intransigent *adj.* hardline, immovable, intractable, irreconcilable, obdurate, obstinate, stubborn, tenacious, tough, unamenable, unbending, unbudgeable, uncompromising, unpersuadable, unyielding, uppity. *antonym* amenable.

intrepid *adj.* audacious, bold, brave, courageous, daring, dashing, dauntless, doughty, fearless, gallant, game, gutsy, heroic, lion-hearted, nerveless, plucky, resolute, stalwart, stout-hearted, unafraid, undashed, undaunted, unflinching, valiant, valorous. *antonyms* cowardly, timid.

intricate *adj.* Byzantine, complex, complicated, convoluted, daedal(e), Daedalian, daedalic, dedal, dedalian, difficult, elaborate, entangled, fancy, Gordian, involved, knotty, labyrinthine, perplexing, rococo, sophisticated, tangled, tortuous. *antonym* simple.

intrigue[1] *v.* attract, charm, fascinate, interest, puzzle, rivet, tantalize, tickle one's fancy, titillate.
antonym bore.

intrigue[2] *n.* affair, amour, brigue, cabal, chicanery, collusion, conspiracy, double-dealing, intimacy, knavery, liaison, machination, machination(s), maneuver, manipulation, plot, romance, ruse, scheme, sharp practice, stratagem, string-pulling, trickery, wheeler-dealing, wile, wire-pulling.
v. connive, conspire, machinate, maneuver, plot, scheme.

intrinsic *adj.* basic, basically, built-in, central, congenital, constitutional, constitutionally, elemental, essential, essentially, fundamental, fundamentally, genuine, inborn, inbred, inherent, intrinsically, inward, native, natural, underlying.
antonym extrinsic.

introduce *v.* acquaint, add, advance, air, announce, begin, bring in, bring up, broach, commence, conduct, establish, familiarize, found, inaugurate, initiate, inject, insert, institute, interpolate, interpose, launch, lead in, lead into, moot, offer, open, organize, pioneer, preface, present, propose, put forward, put in, recommend, set forth, start, submit, suggest, throw in, ventilate.
antonym take away.

introduction *n.* addition, baptism, commencement, debut, establishment, exordium, foreword, inauguration, induction, initiation, insertion, institution, interpolation, intro, launch, lead-in, opening, overture, pioneering, preamble, preface, preliminaries, prelude, presentation, prodrome, prodromus, proem, prolegomena, prolegomenon, prologue, prooemion, prooemium.
antonym withdrawal.
vation, soul-searching.

introverted *adj.* indrawn, intervertive, introspective, introversive, inward-looking, self-centered, self-contained, withdrawn.
antonym extroverted.

intrude *v.* aggress, butt in, encroach, infringe, interfere, interrupt, meddle, obtrude, trespass, violate.
antonyms stand back, withdraw.

intruder *n.* burglar, gate-crasher, infiltrator, interloper, invader, prowler, raider, snooper, trespasser.

intuition *n.* discernment, feeling, gut feeling, hunch, insight, instinct, perception, presentiment, sixth sense.
antonym reasoning.

invade *v.* assail, assault, attack, burst in, come upon, descend upon, encroach, enter, fall upon, infest, infringe, irrupt, occupy, overrun, overspread, penetrate, pervade, raid, rush into, seize, swarm over, violate.
antonym withdraw.

invalid[1] *adj.* ailing, bedridden, disabled, feeble, frail, ill, infirm, invalidish, poorly, sick, sickly, valetudinarian, valetudinary, weak.
antonym healthy.

n. case, convalescent, patient, sufferer, valetudinarian, valetudinary.

invalid[2] *adj.* baseless, fallacious, false, ill-founded, illogical, incorrect, inoperative, irrational, nugatory, null, null and void, unfounded, unscientific, unsound, untrue, void, worthless.
antonym valid.

invalidate *v.* abrogate, annul, cancel, nullify, overrule, overthrow, quash, rescind, undermine, undo, vitiate, weaken.
antonym validate.

invaluable *adj.* costly, exquisite, inestimable, precious, priceless, valuable.
antonym worthless.

invariable *adj.* changeless, consistent, constant, fixed, immutable, inflexible, permanent, regular, rigid, set, static, unalterable, unchangeable, unchanging, unfailing, uniform, unvarying, unwavering.
antonym variable.

invasion *n.* aggression, assault, attack, breach, encroachment, foray, incursion, infiltration, infraction, infringement, inroad, intrusion, irruption, offensive, onslaught, raid, seizure, usurpation, violation.
antonym withdrawal.

invective *n.* abuse, berating, castigation, censure, contumely, denunciation, diatribe, flyting, obloquy, philippic, philippic(s), reproach, revilement, sarcasm, scolding, tirade, tongue-lashing, vilification, vituperation.
antonym praise.

invent *v.* coin, conceive, concoct, contrive, cook up, create, design, devise, discover, dream up, fabricate, formulate, frame, imagine, improvise, make up, originate, think up, trump up.

invention *n.* brainchild, coinage, contraption, contrivance, contrivement, creation, creativeness, creativity, deceit, design, development, device, discovery, excogitation, fabrication, fake, falsehood, fantasy, fib, fiction, figment of (someone's) imagination, forgery, gadget, genius, imagination, ingenuity, inspiration, inventiveness, inveracity, lie, originality, prevarication, resourcefulness, sham, story, tall story, untruth, yarn.
antonym truth.

inventive *adj.* creative, daedal(e), Daedalian, daedalic, dedal, excogitative, fertile, gifted, imaginative, ingenious, innovative, inspired, original, resourceful.
antonym uninventive.

inventor *n.* architect, author, builder, coiner, creator, designer, father, framer, inventress, maker, originator.

inventory *n.* account, catalog, equipment, file, list, listing, record, register, roll, roster, schedule, stock.

invert *v.* capsize, introvert, inverse, overturn, reverse, transpose, turn turtle, turn upside down, upset, upturn.
antonym right.

invest *v.* adopt, advance, authorize, charge, consecrate, devote, empower, endow, endue, enthrone, establish, inaugurate, induct, install, lay out, license, ordain, provide, put in, sanction, sink, spend, supply, vest. *antonym* divest.

investigate *v.* consider, enquire into, examine, explore, go into, inspect, look into, probe, scrutinize, search, see how the land lies, sift, study, suss out.

investigation *n.* analysis, enquiry, examination, exploration, fact finding, hearing, inquest, inquiry, inspection, probe, research, review, scrutiny, search, study, survey, witch-hunt, zetetic.

investment *n.* ante, asset, besieging, blockade, contribution, investing, investiture, siege, speculation, stake, transaction, venture.

invidious *adj.* discriminating, discriminatory, hateful, objectionable, obnoxious, odious, offensive, repugnant, slighting, undesirable. *antonym* desirable.

invigorating *adj.* bracing, energizing, exhilarating, fresh, generous, healthful, inspiriting, refreshing, rejuvenating, rejuvenative, restorative, salubrious, stimulating, tonic, uplifting, vivifying. *antonyms* disheartening, wearying.

invincible *adj.* impenetrable, impregnable, indestructible, indomitable, inseparable, insuperable, invulnerable, irreducible, unassailable, unbeatable, unconquerable, unreducible, unsurmountable, unyielding. *antonym* beatable.

invisible *adj.* concealed, disguised, hidden, imperceptible, inappreciable, inconspicuous, indetectable, indiscernible, infinitesimal, microscopic, out of sight, unperceivable, unseeable, unseen. *antonym* visible.

invite *v.* allure, ask, ask for, attract, beckon, beg, bid, bring on, call, court, draw, encourage, entice, lead, provoke, request, seek, solicit, summon, tempt, welcome. *antonyms* force, order.

inviting *adj.* alluring, appealing, appetizing, attractive, beguiling, captivating, delightful, engaging, enticing, fascinating, intriguing, magnetic, mouthwatering, pleasing, seductive, tantalizing, tempting, warm, welcoming, winning. *antonym* uninviting.

involuntary *adj.* automatic, blind, compulsory, conditioned, forced, instinctive, instinctual, obligatory, reflex, reluctant, spontaneous, unconscious, uncontrolled, unintentional, unthinking, unwilled, unwilling, vegetative. *antonym* voluntary.

involve *v.* absorb, affect, associate, bind, commit, comprehend, comprise, compromise, concern, connect, contain, cover, draw in, embrace, engage, engross, entail, grip, hold, implicate, imply, include, incorporate, incriminate, inculpate, mean, mix up, necessitate, number among, preoccupy, presuppose, require, rivet, take in, touch.

involved *adj.* anfractuous, caught up/in, complex,

complicated, concerned, confusing, convoluted, difficult, elaborate, implicated, in on, intricate, knotty, labyrinthine, mixed up in/with, occupied, participating, sophisticated, tangled, tortuous. *antonyms* simple, uninvolved.

invulnerable *adj.* impenetrable, indestructible, insusceptible, invincible, proof against, safe, secure, unassailable, unwoundable. *antonym* vulnerable.

inward *adj.* confidential, entering, hidden, inbound, incoming, inflowing, ingoing, inly, inmost, inner, innermost, inpouring, inside, interior, internal, penetrating, personal, private, privy, secret. *antonyms* external, outward.

inwardly *adv.* at heart, deep down, in gremio, in pectore, in petto, inly, inside, privately, secretly, to oneself, within. *antonyms* externally, outwardly.

irate *adj.* angered, angry, annoyed, enraged, exasperated, fuming, furibund, furious, gusty, in a paddy, incensed, indignant, infuriated, ireful, irritated, livid, mad, piqued, provoked, riled, up in arms, waxy, worked up, wrathful, wroth. *antonym* calm.

ire *n.* anger, annoyance, choler, displeasure, exasperation, fury, indignation, passion, rage, wax, wrath. *antonym* calmness.

irk *v.* aggravate, annoy, bug, disgust, distress, gall, get, get to, irritate, miff, nettle, peeve, provoke, put out, rile, rub up the wrong way, ruffle, vex, weary. *antonym* please.

irksome *adj.* aggravating, annoying, boring, bothersome, burdensome, disagreeable, exasperating, infuriating, irritating, tedious, tiresome, troublesome, vexatious, vexing, wearisome. *antonym* pleasing.

ironic *adj.* contemptuous, derisive, incongruous, ironical, irrisory, mocking, paradoxical, sarcastic, sardonic, satirical, scoffing, scornful, sneering, wry.

irrational *adj.* aberrant, absurd, alogical, brainless, crazy, demented, foolish, illogical, injudicious, insane, mindless, muddle-headed, nonsensical, preposterous, raving, senseless, silly, unreasonable, unreasoning, unsound, unstable, unthinking, unwise, wild. *antonym* rational.

irreconcilable *adj.* clashing, conflicting, hardline, implacable, incompatible, incongruous, inconsistent, inexorable, inflexible, intransigent, opposed, unappeasable, uncompromising, unreconcilable. *antonym* reconcilable.

irregular *adj.* abnormal, anomalistic(al), anomalous, asymmetrical, broken, bumpy, capricious, craggy, crooked, difform, disconnected, disorderly, eccentric, erratic, exceptional, extraordinary, extravagant, fitful, fluctuating, fragmentary, haphazard, holey, immoderate, improper, inappropriate, incondite, inordinate,

intermittent, jagged, lopsided, lumpy, occasional, odd, patchy, peculiar, pitted, queer, quirky, ragged, random, rough, serrated, shifting, snatchy, spasmodic, sporadic, uncertain, unconventional, unequal, uneven, unofficial, unorthodox, unprocedural, unpunctual, unsteady, unsuitable, unsymmetrical, unsystematic, unusual, variable, wavering.
antonyms conventional, regular, smooth.

irregularity *n.* abberation, abnormality, anomaly, asymmetry, breach, bumpiness, confusion, crookedness, desultoriness, deviation, difformity, disorderliness, disorganization, eccentricity, freak, haphazardness, heterodoxy, jaggedness, lop-sidedness, lumpiness, malfunction, malpractice, oddity, patchiness, peculiarity, raggedness, randomness, roughness, singularity, uncertainty, unconventionality, unevenness, unorthodoxy, unpunctuality, unsteadiness.
antonyms conventionality, regularity, smoothness.

irrelevant *adj.* alien, extraneous, foreign, immaterial, impertinent, inapplicable, inapposite, inappropriate, inapt, inconsequent, inessential, peripheral, tangential, unapt, unconnected, unnecessary, unrelated.
antonym relevant.

irrepressible *adj.* boisterous, bubbling over, buoyant, ebullient, effervescent, inextinguishable, insuppressible, resilient, uncontainable, uncontrollable, ungovernable, uninhibited, unmanageable, unquenchable, unrestrainable, unstoppable.
antonyms depressed, depressive, despondent, resistible.

irresistible *adj.* alluring, beckoning, beguiling, charming, compelling, enchanting, fascinating, imperative, ineluctable, inescapable, inevitable, inexorable, overmastering, overpowering, overwhelming, potent, pressing, ravishing, resistless, seductive, tempting, unavoidable, uncontrollable, urgent. *antonyms* avoidable, resistible.

irresolute *adj.* dithering, doubtful, faint-hearted, fickle, fluctuating, half-hearted, hesitant, hesitating, indecisive, infirm, shifting, shilly-shallying, swithering, tentative, undecided, undetermined, unsettled, unstable, unsteady, vacillating, variable, wavering, weak.
antonym resolute.

irresponsible *adj.* carefree, careless, feather-brained, feckless, flibbertigibbit, flighty, foot-loose, giddy, harebrained, harum-scarum, heedless, ill-considered, immature, lighthearted, madcap, negligent, rash, reckless, scatter-brained, shiftless, thoughtless, undependable, unreliable, untrustworthy, wild.
antonym responsible.

irreverent *adj.* blasphemous, cheeky, contemptuous, derisive, discourteous, disrespectful, flip, flippant, godless, iconoclastic, impertinent, impious, impudent, mocking, profane, rude, sacrilegious, saucy, tongue-in-cheek.
antonym reverent.

irrevocable *adj.* changeless, fated, fixed, hopeless, immutable, inexorable, invariable, irremediable, irrepealable, irretrievable, irreversible, predestined, predetermined, settled, unalterable, unchangeable.
antonyms alterable, flexible, mutable, reversible.

irritable *adj.* bad-tempered, cantankerous, captious, choleric, crabbed, crabby, cross, crotchety, crusty, edgy, feisty, fractious, fretful, hasty, hypersensitive, ill-humored, ill-tempered, impatient, irascible, narky, peevish, petulant, prickly, querulous, short, short-tempered, snappish, snappy, snarling, sore, tense, testy, te(t)chy, thin-skinned, touchy.
antonyms cheerful, complacent.

irritant *n.* annoyance, bore, bother, goad, menace, nuisance, pain, pest, pin-prick, plague, provocation, rankle, tease, thorn in the flesh, trouble, vexation.
antonyms pleasure, sop, sweetness.

irritate *v.* acerbate, aggravate, anger, annoy, bedevil, bother, bug, chafe, emboil, enrage, exacerbate, exasperate, faze, fret, get on one's nerves, get to, give the pip, gravel, grig, harass, incense, inflame, infuriate, intensify, irk, needle, nettle, offend, pain, peeve, pester, pique, provoke, put out, rankle, rile, rouse, rub, ruffle, vex.
antonyms gratify, mollify, placate, please.

irritation *n.* aggravation, anger, annoyance, crossness, displeasure, dissatisfaction, exasperation, fury, goad, impatience, indignation, irritability, irritant, nuisance, pain, pain in the neck, pest, pin-prick, provocation, rankle, resentment, shortness, snappiness, tease, testiness, vexation, wrath.
antonyms pleasure, satisfaction.

isolate *v.* abstract, cut off, detach, disconnect, divorce, exclude, identify, insulate, keep apart, ostracize, pinpoint, quarantine, remove, seclude, segregate, separate, sequester, set apart.
antonyms assimilate, incorporate.

isolated *adj.* abnormal, anomalous, atypical, backwoods, deserted, detached, dissociated, eremitic, exceptional, freak, godforsaken, hermitical, hidden, incommunicado, insular, lonely, monastic, outlying, out-of-the-way, random, reclusive, remote, retired, secluded, single, solitary, special, sporadic, unfrequented, unique, unrelated, untrodden, untypical, unusual, unvisited.
antonyms populous, typical.

isolation *n.* aloofness, detachment, disconnection, dissociation, exile, insularity, insulation, lazaretto, loneliness, quarantine, reclusion, remoteness, retirement, seclusion, segregation, self-sufficiency, separation, solitariness, solitude, withdrawal.

issue[1] *n.* affair, argument, concern, controversy, crux, debate, matter, point, problem, question, subject, topic.

issue[2] *n.* announcement, broadcast, circulation, copy, delivery, dispersal, dissemination, distribution, edition, emanation, flow, granting, handout, impression, instalment, issuance, issuing, number, printing, promulgation, propagation, publication, release, supply, supplying, vent.

v. announce, broadcast, circulate, deal out, deliver, distribute, emit, give out, mint, produce, promulgate, publicize, publish, put out, release, supply.

issue[3] *n.* conclusion, consequence, culmination, dénouement, effect, end, finale, outcome, pay-off, product, result, termination, upshot.

v. arise, burst forth, debouch, emanate, emerge, flow, leak, originate, proceed, rise, spring, stem.

issue[4] *n.* brood, children, descendants, heirs, offspring, progeny, scions, seed, young.

itemize *v.* count, detail, document, enumerate, instance, inventory, list, mention, number, overname, particularize, record, specify, tabulate.

itinerant *adj.* ambulatory, drifting, journeying, migratory, nomadic, peregrinatory, peripatetic, rambling, roaming, rootless, roving, traveling, vagabond, vagrant, wandering, wayfaring.

antonyms settled, stationary.

n. diddicoy, dusty-foot, gypsy, hobo, nomad, perigrinator, peripatetic, piepowder, pilgrim, Romany, tinker, toe-rag, tramp, traveler, vagabond, vagrant, wanderer, wayfarer.

itinerary *n.* circuit, course, journey, line, plan, program, route, schedule, tour.

J

jab v. dig, elbow, jag, lunge, nudge, poke, prod, punch, push, shove, stab, tap, thrust.

jabber v. babble, blather, blether, chatter, drivel, gab, gabble, gash, jaw, mumble, prate, rabbit, ramble, tattle, witter, yap.

jacket n. blouson, case, casing, coat, cover, covering, envelope, folder, jerkin, jupon, mackinaw, sheath, shell, skin, wrap, wrapper, wrapping.

jackpot n. award, big time, bonanza, kitty, pool, pot, prize, reward, stakes, winnings.

jade n. baggage, broad, draggle-tail, floosie, harridan, hussy, nag, shrew, slattern, slut, strumpet, tart, trollop, vixen, wench.

jaded adj. blunted, bored, cloyed, dulled, effete, exhausted, fagged, fatigued, played-out, satiated, spent, surfeited, tired, tired out, weary.
antonyms fresh, refreshed.

jag n. barb, denticle, dentil, notch, point, projection, protrusion, snag, spur, tooth.

jagged adj. barbed, broken, craggy, denticulate, hackly, indented, irregular, notched, pointed, ragged, ridged, rough, saw-edged, serrate, serrated, snagged, snaggy, spiked, spiky, toothed, uneven.
antonyms smooth.

jail, gaol n. borstal, bridewell, brig, calaboose, can, cells, choky, clink, cooler, coop, custody, guardhouse, hoos(e)gow, house of correction, inside, jailhouse, jankers, jug, lock-up, nick, pen, penitentiary, pokey, prison, quod, reformatory, slammer, stir, tollbooth.
v. confine, detain, immure, impound, imprison, incarcerate, intern, lock up, quod, send down.

jailer, gaoler n. captor, guard, keeper, prison officer, screw, turnkey, warden, warder.

jam¹ v. block, clog, compact, confine, congest, cram, crowd, crush, force, obstruct, pack, press, ram, sandwich, squash, squeeze, stall, stick, stuff, throng, thrust, vice, wedge.
n. bottle-neck, concourse, crowd, crush, gridlock, herd, horde, mass, mob, multitude, pack, press, swarm, throng, traffic jam.

jam² n. bind, contretemps, difficulty, dilemma, fix, hitch, hole, hot water, imbroglio, impasse, pickle, plight, predicament, quandary, scrape, spot, straits, tangle, tight corner, trouble.

jam³ n. confiture, confyt, conserve, jelly, marmalade, preserve, spread.

jamboree n. carnival, carouse, celebration, convention, festival, festivity, fête, field day, frolic, gathering, get-together, jubilee, junket, merriment, party, potlatch, rally, revelry, shindig, spree.

jangle v. chime, clank, clash, clatter, jar, jingle, rattle, upset, vibrate.
n. cacophony, clang, clangor, clash, din, dissonance, jar, racket, rattle, reverberation, stridence, stridency, stridor.
antonyms euphony, harmony.

janitor n. caretaker, concierge, custodian, doorkeeper, doorman, janitress, janitrix, ostiary, porter.

jar¹ n. amphora, aquamanile, bellarmine, can, carafe, container, crock, cruet, cruse, ewer, flagon, jug, kang, mug, olla, pitcher, pot, receptacle, stamnos, stoup, urn, vase, vessel.

jar² v. agitate, annoy, clash, convulse, disagree, discompose, disturb, grate, grind, interfere, irk, irritate, jangle, jolt, nettle, offend, quarrel, rasp, rattle, rock, shake, upset, vibrate.
n. clash, disagreement, discord, dissonance, grating, irritation, jangle, jolt, quarrel, rasping, wrangling.

jargon n. argot, balderdash, bunkum, cant, dialect, diplomatese, double-Dutch, drivel, gabble, gibberish, gobbledegook, gobbledygook, Greek, idiom, jive, lingo, mumbojumbo, nonsense, palaver, parlance, patois, rigmarole, slang, tongue, twaddle, vernacular.

jaundiced adj. biased, bitter, cynical, disbelieving, distorted, distrustful, envious, hostile, jaded, jealous, misanthropic, partial, pessimistic, preconceived, prejudiced, resentful, skeptical, suspicious.
antonyms fresh, naïve, optimistic.

jaunty adj. airy, breezy, buoyant, carefree, cheeky, chipper, dapper, debonair, gay, high-spirited, insouciant, lively, perky, self-confident, showy, smart, sparkish, sprightly, spruce, trim.
antonyms anxious, depressed, dowdy, seedy.

jazzy adj. animated, avant-garde, bold, fancy, flashy, gaudy, goey, lively, smart, snazzy, spirited, stylish, swinging, vivacious, wild, zestful.
antonyms conservative, prosaic, square.

jealous adj. anxious, apprehensive, attentive, careful, covetous, desirous, emulous, envious, green, green-eyed, grudging, guarded, heedful, invidious, mistrustful, possessive, proprietorial, protective, resentful, rival, solicitous, suspicious, vigilant, wary, watchful, zealous.

jealousy n. covetousness, distrust, emulation, envy, grudge, heart-burning, ill-will, mistrust, possessiveness, resentment, spite, suspicion, vigilance, watchfulness, zelotypia.

jeer v. banter, barrack, chaff, contemn, deride, explode, fleer, flout, flyte, gibe, heckle, hector, knock, mock, rail, razz, ridicule, scoff, sneer, taunt, twit.

n. abuse, aspersion, catcall, chaff, derision, dig, fleer, flyte, flyting, gibe, hiss, hoot, mockery, raillery, raspberry, ridicule, scoff, sneer, taunt, thrust.

jeopardize *v.* chance, endanger, expose, gamble, hazard, imperil, jeopard, menace, risk, stake, threaten, venture.
antonyms protect, safeguard.

jerk[1] *n.* bounce, jog, jolt, lurch, pluck, pull, shrug, throw, thrust, tug, tweak, twitch, wrench, yank.
v. bounce, flirt, jigger, jog, jolt, jounce, lurch, peck, pluck, pull, shrug, throw, thrust, tug, tweak, twitch, wrench, yank.

jerk[2] *n.* bum, clod, clot, clown, creep, dimwit, dolt, dope, fool, halfwit, idiot, klutz, ninny, prick, schlep, schmo, schmuck, twit.

jerky *adj.* bouncy, bumpy, convulsive, disconnected, fitful, incoherent, jolting, jumpy, rough, shaky, spasmodic, tremulous, twitchy, uncontrolled, unco-ordinated.
antonym smooth.

jest *n.* banter, bon mot, clowning, cod, crack, desipience, foolery, fooling, fun, gag, hoax, jape, jeu d'esprit, joke, josh, kidding, leg-pull, pleasantry, prank, quip, sally, sport, trick, trifling, waggery, wisecrack, witticism.
v. banter, chaff, clown, deride, fool, gibe, jeer, joke, josh, kid, mock, quip, scoff, tease, trifle.

jester *n.* buffoon, clown, comedian, comic, droll, fool, goliard, harlequin, humorist, joculator, joker, juggler, merry-andrew, merryman, motley, mummer, pantaloon, patch, prankster, quipster, wag, wit, zany.

jet[1] *n.* atomizer, flow, fountain, gush, issue, nose, nozzle, rose, rush, spout, spray, sprayer, spring, sprinkler, spurt, squirt, stream, surge.

jet[2] *adj.* atramentous, black, coal-black, ebon, ebony, inky, jetty, pitch-black, pitchy, raven, sable, sloe, sooty.

jetsam *n.* jetsom, jetson, lagan, waif, wreckage.

jettison *v.* abandon, chuck, discard, ditch, dump, eject, expel, heave, offload, scrap, unload.
antonyms load, take on.

jetty *n.* breakwater, dock, groyne, jutty, mole, pier, quay, wharf.

jewel *n.* bijou, brilliant, charm, find, flower, gaud, gem, gemstone, humdinger, locket, masterpiece, ornament, paragon, pearl, precious stone, pride, prize, rarity, rock, sparkler, stone, treasure, wonder.

jib *v.* back off, balk, recoil, refuse, retreat, shrink, stall, stop short.

jibe, gibe *v.* deride, fleer, flout, jeer, mock, rail, ridicule, scoff, scorn, sneer, taunt, twit.
n. barb, crack, derision, dig, fleer, fling, jeer, mockery, poke, quip, raillery, ridicule, sarcasm, scoff, slant, sneer, taunt, thrust.

jig *v.* bob, bobble, bounce, caper, hop, jerk, jiggle, jounce, jump, prance, shake, skip, twitch, wiggle, wobble.

jiggle *v.* agitate, bounce, fidget, jerk, jig, jog, joggle, shake, shift, shimmy, twitch, waggle, wiggle, wobble.

jilt *v.* abandon, betray, brush off, chuck, deceive, desert,

discard, ditch, drop, forsake, reject, repudiate, spurn, throw over.
antonym cleave to.

jingle[1] *v.* chime, chink, clatter, clink, jangle, rattle, ring, tink, tinkle, tintinnabulate.
n. clang, clangor, clink, rattle, reverberation, ringing, tink, tinkle, tintinnabulation.

jingle[2] *n.* chant, chime, chorus, couplet, ditty, doggerel, limerick, melody, poem, rhyme, song, tune, verse.

jinx *n.* black magic, charm, curse, evil eye, gremlin, hex, hoodoo, jettatura, Jonah, plague, spell, voodoo.
v. bedevil, bewitch, curse, doom, hex, hoodoo, plague.

jittery *adj.* agitated, anxious, edgy, fidgety, flustered, jumpy, nervous, panicky, perturbed, quaking, quivering, shaky, shivery, trembling, uneasy.
antonyms calm, composed, confident.

job *n.* activity, affair, allotment, assignment, batch, business, calling, capacity, career, charge, chore, commission, concern, consignment, contract, contribution, craft, duty, employment, enterprise, errand, function, livelihood, lot, message, métier, mission, occupation, office, output, part, piece, place, portion, position, post, proceeding, product, profession, project, province, pursuit, responsibility, role, share, situation, stint, task, trade, undertaking, venture, vocation, work.

jobless *adj.* idle, inactive, laid off, on the dole, out of work, unemployed, unoccupied, unused, workless.
antonym employed.

jocularity *n.* absurdity, comicality, desipience, drollery, facetiousness, fooling, gaiety, hilarity, humor, jesting, jocoseness, jocosity, jolliness, joviality, laughter, merriment, playfulness, pleasantry, roguishness, sport, sportiveness, teasing, waggery, waggishness, whimsicality, whimsy, wit.

jog[1] *v.* activate, arouse, bounce, jar, jerk, joggle, jolt, jostle, jounce, nudge, poke, prod, prompt, push, remind, rock, shake, shove, stimulate, stir.
n. jerk, jiggle, jolt, nudge, poke, prod, push, reminder, shake, shove.

jog[2] *v., n.* bump, canter, dogtrot, jogtrot, lope, lumber, pad, run, trot.

join *v.* abut, accompany, accrete, add, adhere, adjoin, affiliate, alligate, amalgamate, annex, append, associate, attach, border, border on, butt, cement, coincide, combine, compaginate, conglutinate, conjoin, conjugate, connect, couple, dock, enlist, enrol, enter, fasten, knit, link, march with, marry, meet, merge, reach, sign up, splice, team, tie, touch, unite, verge on, yoke.
antonyms leave, separate.

joint[1] *n.* articulation, commissure, connection, geniculation, gimmal, ginglymus, gomphosis, hinge, intersection, junction, juncture, knot, nexus, node, seam, union.
adj. adjunct, amalgamated, collective, combined, communal, concerted, consolidated, co-operative, co-ordinated, joined, mutual, shared, united.

v. articulate, carve, connect, couple, cut up, dismember, dissect, divide, fasten, fit, geniculate, join, segment, sever, sunder, unite.

joint[2] *n.* dance-hall, dive, haunt, honky-tonk, jerry-shop, night-club, place, pub.

joint[3] *n.* reefer, roach, stick.

joke *n.* buffoon, butt, clown, conceit, concetto, frolic, fun, funny, gag, guy, hoot, jape, jest, jeu d'esprit, lark, laughing-stock, play, pun, quip, quirk, sally, simpleton, sport, target, whimsy, wisecrack, witticism, yarn, yell.
v. banter, chaff, clown, deride, fool, frolic, gambol, jest, kid, laugh, mock, quip, ridicule, spoof, taunt, tease, wisecrack.

joker *n.* buffoon, card, character, clown, comedian, comic, droll, humorist, jester, joculator, jokesmith, kidder, prankster, sport, trickster, wag, wit.

jolly *adj.* blithe, blithesome, buxom, carefree, cheerful, cheery, convivial, exuberant, festive, frisky, frolicsome, funny, gay, gladsome, happy, hearty, hilarious, jaunty, jocund, jovial, joyful, joyous, jubilant, merry, mirthful, playful, sportive, sprightly, sunny.
antonym sad.

jolt *v.* astonish, bounce, bump, discompose, disconcert, dismay, disturb, jar, jerk, jog, jostle, jounce, knock, nonplus, perturb, push, shake, shock, shove, stagger, startle, stun, surprise, upset.
n. blow, bolt from the blue, bombshell, bump, hit, impact, jar, jerk, jog, jump, lurch, quiver, reversal, setback, shake, shock, start, surprise, thunderbolt.

jostle *v.* bump, butt, crowd, elbow, force, hustle, jog, joggle, jolt, press, push, rough up, scramble, shake, shoulder, shove, squeeze, throng, thrust.

jot *n.* ace, atom, bit, detail, fraction, gleam, glimmer, grain, hint, iota, mite, morsel, particle, scintilla, scrap, smidgen, speck, tittle, trace, trifle, whit.

journal *n.* book, chronicle, commonplace, daily, day-book, diary, ephemeris, gazette, log, magazine, monthly, newspaper, organ, paper, periodical, publication, record, register, review, tabloid, waste-book, weekly.

journey *n.* career, course, excursion, expedition, eyre, hadj, itinerary, jaunt, odyssey, outing, passage, peregrination, pilgrimage, progress, raik, ramble, route, safari, tour, travel, trek, trip, voyage, wanderings.
v. fare, fly, gallivant, go, jaunt, peregrinate, proceed, ramble, range, roam, rove, safari, tour, tramp, travel, traverse, trek, voyage, wander, wend.

joust *n.* contest, encounter, engagement, pas d'armes, skirmish, tilt, tournament, tourney, trial.

jovial *adj.* affable, airy, animated, blithe, buoyant, cheery, convivial, cordial, ebullient, expansive, Falstaffian, gay, glad, happy, hilarious, jaunty, jocose, jocund, jolly, jubilant, merry, mirthful.
antonyms morose, sad, saturnine.

joy *n.* blessedness, bliss, charm, delight, ecstasy, elation,

exaltation, exultation, felicity, festivity, gaiety, gem, gladness, gladsomeness, glee, gratification, happiness, hilarity, jewel, joyance, joyfulness, joyousness, pleasure, pride, prize, rapture, ravishment, satisfaction, seel, transport, treasure, treat, triumph, wonder.
antonyms mourning, sorrow.

joyful *adj.* blithe, blithesome, delighted, ecstatic, elated, enraptured, glad, gladsome, gratified, happy, jocund, jolly, jovial, jubilant, light-hearted, merry, pleased, rapturous, satisfied, seely, transported, triumphant.
antonyms mournful, sorrowful.

joyous *adj.* cheerful, ecstatic, festal, festive, frabjous, glad, gladsome, gleeful, happy, joyful, jubilant, merry, rapturous.
antonym sad.

jubilant *adj.* celebratory, delighted, elated, enraptured, euphoric, excited, exuberant, exultant, flushed, glad, gratified, joyous, over the moon, overjoyed, rejoicing, thrilled, triumphal, triumphant.
antonyms defeated, depressed.

jubilee *n.* anniversary, carnival, celebration, commemoration, festival, festivity, fête, gala, holiday.

judge *n.* adjudicator, alcalde, arbiter, arbiter elegantiae, arbitrator, arbitratrix, assessor, authority, beak, connoisseur, critic, Daniel, deemster, dempster, doomster, elegantiarum, evaluator, expert, hakim, justice, justiciar, justiciary, Law Lord, magistrate, mediator, moderator, pundit, referee, umpire, virtuoso, wig.
v. adjudge, adjudicate, appraise, appreciate, arbitrate, ascertain, assess, conclude, condemn, consider, criticize, decern, decide, decree, determine, dijudicate, discern, distinguish, doom, esteem, estimate, evaluate, examine, find, gauge, mediate, opine, rate, reckon, refcree, review, rule, sentence, sit, try, umpire, value.

judgment *n.* acumen, appraisal, arbitration, arrêt, assessment, assize, award, belief, common sense, conclusion, conviction, damnation, decision, decree, decreet, deduction, determination, diagnosis, discernment, discretion, discrimination, doom, enlightenment, estimate, expertise, fate, fetwa, finding, intelligence, mediation, misfortune, opinion, order, penetration, perceptiveness, percipience, perspicacity, prudence, punishment, result, retribution, ruling, sagacity, sense, sentence, shrewdness, taste, understanding, valuation, verdict, view, virtuosity, wisdom.

judicial *adj.* critical, decretory, discriminating, distinguished, forensic, impartial, judiciary, juridical, legal, magisterial, magistral, official.

judicious *adj.* acute, astute, canny, careful, cautious, circumspect, considered, diplomatic, discerning, discreet, discriminating, enlightened, expedient, informed, percipient, perspicacious, politic, prescient, prudent, rational, reasonable, sagacious, sage, sane, sapient, sensible, shrewd, skilful, sober, sound, thoughtful, wary, well-advised, well-judged, well-judging, wise.
antonym injudicious.

jug *n.* amphora, aquamanile, bellarmine, blackjack, carafe, churn, container, crock, ewer, flagon, jar, pitcher, stoup, urn, vessel.

juice *n.* essence, extract, fluid, latex, liquid, liquor, nectar, sap, secretion, serum, succus.

jumble *v.* confuse, disarrange, disarray, disorder, disorganize, mingle-mangle, mix, mix up, muddle, shuffle, tangle, tumble, wuzzle.
antonym order.
n. agglomeration, chaos, clutter, collection, confusion, congeries, conglomeration, disarrangement, disarray, disorder, farrago, gallimaufry, hotch-potch, medley, mess, mingle-mangle, miscellany, mishmash, mixture, mix-up, muddle, olio, olla-podrida, pastiche, potpourri, raffle, salad.

jump¹ *v.* bounce, bound, caper, clear, dance, frisk, frolic, gambol, hop, hurdle, jig, leap, pounce, prance, skip, spring, vault.
n. bounce, bound, capriole, curvet, dance, frisk, frolic, gambado, hop, jeté, leap, pounce, prance, saltation, skip, spring, vault.

jump² *v.* avoid, bypass, digress, disregard, evade, ignore, leave out, miss, omit, overshoot, pass over, skip, switch.
n. breach, break, gap, hiatus, interruption, interval, lacuna, lapse, omission, saltation, saltus, switch.

jump³ *v.* advance, appreciate, ascend, boost, escalate, gain, hike, increase, mount, rise, spiral, surge.
n. advance, ascent, augmentation, boost, escalation, increase, increment, mounting, rise, upsurge, upturn.

jump⁴ *v.* flinch, jerk, jump out of one's skin, leap in the air, quail, recoil, resile, shrink, start, wince.
n. jar, jerk, jolt, lurch, quiver, shiver, shock, spasm, start, swerve, twitch, wrench.

jump⁵ *n.* barricade, barrier, fence, gate, hedge, hurdle, impediment, obstacle, pons asinorum, rail.

jumpy *adj.* agitated, anxious, apprehensive, discomposed, edgy, fidgety, jittery, nervous, nervy, restive, restless, shaky, tense, tremulous, uneasy.
antonyms calm, composed.

junction *n.* abutment, combination, confluence, conjunction, connection, coupling, disemboguement, intersection, interstice, join, joining, joint, juncture, linking, meeting-point, nexus, seam, union.

junior *adj.* inferior, lesser, lower, minor, puisne, secondary, subordinate, subsidiary, younger.
antonyms senior.

junk *n.* clutter, debris, detritus, dregs, garbage, litter, oddments, refuse, rejectamenta, rubbish, rummage, scrap, trash, waste, wreckage.

jurisdiction *n.* area, authority, bailiwick, bounds, cognizance, command, control, domination, dominion, field, influence, judicature, orbit, power, prerogative, province, range, reach, rule, scope, sovereignty, sphere, sway, verge, zone.

just *adj.* accurate, apposite, appropriate, apt, blameless, condign, conscientious, correct, decent, deserved, disinterested, due, equitable, even-handed, exact, fair, fairminded, faithful, fitting, four-square, good, honest, honorable, impartial, impeccable, irreproachable, justified, lawful, legitimate, merited, normal, precise, proper, pure, reasonable, regular, right, righteous, rightful, sound, suitable, true, unbiased, unimpeachable, unprejudiced, upright, virtuous, well-deserved.
antonym unjust.

justice¹ *n.* amends, appositeness, appropriateness, compensation, correction, dharma, equitableness, equity, fairness, honesty, impartiality, integrity, justifiableness, justness, law, legality, legitimacy, nemesis, penalty, propriety, reasonableness, recompense, rectitude, redress, reparation, requital, right, rightfulness, rightness, satisfaction.
antonym injustice.

justice² *n.* JP, judge, Justice of the Peace, justiciar, magistrate.

justifiable *adj.* acceptable, allowable, defensible, excusable, explainable, explicable, fit, forgivable, justified, lawful, legitimate, licit, maintainable, pardonable, proper, reasonable, right, sound, tenable, understandable, valid, vindicable, warrantable, warranted, well-founded.
antonyms culpable, illicit, unjustifiable.

justify *v.* absolve, acquit, condone, confirm, defend, establish, exculpate, excuse, exonerate, explain, forgive, legalize, legitimize, maintain, pardon, substantiate, support, sustain, uphold, validate, vindicate, warrant.

jut *v.* beetle, bulge, extend, impend, overhang, poke, project, protrude, stick out.
antonym recede.

juvenile *n.* adolescent, boy, child, girl, halfling, infant, kid, minor, young person, youngster, youth.
antonym adult.
adj. adolescent, babyish, boyish, callow, childish, girlish, immature, impressionable, inexperienced, infantile, jejune, puerile, tender, undeveloped, unsophisticated, young, youthful.
antonym mature.

keen *adj.* acid, acute, anxious, ardent, argute, assiduous, astute, avid, biting, brilliant, canny, caustic, clever, cutting, devoted, diligent, discerning, discriminating, eager, earnest, ebullient, edged, enthusiastic, fervid, fierce, fond, forthright, impassioned, incisive, industrious, intense, intent, mordant, penetrating, perceptive, perfervid, perspicacious, piercing, pointed, pungent, quick, razorlike, sagacious, sapient, sardonic, satirical, scathing, sedulous, sensitive, sharp, shrewd, shrill, tart, trenchant, wise, zealous. *antonyms* apathetic, blunt, dull.

keep[1] *v.* accumulate, amass, carry, collect, conserve, control, deal in, deposit, furnish, garner, hang on to, heap, hold, hold on to, maintain, pile, place, possess, preserve, retain, stack, stock, store.

keep[2] *v.* be responsible for, board, care for, defend, feed, foster, guard, have charge of, have custody of, look after, maintain, manage, mind, nourish, nurture, operate, protect, provide for, provision, safeguard, shelter, shield, subsidize, support, sustain, tend, victual, watch, watch over.
n. board, food, livelihood, living, maintenance, means, nourishment, nurture, subsistence, support, upkeep.

keep[3] *v.* arrest, block, check, constrain, control, curb, delay, detain, deter, hamper, hamstring, hinder, hold, hold back, hold up, impede, inhibit, interfere with, keep back, limit, obstruct, prevent, restrain, retard, shackle, stall, trammel, withhold.

keep[4] *v.* adhere to, celebrate, commemorate, comply with, fulfil, hold, honor, keep faith with, keep up, maintain, obey, observe, perform, perpetuate, recognize, respect, ritualize, solemnize.

keep[5] *n.* castle, citadel, donjon, dungeon, fastness, fort, fortress, motte, peel-house, peel-tower, stronghold, tower.

keeper *n.* attendant, caretaker, conservator, conservatrix, curator, custodian, defender, gaoler, governor, guard, guardian, inspector, jailer, mahout, nab, overseer, steward, superintendent, supervisor, surveyor, warden, warder.

keepsake *n.* emblem, favor, memento, pledge, relic, remembrance, reminder, souvenir, token.

keg *n.* barrel, butt, cask, drum, firkin, hogshead, puncheon, round, rundlet, tierce, tun, vat.

ken *n.* acquaintance, appreciation, awareness, cognizance, compass, comprehension, field, grasp, knowledge, notice, perception, range, reach, realization, scope, sight, understanding, view, vision.

kerchief *n.* babushka, bandana, cravat, fichu, headscarf, headsquare, kaffiyeh, madras, neck-cloth, neckerchief, scarf, shawl, square, sudary, veronica.

kernel *n.* core, essence, germ, gist, grain, heart, marrow, nitty-gritty, nub, pith, seed, substance.

key *n.* answer, clavis, clue, code, crib, cue, digital, explanation, glossary, guide, index, indicator, interpretation, lead, means, pointer, secret, sign, solution, table, translation.
adj. basic, cardinal, central, chief, core, crucial, decisive, essential, fundamental, hinge, important, leading, main, major, pivotal, principal, salient.

keynote *n.* accent, center, core, emphasis, essence, flavor, flavor of the month, gist, heart, kernel, leitmotiv, marrow, motif, pith, stress, substance, theme.

kick *v.* abandon, boot, break, desist from, drop, foot, give up, leave off, leave out, punt, quit, spurn, stop, toe.
n. bite, buzz, dash, élan, enjoyment, excitement, feeling, force, fun, gratification, gusto, intensity, panache, pep, pizzazz, pleasure, power, punch, pungency, relish, snap, sparkle, stimulation, strength, tang, thrill, verve, vitality, zest, zing, zip.

kick-off *n.* beginning, bully-off, commencement, face-off, inception, introduction, opening, outset, start, word go.

kid[1] *n.* babe, baby, bairn, bambino, boy, child, dandiprat, girl, halfling, infant, juvenile, kiddy, lad, nipper, shaver, stripling, teenager, tot, wean, whippersnapper, youngster, youth.

kid[2] *v.* bamboozle, befool, beguile, con, cozen, delude, dupe, fool, gull, have on, hoax, hoodwink, humbug, jest, joke, josh, mock, pretend, pull someone's leg, put one over on, rag, ridicule, tease, trick.

kidnap *v.* abduct, capture, hijack, rape, remove, seize, skyjack, snatch, steal.

kill *v.* abolish, annihilate, assassinate, beguile, bump off, butcher, cancel, cease, deaden, defeat, destroy, dispatch, do away with, do in, do to death, eliminate, eradicate, execute, exterminate, extinguish, extirpate, fill, finish off, halt, kibosh, knock off, knock on the head, liquidate, mar, martyr, massacre, murder, napoo, neutralize, nip in the bud, nullify, obliterate, occupy, pass, pip, put to death, quash, quell, rub out, ruin, scotch, slaughter, slay, smite, smother, spoil, stifle, still, stonker, stop, suppress, top, veto, vitiate, while away, zap.
n. climax, conclusion, coup de grâce, death, death-blow, dénouement, dispatch, end, finish, mop-up, shootout.

killing[1] *n.* assassination, bloodshed, carnage, elimination, ethnocide, execution, extermination, fatality, fratricide, homicide, infanticide, liquidation, mactation, manslaughter, massacre, matricide, murder, parricide, patricide, pogrom, regicide, slaughter, slaying, sororicide, thuggee, uxoricide.

adj. deadly, death-dealing, deathly, debilitating, enervating, exhausting, fatal, fatiguing, final, lethal, lethiferous, mortal, mortiferous, murderous, prostrating, punishing, tiring, vital.

killing[2] *n.* big hit, bonanza, bunce, clean-up, coup, fortune, gain, hit, lucky break, profit, smash, success, windfall, winner.

killing[3] *adj.* absurd, amusing, comical, funny, hilarious, ludicrous, side-splitting, uproarious.

killjoy *n.* complainer, cynic, dampener, damper, grouch, misery, moaner, pessimist, prophet of doom, skeptic, spoilsport, trouble-mirth, wet blanket, whiner.

antonyms enthusiast, optimist, sport.

kin *n.* affines, affinity, blood, clan, connection, connections, consanguinity, cousins, extraction, family, flesh and blood, kindred, kinsfolk, kinship, kinsmen, kith, lineage, people, relations, relationship, relatives, stock, tribe.

adj. affine, akin, allied, close, cognate, congener, connected, consanguine, consanguineous, interconnected, kindred, linked, near, related, similar, twin.

kind[1] *n.* brand, breed, category, character, class, description, essence, family, genus, habit, ilk, kidney, manner, mold, nature, persuasion, race, set, sort, species, stamp, style, temperament, type, variety.

kind[2] *adj.* accommodating, affectionate, altruistic, amiable, amicable, avuncular, beneficent, benevolent, benign, benignant, bonhomous, boon, bounteous, bountiful, brotherly, charitable, clement, compassionate, congenial, considerate, cordial, courteous, diplomatic, fatherly, friendly, generous, gentle, giving, good, gracious, hospitable, humane, indulgent, kind-hearted, kindly, lenient, loving, mild, motherly, neighborly, obliging, philanthropic, propitious, sisterly, soft-boiled, soft-hearted, sweet, sympathetic, tactful, tenderhearted, thoughtful, understanding.

antonyms cruel, inconsiderate, unhelpful.

kindle *v.* activate, actuate, agitate, animate, arouse, awaken, deflagrate, enkindle, exasperate, excite, fan, fire, foment, ignite, incite, induce, inflame, initiate, inspire, inspirit, light, provoke, rouse, set alight, sharpen, stimulate, stir, thrill.

kindly *adj.* benefic, beneficent, beneficial, benevolent, benign, charitable, comforting, compassionate, cordial, favorable, generous, genial, gentle, giving, good-natured, good-willy, hearty, helpful, indulgent, kind, mild, patient, pleasant, polite, sympathetic, tender, warm.

adv. agreeably, charitably, comfortingly, considerately, cordially, generously, gently, graciously, indulgently, patiently, politely, tenderly, thoughtfully.

antonyms cruel, inconsiderate, uncharitable, unpleasant.

kindred *n.* affines, affinity, clan, connections, consanguinity, family, flesh, folk, kin, kinsfolk, kinship, kinsmen, lineage, people, relations, relationship, relatives.

adj. affiliated, affine, akin, allied, cognate, common, congenial, connected, corresponding, kin, like, matching, related, similar.

king *n.* boss, chief, chieftain, doyen, emperor, kingpin, leading light, luminary, majesty, monarch, overlord, paramount, patriarch, potentate, prince, royalet, ruler, sovereign, supremo, suzerain.

kingdom *n.* area, commonwealth, country, division, domain, dominion, dynasty, empire, field, land, monarchy, nation, palatinate, principality, province, realm, reign, royalty, sovereignty, sphere, state, territory, tract.

kingly *adj.* august, basilical, glorious, grand, grandiose, imperial, imperious, imposing, lordly, majestic, monarchical, noble, regal, royal, sovereign, splendid, stately, sublime, supreme.

kink[1] *n.* bend, coil, complication, corkscrew, crick, crimp, defect, dent, difficulty, entanglement, flaw, hitch, imperfection, indentation, knot, loop, tangle, twist, wrinkle.

v. bend, coil, crimp, curl, tangle, twist, wrinkle.

kink[2] *n.* caprice, crotchet, eccentricity, fetish, foible, freak, idiosyncracy, idiosyncrasy, oddity, quirk, singularity, vagary, whim.

kinship *n.* affinity, alliance, association, bearing, community, conformity, connection, consanguinity, correspondence, kin, relation, relationship, similarity.

kismet *n.* destiny, doom, fate, fortune, joss, karma, lot, portion, predestiny, providence, weird.

kiss[1] *v.* buss, canoodle, neck, osculate, peck, salute, smooch, snog.

n. buss, osculation, peck, plonker, salute, smack, smacker, snog.

kiss[2] *v.* brush, caress, fan, glance, graze, lick, scrape, touch.

kit *n.* accouterments, apparatus, appurtenances, baggage, effects, equipage, equipment, gear, impedimenta, implements, instruments, luggage, matériel, muniments, outfit, paraphernalia, provisions, rig, rig-out, set, supplies, tackle, tools, trappings, traps, utensils.

knack *n.* ability, adroitness, aptitude, bent, capacity, dexterity, expertise, expertness, facility, faculty, flair, forte, genius, gift, handiness, hang, ingenuity, propensity, quickness, skilfulness, skill, talent, trick, trick of the trade, turn.

knave *n.* bastard, blackguard, blighter, bounder, cheat, dastard, drôle, fripon, rapscallion, rascal, reprobate, rogue, rotter, scallywag, scamp, scapegrace, scoundrel, stinker, swindler, swine, varlet, villain.

knead *v.* form, knuckle, manipulate, massage, mold, ply, press, rub, shape, squeeze, work.

knick-knack *n.* bagatelle, bauble, bibelot, bric-à-brac, gadget, gaud, gewgaw, gimcrack, gismo, jimjam, kickshaw, object of virtu, plaything, pretty, pretty-pretty, quip, rattle-trap, toy, trifle, trinket, whigmaleerie, whim-wham.

knife *n*. blade, carver, chiv, cutter, dagger, dah, flick-knife, jack-knife, machete, parang, pen-knife, pocket-knife, skean, skene, skene-dhu, skene-occle, switchblade, whittle.

v. cut, impale, lacerate, pierce, rip, slash, stab, wound.

knightly *adj*. bold, chivalrous, courageous, courtly, dauntless, gallant, gracious, heroic, honorable, intrepid, noble, soldierly, valiant, valorous.

antonyms cowardly, ignoble, ungallant.

knit *v*. ally, bind, connect, crease, crotchet, fasten, furrow, heal, interlace, intertwine, join, knot, link, loop, mend, secure, tie, unite, weave, wrinkle.

knob *n*. boll, boss, bump, caput, door-handle, knot, knub, knurl, lump, nub, projection, protrusion, protuberance, snib, stud, swell, swelling, tuber, tumor, umbo.

knock[1] *v*. buffet, clap, cuff, ding, hit, knobble, (k)nubble, punch, rap, slap, smack, smite, strike, thump, thwack.

n. blow, box, chap, clip, clout, con, cuff, hammering, rap, slap, smack, thump.

knock[2] *v*. abuse, belittle, carp, cavil, censure, condemn, criticize, deprecate, disparage, find fault, lambaste, run down, slam, vilify, vilipend.

n. blame, censure, condemnation, criticism, defeat, failure, rebuff, rejection, reversal, setback, stricture.

antonyms boost, praise.

knockout *n*. bestseller, coup de grâce, hit, kayo, KO, sensation, smash, smash-hit, stunner, success, triumph, winner. *antonyms* flop, loser.

knoll *n*. barrow, hill, hillock, hummock, knowe, koppie, mound.

knot *v*. bind, entangle, entwine, knit, loop, secure, tangle, tether, tie, weave.

n. aggregation, bond, bow, braid, bunch, burl, clump, cluster, collection, connection, gnar, gnarl, heap, hitch, joint, knag, knar, knarl, ligature, loop, mass, pile, rosette, tie, tuft.

know *v*. apprehend, comprehend, discern, distinguish, experience, fathom, identify, intuit, ken, learn, make out, notice, perceive, realize, recognize, see, tell, undergo, understand, wist.

knowing *adj*. acute, astute, aware, clever, competent, conscious, cunning, discerning, downy, eloquent, experienced, expert, expressive, gnostic, gnostical, hep, intelligent, meaningful, perceptive, qualified, sagacious, shrewd, significant, skilful, well-informed.

antonyms ignorant, obtuse.

knowledge *n*. ability, acquaintance, acquaintanceship, apprehension, book-learning, booklore, cognition, cognizance, comprehension, consciousness, cum-savvy, discernment, education, enlightenment, erudition, familiarity, gnosis, grasp, information, instruction, intelligence, intimacy, judgment, know-how, learning, multiscience, notice, pansophy, recognition, scholarship, schooling, science, tuition, understanding, wisdom.

antonym ignorance.

knowledgeable *adj*. acquainted, au courant, au fait, aware, book-learned, bright, cognizant, conscious, conversant, educated, erudite, experienced, familiar, in the know, intelligent, learned, lettered, scholarly, well-informed.

antonym ignorant.

kowtow *v*. bow, court, cringe, defer, fawn, flatter, genuflect, grovel, kneel, pander, suck up, toady, truckle.

kudos *n*. acclaim, applause, distinction, esteem, fame, glory, honor, laudation, laurels, plaudits, praise, prestige, regard, renown, repute.

L

label *n.* badge, brand, categorization, characterization, classification, company, description, docket, epithet, mark, marker, sticker, tag, tally, ticket, trademark.
v. brand, call, categorize, characterize, class, classify, define, describe, designate, docket, dub, identify, mark, name, stamp, tag.

labor[1] *n.* chore, donkey-work, drudgery, effort, employees, exertion, grind, hands, industry, job, labor improbus, laborers, moil, pains, painstaking, slog, sweat, task, toil, undertaking, work, workers, workforce, workmen.
antonyms ease, leisure, relaxation, rest.
v. drudge, endeavor, grind, heave, moil, pitch, plod, roll, slave, strive, struggle, suffer, sweat, toil, toss, travail, work.
antonyms idle, laze, loaf, lounge.

labor[2] *n.* birth, childbirth, contractions, delivery, labor pains, pains, parturition, throes, travail.
v. dwell on, elaborate, overdo, overemphasize, overstress, strain.

labored *adj.* affected, awkward, complicated, contrived, difficult, forced, heavy, overdone, overwrought, ponderous, stiff, stilted, strained, studied, unnatural.
antonyms easy, natural.

laborer *n.* drudge, farm-hand, hand, hireling, hobbler, hobo, hodman, hunky, husbandman, manual worker, redneck, worker, working man, workman.

laborious *adj.* arduous, assiduous, backbreaking, burdensome, difficult, diligent, fatiguing, forced, hard, hard-working, heavy, herculean, indefatigable, industrious, labored, onerous, operose, painstaking, persevering, ponderous, sedulous, strained, strenuous, tireless, tiresome, toilsome, tough, unflagging, uphill, wearing, wearisome.
antonyms easy, effortless, relaxing, simple.

labyrinth *n.* circumvolution, coil, complexity, complication, convolution, entanglement, Gordian knot, intricacy, jungle, maze, perplexity, puzzle, riddle, tangle, windings.

lace[1] *n.* crochet, dentelle, filigree, mesh-work, netting, open-work, tatting.

lace[2] *n.* bootlace, cord, lanyard, shoe-lace, string, thong, tie.
v. attach, bind, close, do up, fasten, intertwine, interweave, interwork, string, thread, tie.

lace[3] *v.* add to, fortify, intermix, mix in, spike.

lacerate *v.* afflict, claw, cut, distress, gash, ga(u)nch, harrow, jag, lancinate, maim, mangle, rend, rip, slash, tear, torment, torture, wound.

laceration *n.* cut, gash, injury, lancination, maim, mutilation, rent, rip, slash, tear, wound.

lack *n.* absence, dearth, deficiency, deprivation, destitution, emptiness, insufficiency, need, privation, scantiness, scarcity, shortage, shortcoming, shortness, vacancy, void, want.
antonyms abundance, profusion.
v. miss, need, require, want.

lackey *n.* attendant, creature, fawner, flatterer, flunky, footman, gofer, hanger-on, instrument, manservant, menial, minion, parasite, pawn, servitor, sycophant, toady, tool, valet, yes-man.

lacking *adj.* defective, deficient, flawed, impaired, inadequate, minus, missing, needing, sans, short of, wanting, without.

lackluster *adj.* boring, dim, drab, dry, dull, flat, leaden, lifeless, lusterless, mundane, muted, prosaic, somber, spiritless, unimaginative, uninspired, vapid.
antonyms brilliant, polished.

laconic *adj.* brief, close-mouthed, compact, concise, crisp, curt, pithy, sententious, short, succinct, taciturn, terse.
antonyms garrulous, verbose, wordy.

lad *n.* boy, bucko, callant, chap, fellow, guy, halfling, juvenile, kid, laddie, schoolboy, shaver, stripling, youngster, youth.

laden *adj.* burdened, charged, chock-a-block, chock-full, encumbered, fraught, full, hampered, jammed, loaded, oppressed, packed, stuffed, taxed, weighed down, weighted.
antonym empty.

ladle *v.* bail, dip, dish, lade, scoop, shovel, spoon.

lady *n.* begum, dame, damsel, don(n)a, Frau, gentlewoman, hidalga, madam(e), matron, memsahib, milady, noblewoman, Señora, signora, woman.

ladylike *adj.* courtly, cultured, decorous, elegant, genteel, matronly, modest, polite, proper, queenly, refined, respectable, well-bred.

lag *v.* dawdle, delay, hang back, idle, linger, loiter, mosey, saunter, shuffle, straggle, tarry, trail.
antonym lead.

laggard *n.* dawdler, idler, lingerer, loafer, loiterer, lounger, saunterer, slowcoach, slowpoke, slug-a-bed, sluggard, snail, straggler.
antonyms dynamo, go-getter, livewire.

lair *n.* burrow, den, earth, form, hideout, hole, nest, refuge, retreat, roost, sanctuary, stronghold.

lake *n.* lagoon, loch, lochan, lough, mere, reservoir, tarn.

lambaste *v.* beat, berate, bludgeon, castigate, censure, cudgel, drub, flay, flog, leather, rebuke, reprimand, roast, scold, strike, thrash, upbraid, whip.

lame *adj.* crippled, defective, disabled, disappointing, feeble, flimsy, game, half-baked, halt, handicapped, hobbling, inadequate, insufficient, limping, poor, thin, unconvincing, unsatisfactory, weak.

v. cripple, damage, disable, hamstring, hobble, hurt, incapacitate, injure, maim, wing.

lament *v.* bemoan, bewail, beweep, complain, deplore, grieve, keen, mourn, regret, sorrow, wail, weep, yammer.

antonyms celebrate, rejoice.

n. complaint, coronach, dirge, dumka, elegy, jeremiad, keening, lamentation, moan, moaning, monody, plaint, requiem, threnody, ululation, wail, wailing.

lamentable *adj.* deplorable, disappointing, distressing, funest, grievous, inadequate, insufficient, low, meager, mean, miserable, mournful, pitiful, poor, regrettable, sorrowful, tragic, unfortunate, unsatisfactory, woeful, wretched.

lamp *n.* beacon, flare, floodlight, lampad, lantern, light, limelight, searchlight, torch, veilleuse.

lampoon *n.* burlesque, caricature, mickey-take, parody, Pasquil, Pasquin, pasquinade, satire, send-up, skit, spoof, squib, take-off.

v. burlesque, caricature, make fun of, mock, parody, Pasquil, Pasquin, pasquinade, ridicule, satirize, send up, spoof, squib, take off, take the mickey out of.

land[1] *n.* country, countryside, dirt, district, earth, estate, farmland, fatherland, ground, grounds, loam, motherland, nation, property, province, real estate, realty, region, soil, terra firma, territory, tract.

v. alight, arrive, berth, bring, carry, cause, come to rest, debark, deposit, disembark, dock, drop, end up, plant, touch down, turn up, wind up.

land[2] *v.* achieve, acquire, capture, gain, get, net, obtain, secure, win.

landlord *n.* freeholder, host, hotelier, hotel-keeper, innkeeper, lessor, letter, owner, proprietor, publican.

antonym tenant.

landmark *n.* beacon, boundary, cairn, feature, milestone, monument, signpost, turning-point, watershed.

landscape *n.* aspect, countryside, outlook, panorama, prospect, scene, scenery, view, vista.

landslide *n.* avalanche, earthfall, éboulement, landslip, rock-fall.

adj. decisive, emphatic, overwhelming, runaway.

lane *n.* alley(way), avenue, boreen, byroad, byway, channel, driveway, footpath, footway, gut, loan, passage(way), path(way), towpath, vennel, way, wynd.

language *n.* argot, cant, conversation, dialect, diction, discourse, expression, idiolect, idiom, interchange, jargon, langue, lingo, lingua franca, parlance, parole, patois, phraseology, phrasing, speech, style, talk, terminology, tongue, utterance, vernacular, vocabulary, wording.

languid *adj.* debilitated, drooping, dull, enervated, faint, feeble, heavy, inactive, indifferent, inert, lackadaisical,

languorous, lazy, lethargic, limp, listless, pining, sickly, slow, sluggish, spiritless, torpid, unenthusiastic, uninterested, weak, weary.

antonyms alert, lively, vivacious.

languish *v.* brood, decline, desire, despond, droop, fade, fail, faint, flag, grieve, hanker, hunger, long, mope, pine, repine, rot, sicken, sigh, sink, sorrow, suffer, sulk, want, waste, waste away, weaken, wilt, wither, yearn.

antonym flourish.

languor *n.* apathy, asthenia, calm, debility, dreaminess, drowsiness, enervation, ennui, faintness, fatigue, feebleness, frailty, heaviness, hush, indolence, inertia, lassitude, laziness, lethargy, listlessness, lull, oppressiveness, relaxation, silence, sleepiness, sloth, stillness, torpor, weakness, weariness.

antonyms alacrity, gusto.

lanky *adj.* angular, bony, gangling, gangly, gaunt, loose-jointed, rangy, rawboned, scraggy, scrawny, spare, tall, thin, twiggy, weedy.

antonyms short, squat.

lap[1] *v.* drink, lick, sip, sup, tongue.

lap[2] *v.* gurgle, plash, purl, ripple, slap, slosh, splash, swish, wash.

lap[3] *n.* ambit, circle, circuit, course, distance, loop, orbit, round, tour.

v. cover, encase, enfold, envelop, fold, surround, swaddle, swathe, turn, twist, wrap.

lapse *n.* aberration, backsliding, break, caducity, decline, descent, deterioration, drop, error, failing, fall, fault, gap, indiscretion, intermission, interruption, interval, lull, mistake, negligence, omission, oversight, passage, pause, relapse, slip.

v. backslide, decline, degenerate, deteriorate, drop, end, expire, fail, fall, run out, sink, slide, slip, stop, terminate, worsen.

larceny *n.* burglary, expropriation, heist, misappropriation, pilfering, piracy, purloining, robbery, stealing, theft.

large *adj.* abundant, ample, big, broad, bulky, capacious, colossal, comprehensive, considerable, copious, decuman, enormous, extensive, full, generous, giant, gigantic, goodly, grand, grandiose, great, huge, immense, jumbo, king-sized, liberal, man-sized, massive, monumental, Patagonian, plentiful, plonking, roomy, sizeable, spacious, spanking, substantial, sweeping, swingeing, tidy, vast, wide.

antonyms diminutive, little, slight, small, tiny.

largely *adv.* abundantly, by and large, chiefly, considerably, extensively, generally, greatly, highly, mainly, mostly, predominantly, primarily, principally, widely.

largess(e) *n.* aid, allowance, alms, benefaction, bequest, bounty, charity, donation, endowment, generosity, gift, grant, handout, liberality, munificence, open-handedness, philanthropy, present.

antonym meanness.

lark *n.* antic, caper, escapade, fling, fredaine, frolic, fun, gambol, game, gammock, guy, jape, mischief, prank, revel, rollick, romp, skylark, spree.

v. caper, cavort, frolic, gambol, gammock, play, rollick, romp, skylark, sport.

lascivious *adj.* bawdy, blue, coarse, crude, dirty, horny, indecent, lecherous, lewd, libidinous, licentious, lustful, obscene, offensive, Paphian, pornographic, prurient, randy, ribald, salacious, scurrilous, sensual, smutty, suggestive, tentiginous, unchaste, voluptuous, vulgar, wanton.

lash[1] *n.* blow, cat, cat-o'-nine-tails, hit, quirt, stripe, stroke, swipe, whip.

v. attack, beat, belabor, berate, birch, buffet, castigate, censure, chastize, criticize, dash, drum, flagellate, flay, flog, hammer, hit, horsewhip, knock, lace, lam, lambaste, lampoon, larrup, pound, ridicule, satirize, scold, scourge, smack, strike, tear into, thrash, upbraid, welt, whip.

lash[2] *v.* affix, bind, fasten, join, make fast, rope, secure, strap, tether, tie.

lass *n.* bird, chick, colleen, damsel, girl, lassie, maid, maiden, miss, quean, quine, schoolgirl.

last[1] *adj.* aftermost, closing, concluding, conclusive, definitive, extreme, final, furthest, hindmost, latest, rearmost, remotest, terminal, ultimate, utmost.

antonyms first, initial.

adv. after, behind, finally, ultimately.

antonyms first, firstly.

n. close, completion, conclusion, curtain, end, ending, finale, finish, termination.

antonyms beginning, start.

last[2] *v.* abide, carry on, continue, endure, hold on, hold out, keep (on), perdure, persist, remain, stand up, stay, survive, wear.

latch *n.* bar, bolt, catch, fastening, hasp, hook, lock, sneck.

late[1] *adj.* behind, behind-hand, belated, delayed, dilatory, last-minute, overdue, slow, tardy, unpunctual.

antonyms early, punctual.

adv. behind-hand, belatedly, dilatorily, formerly, recently, slowly, tardily, unpunctually.

antonyms early, punctually.

late[2] *adj.* dead, deceased, defunct, departed, ex-, former, old, past, preceding, previous.

lately *adv.* formerly, heretofore, latterly, recently.

latent *adj.* concealed, delitescent, dormant, hidden, inherent, invisible, lurking, potential, quiescent, secret, underlying, undeveloped, unexpressed, unrealized, unseen, veiled.

antonyms active, live, patent.

lather[1] *n.* bubbles, foam, froth, shampoo, soap, soapsuds, suds.

v. foam, froth, shampoo, soap, whip up.

lather[2] *n.* agitation, dither, fever, flap, fluster, flutter, fuss, pother, state, stew, sweat, tizzy, twitter.

lather[3] *v.* beat, cane, drub, flog, lambaste, lash, leather, strike, thrash, whip.

latitude *n.* breadth, clearance, compass, elbow-room, extent, field, freedom, indulgence, laxity, leeway, liberty, license, play, range, reach, room, scope, space, span, spread, sweep, width.

latter *adj.* closing, concluding, ensuing, last, last-mentioned, later, latest, modern, recent, second, succeeding, successive.

antonym former.

lattice *n.* espalier, fret-work, grate, grating, grid, grille, lattice-work, mesh, network, open-work, reticulation, tracery, trellis, web.

laud *v.* acclaim, applaud, approve, celebrate, extol, glorify, hail, honor, magnify, praise.

antonyms blame, condemn, curse, damn.

laudable *adj.* admirable, commendable, creditable, estimable, excellent, exemplary, meritorious, of note, praiseworthy, sterling, worthy.

antonyms damnable, execrable.

laudation *n.* acclaim, acclamation, accolade, adulation, blessing, celebrity, commendation, devotion, encomion, encomium, eulogy, extolment, glorification, glory, homage, kudos, paean, panegyric, praise, reverence, tribute, veneration.

antonyms condemnation, criticism.

laugh *v.* cachinnate, chortle, chuckle, crease up, fall about, giggle, guffaw, snicker, snigger, split one's sides, te(e)hee, titter.

antonym cry.

n. belly-laugh, card, case, caution, chortle, chuckle, clown, comedian, comic, cure, entertainer, giggle, guffaw, hoot, humorist, joke, lark, scream, snicker, snigger, te(e)hee, titter, wag, wit.

laughable *adj.* absurd, amusing, comical, derisive, derisory, diverting, droll, farcical, funny, gelastic, hilarious, humorous, laughworthy, ludicrous, mirthful, mockable, nonsensical, preposterous, ridiculous, risible.

antonyms impressive, serious, solemn.

launch *v.* begin, cast, commence, discharge, dispatch, embark on, establish, fire, float, found, inaugurate, initiate, instigate, introduce, open, project, propel, send off, set in motion, start, throw.

lavatory *n.* bathroom, bog, can, cloakroom, closet, cludge, comfort station, convenience, dike, draught-house, dunnakin, dunny, dyke, garderobe, Gents, George, head(s), jakes, john, Ladies, latrine, lav, office, powder-room, privy, public convenience, restroom, smallest room, toilet, urinal, washroom, water-closet, WC.

lavish *adj.* abundant, bountiful, copious, effusive, exaggerated, excessive, extravagant, exuberant, free, generous, gorgeous, immoderate, improvident, intemperate, liberal, lush, luxuriant, munificent, open-handed, opulent, plentiful, princely, prodigal, profuse, prolific, sumptuous, thriftless, unlimited, unreasonable, unrestrained, unstinting, wasteful, wild.

antonyms economical, frugal, parsimonious, scanty, sparing, thrifty.

v. bestow, deluge, dissipate, expend, heap, pour, shower, spend, squander, waste.

law *n.* act, axiom, brocard, canon, charter, code, command, commandment, constitution, consuetudinary, covenant, criterion, decree, dharma, edict, enactment, formula, institute, jurisprudence, order, ordinance, precept, principle, regulation, rule, standard, statute.
antonym chance.

lawful *adj.* allowable, authorized, constitutional, hal(l)al, kosher, legal, legalized, legitimate, licit, permissible, proper, rightful, valid, warranted.
antonyms illegal, illicit, lawless, unlawful.

lawless *adj.* anarchic(al), chaotic, disorderly, felonious, insubordinate, insurgent, mutinous, rebellious, reckless, riotous, ruleless, seditious, unbridled, ungoverned, unrestrained, unruly, wild.
antonym lawful.

lawlessness *n.* anarchy, chaos, disorder, insurgency, mobocracy, mob-rule, ochlocracy, piracy, racketeering, rent-a-mob.
antonym order.

lawyer *n.* advocate, attorney, barrister, counsel, counsellor, jurisconsult, law-agent, lawmonger, legist, solicitor.

lax *adj.* broad, careless, casual, derelict, easy-going, flabby, flaccid, general, imprecise, inaccurate, indefinite, inexact, lenient, loose, neglectful, negligent, overindulgent, remiss, shapeless, slack, slipshod, soft, vague, wide, wide-open, yielding.
antonyms rigid, strict, stringent.

lay[1] *v.* advance, allay, alleviate, allocate, allot, appease, apply, arrange, ascribe, assess, assign, assuage, attribute, bet, burden, calm, charge, concoct, contrive, deposit, design, devise, dispose, encumber, establish, gamble, hatch, hazard, impose, impute, leave, locate, lodge, offer, organize, place, plan, plant, plot, posit, position, prepare, present, put, quiet, relieve, risk, saddle, set, set down, set out, settle, soothe, spread, stake, still, submit, suppress, tax, wager, work out.

lay[2] *adj.* amateur, inexpert, laic, laical, non-professional, non-specialist, secular.

lay[3] *n.* ballad, canzone(t), lyric, madrigal, ode, poem, roundelay, song.

lay-off *n.* discharge, dismissal, redundancy, unemployment.

layout *n.* arrangement, blueprint, design, draft, formation, geography, map, outline, plan, sketch.

lazy *adj.* dormant, drowsy, idle, inactive, indolent, inert, languid, languorous, lethargic, otiose, remiss, shiftless, slack, sleepy, slobby, slothful, slow, slow-moving, sluggish, somnolent, torpid, work-shy.
antonyms active, diligent, energetic, industrious.

leach *v.* drain, extract, filter, filtrate, lixiviate, osmose, percolate, seep, strain.

lead *v.* antecede, cause, command, conduct, direct, dispose, draw, escort, exceed, excel, experience, govern, guide, have, head, incline, induce, influence, live, manage, outdo, outstrip, pass, persuade, pilot, precede, preside over, prevail, prompt, spend, steer, supervise, surpass, transcend, undergo, usher.
antonym follow.
n. advance, advantage, clue, direction, edge, example, first place, guidance, guide, hint, indication, leadership, margin, model, precedence, primacy, principal, priority, protagonist, starring role, start, suggestion, supremacy, tip, title role, trace, van, vanguard.
adj. chief, first, foremost, head, leading, main, premier, primary, prime, principal, star.

leader *n.* bell-wether, boss, captain, chief, chieftain, commander, conductor, coryphaeus, counselor, director, doyen, figurehead, flagship, guide, head, mahatma, principal, ringleader, ruler, skipper, superior, supremo.
antonym follower.

leading *adj.* chief, dominant, first, foremost, governing, greatest, highest, main, number one, outstanding, paramount, pre-eminent, primary, principal, ruling, superior, supreme.
antonyms subordinate.

league *n.* alliance, association, band, Bund, cartel, category, class, coalition, combination, combine, compact, confederacy, confederation, consortium, federation, fellowship, fraternity, group, guild, level, partnership, sorority, syndicate, union.
v. ally, amalgamate, associate, band, collaborate, combine, confederate, consort, join forces, unite.

leak *n.* aperture, chink, crack, crevice, disclosure, divulgence, drip, fissure, hole, leakage, leaking, oozing, opening, percolation, perforation, puncture, seepage.
v. discharge, disclose, divulge, drip, escape, exude, give away, let slip, let the cat out of the bag, make known, make public, make water, ooze, pass, pass on, percolate, reveal, seep, spill, spill the beans, tell, trickle, weep.

lean[1] *v.* bend, confide, count on, depend, favor, incline, list, prefer, prop, recline, rely, repose, rest, slant, slope, tend, tilt, tip, trust.

lean[2] *adj.* angular, bare, barren, bony, emaciated, gaunt, inadequate, infertile, lank, meager, pitiful, poor, rangy, scanty, scragged, scraggy, scrawny, skinny, slender, slim, slink(y), spare, sparse, thin, unfruitful, unproductive, wiry.
antonyms fat, fleshy.

lean on force, persuade, pressurize, put pressure on.

leaning *n.* aptitude, bent, bias, disposition, inclination, liking, partiality, penchant, predilection, proclivity, proneness, propensity, susceptibility, taste, tendency, velleity.

leap *v.* advance, bounce, bound, caper, capriole, cavort, clear, curvet, escalate, frisk, gambol, hasten, hop, hurry, increase, jump, jump (over), reach, rocket, rush, skip, soar, spring, surge, vault.
antonyms drop, fall, sink.

n. bound, caper, capriole, curvet, escalation, frisk, hop, increase, jump, rise, sally, skip, spring, surge, upsurge, upswing, vault, volt(e).

learn *v.* acquire, ascertain, assimilate, attain, cognize, con, detect, determine, discern, discover, find out, gather, get off pat, grasp, hear, imbibe, learn by heart, master, memorize, pick up, see, understand.

learned *adj.* academic, adept, blue, cultured, erudite, experienced, expert, highbrow, intellectual, lettered, literate, proficient, sage, scholarly, skilled, versed, well-informed, well-read, wise.
antonyms ignorant, illiterate, uneducated.

learning *n.* acquirements, attainments, culture, edification, education, enlightenment, erudition, information, knowledge, letters, literature, lore, research, scholarship, schoolcraft, schooling, study, tuition, wisdom.

lease *v.* charter, farm out, hire, let, loan, rent, sublet.

leash *n.* check, control, curb, discipline, hold, lead, lyam, rein, restraint, tether.

least *adj.* fewest, last, lowest, meanest, merest, minimum, minutest, poorest, slightest, smallest, tiniest.
antonym most.

leave[1] *v.* abandon, allot, assign, bequeath, cause, cease, cede, commit, consign, decamp, depart, deposit, desert, desist, disappear, do a bunk, drop, entrust, exit, flit, forget, forsake, generate, give over, give up, go, go away, hand down, leave behind, levant, move, produce, pull out, quit, refer, refrain, relinquish, renounce, retire, set out, stop, surrender, take off, transmit, will, withdraw.
antonyms arrive.

leave[2] *n.* allowance, authorization, concession, consent, dispensation, exeat, freedom, furlough, holiday, indulgence, liberty, permission, sabbatical, sanction, time off, vacation.
antonyms refusal, rejection.

lecherous *adj.* carnal, concupiscent, goatish, lascivious, lewd, libidinous, licentious, lickerish, liquorish, lubricous, lustful, prurient, randy, raunchy, salacious, unchaste, wanton, womanizing.

lecture *n.* address, castigation, censure, chiding, discourse, disquisition, dressing-down, going-over, harangue, instruction, lesson, prelection, rebuke, reprimand, reproof, scolding, speech, talk, talking-to, telling-off, wigging.
v. address, admonish, berate, carpet, castigate, censure, chide, discourse, expound, harangue, hold forth, lucubrate, prelect, rate, reprimand, reprove, scold, speak, talk, teach, tell off.

ledge *n.* berm, mantle, projection, ridge, shelf, shelve, sill, step.

leech *n.* bloodsucker, freeloader, hanger-on, parasite, sponger, sycophant, usurer.

leer *v.* eye, fleer, gloat, goggle, grin, ogle, smirk, squint, stare, wink.
n. grin, ogle, smirk, squint, stare, wink.

leeway *n.* elbow-room, latitude, play, room, scope, space.

left-overs *n.* dregs, fag-end, leavings, oddments, odds and ends, orts, refuse, remainder, remains, remnants, residue, scraps, surplus, sweepings.

legacy *n.* bequest, birthright, devise, endowment, estate, gift, heirloom, hereditament, heritage, heritance, inheritance, patrimony.

legal *adj.* above-board, allowable, allowed, authorized, constitutional, forensic, judicial, juridical, lawful, legalized, legitimate, licit, permissible, proper, rightful, sanctioned, valid, warrantable.
antonym illegal.

legalize *v.* allow, approve, authorize, decriminalize, legitimate, legitimize, license, permit, sanction, validate, warrant.

legate *n.* ambassador, delegate, depute, deputy, emissary, envoy, exarch, messenger, nuncio.

legend *n.* caption, celebrity, cipher, code, device, fable, fiction, folk-tale, household name, inscription, key, luminary, marvel, motto, myth, narrative, phenomenon, prodigy, saga, spectacle, story, tale, tradition, wonder.

legendary *adj.* apocryphal, celebrated, fabled, fabulous, famed, famous, fanciful, fictional, fictitious, illustrious, immortal, mythical, renowned, romantic, storied, storybook, traditional, unhistoric(al), well-known.

legible *adj.* clear, decipherable, discernible, distinct, intelligible, neat, readable.
antonym illegible.

legion *n.* army, battalion, brigade, cohort, company, division, drove, force, horde, host, mass, multitude, myriad, number, regiment, swarm, throng, troop.
adj. countless, illimitable, innumerable, multitudinous, myriad, numberless, numerous.

legislation *n.* act, authorization, bill, charter, codification, constitutionalization, enactment, law, law-making, measure, prescription, regulation, ruling, statute.

legislator *n.* law-giver, law-maker, nomothete, parliamentarian.

legitimate *adj.* acknowledged, admissible, authentic, authorized, correct, genuine, just, justifiable, kosher, lawful, legal, legit, licit, logical, proper, real, reasonable, rightful, sanctioned, sensible, statutory, true, true-born, valid, warranted, well-founded.
antonym illegitimate.
v. authorize, charter, entitle, legalize, legitimize, license, permit, sanction.

leisure *n.* breather, ease, freedom, holiday, let-up, liberty, opportunity, pause, quiet, recreation, relaxation, respite, rest, retirement, spare time, time off, vacation.
antonyms toil, work.

leisurely *adj.* carefree, comfortable, deliberate, easy, gentle, indolent, laid-back, lazy, lingering, loose, relaxed, restful, slow, tranquil, unhasty, unhurried.
antonyms hectic, hurried, rushed.

lend *v.* add, advance, afford, bestow, confer, contribute, furnish, give, grant, impart, lease, loan, present, provide, supply.
antonym borrow.

length *n.* distance, duration, elongation, extensiveness, extent, lengthiness, longitude, measure, operoseness, operosity, period, piece, portion, prolixity, protractedness, reach, section, segment, space, span, stretch, tediousness, term.

lengthen *v.* continue, draw out, eke, eke out, elongate, expand, extend, increase, pad out, prolong, prolongate, protract, spin out, stretch.
antonym shorten.

leniency *n.* clemency, compassion, forbearance, gentleness, indulgence, lenience, lenity, mercy, mildness, moderation, permissiveness, soft-heartedness, softness, tenderness, tolerance.
antonym severity.

lenient *adj.* clement, compassionate, easy-going, forbearing, forgiving, gentle, indulgent, kind, merciful, mild, soft, soft-hearted, sparing, tender, tolerant.
antonym severe.

lessen *v.* abate, abridge, bate, contract, curtail, deaden, decrease, de-escalate, degrade, die down, diminish, dwindle, ease, erode, fail, flag, impair, lighten, lower, minimize, moderate, narrow, reduce, shrink, slack, slow down, weaken.
antonym increase.

lesson *n.* admonition, assignment, censure, chiding, class, coaching, deterrent, drill, example, exemplar, exercise, homework, instruction, lection, lecture, message, model, moral, pericope, period, practice, precept, punishment, reading, rebuke, recitation, reprimand, reproof, schooling, scolding, task, teaching, tutorial, tutoring, warning.

let[1] *v.* agree to, allow, authorize, cause, charter, consent to, empower, enable, entitle, give leave, give permission, give the go-ahead, give the green light, grant, hire, lease, make, OK, permit, rent, sanction, tolerate.
antonym forbid.

let[2] *n.* check, constraint, hindrance, impediment, interference, obstacle, obstruction, prohibition, restraint, restriction.
antonym assistance.

let-down *n.* anticlimax, betrayal, blow, desertion, disappointment, disillusionment, frustration, lemon, setback, wash-out.
antonym satisfaction.

lethal *adj.* baleful, dangerous, deadly, deathful, deathly, destructive, devastating, fatal, lethiferous, mortal, mortiferous, murderous, noxious, pernicious, poisonous, virulent.
antonym harmless.

lethargic *adj.* apathetic, comatose, debilitated, drowsy, dull, enervated, heavy, hebetant, hebetated, hebetudinous, inactive, indifferent, inert, languid, lazy, listless, sleepy, slothful, slow, sluggish, somnolent, stupefied, torpid.
antonym lively.

lethargy *n.* apathy, drowsiness, dullness, hebetation, hebetude, hebetudinosity, inaction, indifference, inertia, languor, lassitude, listlessness, sleepiness, sloth, slowness, sluggishness, stupor, torpidity, torpor.
antonym liveliness.

letter[1] *n.* acknowledgment, answer, billet, chit, communication, da(w)k, dispatch, encyclical, epistle, epistolet, line, message, missive, note, reply.

letter[2] *n.* character, grapheme, lexigram, logogram, logograph, sign, symbol.

let-up *n.* abatement, break, breather, cessation, interval, lessening, lull, pause, recess, remission, respite, slackening.
antonym continuation.

level[1] *adj.* aligned, balanced, calm, champaign, commensurate, comparable, consistent, equable, equal, equivalent, even, even-tempered, flat, flush, horizontal, neck and neck, on a par, plain, proportionate, smooth, stable, steady, uniform.
antonyms behind, uneven, unstable.
v. aim, beam, bulldoze, couch, demolish, destroy, devastate, direct, equalize, even out, flatten, flush, focus, knock down, lay low, plane, point, pull down, raze, smooth, tear down, train, wreck.
n. altitude, bed, class, degree, echelon, elevation, floor, grade, height, horizontal, layer, plain, plane, position, rank, stage, standard, standing, status, story, stratum, zone.

level[2] *v.* admit, avow, come clean, confess, divulge, open up, tell.
antonym prevaricate.

level-headed *adj.* balanced, calm, collected, commonsensical, composed, cool, dependable, even-tempered, reasonable, sane, self-possessed, sensible, steady, together, unflappable.

leverage *n.* advantage, ascendancy, authority, clout, force, influence, pull, purchase, rank, strength, weight.

levity *n.* buoyancy, facetiousness, fickleness, flightiness, flippancy, frivolity, giddiness, irreverence, light-heartedness, silliness, skittishness, triviality, whifflery.
antonyms seriousness, sobriety.

levy *v.* assemble, call, call up, charge, collect, conscript, demand, exact, gather, impose, mobilize, muster, press, raise, summon, tax.
n. assessment, collection, contribution, duty, exaction, excise, fee, gathering, imposition, impost, subscription, tariff, tax, toll.

lewd *adj.* bawdy, blue, Cyprian, dirty, harlot, impure, indecent, lascivious, libidinous, licentious, loose, lubric, lubrical, lubricious, lubricous, lustful, obscene, pornographic, profligate, salacious, smutty, unchaste, vile, vulgar, wanton, wicked.
antonyms chaste, polite.

liability *n.* accountability, albatross, answerability, arrears, burden, culpability, debit, debt, disadvantage, drag, drawback, duty, encumbrance, handicap, hindrance, impediment, inconvenience, indebtedness, likeliness, millstone, minus, nuisance, obligation, onus, responsibility.
antonyms asset(s), unaccountability.

liable *adj.* accountable, amenable, answerable, apt, bound, chargeable, disposed, exposed, inclined, likely, obligated, open, predisposed, prone, responsible, subject, susceptible, tending, vulnerable.
antonyms unaccountable, unlikely.

liaison *n.* affair, amour, communication, conjunction, connection, contact, entanglement, interchange, intermediary, intrigue, link, love affair, romance, union.

liar *n.* Ananias, bouncer, deceiver, fabricator, falsifier, fibber, perjurer, prevaricator, storyteller.

libel *n.* aspersion, calumny, defamation, denigration, obloquy, slander, slur, smear, vilification, vituperation.
antonym praise.
v. blacken, calumniate, defame, derogate, malign, revile, slander, slur, smear, traduce, vilify, vilipend, vituperate.
antonym praise.

liberal *adj.* abundant, advanced, altruistic, ample, beneficent, bounteous, bountiful, broad, broad-minded, catholic, charitable, copious, enlightened, flexible, free, free-handed, general, generous, handsome, high-minded, humanistic, humanitarian, indulgent, inexact, kind, large-hearted, latitudinarian, lavish, lenient, libertarian, loose, magnanimous, munificent, open-handed, open-hearted, permissive, plentiful, profuse, progressive, radical, reformist, rich, tolerant, unbiased, unbigoted, unprejudiced, unstinting, verligte, Whig, Whiggish.
antonyms conservative, illiberal, mean, narrow-minded.

liberality *n.* altruism, beneficence, benevolence, bounty, breadth, broad-mindedness, candor, catholicity, charity, free-handedness, generosity, impartiality, kindness, large-heartedness, largess(e), latitude, liberalism, libertarianism, magnanimity, munificence, open-handedness, open-mindedness, permissiveness, philanthropy, progressivism, tolerance, toleration.
antonyms illiberality, meanness.

liberate *v.* affranchise, deliver, discharge, disenthral, emancipate, free, let go, let loose, let out, manumit, ransom, redeem, release, rescue, set free, uncage, unchain, unfetter, unpen, unshackle.
antonyms enslave, imprison, restrict.

liberation *n.* deliverance, emancipation, enfranchisement, freedom, freeing, liberating, liberty, manumission, ransoming, redemption, release, uncaging, unchaining, unfettering, unpenning, unshackling.
antonyms enslavement, imprisonment, restriction.

liberty *n.* authorization, autonomy, carte-blanche, dispensation, emancipation, exemption, franchise, free rein, freedom, immunity, independence, latitude, leave, liberation, license, permission, prerogative, privilege, release, right, sanction, self-determination, sovereignty.
antonyms imprisonment, restriction, slavery.

libretto *n.* book, lines, lyrics, script, text, words.

license[1] *n.* authorization, authority, carte blanche, certificate, charter, dispensation, entitlement, exemption, freedom, immunity, imprimatur, independence, indult, latitude, tude, leave, liberty, permission, permit, privilege, right, self-determination, warrant.
antonyms banning, dependence, restriction.

license[2] *n.* abandon, amorality, anarchy, debauchery, disorder, dissipation, dissoluteness, excess, immoderation, impropriety, indulgence, intemperance, irresponsibility, lawlessness, laxity, profligacy, unruliness.
antonyms decorum, temperance.

license[3] *v.* accredit, allow, authorize, certificate, certify, commission, empower, entitle, permit, sanction, warrant.
antonym ban.

lick[1] *v.* brush, dart, flick, lap, play over, smear, taste, tongue, touch, wash.
n. bit, brush, dab, hint, little, sample, smidgeon, speck, spot, stroke, taste, touch.

lick[2] *v.* beat, best, defeat, excel, flog, outdo, outstrip, overcome, rout, skelp, slap, smack, spank, strike, surpass, thrash, top, trounce, vanquish, wallop.

lick[3] *n.* clip, gallop, pace, rate, speed.

lie[1] *v.* dissimulate, equivocate, fabricate, falsify, fib, forswear oneself, invent, misrepresent, perjure, prevaricate.
n. bam, bounce, caulker, cram, crammer, cretism, deceit, fabrication, falsehood, falsification, falsity, fib, fiction, flam, invention, inveracity, mendacity, plumper, prevarication, stretcher, tar(r)adiddle, untruth, whacker, white lie, whopper.
antonym truth.

lie[2] *v.* be, belong, couch, dwell, exist, extend, inhere, laze, loll, lounge, recline, remain, repose, rest, slump, sprawl, stretch out.

life *n.* activity, animation, autobiography, behavior, being, biography, breath, brio, career, conduct, confessions, continuance, course, creatures, duration, élan vital, energy, entity, essence, existence, fauna, flora and fauna, get-up-and-go, go, growth, heart, high spirits, history, life story, life-blood, life-style, lifetime, liveliness, memoirs, oomph, organisms, sentience, soul, span, sparkle, spirit, story, the world, this mortal coil, time, verve, viability, vigor, vita, vital flame, vital spark, vitality, vivacity, way of life, wildlife, zest.

lift[1] *v.* advance, ameliorate, annul, appropriate, arrest, ascend, boost, buoy up, cancel, climb, collar, copy, countermand, crib, dignify, disappear, disperse, dissipate, draw up, elevate, end, enhance, exalt, half-inch, heft, hoist, improve, mount, nab, nick, pick up, pilfer, pinch, pirate, plagiarize, pocket, promote, purloin, raise, rear, relax, remove, rescind, revoke, rise, steal, stop, take, terminate, thieve, up, upgrade, uplift, upraise, vanish.

antonyms drop, fall, impose, lower.

n. boost, encouragement, fillip, pick-me-up, reassurance, shot in the arm, spur, uplift.

antonym discouragement.

lift[2] *n.* drive, hitch, ride, run, transport.

light[1] *n.* beacon, blaze, brightness, brilliance, bulb, candle, cockcrow, dawn, day, daybreak, daylight, daytime, effulgence, flame, flare, flash, glare, gleam, glim, glint, glow, illumination, incandescence, lambency, lamp, lampad, lantern, lighter, lighthouse, luminescence, luminosity, luster, match, morn, morning, phosphorescence, radiance, ray, refulgence, scintillation, shine, sparkle, star, sunrise, sunshine, taper, torch, window, Yang.

antonym darkness.

v. animate, beacon, brighten, cheer, fire, floodlight, ignite, illuminate, illumine, inflame, irradiate, kindle, light up, lighten, put on, set alight, set fire to, switch on, turn on.

antonyms darken, extinguish.

adj. bleached, blond, bright, brilliant, faded, faint, fair, glowing, illuminated, lightful, lightsome, lucent, luminous, lustrous, pale, pastel, shining, sunny, well-lit.

antonym dark.

light[2] *n.* angle, approach, aspect, attitude, awareness, clue, comprehension, context, elucidation, enlightenment, example, exemplar, explanation, hint, illustration, information, insight, interpretation, knowledge, model, paragon, point of view, slant, understanding, viewpoint.

light[3] *adj.* agile, airy, amusing, animated, blithe, buoyant, carefree, cheerful, cheery, crumbly, delicate, delirious, digestible, diverting, dizzy, easy, effortless, entertaining, facile, faint, fickle, flimsy, friable, frivolous, frugal, funny, gay, gentle, giddy, graceful, humorous, idle, imponderous, inconsequential, inconsiderable, indistinct, insignificant, insubstantial, light-footed, light-headed, light-hearted, lightweight, lithe, lively, loose, manageable, merry, mild, minute, moderate, modest, nimble, pleasing, porous, portable, reeling, restricted, sandy, scanty, simple, slight, small, soft, spongy, sprightly, sunny, superficial, thin, tiny, trifling, trivial, unchaste, undemanding, underweight, unexacting, unheeding, unsteady, unsubstantial, untaxing, volatile, wanton, weak, witty, worthless.

antonyms clumsy, harsh, heavy, important, sad, severe, sober, solid, stiff.

lighten[1] *v.* beacon, brighten, illume, illuminate, illumine, light up, shine.

antonym darken.

lighten[2] *v.* alleviate, ameliorate, assuage, brighten, buoy up, cheer, disburden, disencumber, ease, elate, encourage, facilitate, gladden, hearten, inspire, inspirit, lessen, lift, mitigate, perk up, reduce, relieve, revive, unload, uplift.

antonyms burden, depress, oppress.

light-hearted *adj.* blithe, blithesome, bright, carefree, cheerful, effervescent, elated, frolicsome, gay, glad, gleeful, happy-go-lucky, insouciant, jocund, jolly, jovial, joyful, joyous, light-spirited, merry, perky, playful, sunny, untroubled, upbeat.

antonym sad.

like[1] *adj.* akin, alike, allied, analogous, approximating, cognate, corresponding, equivalent, homologous, identical, parallel, related, relating, resembling, same, similar.

antonym unlike.

n. counterpart, equal, fellow, match, opposite number, parallel, peer, twin.

prep. in the same manner as, on the lines of, similar to.

like[2] *v.* admire, adore, appreciate, approve, care to, cherish, choose, choose to, delight in, desire, dig, enjoy, esteem, fancy, feel inclined, go a bundle on, go for, hold dear, love, prefer, prize, relish, revel in, select, take a shine to, take kindly to, take to, want, wish.

antonym dislike.

n. favorite, liking, love, partiality, penchant, poison, predilection, preference.

antonym dislike.

likely *adj.* acceptable, agreeable, anticipated, appropriate, apt, befitting, believable, bright, credible, disposed, expected, fair, favorite, feasible, fit, foreseeable, hopeful, inclined, liable, odds-on, on the cards, plausible, pleasing, possible, predictable, probable, promising, prone, proper, qualified, reasonable, suitable, tending, up-and-coming, verisimilar.

antonyms unlikely, unsuitable.

adv. doubtlessly, in all probability, like as not, like enough, no doubt, odds on, presumably, probably, very like.

likeness *n.* affinity, appearance, copy, correspondence, counterpart, delineation, depiction, effigies, effigy, facsimile, form, guise, image, model, photograph, picture, portrait, replica, representation, reproduction, resemblance, semblance, similarity, similitude, simulacrum, study.

antonym unlikeness.

likewise *adv.* also, besides, by the same token, eke, further, furthermore, in addition, moreover, similarly, too.

antonym contrariwise.

liking *n.* affection, affinity, appreciation, attraction, bent, bias, desire, favor, fondness, inclination, love, partiality, penchant, predilection, preference, proneness, propensity, satisfaction, soft spot, stomach, taste, tendency, weakness.

antonym dislike.

limb *n.* appendage, arm, bough, branch, extension, extremity, fork, leg, member, offshoot, part, projection, ramus, spur, wing.

limber *adj.* agile, elastic, flexible, flexile, graceful, lissom, lithe, loose-jointed, loose-limbed, plastic, pliable, pliant, supple. *antonym* stiff.

limelight *n.* attention, big time, celebrity, fame, prominence, public notice, publicity, recognition, renown, stardom, the public eye, the spotlight.

limit *n.* bitter end, border, bound, boundary, bourne(e), brim, brink, ceiling, check, compass, confines, curb, cut-off point, deadline, edge, end, extent, frontier, limitation, maximum, mete, obstruction, outrance, perimeter, periphery, precinct, restraint, restriction, rim, saturation point, termination, terminus, terminus a quo, terminus ad quem, threshold, ultimate, utmost, verge. *v.* bound, check, circumscribe, condition, confine, constrain, curb, delimit, delimitate, demarcate, fix, hem in, hinder, ration, restrain, restrict, specify. *antonyms* extend, free.

limp[1] *v.* dot, falter, halt, hamble, hirple, hitch, hobble, hop, shamble, shuffle. *n.* claudication, hitch, hobble, lameness.

limp[2] *adj.* debilitated, drooping, enervated, exhausted, flabby, flaccid, flexible, flexile, floppy, hypotonic, lax, lethargic, limber, loose, pliable, pooped, relaxed, slack, soft, spent, tired, toneless, weak, worn out. *antonym* strong.

limpid *adj.* bright, clear, comprehensible, crystal-clear, crystalline, glassy, hyaline, intelligible, lucid, pellucid, pure, still, translucent, transparent, unruffled, untroubled. *antonyms* muddy, ripply, turbid, unintelligible.

line[1] *n.* band, bar, border, borderline, boundary, cable, chain, channel, column, configuration, contour, cord, crease, crocodile, crow's foot, dash, demarcation, disposition, edge, features, figure, filament, file, firing line, formation, front, front line, frontier, furrow, groove, limit, mark, outline, position, procession, profile, queue, rank, rope, row, rule, score, scratch, sequence, series, silhouette, stipe, strand, streak, string, stroke, tail, thread, trail, trenches, underline, wire, wrinkle. *v.* border, bound, crease, cut, draw, edge, fringe, furrow, hatch, inscribe, mark, rank, rim, rule, score, skirt, verge.

line up align, arrange, array, assemble, dispose, engage, fall in, form ranks, hire, lay on, marshal, obtain, order, organize, prepare, procure, produce, queue up, range, regiment, secure, straighten.

line[2] *n.* activity, approach, area, avenue, axis, belief, business, calling, course, course of action, department, direction, employment, field, forte, ideology, interest, job, line of country, method, occupation, path, policy, position, practice, procedure, profession, province, pursuit, route, scheme, specialism, specialization, specialty, system, track, trade, trajectory, vocation.

line[3] *n.* ancestry, breed, family, lineage, pedigree, race, stirps, stock, strain, succession.

line[4] *n.* card, clue, hint, indication, information, lead, letter, memo, memorandum, message, note, postcard, report, word.

line[5] *v.* ceil, cover, encase, face, fill, reinforce, strengthen, stuff.

lineage *n.* ancestors, ancestry, birth, breed, descendants, descent, extraction, family, forebears, forefathers, genealogy, heredity, house, line, offspring, pedigree, progeny, race, stirp(s), stock, succession.

linger *v.* abide, continue, dally, dawdle, delay, dillydally, endure, hang around, hang on, hold out, idle, lag, last out, loiter, persist, procrastinate, remain, stay, stop, survive, tarry, wait. *antonyms* leave, rush.

lingo *n.* argot, cant, dialect, idiom, jargon, language, parlance, patois, patter, speech, talk, terminology, tongue, vernacular, vocabulary.

link *n.* association, attachment, bond, communication, component, connection, constituent, division, element, joint, knot, liaison, member, part, piece, relationship, tie, tie-up, union. *v.* associate, attach, bind, bracket, catenate, concatenate, connect, couple, fasten, identify, join, relate, tie, unite, yoke. *antonyms* separate, unfasten.

lip[1] *n.* border, brim, brink, edge, margin, rim, verge.

lip[2] *n.* backchat, cheek, effrontery, impertinence, impudence, insolence, rudeness, sauce. *antonym* politeness.

liquid *n.* drink, fluid, juice, liquor, lotion, potation, sap, solution. *adj.* aqueous, clear, convertible, dulcet, flowing, fluid, limpid, liquefied, mellifluent, mellifluous, melted, molten, negotiable, running, runny, serous, shining, smooth, soft, sweet, thawed, translucent, transparent, watery, wet. *antonyms* harsh, solid.

liquidate *v.* abolish, annihilate, annul, assassinate, bump off, cancel, cash, clear, destroy, discharge, dispatch, dissolve, do away with, do in, eliminate, exterminate, finish off, honor, kill, massacre, murder, pay, pay off, realize, remove, rub out, sell off, sell up, settle, silence, square, terminate, wipe out.

liquor[1] *n.* aguardiente, alcohol, booze, drink, fire-water, grog, hard stuff, hooch, intoxicant, juice, jungle juice, potation, rotgut, spirits, strong drink, tape.

liquor[2] *n.* broth, essence, extract, gravy, infusion, juice, liquid, stock.

lissom(e) *adj.* agile, flexible, graceful, light, limber, lithe, lithesome, loose-jointed, loose-limbed, nimble, pliable, pliant, supple, willowy. *antonym* stiff.

list[1] *n.* catalog, directory, enumeration, file, index, inventory, invoice, leet, listing, litany, matricula, record, register, roll, schedule, series, syllabus, table, tabulation, tally.

v. alphabeticize, bill, book, catalog, enrol, enter, enumerate, file, index, itemize, note, record, register, schedule, set down, tabulate, write down.

list² *v.* cant, careen, heel, heel over, incline, lean, slope, tilt, tip.

n. cant, leaning, slant, slope, tilt.

listen *v.* attend, get a load of, give ear, give heed to, hang on (someone's) words, hang on (someone's) lips, hark, hear, hearken, heed, keep one's ears open, lend an ear, mind, obey, observe, pay attention, pin back one's ears, prick up one's ears, take notice.

listless *adj.* apathetic, bored, depressed, enervated, ennuyed, heavy, impassive, inattentive, indifferent, indolent, inert, languid, languishing, lethargic, lifeless, limp, lymphatic, mopish, sluggish, spiritless, supine, torpid, uninterested, vacant.

antonym lively.

literal *adj.* accurate, actual, boring, close, colorless, down-to-earth, dull, exact, factual, faithful, genuine, matter-of-fact, plain, prosaic, prosy, real, simple, strict, true, unexaggerated, unimaginative, uninspired, unvarnished, verbatim, word-for-word.

antonym loose.

literally *adv.* actually, closely, exactly, faithfully, literatim, plainly, precisely, really, simply, strictly, to the letter, truly, verbatim, word for word.

antonym loosely.

literary *adj.* bookish, cultivated, cultured, erudite, formal, learned, lettered, literate, refined, scholarly, well-read.

antonym illiterate.

literature *n.* belles-lettres, blurb, brochure(s), bumf, circular(s), hand-out(s), information, leaflet(s), letters, lore, pamphlet(s), paper(s), writings.

lithe *adj.* double-jointed, flexible, flexile, limber, lissom(e), lithesome, loose-jointed, loose-limbed, pliable, pliant, supple.

antonym stiff.

litigious *adj.* argumentative, belligerent, contentious, disputable, disputatious, quarrelsome.

antonym easy-going.

litter¹ *n.* clutter, confusion, debris, detritus, disarray, disorder, fragments, jumble, mess, muck, refuse, rubbish, scatter, scoria, shreds, untidiness, wastage.

v. bestrew, clutter, derange, disarrange, disorder, mess up, scatter, strew.

antonym tidy.

litter² *n.* brood, family, offspring, progeny, quiverful, young.

litter³ *n.* couch, palanquin, stretcher.

little *adj.* babyish, base, brief, cheap, diminutive, dwarf, elfin, fleeting, hasty, immature, inconsiderable, infant, infinitesimal, insignificant, insufficient, junior, Lilliputian, meager, mean, microscopic, miniature, minor, minute, negligible, paltry, passing, petite, petty, piccaninny, pintsize(d), pygmy, scant, short, short-lived, skimpy, slender, small, sparse, tiny, transient, trifling, trivial, undeveloped, unimportant, wee, young.

antonyms important, large, long.

adv. barely, hardly, infrequently, rarely, scarcely, seldom.

antonyms frequently, greatly.

n. bit, dab, dash, drib, fragment, hint, modicum, particle, pinch, snippet, speck, spot, taste, touch, trace, trifle.

antonym lot.

liturgy *n.* celebration, ceremony, form, formula, office, rite, ritual, sacrament, service, usage, worship.

live¹ *v.* abide, breathe, continue, draw breath, dwell, earn a living, endure, exist, fare, feed, get along, hang out, inhabit, last, lead, lodge, make ends meet, pass, persist, prevail, remain, reside, settle, stay, subsist, survive.

antonyms cease, die.

live² *adj.* active, alert, alight, alive, animate, blazing, breathing, brisk, burning, connected, controversial, current, dynamic, earnest, energetic, existent, glowing, hot, ignited, lively, living, pertinent, pressing, prevalent, relevant, sentient, smoldering, topical, unsettled, vigorous, vital, vivid, wide-awake.

antonyms apathetic, dead, out.

livelihood *n.* employment, income, job, living, maintenance, means, occupation, subsistence, support, sustenance, work.

lively *adj.* active, agile, alert, animated, astir, blithe, blithesome, breezy, bright, brisk, buckish, bustling, busy, buxom, buzzing, canty, cheerful, chipper, chirpy, colorful, crowded, energetic, eventful, exciting, forceful, frisky, frolicsome, galliard, gay, invigorating, keen, lifesome, lightsome, merry, moving, nimble, perky, quick, racy, refreshing, skittish, sparkling, spirited, sprightly, spry, stimulating, stirring, swinging, tit(t)upy, vigorous, vivacious, vivid, zippy.

antonyms apathetic, inactive, moribund.

livid¹ *adj.* angry, beside oneself, boiling, enraged, exasperated, fuming, furibund, furious, incensed, indignant, infuriated, irate, ireful, mad, outraged, waxy.

antonym calm.

livid² *adj.* angry, ashen, black-and-blue, blanched, bloodless, bruised, contused, discolored, doughy, grayish, leaden, pale, pallid, pasty, purple, wan, waxen, waxy.

antonyms healthy, rosy.

living *adj.* active, alive, animated, breathing, existing, live, lively, strong, vigorous, vital.

antonyms dead, sluggish.

n. being, benefice, existence, income, job, life, livelihood, maintenance, occupation, profession, property, subsistence, support, sustenance, way of life, work.

load *n.* affliction, albatross, bale, burden, cargo, consignment, encumbrance, freight, goods, lading, millstone, onus, oppression, pressure, shipment, trouble, weight, worry.

v. adulterate, burden, charge, cram, doctor, drug,

encumber, fill, fortify, freight, hamper, heap, lade, oppress, overburden, pack, pile, prime, saddle with, stack, stuff, trouble, weigh down, weight, worry.

loafer *n.* beachcomber, bludger, bum, bummer, burn, corner-boy, do-nothing, drone, idler, layabout, lazybones, lounge-lizard, lounger, ne'er-do-well, shirker, skiver, sluggard, time-waster, wastrel. *antonym* worker.

loan *n.* accommodation, advance, allowance, calque, credit, lend-lease, loan translation, loan-word, mortgage, touch.
v. accommodate, advance, allow, credit, lend, let out, oblige.
antonym borrow.

loath *adj.* against, averse, backward, counter, disinclined, grudging, hesitant, indisposed, opposed, reluctant, resisting, unwilling.
antonym willing.

loathe *v.* abhor, abominate, despise, detest, dislike, execrate, hate, keck.
antonym like.

loathsome *adj.* abhorrent, abominable, detestable, disgusting, execrable, hateful, horrible, loathful, nasty, nauseating, obnoxious, odious, offensive, repellent, repugnant, repulsive, revolting, vile.
antonym likeable.

lob *v.* chuck, fling, heave, launch, lift, loft, pitch, shy, throw, toss.

lobby[1] *v.* call for, campaign for, demand, influence, persuade, press for, pressure, promote, pull strings, push for, solicit, urge.
n. ginger group, pressure group.

lobby[2] *n.* anteroom, corridor, entrance hall, foyer, hall, hallway, passage, passageway, porch, vestibule, waiting-room.

local *adj.* community, confined, district, limited, narrow, neighborhood, parish, parochial, provincial, pump, regional, restricted, small-town, vernacular, vicinal.
antonym far-away.
n. denizen, inhabitant, native, resident, yokel.
antonym incomer.

locality *n.* area, district, locale, location, neck of the woods, neighborhood, place, position, region, scene, settings, site, spot, vicinity, zone.

locate *v.* detect, discover, establish, find, fix, identify, lay one's hands on, pin-point, place, put, run to earth, seat, set, settle, situate, track down, unearth.

location *n.* bearings, locale, locus, place, point, position, site, situation, spot, ubiety, venue, whereabouts.

lock[1] *n.* bolt, clasp, fastening, padlock, sneck.
v. bolt, clasp, clench, close, clutch, disengage, embrace, encircle, enclose, engage, entangle, entwine, fasten, grapple, grasp, hug, join, latch, link, mesh, press, seal, secure, shut, sneck, unite, unlock.

lock out ban, bar, debar, exclude, keep out, ostracize, refuse admittance to, shut out.

lock together interdigitate, interlock.

lock up cage, close up, confine, detain, enlock, imprison, incarcerate, jail, pen, secure, shut, shut in, shut up.
antonym free.

lock[2] *n.* curl, plait, ringlet, strand, tress, tuft.

locomotion *n.* action, ambulation, headway, motion, movement, moving, progress, progression, travel, traveling.

locution *n.* accent, articulation, cliché, collocation, diction, expression, idiom, inflection, intonation, phrase, phrasing, style, term, turn of phrase, wording.

lodge *n.* abode, assemblage, association, branch, cabin, chalet, chapter, club, cot, cot-house, cottage, den, ganghut, gatehouse, group, haunt, house, hunting-lodge, hut, lair, meeting-place, retreat, shelter, society.
v. accommodate, billet, board, deposit, dig, entertain, file, get stuck, harbor, imbed, implant, lay, place, put, put on record, put up, quarter, register, room, set, shelter, sojourn, stay, stick, stop, submit.

lodger *n.* boarder, guest, inmate, paying guest, renter, resident, roomer, tenant.

lofty *adj.* arrogant, condescending, dignified, disdainful, distinguished, elevated, esteemed, exalted, grand, haughty, high, high and mighty, illustrious, imperial, imposing, lordly, majestic, noble, patronizing, proud, raised, renowned, sky-high, snooty, soaring, stately, sublime, supercilious, superior, tall, toffee-nosed, towering. *antonyms* humble, low(ly), modest.

log[1] *n.* billet, block, bole, chunk, loggat, stump, timber, trunk.

log[2] *n.* account, chart, daybook, diary, journal, listing, logbook, record, tally.
v. book, chart, note, record, register, report, tally, write down, write in, write up.

logic *n.* argumentation, deduction, dialectic(s), ratiocination, rationale, rationality, reason, reasoning, sense.

logistics *n.* co-ordination, engineering, management, masterminding, orchestration, organization, planning, plans, strategy.

loiter *v.* dally, dawdle, delay, dilly-dally, hang about, idle, lag, lallygag, linger, loaf, loll, lollygag, mooch, mouch, saunter, skulk, stroll.

loll *v.* dangle, depend, droop, drop, flap, flop, hang, lean, loaf, lounge, recline, relax, sag, slouch, slump, sprawl.

lone *adj.* deserted, isolated, lonesome, one, only, separate, separated, single, sole, solitary, unaccompanied, unattached, unattended.
antonym accompanied.

loneliness *n.* aloneness, desolation, forlornness, friendlessness, isolation, lonesomeness, seclusion, solitariness, solitude.

lonely *adj.* abandoned, alone, apart, companionless, destitute, estranged, forlorn, forsaken, friendless, isolated, lonely-heart, lonesome, outcast, out-of-the-way, remote, secluded, sequestered, solitary, unfrequented, uninhabited, untrodden.

loner *n.* hermit, individualist, lone wolf, maverick, outsider, pariah, recluse, solitary, solitudinarian.

lonesome *adj.* cheerless, companionless, deserted, desolate, dreary, forlorn, friendless, gloomy, isolated, lone, lonely, solitary.

long *adj.* dragging, elongated, expanded, expansive, extended, extensive, far-reaching, interminable, late, lengthy, lingering, long-drawn-out, marathon, prolonged, protracted, slow, spread out, stretched, sustained, tardy.

antonyms abbreviated, brief, fleeting, short.

long-standing *adj.* abiding, enduring, established, fixed, hallowed, long-established, long-lasting, long-lived, time-honored, traditional.

long-winded *adj.* circumlocutory, diffuse, discursive, garrulous, lengthy, long-drawn-out, overlong, prolix, prolonged, rambling, repetitious, tedious, verbose, voluble, wordy.

antonyms brief, compact, curt, terse.

look *v.* appear, behold, consider, contemplate, display, evidence, examine, exhibit, eye, gape, gawk, gawp, gaze, get a load of, glance, goggle, inspect, observe, ogle, peep, regard, rubberneck, scan, scrutinize, see, seem, show, stare, study, survey, view, watch.

n. air, appearance, aspect, bearing, cast, complexion, countenance, decko, demeanor, effect, examination, expression, eyeful, eye-glance, face, fashion, gaze, glance, glimpse, guise, inspection, look-see, manner, mien, observation, once-over, peek, review, semblance, sight, squint, survey, view.

loom *v.* appear, bulk, dominate, emerge, hang over, hover, impend, materialize, menace, mount, overhang, overshadow, overtop, rise, soar, take shape, threaten, tower.

loop *n.* arc, bend, circle, coil, convolution, curl, curve, eyelet, hoop, kink, loophole, noose, ring, spiral, turn, twirl, twist, whorl.

v. bend, braid, circle, coil, connect, curl, curve round, encircle, fold, gird, join, knot, roll, spiral, turn, twist.

loose[1] *adj.* baggy, crank, diffuse, disconnected, disordered, easy, floating, free, hanging, ill-defined, imprecise, inaccurate, indefinite, indistinct, inexact, insecure, loosened, movable, rambling, random, relaxed, released, shaky, slack, slackened, sloppy, solute, unattached, unbound, unconfined, unfastened, unfettered, unrestricted, unsecured, untied, vague, wobbly.

antonyms close, compact, precise, strict, taut, tense, tight.

v. absolve, detach, disconnect, disengage, ease, free, let go, liberate, loosen, release, set free, slacken, unbind, unbrace, unclasp, uncouple, undo, unfasten, unhand, unleash, unlock, unloose, unmew, unmoor, unpen, untie.

antonyms bind, fasten, fix, secure.

loose[2] *adj.* abandoned, careless, debauched, disreputable, dissipated, dissolute, fast, heedless, immoral, imprudent, lax, lewd, libertine, licentious, negligent, profligate, promiscuous, rash, thoughtless, unchaste, unmindful, wanton.

antonyms strict, stringent, tight.

loosen *v.* deliver, detach, free, let go, let out, liberate, release, separate, set free, slacken, unbind, undo, unfasten, unloose, unloosen, unstick, untie.

antonym tighten.

loot *n.* boodle, booty, cache, goods, haul, plunder, prize, riches, spoils, swag.

v. burglarize, despoil, maraud, pillage, plunder, raid, ransack, ravage, rifle, rob, sack.

lope *v.* bound, canter, gallop, lollop, run, spring, stride.

lop-sided *adj.* askew, asymmetrical, awry, cockeyed, crooked, disproportionate, ill-balanced, off balance, one-sided, out of true, squint, tilting, unbalanced, unequal, uneven, warped.

antonyms balanced, straight, symmetrical.

loquacious *adj.* babbling, blathering, chattering, chatty, gabby, garrulous, gassy, gossipy, multiloquent, multiloquous, talkative, voluble, wordy.

antonyms succinct, taciturn, terse.

lord *n.* baron, commander, count, daimio, duke, earl, governor, Herr, king, leader, liege, liege-lord, master, monarch, noble, nobleman, overlord, peer, potentate, prince, ruler, seigneur, seignior, sovereign, superior, suzerain, viscount.

lore *n.* beliefs, doctrine, erudition, experience, know-how, knowledge, learning, letters, mythus, saws, sayings, scholarship, schooling, teaching, traditions, wisdom.

lose *v.* capitulate, come a cropper, come to grief, consume, default, deplete, displace, dissipate, dodge, drain, drop, duck, elude, escape, evade, exhaust, expend, fail, fall short, forfeit, forget, get the worst of, give (someone) the slip, lap, lavish, leave behind, lose out on, misfile, mislay, misplace, miss, misspend, outdistance, outrun, outstrip, overtake, pass, pass up, shake off, slip away, squander, stray from, suffer defeat, take a licking, throw off, use up, wander from, waste, yield.

antonyms gain, make, win.

loss *n.* bereavement, cost, damage, debit, debt, defeat, deficiency, deficit, depletion, deprivation, destruction, detriment, disadvantage, disappearance, failure, forfeiture, harm, hurt, impairment, injury, losing, losings, misfortune, privation, ruin, shrinkage, squandering, waste, write-off.

antonyms benefit, gain.

lost *adj.* abandoned, abolished, absent, absorbed, abstracted, adrift, annihilated, astray, baffled, bewildered, confused, consumed, corrupt, damned, demolished, depraved, destroyed, devastated, disappeared, disoriented, dissipated, dissolute, distracted, dreamy, engrossed, entranced, eradicated, exterminated, fallen, forfeited, frittered away, irreclaimable, licentious, misapplied, misdirected, mislaid, misplaced, missed, missing, misspent, misused, mystified, obliterated,

off-course, off-track, perished, perplexed, preoccupied, profligate, puzzled, rapt, ruined, spellbound, squandered, strayed, unrecallable, unrecapturable, unrecoverable, untraceable, vanished, wanton, wasted, wayward, wiped out, wrecked.
antonym found.

lot *n.* accident, allowance, assortment, batch, chance, collection, consignment, crowd, cut, destiny, doom, fate, fortune, group, hazard, jing-bang, parcel, part, percentage, piece, plight, portion, quantity, quota, ration, set, share, weird.

lottery *n.* chance, draw, gamble, hazard, raffle, risk, sweep-stake, toss-up, uncertainty, venture.

loud *adj.* blaring, blatant, boisterous, booming, brash, brassy, brazen, clamorous, coarse, crass, crude, deafening, ear-piercing, ear-splitting, flamboyant, flashy, garish, gaudy, glaring, high-sounding, loud-mouthed, lurid, noisy, offensive, ostentatious, piercing, raucous, resounding, rowdy, showy, sonorous, stentorian, streperous, strepitant, strident, strong, tasteless, tawdry, thundering, tumultuous, turbulent, vehement, vocal, vociferous, vulgar.
antonyms low, quiet, soft.

lounge *v.* dawdle, idle, kill time, laze, lie about, lie back, loaf, loiter, loll, potter, recline, relax, slump, sprawl, take it easy, waste time.
n. day-room, drawing-room, parlor, sitting-room.

louring, lowering *adj.* black, brooding, browning, clouded, cloudy, dark, darkening, forbidding, foreboding, gloomy, glowering, gray, grim, heavy, impending, menacing, minatory, ominous, overcast, scowling, sullen, surly, threatening.

lousy *adj.* awful, bad, base, contemptible, crap, despicable, dirty, hateful, inferior, lice-infested, lice-ridden, low, mean, miserable, no good, pedicular, pediculous, poor, rotten, second-rate, shoddy, slovenly, terrible, trashy, vicious, vile.
antonyms excellent, superb.

lovable *adj.* adorable, amiable, attractive, captivating, charming, cuddly, delightful, enchanting, endearing, engaging, fetching, likable, lovely, pleasing, sweet, taking, winning, winsome.
antonym hateful.

love *v.* adore, adulate, appreciate, cherish, delight in, desire, dote on, enjoy, fancy, hold dear, idolize, like, prize, relish, savor, take pleasure in, think the world of, treasure, want, worship.
antonyms detest, hate, loathe.
n. adoration, adulation, affection, agape, aloha, amity, amorosity, amorousness, ardor, attachment, delight, devotion, enjoyment, fondness, friendship, inclination, infatuation, liking, partiality, passion, rapture, regard, relish, soft spot, taste, tenderness, warmth, weakness.
antonyms detestation, hate, loathing.

loveless *adj.* cold, cold-hearted, disliked, forsaken,

friendless, frigid, hard, heartless, icy, insensitive, love-lorn, passionless, unappreciated, uncherished, unfeeling, unfriendly, unloved, unloving, unresponsive, unvalued.
antonym passionate.

lovely *adj.* admirable, adorable, agreeable, amiable, attractive, beautiful, captivating, charming, comely, delightful, enchanting, engaging, enjoyable, exquisite, graceful, gratifying, handsome, idyllic, nice, pleasant, pleasing, pretty, sweet, taking, winning.
antonyms hideous, ugly, unlovely.

lover *n.* admirer, amoretto, amorist, amoroso, beau, beloved, bon ami, boyfriend, Casanova, fancy man, fancy woman, fiancé(e), flame, gigolo, girlfriend, inamorata, inamorato, mistress, paramour, philanderer, suitor, swain, sweetheart.

loving *adj.* affectionate, amative, amatorial, amatorian, amatorious, amorous, ardent, cordial, dear, demonstrative, devoted, doting, fond, friendly, kind, passionate, solicitous, tender, warm, warm-hearted.

low[1] *adj.* abject, base, base-born, blue, brassed off, browned off, cheap, coarse, common, contemptible, crude, dastardly, debilitated, deep, deficient, degraded, dejected, depleted, depraved, depressed, despicable, despondent, disgraceful, disheartened, dishonorable, disreputable, down, down in the dumps, downcast, dying, economical, exhausted, fed up, feeble, forlorn, frail, gloomy, glum, gross, humble, hushed, ignoble, ill, ill-bred, inadequate, inexpensive, inferior, insignificant, little, low-born, low-grade, lowly, low-lying, meager, mean, mediocre, meek, menial, miserable, moderate, modest, morose, muffled, muted, nasty, obscene, obscure, paltry, plain, plebeian, poor, prostrate, puny, quiet, reasonable, reduced, rough, rude, sad, scant, scurvy, second-rate, servile, shallow, shoddy, short, simple, sinking, small, soft, sordid, sparse, squat, stricken, stunted, subdued, substandard, sunken, trifling, unbecoming, undignified, unhappy, unpretentious, unrefined, unworthy, vile, vulgar, weak, whispered, worthless.
antonyms elevated, high, lofty, noble.

lower[1] *adj.* inferior, insignificant, junior, lesser, low-level, lowly, minor, secondary, second-class, smaller, subordinate, subservient, under, unimportant.
v. abase, abate, belittle, condescend, couch, curtail, cut, debase, decrease, degrade, deign, demean, demolish, depress, devalue, diminish, discredit, disgrace, downgrade, drop, fall, humble, humiliate, lessen, let down, minimize, moderate, prune, raze, reduce, sink, slash, soften, stoop, submerge, take down, tone down.
antonyms elevate, increase, raise, rise.

lower[2] *see* **lour**.

low-key *adj.* low-pitched, muffled, muted, quiet, restrained, slight, soft, subdued, understated.

lowly *adj.* average, common, docile, dutiful, homespun, humble, ignoble, inferior, low-born, mean, mean-born,

meek, mild, modest, obscure, ordinary, plain, plebeian, poor, proletarian, simple, submissive, subordinate, unassuming, unexalted, unpretentious.
antonyms lofty, noble.

loyal *adj.* attached, constant, dependable, devoted, dutiful, faithful, honest, leal, patriotic, sincere, staunch,
steadfast, true, true-blue, true-hearted, trustworthy,
trusty, unswerving, unwavering.
antonyms disloyal, traitorous.

loyalty *n.* allegiance, constancy, dependability, devotion, faithfulness, fealty, fidelity, honesty, lealty, patriotism, reliability, sincerity, staunchness, steadfastness, true-heartedness, trueness, trustiness, trustworthiness.
antonyms disloyalty, treachery.

lubricate *v.* grease, lard, oil, smear, wax.

lucid *adj.* beaming, bright, brilliant, clear, clear-cut, clear-
headed, compos mentis, comprehensible, crystalline,
diaphanous, distinct, effulgent, evident, explicit, glassy,
gleaming, intelligible, limpid, luminous, obvious, pellucid, perspicuous, plain, pure, radiant, rational, reasonable, resplendent, sane, sensible, shining, sober,
sound, translucent, transparent.
antonyms dark, murky, unclear.

luck *n.* accident, blessing, break, chance, destiny, fate,
fluke, fortuity, fortune, godsend, good fortune, hap,
happenstance, hazard, jam, joss, prosperity, serendipity, stroke, success, windfall.
antonym misfortune.

lucky *adj.* advantageous, adventitious, auspicious,
blessed, canny, charmed, favored, fluky, fortuitous,
fortunate, jammy, opportune, propitious, prosperous,
providential, serendipitous, successful, timely.
antonyms luckless, unlucky.

lucky dip bran tub, grab-bag.

lucrative *adj.* advantageous, fecund, fertile, fruitful, gainful, paying, productive, profitable, remunerative, well-
paid.
antonym unprofitable.

ludicrous *adj.* absurd, amusing, burlesque, comic, comical, crazy, drôle, droll, farcical, funny, incongruous,
laughable, nonsensical, odd, outlandish, preposterous,
ridiculous, risible, silly, zany.

lug *v.* carry, drag, haul, heave, hump, humph, pull, tote,
tow, yank.

lugubrious *adj.* dismal, doleful, dreary, funereal, gloomy,
glum, melancholy, morose, mournful, sad, sepulchral,
serious, somber, sorrowful, Wertherian, woebegone,
woeful.
antonyms cheerful, jovial, merry.

lukewarm *adj.* apathetic, cold, cool, half-hearted, indifferent, laodicean, Laodicean, lew, phlegmatic, tepid,
unconcerned, unenthusiastic, uninterested, unresponsive, warm.

lull *v.* abate, allay, calm, cease, compose, decrease, diminish, dwindle, ease off, hush, let up, lullaby, moderate,

pacify, quell, quiet, quieten down, sedate, slacken,
soothe, still, subdue, subside, tranquilize, wane.
antonym agitate.
n. calm, calmness, hush, let-up, pause, peace, quiet,
respite, silence, stillness, tranquility.
antonym agitation.

lumber[1] *n.* bits and pieces, clutter, jumble, junk, odds
and ends, refuse, rubbish, trash, trumpery.
v. burden, charge, encumber, hamper, impose, land,
load, saddle.

lumber[2] *v.* clump, galumph, plod, shamble, shuffle,
stump, trudge, trundle, waddle.

luminous *adj.* bright, brilliant, glowing, illuminated,
lighted, lit, lucent, luminescent, luminiferous, lustrous,
radiant, resplendent, shining, vivid.

lump[1] *n.* ball, bulge, bump, bunch, cake, chuck, chump,
chunk, clod, cluster, cyst, dab, daud, dod, gob, gobbet,
group, growth, hunch, hunk, (k)nub, (k)nubble, lob,
mass, nugget, piece, protrusion, protuberance, spot,
swelling, tuber, tumescence, tumor, wedge, wen,
wodge.
v. coalesce, collect, combine, consolidate, group, mass,
unite.

lump[2] *v.* bear (with), brook, endure, put up with, stand,
stomach, suffer, swallow, take, thole, tolerate.

lunacy *n.* aberration, absurdity, craziness, dementia,
derangement, folly, foolhardiness, foolishness, idiocy,
imbecility, insanity, madness, mania, moon-madness,
moonraking, psychosis, senselessness, stupidity, tomfoolery.
antonym sanity.

lunge *v.* bound, charge, cut, dash, dive, fall upon, grab
(at), hit (at), jab, leap, pitch into, plunge, poke, pounce,
set upon, stab, strike (at), thrust.
n. charge, cut, jab, pass, pounce, spring, stab, swing,
swipe, thrust, venue.

lurch *v.* heave, lean, list, pitch, reel, rock, roll, stagger,
stumble, sway, tilt, totter, wallow, weave, welter.

lure *v.* allure, attract, beckon, decoy, draw, ensnare, entice, inveigle, invite, lead on, seduce, tempt, trepan.
n. allurement, attraction, bait, carrot, come-on, decoy,
enticement, inducement, magnet, siren, song, temptation, train.

lurid *adj.* ashen, bloody, disgusting, exaggerated, fiery,
flaming, ghastly, glaring, glowering, gory, graphic, grim,
grisly, gruesome, intense, livid, loud, macabre, melodramatic, pale, pallid, revolting, sallow, sanguine, savage, sensational, shocking, startling, unrestrained, violent, vivid, wan.

lurk *v.* crouch, hide, hide out, lie in wait, lie low, prowl,
skulk, slink, sneak, snook, snoop.

luscious *adj.* appetizing, delectable, delicious, honeyed,
juicy, luxuriant, luxurious, mouth-watering, palatable,
rich, savory, scrumptious, succulent, sweet, tasty,
toothsome, yummy.
antonym austere.

lush *adj.* abundant, dense, elaborate, extravagant, flourishing, grand, green, juicy, lavish, luxuriant, luxurious, opulent, ornate, overgrown, palatial, plush, prolific, rank, ripe, ritzy, succulent, sumptuous, superabundant, teeming, tender, verdant.

lust *n.* appetence, appetency, appetite, avidity, carnality, concupiscence, covetousness, craving, cupidity, desire, greed, Kama, Kamadeva, lasciviousness, lechery, lewdness, libido, licentiousness, longing, passion, prurience, randiness, salaciousness, sensuality, thirst, wantonness.

luster *n.* brightness, brilliance, burnish, dazzle, distinction, effulgence, fame, gleam, glint, glitter, glory, gloss, glow, gorm, honor, illustriousness, lambency, luminousness, prestige, radiance, renown, resplendence, sheen, shimmer, shine, sparkle, water.

lustful *adj.* carnal, concupiscent, craving, goatish, hankering, horny, lascivious, lecherous, lewd, libidinous, licentious, passionate, prurient, randy, raunchy, ruttish, sensual, unchaste, venerous, wanton.

lusty *adj.* blooming, brawny, energetic, gutsy, hale, healthy, hearty, in fine fettle, muscular, powerful, red-blooded, robust, rugged, stalwart, stout, strapping, strong, sturdy, vigorous, virile.
antonyms effete, weak.

luxuriant *adj.* abundant, ample, baroque, copious, dense, elaborate, excessive, extravagant, exuberant, fancy, fecund, fertile, festooned, flamboyant, florid, flowery, lavish, lush, opulent, ornate, overflowing, plenteous, plentiful, prodigal, productive, profuse, prolific, rank, rich, riotous, rococo, sumptuous, superabundant, teeming, thriving.
antonyms barren, infertile.

luxurious *adj.* comfortable, costly, deluxe, epicurean, expensive, hedonistic, lavish, magnificent, opulent, pampered, plush, plushy, rich, ritzy, self-indulgent, sensual, splendid, sumptuous, sybaritic, voluptuous, well-appointed.
antonyms ascetic, austere, economical, frugal, scant(y), spartan.

luxury *n.* affluence, bliss, comfort, delight, dolce vita, enjoyment, extra, extravagance, flesh-pots, flesh-pottery, frill, gratification, hedonism, indulgence, milk and honey, non-essential, opulence, pleasure, richness, satisfaction, splendor, sumptuousness, treat, voluptuousness, well-being.
antonym essential.

lying *adj.* accumbent, deceitful, decumbent, dishonest, dissembling, double-dealing, duplicitous, false, guileful, mendacious, perfidious, treacherous, two-faced, untruthful.
antonyms honest, truthful.
n. deceit, dishonesty, dissimulation, double-dealing, duplicity, fabrication, falsity, fibbing, guile, mendacity, perjury, prevarication, pseudology, untruthfulness.
antonyms honesty, truthfulness.

lyrical *adj.* carried away, ecstatic, effusive, emotional, enthusiastic, expressive, impassioned, inspired, musical, passionate, poetic, rapturous, rhapsodic.

macabre *adj.* cadaverous, deathlike, deathly, dreadful, eerie, frightening, frightful, ghastly, ghostly, ghoulish, grim, grisly, gruesome, hideous, horrible, horrid, morbid, sick, weird.

macerate *v.* blend, liquefy, mash, pulp, soak, soften, steep.

Machiavellian *adj.* amoral, artful, astute, calculating, crafty, cunning, cynical, deceitful, designing, double-dealing, foxy, guileful, intriguing, opportunist, perfidious, scheming, shrewd, sly, underhand, unscrupulous, wily.

machine *n.* agency, agent, apparatus, appliance, automaton, contraption, contrivance, device, engine, gadget, gizmo, instrument, machinery, mechanism, organization, party, puppet, robot, set-up, structure, system, tool, zombi(e).

mad *adj.* abandoned, aberrant, absurd, agitated, angry, ardent, avid, bananas, barmy, bats, batty, berserk, boisterous, bonkers, crackers, crazed, crazy, cuckoo, daft, delirious, demented, deranged, devoted, distracted, dotty, ebullient, enamored, energetic, enraged, enthusiastic, exasperated, excited, fanatical, fond, foolhardy, foolish, frantic, frenetic, frenzied, fuming, furious, gay, have bats in the belfry, hooked, impassioned, imprudent, in a paddy, incensed, infatuated, infuriated, insane, irate, irrational, irritated, keen, livid, loony, loopy, ludicrous, lunatic, madcap, mental, moon-stricken, moon-struck, non compos mentis, nonsensical, nuts, nutty, off one's chump, off one's head, off one's nut, off one's rocker, off one's trolley, out of one's mind, possessed, preposterous, psychotic, rabid, raging, raving, resentful, riotous, round the bend, round the twist, screwball, screwy, senseless, unbalanced, uncontrolled, unhinged, unreasonable, unrestrained, unsafe, unsound, unstable, up the pole, waxy, wild, wrathful, zealous.
antonyms lucid, rational, sane.

madden *v.* annoy, craze, dement, dementate, derange, enrage, exasperate, incense, inflame, infuriate, irritate, provoke, unhinge, upset, vex.
antonyms calm, pacify, please.

madness *n.* abandon, aberration, absurdity, agitation, anger, ardor, craze, craziness, daftness, delusion, dementia, demoniacism, demonomania, derangement, distraction, enthusiasm, exasperation, excitement, fanaticism, folie, folly, fondness, foolhardiness, foolishness, frenzy, furore, fury, infatuation, insanity, intoxication, ire, keenness, lunacy, lycanthropy, mania, monomania, moon-madness, moonraking, nonsense, passion, preposterousness, psychopathy, psychosis, rage, raving, riot, unrestraint, uproar, wildness, wrath, zeal.
antonym sanity.

maelstrom *n.* bedlam, chaos, Charybdis, confusion, disorder, mess, pandemonium, tumult, turmoil, uproar, vortex, whirlpool.

magic *n.* allurement, black art, charm, conjuring, conjury, diablerie, enchantment, fascination, glamor, goety, gramary(e), hocus-pocus, hoodoo, illusion, jiggery-pokery, jugglery, legerdemain, magnetism, medicine, necromancy, occultism, prestidigitation, sleight of hand, sorcery, sortilege, spell, thaumaturgics, thaumaturgism, thaumaturgy, theurgy, trickery, voodoo, witchcraft, wizardry, wonder-work.
adj. bewitching, charismatic, charming, enchanting, entrancing, fascinating, goetic, hermetic, magical, magnetic, marvelous, miraculous, mirific, mirifical, sorcerous, spellbinding, spellful.

magician *n.* archimage, conjurer, conjuror, enchanter, enchantress, genius, illusionist, maestro, mage, Magian, magus, marvel, miracle-worker, necromancer, prestidigitator, prestigiator, sorcerer, spellbinder, thaumaturge, theurgist, virtuoso, warlock, witch, witch-doctor, wizard, wonder-monger, wonder-worker.

magistrate *n.* aedile, bailiff, bail(l)ie, beak, JP, judge, jurat, justice, justice of the peace, mittimus, stipendiary, tribune.

magnanimous *adj.* altruistic, beneficent, big, big-hearted, bountiful, charitable, free, generous, great-hearted, handsome, high-minded, kind, kindly, large-hearted, large-minded, liberal, munificent, noble, open-handed, philanthropic, selfless, ungrudging, unselfish, unstinting.
antonyms mean, paltry, petty.

magnate *n.* aristocrat, baron, bashaw, big cheese, big noise, big shot, big wheel, bigwig, captain of industry, chief, fat cat, grandee, leader, magnifico, merchant, mogul, nabob, noble, notable, personage, plutocrat, prince, tycoon, VIP.

magnet *n.* appeal, attraction, bait, draw, enticement, lodestone, lure, solenoid.
antonym repellent.

magnetic *adj.* absorbing, alluring, attractive, captivating, charismatic, charming, enchanting, engrossing, entrancing, fascinating, gripping, hypnotic, irresistible, mesmerizing, seductive.
antonyms repellent, repugnant, repulsive.

magnetism *n.* allure, appeal, attraction, attractiveness, charisma, charm, draw, drawing power, enchantment, fascination, grip, hypnotism, lure, magic, mesmerism, power, pull, seductiveness, spell.

magnificence *n.* brilliance, glory, gorgeousness, grandeur, grandiosity, impressiveness, luxuriousness, luxury, majesty, nobility, opulence, pomp, resplendence, splendor, stateliness, sublimity, sumptuousness. *antonyms* modesty, plainness, simplicity.

magnificent *adj.* august, brilliant, elegant, elevated, exalted, excellent, fine, glorious, gorgeous, grand, grandiose, imposing, impressive, lavish, luxurious, majestic, noble, opulent, outstanding, plush, posh, princely, regal, resplendent, rich, ritzy, splendid, stately, sublime, sumptuous, superb, superior, transcendent. *antonyms* humble, modest, plain, simple.

magnify *v.* aggrandize, aggravate, amplify, augment, blow up, boost, build up, deepen, dilate, dramatize, enhance, enlarge, exaggerate, expand, greaten, heighten, increase, inflate, intensify, lionize, overdo, overemphasize, overestimate, overplay, overrate, overstate, praise. *antonyms* belittle, play down.

magnitude *n.* amount, amplitude, bigness, brightness, bulk, capacity, consequence, dimensions, eminence, enormousness, expanse, extent, grandeur, greatness, hugeness, immensity, importance, intensity, largeness, mark, mass, measure, moment, note, proportions, quantity, significance, size, space, strength, vastness, volume, weight. *antonym* smallness.

maid *n.* abigail, bonne, damsel, dresser, femme de chambre, fille de chambre, gentlewoman, girl, handmaiden, housemaid, lady's maid, lass, lassie, maiden, maid-of-all-work, maid-servant, miss, nymph, servant, serving-maid, soubrette, tirewoman, tiringwoman, virgin, waitress, wench.

maiden *n.* damozel, damsel, demoiselle, girl, lass, lassie, maid, may, miss, nymph, virgin, wench. *adj.* chaste, female, first, fresh, inaugural, initial, initiatory, intact, introductory, new, pure, unbroached, uncaptured, undefiled, unmarried, unpolluted, untapped, untried, unused, unwed, virgin, virginal. *antonyms* defiled, deflowered, unchaste.

mail *n.* correspondence, da(w)k, delivery, letters, packages, parcels, post. *v.* air-mail, dispatch, forward, post, send.

maim *v.* cripple, disable, hack, haggle, hamstring, hurt, impair, incapacitate, injure, lame, mangle, mar, mutilate, savage, wound. *antonyms* heal, repair.

main[1] *adj.* absolute, brute, capital, cardinal, central, chief, critical, crucial, direct, downright, entire, essential, extensive, first, foremost, general, great, head, leading, mere, necessary, outstanding, paramount, particular, predominant, pre-eminent, premier, primary, prime, principal, pure, sheer, special, staple, supreme, undisguised, utmost, utter, vital. *antonyms* minor, unimportant. *n.* effort, foison, force, might, potency, power, puissance, strength, vigor. *antonym* weakness.

main[2] *n.* cable, channel, conduit, duct, line, pipe.

mainstay *n.* anchor, backbone, bulwark, buttress, linchpin, pillar, prop, support.

maintain *v.* advocate, affirm, allege, argue, assert, asseverate, aver, avouch, avow, back, care for, carry on, champion, claim, conserve, contend, continue, declare, defend, fight for, finance, hold, insist, justify, keep, keep up, look after, make good, nurture, observe, perpetuate, plead for, practice, preserve, profess, prolong, provide, retain, stand by, state, supply, support, sustain, take care of, uphold, vindicate. *antonyms* deny, neglect, oppose.

maintenance *n.* aliment, alimony, allowance, care, conservation, continuance, continuation, defense, food, keep, keeping, livelihood, living, nurture, perpetuation, preservation, prolongation, protection, provision, repairs, retainment, subsistence, supply, support, sustainment, sustenance, sustention, upkeep. *antonym* neglect.

majestic *adj.* august, awesome, dignified, distinguished, elevated, exalted, grand, grandiose, imperial, imperious, imposing, impressive, kingly, lofty, magisterial, magnificent, monumental, noble, pompous, princely, queenly, regal, royal, splendid, stately, sublime, superb. *antonyms* unimportant, unimpressive.

majesty *n.* augustness, awesomeness, dignity, exaltedness, glory, grandeur, impressiveness, kingliness, loftiness, magnificence, majesticness, nobility, pomp, queenliness, regalness, resplendence, royalty, splendor, state, stateliness, sublimity. *antonyms* unimportance, unimpressiveness.

major *adj.* better, bigger, chief, critical, crucial, elder, grave, great, greater, higher, important, key, keynote, larger, leading, main, most, notable, older, outstanding, pre-eminent, radical, senior, serious, significant, superior, supreme, uppermost, vital, weighty. *antonym* minor.

make *v.* accomplish, acquire, act, add up to, amount to, appoint, arrive at, assemble, assign, attain, beget, bring about, build, calculate, carry out, catch, cause, clear, coerce, compel, compose, conclude, constitute, constrain, construct, contract, contribute, convert, create, designate, do, dragoon, draw up, drive, earn, effect, elect, embody, enact, engage in, engender, establish, estimate, execute, fabricate, fashion, fix, flow, force, forge, form, frame, gain, gar, gauge, generate, get, give rise to, impel, induce, install, invest, judge, lead to, manufacture, meet, mold, net, nominate, oblige, obtain, occasion, ordain, originate, pass, perform, practise, press, pressurize, prevail upon, proceed, produce, prosecute, put together, reach, reckon, render, require, secure, shape, smith(y), suppose, synthesize, take in, tend, think, turn, win. *antonyms* dismantle, lose, persuade. *n.* brand, build, character, composition, constitution, construction, cut, designation, disposition, form, formation, humor, kind, make-up, manner, manufacture, mark, model, nature, shape, sort, stamp, structure, style, temper, temperament, texture, type, variety.

make-believe *n.* charade, dream, fantasy, imagination, play-acting, pretense, role-play, unreality.
antonym reality.
adj. dream, fantasized, fantasy, feigned, imaginary, imagined, made-up, mock, pretend, pretended, sham, simulated, unreal.
antonym real.

maker *n.* architect, author, builder, constructor, contriver, creator, director, fabricator, framer, manufacturer, producer.
antonym dismantler.

makeshift *adj.* band-aid, expedient, haywire, improvised, make-do, provisional, rough and ready, stop-gap, substitute, temporary.
antonyms finished, permanent.
n. band-aid, expedient, fig-leaf, shift, stop-gap, substitute.

make-up[1] *n.* cosmetics, fard, fucus, greasepaint, maquillage, paint, powder, war paint, white-face.

make-up[2] *n.* arrangement, assembly, build, cast, character, complexion, composition, configuration, constitution, construction, disposition, figure, form, format, formation, make, nature, organization, stamp, structure, style, temper, temperament.

maladroit *adj.* awkward, bungling, cack-handed, clumsy, gauche, graceless, ham-fisted, ill-timed, inconsiderate, inelegant, inept, incxpert, insensitive, tactless, thoughtless, undiplomatic, unhandy, unskilful, untoward.
antonyms adroit, tactful.

malady *n.* affliction, ailment, breakdown, complaint, disease, disordcr, illness, indisposition, infirmity, malaise, sickness.
antonym health.

malaise *n.* angst, anguish, anxiety, depression, discomfort, disquiet, distemper, doldrums, enervation, future shock, illness, indisposition, lassitude, melancholy, sickness, unease, uneasiness, weakness.
antonyms happiness, well-being.

malcontent *adj.* belly-aching, disaffected, discontented, disgruntled, dissatisfied, dissentious, factious, ill-disposed, morose, rebellious, resentful, restive, unhappy, unsatisfied.
antonym contented.
n. agitator, belly-acher, complainer, grouch, grouser, grumbler, mischief-maker, moaner, rebel, troublemaker.

male *adj.* bull, cock, dog, manlike, manly, masculine, virile.
antonym female.
n. boy, bull, cock, daddy, dog, father, man.
antonym female.

malefactor *n.* convict, criminal, crook, culprit, delinquent, evil-doer, felon, law-breaker, miscreant,

misfeasor, offender, outlaw, transgressor, villain, wrong-doer.

malevolence *n.* bitterness, hate, hatred, hostility, ill-will, malice, maliciousness, malignance, malignancy, malignity, rancor, spite, spitefulness, vengefulness, venom, viciousness, vindictiveness.
antonym benevolence.

malfunction *n.* breakdown, defect, failure, fault, flaw, glitch, impairment.
v. break down, fail, go wrong, misbehave.

malice *n.* animosity, animus, bad blood, bitterness, despite, enmity, hate, hatred, ill-will, malevolence, maliciousness, malignity, rancor, spite, spitefulness, spleen, vengefulness, venom, viciousness, vindictiveness.
antonym kindness.

malicious *adj.* baleful, bitchy, bitter, catty, despiteful, evilminded, hateful, ill-natured, injurious, malevolent, malignant, mischievous, pernicious, rancorous, resentful, sham, spiteful, vengeful, venomous, vicious.
antonyms kind, thoughtful.

malign *adj.* bad, baleful, baneful, deleterious, destructive, evil, harmful, hostile, hurtful, injurious, malevolent, malignant, noxious, pernicious, venomous, vicious, wicked.
antonym benign.
v. abuse, badmouth, blacken the name of, calumniate, defame, denigrate, derogate, disparage, harm, injure, libel, revile, run down, slander, smear, traduce, vilify, vilipend.
antonym praise.

malignant *adj.* baleful, bitter, cancerous, cankered, dangerous, deadly, destructive, devilish, evil, fatal, harmful, hostile, hurtful, inimical, injurious, irremediable, malevolent, malicious, malign, pernicious, spiteful, uncontrollable, venomous, vicious, viperish, viperous, virulent.
antonyms harmless, kind.

malingerer *n.* dodger, lead-swinger, loafer, shirker, skiver, slacker.
antonym toiler.

malleable *adj.* adaptable, biddable, compliant, ductile, governable, impressionable, manageable, plastic, pliable, pliant, soft, tractable, tractile, workable.
antonyms intractable, unworkable.

malodorous *adj.* evil-smelling, fetid, foul-smelling, mephitic, miasmal, miasmatic, miasmatous, miasmic, miasmous, nauseating, niffy, noisome, offensive, putrid, rank, reeking, smelly, stinking.
antonym sweet-smelling.

malpractice *n.* abuse, dereliction, malversation, misbehavior, misconduct, misdeed, mismanagement, negligence, offence, transgression.

maltreat *v.* abuse, bully, damage, harm, hurt, ill-treat, injure, mistreat, misuse, mousle.
antonym care for.

maltreatment *n.* abuse, bullying, harm, ill-treatment, ill-usage, ill-use, injury, mistreatment, misuse.
antonym care.

mammoth *adj.* Brobdingnag, Brobdingnagian, colossal, enormous, formidable, gargantuan, giant, gigantic, herculean, huge, immense, leviathan, massive, mighty, monumental, mountainous, prodigious, rounceval, stupendous, titanic, vast.
antonym small.

man¹ *n.* adult, attendant, beau, bloke, body, boyfriend, cat, chap, employee, fellow, follower, gentleman, guy, hand, hireling, hombre, human, human being, husband, individual, lover, male, manservant, partner, person, retainer, servant, soldier, spouse, subject, subordinate, valet, vassal, worker, workman.
v. crew, fill, garrison, occupy, operate, people, staff, take charge of.

man² *n.* Homo sapiens, human race, humanity, humankind, humans, mankind, mortals, people.

manacle *v.* bind, chain, check, clap in irons, confine, constrain, curb, fetter, gyve, hamper, hamstring, handcuff, inhibit, put in chains, restrain, shackle, trammel.
antonym unshackle.

manage *v.* accomplish, administer, arrange, bring about, bring off, carry on, command, concert, conduct, contrive, control, cope, cope with, deal with, direct, dominate, effect, engineer, fare, get along, get by, get on, govern, guide, handle, influence, make do, make out, manipulate, muddle through, operate, oversee, pilot, ply, preside over, rule, run, shift, solicit, stage-manage, steer, succeed, superintend, supervise, survive, train, use, wield.
antonym fail.

manageable *adj.* amenable, biddable, complaint, controllable, convenient, docile, easy, governable, handy, submissive, tamable, tractable, wieldable, wieldy.
antonym unmanageable.

management *n.* administration, board, bosses, care, charge, command, conduct, control, direction, directorate, directors, employers, executive, executives, governance, government, governors, guidance, handling, managers, manipulation, operation, oversight, rule, running, stewardry, superintendence, supervision, supervisors.

manager *n.* administrator, boss, comptroller, conductor, controller, director, executive, factor, gaffer, governor, head, impresario, organizer, overseer, proprietor, steward, superintendent, supervisor.

mandate *n.* authorization, authority, bidding, charge, command, commission, decree, dedimus, directive, edict, fiat, firman, injunction, instruction, irade, order, precept, rescript, right, sanction, ukase, warrant.

mandatory *adj.* binding, compulsory, imperative, necessary, obligatory, required, requisite.
antonym optional.

maneuver *n.* action, artifice, device, dodge, exercise, gambit, intrigue, machination, move, movement, operation, plan, plot, ploy, ruse, scheme, stratagem, subterfuge, tactic, trick.
v. contrive, deploy, devise, direct, drive, engineer, exercise, guide, handle, intrigue, jockey, machinate, manage, manipulate, move, navigate, negotiate, pilot, plan, plot, pull strings, scheme, steer, wangle.

mangle *v.* butcher, crush, cut, deform, destroy, disfigure, distort, hack, haggle, lacerate, maim, mar, maul, mutilate, rend, ruin, spoil, tear, twist, wreck.

mangy *adj.* dirty, grotty, mean, moth-eaten, ratty, scabby, scruffy, seedy, shabby, shoddy, squalid, tatty.
antonyms clean, neat, spruce.

manhandle *v.* carry, haul, heave, hump, knock about, lift, maltreat, maneuver, maul, mishandle, mistreat, misuse, paw, pull, push, rough up, shove, tug.

manhood *n.* adulthood, bravery, courage, determination, firmness, fortitude, hardihood, machismo, manfulness, manliness, masculinity, maturity, mettle, resolution, spirit, strength, valor, virility.
antonym timidness.

mania *n.* aberration, cacoethes, compulsion, craving, craze, craziness, delirium, dementia, derangement, desire, disorder, enthusiasm, fad, fetish, fixation, frenzy, infatuation, insanity, itch, lunacy, madness, obsession, partiality, passion, preoccupation, rage, thing.

manifest *adj.* apparent, clear, conspicuous, distinct, evident, glaring, noticeable, obvious, open, palpable, patent, plain, unconcealed, undeniable, unmistakable, visible.
antonym unclear.
v. demonstrate, display, establish, evidence, evince, exhibit, expose, illustrate, prove, reveal, set forth, show.
antonym hide.

manifesto *n.* declaration, platform, policies, policy, pronunciamento.

manifold *adj.* abundant, assorted, copious, diverse, diversified, kaleidoscopic, many, multifarious, multifold, multiple, multiplex, multiplied, multitudinous, numerous, varied, various.
antonym simple.

manipulate *v.* conduct, control, cook, direct, employ, engineer, gerrymander, guide, handle, influence, juggle with, maneuver, negotiate, operate, ply, shuffle, steer, use, wield, work.

manly *adj.* bold, brave, courageous, daring, dauntless, fearless, gallant, hardy, heroic, macho, male, manful, masculine, muscular, noble, powerful, resolute, robust, stalwart, stout-hearted, strapping, strong, sturdy, valiant, valorous, vigorous, virile.
antonyms timid, unmanly.

man-made *adj.* artificial, ersatz, imitation, manufactured, simulated, synthetic.
antonym natural.

manner *n.* address, air, appearance, approach, aspect,

bearing, behavior, brand, breed, category, character, comportment, conduct, custom, demeanor, deportment, description, fashion, form, genre, habit, kind, line, look, means, method, mien, mode, nature, practice, presence, procedure, process, routine, sort, style, tack, tenor, tone, type, usage, variety, way, wise, wont.

mannerism *n.* characteristic, feature, foible, habit, idiosyncrasy, peculiarity, quirk, stiltedness, trait, trick.

mannerly *adj.* civil, civilized, courteous, decorous, deferential, formal, genteel, gentlemanly, gracious, ladylike, polished, polite, refined, respectful, well-behaved, well-bred, well-mannered.

antonym unmannerly.

mantle *n.* blanket, canopy, cape, cloak, cloud, cover, covering, curtain, envelope, hood, mantlet, pall, pelerine, pelisse, screen, shawl, shroud, veil, wrap.

manual[1] *n.* bible, book of words, companion, enchi(e)ridion, guide, guide-book, handbook, instructions, primer, vademecum.

manual[2] *adj.* hand, hand-operated, human, physical.

manufacture *v.* assemble, build, churn out, compose, concoct, construct, cook up, create, devise, fabricate, forge, form, hatch, invent, make, make up, mass-produce, mold, process, produce, shape, think up, trump up, turn out.

n. assembly, construction, creation, fabrication, facture, formation, making, mass-production, production.

manure *n.* compost, droppings, dung, fertilizer, guano, muck, ordure.

manuscript *n.* autograph, deed, document, handwriting, holograph, palimpsest, parchment, scroll, text, vellum.

many *adj.* abundant, copious, countless, divers, frequent, innumerable, manifold, multifarious, multifold, multitudinous, myriad, numerous, profuse, sundry, umpteen, umpty, varied, various, zillion.

antonym few.

map *n.* atlas, chart, graph, mappemond, plan, plot, street plan.

mar *v.* blemish, blight, blot, damage, deface, detract from, disfigure, foul up, harm, hurt, impair, injure, maim, mangle, mutilate, pollute, ruin, scar, spoil, stain, sully, taint, tarnish, temper, vitiate, wreck.

antonym enhance.

maraud *v.* depredate, despoil, forage, foray, harry, loot, pillage, plunder, raid, ransack, ravage, reive, sack, spoliate.

march *v.* countermarch, file, flounce, goose-step, pace, parade, slog, stalk, stride, strut, stump, tramp, tread, walk.

n. advance, career, demo, demonstration, development, evolution, footslog, gait, hike, pace, parade, passage, procession, progress, progression, step, stride, tramp, trek, walk.

margin *n.* allowance, border, bound, boundary, brim, brink, compass, confine, edge, extra, latitude, leeway, limit, marge, perimeter, periphery, play, rand, rim, room, scope, side, skirt, space, surplus, verge.

antonyms center, core.

marginal *adj.* bordering, borderline, doubtful, infinitesimal, insignificant, low, minimal, minor, negligible, peripheral, slight, small.

antonyms central, core.

marina *n.* dock, harbor, mooring, port, yacht station.

marine *adj.* maritime, nautical, naval, ocean-going, oceanic, pelagic, salt-water, sea, seafaring, sea-going, thalassian, thalassic.

n. galoot, leather-neck, sailor.

mariner *n.* bluejacket, deckhand, hand, Jack Tar, matelot, matlo(w), navigator, sailor, salt, sea-dog, seafarer, seaman, tar.

marital *adj.* conjugal, connubial, hymeneal, hymenean, married, matrimonial, nuptial, sponsal, sponsal, wedded.

maritime *adj.* coastal, littoral, marine, nautical, naval, oceanic, pelagic, sea, seafaring, seaside, thalassian, thalassic.

mark *n.* aim, badge, blaze, blemish, blot, blotch, brand, bruise, character, characteristic, consequence, criterion, dent, device, dignity, distinction, earmark, emblem, eminence, end, evidence, fame, feature, fingermark, footmark, footprint, goal, hallmark, importance, impression, incision, index, indication, influence, label, level, line, lineament, marque, measure, nick, norm, notability, note, noteworthiness, notice, object, objective, pock, prestige, print, proof, purpose, quality, regard, scar, scratch, seal, sign, smudge, splotch, spot, stain, stamp, standard, standing, streak, symbol, symptom, target, token, trace, track, trail, vestige, yardstick.

v. appraise, assess, attend, betoken, blemish, blot, blotch, brand, bruise, characterize, correct, denote, dent, distinguish, evaluate, evince, exemplify, grade, hearken, heed, identify, illustrate, impress, imprint, label, list, listen, mind, nick, note, notice, observe, print, regard, remark, scar, scratch, show, smudge, splotch, stain, stamp, streak, take to heart, traumatize, watch.

marked *adj.* apparent, clear, considerable, conspicuous, decided, distinct, doomed, emphatic, evident, glaring, indicated, manifest, notable, noted, noticeable, obvious, outstanding, patent, prominent, pronounced, remarkable, salient, signal, striking, strong, suspected, watched.

antonyms slight, unnoticeable.

market *n.* bazaar, demand, fair, market-place, mart, need, outlet, shop, souk.

v. hawk, peddle, retail, sell, vend.

antonym buy.

maroon *v.* abandon, cast away, desert, isolate, leave, put ashore, strand.

antonym rescue.

marriage *n.* alliance, amalgamation, association, confederation, coupling, espousal, link, match, matrimony, matronage, matronhood, merger, nuptials, spousage, spousals, union, wedding, wedlock.
antonym divorce.

marrow *n.* core, cream, essence, gist, heart, kernel, nub, pith, quick, quintessence, soul, spirit, stuff, substance.

marry *v.* ally, bond, espouse, get hitched, get spliced, join, jump the broomstick, knit, link, match, merge, splice, tie, tie the knot, unify, unite, wed, wive, yoke.
antonyms divorce, separate.

marsh *n.* bayou, bog, carr, fen, maremma, marshland, morass, moss, muskeg, quagmire, slough, slump, soak, swale, swamp, wetland.

marshal *v.* align, arrange, array, assemble, collect, conduct, convoy, deploy, dispose, draw up, escort, gather, group, guide, lead, line up, muster, order, organize, rank, shepherd, take, usher.

martial *adj.* bellicose, belligerent, brave, combative, heroic, militant, military, soldierly, warlike.
antonym pacific.

martyrdom *n.* agony, anguish, death, excruciation, ordeal, persecution, suffering, torment, torture, witness.

marvel *n.* genius, miracle, non(e)such, phenomenon, portent, prodigy, sensation, spectacle, whiz, wonder.
v. gape, gaze, goggle, wonder.

marvelous *adj.* amazing, astonishing, astounding, beyond belief, breathtaking, épatant, excellent, extraordinary, fabulous, fantastic, glorious, great, implausible, improbable, incredible, magnificent, miraculous, mirific(al), phenomenal, prodigious, remarkable, sensational, singular, smashing, spectacular, splendid, stupendous, super, superb, surprising, terrific, unbelievable, unlikely, wonderful, wondrous.
antonyms ordinary, plausible, run-of-the-mill.

masculine *adj.* bold, brave, butch, gallant, hardy, macho, male, manlike, manly, mannish, muscular, powerful, redblooded, resolute, robust, stout-hearted, strapping, strong, tomboyish, vigorous, virile.
antonym feminine.

mash *v.* beat, champ, comminute, crush, grind, pound, pulverize, pummel, smash, triturate.

mask *n.* blind, camouflage, cloak, concealment, cover, cover-up, disguise, domino, façade, false face, front, guise, pretense, screen, semblance, show, veil, veneer, visardmask, visor, vizard.
v. camouflage, cloak, conceal, cover, disguise, hide, obscure, screen, shield, veil.
antonym uncover.

masquerade *n.* cloak, costume, costume ball, counterfeit, cover, cover-up, deception, disguise, dissimulation, domino, fancy dress party, front, guise, imposture, mask, masked ball, masque, mummery, pose, pretense, put-on, revel, screen, subterfuge.
v. disguise, dissemble, dissimulate, impersonate, mask, pass oneself off, play, pose, pretend, profess.

mass[1] *n.* accumulation, aggregate, aggregation, assemblage, band, batch, block, body, bulk, bunch, chunk, collection, combination, concretion, congeries, conglomeration, crowd, dimension, entirety, extensity, group, heap, horde, host, hunk, lion's share, load, lot, lump, magnitude, majority, mob, number, piece, pile, preponderance, quantity, size, stack, sum, sum total, throng, totality, troop, welter, whole.
adj. across-the-board, blanket, comprehensive, extensive, general, indiscriminate, large-scale, pandemic, popular, sweeping, wholesale, widespread.
antonym limited.
v. assemble, cluster, collect, congregate, crowd, for(e)gather, gather, muster, rally.
antonym separate.

mass[2] *n.* communion, eucharist, holy communion, Lord's Supper, Lord's Table.

massacre *n.* annihilation, blood bath, butchery, carnage, decimation, extermination, holocaust, killing, murder, slaughter.
v. annihilate, butcher, decimate, exterminate, kill, mow down, murder, slaughter, slay, wipe out.

massage *n.* effleurage, kneading, malaxage, malaxation, manipulation, petrissage, rubbing, rub-down.
v. knead, manipulate, rub, rub down.

massive *adj.* big, bulky, colossal, cyclopean, enormous, extensive, gargantuan, gigantic, great, heavy, hefty, huge, hulking, immense, imposing, impressive, jumbo, mammoth, monster, monstrous, monumental, ponderous, rounceval, solid, substantial, titanic, vast, weighty, whacking, whopping.
antonyms slight, small.

master *n.* ace, adept, baas, boss, bwana, captain, chief, commander, controller, dab hand, deacon, director, doyen, employer, expert, genius, governor, guide, guru, head, Herr, instructor, lord, maestro, manager, overlord, overseer, owner, past master, pedagogue, preceptor, principal, pro, ruler, schoolmaster, skipper, superintendent, swami, teacher, tutor, virtuoso, wizard.
antonyms amateur, learner, pupil, servant, slave.
adj. ace, adept, chief, controlling, crack, expert, foremost, grand, great, leading, main, masterly, predominant, prime, principal, proficient, skilful, skilled.
antonyms copy, subordinate, unskilled.
v. acquire, bridle, check, command, conquer, control, curb, defeat, direct, dominate, get the hang of, govern, grasp, learn, manage, overcome, quash, quell, regulate, rule, subdue, subjugate, suppress, tame, triumph over, vanquish.

masterful *adj.* adept, adroit, arrogant, authoritative, autocratic, bossy, clever, consummate, crack, deft, despotic, dexterous, dictatorial, domineering, excellent, expert, exquisite, fine, finished, first-rate, high-handed, imperious, magisterial, masterly, overbearing, overweening, peremptory, powerful, professional, self-willed, skilful, skilled, superior, superlative, supreme, tyrannical.

antonyms clumsy, humble, unskilful.

masterly *adj.* adept, adroit, clever, consummate, crack, dexterous, excellent, expert, exquisite, fine, finished, first-rate, magistral, masterful, skilful, skilled, superb, superior, superlative, supreme.

antonyms clumsy, poor, unskilled.

mastermind *v.* conceive, design, devise, direct, dream up, forge, frame, hatch, manage, organize, originate, plan. *n.* architect, authority, brain(s), creator, director, engineer, genius, intellect, manager, organizer, originator, planner, prime mover, virtuoso.

masterpiece *n.* chef d'oeuvre, classic, jewel, magnum opus, master-work, museum-piece, pièce de résistance, tour de force.

mastery *n.* ability, acquirement, advantage, ascendancy, attainment, authority, cleverness, command, comprehension, conquest, control, conversancy, deftness, dexterity, domination, dominion, expertise, familiarity, finesse, grasp, know-how, knowledge, pre-eminence, proficiency, prowess, rule, skill, superiority, supremacy, sway, triumph, understanding, upper hand, victory, virtuosity, whip-hand.

antonyms clumsiness, unfamiliarity.

masticate *v.* champ, chew, crunch, eat, knead, manducate, munch, ruminate.

mat *n.* carpet, doormat, drugget, felt, rug, under-felt, underlay.

match[1] *n.* bout, competition, contest, game, main, test, trial, venue.

v. compete, contend, oppose, pit against, rival, vie.

match[2] *n.* affiliation, alliance, combination, companion, complement, copy, counterpart, couple, dead ringer, double, duet, duplicate, equal, equivalent, fellow, like, look-alike, marriage, mate, pair, pairing, parallel, partnership, peer, replica, ringer, rival, spit, spitting image, tally, twin, union.

v. accompany, accord, adapt, agree, ally, blend, combine, compare, co-ordinate, correspond, couple, emulate, equal, fit, gee, go together, go with, harmonize, join, link, marry, mate, measure up to, pair, relate, rival, suit, tally, team, tone with, unite, yoke.

antonyms clash, separate.

match[3] *n.* Congreve-match, fuse, fusee, light, lucifer, lucifer-match, safety match, spill, taper, vesta, vesuvian.

matchless *adj.* consummate, excellent, exquisite, incomparable, inimitable, nonpareil, peerless, perfect, superlative, supreme, unequaled, unique, unmatched, unparalleled, unrivaled, unsurpassed.

antonyms commonplace, poor.

mate *n.* assistant, associate, better half, buddy, china, chum, colleague, companion, compeer, comrade, confidant(e), coworker, crony, double, fellow, fellow-worker, fere, friend, gossip, helper, helpmate, helpmeet, husband, match, pal, partner, repository, side-kick, spouse, subordinate, twin, wife.

v. breed, copulate, couple, join, marry, match, pair, wed, yoke.

material *n.* body, cloth, constituents, data, element, evidence, fabric, facts, information, literature, matter, notes, stuff, substance, textile, work.

adj. applicable, apposite, apropos, bodily, central, concrete, consequential, corporeal, essential, fleshly, germane, grave, gross, hylic, important, indispensable, key, meaningful, momentous, non-spiritual, palpable, pertinent, physical, relevant, serious, significant, substantial, tangible, vital, weighty, worldly.

antonyms ethereal, immaterial.

materialize *v.* appear, arise, happen, occur, take shape, turn up.

antonym disappear.

maternal *adj.* loving, matronal, motherly, protective.

antonym paternal.

matrimony *n.* espousals, marriage, nuptials, sponsalia, spousage, spousal, wedlock.

matron *n.* dame, dowager, matriarch.

matted *adj.* knotted, tangled, tangly, tousled, uncombed.

antonyms tidy, untangled.

matter[1] *n.* affair, amount, argument, body, business, complication, concern, consequence, context, difficulty, distress, episode, event, hyle, import, importance, incident, issue, material, moment, note, occurrence, problem, proceeding, purport, quantity, question, sense, significance, situation, stuff, subject, substance, sum, text, thesis, thing, topic, transaction, trouble, upset, weight, worry.

antonym insignificance.

v. count, make a difference, mean something, signify.

matter[2] *n.* discharge, purulence, pus, secretion, suppuration.

v. discharge, secrete.

mature *adj.* adult, complete, due, fit, full-blown, full-grown, fully fledged, grown, grown-up, matured, mellow, nubile, perfect, perfected, prepared, ready, ripe, ripened, seasoned, well-thought-out.

antonym immature.

v. accrue, age, bloom, come of age, develop, fall due, grow up, maturate, mellow, perfect, ripen, season.

maudlin *adj.* drunk, emotional, fuddled, half-drunk, icky, lachrymose, mawkish, mushy, sentimental, sickly, slushy, soppy, tearful, tipsy, weepy.

antonym matter-of-fact.

maul *v.* abuse, batter, beat, beat up, claw, ill-treat, knock about, lacerate, maltreat, mangle, manhandle, molest, paw, pummel, rough up, thrash.

mawkish *adj.* disgusting, emotional, feeble, flat, foul, gushy, icky, insipid, jejune, loathsome, maudlin, mushy, nauseous, offensive, schmaltzy, sentimental, sickly, slushy, soppy, squeamish, stale, vapid.

antonyms matter-of-fact, pleasant.

maxim *n.* adage, aphorism, apophthegm, axiom, byword, epigram, gnome, mot, motto, precept, proverb, rule, saw, saying, sentence.

maximum *adj.* biggest, greatest, highest, largest, maximal, most, paramount, supreme, topmost, utmost. *antonym* minimum.
n. apogee, ceiling, crest, extremity, height, most, ne plus ultra, peak, pinnacle, summit, top (point), upper limit, utmost, zenith. *antonym* mimimum.

maybe *adv.* haply, happen, mayhap, peradventure, perchance, perhaps, possibly. *antonym* definitely.

maze *n.* confusion, convolutions, imbroglio, intricacy, labyrinth, meander, mesh, mizmaze, puzzle, snarl, tangle, web.

meadow *n.* field, haugh, holm, inch, lea, ley, mead, pasture.

meager *adj.* barren, bony, deficient, emaciated, exiguous, gaunt, hungry, inadequate, infertile, insubstantial, lank, lean, little, negligible, paltry, penurious, poor, puny, scanty, scraggy, scrawny, scrimpy, short, skimpy, skinny, slender, slight, small, spare, sparse, starved, thin, underfed, unfruitful, unproductive, weak. *antonyms* fertile, substantial.

meal[1] *n.* banquet, barbecue, beanfeast, beano, blow-out, breakfast, brunch, collation, déjeuner, déjeuner à la fourchette, dinner, feast, lunch, luncheon, nosh, nosh-up, petit déjeuner, picnic, repast, scoff, snack, supper, tea, tuck-in.

meal[2] *n.* farina, flour, grits, oatmeal, powder.

mean[1] *adj.* abject, bad-tempered, base, base-born, beggarly, callous, cheese-paring, churlish, close, close-fisted, close-handed, common, contemptible, degraded, despicable, disagreeable, disgraceful, dishonorable, down-at-heel, excellent, fast-handed, good, great, hard-hearted, hostile, humble, ignoble, illiberal, inconsiderable, inferior, insignificant, low, low-born, lowly, malicious, malignant, meanspirited, menial, mercenary, mingy, miserable, miserly, modest, narrow-minded, nasty, near, niggardly, obscure, one-horse, ordinary, paltry, parsimonious, penny-pinching, penurious, petty, plebeian, poor, proletarian, pusillanimous, rude, run-down, scrub, scurvy, seedy, selfish, servile, shabby, shameful, skilful, slink, small-minded, snippy, sordid, sour, squalid, stingy, tawdry, tight, tight-fisted, undistinguished, unfriendly, ungenerous, ungiving, unhandsome, unpleasant, vicious, vile, vulgar, wretched.
antonyms generous, kind, noble, superior.

mean[2] *v.* adumbrate, aim, aspire, augur, betoken, cause, connote, contemplate, convey, denote, design, desire, destine, drive at, engender, entail, express, fate, fit, foreshadow, foretell, get at, give rise to, herald, hint, imply, indicate, insinuate, intend, involve, lead to, make, match, necessitate, omen, plan, portend, predestine, preordain, presage, produce, promise, propose, purport, purpose, represent, result in, say, set out, signify, spell, stand for, suggest, suit, symbolize, want, wish.

mean[3] *adj.* average, half-way, intermediate, medial, median, medium, middle, middling, moderate, normal, standard. *antonym* extreme.
n. aurea mediocritas, average, balance, compromise, golden mean, happy medium, median, middle, middle course, middle way, mid-point, norm, via media. *antonym* extreme.

meander *v.* amble, curve, ramble, snake, stravaig, stray, stroll, turn, twist, wander, wind, zigzag.

meaning *n.* aim, connotation, construction, denotation, design, drift, end, explanation, force, gist, goal, idea, implication, import, intention, interpretation, matter, message, object, plan, point, purport, purpose, sense, significance, signification, substance, thrust, trend, upshot, validity, value, worth.

meaningful *adj.* eloquent, expressive, important, material, meaningful, pointed, pregnant, purposeful, relevant, serious, significant, speaking, suggestive, useful, valid, warning, worthwhile.

meaningless *adj.* absurd, aimless, empty, expressionless, futile, hollow, inane, inconsequential, insignificant, insubstantial, nonsense, nonsensical, nugatory, pointless, purposeless, senseless, trifling, trivial, unmeaning, useless, vain, valueless, worthless. *antonym* meaningful.

means *n.* ability, affluence, agency, avenue, capacity, capital, channel, course, estate, expedient, fortune, funds, income, instrument, machinery, measure, medium, method, mode, money, process, property, resources, riches, substance, way, wealth, wherewithal.

measly *adj.* beggarly, contemptible, meager, mean, mingy, miserable, miserly, niggardly, paltry, pathetic, petty, piddling, pitiful, poor, puny, scanty, skimpy, stingy, trivial, ungenerous.

measure *n.* act, action, allotment, allowance, amount, amplitude, beat, bill, bounds, cadence, capacity, control, course, criterion, deed, degree, démarche, enactment, example, expedient, extent, foot, gauge, jigger, law, limit, limitation, magnitude, maneuver, means, method, meter, model, moderation, norm, portion, procedure, proceeding, proportion, quantity, quota, range, ration, reach, resolution, restraint, rhythm, rule, scale, scope, share, size, standard, statute, step, system, test, touchstone, verse, yardstick.
v. admeasure, appraise, assess, calculate, calibrate, choose, compute, determine, estimate, evaluate, fathom, gauge, judge, mark out, measure off, measure out, plumb, quantify, rate, size, sound, step, survey, value, weigh.

measureless *adj.* bottomless, boundless, endless,

immeasurable, immense, incalculable, inestimable, infinite, innumerable, limitless, unbounded, vast. *antonym* measurable.

meat[1] *n.* aliment, charqui, cheer, chow, comestibles, eats, fare, flesh, food, grub, jerk, nourishment, nutriment, provender, provisions, rations, subsistence, sustenance, viands, victuals.

meat[2] *n.* core, crux, essence, fundamentals, gist, heart, kernel, marrow, nub, nucleus, pith, point, substance.

mechanic *n.* artificer, engineer, machinist, mechanician, operative, operator, opificer, repairman, technician.

mechanism *n.* action, agency, apparatus, appliance, components, contrivance, device, execution, functioning, gadgetry, gears, innards, instrument, machine, machinery, means, medium, method, motor, operation, performance, procedure, process, structure, system, technique, tool, workings, works.

medal *n.* award, decoration, gong, honor, medalet, medallion, prize, reward, trophy.

meddle *v.* interfere, interlope, interpose, intervene, intrude, mell, pry, put one's oar in, tamper.

meddlesome *adj.* interfering, intruding, intrusive, meddling, mischievous, officious, prying, ultracrepidarian.

mediate *v.* arbitrate, conciliate, incubate, intercede, interpose, intervene, moderate, negotiate, reconcile, referee, resolve, settle, step in, umpire.

medicinal *adj.* adjuvant, analeptic, curative, healing, homeopathic, medical, medicamental, medicamentary, remedial, restorative, roborant, sanatory, therapeutic.

medicine[1] *n.* cure, diapente, diatessaron, drug, electuary, elixir, febrifuge, Galenical, materia medica, medicament, medication, nostrum, panacea, physic, remedy, specific, tincture, vermifuge.

medicine[2] *n.* acupuncture, allopathy, homeopathy, leechcraft, surgery, therapeutics.

mediocre *adj.* amateurish, average, commonplace, indifferent, inferior, insignificant, mean, medium, middling, ordinary, passable, pedestrian, run-of-the-mill, second-rate, so-so, undistinguished, unexceptional, uninspired. *antonyms* excellent, exceptional, extraordinary.

meditate *v.* be in a brown study, cerebrate, cogitate, consider, contemplate, deliberate, devise, excogitate, intend, mull over, muse, plan, ponder, purpose, reflect, ruminate, scheme, speculate, study, think, think over.

medium[1] *adj.* average, fair, intermediate, mean, medial, median, mediocre, middle, middling, midway, standard.
n. aurea mediocritas, average, center, compromise, golden mean, happy medium, mean, middle, middle ground, midpoint, via media, way.

medium[2] *n.* agency, avenue, base, channel, excipient, form, instrument, instrumentality, means, mode, organ, vehicle, way.

medium[3] *n.* clairvoyant, psychic, spiritist, spiritualist.

medium[4] *n.* ambience, atmosphere, circumstances, conditions, element, environment, habitat, influences, milieu, setting, surroundings.

medley *n.* assortment, collection, confusion, conglomeration, farrago, galimatias, gallimaufry, hodge-podge, hotchpotch, jumble, macaroni, macédoine, mélange, mingle-mangle, miscellany, mishmash, mixture, olio, ollapodrida, omnium-gatherum, pastiche, patchwork, potpourri, quodlibet, salmagundi.

meek *adj.* acquiescent, compliant, deferential, docile, forbearing, gentle, humble, long-suffering, mild, modest, patient, peaceful, resigned, slavish, soft, spineless, spiritless, subdued, submissive, tame, timid, unambitious, unassuming, unpretentious, unresisting, weak, yielding.
antonyms arrogant, rebellious.

meet *v.* abut, adjoin, answer, assemble, bear, bump into, chance on, collect, come across, come together, comply, confront, congregate, connect, contact, convene, converge, cross, discharge, encounter, endure, equal, experience, face, find, forgather, fulfil, gather, go through, gratify, handle, happen on, intersect, join, link up, match, measure up to, muster, perform, rally, rencontre, rencounter, run across, run into, satisfy, suffer, touch, undergo, unite.

melancholy *adj.* blue, dejected, depressed, despondent, disconsolate, dismal, dispirited, doleful, down, down in the dumps, down in the mouth, downcast, downhearted, gloomy, glum, heavy-hearted, hipped, joyless, low, low-spirited, lugubrious, melancholic, miserable, moody, mournful, pensieroso, pensive, sad, somber, sorrowful, splenific, unhappy, woebegone, woeful.
antonyms cheerful, gay, happy, joyful.
n. blues, dejection, depression, despondency, dole, dolor, gloom, gloominess, glumness, low spirits, pensiveness, sadness, sorrow, unhappiness, woe.
antonym exhilaration.

mêlée *n.* affray, battle royal, brawl, broil, dogfight, donnybrook, fight, fracas, fray, free-for-all, ruckus, ruction, rumpus, scrimmage, scrum, scuffle, set-to, stramash, tussle.

mellow *adj.* cheerful, cordial, delicate, dulcet, elevated, expansive, full, full-flavored, genial, happy, jolly, jovial, juicy, mature, mellifluous, melodious, merry, perfect, placid, relaxed, rich, ripe, rounded, serene, smooth, soft, sweet, tipsy, tranquil, well-matured.
antonyms immature, unripe.
v. improve, mature, perfect, ripen, season, soften, sweeten, temper.

melodious *adj.* arioso, canorous, concordant, dulcet, euphonious, harmonious, melodic, musical, silvery, sonorous, sweet-sounding, tuneful.
antonyms discordant, grating, harsh.

melodramatic *adj.* blood-and-thunder, exaggerated, hammy, histrionic, overdone, overdramatic, overemotional, overwrought, sensational, stagy, theatrical.

melody *n.* air, aria, arietta, arriette, euphony, harmony, melisma, melodiousness, music, musicality, refrain, song, strain, theme, tune, tunefulness.

melt *v.* deliquesce, diffuse, disarm, dissolve, flux, fuse, liquate, liquefy, mollify, relax, soften, thaw, touch, uncongeal, unfreeze.
antonyms freeze, harden, solidify.

member *n.* appendage, arm, associate, component, constituent, element, extremity, fellow, initiate, leg, limb, organ, part, portion, representative.

membrane *n.* diaphragm, fell, film, hymen, integument, partition, septum, skin, tissue, veil, velum.

memento *n.* keepsake, memorial, record, relic, remembrance, reminder, souvenir, token, trophy.

memoirs *n.* annals, autobiography, chronicles, confessions, diary, experiences, journals, life, life story, memories, personalia, recollections, records, reminiscences, transactions.

memorable *adj.* catchy, celebrated, distinguished, extraordinary, famous, historic, illustrious, important, impressive, marvelous, momentous, notable, noteworthy, outstanding, remarkable, signal, significant, striking, unforgettable.
antonym forgettable.

memorial *n.* cairn, cromlech, dolmen, martyry, mausoleum, memento, menhir, monument, plaque, record, remembrance, souvenir, stone.
adj. celebratory, commemorative, monumental.

memorize *v.* con, learn, learn by heart, learn by rote, learn off, mug up, swot up.
antonym forget.

memory *n.* celebrity, commemoration, fame, glory, honor, memorial, name, recall, recollection, remembrance, reminiscence, renown, reputation, repute, retention.
antonym forgetfulness.

menace *v.* alarm, browbeat, bully, comminate, cow, frighten, impend, intimidate, loom, lour (lower), terrorize, threaten.
n. annoyance, commination, danger, hazard, intimidation, jeopardy, nuisance, peril, pest, plague, scare, terror, threat, troublemaker, warning.

mend *v.* ameliorate, amend, better, bushel, cobble, convalesce, correct, cure, darn, emend, fix, heal, improve, patch, recover, rectify, recuperate, refit, reform, remedy, renew, renovate, repair, restore, retouch, revise, solder.
antonyms break, destroy, deteriorate.
n. clout, darn, patch, repair, stitch.

mendacious *adj.* deceitful, deceptive, dishonest, duplicitous, fallacious, false, fraudulent, insincere, inveracious, lying, perfidious, perjured, untrue, untruthful, unveracious.
antonyms honest, truthful.

mendicant *adj.* begging, cadging, petitionary, scrounging, supplicant.
n. almsman, beachcomber, beggar, bum, cadger, hobo, moocher, panhandler, pauper, scrounger, tramp, vagabond, vagrant.

menial *adj.* abject, attending, base, boring, degrading, demeaning, dull, fawning, groveling, helping, humble, humdrum, ignoble, ignominious, low, lowly, mean, obsequious, routine, servile, slavish, sorry, subservient, sycophantic, unskilled, vile.
n. attendant, creature, dog's-body, domestic, drudge, eta, flunky, laborer, lackey, peon, serf, servant, skivvy, slave, underling.

mental[1] *adj.* abstract, cerebral, cognitive, conceptual, ideational, ideative, intellectual, noetic, rational, theoretical.
antonym physical.

mental[2] *adj.* crazy, deranged, disturbed, insane, loony, loopy, lunatic, mad, psychiatric, psychotic, unbalanced, unstable.
antonyms balanced, sane.

mentality *n.* attitude, brains, capacity, character, comprehension, disposition, endowment, faculty, frame of mind, intellect, IQ, make-up, mind, outlook, personality, psychology, rationality, understanding, wit.

mentally *adv.* emotionally, intellectually, inwardly, psychologically, rationally, subjectively, temperamentally.

mention *v.* acknowledge, adduce, advise, allude to, apprize, bring up, broach, cite, communicate, declare, disclose, divulge, hint at, impart, intimate, make known, name, point out, recount, refer to, report, reveal, speak of, state, tell, touch on.
n. acknowledgment, allusion, announcement, citation, indication, notification, observation, recognition, reference, remark, tribute.

mentor *n.* adviser, coach, counselor, guide, guru, instructor, pedagogue, swami, teacher, tutor.

merchandise *n.* cargo, commodities, freight, goods, produce, products, shipment, staples, stock, stock in trade, truck, vendibles, wares.
v. carry, deal in, distribute, market, peddle, retail, sell, supply, trade, traffic in, vend.

merchant *n.* broker, dealer, jobber, négociant, retailer, salesman, seller, shopkeeper, trader, tradesman, trafficker, vendor, wholesaler.

merciful *adj.* beneficent, benignant, clement, compassionate, condolent, forbearing, forgiving, generous, gracious, humane, humanitarian, kind, lenient, liberal, mild, pitying, soft, sparing, sympathetic, tender-hearted.
antonyms cruel, merciless.

merciless *adj.* barbarous, callous, cruel, hard, hard-hearted, harsh, heartless, implacable, inexorable, inhuman, inhumane, pitiless, relentless, remorseless, ruthless, severe, unappeasable, unforgiving, unmerciful, unpitying, unsparing.
antonym merciful.

mercurial *adj.* active, capricious, changeable, erratic, fickle, flighty, gay, impetuous, impulsive, inconstant, irrepressible, light-hearted, lively, mobile, spirited, sprightly, temperamental, unpredictable, unstable, variable, volatile.
antonym saturnine.

mercy *n.* benevolence, blessing, boon, charity, clemency, compassion, favor, forbearance, forgiveness, godsend, grace, humanitarianism, kindness, leniency, pity, quarter, relief.
antonyms cruelty, revenge.

mere *adj.* absolute, bare, common, complete, entire, paltry, petty, plain, pure, pure and simple, sheer, simple, stark, unadulterated, unmitigated, unmixed, utter, very.

merge *v.* amalgamate, blend, coalesce, combine, commingle, confederate, consolidate, converge, fuse, incorporate, intermix, join, liquesce, meet, meld, melt into, mingle, mix, unite.

merger *n.* amalgamation, coalescence, coalition, combination, confederation, consolidation, fusion, incorporation, union.

merit *n.* advantage, asset, claim, credit, desert, due, excellence, good, goodness, integrity, justification, quality, right, strong point, talent, value, virtue, worth, worthiness.
antonyms demerit, fault.
v. deserve, earn, incur, justify, rate, warrant.

merited *adj.* appropriate, condign, deserved, due, earned, entitled, fitting, just, justified, rightful, warranted, worthy.
antonyms inappropriate, unjustified.

meritorious *adj.* admirable, commendable, creditable, deserving, estimable, excellent, exemplary, good, honorable, laudable, praiseworthy, right, righteous, virtuous, worthful, worthy.
antonym unworthy.

merry *adj.* amusing, blithe, blithesome, boon, carefree, cheerful, chirpy, comic, comical, convivial, crank, elevated, facetious, festive, frolicsome, fun-loving, funny, gay, glad, gleeful, happy, heartsome, hilarious, humorous, jocular, jocund, jolly, joyful, joyous, light-hearted, mellow, mirthful, rollicking, rorty, saturnalian, sportful, sportive, squiffy, tiddly, tipsy, vivacious.
antonyms gloomy, glum, grave, melancholy, serious, sober, somber.

mesh *n.* entanglement, lattice, net, netting, network, plexus, reticulation, snare, tangle, toils, tracery, trap, web.
v. catch, combine, come together, connect, co-ordinate, dovetail, engage, enmesh, entangle, fit, harmonize, inmesh, interlock, knit.

mesmerize *v.* benumb, captivate, enthral, entrance, fascinate, grip, hypnotize, magnetize, spellbind, stupefy.

mess *n.* botch, chaos, clutter, cock-up, confusion, difficulty, dilemma, dirtiness, disarray, disorder, disorganization, fiasco, fix, guddle, hash, imbroglio, jam, jumble, litter, mishmash, mix-up, muddle, muss(e), perplexity, pickle, plight, predicament, shambles, shemozzle, soss, stew, turmoil, untidiness, yuck.
antonyms order, tidiness.
v. befoul, besmirch, clutter, dirty, disarrange, disarray, dishevel, foul, litter, muss(e), pollute, tousle.
antonyms order, tidy.

message *n.* bulletin, cable, commission, communication, communiqué, dépêche, dispatch, errand, idea, import, intimation, job, letter, meaning, memorandum, mission, missive, moral, note, notice, point, purport, send, task, theme, tidings, word.

messenger *n.* agent, ambassador, bearer, carrier, courier, delivery boy, emissary, envoy, errand-boy, go-between, harbinger, herald, in-between, internuncio, mercury, nuncio, runner, send, vaunt-courier.

messy *adj.* chaotic, cluttered, confused, dirty, disheveled, disordered, disorganized, grubby, littered, muddled, shambolic, sloppy, slovenly, unkempt, untidy, yucky.
antonyms neat, ordered, tidy.

metamorphosis *n.* alteration, change, change-over, conversion, modification, mutation, rebirth, transfiguration, transformation, translation, transmogrification, transmutation, transubstantiation.

mete out administer, allot, apportion, assign, deal out, dispense, distribute, divide out, dole out, hand out, measure out, parcel out, portion, ration out, share out.

meteoric *adj.* brief, brilliant, dazzling, fast, instantaneous, momentary, overnight, rapid, spectacular, speedy, sudden, swift.

method *n.* approach, arrangement, course, design, fashion, form, manner, mode, modus operandi, order, orderliness, organization, pattern, plan, planning, practice, procedure, process, program, purpose, regularity, routine, rule, scheme, structure, style, system, technique, way.

methodical *adj.* business-like, deliberate, disciplined, efficient, meticulous, neat, ordered, orderly, organized, painstaking, planned, precise, punctilious, regular, scrupulous, structured, systematic, tidy.
antonyms confused, desultory, irregular.

meticulous *adj.* accurate, detailed, exact, fastidious, fussy, microscopic, nice, painstaking, particular, perfectionist, precise, punctilious, scrupulous, strict, thorough.
antonyms careless, slapdash.

mettle *n.* ardor, boldness, bottle, bravery, caliber, character, courage, daring, disposition, fire, fortitude, gallantry, gameness, ginger, grit, guts, hardihood, heart, indomitability, kidney, life, make-up, nature, nerve, pith, pluck, quality, resolution, resolve, spirit, spunk, stamp, temper, temperament, valor, vigor.

microscopic *adj.* imperceptible, indiscernible, infinitesimal, invisible, minuscule, minute, negligible, tiny.
antonyms huge, vast.

middle *adj.* central, halfway, inner, inside, intermediate, intervening, mean, medial, median, mediate, medium, mid, middle-bracket.

n. aurea mediocritas, center, focus, golden mean, halfway mark, halfway point, happy medium, heart, inside, mean, middle way, midpoint, midriff, midsection, midst, thick, via media, waist.

antonyms beginning, border, edge, end, extreme.

middleman *n.* broker, distributor, entrepreneur, fixer, go-between, intermediary, negotiator, retailer.

midget *n.* dwarf, gnome, homuncule, homunculus, manikin, minikin, minnow, pygmy, shrimp, Tom Thumb. *antonym* giant.

adj. dwarf, Lilliputian, little, miniature, pocket, pocketsized, pygmy, small, teeny, tiny.

antonym giant.

midst *n.* bosom, center, core, depths, epicenter, heart, hub, interior, middle, mid-point, thick.

midway *adv.* betwixt and between, halfway, in the middle, partially.

mien *n.* air, appearance, aspect, aura, bearing, carriage, complexion, countenance, demeanor, deportment, look, manner, presence, semblance.

miffed *adj.* aggrieved, annoyed, chagrined, disgruntled, displeased, hurt, in a huff, irked, irritated, narked, nettled, offended, piqued, put out, resentful, upset, vexed. *antonyms* chuffed, delighted, pleased.

might *n.* ability, capability, capacity, clout, efficacy, efficiency, energy, force, heftiness, muscularity, potency, power, powerfulness, prowess, puissance, strength, sway, valor, vigor.

mighty *adj.* bulky, colossal, doughty, enormous, forceful, gigantic, grand, great, hardy, hefty, huge, immense, indomitable, large, lusty, manful, massive, monumental, muscular, potent, powerful, prodigious, puissant, robust, stalwart, stout, strapping, strenuous, strong, stupendous, sturdy, titanic, towering, tremendous, vast, vigorous.

antonyms frail, weak.

migrant *n.* drifter, emigrant, globe-trotter, gypsy, immigrant, itinerant, land-louper, nomad, rover, tinker, transient, traveler, vagrant, wanderer.

adj. drifting, globe-trotting, gypsy, immigrant, itinerant, migratory, nomadic, roving, shifting, transient, traveling, vagrant, wandering.

migrate *v.* drift, emigrate, journey, move, roam, rove, shift, transhume, travel, trek, voyage, wander.

migratory *adj.* gipsy, itinerant, migrant, nomadic, peripatetic, roving, shifting, transient, transitory, traveling, vagrant, wandering.

mild *adj.* amiable, balmy, bland, calm, clement, compassionate, docile, easy, easy-going, equable, forbearing, forgiving, gentle, indulgent, kind, lenient, meek, mellow, merciful, moderate, pacific, passive, peaceable, placid, pleasant, serene, smooth, soft, temperate, tender, tranquil, warm. *antonyms* fierce, harsh, stormy, strong, violent.

milieu *n.* arena, background, element, environment, locale, location, medium, scene, setting, sphere, surroundings.

militant *adj.* active, aggressive, assertive, belligerent, combating, combative, contending, embattled, fighting, hawkish, pugnacious, vigorous, warring.

n. activist, aggressor, belligerent, combatant, fighter, partisan, struggler, warrior.

military *adj.* armed, martial, service, soldier-like, soldierly, warlike.

n. armed forces, army, forces, services, soldiers, soldiery.

milksop *n.* chinless wonder, coward, milquetoast, Miss Nancy, molly, mollycoddle, namby-pamby, pansy, sissy, weakling.

mill[1] *n.* ball-mill, crusher, grinder, quern.

v. comminute, crush, granulate, grate, grind, pound, powder, press, pulverize, roll.

mill[2] *n.* factory, foundry, plant, shop, works.

mill[3] *v.* crowd, scurry, seethe, swarm, throng, wander.

millstone *n.* affliction, burden, drag, encumbrance, grindstone, load, quernstone, weight.

mimic *v.* ape, caricature, echo, imitate, impersonate, look like, mirror, parody, parrot, personate, resemble, simulate, take off.

n. caricaturist, copy, copy-cat, imitator, impersonator, impressionist, parodist, parrot.

adj. echoic, fake, imitation, imitative, make-believe, mimetic, mock, pseudo, sham, simulated.

mince[1] *v.* chop, crumble, cut, dice, grind, hash.

n. hachis, hash.

mince[2] *v.* diminish, euphemize, extenuate, hold back, moderate, palliate, play down, soften, spare, suppress, tone down, weaken.

mince[3] *v.* attitudinize, ponce, pose, posture, simper.

mind[1] *n.* attention, attitude, belief, bent, brains, concentration, desire, disposition, fancy, feeling, genius, gray matter, head, imagination, inclination, inner, intellect, intellectual, intelligence, intention, judgment, leaning, marbles, memory, mentality, notion, opinion, outlook, point of view, psyche, purpose, rationality, reason, recollection, remembrance, sanity, sense, senses, sensorium, sensory, sentiment, spirit, tendency, thinker, thinking, thoughts, understanding, urge, view, will, wish, wits.

mind[2] *v.* care, demur, disapprove, dislike, object, resent, take offense.

mind[3] *v.* adhere to, attend, attend to, be careful, be on one's guard, comply with, ensure, follow, guard, have charge of, heed, keep an eye on, listen to, look after, make certain, mark, note, notice, obey, observe, pay attention, pay heed to, regard, respect, take care, take care of, take heed, tend, watch.

mindful *adj.* alert, alive (to), attentive, aware, careful, chary, cognizant, compliant, conscious, heedful, obedient, regardful, remindful, respectful, sensible, thoughtful, wary, watchful.

antonyms heedless, inattentive, mindless.

mine[1] *n.* abundance, coalfield, colliery, deposit, excavation, fund, hoard, lode, pit, reserve, sap, shaft, source, stock, store, supply, treasury, trench, tunnel, vein, wealth, wheal.

v. delve, dig for, dig up, excavate, extract, hew, quarry, remove, sap, subvert, tunnel, undermine, unearth, weaken.

mine[2] *n.* bomb, depth charge, egg, explosive, land-mine.

mingle *v.* alloy, associate, blend, circulate, coalesce, combine, commingle, compound, hobnob, intermingle, intermix, interweave, join, marry, mell, merge, mix, rub shoulders, socialize, unite.

miniature *adj.* baby, diminutive, dwarf, Lilliputian, little, midget, mini, minuscule, minute, pint-size(d), pocket, pocket-sized, pygmy, reduced, scaled-down, small, tiny, toy, wee.

antonym giant.

minimize *v.* abbreviate, attenuate, belittle, curtail, decrease, decry, deprecate, depreciate, diminish, discount, disparage, make light of, make little of, play down, prune, reduce, shrink, underestimate, underrate.

antonym maximize.

minimum *n.* bottom, least, lowest point, nadir, slightest.

antonym maximum.

adj. least, littlest, lowest, minimal, slightest, smallest, tiniest, weeniest, weest.

antonym maximum.

minister *n.* administrator, agent, aide, ambassador, assistant, churchman, clergyman, cleric, delegate, diplomat, divine, ecclesiastic, envoy, executive, Levite, office-holder, official, parson, pastor, plenipotentiary, preacher, priest, servant, subordinate, underling, vicar, vizier.

v. accommodate, administer, attend, cater to, nurse, pander to, serve, take care of, tend.

minor *adj.* inconsequential, inconsiderable, inferior, insignificant, junior, lesser, light, negligible, paltry, petty, piddling, secondary, second-class, slight, small, smaller, subordinate, trifling, trivial, unclassified, unimportant, younger.

antonym major.

minstrel *n.* bard, joculator, jongleur, musician, rhymer, rimer, singer, troubadour.

mint *v.* cast, coin, construct, devise, fabricate, fashion, forge, invent, make, make up, manufacture, monetize, produce, punch, stamp, strike.

adj. brand-new, excellent, first-class, fresh, immaculate, perfect, unblemished, undamaged, untarnished.

n. bomb, bundle, fortune, heap, million, packet, pile, stack.

minute[1] *n.* flash, instant, jiff, jiffy, mo, moment, sec, second, shake, tick, trice.

minute[2] *adj.* close, critical, detailed, diminutive, exact, exhaustive, fine, inconsiderable, infinitesimal, itsy-bitsy, Lilliputian, little, meticulous, microscopic, miniature, minim, minuscule, negligible, painstaking,

paltry, petty, picayune, piddling, precise, punctilious, puny, slender, slight, small, tiny, trifling, trivial, unimportant.

antonyms gigantic, huge, immense.

miraculous *adj.* amazing, astonishing, astounding, extraordinary, incredible, inexplicable, magical, marvelous, otherworldly, phenomenal, preternatural, prodigious, stupendous, superhuman, supernatural, thaumaturgic, unaccountable, unbelievable, wonderful, wondrous.

antonyms natural, normal.

mirage *n.* fata Morgana, hallucination, illusion, optical illusion, phantasm.

mire *n.* bog, difficulties, dirt, fen, glaur, marsh, morass, muck, mud, ooze, quag, quagmire, slime, swamp, trouble.

mirror *n.* copy, double, glass, hand-glass, image, keeking-glass, likeness, looking-glass, pocket-glass, reflection, reflector, replica, representation, speculum, spit and image, spitting image, twin.

v. copy, depict, echo, emulate, follow, imitate, mimic, reflect, represent, show.

mirth *n.* amusement, cheerfulness, festivity, frolic, fun, gaiety, gladness, glee, hilarity, jocosity, jocularity, jocundity, jollity, joviality, joyousness, laughter, levity, merriment, merrymaking, pleasure, rejoicing, revelry, sport.

antonyms gloom, gl&udot;mness, melancholy.

misadventure *n.* accident, calamity, cataclysm, catastrophe, debacle, disaster, failure, ill fortune, ill luck, mischance, misfortune, mishap, reverse, setback, tragedy.

misappropriate *v.* abuse, defalcate, embezzle, misapply, misspend, misuse, peculate, pervert, pocket, steal, swindle.

misbehave *v.* act up, carry on, get up to mischief, kick over the traces, mess about, muck about, offend, transgress, trespass.

antonym behave.

miscalculate *v.* blunder, boob, err, get wrong, misjudge, overestimate, overrate, overvalue, slip up, underestimate, underrate, undervalue.

miscarriage *n.* abortion, botch, breakdown, casualty, disappointment, error, failure, misadventure, mischance, misfire, mishap, mismanagement, perversion, thwarting, undoing.

antonym success.

miscarry *v.* abort, bite the dust, come to grief, come to nothing, fail, fall through, flounder, gang agley, misfire, warp.

antonym succeed.

miscellaneous *adj.* assorted, confused, diverse, diversified, farraginous, heterogeneous, indiscriminate, jumbled, manifold, many, mingled, mixed, motley, multifarious, multiform, omnifarious, promiscuous, sundry, varied, various.

miscellany *n.* anthology, assortment, collection, diversity, farrago, gallimaufry, hash, hotch-potch, jumble, medley, mélange, mixed bag, mixture, olla-podrida, omniumgatherum, pot-pourri, salmagundi, variety.

mischief[1] *n.* bane, damage, detriment, devilment, deviltry, diablerie, disruption, evil, harm, hurt, impishness, injury, misbehavior, misfortune, monkey business, naughtiness, pranks, roguery, roguishness, shenanigans, trouble, waggery, waywardness.

mischief[2] *n.* devil, imp, monkey, nuisance, pest, rapscallion, rascal, rascallion, rogue, scallywag, scamp, tyke, villain.
antonym angel.

mischievous *adj.* arch, bad, damaging, deleterious, destructive, detrimental, elfish, elvan, elvish, evil, exasperating, frolicsome, harmful, hurtful, impish, injurious, malicious, malignant, naughty, pernicious, playful, puckish, rascally, roguish, sinful, spiteful, sportive, teasing, tricksy, troublesome, vexatious, vicious, wayward, wicked.
antonyms good, well-behaved.

misconduct *n.* delinquency, dereliction, hanky-panky, immorality, impropriety, malfeasance, malpractice, malversation, misbehavior, misdemeanor, misfeasance, mismanagement, naughtiness, rudeness, transgression, wrong-doing.

miscreant *n.* blackguard, caitiff, criminal, dastard, evildoer, knave, malefactor, mischief-maker, profligate, rascal, reprobate, rogue, scallywag, scamp, scapegrace, scoundrel, sinner, trouble-maker, vagabond, varlet, villain, wretch, wrong-doer.
antonym worthy.

misdemeanor *n.* delict, fault, indiscretion, infringement, lapse, malfeasance, misbehavior, misconduct, misdeed, offense, peccadillo, transgression, trespass.

miser *n.* cheapskate, curmudgeon, hunks, mammonist, meanie, money-grubber, muck-worm, niggard, penny-pincher, pinchfist, pinchgut, pinchpenny, save-all, screw, Scrooge, skinflint, snudge, tightwad.
antonym spendthrift.

miserable *adj.* abject, anguished, bad, broken-hearted, caitiff, cheerless, contemptible, crestfallen, crushed, dejected, deplorable, depressed, depressive, desolate, despicable, despondent, destitute, detestable, disconsolate, disgraceful, dismal, distressed, doleful, dolorous, down, downcast, dreary, forlorn, gloomy, glum, grief-stricken, hapless, heartbroken, ignominious, impoverished, indigent, joyless, lachrymose, lamentable, low, luckless, lugubrious, meager, mean, melancholic, melancholy, mournful, needy, niggardly, paltry, pathetic, penniless, piteous, pitiable, pitiful, poor, sad, scanty, scurvy, shabby, shameful, sordid, sorrowful, sorrowing, sorry, squalid, star-crossed, stricken, tearful, unhappy, vile, woebegone, worthless, wretched.
antonyms cheerful, comfortable, generous, honorable, noble.

miserly *adj.* avaricious, beggarly, cheese-paring, close,

close-fisted, close-handed, covetous, curmudgeonly, gare, grasping, grudging, illiberal, mean, mercenary, mingy, money-grubbing, near, niggardly, parsimonious, penny-pinching, penurious, sordid, sparing, stingy, thrifty, tight-fisted, ungenerous.
antonyms generous, lavish, prodigal, spendthrift.

misery[1] *n.* abjectness, adversity, affliction, agony, anguish, bale, bane, bitter pill, blow, burden, calamity, catastrophe, cross, curse, depression, desolation, despair, destitution, disaster, discomfort, distress, dole, dolor, extremity, gloom, grief, hardship, heartache, heartbreak, humiliation, indigence, living death, load, melancholia, melancholy, misfortune, mortification, need, oppression, ordeal, penury, poverty, privation, prostration, sadness, sordidness, sorrow, squalor, suffering, torment, torture, trial, tribulation, trouble, unhappiness, want, woe, wretchedness.

misery[2] *n.* grouch, Jeremiah, Job's comforter, killjoy, moaner, pessimist, prophet of doom, ray of sunshine, sourpuss, spoil-sport, Weary Willie, wet blanket, whiner, whinger.
antonym sport.

misfit *n.* drop-out, eccentric, fish out of water, horse marine, individualist, lone wolf, loner, maverick, nonconformist, odd man out, oddball, rogue, square peg in a round hole, weirdo.
antonym conformist.

misfortune *n.* accident, adversity, affliction, bad luck, blow, buffet, calamity, catastrophe, disaster, failure, grief, hardship, harm, ill-luck, infelicity, infortune, loss, misadventure, mischance, misery, mishap, reverse, setback, sorrow, tragedy, trial, tribulation, trouble, woe.
antonyms luck, success.

misgiving *n.* anxiety, apprehension, backward glance, compunction, distrust, doubt, dubiety, fear, hesitation, misdoubt, niggle, presentiment, qualm, reservation, scruple, second thoughts, suspicion, uncertainty, unease, worry.
antonym confidence.

misguided *adj.* deluded, erroneous, foolish, ill-advised, ill-considered, ill-judged, imprudent, incautious, injudicious, misconceived, misled, misplaced, mistaken, rash, unreasonable, unsuitable, unwarranted, unwise.
antonym sensible.

mishap *n.* accident, adversity, balls-up, calamity, contretemps, disaster, hiccup, ill-fortune, ill-luck, misadventure, mischance, misfortune, misventure, setback.

mishmash *n.* conglomeration, farrago, gallimaufry, hash, hotchpotch, jumble, medley, mess, muddle, olio, olla-podrida, pastiche, pot-pourri, salad, salmagundi.

misjudge *v.* miscalculate, miscount, misestimate, misinterpret, misprize, mistake, overestimate, overrate, underestimate, underrate, undervalue.

mislay *v.* lose, lose sight of, misplace, miss.

mislead *v.* beguile, bluff, deceive, delude, fool, give a bum steer, hoodwink, lead up the garden path, misadvise, misdirect, misguide, misinform, mizzle, pull the wool over someone's eyes, snow, take for a ride, take in.

misleading *adj.* ambiguous, biased, casuistical, confusing, deceitful, deceptive, delusive, delusory, disingenuous, distorted, equivocatory, evasive, fallacious, false, falsidical, loaded, mendacious, sophistical, specious, spurious, tricky, unreliable.
antonyms authentic, authoritative, informative, plain, unequivocal.

mismatched *adj.* antipathetic, clashing, discordant, disparate, ill-assorted, incompatible, incongruous, irregular, misallied, mismated, unmatching, unreconcilable, unsuited.
antonyms compatible, matching.

misplace *v.* lose, misapply, misassign, misfile, mislay, miss.

misrepresent *v.* belie, bend, disguise, distort, exaggerate, falsify, garble, load, minimize, miscolor, misconstrue, misinterpret, misquote, misstate, pervert, slant, twist.

miss[1] *v.* avoid, bypass, circumvent, err, escape, evade, fail, forego, jump, lack, leave out, let go, let slip, lose, miscarry, mistake, obviate, omit, overlook, pass over, pass up, side-step, skip, slip, trip.
n. blunder, error, failure, fault, fiasco, flop, lack, lacuna, loss, mistake, need, omission, oversight, want.

miss[2] *v.* grieve for, lack, lament, long for, mourn, need, pine for, regret, sorrow for, want, wish, yearn for.

miss[3] *n.* backfisch, child, damsel, demoiselle, flapper, Fraülein, girl, girly, Jungfrau, junior miss, kid, lass, lassie, mademoiselle, maid, maiden, missy, Ms, nymphet, school-girl, spinster, teenager, young thing.

misshapen *adj.* contorted, crippled, crooked, deformed, distorted, grotesque, ill-made, ill-proportioned, malformed, monstrous, thrawn, twisted, ugly, ungainly, unshapely, unsightly, warped, wry.
antonyms regular, shapely.

missile *n.* arrow, ball, bomb, dart, flying bomb, grenade, projectile, rocket, shaft, shell, shot, torpedo, V-bomb, weapon.

missing *adj.* absent, astray, disappeared, gone, lacking, lost, minus, misgone, mislaid, misplaced, strayed, unaccounted-for, wanting.
antonyms found, present.

mission *n.* aim, assignment, business, calling, campaign, charge, commission, crusade, delegation, deputation, duty, embassy, errand, goal, job, legation, mandate, ministry, object, office, operation, purpose, pursuit, quest, raison d'être, remit, task, task force, trust, undertaking, vocation, work.

missionary *n.* ambassador, apostle, campaigner, champion, crusader, emissary, envoy, evangelist, exponent, gospeller, preacher, promoter, propagandist, proselytizer, teacher.

mist *n.* brume, cloud, condensation, dew, dimness, drizzle,

exhalation, film, fog, haar, haze, mizzle, roke, smir, smog, spray, steam, vapor, veil, water-smoke.
v. becloud, bedim, befog, blur, cloud, dim, film, fog, glaze, obscure, steam up, veil.
antonym clear.

mistake *n.* aberration, bêtise, bish, bloomer, blunder, boner, boob, boo-boo, clanger, clinker, corrigendum, erratum, error, fallacy, false move, fault, faux pas, floater, folly, gaffe, gaucherie, goof, howler, inaccuracy, indiscretion, inexactitude, lapse, lapsus, lapsus calami, lapsus linguae, lapsus memoriae, literal, malapropism, misapprehension, miscalculation, misconception, misjudgment, misprint, misprision, mispronunciation, misreading, misspelling, misunderstanding, mumpsimus, oversight, scape, slip, slip-up, solecism, stumer, tactlessness, trespass.
v. blunder, confound, confuse, err, get the wrong end of the stick, goof, misapprehend, miscalculate, misconceive, misconstrue, misinterpret, misjudge, misobserve, misprize, misrate, misread, misreckon, misunderstand, slip up.

mistaken *adj.* deceived, deluded, erroneous, fallacious, false, faulty, ill-judged, inaccurate, inappropriate, inauthentic, incorrect, inexact, misguided, misinformed, misinstructed, mislead, misprized, off base, unfair, unfounded, unjust, unsound, untrue, wide of the mark, wrong.
antonyms correct, justified.

mistreat *v.* abuse, batter, brutalize, bully, harm, hurt, ill-treat, ill-use, injure, knock about, maltreat, manhandle, maul, mishandle, misuse, molest, rough up.
antonym pamper.

mistrust *n.* apprehension, caution, chariness, distrust, doubt, dubiety, fear, hesitancy, misdoubt, misgiving, reservations, skepticism, suspicion, uncertainty, wariness.
antonym trust.
v. be wary of, beware, disbelieve, distrust, doubt, fear, fight shy of, look askance at, misdoubt, mislippen, question, suspect.
antonym trust.

misunderstand *v.* get the wrong end of the stick, get wrong, misapprehend, miscomprehend, misconceive, misconstrue, misesteem, mishear, misinterpret, misjudge, misknow, misprize, misread, miss the point, mistake, take up wrong(ly).
antonyms grasp, understand.

misunderstanding *n.* argument, breach, clash, conflict, difference, difficulty, disagreement, discord, disharmony, dispute, dissension, error, malentendu, misacceptation, misapprehension, misconception, misconstruction, misinterpretation, misjudgment, misknowledge, misprision, misreading, mistake, mix-up, quarrel, rift, rupture, squabble, variance.
antonyms agreement, reconciliation.

misuse *n.* abusage, abuse, barbarism, catachresis, corruption, desecration, dissipation, distortion, exploitation, harm, ill-treatment, ill-usage, injury, malappropriation, malapropism, maltreatment, manhandling, misapplication, misappropriation, misemployment, mistreatment, misusage, perversion, profanation, prostitution, solecism, squandering, wastage, waste.

v. abuse, brutalize, corrupt, desecrate, dissipate, distort, exploit, harm, ill-treat, ill-use, injure, malappropriate, maltreat, manhandle, maul, misapply, misappropriate, misemploy, mistreat, molest, overload, overtax, pervert, profane, prostitute, squander, strain, waste, wrong.

mite *n.* atom, grain, iota, jot, modicum, morsel, ounce, scrap, smidgen, spark, trace, whit.

mitigate *v.* abate, allay, alleviate, appease, assuage, attemper, blunt, calm, check, decrease, diminish, dull, ease, extenuate, lenify, lessen, lighten, moderate, modify, mollify, pacify, palliate, placate, quiet, reduce, remit, slake, soften, soothe, still, subdue, temper, tone down, weaken.

antonyms aggravate, exacerbate, increase.

mix *v.* allay, alloy, amalgamate, associate, blend, coalesce, combine, commingle, commix, compound, consort, contemper, cross, dash, fold in, fraternize, fuse, hobnob, homogenize, immingle, incorporate, intermingle, intermix, interweave, join, jumble, mell, merge, mingle, shuffle, socialize, synthesize, unite.

antonym separate.

n. alloy, amalgam, assortment, blend, combination, composite, compound, conglomerate, fusion, medley, mishmash, mixture, pastiche, synthesis.

mixture *n.* admixture, alloy, amalgam, amalgamation, association, assortment, blend, brew, coalescence, combination, combine, composite, compost, compound, concoction, conglomeration, cross, fusion, galimatias, gallimaufry, half-breed, hotchpotch, hybrid, jumble, macédoine, medley, mélange, miscegen, miscegenation, miscellany, mix, mixed bag, mongrel, olio, olla-podrida, omnium-gatherum, pastiche, pot-pourri, salad, salmagundi, synthesis, union, variety.

moan *n.* beef, belly-ache, bitch, complaint, gripe, groan, grouch, grouse, grumble, howl, keen, lament, lamentation, sigh, snivel, sob, sough, ululation, wail, whimper, whine, whinge.

v. beef, belly-ache, bemoan, bewail, bitch, carp, complain, deplore, grieve, gripe, groan, grouch, grouse, grumble, howl, keen, lament, mourn, sigh, snivel, sob, sough, ululate, wail, weep, whimper, whine, whinge, wuther.

antonym rejoice.

mob *n.* assemblage, bevy, body, canaille, class, collection, common herd, commonalty, company, crew, crowd, drove, faex populi, flock, galère, gang, gathering, great unwashed, group, herd, hoi polloi, horde, host, jingbang, lot, many-headed beast, many-headed monster, mass, masses, mobile, multitude, pack, plebs, populace, press, rabble, rent-a-crowd, rent-a-mob,

riff-raff, rout, scum, set, swarm, throng, tribe, troop, vulgus.

v. besiege, charge, cram, crowd, crowd round, descend on, fill, jam, jostle, overrun, pack, pester, set upon, surround, swarm round.

antonym shun.

mobile *adj.* active, agile, ambulatory, animated, changeable, changing, energetic, ever-changing, expressive, flexible, fluid, itinerant, lively, locomobile, locomotive, mercurial, migrant, motile, movable, moving, nimble, peripatetic, portable, roaming, roving, supple, traveling, vagile, vivacious, wandering.

antonym immobile.

mock *v.* ape, baffle, befool, burlesque, caricature, chaff, cheat, counterfeit, debunk, deceive, defeat, defy, delude, deride, disappoint, disparage, dupe, elude, explode, fleer, flout, foil, fool, frustrate, guy, imitate, insult, jeer, lampoon, laugh at, laugh in (someone's) face, laugh to scorn, make fun of, make sport of, mimic, parody, parrot, poke fun at, queer, quiz, ridicule, satirize, scoff, scorn, send up, sneer, take the mickey, taunt, tease, thwart, travesty, twit.

antonyms flatter, praise.

adj. artificial, bogus, counterfeit, dummy, ersatz, fake, faked, false, feigned, forged, fraudulent, imitation, phony, pinchbeck, pretended, pseudo, sham, simulated, spurious, synthetic.

mockery *n.* apology, burlesque, caricature, contempt, contumely, deception, derision, disappointment, disdain, disrespect, farce, fleer, gibes, iconoclasm, imitation, insults, invective, irrision, jeering, joke, lampoon, lampoonery, let-down, mickey-taking, mimesis, mimicry, misrepresentation, parody, pasquinade, pretence, quiz, ridicule, sarcasm, satire, scoffing, scorn, send-up, sham, spoof, take-off, travesty, wisecracks.

mode *n.* approach, condition, convention, course, craze, custom, dernier cri, fad, fashion, form, latest thing, look, manner, method, plan, practice, procedure, process, quality, rage, rule, state, style, system, technique, trend, vein, vogue, way.

model *n.* archetype, configuration, copy, criterion, design, draft, dummy, embodiment, epitome, example, exemplar, facsimile, form, gauge, ideal, image, imitation, kind, lodestar, manikin, mannequin, maquette, mark, miniature, mock-up, mode, mold, original, paradigm, paragon, pattern, personification, plan, poser, praxis, prototype, replica, representation, sitter, sketch, standard, style, subject, template, touchstone, type, variety, version, yardstick.

adj. archetypal, complete, consummate, dummy, exemplary, facsimile, ideal, illustrative, imitation, miniature, par excellence, paradigmatic, perfect, prototypal, prototypical, representative, standard, typical.

v. base, carve, cast, create, design, display, fashion, form, make, mold, pattern, plan, sculpt, shape, show off, sport, wear, work.

moderate *adj.* abstemious, average, calm, centrist, continent, controlled, cool, deliberate, disciplined, equable, fair, fairish, frugal, gentle, indifferent, judicious, limited, mediocre, medium, middle-of-the-road, middling, mild, modest, non-extreme, ordinary, passable, peaceable, quiet, rational, reasonable, restrained, sensible, sober, soft-shell(ed), so-so, steady, temperate, unexceptional, well-regulated.
v. abate, allay, alleviate, appease, assuage, attemper, blunt, calm, chasten, check, control, curb, cushion, decrease, diminish, dwindle, ease, lenify, lessen, mitigate, modify, modulate, pacify, palliate, play down, quiet, regulate, repress, restrain, slake, soften, softpedal, subdue, subside, tame, temper, tone down.

moderation *n.* abatement, abstemiousness, alleviation, aurea mediocritas, calmness, caution, chastity, composure, continence, control, coolness, decrease, diminution, discipline, discretion, easing, equanimity, extenuation, fairness, golden mean, judiciousness, justice, justness, let-up, mildness, mitigation, moderateness, modification, modulation, palliation, reasonableness, reduction, restraint, self-control, sobriety, temperance, via media.
antonyms increase, intemperance.

modern *adj.* advanced, avant-garde, contemporary, current, emancipated, fashionable, fresh, go-ahead, goey, innovative, inventive, jazzy, late, latest, mod, modernistic, modish, neoteric, new, newfangled, novel, present, present-day, progressive, recent, stylish, trendy, twentieth-century, up-to-date, up-to-the-minute, with-it.
antonyms antiquated, old.

modernize *v.* do up, improve, modify, neoterize, progress, redesign, reform, refresh, refurbish, regenerate, rejuvenate, remake, remodel, renew, renovate, revamp, streamline, tart up, transform, update.
antonym regress.

modest *adj.* bashful, blushing, chaste, chastened, coy, demure, diffident, discreet, fair, humble, limited, maidenly, meek, middling, moderate, ordinary, proper, quiet, reserved, reticent, retiring, seemly, self-conscious, self-effacing, shamefaced, shy, simple, small, timid, unassuming, unexceptional, unpresuming, unpresumptuous, unpretending, unpretentious, verecund.
antonyms conceited, immodest, pretentious, vain.

modesty *n.* aidos, bashfulness, coyness, decency, demureness, diffidence, discreetness, humbleness, humility, meekness, propriety, quietness, reserve, reticence, seemliness, self-effacement, shamefacedness, shamefastness, shyness, simplicity, timidity, unobtrusiveness, unpretentiousness.
antonyms conceit, immodesty, vanity.

modicum *n.* atom, bit, crumb, dash, drop, fragment, grain, hint, inch, iota, little, mite, ounce, particle, pinch, scrap, shred, speck, suggestion, tinge, touch, trace.

modification *n.* adjustment, alteration, change, limitation, moderation, modulation, mutation, qualification, refinement, reformation, restriction, revision, tempering, variation.

modify *v.* abate, adapt, adjust, allay, alter, attemper, change, convert, improve, lessen, limit, lower, moderate, modulate, qualify, recast, redesign, redo, reduce, refashion, reform, remodel, reorganize, reshape, restrain, restrict, revise, rework, soften, temper, tone down, transform, vary.

modish *adj.* à la mode, all the rage, avant-garde, chic, contemporary, current, fashionable, goey, hip, in, jazzy, latest, mod, modern, modernistic, now, smart, stylish, trendy, up-to-the-minute, vogue, voguish, with-it.
antonyms dowdy, old-fashioned.

modulate *v.* adjust, alter, attune, balance, harmonize, inflect, lower, moderate, regulate, soften, tone, tune, vary.
antonyms increase, raise.

modus operandi manner, method, operation, plan, practice, praxis, procedure, process, rule, rule of thumb, system, technique, way.

mogul *n.* baron, bashaw, big cheese, big gun, big noise, big pot, big shot, big wheel, bigwig, grandee, magnate, magnifico, Mr Big, nabob, notable, panjandrum, personage, potentate, supremo, top dog, tycoon, VIP.
antonym nobody.

moist *adj.* clammy, damp, dampish, dampy, dank, dewy, dripping, drizzly, humid, marshy, muggy, rainy, soggy, swampy, tearful, vaporous, watery, wet, wettish.
antonyms arid, dry.

moisten *v.* bedew, damp, dampen, embrocate, humect, humectate, humidify, humify, imbue, irrigate, lick, madefy, moistify, moisturize, slake, soak, water, wet.
antonym dry.

moisture *n.* damp, dampness, dankness, dew, humidity, humor, liquid, mugginess, perspiration, sweat, tears, vapor, water, wateriness, wet, wetness.
antonym dryness.

mold[1] *n.* arrangement, brand, build, caliber, cast, character, configuration, construction, cut, design, die, fashion, form, format, frame, framework, ilk, kidney, kind, line, make, matrix, model, nature, pattern, quality, shape, sort, stamp, structure, style, template, type. *v.* affect, carve, cast, construct, control, create, design, direct, fashion, fit, forge, form, hew, influence, make, model, sculpt, sculpture, shape, stamp, work.

mold[2] *n.* black, black spot, blight, fungus, mildew, moldiness, must, mustiness, rust.

mold[3] *n.* clods, dirt, dust, earth, ground, humus, loam, soil.

moldy *adj.* bad, blighted, corrupt, decaying, fusty, mildewed, mucedinous, mucid, muggish, muggy, musty, putrid, rotten, rotting, spoiled, stale, vinewed.
antonyms fresh, wholesome.

molest *v.* abuse, accost, afflict, annoy, assail, attack, badger, beset, bother, bug, disturb, faze, harass, harm, harry, hassle, hector, hound, hurt, ill-treat, injure, irritate, maltreat, manhandle, mistreat, persecute, pester, plague, tease, torment, trouble, upset, vex, worry.

mollify *v.* abate, allay, appease, assuage, blunt, calm, compose, conciliate, cushion, ease, lessen, lull, mellow, mitigate, moderate, modify, pacify, placate, propitiate, quell, quiet, relax, relieve, soften, soothe, sweeten, temper.

antonyms aggravate, anger.

moment[1] *n.* breathing-while, flash, hour, instant, jiff, jiffy, juncture, less than no time, minute, mo, point, second, shake, split second, stage, tick, time, trice, twink, twinkling.

moment[2] *n.* concern, consequence, gravity, import, importance, note interest, seriousness, significance, substance, value, weight, weightiness, worth.

antonym insignificance.

momentary *adj.* brief, elusive, ephemeral, evanescent, fleeting, flying, fugitive, hasty, momentaneous, passing, quick, short, short-lived, temporary, transient, transitory.

antonyms lasting, permanent.

momentous *adj.* apocalyptic, consequential, critical, crucial, decisive, earth-shaking, epoch-making, eventful, fateful, grave, historic, important, major, pivotal, serious, significant, tremendous, vital, weighty.

antonym insignificant.

momentum *n.* drive, energy, force, impact, impetus, impulse, incentive, power, propulsion, push, speed, stimulus, strength, thrust, urge, velocity.

monarch *n.* despot, dynast, emperor, empress, king, potentate, prince, princess, queen, ruler, sovereign, tyrant.

money *n.* baksheesh, banco, banknotes, bankroll, boodle, brass, bread, capital, cash, chips, coin, currency, dough, dumps, fat, filthy lucre, fonds, funds, gelt, gold, gravy, greens, hard cash, hard money, legal tender, lolly, loot, mazuma, mint-sauce, money of account, moolah, oof, pelf, readies, ready money, riches, scrip, shekels, siller, silver, specie, spondulix (spondulicks), stumpy, sugar, the needful, the ready, the wherewithal, tin, wealth.

mongrel *n.* bigener, cross, crossbreed, half-breed, hybrid, lurcher, mule, mutt, yellow-dog.

adj. bastard, crossbred, half-breed, hybrid, ill-defined, mixed, mongrelly, nondescript.

antonyms pedigree, pure-bred.

monitor *n.* adviser, detector, guide, invigilator, overseer, prefect, recorder, scanner, screen, supervisor, watchdog.

v. check, detect, follow, keep an eye on, keep track of, keep under surveillance, note, observe, oversee, plot, record, scan, supervise, survey, trace, track, watch.

ite, contemplative, conventual, frate, frater, friar, gyrovague, hermit, mendicant, monastic, religieux, religionary, religioner, religious.

monkey[1] *n.* ape, primate, simian.

monkey[2] *n.* ass, butt, devil, dupe, fool, imp, jackanapes, laughing-stock, mug, rapscallion, rascal, rogue, scallywag, scamp.

v. fiddle, fidget, fool, interfere, meddle, mess, play, potter, tamper, tinker, trifle.

monogamous *adj.* monandrous, monogamic, monogynous.

antonyms bigamous, polygamous.

monologue *n.* harangue, homily, lecture, oration, sermon, soliloquy, speech, spiel.

antonyms conversation, dialogue, discussion.

monomania *n.* bee in one's bonnet, fanaticism, fetish, fixation, hobby-horse, idée fixe, mania, neurosis, obsession, ruling passion, thing.

monopoly *n.* ascendancy, control, corner, domination, exclusive right, monopsony, sole right.

monotonous *adj.* boring, colorless, droning, dull, flat, humdrum, monochrome, plodding, prosaic, repetitious, repetitive, routine, samey, soul-destroying, tedious, tiresome, toneless, unchanging, uneventful, uniform, uninflected, unvaried, unvarying, wearisome.

antonyms colorful, lively, varied.

monster *n.* abortion, barbarian, basilisk, beast, behemoth, bogeyman, brute, centaur, chimera, cockatrice, colossus, Cyclops, demon, devil, fiend, freak, giant, Gorgon, harpy, hellhound, hippocampus, hippogriff, Hydra, jabberwock, kraken, lamia, leviathan, lindworm, mammoth, manticore, Medusa, Minotaur, miscreation, monstrosity, mutant, ogre, ogress, prodigy, rye-wolf, savage, Sphinx, teratism, titan, villain, wivern.

adj. Brobdingnagian, colossal, cyclopean, enormous, gargantuan, giant, gigantic, huge, immense, jumbo, mammoth, massive, monstrous, prodigious, rounceval, stupendous, titanic, tremendous, vast.

antonym minute.

monstrous *adj.* abhorrent, abnormal, atrocious, colossal, criminal, cruel, cyclopean, deformed, devilish, diabolical, disgraceful, dreadful, egregious, elephantine, enormous, evil, fiendish, foul, freakish, frightful, gargantuan, giant, gigantic, great, grotesque, gruesome, heinous, hellish, hideous, horrendous, horrible, horrific, horrifying, huge, hulking, immense, infamous, inhuman, intolerable, loathsome, malformed, mammoth, massive, miscreated, misshapen, monster, obscene, odious, outrageous, prodigious, rounceval, satanic, scandalous, shocking, stupendous, teratoid, terrible, titanic, towering, tremendous, unnatural, vast, vicious, villainous, wicked.

monument *n.* ancient monument, antiquity, barrow, cairn, cenotaph, commemoration, cross, dolmen, evidence, gravestone, headstone, marker, martyry, mausoleum, memento, memorial, obelisk, pillar, prehistoric monument, record, relic, remembrance, reminder, shaft, shrine, statue, testament, token, tombstone, tumulus, witness.

monumental *adj.* abiding, awe-inspiring, awesome, catastrophic, classic, colossal, commemorative, conspicuous, cyclopean, durable, egregious, enduring, enormous, epoch-making, funerary, gigantic, great, historic, horrible, huge, immense, immortal, important, imposing, impressive, indefensible, lasting, magnificent, majestic, massive, memorable, memorial, monolithic, notable, outstanding, overwhelming, prodigious, significant, staggering, statuary, stupendous, terrible, tremendous, vast, whopping.
antonyms insignificant, unimportant.

mood *n.* blues, caprice, depression, disposition, doldrums, dumps, fit, frame of mind, grumps, humor, melancholy, pique, spirit, state of mind, sulk, temper, tenor, the sulks, vein, whim.

moody *adj.* angry, atrabilious, broody, cantankerous, capricious, cast-down, changeable, choleric, crabbed, crabby, cranky, cross, crotchety, crusty, dejected, depressive, dismal, doleful, dour, downcast, erratic, faddish, fickle, fitful, flighty, gloomy, glum, huffish, huffy, ill-humored, impulsive, inconstant, introspective, introvert, irascible, irritable, lugubrious, melancholy, mercurial, miserable, mopy, morose, peevish, pensive, petulant, piqued, sad, saturnine, short-tempered, splenetic, sulky, sullen, temperamental, testy, touchy, unpredictable, unsociable, unstable, unsteady, volatile, waspish.
antonyms cheerful, equable.

moor[1] *v.* anchor, berth, bind, dock, drop anchor, fasten, fix, hitch, lash, secure, tie up.
antonym loose.

moor[2] *n.* brae, downs, fell, heath, moorland, muir, upland, wold.

moot *v.* advance, argue, bring up, broach, debate, discuss, introduce, pose, propose, propound, put forward, submit, suggest, ventilate.
adj. academic, arguable, contestable, controversial, crucial, debatable, disputable, disputed, doubtful, insoluble, knotty, open, open to debate, problematic, questionable, undecided, undetermined, unresolvable, unresolved, unsettled, vexed.

mop *n.* head of hair, mane, mass, mat, shock, sponge, squeegee, swab, tangle, thatch.
v. absorb, clean, soak, sponge, swab, wash, wipe.

mope *v.* agonize, boody, brood, despair, despond, droop, fret, grieve, idle, languish, mooch, moon, pine, sulk.
n. depressive, grouch, grump, introvert, killjoy, melancholy, melancholic, misery, moaner, moper, mopus, pessimist, Weary Willie.

moral *adj.* blameless, chaste, clean-living, decent, equitable, ethical, good, high-minded, honest, honorable, incorruptible, innocent, just, meritorious, moralistic, noble, principled, proper, pure, responsible, right, righteous, square, straight, temperate, upright, upstanding, virtuous. .
antonym immoral.

n. adage, aphorism, apophthegm, dictum, epigram, gnome, import, lesson, maxim, meaning, message, motto, point, precept, proverb, saw, saying, significance, teaching.

morale *n.* confidence, esprit de corps, heart, mettle, mood, resolve, self-esteem, spirit, spirits, state of mind, temper.

morality *n.* chastity, conduct, decency, deontology, equity, ethicality, ethicalness, ethics, ethos, goodness, habits, honesty, ideals, integrity, justice, manners, morals, mores, philosophy, principle, principles, probity, propriety, rationale, rectitude, righteousness, standards, tightness, uprightness, virtue.
antonym immorality.

morals *n.* behavior, conduct, deontics, deontology, equity, ethics, ethos, habits, ideals, integrity, manners, morality, mores, principles, probity, propriety, rectitude, scruples, standards.

morass *n.* bog, can of worms, chaos, clutter, confusion, fen, flow, jam, jumble, marsh, marshland, mess, mire, mix-up, moss, muddle, quag, quagmire, quicksand, slough, swamp, tangle.

morbid *adj.* ailing, brooding, corrupt, deadly, diseased, dreadful, ghastly, ghoulish, gloomy, grim, grisly, gruesome, hideous, horrid, hypochondriacal, infected, lugubrious, macabre, malignant, melancholy, neurotic, pathological, peccant, pessimistic, putrid, sick, sickly, somber, unhealthy, unsalubrious, unsound, unwholesome, vicious, Wertherian.

more *adj.* added, additional, alternative, extra, fresh, further, increased, new, other, renewed, repeated, spare, supplementary.
adv. again, better, further, longer.

moreover *adv.* additionally, also, as well, besides, further, furthermore, in addition, into the bargain, likewise, may I add, more, more to the point, to boot, too, what is more, withal.

moron *n.* ass, blockhead, bonehead, clot, cretin, daftie, dimwit, dolt, dope, dumbbell, dummy, dunce, dunderhead, fool, halfwit, idiot, imbecile, klutz, mental defective, mooncalf, muttonhead, natural, numbskull, schmo, schmuck, simpleton, thickhead, vegetable, zombie.

morose *adj.* blue, cheerless, churlish, crabbed, crabby, cross, crusty, depressed, dour, down, gloomy, glum, grim, grouchy, gruff, grum, huffy, humorless, ill-humored, ill-natured, ill-tempered, low, melancholy, misanthropic, moody, mournful, perverse, pessimistic, saturnine, sour, stern, sulky, sullen, surly, taciturn, testy, unsociable.
antonyms cheerful, communicative.

morsel *n.* atom, bit, bite, bonne-bouche, crumb, fraction, fragment, grain, modicum, morceau, mouthful, nibble, part, piece, scrap, segment, slice, smidgen, snack, soupçon, taste, titbit.

mortal *adj.* agonizing, awful, bodily, corporeal, deadly, deathful, dire, earthly, enormous, ephemeral, extreme,

fatal, fleshly, grave, great, human, impermanent, implacable, intense, irreconcilable, lethal, lethiferous, mortiferous, passing, perishable, relentless, remorseless, severe, sublunary, sworn, temporal, terrible, transient, unrelenting, worldly.
antonym immortal.

n. being, body, creature, earthling, human, human being, individual, man, person, sublunar, sublunary, woman.
antonyms god, immortal.

mortgage *v.* dip, pawn, pledge, put in hock.
n. bond, debenture, lien, loan, pledge, security, wadset.

mortified *adj.* abashed, affronted, annoyed, ashamed, chagrined, chastened, confounded, crushed, dead, decayed, deflated, discomfited, displeased, embarrassed, gangrenous, humbled, humiliated, necrotic, put out, put to shame, putrefied, putrid, rotted, rotten, shamed, vexed.
antonyms elated, jubilant.

mortify *v.* abase, abash, affront, annoy, chagrin, chasten, confound, conquer, control, corrupt, crush, deflate, deny, die, disappoint, discipline, discomfit, embarrass, fester, gangrene, humble, humiliate, macerate, necrose, put to shame, putrefy, shame, subdue, vex.

mortuary *n.* deadhouse, funeral home, funeral parlor, morgue.

mostly *adv.* as a rule, characteristically, chiefly, commonly, customarily, feckly, for the most part, generally, largely, mainly, normally, on the whole, particularly, predominantly, primarily, principally, typically, usually.

mother *n.* dam, generatrix, genetrix, ma, mam, mama, mamma, mammy, mater, materfamilias, mom, momma, mommy, mum, mummy, old lady, old woman.
v. baby, bear, care for, cherish, cosset, foster, fuss over, indulge, nurse, nurture, overprotect, pamper, produce, protect, raise, rear, spoil, tend.
antonym neglect.

motif *n.* concept, decoration, design, device, figure, form, idea, leitmotiv, logo, notion, ornament, pattern, shape, strain, subject, theme.

motion *n.* action, change, dynamics, flow, flux, gesticulation, gesture, inclination, kinesics, kinetics, locomotion, mechanics, mobility, motility, move, movement, nod, passage, passing, progress, proposal, proposition, recommendation, sign, signal, submission, suggestion, transit, travel, wave.
v. beckon, direct, gesticulate, gesture, nod, sign, signal, usher, wave.

motionless *adj.* at a standstill, at rest, calm, fixed, frozen, halted, immobile, inanimate, inert, lifeless, moveless, paralyzed, resting, rigid, stagnant, standing, static, stationary, still, stock-still, transfixed, unmoved, unmoving.
antonym active.

motivate *v.* actuate, arouse, bring, cause, draw, drive, encourage, impel, incite, induce, inspire, inspirit, instigate, kindle, lead, move, persuade, prompt,

propel, provoke, push, spur, stimulate, stir, trigger, urge.
antonyms deter, prevent.

motive *n.* cause, consideration, design, desire, encouragement, ground(s), impulse, incentive, incitement, inducement, influence, inspiration, intention, mainspring, motivation, object, occasion, purpose, rationale, reason, spur, stimulus, thinking, urge.
antonyms deterrent, discouragement, disincentive.
adj. activating, actuating, agential, driving, impelling, initiating, motivating, moving, operative, prompting, propellent.
antonyms deterrent, inhibitory, preventive.

motley *adj.* assorted, checkered, disparate, dissimilar, diverse, diversified, haphazard, heterogeneous, ill-assorted, kaleidoscopic, mingled, miscellaneous, mixed, multicolored, particolored, patchwork, polychromatic, polychrome, polychromous, promiscuous, rainbow, unlike, varied, variegated.
antonyms homogeneous, monochrome, uniform.

mottled *adj.* blotchy, brindled, checkered, dappled, flecked, freaked, freckled, jaspé, marbled, piebald, pied, poikilitic, skewbald, speckled, spotted, stippled, streaked, tabby, variegated, veined, watered.
antonyms monochrome, plain, uniform.

motto *n.* adage, apophthegm, byword, catchword, cry, dictum, epigraph, formula, gnome, golden rule, ichthys, maxim, precept, proverb, rule, saw, saying, sentence, slogan, watchword.

mound *n.* agger, bank, barrow, bing, bulwark, drift, dune, earthwork, elevation, embankment, heap, hill, hillock, hummock, knoll, mote, motte, pile, rampart, rick, ridge, rise, stack, tuffet, tumulus, tussock, yardang.

mount *v.* accumulate, arise, ascend, bestride, build, clamber up, climb, climb on, climb up on, copulate, cover, deliver, display, emplace, enchase, escalade, escalate, exhibit, fit, frame, get astride, get on, get up, get up on, go up, grow, horse, increase, install, intensify, jump on, launch, lift, multiply, pile up, place, position, prepare, produce, put in place, put on, ready, ride, rise, rocket, scale, set, set in motion, set off, set up, soar, stage, straddle, swell, tower, tread.
n. backing, base, fixture, foil, frame, horse, monture, mounting, pedestal, podium, setting, stand, steed, support.

mountain *n.* abundance, alp, backlog, ben, berg, elevation, eminence, fell, heap, height, mass, massif, mound, mount, Munro, peak, pile, reserve, stack, ton.

mountebank *n.* charlatan, cheat, con man, confidence, fake, fraud, huckster, impostor, phony, pretender, pseud, quack, quacksalver, rogue, spieler, swindler, trickster.

mourn *v.* bemoan, bewail, beweep, deplore, grieve, keen, lament, miss, regret, rue, sorrow, wail, weep.
antonyms bless, rejoice.

mournful *adj.* afflicting, broken-hearted, calamitous, cast-down, cheerless, chopfallen, dearnful, dejected, deplorable, depressed, desolate, disconsolate, dismal, distressing, doleful, dolorous, downcast, funereal, gloomy, grief-stricken, grieving, grievous, heartbroken, heavy, heavy-hearted, joyless, lachrymose, lamentable, long-faced, long-visaged, lugubrious, melancholy, miserable, painful, piteous, plaintive, plangent, rueful, sad, somber, sorrowful, stricken, tragic, unhappy, woeful, woesome.

antonyms cheerful, joyful.

mourning *n*. bereavement, black, desolation, grief, grieving, keening, lamentation, sackcloth and ashes, sadness, sorrow, wailing, weeds, weeping, widow's weeds, woe.

antonym rejoicing.

mousy *adj*. brownish, characterless, colorless, diffident, drab, dull, indeterminate, ineffectual, mouse-like, plain, quiet, self-effacing, shy, timid, timorous, unassertive, unforthcoming, uninteresting, withdrawn.

antonyms assertive, bright, extrovert, irrepressible.

move *v*. activate, actuate, adjust, advance, advise, advocate, affect, agitate, budge, carry, cause, change, cover the ground, decamp, depart, disturb, drift, drive, ease, edge, excite, flit, get, give rise to, go, go away, gravitate, impel, impress, incite, induce, influence, inspire, instigate, jiggle, lead, leave, locomote, make strides, march, migrate, motivate, move house, operate, persuade, proceed, progress, prompt, propel, propose, pull, push, put forward, quit, recommend, relocate, remove, rouse, run, set going, shift, shove, start, stimulate, stir, submit, suggest, switch, take, touch, transfer, transport, transpose, turn, urge, walk.

n. act, action, deed, démarche, dodge, draft, flit, flitting, go, maneuver, measure, migration, motion, movement, ploy, relocation, removal, ruse, shift, step, stratagem, stroke, tack, tactic, transfer, turn.

movement *n*. act, action, activity, advance, agitation, beat, cadence, campaign, change, crusade, current, development, displacement, division, drift, drive, evolution, exercise, faction, flow, front, gesture, ground swell, group, grouping, innards, machinery, maneuver, measure, mechanism, meter, motion, move, moving, operation, organization, pace, part, party, passage, progress, progression, rhythm, section, shift, steps, stir, stirring, swing, tempo, tendency, transfer, trend, workings, works.

moving *adj*. affecting, ambulant, ambulatory, arousing, dynamic, emotional, emotive, exciting, impelling, impressive, inspirational, inspiring, locomobile, mobile, motile, motivating, movable, pathetic, persuasive, poignant, portable, propelling, running, stimulating, stimulative, stirring, touching, unfixed.

antonyms fixed, stationary, unemotional.

mow *v*. clip, crop, cut, scythe, shear, trim.

much *adv*. considerably, copiously, decidedly, exceedingly, frequently, greatly, often.

adj. a lot of, abundant, ample, considerable, copious, great, plenteous, plenty of, sizable, substantial.

n. heaps, lashings, loads, lots, oodles, plenty, scads.

antonym little.

muck *n*. dirt, droppings, dung, feces, filth, gunge, gunk, manure, mire, mud, ooze, ordure, scum, sewage, slime, sludge.

muddle *v*. befuddle, bewilder, confound, confuse, daze, disarrange, disorder, disorganize, disorient(ate), fuddle, fuzzle, jumble, make a mess of, mess, mix up, mull, perplex, scramble, spoil, stupefy, tangle.

n. balls up, chaos, clutter, cock-up, confusion, daze, disarray, disorder, disorganization, fankle, guddle, jumble, mess, mix-up, mull, perplexity, pie, plight, predicament, puddle, snarl-up, tangle.

muddled *adj*. at sea, befuddled, bewildered, chaotic, confused, dazed, disarrayed, disordered, disorganized, disorient(at)ed, higgledy-piggledy, incoherent, jumbled, loose, messy, mixed-up, muddle-headed, perplexed, puzzle-headed, scrambled, stupefied, tangled, unclear, vague, woolly.

muff *v*. botch, bungle, fluff, mess up, mishit, mismanage, miss, spoil.

muffle *v*. cloak, conceal, cover, damp down, dampen, deaden, disguise, dull, envelop, gag, hood, hush, mask, mute, muzzle, quieten, shroud, silence, soften, stifle, suppress, swaddle, swathe, wrap up.

antonym amplify.

mug[1] *n*. beaker, cup, flagon, jug, pot, stoup, tankard, toby jug.

mug[2] *n*. chump, fool, gull, innocent, mark, muggins, sap, saphead, simpleton, soft touch, sucker.

mug[3] *n*. clock, countenance, dial, face, features, mush, phiz(og), puss, visage.

mug[4] *v*. attack, bash, batter, beat up, garrotte, jump (on), mill, rob, roll, set upon, steal from, waylay.

muggy *adj*. clammy, close, damp, humid, moist, oppressive, sticky, stuffy, sudorific, sultry, sweltering.

antonym dry.

mulish *adj*. bull-headed, cross-grained, defiant, difficult, headstrong, inflexible, intractable, intransigent, obstinate, perverse, pig-headed, recalcitrant, refractory, rigid, self-willed, stiff-necked, stubborn, unreasonable, wilful, wrong-headed.

multifarious *adj*. different, diverse, diversified, legion, manifold, many, miscellaneous, multiform, multiple, multiplex, multitudinous, numerous, sundry, varied, variegated.

multiply *v*. accumulate, augment, boost, breed, build up, expand, extend, increase, intensify, proliferate, propagate, reproduce, spread.

antonyms decrease, lessen.

multitude *n*. army, assemblage, assembly, collection, commonalty, concourse, congregation, crowd, herd, hive, hoi polloi, horde, host, legion, lot, lots, mass, mob, myriad, people, populace, proletariat, public, rabble, sea, swarm, throng.

antonyms handful, scattering.

mum *adj.* close-lipped, close-mouthed, dumb, mute, quiet, reticent, secretive, silent, tight-lipped, uncommunicative, unforthcoming.

mundane *adj.* banal, commonplace, day-to-day, earthly, everyday, fleshly, human, humdrum, material, mortal, ordinary, prosaic, routine, secular, subastral, sublunar(y), temporal, terrestrial, workaday, worldly. *antonyms* cosmic, extraordinary, supernatural.

municipal *adj.* borough, burgh(al), city, civic, community, public, town, urban.

munificent *adj.* beneficent, benevolent, big-hearted, bounteous, bountiful, free-handed, generous, hospitable, lavish, liberal, magnanimous, open-handed, philanthropical, princely, rich, unstinting. *antonym* mean.

murder *n.* agony, assassination, bloodshed, butchery, carnage, danger, deicide, difficulty, filicide, fractricide, hell, homicide, infanticide, killing, manslaughter, massacre, misery, ordeal, parricide, patricide, slaying, trial, trouble. *v.* abuse, assassinate, bump off, burke, butcher, destroy, dispatch, do in, drub, eliminate, hammer, hit, kill, mangle, mar, massacre, misuse, rub out, ruin, slaughter, slay, spoil, thrash, waste.

murderer *n.* assassin, butcher, cut-throat, filicide, hitman, homicide, killer, matricide, parricide, patricide, slaughterer, slayer.

murky *adj.* cloudy, dark, dim, dismal, dreary, dull, dusky, enigmatic, foggy, gloomy, gray, misty, mysterious, obscure, overcast, veiled. *antonyms* bright, clear.

murmur *n.* babble, brool, burble, buzz, buzzing, complaint, croon, drone, grumble, humming, moan, mumble, muttering, purl, purling, purr, rumble, susurrus, undertone, whisper, whispering. *v.* babble, burble, burr, buzz, drone, gurgle, hum, mumble, mutter, purl, purr, rumble.

muscle *n.* brawn, clout, depressor, force, forcefulness, levator, might, potency, power, sinew, stamina, strength, sturdiness, tendon, thew, weight.

muse *v.* brood, chew, cogitate, consider, contemplate, deliberate, dream, meditate, mull over, ponder, reflect, review, ruminate, speculate, think, think over, weigh.

mushroom *v.* boom, burgeon, expand, flourish, grow, increase, luxuriate, proliferate, shoot up, spread, spring up, sprout. *n.* champignon, chanterelle, fungus, morel, pixy-stool, puffball, toadstool.

musical *adj.* canorous, dulcet, euphonious, Euterpean, harmonious, lilting, lyrical, melodic, melodious, sweet-sounding, tuneful. *antonym* unmusical.

musician *n.* accompanist, bard, composer, conductor, instrumentalist, minstrel, performer, player, singer, vocalist.

musing *n.* absent-mindedness, abstraction, brown study, cerebration, cogitation, contemplation, daydreaming, dreaming, introspection, meditation, ponderment, reflection, reverie, rumination, thinking, wool-gathering.

must *n.* basic, duty, essential, fundamental, imperative, necessity, obligation, prerequisite, provision, requirement, requisite, sine qua non, stipulation.

muster *v.* assemble, call together, call up, collect, come together, congregate, convene, convoke, enrol, gather, group, marshal, mass, meet, mobilize, rally, round up, summon, throng. *n.* assemblage, assembly, collection, concourse, congregation, convention, convocation, gathering, mass, meeting, mobilization, rally, round-up, throng.

musty *adj.* airless, ancient, antediluvian, antiquated, banal, clichéd, dank, decayed, dull, frowsty, fusty, hackneyed, hoary, mildewed, mildewy, moth-eaten, moldy, mucedinous, mucid, obsolete, old, old-fashioned, smelly, stale, stuffy, threadbare, trite, vinewed, worn-out.

mute *adj.* aphonic, dumb, mum, noiseless, silent, speechless, unexpressed, unpronounced, unspeaking, unspoken, voiceless, wordless. *antonyms* articulate, vocal, voluble. *v.* dampen, deaden, lower, moderate, muffle, silence, soften, soft-pedal, subdue, tone down.

mutilate *v.* adulterate, amputate, bowdlerize, butcher, censor, cut, cut to pieces, cut up, damage, detruncate, disable, disfigure, dismember, distort, expurgate, hack, hamble, injure, lacerate, lame, maim, mangle, mar, spoil.

mutinous *adj.* bolshie, bolshy, contumacious, disobedient, insubordinate, insurgent, rebellious, recusant, refractory, revolutionary, riotous, seditious, subversive, turbulent, ungovernable, unmanageable, unruly. *antonyms* compliant, dutiful, obedient.

mutiny *n.* defiance, disobedience, insubordination, insurrection, putsch, rebellion, resistance, revolt, revolution, riot, rising, strike, uprising. *v.* disobey, protest, rebel, resist, revolt, rise up, strike.

mutter *v.* chunter, complain, grouch, grouse, grumble, mumble, murmur, mussitate, rumble.

mutual *adj.* common, communal, complementary, exchanged, interchangeable, interchanged, joint, reciprocal, reciprocated, requited, returned, shared.

muzzle *n.* bit, curb, gag, guard, jaws, mouth, nose, snaffle, snout. *v.* censor, choke, curb, gag, mute, restrain, silence, stifle, suppress.

myopic *adj.* half-blind, near-sighted, short-sighted. *antonym* far-sighted.

myriad *adj.* boundless, countless, immeasurable, incalculable, innumerable, limitless, multitudinous, untold. *n.* army, flood, horde, host, millions, mountain, multitude, scores, sea, swarm, thousands, throng.

mysterious *adj.* abstruse, arcane, baffling, concealed, covert, cryptic, curious, dark, enigmatic, furtive, hidden, impenetrable, incomprehensible, inexplicable, inscrutable, insoluble, mystical, mystifying, obscure, perplexing, puzzling, recondite, secret, secretive, strange, uncanny, unfathomable, unsearchable, veiled, weird.

antonyms comprehensible, frank, straightforward.

mystery *n.* arcanum, conundrum, enigma, problem, puzzle, question, riddle, secrecy, secret.

mystical *adj.* abstruse, arcane, cab(b)alistic(al), cryptic, enigmatical, esoteric, hidden, inscrutable, metaphysical, mysterious, mystic, occult, otherworldly, paranormal, preternatural, supernatural, transcendental.

mystify *v.* baffle, bamboozle, beat, befog, bewilder, confound, confuse, escape, perplex, puzzle, stump.

myth *n.* allegory, delusion, fable, fairy tale, fancy, fantasy, fiction, figment, illusion, legend, old wives' tale, parable, saga, story, superstition, tradition, untruism.

N

nag[1] *v.* annoy, badger, berate, chivvy, goad, harass, harry, henpeck, irritate, kvetch, pain, pester, plague, scold, torment, upbraid, vex.
n. harpy, harridan, kvetch(er), scold, shrew, tartar, termagant, virago.

nag[2] *n.* hack, horse, jade, plug, rip, Rosinante.

nail *v.* apprehend, attach, beat, capture, catch, clinch, collar, fasten, fix, hammer, join, nab, nick, pin, secure, seize, tack.
n. brad, hobnail, peg, pin, rivet, screw, skewer, spike, staple, tack, tacket.

naïve *adj.* artless, callow, candid, childlike, confiding, credulous, dewy-eyed, facile, frank, green, guileless, gullible, ingenuous, innocent, jejune, natural, open, simple, simplistic, trusting, unaffected, uncritical, unpretentious, unsophisticated, unsuspecting, unsuspicious, unworldly, verdant, wide-eyed.
antonyms experienced, sophisticated.

naked *adj.* adamic, bare, blatant, defenseless, denuded, disrobed, divested, evident, exposed, helpless, in puris naturalibus, in the altogether, in the buff, insecure, manifest, mother-naked, nude, open, overt, patent, plain, simple, skyclad, stark, starkers, stark-naked, stripped, unadorned, unarmed, unclothed, unconcealed, uncovered, undisguised, undraped, undressed, unexaggerated, unguarded, unmistakable, unprotected, unqualified, unvarnished, vulnerable.
antonyms clothed, concealed, covered.

name *n.* acronym, agname, agnomen, appellation, character, cognomen, compellation, compellative, credit, denomination, designation, distinction, eminence, epithet, esteem, fame, handle, honor, moni(c)ker, nickname, note, praise, renown, reputation, repute, sobriquet, stage name, term, title, to-name.
v. appoint, baptize, bename, betitle, call, choose, christen, cite, classify, cognominate, commission, denominate, designate, dub, entitle, identify, label, mention, nominate, select, specify, style, term, title.

nap[1] *v.* catnap, doze, drop off, drowse, kip, nod, nod off, rest, sleep, snooze.
n. catnap, forty winks, kip, rest, shuteye, siesta, sleep.

nap[2] *n.* down, downiness, fuzz, grain, pile, shag, weave.

narcissistic *adj.* conceited, egocentric, egomaniacal, ego(-t)istic, self-centered, self-loving, vain.

narcotic *n.* anesthetic, analgesic, anodyne, drug, hop, kef, opiate, pain-killer, sedative, tranquilizer.
adj. analgesic, calming, dulling, hypnotic, Lethean, numbing, pain-killing, sedative, somniferous, somnific, soporific, stupefacient, stupefactive, stupefying.

narrate *v.* chronicle, describe, detail, recite, recount, rehearse, relate, repeat, report, set forth, state, tell, unfold.

narrative *n.* account, chronicle, detail, history, parable, report, statement, story, tale.

narrow *adj.* attenuated, avaricious, biased, bigoted, circumscribed, close, confined, constricted, contracted, cramped, dogmatic, exclusive, fine, illiberal, incapacious, intolerant, limited, meager, mean, mercenary, narrow-minded, near, niggardly, partial, pinched, prejudiced, reactionary, restricted, scanty, select, simplistic, slender, slim, small-minded, spare, straitened, tapering, thin, tight, ungenerous.
antonyms broad, liberal, tolerant, wide.
v. circumscribe, constrict, constringe, diminish, limit, reduce, simplify, straiten, tighten.
antonyms broaden, increase, loosen, widen.
antonyms broadening, widening.

narrow-minded *adj.* biased, bigoted, blinkered, borné, conservative, hidebound, illiberal, insular, intolerant, mean, opinionated, parochial, petty, prejudiced, provincial, reactionary, short-sighted, small-minded, strait-laced.
antonym broad-minded.
antonyms breadth, width.

nascent *adj.* advancing, budding, developing, embryonic, evolving, growing, incipient, naissant, rising, young.
antonym dying.

nasty *adj.* abusive, annoying, bad, bad-tempered, base, critical, dangerous, despicable, dirty, disagreeable, disgusting, distasteful, filthy, foul, gross, horrible, impure, indecent, lascivious, lewd, licentious, loathsome, low-down, malicious, malodorous, mean, mephitic, nauseating, noisome, objectionable, obnoxious, obscene, odious, offensive, painful, polluted, pornographic, repellent, repugnant, ribald, serious, severe, sickening, smutty, spiteful, unappetizing, unpleasant, unsavory, vicious, vile, waspish.
antonyms agreeable, clean, decent, pleasant.

nation *n.* citizenry, commonwealth, community, country, people, population, race, realm, society, state, tribe.

native *adj.* aboriginal, autochthonous, built-in, congenital, domestic, endemic, genuine, hereditary, home, home-born, home-bred, home-grown, home-made, inborn, inbred, indigene, indigenous, ingrained, inherent, inherited, innate, instinctive, intrinsic, inveterate, local, mother, natal, natural, original, real, vernacular.
n. aborigine, autochthon, citizen, countryman, dweller, indigene, inhabitant, national, resident.
antonyms foreigner, outsider, stranger.

natty *adj.* chic, dapper, elegant, fashionable, neat, ritzy, smart, snazzy, spruce, stylish, swanky, trim.

natural *adj.* artless, candid, characteristic, common, congenital, constitutional, essential, everyday, frank, genuine, inborn, indigenous, ingenuous, inherent, innate, instinctive, intuitive, legitimate, logical, natal, native, normal, open, ordinary, organic, plain, pure, real, regular, simple, spontaneous, typical, unaffected, unbleached, unforced, unlabored, unlearned, unmixed, unpolished, unpretentious, unrefined, unsophisticated, unstudied, untaught, usual, whole.
antonyms abnormal, affected, alien, artificial, pretended, unnatural.

naturally *adj.* absolutely, artlessly, as a matter of course, candidly, certainly, customarily, frankly, genuinely, informally, normally, of course, plainly, simply, spontaneously, typically, unaffectedly, unpretentiously.

nature[1] *n.* attributes, category, character, complexion, constitution, cosmos, creation, description, disposition, earth, environment, essence, features, humor, inbeing, inscape, kind, make-up, mood, outlook, quality, sort, species, style, temper, temperament, traits, type, universe, variety, world.

nature[2] *n.* country, countryside, landscape, natural history, scenery.

naught *n.* nil, nothing, nothingness, nought, zero, zilch.

naughty *adj.* annoying, bad, bawdy, blue, disobedient, exasperating, fractious, impish, improper, lewd, misbehaved, mischievous, obscene, off-color, perverse, playful, refractory, remiss, reprehensible, ribald, risqué, roguish, sinful, smutty, teasing, vulgar, wayward, wicked, worthless.
antonyms good, polite, well-behaved.

nausea *n.* abhorrence, aversion, biliousness, disgust, loathing, motion sickness, qualm(s), queasiness, repugnance, retching, revulsion, sickness, squeamishness, vomiting.

nauseating *adj.* abhorrent, detestable, disgusting, distasteful, fulsome, loathsome, nauseous, offensive, repugnant, repulsive, revolting, sickening.

nautical *adj.* boating, marine, maritime, naval, oceanic, sailing, seafaring, sea-going, yachting.

naval *adj.* marine, maritime, nautical, sea.

navigate *v.* con, cross, cruise, direct, drive, guide, handle, helm, journey, maneuver, pilot, plan, plot, sail, skipper, steer, voyage.

near *adj.* accessible, adjacent, adjoining, akin, allied, alongside, approaching, at close quarters, attached, beside, bordering, close, connected, contiguous, dear, familiar, forthcoming, handy, imminent, impending, in the offing, intimate, looming, near-at-hand, nearby, neighboring, next, nigh, on the cards, proximal, related, touching.
antonyms distant, far, remote.

near thing close shave, narrow escape, nasty moment, near miss.

nearly *adv.* about, all but, almost, approaching, approximately, as good as, closely, just about, not quite, practically, pretty much, pretty well, roughly, virtually, well-nigh.

neat *adj.* accurate, adept, adroit, agile, apt, clean-cut, clever, dainty, deft, dexterous, dinky, efficient, effortless, elegant, expert, fastidious, genty, graceful, handy, methodical, nice, nimble, orderly, practiced, precise, pure, shipshape, skilful, smart, spick-and-span, spruce, straight, stylish, systematic, tiddley, tidy, trig, trim, uncluttered, undi *antonyms* disordered, disorderly, messy, untidy.

nebulous *adj.* ambiguous, amorphous, cloudy, confused, dim, fuzzy, hazy, imprecise, indefinite, indeterminate, indistinct, misty, murky, obscure, shadowy, shapeless, uncertain, unclear, unformed, unspecific, vague.
antonym clear.

necessary *adj.* certain, compulsory, de rigueur, essential, fated, imperative, indispensable, ineluctable, inescapable, inevitable, inexorable, mandatory, needed, needful, obligatory, required, requisite, unavoidable, vital.
antonyms inessential, unimportant, unnecessary.

necessity *n.* ananke, compulsion, demand, desideratum, destiny, destitution, essential, exigency, extremity, fate, fundamental, indigence, indispensability, inevitability, inexorableness, necessary, need, needfulness, obligation, penury, poverty, prerequisite, privation, requirement, requisite, sine qua non, want.

necromancy *n.* black art, black magic, conjuration, demonology, divination, enchantment, hoodoo, magic, sorcery, thaumaturgy, voodoo, witchcraft, witchery, wizardry.

need *v.* call for, crave, demand, lack, miss, necessitate, require, want.
n. besoin, demand, deprivation, desideratum, destitution, distress, egence, egency, emergency, essential, exigency, extremity, impecuniousness, inadequacy, indigence, insufficiency, lack, longing, necessity, neediness, obligation, paucity, penury, poverty, privation, requirement, requisite, shortage, urgency, want, wish.
antonym sufficiency.

needed *adj.* called for, compulsory, desired, essential, lacking, necessary, obligatory, required, requisite, wanted.
antonyms unnecessary, unneeded.

needle *v.* aggravate, annoy, bait, goad, harass, irk, irritate, nag, nettle, pester, prick, prod, provoke, rile, ruffle, spur, sting, taunt, torment.

needless *adj.* causeless, dispensable, excessive, expendable, gratuitous, groundless, inessential, non-essential, pointless, purposeless, redundant, superfluous, uncalled-for, unessential, unnecessary, unwanted, useless.
antonyms necessary, needful.

needy *adj.* deprived, destitute, disadvantaged, impecunious,

impoverished, indigent, penniless, penurious, poor, poverty-stricken, underprivileged.
antonyms affluent, wealthy, well-off.

nefarious *adj.* abominable, atrocious, base, criminal, depraved, detestable, dreadful, evil, execrable, foul, heinous, horrible, infamous, infernal, iniquitous, monstrous, odious, opprobrious, satanic, shameful, sinful, unholy, vicious, vile, villainous, wicked. *antonym* exemplary.

negate *v.* abrogate, annul, cancel, contradict, countermand, deny, disallow, disprove, gainsay, invalidate, neutralize, nullify, oppose, quash, refute, repeal, rescind, retract, reverse, revoke, void, wipe out.
antonym affirm.
antonyms optimistic, positive.
n. contradiction, denial, opposite, refusal.

neglect *v.* contemn, disdain, disprovide, disregard, forget, ignore, leave alone, let slide, omit, overlook, pass by, pigeon-hole, rebuff, scorn, shirk, skimp, slight, spurn.
antonyms cherish, nurture, treasure.
n. carelessness, default, dereliction, disdain, disregard, disrespect, failure, forgetfulness, heedlessness, inattention, indifference, laches, laxity, laxness, neglectfulness, negligence, oversight, slackness, slight, slovenliness, unconcern.

negligent *adj.* careless, cursory, disregardful, forgetful, inattentive, indifferent, lax, neglectful, nonchalant, offhand, regardless, remiss, slack, thoughtless, uncareful, uncaring, unmindful, unthinking.
antonyms attentive, careful, heedful, scrupulous.

negligible *adj.* imperceptible, inconsequential, insignificant, minor, minute, neglectable, nugatory, petty, small, trifling, trivial, unimportant.
antonym significant.

negotiate *v.* adjudicate, arbitrate, arrange, bargain, broke, clear, conciliate, confer, consult, contract, cross, deal, debate, discuss, get past, handle, manage, mediate, parley, pass, settle, surmount, transact, traverse, treat, work out.

neighborhood *n.* community, confines, district, environs, locale, locality, precincts, proximity, purlieus, quarter, region, surroundings, vicinage, vicinity.

neighboring *adj.* abutting, adjacent, adjoining, bordering, connecting, contiguous, near, nearby, nearest, next, surrounding, vicinal.
antonyms distant, faraway, remote.

neighborly *adj.* amiable, chummy, civil, companionable, considerate, friendly, genial, helpful, hospitable, kind, obliging, sociable, social, solicitous, well-disposed.

nerve *n.* audacity, boldness, bottle, brass, bravery, brazenness, cheek, chutzpah, coolness, courage, daring, determination, effrontery, endurance, energy, fearlessness, firmness, force, fortitude, gall, gameness, grit, guts, hardihood, impertinence, impudence, insolence,

intrepidity, mettle, might, pluck, resolution, sauce, spirit, spunk, steadfastness, temerity, vigor, will.
antonyms cowardice, weakness.
v. bolster, brace, embolden, encourage, fortify, hearten, invigorate, steel, strengthen.
antonym unnerve.

nervous *adj.* agitated, anxious, apprehensive, edgy, excitable, fearful, fidgety, flustered, hesitant, highly-strung, high-strung, hysterical, jittery, jumpy, nervy, neurotic, on edge, shaky, tense, timid, timorous, twitchy, uneasy, uptight, weak, windy, worried.
antonyms bold, calm, confident, cool, relaxed.

nest *n.* breeding-ground, burrow, den, drey, earth, form, formicary, haunt, hideaway, hotbed, nid(e), nidus, refuge, resort, retreat.

nestle *v.* cuddle, curl up, ensconce, huddle, nuzzle, snuggle.

net[1] *n.* drag, drag-net, drift, drift-net, drop-net, lattice, mesh, netting, network, open-work, reticulum, tracery, web.
v. apprehend, bag, benet, capture, catch, enmesh, ensnare, entangle, nab, trap.

net[2] *adj.* after tax, clear, final, lowest, nett.
v. accumulate, bring in, clear, earn, gain, make, obtain, realize, reap, receive, secure.

nettle *v.* annoy, chafe, discountenance, exasperate, fret, goad, harass, incense, irritate, needle, pique, provoke, ruffle, sting, tease, vex.

neurotic *adj.* abnormal, anxious, compulsive, deviant, disordered, distraught, disturbed, maladjusted, manic, morbid, nervous, obsessive, overwrought, unhealthy, unstable, wearisome.
antonyms normal, stable.

neutral *adj.* colorless, disinterested, dispassionate, dull, even-handed, expressionless, impartial, indeterminate, indifferent, indistinct, indistinguishable, intermediate, non-aligned, non-committal, nondescript, non-partisan, unbia(s)sed, uncommitted, undecided, undefined, uninvolved, unprejudiced.
antonyms biased, prejudiced.

nevertheless *adv.* anyhow, anyway, but, even so, however, nonetheless, notwithstanding, regardless, still, yet.

new *adj.* added, advanced, altered, changed, contemporary, current, different, extra, fresh, improved, latest, modern, modernistic, modernized, modish, more, newborn, newfangled, novel, original, recent, redesigned, renewed, restored, supplementary, topical, trendy, ultra-modern, unfamiliar, unknown, unused, unusual, up-to-date, up-to-the-minute, virgin.
antonyms hackneyed, old, outdated, out-of-date, usual.

newcomer *n.* alien, arrival, arriviste, beginner, colonist, foreigner, immigrant, incomer, Johnny-come-lately, novice, outsider, parvenu, settler, stranger.

news *n.* account, advice, bulletin, communiqué, disclosure, dispatch, exposé, gen, gossip, hearsay, information, intelligence, latest, leak, release, report, revelation, rumor, scandal, statement, story, tidings, update, word.

next *adj.* adjacent, adjoining, closest, consequent, ensuing, following, later, nearest, neighboring, sequent, sequential, subsequent, succeeding.

antonyms preceding, previous.

adv. afterwards, later, subsequently, then, thereafter.

nibble *n.* bit, bite, crumb, morsel, peck, piece, snack, soupçon, taste, titbit.

v. bite, eat, gnaw, knap, knapple, munch, nip, nosh, peck, pickle.

nice *adj.* accurate, agreeable, amiable, attractive, careful, charming, commendable, courteous, critical, cultured, dainty, delicate, delightful, discriminating, exact, exacting, fastidious, fine, finical, friendly, genteel, good, kind, likable, meticulous, neat, particular, pleasant, pleasurable, polite, precise, prepossessing, punctilious, purist, refined, respectable, rigorous, scrupulous, strict, subtle, tidy, trim, virtuous, well-bred, well-mannered.

antonyms careless, disagreeable, haphazard, nasty, unpleasant.

niche[1] *n.* alcove, corner, cubby, cubby-hole, hollow, nook, opening, recess.

niche[2] *n.* calling, métier, pigeon-hole, place, position, slot, vocation.

nick[1] *n.* chip, cut, damage, dent, indent, indentation, mark, notch, scar, score, scratch, snick.

v. chip, cut, damage, dent, indent, mark, notch, scar, score, scratch, snick.

nick[2] *v.* finger, knap, knock off, lag, pilfer, pinch, snitch, steal.

nickname *n.* cognomen, diminutive, epithet, familiarity, label, moni(c)ker, pet name, sobriquet.

niggardly *adj.* avaricious, beggarly, cheese-paring, close, covetous, frugal, grudging, hard-fisted, inadequate, insufficient, meager, mean, mercenary, miserable, miserly, near, paltry, parsimonious, penurious, scanty, skimpy, small, sordid, sparing, stinging, stingy, tight-fisted, ungenerous, ungiving, wretched.

antonyms bountiful, generous.

nightmare *n.* bad dream, ephialtes, hallucination, horror, incubus, ordeal, succubus, torment, trial, tribulation.

nil *n.* duck, goose-egg, love, naught, nihil, none, nothing, zero.

nimble *adj.* active, agile, alert, brisk, deft, dexterous, lightfoot(ed), lissom(e), lively, nippy, proficient, prompt, quick, quick-witted, ready, smart, sprightly, spry, swift, volant.

antonyms awkward, clumsy.

nincompoop *n.* blockhead, dimwit, dolt, dunce, fool, idiot, ignoramus, ninny, nitwit, noodle, numskull, sap, saphead, simpleton.

nip[1] *v.* bite, catch, check, clip, compress, grip, nibble, pinch, snag, snap, sneap, snip, squeeze, tweak, twitch.

nip[2] *n.* dram, draught, drop, finger, mouthful, peg, portion, shot, sip, slug, snifter, soupçon, sup, swallow, taste.

nippy[1] *adj.* astringent, biting, chilly, nipping, pungent, sharp, stinging.

nippy[2] *adj.* active, agile, fast, nimble, quick, speedy, sprightly, spry.

antonym slow.

nit-picking *adj.* captious, carping, caviling, finicky, fussy, hair-splitting, hypercritical, pedantic, pettifogging, quibbling.

noble *n.* aristocrat, baron, gentilhomme, grand seigneur, lord, nobleman, patrician, peer.

antonyms pleb, prole.

adj. aristocratic, august, blue-blooded, dignified, distinguished, elevated, eminent, excellent, generous, gentle, grand, great, high-born, honorable, honored, imposing, impressive, lofty, lordly, magnanimous, magnificent, majestic, patrician, splendid, stately, titled, upright, virtuous, worthy.

antonyms base, ignoble, low-born.

nobody *n.* also-ran, cipher, lightweight, man of straw, menial, minnow, nonentity, no-one, nothing, Walter Mitty.

antonym somebody.

nod *v.* acknowledge, agree, assent, beckon, bob, bow, concur, dip, doze, droop, drowse, duck, gesture, indicate, nap, salute, sign, signal, sleep, slip up, slump.

n. acknowledgment, beck, cue, gesture, greeting, indication, salute, sign, signal.

node *n.* bud, bump, burl, caruncle, growth, knob, knot, lump, nodule, process, protuberance, swelling.

noise *n.* babble, ballyhoo, blare, brattle, chirm, clamor, clash, clatter, coil, commotion, cry, din, fracas, hubbub, outcry, pandemonium, racket, row, sound, talk, tumult, uproar.

antonyms quiet, silence.

v. advertise, announce, bruit, circulate, gossip, publicize, repeat, report, rumor.

noisome *adj.* bad, baneful, deleterious, disgusting, fetid, foul, fulsome, harmful, hurtful, injurious, malodorous, mephitic, mischievous, noxious, offensive, pernicious, pestiferous, pestilential, poisonous, putrid, reeking, smelly, stinking, unhealthy, unwholesome.

antonyms balmy, pleasant, wholesome.

noisy *adj.* boisterous, cacophonous, chattering, clamorous, clangorous, deafening, ear-piercing, ear-splitting, horrisonant, loud, obstreperous, piercing, plangent, rackety, riotous, strepitant, strident, tumultuous, turbulent, uproarious, vocal, vociferous.

antonyms peaceful, quiet, silent.

nomad *n.* drifter, itinerant, migrant, rambler, roamer, rover, traveler, vagabond, vagrant, wanderer.

nominate *v.* appoint, assign, choose, commission, designate, elect, elevate, empower, mention, name, present, propose, put up, recommend, select, submit, suggest, term.

nomination *n.* appointment, choice, designation, election, proposal, recommendation, selection, submission, suggestion.

nominee *n.* appointee, assignee, candidate, contestant, entrant, protégé, runner.

nonchalant *adj.* airy, apathetic, blasé, calm, careless, casual, collected, cool, detached, dispassionate, impassive, indifferent, insouciant, offhand, pococurante, unconcerned, unemotional, unperturbed.
antonyms anxious, careful, concerned, worried.

non-committal *adj.* ambiguous, careful, cautious, circumspect, cunctatious, cunctative, cunctatory, discreet, equivocal, evasive, guarded, indefinite, neutral, politic, reserved, tactful, temporizing, tentative, unrevealing, vague, wary.

nonconformist *n.* deviant, dissenter, dissentient, eccentric, heretic, iconoclast, individualist, maverick, oddball, protester, radical, rebel, seceder, secessionist.
antonym conformist.

nondescript *adj.* commonplace, dull, featureless, indeterminate, mousy, ordinary, plain, unclassified, undistinctive, undistinguished, unexceptional, uninspiring, uninteresting, unmemorable, unremarkable, vague.

nonentity *n.* cipher, dandiprat, drip, drongo, earthworm, gnatling, lightweight, mediocrity, nobody.

non-essential *adj.* dispensable, excessive, expendable, extraneous, extrinsic(al), inessential, peripheral, superfluous, supplementary, unimportant, unnecessary.
antonym essential.

non-existent *adj.* chimerical, fancied, fictional, hallucinatory, hypothetical, illusory, imaginary, imagined, immaterial, incorporeal, insubstantial, legendary, missing, mythical, null, unreal.
antonyms actual, existing, real.

nonplus *v.* astonish, astound, baffle, bewilder, confound, confuse, discomfit, disconcert, discountenance, dismay, dumbfound, embarrass, flabbergast, flummox, mystify, perplex, puzzle, stump, stun, take aback.

nonsense *n.* absurdity, balderdash, balls, baloney, bilge, blah, blather, blethers, bollocks, bombast, bosh, bull, bullshit, bunk, bunkum, claptrap, cobblers, codswallop, crap, double-Dutch, drivel, fadaise, faddle, fandangle, fatuity, fiddle-de-dee, fiddle-faddle, fiddlesticks, flapdoodle, folly, foolishness, fudge, gaff, galimatias, gammon, gas and gaiters, gibberish, gobbledygook, havers, hogwash, hooey, inanity, jabberwock(y), jest, ludicrousness, moonshine, nomeaning, piffle, pulp, ridiculousness, rot, rubbish, senselessness, silliness, squish, squit, stuff, stultiloquence, stupidity, tar(r)adiddle, tommy-rot, tosh, trash, twaddle, twattle, unreason, waffle.
antonym sense.

nonsensical *adj.* absurd, crazy, daft, fatuous, foolish, inane, incomprehensible, irrational, ludicrous, meaningless, ridiculous, senseless, silly.
antonyms logical, sensible.

non-stop *adj.* ceaseless, constant, continuous, direct, endless, incessant, interminable, never-ending, on-going, relentless, round-the-clock, steady, unbroken, unceasing, unending, unfaltering, uninterrupted, unrelenting, unremitting.
antonyms intermittent, occasional.
adv. ceaselessly, constantly, continuously, directly, endlessly, incessantly, interminably, relentlessly, round-the-clock, steadily, unbrokenly, unceasingly, unendingly, unfalteringly, uninterruptedly, unrelentingly, unremittingly.
antonyms intermittently, occasionally.

nook *n.* alcove, cavity, corner, cranny, crevice, cubbyhole, hide-out, ingle-nook, nest, niche, opening, recess, retreat, shelter.

normal *adj.* accustomed, acknowledged, average, common, common-or-garden, conventional, habitual, mainstream, natural, ordinary, par for the course, popular, rational, reasonable, regular, routine, run-of-the-mill, sane, standard, straight, typical, usual, well-adjusted.
antonyms abnormal, irregular, odd, peculiar.

normally *adv.* as a rule, characteristically, commonly, habitually, ordinarily, regularly, straight, typically, usually.
antonym abnormally.

nos(e)y *adj.* curious, eavesdropping, inquisitive, interfering, intermeddling, intrusive, meddlesome, officious, prying, snooping.

nostalgia *n.* homesickness, longing, mal du pays, pining, regret, regretfulness, remembrance, reminiscence, wistfulness, yearning.

notable *adj.* celebrated, conspicuous, distinguished, eminent, evident, extraordinary, famous, impressive, manifest, marked, memorable, noteworthy, noticeable, notorious, outstanding, overt, pre-eminent, pronounced, rare, remarkable, renowned, signal, striking, uncommon, unusual, well-known.
antonyms commonplace, ordinary, usual.
n. celebrity, dignitary, luminary, notability, personage, somebody, VIP, worthy.
antonyms nobody, nonentity.

notch *n.* cleft, cut, degree, grade, incision, indentation, insection, kerf, level, mark, nick, score, sinus, snip, step.
v. cut, gimp, indent, mark, nick, raffle, scallop, score, scratch.

note *n.* annotation, apostil(le), billet, celebrity, character, comment, communication, consequence, distinction, eminence, epistle, epistolet, fame, gloss, heed, indication, jotting, letter, line, mark, memo, memorandum, message, minute, notice, observation, prestige, record, regard, remark, reminder, renown, reputation, signal, symbol, token.
v. denote, designate, detect, enter, indicate, mark, mention, notice, observe, perceive, record, register, remark, see, witness.

noted *adj.* acclaimed, celebrated, conspicuous, distinguished, eminent, famous, great, illustrious, notable, notorious, prominent, recognized, renowned, respected, well-known. **noteworthy** *adj.* exceptional, extraordinary, important, notable, on the map, outstanding, remarkable, significant, unusual, visitable.
antonyms commonplace, ordinary, unexceptional, usual.

notice *v.* descry, detect, discern, distinguish, espy, heed, mark, mind, note, observe, perceive, remark, see, spot.
antonyms ignore, overlook.
n. advertisement, advice, affiche, announcement, attention, bill, civility, cognizance, comment, communication, consideration, criticism, heed, instruction, intelligence, intimation, news, note, notification, observation, order, poster, regard, respect, review, sign, warning.

notify *v.* acquaint, advise, alert, announce, apprize, declare, disclose, inform, publish, reveal, tell, warn.

notion *n.* apprehension, belief, caprice, conceit, concept, conception, concetto, construct, desire, fancy, idea, image, impression, impulse, inclination, inkling, judgment, knowledge, opinion, sentiment, understanding, view, whim, wish.

notorious *adj.* arrant, blatant, dishonorable, disreputable, egregious, flagrant, glaring, infamous, obvious, open, opprobrious, overt, patent, scandalous, undisputed.

nourish *v.* attend, cherish, comfort, cultivate, encourage, feed, foster, furnish, harbor, maintain, nurse, nurture, promote, supply, support, sustain, tend.

nourishment *n.* aliment, diet, food, goodness, nutriment, nutrition, pabulum, provender, sustenance, viands, victuals.

novel *adj.* different, fresh, imaginative, innovative, new, original, rare, singular, strange, surprising, uncommon, unconventional, unfamiliar, unusual.
antonyms familiar, ordinary.
n. fiction, narrative, romance, saga, story, tale, yarn.

novice *n.* amateur, apprentice, beginner, catechumen, convert, cub, griffin, Johnny-raw, learner, neophyte, newcomer, novitiate, probationer, proselyte, pupil, tiro.
antonyms doyen, expert, professional.

now *adv.* at once, at present, directly, immediately, instanter, instantly, next, nowadays, presently, promptly, straightaway, these days.

noxious *adj.* baneful, corrupting, deadly, deleterious, destructive, detrimental, foul, harmful, hurtful, injurious, insalubrious, mephitic(al), morbiferous, morbific, noisome, pernicious, pestilential, poisonous, unhealthy, unwholesome.
antonyms innocuous, wholesome.

nucleus *n.* basis, center, core, crux, focus, heart, heartlet, kernel, nub, pivot.

nude *adj.* au naturel, bare, disrobed, exposed, in one's birthday suit, in puris naturalibus, in the altogether, in the buff, naked, starkers, stark-naked, stripped, unattired, unclad, unclothed, uncovered, undraped, undressed, without a stitch.
antonyms clothed, covered, dressed.

nudge *v., n.* bump, dig, jog, poke, prod, prompt, push, shove, touch.

nugget *n.* chunk, clump, hunk, lump, mass, piece, wodge.

nuisance *n.* annoyance, bore, bother, désagrément, drag, drawback, inconvenience, infliction, irritation, offence, pain, pest, plague, problem, trouble, vexation.

nullify *v.* abate, abolish, abrogate, annul, cancel, counteract, countervail, invalidate, negate, neutralize, quash, repeal, rescind, revoke, undermine, veto, vitiate, void.
antonym validate.

numb *adj.* benumbed, dead, deadened, frozen, immobilized, insensate, insensible, insensitive, paralyzed, stunned, stupefied, torpid, unfeeling.
antonym sensitive.
v. anesthetize, benumb, deaden, dull, freeze, immobilize, obtund, paralyze, stun, stupefy.
antonym sensitize.

number[1] *n.* aggregate, amount, character, collection, company, count, crowd, digit, figure, folio, horde, index, integer, many, multitude, numeral, quantity, several, sum, throng, total, unit.
v. account, add, apportion, calculate, compute, count, enumerate, include, inventory, reckon, tell, total.

number[2] *n.* copy, edition, impression, imprint, issue, printing, volume.

numeral *n.* character, cipher, digit, figure, folio, integer, number.

numerous *adj.* abundant, copious, divers, many, multitudinous, myriad, plentiful, profuse, several, sundry.
antonyms few, scanty.

numskull *n.* blockhead, bonehead, buffoon, clot, dimwit, dolt, dope, dullard, dummy, dunce, dunderhead, fathead, fool, sap, saphead, simpleton, thickhead, twit.

nuptials *n.* bridal, espousal, marriage, matrimony, spousals, wedding.

nurse *v.* breast-feed, care for, cherish, cultivate, encourage, feed, foster, harbor, keep, nourish, nurture, preserve, promote, succor, suckle, support, sustain, tend, treat, wetnurse.
n. amah, district-nurse, home-nurse, mammy, nanny, nursemaid, sister of mercy, wet nurse.

nurture *n.* care, cultivation, development, diet, discipline, education, food, instruction, nourishment, rearing, training, upbringing.
v. bring up, care for, cultivate, develop, discipline, educate, feed, instruct, nourish, nurse, rear, school, support, sustain, tend, train.

nutriment *n.* aliment, diet, food, foodstuff, nourishment, nutrition, pabulum, provender, subsistence, support, sustenance.

nutrition *n.* eutrophy, food, nourishment, nutriment, sustenance.

O

oaf *n.* baboon, blockhead, bonehead, booby, brute, clod, dolt, dullard, dummy, dunce, fool, galoot, gawk, goon, gorilla, half-wit, hick, hobbledehoy, hulk, idiot, imbecile, lout, lummox, moron, nincompoop, oik, sap, schlemiel, schlep, simpleton, yob.

oasis *n.* enclave, haven, island, refuge, resting-place, retreat, sanctuary, sanctum, watering-hole.

oath *n.* affirmation, assurance, avowal, blasphemy, bond, curse, cuss, expletive, imprecation, malediction, pledge, plight, profanity, promise, swear-word, vow, word, word of honor.

obdurate *adj.* adamant, callous, dogged, firm, fixed, flinty, hard, hard-hearted, harsh, immovable, implacable, inexorable, inflexible, intransigent, iron, mulish, obstinate, perverse, pig-headed, relentless, stiff-necked, stony, stubborn, unbending, unfeeling, unrelenting, unshakable, unyielding.
antonyms submissive, tender.

obedience *n.* accordance, acquiescence, agreement, allegiance, amenableness, compliance, conformability, deference, docility, dutifulness, duty, observance, passivity, respect, reverence, submission, submissiveness, subservience, tractability.
antonym disobedience.

obedient *adj.* acquiescent, amenable, biddable, compliant, deferential, docile, duteous, dutiful, law-abiding, observant, passive, regardful, respectful, sequacious, submissive, subservient, tractable, unquestioning, unresisting, well-trained, yielding.
antonyms disobedient, rebellious, refractory, unruly, wilful.

obese *adj.* bulky, corpulent, Falstaffian, fat, fleshy, gross, heavy, outsize, overweight, paunchy, plump, podgy, ponderous, portly, pursy, roly-poly, rotund, stout, tubby.
antonyms skinny, slender, thin.

obey *v.* abide by, act upon, adhere to, be ruled by, bow to, carry out, comply, conform, defer (to), discharge, embrace, execute, follow, fulfil, give in, give way, heed, implement, keep, knuckle under, mind, observe, perform, respond, serve, submit, surrender, take orders from, toe the line, yield.
antonym disobey.

object[1] *n.* aim, article, body, butt, design, end, entity, fact, focus, goal, idea, intent, intention, item, motive, objective, phenomenon, point, purpose, raison d'être, reality, reason, recipient, target, thing, victim, visible.

object[2] *v.* argue, complain, demur, dissent, expostulate, oppose, protest, rebut, refuse, repudiate, take exception.
antonyms accede, acquiesce, agree, assent.

objection *n.* cavil, censure, challenge, complaint, counter-argument, demur, doubt, exception, niggle, opposition, protest, remonstrance, scruple.
antonyms agreement, assent.

objectionable *adj.* abhorrent, antisocial, deplorable, despicable, detestable, disagreeable, dislikable, displeasing, distasteful, exceptionable, indecorous, insufferable, intolerable, loathsome, noxious, obnoxious, offensive, regrettable, repugnant, unacceptable, undesirable, unpleasant, unseemly.
antonyms acceptable, pleasant, welcome.

objective *adj.* calm, detached, disinterested, dispassionate, equitable, even-handed, fair, impartial, impersonal, judicial, just, open-minded, sensible, sober, unbiased, uncolored, unemotional, unimpassioned, uninvolved, unprejudiced.
antonyms biased, subjective.
n. aim, ambition, aspiration, design, destination, end, goal, intention, mark, object, prize, purpose, target.

objectivity *n.* detachment, disinterest, disinterestedness, dispassion, equitableness, even-handedness, impartiality, impersonality, open mind, open-mindedness.
antonyms bias, subjectivity.

obligation *n.* accountability, accountableness, agreement, bond, burden, charge, commitment, compulsion, contract, debt, duty, engagement, indebtedness, liability, must, obstriction, onus, promise, requirement, responsibility, stipulation, trust, understanding.
antonyms choice, discretion.

obligatory *adj.* binding, bounden, coercive, compulsory, de rigueur, enforced, essential, imperative, mandatory, necessary, required, requisite, statutory, unavoidable.
antonym optional.

oblige *v.* accommodate, assist, benefit, bind, coerce, compel, constrain, do a favor, favor, force, gratify, help, impel, indulge, make, necessitate, obligate, please, require, serve.

obliging *adj.* accommodating, agreeable, aidful, amiable, civil, complaisant, considerate, co-operative, courteous, eager, friendly, good-natured, helpful, kind, polite, willing.
antonyms inconsiderate, unhelpful, unkind.

obliterate *v.* annihilate, blot out, cancel, delete, destroy, efface, eradicate, erase, expunge, extirpate, rub out, vaporize, wipe out.

oblivious *adj.* blind, careless, comatose, deaf, disregardful, forgetful, heedless, ignorant, inattentive, insensible, neglectful, negligent, nescient, regardless, unaware, unconcerned, unconscious, unmindful, unobservant.
antonyms aware, conscious.

obloquy *n.* abuse, animadversion, aspersion, attack, bad press, blame, calumny, censure, contumely, criticism, defamation, detraction, discredit, disfavor, disgrace, dishonor, humiliation, ignominy, infamy, invective, odium, opprobrium, reproach, shame, slander, stigma, vilification.

obnoxious *adj.* abhorrent, abominable, detestable, disagreeable, disgusting, dislikable, foul, fulsome, hateful, horrid, insufferable, loathsome, nasty, nauseating, nauseous, noisome, objectionable, odious, offensive, repellent, reprehensible, repugnant, repulsive, revolting, sickening, unpleasant.
antonyms agreeable, likable, pleasant.

obscene *adj.* atrocious, barrack-room, bawdy, blue, coarse, dirty, disgusting, evil, Fescennine, filthy, foul, gross, heinous, immodest, immoral, improper, impure, indecent, lewd, licentious, loathsome, loose, offensive, outrageous, pornographic, prurient, Rabelaisian, ribald, salacious, scabrous, scurrilous, shameless, shocking, sickening, smutty, suggestive, unchaste, unwholesome, vile, wicked.
antonyms clean, decent, decorous.

obscure *adj.* abstruse, ambiguous, arcane, blurred, caliginous, clear as mud, clouded, cloudy, concealed, confusing, cryptic, deep, Delphic, dim, doubtful, dusky, enigmatic, esoteric, faint, gloomy, hazy, hermetic, hidden, humble, incomprehensible, inconspicuous, indefinite, indistinct, inglorious, intricate, involved, little-known, lowly, minor, misty, murky, mysterious, nameless, obfuscated, occult, opaque, oracular, out-of-the-way, recondite, remote, riddling, shadowy, shady, somber, tenebr(i)ous, tenebrose, twilight, unclear, undistinguished, unheard-of, unhonored, unimportant, unknown, unlit, unnoted, unobvious, unrenowned, unseen, unsung, vague, veiled.
antonyms clear, definite, explicit, famous, lucid.
v. bedim, befog, block out, blur, cloak, cloud, conceal, cover, darken, dim, disguise, dull, eclipse, hide, mask, muddy, obfuscate, overshadow, screen, shade, shadow, shroud, veil.
antonyms clarify, illuminate.

obsequious *adj.* abject, cringing, deferential, dough-faced, fawning, flattering, groveling, ingratiating, knee-crooking, menial, oily, servile, slavish, slimy, smarmy, submissive, subservient, sycophantic, toadying, unctuous.
antonym assertive.

observant *adj.* alert, attentive, eagle-eyed, eagle-sighted, falcon-eyed, heedful, mindful, perceptive, percipient, quick, sharp-eyed, vigilant, watchful, wide-awake.
antonyms inattentive, unobservant.

observation *n.* annotation, attention, cognition, comment, consideration, discernment, examination, experience, finding, information, inspection, knowledge, monitoring, note, notice, obiter dictum, opinion, perception, pronouncement, reading, reflection, remark, review, scrutiny, study, surveillance, thought, utterance, watching.

observe *v.* abide by, adhere to, animadvert, celebrate, commemorate, comment, comply, conform to, contemplate, declare, detect, discern, discover, espy, follow, fulfil, heed, honor, keep, keep an eye on, keep tabs on, mention, mind, monitor, note, notice, obey, opine, perceive, perform, regard, remark, remember, respect, say, scrutinize, see, solemnize, spot, state, study, surveille, survey, view, watch, witness.
antonyms break, miss, overlook, violate.

observer *n.* beholder, bystander, commentator, discerner, eyewitness, looker-on, noter, onlooker, spectator, spotter, viewer, watcher, witness.

obsession *n.* bee in one's bonnet, complex, enthusiasm, fetish, fixation, hang-up, idée fixe, infatuation, mania, monomania, phobia, preoccupation, ruling passion, thing, zelotypia.

obsolete *adj.* anachronistic, ancient, antediluvian, antiquated, antique, archaic, bygone, dated, dead, démodé, discarded, disused, extinct, fogram, horse-and-buggy, musty, old, old hat, old-fashioned, out, out of date, outmoded, outworn, passé, superannuated.
antonyms contemporary, current, modern, new, up-to-date.

obstacle *n.* bar, barrier, boyg, catch, check, chicane, difficulty, drawback, hindrance, hitch, hurdle, impediment, interference, interruption, obstruction, pons asinorum, remora, snag, stop, stumbling-block, stumbling-stone.
antonyms advantage, help.

obstinate *adj.* bullet-headed, bull-headed, bullish, camelish, contumacious, determined, dogged, firm, headstrong, immovable, inflexible, intractable, intransigent, mulish, obdurate, opinionated, persistent, pertinacious, perverse, pervicacious, pig-headed, recalcitrant, refractory, restive, rusty, self-willed, steadfast, stomachful, strong-minded, stubborn, sturdy, tenacious, unadvisable, unyielding, uppity, wilful, wrongheaded.
antonyms co-operative, flexible, pliant, submissive.

obstruct *v.* arrest, bar, barricade, block, check, choke, clog, crab, cumber, curb, cut off, frustrate, hamper, hamstring, hide, hinder, hold up, impede, inhibit, interfere with, interrupt, mask, obscure, occlude, prevent, restrict, retard, shield, shut off, slow down, stall, stonewall, stop, stuff, thwart, trammel.
antonym help.

obstruction *n.* bar, barricade, barrier, blockage, check, difficulty, filibuster, hindrance, impediment, snag, stop, stoppage, trammel, traverse.
antonym help.

obtain[1] *v.* achieve, acquire, attain, come by, compass, earn, gain, get, impetrate, procure, secure.

obtain[2] *v.* be in force, be prevalent, be the case, exist, hold, prevail, reign, rule, stand.

obtrusive *adj.* blatant, forward, importunate, interfering, intrusive, manifest, meddling, nosy, noticeable, obvious, officious, prominent, protruding, protuberant, prying, pushy.
antonym unobtrusive.

obtuse *adj.* blunt, boneheaded, crass, dense, dopey, dull, dull-witted, dumb, imperceptive, impercipient, inattentive, insensitive, retarded, rounded, slow, stolid, stupid, thick, thick-skinned, uncomprehending, unintelligent.
antonyms bright, sharp.

obviate *v.* anticipate, avert, counter, counteract, divert, forestall, preclude, prevent, remove.

obvious *adj.* apparent, clear, conspicuous, discernible, distinct, evident, glaring, indisputable, manifest, noticeable, open, open-and-shut, overt, palpable, patent, perceptible, plain, prominent, pronounced, recognizable, self-evident, self-explanatory, straightforward, transparent, unconcealed, undeniable, undisguised, unmistakable, unsubtle, visible.
antonyms obscure, unclear.

obviously *adv.* certainly, clearly, distinctly, evidently, manifestly, of course, palpably, patently, plainly, undeniably, unmistakably, unquestionably, visibly, without doubt.

occasion *n.* affair, call, case, cause, celebration, chance, convenience, event, excuse, experience, ground(s), incident, inducement, influence, instance, justification, moment, motive, occurrence, opening, opportunity, prompting, provocation, reason, time.
v. bring about, bring on, cause, create, effect, elicit, engender, evoke, generate, give rise to, induce, influence, inspire, lead to, make, originate, persuade, produce, prompt, provoke.

occasional *adj.* casual, desultory, fitful, incidental, infrequent, intermittent, irregular, odd, periodic, rare, scattered, sporadic, uncommon.
antonym frequent.

occasionally *adv.* at intervals, at times, every so often, from time to time, infrequently, irregularly, now and again, now and then, off and on, on and off, on occasion, once in a while, periodically, sometimes, sporadically.
antonym frequently.

occult *adj.* abstruse, arcane, cabbalistic, concealed, esoteric, faint, hidden, impenetrable, invisible, magical, mysterious, mystic, mystical, mystifying, obscure, preternatural, recondite, secret, supernatural, unknown, unrevealed, veiled.
v. conceal, cover (up), enshroud, hide, mask, obscure, screen, shroud, veil.
antonym reveal.

occupant *n.* addressee, denizen, holder, householder, incumbent, indweller, inhabitant, inmate, lessee, occupier, resident, squatter, tenant, user.

occupation[1] *n.* absorption, activity, business, calling, craft, employment, job, line, post, profession, pursuit, trade, vocation, walk of life, work.

occupation[2] *n.* billet, conquest, control, habitation, holding, invasion, occupancy, possession, residence, seizure, subjugation, takeover, tenancy, tenure, use.

occupy *v.* absorb, amuse, beguile, busy, capture, conquer, cover, divert, dwell in, employ, engage, engross, ensconce oneself in, entertain, establish oneself in, fill, garrison, hold, immerse, inhabit, interest, invade, involve, keep, keep busy, live in, monopolize, overrun, own, permeate, pervade, possess, preoccupy, reside in, seize, stay in, take over, take possession of, take up, tenant, tie up, use, utilize.

occur *v.* appear, arise, be found, be met with, be present, befall, betide, chance, come about, come off, come to pass, crop up, develop, eventuate, exist, happen, intervene, manifest itself, materialize, obtain, result, show itself, take place, transpire, turn up.

occur to come to mind, come to one, cross one's mind, dawn on, enter one's head, present itself, spring to mind, strike one, suggest itself.

occurrence *n.* action, adventure, affair, appearance, case, circumstance, development, episode, event, existence, happening, incident, instance, manifestation, materialization, proceeding, transaction. **ocean** *n.* briny, main, profound, sea, the deep, the drink.

odd[1] *adj.* abnormal, atypical, bizarre, curious, deviant, different, eccentric, exceptional, extraordinary, fantastic, freak, freakish, freaky, funky, funny, irregular, kinky, outlandish, peculiar, quaint, queer, rare, remarkable, singular, strange, uncanny, uncommon, unconventional, unexplained, unusual, weird, whimsical.
antonym normal.

odd[2] *adj.* auxiliary, casual, fragmentary, ill-matched, incidental, irregular, left-over, lone, miscellaneous, occasional, periodic, random, remaining, seasonal, single, solitary, spare, sundry, surplus, uneven, unmatched, unpaired, varied, various.

odious *adj.* abhorrent, abominable, annoying, detestable, disgusting, execrable, foul, hateful, heinous, horrible, horrid, insufferable, loathsome, obnoxious, offensive, repellent, repugnant, repulsive, revolting, unpleasant, vile.
antonym pleasant.

odium *n.* abhorrence, animosity, antipathy, censure, condemnation, contempt, detestation, disapprobation, disapproval, discredit, disfavor, disgrace, dishonor, dislike, disrepute, execration, hatred, infamy, obloquy, opprobrium, reprobation, shame.

odor *n.* air, aroma, atmosphere, aura, bouquet, breath, emanation, essence, exhalation, flavor, fragrance, perfume, quality, redolence, scent, smell, spirit, stench, stink.

odyssey *n.* journey, travels, wandering.

off *adj.* abnormal, absent, bad, below par, canceled, decomposed, disappointing, disheartening, displeasing, finished, gone, high, inoperative, moldy, poor, postponed, quiet, rancid, rotten, slack, sour, substandard, turned, unavailable, unsatisfactory, wrong.

adv. apart, aside, at a distance, away, elsewhere, out.

off-color *adj.* faded, ill, indecent, indisposed, off form, out of sorts, pasty-faced, peaky, peelie-wally, poorly, queasy, sick, under the weather, unwell.

offend *v.* affront, annoy, disgruntle, disgust, displease, fret, gall, hip, hurt, insult, irritate, miff, nauseate, outrage, pain, pique, provoke, repel, repulse, rile, sicken, slight, snub, transgress, turn off, upset, vex, violate, wound, wrong.

antonym please.

offender *n.* criminal, culprit, delinquent, guilty party, lawbreaker, malefactor, miscreant, misfeasor, sinner, transgressor, wrong-doer.

offense *n.* affront, anger, annoyance, crime, delict, delinquency, displeasure, fault, hard feelings, harm, huff, hurt, indignation, indignity, infraction, infringement, injury, injustice, insult, ire, lapse, misdeed, misdemeanor, needle, outrage, peccadillo, pique, putdown, resentment, sin, slight, snub, transgression, trespass, umbrage, violation, wrath, wrong, wrong-doing.

offensive *adj.* abominable, abusive, aggressive, annoying, attacking, detestable, disagreeable, discourteous, disgusting, displeasing, disrespectful, embarrassing, grisly, impertinent, insolent, insulting, intolerable, invading, irritating, loathsome, nasty, nauseating, noisome, objectionable, obnoxious, odious, rank, repellent, repugnant, revolting, rude, sickening, uncivil, unmannerly, unpalatable, unpleasant, unsavory, vile.

antonyms defensive, pleasing.

n. attack, drive, onslaught, push, raid, sortie, thrust. **offer** *v.* advance, afford, bid, extend, furnish, give, hold out, make available, move, present, proffer, propose, propound, provide, put forth, put forward, show, submit, suggest, tender, volunteer.

n. approach, attempt, bid, endeavor, essay, overture, presentation, proposal, proposition, submission, suggestion, tender.

offhand *adj.* abrupt, aloof, brusque, careless, casual, cavalier, curt, glib, informal, offhanded, perfunctory, take-it-or-leave-it, unappreciative, uncaring, unceremonious, unconcerned, uninterested.

antonyms calculated, planned.

adv. at once, extempore, immediately, off the cuff, off the top of one's head, straightaway.

office *n.* appointment, bath, business, capacity, charge, commission, duty, employment, function, obligation, occupation, place, post, responsibility, role, room, service, situation, station, trust, work.

officiate *v.* adjudicate, chair, conduct, emcee, manage, oversee, preside, referee, serve, superintend, umpire.

offset *v.* balance out, cancel out, compare, compensate for, counteract, counterbalance, counterpoise, countervail, juxtapose, make up for, neutralize.

n. balance, compensation, counterbalance, counterweight, equipoise, equivalent, redress.

offshoot *n.* adjunct, appendage, arm, branch, by-product, development, embranchment, limb, outgrowth, spin-off, sprout, spur.

offspring *n.* brood, child, children, creation, descendant, descendants, family, fry, heir, heirs, issue, kids, litter, progeny, quiverful, result, scion, seed, spawn, successor, successors, young.

antonym parent(s).

often *adv.* again and again, frequently, generally, habitually, many a time, much, oft, over and over, regularly, repeatedly, time after time, time and again.

antonym seldom.

ogle *v.* eye, eye up, leer, look, make eyes at, stare.

ogre *n.* bogey, bogeyman, bogle, boyg, bugaboo, bugbear, demon, devil, giant, humgruffi(a)n, monster, specter.

ointment *n.* balm, balsam, cerate, cream, demulcent, embrocation, emollient, liniment, lotion, salve, unction, unguent.

old *adj.* aboriginal, aged, age-old, ancient, antediluvian, antiquated, antique, archaic, bygone, cast-off, crumbling, dated, decayed, decrepit, done, earlier, early, elderly, erstwhile, ex-, experienced, familiar, former, gray, gray-haired, grizzled, hackneyed, hardened, hoary, immemorial, long-established, long-standing, mature, obsolete, of old, of yore, Ogygian, olden, old-fashioned, one-time, original, out of date, outdated, outmoded, over the hill, passé, patriarchal, practiced, preadamic(al), prehistoric, previous, primeval, primitive, primordial, pristine, quondam, remote, senescent, senile, skilled, stale, superannuated, time-honored, time-worn, traditional, unfashionable, unoriginal, venerable, versed, veteran, vintage, worn-out.

antonym young.

old-fashioned *adj.* ancient, antiquated, archaic, arriéré, behind the times, corny, dated, dead, démodé, fog(e)yish, fusty, horse-and-buggy, musty, neanderthal, obsolescent, obsolete, old hat, old-fog(e)yish, old-time, out of date, outdated, outmoded, passé, past, retro, square, superannuated, unfashionable.

antonyms contemporary, modern, up-to-date.

old-world *adj.* archaic, ceremonious, chivalrous, conservative, courtly, formal, gallant, old-fashioned, picturesque, quaint, traditional.

omen *n.* augury, auspice, boding, foreboding, foretoken, indication, portent, premonition, presage, prognostic, prognostication, sign, straw in the wind, warning, writing on the wall.

ominous *adj.* baleful, bodeful, dark, fateful, inauspicious, menacing, minatory, portentous, premonitory, presageful, sinister, threatening, unpromising, unpropitious.

antonym auspicious.

omission *n.* avoidance, bowdlerization, default, ellipsis, exclusion, failure, forgetfulness, gap, lack, neglect, oversight.
antonyms addition, inclusion.

omit *v.* disregard, drop, edit out, eliminate, exclude, fail, forget, give something a miss, leave out, leave undone, let slide, miss out, neglect, overlook, pass over, pretermit, skip.
antonyms add, include.

omnipotent *adj.* all-powerful, almighty, plenipotent, supreme.
antonym impotent.

omnipresent *adj.* pervasive, ubiquitary, ubiquitous, universal.

omniscient *adj.* all-knowing, all-seeing, pansophic.

once *adv.* at one time, formerly, heretofore, in the old days, in the past, in times gone by, in times past, long ago, once upon a time, previously.

oncoming *adj.* advancing, approaching, forthcoming, gathering, imminent, impending, looming, onrushing, upcoming.

oneness *n.* completeness, consistency, distinctness, identicalness, identity, individuality, sameness, singleness, unicity, unity, wholeness.

onerous *adj.* backbreaking, burdensome, crushing, demanding, difficult, exacting, exhausting, exigent, formidable, grave, hard, heavy, herculean, laborious, oppressive, responsible, taxing, troublesome, weighty.
antonyms easy, light.

one-sided *adj.* asymmetrical, biased, colored, discriminatory, inequitable, lopsided, partial, partisan, prejudiced, unequal, unfair, unilateral, unjust.
antonym impartial.

ongoing *adj.* advancing, continuing, continuous, current, developing, evolving, extant, growing, in progress, lasting, progressing, successful, unfinished, unfolding.

onlooker *n.* bystander, eye-witness, looker-on, observer, rubber-neck, spectator, viewer, watcher, witness.

only *adv.* at most, barely, exclusively, just, merely, purely, simply, solely.
adj. exclusive, individual, lone, single, sole, solitary, unique.

onset *n.* assault, attack, beginning, charge, commencement, inception, kick-off, onrush, onslaught, outbreak, outset, start.
antonyms end, finish.

onslaught *n.* assault, attack, barrage, blitz, bombardment, charge, offensive, onrush, onset.

onus *n.* burden, duty, encumbrance, liability, load, obligation, responsibility, task.

onward(s) *adv.* ahead, beyond, forth, forward, frontward(s), in front, on.
antonym backward(s).

ooze *v.* bleed, discharge, drain, dribble, drip, drop, emit, escape, exude, filter, leach, leak, osmose, overflow with, percolate, seep, strain, sweat, transude, weep.

n. alluvium, deposit, mire, muck, mud, sediment, silt, slime, sludge.

opacity *n.* cloudiness, density, dullness, filminess, impermeability, milkiness, murkiness, obfuscation, obscurity, opaqueness, unclearness.
antonym transparency.

opaque *adj.* abstruse, baffling, clouded, cloudy, cryptic, difficult, dim, dull, enigmatic, filmy, fuliginous, hazy, impenetrable, incomprehensible, inexplicable, lusterless, muddied, muddy, murky, obfuscated, obscure, turbid, unclear, unfathomable, unintelligible.
antonym transparent.

open *adj.* above-board, accessible, agape, airy, ajar, apparent, arguable, artless, available, avowed, bare, barefaced, blatant, bounteous, bountiful, candid, champaign, clear, conspicuous, debatable, disinterested, downright, evident, expanded, exposed, extended, extensive, fair, filigree, flagrant, frank, free, fretted, gaping, general, generous, guileless, holey, honest, honeycombed, impartial, ingenuous, innocent, lacy, liberal, lidless, loose, manifest, moot, munificent, natural, navigable, noticeable, objective, obvious, overt, passable, plain, porous, public, receptive, revealed, rolling, sincere, spacious, spongy, spread out, sweeping, transparent, unbarred, unbiased, unclosed, uncluttered, uncommitted, unconcealed, unconditional, uncovered, uncrowded, undecided, undefended, undisguised, unenclosed, unengaged, unfastened, unfenced, unfolded, unfortified, unfurled, unlidded, unlocked, unobstructed, unoccupied, unprejudiced, unprotected, unqualified, unreserved, unresolved, unrestricted, unroofed, unsealed, unsettled, unsheltered, unwalled, vacant, visible, wide, wide-open, yawning.
antonyms closed, shut.

v. begin, clear, come apart, commence, crack, disclose, divulge, exhibit, explain, expose, inaugurate, initiate, launch, lay bare, ope, pour out, rupture, separate, set in motion, show, split, spread (out), start, throw wide, unbar, unbare, unblock, unclose, uncork, uncover, undo, unfasten, unfold, unfurl, unlatch, unlid, unlock, unroll, unseal, unshutter.
antonyms close, shut.

open-handed *adj.* bountiful, eleemosynary, free, generous, large-hearted, lavish, liberal, munificent, unstinting.
antonym tight-fisted.

opening *n.* adit, aperture, beginning, birth, breach, break, chance, chasm, chink, cleft, commencement, crack, dawn, fissure, fistula, foramen, gap, hole, inauguration, inception, initiation, interstice, kick-off, launch, launching, occasion, onset, opportunity, orifice, ostiole, outset, perforation, place, rent, rupture, slot, space, split, start, vacancy, vent, vista.
antonyms closing, closure.

adj. beginning, commencing, early, first, inaugural,

inauguratory, inceptive, initial, initiatory, introductory, maiden, primary.
antonym closing.

openly *adv.* blatantly, brazenly, candidly, face to face, flagrantly, forthrightly, frankly, glaringly, in full view, in public, overtly, plainly, publicly, shamelessly, unabashedly, unashamedly, unhesitatingly, unreservedly, wantonly.
antonyms secretly, slyly.

open-minded *adj.* broad, broad-minded, catholic, dispassionate, enlightened, free, impartial, latitudinarian, liberal, objective, reasonable, receptive, tolerant, unbiased, unprejudiced. *antonyms* bigoted, intolerant, prejudiced.

operate *v.* act, function, go, handle, manage, maneuver, perform, run, serve, use, utilize, work.

operation *n.* action, activity, affair, agency, assault, business, campaign, course, deal, effect, effort, employment, enterprise, exercise, force, influence, instrumentality, maneuver, manipulation, motion, movement, performance, procedure, proceeding, process, surgery, transaction, undertaking, use, utilization, working.

operative *adj.* active, crucial, current, effective, efficient, engaged, functional, functioning, important, in action, in force, in operation, indicative, influential, key, operational, relevant, serviceable, significant, standing, workable.
antonym inoperative.
n. artisan, employee, hand, laborer, machinist, mechanic, operator, worker.

operator *n.* administrator, conductor, contractor, dealer, director, driver, handler, machinator, machinist, manager, manipulator, mechanic, mover, operant, operative, practitioner, punter, shyster, speculator, technician, trader, wheeler-dealer, worker.

opiate *n.* anodyne, bromide, depressant, downer, drug, narcotic, nepenthe, pacifier, sedative, soporific, stupefacient, tranquilizer.

opinion *n.* assessment, belief, conception, conjecture, conventional wisdom, doxy, estimation, feeling, idea, idée reçue, impression, judgment, mind, notion, perception, persuasion, point of view, sentiment, stance, tenet, theory, view, voice, vox pop, vox populi.

opinionated *adj.* adamant, biased, bigoted, bull-headed, cocksure, dictatorial, doctrinaire, dogmatic, high-dried, inflexible, obdurate, obstinate, overbearing, partisan, pig-headed, prejudiced, self-assertive, single-minded, stubborn, uncompromising, wilful.
antonym open-minded.

opponent *n.* adversary, antagonist, challenger, competitor, contestant, disputant, dissentient, dissident, enemy, foe, objector, opposer, opposition, rival.
antonyms ally, proponent.

opportune *adj.* advantageous, appropriate, apt, auspicious, convenient, favorable, felicitous, fit, fitting, fortunate, good, happy, lucky, pertinent, proper, propitious, seasonable, suitable, timely, well-timed.
antonym inopportune.

opportunity *n.* break, chance, convenience, hour, moment, occasion, opening, scope, shot, time, turn.

oppose *v.* bar, beard, breast, check, combat, compare, confront, contradict, contrary, contrast, contravene, controvert, counter, counterattack, counterbalance, defy, face, fight, fly in the face of, gainsay, hinder, obstruct, pit against, play off, prevent, recalcitrate, resist, stand up to, take a stand against, take issue with, thwart, withstand.
antonyms favor, support.

opposed *adj.* against, agin, antagonistic, anti, antipathetic, antithetical, clashing, conflicting, contrary, contrasted, dissentient, hostile, in opposition, incompatible, inimical, opposing, opposite.
antonym in favor.

opposite *adj.* adverse, antagonistic, antipodal, antipodean, antithetical, conflicting, contradictory, contrary, contrasted, corresponding, different, differing, diverse, facing, fronting, hostile, inconsistent, inimical, irreconcilable, opposed, reverse, unlike.
antonym same. *n.* antipode(s), antipole, antithesis, contradiction, contrary, converse, inverse, reverse.
antonym same.

opposition *n.* antagonism, antagonist, clash, colluctation, competition, contraposition, contrariety, counteraction, counter-stand, counter-time, counter-view, disapproval, foe, hostility, obstruction, obstructiveness, opponent, other side, polarity, prevention, resistance, rival, syzygy, unfriendliness.
antonyms co-operation, support.

oppress *v.* abuse, afflict, burden, crush, depress, dispirit, harass, harry, lie hard on, lie heavy on, maltreat, overpower, overwhelm, persecute, sadden, subdue, subjugate, suppress, torment, trample, tyrannize, vex, weigh heavy.

oppression *n.* abuse, brutality, calamity, cruelty, hardship, harshness, injury, injustice, jackboot, liberticide, maltreatment, misery, persecution, severity, subjection, suffering, tyranny.

oppressive *adj.* airless, brutal, burdensome, close, cruel, despotic, grinding, harsh, heavy, inhuman, intolerable, muggy, onerous, overbearing, overpowering, overwhelming, repressive, severe, stifling, stuffy, suffocating, sultry, torrid, tyrannical, unendurable, unjust.
antonym gentle.

oppressor *n.* autocrat, bully, coercionist, despot, dictator, harrier, intimidator, liberticide, persecutor, scourge, slave-driver, taskmaster, tormentor, tyrant.
olic, vituperative.

opprobrium *n.* calumny, censure, contumely, debasement, degradation, discredit, disfavor, disgrace, dishonor, disrepute, ignominy, infamy, obloquy, odium, reproach, scurrility, shame, slur, stigma.

opt *v.* choose, decide (on), elect, go for, plump for, prefer, select, single out.

optimistic *adj.* assured, bright, bullish, buoyant, cheerful, confident, encouraged, expectant, heartened, hopeful, idealistic, Panglossian, Panglossic, positive, sanguine, upbeat, Utopian.
antonym pessimistic.

option *n.* alternative, choice, election, possibility, preference, selection.

optional *adj.* discretionary, elective, extra, open, possible, unforced, voluntary.
antonym compulsory.

opulence *n.* abundance, affluence, copiousness, cornucopia, easy street, fortune, fullness, lavishness, luxuriance, luxury, plenty, pleroma, profusion, prosperity, riches, richness, sumptuousness, superabundance, wealth.
antonyms penury, poverty.

opulent *adj.* abundant, affluent, copious, lavish, luxuriant, luxurious, moneyed, plentiful, profuse, prolific, prosperous, rich, sumptuous, superabundant, wealthy, well-heeled, well-off, well-to-do.
antonyms penurious, poor.

oracle *n.* adviser, answer, augur, augury, authority, divination, guru, high priest, mastermind, mentor, prediction, prognostication, prophecy, prophet, pundit, python, revelation, sage, seer, sibyl, soothsayer, vision, wizard.

oral *adj.* acroamatic(al), spoken, unwritten, verbal, vocal.
antonym written.

orate *v.* declaim, discourse, harangue, hold forth, pontificate, sermonize, speak, speechify, talk.

oration *n.* address, declamation, discourse, éloge, harangue, homily, lecture, sermon, speech, spiel.

orb *n.* ball, circle, globe, globule, mound, ring, round, sphere, spherule.

orbit *n.* ambit, circle, circumgyration, circumvolution, compass, course, cycle, domain, ellipse, influence, path, range, reach, revolution, rotation, scope, sphere, sphere of influence, sweep, track, trajectory.
v. circle, circumnavigate, circumvolve, encircle, revolve.

orchestrate *v.* arrange, compose, concert, co-ordinate, fix, integrate, organize, prepare, present, score, stage-manage.

ordain *v.* anoint, appoint, call, consecrate, decree, destine, dictate, elect, enact, enjoin, fate, fix, foredoom, foreordain, frock, instruct, intend, invest, lay down, legislate, nominate, order, predestine, predetermine, prescribe, pronounce, require, rule, set, will.

ordeal *n.* affliction, agony, anguish, nightmare, pain, persecution, suffering, test, torture, trial, tribulation(s), trouble(s).

order[1] *n.* application, arrangement, array, behest, booking, calm, categorization, chit, classification, codification, command, commission, control, cosmos, decree, dictate, diktat, direction, directive, discipline, disposal, disposition, eutaxy, grouping, harmony, injunction, instruction, law, law and order, layout, line, line-up, mandate, method, neatness, ordering, orderliness, ordinance, organization, pattern, peace, placement, plan, precept, progression, propriety, quiet, regularity, regulation, request, requisition, reservation, rule, sequence, series, stipulation, structure, succession, symmetry, system, tidiness, tranquility.
antonym disorder.
v. adjure, adjust, align, arrange, authorize, bid, book, catalog, charge, class, classify, command, conduct, control, decree, direct, dispose, enact, engage, enjoin, group, instruct, lay out, manage, marshal, neaten, ordain, organize, prescribe, put to rights, regulate, request, require, reserve, sort out, systematize, tabulate, tidy.
antonym disorder.

order[2] *n.* association, breed, brotherhood, cast, caste, class, community, company, degree, family, fraternity, genre, genus, grade, guild, hierarchy, ilk, kind, league, lodge, organization, pecking order, phylum, position, rank, sect, sisterhood, society, sodality, sort, species, status, subclass, tribe, type, union.

orderly *adj.* businesslike, controlled, cosmic, decorous, disciplined, in order, law-abiding, methodical, neat, nonviolent, peaceable, quiet, regular, restrained, ruly, scientific, shipshape, systematic, systematized, tidy, trim, well-behaved, well-organized, well-regulated.
antonym disorderly.

ordinarily *adv.* as a rule, commonly, conventionally, customarily, familiarly, generally, habitually, in general, normally, usually.

ordinary *adj.* accustomed, average, common, common-or-garden, commonplace, conventional, customary, established, everyday, fair, familiar, habitual, homespun, household, humble, humdrum, inconsequential, indifferent, inferior, mean, mediocre, modest, normal, pedestrian, plain, prevailing, prosaic, quotidian, regular, routine, run-of-the-mill, settled, simple, standard, stock, typical, undistinguished, unexceptional, unmemorable, unpretentious, unremarkable, usual, wonted, workaday.
antonyms extraordinary, special, unusual.

ordnance *n.* arms, artillery, big guns, cannon, guns, matériel, missil(e)ry, munitions, weapons.

organ *n.* agency, channel, device, element, forum, harmonium, hurdy-gurdy, implement, instrument, journal, kist of whistles, means, medium, member, mouthpiece, newspaper, paper, part, periodical, process, publication, structure, tool, unit, vehicle, viscus, voice.

organic *adj.* anatomical, animate, biological, biotic, constitutional, formal, fundamental, inherent, innate, integral, integrated, live, living, methodical, natural, ordered, organized, structural, structured, systematic, systematized.

organization *n.* arrangement, assembling, assembly,

association, body, business, chemistry, combine, company, composition, concern, confederation, configuration, conformation, consortium, constitution, construction, co-ordination, corporation, design, disposal, federation, firm, format, formation, formulation, framework, group, grouping, institution, league, make-up, management, method, methodology, organism, outfit, pattern, plan, planning, regulation, running, standardization, structure, structuring, syndicate, system, unity, whole.
antonym disorganization.

organize *v.* arrange, catalog, classify, codify, constitute, construct, co-ordinate, dispose, establish, form, frame, group, marshal, pigeonhole, regiment, run, see to, set up, shape, structure, systematize, tabulate.
antonym disorganize.

organized *adj.* arranged, neat, orderly, planned.
antonym disorganized.

orient *v.* acclimatize, accommodate, adapt, adjust, align, familiarize, get one's bearings, habituate, orientate.

orifice *n.* aperture, cleft, hole, inlet, mouth, opening, perforation, pore, rent, slit, vent.

origin *n.* ancestry, base, basis, beginning, beginnings, birth, cause, commencement, creation, dawning, derivation, descent, emergence, etymology, etymon, extraction, family, fons et origo, font, foundation, fountain, fountainhead, genesis, heritage, inauguration, inception, incunabula, launch, lineage, occasion, origination, outset, parentage, paternity, pedigree, provenance, root, roots, source, spring, start, stirps, stock, wellspring.
antonyms end, termination.

original *adj.* aboriginal, archetypal, authentic, autochthonous, commencing, creative, earliest, early, embryonic, fertile, first, first-hand, fresh, genuine, imaginative, infant, ingenious, initial, innovative, innovatory, introductory, inventive, master, new, novel, opening, primal, primary, primigenial, primitical, primitive, primordial, pristine, prototypical, resourceful, rudimentary, seminal, starting, unborrowed, unconventional, unhackneyed, unprecedented, unusual.
antonym unoriginal.
n. archetype, case, character, cure, eccentric, master, model, nonconformist, oddity, paradigm, pattern, prototype, queer fish, standard, type, weirdo.

originality *n.* boldness, cleverness, creative spirit, creativeness, creativity, daring, eccentricity, freshness, imagination, imaginativeness, individuality, ingenuity, innovation, innovativeness, inventiveness, newness, novelty, resourcefulness, singularity, unconventionality, unorthodoxy.

originate *v.* arise, be born, begin, come, commence, conceive, create, derive, develop, discover, emanate, emerge, establish, evolve, flow, form, formulate, generate, give birth to, inaugurate, initiate, institute, introduce, invent, issue, launch, pioneer, proceed, produce, result, rise, set up, spring, start, stem.
antonyms end, terminate.

originator *n.* architect, author, creator, designer, father, founder, generator, innovator, inventor, mother, pioneer, prime mover, the brains.

ornament *n.* accessory, adornment, bauble, decoration, doodah, embellishment, fallal, fandangle, figgery, flower, frill, furbelow, garnish, gaud, honor, jewel, leading light, pride, treasure, trimming, trinket.
v. adorn, beautify, bedizen, bespangle, brighten, caparison, deck, decorate, dress up, embellish, festoon, garnish, gild, grace, prettify, prink, trim.

ornamental *adj.* attractive, beautifying, decorative, embellishing, flashy, for show, grandiose, showy.

ornate *adj.* arabesque, aureate, baroque, beautiful, bedecked, busy, convoluted, decorated, elaborate, elegant, fancy, florid, flowery, fussy, ornamented, rococo, sumptuous.
antonyms austere, plain.

orthodox *adj.* accepted, approved, conformist, conventional, correct, customary, doctrinal, established, kosher, official, received, sound, traditional, true, usual, well-established.
antonym unorthodox.

oscillate *v.* fluctuate, librate, seesaw, sway, swing, vacillate, vary, vibrate, waver, wigwag, yo-yo.

ostentation *n.* affectation, boasting, display, exhibitionism, flamboyance, flashiness, flaunting, flourish, foppery, pageantry, parade, pomp, pretension, pretentiousness, show, showiness, showing off, swank, tinsel, trappings, vaunting, window-dressing.
antonym unpretentiousness.

ostentatious *adj.* aggressive, boastful, conspicuous, extravagant, fastuous, flamboyant, flash, flashy, garish, gaudy, loud, obtrusive, pretentious, self-advertising, showy, splashy, swanking, swanky, vain, vulgar.
antonyms quiet, restrained.

ostracize *v.* avoid, banish, bar, black, blackball, blacklist, boycott, cast out, cold-shoulder, cut, debar, disfellowship, exclude, excommunicate, exile, expatriate, expel, reject, segregate, send to Coventry, shun, snub.
antonyms accept, receive, reinstate, welcome.

other *adj.* added, additional, alternative, auxiliary, contrasting, different, differing, dissimilar, distinct, diverse, extra, fresh, further, more, new, remaining, separate, spare, supplementary, unrelated.

oust *v.* depose, disinherit, dislodge, displace, dispossess, drive out, eject, evict, expel, overthrow, replace, supplant, throw out, topple, turn out, unseat, upstage.
antonyms ensconce, install, reinstate, settle.

out[1] *adj.* abroad, absent, away, disclosed, elsewhere, evident, exposed, gone, manifest, not at home, outside, public, revealed.

out[2] *adj.* antiquated, banned, blacked, dated, dead,

démodé, disallowed, ended, excluded, exhausted, expired, extinguished, finished, forbidden, impossible, not on, old hat, old-fashioned, out of date, passé, square, taboo, unacceptable, unfashionable, used up. *antonyms* acceptable, fashionable, in.

outbreak *n.* burst, ebullition, epidemic, eruption, excrescence, explosion, flare-up, flash, outburst, pompholyx, rash, spasm, upsurge.

outburst *n.* access, attack, boutade, discharge, eruption, explosion, fit, fit of temper, flare-up, gale, gush, outbreak, outpouring, paroxysm, seizure, spasm, storm, surge, volley.

outcast *n.* abject, castaway, derelict, exile, leper, outsider, pariah, persona non grata, refugee, reject, reprobate, unperson, untouchable, vagabond, wretch. *antonyms* favorite, idol.

outclass *v.* beat, eclipse, excel over, leave standing, outdistance, outdo, outrank, outrival, outshine, outstrip, overshadow, put in the shade, surpass, top, transcend.

outcome *n.* after-effect, aftermath, conclusion, consequence, effect, end, end result, harvest, issue, pay-off, result, sequel, upshot.

outcry *n.* clamor, commotion, complaint, cry, exclamation, flap, howl, hue and cry, hullaballoo, noise, outburst, protest, row, scream, screech, uproar, vociferation, yell.

outdated *adj.* antediluvian, antiquated, antique, archaic, behind the times, dated, démodé, fogram, obsolescent, obsolete, old-fashioned, out of date, out of style, outmoded, passé, square, unfashionable, unmodish. *antonyms* fashionable, modern, modish.

outdo *v.* beat, best, eclipse, excel over, get the better of, outclass, outdistance, outfox, out-Herod, outmaneuver, outshine, outsmart, outstrip, outwit, overcome, surpass, top, transcend.

outer *adj.* distal, distant, exterior, external, further, outlying, outside, outward, peripheral, remote, superficial, surface. *antonyms* central, inner, mesial, proximal.

outfit[1] *n.* accouterments, clothes, costume, ensemble, equipage, equipment, garb, gear, get-up, kit, paraphernalia, rig, rig-out, set-out, suit, togs, trappings, turn-out.

v. accouter, apparel, appoint, attire, equip, fit out, fit up, furnish, kit out, provision, stock, supply, turn out.

outfit[2] *n.* business, clan, clique, company, corps, coterie, crew, firm, galère, gang, group, organization, set, set-out, set-up, squad, team, unit.

outgoing *adj.* affable, approachable, chatty, communicative, cordial, demonstrative, departing, easy, ex-, expansive, extrovert, former, friendly, genial, gregarious, informal, last, open, past, retiring, sociable, sympathetic, unreserved, warm, withdrawing. *antonyms* incoming, introvert, new, unsociable.

outgrowth *n.* consequence, effect, emanation, excrescence,

offshoot, product, protuberance, shoot, sprout, swelling.

outing *n.* excursion, expedition, jaunt, picnic, pleasure trip, ramble, spin, trip, wayzgoose.

outlandish *adj.* alien, barbarous, bizarre, eccentric, exotic, extraordinary, fantastic, foreign, grotesque, odd, outré, preposterous, queer, strange, unheard-of, weird. *antonyms* familiar, ordinary.

outlandishness *n.* bizarreness, eccentricity, exoticness, grotesqueness, oddness, peregrinity, queerness, strangeness, weirdness. *antonyms* commonplaceness, familiarity.

outlast *v.* come through, outlive, outstay, ride, survive, weather.

outlaw *n.* bandit, brigand, bushranger, cateran, dacoit, desperado, freebooter, fugitive, highwayman, marauder, outcast, outsider, pariah, proscript, robber. *v.* ban, banish, bar, condemn, debar, decitizenize, disallow, embargo, exclude, excommunicate, forbid, illegalize, illegitimate, interdict, prohibit, proscribe, waive. *antonyms* allow, legalize.

outlay *n.* cost, disbursal, disbursement, expenditure, expenses, investment, outgoings, payment, price. *antonym* income.

outlet *n.* avenue, channel, débouché, debouchment, duct, egress, emissary, exit, femerall, market, opening, orifice, outfall, release, safety valve, vent, way out. *antonyms* entry, inlet.

outline *n.* bare facts, configuration, contorno, contour, croquis, delineation, draft, drawing, figure, form, frame, framework, lay-out, lineament(s), plan, profile, recapitulation, résumé, rough, run-down, scenario, schema, shape, silhouette, skeleton, sketch, summary, synopsis, thumbnail sketch, tracing. *v.* adumbrate, delineate, draft, plan, recapitulate, rough out, sketch, summarize, trace.

outlook *n.* angle, aspect, attitude, expectations, forecast, frame of mind, future, look-out, panorama, perspective, point of view, prognosis, prospect, scene, slant, standpoint, vantage-point, view, viewpoint, views, vista.

outlying *adj.* distant, far-away, far-flung, far-off, further, outer, outlandish, peripheral, provincial, remote. *antonyms* central, inner.

outmoded *adj.* anachronistic, antediluvian, antiquated, antique, archaic, behind the times, bygone, dated, démodé, fogram, fossilized, horse-and-buggy, obsolescent, obsolete, olden, old-fashioned, old-fogeyish, out of date, outworn, passé, square, superannuated, superseded, unfashionable, unmodish, unusable. *antonyms* fashionable, fresh, modern, modish, new.

output *n.* achievement, manufacture, outturn, print-out, product, production, productivity, read-out, yield. *antonyms* input, outlay.

outrage *n.* hurt, abuse, affront, anger, atrocity, barbarism, crime, desecration, disgrace, enormity, evil, fury, grand guignol, horror, indignation, indignity, inhumanity,

injury, insult, offence, profanation, rape, ravishing, resentment, scandal, shock, violation, violence, wrath.
v. abuse, affront, astound, defile, desecrate, disgust, épater le bourgeois, incense, infuriate, injure, insult, madden, make someone's blood boil, maltreat, offend, rape, ravage, ravish, repel, scandalize, shock, violate.

outrageous *adj.* abominable, atrocious, barbaric, beastly, disgraceful, egregious, excessive, exorbitant, extortionate, extravagant, flagrant, godless, heinous, horrible, immoderate, infamous, inhuman, iniquitous, inordinate, monstrous, nefarious, offensive, preposterous, scandalous, shocking, steep, turbulent, unconscionable, ungodly, unholy, unreasonable, unspeakable, villainous, violent, wicked.
antonyms acceptable, irreproachable.

outright *adj.* absolute, arrant, categorical, complete, consummate, definite, direct, downright, flat, out-and-out, perfect, point-blank, pure, straightforward, thorough, thoroughgoing, total, uncompromising, unconditional, undeniable, unequivocal, unmitigated, unqualified, utter, wholesale.
antonyms ambiguous, indefinite, provisional.
adv. absolutely, at once, cleanly, completely, directly, explicitly, immediately, instantaneously, instantly, on the spot, openly, positively, straight away, straightaway, straightforwardly, there and then, thoroughly, unhesitatingly, without restraint.

outset *n.* beginning, commencement, early days, forthgoing, inauguration, inception, kick-off, opening, start.
antonyms conclusion, end, finish.

outside[1] *adj.* exterior, external, extramural, extraneous, extreme, outdoor, outer, outermost, outward, superficial, surface.
antonym inside.
n. cover, exterior, façade, face, front, skin, superficies, surface, topside.
antonym inside.
prep. furth, outwith, without.

outside[2] *adj.* distant, faint, infinitesimal, marginal, minute, negligible, remote, slight, slim, small, unlikely.
antonyms likely, real, substantial.

outsider *n.* alien, foreigner, immigrant, incomer, interloper, intruder, layman, misfit, newcomer, non-member, non-resident, observer, odd man out, outcast, outlander, outlier, settler, stranger.
antonyms inhabitant, insider, local, member, native, resident, specialist.

outsmart *v.* beat, best, deceive, dupe, get the better of, outfox, outmaneuver, outperform, out-think, outwit, trick.

outspoken *adj.* abrupt, blunt, candid, direct, explicit, forthright, frank, free, open, plain-spoken, pointed, Rabelaisian, rude, sharp, trenchant, unceremonious, unequivocal, unreserved.
antonyms diplomatic, tactful.

outstanding[1] *adj.* ace, arresting, celebrated, conspicuous, distinguished, egregious, eminent, excellent, exceptional, extraordinary, eye-catching, great, important, impressive, marked, memorable, notable, noteworthy, pre-eminent, prominent, prosilient, remarkable, salient, signal, singular, special, striking, superior, superlative, surpassing.
antonyms ordinary, unexceptional.

outstanding[2] *adj.* due, left, ongoing, open, over, owing, payable, pending, remaining, uncollected, undone, unpaid, unresolved, unsettled.

outward *adj.* alleged, apparent, avowed, evident, exterior, external, noticeable, observable, obvious, ostensible, outer, outside, professed, public, superficial, supposed, surface, visible.
antonyms inner, private.

outweigh *v.* cancel out, compensate for, eclipse, make up for, outbalance, overcome, override, overrule, predominate, preponderate, prevail over, take precedence over, tip the scales in favor of, transcend.

outwit *v.* beat, best, better, cheat, circumvent, deceive, defraud, dupe, get the better of, gull, make a monkey of, outfox, outmaneuver, outsmart, outthink, swindle, trick.

oval *adj.* egg-shaped, ellipsoidal, elliptical, lens-shaped, lenticular, lentiform, lentoid, obovate, obovoid, ovate, oviform, ovoid, ovoidal, vulviform.

ovation *n.* acclaim, acclamation, applause, bravos, cheering, cheers, clapping, éclat, laudation, plaudits, praises, tribute.
antonyms abuse, boos, catcalls, mockery.

over[1] *adj.* accomplished, bygone, closed, completed, concluded, done with, ended, finished, forgotten, gone, in the past, past, settled, up.

over[2] *prep.* above, exceeding, in charge of, in command of, in excess of, more than, on, on top of, superior to, upon.
adv. above, aloft, beyond, extra, in addition, in excess, left, on high, overhead, remaining, superfluous, surplus, unclaimed, unused, unwanted.

overall *adj.* all-embracing, all-inclusive, all-over, blanket, broad, complete, comprehensive, general, global, inclusive, total, umbrella.
antonyms narrow, short-term.
adv. by and large, generally speaking, in general, in the long term, on the whole.

overbearing *adj.* arrogant, autocratic, bossy, cavalier, despotic, dictatorial, dogmatic, domineering, haughty, high and mighty, high-handed, imperious, lordly, magisterial, officious, oppressive, overweening, peremptory, pompous, supercilious, superior, tyrannical.
antonyms modest, unassertive, unassuming.

overcast *adj.* black, clouded, clouded over, cloudy, dark, darkened, dismal, dreary, dull, gray, hazy, leaden, lowering, murky, somber, sunless, threatening.
antonyms bright, clear, sunny.

overcome *v.* beat, best, better, conquer, crush, defeat, expugn, lick, master, overpower, overthrow, overwhelm, prevail, rise above, subdue, subjugate, surmount, survive, triumph over, vanquish, weather, worst.
adj. affected, beaten, bowled over, broken, defeated, exhausted, overpowered, overwhelmed, speechless, swept off one's feet.

over-confident *adj.* arrogant, brash, cocksure, cocky, foolhardy, hubristic, incautious, over-optimistic, overweening, presumptuous, rash, sanguine, temerarious, uppish.
antonyms cautious, diffident.

overdo *v.* do to death, exaggerate, gild the lily, go to extremes, go too far, labor, lay it on thick, overact, overexert, overindulge, overplay, overreach, overstate, overtax, overuse, overwork.
antonyms neglect, underuse.

overdue *adj.* behind schedule, behindhand, belated, delayed, late, owing, slow, tardy, unpunctual.
antonym early.

overemphasize *v.* belabor, exaggerate, labor, overdramatize, overstress.
antonyms belittle, minimize, underplay, understate.

overflow *v.* brim over, bubble over, cover, deluge, discharge, drown, flood, inundate, pour over, shower, soak, spill, spray, submerge, surge, swamp, well over.
n. flood, inundation, overabundance, overspill, spill, superfluity, surplus.

overflowing *adj.* abounding, bountiful, brimful, copious, inundant, plenteous, plentiful, profuse, rife, superabundant, swarming, teeming, thronged.
antonyms lacking, scarce.

overhang *v.* beetle, bulge, extend, impend, jut, loom, menace, project, protrude, stick out, threaten.

overhaul[1] *v.* check, do up, examine, fix, inspect, mend, recondition, re-examine, repair, restore, service, survey.
n. check, check-up, examination, going-over, inspection, reconditioning, repair, restoration, service.

overhaul[2] *v.* gain on, outpace, outstrip, overtake, pass, pull ahead of.

overhead *adv.* above, aloft, on high, up above, upward.
antonyms below, underfoot.
adj. aerial, elevated, overhanging, roof, upper.
antonyms floor, ground, underground.

overjoyed *adj.* delighted, delirious, ecstatic, elated, enraptured, euphoric, in raptures, joyful, jubilant, on cloud nine, over the moon, rapturous, thrilled, tickled pink, transported.
antonyms disappointed, sad.

overlap *v.* coincide, cover, flap over, imbricate, overlay, overlie, shingle.

overload *v.* burden, encumber, oppress, overburden, overcharge, overtax, saddle, strain, surcharge, tax, weigh down.

overlook[1] *v.* condone, disregard, excuse, forget, forgive, ignore, let pass, let ride, miss, neglect, omit, pardon, pass, pass over, skip, slight, turn a blind eye to, wink at.
antonyms animadvert, note, notice, penalize, record, remember.

overlook[2] *v.* command a view of, face, front on to, give upon, look on to.

overly *adv.* exceedingly, excessively, immoderately, inordinately, over, too, unduly, unreasonably.
antonyms inadequately, insufficiently.

overpower *v.* beat, best, conquer, crush, defeat, floor, immobilize, master, overcome, overthrow, overwhelm, quell, subdue, subjugate, vanquish.

overpowering *adj.* compelling, convincing, extreme, forceful, insuppressible, invincible, irrefutable, irrepressible, irresistible, nauseating, oppressive, overwhelming, powerful, sickening, strong, suffocating, telling, unbearable, uncontrollable.

overrate *v.* blow up, magnify, make too much of, overestimate, overpraise, overprize, oversell, overvalue.
antonym underrate.

override *v.* abrogate, annul, cancel, countermand, disregard, ignore, nullify, outweigh, overrule, quash, rescind, reverse, ride roughshod over, set aside, supersede, trample, upset, vanquish.

overrule *v.* abrogate, annul, cancel, countermand, disallow, invalidate, outvote, override, overturn, recall, repeal, rescind, reverse, revoke, set aside, veto, vote down.
antonyms allow, approve.

overrun[1] *v.* choke, infest, inundate, invade, occupy, overflow, overgrow, overspread, overwhelm, permeate, ravage, run riot, spread over, surge over, swamp, swarm over.
antonyms desert, evacuate.

overrun[2] *v.* exceed, overdo, overshoot, overstep.

overseas *adj.* exotic, foreign, outland, outlandish, ultramarine.
antonyms domestic, home.
adv. abroad, in/to foreign climes, in/to foreign parts.
n. foreign climes, foreign parts, outland, outremer.
antonym home.

overseer *n.* boss, chief, foreman, forewoman, gaffer, headman, manager, master, super, superintendent, superior, supervisor, surveyor, workmaster, workmistress.

overshadow *v.* adumbrate, becloud, bedim, blight, cloud, darken, dim, dominate, dwarf, eclipse, excel, mar, obfuscate, obscure, outshine, outweigh, protect, put in the shade, rise above, ruin, shelter, spoil, surpass, tower above, veil.

oversight[1] *n.* administration, care, charge, control, custody, direction, guidance, handling, inspection, keeping, management, responsibility, superintendence, supervision, surveillance.

oversight[2] *n.* blunder, boob, carelessness, delinquency, error, fault, inattention, lapse, laxity, mistake, neglect, omission, slip, slip-up.

overt *adj.* apparent, avowed, evident, manifest, observable, obvious, open, patent, plain, professed, public, unconcealed, undisguised, visible.
antonyms covert, secret.

overtake *v.* befall, catch up with, come upon, draw level with, engulf, happen, hit, outdistance, outdo, outstrip, overhaul, pass, pull ahead of, strike.

overthrow *v.* abolish, beat, bring down, conquer, crush, defeat, demolish, depose, destroy, dethrone, displace, knock down, level, master, oust, overcome, overpower, overturn, overwhelm, raze, ruin, subdue, subjugate, subvert, topple, unseat, upset, vanquish.
antonyms install, reinstate.
n. bouleversement, confounding, defeat, deposition, destruction, dethronement, discomfiture, disestablishment, displacement, dispossession, downfall, end, fall, humiliation, labefactation, labefaction, ousting, prostration, rout, ruin, subjugation, subversion, suppression, undoing, unseating.

overture *n.* advance, approach, introduction, invitation, motion, move, offer, opening, (opening) gambit, opening move, prelude, proposal, proposition, signal, suggestion, tender.

overturn *v.* abolish, abrogate, annul, capsize, countermand, depose, destroy, invalidate, keel over, knock down, knock over, overbalance, overset, overthrow, quash, repeal, rescind, reverse, set aside, spill, tip over, topple, tumble, unseat, upend, upset, upturn.

overweight *adj.* ample, bulky, buxom, chubby, chunky, corpulent, fat, flabby, fleshy, gross, heavy, hefty, huge, massive, obese, outsize, plump, podgy, portly, potbellied, stout, tubby, well-padded, well-upholstered.
antonyms emaciated, skinny, thin, underweight.

overwhelm *v.* bowl over, bury, confuse, crush, cut to pieces, defeat, deluge, destroy, devastate, engulf, floor, inundate, knock for six, massacre, overcome, overpower, overrun, prostrate, rout, snow under, stagger, submerge, swamp.

overwrought *adj.* agitated, beside oneself, distracted, emotional, excited, frantic, keyed up, on edge, overcharged, overexcited, overheated, overworked, stirred, strung up, tense, uptight, worked up, wound up.
antonyms calm, cool, impassive.

owing *adj.* due, in arrears, outstanding, overdue, owed, payable, unpaid, unsettled.

own[1] *adj.* idiosyncratic, individual, inimitable, particular, personal, private.

own[2] *v.* acknowledge, admit, agree, allow, avow, concede, confess, disclose, enjoy, grant, have, hold, keep, possess, recognize, retain.

owner *n.* franklin, freeholder, holder, laird, landlady, landlord, lord, master, mistress, possessor, proprietor, proprietress, proprietrix.

P

pace *n.* celerity, clip, gait, lick, measure, momentum, motion, movement, progress, quickness, rapidity, rate, speed, step, stride, tempo, time, tread, velocity, walk.
v. count, determine, march, mark out, measure, pad, patrol, pound, step, stride, tramp, tread, walk.

pacific *adj.* appeasing, calm, complaisant, conciliatory, diplomatic, dovelike, dovish, eirenic, equable, friendly, gentle, halcyon, irenic, mild, nonbelligerent, nonviolent, pacificatory, pacifist, peaceable, peaceful, peaceloving, peacemaking, placatory, placid, propitiatory, quiet, serene, smooth, still, tranquil, unruffled.
antonyms aggressive, belligerent, contentious, pugnacious.

pacify *v.* allay, ameliorate, appease, assuage, calm, chasten, compose, conciliate, crush, humor, lull, moderate, mollify, placate, propitiate, put down, quell, quiet, repress, silence, smooth down, soften, soothe, still, subdue, tame, tranquilize.
antonyms aggravate, anger.

pack *n.* assemblage, back-pack, bale, band, boodle, bunch, bundle, burden, collection, company, crew, crowd, deck, drove, fardel, flock, galère, gang, group, haversack, herd, kit, kitbag, knapsack, load, lot, Matilda, mob, outfit, package, packet, parcel, rucksack, set, troop, truss.
v. batch, bundle, burden, charge, compact, compress, cram, crowd, empocket, fill, jam, load, mob, package, packet, press, ram, steeve, store, stow, stuff, tamp, throng, thrust, wedge.

package *n.* agreement, amalgamation, arrangement, bale, box, carton, combination, consignment, container, deal, entity, kit, pack, packet, parcel, proposal, proposition, unit, whole.
v. batch, box, pack, pack up, packet, parcel, parcel up, wrap, wrap up.

packed *adj.* brimful, brim-full, chock-a-block, chock-full, congested, cram-full, crammed, crowded, filled, full, hotching, jammed, jam-packed, overflowing, overloaded, seething, swarming.
antonyms deserted, empty.

packet[1] *n.* bag, carton, case, container, pack, package, packing, parcel, poke, wrapper, wrapping.

packet[2] *n.* bomb, bundle, fortune, king's ransom, lot, lots, mint, pile, pot, pots, pretty penny, small fortune, tidy sum.

pact *n.* agreement, alliance, arrangement, bargain, bond, cartel, compact, concord, concordat, contract, convention, covenant, deal, entente, league, protocol, treaty, understanding.
antonyms breach, disagreement, quarrel.

pad[1] *n.* block, buffer, cushion, jotter, notepad, pillow, protection, pulvillus, pulvinar, stiffening, stuffing, tablet, wad, writing-pad.
v. cushion, fill, line, pack, protect, shape, stuff, wrap.

pad[2] *n.* foot, footprint, paw, print, sole.

pad[3] *n.* apartment, flat, hang-out, home, penthouse, place, quarters, room, rooms.

pad[4] *v.* lope, move, run, step, tiptoe, tramp, tread, trudge, walk.

padding *n.* bombast, circumlocution, filling, hot air, packing, perissology, prolixity, stuffing, verbiage, verbosity, wadding, waffle, wordiness.

paddle[1] *n.* oar, scull, sweep.
v. oar, ply, propel, pull, row, scull, steer.

paddle[2] *v.* dabble, plash, slop, splash, stir, trail, wade.

pageant *n.* display, extravaganza, masque, parade, play, procession, representation, ritual, scene, show, spectacle, tableau, tableau vivant.

pain *n.* ache, affliction, aggravation, agony, anguish, annoyance, bitterness, bore, bother, burden, cramp, discomfort, distress, dole, dolor, drag, grief, gyp, headache, heartache, heartbreak, hurt, irritation, lancination, misery, nuisance, pang, pest, smart, soreness, spasm, suffering, tenderness, throb, throe, torment, torture, tribulation, trouble, twinge, vexation, woe, wretchedness.
v. afflict, aggrieve, agonize, annoy, chagrin, cut to the quick, disappoint, disquiet, distress, exasperate, gall, grieve, harass, hurt, irritate, nettle, rile, sadden, torment, torture, vex, worry, wound, wring.
antonyms gratify, please.

painful *adj.* aching, achy, afflictive, agonizing, arduous, difficult, disagreeable, distasteful, distressing, doloriferous, dolorific, excruciating, grievous, hard, harrowing, laborious, lancinating, saddening, severe, smarting, sore, tedious, tender, troublesome, trying, unpleasant, vexatious.
antonyms easy, painless.

painstaking *adj.* assiduous, careful, conscientious, dedicated, devoted, diligent, earnest, exacting, hardworking, industrious, meticulous, perfectionist, persevering, punctilious, scrupulous, sedulous, strenuous, thorough, thoroughgoing.
antonyms careless, negligent.

painting *n.* aquarelle, daubery, depiction, fresco, illustration, kakemono, landscape, miniature, mural, oil, oil-painting, picture, portrait, portraiture, portrayal, representation, scene, seascape, still life, tablature, water-color.

pair *n.* brace, combination, couple, doublet, doubleton, duad, duo, dyad, match, span, twins, two of a kind, two-some, yoke.

v. bracket, couple, join, link, marry, match, match up, mate, pair off, put together, splice, team, twin, wed, yoke.

antonyms dissever, sever.

pal *n.* amigo, buddy, chum, companion, comrade, confidant(e), crony, friend, gossip, intimate, mate, partner, side-kick, soul mate.

antonym enemy.

palatial *adj.* de luxe, grand, grandiose, illustrious, imposing, luxurious, magnificent, majestic, opulent, plush, posh, regal, spacious, splendid, stately, sumptuous, swanky.

antonyms cramped, poky.

pale *adj.* anemic, ashen, ashy, bleached, bloodless, chalky, colorless, dim, etiolated, faded, faint, feeble, inadequate, light, lily-livered, pallid, pasty, poor, sallow, thin, wan, washed-out, waxy, weak, whey-faced, white, white-livered, whitish.

antonym ruddy.

v. blanch, decrease, dim, diminish, dull, etiolate, fade, lessen, whiten.

antonyms blush, color.

pallid *adj.* anemic, ashen, ashy, bloodless, cadaverous, colorless, doughy, etiolated, insipid, lifeless, livid, pale, pasty, pasty-faced, peelie-wally, sallow, spiritless, sterile, tame, tired, uninspired, vapid, wan, waxen, waxy, whey-faced, whitish.

antonyms high-complexioned, ruddy, vigorous.

pally *adj.* affectionate, chummy, close, familiar, friendly, intimate, palsy, palsy-walsy, thick.

antonym unfriendly.

palpable *adj.* apparent, blatant, clear, concrete, conspicuous, evident, manifest, material, obvious, open, overt, patent, plain, real, solid, substantial, tangible, touchable, unmistakable, visible.

antonyms elusive, impalpable, imperceptible, intangible.

paltry *adj.* base, beggarly, contemptible, derisory, despicable, inconsiderable, insignificant, jitney, low, meager, mean, minor, miserable, negligible, pettifogging, petty, picayunish, piddling, piffling, pimping, pitiful, poor, puny, rubbishy, slight, small, sorry, tinpot, trifling, trivial, two-bit, unimportant, worthless, wretched.

antonyms significant, substantial.

pamper *v.* baby, cocker, coddle, cosset, fondle, gratify, humor, indulge, mollycoddle, mother, overindulge, pet, spoil.

antonyms ill-treat, neglect.

pamphlet *n.* booklet, broadside, brochure, chapbook, folder, leaflet, tract, tractate, treatise.

panacea *n.* catholicon, cure-all, diacatholicon, elixir, nostrum, panpharmacon, theriac, treacle.

panache *n.* brio, dash, élan, enthusiasm, flair, flamboyance, flourish, grand manner, ostentation, pizzazz, spirit, style, swagger, theatricality, verve, vigor, zest.

pang *n.* ache, agony, anguish, crick, discomfort, distress, gripe, pain, prick, spasm, stab, sting, stitch, throe, twinge, twitch, wrench.

panic *n.* agitation, alarm, consternation, dismay, fear, fright, hassle, horror, hysteria, scare, terror, tizzy, to-do.

antonyms assurance, confidence.

v. alarm, get one's knickers in a twist, go to pieces, lose one's cool, lose one's nerve, overreact, put the wind up, scare, startle, terrify, unnerve.

antonyms reassure, relax.

pant *v.* ache, blow, breathe, covet, crave, desire, flaff, gasp, hanker, heave, huff, hunger, long, palpitate, pine, puff, sigh, thirst, throb, want, wheeze, yearn, yen.

n. gasp, huff, puff, throb, wheeze.

pants *n.* briefs, drawers, knickers, panties, shorts, slacks, trews, trousers, trunks, underpants, undershorts, Y-fronts.

paper *n.* analysis, archive, article, assignment, authorization, certificate, composition, credential, critique, daily, deed, diary, dissertation, document, dossier, essay, examination, file, gazette, instrument, journal, letter, monograph, news, newspaper, notepaper, organ, rag, record, report, script, stationery, study, thesis, treatise.

papery *adj.* delicate, flimsy, fragile, frail, insubstantial, light, lightweight, paper-thin, thin, translucent.

parable *n.* allegory, apologue, exemplum, fable, homily, lesson, story.

parade *n.* array, cavalcade, ceremony, column, corso, display, exhibition, flaunting, march, motorcade, ostentation, pageant, panache, pizzazz, pomp, procession, promenade, review, show, spectacle, train, vaunting.

v. air, brandish, defile, display, exhibit, flaunt, make a show of, march, peacock, process, show, show off, strut, swagger, vaunt.

paradise *n.* bliss, City of God, delight, Eden, Elysian fields, Elysium, felicity, garden of delights, Garden of Eden, heaven, heavenly kingdom, Land o' the Leal, Olympus, Promised Land, seventh heaven, utopia, Valhalla, Zion.

antonyms Hades, hell.

paradoxical *adj.* absurd, ambiguous, baffling, conflicting, confounding, contradictory, enigmatic, equivocal, Gilbertian, illogical, impossible, improbable, incongruous, inconsistent, puzzling, self-contradictory.

paragon *n.* apotheosis, archetype, crème de la crème, criterion, cynosure, epitome, exemplar, ideal, jewel, masterpiece, model, non(e)such, nonpareil, paradigm, pattern, prototype, quintessence, standard, the bee's knees.

parallel *adj.* akin, aligned, alongside, analogous, co-extensive, collateral, connate, correspondent, corresponding, equidistant, homologous, like, matching, resembling, similar, uniform.

antonyms divergent, separate.

n. analog, analogy, comparison, corollary, correlation, correspondence, counterpart, duplicate, equal, equivalent, homologue, likeness, match, parallelism, resemblance, similarity, twin.

v. agree, compare, conform, correlate, correspond, duplicate, emulate, equal, match.

antonyms diverge, separate.

paramount *adj.* capital, cardinal, chief, dominant, eminent, first, foremost, highest, main, outstanding, predominant, pre-eminent, premier, primary, prime, principal, superior, supreme, topmost, top-rank.

antonyms inferior, last, lowest.

paraphernalia *n.* accessories, accouterments, apparatus, appurtenances, baggage, belongings, bits and pieces, clobber, clutter, effects, equipage, equipment, gear, impedimenta, material, odds and ends, stuff, tackle, things, trappings, traps.

parasite *n.* bloodsucker, cadger, endophyte, endozoon, entozoon, epiphyte, epizoan, epizoon, free-loader, hanger-on, leech, lick-trencher, scrounger, sponge, sponger, sucker.

parcel *n.* band, batch, bunch, bundle, carton, collection, company, crew, crowd, da(w)k, gang, group, lot, pack, package, packet, plot, portion, property, quantity, set, tract.

v. bundle, collect, pack, package, tie up, wrap.

parched *adj.* arid, dehydrated, dried up, drouthy, dry, scorched, shriveled, thirsty, waterless, withered.

pardon *v.* absolve, acquit, amnesty, condone, emancipate, exculpate, excuse, exonerate, forgive, free, let off, liberate, overlook, release, remit, reprieve, respite, vindicate.

n. absolution, acquittal, allowance, amnesty, compassion, condonation, discharge, excuse, exoneration, forgiveness, grace, humanity, indulgence, mercy, release, remission, reprieval, reprieve.

pare *v.* clip, crop, cut, cut back, decrease, diminish, dock, flaught, float, lop, peel, prune, reduce, retrench, shave, shear, skin, skive, trim.

parent *n.* architect, author, begetter, cause, creator, father, forerunner, generant, genetrix, genitor, guardian, mother, origin, originator, procreator, progenitor, progenitress, progenitrix, prototype, root, sire, source.

pariah *n.* black sheep, castaway, exile, Ishmael, leper, outcast, outlaw, undesirable, unperson, untouchable.

parity *n.* affinity, agreement, analogy, conformity, congruence, congruity, consistency, consonance, correspondence, equality, equivalence, likeness, par, parallelism, resemblance, sameness, semblance, similarity, similitude, uniformity, unity.

parley *n.* colloquy, confab, conference, council, deliberation, dialogue, discussion, get-together, meeting, negotiation, palaver, powwow, talk(s), tête-à-tête.

v. confabulate, confer, consult, deliberate, discuss, get together, negotiate, palaver, powwow, speak, talk.

parody *n.* burlesque, caricature, imitation, lampoon, mimicry, pasquinade, satire, send-up, skit, spoof, take-off.

v. burlesque, caricature, lampoon, mimic, pasquinade, satirize, send up, spoof, take off, travesty.

paroxysm *n.* attack, convulsion, eruption, explosion, fit, flare-up, outbreak, outburst, seizure, spasm, tantrum.

parry *v.* avert, avoid, block, circumvent, deflect, divert, dodge, duck, evade, fence, fend off, field, forestall, obviate, rebuff, repel, repulse, shun, sidestep, stave off, ward off.

parsimonious *adj.* cheese-paring, close, close-fisted, close-handed, frugal, grasping, mean, mingy, miserable, miserly, money-grubbing, niggardly, penny-pinching, penny-wise, penurious, saving, scrimpy, sparing, stingy, stinting, tight-fisted.

antonyms generous, liberal, open-handed.

part *n.* airt, area, behalf, bit, branch, business, capacity, cause, character, charge, clause, complement, component, concern, constituent, department, district, division, duty, element, faction, factor, fraction, fragment, function, heft, ingredient, interest, involvement, limb, lines, lot, member, module, neck of the woods, neighborhood, office, organ, particle, partwork, party, piece, place, portion, quarter, region, responsibility, role, scrap, section, sector, segment, share, side, slice, task, territory, tip of the iceberg, unit, vicinity, work.

v. break, break up, cleave, come apart, depart, detach, disband, disconnect, disjoin, dismantle, disperse, disunite, divide, go, go away, leave, part company, quit, rend, scatter, separate, sever, split, split up, sunder, take leave, tear, withdraw.

partake *v.* be involved, engage, enter, participate, share, take part.

partial[1] *adj.* fragmentary, imperfect, incomplete, inexhaustive, limited, part, uncompleted, unfinished.

antonyms complete, exhaustive, total.

partial[2] *adj.* affected, biased, colored, discriminatory, exparte, influenced, interested, one-sided, partisan, predisposed, prejudiced, tendentious, unfair, unjust.

antonyms disinterested, fair, unbiased.

partiality *n.* affinity, bias, discrimination, favoritism, fondness, inclination, liking, love, partisanship, penchant, predilection, predisposition, preference, prejudice, proclivity, propensity, soft spot, taste, weakness.

antonyms dislike, justice.

partially *adv.* fractionally, in part, incompletely, partly, somewhat.

participant *n.* associate, contributor, co-operator, helper, member, partaker, participator, party, shareholder, worker.

participation *n.* a piece of the action, assistance, contribution, co-operation, involvement, mucking in, partaking, partnership, sharing.

particle *n.* atom, atom(y), bit, corn, crumb, drop, electron, grain, iota, jot, kaon, mite, molecule, morsel, mote, neutrino, neutron, piece, pion, proton, scrap, shred, sliver, smidgen, speck, tittle, whit.

particular[1] *adj.* blow-by-blow, circumstantial, detailed, distinct, especial, exact, exceptional, express, itemized, marked, minute, notable, noteworthy, painstaking, peculiar, precise, remarkable, selective, several, singular, special, specific, thorough, uncommon, unique, unusual, very.
antonym general.
n. circumstance, detail, fact, feature, item, point, specific, specification.

particular[2] *adj.* choosy, critical, dainty, demanding, discriminating, exacting, fastidious, finical, finicky, fussy, meticulous, nice, overnice, perjink, pernickety, picky.
antonym casual.

particularity *n.* accuracy, carefulness, characteristic, choosiness, circumstance, detail, distinctiveness, fact, fastidiousness, feature, fussiness, idiosyncrasy, individuality, instance, item, mannerism, meticulousness, peculiarity, point, precision, property, quirk, singularity, thoroughness, trait, uniqueness.

particularly *adv.* decidedly, distinctly, especially, exceptionally, explicitly, expressly, extraordinarily, in particular, markedly, notably, noticeably, outstandingly, peculiarly, remarkably, singularly, specifically, surprisingly, uncommonly, unusually.

partisan *n.* adherent, backer, champion, devotee, disciple, factionary, factionist, follower, guerrilla, irregular, partyman, stalwart, supporter, upholder, votary.
adj. biased, discriminatory, factional, guerrilla, interested, irregular, one-sided, partial, predisposed, prejudiced, resistance, sectarian, tendentious, underground.

partisanship *n.* bias, factionalism, fanaticism, partiality, partyism, sectarianism.

partition[1] *n.* allocation, allotment, apportionment, distribution, dividing, division, part, portion, rationing, out, section, segregation, separation, severance, share, splitting.
v. allocate, allot, apportion, assign, divide, parcel out, portion, section, segment, separate, share, split up, subdivide.

partition[2] *n.* barrier, diaphragm, dissepiment, divider, membrane, room-divider, screen, septum, traverse, wall.
v. bar, divide, fence off, screen, separate, wall off.

partly *adv.* halfway, in part, incompletely, moderately, partially, relatively, slightly, somewhat, to a certain degree, to a certain extent, up to a point.
antonyms completely, in toto, totally.

partner *n.* accomplice, ally, associate, bedfellow, butty, collaborator, colleague, companion, comrade, confederate, consort, co-partner, gigolo, helper, helpmate, helpmeet, husband, mate, participant, side-kick, spouse, team-mate, wife.

party[1] *n.* assembly, at-home, bash, beanfeast, beano, ceilidh, celebration, do, drag, drum, entertainment, -fest, festivity, function, gathering, get-together, hooley,

hoot(e)nanny, housewarming, hurricane, jollification, knees-up, rave-up, reception, rout, shindig, social, soirée, thrash.

party[2] *n.* alliance, association, band, body, bunch, cabal, caucus, clique, coalition, combination, company, confederacy, contingent, contractor, coterie, crew, defendant, detachment, faction, gang, gathering, group, grouping, individual, junto, league, litigant, participant, person, plaintiff, set, side, squad, team, unit.

pass[1] *v.* accept, adopt, answer, approve, authorize, beat, befall, beguile, blow over, cease, come up, come up to scratch, convey, declare, decree, defecate, delate, deliver, depart, develop, devote, die, die away, disappear, discharge, disregard, dissolve, do, dwindle, ebb, elapse, eliminate, employ, empty, enact, end, establish, evacuate, evaporate, exceed, excel, exchange, excrete, expel, experience, expire, express, fade, fall out, fill, flow, get through, give, go, go beyond, go by, go past, graduate, hand, happen, ignore, impersonate, lapse, leave, legislate, melt away, miss, move, neglect, occupy, occur, omit, ordain, outdistance, outdo, outstrip, overlook, overtake, pass muster, proceed, pronounce, qualify, ratify, roll, run, sanction, send, serve as, skip, spend, succeed, suffer, suffice, suit, surmount, surpass, take place, terminate, throw, transcend, transfer, transmit, undergo, utter, validate, vanish, void, waft, wane, while away.

pass[2] *n.* advances, approach, authorization, chit, condition, feint, identification, jab, juncture, laissez-passer, license, lunge, overture, passport, permission, permit, pinch, play, plight, predicament, proposition, push, safe-conduct, situation, stage, state, state of affairs, straits, suggestion, swing, thrust, ticket, warrant.

pass[3] *n.* canyon, col, defile, gap, gorge, nek, ravine.

passable *adj.* acceptable, adequate, admissible, all right, allowable, average, clear, fair, mediocre, middling, moderate, navigable, OK, open, ordinary, presentable, so-so, tolerable, traversable, unblocked, unexceptional, unobstructed.

passage *n.* acceptance, access, adit, advance, allowance, authorization, avenue, change, channel, citation, clause, close, communication, conduit, conversion, corridor, course, crossing, deambulatory, doorway, drift, dromos, duct, enactment, entrance, entrance hall, establishment, excerpt, exit, extract, fistula, flow, freedom, gallery, gut, hall, hallway, journey, lane, legalization, legislation, lobby, motion, movement, opening, orifice, paragraph, part, passageway, passing, path, permission, piece, portion, progress, progression, quotation, ratification, reading, right, road, route, safe-conduct, section, sentence, spiracle, text, thorough, thoroughfare, tour, transit, transition, trek, trip, vent, verse, vestibule, visa, vista, voyage, warrant, way.

passenger *n.* commuter, fare, hitch-hiker, pillionist, pillion-rider, rider, traveler.

passer-by 270 patronize

passer-by *n.* bystander, looker-on, onlooker, spectator, witness.

passion *n.* adoration, affection, anger, animation, ardor, attachment, avidity, bug, chafe, concupiscence, craving, craze, dander, desire, eagerness, emotion, enthusiasm, excitement, fancy, fascination, feeling, fervency, fervor, fire, fit, flare-up, fondness, frenzy, fury, heat, idol, indignation, infatuation, intensity, ire, itch, joy, keenness, love, lust, mania, monomania, obsession, outburst, paroxysm, rage, rapture, resentment, spirit, storm, transport, vehemence, verve, vivacity, warmth, wax, wrath, zeal, zest.
antonyms calm, coolness, self-possession.

passionate *adj.* amorous, animated, ardent, aroused, choleric, desirous, eager, emotional, enthusiastic, erotic, excitable, excited, fervent, fervid, fierce, fiery, frenzied, heart-felt, hot, hot-headed, hot-tempered, impassioned, impetuous, impulsive, incensed, inflamed, inspirited, intense, irascible, irate, irritable, loving, lustful, peppery, quick-tempered, sensual, sexy, stormy, strong, sultry, tempestuous, torrid, vehement, violent, wanton, warm, wild, zealous.
antonyms frigid, laid-back, phlegmatic.

passive *adj.* acquiescent, compliant, docile, enduring, impassive, inactive, indifferent, indolent, inert, lifeless, long-suffering, non-participating, non-violent, patient, quiescent, receptive, resigned, submissive, supine, unaffected, unassertive, uninvolved, unresisting.
antonyms active, involved, lively.

password *n.* countersign, open sesame, parole, shibboleth, signal, watchword.

past *adj.* accomplished, ancient, bygone, completed, defunct, done, early, elapsed, ended, erstwhile, extinct, finished, foregone, forgotten, former, gone, gone by, late, long-ago, no more, olden, over, over and done with, preceding, previous, prior, quondam, recent, spent, vanished.
n. antiquity, auld lang syne, background, days of yore, dossier, experience, former times, good old days, history, life, old times, olden days, track record, yesteryear.

pastiche *n.* blend, composition, farrago, gallimaufry, hotch-potch, medley, mélange, miscellany, mixture, motley, ollapodrida, patchwork, pot-pourri.

pastime *n.* activity, amusement, avocation, distraction, diversion, divertisement, entertainment, game, hobby, play, recreation, relaxation, sport.
antonyms business, employment, occupation, vocation, work.

pat *v.* caress, clap, dab, fondle, pet, rub, slap, stroke, tap, touch.
n. cake, caress, clap, dab, lump, piece, portion, slap, stroke, tap, touch.
adv. exactly, faultlessly, flawlessly, fluently, glibly, just right, off pat, opportunely, perfectly, plumb, precisely, relevantly, seasonably.
antonyms imprecisely, wrongly.

adj. apposite, appropriate, apropos, apt, automatic, easy, facile, felicitous, fitting, glib, happy, neat, pertinent, ready, relevant, right, simplistic, slick, smooth, spot-on, suitable, to the point, well-chosen.
antonyms irrelevant, unsuitable.

patch *n.* area, bit, clout, ground, land, lot, parcel, piece, plot, scrap, shred, spot, stretch, tract.
v. botch, cover, fix, mend, reinforce, repair, sew up, stitch, vamp.

patent *adj.* apparent, blatant, clear, clear-cut, conspicuous, downright, evident, explicit, flagrant, glaring, indisputable, manifest, obvious, open, ostensible, overt, palpable, transparent, unconcealed, unequivocal, unmistakable.
antonyms hidden, opaque.
n. certificate, copyright, invention, license, privilege, registered trademark.

path *n.* avenue, course, direction, footpath, footway, gate, pad, passage, pathway, procedure, ridgeway, road, route, towpath, track, trail, walk, walkway, way.

pathetic *adj.* affecting, contemptible, crummy, deplorable, dismal-looking, distressing, feeble, heartbreaking, heart-rending, inadequate, lamentable, meager, melting, miserable, moving, paltry, petty, piteous, pitiable, pitiful, plaintive, poignant, poor, puny, rubbishy, sad, sorry, tender, touching, trashy, uninteresting, useless, woebegone, woeful, worthless.
antonyms admirable, cheerful.

patience *n.* calmness, composure, constancy, cool, diligence, endurance, equanimity, forbearance, fortitude, long-suffering, perseverance, persistence, resignation, restraint, self-control, serenity, stoicism, submission, sufferance, tolerable, toleration.
antonyms impatience, intolerance.

patient[1] *adj.* accommodating, calm, composed, enduring, even-tempered, forbearing, forgiving, indulgent, lenient, long-suffering, mild, persevering, persistent, philosophical, quiet, resigned, restrained, self-controlled, self-possessed, serene, stoical, submissive, tolerant, uncomplaining, understanding, untiring.
antonyms impatient, intolerant.

patient[2] *n.* case, client, invalid, sufferer.

patriotism *n.* chauvinism, flag-waving, jingoism, loyalty, nationalism.

patrol *n.* defence, garrison, guard, guarding, policing, protecting, roundvigilance, sentinel, surveillance, watch, watching, watchman.
v. cruise, go the rounds, guard, inspect, perambulate, police, range, tour.

patron *n.* advocate, backer, benefactor, buyer, champion, client, customer, defender, fautor, frequenter, friend, guardian, habitué, helper, Maecenas, partisan, philanthropist, protector, regular, shopper, sponsor, subscriber, supporter, sympathizer.

patronize *v.* assist, back, befriend, encourage, foster, frequent, fund, habituate, help, humor, maintain, promote, shop at, sponsor, support, talk down to.

pattern *n.* archetype, arrangement, criterion, cynosure, decoration, delineation, design, device, diagram, examplar, example, figuration, figure, Gestalt, guide, instructions, kind, method, model, motif, norm, order, orderliness, original, ornament, ornamentation, paradigm, paragon, plan, prototype, sample, sequence, shape, sort, specimen, standard, stencil, style, system, template, type, variety.

v. copy, decorate, design, emulate, follow, form, imitate, match, model, mold, order, shape, stencil, style, trim.

paunchy *adj.* adipose, corpulent, fat, podgy, portly, pot-bellied, pudgy, rotund, tubby.

pause *v.* break, cease, cut, delay, desist, discontinue, halt, hesitate, interrupt, rest, take a break, take a breather, take five, wait, waver.

n. abatement, break, breather, caesura, cessation, delay, discontinuance, dwell, gap, halt, hesitation, interlude, intermission, interruption, interval, let-up, lull, respite, rest, slackening, stay, stoppage, suspension, wait.

pawn[1] *n.* cat's-paw, creature, dupe, instrument, plaything, puppet, stooge, tool, toy.

pawn[2] *v.* deposit, dip, gage, hazard, hock, impawn, impignorate, lay in lavender, mortgage, pledge, pop, stake, wager.

n. hostage, security.

pay *v.* ante, benefit, bestow, bring in, clear, compensate, cough up, disburse, discharge, extend, foot, get even with, give, grant, honor, indemnify, liquidate, meet, offer, pay out, present, produce, proffer, profit, punish, reciprocate, recompense, reimburse, remit, remunerate, render, repay, requite, return, reward, serve, settle, square, square up, yield.

n. allowance, compensation, consideration, earnings, emoluments, fee, hire, honorarium, income, payment, recompense, reimbursement, remuneration, reward, salary, stipend, takings, wages.

payable *adj.* due, in arrears, mature, obligatory, outstanding, owed, owing, receivable, unpaid.

peace *n.* accord, agreement, amity, armistice, calm, calmness, cease-fire, composure, conciliation, concord, contentment, frith, harmony, hush, pacification, pax, peacefulness, placidity, quiet, quietude, relaxation, repose, rest, serenity, silence, stillness, tranquility, treaty, truce.

antonyms disagreement, disturbance, war

peace studies irenology.

peaceable *adj.* amiable, amicable, compatible, conciliatory, douce, dovish, easy-going, friendly, gentle, inoffensive, mild, non-belligerent, pacific, peaceful, peace-loving, placid, unwarlike.

antonyms belligerent, offensive.

peaceful *adj.* amicable, at peace, becalmed, calm, conciliatory, friendly, gentle, halcyon, harmonious, irenic (eirenic), non-violent, pacific, peaceable, peace-loving, placatory, placid, quiet, restful, serene, still, tranquil, unagitated, undisturbed, unruffled, untroubled, unwarlike.

antonyms disturbed, noisy, troubled.

peak *n.* acme, aiguille, apex, apogee, brow, climax, crest, crown, culmination, cuspid, high point, maximum, ne plus ultra, pinnacle, point, summit, tip, top, visor, zenith.

antonyms nadir, trough.

v. climax, come to a head, culminate, spire, tower.

peccadillo *n.* boob, delinquency, error, fault, indiscretion, infraction, lapse, misdeed, misdemeanor, slip, slip-up.

peculiar[1] *adj.* abnormal, bizarre, curious, eccentric, exceptional, extraordinary, far-out, freakish, funky, funny, odd, offbeat, outlandish, out-of-the-way, quaint, queer, singular, strange, uncommon, unconventional, unusual, wayout, weird.

antonyms normal, ordinary.

peculiar[2] *adj.* appropriate, characteristic, discriminative, distinct, distinctive, distinguishing, endemic, idiosyncratic, individual, local, particular, personal, private, quintessential, restricted, special, specific, unique.

antonyms general, uncharacteristic.

peculiarity *n.* abnormality, attribute, bizarreness, characteristic, distinctiveness, eccentricity, exception, feature, foible, freakishness, idiosyncrasy, kink, mannerism, mark, oddity, particularity, property, quality, queerness, quirk, singularity, specialty, trait, whimsicality.

pedantic *adj.* abstruse, academic, bookish, caviling, didactic, donnish, erudite, finical, formal, fussy, hair-splitting, learned, nit-picking, particular, pedagogic, perfectionist, pompous, precise, punctilious, scholastic, schoolmasterly, sententious, stilted.

antonyms casual, imprecise, informal.

peddle *v.* dilly-dally, flog, hawk, huckster, idle, loiter, market, piddle, push, retail, sell, tout, trade, trifle, vend.

pedestrian *n.* footslogger, foot-traveler, voetganger, walker.

adj. banal, boring, commonplace, dull, flat, humdrum, indifferent, mediocre, mundane, ordinary, plodding, prosaic, run-of-the-mill, stodgy, tolerable, unimaginative, uninspired, uninteresting.

antonyms bright, brilliant, exciting, imaginative.

pedigree *n.* ancestry, blood, breed, derivation, descent, dynasty, extraction, family, family tree, genealogy, heritage, line, lineage, parentage, race, stemma, stirps, stock, succession.

peek *v.* glance, keek, look, peep, peer, spy.

n. blink, dekko, gander, glance, glimpse, keek, look, look-see, peep.

peel *v.* decorticate, denude, desquamate, flake (off), pare, scale, skin, strip (off), undress.

n. epicarp, exocarp, integument, peeling, rind, skin, zest.

peep *v.* blink, emerge, glimpse, issue, keek, peek, peer. *n.* blink, dekko, gander, glim, glimpse, keek, look, look-see, peek.

peer[1] *v.* appear, blink, emerge, examine, gaze, inspect, peep, scan, scrutinize, snoop, spy, squint.

peer[2] *n.* aristocrat, baron, count, duke, earl, lord, marquess, marquis, noble, nobleman, thane, viscount.

peer[3] *n.* compeer, counterpart, equal, equipollent, equivalent, fellow, like, match.

peevish *adj.* acrimonious, cantankerous, captious, childish, churlish, crabbed, cross, crotchety, crusty, fractious, franzy, fretful, grumpy, hipped, ill-natured, ill-tempered, irritable, miffy, perverse, pettish, petulant, querulous, ratty, short-tempered, snappy, splenetic, sulky, sullen, surly, testy, touchy, waspish. *antonym* good-tempered.

peevishness *n.* acrimony, captiousness, ill-temper, irritability, perversity, pet, petulance, pique, protervity, querulousness, testiness.

peg *v.* attach, control, fasten, fix, freeze, insert, join, limit, mark, pierce, score, secure, set, stabilize. *n.* dowel, hook, knob, marker, pin, post, stake, thole(-pin), toggle.

pejorative *adj.* bad, belittling, condemnatory, damning, debasing, deprecatory, depreciatory, derogatory, detractive, detractory, disparaging, negative, slighting, uncomplimentary, unflattering, unpleasant. *antonyms* complimentary, laudatory.

pen *n.* cage, coop, crib, cru(i)ve, enclosure, fold, hutch, stall, sty. *v.* cage, confine, coop, corral, crib, enclose, fence, hedge, hem in, hurdle, mew (up), shut up.

penalize *v.* amerce, correct, disadvantage, discipline, handicap, mulct, punish. *antonym* reward.

penalty *n.* amende, amercement, disadvantage, fine, forfeit, forfeiture, handicap, mulct, price, punishment, retribution. *antonym* reward.

penchant *n.* affinity, bent, bias, disposition, fondness, inclination, leaning, liking, partiality, predilection, predisposition, preference, proclivity, proneness, propensity, soft spot, taste, tendency, turn. *antonym* dislike.

penetrate *v.* affect, bore, come across, come home, comprehend, decipher, diffuse, discern, enter, fathom, get through to, get to the bottom of, grasp, impress, infiltrate, perforate, permeate, pervade, pierce, prick, probe, seep, sink, stab, strike, suffuse, touch, understand, unravel.

penetrating *adj.* acute, astute, biting, carrying, critical, discerning, discriminating, harsh, incisive, intelligent, intrusive, keen, observant, penetrative, perceptive, percipient, perspicacious, pervasive, piercing, pro-

found, pungent, quick, sagacious, searching, sharp, sharp-witted, shrewd, shrill, stinging, strong. *antonyms* gentle, obtuse, soft.

peninsula *n.* cape, chersonese, doab, mull, point, tongue.

penitent *adj.* abject, apologetic, atoning, conscience-stricken, contrite, humble, in sackcloth and ashes, regretful, remorseful, repentant, rueful, sorrowful, sorry. *antonym* unrepentant.

penniless *adj.* bankrupt, broke, bust(ed), cleaned out, destitute, flat broke, impecunious, impoverished, indigent, moneyless, necessitous, needy, obolary, on one's uppers, on the rocks, penurious, poor, poverty-stricken, ruined, skint, stony-broke, strapped. *antonyms* rich, wealthy.

pensive *adj.* absent-minded, absorbed, cogitative, contemplative, dreamy, grave, meditative, melancholy, musing, preoccupied, reflective, ruminative, serious, sober, solemn, thoughtful, wistful.

penurious *adj.* beggarly, bust(ed), cheeseparing, close, close-fisted, deficient, destitute, flat broke, frugal, grudging, impecunious, impoverished, inadequate, indigent, meager, mean, miserable, miserly, near, needy, niggardly, obolary, paltry, parsimonious, penniless, poor, poverty-stricken, scanty, skimping, stingy, tight-fisted, ungenerous. *antonyms* generous, wealthy.

penury *n.* beggary, dearth, deficiency, destitution, indigence, lack, mendicancy, mendicity, need, paucity, pauperism, poverty, privation, scantiness, scarcity, shortage, sparseness, straitened circumstances, straits, want. *antonym* prosperity.

people *n.* citizens, clan, commonalty, community, crowd, demos, family, folk, general public, gens, grass roots, hoi polloi, human beings, humanity, humans, inhabitants, mankind, many-headed beast, many-headed monster, masses, mob, mortals, multitude, nation, persons, plebs, populace, population, public, punters, rabble, race, rank and file, the herd, the million, tribe. *v.* colonize, inhabit, occupy, populate, settle, tenant.

perceive *v.* appreciate, apprehend, be aware of, behold, catch, comprehend, conclude, deduce, descry, discern, discover, distinguish, espy, feel, gather, get, grasp, intuit, know, learn, make out, note, observe, realize, recognize, remark, see, sense, spot, understand.

perceptible *adj.* apparent, appreciable, clear, conspicuous, detectable, discernible, distinct, distinguishable, evident, noticeable, observable, obvious, palpable, perceivable, recognizable, salient, tangible, visible. *antonym* imperceptible.

perception *n.* apprehension, awareness, conception, consciousness, discernment, feeling, grasp, idea, impression, insight, intellection, notion, observation, recognition, sensation, sense, taste, understanding, uptake.

perceptive *adj.* able to see through a millstone, acute,

alert, astute, aware, discerning, insightful, observant, penetrating, percipient, perspicacious, quick, responsive, sagacious, sapient, sensitive, sharp.
antonym unobservant.

percipient *adj.* alert, alive, astute, aware, discerning, discriminating, intelligent, judicious, knowing, penetrating, perceptive, perspicacious, quick-witted, sharp, wide-awake.
antonyms obtuse, unaware.

perfect *adj.* absolute, accomplished, accurate, adept, blameless, close, complete, completed, consummate, copybook, correct, entire, exact, excellent, experienced, expert, faithful, faultless, finished, flawless, full, ideal, immaculate, impeccable, irreproachable, masterly, model, polished, practiced, precise, pure, right, sheer, skilful, skilled, splendid, spotless, spot-on, strict, sublime, superb, superlative, supreme, true, unadulterated, unalloyed, unblemished, unerring, unimpeachable, unmarred, unmitigated, untarnished, utter, whole.
antonyms flawed, imperfect.
v. accomplish, achieve, carry out, complete, consummate, effect, elaborate, finish, fulfil, perfectionate, perform, realize, refine.

perfection *n.* accomplishment, achievement, acme, completeness, completion, consummation, crown, evolution, exactness, excellence, exquisiteness, flawlessness, fulfilment, ideal, integrity, maturity, nonpareil, paragon, perfectness, pinnacle, precision, purity, realization, sublimity, superiority, wholeness.
antonyms flaw, imperfection.

perfectly *adv.* absolutely, admirably, altogether, completely, consummately, entirely, exquisitely, faultlessly, flawlessly, fully, ideally, impeccably, incomparably, irreproachably, quite, superbly, superlatively, supremely, thoroughly, to perfection, totally, unimpeachably, utterly, wholly, wonderfully.
antonyms imperfectly, partially.

perform *v.* accomplish, achieve, act, appear as, bring about, bring off, carry out, complete, depict, discharge, do, effect, enact, execute, fulfil, function, functionate, manage, observe, play, present, produce, pull off, put on, render, represent, satisfy, stage, transact, work.

performance *n.* accomplishment, account, achievement, act, acting, action, appearance, behavior, bother, business, carrying out, carry-on, completion, conduct, consummation, discharge, efficiency, execution, exhibition, exploit, feat, fulfilment, functioning, fuss, gig, implementation, interpretation, melodrama, operation, play, portrayal, practice, presentation, production, rendition, representation, rigmarole, running, show, to-do, work, working.

performer *n.* actor, actress, artiste, moke, mummer, play-actor, player, Thespian, trouper.

perfume *n.* aroma, attar, balm, balminess, bouquet, cologne, essence, fragrance, incense, odor, redolence, scent, smell, sweetness, toilet water.

perfunctory *adj.* automatic, brief, careless, cursory, heedless, hurried, inattentive, indifferent, mechanical, negligent, offhand, routine, sketchy, slipshod, slovenly, stereo-typed, superficial, wooden.
antonym cordial.

perhaps *adv.* conceivably, feasibly, happen, maybe, mayhap, peradventure, perchance, possibly, you never know.

peril *n.* danger, exposure, hazard, imperilment, insecurity, jeopardy, menace, pitfall, risk, threat, uncertainty, vulnerability.
antonyms safety, security.

perilous *adj.* chancy, dangerous, desperate, dicey, difficult, dire, exposed, hairy, hazardous, menacing, parlous, precarious, risky, threatening, unsafe, unsure, vulnerable.
antonyms safe, secure.

period[1] *n.* age, course, cycle, date, days, end, eon, epoch, era, generation, interval, season, space, span, spell, stage, stint, stop, stretch, term, time, turn, while, years.

period[2] *n.* menses, menstrual flow, menstruation, monthlies, the curse.

periodical *n.* gazette, journal, magazine, monthly, organ, paper, publication, quarterly, review, serial, weekly.

perish *v.* collapse, croak, crumble, decay, decline, decompose, decrease, die, disappear, disintegrate, end, expire, fall, molder, pass away, rot, vanish, waste, wither.

perishable *adj.* biodegradable, corruptible, decomposable, destructible, fast-decaying, fast-deteriorating, short-lived, unstable.

perjury *n.* false oath, false statement, false swearing, false witness, falsification, forswearing, mendacity.

permanent *adj.* abiding, constant, durable, enduring, everlasting, fixed, immutable, imperishable, indestructible, ineffaceable, ineradicable, inerasable, invariable, lasting, long-lasting, perennial, perpetual, persistent, stable, standing, steadfast, unchanging, unfading.
antonyms ephemeral, fleeting, temporary.

permeate *v.* charge, fill, filter through, imbue, impenetrate, impregnate, infiltrate, interfuse, interpenetrate, pass through, penetrate, percolate, pervade, saturate, seep through, soak through.

permissible *adj.* acceptable, admissible, all right, allowable, allowed, authorized, kosher, lawful, leal, legit, legitimate, licit, OK, permitted, proper, sanctioned.
antonym prohibited.

permission *n.* allowance, approval, assent, authorization, consent, dispensation, freedom, go-ahead, green light, imprimatur, indult, leave, liberty, license, permit, sanction, sufferance.
antonym prohibition.

permissive *adj.* acquiescent, complaisant, easy-going, forbearing, free, indulgent, latitudinarian, lax, lenient, liberal, open-minded, overindulgent, tolerant.
antonym strict.

permit *v.* admit, agree, allow, authorize, consent, empower, enable, endorse, endure, give leave, grant, let, warrant.
antonym prohibit.
n. authorization, carnet, liberty, license, pass, passport, permission, sanction, visa, warrant. *antonym* prohibition.

perpetrate *v.* carry out, commit, do, effect, enact, execute, inflict, perform, practice, wreak.

perpetual *adj.* abiding, ceaseless, constant, continual, continuous, deathless, endless, enduring, eternal, everlasting, immortal, incessant, infinite, interminable, lasting, never-ending, never-failing, perennial, permanent, persistent, recurrent, repeated, sempiternal, unceasing, unchanging, undying, unending, unfailing, unflagging, uninterrupted, unremitting, unvarying.
antonyms ephemeral, intermittent, transient.

perpetuate *v.* commemorate, continue, eternalize, immortalize, keep alive, keep up, maintain, preserve, protract, sustain.

perplex *v.* baffle, befuddle, beset, bewilder, complicate, confound, confuse, dumbfound, embrangle, encumber, entangle, gravel, hobble, involve, jumble, mix up, muddle, mystify, nonplus, pother, pudder, puzzle, stump, tangle, thicken, throw.

perplexed *adj.* at a loss, baffled, bamboozled, bewildered, confounded, disconcerted, fuddled, muddled, mystified, puzzled, worried.

perplexing *adj.* amazing, baffling, bewildering, complex, complicated, confusing, difficult, distractive, enigmatic, hard, inexplicable, intricate, involved, knotty, labyrinthine, mysterious, mystifying, paradoxical, puzzling, strange, taxing, thorny, unaccountable, vexatious, weird.
antonyms easy, simple.

persecute *v.* afflict, annoy, badger, bait, bother, castigate, crucify, distress, dragoon, harass, haze, hound, hunt, ill-treat, injure, maltreat, martyr, molest, oppress, pester, pursue, tease, torment, torture, tyrannize, vex, victimize, worry.
antonyms accommodate, humor, indulge, pamper.

persevere *v.* adhere, carry on, continue, endure, go on, hang on, hold fast, hold on, keep going, persist, plug away, pursue, remain, soldier on, stand firm, stick at.
antonyms desist, discontinue, give up, stop.

persist *v.* abide, carry on, continue, endure, insist, keep at it, last, linger, perdure, persevere, remain, stand fast, stand firm.
antonyms desist, stop.

persistence *n.* assiduity, assiduousness, constancy, determination, diligence, doggedness, endurance, grit, indefatigableness, perseverance, pertinacity, pluck, resolution, sedulity, stamina, steadfastness, tenacity, tirelessness.

persistent *adj.* assiduous, constant, continual, continuous, determined, dogged, endless, enduring, fixed, hydra-headed, immovable, incessant, indefatigable, indomitable, interminable, never-ending, obdurate, obstinate, perpetual, persevering, pertinacious, relentless, repeated, resolute, steadfast, steady, stubborn, tenacious, tireless, unflagging, unrelenting, unremitting, zealous.

person *n.* being, bod, body, cat, character, codger, cookie, customer, human, human being, individual, individuum, living soul, party, soul, specimen, type, wight.

personable *adj.* affable, agreeable, amiable, attractive, charming, good-looking, handsome, likable, nice, outgoing, pleasant, pleasing, presentable, warm, winning.
antonyms disagreeable, unattractive.

personal *adj.* bodily, corporal, corporeal, derogatory, disparaging, exclusive, exterior, idiosyncratic, individual, inimitable, insulting, intimate, material, nasty, offensive, own, particular, peculiar, pejorative, physical, private, privy, slighting, special, tête-à-tête. *antonyms* general, public, universal.

personality *n.* attraction, attractiveness, celebrity, character, charisma, charm, disposition, dynamism, humor, identity, individuality, likableness, magnetism, make-up, nature, notable, personage, pleasantness, psyche, selfhood, selfness, star, temper, temperament, traits.

perspicacity *n.* acuity, acumen, acuteness, brains, cleverness, discernment, discrimination, insight, keenness, penetration, perceptiveness, percipience, perspicaciousness, perspicuity, sagaciousness, sagacity, sharpness, shrewdness, wit.

persuade *v.* actuate, advise, allure, bring round, cajole, coax, convert, convince, counsel, entice, impel, incite, induce, influence, inveigle, lead on, lean on, prevail upon, prompt, satisfy, sway, sweet-talk, talk into, urge, win over.
antonyms discourage, dissuade.

persuasion *n.* belief, blandishment, cajolery, camp, certitude, cogency, come-on, conversion, conviction, credo, creed, cult, denomination, enticement, exhortation, faction, faith, force, inducement, influence, inveiglement, opinion, party, persuasiveness, potency, power, pull, school (of thought), sect, side, suasion, sweet talk, tenet, views, wheedling.

persuasive *adj.* cogent, compelling, convincing, credible, effective, eloquent, forceful, honeyed, impelling, impressive, inducing, influential, logical, moving, persuasory, plausible, potent, sound, telling, touching, valid, weighty, whilly, whillywha(w), winning.

pertain *v.* appertain, apply, be appropriate, be part of, be relevant, bear on, befit, belong, come under, concern, refer, regard, relate.

pertinacious *adj.* determined, dogged, headstrong, inflexible, intractable, mulish, obdurate, obstinate, persevering, persistent, perverse, purposeful, relentless, resolute, self-willed, strong-willed, stubborn, tenacious, uncompromising, unyielding, wilful.

pertinent *adj.* ad rem, admissible, analogous, applicable, apposite, appropriate, apropos, apt, befitting, fit, fitting, germane, material, pat, proper, relevant, suitable, to the point, to the purpose.

antonyms inappropriate, irrelevant, unsuitable.

perturbed *adj.* agitated, alarmed, anxious, discomposed, disconcerted, disturbed, fearful, flurried, flustered, nervous, restless, shaken, troubled, uncomfortable, uneasy, unsettled, upset, worried.

antonym unperturbed.

pervade *v.* affect, charge, diffuse, extend, fill, imbue, infuse, osmose, overspread, penetrate, percolate, permeate, saturate, suffuse.

perverse *adj.* abnormal, balky, cantankerous, churlish, contradictory, contrary, contumacious, crabbed, cross, cross-grained, cussed, delinquent, depraved, deviant, disobedient, dogged, fractious, froward, headstrong, ill-natured, ill-tempered, improper, incorrect, intractable, intransigent, miscreant, mulish, obdurate, obstinate, peevish, petulant, pig-headed, rebellious, recalcitrant, refractory, spiteful, stroppy, stubborn, surly, thrawn, thwart, troublesome, unhealthy, unmanageable, unreasonable, unyielding, uppity, wayward, wilful, wrong-headed, wry.

antonyms normal, reasonable.

perversion *n.* aberration, abnormality, anomaly, corruption, debauchery, depravity, deviance, deviancy, deviation, distortion, falsification, immorality, kink, kinkiness, misapplication, misinterpretation, misrepresentation, misuse, paraphilia, twisting, unnaturalness, vice, vitiation, wickedness.

pervert *v.* abuse, bend, corrupt, debase, debauch, degrade, deprave, distort, divert, falsify, garble, lead astray, misapply, misconstrue, misinterpret, misrepresent, misuse, subvert, twist, vitiate, warp, wrest.

n. debauchee, degenerate, deviant, paraphiliac, vert, weirdo.

perverted *adj.* aberrant, abnormal, corrupt, debased, debauched, depraved, deviant, distorted, evil, freakish, immoral, impaired, kinky, misguided, queer, sick, twisted, unhealthy, unnatural, vicious, vitiated, warped, wicked.

pest *n.* annoyance, bane, blight, bore, bother, bug, canker, curse, irritation, nuisance, pain (in the neck), scourge, thorn in one's flesh, trial, vexation.

pester *v.* annoy, badger, bedevil, bother, bug, chivvy, disturb, dog, drive round the bend, drive up the wall, fret, get at, harass, harry, hassle, hector, hound, irk, nag, pick on, plague, ride, torment, worry.

pet *n.* darling, dilling, doll, duck, ewe-lamb, favorite, idol, jewel, treasure, whitehead.

adj. cherished, dearest, favored, favorite, particular, preferred, special.

v. baby, canoodle, caress, coddle, cosset, cuddle, dote on, fondle, indulge, kiss, mollycoddle, neck, pamper, pat, smooch, snog, spoil, stroke.

petition *n.* address, appeal, application, boon, entreaty,

imploration, invocation, plea, prayer, request, rogation, round robin, solicitation, suit, supplication.

v. appeal, ask, beg, beseech, bid, call upon, crave, entreat, implore, memorialize, plead, pray, press, solicit, sue, supplicate, urge.

petrify *v.* amaze, appal, astonish, astound, benumb, calcify, confound, dumbfound, fossilize, gorgonize, harden, horrify, immobilize, numb, paralyze, set, solidify, stun, stupefy, terrify, transfix, turn to stone.

petty *adj.* cheap, contemptible, grudging, inconsiderable, inessential, inferior, insignificant, junior, lesser, little, lower, mean, measly, minor, negligible, one-horse, paltry, picayune, picayunish, piddling, pimping, poking, poky, secondary, shabby, slight, small, small-minded, spiteful, stingy, subordinate, trifling, trivial, ungenerous, unimportant.

antonyms generous, important, large-hearted, significant, vital.

petulant *adj.* bad-tempered, captious, caviling, crabbed, cross, crusty, fretful, ill-humored, impatient, irascible, irritable, moody, peevish, perverse, pettish, procacious, querulous, snappish, sour, sulky, sullen, ungracious, waspish.

phantom *n.* apparition, chimera, eidolon, figment (of the imagination), ghost, hallucination, illusion, manes, phantasm(a), revenant, shade, simulacrum, specter, spirit, spook, vision, wraith.

phase *n.* aspect, chapter, condition, development, juncture, period, point, position, season, spell, stage, state, step, time.

phenomenon *n.* appearance, circumstance, curiosity, episode, event, fact, happening, incident, marvel, miracle, occurrence, prodigy, rarity, sensation, sight, spectacle, wonder.

philanthropy *n.* agape, alms-giving, altruism, beneficence, benevolence, benignity, bounty, brotherly love, charitableness, charity, generosity, humanitarianism, kind-heartedness, liberality, munificence, openhandedness, patronage, public-spiritedness, unselfishness.

philosophical *adj.* abstract, analytical, calm, collected, composed, cool, dispassionate, equanimous, erudite, impassive, imperturbable, learned, logical, metaphysical, patient, philosophic, rational, resigned, sagacious, serene, stoical, theoretical, thoughtful, tranquil, unruffled, wise.

phlegmatic *adj.* apathetic, bovine, cold, dull, frigid, heavy, impassive, imperturbable, indifferent, lethargic, listless, lymphatic, matter-of-fact, nonchalant, placid, sluggish, stoical, stolid, unconcerned, undemonstrative, unemotional.

antonyms demonstrative, passionate.

phony *adj.* affected, assumed, bogus, counterfeit, fake, false, forged, imitation, pseudo, put-on, quack, quacksalving, sham, spurious, trick.

antonyms real, true.

n. counterfeit, fake, faker, forgery, fraud, humbug, impostor, mountebank, pretender, pseud, quack, sham.

phrase *n.* construction, expression, idiom, locution, mention, motto, remark, saying, tag, utterance.

v. couch, express, formulate, frame, present, pronounce, put, say, style, term, utter, voice, word.

physical *adj.* actual, bodily, carnal, concrete, corporal, corporeal, earthly, fleshly, incarnate, material, mortal, natural, palpable, real, sensible, solid, somatic, substantial, tangible, visible.

antonyms mental, spiritual.

physique *n.* body, build, chassis, constitution, figure, form, frame, make-up, shape, structure.

pick *v.* break into, break open, choose, collect, crack, cull, cut, decide on, elect, embrace, espouse, fix upon, foment, gather, harvest, incite, instigate, opt for, pluck, prize, provoke, pull, screen, select, settle on, sift out, single out, start.

antonym reject.

n. best, brightest and best, choice, choicest, choosing, cream, crème de la crème, decision, elect, élite, flower, option, preference, pride, prize, selection, tops.

picket *n.* demonstrator, dissenter, guard, look-out, outpost, pale, paling, palisade, patrol, peg, picketer, post, protester, scout, sentinel, sentry, spotter, stake, stanchion, upright, vedette, watchman.

v. blockade, boycott, corral, demonstrate, enclose, fence, hedge in, palisade, pen in, protest.

pictorial *adj.* diagrammatic, expressive, graphic, illustrated, picturesque, representational, scenic, schematic, striking, vivid.

picture *n.* account, archetype, carbon copy, copy, dead ringer, delineation, depiction, description, double, drawing, duplicate, effigy, embodiment, engraving, epitome, essence, film, flick, graphic, illustration, image, impression, kakemono, likeness, living image, lookalike, motion picture, movie, painting, personification, photograph, portrait, portrayal, print, re-creation, replica, report, representation, ringer, scene, similitude, sketch, spit, spitting image, tablature, table, twin, vraisemblance.

v. conceive of, delineate, depict, describe, draw, envisage, envision, illustrate, image, imagine, paint, photograph, portray, render, represent, see, show, sketch, visualize.

piece *n.* allotment, article, bit, case, chunk, component, composition, constituent, creation, division, element, example, fraction, fragment, instance, item, length, mammock, morsel, mouthful, objet d'art, occurrence, offcut, part, piecemeal, portion, production, quantity, sample, scrap, section, segment, share, shred, slice, snippet, specimen, stroke, study, work, work of art.

piecemeal *adv.* at intervals, bit by bit, by degrees, fitfully, in dribs and drabs, in penny numbers, intermittently, little by little, parcel-wise, partially, slowly.

antonyms completely, entirely, wholly. *adj.* discrete,

fragmentary, intermittent, interrupted, partial, patchy, scattered, unsystematic.

antonyms complete, entire, whole, wholesale.

pierce *v.* affect, barb, bore, comprehend, discern, discover, drift, drill, enter, excite, fathom, grasp, gride, hurt, impale, lancinate, move, pain, penetrate, perforate, pink, prick, probe, prog, puncture, realize, rouse, run through, see, spike, stab, stick into, sting, stir, strike, thrill, thrust, touch, transfix, transpierce, understand, wound.

piercing *adj.* acute, agonizing, alert, algid, arctic, aware, biting, bitter, cold, ear-piercing, ear-splitting, excruciating, exquisite, fierce, freezing, frore, frosty, gelid, high-pitched, intense, keen, loud, nipping, nippy, numbing, painful, penetrating, perceptive, perspicacious, powerful, probing, quick-witted, racking, raw, searching, severe, sharp, shattering, shooting, shrewd, shrill, Siberian, stabbing, wintry.

pig-headed *adj.* bull-headed, contrary, cross-grained, dense, froward, inflexible, intractable, intransigent, mulish, obstinate, perverse, self-willed, stiff-necked, stubborn, stupid, unyielding, wilful, wrong-headed.

antonyms flexible, tractable.

pigment *n.* color, colorant, coloring, coloring matter, dye, dyestuff, hue, paint, stain, tempera, tincture, tint.

pile[1] *n.* accumulation, assemblage, assortment, bing, bomb, building, cock, collection, edifice, erection, fortune, heap, hoard, mass, mint, money, mound, mountain, mow, packet, pot, stack, stockpile, structure, wealth.

v. accumulate, amass, assemble, build up, charge, climb, collect, crowd, crush, flock, flood, gather, heap, hoard, jam, load up, mass, pack, rush, stack, store, stream.

pile[2] *n.* bar, beam, column, foundation, pier, piling, pill, post, rib, stanchion, support, upright.

pile[3] *n.* down, fur, fuzz, fuzziness, hair, nap, plush, shag.

pilgrim *n.* crusader, hadji, palmer, peregrine, traveler, wanderer, wayfarer.

pilgrimage *n.* crusade, excursion, expedition, hadj, journey, mission, odyssey, peregrination, tour, trip.

pillar *n.* balluster, bastion, cippus, column, leader, leading light, mainstay, mast, pier, pilaster, piling, post, prop, rock, shaft, stanchion, support, supporter, tower of strength, upholder, upright, worthy.

pilot *n.* airman, aviator, captain, conductor, coxswain, director, flier, guide, helmsman, hobbler, leader, lodesman, navigator, steersman.

v. boss, conduct, control, direct, drive, fly, guide, handle, lead, manage, navigate, operate, run, shepherd, steer.

adj. experimental, model, test, trial.

pimp *n.* bawd, fancy man, fleshmonger, go-between, mack, pander, panderer, procurer, white-slaver, whoremaster, whoremonger.

pin *v.* affix, attach, fasten, fix, hold down, hold fast, immobilize, join, nail, pinion, press, restrain, secure, tack.

n. bolt, breastpin, brooch, clip, fastener, nail, peg, rivet, screw, spike, spindle, stick pin, tack, tie-pin.

pinch *v.* afflict, apprehend, arrest, bust, chafe, check, collar, compress, confine, cramp, crush, distress, do, economize, filch, grasp, hurt, knap, knock off, lay, lift, nab, nick, nip, oppress, pain, pick up, pilfer, press, prig, pull in, purloin, rob, run in, scrimp, skimp, snaffle, snatch, sneap, snitch, spare, squeeze, steal, stint, swipe, tweak.

n. bit, crisis, dash, difficulty, emergency, exigency, hardship, jam, jot, mite, necessity, nip, oppression, pass, pickle, plight, predicament, pressure, soupçon, speck, squeeze, strait, stress, taste, tweak.

pinion *v.* bind, chain, confine, fasten, fetter, hobble, immobilize, manacle, pin down, shackle, tie, truss.

pinnacle *n.* acme, apex, apogee, cap, cone, crest, crown, eminence, height, needle, obelisk, peak, pyramid, spire, steeple, summit, top, turret, vertex, zenith.

pioneer *n.* colonist, colonizer, developer, explorer, founder, founding father, frontiersman, innovator, leader, settler, trail-blazer, voortrekker, way-maker.

v. blaze a trail, create, develop, discover, establish, found, initiate, instigate, institute, invent, launch, lead, open up, originate, prepare, start.

pious *adj.* dedicated, devoted, devout, God-fearing, godly, good, goody-goody, holier-than-thou, holy, hypocritical, moral, pietistic, religiose, religious, reverent, righteous, saintly, sanctimonious, self-righteous, spiritual, unctuous, virtuous.

antonyms impious.

piquant *adj.* biting, interesting, lively, peppery, poignant, provocative, pungent, racy, salty, savory, scintillating, sharp, sparkling, spicy, spirited, stimulating, stinging, tangy, tart, zesty.

antonyms banal, jejune.

pirate *n.* buccaneer, corsair, filibuster, freebooter, infringer, marauder, marque, picaroon, plagiarist, plagiarizer, raider, rover, sallee-man, sea-rat, sea-robber, sea-rover, sea-wolf, water-rat.

v. appropriate, borrow, copy, crib, lift, nick, pinch, plagiarize, poach, reproduce, steal.

pistol *n.* dag, derringer, gat, gun, hand-gun, iron, Luger, piece, revolver, rod, sidearm, six-shooter.

pit *n.* abyss, alveole, alveolus, cavity, chasm, coal-mine, crater, dent, depression, dimple, excavation, gulf, hole, hollow, indentation, mine, oubliette, pock-mark, pothole, trench, variole.

pitch *v.* bung, cast, chuck, dive, drop, erect, fall headlong, fix, fling, flounder, heave, hurl, launch, lob, locate, lurch, peck, place, plant, plunge, raise, roll, set up, settle, sling, stagger, station, throw, topple, toss, tumble, wallow, welter.

n. angle, cant, degree, dip, gradient, ground, harmonic, height, incline, level, line, modulation, park, patter,

playing-field, point, sales talk, slope, sound, spiel, sports field, steepness, summit, tilt, timbre, tone.

pitcher *n.* bottle, can, container, crock, ewer, jack, jar, jug, urn, vessel.

piteous *adj.* affecting, deplorable, distressing, doleful, doloriferous, dolorific, grievous, heartbreaking, heartrending, lamentable, miserable, mournful, moving, pathetic, pitiable, pitiful, plaintive, poignant, sad, sorrowful, touching, woeful, wretched.

pitfall *n.* catch, danger, difficulty, downfall, drawback, hazard, peril, pit, snag, snare, stumbling-block, trap.

pitiable *adj.* contemptible, distressed, distressful, distressing, doleful, grievous, lamentable, miserable, mournful, pathetic, piteous, poor, sad, sorry, woeful, woesome, wretched.

pitiful *adj.* abject, base, beggarly, contemptible, deplorable, despicable, distressing, grievous, heartbreaking, heart-rending, hopeless, inadequate, insignificant, lamentable, low, mean, miserable, paltry, pathetic, piteous, pitiable, ruthful, sad, scurvy, shabby, sorry, vile, woeful, worthless, wretched.

pitiless *adj.* brutal, callous, cold-blooded, cold-hearted, cruel, flinty, hard-hearted, harsh, heartless, implacable, inexorable, inhuman, merciless, obdurate, relentless, ruthless, uncaring, unfeeling, unmerciful, unpitying, unsympathetic.

antonyms compassionate, gentle, kind, merciful.

pity *n.* charity, clemency, commiseration, compassion, condolence, crime, crying shame, fellow-feeling, forbearance, kindness, mercy, misfortune, regret, ruth, shame, sin, sympathy, tenderness, understanding.

antonyms cruelty, disdain, scorn.

v. absolve, bleed for, commiserate with, condole with, feel for, forgive, grieve for, pardon, reprieve, sympathize with, weep for.

pivotal *adj.* axial, central, climactic, critical, crucial, decisive, determining, focal, vital.

place *n.* abode, accommodation, affair, apartment, appointment, area, berth, billet, charge, city, concern, district, domicile, duty, dwelling, employment, flat, function, grade, home, house, job, locale, locality, location, locus, manor, mansion, neighborhood, pad, point, position, post, prerogative, property, quarter, rank, region, residence, responsibility, right, role, room, seat, site, situation, space, spot, station, status, stead, town, venue, vicinity, village, whereabouts.

v. allocate, appoint, arrange, assign, associate, bung, charge, class, classify, commission, deposit, dispose, dump, entrust, establish, fix, give, grade, group, identify, install, know, lay, locate, order, plant, position, put, put one's finger on, rank, recognize, remember, rest, set, settle, situate, sort, stand, station, stick.

placid *adj.* calm, collected, composed, cool, equable, even, even-tempered, gentle, halcyon, imperturbable, level-headed, mild, peaceful, quiet, reposeful, restful,

self-possessed, serene, still, tranquil, undisturbed, unexcitable, unmoved, unruffled, untroubled.
antonyms agitated, jumpy.

plagiarize *v.* appropriate, borrow, counterfeit, crib, infringe, lift, pirate, reproduce, steal, thieve.

plague *n.* affliction, aggravation, annoyance, bane, blight, bother, calamity, cancer, contagion, curse, death, disease, epidemic, evil, infection, irritant, nuisance, pain, pandemic, pest, pestilence, problem, scourge, thorn in the flesh, torment, trial, vexation, visitation.
v. afflict, annoy, badger, bedevil, bother, distress, disturb, fret, harass, harry, hassle, haunt, hound, molest, pain, persecute, pester, tease, torment, torture, trouble, vex.

plain *adj.* apparent, artless, austere, bare, basic, blunt, candid, clear, clinical, common, commonplace, comprehensible, direct, discreet, distinct, downright, even, everyday, evident, flat, forthright, frank, frugal, guileless, homebred, homely, homespun, honest, ill-favored, ingenuous, legible, level, lowly, lucid, manifest, modest, muted, obvious, open, ordinary, outspoken, patent, penny-plain, plane, pure, restrained, self-colored, severe, simple, sincere, smooth, Spartan, stark, straightforward, transparent, ugly, unadorned, unaffected, unambiguous, unattractive, unbeautiful, understandable, undistinguished, unelaborate, unembellished, unfigured, unhandsome, unlovely, unmistakable, unobstructed, unornamented, unpatterned, unprepossessing, unpretentious, untrimmed, unvarnished, visible, whole-colored, workaday.
antonyms abstruse, attractive, elaborate, exaggerated, ostentatious, rich, striking, unclear.
n. flat, grassland, llano, lowland, maidan, plateau, prairie, steppe, tableland, vega, veld(t).

plan *n.* blueprint, chart, contrivance, delineation, design, device, diagram, drawing, idea, illustration, layout, map, method, plot, procedure, program, project, proposal, proposition, representation, scenario, schedule, scheme, sketch, strategy, suggestion, system.
v. aim, arrange, complot, concoct, conspire, contemplate, contrive, design, devise, draft, envisage, foreplan, foresee, formulate, frame, intend, invent, mean, organize, outline, plot, prepare, propose, purpose, represent, scheme.

plane[1] *n.* class, condition, degree, echelon, footing, level, position, rank, rung, stage, stratum.
adj. even, flat, flush, horizontal, level, plain, planar, regular, smooth, uniform.

plane[2] *n.* aircraft, airliner, airplane, bomber, fighter, glider, jet, jumbo, jumbo jet, sea-plane, swing-wing, VTOL.
v. fly, glide, sail, skate, skim, volplane, wing.

plastic *adj.* compliant, docile, ductile, fictile, flexible, impressionable, malleable, manageable, moldable, pliable, pliant, receptive, responsive, soft, supple, tractable.
antonyms inflexible, rigid.

plasticity *n.* flexibility, malleability, pliability, pliableness, pliancy, softness, suppleness, tractability.
antonyms inflexibility, rigidity.

platform *n.* dais, estrade, gantry, manifesto, objective(s), party line, podium, policy, principle, program, rostrum, stage, stand, tenet(s).

platitude *n.* banality, bromide, chestnut, cliché, common-place, inanity, stereotype, truism.

plausible *adj.* believable, colorable, conceivable, convincing, credible, facile, fair-spoken, glib, likely, persuasive, possible, probable, reasonable, smooth, smooth-talking, smooth-tongued, specious, tenable, voluble.
antonyms implausible, improbable, unlikely.

play *v.* act, bet, caper, challenge, chance, compete, contend, execute, fiddle, fidget, flirt, fool around, frisk, frolic, gamble, gambol, hazard, impersonate, interfere, lilt, participate, perform, personate, portray, punt, represent, revel, risk, rival, romp, speculate, sport, string along, take, take on, take part, take the part of, trifle, vie with, wager.
antonym work.
n. action, activity, amusement, caper, comedy, diversion, doodle, drama, elbowroom, employment, entertainment, exercise, farce, foolery, frolic, fun, function, gambling, gambol, game, gaming, give, humor, jest, joking, lark, latitude, leeway, margin, masque, motion, movement, operation, pastime, performance, piece, prank, range, recreation, romp, room, scope, show, space, sport, sweep, swing, teasing, tragedy, transaction, working.

playful *adj.* arch, cheerful, coltish, coquettish, coy, espiègle, flirtatious, frisky, frolicsome, gamesome, gay, good-natured, humorous, impish, jesting, jokey, joking, joyous, kittenish, kitteny, larkish, larky, lively, merry, mischievous, puckish, reasing, roguish, rollicking, spirited, sportive, sprightly, tongue-in-cheek, toyish, toysome, vivacious, waggish.
antonyms serious, stern.

plaything *n.* amusement, bauble, game, gewgaw, gimcrack, pastime, puppet, toy, trifle, trinket.

playwright *n.* dramatist, dramaturge, dramaturgist, screenwriter, scriptwriter.

plea *n.* action, allegation, apology, appeal, begging, cause, claim, defense, entreaty, excuse, explanation, extenuation, imploration, intercession, invocation, justification, overture, petition, placit(um), prayer, pretext, request, suit, supplication, vindication.

plead *v.* adduce, allege, appeal, argue, ask, assert, beg, beseech, crave, entreat, implore, importune, maintain, moot, petition, put forward, request, solicit, supplicate.

pleasant *adj.* acceptable, affable, agreeable, amene, amiable, amusing, charming, cheerful, cheery, congenial, cool, delectable, delightful, delightsome, engaging, enjoyable, fine, friendly, genial, good-humored, gratifying, likable, listenable, lovely, nice, pleasing, pleasurable, refreshing, satisfying, sunshiny, toothsome, welcome, winsome.

antonyms distasteful, nasty, repugnant, unpleasant.

please *v.* amuse, captivate, charm, cheer, choose, content, delight, desire, enchant, entertain, gladden, go for, gratify, humor, indulge, like, opt, prefer, rejoice, satisfy, see fit, suit, think fit, tickle, tickle pink, want, will, wish.

antonyms anger, annoy, displease.

pleasing *adj.* acceptable, agreeable, amiable, amusing, attractive, charming, congenial, delightful, engaging, enjoyable, entertaining, good, gratifying, likable, nice, pleasurable, polite, satisfying, welcome, winning.

antonym unpleasant.

pleasure *n.* amusement, bliss, choice, comfort, command, complacency, contentment, delectation, delight, desire, diversion, ease, enjoyment, gladness, gratification, happiness, inclination, joy, mind, option, preference, purpose, recreation, satisfaction, solace, will, wish.

antonyms displeasure, pain, sorrow, trouble.

plebiscite *n.* ballot, poll, referendum, straw poll, vote.

pledge *n.* assurance, bail, bond, collateral, covenant, deposit, earnest, gage, guarantee, health, oath, pawn, promise, security, surety, toast, undertaking, vow, warrant, word, word of honor.

v. bind, contract, drink to, engage, ensure, gage, guarantee, mortgage, plight, promise, secure, swear, toast, undertake, vouch, vow.

plentiful *adj.* abounding, abundant, ample, bounteous, bountiful, bumper, complete, copious, fertile, fruitful, generous, inexhaustible, infinite, lavish, liberal, luxuriant, overflowing, plenteous, productive, profuse, prolific.

antonyms rare, scanty, scarce.

plenty *n.* abundance, affluence, copiousness, enough, fertility, fruitfulness, fund, heap(s), lots, luxury, mass, masses, milk and honey, mine, mountain(s), oodles, opulence, pile(s), plenitude, plenteousness, plentifulness, plethora, profusion, prosperity, quantities, quantity, stack(s), store, sufficiency, volume, wealth.

antonyms lack, need, scarcity, want.

pliable *adj.* accommodating, adaptable, bendable, bendy, compliant, docile, ductile, flexible, impressionable, influenceable, limber, lithe, malleable, manageable, persuadable, plastic, pliant, receptive, responsive, suggestible, supple, susceptible, tractable, yielding.

antonyms inflexible, rigid.

pliant *adj.* adaptable, bendable, bendy, biddable, compliant, ductile, easily led, flexible, impressionable, influenceable, lithe, manageable, persuadable, plastic, pliable, supple, susceptible, tractable, whippy, yielding.

antonyms inflexible, intractable.

plight[1] *n.* case, circumstances, condition, difficulty, dilemma, extremity, galère, hole, jam, perplexity, pickle, predicament, quandary, scrape, situation, spot, state, straits, trouble.

plight[2] *n.* affiance, contract, covenant, engage, guarantee, pledge, promise, propose, swear, vouch, vow.

plot[1] *n.* action, cabal, conspiracy, covin, design, intrigue, machination(s), narrative, outline, plan, scenario, scheme, story, story line, stratagem, subject, theme, thread.

v. brew, cabal, calculate, chart, collude, compass, compute, conceive, concoct, conspire, contrive, cook up, design, devise, draft, draw, frame, hatch, imagine, intrigue, lay, locate, machinate, maneuver, map, mark, outline, plan, project, scheme.

plot[2] *n.* allotment, area, green, ground, lot, parcel, patch, tract.

plotter *n.* caballer, conspirator, intriguer, Machiavellian, machinator, schemer, strategist.

ploy *n.* artifice, contrivance, device, dodge, gambit, game, maneuver, move, ruse, scheme, stratagem, subterfuge, tactic, trick, wile.

pluck[1] *n.* backbone, boldness, bottle, bravery, courage, determination, fortitude, gameness, grit, guts, hardihood, heart, intrepidity, mettle, nerve, resolution, spirit, spunk, tenacity.

pluck[2] *v.* catch, clutch, collect, depilate, deplume, displume, draw, evulse, gather, harvest, jerk, pick, plunk, pull, pull off, pull out, snatch, strum, thrum, tug, twang, tweak, unplume, yank.

plug *n.* advert, advertisement, bung, cake, chew, cork, dossil, dottle, good word, hype, mention, pigtail, publicity, puff, push, quid, spigot, spile, stopper, stopple, studdle, tamp(i)on, twist, wad.

v. advertise, block, build up, bung, choke, close, cork, cover, drudge, fill, grind, hype, labor, mention, pack, peg away, plod, promote, publicize, puff, push, seal, slog, stop, stop up, stopper, stopple, stuff, tamp, toil.

plump[1] *adj.* beefy, burly, buxom, chopping, chubby, corpulent, dumpy, embonpoint, endomorphic, fat, fleshy, full, matronly, obese, podgy, portly, roly-poly, rotund, round, stout, tubby, well-upholstered.

antonyms skinny, thin.

plump[2] *v.* collapse, descend, drop, dump, fall, flop, sink, slump.

adv. abruptly, directly, straight.

plunder *v.* depredate, despoil, devastate, loot, pillage, raid, ransack, ravage, reive, rifle, rob, sack, spoil, spoliate, steal, strip.

n. booty, despoilment, ill-gotten gains, loot, pickings, pillage, prey, prize, rapine, spoils, swag.

plunge *v.* career, cast, charge, dash, demerge, demerse, descend, dip, dive, dive-bomb, dook, douse, drop, fall, go down, hurtle, immerse, jump, lurch, nose-dive, pitch, plummet, rush, sink, submerge, swoop, tear, throw, tumble.

n. collapse, descent, dive, dook, drop, fall, immersion, jump, submersion, swoop, tumble.

plurality *n.* bulk, diversity, galaxy, majority, mass, most, multiplicity, multitudinousness, numerousness, preponderance, profusion, variety.

pocketbook *n.* bag, handbag, purse, wallet.

podium *n.* dais, platform, rostrum, stage, stand.

poem *n.* acrostic, ballad(e), dit(t), ditty, eclogue, elegy, epicede, epicedium, epinicion, epithalamion, epithalamium, fabliau, genethliac(on), idyll, jingle, lay, limerick, lipogram, lyric, madrigal, monody, ode, palinode, rhyme, song, sonnet, verse, verselet, verset, versicle.

poetry *n.* free verse, gay science, iambics, lyrics, macaronics, muse, Parnassus, pennill, poems, poesy, rhyme, rhyming, vers libre, verse, versing.

poignant *adj.* acrid, acute, affecting, agonizing, biting, bitter, caustic, distressing, heartbreaking, heart-rending, intense, keen, moving, painful, pathetic, penetrating, piercing, piquant, pointed, pungent, sad, sarcastic, severe, sharp, stinging, tender, touching, upsetting.

point[1] *n.* aim, aspect, attribute, burden, characteristic, circumstance, condition, core, crux, degree, design, detail, dot, drift, end, essence, extent, facet, feature, full stop, gist, goal, import, instance, instant, intent, intention, item, juncture, location, mark, marrow, matter, meaning, moment, motive, nicety, nub, object, objective, particular, peculiarity, period, pith, place, position, property, proposition, purpose, quality, question, reason, respect, score, side, site, speck, spot, stage, station, stop, subject, tally, text, theme, thrust, time, trait, unit, use, usefulness, utility.
v. aim, denote, designate, direct, draw attention to, hint, indicate, level, show, signal, signify, suggest, train.

point[2] *n.* apex, bill, cacumen, cape, end, fastigium, foreland, head, headland, neb, ness, nib, promontory, prong, spike, spur, summit, tang, tine, tip, top.

pointed *adj.* accurate, acicular, aciform, aculeate(d), acuminate, acute, barbed, biting, cuspidate, cutting, edged, fastigiate(d), incisive, keen, lanceolate(d), lancet, lanciform, mucronate, penetrating, pertinent, sharp, telling, trenchant.

pointless *adj.* absurd, aimless, bootless, fruitless, futile, inane, ineffectual, irrelevant, meaningless, nonsensical, profitless, senseless, silly, stupid, unavailing, unbeneficial, unproductive, unprofitable, useless, vague, vain, worthless.
antonyms meaningful, profitable.

poise *n.* aplomb, assurance, calmness, collectedness, composure, cool, coolness, dignity, elegance, equanimity, equilibrium, grace, presence, presence of mind, sangfroid, savoir-faire, self-possession, serenity.
v. balance, float, hang, hold, hover, librate, position, support, suspend.

poison *n.* aconite, aconitum, bane, blight, cancer, canker, contagion, contamination, corruption, malignancy, miasma, toxin, venom, virus.

v. adulterate, contaminate, corrupt, defile, deprave, empoison, envenom, infect, kill, murder, pervert, pollute, subvert, taint, undermine, vitiate, warp.

poke *v.* butt, butt in, dig, elbow, hit, interfere, intrude, jab, meddle, nose, nudge, peek, prod, prog, pry, punch, push, shove, snoop, stab, stick, tamper, thrust.
n. butt, dig, dunt, jab, nudge, prod, punch, shove, thrust.

pole[1] *n.* bar, lug, mast, post, rod, shaft, spar, staff, stake, standard, stang, stick.

pole[2] *n.* antipode, extremity, limit, terminus, (ultima) Thule.

policy *n.* action, approach, code, course, custom, discretion, good sense, guideline, line, plan, position, practice, procedure, program, protocol, prudence, rule, sagacity, scheme, shrewdness, stance, stratagem, theory, wisdom.

polish *v.* brighten, brush up, buff, burnish, clean, correct, cultivate, emend, emery, enhance, file, finish, furbish, improve, luster, perfect, planish, refine, rub, rub up, shine, shine up, slick, slicken, smooth, touch up, wax.
antonyms dull, tarnish.
n. breeding, brightness, brilliance, class, cultivation, elegance, eutrapelia, expertise, finesse, finish, glaze, gloss, grace, luster, perfectionism, politesse, proficiency, refinement, savoir-faire, sheen, smoothness, sophistication, sparkle, style, suavity, urbanity, varnish, veneer, wax.
antonyms clumsiness, dullness, gaucherie.

polished *adj.* accomplished, adept, bright, burnished, civilized, courtly, cultivated, educated, elegant, expert, faultless, fine, finished, flawless, furbished, genteel, glassy, gleaming, glossy, graceful, gracious, impeccable, lustrous, masterly, outstanding, perfected, polite, professional, refined, sheeny, shining, skilful, slippery, smooth, sophisticated, suave, superlative, urbane, well-bred.
antonyms clumsy, dull, gauche, inexpert, tarnished.

polite *adj.* affable, attentive, civil, civilized, complaisant, considerate, cordial, courteous, courtly, cultured, deferential, diplomatic, discreet, elegant, genteel, gentlemanly, gracious, ladylike, mannerly, obliging, polished, refined, respectful, tactful, thoughtful, urbane, well-behaved, well-bred, well-mannered.
antonyms impolite, uncultivated.

politic *adj.* advantageous, advisable, artful, astute, canny, crafty, cunning, designing, diplomatic, discreet, expedient, ingenious, intriguing, judicious, Machiavellian, opportune, prudent, sagacious, sage, scheming, sensible, shrewd, sly, subtle, tactful, unscrupulous, wise.
antonym impolitic.

pollute *v.* adulterate, befoul, besmirch, canker, contaminate, corrupt, debase, debauch, defile, deprave, desecrate, dirty, dishonor, foul, infect, mar, poison, profane, soil, spoil, stain, sully, taint, violate, vitiate.

pomp *n.* ceremonial, ceremoniousness, ceremony, display, éclat, flourish, formality, grandeur, grandiosity, magnificence, ostentation, pageant, pageantry, parade, pomposity, ritual, show, solemnity, splendor, state, vainglory.

antonyms austerity, simplicity.

pompous *adj.* affected, aldermanlike, aldermanly, arrogant, bloated, bombastic, budge, chesty, euphuistic, flatulent, fustian, grandiloquent, grandiose, high-flown, imperious, inflated, magisterial, magniloquent, oro(ro)tund, ostentatious, overbearing, overblown, pontifical, portentous, pretentious, prosy, ranting, self-important, stilted, supercilious, turgid, vainglorious, windy.

antonyms economical, modest, simple, unaffected, unassuming.

ponder *v.* analyze, brood, cerebrate, cogitate, contemplate, consider, deliberate, examine, excogitate, give thought to, incubate, meditate, mull over, muse, ponderate, puzzle over, ratiocinate, reason, reflect, ruminate over, study, think, volve, weigh.

ponderous *adj.* awkward, bulky, clumsy, cumbersome, cumbrous, dreary, dull, elephantine, graceless, heavy, heavy-footed, heavy-handed, hefty, huge, humorless, labored, laborious, lifeless, long-winded, lumbering, massive, pedantic, pedestrian, plodding, portentous, prolix, slow-moving, stilted, stodgy, stolid, tedious, unwieldy, verbose, weighty.

antonyms delicate, light, simple.

pool[1] *n.* dub, lake, lasher, leisure pool, linn, mere, pond, puddle, splash, stank, swimming bath, swimming pool, tarn, water-hole, watering-hole.

pool[2] *n.* accumulation, bank, cartel, collective, combine, consortium, funds, group, jackpot, kitty, pot, purse, reserve, ring, stakes, syndicate, team, trust.

v. amalgamate, chip in, combine, contribute, dob in, merge, muck in, put together, share.

poor[1] *adj.* badly off, bankrupt, beggared, beggarly, broke, deficient, destitute, distressed, embarrassed, exiguous, hard up, impecunious, impoverished, in reduced circumstances, inadequate, indigent, insufficient, lacking, meager, miserable, moneyless, necessitious, needy, niggardly, obolary, on one's beam-ends, on one's uppers, on the rocks, pauperized, penniless, penurious, pinched, pitiable, poverty-stricken, reduced, scanty, skimpy, skint, slight, sparse, stony-broke, straitened, without means, without the where-withal.

antonyms affluent, opulent, rich, wealthy.

poor[2] *adj.* bad, bare, barren, below par, depleted, exhausted, faulty, feeble, fruitless, grotty, humble, imperfect, impoverished, inferior, infertile, insignificant, jejune, lowgrade, lowly, mean, mediocre, modest, paltry, pathetic, pitiful, plain, ropy, rotten, rubbishy, second-rate, shabby, shoddy, sorry, spiritless, sterile, substandard, third-rate, trivial, unfruitful, unimpressive, unproductive, unsatisfactory, valueless, weak, worthless.

antonym superior.

poor[3] *adj.* accursed, cursed, forlorn, hapless, ill-fated, luckless, miserable, pathetic, pitiable, star-crossed, unfortunate, unhappy, unlucky, wretched.

antonym lucky.

poppycock *n.* babble, balderdash, balls, baloney, bullshit, bunk, bunkum, drivel, eyewash, gibberish, gobbledegook, guff, hooey, nonsense, rot, rubbish, tommyrot, tosh, trash, twaddle.

antonym sense.

popular *adj.* accepted, approved, celebrated, common, conventional, current, democratic, demotic, famous, fashionable, favored, favorite, fêted, general, household, idolized, in, in demand, in favor, liked, lionized, modish, overpopular, overused, prevailing, prevalent, public, sought-after, standard, stock, trite, ubiquitous, universal, vernacular, voguey, voguish, vulgar, well-liked, widespread.

antonyms exclusive, unpopular, unusual.

popularity *n.* acceptance, acclaim, adoration, adulation, approbation, approval, celebrity, currency, esteem, fame, favor, glory, idolization, kudos, lionization, mass appeal, recognition, regard, renown, reputation, repute, vogue, worship.

antonym unpopularity.

population *n.* citizenry, citizens, community, denizens, folk, inhabitants, natives, occupants, people, populace, residents, society.

pornographic *adj.* bawdy, blue, coarse, dirty, filthy, girlie, gross, indecent, lewd, nudie, obscene, off-color, offensive, porn, porno, prurient, risqué, salacious, smutty.

antonyms innocent, inoffensive.

port *n.* anchorage, harbor, harborage, haven, hithe, roads, roadstead, seaport.

portable *adj.* carriageable, compact, convenient, handy, light, lightweight, manageable, movable, portatile, portative, transportable.

antonyms fixed, immovable.

portend *v.* adumbrate, announce, augur, bespeak, betoken, bode, forebode, forecast, foreshadow, foretell, foretoken, forewarn, harbinger, herald, indicate, omen, point to, predict, presage, prognosticate, promise, signify, threaten, warn of.

portentous *adj.* alarming, amazing, astounding, awe-inspiring, bloated, charged, consequential, crucial, earth-shaking, epoch-making, extraordinary, fateful, heavy, important, menacing, minatory, miraculous, momentous, ominous, phenomenal, pompous, ponderous, pontifical, pregnant, prodigious, remarkable, significant, sinister, solemn, threatening.

antonyms insignificant, unimportant, unimpressive.

portion *n.* allocation, allotment, allowance, assignment, bit, cup, destiny, division, fate, fortune, fraction, fragment, helping, kismet, lot, luck, measure, meed, moiety, morsel, parcel, part, piece, quantity, quota, rake-off, ration, scrap, section, segment, serving, share, slice, something, tranche, whack.

v. allocate, allot, apportion, assign, carve up, deal, distribute, divide, divvy up, dole, parcel, partion, partition, share out, slice up.

portly *adj.* ample, beefy, bulky, chubby, corpulent, dumpy, embonpoint, fat, fleshy, full, heavy, large, obese, overweight, paunchy, plump, rotund, round, stout, tubby.

antonyms slight, slim.

portrait *n.* account, caricature, characterization, depiction, description, icon, image, likeness, miniature, mug shot, painting, photograph, picture, portraiture, portrayal, profile, representation, sketch, thumbnail, vignette.

portray *v..* act, capture, characterize, delineate, depict, describe, draw emblazon, encapsulate, evoke figure, illustrate, impersonate, limn, paint, personate, personify, picture, play, present, render, represent, sketch, suggest.

pose *v.* advance, affect, arrange, assert, attitudinize, claim, feign, impersonate, masquerade, model, pass oneself off, place, posit, position, posture, present, pretend, profess to be, propound, put, put forward, put on an act, set, sham, sit, state, strike an attitude, submit.

n. act, affectation, air, attitude, bearing, con, façade, front, mark, masquerade, mien, position, posture, pretense, role, sham, stance, take-in.

poseur *n.* attitudinizer, charlatan, con, exhibitionist, impostor, masquerader, mountebank, phony, poser, poseuse, posturer, posturist, pseud, quack.

position *n.* angle, area, arrangement, attitude, bearings, belief, berth, billet, capacity, character, circumstances, condition, deployment, disposition, duty, employment, function, grade, importance, job, level, locale, locality, location, niche, occupation, office, opinion, outlook, pass, perspective, pinch, place, placement, placing, plight, point, point of view, pose, positioning, post, posture, predicament, prestige, rank, reference, reputation, role, set, setting, site, situation, slant, slot, spot, stance, stand, standing, standpoint, state, station, stature, status, ubiety, view, viewpoint, whereabouts.

v. arrange, array, deploy, dispose, fix, lay out, locate, place, pose, put, range, set, settle, stand, stick.

positive *adj.* absolute, actual, affirmative, arrant, assertive, assured, authoritative, beneficial, categorical, certain, clear, clear-cut, cocksure, complete, conclusive, concrete, confident, constructive, consummate, convinced, decided, decisive, definite, direct, dogmatic, downright, effective, efficacious, emphatic, explicit, express, firm, forceful, forward-looking, helpful, hopeful, incontestable, incontrovertible, indisputable, irrefragable, irrefutable, open-and-shut, opinionated, optimistic, out-and-out, peremptory, perfect, practical, productive, progressive, promising, rank, real, realistic, resolute, secure, self-evident, sheer, stubborn, sure, thorough, thoroughgoing, uncompromising, undeniable,

unequivocal, unmistakable, unmitigated, unquestioning, useful, utter.

antonyms indecisive, indefinite, negative, uncertain.

positively *adv.* absolutely, assuredly, authoritatively, categorically, certainly, conclusively, constructively, decisively, definitely, dogmatically, emphatically, expressly, finally, firmly, incontestably, incontrovertibly, indisputably, surely, uncompromisingly, undeniably, unequivocally, unmistakably, unquestionably.

possess *v.* acquire, be endowed with, control, dominate, enjoy, have, hold, obtain, occupy, own, possess oneself of, seize, take, take over, take possession of.

possessed *adj.* bedeviled, berserk, besotted, bewitched, consumed, crazed, cursed, demented, dominated, enchanted, frenzied, hag-ridden, haunted, infatuated, maddened, mesmerized, obsessed, raving.

possession *n.* colony, control, custody, dependency, dominion, enjoyment, fruition, hold, mandate, occupancy, occupation, ownership, proprietorship, protectorate, province, tenure, territory, title.

possessions *n.* assets, belongings, chattels, effects, estate, goods, goods and chattels, junk, meum et tuum, movables, paraphernalia, property, riches, stuff, things, traps, wealth, worldly wealth.

possibility *n.* achievability, chance, conceivability, feasibility, hazard, hope, liability, likelihood, odds, plausibility, potentiality, practicability, probability, prospect, realizability, risk, workableness.

antonym impossibility.

possible *adj.* accomplishable, achievable, alternative, attainable, available, conceivable, credible, doable, feasible, hopeful, hypothetical, imaginable, likely, on, potential, practicable, probable, promising, realizable, tenable, viable, workable.

antonym impossible.

possibly *adv.* at all, by any chance, by any means, Deo volente, DV, God willing, haply, happen, hopefully, in any way, maybe, mayhap, peradventure, perchance, perhaps, very like(ly).

post[1] *n.* baluster, banister, column, leg, newel, pale, palisade, picket, pier, pillar, pin, pole, shaft, stake, stanchion, standard, stock, strut, support, upright.

v. advertise, affix, announce, denounce, display, make known, placard, preconize, proclaim, promulgate, publicize, publish, report, stick up.

post[2] *n.* appointment, assignment, beat, berth, billet, employment, incumbency, job, office, place, position, situation, station, vacancy.

v. appoint, assign, establish, locate, move, place, position, put, second, send, shift, situate, station, transfer.

post[3] *n.* collection, delivery, dispatch, mail, postal service, uplifting.

v. acquaint, advise, apprize, brief, dispatch, fill in on, inform, keep posted, mail, notify, report to, send, transmit.

postpone *v.* adjourn, defer, delay, freeze, hold over,

pigeonhole, prorogue, put back, put off, put on ice, shelve, suspend, table, waive.
antonyms advance, forward.

postulate *v.* advance, assume, hypothesize, lay down, posit, predicate, presuppose, propose, stipulate, suppose, take for granted, theorize.

posture *n.* attitude, bearing, carriage, decubitus, disposition, mien, port, pose, position, set, stance.
v. affect, attitudinize, pose, put on airs, show off, strike attitudes, strut.

potency *n.* authority, capacity, cogency, control, effectiveness, efficaciousness, efficacy, energy, force, headiness, influence, kick, might, muscle, persuasiveness, potential, power, puissance, punch, strength, sway, vigor.
antonyms impotence, weakness.

potential *adj.* budding, concealed, conceivable, dormant, embryonic, future, hidden, imaginable, in embryo, in posse, inherent, latent, likely, possible, probable, promising, prospective, undeveloped, unrealized.
n. ability, aptitude, capability, capacity, flair, possibility, potentiality, power, talent, the makings, what it takes, wherewithal.

potion *n.* beverage, brew, concoction, cup, dose, draught, drink, electuary, elixir, medicine, mixture, philter, potation, tonic, treacle.

pouch *n.* bag, container, marsupium, pocket, poke, purse, reticule, sac, sack, sporran, wallet.

pounce *v.* ambush, attack, dash at, dive on, drop, fall upon, grab, jump, leap at, lunge at, snatch, spring, strike, swoop.
n. assault, attack, bound, dive, grab, jump, leap, lunge, spring, swoop.

pound[1] *v.* bang, bash, baste, batter, beat, belabor, bray, bruise, clobber, clomp, clump, comminute, crush, drum, hammer, levigate, march, palpitate, pelt, powder, pulsate, pulse, pulverize, pummel, smash, stomp, strike, strum, thrash, throb, thrum, thud, thump, thunder, tramp, triturate.

pound[2] *n.* compound, corral, enclosure, fank, fold, pen, yard.

pour *v.* bucket, cascade, course, crowd, decant, effuse, emit, exude, flow, gush, rain, rain cats and dogs, run, rush, sheet, spew, spill, spout, stream, swarm, teem, throng, tumble.

pout *v.* glower, grimace, lower, mope, pull a face, scowl, sulk.
antonyms grin, smile.
n. glower, grimace, long face, moue, scowl.
antonyms grin, smile.

poverty *n.* aridity, bareness, barrenness, beggary, dearth, deficiency, depletion, destitution, distress, exhaustion, hardship, ill-being, impoverishment, inadequacy, indigence, infertility, insolvency, insufficiency, jejuneness, lack, meagerness, necessitousness, necessity, need, paucity, pauperism, pennilessness, penury, poorness,

privation, proletarianism, scarcity, shortage, sterility, thinness, unfruitfulness, want.
antonyms affluence, fertility, fruitfulness, riches, richness.

power *n.* ability, ascendancy, autarchy, authorization, authority, brawn, capability, capacity, clout, clutches, command, competence, competency, control, dominance, domination, dominion, efficience, energy, faculty, force, forcefulness, heavy metal, hegemony, imperium, influence, intensity, juice, kami, license, mana, mastery, might, muscle, omnipotence, plenipotence, potency, potential, prerogative, privilege, right, rule, sovereignty, strength, supremacy, sway, teeth, vigor, virtue, vis, voltage, vroom, warrant, weight.
dominant, effective, effectual, energetic, forceful, forcible, impressive, influential, leading, masterful, mighty, muscular, omnipotent, persuasive, plutocratic, potent, pre-eminent, prepotent, prevailing, puissant, robust, souped-up, sovereign, stalwart, strapping, strong, sturdy, supreme, telling, vigorous, weighty, winning.
antonyms impotent, ineffective, weak.

practical *adj.* accomplished, active, applicative, applied, businesslike, commonsense, commonsensical, down-to-earth, efficient, empirical, everyday, expedient, experienced, experimental, factual, feasible, functional, hard-headed, hard-nosed, material, matter-of-fact, mundane, nuts-and-bolts, ordinary, practicable, practive, pragmatic, proficient, qualified, realistic, seasoned, sensible, serviceable, skilled, sound, trained, unsentimental, useful, utilitarian, workable, workaday, working.
antonym impractical.

practically[1] *adv.* actually, all but, almost, essentially, fundamentally, in effect, in practice, in principle, just about, nearly, not quite, pretty nearly, pretty well, very nearly, virtually, well-nigh.

practically[2] *adv.* clearly, from a commonsense angle, matter-of-factly, rationally, realistically, reasonably, sensibly, unsentimentally.

practice[1] *n.* action, application, business, career, clientèle, convention, custom, discipline, drill, dry run, dummy run, effect, exercise, experience, habit, ism, method, mode, modus operandi, operation, patronage, performance, policy, practic, practicalities, practicum, praxis, preparation, procedure, profession, rehearsal, repetition, routine, rule, run-through, study, system, tradition, training, usage, use, vocation, way, wont, work, work-out.

practice[2] *v.* apply, carry out, discipline, do, drill, enact, engage in, execute, exercise, follow, implement, live up to, observe, perfect, perform, ply, prepare, pursue, put into practice, rehearse, repeat, run through, study, train, undertake, warm up.

practiced *adj.* able, accomplished, consummate, experienced, expert, finished, highly-developed, knowing, knowledgeable, perfected, proficient, qualified, refined, seasoned, skilled, trained, versed, veteran, well-trained. *antonyms* inexpert, unpracticed.

pragmatic *adj.* businesslike, efficient, factual, hard-headed, opportunistic, practical, realistic, sensible, unidealistic, unsentimental, utilitarian. *antonyms* idealistic, romantic, unrealistic.

praise *n.* acclaim, acclamation, accolade, acknowledgment, adoration, adulation, applause, approbation, approval, bouquet, cheering, commend, commendation, compliment, compliments, congratulation, devotion, encomium, eulogium, eulogy, extolment, flattery, glory, homage, honor, kudos, laud, laudation, ovation, panegyric, plaudit, puff, rave, recognition, salvoes, testimonial, thanks, thanksgiving, tribute, worship. *antonyms* criticism, revilement.

v. acclaim, acknowledge, admire, adore, applaud, approve, belaud, bless, celebrate, cheer, compliment, congratulate, cry up, eulogize, exalt, extol, flatter, give thanks to, glorify, hail, honor, laud, magnify, panegyrize, pay tribute to, promote, puff, rave over, recognize, tout, wax lyrical, worship. *antonyms* criticize, revile.

praiseworthy *adj.* admirable, commendable, creditable, deserving, estimable, excellent, exemplary, fine, honorable, laudable, meritorious, reputable, sterling, worthy. *antonyms* discreditable, dishonorable, ignoble.

pray *v.* adjure, ask, beg, beseech, call on, crave, entreat, implore, importune, invoke, obsecrate, petition, plead, press, request, solicit, sue, supplicate, urge.

prayer *n.* appeal, collect, communion, devotion, entreaty, invocation, kyrie, kyrie eleison, litany, orison, paternoster, petition, plea, request, solicitation, suffrage, suit, supplication.

preach *v.* address, admonish, advocate, ethicize, evangelize, exhort, harangue, lecture, moralize, orate, pontificate, pontify, preachify, prose, sermonize, urge.

preamble *n.* exordium, foreword, introduction, lead-in, overture, preface, preliminaries, prelude, preparation, proem, prolegomenon, prologue. *antonyms* epilogue, postscript.

precarious *adj.* chancy, dangerous, delicate, dicey, dodgy, doubtful, dubious, hairy, hazardous, iffy, insecure, parlous, periculous, perilous, problematic, risky, shaky, slippery, ticklish, tricky, uncertain, unpredictable, unreliable, unsafe, unsettled, unstable, unsteady, unsure, vulnerable. *antonyms* certain, safe, secure.

precaution *n.* anticipation, backstop, buffer, care, caution, circumspection, foresight, forethought, insurance, preparation, prophylaxis, protection, providence, provision, prudence, safeguard, safety measure, security, surety, wariness.

precedence *n.* antecedence, first place, lead, pre-eminence, preference, pride of place, primacy, priority, rank, seniority, superiority, supremacy.

precedent *n.* antecedent, authority, citation, criterion, example, exemplar, guideline, instance, judgment, model, paradigm, past instance, pattern, prototype, ruling, standard, yardstick.

precept *n.* axiom, behest, bidding, byword, canon, charge, command, commandment, convention, decree, dictum, direction, directive, guideline, injunction, institute, instruction, law, mandate, maxim, motto, order, ordinance, principle, regulation, rubric, rule, saying, sentence, statute.

precious *adj.* adored, affected, artificial, beloved, cherished, chichi, choice, costly, darling, dear, dearest, expensive, exquisite, fastidious, favorite, fine, flowery, greenery-yallery, idolized, inestimable, invaluable, irreplaceable, loved, namby-pamby, overnice, over-refined, priceless, prized, rare, recherché, treasured, twee, valuable, valued.

precipice *n.* bluff, brink, cliff, cliff face, crag, drop, escarp, escarpment, height, scarp, steep.

precipitate *v.* accelerate, advance, bring on, cast, cause, chuck, discharge, drive, expedite, fling, further, hasten, hurl, hurry, induce, launch, occasion, pitch, press, project, quicken, speed, throw, trigger.

adj. abrupt, breakneck, brief, frantic, Gadarene, hasty, headlong, heedless, hot-headed, hurried, impatient, impetuous, impulsive, incautious, indiscreet, madcap, pell-mell, plunging, precipitous, quick, quixotic, rapid, rash, reckless, rushing, sudden, swift, unannounced, unexpected, violent. *antonym* cautious.

precise *adj.* absolute, accurate, actual, authentic, blow-by-blow, buckram, careful, ceremonious, clear-cut, correct, definite, delimitative, determinate, distinct, exact, explicit, express, expressis verbis, factual, faithful, fastidious, finical, finicky, fixed, formal, identical, literal, meticulous, minute, nice, particular, prim, punctilious, puritanical, rigid, scrupulous, specific, strict, succinct, unequivocal, verbatim, word-for-word. *antonym* imprecise.

precisely *adv.* absolutely, accurately, bang, blow by blow, correctly, dead, distinctly, exactly, expressis verbis, just, just so, literally, minutely, plumb, slap, smack, square, squarely, strictly, verbatim, word for word.

precision *n.* accuracy, care, correctness, definiteness, detail, exactitude, exactness, explicitness, expressness, faithfulness, fastidiousness, fidelity, meticulousness, minuteness, neatness, niceness, nicety, particularity, preciseness, punctilio, punctiliousness, rigor, scrupulosity, specificity. *antonym* imprecision.

preclude *v.* avoid, check, debar, eliminate, exclude, forestall, hinder, inhibit, obviate, prevent, prohibit, restrain, rule out, stop. *antonyms* incur, involve.

precocious *adj.* advanced, ahead, bright, clever, developed,

fast, forward, gifted, mature, precocial, premature, quick, smart.
antonym backward.

predatory *adj.* acquisitive, avaricious, carnivorous, covetous, despoiling, greedy, hunting, lupine, marauding, pillaging, plundering, predacious, predative, preying, rapacious, raptatorial, raptorial, ravaging, ravening, thieving, voracious, vulturine, vulturous, wolfish.

predestination *n.* ananke, destiny, doom, election, fate, foreordainment, foreordination, karma, lot, necessity, portion, predestiny, predetermination, preordainment, preordination, weird.

predicament *n.* can of worms, corner, crisis, dilemma, embarrassment, emergency, fix, galère, hole, hot water, impasse, jam, kettle of fish, mess, pickle, pinch, plight, quandary, scrape, situation, spot, state, trouble.

predict *v.* augur, auspicate, divine, forebode, forecast, foresay, foresee, foreshow, forespeak, foretell, portend, presage, prognosticate, project, prophesy, second-guess, soothsay, vaticinate.

prediction *n.* augury, auspication, divination, forecast, fortune-telling, prognosis, prognostication, prophecy, second sight, soothsaying, vaticination.

predilection *n.* affection, affinity, bent, bias, enthusiasm, fancy, fondness, inclination, leaning, liking, love, partiality, penchant, predisposition, preference, proclivity, proneness, propensity, soft spot, taste, tendency, weakness.
antonyms antipathy, disinclination.

predisposed *adj.* agreeable, amenable, biased, disposed, favorable, inclined, liable, minded, not unwilling, nothing loth, prejudiced, prepared, prone, ready, subject, susceptible, well-disposed, willing.

predominant *adj.* ascendant, capital, chief, controlling, dominant, forceful, important, influential, leading, main, paramount, potent, powerful, prepollent, preponderant, prepotent, prevailing, prevalent, primary, prime, principal, prominent, ruling, sovereign, strong, superior, supreme.
antonyms ineffective, lesser, minor, weak.

predominate *v.* dominate, obtain, outnumber, outweigh, override, overrule, overshadow, preponderate, prevail, reign, rule, tell, transcend.

pre-eminent *adj.* chief, consummate, distinguished, excellent, exceptional, facile princeps, foremost, incomparable, inimitable, leading, matchless, nonpareil, outstanding, paramount, passing, peerless, predominant, prominent, renowned, superior, superlative, supreme, surpassing, transcendent, unequaled, unmatched, unrivaled, unsurpassed.
antonyms undistinguished, unknown.

pre-empt *v.* acquire, anticipate, appropriate, arrogate, assume, bag, forestall, secure, seize, usurp.

preface *n.* exordium, foreword, intro, introduction, preamble, preliminaries, prelims, prelude, proem, prolegomena, prolegomenon, prologue, prooemion, prooemium.

antonyms afterthought, epilogue, postscript.
v. begin, introduce, launch, lead up to, open, precede, prefix, prelude, premise, start.
antonyms append, complete, finish.

prefer[1] *v.* adopt, advocate, back, be partial to, choose, desire, elect, endorse, fancy, favor, go for, incline towards, like better, opt for, pick, plump for, recommend, select, single out, support, want, wish, would rather, would sooner.
antonym reject.

prefer[2] *v.* bring, file, lodge, place, present, press.

prefer[3] *v.* advance, aggrandize, dignify, elevate, exalt, promote, raise, upgrade.
antonym demote.

preference[1] *n.* choice, desire, election, fancy, favorite, first choice, inclination, liking, option, partiality, pick, predilection, selection, wish.

preference[2] *n.* advantage, favor, favoritism, precedence, preferential treatment, priority, special consideration, special treatment.

pregnant[1] *adj.* big, big-bellied, enceinte, expectant, expecting, gravid, impregnated, in an interesting condition, in the club, in the family way, in the pudding club, parturient, preggers, teeming, with child.

pregnant[2] *adj.* charged, eloquent, expressive, full, heavy, loaded, meaning, meaningful, ominous, pithy, pointed, significant, suggestive, telling, weighty.
antonym jejune.

prejudice[1] *n.* bias, bigotry, chauvinism, discrimination, injustice, intolerance, narrow-mindedness, partiality, partisanship, preconception, prejudgment, racism, sexism, unfairness, viewiness, warp.
antonyms fairness, tolerance.
v. bias, color, condition, distort, incline, indoctrinate, influence, jaundice, load, poison, predispose, prepossess, slant, sway, warp, weight.

prejudice[2] *n.* damage, detriment, disadvantage, harm, hurt, impairment, injury, loss, mischief, ruin, vitiation, wreck.
antonyms advantage, benefit.
v. damage, harm, hinder, hurt, impair, injure, mar, ruin, spoil, undermine, vitiate, wreck.
antonyms advance, benefit, help.

prejudiced *adj.* biased, bigoted, chauvinist, conditioned, discriminatory, distorted, ex parte, illiberal, influenced, intolerant, jaundiced, loaded, narrow-minded, one-sided, opinionated, partial, partisan, prepossessed, racist, sexist, subjective, unenlightened, unfair, verkrampte, viewy, warped, weighted.
antonyms fair, tolerant.

preliminary *adj.* earliest, early, embryonic, exordial, experimental, exploratory, first, inaugural, initial, initiative, initiatory, introductory, opening, pilot, precursory, prefatory, prelusive, preparatory, primary, prior, qualifying, test, trial.
antonyms closing, final.

premature *adj.* abortive, early, embryonic, forward, green, half-formed, hasty, ill-considered, ill-timed, immature, imperfect, impulsive, incomplete, inopportune, over-hasty, precipitate, precocious, preterm, previous, rash, raw, undeveloped, unfledged, unripe, unseasonable, untimely.
antonyms late, tardy.

premeditated *adj.* aforethought, calculated, cold-blooded, conscious, considered, contrived, deliberate, intended, intentional, planned, plotted, prearranged, predetermined, prepense, preplanned, studied, wilful.
antonyms spontaneous, unpremeditated.

premeditation *n.* deliberateness, deliberation, design, determination, forethought, intention, malice, afore-thought, planning, plotting, prearrangement, prede-termination, purpose, scheming.
antonyms impulse, spontaneity.

premise *v.* assert, assume, hypothesize, lay down, posit, postulate, predicate, presuppose, state, stipulate, take as true.
n. argument, assertion, assumption, ground, hypoth-esis, postulate, postulation, predication, premiss, pre-supposition, proposition, statement, stipulation, sup-position, thesis.

preoccupied *adj.* absent-minded, absorbed, abstracted, day-dreaming, distracted, distrait, engrossed, entêté, faraway, fixated, heedless, immersed, intent, oblivi-ous, obsessed, pensive, rapt, taken up, unaware, vis-ited, wrapped up.

preparation[1] *n.* alertness, anticipation, arrangement, assignment, basics, development, expectation, fore-sight, foundation, groundwork, homework, imposi-tion, lesson, measure, plan, precaution, preliminaries, prep, preparedness, provision, readiness, revision, rudiments, safeguard, schoolwork, study, task.

preparation[2] *n.* application, composition, compound, concoction, lotion, medicine, mixture, potion, tincture.

prepare *v.* accouter, adapt, adjust, anticipate, arrange, assemble, boun, brace, brief, busk, coach, compose, concoct, confect, construct, contrive, develop, devise, dispose, do one's homework, draft, draw up, dress, equip, fashion, fettle, fit, fit out, fix up, forearm, form, fortify, furnish, get up, gird, groom, instruct, limber up, make, make ready, outfit, plan, practice, predis-pose, prime, produce, provide, psych up, ready, re-hearse, rig out, steel, strengthen, supply, train, trim, warm up.

prepared *adj.* able, arranged, briefed, disposed, expect-ant, fit, forearmed, inclined, minded, planned, predis-posed, primed, psyched up, ready, set, waiting, well-rehearsed, willing, word-perfect.
antonyms unprepared, unready.

preponderance *n.* ascendancy, bulk, dominance, domi-nation, dominion, extensiveness, force, lion's share, majority, mass, power, predominance, prevalence, superiority, supremacy, sway, weight.

prepossessing *adj.* alluring, amiable, appealing, attrac-tive, beautiful, bewitching, captivating, charming, de-lightful, disarming, enchanting, engaging, fair, fasci-nating, fetching, good-looking, handsome, inviting, lik-able, lovable, magnetic, pleasing, striking, taking, win-ning, winsome.
antonyms unattractive, unprepossessing.

preposterous *adj.* absurd, asinine, bizarre, crazy, deri-sory, excessive, exorbitant, extravagant, extreme, fatu-ous, foolish, imbecile, impossible, inane, incredible, insane, intolerable, irrational, laughable, ludicrous, monstrous, nonsensical, outrageous, ridiculous, ris-ible, senseless, shocking, unbelievable, unconscionable, unreasonable, unthinkable.
antonym reasonable.

prerequisite *adj.* basic, essential, fundamental, impera-tive, indispensable, mandatory, necessary, needed, needful, obligatory, required, requisite, vital.
antonym unnecessary.
n. condition, essential, imperative, must, necessity, precondition, provision, proviso, qualification, require-ment, requisite, sine qua non.
antonym extra.

prerogative *n.* advantage, authority, birthright, carte blanche, choice, claim, droit, due, exemption, immu-nity, liberty, license, perquisite, privilege, right, sanc-tion, title.

prescribe *v.* appoint, assign, command, decree, define, dic-tate, direct, enjoin, fix, impose, lay down, limit, ordain, order, require, rule, set, set bounds to, specify, stipulate.

presence *n.* air, apparition, appearance, aspect, attend-ance, aura, bearing, carriage, closeness, companionship, company, comportment, demeanor, ease, existence, ghost, habitation, inhabitance, manifestation, mien, near-ness, neighborhood, occupancy, personality, poise, pro-pinquity, proximity, residence, revenant, self-assurance, shade, specter, spirit, statuesqueness, vicinity.
antonym absence.

present[1] *adj.* at hand, attending, available, contempo-rary, current, existent, extant, here, immediate, instant, near, ready, there, to hand.
antonyms absent, out-of-date, past.

present[2] *v.* acquaint with, adduce, advance, award, be-stow, confer, declare, demonstrate, display, donate, entrust, exhibit, expound, extend, furnish, give, grant, hand over, hold out, introduce, mount, offer, porrect, pose, produce, proffer, put on, raise, recount, relate, show, stage, state, submit, suggest, tender.
antonym take.
n. benefaction, boon, bounty, cadeau, compliment, donation, endowment, favor, gift, grant, gratuity, lar-gess, nuzzer, offering, prezzie, refresher.

presentable *adj.* acceptable, becoming, clean, decent, neat, passable, proper, respectable, satisfactory, suit-able, tidy, tolerable.
antonyms unpresentable, untidy.

presently *adv.* anon, before long, by and by, directly, immediately, in a minute, shortly, soon.

preserve *v.* care for, confect, conserve, continue, defend, embalm, entreasure, guard, keep, maintain, perpetuate, protect, retain, safeguard, save, secure, shelter, shield, store, sustain, uphold.
antonyms destroy, ruin.
n. area, confection, confiture, conserve, domain, field, game park, game reserve, jam, jelly, konfyt, marmalade, realm, reservation, reserve, safari park, sanctuary, specialism, specialty, sphere, thing.

preside *v.* administer, chair, conduct, control, direct, govern, head, lead, manage, officiate, run, supervise.

press[1] *v.* address, afflict, appress, assail, beg, beset, besiege, calendar, clasp, cluster, compel, compress, condense, constrain, crowd, crush, demand, depress, disquiet, dun, embrace, encircle, enfold, enforce, enjoin, entreat, exhort, finish, flatten, flock, force, force down, gather, harass, hasten, herd, hug, hurry, implore, importune, insist on, iron, jam, mangle, mash, mill, petition, plague, plead, pressurize, push, reduce, rush, seethe, smooth, squeeze, steam, stuff, sue, supplicate, surge, swarm, throng, torment, trouble, urge, vex, worry.
antonyms expand, hang back, lighten, relieve.
n. bunch, bustle, crowd, crush, demand, flock, hassle, herd, horde, host, hurry, mob, multitude, pack, pressure, push, strain, stress, swarm, throng, urgency.

press[2] *n.* columnists, correspondents, fourth estate, hacks, journalism, journalists, news media, newsmen, newspapers, paparazzi, papers, photographers, pressmen, reporters, writers.

pressing *adj.* burning, constraining, crowding, crucial, essential, exigent, high-priority, imperative, important, importunate, serious, thronging, urgent, vital.
antonyms trivial, unimportant.

pressure *n.* adversity, affliction, burden, coercion, compressing, compression, compulsion, constraint, crushing, demands, difficulty, distress, exigency, force, hassle, heat, heaviness, hurry, influence, load, obligation, power, press, pression, squeezing, strain, stress, sway, urgency, weight. *v.* browbeat, bulldoze, bully, coerce, compel, constrain, dragoon, drive, force, impel, induce, lean on, oblige, persuade, press, pressurize, squeeze.

prestige *n.* authority, cachet, celebrity, clout, credit, distinction, eminence, esteem, fame, honor, importance, influence, kudos, pull, regard, renown, reputation, standing, stature, status, weight.
antonyms humbleness, unimportance.

presume *v.* assume, bank on, believe, conjecture, count on, dare, depend on, go so far, have the audacity, hypothesize, hypothetize, infer, make bold, make so bold, posit, postulate, presuppose, rely on, suppose, surmise, take for granted, take it, take the liberty, think, trust, undertake, venture.

presumption[1] *n.* assurance, audacity, boldness, brass, brass neck, cheek, effrontery, forwardness, gall, impudence, insolence, neck, nerve, presumptuousness, temerity.
antonyms humility, politeness.

presumption[2] *n.* anticipation, assumption, basis, belief, chance, conjecture, grounds, guess, hypothesis, likelihood, opinion, plausibility, premiss, presupposition, probability, reason, supposition, surmise.

presumptuous *adj.* arrogant, audacious, big-headed, bold, conceited, foolhardy, forward, impertinent, impudent, insolent, over-confident, over-familiar, overweening, presuming, pushy, rash, uppish.
antonym modest.

presupposition *n.* assumption, belief, hypothesis, preconception, premise, premiss, presumption, supposition, theory.

pretend *v.* act, affect, allege, aspire, assume, claim, counterfeit, dissemble, dissimulate, fake, falsify, feign, go through the motions, imagine, impersonate, make believe, pass oneself off, profess, purport, put on, sham, simulate, suppose.

pretense *n.* acting, affectation, aim, allegation, appearance, artifice, blague, bounce, charade, claim, cloak, color, cover, deceit, deception, display, excuse, fabrication, façade, faking, falsehood, feigning, garb, guise, humbug, invention, make-believe, mask, masquerade, posing, posturing, pretentiousness, pretext, profession, pseudery, purpose, ruse, semblance, sham, show, simulation, subterfuge, trickery, veil, veneer, wile.
antonyms honesty, openness, reason.

pretentious *adj.* affected, ambitious, assuming, bombastic, chichi, conceited, euphemistic, exaggerated, extravagant, flaunting, grandiloquent, grandiose, highfalutin, high-flown, high-sounding, hollow, inflated, magniloquent, mannered, oro(ro)tund, ostentatious, overambitious, overassuming, pompous, showy, snobbish, specious, uppish, vainglorious.
antonyms humble, modest, simple, straightforward.

pretty *adj.* appealing, attractive, beautiful, bijou, bonny, charming, comely, cute, dainty, delicate, elegant, fair, fine, good-looking, graceful, lovely, neat, nice, personable, pleasing, sightly, tasteful, trim.
antonyms tasteless, ugly.
adv. fairly, moderately, passably, quite, rather, reasonably, somewhat, tolerably.

prevail *v.* abound, obtain, overcome, overrule, predominate, preponderate, reign, rule, succeed, triumph, win.
antonym lose.

prevailing *adj.* common, controlling, current, customary, dominant, established, fashionable, general, in style, in vogue, influential, main, mainstream, operative, ordinary, popular, predominating, preponderating, prepotent, prevalent, principal, ruling, set, usual, widespread.
antonyms minor, uncommon.

prevalent *adj.* accepted, ascendant, common, commonplace, compelling, current, customary, dominant, epidemic, established, everyday, extensive, frequent, general, governing, habitual, popular, powerful, predominant, prevailing, rampant, regnant, rife, successful, superior, ubiquitous, universal, usual, victorious, widespread.
antonyms subordinate, uncommon.

prevaricate *v.* cavil, deceive, dodge, equivocate, evade, fib, hedge, lie, palter, quibble, shift, shuffle, temporize, tergiversate.

prevent *v.* anticipate, avert, avoid, balk, bar, block, check, counteract, debar, defend against, foil, forestall, frustrate, hamper, head off, hinder, impede, inhibit, intercept, obstruct, obviate, preclude, restrain, stave off, stop, stymie, thwart, ward off.
antonyms cause, foster, help.

preventive *adj.* counteractive, deterrent, hampering, hindering, impeding, inhibitory, obstructive, precautionary, prevenient, preventative, prophylactic, protective, shielding.
antonyms causative, fostering.
n. block, condom, deterrent, hindrance, impediment, neutralizer, obstacle, obstruction, prevention, prophylactic, protection, protective, remedy, safeguard, shield.
antonyms cause, encouragement, incitement.

previous *adj.* antecedent, anterior, arranged, earlier, erstwhile, ex-, foregoing, former, one-time, past, preceding, precipitate, premature, prior, quondam, sometime, umwhile, untimely, whilom.
antonyms later, timely.

prey *n.* booty, dupe, fall guy, game, kill, mark, mug, plunder, quarry, target, victim.

prey on blackmail, bleed, bully, burden, devour, distress, eat, eat away, exploit, feed on, gnaw at, haunt, hunt, intimidate, live off, moth-eat, oppress, seize, take advantage of, terrorize, trouble, victimize, waste, weigh down, weigh heavily, worry.

price *n.* amount, assessment, bill, bounty, charge, consequences, cost, damage, estimate, expenditure, expense, fee, figure, levy, odds, outlay, payment, penalty, rate, reward, sacrifice, sum, toll, valuation, value, worth.
v. assess, cost, estimate, evaluate, offer, put, rate, valorize, value.

priceless[1] *adj.* beyond price, cherished, costly, dear, expensive, incalculable, incomparable, inestimable, invaluable, irreplaceable, precious, prized, rare, rich, treasured, without price.
antonyms cheap, run-of-the-mill.

priceless[2] *adj.* a hoot, a scream, absurd, amusing, comic, droll, funny, hilarious, killing, rib-tickling, ridiculous, riotous, risible, side-splitting.

pride *n.* amour-propre, arrogance, best, big-headedness, boast, choice, conceit, cream, delight, dignity, egotism, élite, flower, gem, glory, gratification, haughtiness, hauteur, high spirits, honor, hubris, jewel, joy, loftiness, magnificence, mettle, morgue, ostentation, pick,

pleasure, presumption, pretension, pretensiousness, pride and joy, prize, satisfaction, self-esteem, self-importance, self-love, self-respect, smugness, snobbery, splendor, superciliousness, treasure, vainglory, vanity.
antonym humility.

prim *adj.* demure, fastidious, formal, fussy, governessy, old-maidish, old-maidist, particular, perjink, po-faced, precise, priggish, prissy, proper, prudish, pudibund, puritanical, school-marmish, sedate, starchy, stiff, strait-laced.
antonyms broad-minded, informal.

primarily *adv.* at first, basically, chiefly, especially, essentially, fundamentally, generally, initially, mainly, mostly, originally, principally.
antonym secondarily.

primary *adj.* aboriginal, basic, beginning, best, capital, cardinal, chief, dominant, earliest, elemental, elementary, essential, first, first-formed, first-made, fundamental, greatest, highest, initial, introductory, leading, main, original, paramount, primal, prime, primeval, primigenial, primitial, primitive, primordial, principal, pristine, radical, rudimentary, simple, top, ultimate, underlying.
antonym secondary.

prime[1] *adj.* basic, best, capital, chief, choice, earliest, excellent, first-class, first-rate, fundamental, highest, leading, main, original, predominant, pre-eminent, primary, principal, pal, quality, ruling, select, selected, senior, superior, top, underlying.
antonyms minor, secondary, second-rate.
n. beginning, flowering, height, heyday, maturity, morning, opening, peak, perfection, spring, springtide, springtime, start, zenith.

prime[2] *v.* brief, charge, clue up, coach, cram, fill, fill in, gen up, groom, inform, notify, post up, prepare, train.

primeval *adj.* ancient, earliest, early, first, Ogygian, old, original, prehistoric, primal, primitial, primitive, primordial, pristine.
antonyms developed, later, modern.

primitive *adj.* aboriginal, barbarian, barbaric, childlike, crude, earliest, early, elementary, first, naïve, neanderthal, original, primal, primary, primeval, primordial, pristine, rough, rude, rudimentary, savage, simple, uncivilized, uncultivated, undeveloped, unrefined, unsophisticated, untrained, untutored.
antonyms advanced, civilized, developed.

primordial *adj.* basic, earliest, elemental, first, first-formed, first-made, fundamental, original, prehistoric, primal, primeval, primigenial, primitial, primitive, pristine, radical.
antonyms developed, later, modern.

principal[1] *adj.* capital, cardinal, chief, controlling, decuman, dominant, essential, first, foremost, highest, key, leading, main, paramount, pre-eminent, primary, prime, strongest, truncal.
antonyms least, lesser, minor.

n. boss, chief, dean, director, first violin, head, head teacher, headmaster, headmistress, lead, leader, master, prima ballerina, prima donna, rector, star, superintendent.

principal[2] *n.* assets, capital, capital funds, money.

principle *n.* assumption, attitude, axiom, belief, canon, code, conscience, credo, criterion, dictum, doctrine, dogma, duty, element, ethic, formula, fundamental, golden rule, honor, institute, integrity, law, maxim, moral, morality, morals, opinion, precept, principium, probity, proposition, rectitude, rule, scruples, standard, tenet, truth, uprightness, verity. *antonyms* corruption, wickedness.

print *v.* engrave, impress, imprint, issue, mark, produce, publish, put to bed, reproduce, run off, stamp, write. *n.* book, characters, copy, dab, engraving, face, fingerprint, font, fount, impression, lettering, letters, magazine, mold, newspaper, newsprint, periodical, photo, photograph, picture, publication, reproduction, stamp, type, typeface, typescript.

prior *adj.* aforementioned, antecedent, anterior, earlier, foregoing, former, preceding, pre-existent, previous. *antonym* later.

prison *n.* bagnio, bastille, brig, cage, calaboose, can, cell, chok(e)y, clink, confinement, cooler, coop, dungeon, glass-house, guardhouse, gulag, hoos(e)gow, house of correction, house of detention, imprisonment, jail, jug, lock-up, panopticon, penal institution, penitentiary, pokey, prison-house, prison-ship, quod, reformatory, slammer, slink, stalag, stir, stockade, tank.

pristine *adj.* earliest, first, former, initial, original, primal, primary, primeval, primigenial, primitial, primitive, primordial, uncorrupted, undefiled, unspoiled, unsullied, untouched, virgin. *antonyms* developed, later, spoiled.

private *adj.* clandestine, closet, concealed, confidential, exclusive, home-felt, hush-hush, in camera, independent, individual, inside, intimate, intraparietal, inward, isolated, off the record, own, particular, personal, privy, reserved, retired, secluded, secret, separate, sequestrated, solitary, special, unofficial, withdrawn. *antonyms* open, public. *n.* buck private, common soldier, enlisted man, private soldier.

privation *n.* affliction, austerity, destitution, distress, hard-ship, indigence, lack, loss, misery, necessary, need, neediness, penury, poverty, suffering, want. *antonyms* affluence, wealth.

privilege *n.* advantage, benefit, birthright, claim, concession, droit, due, entitlement, franchise, freedom, immunity, liberty, license, prerogative, right, sanction, title. *antonym* disadvantage.

prize[1] *n.* accolade, aim, ambition, award, conquest, desire, gain, goal, haul, honor, hope, jackpot, premium, purse, reward, stake(s), trophy, windfall, winnings.

adj. award-winning, best, champion, excellent, first-rate, outstanding, top, top-notch, winning. *antonym* second-rate. *v.* appreciate, cherish, esteem, hold dear, revere, reverence, set store by, treasure, value. *antonyms* despise, undervalue.

prize[2] *n.* booty, capture, loot, pickings, pillage, plunder, spoils, trophy.

prize[3], **prise** *v.* force, jemmy, lever, pry, winkle.

probable *adj.* apparent, credible, feasible, likely, odds-on, on the cards, plausible, possible, presumed, reasonable, seeming, verisimilar. *antonym* improbable.

probe *v.* examine, explore, go into, investigate, look into, pierce, poke, prod, query, scrutinize, search, sift, sound, test, verify. *n.* bore, detection, drill, examination, exploration, inquest, inquiry, investigation, research, scrutiny, study, test.

problem *n.* boyg, brain-teaser, complication, conundrum, difficulty, dilemma, disagreement, dispute, doubt, enigma, no laughing matter, poser, predicament, puzzle, quandary, question, riddle, trouble, vexata quaestio, vexed question. *adj.* delinquent, difficult, intractable, perverse, refractory, uncontrollable, unmanageable, unruly. *antonyms* manageable, well-behaved.

procedure *n.* action, conduct, course, custom, form, formula, method, modus operandi, move, operation, performance, plan of action, policy, practice, process, routine, scheme, step, strategy, system, transaction.

proceed *v.* advance, arise, carry on, come, continue, derive, emanate, ensue, flow, follow, go ahead, issue, move on, originate, press on, progress, result, set in motion, spring, start, stem. *antonyms* retreat, stop.

proceedings *n.* account, action, affair, affairs, annals, archives, business, course of action, dealings, deeds, doings, event(s), matters, measures, minutes, moves, procedure, process, records, report, steps, transactions, undertaking.

proceeds *n.* earnings, emoluments, gain, income, motser, motza, produce, products, profit, receipts, returns, revenue, takings, yield. *antonyms* losses, outlay.

process[1] *n.* action, advance, case, course, course of action, development, evolution, formation, growth, manner, means, measure, method, mode, movement, operation, performance, practice, procedure, proceeding, progress, progression, stage, step, suit, system, transaction, trial, unfolding. *v.* alter, convert, deal with, digitize, dispose of, fulfil, handle, prepare, refine, transform, treat.

process[2] *n.* node, nodosity, nodule, projection, prominence, protuberance, protusion.

procession *n.* cavalcade, column, concatenation, cortege, course, cycle, file, march, motorcade, parade, run, sequence, series, string, succession, train.

proclaim *v.* advertise, affirm, announce, annunciate, blaze, blazon, circulate, declare, enounce, enunciate, give out, herald, indicate, make known, preconize, profess, promulgate, publish, show, testify, trumpet.

proclamation *n.* announcement, annunciation, ban, declaration, decree, edict, indiction, interlocution, irade, manifesto, notice, notification, proclaim, promulgation, pronouncement, pronunciamento, publication, ukase.

procrastinate *v.* adjourn, dally, defer, delay, dilly-dally, drag one's feet, gain time, penelopize, play for time, postpone, prolong, protract, put off, retard, stall, temporize.

antonyms advance, proceed.

procreate *v.* beget, breed, conceive, engender, father, generate, mother, produce, propagate, reproduce, sire, spawn.

procure *v.* acquire, appropriate, bag, buy, come by, earn, effect, find, gain, get, induce, lay hands on, obtain, pander, pick up, pimp, purchase, secure, win.

antonym lose.

prod *v.* dig, drive, egg on, elbow, goad, impel, incite, jab, motivate, move, nudge, poke, prick, prog, prompt, propel, push, rouse, shove, spur, stimulate, urge.

n. boost, cue, dig, elbow, jab, nudge, poke, prog, prompt, push, reminder, shove, signal, stimulus.

prodigious *adj.* abnormal, amazing, astounding, colossal, enormous, exceptional, extraordinary, fabulous, fantastic, flabbergasting, giant, gigantic, huge, immeasurable, immense, impressive, inordinate, mammoth, marvelous, massive, miraculous, monstrous, monumental, phenomenal, remarkable, spectacular, staggering, startling, striking, stupendous, tremendous, unusual, vast, wonderful.

antonyms commonplace, small, unremarkable.

produce[1] *v.* advance, afford, bear, beget, breed, bring forth, cause, compose, construct, create, deliver, demonstrate, develop, direct, effect, engender, exhibit, fabricate, factify, factuate, furnish, generate, give, give rise to, invent, make, manufacture, mount, occasion, offer, originate, present, provoke, put forward, put on, render, result in, show, stage, supply, throw, yield.

antonyms consume, result from. *n.* crop, harvest, product, yield.

produce[2] *v.* continue, elongate, extend, lengthen, prolong, protract.

product *n.* artefact, commodity, concoction, consequence, creation, effect, facture, fruit, goods, invention, issue, legacy, merchandise, offshoot, offspring, outcome, output, produce, production, result, returns, spin-off, upshot, work, yield.

antonym cause.

productive *adj.* advantageous, beneficial, constructive, creative, dynamic, effective, energetic, fecund, fertile,

fructiferous, fructuous, fruitful, gainful, generative, gratifying, inventive, plentiful, producing, profitable, prolific, rewarding, rich, teeming, uberous, useful, valuable, vigorous, voluminous, worthwhile.

antonyms fruitless, unproductive.

profanity *n.* abuse, blasphemy, curse, cursing, execration, expletive, four-letter word, impiety, imprecation, inquination, irreverence, malediction, obscenity, profaneness, sacrilege, swearing, swear-word.

antonyms politeness, reverence.

profess *v.* acknowledge, admit, affirm, allege, announce, assert, asseverate, aver, avow, certify, claim, confess, confirm, declare, enunciate, fake, feign, maintain, make out, own, pretend, proclaim, propose, propound, purport, sham, state, vouch.

profession *n.* acknowledgment, affirmation, assertion, attestation, avowal, business, calling, career, claim, confession, declaration, employment, job, line (of work), manifesto, métier, occupation, office, position, sphere, statement, testimony, vocation, vow, walk of life.

professional *adj.* adept, competent, crack, efficient, experienced, expert, finished, masterly, polished, practiced, proficient, qualified, skilled, slick, trained, virtuose, virtuosic, well-skilled.

antonyms amateur, unprofessional.

n. adept, authority, dab hand, expert, maestro, master, pastmaster, pro, proficient, specialist, virtuoso, wizard.

proffer *v.* advance, extend, hand, hold out, offer, present, propose, propound, submit, suggest, tender, volunteer.

proficient *adj.* able, accomplished, adept, apt, capable, clever, competent, conversant, efficient, experienced, expert, gifted, masterly, qualified, skilful, skilled, talented, trained, versed, virtuose, virtuosic.

antonyms clumsy, incompetent.

profile *n.* analysis, biography, biopic, characterization, chart, contour, diagram, drawing, examination, figure, form, graph, outline, portrait, review, shape, side view, silhouette, sketch, study, survey, table, thumbnail sketch, vignette.

profit *n.* a fast buck, advancement, advantage, avail, benefit, boot, bottom line, bunce, earnings, emoluments, fruit, gain, gelt, good, graft, gravy, grist, interest, melon, percentage, proceeds, receipts, return, revenue, surplus, takings, use, value, velvet, winnings, yield.

antonym loss.

v. advance, advantage, aid, avail, benefit, better, boot, contribute, gain, help, improve, line one's pockets, promote, serve, stand in good stead.

antonyms harm, hinder.

profitable *adj.* advantageable, advantageous, beneficial, commercial, cost-effective, emolumental, emolumentary, fruitful, gainful, lucrative, money-making, paying, plummy, productive, remunerative, rewarding, serviceable, useful, utile, valuable, worthwhile.

antonym unprofitable.

profligate *adj.* abandoned, corrupt, Cyprian, debauched, degenerate, depraved, dissipated, dissolute, extravagant, immoderate, immoral, improvident, iniquitous, libertine, licentious, loose, prodigal, promiscuous, reckless, shameless, spendthrift, squandering, unprincipled, vicious, vitiated, wanton, wasteful, whorish, wicked, wild.

antonyms moral, parsimonious, thrifty, upright.

n. debauchee, degenerate, libertine, prodigal, racketeer, rake, reprobate, roué, spendthrift, squanderer, waster, wastrel.

profound *adj.* abject, absolute, abstruse, abysmal, acute, awful, bottomless, cavernous, complete, consummate, deep, deep-seated, discerning, erudite, exhaustive, extensive, extreme, far-reaching, fathomless, great, heartfelt, heart-rending, hearty, intense, keen, learned, penetrating, philosophical, pronounced, recondite, sagacious, sage, serious, sincere, skilled, subtle, thoroughgoing, thoughtful, total, utter, weighty, wise, yawning.

antonyms mild, shallow, slight.

profuse *adj.* abundant, ample, bountiful, copious, excessive, extravagant, exuberant, fulsome, generous, immoderate, large-handed, lavish, liberal, luxuriant, open-handed, over the top, overflowing, plentiful, prodigal, prolific, teeming, unstinting.

antonyms sparing, sparse.

profusion *n.* abundance, bounty, copiousness, cornucopia, excess, extravagance, exuberance, glut, lavishness, luxuriance, multitude, plenitude, pleroma, plethora, prodigality, quantity, riot, superabundance, superfluity, surplus, wealth.

antonyms sparingness, sparsity.

program *n.* agenda, broadcast, curriculum, design, lineup, list, listing, order of events, order of the day, performance, plan, plan of action, presentation, procedure, production, project, schedule, scheme, show, syllabus, transmission.

v. arrange, bill, book, brainwash, design, engage, formulate, itemize, lay on, line up, list, map out, plan, prearrange, schedule, work out.

progress *n.* advance, advancement, amelioration, betterment, breakthrough, circuit, continuation, course, development, gain, growth, headway, improvement, increase, journey, movement, passage, procession, progression, promotion, step forward, way.

antonyms decline, deterioration.

v. advance, ameliorate, better, blossom, come on, continue, develop, forge ahead, gain, gather momentum, grow, improve, increase, make headway, make strides, mature, proceed, prosper, travel.

antonyms decline, deteriorate.

progression *n.* advance, advancement, chain, concatenation, course, cycle, furtherance, gain, headway, order, progress, sequence, series, string, succession.

antonyms decline, deterioration.

prohibit *v.* ban, bar, constrain, debar, disallow, forbid, hamper, hinder, impede, interdict, obstruct, outlaw, preclude, prevent, proscribe, restrict, rule out, stop, veto.

antonym permit.

prohibition *n.* ban, bar, constraint, disallowance, embargo, exclusion, forbiddal, forbiddance, injunction, interdict, interdiction, negation, obstruction, prevention, proscription, restruction, veto.

antonym permission.

prohibitive *adj.* excessive, exorbitant, extortionate, forbidding, impossible, preposterous, prohibiting, prohibitory, proscriptive, repressive, restraining, restrictive, sky-high, steep, suppressive.

antonyms encouraging, reasonable.

project *n.* activity, assignment, conception, design, enterprise, idea, job, occupation, plan, program, proposal, purpose, scheme, task, undertaking, venture, work.

v. beetle, bulge, calculate, cast, contemplate, contrive, design, devise, discharge, draft, estimate, exsert, extend, extrapolate, extrude, fling, forecast, frame, gauge, hurl, jut, launch, map out, outline, overhang, plan, predetermine, predict, propel, prophesy, propose, protrude, purpose, reckon, scheme, shoot, stand out, stick out, throw, transmit.

prolific *adj.* abounding, abundant, bountiful, copious, fecund, fertile, fertilizing, fruitful, generative, luxuriant, productive, profuse, rank, reproductive, rich, teeming, voluminous.

antonyms infertile, scarce.

prolong *v.* continue, delay, drag out, draw out, extend, lengthen, lengthen out, perpetuate, produce, protract, spin out, stretch.

antonym shorten.

prominent *adj.* beetling, bulging, celebrated, chief, conspicuous, distinguished, eminent, eye-catching, famous, foremost, important, jutting, leading, main, noted, noticeable, obtrusive, obvious, outstanding, popular, pre-eminent, projecting, pronounced, protruding, protrusive, protuberant, remarkable, renowned, respected, salient, standing out, striking, top, unmistakable, weighty, well-known.

antonyms inconspicuous, unimportant.

promiscuity *n.* abandon, amorality, debauchery, depravity, dissipation, immorality, laxity, laxness, lechery, libertinism, licentiousness, looseness, permissiveness, profligacy, promiscuousness, protervity, wantonness, whoredom, whoring, whorishness.

antonym chastity.

promise *v.* assure, augur, bespeak, betoken, bid fair, contract, denote, engage, guarantee, hint at, indicate, look like, pledge, plight, predict, presage, prophesy, stipulate, suggest, swear, take an oath, undertake, vouch, vow, warrant.

n. ability, aptitude, assurance, bond, capability, capacity, commitment, compact, covenant, engagement, flair, guarantee, oath, pledge, pollicitation, potential, talent, undertaking, vow, word, word of honor.

promote *v.* advance, advertise, advocate, aggrandize, aid, assist, back, blazon, boost, champion, contribute to, develop, dignify, elevate, encourage, endorse, espouse, exalt, forward, foster, further, help, honor, hype, kick upstairs, nurture, plug, popularize, prefer, publicize, puff, push, raise, recommend, sell, sponsor, stimulate, support, trumpet, upgrade, urge.

antonyms demote, disparage, obstruct.

prompt[1] *adj.* alert, brisk, eager, early, efficient, expeditious, immediate, instant, instantaneous, on time, punctual, quick, rapid, ready, responsive, smart, speedy, swift, timely, timeous, unhesitating, willing.

antonym slow.

adv. exactly, on the dot, promptly, punctually, sharp, to the minute.

prompt[2] *v.* advise, assist, call forth, cause, cue, elicit, evoke, give rise to, impel, incite, induce, inspire, instigate, motivate, move, occasion, prod, produce, provoke, remind, result in, spur, stimulate, urge.

antonym dissuade. *n.* cue, help, hint, instigation, jog, jolt, prod, reminder, spur, stimulus.

promptly *adv.* directly, forthwith, immediately, instantly, on time, posthaste, pronto, punctually, quickly, speedily, swiftly, unhesitatingly.

promulgate *v.* advertise, announce, broadcast, circulate, communicate, declare, decree, disseminate, issue, notify, preconize, proclaim, promote, publicize, publish, spread.

prone[1] *adj.* apt, bent, disposed, given, inclined, liable, likely, predisposed, propense, subject, susceptible, tending, vulnerable.

antonym unlikely.

prone[2] *adj.* face down, flat, full-length, horizontal, procumbent, prostrate, recumbent, stretched.

antonym upright.

pronounce *v.* accent, affirm, announce, articulate, assert, breathe, declaim, declare, decree, deliver, enunciate, judge, proclaim, say, sound, speak, stress, utter, vocalize, voice.

pronounced *adj.* broad, clear, conspicuous, decided, definite, distinct, evident, marked, noticeable, obvious, positive, striking, strong, unmistakable.

antonyms unnoticeable, vague.

proof *n.* assay, attestation, authentication, certification, confirmation, corroboration, demonstration, documentation, evidence, examination, experiment, ordeal, scrutiny, substantiation, test, testimony, trial, verification, voucher.

adj. impenetrable, impervious, proofed, rainproof, re-pellent, resistant, strong, tight, treated, waterproof, weather-proof, windproof.

antonyms permeable, untreated.

propagate *v.* beget, breed, broadcast, circulate, diffuse, disseminate, engender, generate, increase, multiply, proclaim, procreate, produce, proliferate, promote, promulgate, publicize, publish, reproduce, spawn, spread, transmit.

propel *v.* drive, force, impel, launch, push, send, shoot, shove, start, thrust, waft.

antonyms slow, stop.

propensity *n.* aptness, bent, bias, disposition, foible, inclination, leaning, liability, penchant, predisposition, proclivity, proneness, readiness, susceptibility, tendency, weakness.

antonym disinclination.

proper *adj.* accepted, accurate, appropriate, apt, becoming, befitting, characteristic, conventional, correct, decent, decorous, established, exact, fit, fitting, formal, genteel, gentlemanly, gradely, individual, kosher, ladylike, legitimate, mannerly, meet, orthodox, own, particular, peculiar, perjink, personal, polite, precise, prim, prissy, punctilious, refined, respectable, respective, right, sedate, seemly, special, specific, suitable, suited, well-becoming, well-beseeming.

antonyms common, general, improper.

property[1] *n.* acres, assets, belongings, building(s), capital, chattels, effects, estate, freehold, goods, holding, holdings, house(s), land, means, meum et tuum, possessions, real estate, realty, resources, riches, title, wealth.

property[2] *n.* ability, affection, attribute, characteristic, feature, hallmark, idiosyncrasy, mark, peculiarity, quality, trait, virtue.

prophecy *n.* augury, divination, forecast, foretelling, hariolation, prediction, prognosis, prognostication, revelation, second-sight, soothsaying, taghairm, vaticination.

prophesy *v.* augur, divine, forecast, foresee, foretell, forewarn, hariolate, predict, presage, prognosticate, soothsay, vaticinate.

prophet *n.* augur, Cassandra, clairvoyant, divinator, diviner, forecaster, foreteller, Nostradamus, oracle, prognosticator, prophesier, seer, sibyl, soothsayer, tipster, vaticinator.

propitious *adj.* advantageous, auspicious, beneficial, benevolent, benign, bright, encouraging, favorable, fortunate, friendly, gracious, happy, kindly, lucky, opportune, promising, prosperous, reassuring, rosy, timely, well-disposed.

antonym inauspicious.

proportion *n.* agreement, amount, balance, congruity, correspondence, cut, distribution, division, eurhythmy, fraction, harmony, measure, part, percentage, quota, ratio, relationship, segment, share, symmetry.

antonyms disproportion, imbalance.

proportional *adj.* balanced, commensurate, comparable, compatible, consistent, correspondent, corresponding, equitable, even, fair, just, logistical, proportionate.
antonyms disproportionate, unjust.

proposal *n.* bid, design, draft, manifesto, motion, offer, outline, overture, plan, platform, presentation, proffer, program, project, proposition, recommendation, scheme, sketch, suggestion, suit, tender, terms.

propose *v.* advance, aim, bring up, design, enunciate, have in mind, intend, introduce, invite, lay before, mean, move, name, nominate, pay suit, plan, pop the question, present, proffer, propound, purpose, put forward, put up, recommend, scheme, submit, suggest, table, tender.
antonyms oppose, withdraw.

proposition *n.* manifesto, motion, plan, program, project, proposal, recommendation, scheme, suggestion, tender.
v. accost, solicit.

propound *v.* advance, advocate, contend, enunciate, lay down, move, postulate, present, propose, put forward, set forth, submit, suggest.
antonym oppose.

proprietor *n.* châtelaine, deed holder, freeholder, landlady, landlord, landowner, owner, possessor, proprietary, proprietress, proprietrix, title-holder.

prosaic *adj.* banal, boring, bromidic, commonplace, dry, dull, everyday, flat, hackneyed, humdrum, matter-of-fact, mundane, ordinary, pedestrian, routine, stale, tame, trite, unimaginative, uninspired, uninspiring, unpoetical, vapid, workaday.
antonyms imaginative, interesting.

proscribe *v.* attaint, ban, banish, bar, black, blackball, boycott, censure, condemn, damn, denounce, deport, doom, embargo, exclude, excommunicate, exile, expatriate, expel, forbid, interdict, ostracize, outlaw, prohibit, reject.
antonyms admit, allow.

prosecute *v.* arraign, bring suit against, bring to trial, carry on, conduct, continue, direct, discharge, engage in, execute, follow through, indict, litigate, manage, perform, persevere, persist, practice, prefer charges, pursue, put on trial, see through, sue, summon, take to court, try, work at.
antonym desist.

prospect *n.* calculation, chance, contemplation, expectation, future, hope, landscape, likelihood, odds, opening, outlook, panorama, perspective, plan, possibility, presumption, probability, promise, proposition, scene, sight, spectacle, thought, view, vision, vista.
antonym unlikelihood.
v. explore, fossick, nose, quest, search, seek, survey.

prospective *adj.* anticipated, approaching, awaited, coming, designate, designated, destined, eventual, expected, forthcoming, future, imminent, intended, likely, possible, potential, soon-to-be, to come, -to-be.
antonyms agreed, current.

prosper *v.* advance, bloom, boom, burgeon, fare well, flourish, flower, get on, grow rich, make good, progress, succeed, thrive, turn out well.
antonym fail.

prosperous *adj.* affluent, blooming, booming, burgeoning, flourishing, fortunate, in the money, lucky, moneyed, opulent, palmy, profitable, rich, successful, thriving, wealthy, well-heeled, well-off, well-to-do.
antonym poor.

prostrate *adj.* abject, brought to one's knees, crushed, defenseless, dejected, depressed, desolate, disarmed, done, drained, exhausted, fagged, fallen, flat, helpless, horizontal, impotent, inconsolable, knackered, kowtowing, overcome, overwhelmed, paralyzed, pooped, powerless, procumbent, prone, reduced, shattered, spent, worn out.
antonyms elated, erect, hale, happy, strong, triumphant.
v. crush, depress, disarm, drain, exhaust, fag out, fatigue, knacker, lay low, overcome, overthrow, overturn, overwhelm, paralyze, poop, reduce, ruin, sap, shatter, tire, wear out, weary.
antonyms elate, exalt, strengthen.

protagonist *n.* advocate, champion, chief character, exponent, hero, heroine, lead, leader, mainstay, prime mover, principal, proponent, standard-bearer, supporter.

protect *v.* care for, chaperon, convoy, cover, cover up for, defend, escort, guard, harbor, keep, look after, preserve, safeguard, save, screen, secure, shelter, shield, stand guard over, support, watch over.
antonyms attack, threaten.

protection *n.* aegis, armor, backstop, barrier, buffer, bulwark, care, charge, cover, custody, defense, guard, guardianship, guarding, preservation, protecting, refuge, safe-guard, safekeeping, safety, screen, security, shelter, shield, umbrella, wardship.
antonyms attack, threat.

protest *n.* complaint, declaration, demur, demurral, dharna, disapproval, dissent, formal complaint, objection, obtestation, outcry, protestation, remonstrance.
antonym acceptance.
v. affirm, argue, assert, asseverate, attest, avow, complain, contend, cry out, declare, demonstrate, demur, disagree, disapprove, expostulate, insist, maintain, object, obtest, oppose, profess, remonstrate, squawk, take exception, testify, vow.
antonym accept.

prototype *n.* archetype, example, exemplar, mock-up, model, original, paradigm, pattern, precedent, standard, type.

protract *v.* continue, draw out, extend, keep going, lengthen, prolong, spin out, stretch out, sustain.
antonym shorten.

protuberance *n.* apophysis, bulb, bulge, bump, excrescence, knob, lump, mamelon, mamilla, outgrowth, process, projection, prominence, protrusion, swelling, tuber, tubercle, tumor, umbo, venter, wart, welt.

proud *adj.* appreciative, arrogant, august, boastful, conceited, content, contented, disdainful, distinguished, egotistical, eminent, exalted, glad, glorious, grand, gratified, gratifying, great, haughty, high and mighty, honored, illustrious, imperious, imposing, lofty, lordly, magnificent, majestic, memorable, misproud, noble, orgulous, overbearing, overweening, pleased, pleasing, presumptuous, prideful, red-letter, rewarding, satisfied, satisfying, self-important, self-respecting, snobbish, snobby, snooty, splendid, stately, stuck-up, supercilious, toffee-nosed, vain. *antonym* humble.

prove *v.* analyze, ascertain, assay, attest, authenticate, bear out, check, confirm, corroborate, demonstrate, determine, document, establish, evidence, evince, examine, experience, experiment, justify, show, substantiate, suffer, test, try, turn out, verify. *antonyms* discredit, disprove, falsify.

proverb *n.* adage, aphorism, apophthegm, bromide, byword, dictum, gnome, maxim, precept, saw, saying.

proverbial *adj.* accepted, acknowledged, apophthegmatic, archetypal, axiomatic, bromidic, conventional, current, customary, famed, famous, legendary, notorious, self-evident, time-honored, traditional, typical, unquestioned, well-known.

provide *v.* accommodate, add, afford, anticipate, arrange for, bring, cater, contribute, determine, equip, forearm, furnish, give, impart, lay down, lend, outfit, plan for, prepare for, present, produce, provision, render, require, serve, specify, state, stipulate, stock up, suit, supply, take measures, take precautions, yield. *antonyms* remove, take.

provident *adj.* canny, careful, cautious, discreet, economical, equipped, far-seeing, far-sighted, frugal, imaginative, long-sighted, prudent, sagacious, shrewd, thrifty, vigilant, wary, well-prepared, wise. *antonym* improvident.

provision *n.* accouterment, agreement, arrangement, catering, clause, condition, demand, equipping, fitting out, furnishing, plan, prearrangement, precaution, preparation, prerequisite, providing, proviso, purveyance, purveying, requirement, specification, stipulation, supplying, term, victualing. *antonyms* neglect, removal.

provisions *n.* comestibles, eatables, eats, edibles, fare, food, foodstuff, groceries, grub, piece, prog, provand, provender, proviant, rations, stores, supplies, sustenance, viands, viaticum, victualage, victuals, vittles.

proviso *n.* clause, condition, limitation, provision, qualification, requirement, reservation, restriction, rider, small print, stipulation.

provoke *v.* affront, aggravate, anger, annoy, cause, chafe, elicit, enrage, evoke, exasperate, excite, fire, gall, generate, give rise to, incense, incite, induce, inflame,

infuriate, inspire, instigate, insult, irk, irritate, kindle, madden, motivate, move, occasion, offend, pique, precipitate, produce, promote, prompt, put out, rile, rouse, stimulate, stir, vex. *antonyms* pacify, please, result.

prowess *n.* ability, accomplishment, adeptness, adroitness, aptitude, attainment, bravery, command, daring, dauntlessness, dexterity, doughtiness, excellence, expertise, expertness, facility, genius, heroism, mastery, skill, talent, valor. *antonyms* clumsiness, mediocrity.

prowl *v.* creep, cruise, hunt, lurk, nose, patrol, range, roam, rove, scavenge, search, skulk, slink, sneak, snook, stalk, steal.

proximity *n.* adjacency, closeness, contiguity, juxtaposition, nearness, neighborhood, propinquity, proximation, vicinity. *antonym* remoteness.

proxy *n.* agent, attorney, delegate, deputy, factor, representative, stand-in, substitute, surrogate.

prudence *n.* canniness, care, caution, circumspection, common sense, discretion, economy, far-sightedness, foresight, forethought, frugality, good sense, heedfulness, husbandry, judgment, judiciousness, planning, policy, precaution, preparedness, providence, sagacity, saving, thrift, vigilance, wariness, wisdom. *antonym* imprudence.

prudent *adj.* canny, careful, cautious, circumspect, discerning, discreet, economical, far-sighted, frugal, judicious, politic, provident, sagacious, sage, sensible, shrewd, sparing, thrifty, vigilant, wary, well-advised, wise, wise-hearted. *antonym* imprudent.

prudish *adj.* demure, narrow-minded, old-maidish, overmodest, overnice, po-faced, priggish, prim, prissy, proper, pudibund, puritanical, school-marmish, squeamish, starchy, strait-laced, stuffy, ultra-virtuous, Victorian. *antonyms* easy-going, lax.

pry *v.* delve, dig, ferret, interfere, intrude, meddle, nose, peep, peer, poke, poke one's nose in, snoop. *antonym* mind one's own business.

prying *adj.* curious, inquisitive, interfering, intrusive, meddlesome, meddling, nosy, peering, peery, snooping, snoopy, spying. *antonym* uninquisitive.

psyche *n.* anima, awareness, consciousness, individuality, intellect, intelligence, mind, personality, pneuma, self, soul, spirit, subconscious, understanding.

psychiatrist *n.* analyst, headshrinker, psychoanalyzer, psychoanalyst, psychologist, psychotherapist, shrink, therapist, trick-cyclist.

psychic *adj.* clairvoyant, cognitive, extra-sensory, intellectual, mental, mystic, mystical, occult, preternatural, psychogenic, psychological, spiritual, spiritualistic, supernatural, telekinetic, telepathic.

psychological *adj.* affective, cerebral, cognitive,

emotional, imaginary, intellectual, irrational, mental, psychosomatic, subconscious, subjective, unconscious, unreal.

psychotic *adj.* certifiable, demented, deranged, insane, lunatic, mad, mental, psychopathic, unbalanced.
antonym sane.

public *adj.* accessible, acknowledged, circulating, civic, civil, common, communal, community, exposed, general, important, known, national, notorious, obvious, open, overt, patent, plain, popular, prominent, published, recognized, respected, social, state, universal, unrestricted, well-known, widespread.
antonym private.
n. audience, buyers, citizens, clientèle, commonalty, community, country, electorate, everyone, followers, following, masses, multitude, nation, patrons, people, populace, population, punters, society, supporters, voters.

publicize *v.* advertise, blaze, blazon, broadcast, hype, plug, promote, puff, push, spotlight, spread about, write off.
antonym keep secret.

publish *v.* advertise, announce, bring out, broadcast, circulate, communicate, declare, diffuse, disclose, distribute, divulgate, divulge, evulgate, issue, leak, part, print, proclaim, produce, promulgate, publicize, reveal, spread, vent.
antonym keep secret.

puerile *adj.* babyish, childish, foolish, immature, inane, infantile, irresponsible, jejune, juvenile, naïve, petty, ridiculous, silly, trifling, trivial, weak.
antonym mature.

pugnacious *adj.* aggressive, antagonistic, argumentative, bellicose, belligerent, choleric, combative, contentious, disputatious, hostile, hot-tempered, irascible, petulant, quarrelsome.
antonym easy-going.

pull *v.* attract, cull, dislocate, drag, draw, draw out, entice, extract, gather, haul, jerk, lure, magnetize, pick, pluck, remove, rend, rip, schlep, sprain, strain, stretch, take out, tear, tow, track, trail, tug, tweak, uproot, weed, whang, wrench, yank.
antonyms deter, push, repel.
n. advantage, allurement, attraction, clout, drag, drawing power, effort, exertion, force, forcefulness, influence, inhalation, jerk, leverage, lure, magnetism, muscle, power, puff, seduction, tug, twitch, weight, yank.
antonyms deterring, push, repelling.

pulsate *v.* beat, drum, hammer, oscillate, palpitate, pound, pulse, quiver, throb, thud, thump, tick, vibrate.

pulse *n.* beat, beating, drumming, oscillation, pulsation, rhythm, stroke, throb, throbbing, thudding, vibration.
v. beat, drum, pulsate, throb, thud, tick, vibrate.

pummel *v.* bang, batter, beat, fib, hammer, knock, nevel, pound, punch, strike, thump.

pump *v.* catechize, cross-examine, debrief, drive, force, grill, inject, interrogate, pour, probe, push, question, quiz, send, supply.

pun *n.* clinch, double entendre, equivoke, jeu de mots, paronomasia, paronomasy, play on words, quip, witticism.

punch[1] *v.* bash, biff, bop, box, clout, fib, hit, plug, pummel, slam, slug, smash, sock, strike, wallop.
n. bash, biff, bite, blow, bop, clout, drive, effectiveness, force, forcefulness, hit, impact, jab, knock, knuckle sandwich, lander, muzzler, panache, pizzazz, plug, point, sock, thump, verve, vigor, wallop.
antonym feebleness.

punch[2] *v.* bore, cut, drill, perforate, pierce, pink, prick, puncture, stamp.

punctilious *adj.* careful, ceremonious, conscientious, exact, finicky, formal, formalist, fussy, meticulous, nice, overnice, particular, precise, proper, scrupulous, strict.
antonyms boorish, easy-going, informal.

punctual *adj.* early, exact, in good time, on the dot, on time, precise, prompt, punctilious, strict, timely, up to time.
antonym unpunctual.

pungent *adj.* acid, acrid, acrimonious, acute, aromatic, barbed, biting, bitter, caustic, cutting, fell, hot, incisive, keen, mordant, painful, penetrating, peppery, piercing, piquant, poignant, pointed, sarcastic, scathing, seasoned, sharp, sour, spicy, stinging, stringent, strong, tangy, tart, telling, trenchant.
antonyms feeble, mild, tasteless.

punish *v.* abuse, amerce, batter, beat, castigate, chasten, chastise, correct, crucify, discipline, flog, give a lesson to, give someone laldie, harm, hurt, injure, keelhaul, kneecap, lash, maltreat, manhandle, masthead, misuse, oppress, penalize, rough up, scour, scourge, sort, strafe, trounce.

punishment *n.* abuse, beating, chastening, chastisement, come-uppance, correction, damnation, deserts, discipline, jankers, knee-capping, laldie, maltreatment, manhandling, medicine, pain, pay-off, penalty, penance, punition, retribution, sanction, toco, torture, victimization.

puny *adj.* diminutive, dwarfish, feeble, frail, inconsequential, inferior, insignificant, little, meager, minor, paltry, petty, piddling, pimping, reckling, runted, runtish, runty, sickly, stunted, tiny, trifling, trivial, underfed, undersized, undeveloped, weak, weakly, worthless.
antonyms important, large, strong.

pupil *n.* beginner, catechumen, disciple, learner, neophyte, novice, protégé, scholar, schoolboy, schoolgirl, student, tiro, tutee.
antonym teacher.

purchase *v.* achieve, acquire, attain, buy, earn, gain, invest in, obtain, pay for, procure, ransom, realize, secure, win.
antonym sell.

n. acquisition, advantage, asset, buy, edge, emption, foot-hold, footing, gain, grasp, grip, hold, influence, investment, lever, leverage, possession, property, ransoming, support, toehold.
antonym sale.

pure *adj.* absolute, abstract, academic, antiseptic, authentic, blameless, chaste, clean, clear, disinfected, flawless, genuine, germ-free, guileless, high-minded, honest, hygienic, immaculate, innocent, intemerate, maidenly, modest, natural, neat, pasteurized, perfect, philosophical, real, refined, sanitary, Saturnian, sheer, simple, sincere, snow-white, speculative, spiritous, spotless, stainless, sterile, sterilized, straight, taintless, theoretical, thorough, true, unadulterate, unadulterated, unalloyed, unblemished, uncontaminated, uncorrupted, undefiled, unmingled, unmitigated, unmixed, unpolluted, unqualified, unsoiled, unspoilt, unspotted, unstained, unsullied, untainted, untarnished, upright, utter, virgin, virginal, virginly, virtuous, wholesome.
antonyms adulterated, applied, defiled, immoral, impure, polluted, tainted.

purely *adv.* absolutely, completely, entirely, exclusively, just, merely, only, plainly, sheerly, simply, solely, thoroughly, totally, utterly, wholly.

purify *v.* absolve, beneficiate, catharize, chasten, clarify, clean, cleanse, decontaminate, deodorize, depurate, desalinate, disinfect, epurate, filter, fumigate, furbish, lustrate, mundify, redeem, refine, sanctify, sanitize, shrive, sublimize, wash.
antonyms contaminate, defile, pollute.

purist *n.* Atticist, classicist, formalist, grammaticaster, grammatist, mandarin, nit-picker, pedant, precisian, precisianist, precisionist, quibbler, stickler, vocabularian.
antonym liberal.
adj. austere, captious, fastidious, finicky, fussy, hypercritical, nit-picking, over-exact, over-fastidious, over-meticulous, over-particular, over-precise, pedantic, puristic, quibbling, strict, uncompromising.
antonyms liberal, open-minded, tolerant.

puritanical *adj.* abstemious, abstinent, ascetic, austere, bigoted, disapproving, disciplinarian, fanatical, narrow, narrow-minded, prim, proper, prudish, puritan, rigid, severe, stern, stiff, strait-laced, strict, stuffy, uncompromising, zealous.
antonyms broad-minded, hedonistic, indulgent, liberal.

purity *n.* blamelessness, chasteness, chastity, clarity, classicism, cleanliness, clearness, decency, faultlessness, fineness, genuineness, immaculateness, incorruption, innocence, integrity, morality, piety, pureness, rectitude, refinement, sanctity, simplicity, sincerity, spotlessness, stainlessness, truth, unspottedness, untaintedness, uprightness, virginity, virtue, virtuousness, wholesomeness.
antonyms immorality, impurity.

purloin *v.* abstract, appropriate, filch, finger, half-inch,

lift, nick, nobble, palm, pilfer, pinch, pocket, prig, remove, rob, snaffle, snitch, steal, swipe, take, thieve.

purport *v.* allege, argue, assert, betoken, claim, convey, declare, denote, express, give out, imply, import, indicate, intend, maintain, mean, portend, pose as, pretend, proclaim, profess, seem, show, signify, suggest.
n. bearing, direction, drift, gist, idea, implication, import, meaning, point, significance, spirit, substance, tendency, tenor, theme, thrust.

purpose *n.* advantage, aim, ambition, aspiration, assiduity, avail, benefit, constancy, contemplation, decision, dedication, design, determination, devotion, drive, effect, end, firmness, function, gain, goal, good, hope, idea, ideal, intention, motive, object, objective, outcome, persistence, pertinacity, plan, point, principle, profit, project, rationale, reason, resolution, resolve, result, return, scheme, service, single-mindedness, steadfastness, target, telos, tenacity, use, usefulness, utility, view, vision, will, wish, zeal.
v. aim, aspire, contemplate, decide, design, desire, determine, ettle, intend, mean, meditate, plan, propose, resolve.

purposely *adv..* by design, calculatedly, consciously, deliberately, designedly, expressly, intentionally, knowingly, on purpose, premeditatedly, specifically, wilfully, with malice aforethought.
antonyms impulsively, spontaneously, unpremeditatedly.

pursue *v.* accompany, adhere to, aim at, aim for, aspire to, attend, bedevil, beset, besiege, carry on, chase, check out, conduct, continue, course, court, cultivate, desire, dog, engage in, follow, follow up, go for, gun for, harass, harry, haunt, hold to, hound, hunt, inquire into, investigate, keep on, maintain, perform, persecute, persevere in, persist in, plague, ply, practice, proceed, prosecute, purpose, seek, set one's cap at, shadow, stalk, strive for, tackle, tail, track, trail, try for, wage, woo.
antonyms eschew, shun.

pursuit[1] *n.* chase, chevy, hounding, hue and cry, hunt, hunting, inquiry, investigation, quest, search, seeking, stalking, tracking, trail, trailing.

pursuit[2] *n.* activity, craft, hobby, interest, line, occupation, parergon, pastime, pleasure, side-line, specialty, vocation.

push *v.* advance, advertise, boost, browbeat, bulldoze, bully, coerce, constrain, depress, dragoon, drive, edge, egg on, elbow, encourage, expedite, force, hurry, hype, incite, influence, inveigle, jockey, jog, joggle, jostle, maneuver, manhandle, oblige, peddle, persuade, plug, poke, press, prod, promote, propagandize, propel, publicize, puff, ram, shoulder, shove, speed, spur, squeeze, thrust, urge, wedge, whang.
n. advance, ambition, assault, attack, bunt, butt, charge, determination, discharge, dismissal, drive, dynamism, effort, energy, enterprise, go, impetus, impulse, initia-

tive, jolt, knock, notice, nudge, offensive, one's books, one's cards, one's marching orders, onset, onslaught, poke, pressure, prod, shove, the axe, the boot, the bum's rush, the chop, the sack, thrust, vigor, vim, vitality, zip.

push-over *n.* child's play, cinch, doddle, dupe, easy mark, fall guy, gull, mug, picnic, piece of cake, sinecure, sitting duck, sitting target, soft mark, soft touch, stooge, sucker, walk-over. *antonyms* challenge, labor.

pushy *adj.* aggressive, ambitious, arrogant, assertive, assuming, bold, bossy, brash, bumptious, forceful, forward, loud, obtrusive, offensive, officious, overconfident, presumptuous, pushing, self-assertive. *antonyms* quiet, restrained, unassertive, unassuming.

pusillanimous *adj.* caitiff, chicken, chicken-hearted, cowardly, craven, faint-hearted, fearful, feeble, gutless, lily-livered, mean-spirited, poltroon, recreant, scared, spineless, timid, timorous, unassertive, unenterprising, weak, weak-kneed, yellow. *antonyms* ambitious, courageous, forceful, strong.

put *v.* advance, apply, assign, bring, bring forward, cast, commit, condemn, consign, constrain, couch, deploy, deposit, dispose, drive, employ, enjoin, establish, express, fit, fix, fling, force, formulate, forward, frame, heave, hurl, impel, impose, induce, inflict, land, lay, levy, lob, make, oblige, offer, park, phrase, pitch, place, plonk, pose, position, post, present, propose, push, render, require, rest, send, set, set down, settle, situate, state, station, subject, submit, suggest, tender, throw, thrust, toss, utter, voice, word, write.

putative *adj.* alleged, assumed, conjectural, hypothetical, imputed, presumed, presumptive, reported, reputative, reputed, supposed, suppositional, supposititious.

put-down *n.* affront, dig, disparagement, gibe, humiliation, insult, rebuff, sarcasm, slap in the face, slight, sneer, snub.

putrefy *v.* addle, corrupt, decay, decompose, deteriorate, fester, foost, gangrene, go bad, mortify, mold, necrose, perish, rot, spoil, stink, taint.

putrid *adj.* addle, addled, bad, contaminated, corrupt, decayed, decomposed, fetid, foosty, foul, gangrenous, mephitic, moldy, necrosed, noisome, off, putrefied, rancid, rank, reeking, rotten, rotting, sphacelate(d), spoiled, stinking, tainted. *antonyms* fresh, wholesome.

puzzle[1] *v.* baffle, bamboozle, beat, bewilder, confound, confuse, fickle, floor, flummox, metagrobolize, mystify, non-plus, perplex, pother, stump, worry. *n.* acrostic, anagram, brain-teaser, confusion, conundrum, crossword, difficulty, dilemma, enigma, knot, koan, logogram, logograph, logogriph, maze, mindbender, mystery, paradox, poser, problem, quandary, question, rebus, riddle, Sphinx, tickler.

puzzle[2] *v.* brood, cogitate, consider, deliberate, figure, meditate, mull over, muse, ponder, rack one's brains, ratiocinate, reason, ruminate, study, think, wonder, worry.

puzzled *adj.* at a loss, at sea, baffled, bamboozled, beaten, bemused, bewildered, confounded, confused, disorientated, doubtful, flummoxed, in a haze, lost, mixed up, mizzled, mystified, nonplused, perplexed, stuck, stumped, stymied, uncertain. *antonyms* certain, clear.

puzzling *adj.* abstruse, ambiguous, baffling, bewildering, bizarre, cabalistic, circuitous, confusing, cryptic, curious, enigmatic, equivocal, impenetrable, inexplicable, intricate, involved, knotty, labyrinthine, mindbending, mind-boggling, misleading, mysterious, mystical, mystifying, peculiar, perplexing, queer, riddling, Sphinx-like, strange, tangled, tortuous, unaccountable, unclear, unfathomable.

Q

quack *n.* charlatan, cowboy, empiric, fake, fraud, humbug, impostor, masquerader, medicaster, mountebank, phony, pretender, pseud, quacksalver, sham, spieler, swindler, trickster, witch-doctor.
adj. bogus, counterfeit, fake, false, fraudulent, phony, pretended, sham, so-called, spurious, supposed, unqualified.
antonym genuine.

quackery *n.* charlatanism, charlatanry, empiricism, fraud, fraudulence, humbug, imposture, mountebankery, mountebankism, phoniness, sham.

quaff *v.* booze, carouse, down, drain, drink, gulp, guzzle, imbibe, knock back, swallow, swig, swill, tipple, tope, toss off.
n. bevvy, cup, dram, draught, drink, jorum, slug, snifter, swig.

quagmire *n.* bog, everglade, fen, marsh, mire, morass, moss, mudflat, quag, quicksand, slough, swamp.

quail *v.* back away, blanch, blench, cower, droop, faint, falter, flinch, quake, recoil, shake, shrink, shudder, shy away, tremble, wince.

quaint *adj.* absurd, antiquated, antique, bizarre, charming, curious, droll, eccentric, fanciful, fantastic, freaky, funky, ingenious, odd, old-fashioned, old-time, old-world, peculiar, picturesque, queer, rum, singular, strange, unconventional, unusual, weird, whimsical.

quake *v.* convulse, heave, jolt, move, pulsate, quail, quiver, rock, shake, shiver, shudder, sway, throb, totter, tremble, vibrate, waver, wobble.

qualification[1] *n.* ability, accomplishment, adequacy, aptitude, attribute, capability, capacity, certification, competence, eligibility, fitness, skill, suitability, suitableness, training.

qualification[2] *n.* adaptation, adjustment, allowance, caveat, condition, criterion, exception, exemption, limitation, modification, objection, provision, proviso, reservation, restriction, stipulation.

qualified[1] *adj.* able, accomplished, adept, adequate, capable, certificated, certified, competent, efficient, eligible, equipped, experienced, expert, fit, habilitated, knowledgeable, licensed, practiced, proficient, skilful, talented, trained.
antonym unqualified.

qualified[2] *adj.* bounded, cautious, circumscribed, conditional, confined, contingent, equivocal, guarded, limitative, limited, modificatory, modified, provisional, qualificatory, reserved, restricted.

qualify[1] *v.* authorize, capacitate, certificate, empower, endow, equip, fit, graduate, habilitate, permit, prepare, sanction, shape, train.
antonym unfit.

qualify[2] *v.* abate, adapt, adjust, alleviate, assuage, categorize, characterize, circumscribe, classify, define, delimit, describe, designate, diminish, distinguish, ease, lessen, limit, mitigate, moderate, modify, modulate, reduce, regulate, restrain, restrict, soften, temper, vary, weaken.

quality *n.* aspect, attribute, caliber, character, characteristic, class, complexion, condition, constitution, deal, description, distinction, essence, excellence, feature, fineness, grade, kidney, kind, make, mark, merit, nature, peculiarity, position, pre-eminence, property, rank, refinement, sort, standing, status, superiority, talent, timbre, tone, trait, value, water, worth.

qualm *n.* anxiety, apprehension, compunction, disquiet, doubt, fear, hesitation, misgiving, pang, presentiment, regret, reluctance, remorse, scruple, twinge, uncertainty, unease, uneasiness, worry.

quandary *n.* bewilderment, confusion, corner, difficulty, dilemma, doubt, embarrassment, entanglement, fix, hole, imbroglio, impasse, jam, kettle of fish, mess, perplexity, plight, predicament, problem, puzzle, uncertainty.

quantity *n.* aggregate, allotment, amount, breadth, bulk, capacity, content, dosage, expanse, extent, greatness, length, lot, magnitude, mass, measure, number, part, portion, proportion, quantum, quota, share, size, spread, strength, sum, total, volume, weight.

quarantine *n.* detention, isolation, lazaret, lazaretto, segregation.

quarrel *n.* affray, altercation, argument, barney, beef, bicker, brattle, brawl, breach, breeze, broil, clash, commotion, conflict, contention, controversy, coolness, debate, difference, disagreement, discord, disputation, dispute, dissension, dissidence, disturbance, dust-up, estrangement, feud, fight, fracas, fray, misunderstanding, row, rupture, schism, scrap, shouting match, slanging match, spat, split, squabble, strife, tiff, tumult, vendetta, wrangle.
antonyms agreement, harmony.
v. altercate, argue, be at loggerheads, be at variance, bicker, brawl, carp, cavil, clash, contend, differ, disagree, dispute, dissent, fall out, fight, find fault, object, pick holes, question, row, spar, spat, squabble, take exception, tiff, vitilitigate, wrangle.
antonym agree.

quarrelsome *adj.* altercative, antagonistic, argumentative, bellicose, belligerent, cantankerous, captious, choleric, combative, contentious, contrary, cross, disputatious, fractious, ill-tempered, irascible, irritable, peevish, perverse, petulant, pugnacious, querulous, stroppy, testy, truculent, turbulent, wranglesome.

antonyms peaceable, placid.

quarry *n.* game, goal, kill, object, objective, prey, prize, target, victim.

quarter[1] *n.* area, direction, district, division, locality, location, neighborhood, part, place, point, position, province, quartier, region, section, sector, side, spot, station, territory, vicinity, zone.

quarter[2] *n.* clemency, compassion, favor, forgiveness, grace, indulgence, leniency, mercy, pardon, pity.

quarter[3] *n.* fourth, quartern, term.

v. decussate, divide in four, quadrisect.

quarter[4] *v.* accommodate, bed, billet, board, house, install, lodge, place, post, put up, shelter, station.

quarters *n.* abode, accommodation, apartment, barracks, billet, cantonment, caserne, chambers, digs, domicile, dwelling, habitation, lodging, lodgings, post, quarterage, residence, rooms, station.

quash *v.* annul, cancel, crush, declare null and void, defeat, disannul, disenact, invalidate, nullify, overrule, overthrow, quell, repress, rescind, reverse, revoke, set aside, squash, subdue, suppress, void.

antonyms confirm, justify, reinstate, vindicate.

quaver *v.* break, crack, flicker, flutter, oscillate, pulsate, quake, quiver, shake, shudder, tremble, trill, twitter, vibrate, warble.

n. break, quaveriness, quiver, shake, sob, throb, tremble, trembling, tremolo, tremor, trill, vibration, vibrato, warble.

quay *n.* dock, harbor, jetty, levee, pier, wharf.

queasy *adj.* bilious, dizzy, faint, giddy, green, groggy, ill, indisposed, nauseated, off-color, qualmish, qualmy, queer, sick, sickened, squeamish, unwell.

queen *n.* beauty, belle, consort, diva, doyenne, empress, goddess, grande dame, idol, maharani, mistress, monarch, nonpareil, prima donna, princess, rani, ruler, sovereign, star, sultana, tsarina, Venus.

queer *adj.* aberrant, abnormal, absurd, anomalous, atypical, bizarre, cranky, crazy, curious, daft, demented, deranged, deviant, disquieting, dizzy, doubtful, droll, dubious, eccentric, eerie, eldritch, erratic, exceptional, extraordinary, faint, fanciful, fantastic, fey, fishy, freakish, funny, giddy, grotesque, homosexual, idiosyncratic, ill, irrational, irregular, light-headed, mad, mysterious, odd, offbeat, outlandish, outré, peculiar, preternatural, puzzling, quaint, queasy, questionable, reeling, remarkable, rum, screwy, shady, shifty, singular, strange, suspect, suspicious, touched, unaccountable, unbalanced, uncanny, uncommon, unconventional, uneasy, unhinged, unnatural, unorthodox, unusual, unwell, unwonted, weird.

antonyms common, ordinary, straightforward, unexceptional, usual.

v. botch, cheat, endanger, foil, frustrate, harm, impair, imperil, injure, jeopardize, mar, ruin, spoil, stymie, thwart, upset, wreck.

queerness *n.* aberrance, abnormality, absurdity, anomalousness, atypicalness, bizarreness, crankiness, craziness, curiousness, deviance, drollness, dubiety, dubiousness, eccentricity, eeriness, fishiness, grotesqueness, idiosyncrasy, individuality, irrationality, irregularity, light-headedness, madness, mysteriousness, mystery, oddity, oddness, outlandishness, peculiarity, puzzle, quaintness, shadiness, shiftiness, singularity, strangeness, suspiciousness, uncanniness, uncommonness, unconventionality, unnaturalness, unorthodoxy, unusualness, unwontedness.

quell *v.* allay, alleviate, appease, assuage, blunt, calm, compose, conquer, crush, deaden, defeat, dull, extinguish, hush, mitigate, moderate, mollify, overcome, overpower, pacify, put down, quash, quench, quiet, reduce, silence, soothe, squash, stifle, subdue, subjugate, suppress, vanquish.

quench *v.* allay, appease, check, cool, crush, damp down, destroy, douse, end, extinguish, overcome, put out, quash, quell, sate, satisfy, silence, slake, smother, snuff out, stifle, suppress.

querulous *adj.* cantankerous, captious, carping, caviling, censorious, complaining, crabbed, critical, cross, cross-grained, crusty, discontented, dissatisfied, exacting, fault-finding, fretful, fussy, grouchy, grumbling, hypercritical, intolerant, irascible, irritable, peevish, perverse, petulant, plaintive, quarrelsome, querimonious, sour, testy, thrawn, waspish, whingeing, whining.

antonyms contented, equable, placid, uncomplaining.

query *v.* ask, be skeptical of, call in question, challenge, disbelieve, dispute, distrust, doubt, enquire, misdoubt, mistrust, quarrel with, question, suspect.

antonym accept.

n. demand, doubt, hesitation, inquiry, misdoubt, misgiving, objection, problem, quaere, question, quibble, reservation, skepticism, suspicion, uncertainty.

quest *n.* adventure, crusade, enterprise, expedition, exploration, hunt, inquiry, investigation, journey, mission, pilgrimage, pursuit, search, undertaking, venture, voyage.

question *v.* ask, be skeptical of, catechize, challenge, controvert, cross-examine, debrief, disbelieve, dispute, distrust, doubt, enquire, examine, grill, impugn, interpellate, interrogate, interview, investigate, misdoubt, mistrust, oppose, probe, pump, quarrel with, query, quiz, suspect.

n. argument, confusion, contention, controversy, debate, difficulty, dispute, doubt, dubiety, erotema, erotesis, examination, inquiry, interpellation, interrogation, investigation, issue, misdoubt, misgiving, motion, point, problem, proposal, proposition, quaere, query, quibble, skepsis, subject, theme, topic, uncertainty.

questionable *adj.* arguable, borderline, controversial, debatable, disputable, doubtful, dubious, dubitable, equivocal, fishy, iffy, impugnable, moot, problematical,

queer, shady, suspect, suspicious, uncertain, undetermined, unproven, unreliable, unsettled, vexed.
antonyms certain, indisputable, straightforward.

queue *n.* file, line, line-up, order, procession, sequence, series, string, succession, tail, tail-back, train.

quibble *v.* carp, cavil, chop logic, equivocate, pettifog, prevaricate, shift, split hairs.
n. carriwitchet, casuistry, cavil, complaint, criticism, equivocation, equivoke, evasion, niggle, objection, pettifoggery, prevarication, query, quiddit, quiddity, quillet, quip, quirk, sophism, subterfuge.

quibbler *n.* casuist, caviler, chop-logic, criticaster, equivocator, hair-splitter, logic-chopper, niggler, nitpicker, pettifogger, sophist.

quick *adj.* able, active, acute, adept, adroit, agile, alert, animated, apt, astute, awake, brief, bright, brisk, clever, cursory, deft, dexterous, discerning, energetic, expeditious, express, fast, fleet, flying, hasty, headlong, hurried, immediate, instant, instantaneous, intelligent, keen, lively, nifty, nimble, nippy, penetrating, perceptive, perfunctory, precipitate, prompt, quick-witted, rapid, ready, receptive, responsive, sharp, shrewd, skilful, smart, snappy, speedy, spirited, sprightly, spry, sudden, summary, swift, unhesitating, vivacious, wide-awake, winged.
antonyms dull, slow.

quicken *v.* accelerate, activate, advance, animate, arouse, dispatch, energize, enliven, excite, expedite, galvanize, hasten, hurry, impel, incite, inspire, invigorate, kindle, precipitate, reactivate, refresh, reinvigorate, resuscitate, revitalize, revive, revivify, rouse, sharpen, speed, stimulate, strengthen, vitalize, vivify.
antonyms dull, retard.

quickly *adv.* abruptly, at a rate of knots, at the double, before you can say Jack Robinson, briskly, by leaps and bounds, cursorily, expeditiously, express, fast, hastily, hell for leather, hotfoot, hurriedly, immediately, instantaneously, instantly, lickety-split, like a bat out of hell, perfunctorily, posthaste, promptly, pronto, quick, rapidly, readily, soon, speedily, swiftly, unhesitatingly.
antonyms slowly, tardily, thoroughly.

quickness *n.* acuteness, agility, alertness, aptness, astuteness, briskness, deftness, dexterity, expedition, hastiness, immediacy, instantaneousness, intelligence, keenness, liveliness, nimbleness, penetration, precipitation, promptitude, promptness, quick-wittedness, rapidity, readiness, receptiveness, sharpness, shrewdness, speed, speediness, suddenness, summariness, swiftness, turn of speed.
antonyms dullness, slowness, tardiness.

quick-witted *adj.* acute, alert, astute, bright, clever, crafty, ingenious, intelligent, keen, nimble-witted, penetrating, perceptive, ready-witted, resourceful, sharp, shrewd, smart, wide-awake, witty.
antonyms dull, slow, stupid.

quiescent *adj.* asleep, calm, dormant, in abeyance, inactive, inert, latent, motionless, passive, peaceful, placid, quiet, reposeful, resting, serene, silent, sleeping, smooth, still, tranquil, undisturbed, untroubled.
antonym active.

quiet *adj.* calm, composed, conservative, contemplative, contended, docile, dumb, even-tempered, gentle, hushed, inaudible, isolated, lonely, low, low-pitched, meek, mild, modest, motionless, noiseless, pacific, passive, peaceable, peaceful, placid, plain, private, removed, reserved, restful, restrained, retired, retiring, secluded, secret, sedate, self-contained, sequestered, serene, shy, silent, simple, smooth, sober, soft, soundless, still, stilly, subdued, taciturn, thoughtful, tranquil, uncommunicative, unconversable, undisturbed, uneventful, unexcitable, unexciting, unforthcoming, unfrequented, uninterrupted, unobtrusive, untroubled.
antonyms busy, noisy, obtrusive.
n. calm, calmness, ease, hush, lull, peace, quiescence, quietness, quietude, repose, rest, serenity, silence, stillness, tranquility.
antonyms bustle, disturbance, noise.

quietness *n.* calm, calmness, composure, dullness, hush, inactivity, inertia, lull, peace, placidity, quiescence, quiet, quietude, repose, serenity, silence, still, stillness, tranquility, uneventfulness.
antonyms activity, bustle, commotion, disturbance, noise, racket.

quintessence *n.* core, distillation, embodiment, essence, exemplar, extract, gist, heart, kernel, marrow, pattern, pith, quiddity, soul, spirit, sum and substance.

quip *n.* bon mot, carriwitchet, crack, epigram, gag, gibe, jest, jeu d'esprit, joke, mot, one-liner, pleasantry, quirk, retort, riposte, sally, wisecrack, witticism.
v. gag, gibe, jest, joke, quirk, retort, riposte, wisecrack.

quirk *n.* aberration, caprice, characteristic, curiosity, eccentricity, fancy, fetish, foible, freak, habit, idiosyncrasy, kink, mannerism, oddity, oddness, peculiarity, singularity, trait, turn, twist, vagary, warp, whim.

quit *v.* abandon, abdicate, apostatize, cease, conclude, decamp, depart, desert, disappear, discontinue, drop, end, exit, forsake, give up, go, halt, leave, relinquish, renege, renounce, repudiate, resign, retire, stop, surrender, suspend, vamoose, vanish, withdraw.

quite *adv.* absolutely, comparatively, completely, entirely, exactly, fairly, fully, moderately, perfectly, precisely, rather, relatively, somewhat, totally, utterly, wholly.

quits *adj.* equal, even, level, square.

quitter *n.* apostate, defector, delinquent, deserter, rat, recreant, renegade, shirker, skiver.

quiver *v.* agitate, bicker, convulse, flichter, flicker, flutter, oscillate, palpitate, pulsate, quake, quaver, shake, shiver, shudder, tremble, vibrate, wobble.
n. convulsion, flicker, flutter, oscillation, palpitation, pulsation, shake, shiver, shudder, spasm, throb, tic, tremble, tremor, vibration, wobble.

quixotic *adj.* chivalrous, extravagant, fanciful, fantastical, idealistic, impetuous, impracticable, impulsive, romantic, starry-eyed, unrealistic, unworldly, Utopian, visionary.
antonyms hard-headed, practical, realistic.

quiz *n.* catechism, examination, investigation, questioning, questionnaire, test.
v. ask, catechize, cross-examine, cross-question, debrief, examine, grill, interrogate, investigate, pump, question.

quizzical *adj.* amused, arch, bantering, curious, humorous, inquiring, mocking, questioning, sardonic, satirical, skeptical, teasing, waggish, whimsical.

quota *n.* allocation, allowance, assignment, cut, part, percentage, portion, proportion, quotum, ration, share, slice, whack.

quotation[1] *n.* citation, crib, cutting, excerpt, extract, gobbet, locus classicus, passage, piece, quote, reference, remnant.

quotation[2] *n.* charge, cost, estimate, figure, price, quote, rate, tender.

quote *v.* adduce, attest, cite, detail, echo, instance, name, parrot, recall, recite, recollect, refer to, repeat, reproduce, retell.

R

rabble *n.* canaille, clamjamphrie, colluvies, commonalty, commoners, crowd, doggery, dregs, faex populi, galère, herd, hoi polloi, horde, masses, mob, peasantry, plebs, populace, proles, proletariat, raffle, raggle-taggle, ragtag (and bobtail), rascality, riffraff, scum, swarm, tagrag, throng, trash.
antonyms aristocracy, elite, nobility.

rabid *adj.* berserk, bigoted, crazed, extreme, fanatical, fervent, frantic, frenzied, furious, hydrophobic, hysterical, infuriated, intemperate, intolerant, irrational, mad, maniacal, narrow-minded, obsessive, overzealous, raging, unreasoning, violent, wild, zealous.

race[1] *n.* chase, competition, contention, contest, corso, dash, derby, foot-race, marathon, pursuit, quest, rat race, regatta, rivalry, scramble, sprint, steeplechase.
v. career, compete, contest, dart, dash, fly, gallop, hare, hasten, hurry, run, rush, speed, sprint, tear, zoom.

race[2] *n.* ancestry, blood, breed, clan, descent, family, folk, house, issue, kin, kindred, line, lineage, nation, offspring, people, progeny, seed, stirps, stock, strain, tribe, type.

racial *adj.* ancestral, avital, ethnic, ethnological, folk, genealogical, genetic, inherited, national, tribal.

rack[1] *n.* frame, framework, gantry, gondola, hack, shelf, stand, structure.

rack[2] *n.* affliction, agony, anguish, distress, misery, pain, pangs, persecution, suffering, torment, torture.
v. afflict, agonize, convulse, crucify, distress, excruciate, harass, harrow, lacerate, oppress, pain, shake, strain, stress, stretch, tear, torment, torture, wrench, wrest, wring.

racket[1] *n.* babel, ballyhoo, clamor, clangor, commotion, din, disturbance, fuss, hubbub, hullabaloo, hurly-burly, kerfuffle, noise, outcry, pandemonium, row, shouting, tumult, uproar.

racket[2] *n.* business, con, deception, dodge, fiddle, fraud, game, scheme, swindle, trick.

racy *adj.* animated, bawdy, blue, boisterous, breezy, broad, buoyant, distinctive, doubtful, dubious, dynamic, ebullient, energetic, entertaining, enthusiastic, exciting, exhilarating, gamy, heady, immodest, indecent, indelicate, jaunty, lewd, lively, naughty, piquant, pungent, Rabelaisian, ribald, rich, risqué, salacious, sharp, smutty, sparkling, spicy, spirited, stimulating, strong, suggestive, tangy, tasty, vigorous, zestful.
antonyms dull, ponderous.

radiance *n.* brightness, brilliance, delight, effulgence, gaiety, glare, gleam, glitter, glow, happiness, incandescence, joy, lambency, light, luminosity, luster, pleasure, rapture, refulgence, resplendence, shine, splendor, warmth.

radiant *adj.* aglow, alight, beaming, beamish, beamy, beatific, blissful, bright, brilliant, delighted, ecstatic, effulgent, gleaming, glittering, glorious, glowing, happy, illuminated, incandescent, joyful, joyous, lambent, luminous, lustrous, profulgent, rapturous, refulgent, resplendent, shining, sparkling, splendid, sunny.
antonym dull.

radiate *v.* branch, diffuse, disseminate, divaricate, diverge, emanate, emit, eradiate, gleam, glitter, issue, pour, scatter, shed, shine, spread, spread out.

radical *adj.* basic, complete, comprehensive, constitutional, deep-seated, entire, essential, excessive, extreme, extremist, fanatical, far-reaching, fundamental, inherent, innate, intrinsic, native, natural, organic, primary, profound, revolutionary, rooted, severe, sweeping, thorough, thorough-going, total, violent.
antonym superficial.
n. extremist, fanatic, jacobin, left-winger, militant, reformer, reformist, revolutionary.

rag *v.* badger, bait, bullyrag, chaff, haze, jeer, mock, rib, ridicule, taunt, tease, torment, twit.

ragamuffin *n.* dandiprat, gamin, guttersnipe, mudlark, scarecrow, street arab, tatterdemalion, urchin, waif.

rage *n.* agitation, anger, bate, chafe, conniption, craze, dernier cri, enthusiasm, fad, fashion, frenzy, fury, ire, madness, mania, obsession, paddy, passion, style, tantrum, vehemence, violence, vogue, wrath.
v. chafe, explode, fret, fulminate, fume, inveigh, ramp, rampage, rant, rave, seethe, storm, surge, thunder.

raging *adj.* enraged, fizzing, frenzied, fulminating, fuming, furibund, furious, incensed, infuriated, irate, ireful, mad, rabid, rampageous, raving, seething, wrathful.

raid *n.* attack, break-in, bust, descent, foray, incursion, inroad, invasion, irruption, onset, onslaught, sally, seizure, sortie, strike, swoop.
v. attack, bust, descend on, do, forage, foray, invade, loot, maraud, pillage, plunder, ransack, reive, rifle, rush, sack.

rail *v.* abuse, arraign, attack, castigate, censure, criticize, decry, denounce, fulminate, inveigh, jeer, mock, revile, ridicule, scoff, upbraid, vituperate, vociferate.

railing *n.* balustrade, barrier, fence, paling, parapet, rail, rails.

rain *n.* cloudburst, deluge, downpour, drizzle, fall, flood, hail, mizzle, precipitation, raindrops, rainfall, rains, serein, shower, spate, squall, stream, torrent, volley.
v. bestow, bucket, deluge, deposit, drizzle, drop, expend, fall, heap, lavish, mizzle, pour, shower, spit, sprinkle, teem.

raise *v.* abandon, activate, advance, aggrade, aggrandize,

aggravate, amplify, arouse, assemble, augment, awaken, boost, breed, broach, build, cause, collect, construct, create, cultivate, develop, discontinue, elate, elevate, emboss, embourgeoise, end, engender, enhance, enlarge, erect, escalate, evoke, exaggerate, exalt, excite, foment, form, foster, gather, gentrify, get, grow, heave, heighten, hoist, incite, increase, inflate, instigate, intensify, introduce, kindle, levy, lift, loft, magnify, mass, mobilize, moot, motivate, muster, nurture, obtain, occasion, originate, pose, prefer, produce, promote, propagate, provoke, rally, rear, recruit, reinforce, relinquish, remove, sky, start, strengthen, sublime, suggest, terminate, up, upgrade, uplift.
antonyms debase, decrease, degrade, dismiss, lower, reduce, suppress.

rakish *adj.* abandoned, breezy, dapper, dashing, debauched, debonair, degenerate, depraved, devil-may-care, dissipated, dissolute, flamboyant, flashy, immoral, jaunty, lecherous, libertine, licentious, loose, natty, prodigal, profligate, raffish, sharp, sinful, smart, snazzy, sporty, stylish, wanton.

rally[1] *v.* assemble, bunch, cheer, cluster, collect, congregate, convene, embolden, encourage, gather, hearten, improve, marshal, mass, mobilize, muster, organize, pick up, rally round, reassemble, recover, recuperate, re-form, regroup, reorganize, revive, round up, summon, unite.
n. assembly, comeback, concourse, conference, congregation, convention, convocation, gathering, improvement, jamboree, meeting, recovery, recuperation, regrouping, renewal, reorganization, resurgence, reunion, revival, stand.

rally[2] *v.* chaff, mock, rag, rib, ridicule, send up, taunt, tease, twit.

ramble *v.* amble, babble, chatter, digress, divagate, dodder, drift, expatiate, maunder, meander, perambulate, peregrinate, range, roam, rove, saunter, snake, straggle, stravaig, stray, stroll, traipse, walk, wander, wind, zigzag.
n. divagation, excursion, hike, perambulation, peregrination, roaming, roving, saunter, stroll, tour, traipse, trip, walk.

rambling *adj.* circuitous, desultory, diffuse, digressive, disconnected, discursive, disjointed, excursive, incoherent, irregular, long-drawn-out, long-winded, periphrastic, prolix, sprawling, spreading, straggling, trailing, wordy.
antonym direct.

ramification *n.* branch, complication, consequence, development, dichotomy, divarication, division, excrescence, extension, fork, offshoot, outgrowth, ramulus, ramus, result, sequel, subdivision, upshot.

rampage *v.* rage, rant, rave, run amuck, run riot, run wild, rush, storm, tear.
n. destruction, frenzy, furore, fury, rage, storm, tempest, tumult, uproar, violence.

rampant *adj.* aggressive, dominant, epidemic, erect, excessive, exuberant, fierce, flagrant, luxuriant, outrageous, prevalent, prodigal, profuse, raging, rampaging, rank, rearing, rife, riotous, standing, unbridled, unchecked, uncontrollable, uncontrolled, ungovernable, unrestrained, upright, vehement, violent, wanton, widespread, wild.

ramshackle *adj.* broken-down, crumbling, decrepit, derelict, dilapidated, flimsy, haywire, jerry-built, rickety, shaky, tottering, tumbledown, unsafe, unsteady.
antonyms solid, stable.

rancid *adj.* bad, fetid, foul, frowsty, fusty, musty, off, putrid, rank, reasty, rotten, sour, stale, strong-smelling, tainted.
antonym sweet.

rancor *n.* acrimony, animosity, animus, antipathy, bitterness, enmity, grudge, hate, hatred, hostility, ill-feeling, ill-will, malevolence, malice, malignity, resentfulness, resentment, spite, spleen, venom, vindictiveness.

random *adj.* accidental, adventitious, aimless, arbitrary, casual, chance, desultory, fortuitous, haphazard, incidental, indiscriminate, purposeless, scattershot, spot, stray, unfocused, unplanned, unpremeditated. *antonyms* deliberate, systematic.

range *n.* amplitude, area, assortment, band, bounds, chain, class, collection, compass, confines, diapason, distance, domain, extent, field, file, gamut, kind, latitude, limits, line, lot, orbit, order, palette, parameters, province, purview, radius, raik, rank, reach, row, scale, scope, selection, sequence, series, sort, span, spectrum, sphere, string, sweep, tessitura, tier, variety.
v. aim, align, arrange, array, bracket, catalog, categorize, class, classify, cruise, direct, dispose, explore, extend, file, fluctuate, go, grade, group, level, order, pigeonhole, point, raik, ramble, rank, reach, roam, rove, run, straggle, stravaig, stray, stretch, stroll, sweep, train, traverse, wander.

rank[1] *n.* caste, class, classification, column, condition, degree, dignity, division, echelon, estate, état, file, formation, grade, group, level, line, nobility, order, position, quality, range, row, series, sort, standing, station, status, stratum, tier, type.
v. align, arrange, array, class, classify, dispose, grade, locate, marshal, order, organize, place, position, range, sort.

rank[2] *adj.* absolute, abundant, abusive, arrant, atrocious, bad, blatant, coarse, complete, crass, dense, disagreeable, disgusting, downright, egregious, excessive, extravagant, exuberant, fetid, filthy, flagrant, flourishing, foul, fusty, gamy, glaring, gross, indecent, lush, luxuriant, mephitic, musty, nasty, noisome, noxious, obscene, off, offensive, out-and-out, outrageous, productive, profuse, pungent, putrid, rampant, rancid, repulsive, revolting, scurrilous, sheer, shocking, stale, stinking, strong-smelling, thorough, thoroughgoing, total, undisguised, unmitigated, utter, vigorous, vulgar.
antonyms sparse, sweet.

ransack *v.* comb, depredate, despoil, explore, gut, loot, maraud, pillage, plunder, raid, rake, ravage, rifle, rummage, sack, scour, search, strip.

ransom *n.* deliverance, liberation, money, payment, payoff, price, redemption, release, rescue.
v. buy out, deliver, extricate, liberate, redeem, release, rescue.

rant *v.* bellow, bluster, cry, declaim, mouth it, rave, roar, shout, slang-whang, spout, vociferate, yell.
n. bluster, bombast, declamation, diatribe, fanfaronade, harangue, philippic, rhetoric, storm, tirade, vociferation.

rap *v.* bark, castigate, censure, chat, confabulate, converse, crack, criticize, discourse, flirt, hit, knock, pan, reprimand, scold, strike, talk, tap.
n. blame, blow, castigation, censure, chat, chiding, clout, colloquy, confabulation, conversation, crack, dialogue, discourse, discussion, knock, punishment, rebuke, reprimand, responsibility, sentence, talk, tap.

rapacious *adj.* avaricious, esurient, extortionate, grasping, greedy, insatiable, marauding, plundering, predatory, preying, ravening, ravenous, usurious, voracious, vulturine, vulturish, vulturous, wolfish, wolvish.

rapid *adj.* brisk, expeditious, express, fast, fleet, flying, hasty, headlong, hurried, precipitate, prompt, quick, speedy, swift, tantivy.
antonyms leisurely, slow, sluggish.

rapidity *n.* alacrity, briskness, celerity, dispatch, expedition, expeditiousness, fleetness, haste, hurry, precipitateness, promptitude, promptness, quickness, rush, speed, speediness, swiftness, velocity. *antonym* slowness.

rapids *n.* dalles, white water, wild water.

rapine *n.* depredation, despoilment, despoliation, looting, marauding, pillage, plunder, ransacking, rape, ravaging, robbery, sack, sacking, seizure, spoliation, theft.

rapport *n.* affinity, bond, compatibility, empathy, harmony, link, relationship, sympathy, understanding.

rapture *n.* beatitude, bliss, delectation, delight, ecstasy, enthusiasm, entrancement, euphoria, exaltation, felicity, happiness, joy, ravishment, rhapsody, spell, transport.

rare *adj.* admirable, choice, curious, excellent, exceptional, exquisite, extreme, few, fine, great, incomparable, infrequent, invaluable, peerless, precious, priceless, recherché, rich, scarce, singular, sparse, sporadic, strange, superb, superlative, uncommon, unusual.
antonyms abundant, common, usual.

rarely *adv.* atypically, exceptionally, extraordinarily, finely, hardly, infrequently, little, notably, remarkably, seldom, singularly, uncommonly, unusually.
antonyms frequently, often.

rascal *n.* blackguard, caitiff, cullion, devil, disgrace, good-for-nothing, hellion, imp, knave, loon, miscreant, ne'er-do-well, rake, ra(p)scallion, reprobate, rogue, scallywag, scamp, scoundrel, skeesicks, spalpeen, toe-rag, toe-ragger, varmint, villain, wastrel, wretch.

rash[1] *adj.* adventurous, audacious, brash, careless, foolhardy, harebrained, harum-scarum, hasty, headlong, headstrong, heedless, helter-skelter, hot-headed, ill-advised, ill-considered, impetuous, imprudent, impulsive, incautious, indiscreet, injudicious, insipient, madcap, precipitant, precipitate, premature, reckless, slapdash, temerarious, temerous, thoughtless, unguarded, unthinking, unwary, venturesome.
antonyms calculating, careful, considered, wary.

rash[2] *n.* epidemic, eruption, exanthem(a), flood, hives, nettlerash, outbreak, plague, pompholyx, series, spate, succession, urticaria, wave.

rashness *n.* adventurousness, audacity, brashness, carelessness, foolhardiness, hastiness, heedlessness, incaution, incautiousness, indiscretion, precipitance, precipitation, precipitency, recklessness, temerity, thoughtlessness.
antonyms carefulness, cautiousness.

rasp *n.* croak, grating, grinding, harshness, hoarseness, scrape, scratch.
v. abrade, croak, excoriate, file, grate, grind, irk, irritate, jar, rub, sand, scour, scrape.

rasping *adj.* creaking, croaking, croaky, grating, gravelly, gruff, harsh, hoarse, husky, jarring, raspy, raucous, rough, scratchy, stridulant.

rate[1] *n.* basis, charge, class, classification, cost, degree, dues, duty, fee, figure, gait, grade, hire, measure, pace, percentage, position, price, proportion, quality, rank, rating, ratio, reckoning, relation, scale, speed, standard, status, tariff, tax, tempo, time, toll, value, velocity, worth.
v. adjudge, admire, appraise, assess, class, classify, consider, count, deserve, esteem, estimate, evaluate, figure, grade, judge, measure, measure up, merit, perform, rank, reckon, regard, respect, value, weigh.

rate[2] *v.* admonish, berate, blame, castigate, censure, chide, criticize, lecture, rebuke, reprimand, reprove, roast, scold, tongue-lash, upbraid.

ratify *v.* affirm, approve, authenticate, authorize, bind, certify, confirm, corroborate, endorse, establish, homologate, legalize, recognize, sanction, sign, uphold, validate.
antonyms reject, repudiate.

rating[1] *n.* class, classification, degree, designation, estimate, evaluation, grade, grading, order, placing, position, rank, rate, sort, sorting, standing, status.

rating[2] *n.* castigation, chiding, dressing-down, lecture, rebuke, reprimand, reproof, roasting, row, scolding, telling-off, ticking-off, tongue-lashing, upbraiding, wigging.

ration *n.* allocation, allotment, allowance, amount, dole, helping, measure, part, portion, provision, quota, share.
v. allocate, allot, apportion, budget, conserve, control, deal, dispense, distribute, dole, issue, limit, mete, restrict, save, supply.

rational *adj.* balanced, cerebral, cognitive, compos mentis, dianoetic, enlightened, intelligent, judicious, logical, lucid, normal, ratiocinative, realistic, reasonable, reasoning, sagacious, sane, sensible, sound, thinking, well-founded, well-grounded, wise.

antonyms crazy, illogical, irrational.

rationalize *v.* elucidate, excuse, extenuate, justify, reason out, reorganize, resolve, streamline, trim, vindicate.

raucous *adj.* grating, harsh, hoarse, husky, loud, noisy, rasping, rough, rusty, strident.

ravage *v.* demolish, depredate, desolate, despoil, destroy, devastate, gut, lay waste, loot, pillage, plunder, ransack, raze, ruin, sack, shatter, spoil, wreck.

n. damage, defilement, demolition, depredation, desecration, desolation, destruction, devastation, havoc, pillage, plunder, rapine, ruin, ruination, spoliation, waste, wreckage.

rave *v.* babble, declaim, fulminate, fume, harangue, rage, ramble, rant, roar, splutter, storm, thunder.

adj. ecstatic, enthusiastic, excellent, fantastic, favorable, laudatory, wonderful.

ravenous *adj.* avaricious, covetous, devouring, esurient, famished, ferocious, gluttonous, grasping, greedy, insatiable, insatiate, predatory, rapacious, ravening, starved, starving, voracious, wolfish, wolvish.

ravine *n.* arroyo, canyon, chine, clough, defile, flume, gap, gorge, grike, gulch, gully, kloof, linn, lin(n), pass.

ravish *v.* abuse, captivate, charm, deflorate, deflower, delight, enchant, enrapture, entrance, fascinate, outrage, overjoy, rape, spellbind, transport, violate.

ravishing *adj.* alluring, beautiful, bewitching, charming, dazzling, delightful, enchanting, entrancing, gorgeous, lovely, radiant, seductive, stunning.

raw *adj.* abraded, bare, basic, biting, bitter, bleak, bloody, blunt, brutal, callow, candid, chafed, chill, chilly, coarse, cold, crude, damp, frank, freezing, fresh, grazed, green, harsh, ignorant, immature, inexperienced, naked, natural, new, open, organic, piercing, plain, realistic, rough, scraped, scratched, sensitive, skinned, sore, tender, unadorned, uncooked, undisciplined, undisguised, undressed, unfinished, unpleasant, unpracticed, unprepared, unprocessed, unrefined, unripe, unseasoned, unskilled, untrained, untreated, untried, unvarnished, verdant, wet.

antonyms cooked, experienced, refined.

ray *n.* bar, beam, flash, flicker, gleam, glimmer, glint, hint, indication, scintilla, shaft, spark, stream, trace.

raze *v.* bulldoze, delete, demolish, destroy, dismantle, efface, erase, expunge, extinguish, extirpate, flatten, level, obliterate, remove, ruin. **reach** *v.* amount to, arrive at, attain, contact, drop, fall, get to, grasp, hand, land at, make, move, pass, rise, sink, stretch, strike, touch.

n. ambit, capacity, command, compass, distance, extension, extent, grasp, influence, jurisdiction, latitude, mastery, power, purview, range, scope, spread, stretch, sweep.

react *v.* acknowledge, act, answer, behave, emote, function, operate, proceed, reply, respond, work.

reaction *n.* acknowledgment, answer, antiperistasis, backwash, compensation, conservatism, counteraction, counter-balance, counterbuff, counterpoise, counter-revolution, feedback, obscurantism, recoil, reply, response, swing-back.

readable *adj.* clear, compelling, comprehensible, compulsive, decipherable, enjoyable, entertaining, enthralling, gripping, intelligible, interesting, legible, plain, pleasant, understandable, unputdownable.

antonyms illegible, unreadable.

readily *adv.* cheerfully, eagerly, easily, effortlessly, fain, freely, gladly, lief, promptly, quickly, smoothly, speedily, unhesitatingly, voluntarily, willingly.

ready *adj.* à la main, about, accessible, acute, ad manum, adroit, agreeable, alert, apt, arranged, astute, available, bright, clever, close, completed, convenient, deft, dexterous, disposed, eager, expert, facile, fit, game, glad, handy, happy, inclined, intelligent, keen, liable, likely, minded, near, on call, on tap, organized, overflowing, perceptive, predisposed, prepared, present, primed, prompt, prone, quick, quick-witted, rapid, resourceful, ripe, set, sharp, skilful, smart, willing.

antonyms unprepared, unready.

v. alert, arrange, equip, order, organize, prepare, prime, set.

real *adj.* absolute, actual, authentic, bona fide, certain, dinkum, dinky-di(e), essential, existent, factual, genuine, heartfelt, honest, intrinsic, legitimate, positive, right, rightful, simon-pure, sincere, substantial, substantive, sure-enough, tangible, thingy, true, unaffected, unfeigned, valid, veritable.

antonyms imaginary, unreal.

realization *n.* accomplishment, achievement, actualization, appreciation, apprehension, awareness, cognizance, completion, comprehension, conception, consciousness, consummation, effectuation, fulfilment, grasp, imagination, perception, recognition, understanding.

realize *v.* accomplish, achieve, acquire, actualize, appreciate, apprehend, catch on, clear, complete, comprehend, conceive, consummate, do, earn, effect, effectuate, fulfil, gain, get, grasp, imagine, implement, make, net, obtain, perform, produce, recognize, reify, take in, twig, understand.

really *adv.* absolutely, actually, assuredly, categorically, certainly, essentially, genuinely, indeed, intrinsically, positively, surely, truly, undoubtedly, verily.

realm *n.* area, bailiwick, branch, country, department, domain, dominion, empire, field, jurisdiction, kingdom, land, monarchy, orbit, principality, province, region, sphere, state, territory, world, zone.

reap *v.* acquire, collect, crop, cut, derive, gain, garner, gather, get, harvest, mow, obtain, realize, secure, win.

rear[1] *n.* back, backside, bottom, buttocks, croup, end, hind-quarters, posterior, rearguard, rump, stern, tail. *antonym* front.

adj. aft, after, back, following, hind, hindmost, last. *antonym* front.

rear[2] *v.* breed, build, construct, cultivate, educate, elevate, erect, fabricate, foster, grow, hoist, lift, loom, nurse, nurture, parent, raise, rise, soar, tower, train.

reason *n.* aim, apologia, apology, apprehension, argument, basis, bounds, brains, case, cause, common sense, comprehension, consideration, defense, design, end, excuse, explanation, exposition, goal, ground, grounds, gumption, impetus, incentive, inducement, intellect, intention, judgment, justification, limits, logic, mentality, mind, moderation, motive, nous, object, occasion, propriety, purpose, ratiocination, rationale, rationality, reasonableness, reasoning, sanity, sense, sensibleness, soundness, target, understanding, vindication, warrant, wisdom.

v. conclude, deduce, infer, intellectualize, ratiocinate, resolve, solve, syllogize, think, work out.

reasonable *adj.* acceptable, advisable, arguable, average, believable, credible, equitable, fair, fit, honest, inexpensive, intelligent, judicious, just, justifiable, logical, moderate, modest, OK, passable, plausible, possible, practical, proper, rational, reasoned, right, sane, satisfactory, sensible, sober, sound, tenable, tolerable, viable, well-advised, well-thought-out, wise. *antonyms* crazy, extravagant, irrational, outrageous, unreasonable.

rebel *v.* defy, disobey, dissent, flinch, kick over the traces, mutiny, recoil, resist, revolt, rise up, run riot, shrink.

n. apostate, dissenter, heretic, insurgent, insurrectionary, Jacobin, malcontent, mutineer, nonconformist, revolutionary, revolutionist, schismatic, secessionist.

adj. insubordinate, insurgent, insurrectionary, malcontent(ed), mutinous, rebellious, revolutionary.

rebellion *n.* apostasy, defiance, disobedience, dissent, heresy, insubordination, insurgence, insurgency, insurrection, Jacquerie, mutiny, nonconformity, resistance, revolt, revolution, rising, schism, uprising.

rebellious *adj.* contumacious, defiant, difficult, disaffected, disloyal, disobedient, disorderly, incorrigible, insubordinate, insurgent, insurrectionary, intractable, malcontent(ed), mutinous, obstinate, rebel, recalcitrant, refractory, resistant, revolutionary, seditious, turbulent, ungovernable, unmanageable, unruly. *antonyms* obedient, submissive.

rebirth *n.* reactivation, reanimation, regeneration, reincarnation, rejuvenation, renaissance, renascence, renewal, restoration, resurgence, resurrection, revitalization, revival.

rebuff *v.* cold-shoulder, cut, decline, deny, discourage, put someone's nose out of joint, refuse, reject, repulse, resist, slight, snub, spurn, turn down.

n. brush-off, check, cold shoulder, defeat, denial, discouragement, flea in one's ear, noser, opposition, refusal, rejection, repulse, rubber, set-down, slight, snub.

rebuild *v.* reassemble, reconstruct, re-edify, refashion, remake, remodel, renovate, restore. *antonyms* demolish, destroy.

rebuke *v.* admonish, berate, blame, carpet, castigate, censure, chide, countercheck, jobe, keelhaul, lecture, lesson, rate, reprehend, reprimand, reproach, reprove, scold, slap down, tell off, tick off, trim, trounce, upbraid. *antonyms* compliment, praise.

n. admonition, blame, castigation, censure, countercheck, dressing-down, lecture, reprimand, reproach, reproof, reproval, row, slap, telling-off, ticking-off, tongue-lashing, wigging. *antonyms* compliment, praise.

rebuttal *n.* confutation, defeat, disproof, invalidation, negation, overthrow, refutation.

recall *v.* abjure, annul, cancel, cast one's mind back, countermand, evoke, mind, nullify, place, recognize, recollect, remember, repeal, rescind, retract, revoke, withdraw.

n. abrogation, annulment, cancellation, memory, nullification, recision, recollection, remembrance, repeal, rescission, retraction, revocation, withdrawal.

recapitulate *v.* give a resumé, recap, recount, reiterate, repeat, restate, review, summarize.

recede *v.* abate, decline, decrease, diminish, dwindle, ebb, fade, lessen, regress, retire, retreat, retrogress, return, shrink, sink, slacken, subside, wane, withdraw. *antonyms* advance, proceed.

receive *v.* accept, accommodate, acquire, admit, apprehend, bear, collect, derive, encounter, entertain, experience, gather, get, greet, hear, meet, obtain, perceive, pick up, react to, respond to, suffer, sustain, take, undergo, welcome. *antonyms* donate, give.

recent *adj.* contemporary, current, fresh, late, latter, latter-day, modern, neoteric(al), new, novel, present-day, up-to-date, young. *antonyms* dated, old, out-of-date.

reception *n.* acceptance, acknowledgment, admission, do, durbar, entertainment, function, greeting, levee, party, reaction, receipt, receiving, recipience, recognition, response, shindig, soirée, treatment, welcome.

recess *n.* alcove, apse, apsidiole, bay, break, cavity, cessation, closure, corner, depression, embrasure, holiday, hollow, indentation, intermission, interval, loculus, niche, nook, oriel, respite, rest, vacation.

recession *n.* decline, depression, downturn, slump, stagflation. *antonyms* boom, upturn.

recipe *n.* directions, formula, ingredients, instructions, method, prescription, procedure, process, program, receipt, system, technique.

recital *n.* account, convert, description, detailing, enumeration, interpretation, narration, narrative, performance, reading, recapitulation, recitation, rehearsal, relation, rendering, rendition, repetition, statement, story, tale, telling.

recite *v.* articulate, declaim, deliver, describe, detail, enumerate, itemize, narrate, orate, perform, recapitulate, recount, rehearse, relate, repeat, speak, tell.

reckless *adj.* careless, daredevil, devil-may-care, foolhardy, harebrained, hasty, headlong, heedless, ill-advised, imprudent, inattentive, incautious, indiscreet, irresponsible, madcap, mindless, negligent, precipitate, rantipole, rash, regardless, tearaway, thoughtless, wild.
antonyms calculating, careful, cautious.

recklessness *n.* carelessness, foolhardiness, gallowsness, heedlessness, imprudence, inattention, incaution, irresponsibleness, irresponsibility, madness, mindlessness, negligence, rashness, thoughtlessness.
antonym carefulness.

reckon *v.* account, add up, adjudge, appraise, assess, assume, believe, calculate, compute, conjecture, consider, count, deem, enumerate, esteem, estimate, evaluate, expect, fancy, gauge, guess, hold, imagine, judge, number, opine, rate, regard, suppose, surmise, tally, think, total.

reclaim *v.* impolder, recapture, recover, redeem, reform, regain, regenerate, reinstate, rescue, restore, retrieve, salvage.

recline *v.* couch, lean, lie, loll, lounge, repose, rest, sprawl, stretch out.

recluse *n.* anchoress, anchoret, anchorite, ancress, ascetic, eremite, hermit, monk, solitaire, solitarian, solitary, stylite.

recognize *v.* accept, acknowledge, admit, allow, appreciate, approve, avow, concede, confess, grant, greet, honor, identify, know, notice, own, perceive, place, realize, recall, recollect, remember, respect, salute, see, spot, understand, wot.

recollect *v.* call up, cast one's mind back, mind, place, recall, remember, reminisce.

recollection *n.* image, impression, memory, recall, remembrance, reminiscence, souvenir.

recommend *v.* advance, advise, advocate, approve, commend, counsel, endorse, enjoin, exhort, plug, praise, propose, puff, suggest, urge, vouch for.
antonyms disapprove, veto.

recommendation *n.* advice, advocacy, approbation, approval, blessing, commendation, counsel, endorsement, plug, praise, proposal, puff, reference, sanction, suggestion, testimonial, urging.
antonyms disapproval, veto.

reconcile *v.* accept, accommodate, accord, adjust, appease, compose, conciliate, harmonize, pacify, placate, propitiate, rectify, resign, resolve, reunite, settle, square, submit, yield.
antonym estrange.

recondition *v.* fix, overhaul, refurbish, remodel, renew, renovate, repair, restore, revamp, sort.

reconsider *v.* modify, reassess, re-examine, rethink, review, revise, think better of, think over, think twice.

record *n.* account, album, annals, archives, background, career, chronicle, curriculum vitae, diary, disc, document, documentation, dossier, entry, EP, evidence, file, form, forty-five, gramophone record, history, journal, log, LP, memoir, memorandum, memorial, minute, noctuary, performance, platter, recording, register, release, remembrance, report, single, talkie, testimony, trace, tracing, track record, witness.
v. annalize, chalk up, chronicle, contain, cut, diarize, document, enregister, enrol, enter, indicate, inscribe, log, minute, note, preserve, read, register, report, say, score, show, tape, tape-record, transcribe, video, videotape, wax.

recount *v.* communicate, delineate, depict, describe, detail, enumerate, narrate, portray, recite, rehearse, relate, repeat, report, tell.

recoup *v.* compensate, indemnify, make good, recover, redeem, refund, regain, reimburse, remunerate, repay, requite, retrieve, satisfy.

recover *v.* convalesce, heal, improve, mend, pick up, pull through, rally, recapture, reclaim, recoup, recuperate, redeem, regain, repair, replevy, repossess, restore, retake, retrieve, revive.
antonyms forfeit, lose, worsen.

recreation *n.* amusement, distraction, diversion, enjoyment, entertainment, exercise, fun, games, hobby, leisure activity, pastime, play, pleasure, refreshment, relaxation, relief, sport.

recrimination *n.* accusation, bickering, counter-attack, counterblast, countercharge, name-calling, quarrel, retaliation, retort, squabbling.

recruit *v.* augment, draft, engage, enlist, enrol, gather, headhunt, impress, levy, mobilize, muster, obtain, procure, proselytize, raise, refresh, reinforce, renew, replenish, restore, strengthen, supply, trawl.
n. apprentice, beginner, conscript, convert, draftee, green-horn, helper, initiate, learner, neophyte, novice, proselyte, rookie, trainee, tyro, yob.

recuperate *v.* convalesce, get better, improve, mend, pick up, rally, recoup, recover, regain, revive.
antonym worsen.

recur *v.* persist, reappear, repeat, return.

redeem *v.* absolve, acquit, atone for, cash (in), change, compensate for, defray, deliver, discharge, emancipate, exchange, extricate, free, fulfil, keep, liberate, make good, make up for, meet, offset, outweigh, perform, ransom, reclaim, recoup, recover, recuperate, redress, regain, rehabilitate, reinstate, repossess, repurchase, rescue, retrieve, salvage, satisfy, save, trade in.

redolent *adj.* aromatic, evocative, fragrant, odorous, perfumed, remindful, reminiscent, scented, suggestive, sweet-smelling.

reduce *v.* abate, abridge, bankrupt, break, cheapen, conquer, contract, curtail, cut, debase, decimate, decrease,

degrade, demote, deoxidate, deoxidize, depress, diet, dilute, diminish, discount, downgrade, drive, force, humble, humiliate, impair, impoverish, lessen, lower, master, moderate, overpower, pauperize, rebate, ruin, scant, shorten, slake, slash, slenderize, slim, subdue, trim, truncate, vanquish, weaken.
antonyms boost, fatten, increase, upgrade.

reduction *n.* abbreviation, abridgment, abstraction, alleviation, attenuation, compression, condensation, constriction, contraction, curtailment, cut, cutback, decline, decrease, deduction, degradation, demotion, deoxidation, deoxidization, deposal, depreciation, devaluation, diminution, discount, drop, easing, ellipsis, limitation, loss, miniature, mitigation, moderation, modification, muffling, muting, narrowing, rebate, rebatement, refund, restriction, shortening, shrinkage, slackening, softening, subtraction, summarization, summary, syncope.
antonyms enlargement, improvement, increase.

redundant *adj.* de trop, diffuse, excessive, extra, inessential, inordinate, padded, periphrastic, pleonastical, prolix, repetitious, supererogatory, superfluous, supernumerary, surplus, tautological, unemployed, unnecessary, unneeded, unwanted, verbose, wordy.
antonyms concise, essential, necessary.

reek *v.* exhale, fume, hum, pong, smell, smoke, stink.
n. effluvium, exhalation, fetor, fume(s), malodor, mephitis, odor, pong, smell, smoke, stench, stink, vapor.

refer *v.* accredit, adduce, advert, allude, apply, ascribe, assign, attribute, belong, cite, commit, concern, consign, consult, credit, deliver, direct, go, guide, hint, impute, invoke, look up, mention, pertain, point, recommend, relate, send, speak of, submit, touch on, transfer, turn to.

referee *n.* adjudicator, arbiter, arbitrator, arbitratrix, arbitress, judge, ref, umpire.
v. adjudicate, arbitrate, judge, ref, umpire.

reference *n.* allusion, applicability, bearing, certification, character, citation, concern, connection, consideration, credentials, endorsement, illustration, instance, mention, note, quotation, recommendation, regard, relation, remark, respect, testimonial.

refine *v.* chasten, civilize, clarify, cultivate, distil, elevate, exalt, filter, hone, improve, perfect, polish, process, purify, rarefy, spiritualize, sublimize, subtilize, temper.

refined *adj.* Attic, Augustan, civil, civilized, clarified, clean, courtly, cultivated, cultured, delicate, discerning, discriminating, distilled, elegant, exact, fastidious, filtered, fine, genteel, gentlemanly, gracious, ladylike, nice, polished, polite, precise, processed, punctilious, pure, purified, sensitive, sophisticated, sublime, subtle, urbane, well-bred, well-mannered.
antonyms brutish, coarse, earthy, rude, vulgar.

refinement *n.* breeding, chastity, civilization, civility, clarification, cleansing, courtesy, courtliness, cultivation,

culture, delicacy, discrimination, distillation, elegance, fastidiousness, filtering, fineness, finesse, finish, gentility, grace, graciousness, manners, nicety, nuance, polish, politeness, politesse, precision, processing, purification, rarefaction, rectification, sophistication, style, subtlety, taste, urbanity.
antonyms coarseness, earthiness, vulgarity.

reflect *v.* bespeak, cogitate, communicate, consider, contemplate, deliberate, demonstrate, display, echo, evince, exhibit, express, imitate, indicate, manifest, meditate, mirror, mull (over), muse, ponder, reproduce, return, reveal, ruminate, show, think, wonder.

reflection *n.* aspersion, censure, cerebration, cogitation, consideration, contemplation, counterpart, criticism, deliberation, derogation, echo, idea, image, impression, imputation, meditation, musing, observation, opinion, pondering, reflex, reproach, rumination, slur, study, thinking, thought, view.

reform *v.* ameliorate, amend, better, correct, emend, improve, mend, purge, rebuild, reclaim, reconstitute, reconstruct, rectify, regenerate, rehabilitate, remodel, renovate, reorganize, repair, restore, revamp, revolutionize.
n. amelioration, amendment, betterment, correction, improvement, purge, rectification, rehabilitation, renovation, shake-out.

refractory *adj.* balky, cantankerous, contentious, contumacious, difficult, disobedient, disputatious, headstrong, intractable, mulish, obstinate, perverse, recalcitrant, resistant, restive, stubborn, uncontrollable, unco-operative, unmanageable, unruly, wilful.
antonyms co-operative, malleable, obedient.

refrain[1] *v.* abstain, avoid, cease, desist, eschew, forbear, leave off, quit, renounce, stop, swear off.

refrain[2] *n.* burden, chorus, epistrophe, falderal, melody, song, tune, undersong, wheel.

refresh *v.* brace, cheer, cool, energize, enliven, freshen, inspirit, jog, prod, prompt, reanimate, reinvigorate, rejuvenate, renew, renovate, repair, replenish, restore, revitalize, revive, revivify, stimulate.
antonyms exhaust, tire.

refreshing *adj.* bracing, cooling, different, energizing, fresh, inspiriting, invigorating, new, novel, original, refrigerant, restorative, revivifying, stimulating, thirst-quenching.
antonyms exhausting, tiring.

refreshment *n.* enlivenment, freshening, reanimation, reinvigoration, renewal, renovation, repair, restoration, revitalization, revival, stimulation.

refuge *n.* asylum, bolthole, funk-hole, harbor, haven, hide-away, hideout, holt, protection, resort, retreat, sanctuary, security, shelter.

refuse[1] *v.* decline, deny, nay-say, reject, repel, repudiate, spurn, withhold.
antonyms accept, allow.

refuse[2] *n.* chaff, dregs, dross, excrementa, garbage, hogwash, husks, junk, lag(s), landfill, leavings, lees, left-overs, litter, mullock, offscourings, rejectamenta, riddlings, rubbish, scum, sediment, slops, sordes, sullage, sweepings, tailings, trash, waste, wastrel.

refute *v.* confute, counter, discredit, disprove, give the lie to, negate, overthrow, rebut, silence.

regain *v.* reattain, recapture, reclaim, recoup, recover, redeem, re-establish, repossess, retake, retrieve, return to.

regal *adj.* kingly, magnificent, majestic, monarch(i)al, monarchic(al), noble, princely, proud, queenly, royal, sovereign, stately.

regale *v.* amuse, captivate, delight, divert, entertain, fascinate, feast, gratify, ply, refresh, serve.

regard *v.* account, adjudge, attend, behold, believe, concern, consider, deem, esteem, estimate, eye, heed, hold, imagine, interest, judge, mark, mind, note, notice, observe, pertain to, rate, relate to, remark, respect, scrutinize, see, suppose, think, treat, value, view, watch.
antonyms despise, disregard.
n. account, advertence, advertency, affection, aspect, attachment, attention, bearing, care, concern, connection, consideration, deference, detail, esteem, feature, gaze, glance, heed, honor, item, look, love, matter, mind, note, notice, particular, point, reference, relation, relevance, reputation, repute, respect, scrutiny, stare, store, sympathy, thought.
antonyms contempt, disapproval, disregard.

regardless *adj.* disregarding, heedless, inattentive, inconsiderate, indifferent, neglectful, negligent, nonchalant, rash, reckless, remiss, uncaring, unconcerned, unmindful.
antonyms attentive, heedful, regardful.
adv. anyhow, anyway, come what may, despite everything, in any case, nevertheless, no matter what, nonetheless, willy-nilly.

regards *n.* compliments, devoirs, greetings, respects, salutations.

regenerate *v.* change, inspirit, invigorate, reawaken, reconstitute, reconstruct, re-establish, refresh, reinvigorate, rejuvenate, renew, renovate, reproduce, restore, revive, revivify, uplift.

regime *n.* administration, command, control, establishment, government, leadership, management, reign, rule, system.

regimented *adj.* controlled, co-ordinated, disciplined, methodical, ordered, organized, regulated, severe, standardized, stern, strict, systematic.
antonyms disorganized, free, lax, loose.

region *n.* area, clime, country, district, division, domain, expanse, field, land, locality, neighborhood, part, place, province, quarter, range, realm, scope, section, sector, sphere, terrain, terrene, territory, tract, vicinity, world, zone.

register *n.* almanac, annals, archives, catalog, chronicle, diary, file, ledger, list, log, matricula, memorandum, notitia, record, roll, roster, schedule.

v. bespeak, betray, catalog, chronicle, display, enlist, enrol, enter, exhibit, express, indicate, inscribe, list, log, manifest, mark, note, read, record, reflect, reveal, say, score, show, sign on.

regress *v.* backslide, degenerate, deteriorate, ebb, lapse, recede, relapse, retreat, retrocede, retrogress, return, revert, wane.
antonym progress.

regret *v.* bemoan, bewail, deplore, grieve, lament, miss, mourn, repent, rue, sorrow.
n. bitterness, compunction, contrition, disappointment, grief, lamentation, penitence, remorse, repentance, ruefulness, self-reproach, shame, sorrow.

regrettable *adj.* deplorable, disappointing, distressing, ill-advised, lamentable, pitiable, sad, shameful, sorry, unfortunate, unhappy, unlucky, woeful, wrong.
antonyms fortunate, happy.

regular *adj.* approved, balanced, bona fide, classic, common, commonplace, consistent, constant, consuetudinary, conventional, correct, customary, daily, dependable, efficient, established, even, everyday, fixed, flat, formal, habitual, level, methodical, normal, official, ordered, orderly, ordinary, orthodox, periodic, prevailing, proper, rhythmic, routine, sanctioned, set, smooth, standard, standardized, stated, steady, straight, symmetrical, systematic, time-honored, traditional, typical, uniform, unvarying, usual.
antonyms irregular, sporadic, unconventional.

regulate *v.* adjust, administer, arrange, balance, conduct, control, direct, fit, govern, guide, handle, manage, moderate, modulate, monitor, order, organize, oversee, regiment, rule, run, settle, square, superintend, supervise, systematize, tune.

regulation *n.* adjustment, administration, arrangement, commandment, control, decree, dictate, direction, edict, governance, government, law, management, modulation, order, ordinance, precept, prodecure, regimentation, requirement, rule, statute, supervision, tuning.
adj. accepted, customary, mandatory, normal, official, prescribed, required, standard, stock, usual.

rehabilitate *v.* adjust, clear, convert, mend, normalize, rebuild, recondition, reconstitute, reconstruct, redeem, redintegrate, re-establish, reform, reinstate, reintegrate, reinvigorate, renew, renovate, restore, save.

rehearse *v.* act, delineate, depict, describe, detail, drill, enumerate, list, narrate, practice, prepare, ready, recite, recount, relate, repeat, review, run through, spell out, study, tell, train, trot out.

reign *n.* ascendancy, command, control, dominion, empire, hegemony, influence, monarchy, power, rule, sovereignty, supremacy, sway.
v. administer, authority, command, govern, influence, kingship, obtain, predominate, prevail, rule.

reimburse *v.* compensate, indemnify, recompense, refund, remunerate, repay, requite, restore, return, square up.

rein *n.* brake, bridle, check, check-rein, control, curb, harness, hold, overcheck, restraint, restriction.

v. arrest, bridle, check, control, curb, halt, hold, hold back, limit, restrain, restrict, stop.

reinforce *v.* augment, bolster, buttress, emphasize, fortify, harden, increase, prop, recruit, steel, stiffen, strengthen, stress, supplement, support, toughen, underline.

antonyms undermine, weaken.

reiterate *v.* ding, iterate, recapitulate, repeat, resay, restate, retell.

reject *v.* athetize, condemn, decline, deny, despise, disallow, discard, eliminate, exclude, explode, jettison, jilt, pip, rebuff, refuse, renounce, repel, reprobate, repudiate, repulse, scrap, spike, spurn, veto.

antonyms accept, select.

n. cast-off, discard, failure, second.

rejection *n.* athetesis, brush-off, dear John letter, denial, dismissal, elimination, exclusion, rebuff, refusal, renunciation, repudiation, veto.

antonyms acceptance, selection.

rejoice *v.* celebrate, delight, exult, glory, joy, jubilate, revel, triumph.

rejuvenate *v.* reanimate, recharge, refresh, regenerate, reinvigorate, rekindle, renew, restore, revitalize, revivify.

relapse *v.* backslide, degenerate, deteriorate, fade, fail, lapse, regress, retrogress, revert, sicken, sink, weaken, worsen.

n. backsliding, deterioration, hypostrophe, lapse, recidivism, recurrence, regression, retrogression, reversion, setback, weakening, worsening.

relate *v.* ally, appertain, apply, associate, chronicle, concern, connect, co-ordinate, correlate, couple, describe, detail, empathize, feel for, identify with, impart, join, link, narrate, pertain, present, recite, recount, refer, rehearse, report, sympathize, tell, understand.

relation *n.* account, affiliation, affine, affinity, agnate, agnation, application, bearing, bond, comparison, connection, consanguinity, correlation, description, german, interdependence, kin, kindred, kinship, kinsman, kinswoman, link, narration, narrative, pertinence, propinquity, recital, recountal, reference, regard, relationship, relative, report, sib, similarity, story, tale, tie-in.

relationship *n.* affaire, association, bond, communications, conjunction, connection, contract, correlation, dealings, exchange, intercourse, kinship, liaison, link, parallel, proportion, rapport, ratio, similarity, tie-up.

relative *adj.* allied, applicable, apposite, appropriate, appurtenant, apropos, associated, comparative, connected, contingent, correlative, corresponding, dependent, germane, interrelated, pertinent, proportionate, reciprocal, related, relevant, respective.

n. cognate, connection, german, kinsman, kinswoman, relation, sib.

relatively *adv.* comparatively, fairly, quite, rather, somewhat.

relax *v.* abate, diminish, disinhibit, ease, ebb, lessen, loosen, lower, mitigate, moderate, reduce, relieve, remit, rest, slacken, soften, tranquilize, unbend, unclench, unwind, weaken.

antonyms intensify, tighten.

relaxation *n.* abatement, amusement, délassement, détente, diminution, disinhibition, distraction, easing, emollition, enjoyment, entertainment, fun, leisure, lessening, let-up, moderation, pleasure, recreation, reduction, refreshment, rest, slackening, weakening.

antonyms intensification, tension.

relaxed *adj.* calm, carefree, casual, collected, composed, cool, down-beat, easy-going, even-tempered, happy-go-lucky, informal, insouciant, laid-back, mellow, mild, nonchalant, placid, serene, together, tranquil, unhurried.

antonyms edgy, nervous, stiff, tense, uptight.

release *v.* absolve, acquit, break, circulate, declassify, decontrol, deliver, discage, discharge, disengage, disenthral, disimprison, disinhibit, disoblige, dispense, disprison, disseminate, distribute, drop, emancipate, exempt, excuse, exonerate, extricate, free, furlough, issue, launch, liberate, loose, manumit, present, publish, unbind, uncage, unchain, undo, unfasten, unfetter, unhand, unleash, unloose, unmew, unpen, unshackle, untie, unveil.

antonyms check, detain.

n. absolution, acquittal, acquittance, announcement, deliverance, delivery, discharge, disimprisonment, disinhibition, dispensation, emancipation, exemption, exoneration, freedom, issue, let-off, liberation, liberty, manumission, offering, proclamation, publication, quittance, relief.

antonym detention.

relegate *v.* assign, banish, consign, delegate, demote, deport, dispatch, downgrade, eject, entrust, exile, expatriate, expel, refer, transfer.

antonym promote.

relent *v.* acquiesce, capitulate, drop, ease, fall, forbear, give in, melt, relax, slacken, slow, soften, unbend, weaken, yield.

relentless *adj.* cruel, fierce, grim, hard, harsh, implacable, incessant, inexorable, inflexible, merciless, nonstop, persistent, pitiless, punishing, remorseless, ruthless, stern, sustained, unabated, unbroken, uncompromising, undeviating, unfaltering, unflagging, unforgiving, unrelenting, unrelieved, unremitting, unstoppable, unyielding.

antonyms submissive, yielding.

relevant *adj.* ad rem, admissible, applicable, apposite, appropriate, appurtenant, apt, congruous, fitting, germane, material, pertinent, proper, related, relative, significant, suitable, suited.

antonym irrelevant.

reliable *adj.* certain, constant, copper-bottomed,

dependable, faithful, honest, predictable, regular, responsible, safe, solid, sound, stable, staunch, sure, true, trustworthy, trusty, unfailing, upright, white.
antonyms doubtful, suspect, unreliable, untrustworthy.

reliance *n.* assurance, belief, confidence, credence, credit, dependence, faith, trust.

relic *n.* fragment, keepsake, memento, potsherd, remembrance, remnant, scrap, souvenir, survival, token, trace, vestige.

relief *n.* abatement, aid, alleviation, assistance, assuagement, balm, break, breather, comfort, cure, deliverance, diversion, ease, easement, help, let-up, load off one's mind, mitigation, palliation, refreshment, relaxation, release, remedy, remission, respite, rest, solace, succor, support, sustenance.

relieve *v.* abate, aid, alleviate, appease, assist, assuage, break, brighten, calm, comfort, console, cure, deliver, diminish, discharge, disembarrass, disencumber, dull, ease, exempt, free, help, interrupt, lighten, mitigate, mollify, palliate, relax, release, salve, slacken, soften, solace, soothe, spell, stand in for, substitute for, succor, support, sustain, take over from, take the place of, unburden, vary.
antonyms aggravate, intensify.

religious *adj.* church-going, conscientious, devotional, devout, divine, doctrinal, exact, faithful, fastidious, God-fearing, godly, holy, meticulous, pious, punctilious, pure, reverent, righteous, rigid, rigorous, sacred, scriptural, scrupulous, sectarian, spiritual, strict, theological, unerring, unswerving.
antonyms irreligious, lax, ungodly.

relinquish *n.* abandon, abdicate, cede, desert, discard, drop, forgo, forsake, hand over, leave, quit, release, renounce, repudiate, resign, surrender, vacate, waive, yield.
antonyms keep, retain.

relish *v.* appreciate, degust, enjoy, fancy, lap up, like, prefer, revel in, savor, taste.
n. appetizer, appetite, appreciation, condiment, enjoyment, fancy, flavor, fondness, gout, gusto, liking, love, partiality, penchant, piquancy, predilection, sauce, savor, seasoning, smack, spice, stomach, tang, taste, trace, zest.

reluctance *n.* aversion, backwardness, disinclination, dislike, distaste, hesitancy, indisposition, loathing, recalcitrance, repugnance, unwillingness.
antonyms eagerness, willingness.

reluctant *adj.* averse, backward, disinclined, grudging, hesitant, indisposed, loath, loathful, loth, recalcitrant, renitent, slow, squeamish, unenthusiastic, unwilling.
antonyms eager, willing.

rely *v.* bank, bet, count, depend, lean, reckon, swear by, trust.

remain *v.* abide, bide, cling, continue, delay, dwell, endure, last, linger, persist, prevail, rest, sojourn, stand, stay, survive, tarry, wait.
antonyms depart, go, leave.

remainder *n.* balance, dregs, excess, leavings, remanent, remanet, remnant, residuum, rest, surplus, trace, vestige(s).

remains *n.* ashes, balance, body, cadaver, carcass, corpse, crumbs, debris, detritus, dregs, fragments, leavings, leftovers, oddments, pieces, relics, reliquiae, remainder, remnants, residue, rest, scraps, traces, vestiges.

remark *v.* animadvert, comment, declare, espy, heed, mark, mention, note, notice, observe, perceive, reflect, regard, say, see, state.
n. acknowledgment, assertion, attention, comment, consideration, declaration, heed, mention, notice, observation, opinion, recognition, reflection, regard, say, statement, thought, utterance, word.

remarkable *adj.* amazing, conspicuous, distinguished, exceptional, extraordinary, famous, impressive, miraculous, notable, noteworthy, odd, outstanding, phenomenal, pre-eminent, prominent, rare, signal, singular, strange, striking, surprising, unco, uncommon, unusual, wonderful.
antonyms average, commonplace, ordinary.

remedy *n.* antidote, corrective, counteractive, countermeasure, cure, magistery, medicament, medicine, nostrum, panacea, physic, prescript, redress, relief, restorative, solution, specific, therapy, treatment.
v. alleviate, ameliorate, assuage, control, correct, counteract, cure, ease, fix, heal, help, mitigate, palliate, put right, rectify, redress, reform, relieve, repair, restore, solve, soothe, treat.

remember *v.* commemorate, place, recall, recognize, recollect, reminisce, retain, summon up, think back.
antonym forget.

remembrance *n.* anamnesis, commemoration, keepsake, memento, memorial, memory, mind, monument, recall, recognition, recollection, recordation, regard, relic, remembrancer, reminder, reminiscence, retrospect, souvenir, testimonial, thought, token.

remiss *adj.* careless, culpable, delinquent, derelict, dilatory, fainéant, forgetful, heedless, inattentive, indifferent, lackadaisical, lax, neglectful, negligent, regardless, slack, slipshod, sloppy, slothful, slow, tardy, thoughtless, unmindful.
antonyms careful, scrupulous.

remit *v.* abate, alleviate, cancel, decrease, defer, delay, desist, desist from, diminish, dispatch, dwindle, forbear, forward, halt, mail, mitigate, moderate, post, postpone, put back, reduce, relax, repeal, rescind, send, send back, shelve, sink, slacken, soften, stop, suspend, transfer, transmit, wane, weaken.
n. authorization, brief, guidelines, instructions, orders, responsibility, scope, terms of reference.

remittance *n.* allowance, consideration, dispatch, fee, payment, sending.

remnant *n.* balance, bit, end, fent, fragment, hangover, leftovers, piece, remainder, remains, remane(n)t, residue,

remonstrate312repeat

residuum, rest, rump, scrap, shred, survival, trace, vestige.

remonstrate *v.* argue, challenge, complain, dispute, dissent, expostulate, gripe, object, protest.

remorse *n.* anguish, bad conscience, compassion, compunction, contrition, grief, guilt, penitence, pity, regret, repentance, ruefulness, ruth, self-reproach, shame, sorrow.

remorseless *adj.* callous, cruel, hard, hard-hearted, harsh, implacable, inexorable, inhumane, merciless, pitiless, relentless, ruthless, savage, stern, undeviating, unforgiving, unmerciful, unrelenting, unremitting, unstoppable.

antonyms remorseful, sorry.

remote *adj.* abstracted, alien, aloof, backwoods, cold, detached, distant, doubtful, dubious, extraneous, extrinsic, faint, far, faraway, far-off, foreign, god-forsaken, immaterial, implausible, inaccessible, inconsiderable, indifferent, introspective, introverted, irrelevant, isolated, lonely, meager, negligible, outlying, out-of-the-way, outside, poor, removed, reserved, secluded, slender, slight, slim, small, standoffish, unconnected, uninterested, uninvolved, unlikely, unrelated, withdrawn.

antonyms adjacent, close, nearby, significant.

remove *v.* ablate, abolish, abstract, amove, amputate, assassinate, delete, depart, depose, detach, dethrone, discharge, dislodge, dismiss, displace, doff, efface, eject, eliminate, erase, execute, expunge, extract, flit, flit (move house), guy, kill, liquidate, move, murder, oust, purge, quit, relegate, relocate, shave, shear, shed, shift, sideline, strike, subduct, transfer, transmigrate, transport, unseat, vacate, withdraw.

remuneration *n.* compensation, earnings, emolument, fee, guerdon, income, indemnity, pay, payment, profit, recompense, reimbursement, remittance, reparation, repayment, retainer, return, reward, salary, stipend, wages.

render *v.* act, cede, clarify, construe, contribute, deliver, depict, display, do, evince, exchange, exhibit, explain, furnish, give, give back, give up, hand over, interpret, leave, make, make up, manifest, melt, pay, perform, play, portray, present, provide, put, relinquish, repay, represent, reproduce, restate, restore, return, show, show forth, submit, supply, surrender, swap, tender, trade, transcribe, translate, yield.

rendition *n.* arrangement, construction, delivery, depiction, execution, explanation, interpretation, metaphrase, metaphrasis, performance, portrayal, presentation, reading, rendering, transcription, translation, version.

renegade *n.* apostate, backslider, betrayer, defector, deserter, dissident, mutineer, outlaw, rebel, recreant, renegado, renegate, runaway, tergiversator, traitor, turncoat.

antonyms adherent, disciple, follower.

adj. apostate, backsliding, disloyal, dissident, mutinous, outlaw, perfidious, rebel, rebellious, recreant, runaway, traitorous, unfaithful.

renege *v.* apostatize, cross the floor, default, renegue, renig, repudiate, welsh.

renew *v.* continue, extend, mend, modernize, overhaul, prolong, reaffirm, recommence, recreate, re-establish, refashion, refit, refresh, refurbish, regenerate, rejuvenate, remodel, renovate, reopen, repair, repeat, replace, replenish, restate, restock, restore, resume, revitalize, transform.

renounce *v.* abandon, abdicate, abjure, abnegate, decline, deny, discard, disclaim, disown, disprofess, eschew, forgo, forsake, forswear, put away, quit, recant, reject, relinquish, repudiate, resign, spurn.

renovate *v.* do up, furbish, improve, modernize, overhaul, recondition, reconstitute, recreate, refit, reform, refurbish, rehabilitate, remodel, renew, repair, restore, revamp.

renown *n.* acclaim, celebrity, distinction, eminence, fame, glory, honor, illustriousness, kudos, luster, mark, note, reputation, repute, stardom.

antonyms anonymity, obscurity.

renowned *adj.* acclaimed, celebrated, distinguished, eminent, esteemed, famed, famous, illustrious, notable, noted, pre-eminent, supereminent, well-known.

antonyms anonymous, obscure, unknown.

rent[1] *n.* fee, gale, hire, lease, payment, rental, tariff.
v. charter, farm out, hire, lease, let, sublet, take.

rent[2] *n.* breach, break, chink, cleavage, crack, dissension, disunion, division, flaw, gash, hole, opening, perforation, rift, rip, rupture, schism, slash, slit, split, tear.

repair[1] *v.* debug, fix, heal, mend, patch up, recover, rectify, redress, renew, renovate, restore, retrieve, square.
n. adjustment, condition, darn, fettle, form, improvement, mend, nick, overhaul, patch, restoration, shape, state.

repair[2] *v.* go, wend one's way, move, remove, resort, retire, turn, withdraw.

repartee *n.* badinage, banter, jesting, persiflage, pleasantry, raillery, riposte, sally, waggery, wit, witticism, wittiness, wordplay.

repast *n.* collation, feed, food, meal, nourishment, refection, snack, spread, victuals.

repeal *v.* abolish, abrogate, annul, cancel, countermand, invalidate, nullify, quash, recall, rescind, reverse, revoke, set aside, void, withdraw.

antonyms enact, establish.

n. abolition, abrogation, annulment, cancellation, invalidation, nullification, quashing, rescinding, rescindment, rescission, reversal, revocation, withdrawal.

antonyms enactment, establishment.

repeat *v.* duplicate, echo, iterate, quote, rebroadcast, recapitulate, recite, re-do, rehearse, reiterate, relate, renew, replay, reproduce, rerun, reshow, restate, retell.

n. duplicate, echo, rebroadcast, recapitulation, reiteration, repetition, replay, reproduction, rerun, reshowing.

repeatedly *adv.* again and again, frequently, often, oftentimes, ofttimes, over and over, recurrently, time after time, time and (time) again.

repel *v.* check, confront, decline, disadvantage, disgust, fight, hold off, nauseate, offend, oppose, parry, rebuff, refuse, reject, repulse, resist, revolt, sicken, ward off.
antonym attract.

repellent *adj.* abhorrent, abominable, discouraging, disgusting, distasteful, hateful, horrid, loathsome, nauseating, noxious, obnoxious, odious, offensive, offputting, rebarbative, repugnant, repulsive, revolting, sickening.
antonym attractive.

repent *n.* atone, bewail, deplore, lament, regret, relent, rue, sorrow.

repentance *n.* compunction, contrition, grief, guilt, metanoia, penitence, regret, remorse, self-reproach, sorriness, sorrow.

repentant *adj.* apologetic, ashamed, chastened, compunctious, contrite, penitent, regretful, remorseful, rueful, sorry.
antonym unrepentant.

repetitious *adj.* battological, long-winded, pleonastic(al), prolix, redundant, tautological, tedious, verbose, windy, wordy.

repine *v.* beef, brood, complain, fret, grieve, grouse, grumble, lament, languish, moan, mope, murmur, sulk.

replace *v.* deputize, follow, make good, oust, re-establish, reinstate, restore, substitute, succeed, supersede, supplant, supply.

replacement *n.* double, fill-in, proxy, replacer, stand-in, substitute, succedaneum, successor, surrogate, understudy.

replenish *v.* fill, furnish, provide, recharge, recruit, refill, reload, renew, replace, restock, restore, stock, supply, top up.

replica *n.* clone, copy, duplicate, facsimile, imitation, model, reproduction.

reply *v.* acknowledge, answer, counter, echo, react, reciprocate, rejoin, repartee, respond, retaliate, retort, return, riposte.
n. acknowledgment, answer, comeback, counter, echo, reaction, reciprocation, rejoinder, repartee, response, retaliation, retort, return, riposte.

report *n.* account, announcement, article, bang, blast, boom, bruit, character, communication, communiqué, crack, crash, declaration, description, detail, detonation, discharge, dispatch, esteem, explosion, fame, gossip, hearsay, information, message, narrative, news, noise, note, paper, piece, procès-verbal, recital, record, regard, relation, reputation, repute, reverberation, rumor, sound, statement, story, summary, tale, talk, tidings, version, word, write-up.

v. air, announce, appear, arrive, broadcast, bruit, circulate, come, communicate, cover, declare, describe, detail, document, mention, narrate, note, notify, proclaim, publish, recite, record, recount, relate, relay, state, tell.

reporter *n.* announcer, correspondent, hack, journalist, legman, newscaster, newshound, newspaperman, newspaperwoman, pressman, stringer, writer.

repose[1] *n.* aplomb, calm, calmness, composure, dignity, ease, equanimity, inactivity, peace, poise, quiet, quietness, quietude, relaxation, respite, rest, restfulness, self-possession, serenity, sleep, slumber, stillness, tranquility.
antonyms activity, strain, stress.
v. laze, recline, relax, rest, sleep, slumber.

repose[2] *v.* confide, deposit, entrust, invest, lodge, place, put, set, store.

reprehensible *adj.* bad, blamable, blameworthy, censurable, condemnable, culpable, delinquent, discreditable, disgraceful, errant, erring, ignoble, objectionable, opprobrious, remiss, shameful, unworthy.
antonyms creditable, good, praiseworthy.

represent *v.* act, appear as, be, betoken, delineate, denote, depict, depicture, describe, designate, embody, enact, epitomize, equal, evoke, exemplify, exhibit, express, illustrate, mean, outline, perform, personify, picture, portray, produce, render, reproduce, show, sketch, stage, symbolize, typify.

representation *n.* account, argument, bust, committee, delegates, delegation, delineation, depiction, description, embassy, exhibition, explanation, exposition, expostulation, icon, idol, illustration, image, likeness, model, narration, narrative, performance, petition, picture, play, portrait, portrayal, production, relation, remonstrance, resemblance, show, sight, sketch, spectacle, statue.

representative *n.* agent, archetype, commissioner, congressman, congresswoman, councillor, delegate, depute, deputy, embodiment, epitome, exemplar, member, personification, proxy, rep, representant, salesperson, senator, spokesperson, traveler, type.
adj. archetypal, characteristic, chosen, delegated, elected, elective, emblematic, evocative, exemplary, illustrative, normal, symbolic, typical, usual.
antonyms atypical, unrepresentative.

repress *v.* bottle up, chasten, check, control, crush, curb, hamper, hinder, impede, inhibit, master, muffle, overcome, overpower, quash, quell, reprime, restrain, silence, smother, stifle, subdue, subjugate, suppress, swallow.

reprimand *n.* admonition, blame, castigation, censure, dressing-down, jawbation, jobation, lecture, rebuke, reprehension, reproach, reproof, row, schooling, talking-to, telling-off, ticking-off, tongue-lashing, wigging.
v. admonish, bawl out, blame, bounce, castigate, censure, check, chide, jobe, keelhaul, lecture, lesson,

rebuke, reprehend, reproach, reprove, scold, slate, tongue-lash, upbraid.

reproach *v.* abuse, blame, censure, chide, condemn, criticize, defame, discredit, disparage, dispraise, rebuke, reprehend, reprimand, reprove, scold, upbraid.
n. abuse, blame, blemish, censure, condemnation, contempt, disapproval, discredit, disgrace, dishonor, disrepute, ignominy, indignity, nayword, obloquy, odium, opprobrium, reproof, scorn, shame, slight, slut, stain, stigma, upbraiding.

reproduction *n.* amphimixis, breeding, copy, duplicate, ectype, facsimile, fructuation, gamogenesis, generation, imitation, increase, multiplication, picture, print, procreation, proliferation, propagation, replica.
antonym original.

reproof *n.* admonition, blame, castigation, censure, chiding, condemnation, criticism, dressing-down, rebuke, reprehension, reprimand, reproach, reproval, reproving, scolding, ticking-off, tongue-lashing, upbraiding.
antonym praise.

repugnance *n.* abhorrence, abhorring, antipathy, aversion, disgust, dislike, disrelish, distaste, hatred, inconsistency, loathing, reluctance, repugnancy, repulsion, revulsion.
antonyms liking, pleasure.

repulsive *adj.* abhorrent, abominable, cold, disagreeable, disgusting, distasteful, forbidding, foul, hateful, hideous, horrid, ill-faced, loathsome, nauseating, objectionable, obnoxious, odious, offensive, repellent, reserved, revolting, sickening, ugly, unpleasant, vile.
antonyms friendly, pleasant.

reputable *adj.* creditable, dependable, estimable, excellent, good, honorable, honored, irreproachable, legitimate, principled, reliable, respectable, trustworthy, unimpeachable, upright, worthy.
antonyms disreputable, infamous.

reputation *n.* bad name, character, credit, distinction, esteem, estimation, fame, good name, honor, infamy, name, opinion, renown, repute, standing, stature.

repute *n.* celebrity, distinction, esteem, estimation, fame, good name, name, renown, reputation, standing, stature.
antonym infamy.

request *v.* ask, ask for, beg, beseech, demand, desire, entreat, impetrate, importune, petition, pray, requisition, seek, solicit, supplicate.
n. appeal, application, asking, begging, call, demand, desire, entreaty, impetration, petition, prayer, representation, requisition, solicitation, suit, supplication.

require *v.* ask, beg, beseech, bid, command, compel, constrain, crave, demand, desire, direct, enjoin, exact, force, instruct, involve, lack, make, miss, necessitate, need, oblige, order, request, take, want, wish.

requirement *n.* demand, desideratum, essential, lack, must, necessity, need, precondition, prerequisite,

provision, proviso, qualification, requisite, sine qua non, specification, stipulation, term, want.
antonym inessential.

requisite *adj.* essential, imperative, indispensable, mandatory, necessary, needed, needful, obligatory, prerequisite, required, vital.
antonyms inessential, optional.
n. condition, desiderative, desideratum, essential, must, necessity, need, precondition, prerequisite, requirement, sine qua non.
antonym inessential.

rescind *v.* abrogate, annul, cancel, countermand, invalidate, negate, nullify, overturn, quash, recall, repeal, retract, reverse, revoke, void.
antonym enforce.

rescue *v.* deliver, extricate, free, liberate, ransom, recover, redeem, release, salvage, save.
antonym capture.
n. deliverance, delivery, extrication, liberation, recovery, redemption, release, relief, salvage, salvation, saving.
antonym capture.

research *n.* analysis, delving, examination, experimentation, exploration, fact-finding, groundwork, inquiry, investigation, probe, quest, scrutiny, search, study.
v. analyze, examine, experiment, explore, ferret, investigate, probe, scrutinize, search, study.

resemblance *n.* affinity, analogy, assonance, closeness, comparability, comparison, conformity, correspondence, counterpart, facsimile, image, kinship, likeness, parallel, parity, sameness, semblance, similarity, similitude.
antonym dissimilarity.

resemble *v.* approach, duplicate, echo, favor, mirror, parallel, take after.
antonym differ from.

resentful *adj.* aggrieved, angry, bitter, embittered, exasperated, grudging, huffish, huffy, hurt, incensed, indignant, irate, ireful, jealous, miffed, offended, peeved, piqued, put out, resentive, revengeful, stomachful, unforgiving, wounded.
antonym contented.

resentment *n.* anger, animosity, bitterness, disaffection, discontentment, displeasure, fury, grudge, huff, hurt, ill-feeling, ill-will, indignation, ire, irritation, malice, pique, rage, rancor, umbrage, vexation, vindictiveness, wrath.
antonym contentment.

reservation[1] *n.* arrière pensée, condition, demur, doubt, hesitancy, hesitation, inhibition, proviso, qualification, restraint, scruple, second thought, skepticism, stipulation.

reservation[2] enclave, homeland, park, preserve, reserve, sanctuary, territory, tract.

reserve[1] *v.* bespeak, book, conserve, defer, delay, engage, hoard, hold, husband, keep, postpone, prearrange,

preserve, retain, save, secure, set apart, spare, stockpile, store, withhold.
antonym use up.
n. backlog, cache, capital, fund, hoard, park, preserve, reservation, reservoir, sanctuary, savings, stock, stockpile, store, substitute, supply, tract.
reserve[2] aloofness, constraint, coolness, formality, limitation, modesty, reluctance, reservation, restraint, restriction, reticence, secretiveness, shyness, silence, taciturnity.
antonyms friendliness, informality.
adj. additional, alternate, auxiliary, extra, secondary, spare, substitute.
reserved[1] *adj.* booked, bound, designated, destined, earmarked, engaged, fated, held, intended, kept, meant, predestined, restricted, retained, set aside, spoken for, taken.
antonym unreserved.
reserved[2] aloof, cautious, close-mouthed, cold, cool, demure, formal, modest, prim, restrained, reticent, retiring, secretive, shy, silent, stand-offish, taciturn, unapproachable, unclub(b)able, uncommunicative, uncompanionable, unconversable, undemonstrative, unforthcoming, unresponsive, unsociable.
antonyms friendly, informal.
reside *v.* abide, consist, dwell, exist, inhabit, inhere, lie, live, lodge, remain, settle, sit, sojourn, stay.
residence *n.* abode, country-house, country-seat, domicile, dwelling, habitation, hall, home, house, household, lodging, manor, mansion, occupancy, occupation, pad, palace, place, quarters, seat, sojourn, stay, tenancy, villa.
residue *n.* balance, difference, dregs, excess, extra, leftovers, overflow, overplus, remainder, remains, remnant, residuum, rest, surplus.
antonym core.
resign *v.* abandon, abdicate, cede, forgo, forsake, leave, quit, relinquish, renounce, sacrifice, stand down, surrender, vacate, waive, yield.
antonyms join, maintain.
resignation *n.* abandonment, abdication, acceptance, acquiescence, compliance, defeatism, demission, departure, endurance, forbearing, fortitude, leaving, nonresistance, notice, passivity, patience, relinquishment, renunciation, retirement, submission, sufferance, surrender.
antonym resistance.
resigned *adj.* acquiescent, compliant, defeatist, longsuffering, patient, stoical, subdued, submissive, unprotesting, unresisting.
antonym resisting.
resilience *n.* adaptability, bounce, buoyancy, elasticity, flexibility, give, hardiness, plasticity, pliability, recoil, spring, springiness, strength, suppleness, toughness, unshockability.
antonyms inflexibility, rigidity.

resist *v.* avoid, battle, check, combat, confront, counteract, countervail, curb, defy, dispute, fight back, forbear, forgo, hinder, oppose, recalcitrate, refuse, repel, thwart, weather, withstand.
antonyms accept, submit.
resolute *adj.* bold, constant, determined, dogged, firm, fixed, indissuadable, indivertible, inflexible, obstinate, persevering, purposeful, relentless, set, staunch, steadfast, stout, strong-minded, strong-willed, stubborn, sturdy, tenacious, unbending, undaunted, unflinching, unshakable, unshaken, unwavering.
antonym irresolute.
resolution *n.* aim, answer, boldness, constancy, courage, decision, declaration, dedication, dénouement, determination, devotion, doggedness, earnestness, end, energy, finding, firmness, fortitude, intent, intention, judgment, motion, obstinacy, outcome, perseverance, pertinacity, purpose, relentlessness, resoluteness, resolve, settlement, sincerity, solution, solving, staunchness, steadfastness, stubbornness, tenacity, unraveling, verdict, will power, zeal.
antonym indecision.
resolve *v.* agree, alter, analyze, anatomize, answer, banish, break up, change, clear, conclude, convert, crack, decide, design, determine, disentangle, disintegrate, dispel, dissect, dissipate, dissolve, elucidate, explain, fathom, fix, intend, liquefy, melt, metamorphose, purpose, reduce, relax, remove, separate, settle, solve, transform, transmute, undertake, unravel.
antonyms blend, waver.
n. boldness, conclusion, conviction, courage, decision, design, determination, earnestness, firmness, intention, objective, project, purpose, resoluteness, resolution, sense of purpose, steadfastness, undertaking, will power.
antonym indecision.
resort *v.* frequent, go, haunt, hie, repair, visit.
antonym avoid.
n. alternative, chance, course, expedient, haunt, health resort, hope, howf(f), possibility, recourse, reference, refuge, retreat, spa, spot, watering-place.
resound *v.* boom, echo, re-echo, resonate, reverberate, ring, sound, thunder.
resource *n.* ability, appliance, cache, capability, cleverness, contrivance, course, device, expedient, hoard, ingenuity, initiative, inventiveness, means, quickwittedness, reserve, resort, resourcefulness, shift, source, stockpile, supply, talent.
antonym unimaginativeness.
resourceful *adj.* able, bright, capable, clever, creative, fertile, imaginative, ingenious, innovative, inventive, originative, quick-witted, sharp, slick, talented.
respect *n.* admiration, appreciation, approbation, aspect, bearing, characteristic, connection, consideration, deference, detail, esteem, estimation, facet, feature, homage, honor, matter, particular, point, recognition,

reference, regard, relation, reverence, sense, veneration, way.

antonym disrespect.

v. admire, appreciate, attend, esteem, follow, heed, honor, notice, obey, observe, pay homage to, recognize, regard, revere, reverence, value, venerate.

antonym scorn.

respectable *adj.* admirable, ample, appreciable, clean-living, considerable, decent, decorous, dignified, estimable, fair, good, goodly, honest, honorable, large, passable, presentable, proper, reasonable, reputable, respected, seemly, sizable, substantial, tidy, tolerable, upright, venerable, well-to-do, worthy.

antonyms disreputable, miserly, unseemly.

respectful *adj.* civil, courteous, courtly, deferential, dutiful, filial, gracious, humble, mannerly, obedient, polite, regardful, reverent, reverential, self-effacing, solicitous, submissive, subservient, well-mannered.

antonym disrespectful.

respite *n.* adjournment, break, breather, cessation, delay, gap, halt, hiatus, intermission, interruption, interval, letup, lull, moratorium, pause, postponement, recess, relaxation, relief, remission, reprieve, rest, stay, suspension.

response *n.* acknowledgment, answer, comeback, counterblast, feedback, reaction, rejoinder, reply, respond, retort, return, riposte.

antonym query.

responsibility *n.* accountability, amenability, answerability, authority, blame, burden, care, charge, conscientiousness, culpability, dependability, duty, fault, guilt, importance, level-headedness, liability, maturity, obligation, onus, power, rationality, reliability, sense, sensibleness, soberness, stability, trust, trustworthiness.

antonym irresponsibility.

responsible *adj.* accountable, adult, amenable, answerable, authoritative, bound, chargeable, conscientious, culpable, decision-making, dependable, duty-bound, ethical, executive, guilty, high, important, level-headed, liable, mature, public-spirited, rational, reliable, right, sensible, sober, sound, stable, steady, subject, trustworthy.

antonym irresponsible.

rest[1] *n.* base, break, breather, breathing-space, breathing-time, breathing-while, calm, cessation, cradle, doze, halt, haven, holiday, idleness, inactivity, interlude, intermission, interval, leisure, lie-down, lie-in, lodging, lull, motionlessness, nap, pause, prop, refreshment, refuge, relaxation, relief, repose, retreat, shelf, shelter, shut-eye, siesta, sleep, slumber, snooze, somnolence, spell, stand, standstill, stillness, stop, support, tranquility, trestle, vacation.

antonyms action, activity, restlessness.

v. alight, base, cease, continue, depend, desist, discontinue, doze, found, halt, hang, hinge, idle, keep, land,

lay, laze, lean, lie, lie back, lie down, lie in, perch, prop, recline, relax, rely, remain, repose, reside, settle, sit, sleep, slumber, snooze, spell, stand, stay, stop, turn.

antonyms change, continue, work.

rest[2] *n.* balance, core, excess, left-overs, majority, others, remainder, remains, remnants, residue, residuum, rump, surplus.

restful *adj.* calm, calming, comfortable, easeful, languid, pacific, peaceful, placid, quiet, relaxed, relaxing, serene, sleepy, soothing, tranquil, tranquilizing, undisturbed, unhurried.

antonyms disturbed, disturbing.

restitution *n.* amends, compensation, damages, indemnification, indemnity, recompense, redress, refund, reimbursement, remuneration, reparation, repayment, requital, restoration, restoring, return, satisfaction.

restive *adj.* agitated, edgy, fidgety, fractious, fretful, impatient, jittery, jumpy, nervous, obstinate, recalcitrant, refractory, restless, uneasy, unquiet, unruly.

antonyms calm, relaxed.

restless *adj.* active, agitated, anxious, bustling, changeable, disturbed, edgy, fidgety, fitful, footloose, fretful, hurried, inconstant, irresolute, jumpy, moving, nervous, nomadic, restive, roving, shifting, sleepless, transient, troubled, turbulent, uneasy, unquiet, unresting, unruly, unsettled, unstable, unsteady, wandering, worried.

antonyms calm, relaxed.

restore *v.* fix, mend, reanimate, rebuild, recondition, reconstitute, reconstruct, recover, recruit, redintegrate, re-enforce, re-establish, refresh, refurbish, rehabilitate, reimpose, reinstate, reintroduce, rejuvenate, renew, renovate, repair, replace, retouch, return, revitalize, revive, revivify, strengthen.

antonyms damage, remove, weaken.

restrain *v.* arrest, bind, bit, bridle, chain, check, cohibit, confine, constrain, control, curb, curtail, debar, detain, fetter, govern, hamper, hamshackle, handicap, harness, hinder, hold, imprison, inhibit, jail, keep, limit, manacle, muzzle, pinion, prevent, repress, restrict, stay, subdue, suppress, tie.

antonyms encourage, liberate.

restraint *n.* arrest, ban, bondage, bonds, bridle, captivity, chains, check, coercion, cohibition, command, compulsion, confinement, confines, constraint, control, cramp, curb, curtailment, dam, detention, embargo, fetters, grip, hindrance, hold, imprisonment, inhibition, interdict, lid, limit, limitation, manacles, moderation, pinions, prevention, rein, restriction, self-control, self-discipline, self-possession, self-restraint, stint, straitjacket, suppression, taboo, tie.

antonym freedom.

restrict *v.* astrict, bound, circumscribe, condition, confine, constrain, contain, cramp, demarcate, hamper, handicap, impede, inhibit, limit, regulate, restrain, restringe, scant, thirl, tie.

antonyms broaden, encourage, free.

restriction *n.* check, condition, confinement, constraint, containment, control, curb, demarcation, handicap, inhibition, limitation, regulation, restraint, rule, squeeze, stint, stipulation.
antonyms broadening, encouragement, freedom.

result *n.* conclusion, consequence, decision, development, effect, end, end-product, event, fruit, issue, outcome, produce, reaction, sequel, termination, upshot.
antonyms beginning, cause.

v. appear, arise, culminate, derive, develop, emanate, emerge, end, ensue, eventuate, finish, flow, follow, happen, issue, proceed, spring, stem, terminate.
antonyms begin, cause.

resume *v.* continue, pick up, proceed, recommence, re-institute, reopen, restart, take up.
antonym cease.

resurgence *n.* rebirth, recrudescence, re-emergence, renaissance, renascence, resumption, resurrection, return, revival, revivification, risorgimento.
antonym decrease.

resuscitate *v.* quicken, reanimate, reinvigorate, renew, rescue, restore, resurrect, revitalize, revive, revivify, save.

retain *v.* absorb, commission, contain, detail, employ, engage, grasp, grip, hire, hold, hold back, keep, keep in mind, keep up, maintain, memorize, pay, preserve, recall, recollect, remember, reserve, restrain, save.
antonyms release, spend.

retainer[1] *n.* attendant, dependant, domestic, galloglass, henchman, lackey, minion, servant, satellite, subordinate, supporter.

retainer[2] *n.* advance, deposit, fee, retaining fee.

retaliate *v.* fight back, get back at, get even with, get one's own back, give as good as one gets, hit back, reciprocate, repay in kind, return like for like, revenge oneself, strike back, take revenge.
antonyms accept, submit.

retard *v.* arrest, brake, check, clog, decelerate, defer, delay, detain, encumber, handicap, hinder, impede, keep back, obstruct, slow, stall.
antonym advance.

reticent *adj.* boutonné, close-lipped, close-mouthed, mum, mute, quiet, reserved, restrained, secretive, silent, taciturn, tight-lipped, uncommunicative, unforthcoming, unspeaking.
antonyms communicative, forward, frank.

retire *v.* decamp, depart, draw back, ebb, exit, leave, recede, remove, retreat, withdraw.
antonyms enter, join.

retiring *adj.* bashful, coy, demure, diffident, humble, meek, modest, mousy, quiet, reclusive, reserved, reticent, self-effacing, shamefaced, shrinking, shy, timid, timorous, unassertive, unassuming.
antonyms assertive, forward.

retort *v.* answer, counter, rejoin, repartee, reply, respond, retaliate, return, riposte.

n. answer, backword, come-back, quip, rejoinder, repartee, reply, response, riposte, sally.

retreat *v.* depart, ebb, leave, quit, recede, recoil, retire, shrink, turn tail, withdraw.
antonym advance.

n. asylum, den, departure, ebb, evacuation, flight, funkhole, growlery, haunt, haven, hibernacle, hibernaculum, hideaway, privacy, refuge, resort, retirement, sanctuary, seclusion, shelter, withdrawal.
antonyms advance, company, limelight.

retrench *v.* curtail, cut, decrease, diminish, economize, husband, lessen, limit, pare, prune, reduce, save, slim down, trim.
antonym increase.

retribution *n.* compensation, justice, Nemesis, payment, punishment, reckoning, recompense, redress, repayment, reprisal, requital, retaliation, revenge, reward, satisfaction, talion, vengeance.

retrieve *v.* fetch, make good, recall, recapture, recoup, recover, redeem, regain, repair, repossess, rescue, restore, return, salvage, save.
antonym lose.

retrograde *adj.* backward, declining, degenerative, denigrating, deteriorating, downward, inverse, negative, regressive, relapsing, retreating, retrogressive, reverse, reverting, waning, worsening.
antonym progressive.

return *v.* announce, answer, choose, communicate, convey, deliver, earn, elect, make, net, pick, reappear, rebound, reciprocate, recoil, recompense, recur, redound, re-establish, refund, reimburse, reinstate, rejoin, remit, render, repair, repay, replace, reply, report, requite, respond, restore, retort, retreat, revert, send, submit, transmit, volley, yield.
antonyms leave, take.

n. account, advantage, answer, benefit, comeback, compensation, form, gain, home-coming, income, interest, list, proceeds, profit, quip, reappearance, rebound, reciprocation, recoil, recompense, recrudescence, recurrence, redound, re-establishment, reimbursement, reinstatement, rejoinder, reparation, repayment, replacement, reply, report, requital, response, restoration, retaliation, retort, retreat, revenue, reversion, reward, riposte, sally, statement, summary, takings, yield.
antonyms disappearance, expense, loss, payment.

reveal *v.* announce, bare, betray, broadcast, communicate, disbosom, disclose, dismask, display, divulge, exhibit, expose, impart, leak, lift the lid off, manifest, open, proclaim, publish, show, tell, unbare, unbosom, uncover, unearth, unfold, unmask, unshadow, unveil.
antonym hide.

revel *v.* carouse, celebrate, live it up, make merry, paint the town red, push the boat out, raise the roof, roist, roister, whoop it up.
n. bacchanal, carousal, carouse, celebration, comus,

debauch, festivity, gala, jollification, merry-make, merry-making, party, saturnalia, spree.

revel in bask, crow, delight, gloat, glory, indulge, joy, lap up, luxuriate, rejoice, relish, savor, take pleasure, thrive on, wallow.
antonym dislike.

revelation *n.* announcement, apocalypse, betrayal, broadcasting, communication, disclosure, discovery, display, exhibition, exposé, exposition, exposure, giveaway, leak, manifestation, news, proclamation, publication, telling, uncovering, unearthing, unveiling.

revelry *n.* carousal, carouse, celebration, debauch, debauchery, festivity, fun, jollification, jollity, merry-making, party, revel-rout, riot, roistering, saturnalia, spree, wassail, wassailing, wassailry.
antonym sobriety.

revenge *n.* a dose/taste of one's own medicine, ravanche, reprisal, requital, retaliation, retribution, revengement, satisfaction, ultion, vengeance, vindictiveness.
v. avenge, even the score, get one's own back, get satisfaction, repay, requite, retaliate, vindicate.

revenue *n.* gain, income, interest, proceeds, profits, receipts, returns, rewards, take, takings, yield.
antonym expenditure.

revere *v.* adore, defer to, exalt, honor, pay homage to, respect, reverence, venerate, worship.
antonyms despise, scorn.

reverence *n.* admiration, adoration, awe, deference, devotion, dulia, esteem, genuflection, homage, honor, hyperdulia, latria, respect, veneration, worship.
antonym scorn.
v. acknowledge, admire, adore, honor, respect, revere, venerate, worship.
antonyms despise, scorn.

reverent *adj.* adoring, awed, decorous, deferential, devout, dutiful, humble, loving, meek, pious, respectful, reverential, solemn, submissive.
antonym irreverent.

reverse *v.* alter, annul, back, backtrack, cancel, change, countermand, hark back, invalidate, invert, negate, overrule, overset, overthrow, overturn, quash, repeal, rescind, retract, retreat, revert, revoke, transpose, undo, up-end, upset.
antonym enforce.
n. adversity, affliction, antithesis, back, blow, check, contradiction, contrary, converse, defeat, disappointment, failure, hardship, inverse, misadventure, misfortune, mishap, opposite, rear, repulse, reversal, setback, trial, underside, verso, vicissitude, woman.
adj. backward, contrary, converse, inverse, inverted, opposite, verso.

revert *v.* backslide, lapse, recur, regress, relapse, resume, retrogress, return, reverse.
antonym progress.

review *v.* assess, criticize, discuss, evaluate, examine, inspect, judge, reassess, recall, recapitulate, recollect,

reconsider, re-evaluate, re-examine, rehearse, remember, rethink, revise, scrutinize, study, weigh.
n. analysis, assessment, commentary, criticism, critique, evaluation, examination, journal, judgment, magazine, notice, periodical, reassessment, recapitulation, recension, reconsideration, re-evaluation, re-examination, report, rethink, retrospect, revision, scrutiny, study, survey.

revile *v.* abuse, blackguard, calumniate, defame, denigrate, libel, malign, miscall, reproach, scorn, slander, smear, traduce, vilify, vilipend, vituperate.
antonym praise.

revise *v.* alter, amend, change, correct, edit, emend, memorize, modify, recast, recense, reconsider, reconstruct, redo, re-examine, reread, revamp, review, rewrite, study, swot up, update. **revision** *n.* alteration, amendment, change, correction, editing, emendation, homework, memorizing, modification, recast, recasting, recension, reconstruction, re-examination, rereading, review, rewriting, rifacimento, studying, swotting, updating.

revival *n.* awakening, quickening, reactivation, reanimation, reawakening, rebirth, recrudescence, renaissance, renascence, renewal, restoration, resurgence, resurrection, resuscitation, revitalization, revivification, risorgimento.
antonym suppression.

revive *v.* animate, awaken, cheer, comfort, invigorate, quicken, rally, reactivate, reanimate, recover, refresh, rekindle, renew, renovate, restore, resuscitate, revitalize, revivify, rouse.
antonyms suppress, weary.

revoke *v.* abolish, abrogate, annul, cancel, countermand, disclaim, dissolve, invalidate, negate, nullify, quash, recall, recant, renounce, repeal, repudiate, rescind, retract, reverse, withdraw.
antonym enforce.

revolt[1] *n.* breakaway, defection, insurgency, insurrection, Jacquerie, mutiny, putsch, rebellion, revolution, rising, secession, sedition, uprising.
v. defect, mutiny, rebel, resist, riot, rise.
antonym submit.

revolt[2] *v.* disgust, nauseate, offend, outrage, repel, repulse, scandalize, shock, sicken.
antonym please.

revolting *adj.* abhorrent, abominable, appalling, disgusting, distasteful, fetid, foul, horrible, horrid, loathsome, nasty, nauseating, nauseous, noisome, obnoxious, obscene, offensive, repellent, repugnant, repulsive, shocking, sickening, sickly.
antonym pleasant.

revolution *n.* cataclysm, change, circle, circuit, coup, coup d'état, cycle, gyration, innovation, insurgency, Jacquerie, lap, metamorphosis, metanoia, mutiny, orbit, putsch, rebellion, reformation, revolt, rising, rotation, round, shift, spin, transformation, turn, upheaval, uprising, volution, wheel, whirl.

revolutionary *n.* anarchist, insurgent, insurrectionary, insurrectionist, Jacobin, mutineer, rebel, revolutionist, Trot, Trotskyite.

adj. anarchistic, avant-garde, different, drastic, experimental, extremist, fundamental, innovative, insurgent, insurrectionary, mutinous, new, novel, progressive, radical, rebel, seditious, subversive, thoroughgoing.

antonyms commonplace, establishment.

revolve *v.* circle, circumgyrate, circumvolve, gyrate, orbit, rotate, spin, turn, wheel, whirl.

revolver *n.* air-gun, firearm, gun, hand-gun, heater, peacemaker, piece, pistol, rod, shooter, six-shooter.

revulsion *n.* abhorrence, abomination, aversion, detestation, disgust, dislike, distaste, hatred, loathing, recoil, repugnance, repulsion.

antonym pleasure.

reward *n.* benefit, bonus, bounty, come-up(p)ance, compensation, desert, gain, guerdon, honor, meed, merit, payment, pay-off, premium, prize, profit, punishment, recompense, remuneration, repayment, requital, retribution, return, wages.

antonym punishment.

v. compensate, guerdon, honor, pay, recompense, remunerate, repay, requite.

antonym punish.

rewarding *adj.* advantageous, beneficial, edifying, enriching, fruitful, fulfilling, gainful, gratifying, pleasing, productive, profitable, remunerative, rewardful, satisfying, valuable, worthwhile.

antonym unrewarding.

rhetorical *adj.* artificial, bombastic, declamatory, false, flamboyant, flashy, florid, flowery, grandiloquent, high-flown, high-sounding, hyperbolic, inflated, insincere, linguistic, magniloquent, oratorical, over-decorated, pompous, pretentious, rhetoric, showy, silver-tongued, stylistic, verbal, verbose, windy.

antonyms simple.

rhythm *n.* accent, beat, cadence, cadency, eurhythmy, flow, lilt, measure, meter, movement, pattern, periodicity, pulse, rhythmicity, swing, tempo, time.

ribald *adj.* base, bawdy, blue, broad, coarse, derisive, earthy, filthy, foul-mouthed, gross, indecent, irrisory, jeering, licentious, low, mean, mocking, naughty, obscene, off-color, Rabelaisian, racy, risqué, rude, scurrilous, smutty, vulgar.

antonym polite.

rich *adj.* abounding, abundant, affluent, ample, bright, copious, costly, creamy, deep, delicious, dulcet, elaborate, elegant, expensive, exquisite, exuberant, fatty, fecund, fertile, fine, flavorsome, flush, fruitful, full, full-bodied, full-flavored, full-toned, gay, gorgeous, heavy, highly-flavored, humorous, in the money, intense, juicy, laughable, lavish, loaded, ludicrous, luscious, lush, luxurious, mellifluous, mellow, moneyed, opulent, palatial, pecunious, plenteous, plentiful, plutocratic, precious, priceless, productive, prolific, propertied, property, prosperous, resonant, ridiculous, risible, rolling, savory, side-splitting, spicy, splendid, strong, succulent, sumptuous, superb, sweet, tasty, uberous, valuable, vibrant, vivid, warm, wealthy, well-heeled, well-off, well-provided, well-stocked, well-supplied, well-to-do.

antonyms harsh, miserly, plain, poor, simple, tasteless, thin, unfertile.

rickety *adj.* broken, broken-down, decrepit, derelict, dilapidated, feeble, flimsy, frail, imperfect, infirm, insecure, jerry-built, precarious, ramshackle, shaky, shoogly, tottering, tottery, unsound, unstable, unsteady, weak, wobbly.

antonyms stable, strong.

rid *v.* clear, deliver, disabuse, disburden, disembarrass, disencumber, expel, free, purge, relieve, unburden.

antonym burden.

riddle[1] *n.* brain-teaser, charade, conundrum, enigma, logogram, logograph, logogriph, mystery, poser, problem, puzzle, rebus.

riddle[2] *v.* corrupt, damage, fill, filter, impair, infest, invade, mar, pepper, perforate, permeate, pervade, pierce, puncture, screen, sieve, sift, spoil, strain, winnow.

n. sieve, strainer.

ride *v.* control, dominate, enslave, float, grip, handle, haunt, hurl, journey, manage, move, oppress, progress, sit, survive, travel, weather.

n. drive, hurl, jaunt, journey, lift, outing, spin, trip, whirl.

ridge *n.* arête, band, costa, crinkle, drum, drumlin, escarpment, eskar, hill, hog's back, hummock, lump, reef, ripple, saddle, wale, weal, welt, zastruga.

ridicule *n.* banter, chaff, derision, gibe, irony, irrision, jeering, jeers, laughter, mockery, raillery, sarcasm, satire, scorn, sneers, taunting.

antonym praise.

v. banter, burlesque, caricature, cartoon, chaff, crucify, deride, humiliate, jeer, josh, lampoon, mock, parody, pillory, pooh-pooh, queer, quiz, rib, satirize, scoff, send up, sneer at, take the mickey out of, taunt.

antonym praise.

ridiculous *adj.* absurd, comical, contemptible, damfool, derisory, farcical, foolish, funny, hilarious, incredible, laughable, laughworthy, ludicrous, nonsensical, outrageous, preposterous, risible, silly, stupid, unbelievable.

antonym sensible.

rife *adj.* abounding, abundant, common, commonplace, current, epidemic, frequent, general, plentiful, prevailing, prevalent, raging, rampant, teeming, ubiquitous, universal, widespread.

antonym scarce.

rifle[1] *v.* burgle, despoil, gut, loot, maraud, pillage, plunder, ransack, rob, rummage, sack, strip.

rifle[2] *n.* air-gun, carbine, firearm, firelock, flintlock, fusil, gun, musket, shotgun.

rift *n.* alienation, beach, breach, break, chink, cleavage, cleft, crack, cranny, crevice, difference, disaffection, disagreement, dissure, division, estrangement, fault, flaw, fracture, gap, opening, quarrel, schism, separation, space, split.
antonym unity.

right *adj.* absolute, accurate, admissible, advantageous, appropriate, authentic, balanced, becoming, characteristic, comme il faut, complete, compos mentis, conservative, correct, deserved, desirable, dexter, dextral, direct, done, due, equitable, ethical, exact, factual, fair, favorable, fine, fit, fitting, genuine, good, healthy, honest, honorable, ideal, just, lawful, lucid, moral, normal, opportune, out-and-out, perpendicular, precise, proper, propitious, rational, reactionary, real, reasonable, righteous, rightful, rightist, rightward, right-wing, sane, satisfactory, seemly, sound, spot-on, straight, suitable, thorough, thoroughgoing, Tory, true, unerring, unimpaired, upright, utter, valid, veracious, veritable, virtuous, well.
antonyms left, left-wing, mad, unfit, wrong.
adv. absolutely, accurately, advantageously, altogether, appropriate, aptly, aright, bang, befittingly, beneficially, completely, correctly, directly, entirely, ethically, exactly, factually, fairly, favorably, fittingly, fortunately, genuinely, honestly, honorably, immediately, instantly, justly, morally, perfectly, precisely, promptly, properly, quickly, quite, righteously, rightward(s), satisfactorily, slap-bang, squarely, straight, straightaway, suitably, thoroughly, totally, truly, utterly, virtuously, well, wholly.
antonyms incorrectly, left, unfairly, wrongly.
n. authority, business, claim, droit, due, equity, freedom, good, goodness, honor, integrity, interest, justice, lawfulness, legality, liberty, licence, morality, permission, power, prerogative, privilege, propriety, reason, rectitude, righteousness, rightfulness, rightness, title, truth, uprightness, virtue.
antonyms depravity, wrong.
v. avenge, correct, fix, rectify, redress, repair, righten, settle, stand up, straighten, vindicate.

righteous *adj.* blameless, equitable, ethical, fair, God-fearing, good, guiltless, honest, honorable, incorrupt, just, law-abiding, moral, pure, saintly, sinless, upright, virtuous.
antonym unrighteous.
n. Holy Willies, just, Pharisees, saints, unco guid, welldoers.
antonym unrighteous.

rigid *adj.* adamant, austere, cast-iron, exact, fixed, harsh, inflexible, intransigent, invariable, rigorous, set, severe, starch(y), stern, stiff, stony, strict, stringent, tense, unalterable, unbending, uncompromising, undeviating, unrelenting, unyielding.
antonym flexible.

rigorous *adj.* accurate, austere, challenging, conscientious, demanding, exact, exacting, extreme, firm, hard, harsh, inclement, inflexible, inhospitable, meticulous, nice, painstaking, precise, punctilious, Rhadamanthine, rigid, scrupulous, severe, stern, strict, stringent, thorough, tough, unsparing.
antonyms lenient, mild.

rile *v.* anger, annoy, bug, exasperate, gall, get, irk, irritate, miff, nark, nettle, peeve, pique, provoke, put out, upset, vex.
antonym soothe.

rim *n.* border, brim, brink, circumference, edge, lip, margin, skirt, verge.
antonym center.

rind *n.* crust, epicarp, husk, integument, peel, skin, zest.

ring[1] *n.* annulation, annulet, annulus, arena, association, band, cabal, cartel, cell, circle, circuit, circus, clique, collar, collet, combine, coterie, crew, enclosure, gang, group, gyre, halo, hoop, knot, loop, mob, organization, rink, round, rundle, syndicate.
v. circumscribe, encircle, enclose, encompass, gash, gird, girdle, mark, score, surround.

ring[2] *v.* bell, buzz, call, chime, clang, clink, peal, phone, resonate, resound, reverberate, sound, tang, telephone, ting, tinkle, tintinnabulate, toll.
n. buzz, call, chime, clang, clink, knell, peal, phonecall, tang, ting, tinkle, tintinnabulation.

ringleader *n.* bell-wether, brains, chief, fugleman, leader, spokesman.

rinse *v.* bathe, clean, cleanse, dip, sluice, splash, swill, synd, wash, wet.
n. bath, dip, dye, splash, tint, wash, wetting.

riot *n.* anarchy, bagarre, boisterousness, carousal, commotion, confusion, debauchery, disorder, display, disturbance, Donnybrook, émeute, excess, extravaganza, festivity, flourish, fray, frolic, high, insurrection, jinks, jollification, lawlessness, merry-make, merrymaking, quarrel, revelry, riotousness, riotry, romp, rookery, rout, row, ruction, ruffle, shindig, shindy, show, splash, strife, tumult, turbulence, turmoil, uproar.
antonyms calm, order.
v. carouse, frolic, rampage, rebel, revel, revolt, rise up, roister, romp, run riot, run wild.

riotous *adj.* anarchic, boisterous, disorderly, insubordinate, insurrectionary, lawless, loud, luxurious, mutinous, noisy, orgiastic, rambunctious, rampageous, rebellious, refractory, roisterous, rollicking, rowdy, saturnalian, side-splitting, tumultuous, ungovernable, unrestrained, unruly, uproarious, violent, wanton, wild.
antonyms orderly, restrained.

rip *v.* burst, claw, cut, gash, hack, lacerate, rend, rupture, score, separate, slash, slit, split, tear.
n. cleavage, cut, gash, hole, laceration, rent, rupture, slash, slit, split, tear.

ripe *adj.* accomplished, auspicious, complete, developed, favorable, finished, grown, ideal, mature, mellow, opportune, perfect, prepared, promising, propitious, ready, right, ripened, seasoned, suitable, timely. *antonyms* inopportune, untimely.

ripen *v.* age, burgeon, develop, mature, mellow, prepare, season.

rip-off *n.* cheat, con, con trick, daylight robbery, diddle, exploitation, fraud, robbery, sting, swindle, theft.

riposte *n.* answer, come-back, quip, rejoinder, repartee, reply, response, retort, return, sally.

v. answer, quip, reciprocate, rejoin, reply, respond, retort, return.

ripple *n.* babble, burble, disturbance, eddy, gurgle, lapping, pirl, purl, ripplet, undulation, wave, wimple.

rise *v.* advance, appear, arise, ascend, buoy, climb, crop up, emanate, emerge, enlarge, eventuate, flow, get up, grow, happen, improve, increase, intensify, issue, levitate, lift, mount, mutiny, occur, originate, progress, prosper, rebel, resist, revolt, slope, slope up, soar, spring, spring up, stand up, surface, swell, tower, volume, wax.

antonyms descend, fall.

n. acclivity, advance, advancement, aggrandizement, ascent, climb, elevation, hillock, improvement, incline, increase, increment, origin, progress, promotion, raise, rising, upsurge, upswing, upturn, upward turn.

antonyms descent, fall.

risk *n.* adventure, chance, danger, gamble, hazard, jeopardy, peril, possibility, speculation, uncertainty, venture.

antonyms certainty, safety.

v. adventure, chance, dare, endanger, gamble, hazard, imperil, jeopardize, speculate, venture.

risky *adj.* chancy, dangerous, dicey, dodgy, fraught, hazardous, perilous, precarious, riskful, touch-and-go, tricky, uncertain, unsafe.

antonym safe.

rite *n.* act, ceremonial, ceremony, custom, form, formality, liturgy, mystery, observance, office, ordinance, practice, procedure, ritual, sacrament, service, solemnity, usage, worship.

ritual *n.* ceremonial, ceremony, communion, convention, custom, form, formality, habit, liturgy, mystery, observance, ordinance, practice, prescription, procedure, rite, routine, sacrament, service, solemnity, tradition, usage, wont.

adj. ceremonial, ceremonious, conventional, customary, formal, formulary, habitual, prescribed, procedural, routine, stereotyped.

antonyms informal, unusual.

rival *n.* adversary, antagonist, challenger, collateral, compeer, competitor, contender, contestant, corrival, emulator, equal, equivalent, fellow, match, opponent, peer, rivaless.

antonyms associate, colleague, co-worker.

adj. competing, competitive, conflicting, corrival, emulating, emulous, opposed, opposing.

antonyms associate, co-operating.

v. compete, contend, emulate, equal, match, oppose, rivalize, vie with.

antonym co-operate.

rivalry *n.* antagonism, competition, competitiveness, conflict, contention, contest, duel, emulation, opposition, rivality, rivalship, struggle, vying.

antonym co-operation.

river *n.* beck, burn, creek, ea, flood, flow, gush, riverway, rush, spate, stream, surge, tributary, waterway.

adj. fluvial, riverain, riverine.

riveting *adj.* absorbing, arresting, captivating, engrossing, enthralling, fascinating, gripping, hypnotic, magnetic, spellbinding. *antonym* boring.

road *n.* Autobahn, autopista, autoroute, autostrada, avenue, boulevard, camino real, carriageway, clearway, course, crescent, direction, drift, drive, driveway, freeway, highway, lane, path, pathway, roadway, route, street, thoroughfare, thruway, track, way.

roam *v.* drift, meander, peregrinate, prowl, ramble, range, rove, squander, stravaig, stray, stroll, travel, walk, wander.

antonym stay.

roar *v.* bawl, bay, bell, bellow, blare, clamor, crash, cry, guffaw, hoot, howl, rumble, shout, thunder, vociferate, wuther, yell.

antonym whisper.

n. bellow, belly-laugh, blare, clamor, crash, cry, guffaw, hoot, howl, outcry, rumble, shout, thunder, yell.

antonym whisper.

rob *v.* bereave, bunko, cheat, con, defraud, deprive, despoil, dispossess, do, flake, flimp, gyp, heist, hold up, loot, mill, pillage, plunder, raid, ramp, ransack, reive, rifle, rip off, roll, sack, sting, strip, swindle.

antonyms give, provide.

robbery *n.* burglary, dacoitage, dacoity, depredation, embezzlement, filching, fraud, heist, hold-up, larceny, pillage, plunder, purse-snatching, purse-taking, raid, rapine, rip-off, spoliation, stealing, stick-up, swindle, theft, thievery.

robe *n.* bathrobe, costume, dressing-gown, gown, habit, housecoat, peignoir, vestment, wrap, wrapper.

v. apparel, attire, clothe, drape, dress, garb, vest.

robot *n.* android, automaton, golem, machine, zombie.

robust *adj.* able-bodied, athletic, boisterous, brawny, coarse, down-to-earth, earthy, fit, hale, hard-headed, hardy, healthy, hearty, husky, indecorous, lusty, muscular, over-hearty, powerful, practical, pragmatic, raw, realistic, robustious, roisterous, rollicking, rough, rude, rugged, sensible, sinewy, sound, staunch, sthenic, stout, straight-forward, strapping, strong, sturdy, thick-set, tough, unsubtle, vigorous, well.

antonyms mealy-mouthed, unhealthy, unrealistic, weak.

rock[1] *n.* anchor, boulder, bulwark, cornerstone, danger, foundation, hazard, logan, log(g)an-stone, mainstay, obstacle, pebble, problem, protection, stone, support.

rock[2] *v.* astonish, astound, daze, dumbfound, jar, lurch, pitch, reel, roll, shake, shock, stagger, stun, surprise, sway, swing, tilt, tip, toss, wobble.

rocky[1] *adj.* craggy, flinty, hard, pebbly, rocklike, rough, rugged, stony.
antonyms smooth, soft.

rocky[2] *adj.* dizzy, doubtful, drunk, ill, inebriated, intoxicated, rickety, shaky, sick, sickly, staggering, tipsy, tottering, uncertain, undependable, unpleasant, unreliable, unsatisfactory, unstable, unsteady, unwell, weak, wobbly, wonky.
antonyms dependable, steady, well.

rod *n.* bar, baton, birch, cane, dowel, ferula, ferule, mace, pole, scepter, shaft, spoke, staff, stick, strut, switch, verge, wand.

rogue *n.* blackguard, charlatan, cheat, con man, crook, deceiver, devil, fraud, knave, miscreant, mountebank, nasty piece/bit of work, ne'er-do-well, picaroon, rapscallion, rascal, reprobate, scamp, scapegallows, scoundrel, sharper, swindler, vagrant, villain, wag.
antonym saint.

roguish *adj.* arch, bantering, cheeky, confounded, coquettish, criminal, crooked, deceitful, deceiving, dishonest, espiègle, fraudulent, frolicsome, hempy, impish, knavish, mischievous, playful, puckish, raffish, rascally, roguing, shady, sportive, swindling, unprincipled, unscrupulous, villainous, waggish.
antonyms honest, serious.

roister *v.* bluster, boast, brag, carouse, celebrate, frolic, make merry, paint the town red, revel, roist, rollick, romp, strut, swagger, whoop it up.

role *n.* capacity, character, duty, function, impersonation, job, job of work, part, portrayal, position, post, representation, task.

roll *v.* billow, bind, boom, coil, curl, drum, echo, elapse, enfold, entwine, envelop, even, flatten, flow, furl, grumble, gyrate, level, lumber, lurch, pass, peel, pivot, press, reel, resound, reverberate, revolve, roar, rock, rotate, rumble, run, smooth, spin, spread, stagger, swagger, swathe, sway, swing, swivel, thunder, toss, trill, trindle, trundle, tumble, turn, twirl, twist, undulate, volume, waddle, wallow, wander, welter, wheel, whirl, wind, wrap.
n. annals, ball, bobbin, boom, catalog, census, chronicle, cycle, cylinder, directory, drumming, growl, grumble, gyration, index, inventory, list, notitia, record, reel, register, resonance, reverberation, revolution, roar, roller, roster, rotation, rumble, run, schedule, scroll, spin, spool, table, thunder, turn, twirl, undulation, volume, wheel, whirl.

rollicking *adj.* boisterous, carefree, cavorting, devil-may-care, exuberant, frisky, frolicsome, hearty, jaunty, jovial, joyous, lively, merry, playful, rip-roaring, roisterous, roisting, romping, spirited, sportive, sprightly, swashbuckling.
antonyms restrained, serious.

romance *n.* absurdity, adventure, affair(e), amour, attachment, charm, color, exaggeration, excitement, fabrication, fairy tale, falsehood, fantasy, fascination, fiction, gest(e), glamor, idyll, intrigue, invention, legend, liaison, lie, love affair, love story, melodrama, mystery, novel, passion, relationship, sentiment, story, tale, tear-jerker.
v. exaggerate, fantasize, lie, overstate.

romantic *adj.* amorous, charming, chimerical, colorful, dreamy, exaggerated, exciting, exotic, extravagant, fabulous, fairy-tale, fanciful, fantastic, fascinating, fictitious, fond, glamorous, high-flown, idealistic, idyllic, imaginary, imaginative, impractical, improbable, legendary, lovey-dovey, loving, made-up, mushy, mysterious, passionate, picturesque, quixotic, romantical, sentimental, sloppy, soppy, starry-eyed, tender, unrealistic, utopian, visionary, whimsical, wild.
antonyms humdrum, practical, real, sober, unromantic.
n. Don Quixote, dreamer, idealist, romancer, sentimentalist, utopian, visionary.
antonym realist.

romp *v.* caper, cavort, frisk, frolic, gambol, revel, rig, roister, rollick, skip, sport.
n. caper, frolic, lark, rig, spree.

room *n.* allowance, apartment, area, capacity, chamber, chance, compartment, compass, elbow-room, expanse, extent, house-room, latitude, leeway, margin, occasion, office, opportunity, play, range, salon, saloon, scope, space, territory, volume.

roomy *adj.* ample, broad, capacious, commodious, extensive, generous, large, sizable, spacious, voluminous, wide.
antonym cramped.

root[1] *n.* base, basis, beginnings, bottom, cause, core, crux, derivation, essence, foundation, fountainhead, fundamental, germ, heart, mainspring, more, nub, nucleus, occasion, origin, radicle, radix, rhizome, root-cause, rootlet, seat, seed, source, starting point, stem, tuber.
v. anchor, embed, entrench, establish, fasten, fix, ground, implant, moor, set, sink, stick.

root[2] *v.* burrow, delve, dig, ferret, forage, grout, hunt, nose, poke, pry, rootle, rummage.

rooted *adj.* confirmed, deep, deeply, deep-seated, entrenched, established, felt, firm, fixed, ingrained, radical, rigid, root-fast.
antonyms superficial, temporary.

rope *n.* cable, cord, fake, hawser, lariat, lasso, line, marline, strand, warp, widdy.
v. bind, catch, fasten, hitch, lash, lasso, moor, pinion, tether, tie.

ropy *adj.* below par, deficient, inadequate, indifferent, inferior, off-color, poorly, rough, sketchy, stringy, substandard, unwell.
antonyms good, well.

roster *n.* bead-roll, list, listing, register, roll, rota, schedule, table.

rosy *adj.* auspicious, blooming, blushing, bright, cheerful, encouraging, favorable, fresh, glowing, healthy-looking, hopeful, optimistic, pink, promising, reassuring, red, reddish, rose, roseate, rose-colored, rose-hued, roselike, rose-pink, rose-red, rose-scented, rosy-fingered, rubicund, ruddy, sunny.
antonyms depressed, depressing, sad.

rot *v.* corrode, corrupt, crumble, decay, decline, decompose, degenerate, deteriorate, disintegrate, fester, go bad, languish, molder, perish, putrefy, ret, spoil, taint. *n.* balderdash, blight, bosh, bunk, bunkum, canker, claptrap, codswallop, collapse, corrosion, corruption, decay, decomposition, deterioration, disintegration, drivel, flap-doodle, guff, hogwash, moonshine, mold, nonsense, poppycock, putrefaction, putrescence, rubbish, tommyrot, tosh, twaddle.

rotary *adj.* gyrating, gyratory, revolving, rotating, rotational, rotatory, spinning, turning, whirling.
antonym fixed.

rotate *v.* alternate, gyrate, interchange, pirouette, pivot, reel, revolve, spell, spin, switch, swivel, turn, twiddle, wheel.

rotation *n.* alternation, cycle, gyration, interchanging, orbit, pirouette, reel, revolution, sequence, spin, spinning, succession, switching, turn, turning, volution, wheel.

rotten *adj.* addle(d), bad, base, below par, bent, contemptible, corroded, corrupt, crooked, crumbling, crummy, decayed, decaying, deceitful, decomposed, decomposing, degenerate, deplorable, despicable, dirty, disagreeable, disappointing, dishonest, dishonorable, disintegrating, disloyal, faithless, festering, fetid, filthy, foul, grotty, ill-considered, ill-thought-out, immoral, inadequate, inferior, lousy, low-grade, manky, mean, mercenary, moldering, moldy, nasty, off-color, perfidious, perished, poor, poorly, punk, putid, putrescent, putrid, rank, regrettable, ropy, rough, scurrilous, sick, sorry, sour, stinking, substandard, tainted, treacherous, unacceptable, unfortunate, unlucky, unpleasant, unsatisfactory, unsound, untrustworthy, unwell, venal, vicious, vile, wicked.
antonyms good, honest, practical, sensible, well.

rotund *adj.* bulbous, chubby, corpulent, fat, fleshy, full, globular, grandiloquent, heavy, magniloquent, obese, orbed, orbicular, orby, oro(ro)tund, plump, podgy, portly, resonant, rich, roly-poly, rotundate, round, rounded, sonorous, spheral, spheric, spherical, spherular, sphery, stout, tubby.
antonyms flat, gaunt, slim.

rough *adj.* agitated, amorphous, approximate, arduous, austere, basic, bearish, bluff, blunt, boisterous, bristly, broken, brusque, bumpy, bushy, cacophonous, choppy, churlish, coarse, craggy, crude, cruel, cursory, curt, discordant, discourteous, disheveled, disordered, drastic, estimated, extreme, foggy, formless, fuzzy, general, grating, gruff, hairy, hard, harsh, hasty, hazy, husky, ill, ill-bred, ill-mannered, imperfect, impolite, imprecise, inclement, incomplete, inconsiderate, indelicate, inexact, inharmonious, irregular, jagged, jarring, loutish, nasty, off-color, poorly, quick, rasping, raspy, raucous, raw, rocky, ropy, rotten, rough-and-ready, rowdy, rude, rudimentary, rugged, rusty, scabrous, severe, shaggy, shapeless, sharp, sick, sketchy, spartan, squally, stony, stormy, tangled, tempestuous, tough, tousled, tousy, turbulent, unceremonious, uncivil, uncomfortable, uncouth, uncultured, uncut, undressed, uneven, unfeeling, unfinished, ungracious, unjust, unmannerly, unmusical, unpleasant, unpolished, unprocessed, unrefined, unshaven, unshorn, untutored, unwell, unwrought, upset, vague, violent, wild.
antonyms accurate, calm, harmonious, mild, polite, smooth, well.
n. boor, bruiser, bully, hooligan, keelie, lout, mock-up, model, outline, roughneck, rowdy, ruffian, sketch, thug, tough, yob, yobbo.

round *adj.* ample, annular, ball-shaped, blunt, bowed, bulbous, candid, circular, complete, curved, curvilinear, cylindrical, direct, discoid, disc-shaped, entire, fleshy, frank, full, full-fleshed, globular, mellifluous, orbed, orbicular, orby, orotund, outspoken, plain, plump, resonant, rich, ring-shaped, roly-poly, rotund, rotundate, rounded, solid, sonorous, spheral, spheric, spherical, spherular, sphery, straightforward, unbroken, undivided, unmodified, whole.
antonyms evasive, niggardly, partial, thin.
n. ambit, ball, band, beat, bout, bullet, cartridge, circle, circuit, compass, course, cycle, disc, discharge, division, globe, lap, level, orb, period, ring, routine, schedule, sequence, series, session, shell, shot, sphere, spheroid, spherule, stage, succession, tour, turn.
v. bypass, circle, circumnavigate, encircle, flank, sail round, skirt, turn.

roundabout *adj.* ambagious, circuitous, circumlocutory, devious, discursive, evasive, indirect, meandering, oblique, periphrastic, tortuous, twisting, winding.
antonyms direct, straight, straightforward.

roundly *adv.* bluntly, completely, fiercely, forcefully, frankly, intensely, openly, outspokenly, rigorously, severely, sharply, thoroughly, vehemently, violently.
antonym mildly.

rouse *v.* agitate, anger, animate, arouse, awaken, bestir, call, disturb, enkindle, excite, exhilarating, firk, flush, galvanize, incite, inflame, instigate, move, provoke, rise, start, startle, stimulate, stir, suscitate, unbed, wake, whip up.
antonym calm.

rousing *adj.* brisk, electrifying, excitant, excitative, excitatory, exciting, exhilarating, hypnopompic, inflammatory, inspiring, lively, moving, spirited, stimulating, stirring, vigorous.
antonym calming.

rout *n.* beating, brawl, clamor, crowd, debacle, defeat, disturbance, Donnybrook, drubbing, flight, fracas, fuss, herd, hiding, licking, mob, overthrow, pack, rabble, riot, rookery, ruffle, ruin, shambles, stampede, thrashing. *antonyms* calm, win.

v. beat, best, chase, conquer, crush, defeat, destroy, discomfit, dispel, drub, hammer, lick, overthrow, scatter, thrash, worst.

route *n.* avenue, beat, circuit, course, direction, flightpath, itinerary, journey, passage, path, road, round, run, way. *v.* convey, direct, dispatch, forward, send.

routine *n.* act, bit, custom, formula, grind, groove, heigh, jog-trot, line, method, order, pattern, performance, piece, practice, procedure, program, spiel, usage, way, wont.

adj. banal, boring, clichéd, conventional, customary, day-by-day, dull, everyday, familiar, habitual, hackneyed, humdrum, mundane, normal, ordinary, predictable, run-of-the-mill, standard, tedious, tiresome, typical, unimaginative, uninspired, unoriginal, usual, wonted, workaday.

antonyms exciting, unusual.

rover *n.* drifter, gadabout, gypsy, itinerant, nomad, rambler, ranger, stravaiger, transient, traveler, vagrant, wanderer.

antonym stay-at-home.

row[1] *n.* bank, colonnade, column, file, line, queue, range, rank, sequence, series, string, tier.

row[2] *n.* altercation, brawl, castigation, commotion, controversy, dispute, disturbance, Donnybrook, dressing-down, falling-out, fracas, fray, fuss, lecture, noise, quarrel, racket, rammy, reprimand, reproof, rhubarb, rollicking, rookery, rout, ruckus, ruction, ruffle, rumpus, scrap, shemozzle, shindig, shindy, slanging match, squabble, talking-to, telling-off, ticking-off, tiff, tongue-lashing, trouble, tumult, uproar.

antonym calm.

v. argue, argufy, brawl, dispute, fight, scrap, squabble, wrangle.

rowdy *adj.* boisterous, disorderly, loud, loutish, noisy, obstreperous, roisterous, roisting, rorty, rough, rumbustious, stroppy, unruly, uproarious, wild.

antonyms quiet, restrained.

n. brawler, hoodlum, hooligan, keelie, lout, rough, ruffian, tearaway, tough, yahoo, yob, yobbo.

royal *adj.* august, basilical, grand, imperial, impressive, kinglike, kingly, magnificent, majestic, monarchical, princely, queenlike, queenly, regal, sovereign, splendid, stately, superb, superior.

rub *v.* abrade, apply, caress, chafe, clean, embrocate, fray, grate, knead, malax, malaxate, massage, polish, put, scour, scrape, shine, smear, smooth, spread, stroke, wipe.

n. caress, catch, difficulty, drawback, hindrance, hitch, impediment, kneading, malaxage, malaxation, massage, obstacle, polish, problem, shine, snag, stroke, trouble, wipe.

rubbish *n.* balderdash, balls, baloney, bosh, bunkum, clamjamphrie, claptrap, cobblers, codswallop, crap, dead-wood, debris, draff, drivel, dross, flotsam and jetsam, garbage, gibberish, gobbledegook, guff, havers, hogwash, junk, kibosh, kitsch, landfill, leavings, litter, lumber, moonshine, mullock, nonsense, offal, offscourings, offscum, piffle, poppycock, raffle, refuse, riddlings, rot, scoria, scrap, stuff, sullage, sweepings, tommyrot, tosh, trash, trashery, truck, trumpery, twaddle, vomit, waste.

antonym sense.

ruddy *adj.* blooming, blushing, crimson, flammulated, florid, flushed, fresh, glowing, healthy, pink, red, reddish, roseate, rose-hued, rose-pink, rosy, rosy-cheeked, rubicund, rubineous, rubious, ruby, sanguine, scarlet, sunburnt.

antonyms pale, unhealthy.

rude *adj.* abrupt, abusive, artless, barbarous, blunt, boorish, brusque, brutish, cheeky, churlish, coarse, crude, curt, discourteous, disrespectful, graceless, gross, harsh, ignorant, illiterate, ill-mannered, impertinent, impolite, impudent, inartistic, inconsiderate, inelegant, insolent, insulting, loutish, low, makeshift, oafish, obscene, offhand, peremptory, primitive, raw, rough, savage, scurrilous, sharp, short, simple, startling, sudden, uncivil, uncivilized, uncouth, uncultured, uneducated, ungracious, unmannerly, unpleasant, unpolished, unrefined, untutored, violent, vulgar.

antonyms graceful, polished, polite, smooth.

rudimentary *adj.* abecedarian, basic, early, elementary, embryonic, fundamental, germinal, immature, inchoate, initial, introductory, primary, primitive, primordial, undeveloped, vestigial.

antonyms advanced, developed.

rue *v.* bemoan, bewail, beweep, deplore, grieve, lament, mourn, regret, repent.

antonym rejoice.

ruffian *n.* apache, bruiser, brute, bully, bully-boy, cutthroat, hoodlum, hooligan, keelie, lout, miscreant, Mohock, myrmidon, plug-ugly, rascal, rogue, rough, roughneck, rowdy, scoundrel, thug, tough, villain, yob, yobbo.

ruffle *v.* agitate, annoy, confuse, derange, disarrange, discompose, disconcert, dishevel, disorder, disquiet, disturb, fluster, harass, irritate, mess up, muss up, muss(e), nettle, peeve, perturb, rattle, rumple, stir, torment, tousle, trouble, unsettle, upset, vex, worry, wrinkle.

antonym smooth.

rugged *adj.* arduous, austere, barbarous, beefy, blunt, brawny, broken, bumpy, burly, churlish, crabbed, craggy, crude, demanding, difficult, dour, exacting, graceless, gruff, hale, hard, hard-featured, hardy, harsh, husky, irregular, jagged, laborious, muscular, ragged, rigorous, robust, rocky, rough, rude, severe, sour, stark, stern, strenuous, strong, sturdy, surly, taxing, tough, trying, uncompromising, uncouth, uncultured, uneven, unpolished, unrefined, vigorous, weather-beaten, weathered, worn.

antonyms easy, refined, smooth.

ruin *n.* bankruptcy, bouleversement, breakdown, collapse, crash, damage, decay, defeat, destitution, destruction, devastation, disintegration, disrepair, dissolution, downfall, failure, fall, havoc, heap, insolvency, nemesis, overthrow, ruination, subversion, undoing, Waterloo, wreck, wreckage.

antonyms development, reconstruction.

v. banjax, bankrupt, botch, break, crush, damage, defeat, demolish, destroy, devastate, disfigure, impoverish, injure, jigger, mangle, mar, mess up, overthrow, overturn, overwhelm, pauperize, raze, scupper, scuttle, shatter, smash, spoil, unmake, unshape, wreck.

antonyms develop, restore.

ruinous *adj.* baleful, baneful, broken-down, calamitous, cataclysmic, catastrophic, crippling, deadly, decrepit, deleterious, derelict, destructive, devastating, dilapidated, dire, disastrous, extravagant, fatal, immoderate, injurious, murderous, noxious, pernicious, ramshackle, ruined, shattering, wasteful, withering.

antonym beneficial.

rule *n.* administration, ascendancy, authority, axiom, canon, command, condition, control, convention, course, criterion, custom, decree, direction, domination, dominion, empire, form, formula, governance, government, guide, guideline, habit, influence, institute, jurisdiction, law, leadership, mastery, maxim, method, order, ordinance, policy, power, practice, precept, prescript, principle, procedure, raj, regime, regulation, reign, routine, ruling, standard, supremacy, sway, tenet, way, wont.

v. adjudge, adjudicate, administer, command, control, decide, decree, determine, direct, dominate, establish, find, govern, guide, judge, lead, manage, obtain, predominate, preponderate, prevail, pronounce, regulate, reign, resolve, settle.

ruler *n.* commander, controller, emperor, empress, gerent, governor, gubernator, head of state, imperator, king, leader, lord, monarch, potentate, prince, princess, queen, sovereign, suzerain.

antonym subject.

ruling *n.* adjudication, decision, decree, finding, indiction, interlocution, irade, judgment, pronouncement, resolution, ukase, verdict.

adj. boss, chief, commanding, controlling, dominant, governing, leading, main, predominant, pre-eminent, preponderant, prevailing, prevalent, principal, regnant, reigning, supreme, upper.

ruminate *v.* brood, chew over, chew the cud, cogitate, consider, contemplate, deliberate, meditate, mull over, muse, ponder, reflect, revolve, think.

rummage *v.* delve, examine, explore, hunt, poke around, ransack, root, rootle, rout, search.

rumor *n.* breeze, bruit, bush telegraph, buzz, canard, fame, gossip, grapevine, hearsay, kite, news, on-dit, report, story, talk, tidings, underbreath, whisper, word.

v. bruit, circulate, gossip, publish, put about, report, say, tell, whisper.

rumple *v.* crease, crinkle, crumple, crush, derange, dishevel, disorder, muss up, muss(e), pucker, ruffle, scrunch, tousle, wrinkle.

antonym smooth.

rumpus *n.* bagarre, barney, brouhaha, commotion, confusion, disruption, disturbance, Donnybrook, fracas, furore, fuss, kerfuffle, noise, rhubarb, rookery, rout, row, ruction, shemozzle, shindig, shindy, tumult, uproar.

antonym calm.

run *v.* abscond, administer, bear, beat it, bleed, bolt, boss, career, carry, cascade, challenge, circulate, clear out, climb, compete, conduct, contend, continue, control, convey, co-ordinate, course, creep, dart, dash, decamp, depart, direct, discharge, display, dissolve, drive to, escape, extend, feature, flee, flow, function, fuse, gallop, glide, go, gush, hare, hasten, head, hie, hotfoot, hurry, issue, jog, ladder, last, lead, leak, lie, liquefy, lope, manage, maneuver, mastermind, melt, mix, move, operate, oversee, own, pass, perform, ply, pour, print, proceed, propel, publish, race, range, reach, regulate, roll, rush, scamper, scarper, scramble, scud, scurry, skedaddle, skim, slide, speed, spill, spout, spread, sprint, stand, stream, stretch, superintend, supervise, tear, tick, trail, transport, unravel, work.

antonyms stay, stop.

n. application, category, chain, class, coop, course, current, cycle, dash, demand, direction, drift, drive, enclosure, excursion, flow, gallop, jaunt, jog, journey, joy, kind, ladder, lift, motion, movement, order, outing, passage, path, pen, period, pressure, progress, race, ride, rip, round, rush, season, sequence, series, snag, sort, spell, spin, sprint, spurt, streak, stream, stretch, string, tear, tendency, tenor, tide, trend, trip, type, variety, way.

runaway *n.* absconder, deserter, escapee, escaper, fleer, fugitive, refugee, truant.

adj. escaped, fleeing, fugitive, loose, uncontrolled, wild.

rundown *n.* briefing, cut, decrease, drop, lessening, outline, précis, recap, reduction, résumé, review, runthrough, sketch, summary, synopsis.

run-down *adj.* broken-down, debilitated, decrepit, dilapidated, dingy, drained, enervated, exhausted, fatigued, grotty, peaky, ramshackle, scabby, seedy, shabby, tumble-down, unhealthy, weak, weary, worn-out.

antonym well-kept.

rupture *n.* altercation, breach, break, breaking, burst, bustup, cleavage, cleft, contention, crack, disagreement, disruption, dissolution, estrangement, falling-out, feud, fissure, fracture, hernia, hostility, quarrel, rent, rift, schism, split, splitting, tear.

v. break, burst, cleave, crack, disrupt, dissever, divide, fracture, puncture, rend, separate, sever, split, sunder, tear.

rural *adj.* agrarian, agrestic, agricultural, Arcadian, bucolic, countrified, country, forane, pastoral, predial, rustic, sylvan, yokelish.

antonym urban.

ruse *n.* artifice, blind, deception, device, dodge, hoax, imposture, maneuver, ploy, sham, stall, stratagem, subterfuge, trick, wile.

rush *v.* accelerate, attack, bolt, capture, career, charge, dart, dash, dispatch, expedite, fly, hasten, hightail it, hotfoot, hurry, hustle, overcome, press, push, quicken, race, run, scour, scramble, scurry, shoot, speed, speed up, sprint, stampede, storm, tear, wallop, w(h)oosh.

n. assault, charge, dash, dispatch, expedition, flow, haste, hurry, onslaught, push, race, scramble, speed, stampede, storm, streak, surge, swiftness, tantivy, tear, urgency.

adj. brisk, careless, cursory, emergency, expeditious, fast, hasty, hurried, prompt, quick, rapid, superficial, swift, urgent.

sabotage *v.* cripple, damage, destroy, disable, disrupt, incapacitate, mar, nullify, ratten, scupper, subvert, thwart, undermine, vandalize, vitiate, wreck.

n. damage, destruction, disablement, disruption, impairment, marring, rattening, subversion, treachery, treason, undermining, vandalism, vitiation, wrecking.

sack[1] *v.* axe, discharge, dismiss, fire, lay off, make redundant.

n. discharge, dismissal, notice, one's books, one's cards, one's marching orders, the ax, the boot, the bum's rush, the chop, the elbow, the push.

sack[2] *v.* demolish, depredate, desecrate, despoil, destroy, devastate, lay waste, level, loot, maraud, pillage, plunder, raid, rape, ravage, raze, rifle, rob, ruin, spoil, strip, waste.

n. depredation, desecration, despoliation, destruction, devastation, leveling, looting, marauding, pillage, plunder, plundering, rape, rapine, ravage, razing, ruin, waste.

sacred *adj.* blessed, consecrated, dedicated, devotional, divine, ecclesiastical, godly, hallowed, heavenly, holy, inviolable, inviolate, invulnerable, priestly, protected, religious, revered, sacrosanct, saintly, sanctified, secure, solemn, venerable, venerated.

antonyms mundane, profane, temporal.

sad *adj.* bad, blue, calamitous, cheerless, chopfallen, crestfallen, crushed, dark, dejected, deplorable, depressed, depressing, desolated, despondent, disastrous, disconsolate, dismal, dispirited, distressed, distressing, doleful, dolesome, doloriferous, dolorific, doughy, dour, dowie, downcast, down-hearted, drear, dreary, gloomy, glum, grave, grief-stricken, grieved, grieving, grievous, heart-rending, heavy, heavy-hearted, jaw-fallen, joyless, lachrymose, lamentable, long-faced, low, low-spirited, lugubrious, melancholy, miserable, mournful, moving, painful, pathetic, pensive, piteous, pitiable, pitiful, poignant, regrettable, serious, shabby, sober, sober-minded, somber, sorrowful, sorry, sportless, stiff, tearful, touching, tragic, triste, uncheerful, unfortunate, unhappy, unsatisfactory, upsetting, wan, wistful, woebegone, woeful, wretched.

antonyms cheerful, fortunate, happy, lucky.

safe *adj.* alive and well, all right, cautious, certain, circumspect, conservative, dependable, discreet, foolproof, guarded, hale, harmless, immune, impregnable, innocuous, intact, invulnerable, non-poisonous, non-toxic, OK, out of harm's way, protected, proven, prudent, pure, realistic, reliable, scatheless, secure, sound, sure, tame, tested, tried, trustworthy, unadventurous, uncontaminated, undamaged, unfailing, unharmed, unhurt, uninjured, unscathed, wholesome.

antonyms exposed, harmful, unsafe, vulnerable.

n. cash-box, chest, coffer, deposit box, peter, repository, strongbox, vault.

safeguard *v.* assure, defend, guard, insure, preserve, protect, screen, secure, shelter, shield.

antonyms endanger, jeopardize.

n. armor, assurance, bulwark, convoy, cover, defense, escort, guarantee, guard, insurance, long-stop, Palladium, precaution, preventive, protection, security, shield, surety.

sag *v.* bag, decline, dip, drag, droop, drop, dwindle, fail, fall, flag, give, give way, hang, settle, sink, slide, slip, slump, wane, weaken, wilt.

antonyms bulge, rise.

n. decline, depression, dip, downturn, drop, dwindling, fall, low, low point, reduction, slide, slip, slump.

antonyms peak, rise.

sagacity *n.* acumen, acuteness, astuteness, canniness, discernment, foresight, insight, judgment, judiciousness, knowingness, penetration, percipience, perspicacity, prudence, sapience, sense, sharpness, shrewdness, understanding, wariness, wiliness, wisdom.

antonyms folly, foolishness, obtuseness.

sage *adj.* astute, canny, discerning, intelligent, judicious, knowing, knowledgeable, learned, perspicacious, politic, prudent, sagacious, sapient, sensible, wise.

antonym foolish.

n. authority, elder, expert, guru, hakam, maharishi, mahatma, master, Nestor, oracle, philosopher, pundit, rishi, savant, Solomon, Solon, teacher, wise man.

antonym ignoramus.

saintly *adj.* angelic, beatific, blameless, blessed, blest, celestial, devout, god-fearing, godly, holy, immaculate, innocent, pious, pure, religious, righteous, sainted, saintlike, seraphic, sinless, spotless, stainless, upright, virtuous, worthy.

antonyms godless, unholy, unrighteous, wicked.

sake *n.* account, advantage, aim, behalf, benefit, cause, consideration, end, gain, good, interest, motive, object, objective, principle, profit, purpose, reason, regard, respect, score, welfare, wellbeing.

salary *n.* earnings, emolument, honorarium, income, pay, remuneration, screw, stipend, wage, wages.

salient *adj.* arresting, chief, conspicuous, important, jutting, main, marked, noticeable, obvious, outstanding, principal, projecting, prominent, pronounced, protruding, remarkable, signal, significant, striking.

salubrious *adj.* beneficial, bracing, healthful, health-giving, healthy, hygienic, invigorating, refreshing, restorative, salutary, sanitary, wholesome.

antonyms insalubrious, unwholesome.

salutary *adj.* advantageous, beneficial, good, healthful, healthy, helpful, much-needed, practical, profitable, salubrious, seasonable, timely, useful, valuable, wholesome.

salute *v.* accost, acknowledge, address, bow, greet, hail, honor, kiss, knuckle, nod, recognize, salaam, wave, welcome.
n. acknowledgment, address, bow, gesture, greeting, hail, handclap, handshake, hello, kiss, nod, obeisance, recognition, reverence, salaam, salutation, salve, salvo, tribute, wave.

salvage *v.* conserve, glean, preserve, reclaim, recover, recuperate, redeem, repair, rescue, restore, retrieve, salve, save.
antonyms abandon, lose, waste.

salvation *n.* deliverance, escape, liberation, lifeline, preservation, reclamation, redemption, rescue, restoration, retrieval, safety, saving, soteriology.
antonyms damnation, loss.

same *adj.* aforementioned, aforesaid, alike, analogous, changeless, comparable, consistent, corresponding, duplicate, equal, equivalent, homologous, identical, indistinguishable, interchangeable, invariable, matching, mutual, reciprocal, selfsame, similar, substitutable, synonymous, twin, unaltered, unchanged, undiminished, unfailing, uniform, unvarying, very.
antonyms changeable, different, incompatible, inconsistent, variable.
n. ditto, the above-mentioned, the above-named, the aforementioned, the aforesaid.

sample *n.* cross-section, demonstration, ensample, example, exemplification, foretaste, free sample, freebie, illustration, indication, instance, model, pattern, representative, sign, specimen, swatch.
v. experience, inspect, investigate, pree, sip, taste, test, try.
adj. demonstration, illustrative, pilot, representative, specimen, test, trial.

sanction *n.* accreditation, agreement, allowance, approbation, approval, authorization, authority, backing, cachet, confirmation, countenance, endorsement, go-ahead, green light, imprimatur, license, OK, permission, ratification, seal, support.
antonyms disapproval, veto.
v. accredit, allow, approve, authorize, back, confirm, countenance, countersign, endorse, fiat, license, permit, ratify, support, underwrite, warrant.
antonyms disallow, disapprove, veto.

sanctuary *n.* adytum, altar, ark, asylum, chancel, church, delubrum, frith, grith, harborage, haven, holy of holies, naos, presbytery, protection, refuge, retreat, sacrarium, sanctum, sanctum sanctorum, seclusion, shelter, shrine, tabernacle, temple.

sane *adj.* all there, balanced, compos mentis, dependable, judicious, level-headed, lucid, moderate, normal, rational, reasonable, reliable, right-minded, sensible, sober, sound, stable.

sanguinary *adj.* bloodied, bloodthirsty, bloody, brutal, cruel, fell, gory, grim, merciless, murderous, pitiless, ruthless, savage.

sanguine[1] *adj.* animated, ardent, assured, buoyant, cheerful, confident, expectant, hopeful, lively, optimistic, over-confident, over-optimistic, Panglossian, roseate, spirited, unabashed, unappalled, unbowed.
antonyms cynical, depressive, gloomy, melancholy, pessimistic, realistic.

sanguine[2] *adj.* florid, flushed, fresh, fresh-complexioned, pink, red, rosy, rubicund, ruddy.
antonyms pale, sallow.

sanitary *adj.* aseptic, clean, disinfected, germ- free, healthy, hygienic, pure, salubrious, uncontaminated, unpolluted, wholesome.
antonyms insanitary, unwholesome.

sap *v.* bleed, deplete, devitalize, diminish, drain, enervate, exhaust, impair, reduce, rob, undermine, weaken.
antonyms build up, increase, strengthen.

sarcastic *adj.* acerbic, acid, acrimonious, biting, caustic, contemptuous, cutting, cynical, derisive, disparaging, incisive, ironical, mocking, mordant, sardonic, sarky, satirical, scathing, sharp, sharp-tongued, sneering, taunting, withering.

sardonic *adj.* biting, bitter, cynical, derisive, dry, heartless, ironical, jeering, malevolent, malicious, malignant, mocking, mordant, quizzical, sarcastic, satirical, scornful, sneering, wry.

satanic *adj.* accursed, black, demoniac, demoniacal, demonic, devilish, diabolic, diabolical, evil, fell, fiendish, hellish, infernal, inhuman, iniquitous, malevolent, malignant, Mephistophelian, satanical, wicked.
antonyms benevolent, benign, divine, godlike, godly, heavenly, holy.

sate *v.* cloy, fill, glut, gorge, gratify, overfill, satiate, satisfy, saturate, sicken, slake, surfeit, weary.
antonyms deprive, dissatisfy, starve.

satiate *v.* cloy, engorge, glut, gorge, jade, nauseate, overfeed, overfill, sate, satisfy, slake, stuff, surfeit.
antonyms deprive, dissatisfy, underfeed.

satire *n.* burlesque, caricature, diatribe, invective, irony, lampoon, parody, Pasquil, Pasquin, pasquinade, raillery, ridicule, sarcasm, send-up, skit, spoof, squib, takeoff, travesty, wit.

satirical *adj.* biting, bitter, burlesque, caustic, cutting, cynical, derisive, Hudibrastic, iambic, incisive, ironical, irreverent, mocking, mordant, pungent, sarcastic, sardonic, satiric, taunting.

satisfaction *n.* achievement, amends, appeasing, assuaging, atonement, comfort, compensation, complacency, content, contentedness, contentment, conviction, damages, ease, enjoyment, fulfilment, fullness, gratification, guerdon, happiness, indemnification, justice, payment, pleasure, pride, quittance, recompense, redress, reimbursement, remuneration, reparation, repleteness, repletion, requital, resolution, restitution, reward, satiety, self-satisfaction, sense of achievement, settlement, vindication, well-being.

antonyms discontent, displeasure, dissatisfaction, frustration.

satisfactory *adj.* acceptable, adequate, all right, average, competent, fair, fit, OK, passable, proper, sufficient, suitable, tickety-boo, up to the mark.

antonyms inadequate, unacceptable, unsatisfactory.

satisfy *v.* answer, appease, assuage, assure, atone, compensate, content, convince, delight, discharge, do, fill, fulfil, glut, gratify, guerdon, indemnify, indulge, meet, mollify, pacify, pay, persuade, placate, please, qualify, quench, quiet, reassure, recompense, reimburse, remunerate, replete, requite, reward, sate, satiate, serve, settle, slake, square up, suffice, surfeit.

antonyms disappoint, dissatisfy, fail, frustrate, thwart.

saturate *v.* douse, drench, drouk, imbue, impregnate, infuse, permeate, ret, soak, souse, steep, suffuse, waterlog.

saucy *adj.* arch, audacious, cheeky, dashing, disdainful, disrespectful, flip, flippant, forward, fresh, gay, impertinent, impudent, insolent, irreverent, jaunty, lippy, malapert, natty, perky, pert, presumptuous, provocative, rakish, rude, sassy, sporty.

antonyms polite, respectful.

savage *adj.* barbarous, beastly, bestial, blistering, bloodthirsty, bloody, brutal, brutish, catamountain, cruel, devilish, diabolical, dog-eat-dog, fell, feral, ferocious, fierce, harsh, immane, inhuman, merciless, murderous, pitiless, primitive, ravening, rough, rude, rugged, ruthless, sadistic, sanguinary, uncivilized, uncultivated, undomesticated, uneducated, unenlightened, unsparing, untamed, untaught, vicious, wild.

antonyms benign, civilized, humane.

n. aboriginal, aborigine, ape, autochthon, barbarian, bear, beast, boor, brute, fiend, heathen, illiterate, indigene, lout, monster, native, oaf, philistine, primitive, roughneck, yahoo, yobbo.

v. attack, claw, hammer, lacerate, mangle, maul, pan, scarify, tear.

save *v.* cache, collect, conserve, cut back, deliver, economize, free, gather, guard, hinder, hoard, hold, husband, keep, lay up, liberate, obviate, preserve, prevent, protect, put aside, put by, reclaim, recover, redeem, rescue, reserve, retain, retrench, safeguard, salt away, salvage, screen, shield, spare, squirrel, stash, store.

antonyms discard, spend, squander, waste.

savory *adj.* agreeable, appetizing, aromatic, dainty, decent, delectable, delicious, edifying, full-flavored, gamy, good, gusty, honest, luscious, mouthwatering, palatable, piquant, reputable, respectable, rich, salubrious, scrumptious, spicy, tangy, tasty, toothsome, wholesome.

antonyms insipid, tasteless, unappetizing.

n. appetizer, bonne bouche, canapé, hors d'oeuvre.

say *v.* add, affirm, allege, announce, answer, assert, assume, bruit, claim, comment, communicate, conjecture, convey, declare, deliver, disclose, divulge, do, enunciate, estimate, express, guess, imagine, imply, intimate, judge, maintain, mention, opine, orate, perform, presume, pronounce, read, rec<??>te, reckon, rehearse, rejoin, remark, render, repeat, reply, report, respond, retort, reveal, rumor, signify, speak, state, suggest, surmise, tell, utter, voice.

n. authority, chance, clout, crack, go, influence, power, sway, turn, voice, vote, weight, word.

saying *n.* adage, aphorism, apophthegm, axiom, byword, dictum, gnome, maxim, mot, motto, precept, proverb, remnant, saw, slogan.

scald *v.* blister, burn, sear.

scale[1] *n.* calibration, compass, continuum, degree, degrees, extent, gamut, gradation, grading, graduation, hierarchy, ladder, measure, order, progression, proportion, range, ranking, ratio, reach, register, scope, sequence, series, spectrum, spread, steps.

v. adjust, level, move, proportion, prorate, regulate, shift.

scale[2] *n.* crust, encrustation, film, flake, furfur, lamella, lamina, layer, plate, scutellum, shield, squama, squamella, squamula, squamule.

v. clean, desquamate, exfoliate, flake, peel, scrape.

scale[3] *v.* ascend, clamber, climb, escalade, mount, scramble, shin up, surmount, swarm.

scamp *n.* blighter, caitiff, devil, fripon, imp, knave, mischief-maker, monkey, prankster, rascal, rogue, ruffian, scallywag, scapegrace, tyke, whippersnapper, wretch.

scan *v.* check, con, examine, glance through, investigate, pan, pan over, scrutinize, search, skim, survey, sweep.

n. check, examination, investigation, probe, review, screening, scrutiny, search, survey.

scandal *n.* abuse, aspersion, backbiting, calumniation, calumny, crime, defamation, detraction, dirt, discredit, disgrace, dishonor, embarrassment, enormity, evil, furore, gossip, gossiping, ignominy, infamy, muck-raking, obloquy, odium, offense, opprobrium, outcry, outrage, reproach, rumors, shame, sin, slander, stigma, talk, tattle, traducement, uproar, Watergate, wrongdoing.

scandalize *v.* affront, appal, astound, disgust, dismay, horrify, nauseate, offend, outrage, repel, revolt, shock, sicken.

scandalous *adj.* abominable, atrocious, calumnious, defamatory, disgraceful, disreputable, evil, exorbitant, extortionate, gamy, gossiping, immoderate, improper, infamous, libelous, monstrous, odious, opprobrious, outrageous, scurrilous, shameful, shocking, slanderous, unseemly, unspeakable, untrue.

scant *adj.* bare, deficient, hardly any, inadequate, insufficient, limited, little, little or no, minimal, sparse.

antonyms adequate, ample, sufficient.

scanty *adj.* bare, beggarly, deficient, exiguous, inadequate, insubstantial, insufficient, light, meager, narrow, parsimonious, poor, restricted, scant, scrimp, scrimpy, short, shy, skimped, skimpy, slender, sparing, sparse, thin.

antonyms ample, plentiful, substantial.

scarce *adj.* deficient, few, infrequent, insufficient, lacking, rare, scanty, sparse, thin on the ground, uncommon, unusual, wanting.
antonyms common, copious, plentiful.

scarcely *adv.* barely, hardly, just and no more, not readily, not willingly, only just, scarce.

scarcity *n.* dearth, deficiency, infrequency, insufficiency, lack, niggardliness, paucity, poverty, rareness, rarity, scantiness, shortage, sparseness, uncommonness, want.
antonyms abundance, enough, glut, plenty, sufficiency.

scare *v.* affright, alarm, appal, daunt, dismay, frighten, gally, intimidate, panic, shock, startle, terrify, terrorize, unnerve.
antonym reassure.
n. agitation, alarm, alarm and despondency, alert, consternation, dismay, fright, hysteria, panic, shock, start, terror.
antonym reassurance.

scared *adj.* affrighted, affrightened, agitated, anxious, appalled, dismayed, fearful, frightened, nervous, panicky, panic-stricken, petrified, shaken, startled, terrified, worried.
antonyms confident, reassured.

scarf *n.* babushka, boa, cravat, fichu, headscarf, headsquare, kerchief, muffler, neckerchief, necktie, shawl, stole, tawdry-lace.

scatter *v.* bestrew, break up, broadcast, diffuse, disband, disintegrate, disject, dispel, disperse, disseminate, dissipate, disunite, divide, fling, flurr, litter, propagate, separate, shower, sow, spatter, splutter, spread, sprinkle, squander, strew.
antonyms collect, concentrate.

scene *n.* act, area, arena, backdrop, background, business, carry-on, chapter, circumstances, commotion, confrontation, display, disturbance, division, drama, environment, episode, exhibition, focus, fuss, incident, landscape, locale, locality, location, melodrama, milieu, mise en scène, outburst, pageant, panorama, part, performance, picture, place, position, prospect, representation, row, set, setting, show, sight, site, situation, spectacle, spot, stage, tableau, tantrum, to-do, upset, view, vista, whereabouts, world.

scent *n.* aroma, bouquet, fragrance, fumet, odor, perfume, redolence, smell, spoor, trace, track, trail, waft, whiff.
antonym stink.
v. detect, discern, nose, nose out, perceive, recognize, sense, smell, sniff, sniff out.

schedule *n.* agenda, calendar, catalog, diary, form, inventory, itinerary, list, plan, program, scheme, scroll, table, timetable.
v. appoint, arrange, book, list, organize, plan, program, slot, table, time.

scheme *n.* arrangement, blueprint, chart, codification, configuration, conformation, conspiracy, contrivance, dart, design, device, diagram, disposition, dodge, draft, game, idea, intrigue, lay-out, machinations, maneuver, method, outline, pattern, plan, plot, ploy, procedure, program, project, proposal, proposition, racket, ruse, schedule, schema, shape, shift, stratagem, strategy, subterfuge, suggestion, system, tactics, theory.
v. collude, conspire, contrive, design, devise, frame, imagine, intrigue, machinate, manipulate, maneuver, mastermind, plan, plot, project, pull strings, pull wires, work out.

scheming *adj.* artful, calculating, conniving, crafty, cunning, deceitful, designing, devious, duplicitous, foxy, insidious, Machiavellian, slippery, sly, tricky, underhand, unscrupulous, wily.
antonyms artless, honest, open, transparent.

scholar *n.* academe, academic, authority, bookman, bookworm, egghead, intellectual, man of letters, pupil, savant, scholastic, schoolboy, schoolchild, schoolgirl, schoolman, student.
antonyms dullard, dunce, ignoramus, illiterate, philistine.

scholarly *adj.* academic, analytical, bookish, clerk-like, clerkly, conscientious, critical, erudite, intellectual, knowledgeable, learned, lettered, scholastic, scientific, studious, well-read, wissenschaftlich.
antonyms illiterate, unscholarly.

scholarship[1] *n.* attainments, book-learning, education, erudition, insight, knowledge, learnedness, learning, lore, scholarliness, wisdom, Wissenschaft.

scholarship[2] *n.* award, bursary, endowment, exhibition, fellowship, grant.

science *n.* art, discipline, knowledge, ology, proficiency, skill, specialization, technique, technology, Wissenschaft.

scoff[1] *v.* belittle, deride, despise, fleer, flout, geck, gibe, jeer, knock, mock, poke fun, pooh-pooh, rail, revile, rib, ridicule, scorn, sneer, taunt, twit.
antonyms compliment, flatter, praise.

scoff[2] *v.* bolt, consume, cram, devour, fill one's face, gobble, gulp, guzzle, pig, put away, shift, wolf.
antonym abstain.
n. chow, comestibles, commons, eatables, eats, edibles, fare, feed, fodder, food, grub, meal, nosh, nosh-up, provisions, rations, scran, tuck, victuals.

scold *v.* admonish, bawl out, berate, blame, castigate, censure, chide, find fault with, flyte, jaw, lecture, nag, rate, rebuke, remonstrate, reprimand, reproach, reprove, take to task, tell off, tick off, upbraid, vituperate, wig.
antonyms commend, praise.
n. battle-ax, beldam, fishwife, Fury, harridan, nag, shrew, termagant, virago, vixen, Xanthippe.

scope *n.* ambit, application, area, breadth, capacity, compass, competence, confines, coverage, elbow-room, extent, freedom, latitude, liberty, opportunity, orbit, outlook, purview, range, reach, remit, room, space, span, sphere, terms of reference, tessitura.

scorch *v.* blacken, blister, burn, char, parch, roast, scald, sear, shrivel, singe, sizzle, torrefy, wither.

score *n.* a bone to pick, account, amount, basis, bill, cause, charge, debt, due, gash, grade, gravamen, grievance, ground, grounds, grudge, injury, injustice, line, mark, notch, obligation, outcome, points, reason, reckoning, record, result, scratch, sum total, tab, tally, total, wrong.

v. achieve, adapt, amass, arrange, attain, be one up, benefit, chalk up, count, cut, deface, earn, engrave, furrow, gain, gouge, grave, graze, groove, hatch, have the advantage, have the edge, impress, incise, indent, knock up, make, make a hit, mark, nick, notch, notch up, orchestrate, profit, realize, record, register, scrape, scratch, set, slash, tally, total, win.

scorn *n.* contempt, contemptuousness, contumely, derision, despite, disdain, disgust, dismissiveness, disparagement, geck, mockery, sarcasm, scornfulness, slight, sneer.

antonyms admiration, respect.

v. contemn, deride, despise, disdain, dismiss, flout, hold in contempt, laugh at, laugh in the face of, look down on, misprize, pooh-pooh, refuse, reject, scoff at, slight, sneer at, spurn.

antonyms admire, respect.

scornful *adj.* arrogant, contemptuous, contumelious, defiant, derisive, disdainful, dismissive, disparaging, haughty, insulting, jeering, mocking, sarcastic, sardonic, scathing, scoffing, slighting, sneering, supercilious, withering.

antonyms admiring, complimentary, respectful.

scoundrel *n.* blackguard, blighter, bounder, caitiff, cheat, cur, dastard, good-for-nothing, heel, hound, knave, louse, miscreant, ne'er-do-well, picaroon, rascal, rat, reprobate, rogue, rotter, ruffian, scab, scallywag, scamp, scapegrace, stinker, swine, vagabond, villain.

scour[1] *v.* abrade, buff, burnish, clean, cleanse, flush, furbish, polish, purge, rub, scrape, scrub, wash, whiten.

scour[2] *v.* beat, comb, drag, forage, go over, hunt, rake, ransack, search, turn upside-down.

scourge *n.* affliction, bane, cat, cat-o'-nine-tails, curse, evil, flagellum, infliction, knout, lash, menace, misfortune, penalty, pest, pestilence, plague, punishment, strap, switch, terror, thong, torment, visitation, whip.

antonyms benefit, blessing, boon, godsend.

v. afflict, beat, belt, cane, castigate, chastize, curse, devastate, discipline, excoriate, flagellate, flail, flog, harass, horsewhip, lambaste, lash, lather, leather, plague, punish, tan, terrorize, thrash, torment, trounce, verberate, visit, wallop, whale, whip.

scowl *v.* frown, glare, glower, grimace, lower.

n. frown, glare, glower, grimace, moue.

antonyms beam, grin, smile.

scramble *v.* clamber, climb, contend, crawl, hasten, jostle, jumble, push, run, rush, scale, scrabble, shuffle, sprawl, strive, struggle, swarm, vie.

n. climb, commotion, competition, confusion, contention, free-for-all, hustle, mêlée, muddle, race, rat race, rivalry, rush, strife, struggle, trek, trial, tussle.

scrap[1] *n.* atom, bit, bite, crumb, fraction, fragment, grain, iota, junk, mite, modicum, morsel, mouthful, part, particle, piece, portion, remnant, shard, shred, sliver, snap, snatch, snippet, trace, vestige, waste, whit.

v. abandon, ax, break up, cancel, chuck, demolish, discard, ditch, drop, jettison, junk, shed, throw out, write off.

antonyms reinstate, restore, resume.

scrap[2] *n.* argument, bagarre, barney, battle, brawl, disagreement, dispute, dust-up, fight, quarrel, row, ruckus, ruction, rumpus, scuffle, set-to, shindy, squabble, tiff, wrangle.

antonyms agreement, peace.

v. argue, argufy, bicker, clash, fall out, fight, spat, squabble, wrangle.

antonym agree.

scrape *v.* abrade, bark, claw, clean, erase, file, grate, graze, grind, pinch, rasp, remove, rub, save, scour, scrabble, scratch, screech, scrimp, scuff, skimp, skin, squeak, stint.

n. abrasion, difficulty, dilemma, distress, fix, graze, mess, pickle, plight, predicament, pretty kettle of fish, rub, scratch, scuff, shave, spot, trouble.

scratch *v.* annul, cancel, claw, curry, cut, damage, delete, eliminate, erase, etch, grate, graze, incise, lacerate, mark, race, retire, rub, scarify, score, scrab, scrabble, scrape, withdraw.

n. blemish, claw mark, gash, graze, laceration, mark, race, scrape, streak.

adj. haphazard, impromptu, improvised, rough, rough-and-ready, unrehearsed.

antonym polished.

scrawny *adj.* angular, bony, emaciated, gaunt, lanky, lean, rawboned, scraggy, skeletal, skinny, thin, underfed, under-nourished

antonym plump.

scream[1] *v.* bawl, clash, cry, holler, jar, roar, screak, screech, shriek, shrill, squeal, wail, yell, yelp, yowl.

n. howl, outcry, roar, screak, screech, shriek, squeal, wail, yell, yelp, yowl.

antonym whisper.

scream[2] *n.* card, caution, character, comedian, comic, cure, hoot, joker, laugh, riot, sensation, wit.

antonym bore.

screech *v.* cry, screak, scream, shriek, squawk, squeal, ululate, yelp.

antonym whisper.

screen *v.* broadcast, cloak, conceal, cover, cull, defend, evaluate, examine, filter, gauge, grade, guard, hide, mask, present, process, protect, riddle, safeguard, scan, shade, shelter, shield, show, shroud, sieve, sift, sort, veil, vet.

n. abat-jour, awning, canopy, cloak, concealment, cover, divider, guard, hallan, hedge, hoarding, mantle, mesh, net, partition, shade, shelter, shield, shroud, uncover.

scrimp *v.* curtail, economize, limit, pinch, reduce, restrict, save, scrape, shorten, skimp, stint.
antonym spend.

script *n.* book, calligraphy, cheirography, copy, hand, hand-writing, letters, libretto, lines, longhand, manuscript, penmanship, text, words, writing.

scrounge *v.* beg, bludge, bum, cadge, freeload, purloin, sponge, wheedle.

scrub *v.* abandon, abolish, cancel, clean, cleanse, delete, discontinue, ditch, drop, forget, give up, rub, scour.

scrupulous *adj.* careful, conscientious, conscionable, exact, fastidious, honorable, meticulous, minute, moral, nice, painstaking, precise, principled, punctilious, rigorous, strict, upright.
antonym careless.

scrutinize *v.* analyze, dissect, examine, explore, give a onceover, inspect, investigate, peruse, probe, scan, search, sift, study.

scurrilous *adj.* abusive, coarse, defamatory, Fescennial, foul, foul-mouthed, gross, indecent, insulting, low, nasty, obscene, offensive, Rabelaisian, ribald, rude, salacious, scabrous, scandalous, slanderous, vituperative, vulgar.
antonym polite.

scurry *v.* dart, dash, fly, hurry, race, scamper, scoot, scud, scuttle, skedaddle, skelter, skim, sprint, trot, whisk.
antonym stroll.
n. flurry, hustle and bustle, scampering, whirl.
antonym calm.

scuttle *v.* bustle, hare, hasten, hurry, run, rush, scamper, scoot, scramble, scud, scurry, scutter, trot.
antonym stroll.

seal *v.* assure, attest, authenticate, bung, clinch, close, conclude, confirm, consummate, cork, enclose, establish, fasten, finalize, plug, ratify, secure, settle, shake hands on, shut, stamp, stop, stopper, validate, waterproof.
antonym unseal.
n. assurance, attestation, authentication, bulla, confirmation, imprimatur, insignia, notification, ratification, sigil, signet, stamp.

search *v.* check, comb, examine, explore, ferret, frisk, inquire, inspect, investigate, jerque, look, probe, pry, quest, ransack, rifle, rummage, scour, scrutinize, sift, test.
n. examination, exploration, going-over, hunt, inquiry, inspection, investigation, perquisition, perscrutation, pursuit, quest, researches, rummage, scrutiny, zetetic.

searching *adj.* close, intent, keen, minute, penetrating, piercing, probing, quizzical, severe, sharp, thorough, zetetic.
antonyms superficial, vague.

season *n.* division, interval, period, span, spell, term, time.
v. acclimatize, accustom, anneal, color, condiment, condition, discipline, enliven, flavor, habituate, harden,

imbue, inure, lace, leaven, mature, mitigate, moderate, prepare, qualify, salt, spice, temper, toughen, train.

seasoned *adj.* acclimatized, battle-scarred, experienced, hardened, long-serving, mature, old, practiced, time-served, veteran, weathered, well-versed.
antonym novice.

secede *v.* apostatize, disaffiliate, leave, quit, resign, retire, separate, split off, withdraw.
antonyms join, unite with.

secluded *adj.* claustral, cloistered, cloistral, cut off, isolated, lonely, out-of-the-way, private, reclusive, remote, retired, sequestered, sheltered, solitary, umbratile, umbratilous, unfrequented.
antonyms busy, public.

seclusion *n.* concealment, hiding, isolation, privacy, purdah, recluseness, remoteness, retirement, retreat, shelter, solitude.

secondary *adj.* alternate, auxiliary, back-up, consequential, contingent, derivative, derived, extra, indirect, inferior, lesser, lower, minor, relief, reserve, resultant, resulting, second, second-hand, second-rate, spare, subordinate, subsidiary, supporting, unimportant.
antonym primary.

secret *adj.* abstruse, arcane, back-door, backstairs, cabbalistic(al), camouflaged, clandestine, classified, cloak-and-dagger, close, closet, concealed, conspiratorial, covered, covert, cryptic, deep, discreet, disguised, esoteric, furtive, hidden, hole-and-corner, hush-hush, inly, mysterious, occult, out-of-the-way, private, privy, recondite, reticent, retired, secluded, secretive, sensitive, shrouded, sly, stealthy, tête-à-tête, undercover, underground, underhand, under-the-counter, undisclosed, unfrequented, unknown, unpublished, unrevealed, unseen.
antonyms open, public.
n. arcanum, code, confidence, enigma, formula, key, mystery, recipe.

secrete[1] *v.* appropriate, bury, cache, conceal, cover, disguise, harbor, hide, screen, secure, shroud, stash away, stow, veil.
antonym reveal.

secrete[2] *v.* emanate, emit, extravasate, extrude, exude, osmose, secern, separate.

sect *n.* camp, denomination, division, faction, group, party, school, splinter group, subdivision, wing.

section *n.* area, article, component, cross section, department, district, division, fraction, fractionlet, fragment, instalment, part, passage, piece, portion, region, sample, sector, segment, slice, subdivision, wing, zone.
antonym whole.

secular *adj.* civil, laic, laical, lay, non- religious, profane, state, temporal, worldly.
antonym religious.

secure *adj.* absolute, assured, certain, conclusive, confident, definite, dependable, easy, fast, fastened, firm,

fixed, fortified, immovable, immune, impregnable, on velvet, overconfident, protected, reassured, reliable, safe, sheltered, shielded, solid, stable, steadfast, steady, sure, tight, unassailable, undamaged, unharmed, well-founded.
antonyms insecure, uncertain.

v. acquire, assure, attach, batten down, bolt, chain, ensure, fasten, fix, gain, get, get hold of, guarantee, insure, land, lash, lock, lock up, moor, nail, obtain, padlock, procure, rivet, seize.
antonyms lose, unfasten.

security *n.* assurance, asylum, care, certainty, collateral, confidence, conviction, cover, custody, defense, gage, guarantee, guards, hostage, immunity, insurance, pawn, pledge, positiveness, precautions, preservation, protection, refuge, reliance, retreat, safeguards, safe-keeping, safety, sanctuary, sureness, surety, surveillance, warranty.
antonym insecurity.

sedate *adj.* calm, collected, composed, cool, decorous, deliberate, demure, dignified, douce, earnest, grave, imperturbable, middle-aged, placed, proper, quiet, seemly, serene, serious, slow-moving, sober, solemn, staid, tranquil, unflappable, unruffled.
antonyms flippant, hasty, undignified.

sediment *n.* deposit, draff, dregs, feces, fecula, grounds, lees, precipitate, residium, settlings, warp.

seductive *adj.* alluring, attractive, beguiling, bewitching, captivating, come-hither, come-on, enticing, flirtatious, honeyed, inviting, irresistible, provocative, ravishing, seducing, sexy, siren, specious, tempting. *antonym* unattractive.

see *v.* accompany, anticipate, appreciate, ascertain, attend, behold, comprehend, consider, consult, court, date, decide, deem, deliberate, descry, determine, discern, discover, distinguish, divine, encounter, ensure, envisage, escort, espy, experience, fathom, feel, follow, foresee, foretell, get, glimpse, grasp, guarantee, heed, identify, imagine, interview, investigate, judge, know, lead, learn, look, make out, mark, meet, mind, note, notice, observe, perceive, picture, realize, receive, recognize, reflect, regard, show, sight, spot, take, understand, usher, view, visit, visualize, walk, witness.

seek *v.* aim, ask, aspire to, attempt, beg, busk, desire, endeavor, entreat, essay, follow, hunt, inquire, invite, petition, pursue, request, solicit, strive, try, want.

seem *v.* appear, look, look like, pretend, sound like.

seemly *adj.* appropriate, attractive, becoming, befitting, comely, comme il faut, decent, decorous, fit, fitting, handsome, maidenly, meet, nice, proper, suitable, suited.
antonym unseemly.

segment *n.* articulation, bit, compartment, division, part, piece, portion, section, slice, wedge.
antonym whole.

v. anatomize, cut up, divide, halve, separate, slice, split.

segregate *v.* cut off, discriminate against, dissociate, isolate, quarantine, separate, set apart.
antonym unite.

seize *v.* abduct, annex, apprehend, appropriate, arrest, capture, catch, claw, clutch, cly, collar, commandeer, confiscate, crimp, distrain, distress, fasten, fix, get, grab, grasp, grip, hijack, impound, nab, prehend, smug, snatch, take.
antonym let go.

seldom *adv.* infrequently, occasionally, rarely, scarcely.
antonym often.

select *v.* choose, cull, pick, prefer, single out.
adj. choice, élite, excellent, exclusive, first-class, first-rate, hand-picked, limited, picked, posh, preferable, prime, privileged, rare, selected, special, superior, top, top- notch.
antonyms general, second-rate.

selection *n.* anthology, assortment, choice, choosing, collection, line-up, medley, miscellany, option, palette, pick, potpourri, preference, range, variety.

self-confident *adj.* assured, confident, fearless, poised, secure, self-assured, self-collected, self-possessed, self-reliant.
antonyms humble, unsure.

self-conscious *adj.* affected, awkward, bashful, coy, diffident, embarrassed, ill at ease, insecure, nervous, retiring, self-effacing, shamefaced, sheepish, shrinking, uncomfortable.
antonyms natural, unaffected.

self-denial *n.* abstemiousness, asceticism, moderation, renunciation, self-abandonment, self-abnegation, selflessness, self-renunciation, self-sacrifice, temperance, unselfishness.
antonym self-indulgence.

self-evident *adj.* axiomatic, clear, incontrovertible, inescapable, manifest, obvious, undeniable, unquestionable.

self-important *adj.* arrogant, big-headed, bumptious, cocky, conceited, consequential, overbearing, pompous, pushy, self-consequent, strutting, swaggering, swollen-headed, vain.
antonym humble.

self-indulgence *n.* dissipation, dissoluteness, excess, extravagance, high living, incontinence, intemperance, profligacy, self-gratification, sensualism.
antonym self-denial.

selfish *adj.* egoistic, egoistical, egotistic, egotistical, greedy, mean, mercenary, narrow, self-centered, self-interested, self-seeking, self-serving.
antonym unselfish.

self-possessed *adj.* calm, collected, composed, confident, cool, poised, self-assured, self-collected, together, unruffled.
antonym worried.

self-respect *n.* amour-propre, dignity, pride, self- assurance, self-confidence, self-esteem, self-pride, self-regard.
antonym self-doubt.

self-righteous *adj.* complacent, goody-goody, holier-than-thou, hypocritical, pharisaical, pi, pietistic(al), pious, priggish, sanctimonious, self-satisfied, smug, superior, Tartuffian, Tartuffish.
antonym understanding.

self-sacrifice *n.* altruism, generosity, self- abandonment, self-abnegation, self-denial, selflessness, self- renunciation.
antonym selfishness.

self-satisfied *adj.* complacent, puffed up, self- approving, self-congratulatory, self-righteous, smug.
antonym humble.

self-seeking *adj.* acquisitive, calculating, careerist, fortune-hunting, gold-digging, mercenary, on the make, opportunistic, self-endeared, self-interested, selfish, self- loving, self-serving.
antonym altruistic.

sell *v.* barter, cheat, convince, deal in, exchange, handle, hawk, impose on, market, merchandise, peddle, persuade, promote, retail, sell out, stock, surrender, trade, trade in, traffic in, trick, vend.
antonym buy.

send *v.* broadcast, cast, charm, communicate, consign, convey, delight, deliver, direct, discharge, dispatch, electrify, emit, enrapture, enthrall, excite, exude, fire, fling, forward, grant, hurl, intoxicate, move, please, propel, radiate, ravish, remit, shoot, stir, thrill, titillate, transmit.

senile *adj.* anile, decrepit, doddering, doited, doting, failing, imbecile, senescent.

senior *adj.* aîné(e), elder, first, higher, high- ranking, major, older, superior.
antonym junior.

sensation *n.* agitation, awareness, commotion, consciousness, emotion, Empfindung, excitement, feeling, furore, hit, impression, perception, scandal, sense, stir, surprise, thrill, tingle, vibes, vibrations, wow.

sensational *adj.* amazing, astounding, blood-and- thunder, breathtaking, dramatic, electrifying, excellent, exceptional, exciting, fabulous, gamy, hair-raising, horrifying, impressive, lurid, marvelous, melodramatic, mind-blowing, revealing, scandalous, sensationalistic, shocking, smashing, spectacular, staggering, startling, superb, thrilling.
antonym run-of-the-mill.

sense *n.* advantage, appreciation, atmosphere, aura, awareness, brains, clear-headedness, cleverness, consciousness, definition, denotation, direction, discernment, discrimination, drift, faculty, feel, feeling, gist, good, gumption, implication, import, impression, intelligence, interpretation, intuition, judgment, logic, marbles, meaning, message, mother wit, nous, nuance, opinion, perception, point, premonition, presentiment, purport, purpose, quickness, reason, reasonableness, sagacity, sanity, savvy, sensation, sensibility, sentiment, sharpness, significance, signification, smeddum, substance, tact, understanding, use, value, wisdom, wit(s), worth.
antonym foolishness.
v. appreciate, comprehend, detect, divine, feel, grasp, notice, observe, perceive, realize, suspect, understand.

senseless *adj.* absurd, anesthetized, asinine, crazy, daft, deadened, dotty, fatuous, foolish, halfwitted, idiotic, illogical, imbecilic, inane, incongruous, inconsistent, insensate, insensible, irrational, ludicrous, mad, meaningless, mindless, moronic, nonsensical, numb, numbed, out, out for the count, pointless, ridiculous, silly, simple, stunned, stupid, unconscious, unfeeling, unintelligent, unreasonable, unwise.
antonym sensible.

sensibility *n.* appreciation, awareness, delicacy, discernment, insight, intuition, perceptiveness, responsiveness, sensitiveness, sensitivity, susceptibility, taste.
antonym insensibility.

sensible *adj.* appreciable, canny, considerable, delicate, discernible, discreet, discriminating, down-to-earth, far-sighted, intelligent, judicious, level-headed, matter-of-fact, noticeable, palpable, perceptible, practical, prudent, rational, realistic, reasonable, right-thinking, sagacious, sage, sane, senseful, shrewd, significant, sober, solid, sound, tangible, visible, well-advised, well-thought-out, wise.
antonyms imperceptible, senseless.

sensible of acquainted with, alive to, aware of, cognizant of, conscious of, convinced of, mindful of, observant of, sensitive to, understanding.
antonym unaware of.

sensitive *adj.* acute, controversial, delicate, fine, hyperesthesic, hyperesthetic, hyperconscious, impressionable, irritable, keen, perceptive, precise, reactive, responsive, secret, sensitized, sentient, susceptible, temperamental, tender, thin-skinned, touchy, umbrageous.
antonym insensitive.

sensual *adj.* animal, bodily, carnal, epicurean, erotic, fleshly, lascivious, lecherous, lewd, libidinous, licentious, lustful, luxurious, pandemian, physical, randy, raunchy, self-indulgent, sexual, sexy, voluptuous, worldly.
antonyms ascetic, Puritan.

sentence *n.* aphorism, apophthegm, condemnation, decision, decree, doom, gnome, judgment, maxim, opinion, order, pronouncement, ruling, saying, verdict.
v. condemn, doom, judge, pass judgment on, penalize, pronounce judgment on.

sentiment *n.* attitude, belief, emotion, emotionalism, feeling, idea, judgment, mawkishness, maxim, opinion, persuasion, romanticism, saying, sensibility,

sentimentalism, sentimentality, slush, soft-heartedness, tenderness, thought, view.
antonyms hard-heartedness, straightforwardness.

sentimental *adj.* corny, dewy-eyed, drippy, emotional, gushing, gushy, gutbucket, impressionable, lovey-dovey, maudlin, mawkish, mushy, nostalgic, pathetic, romantic, rose-water, schmaltzy, simpering, sloppy, slushy, soft-hearted, tearful, tear-jerking, tender, too-too, touching, treacly, weepy, Wertherian.
antonym unsentimental.

separate *v.* abstract, bifurcate, deglutinate, departmentalize, detach, disaffiliate, disally, discerp, disconnect, disentangle, disjoin, dislink, dispart, dissever, distance, disunite, divaricate, diverge, divide, divorce, eloi(g)n, estrange, exfoliate, isolate, part, part company, prescind, remove, secede, secern, seclude, segregate, sever, shear, split, split up, sunder, uncouple, winnow, withdraw.
antonyms join, unite.
adj. alone, apart, autonomous, detached, disconnected, discrete, disjointed, disjunct, disparate, distinct, divided, divorced, independent, individual, isolated, particular, several, single, solitary, sundry, unattached, unconnected.
antonyms attached, together.

separation *n.* break, break-up, detachment, diaeresis, dialysis, diaspora, diastasis, discerption, disconnection, disengagement, disgregation, disjunction, disjuncture, disseverance, disseveration, disseverment, dissociation, disunion, division, divorce, estrangement, farewell, gap, leave-taking, parting, rift, segregation, severance, solution, split, split-up.
antonyms togetherness, unification.

sequence *n.* arrangement, chain, consequence, course, cycle, order, procession, progression, series, set, succession, track, train.

serene *adj.* calm, composed, cool, halcyon, imperturbable, peaceful, placid, tranquil, unclouded, undisturbed, unflappable, unruffled, untroubled.
antonym troubled.

serenity *n.* calm, calmness, composure, cool, peace, peacefulness, placidity, quietness, quietude, stillness, tranquility, unflappability.
antonyms anxiety, disruption.

series *n.* arrangement, catena, chain, concatenation, consecution, course, cycle, enfilade, line, order, progression, run, scale, sequence, set, string, succession, train.

serious *adj.* acute, alarming, critical, crucial, dangerous, deep, deliberate, determined, difficult, earnest, far-reaching, fateful, genuine, grave, grim, heavy, honest, humorless, important, long-faced, momentous, pensive, pressing, resolute, resolved, sedate, severe, significant, sincere, sober, solemn, staid, stern, thoughtful, unsmiling, urgent, weighty, worrying.
antonyms facetious, light, slight, smiling, trivial.

servant *n.* aia, amah, ancillary, attendant, ayah, bearer, boy, butler, daily, day, day-woman, domestic, drudge, flunky, footman, garçon, gentleman's gentleman, gossoon, gyp, haiduk, handmaid, handmaiden, help, helper, hind, hireling, Jeeves, kitchen-maid, knave, lackey, lady's maid, livery- servant, maid, maid of all work, maître d'hôtel, major-domo, man, manservant, menial, ministrant, retainer, scout, seneschal, servitor, skivvy, slave, slavey, steward, valet, vassal, woman.
antonyms master, mistress.

serve *v.* act, aid, answer, arrange, assist, attend, avail, complete, content, dance attendance, deal, deliver, discharge, distribute, do, fulfil, further, handle, help, minister to, oblige, observe, officiate, pass, perform, present, provide, satisfy, succor, suffice, suit, supply, undergo, wait on, work for.

service *n.* advantage, assistance, avail, availability, benefit, business, ceremony, check, disposal, duty, employ, employment, expediting, function, help, labor, maintenance, ministrations, observance, office, overhaul, performance, rite, servicing, set, supply, use, usefulness, utility, work, worship.
v. check, maintain, overhaul, recondition, repair, tunc.

serviceable *adj.* advantageous, beneficial, convenient, dependable, durable, efficient, functional, hard- wearing, helpful, operative, plain, practical, profitable, simple, strong, tough, unadorned, usable, useful, utilitarian.
antonym unserviceable.

servile *adj.* abject, base, bootlicking, controlled, craven, cringing, fawning, groveling, humble, low, mean, menial, obsequious, slavish, subject, submissive, subservient, sycophantic, toadying, toadyish, unctuous.
antonyms aggressive, bold.

servitude *n.* bondage, bonds, chains, enslavement, obedience, serfdom, slavery, subjugation, thraldom, thrall, vassalage, villeinage.
antonym freedom.

set[1] *v.* adjust, aim, allocate, allot, apply, appoint, arrange, assign, cake, conclude, condense, congeal, coordinate, crystallize, decline, decree, deposit, designate, determine, dip, direct, disappear, embed, establish, fasten, fix, fix up, gelatinize, harden, impose, install, jell, lay, locate, lodge, mount, name, ordain, park, place, plant, plonk, plump, position, prepare, prescribe, propound, put, rectify, regulate, resolve, rest, schedule, seat, settle, sink, situate, solidify, specify, spread, stake, station, stick, stiffen, subside, synchronize, thicken, turn, vanish.
n. attitude, bearing, carriage, fit, hang, inclination, miseen-scène, position, posture, scene, scenery, setting, turn.
adj. agreed, appointed, arranged, artificial, conventional, customary, decided, definite, deliberate, entrenched, established, firm, fixed, formal, hackneyed, immovable, inflexible, intentional, prearranged,

predetermined, prescribed, regular, rehearsed, rigid, routine, scheduled, settled, standard, stereotyped, stock, strict, stubborn, traditional, unspontaneous, usual.

antonyms free, movable, spontaneous, undecided.

set[2] *n.* apparatus, assemblage, assortment, band, batch, circle, class, clique, collection, company, compendium, coterie, covey, crew, crowd, faction, gang, group, kit, outfit, sect, sequence, series.

settle *v.* adjust, agree, alight, appoint, arrange, bed, calm, choose, clear, colonize, compact, complete, compose, conclude, confirm, decide, decree, descend, determine, discharge, dispose, dower, drop, dwell, endow, establish, fall, fix, found, hush, inhabit, land, light, liquidate, live, lower, lull, occupy, ordain, order, pacify, pay, people, pioneer, plant, plump, populate, quell, quiet, quieten, quit, reassure, reconcile, relax, relieve, reside, resolve, sedate, sink, soothe, square, square up, subside, tranquilize.

settlement[1] *n.* accommodation, adjustment, agreement, allowance, arrangement, clearance, clearing, completion, conclusion, confirmation, decision, defrayal, diktat, discharge, disposition, establishment, income, liquidation, payment, resolution, satisfaction, termination.

settlement[2] *n.* colonization, colony, community, encampment, hamlet, immigration, kibbutz, nahal, occupation, outpost, peopling, plantation, population.

settlement[3] *n.* compacting, drop, fall, sinkage, subsidence.

sever *v.* alienate, bisect, cleave, cut, detach, disconnect, disjoin, dissever, dissociate, dissolve, dissunder, disunite, divide, estrange, part, rend, separate, split, sunder, terminate.

antonyms join, unite.

several *adj.* assorted, different, discrete, disparate, distinct, divers, diverse, individual, many, particular, respective, separate, single, some, some few, specific, sundry, various.

severe *adj.* acute, arduous, ascetic, astringent, austere, biting, bitter, Catonian, caustic, chaste, classic, classical, cold, critical, cruel, cutting, dangerous, demanding, difficult, disapproving, distressing, dour, Draconian, Draconic, Dracontic, eager, exacting, extreme, fierce, flinty, forbidding, functional, grave, grim, grinding, hard, harsh, inclement, inexorable, intense, ironhanded, oppressive, pitiless, plain, punishing, relentless, restrained, Rhadamanthine, rigid, rigorous, satirical, scathing, serious, shrewd, simple, sober, Spartan, stern, strait-laced, strict, stringent, taxing, tight-lipped, tough, trying, unadorned, unbending, unembellished, ungentle, unrelenting, unsmiling, unsparing, unsympathetic, violent.

antonyms compassionate, kind, lenient, mild, sympathetic.

sex *n.* coition, coitus, congress, copulation, desire, fornication, gender, intercourse, intimacy, libido, lovemaking, nookie, reproduction, screw, sexual intercourse, sexual relations, sexuality, union, venery.

sexual *adj.* carnal, coital, erotic, gamic, genital, intimate, procreative, reproductive, sensual, sex, sex-related, venereal.

antonym asexual.

sexy *adj.* arousing, beddable, come-hither, cuddly, curvaceous, epigamic, erotic, flirtatious, inviting, kissable, naughty, nubile, pornographic, provocative, provoking, seductive, sensual, sensuous, slinky, suggestive, titillating, virile, voluptuous.

antonym sexless.

shabby *adj.* cheap, contemptible, dastardly, despicable, dilapidated, dingy, dirty, dishonorable, disreputable, dog-eared, down-at-heel, faded, frayed, ignoble, low, low-down, low-life, low-lived, mangy, mean, motheaten, neglected, paltry, poking, poky, poor, ragged, raunchy, rotten, run-down, scruffy, seedy, shameful, shoddy, tacky, tattered, tatty, threadbare, ungentlemanly, unworthy, worn, worn-out.

antonyms honorable, smart.

shack *n.* bothy, but and ben, cabin, dump, hole, hovel, hut, hutch, lean-to, shanty, shed, shiel, shieling.

shackle *n.* bond, bracelets, chain, darbies, fetter, gyve, hamper, handcuff, hobble, iron, leg-iron, manacle, rope, shackles, tether, trammel.

v. bind, chain, constrain, embarrass, encumber, fetter, gyve, hamper, hamstring, handcuff, handicap, hobble, hogtie, impede, inhibit, limit, manacle, obstruct, pinion, restrain, restrict, secure, tether, thwart, tie, trammel.

shade *n.* amount, apparition, blind, canopy, color, coolness, cover, covering, curtain, darkness, dash, degree, difference, dimness, dusk, eidolon, ghost, gloaming, gloom, gloominess, gradation, hint, hue, manes, murk, nuance, obscurity, phantasm, phantom, screen, semblance, semidarkness, shadiness, shadow, shadows, shelter, shield, shroud, specter, spirit, stain, suggestion, suspicion, tinge, tint, tone, trace, twilight, umbra, umbrage, variation, variety, veil, wraith.

v. cloud, conceal, cover, darken, dim, hide, inumbrate, mute, obscure, overshadow, protect, screen, shadow, shield, shroud, veil.

shadowy *adj.* caliginous, crepuscular, dark, dim, dreamlike, dusky, faint, ghostly, gloomy, half-remembered, hazy, illusory, imaginary, impalpable, indistinct, intangible, murky, nebulous, obscure, shaded, shady, spectral, tenebrious, tenebrose, tenebrous, umbratile, umbratilous, undefined, unreal, unsubstantial, vague, wraithlike.

shady[1] *adj.* bosky, bowery, caliginous, cool, dark, dim, leafy, shaded, shadowy, tenebrous, umbrageous, umbratile, umbratilous, umbriferous, umbrose, umbrous.

antonyms bright, sunlit, sunny.

shady[2] *adj.* crooked, discreditable, dishonest, disreputable, dubious, fishy, louche, questionable, shifty, slippery, suspect, suspicious, underhand, unethical, unscrupulous, untrustworthy.

antonyms honest, trustworthy.

shaggy *adj.* crinose, hairy, hirsute, long-haired, nappy, rough, tousled, tousy, unkempt, unshorn.
antonyms bald, shorn.

shake *n.* agitation, convulsion, disturbance, instant, jar, jerk, jiffy, jolt, jounce, moment, no time, pulsation, quaking, second, shiver, shock, shudder, tick, trembling, tremor, trice, twitch, vellication, vibration.
v. agitate, brandish, bump, churn, concuss, convulse, didder, discompose, distress, disturb, flourish, fluctuate, frighten, heave, impair, intimidate, jar, joggle, jolt, jounce, move, oscillate, quake, quiver, rattle, rock, rouse, shimmy, shiver, shock, shog, shudder, split, stir, succuss, sway, totter, tremble, twitch, undermine, unnerve, unsettle, upset, vellicate, vibrate, wag, waggle, wave, waver, weaken, wobble.

shaky *adj.* dubious, faltering, inexpert, insecure, precarious, questionable, quivery, rickety, rocky, shoogly, suspect, tottering, tottery, uncertain, undependable, unreliable, unsound, unstable, unsteady, unsupported, untrust-worthy, weak, wobbly.
antonyms firm, strong.

shallow *adj.* empty, flimsy, foolish, frivolous, idle, ignorant, meaningless, puerile, simple, skin-deep, slight, superficial, surface, trivial, unanalytical, unintelligent, unscholarly.
antonyms analytical, deep.

sham *n.* charlatan, counterfeit, feint, forgery, fraud, goldbrick, hoax, humbug, imitation, impostor, imposture, mountebank, phony, pretense, pretender, pseud, stumer.
adj. artificial, bogus, counterfeit, ersatz, faked, false, feigned, imitation, mock, pasteboard, phony, pinchbeck, pretended, pseud, pseudo, put-on, simulated, snide, spurious, synthetic.
antonym genuine.
v. affect, counterfeit, fake, feign, malinger, pretend, put on, simulate.

shame *n.* aidos, bashfulness, blot, chagrin, compunction, contempt, degradation, derision, discredit, disgrace, dishonor, disrepute, embarrassment, humiliation, ignominy, infamy, mortification, obloquy, odium, opprobrium, reproach, scandal, shamefacedness, stain, stigma.
antonyms distinction, honor, pride.
v. abash, blot, confound, debase, defile, degrade, discomfit, disconcert, discredit, disgrace, dishonor, embarrass, humble, humiliate, mortify, put to shame, reproach, ridicule, show up, smear, stain, sully, taint.
interj. fi donc, fie, fie upon you, for shame, fy, shame on you.

shameful *adj.* abominable, atrocious, base, contemptible, dastardly, degrading, discreditable, disgraceful, dishonorable, embarrassing, humiliating, ignominious, indecent, infamous, low, mean, mortifying, outrageous, reprehensible, scandalous, shaming, unbecoming, unworthy, vile, wicked.
antonyms creditable, honorable.

shameless *adj.* abandoned, abashless, audacious, barefaced, blatant, brash, brazen, corrupt, defiant, depraved, dissolute, flagrant, hardened, immodest, improper, impudent, incorrigible, indecent, insolent, ithyphallic, profligate, reprobate, unabashed, unashamed, unblushing, unprincipled, unscrupulous, wanton.
antonyms ashamed, contrite, shamefaced.

shape *n.* apparition, appearance, aspect, build, condition, configuration, conformation, contours, cut, dimensions, fettle, figure, form, format, frame, Gestalt, guise, health, kilter, likeness, lines, make, model, mold, outline, pattern, physique, profile, semblance, silhouette, state, template, trim.
v. accommodate, adapt, construct, create, define, develop, devise, embody, fashion, forge, form, frame, guide, make, model, modify, mold, plan, prepare, produce, redact, regulate, remodel.

shapeless *adj.* amorphous, asymmetrical, battered, characterless, dumpy, embryonic, formless, inchoate, indeterminate, indigest, irregular, misshapen, nebulous, undeveloped, unformed, unshapely, unstructured.
antonym shapely.

shapely *adj.* comely, curvaceous, elegant, featous, gainly, graceful, neat, pretty, trim, voluptuous, well-formed, well-proportioned, well-set-up, well-turned.
antonym shapeless.

share *v.* allot, apportion, assign, chip in, distribute, divide, divvy, divvy up, go Dutch, go fifty-fifty, go halves, muck in, partake, participate, split, whack.
n. a piece of the action, allotment, allowance, contribution, cut, dividend, division, divvy, due, finger, lot, part, portion, proportion, quota, ration, snap, snip, stint, whack.

sharp *adj.* abrupt, acerbic, acicular, acid, acidulous, acrid, acrimonious, acute, alert, apt, artful, astute, barbed, biting, bitter, bright, burning, canny, caustic, chic, chiseled, classy, clear, clear-cut, clever, crafty, crisp, cunning, cutting, discerning, dishonest, distinct, dressy, eager, edged, excruciating, extreme, fashionable, fierce, fit, fly, harsh, honed, hot, hurtful, incisive, intense, jagged, keen, knife-edged, knifelike, knowing, long-headed, marked, natty, nimble-witted, noticing, observant, painful, penetrating, peracute, perceptive, piercing, piquant, pointed, pungent, quick, quick-witted, rapid, razor-sharp, ready, sarcastic, sardonic, saw-edged, scathing, serrated, severe, sharpened, shooting, shrewd, sly, smart, snappy, snazzy, sour, spiky, stabbing, stinging, stylish, subtle, sudden, tart, trenchant, trendy, unblurred, undulled, unscrupulous, vinegary, violent, vitriolic, waspish, wily.
antonyms blunt, dull, mild, obtuse, slow, stupid.
adv. abruptly, exactly, on the dot, out of the blue, precisely, promptly, punctually, suddenly, unexpectedly.

sharpen *v.* acuminate, edge, file, grind, hone, strop, taper, whet.
antonym blunt.

shatter *v.* blast, blight, break, burst, crack, crush, demolish, destroy, devastate, disable, disshiver, dumbfound, exhaust, explode, impair, implode, overturn, overwhelm, pulverize, ruin, shiver, smash, split, stun, torpedo, undermine, upset, wreck.

shattered *adj.* all in, crushed, dead beat, devastated, dog-tired, done in, exhausted, jiggered, knackered, overwhelmed, undermined, weary, worn out, zonked.

sheepish *adj.* abashed, ashamed, chagrined, chastened, embarrassed, foolish, mortified, self-conscious, shame-faced, silly, uncomfortable.
antonym unabashed.

sheer[1] *adj.* abrupt, absolute, arrant, complete, downright, mere, out-and-out, perpendicular, precipitous, pure, rank, steep, thorough, thoroughgoing, total, unadulterated, unalloyed, unmingled, unmitigated, unqualified, utter, vertical.

sheer[2] diaphanous, fine, flimsy, gauzy, gossamer, pellucid, see-through, thin, translucent, transparent.
antonyms heavy, thick.

sheet *n.* blanket, broadsheet, broadside, circular, coat, covering, expanse, film, flyer, folio, handbill, handout, lamina, layer, leaf, leaflet, membrane, nappe, newssheet, overlay, pane, panel, piece, plate, shroud, skin, slab, stratum, surface, veneer.

shelf *n.* bank, bar, bench, bracket, ledge, mantel, mantelpiece, platform, projection, reef, sandbank, sand-bar, shoal, step, terrace.

shelter *v.* accommodate, cover, defend, ensconce, guard, harbor, hide, protect, put up, safeguard, screen, shade, shadow, shield, shroud, skug.
antonym expose.

n. accommodation, aegis, asylum, bield, bunker, cover, covert, coverture, defense, dugout, funk-hole, guard, harborage, haven, lean-to, lee, lodging, protection, refuge, retreat, roof, safety, sanctuary, sconce, screen, screening, security, shade, shadow, shiel, umbrage, umbrella.
antonym exposure.

shield *n.* aegis, ancile, buckler, bulwark, cover, defense, escutcheon, guard, pelta, protection, rampart, safeguard, screen, scutum, shelter, targe, ward.
v. cover, defend, guard, protect, safeguard, screen, shade, shadow, shelter.
antonym expose.

shift *v.* adjust, alter, budge, change, dislodge, displace, fluctuate, maneuver, move, quit, rearrange, relocate, remove, reposition, rid, scoff, swallow, swerve, switch, transfer, transpose, vary, veer, wolf.
n. alteration, artifice, change, contrivance, craft, device, displacement, dodge, equivocation, evasion, expedient, fluctuation, maneuver, modification, move, permutation, rearrangement, removal, resource, ruse, shifting, sleight, stratagem, subterfuge, switch, transfer, trick, veering, wile.

shifty *adj.* contriving, crafty, deceitful, devious, dishonest, disingenuous, dubious, duplicitous, evasive, fly-by-night, furtive, scheming, shady, slippery, tricky, underhand, unprincipled, untrustworthy, wily.
antonyms honest, open.

shilly-shally *v.* dilly-dally, dither, falter, fluctuate, haver, hem and haw, hesitate, mess about, prevaricate, seesaw, shuffle, swither, teeter, vacillate, waver.

shimmer *v.* coruscate, gleam, glisten, glitter, phosphoresce, scintillate, twinkle.
n. coruscation, gleam, glimmer, glitter, glow, incandescence, iridescence, luster, phosphorescence.

shine *v.* beam, brush, buff, burnish, coruscate, effulge, excel, flash, glare, gleam, glimmer, glisten, glitter, glow, luster, polish, radiate, resplend, scintillate, shimmer, sparkle, stand out, star, twinkle.
n. brightness, burnish, effulgence, glare, glaze, gleam, gloss, glow, lambency, light, luminosity, luster, patina, polish, radiance, sheen, shimmer, sparkle.

shining *adj.* beaming, bright, brilliant, celebrated, conspicuous, distinguished, effulgent, eminent, fulgent, gleaming, glistening, glittering, glorious, glowing, illustrious, lamping, leading, lucent, luminous, nitid, outstanding, profulgent, radiant, resplendent, rutilant, shimmering, sparkling, splendid, twinkling.

shiny *adj.* agleam, aglow, bright, burnished, gleaming, glistening, glossy, lustrous, nitid, polished, satiny, sheeny, shimmery, sleek.
antonyms dark, dull.

shipshape *adj.* businesslike, neat, orderly, seamanlike, spick-and-span, spruce, tidy, trig, trim, well-organized, well-planned, well-regulated.
antonyms disorderly, untidy.

shiver *v.* palpitate, quake, quiver, shake, shudder, tremble, vibrate.
n. flutter, frisson, grue, quiver, shudder, start, thrill, tremble, trembling, tremor, twitch, vibration.

shock *v.* agitate, appal, astound, confound, disgust, dismay, disquiet, horrify, jar, jolt, nauseate, numb, offend, outrage, paralyze, revolt, scandalize, shake, sicken, stagger, stun, stupefy, traumatize, unnerve, unsettle.
antonyms delight, gratify, please, reassure.
n. blow, bombshell, breakdown, clash, collapse, collision, concussion, consternation, dismay, distress, disturbance, encounter, fright, impact, jarring, jolt, perturbation, prostration, stupefaction, stupor, succussion, thunderbolt, trauma, turn, upset.
antonyms delight, pleasure.

shocking *adj.* abhorrent, abominable, appalling, astounding, atrocious, deplorable, detestable, disgraceful, disgusting, disquieting, distressing, dreadful, execrable, foul, frightful, ghastly, hideous, horrible, horrific, horrifying, insufferable, intolerable, loathsome, monstrous, nauseating, nefandous, odious, offensive, outrageous, repugnant, repulsive, revolting, scandalous, sickening, stupefying, unbearable, unspeakable.
antonyms acceptable, delightful, pleasant, satisfactory.

shore[1] *n.* beach, coast, foreshore, lakeside, littoral, margin, offing, promenade, rivage, sands, seaboard, sea-front, sea-shore, strand, waterfront, water's edge, waterside.

shore[2] *v.* brace, buttress, hold, prop, reinforce, shore up, stay, strengthen, support, underpin.

short *adj.* abbreviated, abridged, abrupt, blunt, brief, brittle, brusque, compendious, compressed, concise, crisp, crumbly, crusty, curt, curtailed, deficient, diminutive, direct, discourteous, dumpy, ephemeral, evanescent, fleeting, friable, gruff, impolite, inadequate, insufficient, lacking, laconic, limited, little, low, meager, momentary, murly, offhand, passing, petite, pithy, poor, précised, sawn-off, scant, scanty, scarce, sententious, sharp, shortened, short-handed, short-lived, short- term, slender, slim, small, snappish, snappy, sparse, squat, straight, succinct, summarized, summary, tart, terse, tight, tiny, transitory, uncivil, understaffed, unplentiful, wanting, wee.
antonyms adequate, ample, expansive, large, lasting, long, long-lived, polite, tall.

shortage *n.* absence, dearth, deficiency, deficit, failure, inadequacy, insufficiency, lack, leanness, meagerness, paucity, poverty, scantiness, scarcity, shortfall, sparseness, want, wantage.
antonyms abundance, sufficiency.

shortcoming *n.* defect, drawback, faible, failing, fault, flaw, foible, frailty, imperfection, inadequacy, weakness.

shorten *v.* abbreviate, abridge, crop, curtail, cut, decrease, diminish, dock, foreshorten, lessen, lop, précis, prune, reduce, take up, telescope, trim, truncate.
antonyms amplify, enlarge, lengthen.

short-lived *adj.* brief, caducous, ephemeral, evanescent, fleeting, fugacious, impermanent, momentary, passing, short, temporary, transient, transitory.
antonyms abiding, enduring, lasting, long-lived.

shortly *adv.* abruptly, anon, briefly, concisely, curtly, directly, laconically, presently, sharply, soon, succinctly, tartly, tersely.

short-sighted *adj.* careless, hasty, ill-advised, ill-considered, impolitic, impractical, improvident, imprudent, injudicious, myopic, near-sighted, unimaginative, unthinking.
antonyms far-sighted, hypermetropic, long-sighted.

short-tempered *adj.* choleric, crusty, fiery, hot- tempered, impatient, irascible, irritable, peppery, quick-tempered, ratty, testy, touchy.
antonyms calm, patient, placid.

shout *n.* bay, bellow, belt, call, cheer, cry, roar, scream, shriek, yell.
v. bawl, bay, bellow, call, cheer, cry, holler, roar, scream, shriek, yell.

shove *v.* barge, crowd, drive, elbow, force, impel, jostle, press, propel, push, shoulder, thrust.

shovel *n.* backhoe, bail, bucket, scoop, spade.

v. convey, dredge, heap, ladle, load, move, scoop, shift, spade, spoon, toss.

show *v.* accompany, accord, assert, attend, attest, bestow, betray, clarify, conduct, confer, demonstrate, disclose, display, divulge, elucidate, escort, evidence, evince, exemplify, exhibit, explain, grant, guide, illustrate, indicate, instruct, lead, manifest, offer, present, prove, register, reveal, teach, usher, witness.
n. affectation, air, appearance, array, dash, demonstration, display, éclat, élan, entertainment, exhibition, exhibitionism, expo, exposition, extravaganza, façade, fair, féerie, flamboyance, gig, illusion, indication, likeness, manifestation, ostentation, pageant, pageantry, panache, parade, performance, pizzazz, plausibility, pose, presentation, pretence, pretext, production, profession, razzle-dazzle, representation, semblance, sight, sign, spectacle, swagger, view.

show-down *n.* clash, climax, confrontation, crisis, culmination, dénouement, exposé, face-off.

show-off *n.* boaster, braggadocio, braggart, egotist, exhibitionist, peacock, self-advertiser, swaggerer, swanker, vaunter.

showy *adj.* epideictic, euphuistic, flamboyant, flash, flashy, florid, flossy, garish, gaudy, glitzy, loud, ostentatious, pompous, pretentious, sparkish, specious, splashy, swanking, swanky, tawdry, tinselly.
antonyms quiet, restrained.

shred *n.* atom, bit, fragment, grain, iota, jot, mammock, mite, piece, rag, ribbon, scrap, sliver, snippet, tatter, trace, whit, wisp.

shrewd *adj.* acute, arch, argute, artful, astucious, astute, calculated, calculating, callid, canny, clever, crafty, cunning, discerning, discriminating, downy, far-seeing, far- sighted, fly, gnostic, intelligent, judicious, keen, knowing, long-headed, observant, perceptive, perspicacious, sagacious, sharp, sly, smart, well-advised, wily.
antonyms naïve, obtuse, unwise.

shriek *v.* bellow, caterwaul, cry, holler, howl, scream, screech, shout, squeal, wail, yell.
n. bellow, caterwaul, cry, howl, scream, screech, shout, squeal, wail.

shrill *adj.* acute, argute, carrying, ear-piercing, ear-splitting, high, high-pitched, penetrating, piercing, piping, screaming, screeching, screechy, sharp, strident, treble.
antonyms gentle, low, soft.

shrink *v.* back away, balk, contract, cower, cringe, decrease, deflate, diminish, dwindle, flinch, lessen, narrow, quail, recoil, retire, shorten, shrivel, shun, shy away, wince, withdraw, wither, wrinkle.
antonyms embrace, expand, stretch, warm to.

shrivel *v.* burn, dehydrate, desiccate, dwindle, frizzle, gizzen, parch, pucker, scorch, sear, shrink, wilt, wither, wizen, wrinkle.

shun *v.* avoid, cold-shoulder, elude, eschew, evade, ignore, ostracize, shy away from, spurn, steer clear of.
antonyms accept, embrace.

shut *v.* bar, bolt, cage, close, fasten, latch, lock, seal, secure, slam, spar.
antonym open.

shy *adj.* backward, bashful, cautious, chary, coy, diffident, distrustful, farouche, hesitant, inhibited, modest, mousy, nervous, reserved, reticent, retiring, self-conscious, self-effacing, shrinking, suspicious, timid, unassertive, wary.
antonyms bold, confident.
v. back away, balk, buck, flinch, quail, rear, recoil, shrink, start, swerve, wince.

sick *adj.* ailing, black, blasé, bored, diseased, disgusted, displeased, dog-sick, fed up, feeble, ghoulish, glutted, ill, indisposed, jaded, laid up, morbid, mortified, nauseated, pining, poorly, puking, qualmish, queasy, sated, satiated, sickly, tired, under the weather, unwell, vomiting, weak, weary.
antonyms healthy, well.

sickness *n.* affliction, ailment, bug, complaint, derangement, disease, disorder, dwam, ill-health, illness, indisposition, infirmity, insanity, malady, nausea, pestilence, qualmishness, queasiness, vomiting.
antonym health.

side *n.* airs, angle, arrogance, aspect, bank, border, boundary, brim, brink, camp, cause, department, direction, division, edge, elevation, face, facet, faction, flank, flitch, fringe, gang, hand, insolence, light, limit, margin, opinion, ostentation, page, part, party, perimeter, periphery, position, pretentiousness, quarter, region, rim, sect, sector, slant, stand, standpoint, surface, team, twist, verge, view, viewpoint.
adj. flanking, incidental, indirect, irrelevant, lateral, lesser, marginal, minor, oblique, roundabout, secondary, subordinate, subsidiary.

sidle *v.* creep, edge, inch, ingratiate, insinuate, slink, sneak, steal, wriggle.

sieve *v.* boult, remove, riddle, separate, sift, strain.
n. boulter, colander, riddle, screen, sifter, strainer.

sight *n.* appearance, apprehension, decko, display, estimation, exhibition, eye, eyes, eye-shot, eyeshot, eyesight, eyesore, field of vision, fright, gander, glance, glimpse, judgment, ken, look, mess, monstrosity, observation, opinion, pageant, perception, range, scene, seeing, show, spectacle, view, viewing, visibility, vision, vista.
v. behold, discern, distinguish, glimpse, observe, perceive, see, spot.

sightseer *n.* excursionist, holidaymaker, rubber- neck, tourist, tripper, visitor.

sign *n.* augury, auspice, badge, beck, betrayal, board, character, cipher, clue, device, emblem, ensign, evidence, figure, foreboding, forewarning, gesture, giveaway, grammalogue, hierogram, hint, indication, indicium, insignia, intimation, lexigram, logo, logogram, logograph, manifestation, mark, marker, miracle, note, notice, omen, placard, pointer, portent, presage, proof, reminder, representation, rune, signal, signature, signification, signpost, spoor, suggestion, symbol, symptom, token, trace, trademark, vestige, warning.
v. autograph, beckon, endorse, gesticulate, gesture, indicate, initial, inscribe, motion, signal, subscribe, wave.

signal *n.* alarm, alert, beacon, beck, cue, flare, flash, gesture, go-ahead, griffin, impulse, indication, indicator, light, mark, OK, password, rocket, sign, tip-off, token, transmitter, waft, warning, watchword.
adj. conspicuous, distinguished, eminent, exceptional, extraordinary, famous, glorious, impressive, memorable, momentous, notable, noteworthy, outstanding, remarkable, significant, striking.
v. beckon, communicate, gesticulate, gesture, indicate, motion, nod, sign, telegraph, waft, wave.

significance *n.* consequence, consideration, force, implication, implications, import, importance, impressiveness, interest, matter, meaning, message, moment, point, purport, relevance, sense, signification, solemnity, weight.
antonym unimportance.

significant *adj.* critical, denoting, eloquent, expressing, expressive, important, indicative, knowing, material, meaning, meaningful, momentous, noteworthy, ominous, pregnant, senseful, serious, solemn, suggestive, symbolic, symptomatic, vital, weighty.
antonyms meaningless, unimportant.

signify *v.* announce, augur, betoken, carry weight, communicate, connote, convey, count, denote, evidence, exhibit, express, imply, indicate, intimate, matter, mean, omen, portend, presage, proclaim, represent, show, stand for, suggest, symbolize, transmit.

silence *n.* calm, dumbness, hush, lull, muteness, noiselessness, obmutescence, peace, quiescence, quiet, quietness, reserve, reticence, secretiveness, speechlessness, stillness, taciturnity, uncommunicativeness.
v. deaden, dumbfound, extinguish, gag, muffle, muzzle, quell, quiet, quieten, stifle, still, strike dumb, subdue, suppress.

silent *adj.* aphonic, aphonous, dumb, hushed, idle, implicit, inaudible, inoperative, mum, mute, muted, noiseless, quiet, reticent, soundless, speechless, still, stilly, tacit, taciturn, tongue-tied, uncommunicative, understood, unexpressed, unforthcoming, unpronounced, unsounded, unspeaking, unspoken, voiceless, wordless.
antonyms loud, noisy, talkative.

silhouette *n.* configuration, delineation, form, outline, profile, shadow-figure, shadowgraph, shape.

silly *adj.* absurd, addled, asinine, benumbed, bird- brained, brainless, childish, cuckoo, daft, dazed, dopey, drippy, fatuous, feather-brained, flighty, foolhardy, foolish, frivolous, giddy, groggy, hen-witted, idiotic, illogical, immature, imprudent, inane, inappropriate, inept, irrational, irresponsible, meaningless, mindless, muzzy, pointless, preposterous, puerile, ridiculous, scatter-brained, senseless, spoony, stunned, stupefied, stupid, unwise, witless.

antonyms collected, mature, sane, sensible, wise.

n. clot, dope, duffer, goose, half-wit, ignoramus, ninny, silly-billy, simpleton, twit, wally.

similar *adj.* alike, analogous, close, comparable, compatible, congruous, corresponding, homogeneous, homogenous, homologous, related, resembling, self-like, uniform.

antonym different.

similarity *n.* affinity, agreement, analogy, closeness, coincidence, comparability, compatibility, concordance, congruence, correspondence, equivalence, homogeneity, likeness, relation, resemblance, sameness, similitude, uniformity.

antonym difference.

simple *adj.* artless, bald, basic, brainless, childlike, classic, classical, clean, clear, credulous, dense, direct, dumb, easy, elementary, feeble, feeble-minded, foolish, frank, green, guileless, half-witted, homely, honest, humble, idiot-proof, inelaborate, ingenuous, innocent, inornate, intelligible, lowly, lucid, manageable, modest, moronic, naïf, naive, naïve, naked, natural, obtuse, one-fold, plain, pure, rustic, Saturnian, shallow, silly, sincere, single, slow, Spartan, stark, straightforward, stupid, thick, unadorned, unaffected, unalloyed, unblended, uncluttered, uncombined, uncomplicated, undeniable, understandable, undisguised, undivided, unelaborate, unembellished, unfussy, uninvolved, unlearned, unmixed, unornate, unpretentious, unschooled, unskilled, unsophisticated, unsuspecting, unvarnished.

antonyms artful, clever, complicated, difficult, fancy, intricate.

simpleton *n.* Abderite, blockhead, booby, daftie, dizzard, dolt, dope, dullard, dunce, dupe, flat, flathead, fool, gaby, gander, gomeril, goon, goop, goose, goose-cap, goosy, Gothamist, Gothamite, green goose, greenhorn, gump, gunsel, idiot, imbecile, jackass, Johnny, juggins, maffling, moron, nincompoop, ninny, ninny-hammer, numskull, soft-head, spoon, stupid, twerp.

antonym brain.

simulate *v.* act, affect, assume, counterfeit, duplicate, echo, fabricate, fake, feign, imitate, mimic, parrot, pretend, put on, reflect, reproduce, sham.

sin *n.* crime, damnation, debt, error, evil, fault, guilt, hamartia, impiety, iniquity, lapse, misdeed, offense, sinfulness, transgression, trespass, ungodliness, unrighteousness, wickedness, wrong, wrongdoing.

v. err, fall, fall from grace, go astray, lapse, misbehave, offend, stray, transgress, trespass.

sincere *adj.* artless, bona fide, candid, deep-felt, earnest, frank, genuine, guileless, heartfelt, heart-whole, honest, natural, open, plain-hearted, plain-spoken, pure, real, serious, simple, simple-hearted, single-hearted, soulful, straightforward, true, true-hearted, truthful, unadulterated, unaffected, unfeigned, unmixed, wholehearted.

antonym insincere.

sincerity *n.* artlessness, bona fides, candor, earnestness, frankness, genuineness, good faith, guilelessness, honesty, plain-heartedness, probity, seriousness, straightforwardness, truth, truthfulness, wholeheartedness.

antonym insincerity.

sinful *adj.* bad, corrupt, criminal, depraved, erring, fallen, guilty, immoral, impious, iniquitous, irreligious, peccable, peccant, ungodly, unholy, unrighteous, unvirtuous, wicked, wrongful.

antonyms righteous, sinless.

sing *v.* betray, bizz, blow the whistle, cantillate, carol, caterwaul, chant, chirp, croon, finger, fink, grass, hum, inform, intone, lilt, melodize, peach, pipe, purr, quaver, rat, render, serenade, spill the beans, squeal, talk, trill, vocalize, warble, whine, whistle, yodel.

singe *v.* blacken, burn, cauterize, char, scorch, sear.

single *adj.* celibate, distinct, exclusive, free, individual, lone, man-to-man, one, one-fold, one-to-one, only, particular, separate, simple, sincere, single-minded, singular, sole, solitary, unattached, unblended, unbroken, uncombined, uncompounded, undivided, unique, unmarried, unmixed, unshared, unwed, wholehearted.

singular *adj.* atypical, conspicuous, curious, eccentric, eminent, exceptional, extraordinary, individual, noteworthy, odd, out-of-the-way, outstanding, peculiar, pre- eminent, private, prodigious, proper, puzzling, queer, rare, remarkable, separate, single, sole, strange, uncommon, unique, unparalleled, unusual.

antonyms normal, usual.

sink *v.* abandon, abate, abolish, bore, collapse, conceal, decay, decline, decrease, defeat, degenerate, degrade, delapse, descend, destroy, dig, diminish, dip, disappear, drill, drive, droop, drop, drown, dwindle, ebb, engulf, excavate, fade, fail, fall, finish, flag, founder, invest, lapse, lay, lessen, lower, merge, overwhelm, pay, penetrate, plummet, plunge, relapse, retrogress, ruin, sag, scupper, slip, slope, slump, stoop, submerge, subside, succumb, suppress, weaken, worsen.

antonyms float, rise, uplift.

sinless *adj.* faultless, guiltless, immaculate, impeccable, innocent, pure, unblemished, uncorrupted, undefiled, unspotted, unsullied, virtuous.

antonym sinful.

sip *v.* delibate, sample, sup, taste.

n. drop, mouthful, spoonful, swallow, taste, thimbleful.

sit *v.* accommodate, assemble, befit, brood, contain, convene, deliberate, hold, meet, officiate, perch, pose, preside, reside, rest, seat, settle.

site *n.* ground, location, lot, place, plot, position, setting, spot, station.

v. dispose, install, locate, place, position, set, situate, station.

situation *n.* ball-game, berth, case, circumstances, condition, employment, galère, job, kettle of fish, lie of the land, locale, locality, location, office, place, plight, position, post, predicament, rank, scenario, seat, setting, setup, site, sphere, spot, state, state of affairs, station, status.

size *n.* amount, amplitude, bigness, bulk, dimensions, extent, greatness, height, hugeness, immensity, largeness, magnitude, mass, measurement(s), proportions, range, vastness, volume.

skeletal *adj.* cadaverous, drawn, emaciated, fleshless, gaunt, haggard, hollow-cheeked, shrunken, skin-and-bone, wasted.

sketch *v.* block out, delineate, depict, draft, draw, outline, paint, pencil, plot, portray, represent, rough out.
n. croquis, delineation, design, draft, drawing, ébauche, esquisse, outline, plan, scenario, skeleton, vignette.

sketchy *adj.* bitty, crude, cursory, imperfect, inadequate, incomplete, insufficient, outline, perfunctory, rough, scrappy, skimpy, slight, superficial, unfinished, vague.
antonym full.

skill *n.* ability, accomplishment, adroitness, aptitude, art, cleverness, competence, dexterity, experience, expertise, expertness, facility, finesse, handiness, ingenuity, intelligence, knack, proficiency, quickness, readiness, savoir-faire, savvy, skilfulness, talent, technique, touch.

skilled *adj.* able, accomplished, crack, experienced, expert, masterly, practiced, professional, proficient, schooled, skilful, trained.
antonym unskilled.

skimpy *adj.* beggarly, exiguous, inadequate, insufficient, meager, measly, miserly, niggardly, scanty, short, sketchy, sparse, thin, tight.
antonym generous.

skin *n.* casing, coating, crust, deacon, epidermis, fell, film, hide, husk, integument, membrane, outside, peel, pellicle, pelt, rind, tegument.
v. abrade, bark, excoriate, flay, fleece, graze, peel, scrape, strip.

skinny *adj.* attenuate(d), emaciated, lean, scragged, scraggy, skeletal, skin-and-bone, thin, twiggy, underfed, under-nourished, weedy.
antonym fat.

skip *v.* bob, bounce, caper, cavort, cut, dance, eschew, flisk, flit, frisk, gambol, hop, miss, omit, overleap, play truant, prance, trip.

skirmish *n.* affair, affray, battle, brush, clash, combat, conflict, contest, dust-up, encounter, engagement, fracas, incident, scrap, scrimmage, set-to, spat, tussle, velitation.
v. clash, collide, pickeer, scrap, tussle.

slack *adj.* baggy, crank, dull, easy, easy-going, flaccid, flexible, idle, inactive, inattentive, lax, lazy, limp, loose, neglectful, negligent, permissive, quiet, relaxed, remiss, slow, slow-moving, sluggish, tardy.

antonyms busy, diligent, quick, rigid, stiff, taut.
n. excess, give, inactivity, leeway, looseness, play, relaxation, room.
v. dodge, idle, malinger, neglect, relax, shirk, slacken.

slander *n.* aspersion, backbiting, calumniation, calumny, defamation, detraction, libel, misrepresentation, muckraking, obloquy, scandal, smear, traducement, traduction.
v. asperse, backbite, calumniate, decry, defame, detract, disparage, libel, malign, muck-rake, scandalize, slur, smear, traduce, vilify, vilipend.
antonyms glorify, praise.

slang *v.* abuse, berate, castigate, excoriate, insult, lambaste, malign, revile, scold, slag, vilify, vituperate.
antonym praise.

slant *v.* angle, bend, bevel, bias, cant, color, distort, incline, lean, list, shelve, skew, slope, tilt, twist, warp, weight.
n. angle, attitude, bias, camber, declination, diagonal, emphasis, gradient, incline, leaning, obliquity, pitch, prejudice, rake, ramp, slope, tilt, viewpoint.

slanting *adj.* angled, askew, aslant, asymmetrical, bent, canted, cater-cornered, diagonal, inclined, oblique, sideways, skew-whiff, slanted, slantwise, sloping, tilted, tilting.
antonyms level.

slap-dash *adj.* careless, clumsy, disorderly, haphazard, hasty, hurried, last-minute, messy, negligent, offhand, perfunctory, rash, slipshod, sloppy, slovenly, thoughtless, thrown-together, untidy.
antonyms careful, orderly.

slash *v.* criticize, cut, drop, gash, hack, lacerate, lash, lower, reduce, rend, rip, score, slit.
n. cut, gash, incision, laceration, lash, rent, rip, slit.

slaughter *n.* battue, blood-bath, bloodshed, butchery, carnage, extermination, holocaust, killing, liquidation, massacre, murder, slaying.
v. butcher, crush, defeat, destroy, exterminate, halal, hammer, kill, liquidate, massacre, murder, overwhelm, rout, scupper, slay, thrash, trounce, vanquish. **slave** *n.* abject, bondservant, bond-slave, bond(s)man, bond(s)woman, captive, drudge, peon, scullion, serf, servant, skivvy, slavey, thrall, vassal, villein.
v. drudge, grind, labor, skivvy, slog, struggle, sweat, toil.

slavery *n.* bondage, captivity, duress(e), enslavement, impressment, serfdom, servitude, subjugation, thraldom, thrall, vassalage, yoke.
antonym freedom.

slay *v.* amuse, annihilate, assassinate, butcher, destroy, dispatch, eliminate, execute, exterminate, impress, kill, massacre, murder, rub out, slaughter, wow.

sleek *adj.* glossy, insinuating, lustrous, plausible, shiny, smooth, smug, well-fed, well-groomed.

sleep *v.* catnap, doss (down), doze, drop off, drowse, hibernate, nod off, repose, rest, slumber, snooze, snore.

n. coma, dormancy, doss, doze, forty winks, hibernation, nap, repose, rest, shut-eye, siesta, slumber(s), snooze, sopor.

sleepy *adj.* drowsy, dull, heavy, hypnotic, inactive, lethargic, quiet, slow, sluggish, slumb(e)rous, slumbersome, slumbery, somnolent, soporific, soporose, soporous, torpid.
antonyms alert, awake, restless, wakeful.

slender *adj.* acicular, faint, feeble, flimsy, fragile, gracile, inadequate, inconsiderable, insufficient, lean, little, meager, narrow, poor, remote, scanty, slight, slim, small, spare, svelte, sylph-like, tenuous, thin, thready, wasp- waisted, weak, willowish, willowy.
antonyms considerable, fat, thick.

slide *v.* coast, glide, glissade, lapse, skate, skim, slidder, slip, slither, toboggan, veer.

slight *adj.* delicate, feeble, flimsy, fragile, gracile, inconsiderable, insignificant, insubstantial, meager, minor, modest, negligible, paltry, scanty, slender, slim, small, spare, superficial, trifling, trivial, unimportant, weak.
antonyms considerable, large, major, significant.
v. affront, cold-shoulder, cut, despise, disdain, disparage, disrespect, ignore, insult, neglect, scorn, snub.
antonyms compliment, flatter.
n. affront, contempt, discourtesy, disdain, disregard, disrespect, inattention, indifference, insult, neglect, rebuff, rudeness, slur, snub.

slim *adj.* ectomorphic, faint, gracile, lean, narrow, poor, remote, slender, slight, svelte, sylph-like, thin, trim.
antonyms chubby, fat, strong.
v. bant, diet, lose weight, reduce, slenderize.

slip[1] *v.* blunder, boob, conceal, creep, disappear, discharge, dislocate, elude, err, escape, fall, get away, glide, hide, lapse, loose, miscalculate, misjudge, mistake, skate, skid, slidder, slide, slink, slither, sneak, steal, trip.
n. bloomer, blunder, boob, error, failure, fault, imprudence, indiscretion, lapsus, lapsus calami, lapsus linguae, lapsus memoriae, mistake, omission, oversight, slip-up.

slip[2] *n.* certificate, coupon, cutting, offshoot, pass, piece, runner, scion, shoot, sliver, sprig, sprout, strip.

slipshod *adj.* careless, casual, loose, negligent, slap-dash, sloppy, slovenly, unsystematic, untidy.
antonyms careful, fastidious, neat, tidy.

slit *v.* cut, gash, knife, lance, pierce, rip, slash, slice, split.
n. cut, fent, fissure, gash, incision, opening, rent, split, tear, vent. *adj.* cut, pertusate, pertuse(d), rent, split, torn.

slogan *n.* battle-cry, catch-phrase, catchword, chant, jingle, motto, rallying-cry, war cry, watchword.

slope *v.* batter, delve, fall, incline, lean, pitch, rise, slant, tilt, verge, weather.
n. bajada, brae, cant, declination, declivity, descent, downgrade, escarp, glacis, gradient, inclination, incline, ramp, rise, scarp, slant, tilt, versant.

sloth *n.* accidie, acedia, fainéance, idleness, inactivity, indolence, inertia, laziness, listlessness, slackness, slothfulness, sluggishness, torpor.
antonyms diligence, industriousness, sedulity.

slothful *adj.* do-nothing, fainéant, idle, inactive, indolent, inert, lazy, listless, slack, sluggish, torpid, workshy.
antonyms diligent, industrious, sedulous.

slouching *adj.* careless, disorderly, heedless, loose, negligent, shambling, shuffling, slack, slap-dash, slatternly, slipshod, sloppy, unkempt, untidy.

slow *adj.* adagio, backward, behind, behindhand, boring, bovine, conservative, creeping, dawdling, dead, dead-and- alive, delayed, deliberate, dense, dilatory, dim, dull, dull- witted, dumb, easy, gradual, inactive, lackadaisical, laggard, lagging, late, lazy, leaden, leisurely, lingering, loitering, long-drawn-out, measured, obtuse, one-horse, pedetentous, plodding, ponderous, prolonged, protracted, quiet, retarded, slack, sleepy, slow-moving, slow-witted, sluggardly, sluggish, stagnant, stupid, tame, tardy, tedious, thick, time-consuming, uneventful, unhasty, unhurried, uninteresting, unproductive, unprogressive, unpunctual, unresponsive, wearisome.
antonyms active, fast, quick, rapid, swift.
v. brake, check, curb, decelerate, delay, detain, draw rein, handicap, hold up, lag, relax, restrict, retard.

sluggish *adj.* dull, heavy, inactive, indolent, inert, lethargic, lifeless, listless, lurdan, lymphatic, phlegmatic, slothful, slow, slow-moving, torpid, unresponsive.
antonyms brisk, dynamic, eager, quick, vigorous.

slumber *v.* doze, drowse, nap, repose, rest, sleep, snooze.

slump *v.* bend, collapse, crash, decline, deteriorate, droop, drop, fall, hunch, loll, plummet, plunge, sag, sink, slip, slouch, worsen.
n. collapse, crash, decline, depreciation, depression, downturn, drop, failure, fall, falling-off, low, recession, reverse, stagnation, trough, worsening.
antonym boom.

sly *adj.* arch, artful, astute, canny, clever, conniving, covert, crafty, cunning, devious, foxy, furtive, guileful, impish, insidious, knowing, mischievous, peery, roguish, scheming, secret, secretive, shifty, sleeky, stealthy, subtle, surreptitious, underhand, vulpine, wily.
antonyms frank, honest, open, straightforward.

small *adj.* bantam, base, dilute, diminutive, dwarf(ish), grudging, humble, illiberal, immature, inadequate, incapacious, inconsiderable, insignificant, insufficient, itsybitsy, lesser, limited, little, meager, mean, mignon(ne), mini, miniature, minor, minuscule, minute, modest, narrow, negligible, paltry, petite, petty, pigmean, pintsize(d), pocket, pocket-sized, puny, pygmaean, pygmean, scanty, selfish, slight, small-scale, tiddl(e)y, tiny, trifling, trivial, undersized, unimportant, unpretentious, wee, young.
antonyms big, huge, large.

smart[1] *adj.* acute, adept, agile, apt, astute, bright, brisk, canny, chic, clever, cracking, dandy, effective, elegant, fashionable, fine, impertinent, ingenious, intelligent, jaunty, keen, lively, modish, natty, neat, nimble, nimble-witted, nobby, pert, pointed, quick, quick-witted, rattling, ready, ready-witted, saucy, sharp, shrewd, smart-alecky, snappy, spanking, spirited, spruce, stylish, swagger, swish, tippy, trim, vigorous, vivacious, well-appointed, witty.
antonyms dowdy, dumb, slow, stupid, unfashionable, untidy.

smart[2] *v.* burn, hurt, nip, pain, sting, throb, tingle, twinge.
adj. hard, keen, nipping, nippy, painful, piercing, resounding, sharp, stinging.
n. nip, pain, pang, smarting, soreness, sting, twinge.

smash *v.* break, collide, crash, crush, defeat, demolish, destroy, disintegrate, lay waste, overthrow, prang, pulverize, ruin, shatter, shiver, squabash, wreck.
n. accident, collapse, collision, crash, defeat, destruction, disaster, downfall, failure, pile-up, prang, ruin, shattering, smash-up.

smear *v.* asperse, bedaub, bedim, besmirch, blacken, blur, calumniate, coat, cover, dab, daub, dirty, drag (someone's) name through the mud, gaum, malign, patch, plaster, rub on, slubber, smarm, smudge, soil, spread over, stain, sully, tarnish, traduce, vilify.
n. blot, blotch, calumny, daub, defamation, gaum, libel, mudslinging, slander, smudge, splodge, streak, vilification, whispering campaign.

smell *n.* aroma, bouquet, fetor, fragrance, fumet(te), funk, malodor, mephitis, nose, odor, perfume, pong, redolence, scent, sniff, stench, stink, whiff.
v. be malodorous, hum, inhale, nose, pong, reek, scent, sniff, snuff, stink, stink to high heaven, whiff.

smelly *adj.* bad, evil-smelling, fetid, foul, foul-smelling, frowsty, funky, graveolent, high, malodorous, mephitic, noisome, off, pongy, putrid, reeking, stinking, strong, strong-smelling, whiffy.

smitten *adj.* afflicted, beguiled, beset, bewitched, bowled over, burdened, captivated, charmed, enamored, infatuated, plagued, struck, troubled.

smoke *n.* exhaust, film, fog, fume, funk, gas, mist, reek, roke, smog, vapor.
v. cure, dry, fume, fumigate, reek, roke, smolder, vent.

smooth *adj.* agreeable, bland, calm, classy, easy, effortless, elegant, equable, even, facile, fair-spoken, flat, flowing, fluent, flush, frictionless, glassy, glib, glossy, hairless, horizontal, ingratiating, level, levigate, mellow, mild, mirror-like, peaceful, persuasive, plain, plane, pleasant, polished, regular, rhythmic, serene, shiny, silken, silky, sleek, slick, slippery, smarmy, smug, soft, soothing, steady, suave, tranquil, unbroken, unctuous, undisturbed, uneventful, uniform, uninterrupted, unpuckered, unruffled, unrumpled, untroubled, unwrinkled, urbane, velvety, well-ordered.
antonyms coarse, harsh, irregular, rough, unsteady.

v. allay, alleviate, appease, assuage, calm, dub, ease, emery, extenuate, facilitate, flatten, iron, level, levigate, mitigate, mollify, palliate, plane, polish, press, slicken, soften, unknit, unwrinkle.
antonym roughen.

smother *v.* choke, cocoon, conceal, cover, envelop, extinguish, heap, hide, inundate, muffle, overlie, overwhelm, repress, shower, shroud, snuff, stifle, strangle, suffocate, suppress, surround.

smug *adj.* cocksure, complacent, conceited, holier-thanthou, priggish, self-opinionated, self-righteous, self-satisfied, superior, unctuous. *antonym* modest.

smutty *adj.* bawdy, blue, coarse, crude, dirty, filthy, gross, improper, indecent, indelicate, lewd, obscene, off-color, pornographic, prurient, racy, raunchy, ribald, risqué, salacious, suggestive, vulgar.
antonyms clean, decent.

snag *n.* bug, catch, complication, difficulty, disadvantage, drawback, hitch, inconvenience, obstacle, problem, snub, stick, stumbling block.
v. catch, hole, ladder, rip, tear.

snap *v.* bark, bite, break, catch, chop, click, crack, crackle, crepitate, flash, grip, growl, knap, nip, pop, retort, seize, separate, snarl, snatch.
n. bite, break, crack, crackle, energy, fillip, flick, get-up-and-go, go, grabe, liveliness, nip, pizazz, pop, vigor, zip.
adj. abrupt, immediate, instant, offhand, on-the-spot, sudden, unexpected, unpremeditated.

snappy *adj.* brusque, chic, crabbed, cross, dapper, edgy, fashionable, hasty, ill-natured, irritable, modish, natty, quick-tempered, smart, snappish, stylish, tart, testy, touchy, trendy, up-to-the-minute, waspish.

snare *v.* catch, ensnare, entrap, illaqueate, net, seize, springe, trap, trepan, wire.
n. catch, cobweb, gin, lime, lime-twig, net, noose, pitfall, springe, springle, toils, trap, wire.

snarl[1] *v.* complain, gnarl, gnar(r), growl, grumble, knar.

snarl[2] *v.* complicate, confuse, embroil, enmesh, entangle, entwine, jam, knot, muddle, ravel, tangle.

snatch *v.* clutch, gain, grab, grasp, grip, kidnap, nab, pluck, pull, ramp, rap, rescue, seize, spirit, take, win, wrench, wrest.
n. bit, fraction, fragment, part, piece, section, segment, smattering, snippet, spell.

sneak *v.* cower, cringe, grass on, inform on, lurk, pad, peach, sidle, skulk, slink, slip, smuggle, spirit, steal, tell tales.
n. informer, snake in the grass, sneaker, telltale.
adj. clandestine, covert, furtive, quick, secret, stealthy, surprise, surreptitious.

sneer *v.* deride, disdain, fleer, gibe, jeer, laugh, look down on, mock, ridicule, scoff, scorn, sniff at, snigger.
n. derision, disdain, fleer, gibe, jeer, mockery, ridicule, scorn, smirk, snidery, snigger.

sniff *v.* breathe, inhale, nose, smell, snuff, snuffle, vent.

snigger *v., n.* giggle, laugh, sneer, snicker, snort, titter.

sniveling *adj.* blubbering, crying, girning, grizzling, mewling, moaning, sniffling, snuffling, weeping, whimpering, whingeing, whining.

snobbish *adj.* arrogant, condescending, high and mighty, high-hat, hoity-toity, lofty, lordly, patronizing, pretentious, snooty, stuck-up, superior, toffee-nosed, uppish, uppity, upstage.

snoop *v.* interfere, pry, sneak, spy.

snooze *v.* catnap, doze, drowse, kip, nap, nod off, sleep. *n.* catnap, doze, forty winks, kip, nap, shut-eye, siesta, sleep.

snub *v.* check, cold-shoulder, cut, humble, humiliate, mortify, rebuff, rebuke, shame, slight, sneap, squash, squelch, wither.

n. affront, brush-off, check, humiliation, insult, putdown, rebuff, rebuke, slap in the face, sneap.

snug *adj.* close, close-fitting, comfortable, comfy, compact, cosy, homely, intimate, neat, sheltered, trim, warm.

soak *v.* bathe, damp, drench, imbue, immerse, infuse, interfuse, marinate, moisten, penetrate, permeate, saturate, sog, souse, steep, wet.

soar *v.* ascend, climb, escalate, fly, mount, plane, rise, rocket, tower, wing.

antonym plummet.

sob *v.* bawl, blubber, boohoo, cry, greet, howl, mewl, moan, shed tears, snivel, weep.

sober *adj.* abstemious, abstinent, calm, clear-headed, cold, composed, cool, dark, dispassionate, douce, drab, grave, level-headed, lucid, moderate, peaceful, plain, practical, quiet, rational, realistic, reasonable, restrained, sedate, serene, serious, severe, solemn, somber, sound, staid, steady, subdued, temperate, unexcited, unruffled.

antonyms drunk, excited, frivolous, gay, intemperate, irrational.

sobriety *n.* abstemiousness, abstinence, calmness, composure, continence, coolness, gravity, levelheadedness, moderation, reasonableness, restraint, sedateness, self-restraint, seriousness, soberness, solemnity, staidness, steadiness, temperance.

antonyms drunkenness, excitement, frivolity.

social *adj.* collective, common, communal, community, companionable, friendly, general, gregarious, group, neighborly, organized, public, sociable, societal.

n. ceilidh, do, gathering, get-together, hoolly, hoot(e)nanny, party.

society *n.* association, beau monde, brotherhood, camaraderie, circle, civilization, club, companionship, company, corporation, culture, elite, fellowship, fraternity, fratry, friendship, gentry, Gesellschaft, group, guild, haut monde, humanity, institute, league, mankind, organization, people, population, sisterhood, the public, the smart set, the swells, the top drawer, the world, union, upper classes, upper crust, Verein.

soft *adj.* balmy, bendable, bland, caressing, comfortable, compassionate, cottony, creamy, crumby, cushioned, cushiony, cushy, daft, delicate, diffuse, diffused, dim, dimmed, doughy, downy, ductile, dulcet, easy, easygoing, effeminate, elastic, faint, feathery, feeble-minded, flabby, flaccid, fleecy, flexible, flowing, fluid, foolish, furry, gelatinous, gentle, impressible, indulgent, kind, lash, lax, lenient, liberal, light, limp, low, malleable, mellifluous, mellow, melodious, mild, moldable, murmured, muted, namby-pamby, non-alcoholic, overindulgent, pale, pampered, pastel, permissive, pitying, plastic, pleasant, pleasing, pliable, pulpy, quaggy, quiet, restful, sensitive, sentimental, shaded, silky, silly, simple, smooth, soothing, soppy, spineless, spongy, squashy, subdued, supple, swampy, sweet, sympathetic, temperate, tender, tender-hearted, undemanding, understated, unprotected, velvety, weak, whispered, yielding.

antonyms hard, harsh, heavy, loud, rigid, rough, severe, strict.

soften *v.* abate, allay, alleviate, anneal, appease, assuage, calm, cushion, digest, diminish, ease, emolliate, intenerate, lessen, lighten, lower, macerate, malax, malaxate, melt, mitigate, moderate, modify, mollify, muffle, palliate, quell, relax, soothe, still, subdue, temper.

soil[1] *n.* clay, country, dirt, dust, earth, glebe, ground, humus, land, loam, region, terra firma.

soil[2] *v.* bedaggle, bedraggle, befoul, begrime, besmirch, besmut, defile, dirty, foul, maculate, muddy, pollute, smear, spatter, spot, stain, sully, tarnish.

solace *n.* alleviation, assuagement, comfort, consolation, relief, succor, support.

v. allay, alleviate, comfort, console, mitigate, soften, soothe, succor, support.

sole *adj.* alone, exclusive, individual, one, only, single, singular, solitary, unique.

antonyms multiple, shared.

solemn *adj.* august, awed, awe-inspiring, ceremonial, ceremonious, devotional, dignified, earnest, formal, glum, grand, grave, hallowed, holy, imposing, impressive, majestic, momentous, pompous, portentous, religious, reverential, ritual, sacred, sanctified, sedate, serious, sober, somber, staid, stately, thoughtful, venerable.

antonyms frivolous, gay, light-hearted.

solicit *v.* ask, beg, beseech, canvass, crave, entreat, implore, importune, petition, pray, seek, sue, supplicate.

solicitous *adj.* anxious, apprehensive, ardent, attentive, careful, caring, concerned, eager, earnest, fearful, troubled, uneasy, worried, zealous.

solicitude *n.* anxiety, attentiveness, care, concern, considerateness, consideration, disquiet, regard, uneasiness, worry.

solid *adj.* agreed, compact, complete, concrete, constant, continuous, cubic(al), decent, dense, dependable, estimable, firm, genuine, good, hard, law-abiding, level-headed, massed, pure, real, reliable, sensible, serious, sober, sound, square, stable, stocky, strong, sturdy, substantial, trusty, unalloyed, unanimous, unbroken, undivided, uninterrupted, united, unmixed, unshakeable, unvaried, upright, upstanding, wealthy, weighty, worthy.

antonyms broken, insubstantial, liquid.

solitary *adj.* alone, cloistered, companionless, de(a)rnful, desolate, friendless, hermitical, hidden, isolated, lone, lonely, lonesome, out-of-the-way, reclusive, remote, retired, secluded, separate, sequestered, single, sole, unfrequented, unsociable, unsocial, untrodden, unvisited.

antonyms accompanied, gregarious.

solitude *n.* aloneness, desert, emptiness, isolation, loneliness, privacy, reclusiveness, retirement, seclusion, waste, wasteland, wilderness.

antonym companionship.

solution *n.* answer, blend, clarification, compound, decipherment, dénouement, disconnection, dissolution, elucidation, emulsion, explanation, explication, key, liquefaction, melting, mix, mixture, resolution, result, solvent, solving, suspension, unfolding, unraveling.

solve *v.* answer, clarify, crack, decipher, disentangle, dissolve, elucidate, explain, expound, interpret, resolve, settle, unbind, unfold, unravel, work out.

somber *adj.* dark, dim, dismal, doleful, drab, dull, dusky, funereal, gloomy, grave, joyless, lugubrious, melancholy, mournful, obscure, sad, sepulchral, shadowy, shady, sober, sombrous, subfusc.

antonyms bright, cheerful, happy.

sometimes *adv.* at times, from time to time, now and again, now and then, occasionally, off and on, once in a while, otherwhiles.

antonyms always, never.

soon *adv.* anon, betimes, in a minute, in a short time, in the near future, presently, shortly.

soothe *v.* allay, alleviate, appease, assuage, calm, coax, comfort, compose, ease, hush, lull, mitigate, mollify, pacify, quiet, relieve, salve, settle, soften, still, tranquilize.

antonyms annoy, irritate, vex.

soothing *adj.* anetic, assuasive, balmy, balsamic, calming, demulcent, easeful, emollient, lenitive, palliative, relaxing, restful.

antonyms annoying, irritating, vexing.

sophisticated *adj.* advanced, blasé, citified, complex, complicated, cosmopolitan, couth, cultivated, cultured, delicate, elaborate, highly-developed, intricate, jet-set, multifaceted, refined, seasoned, subtle, urbane, worldly, worldlywise, world-weary.

antonyms artless, naïve, simple, unsophisticated.

sorcery *n.* black art, black magic, charm, diablerie, divination, enchantment, hoodoo, incantation, magic, necromancy, pishogue, spell, voodoo, warlockry, witchcraft, witchery, witching, wizardry.

sordid *adj.* avaricious, base, corrupt, covetous, debauched, degenerate, degraded, despicable, dingy, dirty, disreputable, filthy, foul, grasping, low, mean, mercenary, miserly, niggardly, rapacious, seamy, seedy, selfish, self- seeking, shabby, shameful, sleazy, slovenly, slummy, squalid, tawdry, unclean, ungenerous, venal, vicious, vile, wretched.

sore *adj.* acute, afflicted, aggrieved, angry, annoyed, annoying, burning, chafed, critical, desperate, dire, distressing, extreme, grieved, grievous, harrowing, hurt, inflamed, irked, irritable, irritated, pained, painful, peeved, pressing, raw, reddened, resentful, sensitive, severe, sharp, smarting, stung, tender, touchy, troublesome, upset, urgent, vexed.

n. abscess, boil, canker, carbuncle, chafe, gathering, inflammation, swelling, ulcer, wound.

sorrow *n.* affliction, anguish, blow, distress, dole, grief, hardship, heartache, heartbreak, lamentation, misery, misfortune, mourning, regret, ruth, sadness, trial, tribulation, trouble, unhappiness, woe, worry.

antonyms happiness, joy.

v. agonize, bemoan, bewail, beweep, grieve, lament, moan, mourn, pine, weep.

antonym rejoice.

sorrowful *adj.* affecting, afflicted, dejected, depressed, disconsolate, distressing, doleful, grievous, heartbroken, heart-rending, heavy-hearted, lamentable, lugubrious, melancholy, miserable, mournful, painful, piteous, rueful, ruthful, sad, sorry, tearful, unhappy, wae, woebegone, woeful, wretched.

antonyms happy, joyful.

sorry *adj.* abject, apologetic, base, commiserative, compassionate, conscience-stricken, contrite, deplorable, disconsolate, dismal, distressed, distressing, grieved, guiltridden, mean, melancholy, miserable, mournful, moved, paltry, pathetic, penitent, piteous, pitiable, pitiful, pitying, poor, regretful, remorseful, repentant, ruthful, sad, self- reproachful, shabby, shamefaced, sorrowful, sympathetic, unhappy, unworthy, vile, wretched.

antonym glad.

sort *n.* brand, breed, category, character, class, denomination, description, family, genre, genus, group, ilk, kidney, kind, make, nature, order, quality, race, species, stamp, style, type, variety.

v. arrange, assort, catalog, categorize, choose, class, classify, distribute, divide, file, grade, group, neaten, order, rank, screen, select, separate, systematize, tidy.

sound[1] *n.* description, din, earshot, hearing, idea, implication, impression, look, noise, range, report, resonance, reverberation, tenor, tone, utterance, voice. *v.* announce, appear, articulate, chime, declare, echo, enunciate, express, knell, look, peal, pronounce, resonate, resound, reverberate, ring, seem, signal, toll, utter, voice.

sound[2] *adj.* complete, copper-bottomed, correct, deep, entire, established, fair, fere, firm, fit, hale, healthy, hearty, intact, just, level-headed, logical, orthodox, peaceful, perfect, proper, proven, prudent, rational, reasonable, recognized, reliable, reputable, responsible, right, right- thinking, robust, safe, secure, sensible, solid, solvent, stable, sturdy, substantial, thorough, tried-and-true, true, trustworthy, unbroken, undamaged, undisturbed, unhurt, unimpaired, uninjured, untroubled, valid, vigorous, wakeless, well-founded, well- grounded, whole, wise.

antonyms shaky, unfit, unreliable, unsound.

sound³ *v.* examine, fathom, inspect, investigate, measure, plumb, probe, test.

sound⁴ *n.* channel, estuary, firth, fjord, inlet, passage, strait, voe.

sour *adj.* acerb(ic), acetic, acid, acidulated, acrid, acrimonious, bad, bitter, churlish, crabbed, curdled, cynical, disagreeable, discontented, embittered, fermented, grouchy, grudging, ill-natured, ill-tempered, inharmonious, jaundiced, off, peevish, pungent, rancid, rank, sharp, tart, turned, ungenerous, unpleasant, unsavory, unsuccessful, unsweet, unwholesome, vinegarish, vinegary, waspish.

antonyms good-natured, sweet.

v. alienate, curdle, disenchant, embitter, envenom, exacerbate, exasperate, spoil.

source *n.* author, authority, begetter, beginning, cause, commencement, derivation, fons et origo, fountainhead, informant, klondike, milch-cow, mine, origin, originator, primordium, quarry, rise, spring, waterhead, well-head, ylem.

souvenir *n.* fairing, gift, keepsake, memento, memory, relic, remembrance(r), reminder, token.

sovereign *n.* autarch, chief, dynast, emperor, empress, kaiser, king, monarch, potentate, prince, queen, ruler, shah, tsar.

adj. absolute, august, chief, dominant, effectual, efficacious, efficient, excellent, imperial, kingly, majestic, monarch(ic)al, paramount, predominant, principal, queenly, regal, royal, ruling, supreme, unlimited.

sovereignty *n.* ascendancy, domination, imperium, kingship, primacy, raj, regality, supremacy, suzerainty, sway.

space *n.* accommodation, amplitude, berth, blank, capacity, chasm, diastema, distance, duration, elbowroom, expanse, extension, extent, gap, house-room, interval, lacuna, leeway, margin, omission, period, place, play, room, scope, seat, spaciousness, span, time, volume.

spacious *adj.* ample, big, broad, capacious, comfortable, commodious, expansive, extensive, huge, large, roomy, sizable, uncrowded, vast, wide.

antonyms confined, cramped, narrow, small.

span *n.* amount, compass, distance, duration, extent, length, period, reach, scope, spell, spread, stretch, term.

v. arch, bridge, cover, cross, encompass, extend, link, overarch, traverse, vault.

spare *adj.* additional, economical, emergency, extra, free, frugal, gash, gaunt, lank, lean, leftover, meager, modest, odd, over, remaining, scanty, slender, slight, slim, sparing, superfluous, supernumerary, surplus, unoccupied, unused, unwanted, wiry.

antonyms corpulent, necessary, profuse.

v. afford, allow, bestow, give quarter, grant, leave, let off, pardon, part with, refrain from, release, relinquish.

sparing *adj.* careful, chary, cost-conscious, economical, frugal, lenten, prudent, saving, thrifty.

antonyms lavish, liberal, unsparing.

sparkle *v.* beam, bubble, coruscate, dance, effervesce, emicate, fizz, fizzle, flash, gleam, glint, glisten, glister, glitter, glow, scintillate, shimmer, shine, spark, twinkle, wink.

n. animation, brilliance, coruscation, dash, dazzle, effervescence, élan, emication, flash, flicker, gaiety, gleam, glint, glitter, life, panache, pizzazz, radiance, scintillation, spark, spirit, twinkle, vim, vitality, vivacity, wit, zip.

spartan *adj.* abstemious, abstinent, ascetic, austere, bleak, disciplined, extreme, frugal, hardy, joyless, plain, rigorous, self-denying, severe, stern, strict, stringent, temperate, unflinching.

spasm *n.* access, burst, contraction, convulsion, eruption, fit, frenzy, jerk, outburst, paroxysm, seizure, throe, twitch.

speak *v.* address, advert to, allude to, argue, articulate, breathe, comment on, communicate, converse, deal with, declaim, declare, discourse, discuss, enunciate, express, harangue, lecture, mention, plead, pronounce, refer to, say, speechify, spiel, state, talk, tell, utter, voice.

special *adj.* appropriate, certain, characteristic, chief, choice, detailed, distinctive, distinguished, especial, exceptional, exclusive, extraordinary, festive, gala, important, individual, intimate, main, major, memorable, momentous, particular, peculiar, precise, primary, red-letter, select, significant, specialized, specific, uncommon, unique, unusual.

antonyms common, normal, ordinary, usual.

specialist *n.* adept, authority, connoisseur, consultant, expert, master, professional, proficient.

species *n.* breed, category, class, collection, denomination, description, genus, group, kind, sort, type, variety.

specific *adj.* characteristic, clear-cut, definite, delimitative, distinguishing, especial, exact, explicit, express, limited, particular, peculiar, precise, special, unambiguous, unequivocal.

antonyms general, vague.

specify *v.* cite, define, delineate, describe, designate, detail, enumerate, indicate, individualize, itemize, list, mention, name, particularize, spell out, stipulate.

specimen *n.* copy, embodiment, ensample, example,

exemplar, exemplification, exhibit, illustration, individual, instance, model, paradigm, pattern, person, proof, representative, sample, type.

speck *n.* atom, bit, blemish, blot, defect, dot, fault, flaw, fleck, grain, iota, jot, macula, mark, mite, modicum, mote, particle, shred, speckle, spot, stain, tittle, trace, whit.

spectacle *n.* curiosity, display, event, exhibition, extravaganza, marvel, pageant, parade, performance, phenomenon, scene, show, sight, wonder.

spectator *n.* beholder, bystander, eye-witness, looker-on, observer, onlooker, passer-by, viewer, watcher, witness.

antonyms contestant, participant, player.

speculate *v.* cogitate, conjecture, consider, contemplate, deliberate, gamble, guess, hazard, hypothesize, meditate, muse, reflect, risk, scheme, suppose, surmise, theorize, venture, wonder.

speech *n.* address, articulation, colloquy, communication, conversation, dialect, dialogue, diction, discourse, discussion, disquisition, enunciation, harangue, homily, idiom, intercourse, jargon, language, lecture, lingo, oration, parlance, parole, peroration, say, spiel, talk, tongue, utterance, voice, winged words.

speed *n.* acceleration, celerity, dispatch, expedition, fleetness, haste, hurry, lick, momentum, pace, precipitation, quickness, rapidity, rush, swiftness, tempo, velocity.

v. advance, aid, assist, belt, bomb, boost, bowl along, career, dispatch, expedite, facilitate, flash, fleet, further, gallop, hasten, help, hurry, impel, lick, press on, promote, put one's foot down, quicken, race, rush, sprint, step on it, step on the gas, step on the juice, tear, urge, vroom, zap, zoom.

antonyms delay, hamper, restrain, slow.

spell[1] *n.* bout, course, innings, interval, patch, period, season, stint, stretch, term, time, turn.

spell[2] *n.* abracadabra, allure, bewitchment, charm, conjuration, enchantment, exorcism, fascination, glamor, hex, incantation, jettatura, love-charm, magic, open sesame, paternoster, philter, rune, sorcery, trance, weird, witchery.

spell[3] *v.* augur, herald, imply, indicate, mean, portend, presage, promise, signal, signify, suggest.

spellbound *adj.* bemused, bewitched, captivated, charmed, enchanted, enthralled, entranced, fascinated, gripped, hooked, mesmerized, possessed, rapt, transfixed, transported.

spend *v.* apply, bestow, blow, blue, concentrate, consume, cough up, deplete, devote, disburse, dispense, dissipate, drain, employ, empty, exhaust, expend, fill, fork out, fritter, invest, lavish, lay out, occupy, pass, pay out, shed, shell out, splash out, squander, use, use up, waste.

antonyms hoard, save.

spendthrift *n.* big spender, prodigal, profligate, spendall,

spender, squanderer, unthrift, waster, wastrel.

antonyms hoarder, miser, saver.

adj. extravagant, improvident, prodigal, profligate, thriftless, wasteful.

sphere *n.* ball, capacity, circle, compass, department, domain, employment, field, function, globe, globule, milieu, orb, province, range, rank, realm, scope, spheroid, spherule, station, stratum, territory.

spherical *adj.* globate, globed, globe-shaped, globoid, globose, globular, orbicular, rotund, round.

spicy *adj.* aromatic, flavorsome, fragrant, hot, improper, indecorous, indelicate, off-color, piquant, pointed, pungent, racy, ribald, risqué, savory, scandalous, seasoned, sensational, showy, suggestive, tangy, titillating, unseemly.

antonym bland.

spin *v.* birl, concoct, develop, gyrate, gyre, hurtle, invent, narrate, pirouette, purl, recount, reel, relate, revolve, rotate, spirt, swim, swirl, tell, turn, twirl, twist, unfold, wheel, whirl.

n. agitation, commotion, drive, flap, gyration, hurl, panic, pirouette, revolution, ride, roll, run, state, tizzy, turn, twist, whirl.

spine *n.* backbone, barb, needle, quill, rachis, ray, spicule, spiculum, spike, spur, vertebrae, vertebral column.

spineless *adj.* cowardly, faint-hearted, feeble, gutless, inadequate, ineffective, irresolute, lily-livered, soft, spiritless, squeamish, submissive, vacillating, weak, weak-kneed, weak-willed, wet, wishy-washy, yellow.

antonyms brave, strong.

spirit *n.* air, animation, apparition, ardor, Ariel, atmosphere, attitude, backbone, bravura, breath, brio, character, complexion, courage, daemon, dauntlessness, deva, disposition, div, djinni, earnestness, energy, enterprise, enthusiasm, entrain, Erdgeist, esprit follet, essence, familiar, faun, feeling, feelings, fire, foison, force, gameness, geist, genie, genius, genius loci, ghost, ghoul, gist, grit, guts, humor, intent, intention, jinnee, jinni, ka, kobold, life, liveliness, manito(u), marid, meaning, mettle, mood, morale, motivation, outlook, phantom, pneuma, psyche, purport, purpose, python, quality, resolution, resolve, revenant, sense, shade, shadow, soul, sparkle, specter, spook, sprite, spunk, stout-heartedness, substance, sylph, temper, temperament, tenor, tone, verve, vigor, vision, vivacity, warmth, water-horse, water-nymph, water-rixie, water-sprite, Weltgeist, wili, will, will power, Zeitgeist, zest.

v. abduct, abstract, capture, carry, convey, kidnap, purloin, remove, seize, snaffle, steal, whisk.

spirited *adj.* active, animated, ardent, bold, courageous, energetic, game, gamy, high-spirited, lively, mettlesome, plucky, sparkling, sprightly, spunky, stomachful, vigorous, vivacious.

antonyms lazy, spiritless, timid.

spiritless *adj.* anemic, apathetic, dejected, depressed, despondent, dispirited, droopy, dull, lackluster, languid, lifeless, listless, low, melancholic, melancholy, mopy, torpid, unenthusiastic, unmoved, wishy-washy. *antonym* spirited.

spiritual *adj.* aery, devotional, divine, ecclesiastical, ethereal, ghostly, holy, immaterial, incorporeal, otherwordly, pneumatic, pure, religious, sacred, unfleshly, unworldly.
antonyms material, physical.

spit *v.* discharge, drizzle, eject, expectorate, hawk, hiss, spew, splutter, sputter.
n. dribble, drool, expectoration, phlegm, saliva, slaver, spittle, sputum.

spite *n.* animosity, bitchiness, despite, gall, grudge, hate, hatred, ill-nature, malevolence, malice, malignity, pique, rancor, spitefulness, spleen, venom, viciousness.
antonyms affection, goodwill.
v. annoy, discomfit, gall, harm, hurt, injure, irk, irritate, needle, nettle, offend, peeve, pique, provoke, put out, vex.

spiteful *adj.* barbed, bitchy, catty, cruel, ill- disposed, ill-natured, malevolent, malicious, malignant, nasty, rancorous, snide, splenetic, vengeful, venomous, vindictive, waspish.
antonyms affectionate, charitable.

splendid *adj.* admirable, beaming, bright, brilliant, costly, dazzling, excellent, exceptional, fantastic, fine, first-class, glittering, glorious, glowing, gorgeous, grand, great, heroic, illustrious, imposing, impressive, lavish, lustrous, luxurious, magnificent, marvelous, ornate, outstanding, pontific(al), radiant, rare, refulgent, remarkable, renowned, resplendent, rich, splendiferous, splend(o)rous, sterling, sublime, sumptuous, superb, supreme, tiptop, top-hole, top-notch, topping, wonderful.
antonyms drab, ordinary, run-of-the-mill.

splendor *n.* brightness, brilliance, ceremony, dazzle, display, effulgence, fulgor, glory, gorgeousness, grandeur, luster, magnificence, majesty, pomp, radiance, refulgence, renown, resplendence, richness, show, solemnity, spectacle, stateliness, sumptuousness.

splinter *n.* chip, flake, flinder, fragment, needle, paring, shaving, sliver, spall, spicule, stob.
v. disintegrate, fracture, fragment, shatter, shiver, smash, split.

split *v.* allocate, allot, apportion, betray, bifurcate, branch, break, burst, cleave, crack, delaminate, disband, distribute, disunite, divaricate, diverge, divide, divulge, fork, gape, grass, halve, inform on, open, parcel out, part, partition, peach, rend, rip, separate, share out, slash, slice up, slit, sliver, snap, spell, splinter, squeal.
n. breach, break, break-up, cleft, crack, damage, dichotomy, difference, discord, disruption, dissension, disunion, divergence, division, estrangement, fissure, gap, partition, race, rent, rift, rip, rupture, schism, scissure, separation, slash, slit, tear.

adj. ambivalent, bisected, broken, cleft, cloven, cracked, divided, dual, fractured, ruptured, twofold.

spoil *v.* addle, baby, blemish, bugger, butcher, cocker, coddle, cosset, curdle, damage, debase, decay, decompose, deface, despoil, destroy, deteriorate, disfigure, go bad, go off, harm, impair, indulge, injure, jigger, louse up, mar, mildew, mollycoddle, pamper, plunder, putrefy, queer, rot, ruin, screw, spoon-feed, turn, upset, wreck.

spoken *adj.* declared, expressed, oral, phonetic, said, stated, told, unwritten, uttered, verbal, viva voce, voiced.
antonyms unspoken, written.

spontaneous *adj.* extempore, free, impromptu, impulsive, instinctive, natural, ultroneous, unbidden, uncompelled, unconstrained, unforced, unhesitating, unlabored, unpremeditated, unprompted, unstudied, untaught, voluntary, willing.
antonyms forced, planned, studied.

sport *n.* activity, amusement, badinage, banter, brick, buffoon, butt, dalliance, derision, diversion, entertainment, exercise, fair game, frolic, fun, game, jest, joking, kidding, laughing-stock, merriment, mirth, mockery, pastime, play, plaything, raillery, recreation, ridicule, sportsman, teasing.
v. caper, dally, display, disport, exhibit, flirt, frolic, gambol, philander, play, romp, show off, toy, trifle, wear.

sporting *adj.* considerate, fair, gentlemanly, sportsmanlike.
antonyms unfair, ungentlemanly, unsporting.

spot *n.* bit, blemish, blot, blotch, daub, difficulty, discoloration, flaw, little, locality, location, macula, maculation, macule, mark, mess, morsel, pimple, place, plight, plook, point, position, predicament, pustule, quandary, scene, site, situation, smudge, speck, splash, stain, stigma, taint, trouble.
v. besmirch, blot, descry, detect, dirty, discern, dot, espy, fleck, identify, maculate, mark, mottle, observe, recognize, see, sight, soil, spatter, speckle, splodge, splotch, stain, sully, taint, tarnish.

spotty *adj.* blotchy, pimpled, pimply, plooky, speckled, spotted.

spout *v.* declaim, discharge, emit, erupt, expatiate, gush, jet, orate, pontificate, rabbit on, ramble (on), rant, sermonize, shoot, speechify, spiel, spray, spurt, squirt, stream, surge.
n. chute, fistula, fountain, gargoyle, geyser, jet, nozzle, outlet, rose, spray.

spray[1] *v.* atomize, diffuse, douse, drench, scatter, shower, sprinkle, wet.
n. aerosol, atomizer, drizzle, droplets, foam, froth, mist, moisture, spindrift, spoondrift, sprinkler.

spray[2] *n.* bough, branch, corsage, garland, shoot, sprig, wreath.

spread *v.* advertise, arrange, array, blazon, bloat, broadcast, broaden, bruit, cast, circulate, couch, cover, diffuse,

dilate, dispread, disseminate, distribute, divulgate, divulge, effuse, escalate, expand, extend, fan out, furnish, lay, metastasize, multiply, mushroom, open, overlay, prepare, proclaim, proliferate, promulgate, propagate, publicize, publish, radiate, scatter, set, shed, sprawl, stretch, strew, swell, transmit, unfold, unfurl, unroll, widen.
antonyms close, compress, contain, fold.
n. advance, advancement, array, banquet, blow-out, compass, cover, development, diffusion, dispersion, dissemination, divulgation, divulgence, escalation, expanse, expansion, extent, feast, increase, period, proliferation, ranch, reach, repast, span, spreading, stretch, suffusion, sweep, term, transmission.

sprightly *adj.* active, agile, airy, alert, animated, blithe, brisk, cheerful, energetic, frolicsome, gamesome, gay, hearty, jaunty, joyous, lively, nimble, perky, playful, spirited, sportive, spry, vivacious.
antonym inactive.

spring[1] *v.* appear, arise, bounce, bound, burgeon, come, dance, derive, descend, develop, emanate, emerge, grow, hop, issue, jump, leap, mushroom, originate, proceed, rebound, recoil, shoot up, sprout, start, stem, vault.
n. bounce, bounciness, bound, buck, buoyancy, elasticity, flexibility, gambado, give, hop, jump, leap, rebound, recoil, resilience, saltation, springiness, vault.

spring[2] *n.* beginning, cause, eye, fountain-head, origin, root, source, well, well-spring.

sprinkle *v.* asperge, diversify, dot, dredge, dust, pepper, powder, scatter, seed, shower, sparge, spatter, spray, strew.

spruce *adj.* dainty, dapper, elegant, natty, neat, sleek, slick, smart, smirk, trig, trim, well-groomed, well-turned-out.
antonyms disheveled, untidy.

spry *adj.* active, agile, alert, brisk, energetic, nimble, nippy, peppy, quick, ready, sprightly, supple.
antonyms doddering, inactive, lethargic.

spur *v.* animate, drive, goad, impel, incite, poke, press, prick, prod, prompt, propel, stimulate, urge.
antonym curb.
n. fillip, goad, impetus, impulse, incentive, incitement, inducement, motive, prick, rowel, stimulus.
antonym curb.

spurious *adj.* adulterate, adulterine, apocryphal, artificial, bastard, bogus, contrived, counterfeit, deceitful, dog, fake, false, feigned, forged, illegitimate, imitation, mock, phony, pretended, pseudo, sham, simulated, specious, supposititious, unauthentic.
antonyms authentic, genuine, real.

squabble *v.* argue, bicker, brawl, clash, dispute, fall out, fight, quarrel, row, scrap, spat, tiff, wrangle.
n. argument, barney, clash, disagreement, dispute, fight, rhubarb, row, scrap, set-to, spat, tiff.

squalid *adj.* broken-down, decayed, dingy, dirty, disgusting, fetid, filthy, foul, low, nasty, neglected, poverty-stricken, repulsive, run-down, seedy, sleazy, slovenly, slummy, sordid, uncared-for, unclean, unkempt.
antonyms clean, pleasant.

squander *v.* blow, blue, consume, dissipate, expend, fritter away, lavish, misspend, misuse, scatter, spend, splurge, throw away, waste.

square *v.* accommodate, accord, adapt, adjust, agree, align, appease, balance, bribe, conform, correspond, corrupt, discharge, fit, fix, harmonize, level, liquidate, match, quit, reconcile, regulate, rig, satisfy, settle, suborn, suit, tailor, tally, true.
adj. above-board, bourgeois, broad, complete, conservative, conventional, decent, equitable, ethical, even, exact, fair, fitting, full, genuine, honest, just, old-fashioned, on the level, opposed, orthodox, quadrate, right-angled, satisfying, solid, straight, straightforward, strait-laced, stuffy, suitable, thick-set, traditional, true, unequivocal, upright.
n. antediluvian, conformer, conformist, conservative, conventionalist, die-hard, fuddy-duddy, (old) fogy, stick-in-the- mud, traditionalist.

squeamish *adj.* coy, delicate, fastidious, finicky, nauseous, particular, prissy, prudish, punctilious, qualmish, queasy, queer, reluctant, scrupulous, sick, sickish, strait- laced.

squeeze *v.* bleed, chirt, clasp, clutch, compress, cram, crowd, crush, cuddle, embrace, enfold, extort, force, grip, hug, jam, jostle, lean on, milk, nip, oppress, pack, pinch, press, pressurize, ram, scrounge, squash, strain, stuff, thrust, wedge, wrest, wring.
n. clasp, congestion, crowd, crush, embrace, grasp, handclasp, hold, hug, jam, press, pressure, restriction, squash.

stability *n.* constancy, durability, firmness, fixity, permanence, solidity, soundness, steadfastness, steadiness, strength, sturdiness.
antonyms insecurity, instability, unsteadiness, weakness.

stable *adj.* abiding, constant, deep-rooted, durable, enduring, established, fast, firm, fixed, immutable, invariable, lasting, permanent, reliable, secure, self-balanced, sound, static, steadfast, steady, strong, sturdy, sure, unalterable, unchangeable, unwavering, well-founded.
antonyms shaky, unstable, weak, wobbly.

stack *n.* accumulation, clamp, cock, heap, hoard, load, mass, mound, mountain, pile, ruck, stockpile.
v. accumulate, amass, assemble, gather, load, pile, save, stockpile, store.

staff *n.* caduceus, cane, crew, employees, lecturers, lituus, officers, organization, personnel, pole, prop, rod, stave, teachers, team, wand, workers, workforce.

stage *n.* division, floor, juncture, lap, leg, length, level, period, phase, point, shelf, step, story, subdivision, tier.

v. arrange, do, engineer, give, mount, orchestrate, organize, perform, present, produce, put on, stage-manage.

stagger *v.* alternate, amaze, astonish, astound, confound, daddle, daidle, dumbfound, falter, flabbergast, hesitate, lurch, nonplus, overlap, overwhelm, reel, shake, shock, step, stun, stupefy, surprise, sway, teeter, titubate, totter, vacillate, waver, wobble, zigzag.

staid *adj.* calm, composed, decorous, demure, grave, quiet, sedate, self-restrained, serious, sober, sober-blooded, solemn, steady, Victorian.

antonyms debonair, frivolous, jaunty, sportive.

stain *v.* bedye, besmirch, blacken, blemish, blot, color, contaminate, corrupt, defile, deprave, dirty, discolor, disgrace, distain, dye, imbue, mark, smutch, soil, spot, sully, taint, tarnish, tinge.

n. blemish, blot, discoloration, disgrace, dishonor, dye, infamy, reproach, shame, slur, smirch, smutch, soil, splodge, spot, stigma, tint.

stake[1] *n.* loggat, pale, paling, picket, pile, pole, post, spike, standard, stang, stave, stick.

v. brace, fasten, pierce, prop, secure, support, tether, tie, tie up.

stake[2] *n.* ante, bet, chance, claim, concern, hazard, interest, investment, involvement, peril, pledge, prize, risk, share, venture, wager.

v. ante, bet, chance, gage, gamble, hazard, imperil, jeopardize, pledge, risk, venture, wager.

stale *adj.* antiquated, banal, cliché'd, cliché-ridden, common, commonplace, decayed, drab, dry, effete, faded, fetid, flat, fozy, fusty, hackneyed, hard, insipid, musty, old, old hat, overused, platitudinous, repetitious, sour, stagnant, stereotyped, tainted, tasteless, threadbare, trite, unoriginal, vapid, worn-out.

antonym fresh.

stalk[1] *v.* approach, follow, haunt, hunt, march, pace, pursue, shadow, stride, strut, tail, track.

stalk[2] *n.* bole, branch, kex, shoot, spire, stem, sterigma, trunk.

stall[1] *v.* delay, equivocate, hedge, obstruct, penelopize, play for time, prevaricate, stonewall, temporize.

antonym advance.

stall[2] *n.* bay, bench, booth, compartment, cowshed, pew, seat, stable, table.

stammer *v.* falter, gibber, hesitate, splutter, stumble, stutter.

stamp *v.* beat, brand, bray, categorize, characterize, crush, engrave, exhibit, fix, identify, impress, imprint, inscribe, label, mark, mint, mold, pound, print, pronounce, reveal, strike, trample.

n. attestation, authorization, brand, breed, cast, character, cut, description, earmark, evidence, fashion, form, hallmark, impression, imprint, incuse, kind, mark, mold, sign, signature, sort, stomp, type.

stand *v.* abide, allow, bear, belong, brook, continue, cost, countenance, demur, endure, erect, exist, experience, halt, handle, hold, mount, obtain, pause, place, position,

prevail, put, rank, remain, rest, rise, scruple, set, stay, stomach, stop, suffer, support, sustain, take, thole, tolerate, undergo, wear, weather, withstand.

antonym advance.

n. attitude, base, booth, bracket, cradle, dais, determination, erection, frame, grandstand, halt, holder, loss, opinion, place, platform, position, rack, rank, resistance, rest, stage, staging, stall, stance, standpoint, standstill, stay, stop, stop-over, stoppage, support, table, tub, vat, witness-box.

antonym progress.

standard[1] *n.* average, bench-mark, canon, criterion, example, exemplar, gauge, grade, guide, guideline, level, measure, model, norm, norma, pattern, principle, requirement, rule, sample, specification, touchstone, type, yardstick.

adj. accepted, approved, authoritative, average, basic, classic, customary, definitive, established, mainstream, normal, official, orthodox, popular, prevailing, recognized, regular, set, staple, stock, typical, usual.

antonyms abnormal, irregular, unusual.

standard[2] *n.* banner, colors, ensign, flag, gonfalon, gonfanon, labarum, pennant, pennon, rallying-point, streamer, vexillum.

standing *n.* condition, continuance, credit, duration, eminence, estimation, existence, experience, footing, position, rank, reputation, repute, seniority, station, status.

adj. erect, fixed, lasting, on one's feet, permanent, perpendicular, perpetual, rampant, regular, repeated, upended, upright, vertical.

antonyms horizontal, lying.

standpoint *n.* angle, point of view, position, post, stance, station, vantage-point, viewpoint, Weltanschauung.

staple *adj.* basic, chief, essential, fundamental, key, leading, main, major, predominant, primary, principle.

antonym minor.

stare *v.* gape, gawk, gawp, gaze, glare, goggle, look, watch.

n. fish-eye, gaze, glare, glower, leer, look, ogle, scowl.

stark *adj.* absolute, arrant, austere, bald, bare, barren, bleak, blunt, cold, consummate, depressing, desolate, downright, drear, dreary, entire, flagrant, forsaken, grim, harsh, out-and-out, palpable, patent, plain, pure, severe, sheer, simple, solitary, stern, stiff, strong, unadorned, unalloyed, unmitigated, unyielding, utter.

antonyms mild, slight.

adv. absolutely, altogether, clean, completely, entirely, quite, stoutly, totally, utterly, wholly.

antonyms mildly, slightly.

start *v.* activate, appear, arise, begin, blench, break away, commence, create, dart, depart, engender, establish, father, flinch, found, inaugurate, initiate, instigate, institute, introduce, issue, jerk, jump, kick off, launch, leave, open, originate, pioneer, recoil, sally forth, set off, set out, set up, shoot, shy, spring forward, twitch.

antonyms finish, stop.

n. advantage, backing, beginning, birth, break, chance, commencement, convulsion, dawn, edge, fit, foundation, inauguration, inception, initiation, introduction, jar, jump, kick-off, lead, onset, opening, opportunity, outburst, outset, spasm, sponsorship, spurt, twitch. *antonyms* finish, stop.

startle *v.* affray, agitate, alarm, amaze, astonish, astound, electrify, flush, frighten, scare, shock, spook, start, surprise. *antonym* calm.

starving *adj.* famished, hungering, hungry, ravenous, sharpset, starved, underfed, undernourished. *antonym* fed.

state[1] *v.* affirm, articulate, assert, asseverate, aver, declare, enumerate, explain, expound, express, formalize, formulate, formulize, present, propound, put, report, say, specify, voice.
n. attitude, bother, case, category, ceremony, circumstances, condition, dignity, display, flap, glory, grandeur, humor, majesty, mode, mood, panic, pass, phase, plight, pomp, position, pother, predicament, shape, situation, spirits, splendor, stage, station, style, tizzy. *antonym* calmness.

state[2] *n.* body politic, commonwealth, country, federation, government, kingdom, land, leviathan, nation, republic, territory.
adj. ceremonial, ceremonious, formal, governmental, magnificent, national, official, pompous, public, solemn.

stately *adj.* august, ceremonious, deliberate, dignified, elegant, grand, imperial, imposing, impressive, Junoesque, kingly, lofty, majestic, measured, noble, pompous, princely, queenly, regal, royal, solemn. *antonyms* informal, unimpressive.

statement *n.* account, announcement, bulletin, communication, communiqué, constatation, declaration, explanation, ipse dixit, ipsissima verba, proclamation, recital, relation, report, testimony, utterance, verbal.

station *n.* appointment, base, business, calling, depot, employment, grade, habitat, head-quarters, location, occupation, office, place, position, post, rank, seat, situation, sphere, stance, standing, standing-place, status, stopping-place.
v. appoint, assign, establish, fix, garrison, install, locate, post, send, set.

statuesque *adj.* dignified, imposing, majestic, regal, stately, statuary. *antonym* small.

status *n.* character, condition, consequence, degree, distinction, eminence, grade, importance, position, prestige, rank, standing, state, weight. *antonym* unimportance.

statute *n.* act, decree, edict, enactment, indiction, interlocution, irade, law, ordinance, regulation, rescript, rule, ukase.

staunch[1] *adj.* constant, dependable, faithful, firm, hearty, loyal, reliable, resolute, sound, steadfast, stout, strong, sure, true, true-blue, trustworthy, trusty, watertight, yeomanly, zealous. *antonyms* unreliable, wavering, weak.

staunch[2] *same as* **stanch**.

stay[1] *v.* abide, adjourn, allay, arrest, check, continue, curb, defer, delay, detain, discontinue, dwell, endure, halt, hinder, hold, hold out, hover, impede, last, linger, live, lodge, loiter, obstruct, pause, prevent, prorogue, remain, reside, restrain, settle, sojourn, stand, stop, suspend, tarry, visit, wait. *antonyms* advance, leave.
n. continuance, deferment, delay, halt, holiday, pause, postponement, remission, reprieve, sojourn, stop, stopover, stopping, suspension, visit.

stay[2] *n.* brace, buttress, prop, reinforcement, shoring, stanchion, support.
v. buttress, prop, prop up, shore up, support, sustain.

steadfast *adj.* constant, dedicated, dependable, established, faithful, fast, firm, fixed, intent, loyal, perseverant, persevering, reliable, resolute, singleminded, stable, staunch, steady, unfaltering, unflinching, unswerving, unwavering. *antonyms* unreliable, wavering, weak.

steady *adj.* balanced, calm, ceaseless, confirmed, consistent, constant, continuous, dependable, equable, even, faithful, firm, fixed, habitual, immovable, imperturbable, incessant, industrious, level-headed, nonstop, persistent, regular, reliable, rhythmic, safe, sedate, sensible, serene, serious-minded, settled, sober, stable, staid, steadfast, substantial, unbroken, unchangeable, unfaltering, unfluctuating, unhasting, unhasty, unhurried, uniform, uninterrupted, unremitting, unswerving, unvarying, unwavering. *antonyms* unsteady, wavering.
v. balance, brace, firm, fix, secure, stabilize, support.

steal *v.* appropriate, bone, cly, convey, creep, embezzle, filch, flit, half-inch, heist, knap, knock off, lag, lift, mill, misappropriate, nab, nick, peculate, pilfer, pinch, pirate, plagiarize, poach, purloin, relieve someone of, rip off, shoplift, slink, slip, smouch, smug, snaffle, snatch, sneak, snitch, swipe, take, thieve, tiptoe. *antonym* return.

stealthy *adj.* cat-like, clandestine, covert, furtive, quiet, secret, secretive, skulking, sly, sneaking, sneaky, surreptitious, underhand. *antonym* open.

steamy *adj.* close, damp, gaseous, hazy, humid, misty, muggy, roky, steaming, stewy, sticky, sultry, sweaty, sweltering, vaporiform, vaporous, vaporish, vapory.

steep[1] *adj.* abrupt, bluff, excessive, exorbitant, extortionate, extreme, headlong, high, overpriced, precipitous, sheer, stiff, uncalled-for, unreasonable. *antonyms* gentle, moderate.

steep[2] *v.* brine, damp, drench, fill, imbrue, imbue, immerse, infuse, macerate, marinate, moisten, permeate, pervade, pickle, saturate, seethe, soak, souse, submerge, suffuse.

steer v. con, conduct, control, direct, govern, guide, pilot.

stem[1] n. axis, branch, family, house, line, lineage, peduncle, race, shoot, stalk, stock, trunk.

stem[2] v. check, contain, curb, dam, oppose, resist, restrain, stanch, stay, stop, tamp.
antonyms encourage, increase.

stench n. mephitis, odor, pong, reek, stink, whiff.

step n. act, action, advance, advancement, deed, degree, demarche, doorstep, expedient, footfall, footprint, footstep, gait, halfpace, impression, level, maneuver, means, measure, move, pace, phase, point, print, procedure, proceeding, process, progression, rank, remove, round, rung, stage, stair, stride, trace, track, tread, walk.
v. move, pace, stalk, stamp, tread, walk.

stereotyped adj. banal, cliché'd, cliché-ridden, conventional, corny, hackneyed, mass-produced, overused, platitudinous, stale, standard, standardized, stock, threadbare, tired, trite, unoriginal.
antonyms different, unconventional.

sterile adj. abortive, acarpous, antiseptic, aseptic, bare, barren, disinfected, dry, empty, fruitless, germ- free, infecund, pointless, sterilized, unfruitful, unimaginative, unproductive, unprofitable, unprolific.
antonyms fruitful, septic.

stern adj. austere, authoritarian, bitter, cruel, flinty, forbidding, frowning, grim, hard, harsh, inflexible, relentless, rigid, rigorous, serious, severe, stark, steely, strict, unrelenting, unsmiling, unsparing, unyielding.
antonym mild.

stew v. agonize, boil, braise, fret, fricassee, fuss, jug, perspire, seethe, simmer, sweat, swelter, worry.
n. agitation, bother, bouillabaisse, chowder, daube, fluster, fret, fuss, goulash, hash, lobscouse, pot-au-feu, pother, ragout, tizzy, worry.

stick[1] v. abid, adhere, affix, attach, bind, bond, bulge, catch, cement, cleave, cling, clog, deposit, dig, drop, endure, extend, fasten, fix, fuse, glue, gore, hold, insert, install, jab, jam, join, jut, lay, linger, lodge, obtrude, paste, penetrate, persist, pierce, pin, place, plant, plonk, poke, position, prod, project, protrude, puncture, put, put up with, remain, set, show, snag, spear, stab, stand, stay, stomach, stop, store, stuff, take, thole, thrust, tolerate, transfix, weld.
antonym unstick.

stick[2] n. baton, bavin, birch, bludgeon, branch, cane, lathi, lug, pole, quarterstaff, rod, scepter, staff, stake, stave, switch, twig, wand, whip, withy.

stick[3] n. abuse, blame, criticism, flak, hostility, punishment, reproof.
antonym praise.

stickler n. fanatic, fusspot, maniac, martinet, nut, pedant, perfectionist, precisianist, purist.

sticky adj. adhesive, awkward, claggy, clammy, clinging, clingy, cloggy, close, dauby, delicate, difficult, discomforting, embarrassing, gluey, glutinous, gooey, gummy, hairy, humid, muggy, nasty, oppressive, painful, smeary, sultry, sweltering, syrupy, tacky, tenacious, thorny, tricky, unpleasant, viscid, viscous.
antonyms cool, dry, easy.

stiff adj. arduous, arthritic, artificial, austere, awkward, brisk, brittle, buckram, budge, ceremonious, chilly, clumsy, cold, constrained, creaky, crude, cruel, difficult, drastic, exacting, excessive, extreme, fatiguing, firm, forced, formal, formidable, fresh, graceless, great, hard, hardened, harsh, heavy, inelastic, inelegant, inexorable, inflexible, jerky, laborious, labored, mannered, oppressive, pertinacious, pitiless, pokerish, pompous, powerful, priggish, prim, punctilious, resistant, rheumaticky, rigid, rigorous, severe, sharp, solid, solidified, stand-offish, starch(y), stark, stilted, strict, stringent, strong, stubborn, taut, tense, tight, toilsome, tough, trying, unbending, uneasy, ungainly, ungraceful, unnatural, unrelaxed, unsupple, unyielding, uphill, vigorous, wooden.
antonyms flexible, graceful, informal, mild.

stifle v. asphyxiate, check, choke, curb, dampen, extinguish, hush, muffle, prevent, repress, restrain, silence, smother, stop, strangle, suffocate, suppress.
antonym encourage.

stigma n. blemish, blot, brand, disgrace, dishonor, imputation, mark, reproach, shame, slur, smirch, spot, stain.
antonym credit.

still adj. calm, hushed, inert, lifeless, motionless, noiseless, pacific, peaceful, placid, quiet, restful, serene, silent, smooth, stagnant, stationary, stilly, tranquil, undisturbed, unruffled, unstirring.
antonyms agitated, busy, disturbed, noisy.
v. allay, alleviate, appease, calm, hold back, hush, lull, pacify, quiet, quieten, restrain, settle, silence, smooth, soothe, subdue, tranquilize.
antonyms agitate, stir up.
n. hush, peace, peacefulness, quiet, quietness, silence, stillness, tranquility.
antonyms agitation, disturbance, noise.
adv. but, even so, even then, however, nevertheless, nonetheless, notwithstanding, yet.

stimulate v. animate, arouse, encourage, fan, fire, foment, get psyched up, goad, hop up, hype up, impel, incite, inflame, instigate, jog, prompt, provoke, psych oneself up, quicken, rouse, spur, titillate, urge, whet.
antonym discourage.

stimulus n. carrot, encouragement, fillip, ginger, goad, incentive, incitement, inducement, prick, provocation, spur.
antonym discouragement.

stingy adj. avaricious, cheeseparing, close-fisted, covetous, illiberal, inadequate, insufficient, meager, mean, measly, mingy, miserly, near, niggardly, parsimonious,

penny- pinching, penurious, save-all, scanty, scrimping, small, tightfisted, ungenerous, ungiving.
antonym generous.

stinking *adj.* boozed, canned, contemptible, disgusting, drunk, fetid, foul-smelling, graveolent, grotty, ill- smelling, intoxicated, low, low-down, malodorous, mean, mephitic, noisome, pissed, plastered, pongy, reeking, rotten, smashed, smelly, sozzled, stenchy, stewed, stoned, unpleasant, vile, whiffy, wretched.
antonyms good, pleasant, sober.

stipulate *v.* agree, contract, covenant, engage, guarantee, insist upon, lay down, pledge, postulate, promise, provide, require, settle, specify.
antonym imply.

stir *v.* affect, agitate, beat, bestir, budge, disturb, electrify, emove, excite, fire, flutter, hasten, inspire, look lively, mix, move, quiver, rustle, shake, shake a leg, thrill, touch, tremble.
antonyms bore, calm, stay.
n. activity, ado, agitation, bustle, commotion, disorder, disturbance, excitement, ferment, flurry, fuss, hustle and bustle, movement, to-do, toing and froing, tumult, uproar.
antonym calm.

stock *n.* ancestry, array, assets, assortment, background, beasts, block, breed, cache, capital, cattle, choice, commodities, descent, equipment, estimation, extraction, family, flocks, forebears, fund, funds, goods, handle, herds, hoard, horses, house, inventory, investment, kindred, line, lineage, livestock, log, merchandise, parentage, pedigree, post, property, race, range, repertoire, repute, reserve, reservoir, selection, sheep, source, stem, stockpile, store, strain, stump, supply, trunk, type, variety, wares.
adj. banal, basic, bromidic, clichéd, commonplace, conventional, customary, formal, hackneyed, ordinary, overused, regular, routine, run-of-the-mill, set, standard, staple, stereotyped, traditional, trite, usual, worn-out.
antonym original.
v. deal in, handle, keep, sell, supply, trade in.

stoical *adj.* calm, cool, dispassionate, impassive, imperturbable, indifferent, long-suffering, patient, philosophic(al), phlegmatic, resigned, stoic, stolid.
antonyms anxious, depressed, furious, irascible.

stolid *adj.* apathetic, beefy, blockish, bovine, doltish, dull, heavy, impassive, lumpish, obtuse, slow, stoic(al), stupid, unemotional, wooden.
antonyms interested, lively.

stone *n.* boulder, cobble, concretion, endocarp, flagstone, gem, gemstone, gravestone, headstone, jewel, kernel, lapis, pebble, pip, pit, rock, seed, set(t), slab, tombstone.

stony *adj.* adamant, blank, callous, chilly, expressionless, frigid, hard, heartless, hostile, icy, indifferent, inexorable, lapideous, lapilliform, lithoid(al), merciless, obdurate, pitiless, steely, stonelike, unfeeling, unforgiving, unresponsive.

antonyms forgiving, friendly, soft-hearted.

stoop *v.* bend, bow, couch, crouch, descend, duck, hunch, incline, kneel, lean, squat.
n. droop, inclination, round-shoulderedness, sag, slouch, slump.

stop *v.* arrest, bar, block, break, cease, check, close, conclude, desist, discontinue, embar, end, finish, forestall, frustrate, halt, hinder, impede, intercept, intermit, interrupt, knock off, leave off, lodge, obstruct, pack (it) in, pack in, pack up, pause, plug, poop out, prevent, quit, refrain, repress, rest, restrain, scotch, seal, silence, sojourn, stall, staunch, stay, stem, stymie, suspend, tarry, terminate.
antonyms advance, continue, start.
n. bar, block, break, bung, cessation, check, conclusion, control, depot, destination, discontinuation, end, finish, halt, hindrance, impediment, plug, rest, sojourn, stage, standstill, station, stay, stop-over, stoppage, termination, terminus, ventage, visit.
antonyms continuation, start.
interj. avast, cease, cut it out, desist, easy, give over, halt, hang on, hold it, hold on, hold your horses, lay off, leave it out, refrain, stop it, wait, wait a minute, whoa.

store *v.* accumulate, cupboard, deposit, garner, hive, hoard, husband, keep, lay aside, lay by, lay in lavender, lay up, put aside, reserve, salt away, save, stash, stock, stockpile, treasure.
antonym use.
n. abundance, accumulation, cache, cupboard, depository, emporium, esteem, fund, hoard, keeping, lot, market, mart, mine, outlet, panary, plenty, plethora, provision, quantity, repository, reserve, reservoir, shop, stock, stockpile, storehouse, storeroom, supermarket, supply, value, warehouse, wealth.
antonym scarcity.

storm *n.* agitation, anger, assault, attack, blast, blitz, blitzkrieg, blizzard, clamor, commotion, cyclone, disturbance, dust-devil, furore, gale, gust, hubbub, hurricane, offensive, onset, onslaught, outbreak, outburst, outcry, paroxysm, passion, roar, row, rumpus, rush, sandstorm, squall, stir, strife, tempest, tornado, tumult, turmoil, violence, whirlwind.
antonym calm.
v. assail, assault, beset, bluster, charge, complain, expugn, flounce, fly, fume, rage, rant, rave, rush, scold, stalk, stamp, stomp, thunder.

stormy *adj.* blustering, blustery, boisterous, choppy, dirty, foul, gustful, gusty, oragious, raging, rough, squally, tempestuous, turbulent, wild, windy.
antonym calm.

story[1] *n.* account, ancedote, article, chronicle, episode, fable, fairy-tale, falsehood, feature, fib, fiction, historiette, history, legend, lie, Märchen, myth, narration, narrative, news, novel, plot, recital, record, relation, report, romance, scoop, spiel, tale, untruth, version, yarn.

story[2] *n.* deck, étage, flight, floor, level, stage, stratum, tier.

stout *adj.* able-bodied, athletic, beefy, big, bold, brave, brawny, bulky, burly, chopping, corpulent, courageous, dauntless, doughty, embonpoint, enduring, fat, fearless, fleshy, gallant, hardy, heavy, hulking, husky, intrepid, lion-hearted, lusty, manly, muscular, obese, overweight, plucky, plump, portly, resolute, robust, rotund, stalwart, strapping, strong, sturdy, substantial, thick, tough, tubby, valiant, valorous, vigorous.
antonyms slim, timid, weak.

straight *adj.* accurate, aligned, arranged, authentic, balanced, blunt, bourgeois, candid, consecutive, conservative, continuous, conventional, decent, direct, downright, equitable, erect, even, fair, forthright, frank, honest, honorable, horizontal, just, law-abiding, level, near, neat, nonstop, normal, orderly, organized, orthodox, outright, perpendicular, plain, plumb, point-blank, pure, reliable, respectable, right, running, settled, shipshape, short, smooth, solid, square, straightforward, successive, sustained, through, tidy, traditional, true, trustworthy, unadulterated, undeviating, undiluted, uninterrupted, unmixed, unqualified, unrelieved, unswerving, upright, vertical.
antonyms circuitous, dilute, dishonest, evasive, indirect, roundabout.
adv. candidly, directly, frankly, honestly, outspokenly, point-blank, upright.

straightforward *adj.* candid, clear-cut, direct, easy, elementary, forthright, genuine, guileless, honest, open, open-and-shut, penny-plain, routine, simple, sincere, truthful, uncomplicated, undemanding.
antonyms complicated, devious, evasive.

strain[1] *v.* compress, distend, drive, embrace, endeavor, exert, express, extend, fatigue, filter, injure, labor, overtax, overwork, percolate, pull, purify, restrain, retch, riddle, screen, seep, separate, sieve, sift, sprain, squeeze, stretch, strive, struggle, tauten, tax, tear, tighten, tire, tug, twist, weaken, wrench, wrest, wrick.
n. anxiety, burden, effort, exertion, force, height, injury, key, pitch, pressure, pull, sprain, stress, struggle, tautness, tension, wrench.

strain[2] *n.* ancestry, blood, descent, extraction, family, humor, lineage, manner, pedigree, race, spirit, stem, stock, streak, style, suggestion, suspicion, temper, tendency, tone, trace, trait, vein, way.

strained *adj.* artificial, awkward, constrained, difficult, embarrassed, epitonic, false, forced, labored, self-conscious, stiff, tense, uncomfortable, uneasy, unnatural, unrelaxed.
antonym natural.

straitened *adj.* difficult, distressed, embarrassed, impoverished, limited, poor, reduced, restricted.
antonyms easy, well-off.

strait-laced *adj.* moralistic, narrow, narrow-minded, oldmaidish, prim, proper, prudish, puritanical, strict, stuffy, upright, Victorian.
antonyms broad-minded, easy-going.

strange *adj.* abnormal, alien, astonishing, awkward, bewildered, bizarre, curious, disorientated, disoriented, eccentric, eerie, exceptional, exotic, extraordinary, fantastic(al), foreign, funny, irregular, lost, marvelous, mystifying, new, novel, odd, out-of-the-way, peculiar, perplexing, queer, rare, remarkable, remote, singular, sinister, unaccountable, unacquainted, uncanny, unco, uncomfortable, uncommon, unexplained, unexplored, unfamiliar, unheard of, unknown, untried, unversed, weird, wonderful.
antonyms comfortable, common, familiar, ordinary.

stranger *n.* alien, foreigner, guest, incomer, newcomer, non-member, outlander, unknown, visitor.
antonyms local, native.

strap *n.* belt, leash, thong, tie, vitta.
v. beat, belt, bind, buckle, fasten, flog, lash, scourge, secure, tie, truss, whip.

stratagem *n.* artifice, device, dodge, feint, fetch, intrigue, maneuver, plan, plot, ploy, ruse, ruse de guerre, scheme, subterfuge, trick, wile.

strategy *n.* approach, design, maneuvering, plan, planning, policy, procedure, program, scheme, way.

stray *v.* deviate, digress, diverge, drift, err, get lost, meander, ramble, range, roam, rove, straggle, wander (off).
adj. abandoned, accidental, chance, erratic, forwandered, freak, homeless, lost, odd, random, roaming, scattered, vagrant.

stream *n.* beck, brook, burn, course, creek, current, drift, flow, freshet, ghyll, gill, gush, outpouring, rill, rillet, river, rivulet, run, runnel, rush, surge, tide, torrent, tributary.
v. cascade, course, emit, flood, flow, glide, gush, issue, pour, run, shed, spill, spout, surge, well out.

streamer *n.* banner, ensign, flag, gonfalon, gonfanon, pennant, pennon, plume, ribbon, standard.

street *n.* avenue, boulevard, corso, crescent, drive, expressway, freeway, highway, lane, main drag, parkway, road, roadway, row, terrace, thoroughfare, thruway, turnpike.

strength *n.* advantage, anchor, asset, backbone, brawn, brawniness, cogency, concentration, courage, effectiveness, efficacy, energy, firmness, foison, force, fortitude, fushion, health, intensity, lustiness, mainstay, might, muscle, potency, power, resolution, robustness, security, sinew, spirit, stamina, stoutness, sturdiness, thew, toughness, vehemence, vigor, virtue.
antonyms timidness, weakness.

strengthen *v.* afforce, bolster, brace, buttress, confirm, consolidate, corroborate, edify, encourage, enhance, establish, fortify, harden, hearten, heighten, increase, intensify, invigorate, justify, nerve, nourish, reinforce, rejuvenate, restore, steel, stiffen, substantiate, support, toughen.
antonym weaken.

strenuous *adj.* active, arduous, bold, demanding, determined, eager, earnest, energetic, exhausting, hard, Herculean, laborious, persistent, resolute, spirited, strong, taxing, tireless, toilful, toilsome, tough, uphill, urgent, vigorous, warm, zealous.

antonyms easy, effortless.

stress *n.* accent, accentuation, anxiety, beat, burden, emphasis, emphaticalness, force, hassle, importance, oppression, pressure, significance, strain, tautness, tension, trauma, urgency, weight, worry.

antonym relaxation.

v. accentuate, belabor, emphasize, repeat, strain, tauten, underline, underscore.

antonym relax.

stretch *n.* area, bit, distance, exaggeration, expanse, extensibility, extension, extent, period, reach, run, space, spell, spread, stint, strain, sweep, term, time, tract.

v. cover, distend, elongate, expand, extend, inflate, lengthen, pull, rack, reach, spread, strain, swell, tauten, tighten, unfold, unroll.

antonyms relax, squeeze.

strict *adj.* absolute, accurate, austere, authoritarian, close, complete, exact, faithful, firm, harsh, meticulous, nononsense, particular, perfect, precise, religious, restricted, rigid, rigorous, scrupulous, severe, stern, stringent, thoroughgoing, total, true, unsparing, utter, Victorian.

antonyms easy-going, flexible, mild.

strident *adj.* cacophonous, clamorous, clashing, discordant, grating, harsh, jangling, jarring, loud, rasping, raucous, screeching, shrill, stridulant, stridulous, unmusical, vociferous.

antonyms quiet, sweet.

strife *n.* animosity, battle, bickering, brigue, colluctation, combat, conflict, contention, contest, contestation, controversy, discord, dissension, friction, quarrel, rivalry, row, squabbling, struggle, warfare, wrangling.

antonym peace.

strike *n.* attack, buffet, hit, mutiny, raid, refusal, stoppage, thump, walk-out, wallop, work-to-rule.

v. achieve, affect, afflict, arrange, assail, assault, assume, attack, attain, bang, beat, bop, box, buff, buffet, cancel, chastise, clap, clash, clobber, clout, clump, cob, coin, collide with, cuff, dart, dash, delete, devastate, discover, dismantle, douse, down tools, drive, dunt, effect, encounter, find, force, hammer, hit, impel, impress, interpose, invade, knock, mutiny, penetrate, pierce, pound, print, punish, ratify, reach, register, remove, revolt, seem, shoot, slap, slat, smack, smite, sock, stamp, stumble across, stumble upon, surrender, swap, swipe, swop, thrust, thump, touch, trap, turn up, uncover, unearth, walk out, wallop, wham, work to rule, zap.

striking *adj.* arresting, astonishing, conspicuous, dazzling, distingué(e), extraordinary, forcible, foudroyant, frappant, impressive, memorable, noticeable, outstanding, salient, stunning, wonderful.

antonym unimpressive.

stringent *adj.* binding, demanding, exacting, flexible, inflexible, mild, rigid, rigorous, severe, strict, tight, tough.

strip[1] *v.* bare, clear, defoliate, denude, deprive, despoil, devest, disadorn, disembellish, disgarnish, disinvest, disleaf, disleave, dismantle, displenish, disrobe, divest, doff, empty, excoriate, excorticate, expose, gut, husk, lay bare, loot, peel, pillage, plunder, ransack, rob, sack, skin, spoil, unclothe, uncover, undress, widow.

antonyms cover, provide.

strip[2] *n.* band, belt, bit, fillet, lath, list, piece, ribbon, sash, screed, shred, slat, slip, spline, strake, strap, swathe, thong, tongue, vitta.

stripe *n.* band, bar, belt, chevron, flash, fleck, striation, vitta.

strive *v.* attempt, compete, contend, endeavor, fight, labor, push oneself, strain, struggle, toil, try, work.

stroke *n.* accomplishnment, achievement, apoplexy, attack, blow, clap, collapse, effleurage, feat, fit, flourish, hit, knock, move, movement, pat, rap, seizure, shock, swap, swop, thump.

v. caress, clap, fondle, pat, pet, rub.

stroll *v.* amble, dander, dawdle, mosey, promenade, ramble, saunter, stooge, toddle, wander.

n. airing, constitutional, dawdle, excursion, promenade, ramble, saunter, toddle, turn, walk.

strong *adj.* acute, aggressive, athletic, beefy, biting, bold, brave, brawny, bright, brilliant, burly, capable, clear, clear-cut, cogent, compelling, competent, concentrated, convincing, courageous, dazzling, dedicated, deep, deep-rooted, determined, distinct, drastic, durable, eager, effective, efficient, emphasized, excelling, extreme, fastmoving, fervent, fervid, fierce, firm, forceful, forcible, formidable, glaring, great, grievous, gross, hale, hard, hard-nosed, hard-wearing, hardy, heady, healthy, hearty, heavy-duty, Herculean, highly-flavored, highly-seasoned, hot, intemperate, intense, intoxicating, keen, loud, lusty, marked, muscular, nappy, numerous, offensive, overpowering, persuasive, petrous, piquant, pithy, plucky, pollent, potent, powerful, pungent, pure, rank, redoubtable, reinforced, resilient, resolute, resourceful, robust, self-assertive, severe, sharp, sinewy, sound, spicy, stalwart, stark, staunch, steadfast, sthenic, stout, stout-hearted, strapping, stressed, sturdy, substantial, telling, tenacious, thewy, tough, trenchant, undiluted, unmistakable, unseemly, unyielding, urgent, vehement, violent, virile, vivid, weighty, well-armed, well-built, well-established, well-founded, well-knit, well-protected, well-set, well-versed, zealous.

antonyms mild, weak.

structure *n.* arrangement, building, compages, configuration, conformation, construction, contexture, design, edifice, erection, fabric, form, formation, make-up, organization, pile, set-up.

v. arrange, assemble, build, construct, design, form, organize, shape.

struggle *v.* agonize, battle, compete, contend, fight, grapple, labor, scuffle, strain, strive, toil, work, wrestle.

antonyms give in, rest.

n. agon, agony, battle, brush, clash, combat, conflict, contest, effort, encounter, exertion, grind, hostilities, labor, luctation, pains, scramble, skirmish, strife, toil, tussle, work. *antonyms* ease, submission.

stubborn *adj.* bull-headed, contumacious, cross- grained, difficult, dogged, dour, fixed, headstrong, inflexible, intractable, intransigent, mulish, obdurate, obstinate, opinionated, persistent, pertinacious, pig-headed, recalcitrant, refractory, rigid, self-willed, stiff, stiff-necked, tenacious, unbending, unmanageable, unshakable, unyielding, wilful.
antonym compliant.

student *n.* apprentice, bajan, bejant, bookman, chela, coed, collegianer, contemplator, disciple, fresher, freshman, learner, observer, pupil, scholar, seminarist, soph, sophomore, undergraduate, undergraduette.

studio *n.* atelier, school, workroom, workshop.

study *v.* analyze, cogitate, con, consider, contemplate, cram, deliberate, dig, examine, investigate, learn, lucubrate, meditate, mug up, peruse, ponder, pore over, read, read up, research, scan, scrutinize, survey, swot. *n.* analysis, application, attention, cogitation, consideration, contemplation, cramming, critique, examination, inclination, inquiry, inspection, interest, investigation, learning, lessons, lucubration, memoir, monograph, prolusion, reading, report, research, reverie, review, scrutiny, survey, swotting, thesis, thought, zeal.

stuff *v.* binge, bombast, compress, cram, crowd, fill, force, gobble, gorge, gormandize, guzzle, jam, load, overindulge, pack, pad, push, ram, sate, satiate, shove, squeeze, steeve, stodge, stow, trig, wedge. *antonyms* nibble, unload.
n. belongings, clobber, cloth, effects, equipment, essence, fabric, furniture, gear, goods, impedimenta, junk, kit, luggage, material, materials, matériel, matter, objects, paraphernalia, pith, possessions, provisions, quintessence, staple, substance, tackle, textile, things, trappings.

stumble *v.* blunder, fall, falter, flounder, fluff, hesitate, lurch, reel, slip, stagger, stammer, stutter, titubate, trip.

stun *v.* amaze, astonish, astound, bedeafen, bewilder, confound, confuse, daze, deafen, dumbfound, flabbergast, overcome, overpower, shock, stagger, stupefy.

stunning *adj.* beautiful, brilliant, dazing, dazzling, devastating, gorgeous, great, heavenly, impressive, lovely, marvelous, ravishing, remarkable, sensational, smashing, spectacular, stotting, striking, wonderful. *antonyms* poor, ugly.

stunt[1] *n.* act, campaign, deed, enterprise, exploit, feat, feature, gest(e), performance, tour de force, trick, turn.

stunt[2] *v.* arrest, check, dwarf, hamper, hinder, impede, restrict, slow, stop.
antonym promote.

stupefy *v.* amaze, astound, baffle, benumb, bewilder, confound, daze, drowse, dumbfound, hocus, numb, shock, stagger, stun.

stupid *adj.* anserine, asinine, beef-brained, beef- witted, blockish, Boeotian, boobyish, boring, bovine, brainless, clueless, crackbrained, cretinous, cuckoo, damfool, dazed, deficient, dense, dim, doltish, dopey, dovie, dozy, drippy, dull, dumb, fat-witted, foolish, fozy, futile, gaumless, glaikit, gormless, groggy, gullible, half-baked, half-witted, hammer- headed, idiotic, ill-advised, imbecilic, inane, indiscreet, insensate, insensible, insulse, irrelevant, irresponsible, laughable, ludicrous, lumpen, lurdan, meaningless, mindless, moronic, naïve, nonsensical, obtuse, opaque, pointless, puerile, punch-drunk, rash, semiconscious, senseless, short-sighted, simple, simple-minded, slow, slow-witted, sluggish, stolid, stunned, stupefied, thick, thick-headed, thick-witted, trivial, unintelligent, unthinking, vacuous, vapid, witless, wooden- headed.
antonyms alert, clever.

stupor *n.* coma, daze, inertia, insensibility, kef, lethargy, numbness, stupefaction, torpor, trance, unconsciousness, wonder.
antonym alertness

sturdy *adj.* athletic, brawny, determined, durable, firm, flourishing, hardy, hearty, husky, lusty, muscular, obstinate, powerful, resolute, robust, secure, solid, stalwart, staunch, steadfast, stout, strong, substantial, vigorous, well- built, well-made.
antonyms decrepit, puny.

style *n.* affluence, appearance, approach, bon ton, category, chic, comfort, cosmopolitanism, custom, cut, dash, design, diction, dressiness, dress-sense, ease, élan, elegance, expression, fashion, fashionableness, flair, flamboyance, form, genre, grace, grandeur, hand, haut ton, kind, luxury, manner, method, mode, panache, pattern, phraseology, phrasing, pizzazz, polish, rage, refinement, savoir-faire, smartness, sophistication, sort, spirit, strain, stylishness, taste, technique, tenor, tone, treatment, trend, type, urbanity, variety, vein, vogue, way, wording.
antonym inelegance.
v. adapt, address, arrange, call, christen, create, cut, denominate, design, designate, dress, dub, entitle, fashion, label, name, shape, tailor, term, title.

suave *adj.* affable, agreeable, bland, charming, civilized, courteous, diplomatic, gracious, obliging, pleasing, polite, smooth, smooth-tongued, soft-spoken, sophisticated, unctuous, urbane, worldly.
antonym unsophisticated.

subdue *v.* allay, break, check, conquer, control, crush, damp, dampen, daunt, defeat, discipline, humble, master, mellow, moderate, overcome, overpower, overrun, quell, quieten, reduce, repress, soften, soft-pedal, subact, subject, suppress, tame, trample, vanquish.
antonym arouse.

subject *n.* affair, business, case, chapter, citizen, client, dependant, ground, issue, liegeman, matter, mind, national, object, participant, patient, point, question, subordinate, substance, theme, topic, vassal, victim. *antonym* master.

adj. answerable, captive, cognizable, conditional, contingent, dependent, disposed, enslaved, exposed, heteronomous, inferior, liable, obedient, open, prone, satellite, subjugated, submissive, subordinate, subservient, susceptible, vulnerable.

antonyms free, insusceptible, superior.

v. expose, lay open, subdue, submit, subordinate, treat.

sublime *adj.* Dantean, Dantesque, elevated, eminent, empyreal, empyrean, exalted, glorious, grand, great, high, imposing, lofty, magnificent, majestic, noble, transcendent. *antonym* lowly.

submerge *v.* deluge, demerge, dip, drown, duck, dunk, engulf, flood, immerse, implunge, inundate, overflow, overwhelm, plunge, sink, submerse, swamp.

antonym surface.

submissive *adj.* abject, accommodating, acquiescent, amenable, biddable, bootlicking, complaisant, compliant, deferential, docile, dutiful, humble, ingratiating, malleable, meek, obedient, obeisant, obsequious, passive, patient, pliant, resigned, subdued, subservient, supine, tractable, uncomplaining, unresisting, yielding. *antonym* intractable.

submit *v.* accede, acquiesce, advance, agree, argue, assert, bend, bow, capitulate, claim, commit, comply, contend, defer, endure, knuckle under, move, present, proffer, propose, propound, put, refer, state, stoop, succumb, suggest, surrender, table, tender, tolerate, volunteer, yield.

antonym struggle.

subordinate *adj.* ancillary, auxiliary, dependent, inferior, junior, lesser, lower, menial, minor, secondary, servient, subject, subservient, subsidiary, supplementary. *antonym* superior.

n. adjunct, aide, assistant, attendant, dependant, inferior, junior, second, second banana, stooge, sub, subaltern, underdog, underling, underman, under-workman, weakling.

antonym superior.

antonym superiority.

subpoena *n.* court order, decree, summons, writ.

subsequent *adj.* after, consequent, consequential, ensuing, following, later, postliminary, postliminous, resulting, succeeding.

antonym previous.

subside *v.* abate, collapse, decline, decrease, descend, diminish, drop, dwindle, ease, ebb, fall, lessen, lower, moderate, quieten, recede, settle, sink, slacken, slake, wane.

antonym increase.

subsidy *n.* aid, allowance, assistance, backing, contribution, finance, grant, help, sponsorship, subvention, support.

subsist *v.* continue, endure, exist, hold out, inhere, last, live, remain, survive.

substance *n.* actuality, affluence, assets, body, burden, concreteness, consistence, element, entity, essence, estate, fabric, force, foundation, gist, gravamen, ground, hypostasis, import, material, matter, meaning, means, nitty- gritty, pith, property, reality, resources, significance, solidity, stuff, subject, subject-matter, texture, theme, wealth.

substantial *adj.* actual, ample, big, bulky, considerable, corporeal, durable, enduring, essential, existent, firm, full-bodied, generous, goodly, hefty, important, large, massive, material, positive, real, significant, sizable, solid, sound, stout, strong, sturdy, tidy, true, valid, weighty, well- built, worthwhile.

antonyms insignificant, small.

substantiate *v.* affirm, authenticate, confirm, corroborate, embody, establish, prove, support, validate, verify. *antonym* disprove.

substitute *v.* change, commute, exchange, interchange, replace, subrogate, swap, switch.

n. agent, alternate, depute, deputy, equivalent, ersatz, locum, locum tenens, makeshift, proxy, relief, replacement, replacer, reserve, stand-by, stop-gap, sub, succedaneum, supply, surrogate, temp, vicar.

adj. acting, additional, alternative, ersatz, proxy, replacement, reserve, second, surrogate, temporary, vicarious.

substitution *n.* change, exchange, interchange, replacement, swap, swapping, switch, switching.

subterfuge *n.* artifice, deception, deviousness, dodge, duplicity, evasion, excuse, expedient, machination, maneuver, ploy, pretense, pretext, quibble, ruse, scheme, shift, stall, stratagem, trick.

antonyms honesty, openness.

subtle *adj.* artful, astute, crafty, cunning, deep, delicate, designing, devious, discriminating, elusive, faint, fine-drawn, fine-spun, impalpable, implied, indirect, ingenious, insinuated, intriguing, keen, Machiavellian, nice, obstruse, over-refined, penetrating, profound, rarefied, refined, scheming, shrewd, slight, sly, sophisticated, tenuous, understated, wily.

antonyms open, unsubtle.

subtract *v.* debit, deduct, detract, diminish, remove, withdraw.

antonyms add, add to.

subvert *v.* confound, contaminate, corrupt, debase, demolish, demoralize, deprave, destroy, disrupt, invalidate, overturn, pervert, poison, raze, ruin, sabotage, undermine, upset, vitiate, wreck.

antonyms boost, uphold.

succeed *v.* arrive, ensue, fadge, flourish, follow, make good, make it, prosper, result, supervene, thrive, triumph, work.

antonyms fail, precede.

success *n.* ascendancy, bestseller, celebrity, eminence, fame, fortune, happiness, hit, luck, prosperity, sensation, somebody, star, triumph, VIP, well-doing, winner. *antonym* failure.

successful *adj.* acknowledged, bestselling, booming, efficacious, favorable, flourishing, fortunate, fruitful, lucky, lucrative, moneymaking, paying, profitable, prosperous, rewarding, satisfactory, satisfying, thriven, thriving, top, unbeaten, victorious, wealthy, well-doing. *antonym* unsuccessful.

succession *n.* accession, assumption, chain, concatenation, continuation, course, cycle, descendants, descent, elevation, flow, inheritance, line, lineage, order, procession, progression, race, run, sequence, series, train.

successive *adj.* consecutive, following, in succession, sequent, succeeding.

succinct *adj.* brief, compact, compendious, concise, condensed, gnomic, laconic, pithy, short, summary, terse. *antonym* wordy.

succor *v.* aid, assist, befriend, comfort, encourage, foster, help, help out, nurse, relieve, support. *antonym* undermine.
n. aid, assistance, comfort, help, helping hand, ministrations, relief, support.

sudden *adj.* abrupt, hasty, hurried, impulsive, prompt, quick, rapid, rash, snap, startling, subitaneous, swift, unexpected, unforeseen, unusual. *antonym* slow.

suffer *v.* ache, agonize, allow, bear, brook, deteriorate, endure, experience, feel, grieve, hurt, let, permit, sorrow, support, sustain, tolerate, undergo.

suffering *n.* ache, affliction, agony, anguish, discomfort, distress, hardship, martyrdom, misery, ordeal, pain, pangs, torment, torture.

sufficient *adj.* adequate, competent, effective, enough, satisfactory, sufficing, well-off, well-to-do. *antonyms* insufficient, poor.

suffocate *v.* asphyxiate, choke, smother, stifle, strangle, throttle.

suggest *v.* advise, advocate, connote, evoke, hint, imply, indicate, inkle, innuendo, insinuate, intimate, move, propose, recommend. *antonyms* demonstrate, order.

suggestion *n.* breath, hint, incitement, indication, innuendo, insinuation, intimation, motion, plan, proposal, proposal, proposition, recommendation, suspicion, temptation, trace, whisper. *antonyms* demonstration, order.

suit *v.* accommodate, adapt, adjust, agree, answer, become, befit, correspond, do, fashion, fit, gee, gratify, harmonize, match, modify, please, proportion, satisfy, tailor, tally. *antonyms* clash, displease.
n. action, addresses, appeal, attentions, case, cause, clothing, costume, courtship, dress, ensemble, entreaty,

get-up, habit, invocation, kind, lawsuit, outfit, petition, prayer, proceeding, prosecution, request, rig-out, series, trial, type.

suitable *adj.* acceptable, accordant, adequate, applicable, apposite, appropriate, apt, becoming, befitting, competent, conformable, congenial, congruent, consonant, convenient, correspondent, due, fit, fitting, opportune, pertinent, proper, relevant, right, satisfactory, seemly, square, suited, well-becoming, well-beseeming. *antonym* unsuitable.

sulky *adj.* aloof, churlish, cross, disgruntled, grouty, ill-humored, moody, morose, perverse, pettish, petulant, put out, resentful, sullen. *antonym* cheerful.

sullen *adj.* baleful, brooding, cheerless, cross, dark, dismal, dull, farouche, gloomy, glowering, glum, heavy, lumpish, malignant, moody, morose, obstinate, perverse, silent, somber, sour, stubborn, sulky, surly, unsociable. *antonym* cheerful.

sultry *adj.* close, come-hither, erotic, hot, humid, indecent, lurid, muggy, oppressive, passionate, provocative, seductive, sensual, sexy, sticky, stifling, stuffy, sweltering, torrid, voluptuous. *antonyms* cold, cool.

sum *n.* aggregate, amount, completion, culmination, entirety, height, quantity, reckoning, result, score, substance, sum total, summary, tally, total, totality, whole.

summarize *v.* abbreviate, abridge, condense, encapsulate, epitomize, outline, précis, review, shorten, sum up. *antonym* expand (on).

summary *n.* abridgment, abstract, compendium, digest, epitome, essence, extract, outline, précis, recapitulation, résumé, review, rundown, summation, summing-up, synopsis.
adj. arbitrary, brief, compact, compendious, concise, condensed, cursory, expeditious, hasty, laconic, perfunctory, pithy, short, succinct. *antonym* lengthy.

summit *n.* acme, apex, apogee, crown, culmination, head, height, peak, pinnacle, point, top, zenith. *antonyms* bottom, nadir.

summon *v.* accite, arouse, assemble, beckon, bid, call, cite, convene, convoke, gather, hist, invite, invoke, mobilize, muster, preconize, rally, rouse. *antonym* dismiss.

sundry *adj.* a few, assorted, different, divers, miscellaneous, separate, several, some, varied, various.

sunny *adj.* beaming, blithe, bright, brilliant, buoyant, cheerful, cheery, clear, cloudless, fine, genial, happy, joyful, light-hearted, luminous, optimistic, pleasant, radiant, smiling, summery, sun-bright, sunlit, sunshiny. *antonym* gloomy.

superannuated *adj.* aged, antiquated, decrepit, fogram,

moribund, obsolete, old, past it, pensioned off, put out to grass, retired, senile, superannuate.
antonym young.

superb *adj.* admirable, breathtaking, choice, clipping, excellent, exquisite, fine, first-rate, gorgeous, grand, magnificent, marvelous, splendid, superior, unrivaled.
antonym poor.

supercilious *adj.* arrogant, condescending, contemptuous, disdainful, haughty, highty-tighty, hoity-toity, imperious, insolent, lofty, lordly, overbearing, patronizing, proud, scornful, snooty, snotty, snouty, stuck-up, toffee-nosed, uppish, uppity, upstage, vainglorious.
antonym humble.

superficial *adj.* apparent, casual, cosmetic, cursory, desultory, empty, empty-headed, evident, exterior, external, frivolous, hasty, hurried, lightweight, nodding, ostensible, outward, passing, perfunctory, peripheral, seeming, shallow, silly, sketchy, skin-deep, slapdash, slight, surface, trivial, unanalytical, unreflective.
antonym detailed.

superintend *v.* administer, control, direct, guide, inspect, manage, overlook, oversee, run, steer, supervise.

superintendence *n.* administration, care, charge, control, direction, government, guidance, inspection, management, supervision, surveillance.

superintendent *n.* administrator, chief, conductor, controller, curator, director, gaffer, governor, inspector, manager, overseer, supervisor.

superior *adj.* admirable, airy, better, choice, condescending, de luxe, disdainful, distinguished, excellent, exceptional, exclusive, fine, first-class, first-rate, good, grander, greater, haughty, high-class, higher, highty-tighty, hoity-toity, lofty, lordly, par excellence, patronizing, predominant, preferred, pretentious, prevailing, respectable, snobbish, snooty, snotty, snouty, stuck-up, supercilious, superordinate, surpassing, top-flight, top-notch, transcendent, unrivaled, upper, uppish, uppity, upstage, worthy.
antonyms humble, inferior.
n. boss, chief, director, foreman, gaffer, manager, principal, senior, supervisor.
antonyms inferior, junior.

superiority *n.* advantage, ascendancy, edge, excellence, lead, predominance, pre-eminence, preponderance, prevalence, supremacy, vis major.
antonym inferiority.

superlative *adj.* consummate, crack, excellent, greatest, highest, magnificent, matchless, nonpareil, outstanding, peerless, supreme, surpassing, transcendent, unbeatable, unbeaten, unparalleled, unrivaled, unsurpassed.
antonym poor.

supernatural *adj.* abnormal, dark, ghostly, hidden, hyperphysical, metaphysical, miraculous, mysterious, mystic, occult, paranormal, phantom, preternatural, psychic, spectral, spiritual, superlunary,

supersensible, supersensory, uncanny, unearthly, unnatural.
antonym natural.

supervise *v.* administer, conduct, control, direct, general, handle, inspect, keep tabs on, manage, oversee, preside over, run, superintend.

supervision *n.* administration, auspices, care, charge, control, direction, guidance, instruction, leading-strings, management, oversight, stewardship, superintendence, surveillance.

supervisor *n.* administrator, boss, chief, foreman, gaffer, inspector, manager, overseer, steward, superintendent.

supplant *v.* displace, dispossess, oust, overthrow, remove, replace, supersede, topple, undermine, unseat.

supple *adj.* bending, double-jointed, elastic, flexible, limber, lithe, loose-limbed, plastic, pliable, pliant, whippy, willowish, willowy.
antonym rigid.

supplement *n.* addendum, addition, appendix, codicil, complement, extra, insert, postscript, pull-out, sequel, supplemental, supplementary, suppletion.
v. add, add to, augment, complement, eke, eke out, extend, fill up, reinforce, supply, top up.
antonym deplete.

supplication *n.* appeal, entreaty, invocation, orison, petition, plea, pleading, prayer, request, rogation, solicitation, suit, supplicat.

supply *v.* afford, contribute, endow, equip, fill, furnish, give, grant, minister, outfit, produce, provide, purvey, replenish, satisfy, stock, store, victual, yield.
antonym take.
n. cache, fund, hoard, materials, necessities, provender, provisions, quantity, rations, reserve, reservoir, service, source, stake, stock, stockpile, store, stores.
antonym lack.

support *v.* adminiculate, advocate, aid, appui, appuy, assist, authenticate, back, bear, bolster, brace, brook, buttress, carry, champion, cherish, confirm, corroborate, countenance, crutch, defend, document, endorse, endure, finance, foster, fund, help, hold, keep, maintain, nourish, promote, prop, rally round, reinforce, second, stand (for), stay, stomach, strengthen, strut, submit, subsidize, substantiate, succor, suffer, sustain, take (someone's) part, thole, tolerate, underpin, underwrite, uphold, verify.
antonyms contradict, oppose.
n. abutment, adminicle, aid, aidance, approval, appui, assistance, back, backbone, backer, backing, backstays, backstop, blessing, brace, championship, comfort, comforter, crutch, encouragement, foundation, friendship, fulcrum, furtherance, help, jockstrap, keep, lining, livelihood, loyalty, mainstay, maintenance, patronage, pillar, post, prop, protection, relief, second, sheet-anchor, shore, stanchion, stay, stiffener, subsistence, succor, supporter, supportment, supporture,

sustenance, sustenance, underpinning, upkeep.
antonym opposition.

supporter *n.* adherent, advocate, ally, apologist, bottle-holder, champion, co-worker, defender, fan, follower, friend, heeler, helper, patron, seconder, sponsor, upholder, well-wisher.
antonym opponent.

suppose *v.* assume, believe, calculate, conceive, conclude, conjecture, consider, expect, fancy, guess, hypothesize, hypothetize, imagine, infer, judge, opine, posit, postulate, presume, presuppose, pretend, surmise, think.
antonym know.

supposition *n.* assumption, conjecture, doubt, guess, guesstimate, guesswork, hypothesis, idea, notion, opinion, postulate, presumption, speculation, surmise, theory.
antonym knowledge.

suppress *v.* censor, check, conceal, conquer, contain, crush, extinguish, muffle, muzzle, overpower, overthrow, quash, quell, repress, restrain, silence, smother, snuff out, squelch, stamp out, stifle, stop, strangle, subdue, submerge, vote down, withhold.
antonyms encourage, incite.

supremacy *n.* ascendancy, dominance, domination, dominion, hegemony, lordship, mastery, paramountcy, predominance, pre-eminence, primacy, sovereignty, sway.

supreme *adj.* cardinal, chief, consummate, crowning, culminating, extreme, final, first, foremost, greatest, head, highest, incomparable, leading, matchless, nonpareil, paramount, peerless, predominant, pre-eminent, prevailing, prime, principal, second-to-none, sovereign, superlative, surpassing, top, transcendent, ultimate, unbeatable, unbeaten, unsurpassed, utmost, world-beating. *antonyms* lowly, poor, slight.

sure *adj.* accurate, assured, bound, certain, clear, confident, convinced, decided, definite, dependable, effective, fast, firm, fixed, foolproof, guaranteed, honest, indisputable, ineluctable, inescapable, inevitable, infallible, irrevocable, persuaded, positive, precise, reliable, safe, satisfied, secure, solid, stable, steadfast, steady, sure-fire, trustworthy, trusty, undeniable, undoubted, unerring, unfailing, unmistakable, unswerving, unwavering.
antonyms doubtful, unsure.

surface *n.* covering, day, exterior, façade, face, facet, grass, outside, plane, side, skin, superficies, top, veneer, working-surface, worktop.
antonym interior.
adj. apparent, exterior, external, outer, outside, outward, superficial.
antonym interior.
v. appear, come to light, emerge, materialize, rise, transpire.
antonyms disappear, sink.

surge *v.* billow, eddy, gush, heave, rise, roll, rush, seethe, swell, swirl, tower, undulate.
n. access, billow, breaker, efflux, flood, flow, gurgitation, gush, intensification, outpouring, roller, rush, swell, uprush, upsurge, wave.

surly *adj.* bearish, brusque, chuffy, churlish, crabbed, cross, crusty, curmudgeonly, grouchy, gruff, grum, gurly, ill-natured, morose, perverse, sulky, sullen, testy, uncivil, ungracious.
antonym pleasant.

surmise *v.* assume, conclude, conjecture, consider, deduce, fancy, guess, imagine, infer, opine, presume, speculate, suppose, suspect.
antonym know.
n. assumption, conclusion, conjecture, deduction, guess, hypothesis, idea, inference, notion, opinion, possibility, presumption, speculation, supposition, suspicion, thought.
antonym certainty.

surmount *v.* conquer, exceed, get over, master, overcome, surpass, triumph over, vanquish.

surpass *v.* beat, best, ding, eclipse, exceed, excel, outdo, outshine, outstrip, override, overshadow, surmount, top, tower above, transcend.

surplus *n.* balance, excess, overplus, remainder, residue, superabundance, superfluity, surfeit, surplusage.
antonym lack.
adj. excess, extra, odd, redundant, remaining, spare, superfluous, unused.
antonym essential.

surprise *v.* amaze, astonish, astound, bewilder, confuse, disconcert, dismay, flabbergast, nonplus, stagger, startle, stun.
n. amazement, astonishment, bewilderment, bombshell, dismay, eye-opener, incredulity, jolt, revelation, shock, start, stupefaction, wonder.
antonym composure.

surrender *v.* abandon, capitulate, cede, concede, forego, give in, give up, quit, relinquish, remise, renounce, resign, submit, succumb, waive, yield.
antonyms fight on.
n. appeasement, capitulation, déchéance, delivery, Munich, relinquishment, remise, rendition, renunciation, resignation, submission, white flag, yielding.

surreptitious *adj.* behind-door, clandestine, covert, fraudulent, furtive, secret, sly, sneaking, stealthy, unauthorized, underhand, veiled.
antonym open.

surround *v.* begird, besiege, compass, embosom, encase, encincture, encircle, enclose, encompass, envelop, environ, girdle, invest, ring.

surveillance *n.* care, charge, check, control, direction, guardianship, inspection, monitoring, observation, regulation, scrutiny, stewardship, superintendence, supervision, vigilance, watch.

survey *v.* appraise, assess, consider, contemplate, estimate, examine, inspect, measure, observe, peruse, plan, plot, prospect, reconnoiter, research, review, scan, scrutinize, study, supervise, surview, triangulate, view.

n. appraisal, assessment, conspectus, examination, geodesy, inquiry, inspection, measurement, overview, perusal, review, sample, scrutiny, study, triangulation.

survive *v.* endure, exist, last, last out, live, live out, live through, outlast, outlive, ride, stay, subsist, weather, withstand.

antonym succumb.

susceptible *adj.* defenseless, disposed, given, impressible, impressionable, inclined, liable, open, predisposed, pregnable, prone, receptive, responsive, sensitive, subject, suggestible, tender, vulnerable.

antonyms impregnable, resistant.

suspect *v.* believe, call in question, conclude, conjecture, consider, distrust, doubt, fancy, feel, guess, infer, mistrust, opine, speculate, suppose, surmise.

adj. debatable, dodgy, doubtful, dubious, fishy, questionable, suspicious, unauthoritative, unreliable.

antonyms acceptable, innocent, straightforward.

suspend *v.* adjourn, append, arrest, attach, cease, dangle, debar, defer, delay, disbar, discontinue, dismiss, expel, freeze, hang, hold off, interrupt, postpone, shelve, sideline, stay, swing, unfrock, withhold.

antonyms continue, expedite, reinstate, restore.

suspicious *adj.* apprehensive, chary, distrustful, dodgy, doubtful, dubious, fishy, incredulous, irregular, jealous, louche, mistrustful, peculiar, queer, questionable, shady, skeptical, suspect, suspecting, unbelieving, uneasy, wary.

antonyms innocent, trustful, unexceptionable.

sustain *v.* aid, approve, assist, bear, carry, comfort, confirm, continue, endorse, endure, experience, feel, foster, help, hold, keep going, maintain, nourish, nurture, prolong, protract, provide for, ratify, relieve, sanction, stay, suffer, support, survive, sustenate, undergo, uphold, validate, verify, withstand.

sustenance *n.* aliment, board, comestibles, commons, eatables, edibles, étape, fare, food, freshments, livelihood, maintenance, nourishment, nutriment, pabulum, provender, provisions, rations, refection, subsistence, support, viands, victuals.

swagger *v.* bluster, boast, brag, brank, bully, cock, crow, gasconade, hector, parade, prance, roist, roister, strut, swank.

n. arrogance, bluster, boastfulness, boasting, braggadocio, display, fanfaronade, gasconade, gasconism, ostentation, rodomontade, show, showing off, swank, vainglory.

antonyms diffidence, modesty, restraint.

swallow *v.* absorb, accept, assimilate, believe, buy, consume, devour, down, drink, eat, englut, engulf, gulp, imbibe, ingest, ingurgitate, knock back, quaff, stifle, suppress, swig, swill, wash down.

swamp *n.* bog, dismal, everglades, fen, marsh, mire, morass,

moss, quagmire, quicksands, slough, vlei. *v.* beset, besiege, capsize, deluge, drench, engulf, flood, inundate, overload, overwhelm, saturate, sink, submerge, waterlog.

swank *v.* attitudinize, boast, parade, posture, preen oneself, show off, strut, swagger.

n. boastfulness, conceit, conceitedness, display, ostentation, pretentiousness, self-advertisement, show, showing- off, swagger, vainglory.

antonyms modesty, restraint.

swarm *n.* army, bevy, concourse, crowd, drove, flock, herd, horde, host, mass, mob, multitude, myriad, shoal, throng.

v. congregate, crowd, flock, flood, mass, stream, throng.

swarthy *adj.* black, brown, dark, dark-complexioned, dark-skinned, dusky, swart, swarth, tawny.

antonyms fair, pale.

sway *v.* affect, bend, control, direct, divert, dominate, fluctuate, govern, guide, incline, induce, influence, lean, lurch, oscillate, overrule, persuade, rock, roll, swerve, swing, titter, veer, wave.

n. ascendency, authority, cloud, command, control, dominion, government, hegemony, influence, jurisdiction, leadership, power, predominance, preponderance, rule, sovereignty, sweep, swerve, swing.

swear[1] *v.* affirm, assert, asseverate, attest, avow, declare, depose, insist, promise, testify, vow, warrant.

swear[2] *v.* blaspheme, blind, curse, cuss, eff, imprecate, maledict, take the Lord's name in vain, turn the air blue.

sweat *n.* agitation, anxiety, chore, dew, diaphoresis, distress, drudgery, effort, exudation, fag, flap, hidrosis, labor, panic, perspiration, strain, sudation, sudor, worry.

v. agonize, chafe, exude, fret, glow, perspirate, perspire, swelter, worry.

sweeping *adj.* across-the-board, all-embracing, all- inclusive, blanket, broad, comprehensive, exaggerated, extensive, far-reaching, global, indiscriminate, overdrawn, oversimplified, overstated, radical, simplistic, thoroughgoing, unanalytical, unqualified, wholesale, wide, wide-ranging.

sweet[1] *adj.* affectionate, agreeable, amiable, appealing, aromatic, attractive, balmy, beautiful, beloved, benign, charming, cherished, clean, cloying, darling, dear, dearest, delightful, dulcet, engaging, euphonic, euphonious, fair, fragrant, fresh, gentle, gracious, harmonious, honeyed, icky, kin, lovable, luscious, mellow, melodious, melting, mild, musical, new, perfumed, pet, precious, pure, redolent, saccharine, sickly, silver-toned, silvery, soft, suave, sugary, sweetened, sweet-smelling, sweet-sounding, sweet- tempered, syrupy, taking, tender, toothsome, treasured, tuneful, unselfish, wholesome, winning, winsome.

antonyms acid, bitter, cacophonous, discordant, malodorous, salty, sour, unpleasant.

n. afters, dessert, pudding, second course, sweet course.

sweet[2] *n.* bonbon, candy, comfit, confect, confection, confectionery, sweetie, sweetmeat.

swell[1] *v.* aggravate, augment, balloon, belly, billow, blab, bloat, boll, bulb, bulge, dilate, distend, enhance, enlarge, expand, extend, fatten, grow, heave, heighten, hove, increase, intensify, intumesce, louden, mount, protrude, reach a crescendo, rise, strout, surge, tumefy, volume.

antonyms contract, dwindle, shrink. *n.* billow, bore, bulge, distension, eagre, enlargement, loudening, rise, surge, swelling, undulation, wave.

swell[2] *n.* adept, beau, bigwig, blade, cockscomb, dandy, dude, fop, nob, popinjay, toff.

antonyms down-and-out, scarecrow, tramp.

adj. de luxe, dude, exclusive, fashionable, flashy, grand, posh, ritzy, smart, stylish, swanky.

antonyms seedy, shabby.

swift *adj.* abrupt, agile, expeditious, express, fast, fleet, fleet-footed, flying, hurried, light-heeled, light-legged, limber, nimble, nimble-footed, nippy, precipitate, prompt, quick, rapid, ready, short, spanking, speedy, sudden, winged.

antonyms slow, sluggish, tardy.

swindle *v.* bamboozle, bilk, bunko, cheat, chicane, chouse, con, deceive, defraud, diddle, do, dupe, finagle, financier, fleece, grift, gyp, hand someone a lemon, hornswoggle, overcharge, ramp, rip off, rook, sell smoke, sell someone a pup, skelder, trick.

n. chicanery, con, deceit, deception, double-dealing, fiddle, fraud, gold-brick, grift, gyp, imposition, knavery, racket, rip-off, roguery, scam, sharp practice, shenanigans, skingame, swizz, swizzle, trickery.

swing *v.* arrange, brandish, control, dangle, fix, fluctuate, hang, hurl, influence, librate, oscillate, pendulate, rock, suspend, sway, swerve, vary, veer, vibrate, wave, whirl.

n. fluctuation, impetus, libration, motion, oscillation, rhythm, scope, stroke, sway, swaying, sweep, sweeping, vibration, waving.

switch[1] *v.* change, change course, change direction, chop and change, deflect, deviate, divert, exchange, interchange, put, rearrange, replace, shift, shunt, substitute, swap, trade, turn, veer.

n. about-turn, alteration, change, change of direction, exchange, interchange, shift, substitution, swap.

switch[2] *v.* birch, flog, jerk, lash, swish, twitch, wave, whip, whisk.

n. birch, cane, jerk, rod, whip, whisk.

swivel *v.* gyrate, pirouette, pivot, revolve, rotate, spin, swing round, turn, twirl, wheel.

sycophantic *adj.* ass-licking, backscratching, bootlicking, cringing, fawning, flattering, groveling, ingratiating, obsequious, parasitical, servile, slavish, slimy, smarmy, timeserving, toad-eating, toadying, truckling, unctuous.

symbol *n.* badge, character, emblem, figure, grammalogue, ideogram, ideograph, image, logo, logogram, logograph, mandala, mark, representation, rune, sign, token, type.

symmetry *n.* agreement, balance, correspondence, evenness, form, harmony, isometry, order, parallelism, proportion, regularity.

antonyms asymmetry, irregularity.

sympathetic *adj.* affectionate, agreeable, appreciative, caring, comforting, commiserating, companionable, compassionate, compatible, concerned, congenial, consoling, empathetic, empathic, exorable, feeling, friendly, interested, kind, kindly, like-minded, pitying, responsive, supportive, tender, understanding, warm, warm-hearted, well-intentioned.

antonyms antipathetic, callous, indifferent, unsympathetic.

sympathize *v.* agree, commiserate, condole, empathize, feel for, identify with, pity, rap, respond to, side with, understand.

antonyms disapprove, dismiss, disregard, ignore, oppose.

sympathy *n.* affinity, agreement, comfort, commiseration, compassion, condolement, condolence, condolences, congeniality, correspondence, empathy, fellow-feeling, harmony, pity, rapport, responsiveness, tenderness, thoughtfulness, understanding, warmth.

antonyms callousness, disharmony, incompatibility, indifference.

symptom *n.* concomitant, diagnostic, evidence, expression, feature, indication, manifestation, mark, note, sign, syndrome, token, warning.

symptomatic *adj.* associated, characteristic, indicative, suggestive, typical.

synonymous *adj.* co-extensive, comparable, corresponding, equal, equivalent, exchangeable, identical, identified, interchangeable, parallel, similar, substitutable, tantamount, the same.

antonyms antonymous, dissimilar, opposite.

synopsis *n.* abridgment, abstract, aperçu, compendium, condensation, conspectus, digest, epitome, outline, précis, recapitulation, résumé, review, run-down, sketch, summary, summation.

synthetic *adj.* artificial, bogus, ersatz, fake, imitation, manmade, manufactured, mock, pseud, pseudo, put-on, sham, simulated.

antonyms genuine, real.

system *n.* arrangement, classification, co-ordination, logic, method, methodicalness, methodology, mode, modus operandi, orderliness, organization, plan, practice, procedure, process, regularity, routine, rule, scheme, set-up, structure, systematization, tabulation, taxis, taxonomy, technique, theory, usage.

systematic *adj.* businesslike, efficient, habitual, intentional, logical, methodical, ordered, orderly, organized, planned, precise, standardized, systematical, systematized, well-ordered, well-planned.

antonyms disorderly, inefficient, unsystematic.

T

table *n.* agenda, altar, bench, board, catalog, chart, counter, diagram, diet, digest, fare, flat, flatland, food, graph, index, inventory, list, mahogany, paradigm, plain, plan, plateau, record, register, roll, schedule, slab, spread, stall, stand, syllabus, synopsis, tableland, victuals.
v. postpone, propose, put forward, submit, suggest.

tableau *n.* diorama, picture, portrayal, representation, scene, spectacle, tableau vivant, vignette.

taboo *adj.* accursed, anathema, banned, forbidden, inviolable, outlawed, prohibited, proscribed, sacrosanct, unacceptable, unmentionable, unthinkable, verboten.
antonym acceptable.
n. anathema, ban, curse, disapproval, interdict, interdiction, prohibition, proscription, restriction.

tacit *adj.* implicit, implied, inferred, silent, ulterior, undeclared, understood, unexpressed, unprofessed, unspoken, unstated, unuttered, unvoiced, voiceless, wordless.
antonyms explicit, express, spoken, stated.

taciturn *adj.* aloof, antisocial, cold, distant, dumb, mute, quiet, reserved, reticent, saturnine, silent, tight- lipped, uncommunicative, unconversable, unforthcoming, withdrawn.
antonyms communicative, forthcoming, sociable, talkative.

tack *n.* approach, attack, bearing, course, direction, drawing-pin, heading, line, loop, method, nail, path, pin, plan, procedure, route, staple, stitch, tactic, thumbtack, tin-tack, way. *v.* add, affix, annex, append, attach, baste, fasten, fix, join, nail, pin, staple, stitch, tag.

tackle[1] *n.* accouterments, apparatus, equipment, gear, harness, implements, outfit, paraphernalia, rig, rigging, tackling, tools, trappings.
v. harness.

tackle[2] *n.* attack, block, challenge, interception, intervention, stop.
v. attempt, begin, block, challenge, clutch, confront, deal with, embark upon, encounter, engage in, essay, face up to, grab, grapple with, grasp, halt, intercept, seize, set about, stop, take on, throw, try, undertake, wade into.
antonyms avoid, side-step.

tacky *adj.* adhesive, cheap, gimcrack, gluey, gummy, messy, nasty, scruffy, seedy, shabby, shoddy, sleazy, sticky, tasteless, tatty, tawdry, vulgar, wet.

tact *n.* address, adroitness, consideration, delicacy, diplomacy, discernment, discretion, finesse, grace, judgment, perception, prudence, savoir-faire, sensitivity, skill, thoughtfulness, understanding.
antonyms clumsiness, indiscretion, tactlessness.

tactful *adj.* careful, considerate, delicate, diplomatic, discerning, discreet, graceful, judicious, perceptive, polished, polite, politic, prudent, sensitive, skilful, subtle, thoughtful, understanding.
antonym tactless.

tactical *adj.* adroit, artful, calculated, clever, cunning, diplomatic, judicious, politic, prudent, shrewd, skilful, smart, strategic.
antonym impolitic.

tactics *n.* approach, campaign, game plan, line of attack, maneuvers, moves, plan, plan of campaign, plans, ploys, policy, procedure, shifts, stratagems, strategy.

tag[1] *n.* aglet, aiglet, aiguillette, appellation, dag, designation, docket, epithet, flap, identification, label, mark, marker, name, note, slip, sticker, tab, tally, ticket.
v. add, adjoin, affix, annex, append, call, christen, designate, dub, earmark, fasten, identify, label, mark, name, nickname, style, tack, term, ticket.

tag[2] *n.* dictum, fadaise, gnome, gobbet, maxim, moral, motto, proverb, quotation, quote, remnant, saw, saying.

tail *n.* appendage, backside, behind, bottom, bum, buttocks, conclusion, croup, detective, empennage, end, extremity, file, follower, fud, line, posterior, queue, rear, rear end, retinue, rump, scut, suite, tailback, tailpiece, tailplane, train.
v. dog, follow, keep with, shadow, spy on, stalk, track, trail.

tailor *n.* clothier, costumer, costumier, couturier, couturière, dressmaker, modiste, outfitter, seamstress, whipcat, whip-stitch.
v. accommodate, adapt, adjust, alter, convert, cut, fashion, fit, modify, mold, shape, style, suit, trim.

taint *v.* adulterate, besmirch, blacken, blemish, blight, blot, brand, contaminate, corrupt, damage, defile, deprave, dirty, disgrace, dishonor, envenom, foul, infect, muddy, poison, pollute, ruin, shame, smear, smirch, soil, spoil, stain, stigmatize, sully, tarnish, vitiate.
n. blemish, blot, contagion, contamination, corruption, defect, disgrace, dishonor, fault, flaw, infamy, infection, obloquy, odium, opprobium, pollution, shame, smear, smirch, spot, stain, stigma.

take *v.* abduct, abide, abstract, accept, accommodate, accompany, acquire, adopt, appropriate, arrest, ascertain, assume, attract, bear, believe, betake, bewitch, blight, book, brave, bring, brook, buy, call for, captivate, capture, carry, cart, catch, charm, clutch, conduct, consider, consume, contain, convey, convoy, deduct, deem, delight, demand, derive, detract, do, drink, eat, effect, eliminate, enchant, endure, engage,

ensnare, entrap, escort, execute, fascinate, ferry, fetch, filch, gather, glean, grasp, grip, guide, haul, have, have room for, hire, hold, imbibe, ingest, inhale, lead, lease, make, measure, misappropriate, necessitate, need, nick, observe, obtain, operate, perceive, perform, photograph, pick, pinch, please, pocket, portray, presume, purchase, purloin, receive, regard, remove, rent, require, reserve, secure, seize, select, stand, steal, stomach, strike, subtract, succeed, suffer, swallow, swipe, thole, tolerate, tote, transport, undergo, understand, undertake, usher, weather, win, withstand, work.
n. catch, gate, haul, income, proceeds, profits, receipts, return, revenue, takings, yield.

take-off *n.* burlesque, caricature, imitation, lampoon, mickey-take, mimicry, parody, spoof, travesty.

taking *adj.* alluring, appealing, attractive, beguiling, captivating, catching, charming, compelling, delightful, enchanting, engaging, fascinating, fetching, intriguing, pleasing, prepossessing, winning, winsome.
antonyms repellent, repulsive, unattractive.
n. agitation, alarm, coil, commotion, consternation, flap, fuss, panic, passion, pother, state, sweat, tiz-woz, tizzy, turmoil, wax.

tale *n.* account, anecdote, fable, fabrication, falsehood, fib, fiction, legend, lie, Märchen, Munchausen, myth, narration, narrative, old wives' tale, relation, report, rigmarole, romance, rumor, saga, spiel, story, superstition, tall story, tradition, untruth, yarn.

talent *n.* ability, aptitude, bent, capacity, endowment, faculty, feel, flair, forte, genius, gift, knack, long suit, nous, parts, power, strength.
antonyms inability, ineptitude, weakness.

talented *adj.* able, accomplished, adept, adroit, apt, artistic, brilliant, capable, clever, deft, gifted, ingenious, inspired, well-endowed.
antonyms clumsy, inept, maladroit.

talk *v.* articulate, blab, blether, chat, chatter, chinwag, commune, communicate, confabulate, confer, converse, crack, gab, gossip, grass, inform, jaw, natter, negotiate, palaver, parley, prate, prattle, rap, say, sing, speak, squeak, squeal, utter, verbalize, witter.
n. address, argot, bavardage, blather, blether, causerie, chat, chatter, chinwag, chitchat, clash, claver, colloquy, conclave, confab, confabulation, conference, consultation, conversation, crack, dialect, dialogue, discourse, discussion, disquisition, dissertation, gab, gossip, harangue, hearsay, jargon, jaw, jawing, language, lecture, lingo, meeting, natter, negotiation, oration, palabra, palaver, parley, patois, rap, rumor, seminar, sermon, slang, speech, spiel, symposium, tittle-tattle, utterance, words.

talkative *adj.* chatty, communicative, conversational, effusive, expansive, forthcoming, gabby, garrulous, gossipy, long-tongued, long-winded, loquacious, prating, prolix, unreserved, verbose, vocal, voluble, wordy.
antonyms reserved, taciturn.

tall *adj.* absurd, big, dubious, elevated, embellished, exaggerated, far-fetched, giant, grandiloquent, great, high, implausible, improbable, incredible, lanky, leggy, lofty, overblown, preposterous, remarkable, soaring, steep, topless, towering, unbelievable, unlikely. *antonyms* low, reasonable, short, small.

tally *v.* accord, agree, coincide, compute, concur, conform, correspond, figure, fit, harmonize, jibe, mark, match, parallel, reckon, record, register, square, suit, tie in, total.
antonyms differ, disagree.
n. account, count, counterfoil, counterpart, credit, duplicate, label, mark, match, mate, notch, reckoning, record, score, stub, tab, tag, tick, total.

tame *adj.* amenable, anemic, biddable, bland, bloodless, boring, broken, compliant, cultivated, disciplined, docile, domesticated, dull, feeble, flat, gentle, humdrum, insipid, lifeless, manageable, meek, obedient, prosaic, spiritless, subdued, submissive, tedious, tractable, unadventurous, unenterprising, unexciting, uninspired, uninspiring, uninteresting, unresisting, vapid, wearisome.
antonyms exciting, rebellious, unmanageable, wild.
v. break in, bridle, calm, conquer, curb, discipline, domesticate, enslave, gentle, house-train, humble, master, mellow, mitigate, mute, pacify, quell, repress, soften, subdue, subjugate, suppress, temper, train.

tamper *v.* alter, bribe, cook, corrupt, damage, fiddle, fix, influence, interfere, intrude, juggle, manipulate, meddle, mess, rig, tinker.

tang *n.* aroma, bite, flavor, hint, kick, overtone, piquancy, pungency, reek, savor, scent, smack, smell, suggestion, taste, tinge, touch, trace, whiff.

tangible *adj.* actual, concrete, corporeal, definite, discernible, evident, manifest, material, objective, observable, palpable, perceptible, physical, positive, real, sensible, solid, substantial, tactile, touchable.
antonym intangible.

tangle *n.* burble, coil, complication, confusion, convolution, embroglio, embroilment, entanglement, fankle, fix, imbroglio, jam, jumble, jungle, knot, labyrinth, mass, mat, maze, mesh, mess, mix-up, muddle, raffle, snarl, snarl-up, twist, web.
v. catch, coil, confuse, convolve, embroil, enmesh, ensnare, entangle, entrap, hamper, implicate, interlace, interlock, intertwine, intertwist, interweave, involve, jam, knot, mat, mesh, muddle, snarl, trap, twist.
antonym disentangle.

tangy *adj.* biting, bitter, fresh, gamy, piquant, pungent, savory, sharp, spicy, strong, tart.
antonym insipid.

tantalize *v.* baffle, bait, balk, disappoint, entice, frustrate, lead on, play upon, provoke, taunt, tease, thwart, titillate, torment, torture.
antonym satisfy.

tantrum *n.* bate, fit, flare-up, fury, hysterics, outburst, paddy, paroxysm, rage, scene, storm, temper, wax.

tap[1] *v.* beat, chap, drum, knock, pat, rap, strike, tat, touch.
n. beat, chap, knock, pat, rap, rat-tat, touch.

tap[2] *n.* bug, bung, faucet, plug, receiver, spigot, spile, spout, stop-cock, stopper, valve.
v. bleed, broach, bug, drain, exploit, milk, mine, open, pierce, quarry, siphon, unplug, use, utilize, wiretap.

tape *n.* band, binding, magnetic tape, riband, ribbon, strip, tape-measure.
v. assess, bind, measure, record, seal, secure, stick, tape-record, video, wrap.

taper[1] *v.* attenuate, decrease, die away, die out, dwindle, fade, lessen, narrow, peter out, reduce, slim, subside, tail off, thin, wane, weaken.
antonyms increase, swell, widen.

taper[2] *n.* bougie, candle, spill, wax- light, wick.

tardy *adj.* backward, behindhand, belated, dawdling, delayed, dilatory, eleventh-hour, lag, last-minute, late, loitering, overdue, procrastinating, retarded, slack, slow, sluggish, unpunctual.
antonyms prompt, punctual.

target *n.* aim, ambition, bull's-eye, butt, destination, end, goal, intention, jack, mark, object, objective, prey, prick, purpose, quarry, scapegoat, victim.

tariff *n.* assessment, bill of fare, charges, customs, duty, excise, impost, levy, menu, price list, rate, schedule, tax, toll.

tarnish *v.* befoul, blacken, blemish, blot, darken, dim, discolor, disluster, dull, mar, rust, soil, spoil, spot, stain, sully, taint.
antonyms brighten, enhance, polish up.
n. blackening, blemish, blot, discoloration, film, patina, rust, spot, stain, taint.
antonyms brightness, polish.

tarry *v.* abide, bide, dally, dawdle, delay, dwell, lag, linger, loiter, pause, remain, rest, sojourn, stay, stop, wait.

tart[1] *n.* pastry, pie, quiche, tartlet.

tart[2] *adj.* acerb, acerbic, acid, acidulous, acrimonious, astringent, barbed, biting, bitter, caustic, cutting, incisive, piquant, pungent, sardonic, scathing, sharp, short, sour, tangy, trenchant, vinegary.

tart[3] *n.* broad, call girl, drab, fallen woman, fille de joie, fille publique, floosie, harlot, hooker, prostitute, slut, street-walker, strumpet, tramp, trollop, whore.

task *n.* assignment, aufgabe, burden, business, charge, chore, darg, duty, employment, enterprise, exercise, imposition, job, job of work, labor, mission, occupation, pensum, toil, undertaking, work.
v. burden, charge, commit, encumber, entrust, exhaust, load, lumber, oppress, overload, push, saddle, strain, tax, test, weary.

taste *n.* appetite, appreciation, bent, bit, bite, choice, correctness, cultivation, culture, dash, decorum, delicacy, desire, discernment, discretion, discrimination, drop, elegance, experience, fancy, finesse, flavor, fondness, gout, grace, gustation, inclination, judgment, leaning, liking, morsel, mouthful, nibble, nicety, nip, palate, partiality, penchant, perception, polish, politeness, predilection, preference, propriety, refinement, relish, restraint, sample, sapor, savor, sensitivity, sip, smack, smatch, soupçon, spoonful, style, swallow, tact, tactfulness, tang, tastefulness, titbit, touch.
v. assay, degust, degustate, differentiate, discern, distinguish, encounter, experience, feel, know, meet, nibble, perceive, relish, sample, savor, sip, smack, test, try, undergo.

tasteful *adj.* aesthetic, artistic, beautiful, charming, comme il faut, correct, cultivated, cultured, delicate, discreet, discriminating, elegant, exquisite, fastidious, graceful, handsome, harmonious, judicious, polished, refined, restrained, smart, stylish, well-judged.
antonym tasteless.

tasteless *adj.* barbaric, bland, boring, cheap, coarse, crass, crude, dilute, dull, flashy, flat, flavorless, garish, gaudy, graceless, gross, improper, inartistic, indecorous, indelicate, indiscreet, inelegant, inharmonious, insipid, low, mild, rude, stale, tacky, tactless, tame, tatty, tawdry, thin, uncouth, undiscriminating, uninspired, uninteresting, unseemly, untasteful, vapid, vulgar, watered-down, watery, weak, wearish.
antonym tasteful.

tasty *adj.* appetizing, delectable, delicious, flavorful, flavorous, flavorsome, gusty, luscious, mouthwatering, palatable, piquant, sapid, saporous, savory, scrumptious, succulent, toothsome, yummy.
antonyms disgusting, insipid, tasteless.

tattered *adj.* duddie, frayed, in shreds, lacerated, ragged, raggy, rent, ripped, tatty, threadbare, torn.
antonyms neat, trim.

tattle *v.* babble, blab, blather, blether, chat, chatter, clash, claver, gab, gash, gossip, jabber, natter, prate, prattle, talk, tittle-tattle, yak, yap.
n. babble, blather, blether, chat, chatter, chitchat, clash, claver, gossip, hearsay, jabber, prattle, rumor, talk, tittle-tattle, yak, yap.

taunt *v.* bait, chiack, deride, fleer, flout, flyte, gibe, insult, jeer, mock, provoke, reproach, revile, rib, ridicule, sneer, tease, torment, twit.
n. barb, catcall, censure, cut, derision, dig, fling, gibe, insult, jeer, poke, provocation, reproach, ridicule, sarcasm, sneer, teasing.

taut *adj.* contracted, rigid, strained, stressed, stretched, tense, tensed, tight, tightened, unrelaxed.
antonyms loose, relaxed, slack.

tautology *n.* duplication, iteration, otioseness, perissology, pleonasm, redundancy, repetition, repetitiousness, repetitiveness, superfluity.
antonyms economy, succinctness.

tavern *n.* alehouse, bar, boozer, bush, dive, doggery, fonda, hostelry, inn, joint, local, pub, roadhouse, saloon, taphouse.

tawdry *adj.* cheap, cheap-jack, flashy, garish, gaudy, gimcrack, gingerbread, glittering, meretricious, pinchbeck, plastic, raffish, showy, tacky, tasteless, tatty, tinsel, tinsely, vulgar.

antonyms excellent, fine, superior.

tax *n.* agistment, assessment, burden, charge, contribution, customs, demand, drain, duty, excise, geld, imposition, impost, levy, load, octroi, pressure, rate, scat, scot, strain, tariff, tithe, toll, tribute, weight.

v. accuse, arraign, assess, blame, burden, censure, charge, demand, drain, enervate, exact, exhaust, extract, geld, impeach, impose, impugn, incriminate, load, overburden, overtax, push, rate, reproach, sap, strain, stretch, task, tithe, try, weaken, weary.

taxi *n.* cab, fiacre, hack, hansom-cab, taxicab.

teach *v.* accustom, advise, coach, counsel, demonstrate, direct, discipline, drill, edify, educate, enlighten, ground, guide, impart, implant, inculcate, inform, instil, instruct, school, show, train, tutor, verse.

teacher *n.* abecedarian, coach, dominie, don, educator, guide, guru, instructor, khodja, kindergartener, kindergärtner, lecturer, luminary, maharishi, master, mentor, mistress, pedagogue, professor, pundit, school-marm, schoolmaster, schoolmistress, schoolteacher, trainer, tutor, usher.

team *n.* band, body, bunch, company, crew, écurie, équipe, gang, group, line-up, pair, set, shift, side, span, squad, stable, troupe, yoke.

v. combine, couple, join, link, match, yoke.

teamwork *n.* collaboration, co-operation, co- ordination, esprit de corps, fellowship, joint effort, team spirit.

antonyms disharmony, disunity.

tear *v.* belt, bolt, career, charge, claw, dart, dash, dilacerate, divide, drag, fly, gallop, gash, grab, hurry, lacerate, mangle, mutilate, pluck, pull, race, rend, rip, rive, run, rupture, rush, scratch, seize, sever, shoot, shred, snag, snatch, speed, split, sprint, sunder, wrench, wrest, yank, zoom.

n. hole, laceration, rent, rip, run, rupture, scratch, snag, split.

tearful *adj.* blubbering, crying, distressing, dolorous, emotional, lachrymose, lamentable, maudlin, mournful, pathetic, pitiable, pitiful, poignant, sad, sobbing, sorrowful, upsetting, weeping, weepy, whimpering, woeful.

tease *v.* aggravate, annoy, badger, bait, banter, bedevil, chaff, chip, gibe, goad, grig, guy, irritate, josh, mock, needle, pester, plague, provoke, rag, rib, ridicule, take a rise out of, tantalize, taunt, torment, twit, vex, worry.

technique *n.* address, adroitness, approach, art, artistry, course, craft, craftsmanship, delivery, executancy, execution, expertise, facility, fashion, knack, know-how, manner, means, method, mode, modus operandi, performance, procedure, proficiency, skill, style, system, touch, way.

tedious *adj.* annoying, banal, boring, deadly, drab, dreary, dreich, dull, fatiguing, humdrum, irksome, laborious, lifeless, long-drawn-out, longsome, long-spun, monotonous, prosaic, prosy, soporific, tiring, unexciting, uninteresting, vapid, wearisome.

antonyms exciting, interesting.

tedium *n.* banality, boredom, drabness, dreariness, dullness, ennui, lifelessness, monotony, prosiness, routine, sameness, tediousness, vapidity.

teem *v.* abound, bear, brim, bristle, burst, increase, multiply, overflow, overspill, produce, proliferate, pullulate, swarm.

antonyms lack, want.

teeming *adj.* abundant, alive, brimful, brimming, bristling, bursting, chock-a-block, chock-full, crawling, fruitful, full, numerous, overflowing, packed, pregnant, proliferating, pullulating, replete, swarming, thick.

antonyms lacking, rare, sparse.

teeter *v.* balance, lurch, pitch, pivot, rock, seesaw, stagger, sway, titubate, totter, tremble, waver, wobble.

teetotaller *n.* abstainer, nephalist, non-drinker, Rechabite, water-drinker.

telephone *n.* blower, handset, line, phone.

v. buzz, call, call up, contact, dial, get in touch, get on the blower, give someone a tinkle, phone, ring (up).

telescope *v.* abbreviate, abridge, compress, concertina, condense, contract, crush, curtail, cut, reduce, shorten, shrink, squash, trim, truncate.

television *n.* boob tube, goggle-box, idiot box, receiver, set, small screen, the box, the tube, TV, TV set.

tell *v.* acquaint, announce, apprize, authorize, bid, calculate, chronicle, command, communicate, comprehend, compute, confess, count, depict, describe, differentiate, direct, discern, disclose, discover, discriminate, distinguish, divulge, enjoin, enumerate, express, foresee, identify, impart, inform, instruct, mention, militate, narrate, notify, number, order, portray, predict, proclaim, reckon, recount, register, rehearse, relate, report, require, reveal, say, see, speak, state, summon, tally, understand, utter, weigh.

temerity *n.* assurance, audacity, boldness, brass neck, chutzpah, daring, effrontery, forwardness, gall, heedlessness, impudence, impulsiveness, intrepidity, nerve, pluck, rashness, recklessness.

antonym caution.

temper *n.* anger, annoyance, attitude, bate, calm, calmness, character, composure, constitution, cool, coolness, disposition, equanimity, fury, heat, humor, ill-humor, irascibility, irritability, irritation, mind, moderation, mood, nature, paddy, passion, peevishness, pet, petulance, rage, resentment, sang-froid, self-control, surliness, taking, tantrum, temperament, tenor, tranquility, vein, wax, wrath.

v. abate, admix, allay, anneal, assuage, calm, harden, indurate, lessen, mitigate, moderate, modify, mollify, palliate, restrain, soften, soothe, strengthen, toughen.

temperament *n.* anger, bent, character, complexion,

constitution, crasis, disposition, excitability, explosiveness, hot-headedness, humor, impatience, make-up, mettle, moodiness, moods, nature, outlook, personality, petulance, quality, soul, spirit, stamp, temper, tendencies, tendency, volatility.

temperamental *adj.* capricious, congenital, constitutional, emotional, erratic, excitable, explosive, fiery, highly-strung, hot-headed, hypersensitive, impatient, inborn, inconsistent, ingrained, inherent, innate, irritable, mercurial, moody, natural, neurotic, over-emotional, passionate, petulant, sensitive, touchy, undependable, unpredictable, unreliable, volatile, volcanic.
antonyms calm, serene, steady.

temperance *n.* abstemiousness, abstinence, continence, discretion, forbearance, moderation, prohibition, restraint, self-abnegation, self-control, self-denial, self-discipline, self-restraint, sobriety, teetotalism.
antonyms excess, intemperance.

temperate *adj.* abstemious, abstinent, agreeable, balanced, balmy, calm, clement, composed, continent, controlled, cool, dispassionate, equable, even-tempered, fair, gentle, mild, moderate, pleasant, reasonable, restrained, sensible, sober, soft, stable.
antonyms excessive, extreme, intemperate.

tempest *n.* bourasque, commotion, cyclone, disturbance, ferment, furore, gale, hurricane, squall, storm, tornado, tumult, typhoon, upheaval, uproar.

tempo *n.* beat, cadence, measure, meter, pace, pulse, rate, rhythm, speed, time, velocity.

temporal *adj.* carnal, civil, earthly, evanescent, fleeting, fleshly, fugacious, fugitive, impermanent, lay, material, momentary, mortal, mundane, passing, profane, secular, short-lived, sublunary, temporary, terrestrial, transient, transitory, unspiritual, worldly.
antonym spiritual.

temporary *adj.* brief, ephemeral, evanescent, fleeting, fugacious, fugitive, impermanent, interim, makeshift, momentary, passing, pro tem, pro tempore, provisional, short- lived, stop-gap, transient, transitory.
antonyms everlasting, permanent.

tempt *v.* allure, attract, bait, coax, dare, decoy, draw, enamor, entice, incite, inveigle, invite, lure, provoke, risk, seduce, tantalize, test, try, woo.
antonyms discourage, dissuade.

tenacious *adj.* adamant, adhesive, clinging, coherent, cohesive, determined, dogged, fast, firm, forceful, gluey, glutinous, inflexible, intransigent, mucilaginous, obdurate, obstinate, persistent, pertinacious, resolute, retentive, single-minded, solid, staunch, steadfast, sticky, strong, strong-willed, stubborn, sure, tight, tough, unshakeable, unswerving, unwavering, unyielding, viscous.
antonyms loose, slack, weak.

tenacity *n.* adhesiveness, application, clinginess, coherence, cohesiveness, determination, diligence, doggedness,

fastness, firmness, force, forcefulness, indomitability, inflexibility, intransigence, obduracy, obstinacy, perseverance, persistence, pertinacity, power, resoluteness, resolution, resolve, retention, retentiveness, single-mindedness, solidity, solidness, staunchness, steadfastness, stickiness, strength, stubbornness, toughness, viscosity.
antonyms looseness, slackness, weakness.

tenant *n.* gavelman, inhabitant, landholder, leaseholder, lessee, occupant, occupier, renter, resident.

tend[1] *v.* affect, aim, bear, bend, conduce, contribute, go, gravitate, head, incline, influence, lead, lean, move, point, trend, verge.

tend[2] *v.* attend, comfort, control, cultivate, feed, guard, handle, keep, maintain, manage, minister to, nurse, nurture, protect, serve, succor.
antonym neglect.

tendency *n.* bearing, bent, bias, conatus, course, direction, disposition, drift, drive, heading, inclination, leaning, liability, movement, partiality, penchant, predilection, predisposition, proclivity, proneness, propensity, purport, readiness, susceptibility, tenor, thrust, trend, turning.

tender[1] *adj.* aching, acute, affectionate, affettuoso, amoroso, amorous, benevolent, breakable, bruised, callow, caring, chary, compassionate, complicated, considerate, dangerous, delicate, difficult, emotional, evocative, feeble, fond, fragile, frail, gentle, green, humane, immature, impressionable, inexperienced, inflamed, irritated, kind, loving, merciful, moving, new, painful, pathetic, pitiful, poignant, raw, risky, romantic, scrupulous, sensitive, sentimental, smarting, soft, soft-hearted, sore, sympathetic, tender-hearted, ticklish, touching, touchy, tricky, vulnerable, warm, warm-hearted, weak, young, youthful.
antonyms callous, chewy, hard, harsh, rough, severe, tough.

tender[2] *v.* advance, extend, give, offer, present, proffer, propose, submit, suggest, volunteer.
n. bid, currency, estimate, medium, money, offer, payment, proffer, proposal, proposition, specie, submission, suggestion.

tender-hearted *adj.* affectionate, benevolent, benign, caring, compassionate, considerate, feeling, fond, gentle, humane, kind, kind-hearted, kindly, loving, merciful, mild, pitying, responsive, sensitive, sentimental, soft-hearted, sympathetic, warm, warm-hearted.
antonyms callous, cruel, hard-hearted, unfeeling.

tenderness *n.* ache, aching, affection, amorousness, attachment, benevolence, bruising, callowness, care, compassion, consideration, delicateness, devotion, discomfort, feebleness, fondness, fragility, frailness, gentleness, greenness, humaneness, humanity, immaturity, impressionableness, inexperience, inflammation, irritation, kindness, liking, love, loving-kindness, mercy, newness, pain, painfulness, pity, rawness, sensitiveness, sensitivity, sentimentality, soft- heartedness, softness, soreness, sweetness, sympathy, tender- heartedness, vulnerability, warm-heartedness, warmth, weakness, youth, youthfulness.

antonyms cruelty, hardness, harshness.

tenet *n*. article of faith, belief, canon, conviction, credo, creed, doctrine, dogma, maxim, opinion, precept, presumption, principle, rule, teaching, thesis, view.

tense *adj*. anxious, apprehensive, edgy, electric, exciting, fidgety, jittery, jumpy, moving, nerve-racking, nervous, overwrought, restless, rigid, strained, stressful, stretched, strung up, taut, tight, uneasy, uptight, worrying.

antonyms calm, lax, loose, relaxed.

v. brace, contract, strain, stretch, tauten, tighten.

antonyms loosen, relax.

tension *n*. anxiety, apprehension, edginess, hostility, nervousness, pressure, restlessness, rigidity, stiffness, strain, straining, stress, stretching, suspense, tautness, tightness, tone, unease, worry.

antonyms calm(ness), laxness, looseness, relaxation.

tentative *adj*. cautious, conjectural, diffident, doubtful, experimental, faltering, hesitant, indefinite, peirastic, provisional, speculative, timid, uncertain, unconfirmed, undecided, unformulated, unsettled, unsure.

antonyms conclusive, decisive, definite, final.

tenure *n*. habitation, holding, incumbency, occupancy, occupation, possession, proprietorship, residence, tenancy, term, time.

tepid *adj*. apathetic, cool, half-hearted, indifferent, lew, lukewarm, unenthusiastic, warmish.

antonyms animated, cold, hot, passionate.

term[1] *n*. appellation, denomination, designation, epithet, epitheton, expression, locution, name, phrase, title, word.

v. call, denominate, designate, dub, entitle, label, name, style, tag, title.

term[2] *n*. bound, boundary, close, conclusion, confine, course, culmination, duration, end, finish, fruition, half, interval, limit, period, season, semester, session, space, span, spell, terminus, time, while.

terminal *adj*. bounding, concluding, deadly, desinent, desinential, extreme, fatal, final, incurable, killing, last, lethal, limiting, mortal, ultimate, utmost.

antonym initial.

n. boundary, depot, end, extremity, limit, termination, terminus.

terminate *v*. abort, cease, close, complete, conclude, cut off, discontinue, drop, end, expire, finish, issue, lapse, result, stop, wind up.

antonyms begin, initiate, start.

terminology *n*. argot, cant, jargon, language, lingo, nomenclature, patois, phraseology, terms, vocabulary, words.

terms *n*. agreement, charges, compromise, conditions, fees, footing, language, particulars, payment, phraseology, position, premises, price, provisions, provisos, qualifications, rates, relations, relationship, specifications, standing, status, stipulations, terminology, understanding.

terrible *adj*. abhorrent, appalling, awful, bad, beastly, dangerous, desperate, dire, disgusting, distressing, dread, dreaded, dreadful, extreme, fearful, foul, frightful, godawful, gruesome, harrowing, hateful, hideous, horrendous, horrible, horrid, horrific, horrifying, loathsome, monstrous, obnoxious, odious, offensive, outrageous, poor, repulsive, revolting, rotten, serious, severe, shocking, unpleasant, vile.

antonyms great, pleasant, superb, wonderful.

terrific *adj*. ace, amazing, awesome, awful, breathtaking, brilliant, dreadful, enormous, excellent, excessive, extreme, fabulous, fantastic, fearful, fierce, fine, gigantic, great, harsh, horrific, huge, intense, magnificent, marvelous, monstrous, outstanding, prodigious, sensational, severe, smashing, stupendous, super, superb, terrible, tremendous, wonderful.

terrify *v*. affright, alarm, appal, awe, dismay, frighten, horrify, intimidate, petrify, scare, shock, terrorize.

territory *n*. area, bailiwick, country, dependency, district, domain, jurisdiction, land, park, preserve, province, region, sector, state, terrain, tract, zone.

terror *n*. affright, alarm, anxiety, awe, blue funk, bogeyman, bugbear, consternation, devil, dismay, dread, fear, fiend, fright, horror, intimidation, monster, panic, rascal, rogue, scourge, shock, tearaway. **terse** *adj*. abrupt, aphoristic, brief, brusque, clipped, compact, concise, condensed, crisp, curt, economical, elliptical, epigrammatic, gnomic, incisive, laconic, neat, pithy, sententious, short, snappy, succinct.

antonyms long-winded, prolix, repetitious.

test *v*. analyze, assay, assess, check, examine, experiment, investigate, prove, screen, try, verify.

n. analysis, assessment, attempt, catechism, check, evaluation, examination, hurdle, investigation, moment of truth, ordeal, pons asinorum, probation, proof, shibboleth, trial, try- out.

testify *v*. affirm, assert, asseverate, attest, avow, certify, corroborate, declare, depone, depose, evince, show, state, swear, vouch, witness.

testimony *n*. affidavit, affirmation, asseveration, attestation, avowal, confirmation, corroboration, declaration, demonstration, deposition, evidence, indication, information, manifestation, profession, proof, statement, submission, support, verification, witness.

testy *adj*. bad-tempered, cantankerous, captious, carnaptious, crabbed, cross, crusty, fretful, grumpy, impatient, inflammable, irascible, irritable, peevish, peppery, petulant, quarrelsome, quick-tempered, short-tempered, snappish, snappy, splenetic, sullen, tetchy, touchy, waspish.

antonyms even-tempered, good-humored.

tether *n*. bond, chain, cord, fastening, fetter, halter, lead, leash, line, restraint, rope, shackle.

v. bind, chain, fasten, fetter, lash, leash, manacle, picket, restrain, rope, secure, shackle, tie.

text *n.* argument, body, contents, lection, libretto, matter, motif, paragraph, passage, reader, reading, script, sentence, source, subject, textbook, theme, topic, verse, wordage, wording, words.

texture *n.* character, composition, consistency, constitution, fabric, feel, grain, quality, structure, surface, tissue, weave, weftage, woof.

thankful *adj.* appreciative, beholden, contented, grateful, indebted, obliged, pleased, relieved.
antonyms thankless, unappreciative, ungrateful.

thaw *v.* defreeze, defrost, dissolve, liquefy, melt, soften, unbend, uncongeal, unfreeze, unthaw, warm.
antonym freeze.

theater *n.* amphitheater, auditorium, hall, lyceum, odeon, opera house, playhouse.

theatrical *adj.* affected, artificial, ceremonious, dramatic, dramaturgic, exaggerated, extravagant, hammy, histrionic, mannered, melodramatic, ostentatious, overdone, pompous, scenic, showy, stagy, stilted, theatric, Thespian, unreal.

theft *n.* abstraction, embezzlement, fraud, heist, kleptomania, larceny, pilfering, plunderage, purloining, rip-off, robbery, stealing, thievery, thieving.

theme *n.* argument, burden, composition, dissertation, essay, exercise, idea, keynote, leitmotiv, lemma, matter, motif, mythos, paper, subject, subject-matter, text, thesis, topic, topos.

theoretical *adj.* abstract, academic, conjectural, doctrinaire, doctrinal, hypothetical, ideal, impractical, on paper, pure, speculative.
antonyms applied, concrete, practical.

theory *n.* abstraction, assumption, conjecture, guess, hypothesis, ism, philosophy, plan, postulation, presumption, proposal, scheme, speculation, supposition, surmise, system, thesis.
antonyms certainty, practice.

therefore *adv.* accordingly, as a result, consequently, ergo, for that reason, hence, so, then, thence, thus.

thick *adj.* abundant, brainless, brimming, bristling, broad, bulky, bursting, chock-a-block, chock-full, chummy, close, clotted, coagulated, compact, concentrated, condensed, confidential, covered, crass, crawling, crowded, decided, deep, dense, devoted, dim-witted, distinct, distorted, dopey, dull, excessive, familiar, fat, foggy, frequent, friendly, full, gross, guttural, heavy, hoarse, husky, impenetrable, inarticulate, indistinct, insensitive, inseparable, intimate, marked, matey, moronic, muffled, numerous, obtuse, opaque, packed, pally, pronounced, replete, rich, slow, slow-witted, solid, soupy, squabbish, strong, stupid, substantial, swarming, teeming, thick-headed, throaty, turbid, wide.
antonyms brainy, clever, slender, slight, slim, thin, watery.
n. center, focus, heart, hub, middle, midst.

thief *n.* abactor, Autolycus, bandit, burglar, cheat, cracksman, crook, cut-purse, embezzler, filcher, housebreaker, kleptomaniac, ladrone, land-rat, larcener, larcenist, latron, mugger, pickpocket, pilferer, plunderer, prigger, purloiner, robber, shop-lifter, snatch-purse, St Nicholas's clerk, stealer, swindler.

thin *adj.* attenuate, attenuated, bony, deficient, delicate, diaphanous, dilute, diluted, emaciated, feeble, filmy, fine, fine-drawn, flimsy, gaunt, gossamer, inadequate, insubstantial, insufficient, lanky, lean, light, meager, narrow, poor, rarefied, runny, scant, scanty, scarce, scattered, scragged, scraggy, scrawny, see-through, shallow, sheer, skeletal, skimpy, skinny, slender, slight, slim, spare, sparse, spindly, superficial, tenuous, translucent, transparent, unconvincing, undernourished, underweight, unsubstantial, washy, watery, weak, wishy-washy, wispy.
antonyms broad, dense, fat, solid, strong, thick.
v. attenuate, decrassify, dilute, diminish, emaciate, extenuate, prune, rarefy, reduce, refine, trim, water down, weaken, weed out.

think *v.* anticipate, be under the impression, believe, brood, calculate, cerebrate, cogitate, conceive, conclude, consider, contemplate, deem, deliberate, design, determine, envisage, esteem, estimate, expect, foresee, hold, ideate, imagine, intellectualize, judge, meditate, mull over, muse, ponder, presume, purpose, ratiocinate, reason, recall, reckon, recollect, reflect, regard, remember, revolve, ruminate, suppose, surmise.
n. assessment, cogitation, consideration, contemplation, deliberation, meditation, reflection.

thirst *n.* appetite, craving, desire, drought, drouth, drouthiness, dryness, eagerness, hankering, hunger, hydromania, keenness, longing, lust, passion, thirstiness, yearning, yen.

thirsty *adj.* adry, appetitive, arid, athirst, avid, burning, craving, dehydrated, desirous, drouthy, dry, dying, eager, greedy, hankering, hungry, hydropic, itching, longing, lusting, parched, thirsting, yearning.

thorn *n.* acantha, affliction, annoyance, bane, barb, bother, curse, doorn, irritant, irritation, nuisance, pest, plague, prickle, scourge, spike, spine, torment, torture, trouble.

thorough *adj.* absolute, all-embracing, all-inclusive, arrant, assiduous, careful, complete, comprehensive, conscientious, deep-seated, downright, efficient, entire, exhaustive, full, in-depth, intensive, meticulous, out-and-out, pains-taking, perfect, pure, root-and-branch, scrupulous, sheer, sweeping, thoroughgoing, total, unmitigated, unqualified, utter.
antonyms careless, haphazard, partial.

thoroughfare *n.* access, avenue, boulevard, concourse, expressway, freeway, highway, motorway, passage, passageway, road, roadway, street, thruway, turnpike, way.

though *conj.* albeit, allowing, although, even if, granted, howbeit, notwithstanding, while.

adv. all the same, even so, for all that, however, in spite of that, nevertheless, nonetheless, notwithstanding, still, yet.

thought *n.* aim, anticipation, anxiety, aspiration, assessment, attention, attentiveness, belief, brainwork, care, cerebration, cogitation, compassion, concept, conception, concern, conclusion, conjecture, considerateness, consideration, contemplation, conviction, dash, deliberation, design, dream, estimation, excogitation, expectation, heed, hope, idea, intention, introspection, jot, judgment, kindness, little, meditation, mentation, muse, musing, notion, object, opinion, plan, prospect, purpose, reflection, regard, resolution, rumination, scrutiny, solicitude, study, sympathy, thinking, thoughtfulness, touch, trifle, view, whisker.

thoughtful *adj.* absorbed, abstracted, astute, attentive, canny, careful, caring, cautious, circumspect, considerate, contemplative, deliberate, deliberative, discreet, heedful, helpful, introspective, kind, kindly, meditative, mindful, musing, pensieroso, pensive, prudent, rapt, reflective, ruminative, serious, solicitous, studious, thinking, unselfish, wary, wistful.
antonym thoughtless.

thoughtless *adj.* absent-minded, careless, étourdi(e), foolish, heedless, ill-considered, impolite, imprudent, inadvertent, inattentive, inconsiderate, indiscreet, injudicious, insensitive, mindless, neglectful, negligent, rash, reckless, regardless, remiss, rude, selfish, silly, stupid, tactless, uncaring, undiplomatic, unkind, unmindful, unobservant, unreflecting, unthinking.
antonym thoughtful.

thrash *v.* beat, belt, bethump, bethwack, birch, cane, chastise, clobber, crush, defeat, drub, flagellate, flail, flog, hammer, heave, horse-whip, jerk, lam, lambaste, larrup, lather, lay into, leather, maul, overwhelm, paste, plunge, punish, quilt, rout, scourge, slaughter, spank, squirm, swish, tan, thresh, toss, towel, trim, trounce, wallop, whale, whap, whip, writhe.

thread *n.* cotton, course, direction, drift, fiber, filament, film, fimbria, line, motif, plot, story-line, strain, strand, string, tenor, theme, yarn.
v. ease, inch, meander, pass, string, weave, wind.

threadbare *adj.* clichéd, cliché-ridden, commonplace, conventional, corny, down-at-heel, frayed, hackneyed, moth-eaten, old, overused, overworn, ragged, scruffy, shabby, stale, stereotyped, stock, tattered, tatty, tired, trite, used, well-worn, worn, worn-out.
antonyms fresh, luxurious, new, plush.

threat *n.* commination, danger, foreboding, foreshadowing, frighteners, hazard, menace, omen, peril, portent, presage, risk, saber-rattling, warning.

threaten *v.* browbeat, bully, comminate, cow, endanger, forebode, foreshadow, impend, imperil, intimidate, jeopardize, menace, portend, presage, pressurize, terrorize, warn.

threatening *adj.* baleful, bullying, cautionary, comminatory, Damoclean, grim, inauspicious, intimidatory, menacing, minacious, minatory, ominous, sinister, terrorizing, warning.

threshold *n.* beginning, brink, dawn, door, door-sill, door-stead, doorstep, doorway, entrance, inception, minimum, opening, outset, sill, start, starting-point, verge.

thrift *n.* carefulness, conservation, economy, frugality, husbandry, parsimony, prudence, saving, thriftiness.
antonyms profligacy, waste.

thrifty *adj.* careful, conserving, economical, frugal, parsimonious, provident, prudent, saving, sparing.
antonyms prodigal, profligate, thriftless, wasteful.

thrill *n.* adventure, buzz, charge, flutter, fluttering, frisson, glow, kick, pleasure, quiver, sensation, shudder, stimulation, throb, tingle, titillation, tremble, tremor, vibration.
v. arouse, electrify, excite, flush, flutter, glow, move, quake, quiver, send, shake, shudder, stimulate, stir, throb, tingle, titillate, tremble, vibrate, wow.

thrive *v.* advance, bloom, blossom, boom, burgeon, develop, flourish, gain, grow, increase, profit, prosper, succeed, wax.
antonyms die, fail, languish, stagnate.

throb *v.* beat, palpitate, pound, pulsate, pulse, thump, vibrate.
n. beat, palpitation, pounding, pulsating, pulsation, pulse, thump, thumping, vibration, vibrato.

throe *n.* convulsion, fit, pain, pang, paroxysm, seizure, spasm, stab.

throng *n.* assemblage, bevy, concourse, congregation, crowd, crush, flock, herd, horde, host, jam, mass, mob, multitude, pack, press, swarm.
v. bunch, congregate, converge, cram, crowd, fill, flock, herd, jam, mill around, pack, press, swarm.

throttle *v.* asphyxiate, choke, control, gag, garrotte, inhibit, silence, smother, stifle, strangle, strangulate, suppress.

through *prep.* as a result of, because of, between, by, by means of, by reason of, by virtue of, by way of, during, in, in and out of, in consequence of, in the middle of, past, thanks to, throughout, using, via.
adj. completed, direct, done, ended, express, finished, nonstop, terminated.

throughout *adv.* everywhere, extensively, ubiquitously, widely.

throw *v.* astonish, baffle, bemuse, bring down, cast, chuck, confound, confuse, defeat, discomfit, disconcert, dislodge, dumbfound, elance, execute, fell, fling, floor, heave, hurl, jaculate, launch, lob, overturn, perform, perplex, pitch, produce, project, propel, put, send, shy, sling, slug, toss, unhorse, unsaddle, unseat, upset, whang.
n. attempt, cast, chance, essay, fling, gamble, hazard, heave, lob, pitch, projection, put, shy, sling, spill, toss, try, venture, wager.

thrust *v.* bear, butt, drive, force, impel, intrude, jab, jam, lunge, pierce, plunge, poke, press, prod, propel, push, ram, shove, stab, stick, urge, wedge.

n. drive, flanconade, impetus, lunge, momentum, poke, prod, prog, push, shove, stab, stoccado.

thug *n.* animal, assassin, bandit, bangster, bruiser, bullyboy, cut-throat, gangster, goon, gorilla, heavy, highbinder, hood, hoodlum, hooligan, killer, mugger, murderer, robber, ruffian, tough.

thump *n.* bang, blow, box, clout, clunk, crash, cuff, knock, rap, smack, thud, thwack, wallop, whack.

v. bang, batter, beat, belabor, box, clout, crash, cuff, daud, ding, dunt, dush, hit, knock, lambaste, pound, rap, smack, strike, thrash, throb, thud, thwack, wallop, whack.

thunderstruck *adj.* agape, aghast, amazed, astonished, astounded, dazed, dumbfounded, flabbergasted, floored, flummoxed, nonplused, open-mouthed, paralyzed, petrified, shocked, staggered, stunned.

thus *adv.* accordingly, as follows, consequently, ergo, hence, in this way, like so, like this, so, then, therefore, thuswise.

thwart *v.* baffle, balk, check, defeat, foil, frustrate, hinder, impede, obstruct, oppose, outwit, prevent, spite, stonker, stop, stymie, transverse, traverse.

antonyms abet, aid, assist.

ticket *n.* card, certificate, coupon, docket, label, marker, pass, slip, sticker, tab, tag, tessera, token, voucher.

tickle *v.* amuse, cheer, delight, divert, enchant, entertain, excite, gratify, please, thrill, titillate.

ticklish *adj.* awkward, critical, delicate, difficult, dodgy, hazardous, nice, precarious, risky, sensitive, thorny, touchy, tricky, uncertain, unstable, unsteady.

antonyms easy, straightforward.

tidings *n.* advice, bulletin, communication, dope, gen, greetings, information, intelligence, message, news, report, word.

tidy *adj.* ample, businesslike, clean, cleanly, considerable, fair, generous, good, goodly, handsome, healthy, large, largish, methodical, neat, ordered, orderly, respectable, shipshape, sizable, spick, spick-and-span, spruce, substantial, systematic, trim, uncluttered, well-groomed, well-kept.

antonyms disorganized, untidy.

v. arrange, clean, fettle, groom, neaten, order, spruce up, straighten.

tie *v.* attach, bind, confine, connect, draw, equal, fasten, hamper, hinder, hold, interlace, join, knot, lash, ligature, limit, link, match, moor, oblige, restrain, restrict, rope, secure, strap, tether, truss, unite.

n. affiliation, allegiance, band, bond, commitment, connection, contest, copula, cord, dead heat, deadlock, draw, duty, encumbrance, fastening, fetter, fixture, game, hindrance, joint, kinship, knot, liaison, ligature, limitation, link, match, obligation, relationship, restraint, restriction, rope, stalemate, string.

tier *n.* band, belt, echelon, floor, gradin(e), layer, level, line, rank, row, stage, story, stratification, stratum, zone.

tiff *n.* barney, difference, disagreement, dispute, falling-out, huff, ill-humor, pet, quarrel, row, scrap, set-to, spat, squabble, sulk, tantrum, temper, words.

tight[1] *adj.* close, close-fitting, compact, competent, constricted, cramped, dangerous, difficult, even, evenly-balanced, fast, firm, fixed, grasping, harsh, hazardous, hermetic, impervious, inflexible, mean, miserly, narrow, near, niggardly, parsimonious, penurious, perilous, precarious, precise, problematic, proof, rigid, rigorous, sealed, secure, severe, snug, sound, sparing, stern, sticky, stiff, stingy, stretched, strict, stringent, taut, tense, ticklish, tight-fisted, tough, tricky, trig, troublesome, uncompromising, unyielding, watertight, well-matched, worrisome.

antonyms lax, loose, slack.

tight[2] *adj.* blotto, drunk, half cut, half-seas-over, in one's cups, inebriated, intoxicated, pickled, pie-eyed, pissed, plastered, smashed, sozzled, stewed, stoned, three sheets in the wind, tiddly, tipsy, under the influence.

antonym sober.

till *v.* cultivate, dig, dress, plow, work.

tilt *v.* attack, cant, clash, contend, duel, encounter, fight, heel, incline, joust, lean, list, overthrow, pitch, slant, slope, spar, tip.

n. angle, cant, clash, combat, duel, encounter, fight, inclination, incline, joust, list, lists, pitch, set-to, slant, slope, thrust, tournament, tourney.

timber *n.* beams, boarding, boards, forest, logs, planking, planks, trees, wood.

time *n.* age, beat, chronology, date, day, duration, epoch, era, generation, heyday, hour, instance, interval, juncture, life, lifespan, lifetime, measure, meter, occasion, peak, period, point, rhythm, season, space, span, spell, stage, stretch, tempo, term, tide, while.

v. clock, control, count, judge, measure, meter, regulate, schedule, set.

timeless *adj.* abiding, ageless, amaranthine, ceaseless, changeless, deathless, endless, enduring, eternal, everlasting, immortal, immutable, imperishable, indestructible, lasting, permanent, perpetual, persistent, undying.

timely *adj.* appropriate, convenient, judicious, opportune, prompt, propitious, punctual, seasonable, suitable, tempestive, well-timed.

antonym ill-timed, inappropriate, unfavorable.

timetable *n.* agenda, calendar, curriculum, diary, list, listing, program, roster, rota, schedule.

time-worn *adj.* aged, ancient, broken-down, bromidic, clichéd, dated, decrepit, dog-eared, hackneyed, hoary, lined, old hat, out of date, outworn, passé, ragged, ruined, rundown, shabby, stale, stock, threadbare, tired, trite, weathered, well-worn, worn, wrinkled.

antonyms fresh, new.

timid *adj*. afraid, apprehensive, bashful, cowardly, coy, diffident, faint-hearted, fearful, hen-hearted, irresolute, modest, mousy, nervous, pavid, pusillanimous, retiring, shrinking, shy, spineless, timorous.
antonyms audacious, bold, brave.

tinge *n*. bit, cast, color, dash, drop, dye, flavor, pinch, shade, smack, smatch, smattering, sprinkling, stain, suggestion, tinct, tincture, tint, touch, trace, wash.
v. color, dye, encolor, imbue, shade, stain, suffuse, tint.

tingle *v*. dindle, itch, prickle, ring, sting, thrill, throb, tickle, vibrate.
n. frisson, gooseflesh, goose-pimples, itch, itching, pins and needles, prickling, quiver, shiver, stinging, thrill, tickle, tickling.

tinker *v*. dabble, fiddle, meddle, monkey, play, potter, putter, toy, trifle.
n. botcher, bungler, diddicoy, fixer, itinerant, mender.

tint *n*. cast, color, dye, hint, hue, rinse, shade, stain, streak, suggestion, tinct, tincture, tinge, tone, touch, trace, wash.
v. affect, color, dye, influence, rinse, stain, streak, taint, tincture, tinge.

tiny *adj*. diminutive, dwarfish, infinitesimal, insignificant, itsy-bitsy, Lilliputian, little, microscopic, mini, miniature, minute, negligible, petite, pint-size(d), pocket, puny, pygmy, slight, small, teensy, teentsy, teeny, teeny-weeny, tiddl(e)y, tottie, totty, trifling, wee, weeny.
antonyms big, immense.

tip[1] *n*. acme, apex, cap, crown, end, extremity, ferrule, head, nib, peak, pinnacle, point, summit, top.
v. cap, crown, finish, pinnacle, poll, pollard, prune, surmount, top.

tip[2] *v*. cant, capsize, ditch, dump, empty, heel, incline, lean, list, overturn, pour out, slant, spill, tilt, topple over, unload, up-end, upset.
n. bing, coup, dump, midden, refuse-heap, rubbish-heap, slag-heap.

tip[3] *n*. baksheesh, clue, forecast, gen, gift, gratuity, hint, information, inside information, lagniappe, perquisite, pointer, pourboire, refresher, suggestion, tip-off, warning, word, word of advice, wrinkle.
v. advise, caution, forewarn, inform, remunerate, reward, suggest, tell, warn.

tipsy *adj*. a peg too low, a pip out, cockeyed, corny, drunk, elevated, fuddled, happy, mellow, merry, moony, moppy, mops and brooms, nappy, pixil(l)ated, rocky, screwed, screwy, slewed, sprung, squiff(y), tiddled, tiddley, tiddly, tight, totty, wet, woozy.
antonym sober.

tirade *n*. abuse, denunciation, diatribe, fulmination, harangue, invective, lecture, outburst, philippic, rant.

tire *v*. annoy, betoil, bore, cook, drain, droop, enervate, exasperate, exhaust, fag, fail, fatigue, flag, harass, irk, irritate, jade, knacker, sink, weary.

antonyms energize, enliven, exhilarate, invigorate, refresh.

tired *adj*. all in, awearied, aweary, beat, bone- weary, bushed, clapped-out, clichéd, conventional, corny, dead- beat, disjaskit, dog-tired, drained, drooping, drowsy, enervated, épuisé(e), exhausted, fagged, familiar, fatigued, flagging, forfairn, forfough(t)en, forjeskit, hackneyed, jaded, knackered, old, outworn, shagged, shattered, sleepy, spent, stale, stock, threadbare, trite, weary, well-worn, whacked, worn out.
antonyms active, energetic, fresh, lively, rested.

tireless *adj*. determined, diligent, energetic, indefatigable, industrious, resolute, sedulous, unflagging, untiring, unwearied, vigorous.
antonyms tired, unenthusiastic, weak.

tiresome *adj*. annoying, boring, bothersome, dull, exasperating, fatiguing, flat, irksome, irritating, laborious, monotonous, pesky, tedious, troublesome, trying, uninteresting, vexatious, wearing, wearisome.
antonyms easy, interesting, stimulating.

tiring *adj*. arduous, demanding, draining, enervating, enervative, exacting, exhausting, fagging, fatiguing, laborious, strenuous, tough, wearing, wearying.

titan *n*. Atlas, colossus, giant, Hercules, leviathan, superman.

titillating *adj*. arousing, captivating, exciting, interesting, intriguing, lewd, lurid, provocative, sensational, stimulating, suggestive, teasing, thrilling.

title *n*. appellation, caption, championship, claim, crown, denomination, designation, entitlement, epithet, handle, heading, inscription, label, laurels, legend, letterhead, moniker, name, nickname, nom de plume, ownership, prerogative, privilege, pseudonym, right, sobriquet, style, term.
v. call, christen, designate, dub, entitle, label, name, style, term.

toast[1] *v*. broil, brown, grill, heat, roast, warm.

toast[2] *n*. compliment, darling, drink, favorite, grace cup, health, hero, heroine, pledge, salutation, salute, tribute, wassail.

together *adv*. all at once, arranged, as one, as one man, at the same time, cheek by jowl, closely, collectively, concurrently, consecutively, contemporaneously, continuously, en masse, fixed, hand in glove, hand in hand, in a body, in a row, in concert, in co-operation, in fere, in mass, in succession, in unison, jointly, mutually, on end, ordered, organized, pari passu, settled, shoulder to shoulder, side by side, simultaneously, sorted out, straight, successively.
antonym separately.
adj. calm, commonsensical, composed, cool, down-to- earth, level-headed, sensible, stable, well-adjusted, well- balanced, well-organized.

toil *n*. application, donkey-work, drudgery, effort, elbow grease, exertion, graft, industry, labor, labor improbus, pains, slog, sweat, travail.

v. drudge, graft, grind, grub, labor, persevere, plug away, slave, slog, strive, struggle, sweat, tew, work.

token *n.* badge, clue, demonstration, earnest, evidence, expression, index, indication, keepsake, manifestation, mark, memento, memorial, note, proof, remembrance, reminder, representation, sign, souvenir, symbol, tessera, testimony, voucher, warning.
adj. emblematic, hollow, inconsiderable, minimal, nominal, perfunctory, superficial, symbolic.

tolerant *adj.* biddable, broad-minded, catholic, charitable, complaisant, compliant, easy-going, fair, forbearing, indulgent, kind-hearted, latitudinarian, lax, lenient, liberal, long-suffering, magnanimous, open-minded, patient, permissive, soft, sympathetic, understanding, unprejudiced.
antonyms biased, bigoted, intolerant, prejudiced, unsympathetic.

tolerate *v.* abear, abide, accept, admit, allow, bear, brook, condone, connive at, countenance, endure, indulge, permit, pocket, put up with, receive, sanction, stand, stomach, suffer, swallow, take, thole, turn a blind eye to, undergo, wear, wink at.

toll[1] *v.* announce, call, chime, clang, knell, peal, ring, send, signal, sound, strike, summon, warn.

toll[2] *n.* assessment, charge, cost, customs, damage, demand, duty, fee, impost, inroad, levy, loss, payment, penalty, rate, tariff, tax, tithe, tribute.

tomb *n.* burial-place, catacomb, cenotaph, crypt, dolmen, grave, mastaba, mausoleum, sepulcher, sepulture, speos, vault.

tone *n.* accent, air, approach, aspect, attitude, cast, character, color, drift, effect, emphasis, feel, force, frame, grain, harmony, hue, inflection, intonation, klang, manner, modulation, mood, note, pitch, quality, shade, spirit, strength, stress, style, temper, tenor, timbre, tinge, tint, tonality, vein, volume.
v. blend, harmonize, intone, match, sound, suit.

tongue *n.* argot, articulation, clack, clapper, dialect, discourse, idiom, language, languet(te), lath, lingo, parlance, patois, red rag, speech, talk, utterance, vernacular, voice.

tongue-tied *adj.* dumb, dumbstruck, inarticulate, mute, silent, speechless, voiceless.
antonyms garrulous, talkative, voluble.

too[1] *adv.* also, as well, besides, further, in addition, into the bargain, likewise, moreover, to boot, what's more.

too[2] *adv.* excessively, exorbitantly, extremely, immoderately, inordinately, over, overly, ridiculously, to excess, to extremes, unduly, unreasonably, very.

tool *n.* agency, agent, apparatus, appliance, cat's-paw, contraption, contrivance, creature, device, dupe, flunkey, front, gadget, hireling, implement, instrument, intermediary, jackal, lackey, machine, means, medium, minion, pawn, puppet, stooge, toady, utensil, vehicle, weapon, widget. *v.* chase, cut, decorate, fashion, machine, ornament, shape, work.

top *n.* acme, apex, apogee, cacumen, cap, cop, cork, cover, crest, crown, culmen, culmination, head, height, high point, hood, lead, lid, meridian, peak, pinnacle, roof, stopper, summit, upside, vertex, zenith.
antonyms base, bottom, nadir.
adj. best, chief, crack, crowning, culminating, dominant, elite, finest, first, foremost, greatest, head, highest, lead, leading, pre-eminent, prime, principal, ruling, sovereign, superior, topmost, upmost, upper, uppermost.
v. ascend, beat, best, better, cap, climb, command, cover, crest, crown, decorate, eclipse, exceed, excel, finish, finish off, garnish, head, lead, outdo, outshine, outstrip, roof, rule, scale, surmount, surpass, tip, transcend.

topic *n.* issue, lemma, matter, motif, point, question, subject, subject-matter, talking-point, text, theme, thesis.

topical *adj.* contemporary, current, familiar, newsworthy, popular, relevant, up-to-date, up-to-the-minute.

topple *v.* capsize, collapse, oust, overbalance, overthrow, overturn, totter, tumble, unseat, upset.

torment *v.* afflict, agitate, agonize, annoy, bedevil, bother, chivvy, crucify, devil, distort, distress, excruciate, harass, harrow, harry, hound, irritate, nag, pain, persecute, pester, plague, provoke, rack, tease, torture, trouble, vex, worry, wrack.
n. affliction, agony, angst, anguish, annoyance, bane, bother, distress, harassment, hassle, hell, irritation, misery, nag, nagging, nuisance, pain, persecution, pest, plague, provocation, scourge, suffering, torture, trouble, vexation, worry.

torpid *adj.* apathetic, benumbed, dormant, drowsy, dull, fainéant, hebetudinous, inactive, indolent, inert, lackadaisical, languid, languorous, lazy, lethargic, listless, lymphatic, motionless, numb, passive, slothful, slow, slow- moving, sluggish, somnolent, stagnant, supine.
antonyms active, lively, vigorous.

torpor *n.* accidie, acedia, apathy, dormancy, drowsiness, dullness, hebetude, inactivity, inanition, indolence, inertia, inertness, languor, laziness, lethargy, listlessness, numbness, passivity, sloth, sluggishness, somnolence, stagnancy, stupidity, stupor, torpidity.
antonyms activity, animation, vigor.

torrent *n.* barrage, cascade, deluge, downpour, effusion, flood, flow, gush, outburst, rush, spate, stream, tide, volley.

torrid *adj.* ardent, arid, blistering, boiling, broiling, burning, dried, dry, emotional, erotic, fervent, fiery, hot, intense, parched, parching, passionate, scorched, scorching, sexy, sizzling, steamy, stifling, sultry, sweltering, tropical.
antonym arctic.

tortuous *adj.* ambagious, ambiguous, bent, Byzantine, circuitous, complicated, convoluted, crooked, cunning, curved, deceptive, devious, indirect, involved, mazy,

meandering, misleading, roundabout, serpentine, sinuous, tricky, twisted, twisting, winding, zigzag.
antonyms straight, straightforward.

torture *v.* afflict, agonize, crucify, distress, excruciate, harrow, lacerate, martyr, martyrize, pain, persecute, rack, torment, wrack.
n. affliction, agony, anguish, distress, gyp, hell, laceration, martyrdom, misery, pain, pang(s), persecution, rack, suffering, torment.

toss *v.* agitate, cant, cast, chuck, disturb, fling, flip, heave, hurl, jiggle, joggle, jolt, labor, launch, lob, lurch, pitch, project, propel, rock, roll, shake, shy, sling, thrash, throw, tumble, wallow, welter, wriggle, writhe.
n. cast, chuck, fling, lob, pitch, shy, sling, throw.

total *n.* aggregate, all, amount, ensemble, entirety, lot, mass, sum, totality, whole.
adj. absolute, all-out, complete, comprehensive, consummate, downright, entire, full, gross, integral, out-and- out, outright, perfect, root-and-branch, sheer, sweeping, thorough, thoroughgoing, unconditional, undisputed, undivided, unmitigated, unqualified, utter, whole, whole-hog.
antonyms limited, partial, restricted.
v. add (up), amount to, come to, count (up), reach, reckon, sum (up), tot up.

totalitarian *adj.* authoritarian, despotic, dictatorial, monocratic, monolithic, omnipotent, one-party, oppressive, tyrannous, undemocratic.
antonym democratic.

totter *v.* daddle, daidle, falter, lurch, quiver, reel, rock, shake, stagger, stumble, sway, teeter, titter, tremble, waver.

touch *n.* ability, acquaintance, adroitness, approach, art, artistry, awareness, bit, blow, brush, caress, characteristic, command, communication, contact, correspondence, dash, deftness, detail, direction, drop, effect, facility, familiarity, feel, feeling, flair, fondling, hand, handiwork, handling, hint, hit, influence, intimation, jot, knack, manner, mastery, method, palpation, pat, pinch, push, skill, smack, smattering, soupçon, speck, spot, stroke, style, suggestion, suspicion, tactility, tap, taste, technique, tig, tincture, tinge, trace, trademark, understanding, virtuosity, way, whiff.
v. abut, adjoin, affect, attain, border, brush, caress, cheat, compare with, concern, consume, contact, converge, disturb, drink, eat, equal, feel, finger, fondle, graze, handle, hit, hold a candle to, impress, influence, inspire, interest, mark, match, meet, melt, move, palp, palpate, parallel, pat, pertain to, push, reach, regard, rival, soften, stir, strike, stroke, tap, tat, tinge, upset, use, utilize.

touch-and-go *adj.* close, critical, dangerous, dodgy, hairy, hazardous, near, nerve-racking, offhand, parlous, perilous, precarious, risky, sticky, tricky.

touching *adj.* affecting, emotional, emotive, haptic, heartbreaking, libant, melting, moving, pathetic, piteous, pitiable, pitiful, poignant, sad, stirring, tender.

touchy *adj.* bad-tempered, captious, crabbed, cross, feisty, grouchy, grumpy, huffy, irascible, irritable, miffy, peevish, pettish, petulant, querulous, quick-tempered, snippety, snuffy, sore, splenetic, surly, testy, tetchy, thin-skinned.
antonyms calm, imperturbable, serene, unflappable.

tough *adj.* adamant, arduous, bad, baffling, brawny, butch, callous, cohesive, difficult, durable, exacting, exhausting, firm, fit, hard, hard-bitten, hard-boiled, hardened, hardnosed, hardy, herculean, inflexible, intractable, irksome, knotty, laborious, lamentable, leathery, merciless, obdurate, obstinate, perplexing, pugnacious, puzzling, refractory, regrettable, resilient, resistant, resolute, rigid, rough, ruffianly, rugged, ruthless, seasoned, severe, solid, stalwart, stern, stiff, stout, strapping, strenuous, strict, strong, stubborn, sturdy, tenacious, thorny, troublesome, unbending, unforgiving, unfortunate, unlucky, unyielding, uphill, vicious, vigorous, violent.
antonyms brittle, delicate, fragile, liberal, soft, tender, vulnerable, weak.
n. bravo, bruiser, brute, bully, bully-boy, bully- rook, gorilla, hooligan, rough, roughneck, rowdy, ruffian, thug, yob, yobbo.

toughness *n.* arduousness, callousness, difficulty, durability, firmness, fitness, grit, hardiness, hardness, inflexibility, intractability, laboriousness, obduracy, obstinacy, pugnacity, resilience, resistance, rigidity, roughness, ruggedness, ruthlessness, severity, solidity, sternness, stiffness, strength, strenuousness, strictness, sturdiness, tenacity, viciousness.
antonyms fragility, liberality, softness, vulnerability, weakness.

tour *n.* circuit, course, drive, excursion, expedition, jaunt, journey, outing, peregrination, progress, ride, round, trip.
v. drive, explore, journey, ride, sightsee, travel, visit.

tourist *n.* excursionist, globe-trotter, holidaymaker, journeyer, rubber-neck, sightseer, sojourner, traveler.

tournament *n.* championship, competition, contest, event, joust, lists, match, meeting, series, tourney.

tousled *adj.* disarranged, disheveled, disordered, messed up, ruffled, rumpled, tangled, tumbled.

tow *v.* drag, draw, haul, lug, pull, tote, trail, transport, trawl, tug, yank.

towering *adj.* burning, colossal, elevated, excessive, extra-ordinary, extreme, fiery, gigantic, great, high, immoderate, imposing, impressive, inordinate, intemperate, intense, lofty, magnificent, mighty, monumental, outstanding, overpowering, paramount, passionate, prodigious, soaring, sublime, superior, supreme, surpassing, tall, transcendent, vehement, violent.
antonyms minor, small, trivial.

town *n.* borough, bourg, burg, burgh, city, metropolis, municipality, settlement, township.
antonym country.

toxic *adj.* baneful, deadly, harmful, lethal, morbific, noxious, pernicious, pestilential, poisonous, septic, unhealthy.
antonym harmless.

toy *n.* bauble, doll, game, gewgaw, kickshaw(s), knick-knack, plaything, trifle, trinket.
v. dally, fiddle, flirt, play, potter, putter, sport, tinker, trifle, wanton.

trace *n.* bit, dash, drop, evidence, footmark, footprint, footstep, hint, indication, iota, jot, mark, path, record, relic, remains, remnant, scintilla, shadow, sign, smack, soupçon, spoor, spot, suggestion, survival, suspicion, tincture, tinge, token, touch, track, trail, trifle, vestige, whiff.
v. ascertain, chart, copy, delineate, depict, detect, determine, discover, draw, find, follow, map, mark, outline, pursue, record, seek, shadow, show, sketch, stalk, track, trail, traverse, unearth, write.

track *n.* course, drift, footmark, footprint, footstep, line, mark, orbit, path, pathway, piste, rail, rails, ridgeway, road, scent, sequence, slot, spoor, tack, trace, trail, train, trajectory, wake, wavelength, way.
v. chase, dog, follow, hunt, pursue, shadow, spoor, stalk, tail, trace, trail, travel, traverse.

tract[1] *n.* area, district, estate, expanse, extent, lot, plot, quarter, region, section, stretch, territory, zone.

tract[2] *n.* booklet, brochure, discourse, disquisition, dissertation, essay, homily, leaflet, monograph, pamphlet, sermon, tractate, treatise.

tractable *adj.* amenable, biddable, complaisant, compliant, controllable, docile, ductile, fictile, governable, malleable, manageable, obedient, persuadable, plastic, pliable, pliant, submissive, tame, tractile, willing, workable, yielding.
antonyms headstrong, intractable, obstinate, refractory, stubborn, unruly, wilful.

trade *n.* avocation, barter, business, calling, clientele, commerce, commodities, craft, custom, customers, deal, dealing, employment, exchange, interchange, job, line, market, métier, occupation, patrons, profession, public, pursuit, shopkeeping, skill, swap, traffic, transactions, truck.
v. bargain, barter, commerce, deal, do business, exchange, peddle, swap, switch, traffic, transact, truck.

trademark *n.* badge, brand, crest, emblem, hallmark, identification, idiograph, insignia, label, logo, logotype, name, sign, symbol.

tradition *n.* convention, custom, customs, folklore, habit, institution, lore, praxis, ritual, usage, usance, way, wony.

traduce *v.* abuse, asperse, blacken, calumniate, decry, defame, denigrate, deprecate, depreciate, detract, disparage, knock, malign, misrepresent, revile, run down, slag, slander, smear, vilify.

tragedy *n.* adversity, affliction, blow, calamity, catastrophe, disaster, misfortune, unhappiness.
antonyms prosperity, success, triumph.

tragic *adj.* anguished, appalling, awful, calamitous, catastrophic, deadly, dire, disastrous, doleful, dreadful, fatal, grievous, heartbreaking, heart-rending, ill-fated, ill-starred, lamentable, miserable, mournful, pathetic, pitiable, ruinous, sad, shocking, sorrowful, thespian, unfortunate, unhappy, woeful, wretched.
antonyms comic, successful, triumphant.

trail *v.* chase, dangle, dawdle, drag, draw, droop, extend, follow, hang, haul, hunt, lag, linger, loiter, pull, pursue, shadow, stalk, straggle, stream, sweep, tail, tow, trace, track, traipse.
n. abature, appendage, drag, footpath, footprints, footsteps, mark, marks, path, road, route, scent, spoor, stream, tail, trace, track, train, wake, way.

train *v.* aim, coach, direct, discipline, drill, educate, exercise, focus, guide, improve, instruct, lesson, level, point, prepare, rear, rehearse, school, teach, tutor.
n. appendage, attendants, caravan, chain, choo-choo, column, concatenation, convoy, cortege, course, court, entourage, file, followers, following, household, lure, order, process, procession, progression, retinue, sequence, series, set, staff, string, succession, suite, tail, trail.

traipse *v.* plod, slouch, trail, tramp, trudge.
n. plod, slog, tramp, trek, trudge.

trait *n.* attribute, characteristic, feature, idiosyncrasy, lineament, mannerism, peculiarity, quality, quirk, thew.

traitor *n.* apostate, back-stabber, betrayer, deceiver, defector, deserter, double-crosser, fifth columnist, informer, Judas, miscreant, nithing, proditor, quisling, rebel, renegade, turncoat.

traitorous *adj.* apostate, dishonorable, disloyal, double-crossing, double-dealing, faithless, false, perfidious, proditorious, renegade, seditious, treacherous, treasonable, unfaithful, untrue.
antonyms faithful, loyal, patriotic.

trajectory *n.* course, flight, line, path, route, track, trail.

tramp *v.* crush, footslog, hike, march, plod, ramble, range, roam, rove, slog, stamp, stomp, stump, toil, traipse, trample, tread, trek, trudge, walk, yomp.
n. call girl, clochard, derelict, dosser, down-and-out, drifter, drummer, footfall, footstep, hike, hobo, hooker, march, piker, plod, ramble, slog, stamp, street walker, toerag(ger), tread, trek, vagabond, vagrant, weary willie.

trample *v.* crush, flatten, hurt, infringe, insult, squash, stamp, tread, violate.

tranquil *adj.* at peace, calm, composed, cool, disimpassioned, dispassionate, pacific, peaceful, placid, quiet, reposeful, restful, sedate, serene, still, undisturbed, unexcited, unperturbed, unruffled, untroubled.
antonyms agitated, disturbed, noisy, troubled.

tranquility *n.* ataraxia, ataraxy, calm, calmness, composure, coolness, equanimity, hush, imperturbability, peace, peacefulness, placidity, quiet, quietness, quietude, repose, rest, restfulness, sedateness, serenity, silence, stillness.
antonyms agitation, disturbance, noise.

transact *v.* accomplish, carry on, carry out, conclude, conduct, discharge, dispatch, do, enact, execute, handle, manage, negotiate, perform, prosecute, settle.

transaction *n.* action, affair, arrangement, bargain, business, coup, deal, deed, enterprise, event, execution, matter, negotiation, occurrence, proceeding, undertaking.

transcend *v.* eclipse, exceed, excel, outdo, outrival, outshine, outstrip, overleap, overstep, overtop, surmount, surpass.

transcribe *v.* copy, engross, exemplify, interpret, note, record, render, reproduce, rewrite, take down, tape, tape- record, transfer, translate, transliterate.

transfer *v.* carry, cede, change, consign, convey, decal, decant, demise, displace, grant, hand over, move, relocate, remove, second, shift, translate, transmit, transplant, transport, transpose.

n. change, changeover, crossover, decantation, displacement, handover, move, relocation, removal, shift, switch, switch-over, transference, translation, transmission, transposition, virement.

transform *v.* alter, change, convert, metamorphose, reconstruct, remodel, renew, revolutionize, transfigure, translate, transmogrify, transmute, transverse.
antonym preserve.

transgression *n.* breach, contravention, crime, debt, encroachment, error, fault, infraction, infringement, iniquity, lapse, misbehavior, misdeed, misdemeanor, offence, peccadillo, peccancy, sin, trespass, violation, wrong, wrongdoing.

transient *adj.* brief, caducous, deciduous, ephemeral, evanescent, fleeting, flying, fugacious, fugitive, impermanent, momentary, passing, short, short-lived, short-term, temporary, transitory.
antonym permanent.

transition *n.* alteration, change, changeover, conversion, development, evolution, flux, metabasis, metamorphosis, metastasis, passage, passing, progress, progression, shift, transformation, transit, transmutation, upheaval.
antonyms beginning, end.

translate *v.* alter, carry, change, construe, convert, convey, decipher, decode, do, do up, elucidate, enrapture, explain, improve, interpret, metamorphose, move, paraphrase, remove, render, renovate, send, simplify, spell out, transcribe, transfer, transfigure, transform, transliterate, transmogrify, transmute, transplant, transport, transpose, turn.

translucent *adj.* clear, diaphanous, limpid, lucent, pellucid, translucid, transparent.
antonym opaque.

transmit *v.* bear, broadcast, carry, communicate, convey, diffuse, dispatch, disseminate, forward, impart, network, radio, relay, remit, send, spread, traject, transfer, transport.
antonym receive.

transparent *adj.* apparent, candid, clear, crystalline, diaphanous, dioptric, direct, distinct, easy, evident, explicit, filmy, forthright, frank, gauzy, hyaline, hyaloid, ingenuous, limpid, lucent, lucid, manifest, obvious, open, patent, pellucid, perspicuous, plain, plain-spoken, recognizable, see-through, sheer, straight, straightforward, translucent, transpicuous, unambiguous, understandable, undisguised, unequivocal, visible.
antonyms ambiguous, opaque, unclear.

transpire *v.* appear, arise, befall, betide, chance, come out, come to light, emerge, happen, leak out, occur, take place, turn up.

transport *v.* banish, bear, bring, captivate, carry, carry away, convey, delight, deport, ecstasize, electrify, enchant, enrapture, entrance, exile, fetch, haul, move, ravish, remove, run, ship, spellbind, take, transfer, waft.
antonyms bore, leave.
n. bliss, carriage, cartage, carting, conveyance, delight, ecstasy, enchantment, euphoria, happiness, haulage, heaven, rapture, ravishment, removal, shipment, shipping, transference, transportation, vehicle, waterage.
antonym boredom.

transpose *v.* alter, change, exchange, interchange, metathesize, move, rearrange, relocate, reorder, shift, substitute, swap, switch, transfer.
antonym leave.

trap *n.* ambush, artifice, bunker, danger, deception, device, gin, hazard, net, noose, pitfall, ruse, snare, spring, springe, springle, strategem, subterfuge, toils, trapdoor, trepan, trick, trickery, wile.
v. ambush, beguile, benet, catch, corner, deceive, dupe, enmesh, ensnare, entrap, illaqueate, inveigle, lime, snare, take, tangle, trepan, trick.

trash *n.* balderdash, draff, dregs, drivel, dross, garbage, hogwash, inanity, junk, kitsch, litter, nonsense, offscourings, offscum, refuse, riddlings, rot, rubbish, scoria, sullage, sweepings, trashery, tripe, trumpery, twaddle, waste.
antonym sense.

trashy *adj.* catchpenny, cheap, cheap-jack, flimsy, grotty, inferior, kitschy, meretricious, pinchbeck, rubbishy, shabby, shoddy, tawdry, third-rate, tinsel, worthless.
antonym first-rate.

trauma *n.* agony, anguish, damage, disturbance, hurt, injury, jolt, lesion, ordeal, pain, scar, shock, strain, suffering, torture, upheaval, upset, wound.
antonyms healing, relaxation.

travail *n.* birth-pangs, childbirth, distress, drudgery, effort, exertion, grind, hardship, labor, labor pains, pain, slavery, slog, strain, stress, suffering, sweat, tears, throes, toil, tribulation.
antonym rest.

travel *v.* carry, commute, cross, excursionize, go, journey, locomote, move, peregrinate, proceed, progress, ramble, roam, rove, tour, traverse, trek, voyage, walk, wander, wayfare, wend.
antonym stay.

travesty *n*. apology, botch, burlesque, caricature, distortion, lampoon, mockery, parody, perversion, send-up, sham, take-off. *v.* burlesque, caricature, deride, distort, lampoon, mock, parody, pervert, pillory, ridicule, send up, sham, spoof, take off.

treachery *n*. betrayal, disloyalty, double-cross, double-dealing, duplicity, faithlessness, falseness, infidelity, Judaskiss, laesa majestas, Medism, perfidiousness, perfidy, Punic faith, Punica fides, trahison, treason. *antonyms* dependability, loyalty.

treason *n*. disaffection, disloyalty, duplicity, laesa majestas, lese-majesty, mutiny, perfidy, sedition, subversion, trahison, traitorousness, treachery. *antonym* loyalty.

treasure *n*. cash, darling, ewe-lamb, flower, fortune, funds, gem, gold, jewel, jewels, money, nonpareil, paragon, pearl, precious, pride and joy, prize, riches, valuables, wealth. *v.* adore, cherish, esteem, idolize, love, preserve, prize, revere, value, venerate, worship. *antonym* disparage.

treat *n*. banquet, celebration, delight, enjoyment, entertainment, excursion, feast, fun, gift, gratification, joy, outing, party, pleasure, refreshment, satisfaction, surprise, thrill, wayzgoose. *antonym* drag. *v.* attend to, bargain, care for, confer, consider, contain, deal with, discourse upon, discuss, doctor, entertain, feast, give, handle, manage, medicament, medicate, medicine, negotiate, nurse, parley, provide, regale, regard, stand, use.

treaty *n*. agreement, alliance, bargain, bond, compact, concordat, contract, convention, covenant, entente, negotiation, pact.

trek *n*. expedition, footslog, hike, journey, march, migration, odyssey, safari, slog, tramp, walk. *v.* footslog, hike, journey, march, migrate, plod, range, roam, rove, slog, traipse, tramp, trudge, yomp.

tremble *v.* heave, oscillate, quake, quiver, rock, shake, shiver, shudder, teeter, totter, vibrate, wobble. *n.* heart-quake, oscillation, quake, quiver, shake, shiver, shudder, tremblement, tremor, vibration. *antonym* steadiness.

trembling *n*. heart-quake, oscillation, quaking, quavering, quivering, rocking, shakes, shaking, shivering, shuddering, tremblement, trepidation, vibration. *antonym* steadiness.

tremendous *adj.* ace, amazing, appalling, awe- inspiring, awesome, awful, colossal, deafening, dreadful, enormous, excellent, exceptional, extraordinary, fabulous, fantastic, fearful, formidable, frightful, gargantuan, gigantic, great, herculean, huge, immense, incredible, mammoth, marvelous, monstrous, prodigious, sensational, spectacular, stupendous, super, terrible, terrific, titanic, towering, vast, whopping, wonderful. *antonyms* boring, dreadful, run-of-the-mill, tiny.

tremor *n*. agitation, earthquake, quake, quaking, quaver, quavering, quiver, quivering, shake, shaking, shiver, shock, thrill, tremble, trembling, trepidation, trillo, vibration, wobble. *antonym* steadiness.

tremulous *adj.* afraid, agitated, agog, anxious, aspen, excited, fearful, frightened, jittery, jumpy, nervous, quavering, quivering, quivery, scared, shaking, shivering, timid, trembling, trembly, tremulant, trepid, trepidant, vibrating, wavering. *antonyms* calm, firm.

trenchant *adj.* acerbic, acid, acidulous, acute, astringent, biting, caustic, clear, clear-cut, cogent, crisp, cutting, distinct, driving, effective, effectual, emphatic, energetic, explicit, forceful, forthright, hurtful, incisive, keen, mordant, penetrating, piquant, pointed, potent, powerful, pungent, sarcastic, scratching, severe, sharp, strong, tart, unequivocal, vigorous. *antonym* woolly.

trend *n*. bias, course, crazed, current, dernier cri, direction, fad, fashion, flow, inclination, leaning, look, mode, rage, style, tendency, thing, vogue.

trendy *adj.* fashionable, funky, groovy, in, latest, modish, stylish, up to the minute, voguish, with it. *antonym* unfashionable.

trepidation *n*. agitation, alarm, anxiety, apprehension, butterflies, cold sweat, consternation, dismay, disquiet, disturbance, dread, emotion, excitement, fear, fright, jitters, misgivings, nervousness, palpitation, perturbation, qualms, quivering, shaking, trembling, tremor, unease, uneasiness, worry. *antonym* calm.

trespass *v.* encroach, err, infringe, injure, intrude, invade, obtrude, offend, poach, sin, transgress, violate, wrong. *antonyms* keep to, obey. *n.* breach, contravention, crime, debt, delinquency, encroachment, error, evil-doing, fault, infraction, infringement, iniquity, injury, intrusion, invasion, misbehavior, misconduct, misdeed, misdemeanor, offense, poaching, sin, transgression, wrong-doing.

trespasser *n*. criminal, debtor, delinquent, evil- doer, infringer, interloper, intruder, invader, malefactor, offender, poacher, sinner, transgressor, wrong-doer.

tribe *n*. blood, branch, caste, clan, class, division, dynasty, family, gens, group, house, ilk, nation, people, phratry, race, seed, sept, stock.

tribulation *n*. adversity, affliction, blow, burden, care, curse, distress, grief, heartache, misery, misfortune, ordeal, pain, reverse, sorrow, suffering, travail, trial, trouble, unhappiness, vexation, woe, worry, wretchedness. *antonyms* happiness, rest.

tribunal *n*. bar, bench, court, examination, hearing, inquisition, trial.

tribute *n*. accolade, acknowledgment, annates, applause,

charge, commendation, compliment, contribution, cornage, credit, customs, duty, encomium, esteem, eulogy, excise, first-fruits, gavel, gift, gratitude, homage, honor, horngeld, impost, laudation, offering, panegyric, payment, praise, ransom, recognition, respect, subsidy, tax, testimonial, testimony, toll.
antonyms blame.

trick *n.* antic, art, artifice, cantrip, caper, characteristic, chicane, command, con, craft, deceit, deception, device, dodge, dog-trick, expedient, expertise, feat, feint, foible, fraud, frolic, gag, gambol, gift, gimmick, habit, hang, hoax, idiosyncrasy, imposition, imposture, jape, joke, josh, knack, know-how, legerdemain, leg-pull, maneuver, mannerism, peculiarity, ploy, practical joke, practice, prank, put-on, quirk, quiz, rig, ruse, secret, shot, skill, sleight, spell, stall, stratagem, stunt, subterfuge, swindle, technique, toy, trait, trap, trinket, turn, wile.
adj. artificial, bogus, counterfeit, ersatz, fake, false, feigned, forged, imitation, mock, pretend, sham.
antonym genuine.
v. bamboozle, beguile, cheat, con, cozen, deceive, defraud, delude, diddle, dupe, fool, gull, hoax, hocus-pocus, hoodwink, hornswoggle, illude, lead on, mislead, outwit, pull a fast one on, pull someone's leg, sell, swindle, trap.

trickle *v.* dribble, drip, drop, exude, filter, gutter, leak, ooze, percolate, run, seep.
antonyms gush, stream.
n. drib, dribble, driblet, dribs and drabs, drip, seepage.
antonyms gush, stream.

tricky *adj.* artful, complicated, crafty, cunning, deceitful, deceptive, delicate, devious, difficult, foxy, Gordian, knotty, legerdemain, problematic, risky, scheming, slippery, sly, sticky, subtle, thorny, ticklish, touch-and-go, trickish, tricksome, tricksy, wily.
antonyms easy, honest.

trifling *adj.* empty, footling, foozling, fribbling, fribblish, frivolous, idle, inconsiderable, insignificant, minuscule, negligible, nugatory, paltry, petty, piddling, piffling, puny, shallow, silly, slight, small, tiny, trivial, unimportant, valueless, worthless.
antonym important.
n. desipience, fiddling, fooling, footling, frivolity, piddling, piffling, whifflery.

trigger *v.* activate, actuate, cause, elicit, generate, initiate, produce, prompt, provoke, set off, spark off, start.
n. catch, goad, lever, release, spur, stimulus, switch.

trim *adj.* clean-limbed, compact, dapper, natty, neat, orderly, shipshape, slender, slim, smart, smirk, soigné, spick-and-span, spruce, streamlined, svelte, trig, well-dressed, well-groomed, willowy.
antonym scruffy.
v. adjust, adorn, arrange, array, balance, barb, barber, beautify, bedeck, clip, crop, curtail, cut, decorate, distribute, dock, dress, dub, embellish, embroider, garnish,

lop, order, ornament, pare, prepare, prune, settle, shave, shear, tidy, trick.
n. adornment, array, attire, border, clipping, condition, crop, cut, decoration, disposition, dress, edging, embellishment, equipment, fettle, fitness, fittings, form, frill, fringe, garnish, gear, health, humor, nick, order, ornament, ornamentation, piping, pruning, repair, shape, shave, shearing, situation, state, temper, trappings, trimming.

trimmings *n.* accessories, accompaniments, additions, appurtenances, clippings, cuttings, ends, extras, frills, garnish, ornaments, paraphernalia, parings, remnants, shavings, trappings.

trinket *n.* bagatelle, bauble, bibelot, bijou, doodad, fairing, gewgaw, gimcrack, kickshaws, knick-knack, nothing, ornament, toy, trifle, trinkum-trankum, whigmaleerie, whim-wham.

trio *n.* terzetto, threesome, triad, trilogy, trine, trinity, triple, triplet, triptych, triumvirate, triune.

trip *n.* blunder, boob, errand, error, excursion, expedition, fall, faux pas, foray, indiscretion, jaunt, journey, lapse, misstep, outing, ramble, run, skip, slip, step, stumble, tour, travel, voyage.
v. activate, blunder, boob, caper, confuse, dance, disconcert, engage, err, fall, flip, flit, frisk, gambol, go, hop, lapse, miscalculate, misstep, pull, ramble, release, set off, skip, slip, slip up, spring, stumble, switch on, throw, tilt up, tip up, tour, trap, travel, tumble, unsettle, voyage.

trite *adj.* banal, bromidic, clichéd, common, commonplace, corny, dull, hack, hackneyed, Mickey Mouse, ordinary, overworn, pedestrian, routine, run-of-the-mill, stale, stereotyped, stock, threadbare, tired, uninspired, unoriginal, well-trodden, well-worn, worn, worn out.
antonym original.

triumph *n.* accomplishment, achievement, ascendancy, attainment, conquest, coup, elation, exultation, feat, happiness, hit, joy, jubilation, masterstroke, mastery, pride, rejoicing, sensation, smash, smash-hit, success, tour de force, victory, walk-away, walk-over, win.
antonym disaster.
v. best, celebrate, crow, defeat, dominate, exult, gloat, glory, have the last laugh, humble, humiliate, jubilate, overcome, overwhelm, prevail, prosper, rejoice, revel, subdue, succeed, swagger, vanquish, win.
antonym fail.

triumphant *adj.* boastful, celebratory, cock-a-hoop, conquering, dominant, elated, epinikian, exultant, gloating, glorious, joyful, jubilant, proud, rejoicing, successful, swaggering, triumphal, undefeated, victorious, winning.
antonyms defeated, humble.

trivial *adj.* commonplace, dinky, everyday, frivolous, incidental, inconsequential, inconsiderable, insignificant, little, meaningless, Mickey Mouse, minor, negligible, nugatory, paltry, pettifogging, petty, piddling,

piffling, puny, slight, small, snippety, trifling, trite, unimportant, valueless, worthless.
antonym significant.

troops *n.* army, forces, men, military, servicemen, soldiers, soldiery.

trophy *n.* award, booty, cup, laurels, memento, memorial, prize, souvenir, spoils.

tropical *adj.* equatorial, hot, humid, lush, luxuriant, steamy, stifling, sultry, sweltering, torrid.
antonyms arctic, cold, cool, temperate.

trouble *n.* affliction, agitation, ailment, annoyance, anxiety, attention, bother, care, commotion, complaint, concern, danger, defect, difficulty, dilemma, disability, discontent, discord, disease, disorder, disquiet, dissatisfaction, distress, disturbance, effort, exertion, failure, grief, heartache, illness, inconvenience, irritation, labor, malfunction, mess, misfortune, nuisance, pain, pains, pest, pickle, predicament, problem, row, scrape, solicitude, sorrow, spot, strife, struggle, suffering, thought, torment, travail, trial, tribulation, tumult, uneasiness, unrest, upheaval, upset, vexation, woe, work, worry.
antonyms calm, peace.
v. afflict, agitate, annoy, bother, burden, discomfort, discommode, discompose, disconcert, disquiet, distress, disturb, fash, fret, grieve, harass, incommode, inconvenience, molest, muddy, pain, perplex, perturb, pester, plague, sadden, torment, upset, vex, worry.
antonyms help, reassure.

troublemaker *n.* agent provocateur, agitator, bellwether, bolshevik, firebrand, heller, incendiary, instigator, meddler, mischief-maker, rabble-rouser, ringleader, stirrer, tub- thumper.
antonym peace-maker.

troublesome *adj.* annoying, arduous, bothersome, burdensome, demanding, difficult, disorderly, fashious, harassing, hard, importunate, inconvenient, insubordinate, irksome, irritating, laborious, oppressive, pestilential, plaguesome, plaguey, rebellious, recalcitrant, refractory, rowdy, spiny, taxing, thorny, tiresome, tricky, trying, turbulent, uncooperative, undisciplined, unruly, upsetting, vexatious, violent, wearisome, worrisome, worrying.
antonyms easy, helpful, polite.

trounce *v.* beat, best, censure, clobber, crush, drub, hammer, lick, overwhelm, paste, punish, rebuke, rout, slaughter, thrash, whale, whitewash.

truant *n.* absentee, deserter, dodger, hookey, malingerer, runaway, shirker, skiver, wag.
adj. absent, malingering, missing, runaway, skiving.
v. desert, dodge, malinger, play truant, shirk.

truce *n.* armistice, break, cease-fire, cessation, intermission, interval, let-up, lull, moratorium, peace, respite, rest, stay, suspension, treaty, Truce of God.
antonym hostilities.

truculent *adj.* aggressive, antagonistic, bad- tempered,

bellicose, belligerent, combative, contentious, cross, defiant, fierce, hostile, ill-tempered, obstreperous, pugnacious, quarrelsome, savage, scrappy, sullen, violent.
antonyms co-operative, good-natured.

trudge *v.* clump, footslog, hike, labor, lumber, march, mush, plod, slog, stump, traipse, tramp, trek, walk.
n. footslog, haul, hike, march, mush, slog, traipse, tramp, trek, walk.

true *adj.* absolute, accurate, actual, apod(e)ictic, authentic, bona fide, confirmed, conformable, constant, correct, corrected, dedicated, devoted, dutiful, exact, factual, faithful, fast, firm, genuine, honest, honorable, legitimate, loyal, natural, perfect, precise, proper, pure, real, right, rightful, sincere, sooth, spot-on, square, staunch, steady, true-blue, true-born, true-hearted, trustworthy, trusty, truthful, typical, unerring, unswerving, upright, valid, veracious, veridical, veritable.
antonyms faithless, false, inaccurate.
adv. accurately, correctly, exactly, faithfully, honestly, perfectly, precisely, properly, rightly, truly, truthfully, unerringly, veraciously, veritably.
antonyms falsely, inaccurately.

truly *adv.* accurately, authentically, constantly, correctly, devotedly, dutifully, en verité, exactly, exceptionally, extremely, factually, faithfully, firmly, genuinely, greatly, honestly, honorably, in good sooth, in reality, in truth, indeed, indubitably, legitimately, loyally, precisely, properly, really, rightly, sincerely, soothly, staunchly, steadfastly, steadily, truthfully, undeniably, veraciously, verily, veritably, very.
antonyms faithlessly, falsely, incorrectly, slightly.

truncate *v.* abbreviate, clip, crop, curtail, cut, cut short, lop, maim, pare, prune, shorten, trim.
antonym lengthen.

truss *v.* bind, bundle, fasten, hogtie, pack, pinion, secure, strap, tether, tie.
antonym untie.
n. bale, bandage, beam, binding, brace, bundle, buttress, joist, prop, shore, stanchion, stay, strut, support.

trust *n.* affiance, assurance, belief, care, certainty, certitude, charge, confidence, conviction, credence, credit, custody, duty, expectation, faith, fidelity, guard, guardianship, hope, obligation, protection, reliance, responsibility, safe-keeping, trusteeship, uberrima fides.
antonym mistrust.
v. assign, assume, bank on, believe, command, commit, confide, consign, count on, credit, delegate, depend on, entrust, expect, give, hope, imagine, presume, rely on, suppose, surmise, swear by.
antonym mistrust.

trusting *adj.* confiding, credulous, gullible, innocent, naïve, optimistic, simple, trustful, unguarded, unquestioning, unsuspecting, unsuspicious, unwary.
antonyms cautious, distrustful.

trustworthy *adj.* authentic, dependable, ethical, foursquare, honest, honorable, level-headed, mature, principled, reliable, responsible, righteous, sensible, steadfast, true, trusty, truthful, upright.
antonym unreliable.

truth *n.* accuracy, actuality, axiom, candor, certainty, constancy, dedication, devotion, dutifulness, exactness, fact, facts, factuality, factualness, faith, faithfulness, fidelity, frankness, genuineness, historicity, honesty, integrity, law, legitimacy, loyalty, maxim, naturalism, precision, realism, reality, sooth, truism, truthfulness, uprightness, validity, veracity, verdicality, verity.
antonym falsehood.

truthful *adj.* accurate, candid, correct, exact, faithful, forthright, frank, honest, literal, naturalistic, plainspoken, precise, realistic, reliable, sincere, sooth, soothfast, soothful, straight, straightforward, true, trustworthy, veracious, veridicous, verist, veristic, veritable.
antonym untruthful.

try *v.* adjudge, adjudicate, afflict, aim, annoy, appraise, attempt, catechize, endeavor, essay, evaluate, examine, experiment, hear, inconvenience, inspect, investigate, irk, irritate, pain, plague, prove, sample, seek, strain, stress, strive, struggle, taste, tax, test, tire, trouble, undertake, upset, venture, vex, wear out, weary.
n. appraisal, attempt, bash, crack, effort, endeavor, essay, evaluation, experiment, fling, go, inspection, sample, shot, stab, taste, taster, test, trial, whack.

trying *adj.* aggravating, annoying, arduous, bothersome, difficult, distressing, exasperating, fatiguing, hard, irksome, irritating, searching, severe, stressful, taxing, testing, tiresome, tough, troublesome, upsetting, vexing, wearisome.
antonym calming.

tub *n.* back, barrel, basin, bath, bathtub, bucket, butt, cask, hogshead, keeve, keg, kid, kit, pail, puncheon, stand, tun, vat.

tube *n.* channel, conduit, cylinder, duct, hose, inlet, main, outlet, pipe, shaft, spout, trunk, valve, vas.

tubular *adj.* pipelike, pipy, tubate, tubelike, tubiform, tubulate, tubulous, vasiform.

tuck[1] *v.* cram, crease, fold, gather, insert, push, stuff.
n. crease, fold, gather, pinch, pleat, pucker.

tuck[2] *n.* comestibles, eats, food, grub, nosh, prog, scoff, victuals, vittles.

tuft *n.* beard, bunch, clump, cluster, collection, crest, dag, daglock, dollop, floccule, flocculus, floccus, flock, knot, shock, tassle, topknot, truss, tussock.

tug *v.* drag, draw, haul, heave, jerk, jigger, lug, pluck, pull, tow, wrench, yank.
n. drag, haul, heave, jerk, pluck, pull, tow, traction, wrench, yank.

tuition *n.* education, instruction, lessons, pedagogics, pedagogy, schooling, teaching, training, tutelage, tutoring.

tumble *v.* disorder, drop, fall, flop, jumble, overthrow, pitch, plummet, roll, rumple, stumble, topple, toss, trip up.
n. collapse, drop, fall, flop, plunge, roll, spill, stumble, toss, trip.

tumbledown *adj.* broken-down, crumbling, crumbly, decrepit, dilapidated, disintegrating, ramshackle, rickety, ruined, ruinous, shaky, tottering.
antonym well-kept.

tumult *n.* ado, affray, agitation, altercation, bedlam, brattle, brawl, brouhaha, bustle, clamor, coil, commotion, deray, din, disorder, disturbance, Donnybrook, émeute, excitement, fracas, hubbub, hullabaloo, outbreak, pandemonium, quarrel, racket, riot, rookery, rout, row, ruction, ruffle, stir, stramash, strife, turmoil, unrest, upheaval, uproar.
antonym calm.

tune *n.* agreement, air, attitude, concert, concord, consonance, demeanor, disposition, euphony, frame of mind, harmony, melisma, melody, mood, motif, pitch, song, strain, sympathy, temper, theme, unison.
v. adapt, adjust, attune, harmonize, pitch, regulate, set, synchronize, temper.

tunnel *n.* burrow, channel, chimney, drift, flue, gallery, hole, passage, passageway, sap, shaft, subway, underpass.
v. burrow, dig, excavate, mine, penetrate, sap, undermine.

turbid *adj.* clouded, cloudy, confused, dense, dim, disordered, feculent, foggy, foul, fuzzy, hazy, impure, incoherent, muddled, muddy, murky, opaque, roily, thick, unclear, unsettled.
antonym clear.

turbulent *adj.* agitated, anarchic, blustery, boiling, boisterous, choppy, confused, disordered, disorderly, foaming, furious, insubordinate, lawless, mutinous, obstreperous, raging, rebellious, refractory, riotous, rough, rowdy, seditious, stormy, tempestuous, tumultuous, unbridled, undisciplined, ungovernable, unruly, unsettled, unstable, uproarious, violent, wild.
antonym calm.

turf *n.* clod, divot, glebe, grass, green, sod, sward.

turmoil *n.* agitation, bedlam, brouhaha, bustle, chaos, combustion, commotion, confusion, disorder, disquiet, disturbance, Donnybrook, dust, émeute, ferment, flurry, hubbub, hubbuboo, noise, pandemonium, pother, pudder, rookery, rout, row, ruffle, stir, stour, stramash, strife, tracasserie, trouble, tumult, turbulence, uproar, violence, welter.
antonym calm.

turn *v.* adapt, alter, apostatize, appeal, apply, approach, become, caracol, change, circle, construct, convert, corner, curdle, defect, deliver, depend, desert, divert, double, execute, fashion, fit, form, frame, go, gyrate, hang, hinge, infatuate, influence, issue, look, make, metamorphose, mold, move, mutate, nauseate, negotiate, pass, perform, persuade, pivot, prejudice, remodel, renege, resort, retract, return, reverse, revolve, roll, rotate, shape, shift, sicken, sour, spin, spoil, swerve, switch, swivel, taint, transfigure, transform, translate, transmute, twirl, twist, upset, veer, wheel, whirl, write. *n.* act, action, airing, aptitude, bend, bent, bias, bout, caracol, cast, chance, change, circle, circuit, constitutional, crack, crankle, crisis, culmination, curve, cycle, deed, departure, deviation, direction, distortion, drift, drive, excursion, exigency, fashion, favor, fling, form, format, fright, gesture, go, guise, gyration, heading, innings, jaunt, make-up, manner, mode, mold, occasion, opportunity, outing, performance, performer, period, pivot, promenade, reversal, revolution, ride, rotation, round, saunter, scare, service, shape, shift, shock, shot, spell, spin, start, stint, stroll, style, succession, surprise, swing, tendency, time, trend, trick, try, turning, twist, uey, U-turn, vicissitude, walk, warp, way, whack, whirl.

turncoat *n.* apostate, backslider, blackleg, defector, deserter, fink, rat, recreant, renegade, renegate, scab, seceder, tergiversator, traitor.

turning *n.* bend, crossroads, curve, flexure, fork, junction, turn, turn-off.

turning-point *n.* change, climacteric, crisis, crossroads, crux, cusp, moment of truth, watershed.

turnover *n.* business, change, flow, income, movement, output, outturn, production, productivity, profits, replacement, volume, yield.

tussle *v.* battle, brawl, compete, contend, fight, grapple, scramble, scrap, scuffle, struggle, vie, wrestle. *n.* battle, bout, brawl, competition, conflict, contention, contest, dust-up, fight, fracas, fray, mêlée, punch-up, race, scramble, scrap, scrimmage, scrum, scuffle, set-to, struggle.

tutor *n.* coach, director of studies, educator, governor, guardian, guide, guru, instructor, lecturer, master, mentor, preceptor, répétiteur, supervisor, teacher. *v.* coach, control, direct, discipline, drill, edify, educate, guide, instruct, lecture, school, supervise, teach, train.

tweak *v., n.* jerk, nip, pull, punch, snatch, squeeze, tug, twist, twitch.

twig[1] *n.* branch, offshoot, ramulus, shoot, spray, spring, stick, wattle, whip, withe, withy.

twig[2] *v.* catch on, comprehend, cotton on, fathom, get, grasp, rumble, savvy, see, tumble to, understand.

twilight *n.* crepuscle, crepuscule, decline, demi- jour, dimness, dusk, ebb, evening, eventide, gloaming, half-light, sundown, sunset. *adj.* crepuscular, darkening, declining, dim, dying, ebbing, evening, final, last, shadowy.

twin *n.* clone, corollary, counterpart, doppelgänger, double, duplicate, fellow, gemel, likeness, lookalike, match, mate, ringer. *adj.* balancing, corresponding, didymous, double, dual,

duplicate, geminate, geminous, identical, matched, matching, paired, parallel, symmetrical, twofold. *v.* combine, couple, join, link, match, pair, yoke.

twine *n.* cord, string, twist, yarn. *v.* bend, braid, coil, curl, encircle, entwine, interlace, interweave, knit, loop, meander, plait, snake, spiral, splice, surround, tie, twist, weave, wind, wrap, wreathe, wriggle, zigzag.

twinge *n.* bite, gripe, pain, pang, pinch, prick, qualm, spasm, stab, stitch, throb, throe, tweak, twist, twitch.

twinkle *v.* blink, coruscate, flash, flicker, gleam, glint, glisten, glitter, scintillate, shimmer, shine, sparkle, vibrate, wink. *n.* amusement, blink, coruscation, flash, flicker, gleam, glimmer, glistening, glitter, glittering, light, quiver, scintillation, shimmer, shine, spark, sparkle, wink.

twirl *v.* birl, coil, gyrate, gyre, pirouette, pivot, revolve, rotate, spin, swivel, turn, twiddle, twist, wheel, whirl, wind. *n.* coil, convulution, gyration, gyre, helix, pirouette, revolution, rotation, spin, spiral, turn, twiddle, twist, wheel, whirl, whorl.

twist *v.* alter, change, coil, contort, corkscrew, crankle, crinkle, crisp, curl, distort, encircle, entangle, entwine, garble, intertwine, misquote, misrepresent, pervert, pivot, revolve, rick, screw, spin, sprain, squirm, strain, swivel, turn, tweak, twine, warp, weave, wigwag, wind, wrap, wreathe, wrench, wrest, wrick, wriggle, wring, writhe. *n.* aberration, arc, bend, bent, braid, break, change, characteristic, coil, confusion, contortion, convolution, crankle, curl, curlicue, curve, defect, deformation, development, distortion, eccentricity, entanglement, fault, flaw, foible, hank, idiosyncrasy, imperfection, intortion, jerk, kink, knot, meander, mess, mix-up, nuance, oddity, peculiarity, plug, proclivity, pull, quid, quirk, revelation, roll, screw, slant, snarl, spin, sprain, squiggle, surprise, swivel, tangle, tortion, trait, turn, twine, undulation, variation, warp, wind, wrench, wrest, zigzag.

twitch *v.* blink, flutter, jerk, jump, pinch, pluck, pull, snatch, tug, tweak, vellicate, yank. *n.* blink, convulsion, flutter, jerk, jump, pluck, pull, spasmytic, subsultus, tremor, tweak, twinge, vellication.

two-faced *adj.* deceitful, deceiving, devious, dissembling, double-dealing, double-tongued, duplicitous, false, hypocritical, insincere, Janus-faced, lying, mendacious, perfidious, treacherous, untrustworthy. *antonyms* candid, frank, honest.

tycoon *n.* baron, big cheese, big noise, big shot, capitalist, captain of industry, Croesus, Dives, entrepreneur, fat cat, financier, gold-bug, industrialist, magnate, mogul, nabob, plutocrat, potentate, supremo.

type[1] *n.* archetype, breed, category, class, classification, description, designation, emblem, embodiment, epitome, essence, example, exemplar, form, genre, group, ilk, insignia, kidney, kind, mark, model, order, original, paradigm, pattern, personification, prototype, quintessence, sort, species, specimen, stamp, standard, strain, subdivision, variety.

type[2] *n.* case, characters, face, font, fount, lettering, print, printing.

typhoon *n.* baguio, cordonazo, cyclone, hurricane, squall, storm, tempest, tornado, twister, whirlwind, willy-willy.

typical *adj.* archetypal, average, characteristic, classic, conventional, distinctive, essential, illustrative, indicative, model, normal, orthodox, quintessential, representative, standard, stock, symptomatic, usual, vintage.
antonyms atypical, untypical.

typify *v.* characterize, embody, encapsulate, epitomize, exemplify, illustrate, incarnate, personify, represent, symbolize.

tyrannical *adj.* absolute, arbitrary, authoritarian, autocratic, coercive, despotic, dictatorial, domineering, high-handed, imperious, inexorable, iron-handed, magisterial, Neronian, oppressive, overbearing, overpowering, overweening, peremptory, ruthless, severe, tyrannous, unjust, unreasonable.
antonyms liberal, tolerant.

tyrannize *v.* browbeat, bully, coerce, crush, dictate, domineer, enslave, intimidate, lord it, oppress, subjugate, terrorize.

U

ubiquitous *adj*. all-over, common, commonly- encountered, ever-present, everywhere, frequent, global, omnipresent, pervasive, universal.
antonym rare.

ugly *adj*. angry, bad-tempered, dangerous, dark, disagreeable, disgusting, distasteful, evil, evil-favored, forbidding, frightful, hagged, haggish, hard-favored, hard-featured, hideous, homely, horrid, ill-faced, ill-favored, ill- looking, malevolent, menacing, misshapen, monstrous, nasty, objectionable, offensive, ominous, plain, repugnant, repulsive, revolting, shocking, sinister, spiteful, sullen, surly, terrible, threatening, truculent, unattractive, unlovely, unpleasant, unprepossessing, unsightly, vile.
antonyms beautiful, charming, good, pretty.

ultimate *adj*. basic, conclusive, consummate, decisive, elemental, end, eventual, extreme, final, fundamental, furthest, greatest, highest, last, maximum, paramount, perfect, primary, radical, remotest, superlative, supreme, terminal, topmost, utmost.
n. consummation, culmination, daddy of them all, dinger, epitome, extreme, granddaddy, greatest, height, peak, perfection, summit.

umbrage *n*. anger, chagrin, disgruntlement, displeasure, grudge, high dudgeon, huff, indignation, offence, pique, resentment, sulks.

umpire *n*. adjudicator, arbiter, arbitrator, daysman, judge, linesman, mediator, moderator, ref, referee.
v. adjudicate, arbitrate, call, control, judge, moderate, ref, referee.

umpteen *adj*. a good many, a thousand, considerable, countless, innumerable, millions, numerous, plenty, uncounted.
antonym few.

unabashed *adj*. blatant, bold, brazen, composed, confident, unawed, unblushing, unconcerned, undaunted, undismayed, unembarrassed.
antonyms abashed, sheepish.

unaccountable *adj*. astonishing, baffling, extraordinary, impenetrable, incomprehensible, inexplicable, inscrutable, mysterious, odd, peculiar, puzzling, singular, strange, uncommon, unexplainable, unfathomable, unheard-of, unintelligible, unusual, unwonted.
antonyms accountable, explicable.

unaffected[1] *adj*. aloof, impervious, naïf, natural, proof, spontaneous, unaltered, unchanged, unimpressed, unmoved, unresponsive, untouched.
antonyms affected, unnatural.

unaffected[2] *adj*. artless, blasé, genuine, honest, indifferent, ingenuous, naive, plain, simple, sincere, straightforward, unassuming, unconcerned, unpretentious, unsophisticated, unspoilt, unstudied.
antonyms affected, impressed, moved.

unalterable *adj*. final, fixed, immutable, inflexible, invariable, permanent, rigid, steadfast, unchangeable, unchanging, unyielding.
antonyms alterable, flexible.

unanimous *adj*. agreed, common, concerted, concordant, harmonious, in accord, in agreement, joint, united.
antonyms disunited, split.

unapproachable *adj*. aloof, distant, forbidding, formidable, frigid, godforsaken, inaccessible, remote, reserved, standoffish, unbending, unfriendly, un-get-at-able, unreachable, unsociable, withdrawn.
antonym approachable.

unassailable *adj*. absolute, conclusive, impregnable, incontestable, incontrovertible, indisputable, invincible, inviolable, invulnerable, irrefutable, positive, proven, sacrosanct, secure, sound, undeniable, well-armed, well- fortified.
antonym assailable.

unassuming *adj*. diffident, humble, meek, modest, natural, quiet, restrained, retiring, self-effacing, simple, unassertive, unobtrusive, unostentatious, unpresuming, unpretentious.
antonyms assuming, presumptuous, pretentious.

unattached *adj*. autonomous, available, fancy-free, footloose, free, independent, non-aligned, single, unaffilated, uncommitted, unengaged, unmarried, unspoken for. *antonyms* attached, committed, engaged.

unavailing *adj*. abortive, barren, bootless, fruitless, futile, idle, ineffective, ineffectual, inefficacious, pointless, unproductive, unprofitable, unsuccessful, useless, vain.
antonyms productive, successful.

unavoidable *adj*. certain, compulsory, fated, ineluctable, inescapable, inevitable, inexorable, mandatory, necessary, obligatory.
antonym avoidable.

unawares *adv*. aback, abruptly, accidentally, by surprise, imperceptibly, inadvertently, insidiously, mistakenly, off guard, on the hop, suddenly, unconsciously, unexpectedly, unintentionally, unknowingly, unprepared, unthinkingly, unwittingly.

unbalanced *adj*. asymmetrical, biased, crazy, demented, deranged, disturbed, dysharmonic, eccentric, erratic, inequitable, insane, irrational, irregular, lopsided, lunatic, mad, off-balance, off-center, one-sided, partial, partisan, prejudiced, shaky, touched, unequal, uneven, unfair, unhinged, unjust, unsound, unstable, unsteady, wobbly.
antonym balanced.

unbearable *adj.* insufferable, insupportable, intolerable, outrageous, unacceptable, unendurable, unspeakable. *antonyms* acceptable, bearable.

unbecoming *adj.* discreditable, dishonorable, ill- suited, improper, inappropriate, incongruous, indecorous, indelicate, offensive, tasteless, unattractive, unbefitting, unfit, unflattering, unmaidenly, unmeet, unseemly, unsightly, unsuitable, unsuited. *antonyms* becoming, seemly.

unbelievable *adj.* astonishing, far-fetched, implausible, impossible, improbable, inconceivable, incredible, outlandish, preposterous, questionable, staggering, unconvincing, unimaginable, unlikely, unthinkable. *antonyms* believable, credible.

unbending *adj.* aloof, distant, firm, forbidding, formal, formidable, hard-line, inflexible, intransigent, reserved, resolute, Rhadamanthine, rigid, severe, stiff, strict, stubborn, tough, uncompromising, unyielding. *antonyms* approachable, friendly, relaxed.

unbiased *adj.* disinterested, dispassionate, equitable, evenhanded, fair, fair-minded, impartial, independent, just, neutral, objective, open-minded, uncolored, uninfluenced, unprejudiced. *antonym* biased.

unbidden *adj.* free, spontaneous, unasked, unforced, uninvited, unprompted, unsolicited, unwanted, unwelcome, voluntary, willing. *antonyms* invited, solicited.

unblemished *adj.* clear, flawless, immaculate, irreproachable, perfect, pure, spotless, unflawed, unimpeachable, unspotted, unstained, unsullied, untarnished. *antonyms* blemished, flawed, imperfect.

unbosom *v.* admit, bare, confess, confide, disburden, disclose, divulge, lay bare, let out, pour out, reveal, tell, unburden, uncover. *antonyms* conceal, suppress.

unbridled *adj.* excessive, immoderate, intemperate, licentious, profligate, rampant, riotous, unchecked, unconstrained, uncontrolled, uncurbed, ungovernable, ungoverned, unrestrained, unruly, violent, wanton.

unbroken *adj.* ceaseless, complete, constant, continuous, endless, entire, incessant, intact, integral, perpetual, progressive, serried, solid, successive, total, unbowed, unceasing, undivided, unimpaired, uninterrupted, unremitting, unsubdued, untamed, whole. *antonyms* cowed, fitful, intermittent.

unburden *v.* confess, confide, disburden, discharge, disclose, discumber, disencumber, empty, lay bare, lighten, offload, pour out, relieve, reveal, tell all, unbosom, unload. *antonyms* conceal, hide, suppress.

uncalled-for *adj.* gratuitous, inappropriate, needless, undeserved, unheeded, unjust, unjustified, unmerited, unnecessary, unprovoked, unwanted, unwarranted, unwelcome. *antonym* timely.

uncanny *adj.* astonishing, astounding, bizarre, creepy, eerie, eldritch, exceptional, extraordinary, fantastic, incredible, inspired, miraculous, mysterious, preternatural, prodigious, queer, remarkable, scary, singular, spooky, strange, supernatural, unaccountable, unco, unearthly, unerring, unheard- of, unnatural, unusual, weird.

uncertain *adj.* ambiguous, ambivalent, chancy, changeable, conjectural, dicky, doubtful, dubious, erratic, fitful, hazardous, hazy, hesitant, iffy, in the lap of the gods, incalculable, inconstant, indefinite, indeterminate, indistinct, insecure, irregular, irresolute, on the knees of the gods, precarious, problematic, questionable, risky, shaky, slippy, speculative, unclear, unconfirmed, undecided, undetermined, unfixed, unforeseeable, unpredictable, unreliable, unresolved, unsettled, unsure, vacillating, vague, variable, wavering. *antonym* certain.

uncertainty *n.* ambiguity, bewilderment, confusion, diffidence, dilemma, doubt, dubiety, hesitancy, hesitation, incalculability, inconclusiveness, indecision, insecurity, irresolution, misgiving, peradventure, perplexity, puzzlement, qualm, quandary, risk, skepticism, unpredictability, vagueness. *antonym* certainty.

uncharitable *adj.* callous, captious, cruel, hard- hearted, hypercritical, inhumane, insensitive, mean, merciless, pitiless, stingy, unchristian, unfeeling, unforgiving, unfriendly, ungenerous, unkind, unsympathetic. *antonym* charitable.

uncharted *adj.* foreign, mysterious, new, novel, strange, undiscovered, unexplored, unfamiliar, unknown, unplumbed, virgin. *antonyms* familiar, well-known.

uncivil *adj.* abrupt, bad-mannered, bearish, boorish, brusque, churlish, curt, discourteous, disrespectful, gruff, ill-bred, ill-mannered, impolite, rude, surly, uncouth, ungracious, unmannerly. *antonym* civil.

uncivilized *adj.* antisocial, barbarian, barbaric, barbarous, boorish, brutish, churlish, coarse, gross, heathenish, ill-bred, illiterate, philistine, primitive, savage, tramontane, uncouth, uncultivated, uncultured, uneducated, unpolished, unsophisticated, untamed, vulgar, wild. *antonym* civilized.

unclean *adj.* contaminated, corrupt, defiled, dirty, evil, filthy, foul, impure, insalubrious, nasty, polluted, soiled, spotted, stained, sullied, tainted, unhygienic, unwholesome. *antonym* clean.

uncomfortable *adj.* awkward, bleak, confused, conscience-stricken, cramped, disagreeable, discomfited, discomfortable, discomposed, disquieted, distressed, disturbed, embarrassed, hard, ill-fitting, incommodious, irritating, painful, poky, self-conscious, sheepish, troubled, troublesome, uneasy. *antonyms* comfortable, easy.

uncommon *adj.* abnormal, atypical, bizarre, curious, distinctive, exceptional, extraordinary, incomparable, infrequent, inimitable, notable, noteworthy, novel, odd, outstanding, peculiar, queer, rare, recherché, remarkable, scarce, singular, special, strange, superior, unfamiliar, unparalleled, unprecedented, unusual, unwonted. *antonym* common.

uncompromising *adj.* decided, die-hard, firm, hard-core, hard-line, hardshell, inexorable, inflexible, intransigent, obdurate, obstinate, rigid, steadfast, strict, stubborn, tough, unaccommodating, unbending, unyielding. *antonyms* flexible, open-minded.

unconcerned *adj.* aloof, apathetic, blithe, callous, carefree, careless, complacent, composed, cool, detached, dispassionate, distant, easy, incurious, indifferent, insouciant, joco, nonchalant, oblivious, pococurante, relaxed, serene, uncaring, uninterested, uninvolved, unmoved, unperturbed, unruffled, unsympathetic, untroubled, unworried. *antonym* concerned.

unconditional *adj.* absolute, categorical, complete, downright, entire, full, implicit, out-and-out, outright, plenary, positive, thoroughgoing, total, unequivocal, unlimited, unqualified, unreserved, unrestricted, utter, whole-hearted. *antonym* conditional.

uncongenial *adj.* antagonistic, antipathetic, disagreeable, discordant, displeasing, distasteful, incompatible, unappealing, unattractive, uninviting, unpleasant, unsavory, unsuited, unsympathetic. *antonym* congenial.

unconscious *adj.* accidental, automatic, blind to, comatose, concussed, deaf to, heedless, ignorant, inadvertent, innate, insensible, instinctive, involuntary, knocked out, latent, oblivious, out, out cold, out for the count, reflex, repressed, senseless, stunned, subconscious, subliminal, suppressed, unaware, unintended, unintentional, unknowing, unmindful, unsuspecting, unwitting. *antonym* conscious.

unconventional *adj.* abnormal, alternative, atypical, bizarre, bohemian, different, eccentric, freakish, idiosyncratic, individual, individualistic, informal, irregular, nonconforming, odd, offbeat, original, spacy, unconformable, unorthodox, unusual, way-out, wayward. *antonym* conventional.

uncouth *adj.* awkward, barbarian, barbaric, boorish, clownish, clumsy, coarse, crude, gauche, gawky, graceless, gross, ill-mannered, loutish, lubberly, oafish, rough, rude, rustic, uncivilized, uncultivated, ungainly, unrefined, unseemly, vulgar. *antonyms* polished, polite, refined, urbane.

uncover *v.* bare, detect, disclose, discover, dismask, disrobe, divulge, exhume, expose, leak, lift the lid off, open, reveal, show, strip, unearth, unmask, unveil, unwrap. *antonyms* conceal, cover, suppress.

unctuous *adj.* fawning, glib, greasy, gushing, ingratiating, insincere, obsequious, oily, pietistic, plausible, religiose, sanctimonious, slick, smarmy, smooth, suave, sycophantic.

undaunted *adj.* bold, brave, courageous, dauntless, fearless, gallant, indomitable, intrepid, resolute, steadfast, unbowed, undashed, undeterred, undiscouraged, undismayed, unfaltering, unflinching, unperturbed, unshrinking. *antonyms* cowed, timorous.

undefined *adj.* formless, hazy, ill-defined, imprecise, indefinite, indeterminate, indistinct, inexact, nebulous, shadowy, tenuous, unclear, unexplained, unspecified, vague, woolly. *antonyms* definite, precise.

undependable *adj.* capricious, changeable, erratic, fairweather, fickle, inconsistent, inconstant, irresponsible, mercurial, treacherous, uncertain, unpredictable, unreliable, unstable, untrustworthy, variable. *antonyms* dependable, reliable.

under *prep.* belonging to, below, beneath, governed by, included in, inferior to, junior to, lead by, less than, lower than, secondary to, subject to, subordinate to, subservient to, underneath. *adv.* below, beneath, down, downward, less, lower.

undercover *adj.* clandestine, concealed, confidential, covert, furtive, hidden, hush-hush, intelligence, private, secret, spy, stealthy, surreptitious, underground. *antonyms* open, unconcealed.

undercurrent *n.* atmosphere, aura, cross-current, drift, eddy, feeling, flavor, hint, movement, murmur, overtone, rip, riptide, sense, suggestion, tendency, tenor, tide, tinge, trend, underflow, undertone, undertow, vibes, vibrations.

undergo *v.* bear, brook, endure, experience, run the gauntlet, stand, submit to, suffer, sustain, weather, withstand.

underhand *adj.* clandestine, crafty, crooked, deceitful, deceptive, devious, dishonest, dishonorable, fraudulent, furtive, immoral, improper, shady, shifty, sly, sneaky, stealthy, surreptitious, treacherous, underhanded, unethical, unscrupulous. *antonym* above board.

undermine *v.* debilitate, disable, erode, excavate, impair, mar, mine, sabotage, sap, subvert, threaten, tunnel, undercut, vitiate, weaken, wear away. *antonyms* fortify, strengthen.

underprivileged *adj.* deprived, destitute, disadvantaged, impecunious, impoverished, needy, poor, poverty-stricken. *antonyms* affluent, fortunate, privileged.

understand *v.* accept, appreciate, apprehend, assume, believe, commiserate, comprehend, conceive, conclude, cotton on, discern, fathom, follow, gather, get, get the message, get the picture, grasp, hear, know, learn, penetrate, perceive, presume, realize, recognize, savvy, see, see daylight, suppose, sympathize, think, tolerate, tumble, twig. *antonym* misunderstand.

understanding *n.* accord, agreement, appreciation, awareness, belief, comprehension, conclusion, discernment, estimation, grasp, idea, impression, insight, intellect, intellection, intelligence, interpretation, judgment, knowledge, notion, opinion, pact, penetration, perception, reading, sense, view, viewpoint, wisdom. *adj.* accepting, compassionate, considerate, discerning, forbearing, forgiving, kind, kindly, loving, patient, perceptive, responsive, sensitive, sympathetic, tender, tolerant.
antonyms impatient, insensitive, intolerant, unsympathetic.

understudy *n.* alternate, deputy, double, fill-in, replacement, reserve, stand-in, substitute.

undertake *v.* accept, agree, assume, attempt, bargain, begin, commence, contract, covenant, embark on, endeavor, engage, guarantee, pledge, promise, shoulder, stipulate, tackle, try.

undertaking *n.* adventure, affair, assurance, attempt, business, commitment, effort, emprise, endeavor, enterprise, game, operation, pledge, project, promise, task, venture, vow, word.

undervalue *v.* depreciate, discount, dismiss, disparage, disprize, minimize, misjudge, misprice, misprize, underestimate, underrate.
antonyms exaggerate, overrate.

underwrite *v.* approve, authorize, back, consent, countenance, countersign, endorse, finance, fund, guarantee, initial, insure, okay, sanction, sign, sponsor, subscribe, subsidize, validate.

undesirable *adj.* disagreeable, disliked, disreputable, distasteful, dreaded, objectionable, obnoxious, offensive, repugnant, unacceptable, unattractive, unpleasant, unpopular, unsavory, unsuitable, unwanted, unwelcome, unwished-for.
antonym desirable.

undignified *adj.* foolish, improper, inappropriate, indecorous, inelegant, infra dig, petty, unbecoming, ungentlemanly, unladylike, unrefined, unseemly, unsuitable.
antonym dignified.

undisciplined *adj.* disobedient, disorganized, obstreperous, uncontrolled, unpredictable, unreliable, unrestrained, unruly, unschooled, unsteady, unsystematic, untrained, wayward, wild, wilful.
antonym disciplined.

undivided *adj.* combined, complete, concentrated, concerted, entire, exclusive, full, individuate, solid, thorough, tight-knit, unanimous, unbroken, united, whole, whole-hearted.

undoing *n.* besetting sin, blight, collapse, curse, defeat, destruction, disgrace, downfall, hamartia, humiliation, misfortune, overthrow, overturn, reversal, ruin, ruination, shame, tragic fault, trouble, weakness.

undoubtedly *adv.* assuredly, certainly, definitely, doubtless, indubitably, of course, surely, undeniably, unmistakably, unquestionably.

undreamed-of *adj.* astonishing, inconceivable, incredible, miraculous, undreamt, unexpected, unforeseen, unheardof, unhoped-for, unimagined, unsuspected.

undulating *adj.* billowing, flexuose, flexuous, rippling, rolling, sinuous, undate, undulant, wavy.
antonym flat.

unduly *adv.* disproportionately, excessively, extravagantly, immoderately, inordinately, over, overly, overmuch, too, unjustifiably, unnecessarily, unreasonably.
antonym reasonably.

undying *adj.* abiding, constant, continuing, deathless, eternal, everlasting, immortal, imperishable, indestructible, inextinguishable, infinite, lasting, perennial, permanent, perpetual, sempiternal, undiminished, unending, unfading.
antonyms impermanent, inconstant.

unearthly *adj.* abnormal, eerie, eldritch, ethereal, extraordinary, ghostly, haunted, heavenly, nightmarish, otherworldly, phantom, preternatural, spectral, spine-chilling, strange, sublime, supernatural, uncanny, ungodly, unreasonable, weird.

uneasy *adj.* agitated, anxious, apprehensive, awkward, constrained, discomposed, disquieting, disturbed, disturbing, edgy, impatient, insecure, jittery, nervous, niggling, on edge, perturbed, precarious, restive, restless, shaky, strained, tense, troubled, troubling, uncomfortable, unquiet, unsettled, unstable, upset, upsetting, worried, worrying.
antonyms calm, composed.

uneconomic *adj.* loss-making, non-profit-making, uncommercial, unprofitable.
antonyms economic, profitable.

unemotional *adj.* apathetic, cold, cool, dispassionate, impassive, indifferent, laid-back, low-key, objective, passionless, phlegmatic, reserved, undemonstrative, unexcitable, unfeeling, unimpassioned, unresponsive.
antonyms emotional, excitable.

unemployed *adj.* idle, jobless, out of employ, out of work, redundant, resting, unoccupied, workless.
antonym employed.

unenviable *adj.* disagreeable, painful, thankless, uncomfortable, uncongenial, undesirable, unpalatable, unpleasant, unsavory.
antonyms desirable, enviable.

unequal *adj.* asymmetrical, different, differing, disparate, disproportionate, dissimilar, ill-equipped, ill-matched, inadequate, incapable, incompetent, insufficient, irregular, unbalanced, uneven, unlike, unmatched, variable, varying.
antonym equal.

unequivocal *adj.* absolute, certain, clear, clear-cut, crystal-clear, decisive, definite, direct, distinct, evident, explicit, express, incontrovertible, indubitable, manifest, plain, positive, straight, unambiguous, uncontestable, unmistakable.
antonyms ambiguous, vague.

unerring *adj.* accurate, certain, dead, exact, faultless, impeccable, infallible, perfect, sure, uncanny, unfailing.
antonym fallible.

unethical *adj.* dirty, discreditable, dishonest, dishonorable, disreputable, illegal, illicit, immoral, improper, shady, underhand, unfair, unprincipled, unprofessional, unscrupulous, wrong.
antonym ethical.

uneven *adj.* accidented, asymmetrical, broken, bumpy, changeable, desultory, disparate, erratic, fitful, fluctuating, ill-matched, inconsistent, intermittent, irregular, jerky, lopsided, odd, one-sided, patchy, rough, spasmodic, unbalanced, unequal, unfair, unsteady, variable.
antonym even.

unexceptional *adj.* average, commonplace, conventional, indifferent, insignificant, mediocre, normal, ordinary, pedestrian, run-of-the-mill, typical, undistinguished, unimpressive, unmemorable, unremarkable, usual.
antonyms exceptional, impressive.

unexpected *adj.* abrupt, accidental, amazing, astonishing, chance, fortuitous, startling, sudden, surprising, unaccustomed, unanticipated, unforeseen, unlooked-for, unpredictable, unusual, unwonted.
antonyms expected, normal, predictable.

unfair *adj.* arbitrary, biased, bigoted, crooked, discriminatory, dishonest, dishonorable, inequitable, one-sided, partial, partisan, prejudiced, uncalled-for, undeserved, unethical, unjust, unmerited, unprincipled, unscrupulous, unsporting, unwarranted, wrongful.
antonym fair.

unfaithful *adj.* adulterous, deceitful, dishonest, disloyal, faithless, false, false-hearted, fickle, godless, inconstant, perfidious, recreant, traitorous, treacherous, treasonable, two-timing, unbelieving, unchaste, unreliable, untrue, untrustworthy.
antonyms faithful, loyal.

unfamiliar *adj.* alien, curious, different, foreign, new, novel, out-of-the-way, strange, unaccustomed, unacquainted, uncharted, uncommon, unconversant, unexplored, unknown, unpracticed, unskilled, unusual, unversed.
antonyms customary, familiar.

unfasten *v.* detach, disconnect, loosen, open, separate, uncouple, undo, unlace, unlock, unloose, unloosen, untie.
antonym fasten.

unfavorable *adj.* adverse, bad, contrary, critical, disadvantageous, discouraging, hostile, ill-suited, inauspicious, infelicitous, inimical, inopportune, low, negative, ominous, poor, threatening, uncomplimentary, unfortunate, unfriendly, unlucky, unpromising, unpropitious, unseasonable, unsuited, untimely, untoward.
antonym favorable.

unfeeling *adj.* apathetic, callous, cold, cruel, hard, hardened, hard-hearted, harsh, heartless, inhuman, insensitive, pitiless, soulless, stony, uncaring, unsympathetic.
antonym concerned.

unfeigned *adj.* frank, genuine, heartfelt, natural, pure, real, sincere, spontaneous, unaffected, unforced, whole- hearted.
antonyms feigned, insincere, pretended.

unfit *adj.* debilitated, decrepit, feeble, flabby, flaccid, hypotonic, ill-adapted, ill-equipped, inadequate, inappropriate, incapable, incompetent, ineffective, ineligible, unequal, unhealthy, unprepared, unqualified, unsuitable, unsuited, untrained, useless.
antonyms competent, fit, suitable.

unfold *v.* clarify, describe, develop, disclose, disentangle, divulge, elaborate, evolve, expand, explain, flatten, grow, illustrate, mature, open, present, reveal, show, spread, straighten, stretch out, uncoil, uncover, undo, unfurl, unravel, unroll, unwrap.
antonyms fold, suppress, withhold, wrap.

unforeseen *adj.* abrupt, accidental, fortuitous, startling, sudden, surprise, surprising, unanticipated, unavoidable, unexpected, unheralded, unlooked-for, unpredicted.
antonyms expected, predictable.

unfortunate *adj.* adverse, calamitous, cursed, deplorable, disadventurous, disastrous, doomed, hapless, hopeless, ill-advised, ill-fated, ill-starred, ill-timed, inappropriate, infelicitous, inopportune, lamentable, luckless, poor, regrettable, ruinous, star-crossed, tactless, unbecoming, unfavorable, unhappy, unlucky, unprosperous, unsuccessful, unsuitable, untimely, untoward, wretched.
antonym fortunate.

unfriendly *adj.* alien, aloof, antagonistic, chilly, cold, critical, disagreeable, distant, hostile, ill-disposed, inauspicious, inhospitable, inimical, quarrelsome, sour, stand- offish, surly, unapproachable, unbending, uncongenial, unfavorable, unneighborly, unsociable, unwelcoming.
antonyms agreeable, amiable, friendly.

ungainly *adj.* awkward, clumsy, gangling, gauche, gawky, inelegant, loutish, lubberly, lumbering, slouching, uncoordinated, uncouth, unwieldy.
antonyms elegant, graceful.

ungodly *adj.* blasphemous, corrupt, depraved, dreadful, godless, horrendous, immoral, impious, intolerable, irreligious, outrageous, profane, sinful, unearthly, unreasonable, unseasonable, unseemly, unsocial, vile, wicked.

ungrateful *adj.* heedless, ill-mannered, ingrate, selfish, thankless, unappreciative, ungracious, unmindful.
antonym grateful.

unguarded[1] *adj.* careless, foolhardy, foolish, heedless, ill-considered, impolitic, imprudent, incautious, indiscreet, rash, thoughtless, uncircumspect, undiplomatic, un-heeding, unthinking, unwary.

antonyms cautious, guarded.

unguarded[2] *adj*. defenseless, exposed, pregnable, unde-fended, unpatrolled, unprotected, vulnerable.

antonyms guarded, protected.

unhappy *adj*. awkward, blue, clumsy, contentless, crest-fallen, cursed, dejected, depressed, despondent, dis-consolate, dismal, dispirited, down, downcast, gauche, gloomy, hapless, ill-advised, ill-chosen, ill-fated, ill-omened, ill- timed, inappropriate, inapt, inept, infe-licitous, injudicious, long-faced, luckless, lugubrious, malapropos, melancholy, miserable, mournful, sad, sorrowful, sorry, tactless, uneasy, unfortunate, un-lucky, unsuitable, wretched.

antonyms fortunate, happy.

unhealthy *adj*. ailing, bad, baneful, corrupt, corrupting, degrading, deleterious, delicate, demoralizing, detrimen-tal, epinosic, feeble, frail, harmful, infirm, insalubri-ous, insalutary, insanitary, invalid, morbid, noisome, noxious, polluted, poorly, sick, sickly, undesirable, unhygienic, unsound, unwell, unwholesome, weak.

antonyms healthy, hygienic, robust, salubrious.

unheard-of *adj*. disgraceful, extreme, inconceivable, new, novel, obscure, offensive, out of the question, outra-geous, preposterous, shocking, singular, unacceptable, unbelievable, undiscovered, undreamed-of, unexampled, unfamiliar, unimaginable, unique, un-known, unprecedented, unregarded, unremarked, un-sung, unthinkable, unthought-of, unusual.

antonyms famous, normal, usual.

unhurried *adj*. calm, deliberate, easy, easy-going, laid-back, leisurely, relaxed, sedate, slow.

antonyms hasty, hurried.

uniform *n*. costume, dress, garb, gear, habit, insignia, livery, outfit, regalia, regimentals, rig, robes, suit.

adj. alike, consistent, constant, equable, equal, even, homochromous, homogeneous, homomorphic, homomorphous, identical, like, monochrome, montonous, of a piece, regular, same, selfsame, simi-lar, smooth, unbroken, unchanging, undeviating, un-varying.

antonyms changing, colorful, varied.

unify *v*. amalgamate, bind, combine, confederate, con-solidate, federate, fuse, join, marry, merge, unite, weld.

antonyms separate, split.

unimaginable *adj*. fantastic, impossible, inconceivable, incredible, indescribable, ineffable, mind- boggling, unbelievable, undreamed-of, unheard-of, unhoped-for, unknowable, unthinkable.

unimportant *adj*. immaterial, inconsequential, insignifi-cant, irrelevant, low-ranking, Mickey Mouse, minor, minuscule, negligible, nugatory, off the map, paltry, paravail, petty, slight, small-time, trifling, trivial, worthless.

antonym important.

unimpressive *adj*. average, commonplace, dull, indif-ferent, mediocre, undistinguished, unexceptional, un-interesting, unremarkable, unspectacular.

antonyms impressive, memorable, notable.

uninhibited *adj*. abandoned, candid, emancipated, frank, free, informal, instinctive, liberated, natural, open, re-laxed, spontaneous, unbridled, unchecked, uncon-strained, uncontrolled, uncurbed, unrepressed, unre-served, unrestrained, unrestricted, unselfconscious.

antonyms constrained, inhibited, repressed.

uninspired *adj*. boring, commonplace, dull, humdrum, indifferent, ordinary, pedestrian, prosaic, stale, stock, trite, undistinguished, unexciting, unimaginative, un-inspiring, uninteresting, unoriginal.

antonyms inspired, original.

unintelligent *adj*. brainless, dense, dull, dumb, empty-headed, fatuous, foolish, gormless, half-witted, ob-tuse, silly, slow, stupid, thick, unreasoning, unthink-ing.

antonym intelligent.

unintelligible *adj*. double Dutch, garbled, illegible, in-apprehensible, inarticulate, incoherent, incomprehen-sible, indecipherable, indistinct, jumbled, meaningless, muddled, unfathomable.

antonym intelligible.

unintentional *adj*. accidental, fortuitous, inadvertent, involuntary, unconscious, undeliberate, unintended, unpremeditated, unthinking, unwitting.

antonyms deliberate, intentional.

uninviting *adj*. disagreeable, distasteful, offensive, off-putting, repellent, repulsive, unappealing, unappetiz-ing, unattractive, undesirable, unpleasant, unsavory, unwelcoming.

antonyms inviting, welcome.

union *n*. accord, agreement, alliance, amalgam, amalga-mation, Anschluss, association, blend, Bund, coali-tion, coition, coitus, combination, compact, concord, concrescence, concurrence, confederacy, confederation, conjugation, conjunction, copulation, couplement, cou-pling, enosis, federation, fusion, harmony, intercourse, junction, juncture, league, marriage, matrimony, mix-ture, symphysis, synthesis, unanimity, unison, unit-ing, unity, wedlock.

antonyms alienation, disunity, estrangement, separation.

unique *adj*. incomparable, inimitable, lone, matchless, nonpareil, one-off, only, peerless, single, sole, soli-tary, sui generis, unequaled, unexampled, unmatched, unparalleled, unprecedented, unrivaled.

antonym commonplace.

unison *n*. accord, accordance, aggreement, concert, con-cord, co-operation, harmony, homophony, monophony, unanimity, unity.

antonyms disharmony, polyphony.

unit *n*. ace, assembly, component, constituent, detach-ment, element, entity, Gestalt, group, item, measure, measurement, member, module, monad, monas, one, part, piece, portion, quantity, section, segment, system, whole.

unite *v.* accrete, ally, amalgamate, associate, band, blend, coadunate, coalesce, combine, confederate, conglutinate, conjoin, conjugate, consolidate, cooperate, couple, fay, fuse, incorporate, join, join forces, league, link, marry, merge, pool, splice, unify, wed. *antonyms* separate, sever.

universal *adj.* across-the-board, all-embracing, all-inclusive, all-round, catholic, common, ecumenic, ecumenical, entire, general, global, omnipresent, total, ubiquitous, unlimited, whole, widespread, worldwide.

unjustifiable *adj.* excessive, immoderate, indefensible, inexcusable, outrageous, steep, unacceptable, unforgivable, unjust, unpardonable, unreasonable, unwarrantable, wrong. *antonym* justifiable.

unkempt *adj.* bedraggled, blowsy, disarranged, disheveled, disordered, frowsy, mal soigné, messy, mop-headed, ratty, rumpled, scruffy, shabby, shaggy, slatternly, sloppy, slovenly, sluttish, tousled, uncombed, ungroomed, untidy. *antonyms* neat, tidy.

unkind *adj.* callous, cruel, disobliging, hard-hearted, harsh, inconsiderate, inhuman, inhumane, insensitive, malevolent, malicious, mean, nasty, spiteful, thoughtless, unamiable, uncaring, uncharitable, unchristian, unfeeling, unfriendly, unsympathetic. *antonyms* considerate, kind.

unknown *adj.* alien, anonymous, concealed, dark, foreign, hidden, humble, incognito, mysterious, nameless, new, obscure, secret, strange, uncharted, undisclosed, undiscovered, undistinguished, unexplored, unfamiliar, unheard-of, unidentified, unnamed, unrecognized, unsung, untold. *antonyms* familiar, known.

unlawful *adj.* actionable, banned, criminal, forbidden, illegal, illegitimate, illicit, outlawed, prohibited, unauthorized, unconstitutional, unlicensed, unsanctioned. *antonym* lawful.

unlike *adj.* contrasted, different, difform, disparate, dissimilar, distinct, divergent, diverse, ill-matched, incompatible, opposed, opposite, unequal, unrelated. *antonyms* related, similar.

unlimited *adj.* absolute, all-encompassing, boundless, complete, countless, endless, extensive, full, great, illimitable, immeasurable, immense, incalculable, infinite, limitless, total, unbounded, uncircumscribed, unconditional, unconstrained, unfettered, unhampered, unqualified, unrestricted, vast. *antonyms* circumscribed, limited.

unlooked-for *adj.* chance, fortuitous, fortunate, lucky, surprise, surprising, unanticipated, undreamed-of, unexpected, unforeseen, unhoped-for, unpredicted, unthought-of. *antonyms* expected, predictable.

unlucky *adj.* cursed, disastrous, doomed, hapless, ill-fated, ill-omened, ill-starred, inauspicious, infaust, jinxed, left-handed, luckless, mischanceful, miserable, ominous, unfavorable, unfortunate, unhappy, unsuccessful, untimely, wretched. *antonym* lucky.

unmanageable *adj.* awkward, bulky, cumbersome, difficult, disorderly, fractious, inconvenient, intractable, obstreperous, recalcitrant, refractory, stroppy, uncontrollable, unco-operative, unhandy, unruly, unwieldy, wild. *antonyms* docile, manageable.

unmannerly *adj.* badly-behaved, bad-mannered, boorish, discourteous, disrespectful, graceless, ill-bred, ill-mannered, impolite, low-bred, rude, uncivil, uncouth, ungracious. *antonym* polite.

unmatched *adj.* beyond compare, consummate, incomparable, matchless, nonpareil, paramount, peerless, supreme, unequaled, unexampled, unparalleled, unrivaled, unsurpassed.

unmerciful *adj.* brutal, callous, cruel, hard, heartless, implacable, merciless, pitiless, relentless, remorseless, ruthless, sadistic, uncaring, unfeeling, unrelenting, unsparing. *antonym* merciful.

unmistakable *adj.* certain, clear, conspicuous, crystal-clear, decided, distinct, evident, explicit, glaring, indisputable, manifest, obvious, palpable, patent, plain, positive, pronounced, sure, unambiguous, undeniable, undisputed, unequivocal, unquestionable. *antonyms* ambiguous, unclear.

unmitigated *adj.* absolute, arrant, complete, consummate, downright, grim, harsh, intense, oppressive, out-and-out, outright, perfect, persistent, pure, rank, relentless, sheer, thorough, thoroughgoing, unabated, unalleviated, unbroken, undiminished, unmodified, unqualified, unredeemed, unrelenting, unrelieved, unremitting, utter.

unnatural *adj.* aberrant, abnormal, absonant, affected, anomalous, artificial, assumed, bizarre, brutal, callous, cataphysical, cold-blooded, contrived, cruel, disnatured, evil, extraordinary, factitious, false, feigned, fiendish, forced, freakish, heartless, inhuman, insincere, irregular, labored, mannered, monstrous, odd, outlandish, perverse, perverted, phony, queer, ruthless, sadistic, savage, self-conscious, stagy, stiff, stilted, strained, strange, studied, supernatural, theatrical, unaccountable, uncanny, unfeeling, unspontaneous, unusual, wicked. *antonyms* acceptable, natural, normal.

unnecessary *adj.* dispensable, expendable, inessential, needless, non-essential, otiose, pleonastic, redundant, supererogatory, superfluous, supernumerary, tautological, uncalled-for, unjustified, unneeded, useless. *antonyms* indispensable, necessary.

unobtrusive *adj.* humble, inconspicuous, low-key, meek, modest, quiet, restrained, retiring, self-effacing, subdued, unassertive, unassuming, unemphatic, unnoticeable, unostentatious, unpretentious.
antonyms obtrusive, ostentatious.

unoccupied *adj.* disengaged, empty, free, idle, inactive, jobless, unemployed, uninhabited, untenanted, vacant, workless.
antonyms busy, occupied.

unofficial *adj.* confidential, illegal, informal, personal, private, ulterior, unauthorized, unconfirmed, undeclared, wildcat.
antonym official.

unorthodox *adj.* abnormal, alternative, fringe, heterodox, irregular, nonconformist, unconventional, unusual, unwonted.
antonyms conventional, orthodox.

unparalleled *adj.* consummate, exceptional, incomparable, matchless, peerless, rare, singular, superlative, supreme, surpassing, unequaled, unexampled, unique, unmatched, unprecedented, unrivaled, unsurpassed.

unpleasant *adj.* abhorrent, bad, disagreeable, displeasing, distasteful, god-awful, ill-natured, irksome, nasty, objectionable, obnoxious, repulsive, rocky, sticky, traumatic, troublesome, unattractive, unpalatable.
antonym pleasant.

unpopular *adj.* avoided, detested, disliked, hated, neglected, rejected, shunned, undesirable, unfashionable, unloved, unsought-after, unwanted, unwelcome.
antonyms fashionable, popular.

unprecedented *adj.* abnormal, exceptional, extraordinary, freakish, new, novel, original, remarkable, revolutionary, singular, unexampled, unheard-of, unknown, unparalleled, unrivaled, unusual.

unpredictable *adj.* chance, changeable, doubtful, erratic, fickle, fluky, iffy, in the lap of the gods, inconstant, on the knees of the gods, random, scatty, unforeseeable, unreliable, unstable, variable.
antonym predictable.

unprejudiced *adj.* balanced, detached, dispassionate, enlightened, even-handed, fair, fair-minded, impartial, just, non-partisan, objective, open-minded, unbiased, uncolored.
antonyms narrow-minded, prejudiced.

unpremeditated *adj.* extempore, fortuitous, impromptu, impulsive, offhand, off-the-cuff, spontaneous, spur-of-the-moment, unintentional, unplanned, unprepared, unrehearsed.
antonym premeditated.

unprincipled *adj.* amoral, corrupt, crooked, deceitful, devious, discreditable, dishonest, dishonorable, immoral, underhand, unethical, unprofessional, unscrupulous.
antonym ethical.

unprofessional *adj.* amateur, amateurish, improper, inadmissible, incompetent, inefficient, inexperienced, inexpert, lax, negligent, unacceptable, unbecoming, unethical, unfitting, unprincipled, unseemly, unskilled, untrained, unworthy.
antonyms professional, skilful.

unprotected *adj.* defenseless, exposed, helpless, inerm, liable, naked, open, pregnable, unarmed, unattended, undefended, unfortified, unguarded, unsheltered, unshielded, unvaccinated, vulnerable.
antonyms immune, protected, safe.

unqualified *adj.* absolute, categorical, complete, consummate, downright, ill-equipped, incapable, incompetent, ineligible, out-and-out, outright, thorough, thoroughgoing, total, uncertificated, unconditional, unfit, unmitigated, unmixed, unprepared, unreserved, unrestricted, untrained, utter, whole-hearted.
antonyms conditional, tentative.

unreal *adj.* academic, artificial, chimerical, fabulous, fairytale, fake, false, fanciful, fantastic, fictitious, hypothetical, illusory, imaginary, immaterial, impalpable, insincere, insubstantial, intangible, made-up, make-believe, mock, moonshiny, mythical, nebulous, ostensible, phantasmagorical, pretended, seeming, sham, storybook, synthetic, vaporous, visionary.
antonyms genuine, real.

unrealistic *adj.* half-baked, idealistic, impracticable, impractical, improbable, quixotic, romantic, starry-eyed, theoretical, unworkable.
antonyms pragmatic, realistic.

unreasonable *adj.* absurd, arbitrary, biased, blinkered, capricious, cussed, erratic, excessive, exorbitant, extortionate, extravagant, far-fetched, foolish, froward, headstrong, illogical, immoderate, inconsistent, irrational, mad, nonsensical, opinionated, perverse, preposterous, quirky, senseless, silly, steep, stupid, thrawn, uncalled-for, undue, unfair, unjust, unjustifiable, unjustified, unwarranted.
antonyms moderate, rational, reasonable.

unregenerate *adj.* abandoned, hardened, impenitent, incorrigible, intractable, obdurate, obstinate, persistent, recalcitrant, refractory, shameless, sinful, stubborn, unconverted, unreformed, unrepentant, wicked.
antonyms reformed, repentant.

unrelenting *adj.* ceaseless, constant, continual, continuous, cruel, endless, implacable, incessant, inexorable, insistent, intransigent, merciless, perpetual, pitiless, relentless, remorseless, ruthless, steady, stern, tough, unabated, unalleviated, unbroken, unceasing, uncompromising, unmerciful, unremitting, unsparing.
antonyms intermittent, spasmodic.

unreliable *adj.* deceptive, delusive, disreputable, erroneous, fair-weather, fallible, false, implausible, inaccurate, inauthentic, irresponsible, mistaken, specious, uncertain, unconvincing, undependable, unsound, unstable, untrustworthy.
antonym reliable.

unrepentant *adj.* callous, hardened, impenitent,

incorrigible, obdurate, shameless, unabashed, unashamed, unregenerate, unremorseful, unrepenting.
antonyms penitent, repentant.

unresponsive *adj*. aloof, apathetic, cool, echoless, indifferent, unaffected, uninterested, unmoved, unsympathetic.
antonyms responsive, sympathetic.

unrest *n*. agitation, anxiety, apprehension, disaffection, discontent, discord, disquiet, dissatisfaction, dissension, distress, perturbation, protest, rebellion, restlessness, sedition, strife, tumult, turmoil, unease, uneasiness, worry.
antonyms calm, peace.

unrestrained *adj*. abandoned, boisterous, free, immoderate, inordinate, intemperate, irrepressible, natural, rampant, unbounded, unbridled, unchecked, unconstrained, uncontrolled, unhindered, uninhibited, unrepressed, unreserved, uproarious.
antonym inhibited.

unruffled *adj*. calm, collected, composed, cool, even, imperturbable, level, peaceful, placid, serene, smooth, tranquil, unbroken, undisturbed, unflustered, unmoved, unperturbed, untroubled.
antonyms anxious, troubled.

unruly *adj*. camstairy, disobedient, disorderly, fractious, headstrong, insubordinate, intractable, lawless, mutinous, obstreperous, rebellious, refractory, riotous, rowdy, ruleless, turbulent, uncontrollable, ungovernable, unmanageable, wayward, wild, wilful.
antonym manageable.

unsafe *adj*. dangerous, exposed, hazardous, insecure, parlous, perilous, precarious, risky, threatening, treacherous, uncertain, unreliable, unsound, unstable, vulnerable.
antonyms safe, secure.

unsatisfactory *adj*. deficient, disappointing, displeasing, dissatisfying, frustrating, inadequate, inferior, insufficient, leaving a lot to be desired, mediocre, poor, rocky, thwarting, unacceptable, unsatisfying, unsuitable, unworthy, weak.
antonym satisfactory.

unscrupulous *adj*. corrupt, crooked, cynical, discreditable, dishonest, dishonorable, immoral, improper, ruthless, shameless, unethical, unprincipled.
antonym scrupulous.

unseemly *adj*. discreditable, disreputable, improper, inappropriate, indecorous, indelicate, shocking, unbecoming, unbefitting, undignified, undue, ungentlemanly, unlady-like, unrefined, unsuitable.
antonyms decorous, seemly.

unselfish *adj*. altruistic, charitable, dedicated, devoted, dis-interested, generous, humanitarian, kind, liberal, magnanimous, noble, philanthropic, self-denying, selfless, self- sacrificing, single-eyed, ungrudging, unstinting.
antonym selfish.

unsentimental *adj*. cynical, hard as nails, hard- headed, level-headed, practical, pragmatic, realistic, shrewd, tough.
antonyms sentimental, soft.

unsettled *adj*. agitated, anxious, changeable, changing, confused, debatable, disorderly, disoriented, disturbed, doubtful, due, edgy, flustered, iffy, inconstant, insecure, moot, open, outstanding, overdue, owing, payable, pending, perturbed, problematical, restive, restless, shaken, shaky, tense, troubled, uncertain, undecided, undetermined, uneasy, unnerved, unpredictable, unresolved, unstable, unsteady, upset, variable.
antonyms certain, composed, settled.

unsightly *adj*. disagreeable, displeasing, hideous, horrid, off-putting, repellent, repugnant, repulsive, revolting, ugly, unattractive, unpleasant, unprepossessing.
antonym pleasing.

unsolicited *adj*. gratuitous, spontaneous, unasked, uncalled-for, unforced, uninvited, unrequested, unsought, unwanted, unwelcome, voluntary.
antonyms invited, solicited.

unsophisticated *adj*. artless, childlike, funky, guileless, hick, homespun, inexperienced, ingenuous, innocent, naïve, natural, plain, simple, straightforward, unaffected, uncomplicated, uninvolved, unpretentious, unrefined, unspecialized, unspoilt, untutored, unworldly.
antonyms complex, pretentious, sophisticated.

unsound *adj*. ailing, defective, delicate, deranged, dicky, diseased, erroneous, fallacious, fallible, false, faulty, flawed, frail, ill, ill-founded, illogical, insecure, invalid, shaky, specious, unbalanced, unhealthy, unhinged, unreliable, unsafe, unstable, unsteady, unwell, weak, wobbly.
antonyms safe, sound.

unspeakable *adj*. abhorrent, abominable, appalling, dreadful, evil, execrable, frightful, heinous, horrible, inconceivable, indescribable, ineffable, inexpressible, loathsome, monstrous, nefandous, odious, overwhelming, repellent, shocking, unbelievable, unimaginable, unutterable, wonderful.

unstable *adj*. astable, capricious, changeable, erratic, fitful, fluctuating, inconsistent, inconstant, insecure, irrational, labile, precarious, rickety, risky, shaky, shoogly, slippy, ticklish, tottering, unpredictable, unsettled, unsteady, untrustworthy, vacillating, variable, volatile, wobbly.
antonyms stable, steady.

unsteady *adj*. changeable, dicky, erratic, flickering, flighty, fluctuating, frail, inconstant, infirm, insecure, irregular, precarious, reeling, rickety, shaky, shoogly, skittish, tittupy, tottering, totty, treacherous, tremulous, unreliable, unsafe, unstable, unsteeled, vacillating, variable, volatile, wavering, wobbly.
antonyms firm, steady.

unsubstantiated *adj.* debatable, dubious, questionable, unattested, unconfirmed, uncorroborated, unestablished, unproved, unproven, unsupported, unverified.
antonyms proved, proven.

unsuccessful *adj.* abortive, bootless, failed, foiled, fruitless, frustrated, futile, ill-fated, inadequate, ineffective, ineffectual, losing, luckless, manqué, otiose, sterile, thwarted, unavailing, unfortunate, unlucky, unproductive, unsatisfactory, useless, vain.
antonyms effective, successful.

unsuitable *adj.* improper, inapposite, inappropriate, inapt, incompatible, incongruous, inconsistent, indecorous, ineligible, infelicitous, malapropos, unacceptable, unbecoming, unbefitting, unfitting, unlikely, unseasonable, unseemly, unsuited.
antonyms seemly, suitable.

unsuspecting *adj.* childlike, confiding, credulous, green, gullible, inexperienced, ingenuous, innocent, naïve, trustful, trusting, unconscious, uncritical, unsuspicious, unwary, unwitting.
antonyms conscious, knowing.

unswerving *adj.* constant, dedicated, devoted, direct, firm, fixed, immovable, resolute, single-minded, staunch, stead-fast, steady, sure, true, undeviating, unfaltering, unflagging, untiring, unwavering.
antonyms irresolute, tentative.

unsympathetic *adj.* antagonistic, antipathetic, apathetic, callous, cold, compassionless, cruel, hard, hard as nails, hard-hearted, harsh, heartless, indifferent, inhuman, insensitive, soulless, stony, uncharitable, uncompassionate, unconcerned, unfeeling, unkind, unmoved, unpitying, unresponsive.
antonyms compassionate, sympathetic.

untamed *adj.* barbarous, ferae naturae, feral, fierce, haggard, savage, unbroken, undomesticated, unmellowed, untameable, wild. *antonyms* domesticated, tame.

untenable *adj.* fallacious, flawed, illogical, indefensible, insupportable, rocky, shaky, unmaintainable, unreasonable, unsound, unsustainable.
antonyms sound, tenable.

untidy *adj.* bedraggled, chaotic, cluttered, disheveled, disorderly, higgledy-piggledy, jumbled, littered, messy, muddled, ratty, raunchy, rumpled, scruffy, shambolic, slatternly, slipshod, sloppy, slovenly, sluttish, topsy-turvy, unkempt, unsystematic.
antonyms systematic, tidy.

untimely *adj.* awkward, early, ill-timed, inappropriate, inauspicious, inconvenient, inopportune, intempestive, malapropos, mistimed, premature, unfortunate, unseasonable, unsuitable.
antonyms opportune, timely.

untold *adj.* boundless, countless, hidden, incalculable, indescribable, inexhaustible, inexpressible, infinite, innumerable, measureless, myriad, numberless, private, secret, uncountable, uncounted, undisclosed, undreamed-of, unimaginable, unknown, unnumbered, unpublished, unreckoned, unrecounted, unrelated, unrevealed, unthinkable, unutterable.

untoward *adj.* adverse, annoying, awkward, contrary, disastrous, ill-timed, improper, inappropriate, inauspicious, inconvenient, indecorous, inimical, inopportune, irritating, ominous, troublesome, unbecoming, unexpected, unfavorable, unfitting, unfortunate, unlucky, unpropitious, unseemly, unsuitable, untimely, vexatious, worrying.
antonyms auspicious, suitable.

untrustworthy *adj.* capricious, deceitful, devious, dishonest, disloyal, dubious, duplicitous, fair-weather, faithless, false, fickle, fly-by-night, shady, slippery, treacherous, tricky, two-faced, undependable, unfaithful, unreliable, unsafe, untrue, untrusty.
antonyms reliable, trustworthy.

untruthful *adj.* crooked, deceitful, deceptive, dishonest, dissembling, false, hypocritical, lying, mendacious, untrustworthy, unveracious.
antonym truthful.

untutored *adj.* artless, ignorant, illiterate, inexperienced, inexpert, simple, uneducated, unlearned, unlessoned, unpracticed, unrefined, unschooled, unsophisticated, untrained, unversed.
antonyms educated, trained.

unusual *adj.* abnormal, anomalous, atypical, bizarre, curious, different, eccentric, exceptional, extraordinary, odd, phenomenal, queer, rare, remarkable, singular, strange, surprising, uncommon, unconventional, unexpected, unfamiliar, unwonted.
antonyms normal, usual.

unutterable *adj.* egregious, extreme, indescribable, ineffable, nefandous, overwhelming, unimaginable, unspeakable.

unwarranted *adj.* baseless, gratuitous, groundless, indefensible, inexcusable, uncalled-for, unjust, unjustified, unprovoked, unreasonable, vain, wrong.
antonyms justifiable, warranted.

unwary *adj.* careless, credulous, hasty, heedless, imprudent, incautious, indiscreet, rash, reckless, thoughtless, unchary, uncircumspect, unguarded, unthinking, unwatchful.
antonyms cautious, wary.

unwieldy *adj.* awkward, bulky, burdensome, clumsy, cumbersome, cumbrous, gangling, hefty, hulking, inconvenient, massive, ponderous, ungainly, unhandy, unmanageable, weighty.
antonyms dainty, neat, petite.

unwilling *adj.* averse, disinclined, grudging, indisposed, laggard, loath, loathful, opposed, reluctant, resistant, slow, unenthusiastic.
antonyms enthusiastic, willing.

unwise *adj.* foolhardy, foolish, ill-advised, ill-considered, ill-judged, impolitic, improvident, imprudent, inadvisable, indiscreet, inexpedient, injudicious,

irresponsible, rash, reckless, senseless, short-sighted, silly, stupid, thoughtless, unintelligent.
antonyms prudent, wise.

unwitting *adj.* accidental, chance, ignorant, inadvertent, innocent, involuntary, unaware, unconscious, unintended, unintentional, unknowing, unmeant, unplanned, unsuspecting, unthinking.
antonyms conscious, deliberate, knowing, witting.

unwonted *adj.* atypical, exceptional, extraordinary, infrequent, peculiar, rare, singular, strange, unaccustomed, uncommon, uncustomary, unexpected, unfamiliar, unheard-of, unusual.
antonyms usual, wonted.

unyielding *adj.* adamant, determined, firm, hardline, immovable, implacable, inexorable, inflexible, intractable, intransigent, obdurate, obstinate, relentless, resolute, rigid, solid, staunch, steadfast, stubborn, tough, unbending, uncompromising, unrelenting, unwavering.
antonyms flexible, yielding.

upbeat *adj.* bright, bullish, buoyant, cheerful, cheery, encouraging, favorable, forward-looking, heartening, hopeful, optimistic, positive, promising, rosy.
antonyms down-beat, gloomy.

upbraid *v.* admonish, berate, blame, carpet, castigate, censure, chide, condemn, criticize, dress down, jaw, lecture, rate, rebuke, reprimand, reproach, reprove, scold, take to task, tell off, tick off.
antonyms commend, praise.

upbringing *n.* breeding, bringing-up, care, cultivation, education, instruction, nurture, parenting, raising, rearing, tending, training.

upgrade *v.* advance, ameliorate, better, elevate, embourgeoise, enhance, gentilize, gentrify, improve, promote, raise.
antonyms degrade, downgrade.

uphold *v.* advocate, aid, back, champion, countenance, defend, encourage, endorse, fortify, hold to, justify, maintain, promote, stand by, stengthen, support, sustain, vindicate.

upkeep *n.* care, conservation, expenditure, expenses, keep, maintenance, oncosts, operating costs, outgoing, outlay, overheads, preservation, repair, running, running costs, subsistence, support, sustenance.
antonym neglect.

uppish *adj.* affected, arrogant, assuming, big-headed, bumptious, cocky, conceited, hoity-toity, impertinent, overweening, presumptuous, self-important, snobbish, stuck-up, supercilious, swanky, toffee-nosed, uppity.
antonyms diffident, unassertive.

upright *adj.* arrect, bluff, conscientious, erect, ethical, faithful, four-square, good, high-minded, honest, honorable, incorruptible, just, noble, perpendicular, principled, righteous, straight, straightforward, true, trustworthy, unimpeachable, upstanding, vertical, virtuous.

antonyms dishonest, flat, horizontal, prone, supine.

uprising *n.* insurgence, insurgency, insurrection, mutiny, putsch, rebellion, revolt, revolution, rising, sedition, upheaval.

uproar *n.* brawl, brouhaha, clamor, commotion, confusion, din, disorder, furore, hubbub, hullabaloo, hurly-burly, katzenjammer, noise, outcry, pandemonium, racket, rammy, randan, riot, ruckus, ruction, rumpus, stramash, tumult, turbulence, turmoil.

uproarious *adj.* boisterous, clamorous, confused, convulsive, deafening, disorderly, gleeful, hilarious, hysterical, killing, loud, noisy, rib-tickling, riotous, rip-roaring, roistering, rollicking, rowdy, rowdy-dowdy, side-splitting, tempestuous, tumultuous, turbulent, unrestrained, wild.
antonym sedate.

upset *v.* agitate, bother, capsize, change, conquer, defeat, destabilize, discombobulate, discompose, disconcert, dismay, disorder, disorganize, disquiet, distress, disturb, fluster, grieve, hip, overcome, overset, overthrow, overturn, perturb, ruffle, shake, spill, spoil, tip, topple, trouble, unnerve, unsteady.
n. agitation, bother, bug, complaint, defeat, disorder, disruption, disturbance, illness, indisposition, malady, purl, reverse, shake-up, shock, sickness, surprise, trouble, upheaval, worry.
adj. agitated, bothered, capsized, chaotic, choked, confused, disconcerted, dismayed, disordered, disquieted, distressed, disturbed, frantic, gippy, grieved, hurt, ill, messed up, muddled, overturned, overwrought, pained, poorly, qualmish, queasy, ruffled, shattered, sick, spilled, toppled, topsy-turvy, troubled, tumbled, worried.

upshot *n.* conclusion, consequence, culmination, end, event, finale, finish, issue, outcome, pay-off, result.

urbane *adj.* bland, civil, civilized, cosmopolitan, courteous, cultivated, cultured, debonair, easy, elegant, mannerly, polished, refined, smooth, sophisticated, suave, well-bred, well-mannered.
antonyms gauche, uncouth.

urge *v.* advise, advocate, beg, beseech, champion, compel, constrain, counsel, drive, emphasize, encourage, entreat, exhort, force, goad, hasten, hist, impel, implore, incite, induce, instigate, nag, plead, press, propel, push, recommend, solicit, spur, stimulate, support, underline, underscore.
antonyms deter, dissuade.
n. compulsion, desire, drive, eagerness, fancy, impulse, inclination, itch, libido, longing, wish, yearning, yen.
antonym disinclination.

urgency *n.* exigence, exigency, extremity, gravity, hurry, imperativeness, importance, importunity, instancy, necessity, need, pressure, seriousness, stress.

urgent *adj.* clamorous, cogent, compelling, critical, crucial, eager, earnest, emergent, exigent, immediate, imperative, important, importunate, insistent, instant, intense, persistent, persuasive, pressing, top-priority.

usage *n.* application, control, convention, custom, employment, etiquette, form, habit, handling, management, method, mode, operation, practice, procedure, protocol, régime, regulation, routine, rule, running, tradition, treatment, use, wont.

use *v.* apply, bring, consume, employ, enjoy, exercise, exhaust, expend, exploit, handle, manipulate, misuse, operate, ply, practice, spend, treat, usufruct, utilize, waste, wield, work.

n. advantage, application, avail, benefit, call, cause, custom, employment, end, enjoyment, exercise, good, habit, handling, help, meaning, mileage, necessity, need, object, occasion, operation, point, practice, profit, purpose, reason, service, treatment, usage, usefulness, usufruct, utility, value, way, wont, worth.

useful *adj.* advantageous, all-purpose, beneficial, convenient, effective, fruitful, general-purpose, handy, helpful, practical, productive, profitable, salutary, serviceable, valuable, worthwhile.

antonym useless.

useless *adj.* bootless, clapped-out, disadvantageous, effectless, feckless, fruitless, futile, hopeless, idle, impractical, incompetent, ineffective, ineffectual, inefficient, inept, of no use, pointless, profitless, shiftless, stupid, unavailing, unproductive, unworkable, vain, valueless, weak, worthless.

antonym useful.

usher *n.* attendant, doorkeeper, escort, guide, huissier, usherette.

v. conduct, direct, escort, guide, lead, pilot, shepherd, steer.

usual *adj.* accepted, accustomed, common, constant, conventional, customary, everyday, expected, familiar, fixed, general, habitual, nomic, normal, ordinary, recognized, regular, routine, standard, stock, typical, unexceptional, wonted.

antonyms unheard-of, unusual.

usually *adv.* as a rule, by and large, chiefly, commonly, customarily, generally, generally speaking, habitually, in the main, mainly, mostly, normally, on the whole, ordinarily, regularly, routinely, traditionally, typically.

antonym exceptionally.

utensil *n.* apparatus, contrivance, device, gadget, gismo, implement, instrument, tool.

utility *n.* advantage, advantageousness, avail, benefit, convenience, efficacy, expedience, fitness, point, practicality, profit, satisfactoriness, service, serviceableness, use, usefulness, value.

antonym inutility.

utilize *v.* adapt, appropriate, employ, exploit, make use of, put to use, resort to, take advantage of, turn to account, use.

Utopian *adj.* airy, chimerical, dream, Elysian, fanciful, fantastic, ideal, idealistic, illusory, imaginary, impractical, perfect, romantic, unworkable, visionary, wishful.

utter[1] *adj.* absolute, arrant, complete, consummate, dead, downright, entire, out-and-out, perfect, sheer, stark, thorough, thoroughgoing, total, unalleviated, unmitigated, unqualified.

utter[2] *v.* articulate, declare, deliver, divulge, enounce, enunciate, express, proclaim, promulgate, pronounce, publish, reveal, say, sound, speak, state, tell, tongue, verbalize, vocalize, voice.

V

vacancy *n.* accommodation, emptiness, gap, job, opening, opportunity, place, position, post, room, situation, space, vacuity, vacuousness, vacuum, void.

vacant *adj.* absent, absent-minded, abstracted, available, blank, disengaged, dreaming, dreamy, empty, expressionless, free, idle, inane, inattentive, incurious, thoughtless, to let, unemployed, unengaged, unfilled, unoccupied, untenanted, unthinking, vacuous, void.
antonyms engaged, occupied.

vacate *v.* abandon, depart, evacuate, leave, quit, withdraw.

vacillate *v.* fluctuate, haver, hesitate, oscillate, shilly-shally, shuffle, sway, swither, temporize, tergiversate, waver.

vacillating *adj.* hesitant, irresolute, oscillating, shilly-shallying, shuffling, swithering, temporizing, uncertain, unresolved, wavering.
antonyms resolute, unhesitating.

vacuity *n.* apathy, blankness, emptiness, inanity, incognizance, incomprehension, incuriosity, nothingness, space, vacuousness, vacuum, void.

vacuous *adj.* apathetic, blank, empty, idle, inane, incurious, stupid, uncomprehending, unfilled, unintelligent, vacant, void.

vacuum *n.* chasm, emptiness, gap, nothingness, space, vacuity, void.

vagabond *n.* beggar, bo, bum, down-and-out, hobo, itinerant, knight of the road, migrant, nomad, outcast, rascal, rover, runabout, runagate, tramp, vagrant, wanderer, wayfarer.

vagary *n.* caprice, crotchet, fancy, fegary, humor, megrim, notion, prank, quirk, whim, whimsy.

vagrant *n.* beggar, bum, gangrel, hobo, itinerant, rolling stone, stroller, tramp, wanderer.
adj. footloose, homeless, itinerant, nomadic, roaming, rootless, roving, shiftless, traveling, vagabond, wandering.

vague *adj.* amorphous, blurred, dim, doubtful, evasive, fuzzy, generalized, hazy, ill-defined, imprecise, indefinite, indeterminate, indistinct, inexact, lax, loose, misty, nebulous, obscure, shadowy, uncertain, unclear, undefined, undetermined, unknown, unspecific, unspecified, woolly.
antonyms certain, clear, definite.

vain *adj.* abortive, affected, arrogant, baseless, bigheaded, conceited, egotistical, empty, fruitless, futile, groundless, hollow, idle, inflated, mindless, narcissistic, nugatory, ostentatious, overweening, peacockish, pointless, pretentious, proud, purposeless, self-important, self-satisfied, senseless, stuck-up, swaggering, swanky, swollen-headed, time- wasting, trifling, trivial, unavailing, unimportant, unproductive, unprofitable, unsubstantial, useless, vain- glorious, vaporous, worthless.
antonyms modest, self-effacing.

valet *n.* body servant, gentleman's gentleman, man, manservant, valet de chambre.

valiant *adj.* bold, brave, courageous, dauntless, doughty, fearless, gallant, heroic, indomitable, intrepid, plucky, redoubtable, stalwart, staunch, stout, stout-hearted, valorous, worthy.
antonym cowardly.

valid *adj.* approved, authentic, binding, bona fide, cogent, conclusive, convincing, efficacious, efficient, genuine, good, just, lawful, legal, legitimate, logical, official, potent, powerful, proper, rational, reliable, sound, substantial, telling, weighty, well-founded, well-grounded.
antonym invalid.

validate *v.* attest, authenticate, authorize, certify, confirm, corroborate, endorse, legalize, ratify, substantiate, underwrite.

validity *n.* authority, cogency, force, foundation, grounds, justifiability, lawfulness, legality, legitimacy, logic, point, power, soundness, strength, substance, weight.
antonym invalidity.

valley *n.* arroyo, canyon, cwm, dale, dell, depression, dingle, draw, glen, gorge, gulch, hollow, hope, slade, strath, vale.

valor *n.* boldness, bravery, courage, derring-do, doughtiness, fearlessness, fortitude, gallantry, hardiness, heroism, intrepidity, lion-heartedness, mettle, spirit.
antonyms cowardice, weakness.

valuable *adj.* advantageous, beneficial, blue-chip, cherished, costly, dear, esteemed, estimable, expensive, fruitful, handy, helpful, high-priced, important, invaluable, precious, prizable, prized, productive, profitable, serviceable, treasured, useful, valued, worthwhile, worthy.
antonyms useless, valueless.

value *n.* account, advantage, avail, benefit, cost, desirability, equivalent, good, help, importance, merit, price, profit, rate, significance, use, usefulness, utility, worth.
v. account, appraise, appreciate, apprize, assess, cherish, compute, esteem, estimate, evaluate, hold dear, price, prize, rate, regard, respect, survey, treasure.
antonyms disregard, neglect, undervalue.

vanish *v.* dematerialize, depart, die out, disappear, disperse, dissolve, evanesce, evaporate, exit, fade, fizzle out, melt, peter out.
antonyms appear, materialize.

vanity *n.* affectation, airs, arrogance, bigheadedness, conceit, conceitedness, egotism, emptiness, frivolity, fruitlessness, fume, futility, hollowness, idleness, inanity, narcissism, ostentation, peacockery, pointlessness, pretension, pride, self-admiration, self-conceit, self-love, self-satisfaction, swollen-headedness, triviality, unreality, unsubstantiality, uselessness, vainglory, worthlessness.
antonyms modesty, worth.

vanquish *v.* beat, confound, conquer, crush, defeat, humble, master, overcome, overpower, overwhelm, quell, reduce, repress, rout, subdue, subjugate, triumph over.

vapid *adj.* banal, bland, bloodless, boring, colorless, dead, dull, flat, flavorless, insipid, jejune, lifeless, limp, stale, tame, tasteless, tedious, tiresome, trite, uninspiring, uninteresting, watery, weak, wishy-washy.
antonyms interesting, vigorous.

vapor *n.* breath, brume, damp, dampness, exhalation, fog, fumes, halitus, haze, miasm, miasma, mist, reek, roke, smoke, steam.

variable *adj.* capricious, chameleonic, changeable, fickle, fitful, flexible, fluctuating, inconstant, mercurial, moonish, mutable, protean, shifting, temperamental, unpredictable, unstable, unsteady, vacillating, varying, versiform, wavering.
antonym invariable.
n. factor, parameter.

variant *adj.* alternative, derived, deviant, different, divergent, exceptional, modified.
antonyms normal, standard, usual.
n. alternative, development, deviant, modification, rogue, sport, variation.

variation *n.* alteration, change, departure, deviation, difference, discrepancy, diversification, diversity, elaboration, inflection, innovation, modification, modulation, novelty, variety.
antonyms monotony, similitude, uniformity.

variety *n.* array, assortment, brand, breed, category, change, class, collection, difference, discrepancy, diversification, diversity, intermixture, kind, make, manifoldness, many-sidedness, medley, miscellany, mixture, multifariousness, multiplicity, olio, olla-podrida, order, pot-pourri, range, sort, species, strain, type, variation.
antonyms monotony, similitude, uniformity.

various *adj.* assorted, different, differing, disparate, distinct, divers, diverse, diversified, heterogeneous, many, many-sided, miscellaneous, multifarous, omnifarous, several, sundry, varied, variegated, varying.

vary *v.* alter, alternate, change, depart, differ, disagree, diverge, diversify, fluctuate, inflect, intermix, modify, modulate, permutate, reorder, transform.

vassalage *n.* bondage, dependence, serfdom, servitude, slavery, subjection, subjugation, thraldom, villeinage.

vast *adj.* astronomical, boundless, capacious, colossal, cyclopean, enormous, extensive, far-flung, fathomless,

gigantic, great, huge, illimitable, immeasurable, immense, limitless, mammoth, massive, measureless, monstrous, monumental, never-ending, prodigious, stupendous, sweeping, tremendous, unbounded, unlimited, vasty, voluminous, wide.

vault[1] *v.* bound, clear, hurdle, jump, leap, leap-frog, spring.

vault[2] *n.* arch, camera, cavern, cellar, concave, crypt, depository, mausoleum, repository, roof, span, strongroom, tomb, undercroft, wine-cellar.

vaunt *v.* blazon, boast, brag, crow, exult in, flaunt, parade, show off, trumpet.
antonyms belittle, minimize.

veer *v.* change, sheer, shift, swerve, tack, turn, wheel.

vehement *adj.* animated, ardent, eager, earnest, emphatic, enthusiastic, fervent, fervid, fierce, forceful, forcible, heated, impassioned, impetuous, intense, passionate, powerful, strong, urgent, violent, zealous.
antonyms apathetic, indifferent.

veil *v.* cloak, conceal, cover, dim, disguise, dissemble, dissimulate, hide, mantle, mask, obscure, screen, shade, shadow, shield.
antonyms expose, uncover.
n. blind, cloak, cover, curtain, disguise, film, humeral, integument, mask, screen, shade, shroud, velum.

venal *adj.* bent, bribable, buyable, corrupt, corruptible, grafting, mercenary, purchasable, simoniacal.
antonym incorruptible.

venerable *adj.* aged, august, dignified, esteemed, grave, honored, respected, revered, reverenced, reverend, sage, sedate, venerated, wise, worshipful.

venerate *v.* adore, esteem, hallow, honor, respect, revere, reverence, worship.
antonyms anathematize, disregard, execrate.

vengeance *n.* avengement, lex talionis, reprisal, requital, retaliation, retribution, revanche, revenge, talion, tit for tat.
antonym forgiveness.

venom *n.* acrimony, bane, bitterness, gall, grudge, hate, hatred, ill-will, malevolence, malice, maliciousness, malignity, poison, rancor, spite, spitefulness, spleen, toxin, venin, vindictiveness, virulence, virus, vitrio.

vent *n.* aperture, blowhole, duct, hole, opening, orifice, outlet, passage, spiracle, split.
v. air, discharge, emit, express, let fly, release, unloose, utter, voice.

venture *v.* advance, adventure, chance, dare, endanger, hazard, imperil, jeopardize, make bold, presume, put forward, risk, speculate, stake, suggest, take the liberty, volunteer, wager.
n. adventure, chance, endeavor, enterprise, fling, gamble, hazard, operation, project, risk, speculation, undertaking.

verbal *adj.* lexical, oral, spoken, unwritten, verbatim, word-of-mouth.

verbatim *adv.* exactly, literally, precisely, to the letter, (verbatim et) literatim, word for word.

verbose *adj.* ambagious, circumlocutory, diffuse, garrulous, long-winded, loquacious, multiloquent, periphrastic, phrasy, pleonastic, prolix, windy, wordy.
antonyms economical, laconic, succinct.

verbosity *n.* garrulity, logorrhoea, long-windedness, loquaciousness, loquacity, multiloquy, prolixity, verbiage, verboseness, windiness, wordiness.
antonyms economy, succinctness.

verdict *n.* adjudication, assessment, conclusion, decision, finding, judgment, opinion, sentence.

verge *n.* border, boundary, brim, brink, edge, edging, extreme, limit, lip, margin, roadside, threshold.

verification *n.* attestation, authentication, checking, confirmation, corroboration, proof, substantiation, validation.

verify *v.* attest, authenticate, check, confirm, corroborate, prove, substantiate, support, testify, validate.
antonyms discredit, invalidate.

vernacular *adj.* colloquial, common, endemic, indigenous, informal, local, mother, native, popular, vulgar.
n. argot, cant, dialect, idiom, jargon, language, lingo, parlance, patois, speech, tongue.

versatile *adj.* adaptable, adjustable, all-round, flexible, functional, general-purpose, handy, many-sided, multifaceted, multipurpose, protean, Renaissance, resourceful, variable.
antonym inflexible.

versed *adj.* accomplished, acquainted, au fait, competent, conversant, experienced, familiar, knowledgeable, learned, practiced, proficient, qualified, seasoned, skilled.

version *n.* account, adaptation, design, form, interpretation, kind, model, paraphrase, portrayal, reading, rendering, rendition, style, translation, type, variant.

vertical *adj.* erect, on end, perpendicular, upright, upstanding.
antonym horizontal.

verve *n.* animation, brio, dash, élan, energy, enthusiasm, force, gusto, life, liveliness, pizzazz, punch, relish, sparkle, spirit, vigor, vim, vitality, vivacity, zeal, zip.
antonym apathy.

very *adv.* absolutely, acutely, awfully, decidedly, deeply, dogged, dooms, eminently, exceeding(ly), excessively, extremely, fell, gey, greatly, highly, jolly, noticeably, particularly, passing, rattling, really, remarkably, superlatively, surpassingly, terribly, truly, uncommonly, unusually, wonderfully.
antonyms hardly, scarcely, slightly.
adj. actual, appropriate, bare, exact, express, identical, mere, perfect, plain, precise, pure, real, same, selfsame, sheer, simple, unqualified, utter.

vessel *n.* barque, boat, canister, container, craft, holder, jar, pot, receptacle, ship, utensil.

vestige *n.* evidence, glimmer, hint, indication, print, relic, remainder, remains, remnant, residue, scrap, sign, suspicion, token, trace, track, whiff.

veto *v.* ban, blackball, disallow, forbid, interdict, kill, negative, prohibit, reject, rule out, turn down.
antonyms approve, sanction.
n. ban, embargo, interdict, prohibition, rejection, thumbs down.
antonyms approval, assent.

vex *v.* afflict, aggravate, agitate, annoy, bother, bug, chagrin, deave, displease, distress, disturb, exasperate, fret, gall, get (to), harass, hump, irritate, molest, needle, nettle, offend, peeve, perplex, pester, pique, plague, provoke, rile, spite, tease, torment, trouble, upset, worry.
antonym soothe.

vexation *n.* aggravation, anger, annoyance, bore, bother, chagrin, difficulty, displeasure, dissatisfaction, exasperation, frustration, fury, headache, irritant, misfortune, nuisance, pique, problem, trouble, upset, worry.

viable *adj.* achievable, applicable, feasible, operable, possible, practicable, usable, workable.
antonyms impossible, unworkable.

vibrate *v.* fluctuate, judder, oscillate, pendulate, pulsate, pulse, quiver, resonate, reverberate, shake, shimmy, shiver, shudder, sway, swing, throb, tremble, undulate.

vice *n.* bad habit, besetting sin, blemish, corruption, defect, degeneracy, depravity, evil, evil-doing, failing, fault, hamartia, immorality, imperfection, iniquity, profligacy, shortcoming, sin, venality, weakness, wickedness.
antonym virtue.

vicinity *n.* area, circumjacency, district, environs, locality, neighborhood, precincts, propinquity, proximity, purlieus, vicinage.

vicious *adj.* abhorrent, atrocious, backbiting, bad, barbarous, bitchy, brutal, catty, corrupt, cruel, dangerous, debased, defamatory, depraved, diabolical, fiendish, foul, heinous, immoral, infamous, malicious, mean, monstrous, nasty, perverted, profligate, rancorous, savage, sinful, slanderous, spiteful, unprincipled, venomous, vile, vindictive, violent, virulent, vitriolic, wicked, worthless, wrong.
antonyms gentle, good, virtuous.

victimize *v.* bully, cheat, deceive, defraud, discriminate against, dupe, exploit, fool, gull, hoodwink, oppress, persecute, pick on, prey on, swindle, use.

victor *n.* champ, champion, conqueror, first, prize-winner, subjugator, top dog, vanquisher, victor ludorum, victrix, winner.
antonyms loser, vanquished.

victory *n.* conquest, laurels, mastery, palm, prize, subjugation, success, superiority, triumph, vanquishment, win.
antonyms defeat, loss.

view *n.* aspect, attitude, belief, contemplation, conviction, display, estimation, examination, feeling, glimpse, impression, inspection, judgment, landscape, look, notion, opinion, outlook, panorama, perception, perspective, picture, prospect, scan, scene, scrutiny, sentiment, sight, spectacle, survey, viewing, vision, vista. *v.* behold, consider, contemplate, deem, examine, explore, eye, inspect, judge, observe, perceive, read, regard, scan, speculate, survey, watch, witness.

viewpoint *n.* angle, Anschauung, attitude, feeling, opinion, perspective, position, slant, stance, standpoint.

vigilant *adj.* alert, Argus-eyed, attentive, careful, cautious, circumspect, guarded, on one's guard, on one's toes, on the alert, on the lookout, on the qui vive, sleepless, unsleeping, wakeful, watchful, wide-awake. *antonyms* careless, forgetful, lax, negligent.

vigor *n.* activity, animation, dash, dynamism, energy, force, forcefulness, gusto, health, liveliness, might, oomph, pep, potency, power, punch, robustness, snap, soundness, spirit, stamina, strength, verve, vim, virility, vitality, zip.
antonyms impotence, sluggishness, weakness.

vigorous *adj.* active, brisk, dynamic, effective, efficient, energetic, enterprising, flourishing, forceful, forcible, full-blooded, hale, hardy, healthy, hearty, intense, lively, lusty, mettlesome, powerful, red-blooded, robust, sound, spanking, spirited, stout, strenuous, strong, virile, vital, zippy.
antonyms feeble, lethargic, weak.

vile *adj.* abandoned, abject, appalling, bad, base, coarse, contemptible, corrupt, debased, degenerate, degrading, depraved, despicable, disgraceful, disgusting, earthly, evil, foul, horrid, humiliating, ignoble, impure, loathsome, low, mean, miserable, nasty, nauseating, nefarious, noxious, offensive, perverted, repellent, repugnant, repulsive, revolting, scabbed, scabby, scandalous, scurvy, shocking, sickening, sinful, ugly, vicious, vulgar, wicked, worthless, wretched.

vilify *v.* abuse, asperse, bad-mouth, berate, calumniate, criticize, debase, decry, defame, denigrate, denounce, disparage, malign, revile, slander, smear, stigmatize, traduce, vilipend, vituperate.
antonyms adore, compliment, eulogize, glorify.

village *n.* clachan, community, district, dorp, hamlet, kraal, pueblo, settlement, township.

villain *n.* anti-hero, baddy, blackguard, bravo, caitiff, criminal, devil, evil-doer, heavy, knave, libertine, malefactor, miscreant, profligate, rapscallion, rascal, reprobate, rogue, scoundrel, wretch.
antonyms angel, goody, hero, heroine.

villainous *adj.* atrocious, bad, base, blackguardly, criminal, cruel, debased, degenerate, depraved, detestable, diabolical, disgraceful, evil, fiendish, hateful, heinous, ignoble, infamous, inhuman, malevolent, mean, nefarious, opprobrious, outrageous, ruffianly, scoundrelly, sinful, terrible, thievish, vicious, vile, wicked.
antonyms angelic, good, heroic.

vindication *n.* apology, assertion, defence, exculpation, excuse, exoneration, extenuation, justification,

maintenance, plea, rehabilitation, substantiation, support, verification.
antonyms accusation, conviction.

violate *v.* abuse, assault, befoul, break, contravene, debauch, defile, desecrate, dishonor, disobey, disregard, flout, infract, infringe, invade, outrage, pollute, profane, rape, ravish, transgress.
antonyms obey, observe, uphold.

violence *n.* abandon, acuteness, bestiality, bloodshed, bloodthirstiness, boisterousness, brutality, conflict, cruelty, destructiveness, ferocity, fervor, fierceness, fighting, force, frenzy, fury, harshness, hostilities, intensity, murderousness, passion, power, roughness, savagery, severity, sharpness, storminess, terrorism, thuggery, tumult, turbulence, vehemence, wildness.
antonyms passivity, peacefulness.

violent *adj.* acute, agonizing, berserk, biting, bloodthirsty, blustery, boisterous, brutal, cruel, destructive, devastating, excruciating, extreme, fiery, forceful, forcible, furious, harsh, headstrong, homicidal, hot-headed, impetuous, intemperate, intense, maddened, maniacal, murderous, outrageous, painful, passionate, peracute, powerful, raging, riotous, rough, ruinous, savage, severe, sharp, strong, tempestuous, tumultuous, turbulent, uncontrollable, ungovernable, unrestrained, vehement, vicious, wild.
antonyms calm, gentle, moderate, passive, peaceful.

virgin *n.* bachelor, celibate, damsel, girl, maid, maiden, spinster, vestal, virgo intacta.
adj. chaste, fresh, immaculate, intact, maidenly, modest, new, pristine, pure, snowy, spotless, stainless, uncorrupted, undefiled, unsullied, untouched, unused, vestal, virginal.

virile *adj.* forceful, husky, lusty, macho, male, man-like, manly, masculine, potent, red-blooded, robust, rugged, strong, vigorous.
antonyms effeminate, impotent, weak.

virtue *n.* advantage, asset, attribute, chastity, credit, excellence, goodness, high-mindedness, honor, incorruptibility, innocence, integrity, justice, merit, morality, plus, probity, purity, quality, rectitude, redeeming feature, righteousness, strength, uprightness, virginity, worth, worthiness.
antonym vice.

virtuous *adj.* blameless, celibate, chaste, clean-living, continent, ethical, excellent, exemplary, good, high-principled, honest, honorable, incorruptible, innocent, irreproachable, moral, praiseworthy, pure, righteous, spotless, unimpeachable, upright, virginal, worthy.
antonyms bad, dishonest, immoral, vicious, wicked.

virulent *adj.* acrimonious, baneful, bitter, deadly, envenomed, hostile, infective, injurious, lethal, malevolent, malicious, malignant, noxious, pernicious, poisonous, rancorous, resentful, septic, spiteful, splenetic, toxic, venomous, vicious, vindictive, vitriolic.

vision *n.* apparition, chimera, concept, conception,

construct, daydream, delusion, discernment, dream, eyes, eyesight, fantasy, far-sightedness, foresight, ghost, hallucination, idea, ideal, illusion, image, imagination, insight, intuition, mirage, penetration, perception, phantasm, phantasma, phantom, picture, prescience, revelation, seeing, sight, spectacle, specter, view, wraith.

visionary *adj.* chimerical, delusory, dreaming, dreamy, fanciful, fantastic, ideal, idealized, idealistic, illusory, imaginary, impractical, moonshiny, prophetic, quixotic, romantic, speculative, starry-eyed, unreal, unrealistic, unworkable, utopian.

n. daydreamer, Don Quixote, dreamer, enthusiast, fantasist, idealist, mystic, prophet, rainbow-chaser, romantic, seer, theorist, utopian, zealot.

antonym pragmatist.

visit *v.* afflict, assail, attack, befall, call in, call on, drop in on, haunt, inspect, look in, look up, pop in, punish, see, smite, stay at, stay with, stop by, take in, trouble.

n. call, excursion, sojourn, stay, stop.

visitor *n.* caller, company, guest, holidaymaker, tourist, visitant.

vista *n.* enfilade, panorama, perspective, prospect, view.

vital *adj.* alive, animate, animated, animating, basic, cardinal, critical, crucial, decisive, dynamic, energetic, essential, forceful, fundamental, generative, imperative, important, indispensable, invigorating, key, life-giving, life- or-death, live, lively, living, necessary, quickening, requisite, significant, spirited, urgent, vibrant, vigorous, vivacious, zestful.

antonyms inessential, peripheral, unimportant.

vitality *n.* animation, energy, exuberance, foison, go, life, liveliness, lustiness, oomph, pep, robustness, sparkle, stamina, strength, vigor, vim, vivaciousness, vivacity.

vitiate *v.* blemish, blight, contaminate, corrupt, debase, defile, deprave, deteriorate, devalue, harm, impair, injure, invalidate, mar, nullify, pervert, pollute, ruin, spoil, sully, taint, undermine.

antonym purify.

vituperation *n.* abuse, blame, castigation, censure, contumely, diatribe, fault-finding, flak, invective, objurgation, obloquy, phillipic, rebuke, reprimand, reproach, revilement, scurrility, stick, vilification.

antonyms acclaim, eulogy, praise.

vivacious *adj.* animated, bubbling, bubbly, cheerful, chipper, ebullient, effervescent, frisky, frolicsome, gay, high-spirited, jolly, light-hearted, lively, merry, scintillating, sparkling, spirited, sportive, sprightly, vital.

antonym languid.

vivid *adj.* active, animated, bright, brilliant, clear, colorful, distinct, dramatic, dynamic, eidetic, energetic, expressive, flamboyant, glowing, graphic, highly-colored, intense, lifelike, lively, memorable, powerful, quick, realistic, rich, sharp, spirited, stirring, striking, strong, telling, vibrant, vigorous.

antonyms dull, lifeless.

vocal *adj.* articulate, clamorous, eloquent, expressive, forthright, frank, free-spoken, noisy, oral, outspoken, plain-spoken, said, shrill, spoken, strident, uttered, vociferous, voiced.

antonyms inarticulate, quiet.

vocation *n.* bag, business, calling, career, employment, job, métier, mission, niche, office, post, profession, pursuit, role, trade, work.

void *adj.* bare, blank, canceled, clear, dead, drained, emptied, empty, free, inane, ineffective, ineffectual, inoperative, invalid, nugatory, null, tenantless, unenforceable, unfilled, unoccupied, useless, vacant, vain, worthless.

antonyms full, valid.

n. blank, blankness, cavity, chasm, emptiness, gap, hiatus, hollow, lack, opening, space, vacuity, vacuum, want.

v. abnegate, annul, cancel, defecate, discharge, drain, eject, elimate, emit, empty, evacuate, invalidate, nullify, rescind.

antonyms fill, validate.

volatile *adj.* airy, changeable, erratic, explosive, fickle, flighty, gay, giddy, hot-headed, hot-tempered, inconstant, lively, mercurial, sprightly, temperamental, unsettled, unstable, unsteady, variable, volcanic.

antonyms constant, steady.

volition *n.* choice, choosing, determination, discretion, election, option, preference, purpose, resolution, taste, velleity, will.

voluble *adj.* articulate, fluent, forthcoming, garrulous, glib, loquacious, talkative.

volume *n.* aggregate, amount, amplitude, bigness, body, book, bulk, capacity, compass, dimensions, fascic(u)le, heft, mass, part, publication, quantity, tome, total, treatise.

voluminous *adj.* abounding, ample, big, billowing, bulky, capacious, cavernous, commodious, copious, full, large, massive, prolific, roomy, vast.

antonyms scanty, slight.

voluntary *adj.* conscious, deliberate, discretional, free, gratuitous, honorary, intended, intentional, optional, purposeful, purposive, spontaneous, unconstrained, unforced, unpaid, volunteer, wilful, willing.

antonyms compulsory, forced, involuntary, unwilling.

voluptuous *adj.* ample, buxom, curvaceous, effeminate, enticing, epicurean, erotic, goluptious, hedonistic, licentious, luscious, luxurious, pleasure-loving, provocative, seductive, self-indulgent, sensual, shapely, sybaritic.

antonym ascetic.

voracious *adj.* acquisitive, avid, devouring, edacious, gluttonous, greedy, hungry, insatiable, omnivorous, pantophagous, prodigious, rapacious, ravening, ravenous, uncontrolled, unquenchable.

vouch for affirm, assert, asseverate, attest to, avouch, back, certify, confirm, endorse, guarantee, support, swear to, uphold.

vouchsafe *v.* accord, bestow, cede, confer, deign, grant, impart, yield.

vow *v.* affirm, avouch, bename, consecrate, dedicate, devote, maintain, pledge, profess, promise, swear.
n. avouchment, oath, pledge, promise, troth.

voyage *n.* crossing, cruise, expedition, journey, passage, peregrination, travels, trip.

vulgar *adj.* banausic, blue, boorish, cheap and nasty, coarse, common, crude, dirty, flashy, gaudy, general, gross, ill-bred, impolite, improper, indecent, indecorous, indelicate, low, low-life, low-lived, low-minded, low-thoughted, nasty, native, naughty, ordinary, pandemian, plebby, plebeian, ribald, risqué, rude, suggestive, tacky, tasteless, tawdry, uncouth, unmannerly, unrefined, vernacular.
antonyms correct, decent, elegant, noble, polite, refined.

vulnerable *adj.* accessible, assailable, defenseless, exposed, expugnable, pregnable, sensitive, susceptible, tender, thin-skinned, unprotected, weak, wide open.
antonyms protected, strong.

W

wacky *adj*. crazy, daft, eccentric, erratic, goofy, irrational, loony, loopy, nutty, odd, screwy, silly, unpredictable, wild, zany.
antonym sensible.

wad *n*. ball, block, bundle, chunk, hump, hunk, mass, pledget, plug, roll.

waffle *v*. blather, fudge, jabber, prate, prattle, prevaricate, rabbit on, spout, witter on.
n. blather, gobbledegook, guff, jabber, nonsense, padding, prating, prattle, prolixity, verbiage, verbosity, wordiness.

waft *v*. bear, carry, convey, drift, float, ride, transmit, transport, whiffle, winnow.
n. breath, breeze, current, draft, puff, scent, whiff.

wage *n*. allowance, compensation, earnings, emolument, fee, guerdon, hire, pay, payment, penny-fee, recompense, remuneration, reward, salary, screw, stipend, wage- packet, wages.
v. carry on, conduct, engage in, practice, prosecute, pursue, undertake.

wager *n*. bet, flutter, gage, gamble, hazard, pledge, punt, speculation, stake, venture.
v. bet, chance, gamble, hazard, lay, lay odds, pledge, punt, risk, speculate, stake, venture.

waggish *adj*. amusing, arch, bantering, comical, droll, espiègle, facetious, frolicsome, funny, humorous, impish, jesting, jocose, jocular, merry, mischievous, playful, puckish, risible, roguish, sportive, witty.
antonyms grave, serious, staid.

wagon *n*. buggy, carriage, cart, float, pushcart, train, truck, wain.

waif *n*. foundling, orphan, stray, wastrel.

wail *v*. bemoan, bewail, complain, cry, deplore, grieve, howl, keen, lament, mewl, moan, ululate, weep, yammer, yowl.
n. caterwaul, complaint, cry, grief, howl, keen, lament, lamentation, moan, ululation, weeping, yowl.

wait *v*. abide, dally, delay, hang fire, hesitate, hold back, hover, linger, loiter, mark time, pause, remain, rest, stay, tarry.
antonyms depart, go, leave.
n. delay, halt, hesitation, hiatus, hold-up, interval, pause, rest, stay.

waive *v*. abandon, defer, disclaim, forgo, postpone, relinquish, remit, renounce, resign, surrender.
antonyms claim, maintain.

wake[1] *v*. activate, animate, arise, arouse, awake, awaken, bestir, enliven, excite, fire, galvanize, get up, kindle, provoke, quicken, rise, rouse, stimulate, stir, unbed.
antonyms relax, sleep.
n. death-watch, funeral, pernoctation, vigil, watch.

wake[2] *n*. aftermath, backwash, path, rear, track, trail, train, wash, waves.

waken *v*. activate, animate, arouse, awake, awaken, enliven, fire, galvanize, get up, ignite, kindle, quicken, rouse, stimulate, stir, whet.

walk *v*. accompany, advance, amble, convoy, escort, go by Shanks's pony, hike, hoof it, march, move, pace, pedestrianize, perambulate, plod, promenade, saunter, step, stride, stroll, take, traipse, tramp, tread, trek, trog, trudge.
n. aisle, alley, ambulatory, avenue, carriage, constitutional, esplanade, footpath, frescade, gait, hike, lane, mall, march, pace, path, pathway, pavement, pawn, perambulation, promenade, ramble, saunter, sidewalk, step, stride, stroll, trail, traipse, tramp, trek, trudge, turn.

wall *n*. bailey, barricade, barrier, block, breastwork, bulkhead, bulwark, dike, divider, dyke, embankment, enclosure, fence, fortification, hedge, impediment, membrane, obstacle, obstruction, palisade, panel, parapet, partition, rampart, screen, septum, stockade.

wallow *v*. bask, delight, enjoy, flounder, glory, indulge, lie, lurch, luxuriate, relish, revel, roll, splash, stagger, stumble, tumble, wade, welter.

wan *adj*. anemic, ashen, bleak, bloodless, cadaverous, colorless, dim, discolored, faint, feeble, ghastly, livid, lurid, mournful, pale, pallid, pasty, sickly, waxen, weak, weary, whey-faced, white.

wander *v*. aberrate, babble, cruise, depart, deviate, digress, divagate, diverge, drift, err, hump the bluey, lapse, meander, mill around, peregrinate, ramble, range, rave, roam, rove, saunter, squander, straggle, stravaig, stray, stroll, swerve, traipse, veer, wilder.
n. cruise, excursion, meander, peregrination, ramble, saunter, stroll, traipse.

wane *v*. abate, atrophy, contract, decline, decrease, dim, diminish, droop, drop, dwindle, ebb, fade, fail, lessen, shrink, sink, subside, taper off, weaken, wither.
antonyms increase, wax.
n. abatement, atrophy, contraction, decay, decline, decrease, diminution, drop, dwindling, ebb, fading, failure, fall, lessening, sinking, subsidence, tapering off, weakening.
antonym increase.

want *v*. call for, covet, crave, demand, desiderate, desire, fancy, hanker after, hunger for, lack, long for, miss, need, pine for, require, thirst for, wish, yearn for, yen.
n. absence, appetite, besoin, craving, dearth, default, deficiency, demand, desideratum, desire, destitution,

famine, fancy, hankering, hunger, indigence, insufficiency, lack, longing, necessity, need, neediness, paucity, pauperism, penury, poverty, privation, requirement, scantiness, scarcity, shortage, thirst, wish, yearning, yen.

antonyms abundance, plenty, riches.

wanton *adj.* abandoned, arbitrary, careless, coltish, cruel, dissipated, dissolute, evil, extravagant, fast, gratuitous, groundless, heedless, immoderate, immoral, intemperate, lavish, lecherous, lewd, libertine, libidinous, licentious, loose, lubricious, lustful, malevolent, malicious, motiveless, needless, outrageous, promiscuous, rakish, rash, reckless, senseless, shameless, spiteful, uncalled-for, unchaste, unjustifiable, unjustified, unprovoked, unrestrained, vicious, wicked, wild, wilful.
n. baggage, Casanova, debauchee, Don Juan, floozy, harlot, hussy, lecher, libertine, loose woman, profligate, prostitute, rake, roué, slut, strumpet, tart, trollop, voluptuary, wench, whore.

war *n.* battle, bloodshed, combat, conflict, contention, contest, enmity, fighting, hostilities, hostility, jihad, strife, struggle, ultima ratio regum, warfare.
antonym peace.
v. battle, clash, combat, contend, contest, fight, skirmish, strive, struggle, take up arms, wage war.

ward *n.* apartment, area, care, charge, cubicle, custody, dependant, district, division, guardianship, keeping, minor, precinct, protection, protégé, pupil, quarter, room, safe- keeping, vigil, watch, zone.

warden *n.* administrator, captain, caretaker, castellan, châtelaine, concierge, curator, custodian, guardian, janitor, keeper, ranger, steward, superintendent, warder, watchman.

wardrobe *n.* apparel, attire, closet, clothes, cupboard, garderobe, outfit.

warehouse *n.* depository, depot, entrepot, freightshed, godown, hong, repository, stockroom, store, storehouse.

wares *n.* commodities, goods, lines, manufactures, merchandise, produce, products, stock, stuff, vendibles.

wariness *n.* alertness, apprehension, attention, caginess, care, carefulness, caution, circumspection, discretion, distrust, foresight, heedfulness, hesitancy, mindfulness, prudence, suspicion, unease, vigilance, watchfulness.
antonyms heedlessness, recklessness, thoughtlessness.

warlike *adj.* aggressive, antagonistic, bellicose, belligerent, bloodthirsty, combative, hawkish, hostile, inimical, jingoistic, martial, militaristic, military, pugnacious, saber- rattling, truculent, unfriendly.
antonym peaceable.

warm *adj.* affable, affectionate, amiable, amorous, animated, ardent, balmy, calid, cheerful, cordial, dangerous, disagreeable, earnest, effusive, emotional, enthusiastic, excited, fervent, friendly, genial, glowing, happy, hazardous, hearty, heated, hospitable, impassioned, incalescent, intense, irascible, irritable, keen, kindly,
lively, loving, lukewarm, passionate, perilous, pleasant, quick, sensitive, short, spirited, stormy, sunny, tender, tepid, thermal, touchy, tricky, uncomfortable, unpleasant, vehement, vigorous, violent, zealous.
antonyms cool, indifferent, unfriendly.
v. animate, awaken, excite, heat, heat up, interest, melt, mull, put some life into, reheat, rouse, stimulate, stir, thaw, turn on.
antonym cool.

warm-hearted *adj.* affectionate, ardent, compassionate, cordial, generous, genial, kind-hearted, kindly, loving, sympathetic, tender, tender-hearted.
antonyms cold, unsympathetic.

warmth *n.* affability, affection, amorousness, animation, ardor, calidity, cheerfulness, cordiality, eagerness, earnestness, effusiveness, empressement, enthusiasm, excitement, fervency, fervor, fire, happiness, heartiness, heat, hospitableness, hotness, intensity, kindliness, love, passion, spirit, tenderness, transport, vehemence, vigor, violence, warmness, zeal, zest.
antonyms coldness, coolness, unfriendliness.

warn *v.* admonish, advise, alert, apprize, caution, counsel, forewarn, inform, notify, put on one's guard, tip off.

warning *n.* admonishment, admonition, advance notice, advice, alarm, alert, augury, caution, caveat, forenotice, foretoken, forewarning, griffin, hint, larum, larum-bell, lesson, monition, notice, notification, omen, premonition, presage, prodrome, sign, signal, siren, threat, tip, tip-off, token, vigia, word, word to the wise.
adj. admonitory, aposematic, cautionary, in terrorem, monitive, monitory, ominous, premonitory, prodromal, prodromic, threatening.

warp *v.* bend, contort, deform, deviate, distort, kink, misshape, pervert, twist.
antonym straighten.
n. bend, bent, bias, contortion, deformation, deviation, distortion, irregularity, kink, perversion, quirk, turn, twist.

warranty *n.* assurance, authorization, bond, certificate, contract, covenant, guarantee, justification, pledge.

warrior *n.* champion, combatant, fighter, fighting man, knight, man-at-arms, soldier, wardog, war-horse.

wary *adj.* alert, apprehensive, attentive, cagey, careful, cautious, chary, circumspect, distrustful, guarded, hawk-eyed, heedful, leery, on one's guard, on the lookout, on the qui vive, prudent, suspicious, vigilant, watchful, wide- awake.
antonyms careless, foolhardy, heedless, reckless, unwary.

wash[1] *v.* bath, bathe, clean, cleanse, launder, moisten, rinse, scrub, shampoo, shower, sluice, swill, wet.
n. a lick and a promise, ablution, bath, bathe, cleaning, cleansing, coat, coating, ebb and flow, film, flow, laundering, layer, overlay, rinse, roll, screen, scrub, shampoo, shower, souse, stain, suffusion, surge, sweep, swell, washing, wave.

wash[2] *v.* bear examination, bear scrutiny, carry weight, hold up, hold water, pass muster, stand up, stick.

washed-out *adj.* all in, blanched, bleached, colorless, dead on one's feet, dog-tired, drained, drawn, etiolated, exhausted, faded, fatigued, flat, haggard, knackered, lackluster, mat, pale, pallid, peelie-wally, spent, tired-out, wan, weary, worn-out.

waspish *adj.* bad-tempered, bitchy, cantankerous, captious, crabbed, crabby, cross, crotchety, fretful, grouchy, grumpy, ill-tempered, irascible, irritable, peevish, peppery, pettish, petulant, prickly, snappish, splenetic, testy, touchy, waxy.

waste *v.* atrophy, blow, consume, corrode, crumble, debilitate, decay, decline, deplete, despoil, destroy, devastate, disable, dissipate, drain, dwindle, eat away, ebb, emaciate, enfeeble, exhaust, fade, fritter away, gnaw, lavish, lay waste, misspend, misuse, perish, pillage, prodigalize, rape, ravage, raze, rig, ruin, sack, sink, spend, spoil, squander, tabefy, throw away, undermine, wane, wanton, wear out, wither.
n. debris, desert, desolation, destruction, devastation, dissipation, dregs, dross, effluent, expenditure, extravagance, garbage, havoc, leavings, leftovers, litter, loss, misapplication, misuse, mullock, offal, offscouring(s), prodigality, ravage, recrement, refuse, rubbish, ruin, scrap, slops, solitude, spoilage, squandering, sweepings, trash, void, wastefulness, wasteland, wild, wilderness.
adj. bare, barren, desolate, devastated, dismal, dreary, empty, extra, left-over, superfluous, supernumerary, uncultivated, uninhabited, unproductive, unprofitable, unused, unwanted, useless, wild, worthless.

wasteful *adj.* dissipative, extravagant, improvident, lavish, prodigal, profligate, ruinous, spendthrift, thriftless, uneconomical, unthrifty.
antonyms economical, frugal, thrifty.

watch[1] *v.* attend, contemplate, eye, gaze at, guard, keep, keep an eye open, look, look after, look at, look on, look out, mark, mind, note, observe, ogle, pay attention, peer at, protect, regard, see, spectate, stare at, superintend, take care of, take heed, tend, view, wait.
n. alertness, attention, eye, heed, inspection, lookout, notice, observation, pernoctation, supervision, surveillance, vigil, vigilance, wake, watchfulness.

watch[2] *n.* chronometer, clock, ticker, tick-tick, tick-tock, timepiece, wristwatch.

watch-dog *n.* custodian, guard dog, guardian, house- dog, inspector, monitor, ombudsman, protector, scrutineer, vigilante.

watchful *adj.* alert, attentive, cautious, circumspect, guarded, heedful, observant, on one's guard, on the lookout, on the qui vive, on the watch, suspicious, unmistaking, vigilant, wary, wide awake.
antonym inattentive.

water *n.* Adam's ale, Adam's wine, aqua, lake, ocean, rain, river, saliva, sea, stream, sweat, tears, urine.

v. adulterate, damp, dampen, dilute, douse, drench, drink, flood, hose, irrigate, moisten, soak, souse, spray, sprinkle, thin, water down, weaken.
antonyms dry out, purify, strengthen.

waterfall *n.* cascade, cataract, chute, fall, force, lash, lin(n), torrent.

watery *adj.* adulterated, aqueous, damp, dilute, diluted, flavorless, fluid, humid, hydatoid, insipid, liquid, marshy, moist, poor, rheumy, runny, soggy, squelchy, tasteless, tear-filled, tearful, thin, washy, watered-down, waterish, weak, weepy, wet, wishy-washy.
antonyms solid, strong.

wave[1] *v.* beckon, brandish, direct, flap, flourish, flutter, gesticulate, gesture, indicate, oscillate, quiver, ripple, shake, sign, signal, stir, sway, swing, undulate, waft, wag, waver, weave, wield.

wave[2] *n.* billow, breaker, comber, current, drift, flood, ground swell, movement, outbreak, rash, ripple, roller, rush, stream, surge, sweep, swell, tendency, tidal wave, trend, tsunami, undulation, unevenness, upsurge, water-wave, wavelet, white horse.

waver *v.* blow hot and cold, dither, falter, flicker, fluctuate, haver, hesitate, hum and haw, quiver, reel, rock, seesaw, shake, shilly-shally, sway, swither, totter, tremble, undulate, vacillate, vary, waffle, wave, weave, wobble.
antonyms decide, stand.

wavering *adj.* dithering, dithery, doubtful, doubting, havering, hesitant, in two minds, shilly-shallying.
antonym determined.

wavy *adj.* curly, curvy, flamboyant, ridged, ridgy, rippled, ripply, sinuate(d), sinuous, undate, undulate, undulated, winding, wrinkled, zigzag.
antonyms flat, smooth.

wax *v.* become, develop, dilate, enlarge, expand, fill out, grow, increase, magnify, mount, rise, swell.
antonym wane.

way *n.* access, advance, aim, ambition, approach, aspect, avenue, channel, characteristic, choice, circumstance, condition, conduct, course, custom, demand, desire, detail, direction, distance, elbow-room, fashion, feature, fettle, gate, goal, habit, headway, highway, idiosyncrasy, journey, lane, length, manner, march, means, method, mode, movement, nature, opening, particular, passage, path, pathway, personality, plan, pleasure, point, practice, procedure, process, progress, respect, road, room, route, scheme, sense, shape, situation, space, state, status, street, stretch, style, system, technique, thoroughfare, track, trail, trait, usage, will, wish, wont.

waylay *v.* accost, ambush, attack, buttonhole, catch, hold up, intercept, lie in wait for, seize, set upon, surprise.

way-out *adj.* advanced, amazing, avant-garde, bizarre, crazy, eccentric, excellent, experimental, fantastic, far-out, freaky, great, marvelous, off-beat, outlandish, progressive, satisfying, tremendous, unconventional, unorthodox, unusual, weird, wild, wonderful.

antonym ordinary.

wayward *adj.* capricious, changeable, contrary, contumacious, cross-grained, disobedient, erratic, fickle, flighty, froward, headstrong, inconstant, incorrigible, insubordinate, intractable, mulish, obdurate, obstinate, perverse, rebellious, refractory, self-willed, stubborn, undependable, ungovernable, unmanageable, unpredictable, unruly, uppity, wilful.

antonyms complaisant, good-natured.

weak *adj.* anemic, asthenic, atonic, cowardly, debile, debilitated, decrepit, defenseless, deficient, delicate, diluted, disturbant, dull, effete, enervated, exhausted, exposed, faint, faulty, feeble, fiberless, flimsy, fragile, frail, helpless, hollow, imperceptible, impotent, inadequate, inconclusive, indecisive, ineffective, ineffectual, infirm, insipid, invalid, irresolute, lacking, lame, languid, low, milk- and-water, muffled, namby-pamby, pathetic, poor, powerless, puny, quiet, runny, shaky, shallow, sickly, slight, small, soft, spent, spineless, substandard, tasteless, tender, thin, timorous, toothless, unconvincing, under-strength, unguarded, unprotected, unresisting, unsafe, unsatisfactory, unsound, unsteady, unstressed, untenable, vulnerable, wanting, wasted, watery, weak- hearted, weak-kneed, weakly, weak-minded, weak-spirited, wishy- washy.

antonym strong.

weaken *v.* abate, adulterate, craze, cut, debase, debilitate, depress, dilute, diminish, disinvigorate, droop, dwindle, ease up, effeminate, effeminize, emasculate, enervate, enfeeble, fade, fail, flag, give way, impair, invalidate, lessen, lower, mitigate, moderate, reduce, sap, soften up, temper, thin, tire, undermine, wane, water down.

antonym strengthen.

weakling *n.* coward, doormat, drip, milksop, mouse, namby-pamby, puff, pushover, sissy, softling, underdog, underling, wally, weed, wet, wimp, wraith.

antonyms hero, stalwart.

weakness *n.* Achilles' heel, asthenia, atonicity, atony, blemish, debility, decrepitude, defect, deficiency, enervation, enfeeblement, faible, failing, faintness, fault, feebleness, flaw, foible, fondness, fragility, frailty, imperfection, impotence, inclination, infirmity, irresolution, lack, liking, passion, penchant, powerlessness, predilection, proclivity, proneness, shortcoming, soft spot, soft underbelly, underbelly, vulnerability, weakpoint, weediness.

antonyms dislike, strength.

wealth *n.* abundance, affluence, assets, bounty, capital, cash, copiousness, cornucopia, estate, fortune, fullness, funds, golden calf, goods, klondike, lucre, mammon, means, money, opulence, pelf, plenitude, plenty, possessions, profusion, property, prosperity, resources, riches, richness, store, substance.

antonym poverty.

wealthy *adj.* affluent, comfortable, easy, filthy rich, flush, living in clover, loaded, moneyed, opulent, prosperous, rich, rolling in it, well-heeled, well-off, well-to- do.

antonym poor.

wear *v.* abrade, accept, allow, annoy, bear, bear up, believe, brook, carry, consume, corrode, countenance, deteriorate, display, don, drain, dress in, endure, enervate, erode, exasperate, exhibit, fall for, fatigue, fly, fray, grind, harass, have on, hold up, irk, last, permit, pester, put on, put up with, rub, show, sport, stand for, stand up, stomach, swallow, take, tax, tolerate, undermine, use, vex, waste, weaken, weary.

n. abrasion, apparel, attire, attrition, clothes, corrosion, costume, damage, depreciation, deterioration, dress, durability, employment, erosion, friction, garb, garments, gear, habit, mileage, outfit, service, things, use, usefulness, utility, wear and tear.

weariness *n.* drowsiness, enervation, ennui, exhaustion, fatigue, languor, lassitude, lethargy, listlessness, prostration, sleepiness, tiredness.

antonym freshness.

wearisome *adj.* annoying, boring, bothersome, burdensome, dreary, dull, ennuying, exasperating, exhausting, fatiguing, humdrum, irksome, monotonous, oppressive, pestilential, prolix, prosaic, protracted, tedious, troublesome, trying, vexatious, weariful, wearing.

antonym refreshing.

weary *adj.* all in, arduous, aweared, aweary, beat, bored, browned-off, dead beat, dead on one's feet, discontented, dog-tired, drained, drooping, drowsy, enervated, enervative, ennuied, ennuyé, exhausted, fagged, fatigued, fed up, flagging, impatient, indifferent, irksome, jaded, knackered, laborious, sick, sick and tired, sleepy, spent, taxing, tired, tiresome, tiring, wayworn, wearied, wearing, wearisome, whacked, worn out.

antonyms excited, fresh, lively.

v. annoy, betoil, bore, bug, burden, debilitate, drain, droop, enervate, ennui, exasperate, fade, fag, fail, fatigue, irk, irritate, jade, plague, sap, sicken, tax, tire, tire out, wear out.

weather *n.* climate, conditions, rainfall, temperature.

v. brave, come through, endure, expose, harden, live through, overcome, pull through, resist, ride out, rise above, season, stand, stick out, suffer, surmount, survive, toughen, weather out, withstand.

antonym succumb.

weave *v.* blend, braid, build, construct, contrive, create, criss-cross, entwine, fabricate, fuse, incorporate, intercross, interdigitate, interlace, intermingle, intertwine, introduce, knit, make, mat, merge, plait, put together, spin, twist, unite, wind, zigzag.

web *n.* interlacing, lattice, mesh, mesh-work, net, netting, network, palama, screen, snare, tangle, tela, texture, toils, trap, weave, webbing, weft.

wed *v.* ally, blend, coalesce, combine, commingle, dedicate, espouse, fuse, get hitched, interweave, join, jump the broomstick, link, marry, merge, splice, tie the knot, unify, unite, wive, yoke.
antonym divorce.

wedlock *n.* holy matrimony, marriage, matrimony, union.

wee *adj.* diminutive, insignificant, itsy-bitsy, Lilliputian, little, microscopic, midget, miniature, minuscule, minute, negligible, small, teeny, teeny-weeny, tiny, weeny.
antonym large.

weep *v.* bemoan, bewail, blub, blubber, boo-hoo, bubble, complain, cry, drip, exude, greet, keen, lament, leak, moan, mourn, ooze, pipe, pipe one's eye, pour forth, pour out, rain, snivel, sob, tune one's pipes, ululate, whimper, whinge.
antonym rejoice.

n. blub, bubble, cry, greet, lament, moan, snivel, sob.

weigh *v.* bear down, burden, carry weight, consider, contemplate, count, deliberate, evaluate, examine, give thought to, impress, matter, meditate on, mull over, oppress, ponder, ponderate, prey, reflect on, study, tell, think over.
antonyms cut no ice, hearten.

weight *n.* authority, avoirdupois, ballast, burden, clout, consequence, consideration, efficacy, emphasis, force, gravity, heaviness, heft, impact, import, importance, impressiveness, influence, load, mass, millstone, moment, onus, oppression, persuasiveness, ponderance, ponderancy, poundage, power, preponderance, pressure, significance, strain, substance, tonnage, value.
antonym lightness.

v. ballast, bias, burden, charge, encumber, freight, handicap, hold down, impede, keep down, load, oppress, overburden, slant, unbalance, weigh down.
antonym lighten.

weird *adj.* bizarre, creepy, eerie, eldritch, freakish, ghostly, grotesque, mysterious, odd, outlandish, preternatural, queer, spooky, strange, superlunar, supernatural, uncanny, unco, unearthly, unnatural, witching.
antonym normal.

welcome *adj.* able, acceptable, accepted, agreeable, allowed, appreciated, delightful, desirable, entitled, free, gratifying, permitted, pleasant, pleasing, refreshing.
antonym unwelcome.

n. acceptance, greeting, hospitality, reception, red carpet, salaam, salutation.

v. accept, approve of, embrace, greet, hail, meet, receive, roll out the red carpet for.
antonyms reject, snub.

weld *v.* bind, bond, cement, connect, fuse, join, link, seal, solder, unite.
antonym separate.

n. bond, joint, seal, seam.

welfare *n.* advantage, benefit, good, happiness, heal, health, interest, profit, prosperity, success, weal, well-being.
antonym harm.

well[1] *n.* bore, cavity, fount, fountain, hole, lift-shaft, mine, pit, pool, repository, shaft, source, spring, waterhole, well-spring.

v. brim over, flood, flow, gush, jet, ooze, pour, rise, run, seep, spout, spring, spurt, stream, surge, swell, trickle.

well[2] *adv.* ably, abundantly, accurately, adeptly, adequately, admirably, agreeably, amply, approvingly, attentively, capitally, carefully, clearly, closely, comfortably, completely, conscientiously, considerably, correctly, deeply, easily, effectively, efficiently, expertly, fairly, famously, favorably, fittingly, flourishingly, fully, glowingly, graciously, greatly, happily, heartily, highly, intimately, justly, kindly, nicely, personally, pleasantly, possibly, proficiently, profoundly, properly, prosperously, readily, rightly, satisfactorily, skilfully, smoothly, splendidly, substantially, successfully, sufficiently, suitably, thoroughly, warmly.
antonym badly.

adj. A1, able-bodied, advisable, agreeable, bright, fine, fit, fitting, flourishing, fortunate, good, great, hale, happy, healthy, hearty, in fine fettle, in good health, lucky, on the top of the world, pleasing, profitable, proper, prudent, right, robust, satisfactory, sound, strong, thriving, up to par, useful.
antonyms bad, ill.

well-being *n.* comfort, contentment, good, happiness, prosperity, weal, welfare.
antonyms discomfort, harm.

well-bred *adj.* aristocratic, blue-blooded, civil, courteous, courtly, cultivated, cultured, gallant, genteel, gentle, gentlemanly, highborn, ladylike, mannerly, noble, patrician, polished, polite, refined, titled, upper-crust, urbane, well-born, well-brought-up, well-mannered.
antonym ill-bred.

well-known *adj.* celebrated, famed, familiar, famous, illustrious, notable, noted, popular, renowned.
antonym unknown.

well-off *adj.* affluent, comfortable, flourishing, flush, fortunate, in the money, loaded, lucky, moneyed, prosperous, rich, successful, thriving, warm, wealthy, well-heeled, well-to-do.
antonym poor.

well-thought-of *adj.* admired, esteemed, highly regarded, honored, reputable, respected, revered, venerated, weighty.
antonym despised.

well-to-do *adj.* affluent, comfortable, flush, loaded, moneyed, prosperous, rich, warm, wealthy, well-heeled, well-off.
antonym poor.

welsh *v.* cheat, defraud, diddle, do, swindle, welch.

wet *adj.* boggy, clammy, damp, dank, drenched, dripping, drizzling, effete, feeble, foolish, humid, ineffectual, irresolute, misty, moist, moistened, namby-pamby, pouring, raining, rainy, saturated, showery, silly, sloppy, soaked, soaking, sodden, soft, soggy, sopping, soppy, soused, spineless, spongy, teeming, timorous, waterlogged, watery, weak, weedy.
antonyms dry, resolute, strong.
n. clamminess, condensation, damp, dampness, drip, drizzle, humidity, liquid, milksop, moisture, rain, rains, sap, water, weakling, weed, wetness, wimp.
antonyms dryness.
v. bedabble, bedew, bedrench, damp, dampen, dip, douse, drench, humidify, imbue, irrigate, moisten, saturate, sluice, soak, splash, spray, sprinkle, steep, water.
antonym dry.

wharf *n.* dock, dockyard, jetty, landing-stage, marina, pier, quay, quayside.

wheedle *v.* cajole, charm, coax, court, draw, entice, flatter, importune, inveigle, persuade, whilly, whillywha(w).
antonym force.

whereabouts *n.* location, place, position, site, situation, vicinity.

wherewithal *n.* capital, cash, funds, means, money, necessary, readies, resources, supplies.

whim *n.* caprice, chimera, conceit, concetto, crank, craze, crotchet, fad, fancy, fizgig, flam, freak, humor, impulse, maggot, notion, quirk, sport, urge, vagary, whims(e)y.

whimper *v.* blub, blubber, cry, girn, grizzle, mewl, moan, pule, snivel, sob, weep, whine, whinge.
n. girn, moan, snivel, sob, whine.

whimsical *adj.* capricious, chimeric(al), crotchety, curious, dotty, droll, eccentric, fanciful, fantastic(al), freakish, funny, maggoty, mischievous, odd, peculiar, playful, quaint, queer, singular, unusual, waggish, weird, whimmy.
antonym sensible.

whine *n.* beef, belly-ache, complaint, cry, girn, gripe, grouch, grouse, grumble, moan, sob, wail, whimper.
v. beef, belly-ache, carp, complain, cry, girn, gripe, grizzle, grouch, grouse, grumble, kvetch, moan, sob, wail, whimper, whinge.

whip *v.* agitate, beat, best, birch, cane, castigate, clobber, compel, conquer, dart, dash, defeat, dive, drive, drub, flagellate, flash, flit, flog, flounce, fly, foment, goad, hammer, hound, incite, instigate, jambok, jerk, knout, lash, leather, lick, outdo, overcome, overpower, overwhelm, paddle, prick, prod, produce, provoke, pull, punish, push, quirt, remove, rout, rush, scourge, shoot, sjambok, snatch, spank, spur, stir, strap, switch, tan, tear, thrash, trounce, urge, whale, whisk, whop, worst.
n. birch, bullwhip, cane, cat, cat-o'-nine-tails, crop, flagellum, horsewhip, jambok, knout, lash, paddle, quirt, rawhide, riding-crop, scourge, sjambok, switch, thong.

whirl *v.* birl, circle, gyrate, gyre, pirouette, pivot, reel, revolve, roll, rotate, spin, swirl, swivel, turn, twirl, twist, wheel.
n. agitation, birl, bustle, circle, commotion, confusion, daze, dither, flurry, giddiness, gyration, gyre, hubbub, hubbuboo, hurly-burly, merry-go-round, pirouette, reel, revolution, roll, rotation, round, series, spin, stir, succession, swirl, tumult, turn, twirl, twist, uproar, vortex, wheel, whorl.
antonym calm.

whisk *v.* beat, brush, dart, dash, flick, fly, grab, hasten, hurry, race, rush, scoot, shoot, speed, sweep, swipe, tear, twitch, whip, wipe.
n. beater, brush, swizzle-stick.

whisk(e)y *n.* barley-bree, bourbon, Canadian, corn, John Barleycorn, Irish, malt, mountain dew, peat-reek, rye, Scotch, usquebaugh.

whisper *v.* breathe, buzz, divulge, gossip, hint, hiss, insinuate, intimate, murmur, rustle, sigh, sough, susurrate, tittle.
antonym shout.
n. breath, buzz, gossip, hint, hiss, innuendo, insinuation, murmur, report, rumor, rustle, shadow, sigh, sighing, soughing, soupçon, suggestion, suspicion, susurration, susurrus, swish, tinge, trace, underbreath, undertone, whiff, word.
antonym roar.

whistle *n.* call, cheep, chirp, hooter, siren, song, warble.
v. call, cheep, chirp, pipe, siffle, sing, warble, wheeze, whiss.

whole *adj.* better, complete, cured, entire, faultless, fit, flawless, full, good, hale, healed, healthy, in one piece, intact, integral, integrate, inviolate, mint, perfect, recovered, robust, sound, strong, total, unabbreviated, unabridged, unbroken, uncut, undamaged, undivided, unedited, unexpurgated, unharmed, unhurt, unimpaired, uninjured, unmutilated, unscathed, untouched, well.
antonyms damaged, ill, partial.
n. aggregate, all, ensemble, entirety, entity, everything, fullness, Gestalt, lot, piece, total, totality, unit, unity.
antonym part.

wholesome *adj.* advantageous, beneficial, clean, decent, edifying, exemplary, good, healthful, health-giving, healthy, helpful, honorable, hygienic, improving, innocent, invigorating, moral, nice, nourishing, nutritious, propitious, pure, respectable, righteous, salubrious, salutary, sanitary, uplifting, virtuous, worthy.
antonym unwholesome.

wholly *adv.* absolutely, all, altogether, completely, comprehensively, entirely, exclusively, fully, in toto, only, perfectly, solely, thoroughly, through and through, totally, utterly.
antonym partly.

wicked *adj.* abandoned, abominable, acute, agonizing, amoral, arch, atrocious, awful, bad, black-hearted,

bothersome, corrupt, debased, depraved, destructive, devilish, difficult, dissolute, distressing, dreadful, egregious, evil, facinorous, fearful, fiendish, fierce, flagitious, foul, galling, guilty, harmful, heinous, immoral, impious, impish, incorrigible, inexpiable, iniquitous, injurious, intense, irreligious, mighty, mischievous, nasty, naughty, nefarious, nefast, offensive, painful, piacular, rascal-like, rascally, roguish, scandalous, severe, shameful, sinful, spiteful, terrible, troublesome, trying, ungodly, unpleasant, unprincipled, unrighteous, vicious, vile, villainous, worthless.
antonyms good, harmless, modest, upright.

wide *adj.* ample, away, baggy, broad, capacious, catholic, commodious, comprehensive, diffuse, dilated, distant, distended, encyclopedic, expanded, expansive, extensive, far- reaching, full, general, immense, inclusive, large, latitudinous, loose, off, off-course, off-target, outspread, outstretched, remote, roomy, spacious, sweeping, vast.
antonyms limited, narrow.
adv. aside, astray, off course, off target, off the mark, out.
antonym on target.

wide-awake *adj.* alert, astute, aware, conscious, fully awake, heedful, keen, observant, on one's toes, on the alert, on the ball, on the qui vive, quick-witted, roused, sharp, vigilant, wakened, wary, watchful.
antonym asleep.

width *n.* amplitude, beam, breadth, compass, diameter, extent, girth, measure, range, reach, scope, span, thickness, wideness.

wield *v.* apply, brandish, command, control, employ, exercise, exert, flourish, handle, have, hold, maintain, manage, manipulate, ply, possess, swing, use, utilize, wave, weave.

wild *adj.* agrest(i)al, brabaric, barbarous, berserk, blustery, boisterous, brutish, chaotic, chimeric(al), choppy, crazed, crazy, daft, delirious, demented, desert, deserted, desolate, disheveled, disordered, disorderly, eager, empty, enthusiastic, excited, extravagant, fantastic, ferae naturae, feral, feralized, ferine, ferocious, fierce, flighty, foolhardy, foolish, frantic, free, frenzied, furious, giddy, god- forsaken, howling, hysterical, ill-considered, impetuous, impracticable, imprudent, inaccurate, indigenous, intense, irrational, lawless, mad, madcap, maniacal, native, natural, noisy, nuts, outrageous, potty, preposterous, primitive, rabid, raging, rash, raving, reckless, riotous, rough, rowdy, rude, savage, self-willed, tempestuous, tousled, trackless, turbulent, unbridled, unbroken, uncheated, uncivilized, uncontrollable, uncontrolled, uncultivated, undisciplined, undomesticated, unfettered, ungovernable, uninhabited, unjustified, unkempt, unmanageable, unpopulated, unpruned, unrestrained, unruly, unsubstantiated, untamed, untidy, uproarious, violent, virgin, wayward, woolly.

antonyms civilized, peaceful, sane, sensible, tame, unenthusiastic.

wilderness *n.* clutter, confusion, congeries, desert, jumble, jungle, mass, maze, muddle, tangle, waste, wasteland, welter, wild, wild-land.

wile *n.* artfulness, artifice, cheating, chicanery, contrivance, craft, craftiness, cunning, deceit, device, dodge, expedient, fraud, guile, hanky-panky, imposition, lure, maneuver, ploy, ruse, slyness, stratagem, subterfuge, trick, trickery.
antonym guilelessness.

wilful *adj.* adamant, bloody-minded, bull-headed, conscious, deliberate, determined, dogged, froward, headstrong, inflexible, intended, intentional, intractable, intransigent, mulish, obdurate, obstinate, persistent, perverse, pig-headed, purposeful, refractory, self-willed, stubborn, thrawn, uncompromising, unyielding, volitional, voluntary.
antonyms complaisant, good-natured.

will *n.* aim, attitude, choice, command, decision, declaration, decree, desire, determination, discretion, disposition, fancy, feeling, inclination, intention, mind, option, pleasure, preference, prerogative, purpose, resolution, resolve, testament, velleity, volition, will power, wish, wishes.
v. bequeath, bid, cause, choose, command, confer, decree, desire, determine, devise, direct, dispose of, elect, give, leave, opt, ordain, order, pass on, resolve, transfer, want, wish.

willing *adj.* agreeable, amenable, biddable, compliant, consenting, content, desirous, disposed, eager, enthusiastic, favorable, game, happy, inclined, nothing lo(a)th, pleased, prepared, ready, so-minded, volitient, willing-hearted.
antonym unwilling.

wilt *v.* atrophy, diminish, droop, dwindle, ebb, fade, fail, flag, flop, languish, melt away, sag, shrivel, sink, wane, weaken, wither.
antonym perk up.

wily *adj.* arch, artful, astute, cagey, crafty, crooked, cunning, deceitful, deceptive, designing, fly, foxy, guileful, intriguing, long-headed, Machiavellian, scheming, sharp, shifty, shrewd, sly, tricky, underhand, versute, wileful.
antonym guileless.

win *v.* accomplish, achieve, acquire, attain, bag, capture, catch, collect, come away with, conquer, earn, gain, get, net, obtain, overcome, pick up, prevail, procure, receive, secure, succeed, sweep the board, triumph.
antonym lose.
n. conquest, mastery, success, triumph, victory.
antonym defeat.

wind[1] *n.* air, air-current, babble, blast, blather, bluster, boasting, breath, breeze, clue, current, cyclone, draft, flatulence, flatus, gab, gale, gas, gust, hint, hot air, humbug, hurricane, idle talk, inkling, intimation, northeaster, notice, puff, report, respiration, rumor, sirocco, southwester, suggestion, talk, tidings, tornado, twister, typhoon, warning, whisper, williwaw, windiness, zephyr.

wind[2] *v.* bend, coil, curl, curve, deviate, encircle, furl, loop, meander, ramble, reel, roll, serpent, serpentine, serpentinize, snake, spiral, turn, twine, twist, wreath, zigzag.

n. bend, curve, meander, turn, twist, zigzag.

windfall *n.* bonanza, find, godsend, jackpot, manna, pennies from heaven, stroke of luck, treasure-trove.

windy *adj.* afraid, blowy, blustering, blustery, boastful, boisterous, bombastic, breezy, changeable, chicken, conceited, cowardly, diffuse, empty, fearful, flatulent, flatuous, frightened, garrulous, gusty, long-winded, loquacious, meandering, nervous, pompous, prolix, rambling, scared, squally, stormy, tempestuous, thrasonic, timid, turgid, ventose, verbose, wild, wind-swept, wordy.

antonyms calm, fearless, modest.

wing *n.* adjunct, annexe, arm, branch, circle, clique, coterie, extension, faction, fender, flank, group, grouping, pinion, protection, section, segment, set, side.

v. clip, fleet, flit, fly, glide, hasten, hit, hurry, move, nick, pass, race, soar, speed, travel, wound, zoom.

wink *v.* bat, blink, flash, flicker, flutter, gleam, glimmer, glint, nictate, nictitate, pink, sparkle, twinkle.

n. blink, flash, flutter, gleam, glimmering, glint, hint, instant, jiffy, moment, nictation, nictitation, second, sparkle, split second, twinkle, twinkling.

winnow *v.* comb, cull, diffuse, divide, fan, part, screen, select, separate, sift, waft.

winsome *adj.* agreeable, alluring, amiable, attractive, bewitching, captivating, charming, cheerful, comely, delectable, disarming, enchanting, endearing, engaging, fair, fascinating, fetching, graceful, pleasant, pleasing, prepossessing, pretty, sweet, taking, winning.

antonym unattractive.

wire-pulling *n.* clout, conspiring, influence, intrigue, Machiavellianism, manipulation, plotting, pull, scheming.

wisdom *n.* anthroposophy, astuteness, circumspection, comprehension, discernment, enlightenment, erudition, foresight, gnosis, intelligence, judgment, judiciousness, knowledge, learning, penetration, prudence, reason, sagacity, sapience, sense, sophia, understanding.

antonym folly.

wise *adj.* aware, clever, discerning, enlightened, erudite, informed, intelligent, judicious, knowing, long-headed, long-sighted, perceptive, politic, prudent, rational, reasonable, sagacious, sage, sapient, sensible, shrewd, sound, understanding, well-advised, well-informed.

antonym foolish.

wish *v.* ask, aspire, bid, command, covet, crave, desiderate, desire, direct, greet, hanker, hope, hunger, instruct, long, need, order, require, thirst, want, whim, yearn, yen.

antonyms dislike, fear.

n. aspiration, bidding, command, desire, hankering, hope, hunger, inclination, intention, liking, order, request, thirst, urge, velleity, voice, want, whim, will, yearning, yen.

antonyms dislike, fear.

wispy *adj.* attenuate, attenuated, delicate, diaphanous, ethereal, faint, fine, flimsy, flyaway, fragile, frail, gossamer, insubstantial, light, thin, unsubstantial.

antonym substantial.

wistful *adj.* contemplative, disconsolate, dreaming, dreamy, forlorn, longing, meditative, melancholy, mournful, musing, pensive, reflective, sad, soulful, thoughtful, wishful, yearning.

wit *n.* acumen, badinage, banter, brains, card, cleverness, comedian, common sense, comprehension, conceit, discernment, drollery, epigrammatist, eutrapelia, facetiousness, farceur, fun, homme d'esprit, humorist, humor, ingenuity, insight, intellect, intelligence, jocularity, joker, judgment, levity, merum sal, mind, nous, perception, pleasantry, punster, quipster, raillery, reason, repartee, sense, smeddum, understanding, wag, wisdom, wit-cracker, wordplay. *antonyms* seriousness, stupidity.

witch *n.* enchantress, hag, hex, lamia, magician, necromancer, occultist, pythoness, sorceress, sortileger, weird, wise woman, witch-wife.

witchcraft *n.* black magic, conjuration, divination, enchantment, glamor, goety, incantation, invultuation, magic, myalism, necromancy, occultism, pishogue, sorcery, sortilege, sortilegy, spell, the black art, the occult, voodoo, witchery, witching, wizardry.

withdraw *v.* abjure, absent oneself, back out, depart, disavow, disclaim, disengage, disenrol, disinvest, draw back, draw out, drop out, extract, fall back, go, go away, hive off, leave, pull back, pull out, recall, recant, remove, repair, rescind, retire, retract, retreat, revoke, secede, subduct, subtract, take away, take back, take off, unsay, waive.

antonyms advance, deposit, persist.

wither *v.* abash, blast, blight, decay, decline, desiccate, disintegrate, droop, dry, fade, humiliate, languish, miff, mortify, perish, put down, shame, shrink, shrivel, snub, wane, waste, welt, wilt.

antonyms boost, thrive.

withhold *v.* check, conceal, deduct, detain, hide, keen, keep back, refuse, repress, reserve, resist, restrain, retain, sit on, suppress, suspend.

antonyms accord, give.

withstand *v.* bear, brave, combat, confront, cope with, defy, endure, face, grapple with, hold off, hold one's ground, hold out, last out, oppose, put up with, resist, stand, stand fast, stand one's ground, stand up to, survive, take, take on, thwart, tolerate, weather.

antonyms collapse, yield.

witness *n.* attestant, beholder, bystander, corroborator, deponent, eye-witness, looker-on, observer, onlooker, spectator, testifier, viewer, vouchee, voucher, watcher, witnesser.

v. attend, attest, bear out, bear witness, confirm, corroborate, countersign, depone, depose, endorse, look on, mark, note, notice, observe, perceive, see, sign, testify, view, watch.

wits *n.* acumen, astuteness, brains, cleverness, comprehension, faculties, gumption, ingenuity, intelligence, judgment, marbles, mother-wit, nous, reason, sense, understanding.

antonym stupidity.

witty *adj.* amusing, brilliant, clever, comic, droll, epigrammatic, facetious, fanciful, funny, humorous, ingenious, jocular, lively, original, piquant, salty, sparkling, waggish, whimsical.

antonyms dull, unamusing.

wizard[1] *n.* conjurer, enchanter, mage, magician, magus, necromancer, occultist, shaman, sorcerer, sortileger, thaumaturge, warlock, witch.

wizard[2] *n.* ace, adept, dabster, deacon, expert, genius, hotshot, maestro, master, prodigy, star, virtuoso, whiz.

antonym duffer.

adj. ace, brilliant, enjoyable, fab, fantastic, good, great, marvelous, sensational, smashing, super, superb, terrif, terrific, tiptop, topping, tremendous, wonderful.

antonym rotten.

wizardry *n.* black magic, conjuration, divination, enchantment, glamor, goety, incantation, invultuation, magic, myalism, necromancy, occultism, pishogue, sorcery, sortilege, sortilegy, the black art, the occult, voodoo, warlockry, witchcraft, witchery, witching.

woe *n.* adversity, affliction, agony, anguish, burden, curse, dejection, depression, disaster, distress, dole, dolor, dule, gloom, grief, hardship, heartache, heartbreak, melancholy, misery, misfortune, pain, sadness, sorrow, suffering, tears, trial, tribulation, trouble, unhappiness, wretchedness.

antonym joy.

woebegone *adj.* blue, crestfallen, dejected, disconsolate, dispirited, doleful, down in the mouth, downcast, down-hearted, forlorn, gloomy, grief-stricken, hangdog, long-faced, lugubrious, miserable, mournful, sad, sorrowful, tearful, tear-stained, troubled, wretched.

antonym joyful.

woman *n.* bride, broad, chambermaid, char, charwoman, chick, dame, daughter, domestic, fair, female, feme, femme, Frau, girl, girlfriend, handmaiden, housekeeper, kept woman, lady, lady-in-waiting, ladylove, lass, lassie, maid, maiden, maidservant, mate, miss, mistress, old lady, partner, piece, she, sheila, spouse, sweetheart, vrouw, wife, woman-body.

antonym man.

womanly *adj.* female, feminine, ladylike, matronly, motherly, weak, womanish.

antonym manly.

wonder *n.* admiration, amaze, amazement, astonishment, awe, bewilderment, curiosity, fascination, marvel, miracle, nonpareil, phenomenon, portent, prodigy, rarity, sight, spectacle, stupefaction, surprise, wonderment, wunderkind.

antonyms disinterest, ordinariness.

v. ask oneself, boggle, conjecture, doubt, gape, gaup, gawk, inquire, marvel, meditate, ponder, puzzle, query, question, speculate, stare, think.

wonderful *adj.* ace, admirable, amazing, astonishing, astounding, awe-inspiring, awesome, brilliant, épatant, excellent, extraordinary, fab, fabulous, fantastic, great, incredible, magnificent, marvelous, miraculous, mirific(al), odd, oustanding, peculiar, phenomenal, remarkable, sensational, smashing, staggering, startling, strange, stupendous, super, superb, surprising, terrif, terrific, tiptop, top-hole, topping, tremendous, unheard-of, wizard, wondrous.

antonyms ordinary, rotten.

wont *adj.* accustomed, given, habituated, used.

n. custom, habit, practice, routine, rule, use, way.

wooden *adj.* awkward, blank, clumsy, colorless, deadpan, dense, dim, dim-witted, dull, dull-witted, emotionless, empty, expressionless, gauche, gawky, glassy, graceless, inelegant, inflexible, lifeless, ligneous, maladroit, muffled, oaken, obstinate, obtuse, rigid, slow, spiritless, stiff, stupid, thick, timber, treen, unbending, unemotional, ungainly, unresponsive, unyielding, vacant, woody, xyloid.

antonyms bright, lively.

word *n.* account, advice, affirmation, assertion, assurance, bidding, bulletin, chat, colloquy, command, commandment, comment, communication, communiqué, confab, confabulation, consultation, conversation, countersign, declaration, decree, discussion, dispatch, edict, expression, firman, go-ahead, green light, guarantee, hint, information, intelligence, interlocution, intimation, lexigram, locution, mandate, message, news, notice, oath, order, palabra, parole, password, pledge, promise, remark, report, rescript, rumor, sign, signal, slogan, talk, term, tête-à-tête, tidings, ukase, undertaking, utterance, vocable, vow, warcry, watch-word, will.

v. couch, explain, express, phrase, put, say, write.

wordy *adj.* diffuse, discursive, garrulous, longiloquent, long-winded, loquacious, phrasy, pleonastic, prolix, rambling, verbose, windy.

antonyms concise, laconic.

work *n.* achievement, art, assignment, book, business, calling, chore, commission, composition, craft, creation, darg, deed, doings, drudgery, duty, effort, elbow grease, employ, employment, exertion, graft, grind, handiwork, industry, job, labor, line, livelihood, métier, occupation, oeuvre, office, opus, ouvrage, performance, piece, play, poem, production, profession, pursuit, service, skill, slog, stint, sweat, task, toil, trade, travail, undertaking, workload, workmanship.

antonyms hobby, play, rest.

v. accomplish, achieve, act, arrange, beaver, bring about, bring off, cause, contrive, control, convulse, create, cultivate, dig, direct, drive, drudge, effect, encompass, execute, exploit, farm, fashion, fiddle, fix, force, form, function, go, graft, handle, implement, knead, labor, make, manage, maneuver, manipulate, mold, move, operate, peg away, perform, ply, process, progress, pull off, run, shape, slave, slog, sweat, swing, till, toil, twitch, use, wield, writhe. *antonyms* fail, play, rest.

workable *adj.* doable, effectible, feasible, possible, practicable, practical, realistic, viable. *antonym* unworkable.

working *n.* action, functioning, manner, method, operation, routine, running. *adj.* active, employed, functioning, going, laboring, operational, operative, running. *antonyms* idle, inoperative, retired, unemployed.

workmanlike *adj.* adept, careful, efficient, expert, masterly, painstaking, professional, proficient, satisfactory, skilful, skilled, thorough, workmanly. *antonym* amateurish.

workmanship *n.* art, artistry, craft, craftsmanship, execution, expertise, facture, finish, handicraft, handiwork, manufacture, skill, technique, work.

world *n.* age, area, class, creation, days, division, domain, earth, environment, epoch, era, existence, field, globe, human race, humanity, humankind, kingdom, life, man, mankind, men, nature, people, period, planet, province, public, realm, society, sphere, star, system, terrene, times, universe, Welt.

worldly *adj.* ambitious, avaricious, blasé, carnal, cosmopolitan, covetous, earthly, experienced, fleshly, grasping, greedy, knowing, lay, materialistic, mundane, physical, politic, profane, secular, selfish, sophisticated, sublunary, temporal, terrene, terrestrial, unspiritual, urbane, worldly-minded, worldly-wise. *antonym* unworldly.

worn *adj.* attrite, bromidic, careworn, clichéd, drawn, exhausted, fatigued, frayed, hackneyed, haggard, jaded, lined, pinched, played-out, ragged, shabby, shiny, spent, tattered, tatty, threadbare, tired, trite, wearied, weary, wizened, woe-wearied, woe-worn, worn-out. *antonyms* fresh, new.

worried *adj.* afraid, agonized, anxious, apprehensive, bothered, concerned, distracted, distraught, distressed, disturbed, fearful, frabbit, fretful, frightened, ill at ease, nervous, on edge, overwrought, perturbed, strained, tense, tormented, troubled, uneasy, unquiet, upset. *antonyms* calm, unconcerned, unworried.

worry *v.* agonize, annoy, attack, badger, bite, bother, brood, disquiet, distress, disturb, faze, fret, get one's knickers in a twist, gnaw at, go for, harass, harry, hassle, hector, importune, irritate, kill, lacerate, nag, perturb, pester, plague, savage, tantalize, tear, tease, torment, trouble, unsettle, upset, vex.

antonyms comfort, reassure. *n.* agitation, annoyance, anxiety, apprehension, care, concern, disturbance, fear, irritation, misery, misgiving, perplexity, pest, plague, problem, stew, tew, tizz, tizzy, torment, trial, trouble, unease, vexation, woe, worriment. *antonyms* comfort, reassurance.

worsen *v.* aggravate, damage, decay, decline, degenerate, deteriorate, disimprove, exacerbate, go downhill, pejorate, retrogress, sink, take a turn for the worse. *antonym* improve.

worship *v.* adore, adulate, deify, exalt, glorify, honor, idolatrize, idolize, kanticoy, laud, love, misworship, praise, pray to, respect, revere, reverence, venerate. *antonym* despise. *n.* adoration, adulation, deification, devotion(s), dulia, exaltation, glorification, glory, homage, honor, hyperdulia, image-worship, knee-drill, latria, latry, laudation, love, misdevotion, misworship, monolatry, praise, prayer(s), regard, respect, reverence, will-worship. *antonym* vilification.

worth *n.* aid, assistance, avail, benefit, cost, credit, desert(s), excellence, goodness, help, importance, merit, price, quality, rate, significance, use, usefulness, utility, value, virtue, worthiness. *antonym* worthlessness.

worthless *adj.* abandoned, abject, base, beggarly, contemptible, depraved, despicable, draffish, draffy, futile, good-for-nothing, grotty, ignoble, ineffectual, insignificant, littleworth, meaningless, miserable, no use, no-account, nugatory, paltry, pointless, poor, rubbishy, scabbed, scabby, screwy, stramineous, trashy, trifling, trivial, unavailing, unimportant, unusable, useless, valueless, vaurien, vile, wretched. *antonym* valuable.

worthy *adj.* admirable, appropriate, commendable, creditable, decent, dependable, deserving, estimable, excellent, fit, good, honest, honorable, laudable, meritorious, praise- worthy, reliable, reputable, respectable, righteous, suitable, upright, valuable, virtuous, worthwhile. *antonyms* disreputable, unworthy. *n.* big cheese, big noise, big pot, big shot, big-wig, dignitary, luminary, name, notable, personage.

wound *n.* anguish, cut, damage, distress, gash, grief, harm, heartbreak, hurt, injury, insult, laceration, lesion, offense, pain, pang, scar, shock, slash, slight, torment, torture, trauma. *v.* annoy, bless, cut, cut to the quick, damage, distress, gash, grieve, harm, hit, hurt, injure, irritate, lacerate, mortify, offend, pain, pierce, pip, shock, slash, sting, traumatize, wing, wring someone's withers.

wrangle *n.* altercation, argument, argy-bargy, barney, bickering, brawl, clash, contest, controversy, dispute, quarrel, row, set-to, slanging match, squabble, tiff, tussle. *antonym* agreement.

v. altercate, argue, argufy, bicker, brawl, contend, digladiate, disagree, dispute, ergotize, fall out, fight, quarrel, row, scrap, squabble.

antonym agree.

wrap *v.* absorb, bind, bundle up, cloak, cocoon, cover, encase, enclose, enfold, envelop, fold, hap, immerse, muffle, pack, package, roll up, sheathe, shroud, surround, swathe, wind.

antonym unwrap.

n. cape, cloak, mantle, pelisse, robe, shawl, stole.

wrath *n.* anger, bitterness, choler, displeasure, exasperation, fury, indignation, ire, irritation, passion, rage, resentment, spleen, temper.

antonyms calm, pleasure.

wreck *v.* break, crab, demolish, destroy, devastate, mar, play havoc with, ravage, ruin, shatter, smash, spoil, torpedo, write off.

antonyms repair, save.

n. derelict, desolation, destruction, devastation, disruption, hulk, mess, overthrow, ruin, ruination, shipwreck, undoing, write-off.

wrench *v.* distort, force, jerk, pull, rax, rick, rip, sprain, strain, tear, tug, twist, wrest, wring, yank.

n. ache, blow, jerk, monkey-wrench, pain, pang, pliers, pull, sadness, shock, sorrow, spanner, sprain, tear, tug, twist, upheaval, uprooting.

wrestle *v.* battle, combat, contend, contest, fight, grapple, scuffle, strive, struggle, tussle, vie.

wretch *n.* blackguard, cad, caitiff, cullion, cur, good-for-nothing, insect, miscreant, outcast, profligate, rapscallion, rascal, rascallion, rat, rogue, rotter, ruffian, scoundrel, swine, vagabond, villain, wight, worm.

wretched *adj.* abject, base, broken-hearted, caitiff, calamitous, cheerless, comfortless, contemptible, crestfallen, dejected, deplorable, depressed, despicable, disconsolate, distressed, doggone, doleful, downcast, forlorn, gloomy, grotty, hapless, hopeless, inferior, low, low-down, mean, melancholy, miserable, paltry, pathetic, pesky, pitiable, pitiful, poor, ratty, scurvy, shabby, shameful, sorry, unfortunate, unhappy, vile, woebegone, woeful, worthless.

antonyms excellent, happy.

writ *n.* court order, decree, subpoena, summons.

write *v.* compose, copy, correspond, create, draft, draw up, indite, inscribe, jot down, pen, record, screeve, scribble, scribe, set down, take down, tell, transcribe.

writer *n.* amanuensis, author, authoress, clerk, columnist, copyist, crime writer, detectivist, dialogist, diarist, diatribist, dramatist, dramaturg, dramaturgist, elegiast, elegist, encomiast, epigrammatist, epistler, epistolarian, epistoler, epistolist, epitapher, epitaphist, epitomist, essayist, farceur, fictionist, hack, librettist, littérateur, man of letters, memoirist, novelist, panegyrist, paper-stainer, pen, penman, penny-a-liner, penpusher, penwoman, periodicalist, playwright, prosaist, proseman, proser, prose-writer, quill-driver, scribbler, scribe, secretary, wordsmith, writeress.

writhe *v.* coil, contort, jerk, squirm, struggle, thrash, thresh, toss, twist, wiggle, wreathe, wriggle.

wrong *adj.* abusive, amiss, askew, awry, bad, blameworthy, criminal, crooked, defective, dishonest, dishonorable, erroneous, evil, fallacious, false, faulty, felonious, funny, illegal, illicit, immoral, improper, in error, in the wrong, inaccurate, inappropriate, inapt, incongruous, incorrect, indecorous, infelicitous, iniquitous, inner, inside, inverse, malapropos, misinformed, mistaken, off beam, off target, off-base, opposite, out, out of commission, out of order, reprehensible, reverse, sinful, unacceptable, unbecoming, unconventional, under, undesirable, unethical, unfair, unfitting, unhappy, unjust, unlawful, unseemly, unsound, unsuitable, untrue, wicked, wide of the mark, wrongful, wrongous.

antonym right.

adv. amiss, askew, astray, awry, badly, erroneously, faultily, improperly, inaccurately, incorrectly, mistakenly, wrongly.

antonym right.

n. abuse, crime, error, grievance, immorality, inequity, infraction, infringement, iniquity, injury, injustice, misdeed, offense, sin, sinfulness, transgression, trespass, unfairness, wickedness, wrong-doing.

antonym right.

v. abuse, cheat, discredit, dishonor, harm, hurt, illtreat, ill-use, impose on, injure, malign, maltreat, misrepresent, mistreat, oppress, traduce.

wry *adj.* askew, aslant, awry, contorted, crooked, deformed, distorted, droll, dry, ironic, mocking, pawky, perverse, sarcastic, sardonic, thrawn, twisted, uneven, warped.

antonym straight.

yank *v., n.* haul, heave, jerk, pull, snatch, tug, wrench.

yap *v.* babble, blather, chatter, go on, gossip, jabber, jaw, prattle, talk, tattle, twattle, ya(c)k, yammer, yatter, yelp, yip.

yard *n.* court, court-yard, garden, garth, Hof, hypaethron, quad, quadrangle.

yardstick *n.* benchmark, comparison, criterion, gauge, measure, standard, touchstone.

yarn[1] *n.* abb, fiber, fingering, gimp, lisle, thread.

yarn[2] *n.* anecdote, cock-and-bull story, fable, fabrication, story, tale, tall story.

yawn *v.* gape, ga(u)nt, open, split.

yearly *adj.* annual, per annum, per year.
adv. annually, every year, once a year.

yearn for ache for, covet, crave, desire, hanker for, hunger for, itch for, languish for, long for, lust for, pant for, pine for, want, wish for, yen for.
antonym dislike.

yell *v.* bawl, bellow, holler, hollo, howl, roar, scream, screech, shout, shrick, squawl, squeal, whoop, yelp, yowl.
antonym whisper.
n. bellow, cry, holler, hollo, howl, roar, scream, screech, shriek, squawl, whoop, yelp.
antonym whisper.

yellow *adj.* flavescent, flaxen, fulvid, fulvous, gold, golden, lemon, primrose, saffron, vitellary, vitelline, xanthic, xanthochroic, xanthomelanous, xanthous.

yelp *v.* bark, bay, cry, yap, yell, yip, yowl.
n. bark, cry, yap, yell, yip, yowl.

yen *n.* craving, desire, hankering, hunger, itch, longing, lust, passion, thing, yearning.
antonym dislike.

yield[1] *v.* abandon, abdicate, accede, acquiesce, admit defeat, agree, allow, bow, capitulate, cave in, cede, comply, concede, consent, cry quits, give, give in, give way, go along with, grant, knuckle under, part with, permit, relinquish, resign, resign oneself, submit, succumb, surrender, throw in the towel.
antonym withstand.

yield[2] *v.* afford, bear, bring forth, bring in, earn, fructify, fructuate, fruit, furnish, generate, give, net, pay, produce, provide, return, supply.

n. crop, earnings, harvest, income, output, proceeds, produce, product, profit, return, revenue, takings.

yielding *adj.* accommodating, acquiescent, amenable, biddable, complaisant, compliant, docile, easy, elastic, flexible, obedient, obliging, pliable, pliant, quaggy, resilient, soft, spongy, springy, submissive, supple, tractable, unresisting.
antonyms obstinate, solid.

yoke *n.* bond, bondage, burden, chain, coupling, enslavement, helotry, ligament, link, oppression, serfdom, service, servility, servitude, slavery, subjugation, thraldom, tie, vassalage.
v. bracket, connect, couple, enslave, harness, hitch, inspan, join, link, tie, unite.
antonym unhitch.

yokel *n.* boor, bucolic, bumpkin, clodhopper, corn-ball, country cousin, hick, hillbilly, jake, peasant, rustic.
antonyms sophisticate, towny.

young *adj.* adolescent, baby, callow, cub, early, fledgling, green, growing, immature, infant, junior, juvenile, little, new, recent, unblown, unfledged, youthful.
antonym old.
n. babies, brood, chicks, cubs, family, fledglings, issue, litter, little ones, offspring, progeny, quiverful.
antonym parents.

youngster *n.* boy, girl, juvenile, kid, lad, laddie, lass, lassie, nipper, shaver, teenybopper, urchin, young pup, youth.
antonym oldie.

youthful *adj.* active, boyish, childish, ephebic, fresh, girlish, immature, inexperienced, juvenescent, juvenile, lively, pubescent, puerile, sprightly, spry, vigorous, vivacious, well-preserved, young.
antonyms aged, languorous.

youthfulness *n.* freshness, juvenileness, juvenility, liveliness, sprightliness, spryness, vigor, vivaciousness, vivacity.
antonyms agedness, languor.

yowl *v.* bay, caterwaul, cry, howl, screech, squall, ululate, wail, yell, yelp.
n. cry, howl, screech, wail, yell, yelp.

Z

zany *adj.* amusing, clownish, comical, crazy, daft, droll, eccentric, funny, goofy, kooky, loony, madcap, nutty, screwy, wacky.

antonym serious.

n. buffoon, card, clown, comedian, cure, droll, fool, jester, joker, kook, laugh, merry-andrew, nut, nutcase, nutter, screwball, wag.

zeal *n.* ardor, dedication, devotion, eagerness, earnestness, enthusiasm, fanaticism, fervency, fervor, fire, gusto, keenness, militancy, passion, spirit, verve, warmth, zelotypia, zest.

antonym apathy.

zealot *n.* bigot, devotee, enthusiast, extremist, fanatic, fiend, freak, maniac, militant.

zealous *adj.* ardent, burning, devoted, eager, earnest, enthusiastic, fanatical, fervent, fervid, fired, gung-ho, impassioned, keen, militant, passionate, rabid, spirited.

antonym apathetic.

zenith *n.* acme, apex, apogee, climax, culmination, height, high point, meridian, peak, pinnacle, summit, top, vertex.

antonym nadir.

zero *n.* bottom, cipher, duck, goose-egg, love, nadir, naught, nil, nothing, nought.

zest *n.* appetite, charm, delectation, élan, enjoyment, flavor, gusto, interest, joie de vivre, keenness, kick, peel, piquancy, pungency, relish, rind, savor, smack, spice, tang, taste, zeal, zing.

antonym apathy.

zip *n.* brio, drive, élan, energy, enthusiasm, get-up-and-go, go, gusto, life, liveliness, oomph, pep, pizzazz, punch, sparkle, spirit, verve, vigor, vim, vitality, zest, zing.

antonym listlessness.

v. dash, flash, fly, gallop, hurry, race, rush, scoot, shoot, speed, tear, whiz, whoosh, zoom.

zone *n.* area, belt, district, region, section, sector, sphere, stratum, territory, tract, zona, zonule, zonulet.

zoo *n.* animal park, aquarium, aviary, menagerie, safari park, zoological gardens.

APPENDICES

Abbreviations

A

a at; o, in algebra, known quantity, constant

A1 first class

A ace, acre, America, American, April, argon

A angstrom unit

AA Alcoholics Anonymous, Associate of Arts, anti-aircraft

AAA Agricultural Adjustment Administration, Amateur Athletic Association, American Automobile Association

AAAL American Academy of Arts and Letters

AAAS American Association for the Advancement of Science

AAG Assistant Adjutant General

A and M agricultural and mechanical, ancient and modern

AAR against all risks

AAU Amateur Athletic Union

AAUP American Association of University Professors

AAUW American Association of University Women

AB able-bodied seaman, airman basic. Alberta. [*artium baccalaureus*] bachelor of arts

ABA American Bankers Association, American Bar Association, American Basketball Association, American Booksellers Association

abbr abbreviation

ABC American Bowling Congress, American Broadcasting Company, Australian Broadcasting Company

ABCD accelerated business collection and delivery

abd or **abdom** abdomen, abdominal

abl ablative

abn airborne

abp archbishop

abr abridged, abridgment

abs absolute, abstract

ABS American Bible Society

abstr abstract

abt about

ac account, acre

Ac actinium

AC air-conditioning, alternating current, (*ante Christum*) before Christ

acad academic, academy

AC and U Association of Colleges and Universities

acc accusative

accel accelerando

acct account, accountant

accus accusative

ACE American Council on Education

ack acknowledge, acknowledgment

ACLU American Civil Liberties Union

ACP American College of Physicians

acpt acceptance

ACS American Chemical Society, American College of Surgeons

act active, actor, actual

ACT American College Test, Association of Classroom Teachers, Australian Capital Territory

actg acting

ACW alternating continuous waves

AD active duty, after date, [*anno domini*] in the year of our Lord

ad advertisement

ADA American Dental Association, average daily attendance

ADC aide-de-camp. Air Defense Command

ADD American Dialect Dictionary

addn addition

addnl additional

ADF automatic direction finder

ADH antidiuretic hormone

ad inf to infinity [*ad infinitum*]

ad int ad interim

ADIZ air defense identification zone

adj adjective, adjunct, adjustment, adjutant

ad loc [*ad locum*] to or at the place

adm administration, administrative

admin administration

admrx administratrix

ADP automatic data processing

adv advert. (*adversus*) against

ad val ad valorem

advt advertisement

AEC Atomic Energy Commission

AEF American Expeditionary Force

aeq (*aequalis*) equal

aero aeronautical, aeronautics

aet or **aetat** (*aetatis*) of age, aged

af affix

AF air force, audio frequency

Af Africa, African

AFB air force base

AFBS American and Foreign Bible Society
AFC American Football Conference, automatic
frequency control
aff affirmative
afft affidavit
AFL American Football League, American Federation
of Labor
AFL—CIO American Federation of Labor and
Congress of Industrial Organizations
aft afternoon
AFT American Federation of Teachers, automatic fine
tuning
AFTRA American Federation of Television and Radio
Artists
Ag (L. *argentum*) silver
AG adjutant general, attorney general
agcy agency
AGR advanced gas-cooled reactor
agr *or* **agric** agricultural, agriculture
agt agent
AH ampere-hour, (*anno hegirae*) in the year of the
Hegira (flight of Mohammed from Mecca to Medina,
622 A.D.)
AHC Army Hospital Corps
AHL American Hockey League
AI ad interim, artificial insemination, artificial intelli-
gence
AIA Associate of the Institute of Actuaries
AID Agency for International Development
AIDS acquired immune (or immuno-) deficiency
syndrome
AIM American Indian Movement
AIME American Institute of Mining Engineers,
Associate of the Institute of Mechanical Engineers
AK Alaska
aka also known as
AKC American Kennel Club
Al aluminium
AL Alabama, American League, American Legion
Ala Alabama
ALA American Library Association
alc alcohol
alk alkaline
allo allegro
alt alternate, altitude
Alta Alberta
alw allowance
Am America, American, americium
AM (*ante meridiem*) before midday, (*artium magister*)
master of arts
AMA American Medical Association
AMD Army Medical Department
Amer America, American
Amer Ind American Indian
Amn airman
amp ampere

amp hr ampere-hour
AMS Agricultural Marketing Service, Army Medical
Staff
amnt amount
AMU atomic mass unit
AMVETS American Veteran (of World War I)
AN airman (Navy)
ANA American Newspaper Association, American
Nurses Association
anat anatomical, anatomy
ANC Army Nurse Corps
Angl Anglican
anhyd anhydrous
ann annals, annual
anon anonymous
ANOVA analysis of variance
AO account of
AP additional premium, antipersonnel, Associated
Press, author's proof
APB all points bulletin
APC armored personnel carrier, Army Pay Corps
API air position indicator
APO army post office
appl applied
approx approximate, approximately
appt appoint, appointed, appointment
apptd appointed
Apr April
APR annual percentage rate
apt apartment, aptitude
aq aqua, aqueous
Ar argon
AR accounts receivable, acknowledgment of receipt, all
risks, Arkansas
ARC American Red Cross
arch archaic, architect, architecture
Arch Archbishop
arg argent, argument
arith arithmetic, arithmetical
Ariz Arizona
Ark Arkansas
ARP air-raid precautions
arr arranged, arrival, arrive
art article, artificial
As arsenic
AS after sight, American Samoa, Anglo-Saxon
ASA American Standards Association
ASAP as soon as possible
asb asbestos
ASCAP American Society of Composers, Authors
and Publishers
ASCU Association of State Colleges and Universities
ASF American Stock Exchange
ASEAN Association of Southeast Asian Nations
ASI airspeed indicator
ASL American Sign Language

ASR airport surveillance radar, air-sea rescue
assn association
assoc associate, associated, association
ASSR Autonomous Soviet Socialist Republic
asst assitant
Assyr Assyrian
ATS American Tract Society, American Temperance
  Society
astrol astrologer, astrology
astron astronomer, astronomy
ASV American Standard Version
Atl Atlantic
atm atmosphere, atmospheric
attn attention
atrib attributive, attributively
AUA American Unitarian Association
Au (*aurum*) gold
aud audit, auditor
Aug August
Aus Austria, Austrian, Australia, Australian
AUS Army of the United States
Austral Australia
auth authentic, authorized
auto automatic
av avenue, average, avoidupois
AV ad valorem, audiovisual, Authorized Version
AVC automatic volume control
avdp avoirdupois
ave avenue
avg average
AWACS airborne warning and control system
AYC American Youth Congress
AYD American Youth for Democracy
AZ Arizona

B

B boron
Ba barium
BA Bachelor of Arts
BAEd Bachelor of Arts in Education
BAg Bachelor of Agriculture
bal balance
B and B bed-and-breakfast
b and w black and white
Bapt Baptist
bar barometer, barometric
BAr Bachelor of Architecture
BAS Bachelor of Agricultural Science, Bachelor of
  Applied Science
Bart baronet
BBC British Broadcasting Corporation
bbl barrel, barrels
BC before Christ, British Columbia
BCD binary-coded decimal
BCh Bachelor of Chemistry
bcn beacon

BCSE Board of Civil Service Examiners
bd ft board foot
bdl *or* **bdle** bundle
bdrm bedroom
Be beryllium
BE Bachelor of Education, Bachelor of Engineering, bill
  of exchange
BEC Bureau of Employees' Compensation
BEd Bachelor of Education
BEF British Expeditionary Force
beg begin, beginning
Belg Belgian, Belgium
BEM British Empire Medal
BEngr Bachelor of Engineering
BFA Bachelor of Fine Arts
BG *or* **B Gen** brigadier general
BH bill of health
bhd bulkhead
BHE Bureau of Higher Education
bhp bishop
BIA Bachelor of Industrial Arts, Braille Institute of
  America, Bureau of Indian Affairs
bib Bible, biblical
biog biographer, biographical, biography
biol biologic, biological, biologist, biology
Bk berkelium
bkg banking, bookkeeping, breakage
bkgd background
bks barracks
bkt basket, bracket
bl bale, barrel, block
BL Bachelor of Law, Bachelor of Letters, bill of lading,
  breadth/length
bldg building
bldr builder
Blitt *or* **BLit** (*baccalaureus litterarum*) Bachelor of
  Letters, Bachelor of Literature
blk black, block, bulk
blvd boulevard
BMR basal metabolic rate
BNDD Bureau of Narcotics and Dangerous Drugs
BO back order, body odor, branch office, buyer's
  option
BOD biochemical oxygen demand, biological oxygen
  demand
bor borough
bot botanical, botanist, botany, bottle, bottom, bought
BP bills payable, blood pressure, blueprint, boiling
  point
BPD barrels per day
bpi bits per inch, bytes per inch
Br Britain, British, bromine
BR bills receivable
brig brigade, brigadier
Brig Gen brigadier general
Brit Britain, British

brl barrel
bro brother, brothers
bros brothers
BS Bachelor of Science, balance sheet, bill of sale, British Standard
BSA Boy Scouts of America
BSI British Standards Institution
bskt basket
Bt baronet
btry battery
Btu British thermal unit
bu bureau, bushel
bur bureau
bus business
BV Blessed Virgin
BW bacteriological warfare, biological warfare, black and white
BWI British West Indies
BYO bring your own

C

C carbon
ca circa
Ca calcium
CA California, chartered accountant, chief accountant
CAB Civil Aeronautics Board
CAD computer-aided design
CAF cost and freight
CAGS Certificate Advanced Graduate Study
CAI computer-aided instruction, computer-associated instruction
cal calendar, caliber, calorie, small calorie
Cal California, large calorie
calc calculate, calculated
Calif California
CAM computer-aided manufacturing
can canceled, cancellation
Can or **Canad** Canada, Canadian
canc canceled
C and F cost and freight
C and W country and western
cap capacity, capital, capitalize
CAP Civil Air Patrol
caps capitals, capsule
Capt captain
card cardinal
CAS certificate of advanced study
cat catalog, catalyst
cath cathedral, cathode
CATV community antenna television
caus causative
cav cavalry, cavity
Cb columbium
CBC Canadian Broadcasting Corporation
CBD cash before delivery
CBI computer-based instruction, Cumulative Book Index

CBS Columbia Broadcasting System
CBW chemical and biological warfare
cc cubic centimeter
CC carbon copy, chief clerk
CCF Cooperative Commonwealth Federation (of Canada)
cckw counterclockwise
CCTV closed-circuit television
CCU cardiac care unit, coronary care unit, critical care unit
ccw counterclockwise
cd candela
Cd cadmium
CD carried down, certificate of deposit, civil defense, (*corps diplomatique*) diplomatic corps
CDD certificate of disability for discharge
cdg commanding
CDR commander
CDT central daylight time
Ce cerium
ce chemical engineer, civil engineer
CEA College English Association, Council of Economic Advisors
CED Committee for Economic Development
cem cement
cent centigrade, central, centium, century
Cent Central
CENTO Central Treaty Organization
CEO chief executive officer
CER conditioned emotional response
cert certificate, certified
CETA Comprehensive Employment and Training Act
cf (*confer*) compare
Cf californium
CF carried forward, cost and freight, cystic fibrosis
CFI cost, freight, and insurance
cfm cubic feet per minute
cfs cubic feet per second
CG center of gravity, coast guard, commanding general
cg or **cgm** centigram
CGT (*Confederation Generale du Travail*) General Confederation of Labor
ch chain, chapter, church
CH clearinghouse, courthouse, customhouse
chan channel
chap chapter
chem chemical, chemist, chemistry
chg change, charge
chm chairman, checkmate
Chmn chairman
chron chronicle, chronological, chronology
Ci curie
CI certificate of insurance, cost and insurance
CIA Central Intelligence Agency
CIC Commander in Chief
CID Criminal Investigation Department

cie (*compagnie*) company
CIF cost, insurance and freight
C in C commander in chief
CIP Cataloging in Publication
cir circle, circuit, circumference
circ circular
cit citation, cited, citizen
civ civil, civilian
CJ chief justice
ck cask, check
cl centiliter, class
Cl chlorine
CL center line, civil law, common law
cld called, cleared
Clev Cleveland
clin clinical
clk clerk
clr clear, clearance
CLU chartered life underwriter
cm centimeter, cumulative
Cm curium
CMA certified medical assistant
cmd command
cmdg commanding
cmdr commander
CMG Companion of the Order of St Michael and St
  George
cml commercial
CMSgt chief master sergeant
CN credit note
CNO chief of naval operations
CNS central nervous system
co company, county
Co cobalt
CO cash order, Colorado, commanding officer,
  conscientious objector
c/o care of
cod codex
COD cash on delivery
C of S chief of staff
col color, colored, column
col *or* coll collateral, college
Col colonel, Colorado
COL colonel, cost of living
collat collateral
colloq colloquial
Colo Colorado
comb combination, combined
comd command
comdg commanding
comdr commander
comdt commandant
COMECON Council for Mutual Economic Assistance
coml commercial
comm command, commerce, commission, committee,
  communication

commo commodore
comp compare, complex
compd compound
comr commissioner
conc concentrate, concentrated
conf conference, confidential
Confed Confederate
cong congress, congressional
Conn Connecticut
consol consolidated
cont containing, contents, continent, continued
contd continued
contg containing
contrib contribution, contributor
CORE Congress of Racial Equality
corp corporal, corporation
corr correct, corrected, corresponding
cos cosine
COS cash on shipment, chief of staff
cp compare, coupon
CP candlepower, charter party, communist party
CPA certified public accountant
CPB Corporation for Public Broadcasting
CPCU chartered property and casualty underwriter
cpd compound
CPFF cost plus fixed fee
CPI consumer price index
Cpl corporal
CPO chief petty officer
CPOM master chief petty officer
CPOS senior chief petty officer
CPS characters per second, cycle per second
CPT captain
cpu central processing unit
Cr chromeum
CR carrier's risk, cathode ray
CRC Civil Rights Commission
cresc crescendo
crim criminal
crit critical, criticism, criticized
CRT cathode-ray tube
cryst crystalline, crystallized
Cs cesium
CS capital stock, chief of staff, Christian Science, civil
  service
C/S cycles per second
CSA Confederate States of America
CSC Civil Service Commission
CSM command sergeant major
CSO chief signal officer, chief staff officer
CST central standard time
ct carat, cent, count, county, court
CT central time, certificated teacher, Connecticut
CTC centralized traffic control
ctf certificate
ctg *or* ctge cartage

ctn carton
cto concerto
c to c center to center
ctr center, counter
cu cubic, cumulative
Cu (*cuprum*) copper
CU close-up
cum cumulative
cur currency, current
CV cardiovascular, curriculum vitae
cvt convertible
cw clockwise
CW chemical warfare, chief warrant officer
CWO cash with order, chief warrant officer
cwt hundred weight
CY calendar year
cyl cylinder
CYO Catholic Youth Organization
CZ Canal Zone

D

d deceased, penny
D Democrat, deuterium
da deka-
DA days after acceptance, deposit account, district
   attorney
DAB Dictionary of American Biography
dag dekagram
dal dekaliter
dam dekameter
DAR Daughters of the American Revolution
dat dative
DAV Disabled American Veterans
db debenture
db *or* dB decibel
DB daybook
DBE Dame Commander of the Order of the British
   Empire
dbl double
DBMS data base management system
DC direct current, District of Columbia
dd dated, delivered
DD days after date, demand draft, dishonorable
   discharge, due date
DDC Dewey Decimal Classification
DDD direct distance dialing
DDS Doctor of Dental Science, Doctor of Dental
   Surgery
DE Delaware
deb debenture
dec deceased, declaration, declared, decorative,
   decrease
Dec December
def defendant, defense, deferred, defined, definite
deg degree
del delegate, delegation, delete

Del Delaware
dely delivery
dem demonstrative, demurrage
Dem Democrat, Democratic
Den Denmark
dent dental, dentist, dentistry
dep depart, department, departure, deposit, depot,
   deputy
dept department
der *or* deriv derivation, derivative
DEW distant early warning
DF damage free, direction finder
DFC Distinguished Flying Cross
DFM Distinguished Flying Medal
dft defendant, draft
dg decigram
DG director general, (*Dei gratia*) by the grace of God
dia diameter
diag diagonal, diagram
dial dialect
diam diameter
dict dictionary
dim diminutive
dip diploma
dir director
disc discount
dist distance, district
distr distribute, distribution
div dividend, division
DJ disc jockey, district judge, Doctor of Jurisprudence
DJIA Dow-Jones Industrial Average
dkg dekagram
dkl dekaliter
dkm dekameter
dl deciliter
DLitt *or* DLit (*doctor litterarum*) Doctor of Letters,
   Doctor of Literature
DLO dead letter office, dispatch loading only
dm decimeter
DM deutsche Mark
DMZ demilitarized zone
dn down
DNB Dictionary of National Biography
do ditto
DOA dead on arrival
DOB date of birth
doc document
DOD Department of Defense
DOE Department of Energy
dol dollar
DOM (*Deo optimo maximo*) to God, the best and
   greatest
DOS disk operating system
DOT Department of Transportation
doz dozen
DP data processing, dew point

DPH department of public health
dr dram
Dr doctor
DR dead reckoning
DSM Distinguished Service Medal
DSO Distinguished Service Order
DSP (*decessit sine prole*) died without issue
DST daylight time, double time
dup duplex, duplicate
DV (*Deo volente*) God willing
DVM Doctor of Veterinary Medicine
DW deadweight
dwt deadweight ton, pennyweight
DX distance
dy delivery, deputy, duty
Dy dysprosium
dynam dynamics
dz dozen

E

ea each
E Earl, Easter, English
E and OE errors and omissions excepted
EB eastbound
eccl ecclesiastic, ecclesiastical
ECG electrocardiogram
ECM European Common Market
ecol ecological, ecology
econ economics, economist, economy
ed edited, edition, editor, education
EDP electronic data processing
EDT eastern daylight time
educ education, educational
EEC European Economic Community
EEG electroencephalogram, electroencephalograph
EENT eye, ear, nose, and throat
EEO equal employment opportunity
eff efficiency
EFT *or* EFTS electronic funds transfer (system)
eg (*exempli gratia*) for example
EHF extremely high frequency
EHP effective horsepower, electric horsepower
EHV extra high voltage
elec electric, electrical, electricity
elem elementary
elev elevation
ELF extremely low frequency
ELSS extravehicular life support system
EM electromagnetic, electron microscope
emer emeritus
emf electromotive force
emp emperor, empress
enc *or* encl enclosure
ENE east-northeast
eng engine, engineer, engineering
Eng England, English

ENS ensign
env envelope
EO executive order
EOM end of month
EP extended play
EPA Environmental Protection Agency
eq equal, equation
equip equipment
equiv equivalency, equivalent
Er erbium
Es einsteinium
ESE east-southeast
ESL English as a second language
esp especially
Esq esquire
est established, estimate, estimated
EST eastern standard time
esu electrostatic unit
ESV earth satellite vehicle
ET eastern time, extra-terrestrial
ETA estimated time of arrival
et al *et alii* (masc.), *et aliae* (fem.) or *et alia* (neut.) and
others
etc et cetera, and the rest
ETD estimated time of departure
ETO European theater of operations
et seq (*et sequens*) and the following one
et ux (*et uxor*) and wife
Eu europium
Eur Europe, European
EVA extravehicular activity
ex example, exchange, excluding, executive, express,
extra
exch exchange, exchanged
exec executive
exhbn exhibition
exor executor
expy expressway
ext extension, exterior, external

F

f Fahrenheit, farad, faraday, and the following one
F fluorine
FA field artillery, fielding average, football association
FAA Federal Aviation Administration, free of all
average
fac facsimile, faculty
FADM fleet admiral
fam familiar, family
F and A fore and aft
FAO Food and Agriculture Organization of the United
Nations
FAQ fair average quality
far farthing
FAS free alongside ship
fath fathom

FBI Federal Bureau of Investigation
FCA Farm Credit Administration
FCC Federal Communications Commission
fcp foolscap
FDA Food and Drug Administration
FCIC Federal Deposit Insurance Corporation
Fe (*ferrum*) iron
Feb February
fec (*fecit*) he made it
fed federal, federation
fem female, feminine
FERA Federal Emergency Relief Administration
ff folios, and the following ones, fortissimo
FHA Federal Housing Administration
fict fiction, fictitious
FIFO first in, first out
fig figurative, figuratively, figure
fin finance, financial, finish
FIO free in and out
fir firkin
fl florin (*floruit*) flourished
FL Florida
Fla Florida
fl oz fluid ounce
FLSA Fair Labor Standards Act
fm fathom
Fm fermium
FM field manual
FMB Federal Maritime Board
FMCS Federal Mediation and Conciliation Service
fn footnote
fo *or* **fol** folio
FO foreign office
FOB free on board
FOC free of charge
fp freezing point
FPA Foreign Press Association, free of particular average
FPC Federal Power Commission
fps feet per second, foot-pound-second, frames per second
fr father, franc, from
Fr francium
freq frequency
Fri Friday
FRS Federal Reserve System
frt freight
frwy freeway
FS Foreign Service
FSLIC Federal Savings and Loan Insurance Corporation
FSP Food Stamp Program
ft feet, foot
FTC Federal Trade Commission
fth fathom
ft lb foot-pound
fur furlong

fut future
fwd foreword, forward
FWD front-wheel drive
FX foreign exchange
FY fiscal year
FYI for your information
fz (*forzando, forzato*) accented

G

g gauge, gold, grain, acceleration of gravity, gram, gravity
Ga gallium, Georgia
GA general assembly, general average, Georgia
gal gallery, gallon
galv galvanized
GAO General Accounting Office
gar garage
GATT General Agreement on Tariffs and Trade
GAW guaranteed annual wage
gaz gazette
GB Great Britain
GCA ground-controlled approach
GCB Knight Grand Cross of the Bath
Gd gadolinium
GDR German Democratic Republic
Ge germanium
GE gilt edges
gen general, genitive, genus
Gen AF general of the air force
Gent gentleman, gentlemen
genl general
geog geographic, geographical, geography
geol geologic, geological, geology
geom geometric, geometrical, geometry
ger gerund
GGPA graduate grade-point average
GHQ general headquarters
hi gill
GI gastrointestinal, general issue, government issue
GM general manager, grand master, guided missile
GMT Greenwich mean time
GMW gram-molecular weight
gn guinea
GNI Gross national income
GNP gross national product
GO general order
GOP Grand Old Party (Republican)
gov government, governor
govt government
gp group
GP general practice
GPD gallons per day
GPH gallons per hour
GPM gallons per minute
GPO general post office, Government Printing Office
GPS gallons per second

gr grade, grain, gram, gravity, gross
grad graduate, graduated
gram grammar, grammatical
gro gross
gr wt gross weight
GSA General Services Administration, Girl Scouts of America
GSC general staff corps
GSO general staff officer
GSV guided space vehicle
GT gross ton
Gt Brit Great Britain
gtd guaranteed
gyn gynecology

H

ha hectare
hab corp habeas corpus
Hb hemoglobin
hc (*honoris causa*) for the sake of honor
HC Holy Communion, House of Commons
HCF highest common factor
hd head
HD heavy duty
hdbk handbook
He helium
HE Her Excellency, His Excellency
HEW Department of Health, Education and Welfare
hf half
Hf hafnium
HF high frequency
hg hectogram
Hg (*hydrargyrum*) mercury
HH Her Highness, His Highness, His Holiness
HI Hawaii
Hind Hindustani
hist historian, historical, history
hl hectoliter
HL House of Lords
hld hold
HLS (*hoc loco situs*) laid in this place, holograph letter signed
hlt halt
hm hectometer
HM Her Majesty, Her Majesty's, His Majesty, His Majesty's
HMC Her Majesty's Customs, His Majesty's Customs
HMS Her Majesty's ship, His Majesty's ship
HN head nurse
Ho holmium
hon honor, honorable, honorary
hor horizontal
hort horticultural, horticulture
hosp hospital
HP high pressure, hire purchase, horsepower

HQ headquarters
hr hour
HR House of Representatives
HRH Her Royal Highness, His Royal Highness
HRIP here rests in peace
hrzn horizon
HS high school
HSGT high-speed ground transport
HST Hawaiian standard time
ht height
HUD Department of Housing and Urban Development
HV high velocity, high-voltage
hvy heavy
HWM high-water mark
hwy highway
Hz hertz

I

Ia *or* **IA** Iowa
IAAF International Amateur Athletic Federation
IABA International Amateur Boxing Association
IAEA International Atomic Energy Agency
IALC instrument approach and landing chart
IATA International Air Transport Association
ib *or* **ibid** ibidem
IBM intercontinental ballistic missile
IBRD International Bank for Reconstruction and Development
ICA International Cooperation Administration, International Cooperative Alliance
ICAO International Civil Aviation Organization
ICBM intercontinental ballistic missile
ICC Indian Claims Commission, International Chamber of Commerce, Interstate Commerce Commission
ICFTU International Confederation of Free Trade Unions
ICJ International Court of Justice
ICRC International Committee of the Red Cross
ICU intensive care unit
id idem
ID Idaho, identification
i e (*id est*) that is
IFC International Finance Corporation
IG inspector general
Il Illinois
ill illustrated, illustration, illustrator
IL Illinois
illust *or* **illus** illustrated, illustration
ILO International Labor Organization
ILS instrument landing system
IMF International Monetary Fund
imit imitative
immun immunity, immunization
imp imperative, imperfect, import
in inch

In indium
IN Indiana
inc including, incorporated, increase
incl including, inclusive
incog incognito
ind independent, industrial, industry
Ind Indian, Indiana
inf infantry, infinitive
infl influenced
inq inquire
INRI (*Jesus Nazarenus Rex Iudaeorum*) Jesus of
  Nazareth, King of the Jews
ins inches, insurance
INS Immigration and Naturalization Service
intl *or* **intnl** international
intrans intransitive
in trans (*in transitu*) in transit
intsv intensive
IOC International Olympic Committee
IPA International Phonetic Alphabet, International
  Phonetic Association
ipm inches per minute
IPPF International Planned Parenthood Federation
ips inches per second
iq (*idem quod*) the same as
Ir iridium
IR infrared, inland revenue, intelligence ratios, internal
  revenue
IRA Irish Republican Army
IRBM intermediate range ballistic missile
irreg irregular
IRS Internal Revenue Service
ISBN International Standard Book Number
ISC interstate commerce
ISSN International Standard Serial Number
ital italic, italicized
ITO International Trade Organization
IU international unit
IV intravenous, intravenously
IWW Industrial Workers of the World

J

j joule
JA joint account, judge advocate
JAG judge advocate general
Jan January
Jap Japan, Japanese
Jav Javanese
JBS John Birch Society
JCS joint chiefs of staff
jct junction
JD justice department, juvenile delinquent, (*juris
  doctor*) doctor of jurisprudence, doctor of law
JP justice of the peace
Jr junior
jt *or* **jnt** joint

jun junior
Jun June
junc junction
juris jurisprudence
juv juvenile

K

k karat, kilogram, king, knight, kopeck, krona, kronor
K (*kalium*) potassium, Kelvin
Kan *or* **Kans** Kansas
kb *or* **kbar** kilobar
KB kilobyte
KC Kansas City, King's Counsel, Knights of
  Columbus
kcal kilocalorie, kilogram calorie
KCB Knight Commander of the Order of the Bath
kc/s kilocycles per second
KD knocked down
Ken Kentucky
kg kilogram
KG Knight of the Order of the Garter
KGB (*Komitet Gosudarstvennoi Bezopasnosti*)
  (Soviet) State Security Committee
kHz kilohertz
KIA killed in action
KJV King James Version
KKK Ku Klux Klan
kl kiloliter
km kilometer
KMPS kilometers per second
kn knot
K of C Knights of Columbus
kph kilometers per hour
Kr Krypton
KS Kansas
kt karat, knight
kv kilovolt
kw kilowatt
kwhr *or* **kwh** kilowatt-hour
Ky *or* **KY** Kentucky

L

L lady, lake, land, latitude, law, leaf, league, left, length,
  liberal, lira, liter, lodge, lord
La lanthanum, Louisiana
LA law agent, Los Angeles, Louisiana
Lab Labrador
lam laminated
lang language
lat latitude
Lat Latin, Latvia
LAT local apparent time
lb (*libra*) pound
LB Labrador
lc lowercase
LC landing craft, letter of credit, Library of Congress

LCD lowest common denominator
LCF lowest common factor
LCJ Lord Chief Justice
LCM lowest common multiple
LD lethal dose
LDC less developed country
ldg landing, loading
LDS Latter-day Saints
lect lecture, lecturer
leg legal, legislative, legislation
legis legislation, legislative, legislature
lex lexicon
lexicog lexicography
LF low frequency
lg large, long
LH left hand
Li lithium
LI Long Island
lib liberal, librarian, theory
lieut lieutenant
LIFO last in, first out
lin lineal, linear
ling linguistics
liq liquid, liquor
lit liter, literal, literally, literary, literature
llth lithographic, lithography
ll lines
LL limited liability
LM Legion of Merit, lunar module
LMT local mean time
lndg landing
LNG liquefied natural gas
loc cit (*loco citato*) in the place cited
LP low pressure
LPG liquified petroleum gas
LPGA Ladies Professional Golf Association
Lr lawrencium
LS (*locus sigilli*) place of the seal
LSS lifesaving station, life-support system
Lt lieutenant
LT long ton
LTC *or* **Lt Col** lieutenant colonel
Lt Comdr lieutenant commander
ltd limited
LTG *or* **Lt Gen** lieutenant general
lt gov lieutenant governor
LTJG lieutenant, junior grade
Lu lutetium
lub lubricant, lubricating
LVT landing vehicle, tracked
LWM low-water mark
LWV League of Women Voters
LZ landing zone

M

m much, meter (*mille*) thousand

M monsieur
ma *or* **mA** miliampere
MA Massachusetts, (*magister artium*) master of arts
MAD mutual assured destruction
MAE *or* **MA Ed** master of arts in education
mag magnesium, magnetism, magnitude
Maj major
Maj Gen major general
man manual
Man Manitoba
manuf manufacture, manufacturing
MAP modified American plan
mar maritime
Mar March
masc masculine
MASH mobile army surgical hospital
Mass Massachusetts
math mathematical, mathematician
matric matriculated, matriculation
max maximum
mb millibar
MB bachelor of medicine, Manitoba, megabyte
MBA master of business administration
mbd million barrels per day
MBE Member of the Order of the British Empire
MBS Mutual Broadcasting System
mc megacycle, millicurie
MC Member of Congress
mcf thousand cubic feet
mig microgram
MCPO master chief petty officer
Md Maryland
MD Maryland, (*medicinae doctor*) doctor of medicine
mdse merchandise
MDT mountain daylight time
Me Maine, methyl
ME Maine
meas measure
mech mechanical, mechanics
med medicine, medieval medium
Med Mediterranean
MEd master of education
met meteorological, meteorology, metropolitan
METO Middle East Treaty Organization
Mex Mexican, Mexico
MF medium frequency, mezzo forte, microfiche
mfd manufactured
mfg manufacturing
MFN most favored nation
mfr manufacture, manufacturer
mg milligram
Mg magnesium
mgd million gallons per day
mgr manager, monseigneur, monsignor
mgt management
MH medal of honor, mobile home

MHz megahertz
mi mile, mileage, mill
MI Michigan, military intelligence
MIA missing in action
Mich Michigan
mid middle
midn midshipman
mil military, million
min minimum, minute
Minn Minnesota
misc miscellaneous
Miss Mississippi, mistress, (unmarried woman)
Mk Mark
mks meter-kilogram-second
mktg marketing
ml milliliter
MLA Member of the Legislative Assembly
MLD median lethal dose, minimum lethal dose
MLF multilateral force
Mlle mademoiselle
Mlles mesdemoiselles
mm millimeter
MM messieurs, mutatis mutandis
Mme madame
Mm manganese
MN Minnesota
mo month
Mo Missouri, molybdenum
MO mail order, medical officer, Missouri, modus operandi, money order
mod moderate, modern, modification, modified, modulo, modulus
modif modification
mol molecular, molecule
MOl manned orbiting laboratory
Mont Montana
MP melting point, member of parliament, metropolitan police, military police, military policeman
mpg miles per gallon
mph miles per hour
MR map reference, mentally retarded
Mr mister
mRNA messenger RNA
Mrs mistress (married woman)
ms millisecond
MS manuscript, master of science, military science, Mississippi, motorship, multiple sclerosis
Ms mistress (woman, marital status unmarked)
MSc master of science
msec millisecond
msg message
MSG master sergeant, monosodium glutamate
msgr monseigneur, monsignor
MSgt master sergeant
MSS manuscripts
MST mountain standard time

mt mount, mountain
MT Montana, mountain time
mtg meeting, mortgage
mtge mortgage
mun *or* munic municipal
mus museum, music, musical, musician
mv *or* mV millivolt
MV motor vessel
MVA Missouri Valley Authority
MW megawatt
MWe megawatts electric
mxd mixed

N

n neuter, neutron, north, northern, noun, number
N newton, nitrogen
Na (*natrium*) sodium
NA no account, North America, not applicable
NAACP National Association for the Advancement of Colored People
NAB New American Bible
NACU National Association of Colleges and Universities
NAM National Association of Manufacturers
NAMH National Association for Mental Health
NAS National Academy of Sciences, naval air station
NASA National Aeronautics and Space Administration
nat national native, natural
NATO North Atlantic Treaty Organization
naut nautical
Nb niobium
NB New Brunswick, northbound, nota bene
NBA National Basketball Association, National Boxing Association
NBC National Broadcasting Company
NBS National Bureau of Standards
NC no charge, no credit, North Carolina
NCAA National Collegiate Athletic Association
ncv no commercial value
Nd neodymium
ND North Dakota
N Dak North Dakota
Ne neon
NE Nebraska, New England, northeast
NEA National Education Association
Neb *or* Nebr Nebraska
NEB New English Bible
neg negative
nem con (*nemine contradicente*) no one contradicting
nem diss (*nemine dissentiente*) no one dissenting
neut neuter
Nev Nevada
New Eng New England
NF Newfoundland, no funds
NFC National Football Conference

NFL National Football League
Nfld Newfoundland
NFS not for sale
ng nanogram
NG national guard, no good
NH New Hampshire
NHL National Hockey League
NHP nominal horsepower
Ni nickel
NIH National Institutes of Health
NJ New Jersey
NL National League, new line, (*non licet*) it is not permitted
NLF National Liberation Front
NLRB National Labor Relations Board
NLT night letter
NM nautical mile, New Mexico, no mark
N Mex New Mexico
NMI no middle initial
NMR nuclear magnetic resonance
NNE north-northeast
NNW north-northwest
no north, northern, (*numero*) number
No nobelium
nom nominative
non seq (*non sequitur*) it does not follow
NOP not otherwise provided for
Nor Norway, Norwegian
NORAD North American Air Defense Command
norm normal
nos numbers
NOS not otherwise specified
Nov November
Np neptunium
NP Notary Public
NPR National Public Radio
nr near
NRA National Recovery Administration, National Rifle Association
NRC National Research Council, Nuclear Regulatory Commission
NS new style, not specified, not sufficient, Nova Scotia
NSA National Security Agency
NSC National Security Council
NSW New South Wales
NT New Testament, Northern Territory, Northwest Territories
NTP normal temperature and pressure
nt wt *or* **n wt** net weight
NV Nevada, nonvoting
NW northwest
NWT Northwest Territories
NY New York
NYA National Youth Administration
NYC New York City

NYSE New York Stock Exchange
NZ New Zealand

O

o ohm
O Ohio, oxygen
o/a on or about
OAS Organization of American States
OAU Organization of African Unity
ob (*obit*) he died, she died
OBE Officer of the Order of the British Empire
obj object, objective
OCR optical character reader, optical character recognition
oct octavo
Oct October
OD on demand, overdose, overdrawn
OE Old English
OECD Organization for Economic Cooperation and Development
OED Oxford English Dictionary
OF outfield
off office, officer, official
offic official
OH Ohio
OHMS on Her Majesty's service, on His Majesty's service
OIT Office of International Trade
OK Oklahoma
Okla Oklahoma
OM order of merit
On *or* **ONT** Ontario
OP out of print
op cit (*opere citato*) in the work cited
OPEC Organization of Petroleum Exporting Countries
opp opposite
opt optical, optician
OR Oregon, owner's risk
orch orchestra
ord order, ordinance
Oreg *or* **Ore** Oregon
org organic, organization, organized
orig original, originally, originator
Os osmium
OS old style, ordinary seaman, out of stock
OT occupational therapy, Old Testament, overtime
OTC over-the-counter
OTS officers' training school
OW one-way
Oxon (*Oxonia*) Oxford
oz (*onza*) ounce, ounces

P

p page, penny, peseta, peso
P phosphorus
Pa Pennsylvania, protactinium

PA particular average, Pennsylvania, per annum, personal appearance, power of attorney, press agent, private account

p and h postage and handling

P and L profit and loss

par paragraph, parallel

part participle, particular

pass passenger, passive

pat patent

path or **pathol** pathological, pathology

PAU Pan American Union

PAYE pay as you earn, pay as you enter

payt payment

Pb (*plumbum*) lead

PB power brakes

PBS Public Broadcasting Service

PBX private branch exchange

PC Peace Corps, percent, percentage, personal computer, postcard

pct percent, percentage

pd paid

Pd palladium

PD per diem, police department

PDD past due date

PDT Pacific daylight time

PE physical education, printer's error, probable error

P/E price/earnings

pen peninsula

PEN International Association of Poets, Playwrights, Editors, Essayists and Novelists

Penn Pennsylvania

per period, person

perf perfect, perforated, performance

perh perhaps

perm permanent

perp perpendicular

pers person, personal, personnel

pert pertaining

pfd preferred

PGA Professional Golfers' Association

ph phase

PH public health, Purple Heart

phar pharmacy

pharm pharmaceutical, pharmacist, pharmacy

PhB (*philosophiae doctor*) Bachelor of Philosophy

PhD (*philosophiae doctor*) Doctor of Philosophy

phon phonetics

photog photographic, photography

phr phrase

phys physics

pinx (*pinxit*) he painted it, she painted it

pk park, peak, peck, pike

PK psychokinesis

pkg package

pkng packaging

pkt packet, pocket

pkwy parkway

pl place, plate, plural

PL partial loss, private line

plat plateau, platoon

plf plaintiff

PLO Palestine Liberation Organization

PLSS portable life-support system

pm phase modulation, premium

Pm promethium

PM paymaster, permanent magnet, police magistrate, postmaster, (*post meridiem*) after midday, postmortem, prime minister, provost marshal

pmk postmark

pmt payment

PN promissory note

Po polonium

PO petty officer, postal order, post office, purchase order

POC port of call

POD pay on delivery, post office department

POE port of embarkation, port of entry

poly polytechnic

POO post office order

pop popular, population

por portrait

POR pay on return

Port Portugal, Portuguese

pos position, positive

poss possessive

pp pages, (*per procurationem*) by proxy

PP parcel post, past participle, postpaid, prepaid

ppd post paid, prepaid

ppm parts per million

PPS (*post postscriptum*) an additional postscript

ppt parts per thousand, parts per trillion

pptn precipitation

PQ previous question, Province of Quebec

pr pair, price, printed

Pr praseodymium

PR payroll, proportional representation, public relations

PRC People's Republic of China

prec preceding

pred predicate

pref preface, preferred, prefix

prem premium

prep preparatory, preposition

pres present, president

Presb Presbyterian

prev previous, previously

prf proof

prim primary, primitive

prin principal, principle

priv private, privately, privative

PRN (*pro re nata*) for the emergency, as needed

PRO public relations officer

prob probable, probably, probate, problem
proc proceedings
prod product, production
prof professional, professor
prom promontory
pron pronoun, pronounced, pronunciation
prop property, proposition, proprietor
pros prosody
Prot Protestant
prov province, provincial, provisional
PS (*postscriptum*) postscript
pseud pseudonym, pseudonymous
psi pounds per square inch
PST Pacific standard time
psych psychology
psychol psychologist, psychology
pt part, payment, pint, point, port
Pt platinum
PT Pacific time, part-time, physical therapy, physical training
pta peseta
PTA Parent-Teacher Association
ptg printing
PTO Parent-Teacher Organization, please turn over
Pu plutonium
pub public, publication, published, publisher, publishing
publ publication, published, publisher
PUD pickup and delivery
PVA polyvinyl acetate
PVC polyvinyl chloride
pvt private
PVT pressure, volume, temperature
PW prisoner of war
pwr power
pwt pennyweight
PX please exchange, post exchange

Q

q quart, quartile, quarto, query, question
QB queen's bench
QC quality control, queen's counsel
QED (*quod erat demonstrandum*) which was to be demonstrated
QEF (*quod erat faciendum*) which was to be done
QEI (*quod erat inveniendum*) which was to be found out
QMG quartermaster general
qp or **q pl** (*quantum placet*) as much as you please
qq questions
qr quarter, quire
qs (*quantum sufficit*) as much as suffices
qt quantity, quart
qtd quartered
qto quarto
qty quantity

qu or **ques** question
quad quadrant
qual qualitative, quality
quant quantitative
quar quarterly
Que Quebec
quot quotation
qv (*quod vide*) which see

R

r radius, repeat, Republican, ruble, rupee
R radical, registered trademark
Ra radium
RA regular army, Royal Academician, Royal Academy
RAAF Royal Australian Air Force
rad radical, radian, radiator, radio, radius, radix
RAF Royal Air Force
RAM random access memory
R & B rhythm and blues
R & D research and development
R & R rest and recreation, rest and recuperation
Rb rubidium
RBC red blood cells, red blood count
RBE relative biological effectiveness
RC Red Cross, Roman Catholic
RCAF Royal Canadian Air Force
RCMP Royal Canadian Mounted Police
RCN Royal Canadian Navy
rct recruit
rd road, rod, round
RD refer to drawer
RDA recommended daily allowance, recommended dietary allowance
RDF radio direction finder, radio direction finding
Re rhenium
rec receipt, record, recording, recreation
recd received
recip reciprocal, reciprocity
rec sec recording secretary
rect receipt, rectangle, rectangular, rectified
red reduce, reduction
ref reference, referred, refining, reformed, refunding
refl reflex, reflexive
refrig refrigerating, refrigeration
reg region, register, registered, registration, regular
regd registered
regt regiment
rel relating, relative, released, religion, religious
relig religion
rep report, representative, republic
Rep Republican
repl replace, replacement
req request, require, required, requisition
reqd required
res research, reservation, reserve, residence, resolution
resp respective, respectively

retd retained, retired, returned
rev revenue, reverse, review, reviewed, revised, revision, revolution
Rev reverend
rf refunding
RF radio frequency
rh relative humidity
Rh rhodium
rhet rhetoric
RI refractive index, Rhode Island
RIP (*requiescat in pace*) may he rest in peace, may she rest in peace
rit ritardando
riv river
rm ream, room
RMS Royal Mail Service, Royal Mail Steamship
Rn radon
RN registered nurse, Royal Navy
rnd round
ROG receipt of goods
ROI return of investment
Rom Roman, Romance, Romania, Romanian
ROM read-only memory
ROP record of production
rot rotating, rotation
ROTC Reserve Officers' Training Corps
RP Received Pronunciation, reply paid, reprint, reprinting
RPM revolutions per minute
RPO railways post office
RPS revolutions per second
rpt repeat, report
RR railroad
RS Royal Society
RSV Revised Standard Version
RSVP (*répondez s'il vous plaît*) please reply
RSWC right side up with care
rt right
RT radiotelephone, room temperature
rte route
rtw ready-to-wear
Ru ruthenium
RV recreational vehicle
rwy *or* **ry** railway

S

s saint, schilling, senate, shilling, sine, singular, small, south, southern
S sulfur
SA Salvation Army, seaman apprentice, (*sine anno*) without year, without dates, South Africa, South America, South Australia
SAC Strategic Air Command
SAE self-addressed envelope, stamped addressed envelope
SALT Strategic Arms Limitation Talks

SAM surface-to-air missile
S & M sadism and masochism
sanit sanitary, sanitation
SASE self-addressed stamped envelope
Sask Saskatchewan
sat saturate, saturated, saturation
Sat Saturday
satd saturated
S Aust South Australia
sb substantive
Sb (*stibium*) antimony
SBA Small Business Administration
SBN Standard Book Number
sc scale, scene, science, (*sculpsit*) he carved it, she carved it, he engraved it, she engraved it
Sc scandium, Scots
SC small capitals, South Carolina, supreme court
sch school
sci science, scientific
SCP single-cell protein
SCPO senior chief petty officer
sct scout
SD South Dakota, special delivery, stage direction
SDA specific dynamic action
S Dak South Dakota
SDI Strategic Defense Initiative
SDR special drawing rights
Se selenium
SE southeast, Standard English, stock exchange
SEATO Southeast Asia Treaty Organization
sec second, secretary, (*secundum*) according to
sect section, sectional
secy secretary
sed sediment, sedimentation
sel selected, selection
sen senate, senator, senior
sep separate, separated
Sep September
sepd separated
Sept September
seq (*sequens*) the following
serg *or* **sergt** sergeant
serv service
sf *or* **sfz** sforzando
SF science fiction, sinking fund
SFC sergeant first class
SG sergeant, solicitor general, specific gravity
sgd signed
Sgt sergeant
Sgt Maj sergeant major
sh share
shipt shipment
shpt shipment
sht sheet
shtg shortage
Si silicon

SI (*Système International d'Unitéds*) International System of Units
SIDS sudden infant death syndrome
sig signal, signature, signor
SIG special interest group
sigill (*sigillum*) seal
sin sine
sing singular
SJ Society of Jesus
SK Saskatchewan
sl slightly, slow
SL salvage loss, sea level, south latitude
SLBM submarine-launched ballistic missile
sld sailed, sealed, sold
SLR single lens reflex
Sm samarium
SMaj sergeant major
SMSgt senior master sergeant
SMV slow-moving vehicle
Sn [*stannum*] tin
SNG substitute natural gas, synthetic natural gas
so south, southern
SO seller's option, strikeout
soc social, society
sociol sociologist, sociology
soln solution
SOP standard operating procedure
soph sophomore
sp species, specific, specimen, spelling
SP self-propelled, shore patrol
SPCA Society for the Prevention of Cruelty to Animals
SPCC Society for the Prevention of Cruelty to Children
spec special, specifically
specif specific, specifically
sp gr specific gravity
SPOT satellite positioning and tracking
SPQR (*senatus populusque Romanus*) the senate and the people of Rome
sq squadron, square
Sr senior, senor, señor, sister, strontium
Sra senora, señora
SRO standing room only
Srta senorita, señorita
SS saints, same size, Social Security, steamship
SSA Social Security Administration
SSE south-southeast
SSG *or* **SSgt** staff sergeant
SSM staff sergeant major
SSW south-southwest
st stanza, state, street
St saint, stratus
ST short ton, single throw, standard time
sta station, stationary
stat (*statim*) immediately

stbd starboard
std standard
Ste (*sainte*) saint (*fem.*)
ster *or* **stg** sterling
stge storage
stk stock
STOL short takeoff and landing
stor storage
STP standard temperature and pressure
STV subscription television
sub subaltern, subtract, suburb
subj subject, subjunctive
suff sufficient, suffix
Sun Sunday
supp *or* **suppl** supplement, supplementary
supr supreme
supt superintendent
sur surface
surg surgeon, surgery, surgical
surv survey, surveying, surveyor
sv sailing vessel, saves, (*sub verbo* or *sub voce*) under the word
svgs savings
sw switch
SW shortwave, southwest
sym symbol, symmetrical
syn synonym, synonymous
syst system

T

T tritium
Ta tantalum
TA teaching assistant
TAC Tactical Air Command
tan tangent
tb tablespoon, tablespoonful
Tb terbium
TB trial balance, tubercle bacillus
tbs *or* **tbsp** tablespoon, tablespoonful
Tc technetium
tchr teacher
TD touchdown, Treasury Department
TDN total digestible nutrients
TE tellurium
tech technical, technically, technician, technological, technology
TEFL teaching English as a foreign language
tel telegram, telegraph, telephone
teleg telegraphy
temp temperance, temperature, template, temporal, temporary
Tenn Tennessee
TESL teaching English as a second language
TESOL Teachers of English to speakers of Other Languages
Test Testament

Tex Texas
TG transformational grammar, type genus
Th thorium, Thursday
Thurs *or* **Thu** Thursday
Ti titanium
tk tank, truck
tkt ticket
TL total loss, truckload
TLC tender loving care
TLO total loss only
tlr tailor, trailer
Tm thulium
TM trademark, transcendental meditation
TMO telegraph money order
tn ton, town, train
TN Tennessee, true north
tng training
tnpk turnpike
topog topography
tot total
tpk *or* **tpke** turnpike
tps townships, troops
tr translated, translation, translator, transpose
trans transaction, transitive, translated, translation,
    translator
transl translated, translation
transp transportation
trib tributary
trop tropic, tropical
ts tensile strength
tsp teaspoon, teaspoonful
TT telegraphic transfer, Trust Territories
Tu Tuesday
TU trade union, transmission unit
TUC Trades Union Congress
Tues *or* **Tue** Tuesday
TV television, terminal velocity, transvestite
TX Texas

U

U university, uranium
UAE United Arab Emirates
UAR United Arab Republic
UC undercharge, uppercase
ugt urgent
UHF ultrahigh frequency
UK United Kingdom
ult ultimate, ultimo
UN United Nations
unan unanimous
UNESCO United Nations Educational, Scientific, and
    Cultural Organization
UNICEF United Nations International Children's
    Emergency Fund
univ universal, university
UNRWA United Nations Relief and Works Agency

uns unsymmetrical
UPC Universal Product Code
UPI United Press International
US United States Army, United States of America
USAF United States Air Force
USCG United States Coast Guard
USDA United States Department of Agriculture
USIA United States Information Agency
USM United States Mail
USMC United States Maritime Corps
USN United States Navy
USO United Service Organizations
USPS United States Postal Service
USS United States ship
USSR Union of Soviet Socialist Republics
usu usual, usually
UT Universal time, Utah
util utility
UV ultraviolet
UW underwriter
ux wife
UXB unexploded bomb

V

v vector, verb, versus, very, volt, voltage, vowel
V vanadium
Va Virginia
VA Veterans Administration, vice admiral, Virginia,
    visual aid, volt-ampere
vac vacuum
VADM vice admiral
val value, valued
var variant, variety, various
VAT value-added tax
vb verb, verbal
VC veterinary corps, vice-chancellor, vice-consul,
    Victoria Cross, Vietcong
VD vapor density, venereal disease
VDT video display terminal
VDU visual display unit
veg vegetable
vel vellum, velocity
vert vertebrate, vertical
VFD volunteer fire department
VG very good, vicar-general
VHF very high frequency
vi verb intransitive
VI Virgin Islands, viscosity index, volume indicator
vic vicinity
Vic Victoria
vil village
vis visibility, visual
VISTA Volunteers in Service to America
viz vicelicet
VLF very low frequency

VOA Voice of America
voc vocational, vocative
vocab vocabulary
vol volcano, volume, volunteer
VOLAR volunteer army
VOM volt ohm meter
VP variable pitch, various places, verb phrase, vice president
VRM variable rate mortgage
vs verse, versus
VS veterinary surgeon
vss verses, versions
V/STOL vertical short takeoff and landing
Vt Vermont
VT vacuum tube, variable time, Vermont
VTOL vertical takeoff and landing
VTR video tape recorder, video tape recording
VU volume unit
Vulg Vulgate
vv verses, vice versa

W

W (*Wolfram*) tungsten
WA Washington, Western Australia
war warrant
W Aust Western Australia
WC water closet, without charge
Wed Wednesday
WFTU World Federation of Trade Unions
WH watt-hour
WHA World Hockey Association
whf wharf
WHO World Health Organization
whr watt-hour
whs *or* **whse** warehouse
whsle wholesale
wi when issued
WI West Indies, Wisconsin
WIA wounded in action
wid widow, widower
wk week, work
wkly weekly
WL waterline, wavelength
WNW west-northwest
WO warrant officer

w/o without
W/O water-in-oil
WOC without compensation
WP without prejudice
WPM words per minute
wpn weapon
WR warehouse receipt
WRAC Women's Royal Army Corps
WRAF Women's Royal Air Force
WRNS Women's Royal Naval Service
wrnt warrant
WSW west-southwest
wt weight
WT watertight, wireless telegraphy
WV *or* **W Va** West Virginia
WVS Women's Voluntary Services
WW warehouse warrant, with warrants, world war
w/w wall-to-wall
Wy *or* **Wyo** Wyoming

X

x cross, ex, experimental, extra
XC ex coupon
XD *or* **x div** ex dividend
Xe xenon
XI *or* **x in** *or* **x int** ex interest
XL extra large, extra long

Y

y yard, year, yen
Y ytrium
Yb ytterbium
YB yearbook
yd yard
YO year old
YOB year of birth
yr year, younger, your
yrbk yearbook
Yug Yugoslavia

Z

z zero, zone
Zn zinc
ZPG zero population growth

Phrases and Quotations from Latin, Greek and Modern Foreign Languages

A

abiit, excessit, evasit, erupit (L.) he is gone, he is off, he has escaped, he has broken away. — Cicero, *In Catilinam*, II. i. 1.

ab imo pectore (L.) from the bottom of the heart.

à bon chat, bon rat (Fr.) to a good cat, a good rat — well matched: set a thief to catch a thief.

ab ovo usque ad mala (L.) from the egg to the apples — of a Roman banquet: from the beginning to the end.

absens haeres non erit (L.) the absent one will not be the heir — out of sight, out of mind.

ab uno disce omnes (L.) from one (offense) learn all (the race). — Virgil, *Aen.*, I. 65–66: hence, from one example you may know the rest.

abusus non tollit usum (L.) abuse does not do away with use — i.e. an abuse is not a reason for giving up the legitimate use of a thing.

a capite ad calcem (L.) from head to heel.

à chacun son goût (Fr.) to everyone his own taste. See also **chacun (à) son goût**.

à chaque saint sa chandelle (Fr.) every saint his candle: to every patron his meed of service.

Acherontis pabulum (L.) food for Acheron — of a bad person. — Plautus, *Casina*, II. i. 12.

actum est de republica (L.) it is all up with the state.

actum ne agas (L.) do not do what is already done — quoted as a proverb by Terence, *Phormio.*, II. iii. 72 (or 1. 419).

ad Calendas Graecas (L.) at the Greek Calends — i.e. never, as the Greeks had no Calends.

adhuc sub judice lis est (L.) the dispute is still before the court. — Horace, *A.P.*, 78.

ad majorem Dei gloriam (L.) for the greater glory of God — the Jesuit motto.

adscriptus glebae (L.) bound to the soil — of serfs.

ad utrumque paratus (L.) prepared for either case.

ad vitam aut culpam (L.) for life or till fault: of appointments, for life unless misconduct necessitates dismissal.

advocatus diaboli (L.) devil's advocate. See Dict.

aequam memento rebus in arduis servare mentem (L.) remember to keep a calm mind in difficulties. — Horace, *Od.*, II. iii. 1.

aequitas sequitur legem (L.) equity follows law.

age quod agis (L.) do what you are doing — i.e. with all your powers.

aide-toi, le ciel t'aidera (Fr.) help yourself and Heaven will help you.

aliquando bonus dormitat Homerus (L.) See **indignor**.

aliquid haeret (L.) something sticks.

Allah il Allah, a corr. of Ar. *laa ilaaha illaa 'llaah* = there is no God but the God.

Allahu akbar (Ar.) God is great.

alter ipse amicus (L.) a friend is another self.

amabilis insania (L.) a pleasing madness or rapture. — Horace, *Od.*, III. 4. 5–6.

amantium irae amoris integratio est (L.) lovers' quarrels are a renewal of love. — Terence, *Andr.*, III. iii. 23.

amare et sapere vix deo conceditur (L.) to be in love and to be wise is scarce granted even to a god. — Laberius.

amari aliquid (L.) some touch of bitterness. — Lucretius, *De Rer. Nat.*, iv. 1130.

a mensa et toro (L.) from bed and board.

amicus Plato, amicus Socrates, sed magis amica veritas (L.) Plato is dear to me (or is my friend), Socrates is dear, but truth is dearer still. — L. version of saying attributed to Aristotle.

amicus usque ad aras (L.) a friend as far as the altars — i.e. as far as may be without offense to the gods.

amor sceleratus habendi (L.) the accursed love of possessing. — Ovid, *Met.*, I. 131.

amor vincit omnia (L.). See **omnia**.

anathema sit (L.) let him be accursed. — 1 Cor. xvi. 22.

anch' io son pittore (It.) I, too, am a painter (said by Correggio on looking at Raphael's 'St Cecilia').

anearithmon gelasma. See **kymatoan anearithmon gelasma**.

anguis in herba (L.) a snake in the grass. — Virgil, *Ecl.*, III. 93.

anima naturaliter Christiana (L.) a soul naturally Christian, i.e. one who behaves like a Christian without the benefit of Christian revelation. — Tertullian, *Apologia*, xvii.

animula vagula (L.) little soul flitting away — beginning of a poem ascribed to the dying Hadrian, translated or paraphrased by Prior, Pope, Byron, and Dean Merivale.

à nos moutons. See **revenons**.

ante Agamemnona. See **vixere fortes**.

a parte ante (L.) on the side before, from past eternity — opp. to **a parte post**, in future eternity.

a posse ad esse (L.) from the possible to the actual. **après moi (nous) le déluge** (Fr.) after me (us) the deluge: then the deluge may come when it likes — attributed to Mme. de Pompadour and to Louis XV. Cf. **emou thanontos**.

aquila non capit muscas (L.) an eagle does not catch flies.

arbiter elegantiae (L.) judge of good taste — said by Tacitus, *Annals*, XVI. 18, of Gaius Petronius, an exquisite at the court of Nero (prob. same as Petronius Arbiter). — Also quoted as **arbiter elegantiarum**.

Arcades ambo (L.) Arcadians both: two of the same stamp. — Virgil, *Ecl.*, VII. 4. — Rendered by Byron blackguards both, *Don Juan*, IV. xciii.

ariston men hydoar (Gr.) water is best. — Pindar, *Olympian Odes*, i. 1.

ars est celare artem (L.) true art is to conceal art.

ars longa, vita brevis (L.) art is long, life is short. — Seneca, *De Brevitate Vitae*, 1. Cf. **ho bios brachys**.

asbestos geloas (Gr.) inextinguishable laughter. — Homer, *Iliad*, I. 599, etc.

asinus ad lyram (L.) an ass at the lyre, one ignorant of music or art: one unsuited to an occupation. — From a Greek proverbial expression *onos pros lyran*.

astra castra, numen lumen (L.) the stars my camp, God my lamp.

Athanasius contra mundum (L.) Athanasius against the world: one resolute man facing universal opposition.

atra cura (L.) black care. See **post equitem**.

at spes non fracta (L.) but hope is not yet crushed.

au bout de son latin (Fr.) at the end of his Latin, at the end of his knowledge, at his wits' end.

auctor quae pretiosa facit (L.) gifts that the giver adds value to. — Ovid, *Her.*, XVII. 71–2.

audentes fortuna Juvat (L.) fortune favors the daring. — Virgil, *Aen.*, X. 284.

audi alteram partem (L.) hear the other side. — St Augustine, *De Duabus Animabus*, XIV. 2.

auditque vocatus Apollo (L.) and Apollo hears when invoked. — Virgil, *Georg.*, IV. 7.

aufgeschoben ist nicht aufgehoben (Ger.) put off is not given up.

aujourd'hui roi, demain rien (Fr.) king today, nothing tomorrow.

au plaisir de vous revoir (Fr.) till I have the pleasure of seeing you again.

auribus teneo lupum (L.) I am holding a wolf by the ears. — Terence, *Phormio*, III. ii. 21.

auri sacra fames (L.) accursed hunger for gold. — Virgil, *Aen.*, III. 57.

au royaume des aveugles les borgnes sont rois (Fr.) in the kingdom of the blind the one-eyed are kings. — As a Latin proverb, *beati monoculi in regione caecorum*.

aurum omnes, victa jam pietate, colunt (L.) all worship gold, piety being overthrown. — Propertius, III. xiii. 48.

auspicium melioris aevi (L.) augury of a better age.

aussitôt dit, aussitôt fait (Fr.) no sooner said than done.

Austriae est imperare orbi universo (L.) it is Austria's part to command the whole world — often **A.E.I.O.U.**

aut amat aut odit mulier, nihil est tertium (L.) a woman either loves or hates, there is no third course. — Syrus, 42.

autant d'hommes (or **de têtes**), **autant d'avis** (Fr.) so many men, so many minds. Cf. **quot homines**.

aut Caesar aut nullus, or **nihil** (L.) either Caesar or nobody (nothing): all or nothing.

aut insanit homo aut versus facit (L.) either the man is mad or he is making verses. — Horace, *Sat.*, II. vii. 117.

aut inveniam viam aut faciam (L.) I shall either find a way or make one.

aut non tentaris aut perfice (L.) either do not attempt or else achieve. — Ovid, *A.A.*, I. 389.

aut prodesse volunt aut delectare poetae (L.) poets seek either to profit or to please. — Horace, *A.P.*, 333.

aut regem aut fatuum nasci oportet (L.) one should be born either king or fool. — Proverb; quoted by Seneca.

autres temps, autres mœurs (Fr.) other times, other manners.

aut vincere aut mori (L.) to conquer or die.

aut vitam aut culpam. An incorrect variant of **ad vitam aut culpam** (q.v.).

aux absents les os (Fr.) the bones to the absent.

aux grands maux les grands remèdes (Fr.) to desperate evils, desperate remedies.

auxilium ab alto (L.) help from on high.

ave, Caesar (or **imperator**), **morituri te salutant** (L.) hail, Caesar, men doomed to die salute thee (said by gladiators).

a verbis ad verbera (L.) from words to blows.

à vieux comptes nouvelles disputes (Fr.) old accounts breed new disputes.

a vinculo matrimonii (L.) from the bond of matrimony.

avi numerantur avorum (L.) ancestors of ancestors are counted [to me].

avis au lecteur (Fr.) notice to the reader.

avise la fin (Fr.) weigh well the end.

avito viret honore (L.) he is green with ancestral honours.

avoir la langue déliée (Fr.) to have the tongue unbound, to be glib of speech.

B

barba tenus sapientes (L.) sages as far as the beard — i.e. with an appearance of wisdom only.

battre la campagne (Fr.) to scour the country, to beat the bush.

bayer aux corneilles (Fr.) to gape at the crows, to stare vacantly.

beatus ille qui procul negotiis . . . paterna rura bobus exercet suis (L.) happy he who, far removed from business . . . tills with his own oxen the fields that were his father's.— Horace, *Epod.*, ii. 1.

bella gerant alii, tu, felix Austria, nube (L.) let others wage wars; do thou, lucky Austria, make marriages. — Matthias Corvinus of Hungary.

bella, horrida bella (L.) wars, horrid wars. — Virgil, *Aen.*, VI. 86.

bellaque matribus detestata (L.) and wars abhorred by mothers. — Horace, *Od.*, I. i. 24–5.

bellum nec timendum nec provacandum (L.) war is neither to be feared nor provoked (Pliny the Younger, *Panegyricus*, 16, **nec times bellum, nec provocas**).

belua multorum capitum (L.) monster with many heads— the irrational mob. — Horace, *Epistolae*, I. i. 76.

beneficium accipere libertatem est vendere (L.) to accept a favor is to sell one's liberty. — Syrus, 49.

bene orasse est bene studuisse (L.) to have prayed well is to have endeavored well.

bene qui latuit bene vixit (L.) he has lived well who has lived obscure. — Ovid, *Trist.*, III. iv. 25.

benigno numine (l.) with favoring godhead. — Horace, *Od.*, III. iv. 74.

bibere venenum in auro (L.) to drink poison from a cup of gold.

biblia abiblia (Gr.) books that are no books.

bis dat qui cito dat (L.) he gives twice who gives promptly. — Proverb; by Bacon.

bis peccare in bello non licet (L.) in war one may not blunder twice.

bis pueri senes (L.) old men are twice boys.

blandae mendacia linguae (L.) falsehoods of a smooth tongue.

bon avocat, mauvais voisin (Fr.) a good lawyer is a bad neighbor.

bon jour, bonne œuvre (Fr.) better day, better deed.

bonnes nouvelles adoucissent le sang (Fr.) good news sweetens the blood.

borgen macht sorgen (Ger.) borrowing makes sorrowing.

boutez en avant (Fr.) push forward.

brevis esse laboro, obscurus fio (L.) I labor to be brief, and I become obscure. — Horace, *A.P.*, 25–26.

briller par son absence (Fr.) to be conspicuous by its absence.

brûler la chandelle par les deux bouts (Fr.) to burn the candle at both ends.

buen principio, la mitad es hecha (Sp.) well begun is half-done.

C

cadit quaestio (L.) the question drops.

caeca invidia est (L.) envy is blind. — Livy, xxxviii. 49.

caelebs quid agam (L.) (you wonder) what I, a bachelor, am about. — Horace, *Od.*, III. viii. 1.

caelum non animum mutant qui trans mare currunt (L.) they change their sky, not their mind, who scour across the sea. — Horace, *Epist.*, I. xi. 27.

Caesar non supra grammaticos (L.) Caesar has no authority over the grammarians.

ça ira (Fr.) it will go — refrain of a famous song of the French Revolution.

callida junctura (L.) a skilful connection. — Horace, *A.P.*, 47–48.

candida Pax (L.) white-robed Peace. — Tibullus, I. x. 45.

cantabit vacuus coram latrone viator (L.) the empty-handed traveler will sing in presence of the robber. — Juvenal, X. 22.

carent quia vate sacro (L.) because they lack a sacred bard. — Horace, *Od.*, IV. ix. 28.

carpe diem, quam minimum credula postero (L.) enjoy the present day, trust the least possible to the future. — Horace, *Od.*, I. xi. 8.

causa sine qua non (L.) an indispensable cause.

cave quid dicis, quando, et cui (L.) beware what you say, when, and to whom.

cedant arma togae (L.) let arms yield to the gown: let military authority yield to civil. — Cicero, *De Officiis*, I. xxii. 77, *in Pisonem*, xxx. 73.

cela va sans dire (Fr.) that goes without saying: of course.

cela viendra (Fr.) that will come.

celui qui veut, peut (Fr.) who will, can.

ce monde est plein de fous (Fr.) this world is full of madmen.

c'en est fait de lui (Fr.) it is all up with him.

ce n'est que le premier pas qui coûte (Fr.). See **il n'ya. certum est quia impossibile est** (L.) it is certain because it is impossible. — Tertullian.

c'est-à-dire (Fr.) that is to say.

c'est égal (Fr.) it's all one (to me): it makes no odds.

c'est le commencement de la fin (Fr.) it is the beginning of the end. — Attrib. to Talleyrand.

c'est magnifique, mais ce n'est pas la guerre (Fr.) it is magnificent, but it is not war (said at Balaklava by a French general watching the charge of the Light Brigade).

c'est pire (or **plus**) **qu'un crime, c'est une faute** (Fr.) it is worse than a crime, it is a blunder (on the execution of the Duc d'Enghien; attributed to various persons, incl. Boulay de la Meurthe).

c'est selon (Fr.) that is according to the circumstances.

c'est (une) autre chose (Fr.) that is quite another thing.

ceterum censeo (L.) but I think (said of persistent obstruction like that of Cato).

chacun (à) son goût (Fr.) everyone to his taste. Also **à chacun son goût**.

chapeaux bas (Fr.) hats off.

cherchez la femme (Fr.) look for the woman: there's a woman at the bottom of it. — Dumas *père*.

che sarà sarà (It.) what will be will be.

chiesa libera in libero stato (It.) a free church in a free state (Cavour's ideal for Italy).

chi tace confessa (It.) who keeps silence, confesses.

circulus in probando (L.) arguing in a circle, using the conclusion as one of the arguments.

civis Romanus sum (L.) I am a Roman citizen. — Cicero, *In Verrem*, VI. 57.

clarior e tenebris (L.) the brighter from the darkness.

clarum et venerabile nomen (L.) an illustrious and venerable name. — Lucan, IX. 202.

cogito, ergo sum (L.) I think, therefore I am. (Descartes's fundamental basis of philosophy.)

comitas inter gentes, or **comitas gentium** (L.) See **comity** in Dict.

conditio sine qua non (L.) an indispensable condition.

conjunctis viribus (L.) with united powers.

conquiescat in pace (L.) may he [or she] rest in peace.

conscia mens recti (L.) a mind conscious of rectitude. — Ovid, *Fast.*, IV. 311. Cf. **mens sibi**.

consensus facit legem (L.) consent makes law or rule.

consuetudo pro lege servatur (L.) custom is held as a law.

consule Planco (L.) when Plancus was consul, when I was a young man. — Horace, *Od.*, III. xiv. 28.

contraria contrariis curantur (L.) opposites are cured by opposites.

corruptio optimi pessima (L.) the corruption of the best is the worst of all.

cosi fan tutte (It.) so do they all (of women): they are all like that.

coûte que coûte (Fr.) cost what it may.

crambe repetita (L.) cauld kale het again — cold cabbage warmed up. — Juvenal, VII. 154.

credat Judaeus Apella, non ego (L.) let the Jew Apella believe that, for I don't. — Horace, *Sat.*, I. v. 100.

credo quia absurdum (L.) I believe it because it is absurd; — **quia impossibile** because it is impossible (based on Tertullian; see **certum est quia impossibile est**).

crescit eundo (L.) it grows as it goes. — Lucretius VI. 341.

cucullus non facit monachum (L.) the cowl does not make the monk.

cuilibet (or **cuicunque**) **in arte sua** (**perito**) **credendum est** (L.) every (skilled) person is to be trusted in his own art. — Coke.

cujus regio, ejus religio (L.) whose the region, his the religion — the principle that the established religion should be that of the prince in each state.

curiosa felicitas (L.) studied felicity of expression — said by Petronius Arbiter, *Saturae* (*Satyricon*), 118, 5 of Horace's style: (*loosely*) curious felicity.

D

da dextram misero (L.) give the right hand to the unhappy.

da locum melioribus (L.) give place to your betters. — Terence, *Phormio*, III. ii. 37.

damnosa haereditas (L.) an inheritance of debts (*Roman law*): any hurtful inheritance. — Gaius, *Institutes*, ii. 163.

damnum absque injuria (L.) loss without legal injury.

das Ding an sich (Ger.) the thing in itself.

das Ewig-Weibliche zieht uns hinan (Ger.) the eternal feminine draws us upward. — Goethe, *Faust*, at end.

data et accepta (L.) expenditures and receipts.

date obolum Belisario (L.) give a penny to Belisarius (ascribed to the great general when reduced to beggary).

Davus sum, non Oedipus (L.) I am Davus, not Oedipus — no good at riddles. — Terence, *Andria.*, I. ii. 23.

de die in diem (L.) from day to day.

de gustibus non est disputandum (L.) there is no disputing about tastes.

de l'audace, encore de l'audace, et toujours de l'audace (Fr.) to dare, still to dare, and ever to dare (Danton's famous phrase).

delenda est Carthago (L.) Carthage must be wiped out (a saying constantly repeated by Cato).

de mal en pis (Fr.) from bad to worse.

de minimis non curat lex (L.) the law does not concern itself about very small matters. — Bacon, Letter cclxxxii.

de mortuis nil nisi bonum (L.) say nothing but good of the dead.

de nihilo nihilum. See **gigni**.

de omni re scibili et quibusdam aliis (L.) about all things knowable, and some others.

de pis en pis (Fr.) worse and worse.

der grosse Heide (Ger.) the great pagan (Heine's name for Goethe).

desipire in loco. See **dulce**.

desunt cetera (L.) the rest is wanting.

de te fabula narratur (L.) the story is about you. — Horace, *Sat.*, I. i. 69–70.

detur digniori (L.) let it be given to the more worthy; **detur pulchriori** let it be given to the fairer.

deus nobis haec otia fecit (L.) it is a god that hath given us this ease. — Virgil, *Ecl.*, I. 6.

dicamus bona verba (L.) let us speak words of good omen. — Tibullus, II, ii. 1.

Dichtung und Wahrheit (Ger.) poetry and truth.

dictum de dicto (L.) hearsay report.

dictum sapienti sat est (L.) a word to the wise is enough (usu. quoted as **verbum**). — Plautus, *Persa*, IV. vii. 19.

diem perdidi (L.) I have lost a day (said by the Emperor Titus). **Dieu défend le droit** (Fr.) God defends the right; **Dieu vous garde** God keep you.

Die Wacht am Rhein (Ger.) the Watch on the Rhine (a famous German patriotic song).

digito monstrari (L.) to be pointed out with the finger: to be famous. — Persius, I. 28.

dignus vindice nodus (L.) See **nec deus intersit**.

di grado in grado (It.) by degrees.

dis aliter visum (L.) the gods have adjudged otherwise. — Virgil, *Aen.*, II. 428.

disjecta membra (L.) scattered limbs (after Ovid, *Met.*, III. 724); **disjecti membra poetae** limbs of the dismembered poet. — Horace, *Sat.*, I. iv. 62.

distinguo (L.) I distinguish.

divide et impera (L.) divide and rule.

docendo discimus (L.) we learn by teaching.

doctor utriusque legis (L.) doctor of both laws (civil and canon).

doli capax (L.) capable of committing a wrong — opp. to *doli incapax*.

Domine. dirige nos (L.) Lord, direct us (the motto of London).

Dominus illuminatio mea (L.) the Lord is my light.

domus et placens uxor (L.) a home and a pleasing wife. — Horace, *Od.*, II. xiv. 21–22.

dorer la pilule (Fr.) to gild the pill.

dormitat Homerus (L.) See **indignor**.

dos moi pou stoa kai tean gean kineasoa (Gr.) give me where to stand, and I will move the earth (attributed to Archimedes).

do ut des (L.) I give that you may give.

dulce, 'Domum' (L.) sweet strain, 'Homeward' — from a Winchester school song sung before the holidays; **dulce est desipire in loco** it is pleasant to play the fool on occasion. — Horace, *Od.*, IV. xii. 28; **dulce et decorum est pro patria mori** it is sweet and glorious to die for one's country. — Horace, *Od.*, III. ii. 13.

dum casta (L.) while (she is) chaste.

dum spiro, spero (L.) while I breathe, I hope.

dum vivimus, vivamus (L.) let us live while we live.

dux femina facti (L.) a woman was leader in the deed. — Virgil, *Aen.*, I. 364.

E

écrasez l'infâme (Fr.) crush the vile thing. Voltaire against the Roman Catholic Church of his time.

edax rerum. See **tempus**.

ego et rex meus (L.) I and my kng. — Cardinal Wolsey.

ebeu fugaces ... labuntur anni (L.) alas! the fleeting years slip away. — Horace, *Od.*, II. xiv. 1–2.

eile mit Weile (Ger.) make speed with leisure. Cf. **festina lente**.

ein Mal, kein Mal (Ger.) just once counts nothing.

ek parergou (Gr.) as a by-work.

eali, eali, lama sabachthani (Matt. xxvii. 46), **Eloi, Eloi, lamma sabachthani** (Mark xv. 34) (Gr. transliterations of Aramic) my God, my God, why hast thou forsaken mc?

emou thanontos gaia michtheatoa pyri (Gr.) when I am dead let earth be mingled with fire. Cf. **après moi le déluge**.

entbehren sollst du, sollst entbehren (Ger.) thou must abstain, abstain thou must. — Goethe, *Faust*, Part I. (Studierzimmer, ii).

en toutoai nika (Gr.) conquer in this (sign). See **in hoc (signo) vinces**.

epea pteroenta (Gr.) winged words. — Homer (*Iliad*, I, 201, etc.).

ephphatha (Aramaic) be opened (Mark vii. 34).

e pluribus unum (L.) one out of many — before 1956 regarded as motto of the United States.

eppur si muove (It.) it does move all the same (attrib. to Galileo after he had recanted his doctrine that the earth moves round the sun).

erectos ad sidera tollere vultus (L.). See **os homini**.

ergo bibamus (L.) therefore let us drink.

Erin go bragh (Ir.) Erin forever.

errare est humanum (L.) to err is human.

es korakas (Gr.) to the ravens: go and be hanged.

esse quam videri (L.) to be, rather than to seem.

est modus in rebus (L.) there is a mean in (all) things. — Horace, *Sat.*, I. i. 106.

esto perpetua (L.) be lasting.

est quaedam flere voluptas (L.) there is in weeping a certain pleasure. — Ovid, *Trist.*, IV. iii. 37.

et hoc (or **id**) **genus omne** (L.) and all that sort of thing.

et in Arcadia ego (L.) I, too, lived in Arcadia. (Inscription from tomb, used in Poussin's picture 'The Arcadian Shepherds').

et tu, Brute (L.) you too, Brutus. (Caesar's alleged exclamation when he saw Brutus amongst his assassins.)

eventus stultorum magister (L.) the outcome is the schoolmaster of fools. — Livy, XXII, 39.

ex abusu non arguitur ad usum (L.) from the abuse no argument is drawn against the use. Cf. **abusus non**.

exceptio confirmat (or **probat**) **regulam** (L.) the exception proves the rule. (See **except** in Dict.)

exegi monumentum aere perennius (L.) I have reared a monument more lasting than brass. — Horace, *Od.*, III. xxx. 1.

exempla sunt odiosa (L.) examples are hateful.

exitus acta probat (L.) the outcome justifies the deed. — Ovid, *Her.*, II. 85.

ex nihilo (or **nilo**) **nihil** (or **nil**) **fit** (L.) out of nothing nothing comes. See **gigni**.

ex pede Herculem (L.) (we recognise) Hercules from his foot.

experientia docet stultos (L.) experience teaches fools.

experto crede, or (Virgil, *Aen.*, XI. 283) **credite** (L.) trust one who has tried, or had experience.

expertus metuet, or **metuit** (L.) he who has experienced it will fear (or fears). — Horace, *Epist.*, I. xviii, 87.

exstinctus amabitur idem (L.) the same man (maligned living) when dead will be loved. — Horace, *Epist.*, II. i. 14.

ex ungue leonem (L.) (judge, or infer) the lion from his claws.

F

faber est quisque fortunae suae (L.) every man is the fashioner of his own fortunes. — Proverb quoted by Sallust, *De Republica*. I.

fable convenue (Fr.) fable agreed upon — Voltaire's name for history.

facile est inventis addere (L.) it is easy to add to things invented already.

facilis descensus Averno, or **Averni** (L.) descent to Avernus is easy. — Virgil, *Aen.*, VI. 126.

facinus majoris abollae (L.) the crime of a larger cloak, i.e. of a philosopher. — Juvenal, III. 115.

facit indignatio versum (L.) indignation makes verse. — Juvenal. I. 79.

facta non verba (L.) deeds, not words.

factum est (L.) it is done.

facundi. See **fecundi**.

faire bonne mine (Fr.) to put a good face on the matter.

falsus in uno, falsus in omnibus (L.) false in one thing, false in all.

fama nihil est celerius (L.) nothing is swifter than rumour. — Livy.

fama semper vivat (L.) may his (or her) fame live for ever.

far niente (It.) doing nothing.

farrago libelli. See **quicquid**.

fas est et ab hoste doceri (L.) it is right to learn even from an enemy. — Ovid, *Met.*, IV. 428.

Fata obstant (L.) the Fates oppose. — Virgil, *Aen.*, IV. 440.

Fata viam invenient (L.) the Fates will find out a way. — Virgil, *Aen.*, X. 113.

favete linguis (L.) favor me with your tongues — keep silent to avoid ill omen. — Horace, *Od.*, III. i. 2.

fecundi (or **facundi**) **calices quem non fecere disertum**? (L.) whom have not full cups made eloquent? — Horace, *Epist.*, I. v. 19.

felicitas multos habet amicos (L.) prosperity has many friends.

felix qui potuit rerum congnoscere causas (L.) happy is he who has been able to understand the causes of things. — Virgil, *Georg.*, II. 490.

fendre un cheveu en quatre (Fr.) to split a hair in four.

fenum (or **foenum**) **habet in cornu** (L.) he has hay on his horn (sign of a dangerous bull). — Horace, *Sat.*, I. iv. 34.

festina lente (L.) hasten gently.

fiat experimentum in corpore vili (L.) let experiment be made on a worthless body.

fiat justitia, ruat caelum (L.) let justice be done, though the heavens should fall.

fiat lux (L.) let there be light.

fide, sed cui vide (L.) trust, but take care in whom.

fidus Achates (L.) faithful Achates (friend of Aeneas): hence, a close friend. — Virgil.

finem respice (L.) See **respice finem**.

finis coronat opus (L.) the end crowns the work.

fin mot de l'affaire (Fr.) the bottom of the matter, the explanation.

flectere si nequeo superos, Acheronta movebo (L.) if I can't move the gods, I'll stir up hell. — Virgil, *Aen.*, VII. 312.

foenum. See **fenum**.

forsan et haec olim meminisse juvabit (L.) perhaps some day we shall like to remember even these things. — Virgil, *Aen.*, I. 203.

Fors Clavigera (L.) Fortune the club-bearer (used as a title by Ruskin).

fortes Fortuna adjuvat (L.) Fortune helps the brave (Terence, *Phorm.*, I. iv. 26): **forti et fideli nihil difficile** to the brave and faithful nothing is difficult; **fortis cadere, cedere non potest** the brave man may fall, he cannot yield.

fortiter in re, suaviter in modo (L.). See **suaviter**.

Fortuna favet fatuis (L.) Fortune favors fools; **Fortuna favet fortibus** Fortune favors the bold.

frangas, non flectes (L.) you may break, you shall not bend.

fraus est celare fraudem (L.) it is a fraud to conceal a fraud.

frontis nulla fides (L.) no reliance on the face, no trusting appearances. — Juvenal, II. 8.
fruges consumere nati (L.) born to consume the fruits of the soil. — Horace, *Epist.*, I. ii. 27.
fugit hora (L.) the hour flies. — Persius, V. 153.
fuimus Troes; fuit Ilium (L.) we were Trojans; Troy was. — Virgil, *Aen.*, II. 325.
fulmen brutum (L.) a harmless thunderbolt.
furor arma ministrat (L.) rage supplies arms. — Virgil, *Aen.*, I. 150.

G

gaudet tentamine virtus (L.) virtue rejoices in trial.
geflügelte Worte (Ger.) winged words. See **epea**.
genus irritabile vatum (L.) the irritable tribe of poets. — Horace, *Epist.*, II. ii. 102.
gibier de potence (Fr.) gallows-bird.
gigni de nihilo nihilum, in nihilum nil posse reverti (L.) from nothing nothing can come, into nothing nothing can return. — Persius, III. 84.
giovine santo, diavolo vecchio (It.) young saint, old devil.
gli assenti hanno torto (It.) the absent are in the wrong.
gloria virtutis umbra (L.) glory (is) the shadow of virtue.
glückliche Reise (Ger.) prosperous journey to you.
gnoathi seauton (Gr.) know thyself.— Inscribed on the temple of Apollo at Delphi. See also **nosce teipsum**.
Gott mit uns (Ger.) God with us — Hohenzollern motto.
gradu diverso, via una (L.) with different step on the one way.
gradus ad Parnassum (L.) a step, or stairs, to Parnassus, a Latin or Greek poetical dictionary.
Graeculus esuriens (L.) the hungry Greekling. — Juvenal III. 78.
Graecum est: non legitur (L.) this is Greek; it is not read (placed against a Greek word in mediaeval MSS, a permission to skip the hard words).
grande chère et beau feu (Fr.) ample cheer and a fine fire; **grande fortune, grande servitude** great wealth, great slavery.
gratia placendi (L.) the delight of pleasing.
graviora manent (L.) greater dangers remain (Virgil, *Aen.*, VI. 84); **graviora quaedam sunt remedia periculis** some remedies are more grievous than the perils (Syrus).
gravis ira regum est semper (L.) the anger of kings is always serious.
grosse Seelen dulden still (Ger.) great souls suffer in silence. — Schiller, *Don Carlos*, I. iv., end of scene.
grosse tête et peu de sens (Fr.) big head and little wit.
gutta cavat lapidem (L.) the drop wears away the stone. — Ovid, *Pont.*, IV. x. 5.

H

habendum et tenendum (L.) to have and to hold.
habent sua fata libelli (L.) books have their destinies. — Maurus, *De Litteris, Syllabis et Metris*. **hanc veniam petimusque damusque vicissim** (L.) this liberty we ask and grant in turn. — Horace, *A.P.*, 11.
Hannibal ad portas (L.) Hannibal at the gates. — Cicero, *Philippica*, I. v. 11.
haud longis intervallis (L.) at no long intervals.
helluo librorum (L.) a glutton of books.
heu pietas! heu prisca fides! (L.) alas for piety! alas for the ancient faith! — Virgil, *Aen.*, VI. 879.
hiatus valde deflendus (L.) a gap deeply to be deplored.
hic finis fandi (L.) here (was, or let there be) an end of the speaking.
hinc illae lacrumae (L.) hence [came] those tears. — Terence, *Andria*, I. i. 99; also Horace, *Epist.*, I. xix. 41.
hinc lucem et pocula sacra (L.) from this source [we draw] light and draughts of sacred learning.
ho bios brachys, hea de technea makrea (Gr.) life is short and art is long. — Attributed to Hippocrates.
hoc age (L.) this do.
hoc erat in votis (L.) this was the very thing I prayed for. — Horace, *Sat.*, II. vi. 1.
hoc opus, hic labor est (L.) this is the toil, this the labor. — Virgil, *Aen.*, VI. 129.
hoc saxum posuit (L.) placed this stone.
hoc (or **sic**) **volo, sic jubeo, sit pro ratione voluntas** (L.) this (thus) I will, thus I command, be my will sufficient reason. — Juvenal, VI. 223.
hodie mihi, cras tibi (L.) me today, you tomorrow.
hominibus plenum, amicis vacuum (L.) full of men, empty of friends.

hominis est errare (L.) it belongs to man to err.

homo alieni juris (L.) one under control of another; **homo antiqua virtute ac fide** a man of the antique virtue and loyalty (Terence, *Adelphi*, III. iii. 88 or 1. 442); **homo homini lupus** man is a wolf to man; **homo multarum literarum** a man of many literary accomplishments; **homo mullius coloris** a man of no color, one who does not commit himself; **homo sui juris** one who is his own master; **homo sum: humani nihil a me alienum puto** I am a man: I count nothing human indifferent to me (Terence, *Heaut.*, I. i. 25); **homo trium litterarum** man of three letters — i.e. *fur* = thief; **homo unius libri** a man of one book.

hon hoi theoi philousi apothneaskei neos (Gr.) whom the gods love dies young. — Menander. Cf. **quem di diligunt . . .**

honi soit qui mal y pense (O.Fr.) the shame be his who thinks ill of it — the motto of the Order of the Garter.

honneur et patrie (Fr.) honor and native land.

honores mutant mores (L.) honors change manners.

honor virtutis praemium (L.) honor is the reward of virtue.

honos alit artes (L.) honor nourishes the arts (Cicero, *Tusculanae Disputationes*, I. ii. 4); **honos habet onus** honor has its burden.

hora fugit (L.) the hour flies.

horas non numero nisi serenas (L.) I number none but shining hours. [Common on sundials.]

horresco referens (L.) I shudder in relating. — Virgil, *Aen.*, II, 204.

horribile dictu (L.) horrible to relate.

hostis honori invidia (L.) envy is an enemy to honor; **hostis humani generis** enemy of the human race.

humanum est errare (L.) to err is human.

hurtar para dar por Dios (Sp.) to steal in order to give to God.

hypage Satana (Gr.) away Satan. — Matt. iv. 10. **hypotheses non fingo** (L.) I do not frame hypotheses (i.e. unverifiable speculations). — Newton.

I

ich dien (Ger.) I serve.

ici on parle français (Fr.) here French is spoken.

idem velle atque idem nolle ea demum firma amicitia est (L.) to like and dislike the same things is indeed true friendship. — Sallust, *Catalina*, 20.

Iesus Hominum Salvator (L.) Jesus, Saviour of men.

ignorantia legis neminem excusat (L.) ignorance of the law excuses nobody.

ignoti nulla cupido (L.) for a thing unknown there is no desire. — Ovid, *A.A.*, III. 397.

ignotum per ignotius (L.) the unknown by the still more unknown.

i gran dolori sono muti (It.) great griefs are mute.

il a inventé l'histoire (Fr.) he has invented history.

il a le diable au corps (Fr.) the devil is in him: he is full of devilment, or of vivacity, wit, enthusiasm, etc.: he can't sit still.

il a les défauts de ses qualités (Fr.) he has the defects that answer to his good qualities.

il faut de l'argent (Fr.) money is necessary.

il faut laver son linge sale en famille (Fr.) one should wash one's dirty linen in private.

il gran rifiuto (It.) the great refusal (the abdication of Pope Celestine V). — Dante, *Inferno*, III. 60.

Ilias malorum (L.) an Iliad of woes.

ille crucem sceleris pretium tulit, hic diadema (L.) that man got a cross, this man a crown, as the price of his crime. — Juvenal, XIII. 105.

ille terrarum mihi praeter omnes angulus ridet (L.) that corner of the earth to me smiles sweetest of all. — Horace, *Od.*, II. vi. 13–14.

il meglio è l'inimico del bene (It.) the better is the enemy of the good.

il n'y a pas à dire (Fr.) there is nothing to be said.

il n'y a que le premier pas qui coûte (Fr.) it is only the first step that counts. (Mme du Deffand on St Denis walking after decapitation.)

ils n'ont rien appris ni rien oublié (Fr.) they have learned nothing and forgotten nothing [said of the French *Émigrés*, often of the Bourbons].

impar congressus Achilli (L.) unequally matched against Achilles. — Virgil, *Aen.*, I. 475.

incedis per ignis suppositos cineri doloso (L.) you walk on fires covered with treacherous ash. — Horace, *Od.*, II. i. 7–8.

incidis in Scyllam cupiens vitare Charybdim (L.) you fall into Scylla trying to avoid Charybdis. — Philip Gaultier de Lille.

incredulus odi (L.) I hate and disbelieve. — Horace, *A.P.*, 188.

indignor quandoque bonus dormitat Homerus (L.) I am annoyed whenever good Homer slumbers. — Horace, *A.P.*, 359. Usually cited as **aliquando** (=sometimes) **bonus**, etc.

infandum, regina, jubes renovare dolorem (L.) thou bidst me, queen, renew unspeakable woes. — Virgil, *Aen.*, II. 3.

in hoc (signo) vinces (L.) in this sign thou wilt conquer — i.e. in the Cross [the motto of Constantine the Great]. See **en toutoai nika**.

in magnis et voluisse sat est (L.) in great things even to have wished is enough. — Propertius, II. x. 6. **in meditatione fugae** (L.) in contemplation of flight.

inopen me copia fecit (L.) plenty has made me poor. — Ovid, *M.*, III. 466.

integer vitae scelerisque purus (L.) blameless in life and clear of offense. — Horace, *Od.*, I. xxii. 1.

inter arma silent leges (L.) amid wars laws are silent (Cicero).

interdum stultus bene loquitur (L.) sometimes a fool speaks a right.

invita Minerva (L.) against the will of Minerva: uninspired. — Horace, *A.P.*, 385.

ira furor brevis est (L.) rage is a brief madness. — Horace, *Epist.*, I. ii. 62.

Italia irredenta (It.) unredeemed Italy — the parts of Italy still under foreign domination after the war of 1866 — South Tirol, etc.

J

jacta est alea (L.) the die is cast (quoted as said by Caesar at the crossing of the Rubicon).

je n'en vois pas la nécessité (Fr.) I don't see the necessity for that [said by the Comte d'Argental in reply to a man who pleaded, 'But one must live somehow'].

joci causa (L.) for the joke.

judex damnatur cum nocens absolvitur (L.) the judge is condemned when the guilty is acquitted. — Syrus, 247.

Jup(p)iter optimus maximus (L.) Jupiter best and greatest; **Jup(p)iter Pluvius** rain-bringing Jupiter; **Jup(p)iter Tonans** Jupiter the thunderer.

justum et tenacem propositi virum (L.) a man upright and tenacious of purpose. — Horace, *Od.*, III. iii. 1.

j'y suis, j'y reste (Fr.) here I am, here I stay [said by Macmahon at the Malakoff].

K

kai ta leipomena, kai ta loipa (Gr.) and the rest: and so on.

kalos kagathos, kalokagathos (Gr.) good and honorable: a perfect gentleman.

kat' cxochean (Gr.) pre-eminently: *par excellence*.

keine Antwort is auch eine Antwort (Ger.) no answer is still an answer: silence gives consent.

Kirche, Küche, Kinder (Ger). church, kitchen, children — said, e.g. during the Nazi period, to be the proper interests of a German woman.

kteama es aei (Gr.) a possession for ever.

kymatoan anearithmon gelasma (Gr.) innumerable smiles of the waves. — Aeschylus, *Prom.*, 89–90.

L

laborare est orare (L.) work is prayer.

labore et honore (L.) by labor and honor.

labuntur et imputantur (L.) [the moments] slip away and are laid to our account (inscription on sundials). Also **pereunt et imputantor** (q.v.).

la donna è mobile (It.) woman is changeable.

la garde meurt et ne se rend pas (Fr.) the guard dies, it does not surrender.

la grande nation (Fr.) the great nation — i.e. France.

laa ilaaha illaa 'llaah (Ar.) there is no god but God.

langage des halles (Fr.) language of the market-place.

l'appétit vient en mangeant (Fr.) appetite comes as you eat.

la propriété c'est le vol (Fr.) property is theft [from Proudhon].

la reyne le veult (s'avisera) (Norm. Fr.). See **le roy**.

lasciate ogni speranza, voi che'ntrate (It.) abandon all hope ye who enter. — Dante, *Inferno*, III. 9. From the inscription over the gate of hell.

latet anguis in herba (L.) there is a snake hidden in the grass. — Virgil, *Ecl.*, III. 93.

laudator temporis acti (L.) one who praises past times. — Horace, *A.P.*, 173.

le génie n'est qu'une grande aptitude à la patience (Fr.) genius is merely a great aptitude for patience (attributed to Buffon).

le grand monarque (Fr.) the great king — i.e. Louis XIV.

le jeu ne vaut pas la chandelle (Fr.) the game is not worth the candle.

l'empire c'est la paix (Fr.) the empire means peace [said by Louis Napoleon in 1852].

le roy (or la reyne) le veult (Norm. Fr.) the king (or queen) wills it — form of royal assent.

le roy (la reyne) s'avisera (Norm. Fr.) the king (or queen) will deliberate — form of refusal.

le style est l'homme (même) (Fr.) the style is the man himself (from Buffon).

l'état, c'est moi (Fr.) I am the state [alleged to have been said by Louis XIV].

liberté, égalité, fraternité (Fr.) liberty, equality, fraternity — a slogan of the French Revolution.

limae labor (L.) the labor of the file, of polishing. — Horace, *A.P.*, 291.

littera scripta manet (L.) what is written down is permanent. See **vox audita**.

lucri causa (L.) for the sake of gain.

lucus a non lucendo (L.) the grove (*lucus*) (is so named) from its *not* shining (*lucendo*).

ludere cum sacris (L.) to trifle with sacred things.

l'union fait la force (Fr.) union makes strength.

lupus in fabula (L.) the wolf in the fable: talk of the devil. — Terence, *Adelphi.*, IV. i. 21.

M

macte virtute (L.) be honored in your valor, virtue — used by Cicero, Virgil, Livy (**macte virtute esto** — Cato to one coming out of a resort of vice, acc. to Horace, *Sat.*, I. ii. 31–32).

magna est veritas et praevalebit (L.) truth is great and will prevail (Vulgate, **et prevalet**).

magni nominis umbra (L.) the mere shadow of a mighty name. — Lucan, I. 135.

man spricht Deutsch (Ger.) German spoken here.

matre pulchra filia pulchrior (L.) a daughter fairer than her fair mother. — Horace, *Od.*, I. xvi. 1.

maxima debetur puero reverentia (L.) the greatest reverence is due to the boy — i.e. to the innocence of his age. — Juvenal, XIV, 47.

mea virtute me involvo (L.) I wrap myself in my virtue. — Horace, *Od.*, III. xxix. 54–55.

meaden agan (Gr.) [let there be] nothing in excess.

medio tutissimus ibis (L.) thou wilt go safest in the middle. — Ovid, *Met.*, II. 137.

mega biblion, mega kakon (Gr.) big book, great evil.

mea kinei Kamarinan (Gr.) do not stir up Kamarina (a pestilent marsh in Sicily): let well alone.

mens sana in corpore sano (L.) a sound mind in a sound body.— Juvenal, X. 356. **mens sibi conscia recti** (L.) a mind conscious of rectitude. — Virgil, *Aen.*, I. 604. Cf. **conscia mens recti**.

mirabile dictu (L.) wonderful to tell; **mirabile visu**, wonderful to see.

mole ruit sua (L.) falls by its own weight. — Horace, *Od.*, III. iv. 65.

monstrum horrendum, informe, ingens (L.) a frightful monster, ill-shapen, huge. — Virgil, *Aen.*, III. 658.

morituri te salutant. See **ave**.

muet comme un poisson (Fr.) dumb as a fish.

N

natura abhorret vacuum (L.) nature abhors a vacuum.

naturam expellas furca, tamen usque recurret (L.) though you drive out nature with a pitchfork, yet will she always return. — Horace, *Epist.*, I. x. 24.

natura non facit saltus (or **saltum**) (L.) nature does not make leaps (or a leap).

naviget Anticyram (L.) let him sail to Anticyra [where hellebore could be had, to cure madness]. — Horace, *Sat.*, II. iii. 166.

nec cupias, nec metuas (L.) neither desire nor fear.

nec deus intersit nisi dignus vindice nodus inciderit (L.) let not a god intervene unless a knot occur worthy of the untier. — Horace, *A.P.*, 191–2.

ne cede malis (L.) yield not to misfortune. — Virgil, *Aen.*, VI. 95.

necessitas non habet legem (L.) necessity has no law.

nec pluribus impar (L.) no unequal match for several (suns). — Louis XIV's motto.

nec scire fas est omnia (L.) it is not permitted to know all things. — Horace, *Od.*, IV. iv. 22.

ne exeat (L.) let him not depart.

negatur (L.) it is denied.

nemo me impune lacessit (L.) no one provokes me with impunity — the motto of the kings of Scotland and of the Order of the Thistle; **nemo repente fuit turpissimus** no one ever became utterly bad all at once. — Juvenal, II 83.

ne obliviscaris (L.) do not forget.

neque semper arcum tendit Apollo (L.) Apollo does not always bend his bow. — Horace, *Od.*, II. x. 19–20.

ne quid nimis (L.) [let there be] nothing in excess.

nescis, mi fili, quantilla prudentia mundus regatur (L.) you know not, my son, with what a small stock of wisdom the world is governed. — Attributed to Oxenstierna and others.

nescit vox missa reverti (L.) a word published cannot be recalled. — Horace, *A.P.*, 390.

n'est-ce-pas? (Fr.) is it not so?

ne sutor ultra crepidam (L.). See **sutor**.

ne temere (L.) not rashly — a papal decree of 1907 denying recognition to the marriage of a Catholic unless contracted before a priest.

nicht wahr? (Ger.) is it not true? isn't that so?

nihil tetigit quod non ornavit. See **nullum**.

nil actum credens dum quid superesset agendum (L.) thinking nothing done while anything was yet to do. — Lucan, II. 657; **nil admirari** to wonder at nothing. — Horace, *Epist.*, I. vi. 1; **nil desperandum** nothing is to be despaired of. — Horace, *Od.*, I. vii. 27.

n'importe (Fr.) no matter.

nisi Dominus frustra (L.) except the Lord (keep the city, the watchman waketh but) in vain. — Ps. cxxvii — the motto of Edinburgh.

nitor in adversum (L.) I strive in opposition. — Ovid, *Met.*, II. 72.

non amo te, Sabidi, nec possum dicere quare (L.) I do no love thee, Sabidius, nor can I tell you why. — Martial, I. xxxiii.

non compos mentis (L.) not of sound mind.

non est inventus (L.) he has not been found (he has absconded).

non licet (L.) it is not allowed.

non liquet (L.) it is not clear.

non mi ricordo (It.) I don't remember.

non multa, sed multum (L.) not many, but much.

non nobis, Domine (L.) not unto us, O Lord. — Psalm cxv.

non olet pecunia (L.) the money does not stink. — Attributed to Vespasian, of revenue from an unsavoury source.

non omnia possumus omnes (L.) we cannot all do everything. — Virgil, *Ecl.*, viii. 63.

non omnis moriar (L.) I shall not wholly die. — Horace, *Od.*, III. xxx. 6.

non placet (L.) it does not please — a negative vote.

non possumus (L.) we cannot — a form of refusal.

non tali auxilio nec defensoribus istis tempus eget (L.) not for such aid nor for these defenders does the time call. — Virgil, *Aen.*, II. 521.

nonumque prematur in annum (L.) and let it be kept unpublished till the ninth year. — Horace, *A.P.*, 388.

non ut edam vivo sed ut vivam edo (L.) I do not live to eat, but eat to live. — Quintilian.

nosce teipsum (L.) know thyself — a translation of **gnoathi seauton** (q.v.).

nous avons changé tout cela (Fr.) we have changed all that. — Molière, *Le Médecin malgré lui*, II. iv.

nous verrons (ce que nous verrons) (Fr.) we shall see (what we shall see).

nulla dies sine linea (L.) no day without a line, without painting (or writing) a little.

nulla nuova, buona nuova (It.) no news is good news.

nullius addictus (or **adductus**) **jurare in verba magistri** (L.) bound to swear to the words of no master, to follow no one blindly or slavishly. — Horace, *Epist.*, I. i. 14.

nullum (scil. **scribendi genus**) **quod tetigit non ornavit** (L.) he touched no form of literature without adorning it. From Johnson's epitaph on Goldsmith.

nunc est bibendum (L.) now is the time to drink. — Horace, *Od.*, I. xxxvii. 1.

O

obscurum per obscurius (L.) (explaining) the obscure by means of the more obscure.

oderint dum metuant (L.) let them hate so long as they fear. — Accius, *Atreus*, Fragment IV; quoted in Cicero, *Philippica*, I. xiv.

odi profanum vulgus et arceo (L.) I loathe and shun the profane rabble. — Horace, *Od.*, iii. i. 1.

O fortunatos nimium, sua si bona norint, agricolas (L.) Oh too happy farmers, if they but knew their luck. — Virgil, *Georg.*, II. 458.

ohe! jam satis (L.) hold! enough now (a common phrase).

ohne Hast, ohne Rast (Ger.) without haste, without rest. — Goethe's motto.

olim meminisse juvabit. See **forsan**.

omne ignotum pro magnifico (L.) everything unknown (is taken to be) magnificent. — Tacitus, *Agric.*, 30.

omnem crede diem tibi diluxisse supremum (L.) believe each day to have dawned as your last. — Horace, *Epist.*, I. iv. 13.

omne tulit punctum qui miscuit utile dulci (L.) he has carried every vote who has combined the useful with the pleasing. — Horace, *A.P.*, 343.

omne vivum ex ovo (L.) every living thing comes from an egg. — Attributed to Harvey.

omnia mea mecum porto (L.) all I have I carry with me.

omnia mutantur. See **tempora mutantur**.

omnia vincit amor, et nos cedamus amori (L.) love overcomes all things, let us too yield to love. — Virgil, *Ecl.*, X. 69.

ore rotunda (L.) with round, full voice (mouth). — Horace, *A.P.*, 323.

O sancta simplicitas! (L.) O holy simplicity!

os homini sublime dedit caelumque tueri jussit et erectos ad sidera tollere vultus (L.) he gave man an up-turned face and bade contemplate the heavens and raise looks to the stars. — Ovid, *Met.*, I. 85.

O si sic omnia! (L.) Oh that he had done all things thus, or Oh that all things were thus!

O tempora! O mores! (L.) O the times! O the manners! Occurs in Cicero's first speech against Catiline.

otia dant vitia (L.) idleness begets vice.

otium cum dignitate (L.) dignified leisure.

ouk esti? (Gr.) is it not so?

ovem lupo committere (L.) to entrust the sheep to the wolf.

P

pace tua (L.) by your leave.

pallida Mors aequo pulsat pede pauperum tabernas regumque turres (L.) pale Death knocks with impartial foot at poor men's huts and kings' castles. — Horace, *Od.*, I. iv. 13–14.

palmam qui meruit ferat (L.) let him who has won the palm wear it. — Dr Jortin, *Lusus Poetici*, viii. 20.

panem et circenses (L.) bread and (Roman) circus-games — food and amusements at public expense. — Juvenal, X. 81.

panta men kathara tois katharois (Gr.) all things are pure to the pure. — Titus, I. 15.

panta rhei (Gr.) all things are in a flux (a saying of Heraclitus).

parcere subjectis et debellare superbos (L.) to spare the vanquished and put down the proud. — Virgil, *Aen.*, VI. 854.

par nobile fratrum (L.) a noble pair of brothers. — Horace, *Sat.*, II. iii. 243.

parturiunt montes, nascetur ridiculus mus (L.) the mountains are in travail, an absurd mouse will be born. — Horace, *A.P.*, 139.

parva componere magnis. See **si parva**.

pas op (Afrik.) look out.

patheamata matheamata (Gr.) sufferings [are] lessons.

paulo majora canamus (L.) let us sing of rather greater things. — Virgil, *Ecl.*, IV. 1.

pax vobiscum (L.) peace be with you.

peccavi (L.) I have sinned.

pecunia non olet. See **non olet pecunia**.

pereant qui ante nos nostra dixerunt (L.) perish those who have said our good things before us. — Attributed to Donatus and to Augustine.

pereunt et imputantur (L.) [the moments, hours] pass away and are reckoned to our account.

perfervida. See **praefervida**. **per varios casus, per tot discrimina rerum** (L.) through various chances, through so many crises of fortune. — Virgil, *Aen.*, I. 204.

pleon heamisy pantos (Gr.) the half is more than the whole. — Hesiod, *Erga*, 40.

plus ça change, plus c'est la même chose (Fr.) the more that changes the more it is the same thing (no superficial or apparent change alters its essential nature).

poeta nascitur, non fit (L.) the poet is born, not made.

polloan onomatoan mia morphea (Gr.) one shape of many names. — Aeschylus, *Prometheus*, 210.

polyphloisboio thalasseas (Gr.) of the much-sounding sea. — Homer, *Il.*, I. 34; also Hesiod, *Erga*, 648.

populus vult decipi, ergo decipiatur (L.) the public wishes to be fooled, therefore let it be fooled. — Ascribed to Cardinal Caraffa.

poscimur (L.) we are called on [to sing, etc.].

post equitem sedet atra cura (L.) behind the horseman sits black care. — Horace, *Odes*, III. i. 40.

post hoc, ergo propter hoc (L.) after this, therefore because of this (a fallacious reasoning).

pour encourager les autres (Fr.) to encourage the others (Voltaire, *Candide*, on the shooting of Admiral Byng); **pour faire rire**, to raise a laugh; **pour mieux sauter** see **reculer** below; **pour passer le temps** to pass away the time; **pour prendre congé**, or **PPC**, to take leave.

praefervida (misquoted as **perfervida**). See **Scotorum**.

principiis obsta (L.) resist the first beginnings. — Ovid, *R.A.*, 91. Cf. **yenienti**, etc.

probatum est (L.) it has been proved.

probitas laudatur et alget (L.) honesty is commended and left out in the cold. — Juvenal, I. 74.

procul este, profani (L.) keep your distance, uninitiated ones. — Virgil, *Aen.*, VI. 258.

proh pudor! (L.) oh, for shame!

proxime accessit (*pl.* **accesserunt**) (L.) came next [to the prizeman].

pulvis et umbra sumus (L.) we are dust and a shadow. — Horace, *Od.*, IV. vii. 16.

purpureus pannus (L.) a purple patch. — From Horace, *A.P.*, 15–16.

Q

quamdiu se bene gesserit (L.) during good behavior.

quantum mutatus ab illo (L.) how changed from that (Hector who came back clad in Achilles's spoils). — Virgil, *Aen.*, II. 274.

que diable allait-il faire dans cette galère? (Fr.) what the devil was he doing in that galley? — Molière, *Les Fourberies de Scapin*, II. vii.

quem di diligunt adolescens moritur (L.) whom the gods love dies young. — Plautus's translation of **hon hoi theoi** . . .

quem lupiter vult perdere dementat prius, or **quem deus perdere vult, prius dementat** (L.) whom Jupiter (a god) wishes to destroy, he first makes mad.

que sais-je (sçai-je)? (Fr.) what do I know? — Montaigne's motto.

que voulez-vous? (Fr.) what would you?

quicquid agunt homines . . . nostri est farrago libelli (L.) whatever men do is the medley of our little book. — Juvenal, I. 85–86.

quicquid delirant reges plectuntur Achivi (L.) whatever madness possesses the chiefs, it is (the common soldiers or people of) the Achaeans who suffer. — Horace, *Epist.*, I. ii. 14.

quicunque vult salvus esse (L.) whosoever will be saved (the beginning of the Athanasian creed).

quid hoc sibi vult? (L.) what does this mean?

quid rides? mutato nomine de te fabula narratur (L.) why do you laugh? with change of name the story is about you. — Horace, *Sat.*, I. i. 69–70.

quién sabe? (Sp.) who knows?

quieta non movere (L.) not to move things that are at rest — to let sleeping dogs lie.

qui facit per alium facit per se (L.) he who acts through another is himself responsible.

quis custodiet ipsos custodes? (L.) who will guard the guards themselves? — Juvenal, VI. 347–8.

quis desiderio sit pudor aut modus tam cari capitis? (L.) what shame or stint should there be in mourning for one so dear? — Horace, *Od.*, I. xxiv. 1.

qui s'excuse s'accuse (Fr.) he who excuses himself accuses himself.

quis separabit? (L.) who shall separate [us]?

qui tacet consentit (L.) who keeps silence consents.

qui va là? (Fr.) who goes there?

quod avertat Deus (L.) which may God avert.

quod bonum, felix, faustumque sit (L.) may it be right, happy, and of good omen.

quod erat demonstrandum (L.), or **Q.E.D.**, which was to be proved or demonstrated; **quod erat faciendum**, or **Q.E.F.**, which was to be done.

quod ubique, quod semper, quod ab omnibus (L.) what everywhere, what always, what by all (has been believed). — St Vincent of Lérin's definition of orthodoxy.

quorum pars magna fui (L.) in which I bore a great share. — Virgil, *Aen.*, II. 6.

quot homines, tot sententiae (L.) as many men, so many minds or opinions. — Terence, *Phormio*, II. iv. 14 (or 1. 454).

quousque tandem abutere, Catilina, patientia nostra? (L.) how far, O Catiline, will you abuse our patience?— Cicero, *In Catilinam*.

quo vadis? (L.) whither goest thou?

R

rara avis (L.) a rare bird, rare person or thing. — Juvenal, VI. 165.

rari nantes in gurgite vasto (L.) here and there some swimming in a vast whirlpool. — Virgil, *Aen.*, I. 118.

reculer pour mieux sauter (Fr.) to draw back to take a better leap.

redolet lucerna (L.) it smells of the lamp.

re galantuomo (It.) the honest king — king and gentleman [said of Victor Emmanuel II].

religio loci (L.) the religious spirit of the place. — Virgil, *Aen.*, VIII. 349.

rem acu tetigisti (L.) you have touched the thing with a needle, hit it exactly. — Proverbial expression used by Plautus.

remis velisque (L.) with oars and sails; also **remis ventisque** with oars and winds (Virgil, etc.): with all vigor.

res angusta domi (L.) straitened circumstances at home. — Juvenal, III. 165.

res ipsa loquitur (L.) the thing speaks for itself: the accident is in itself evidence of negligence.

respice finem (L.) look to the end. — Playfully perverted into **respice funem**, beware of the (hangman's) rope.

resurgam (L.) I shall rise again.

retro me, satana (L.) in Vulgate, **vade retro me, satana**, get thee behind me, Satan (Matt. xvi. 23, Mark viii. 33, Luke iv. 8): stop trying to tempt me.

revenons à nos moutons (Fr.) let us return to our sheep, i.e. our subject. — From the mediaeval farce, *L'Avocat Pathelin*.

rhododaktylos Eoas (Gr.) rosy-fingered Dawn. — Homer, *Odyssey*, II. 1.

rien ne va plus (Fr.) lit. nothing goes any more — used by croupiers to indicate that no more bets may be made.

risum teneatis, amici? (L.) could you keep from laughing, friends? — Horace, *A.P.*, 5.

Roma locuta, causa finita (L.) Rome has spoken, the cause is ended.

ruat caelum. See **fiat justitia**.

rudis indigestaque moles (L.) a rude and shapeless mass. — Ovid, *Met.*, I. 7.

ruit. See **mole**.

rus in urbe (L.) the country in town. — Martial, XII. 57, 21.

rusticus expectat dum defluat amnis (L.) waits like the yokel for the river to run by. — Horace, *Epist.*, I. ii. 42.

S

salaam aleikum (Ar.) peace be upon you.

salus populi suprema lex esto (L.) let the welfare of the people be the final law (Cicero, *De Legibus*, III. iiii: **suprema est lex**).

sans peur et sans reproche (Fr.) without fear and without reproach.

sapere aude (L.) dare to be wise. — Horace, *Epist.*, I. ii. 40.

sartor resartus (L.) the tailor retailored.

sauter à pieds joints (Fr.) to take a standing jump.

sauve qui peut (Fr.) save himself who can: every man for himself.

Scotorum praefervida ingenia (L.) the ardent tempers of the Scots. — Buchanan, *Hist. Scot.*, XVI. li.

selon les règles (Fr.) according to the rules.

semel insanivimus omnes (L.) we have all played the fool once. — J. B. Mantuanus, *Ecl.*, i. 217.

se non è vero, è ben trovato (It.) if it is not true, it is cleverly invented.

sero venientibus ossa (L.) the bones to the late-comers.

sic itur ad astra (L.) such is the way to the stars. — Virgil, *Aen.*, IX. 641.

si componere magnis parva, etc. See **si parva**, etc.

sic transit gloria mundi (L.) so passes away earthly glory.

sic volo. See **hoc volo**.

sic vos non vobis (L.) thus do you, not for yourselves. — Ascribed to Virgil.

Sieg heil (Ger.) victory hail!

si jeunesse savait, si vieillesse pouvait (Fr.) if youth but knew, if age but could.

s'il vous plaît (Fr.) if you please.

similia similibus curantur (L.) likes are cured by likes — a hair of the dog that bit one.

si monumentum requiris, circumspice (L.) if you seek (his) monument, look round you (inscription for the architect Christopher Wren's tomb in St Paul's).

simplex munditiis (L.) elegant in simplicity. — Horace, *Od.*, I. v. 5. **sine Cerere et Libero friget Venus** (L.) without Ceres and Bacchus (food and drink) Venus (love) is cold. — Terence, *Eun.*, IV. v. 6.

sine ira et studio (L.) without ill-will and without favor.

sint ut sunt aut non sint (L.) let them be as they are or not at all.

si parla Italiano (It.) Italian spoken.

si parva licet componere magnis (L.; Virgil, *Georg.*, IV. 176); **si componere magnis parva mihi fas est** (Ovid, *Met.*, V. 416–7) if it is permissible to compare small things to great.

siste, viator (L.) stop, traveler.

si vis pacem, para bellum (L.) if you would have peace, be ready for war.

skias onar anthroapos (Gr.) man is a dream of a shadow. — Pindar., *Pyth.*, VIII. 95.

solitudinem faciunt, pacem appellant (L.) they make a desert and call it peace. — Tacitus, *Agric.*, 30.

solventur risu tabulae: tu missus abibis (L.) the bills will be dismissed with laughter — you will be laughed out of court. — Horace, *Sat.*, II. i. 86.

solvitur ambulando (L.) (the problem of reality of motion) is solved by walking — by practical experiment, by actual performance.

spero meliora (L.) I hope for better things.

splendide mendax (L.) splendidly false, nobly lying. — Horace, *Od.*, III. xi. 35.

spretaeque injuria formae (L.) (and) the insult of beauty slighted. — Virgil, *Aen.*, I. 27.

stans pede in uno (L.) standing on one foot. — Horace, *Sat.*, I. iv. 10.

stat pro ratione voluntas (L.) See **hoc volo**.

stet fortuna domus (L.) may the fortune of the house last long.

Sturm und Drang (Ger.) storm and stress.

sua si bona. See **O fortunatos**, etc.

suaviter in modo, fortiter in re (L.) gentle in manner, resolute in deed.

suggestio falsi. See **suppressio veri**, etc.

sunt lacrimae rerum (L.) there are tears for things (unhappy). — Virgil, *Aen.*, I. 462.

suo motu on one's own initiative.

suppressio veri suggestio falsi (L.) suppression of truth is suggestion of the false. (In law, **suppressio veri** is passive, **suggestio falsi** active, misrepresentation.)

sursum corda (L.) lift up your hearts.

surtout, pas de zèle (Fr.) above all, no zeal.

sutor ne supra crepidam judicaret (L.) let not the cobbler criticise (a work of art) above the sandal. See **ultracrepidate** in Dict.

T

tacent, satis laudant (L.) their silence is praise enough. — Terence, *Eun.*, III. ii. 23.

tantae molis erat Romanam condere gentem (L.) a task of such difficulty was it to found the Roman race. — Virgil, *Aen.*, I. 33.

tantaene animis caelestibus irae? (L.) are there such violent passions in celestial minds? — Virgil, *Aen.*, I. 11.

tempora (orig. **omnia**) **mutantur, nos et mutamur in illis** (L.) the times (all things) change, and we with them.

tempus edax rerum (L.) time, consumer of things. — Ovid, *Met.*, XV. 234.

tempus fugit (L.) time flies.

thalassa, thalassa! or **thalatta thalatta!** (Gr.) the sea, the sea! (the exulting cry of Xenophon's men on beholding the sea). — Xenophon, *Anabasis*, IV. 7.

timeo Danaos et dona ferentes (L.) I fear the Greeks, even when bringing gifts. — Virgil, *Aen.*, II. 49.

tiré à quatre épingles (Fr.) as neat as can be.

ton d'apameibomenos prosephea (Gr.) addressed him in reply. — Homer (*passim*).

totus, teres, atque rotundus (L.) complete, smooth, and round. — Horace, *Satires*, II. vii. 86.

toujours perdrix (Fr.) partridge every day — too much of a good thing.

tout comprendre c'est tout pardonner (Fr.) to understand all is to pardon all; **tout est perdu fors l'honneur** all is lost but honor [attrib. to Francis I after Pavia]; **tout vient (à point) à qui sait attendre** all things come to him who can wait.

traduttore traditore (It.) a translator is a traitor or betrayer: *pl.* **traduttori traditori**.

tria juncta in uno (L.) three things in one.

U

ubi bene, ibi patria (L.) where it goes well with me, there is my fatherland.

ubi saeva indignatio ulterious cor lacerare nequit (L.) where fierce indignation can tear his heart no longer. — Part of Swift's epitaph.

und so weiter (Ger.), or **u.s.w.**, and so forth.

urbi et orbi (L.) to the city (Rome) and to the world, to everyone.

uti possidetis (L.) lit. as you possess — the principle of letting e.g. belligerents keep what they have acquired.

V

vade in pace (L.) go in peace.

vade retro me, satana. See **retro**.

varium et mutabile semper femina (L.) woman is ever a fickle and changeable thing. — Virgil, *Aen.*, IV. 569.

vedi Napoli, e poi muori (It.) see Naples, and die.

veni Creator Spiritus (L.) come, Creator Spirit — the beginning of an early Latin hymn.

venienti occurrite morbo (L.) run to meet disease as it comes. — Persius, III. 63.

veni, vidi, vici (L.) I came, I saw, I conquered. — Ascribed to Caesar on his victory over Pharnaces.

vera incessu patuit dea (L.) the true goddess was revealed by her gait. — Virgil, *Aen.*, I. 405.

verbum sapienti sat est (L.) a word to the wise is enough — often abbrev. *verb. sap.* and *verb. sat.* See **dictum**.

veritas odium parit (L.) truth begets hatred. — Terence, *Andria*, I. i. 41.

vestigia . . . nulla retrorsum (L.) no footprints backwards (at the lion's den): sometimes used to mean no going back. — Horace, *Epist.*, I. i. 74–75.

victrix causa deis placuit, sed victa Catoni (L.) the gods preferred the winning cause, but Cato the losing. — Lucan, I. 128.

video meliora proboque, deteriora sequor (L.) I see the better course and approve it, I follow the worse. — Ovid, *Met.*, VII. 20.

vigilate et orate (L.) watch and pray.

viresque acquirit eundo (L.) (Fama, hearsay personified) gains strenght as she goes. — Virgil, *Aen.*, IV. 175.

Virgilium vidi tantum (L.) I just saw Virgil [and no more]. — Ovid, *Trist.*, IV. x. 51.

virginibus puerisque canto (L.) I sing for maidens and boys — for the young person. — Horace, *Od.*, III. i. 4.

virtus post nummos (L.) virtue after money — i.e. money first. — Horace, *Epist.*, I. i. 54.

vita brevis, ars longa (L.) life is short, art is long (see **ho bios**, etc.); **vita sine litteris mors est** life without literature is death.

vive la bagatelle (quasi-Fr.) long live folly.

vive ut vivas (L.) live that you may live; **vive, valeque** life and health to you

vivit post funera virtus (L.) virtue lives beyond the grave.

vixere fortes ante Agamemnona multi (L.) many brave men lived before Agamemnon. — Horace, *Od.*, IV. ix. 25–26.

vogue la galère! (Fr.) row the boat: row on: come what may!

volenti non fit injuria (L.) no wrong is done to one who consents.

volo, non valeo (L.) I am willing, but unable.

volto sciolto e pensieri stretti (It.) open face, close thoughts.

vous l'avez voulu, George Dandin (Fr.) you would have it so. — Molière, *George Dandin*, Act 1.

vox audita perit, littera scripta manet (L.) the heard word is lost, the written letter abides; **vox et praeterea nihil** a voice and nothing more (of a nightingale).

W

Wahrheit und Dichtung (Ger.) truth and poetry.

Wein, Weib, und Gesang (Ger.) wine, women and song.

wer da? (Ger.) who is there?

wie geht's? (Ger.) how are you?

Z

zonam perdidit (L.) he has lost his money-belt: he is in needy circumstances; **zonam solvere** to loose the virgin zone, i.e. marry.

Words Listed by Suffix

-ast chiliast, diaskeuast, dicast, dikast, dynast, ecclesiast, ecdysiast, elegiast, encomiast, enthusiast, fantast, gymnasiast, gymnast, Hesychast, hypochondriast, iconoclast, idoloclast, metaphrast, orgiast, pancratiast, paraphrast, pederast, peltast, phantasiast, pleonast, scholiast, utopiast.

-aster criticaster, grammaticaster, medicaster, philosophaster, poetaster, politicaster, theologaster.

-cide aborticide, acaricide, algicide, aphicide, aphidicide, bacillicide, bactericide, biocide, deicide, ecocide, ethnocide, feticide, filicide, foeticide, fratricide, fungicide, genocide, germicide, giganticide, herbicide, homicide, infanticide, insecticide, larvicide, liberticide, matricide, menticide, molluscicide, ovicide, parasiticide, parasuicide, parricide, patricide, pesticide, prolicide, regicide, rodenticide, sororicide, spermicide, suicide, taeniacide, trypanocide, tyrannicide, uxoricide, vaticide, verbicide, vermicide, viricide, viticide, vulpicide, weedicide,

-cracy aristocracy, autocracy, bureaucracy, chrysocracy, cottonocracy, democracy, demonocracy, despotocracy, dollarocracy, doulocracy, dulocracy, ergatocracy, Eurocracy, gerontocracy, gynecocracy, hagiocracy, hierocracy, isocracy, kakistocracy, meritocracy, millocracy, mobocracy, monocracy, nomocracy, ochlocracy, pantisocracy, pedantocracy, physiocracy, plantocracy, plutocracy, plutodemocracy, pornocracy, ptochocracy, slavocracy, snobocracy, squattocracy, stratocracy, technocracy, thalassocracy, thalattocracy, theocracy, timocracy.

-crat aristocrat, autocrat, bureaucrat, cosmocrat, democrat, hierocrat, meritocrat, millocrat, mobocrat, monocrat, ochlocrat, pantisocrat, pedantocrat, physiocrat, plutocrat, slavocrat, stratocrat, technocrat, theocrat.

-cratic aristocratic, autocratic, bureaucratic, cosmocratic, democratic, Eurocratic, gerontocratic, gynecocratic, hierocratic, isocratic, meritocratic, mobocratic, monocratic, ochlocratic, pancratic, pantisocratic, pedantocratic, physiocratic, plutocratic, stratocratic, technocratic, theocratic, timocratic, undemocratic.

-cultural accultural, agricultural, arboricultural, crinicultural, cultural, floricultural, horticultural, piscicultural, subcultural, vinicultural, vocicultural.

-culture agriculture, apiculture, aquaculture, aquiculture, arboriculture, aviculture, culture, electroculture, floriculture, horticulture, mariculture, monoculture, ostreiculture, pisciculture, pomiculture, self-culture, sericiculture, sericulture, silviculture, stirpiculture, subculture, sylviculture, viniculture, viticulture, water-culture, zooculture.

-cyte athrocyte, cyte, erythrocyte, fibrocyte, gonocyte, granulocyte, hemocyte, leucocyte, lymphocyte, macrocyte, microcyte, oocyte, phagocyte, poikilocyte, spermatocyte, thrombocyte, thymocyte.

-dom Anglo-Saxondom, apedom, archdukedom, attorneydom, babeldom, babudom, bachelordom, beadledom, beggardom, birthdom, bishopdom, boredom, Bumbledom, chiefdom, Christendom, clerkdom, cockneydom, crippledom, cuckoldom, czardom, demirepdom, devildom, Dogberrydom, dolldom, dufferdom, dukedom, dancedom, earldom, enthraldom, fairydom, fandom, filmdom, flunkeydom, fogydom, freedom, fresherdom, Greekdom, gypsydom, halidom, heathendom, heirdom, hobbledehoydom, hobodom, junkerdom, kaiserdom, kingdom, kitchendom, leechdom, liegedom, mandom, martyrdom, masterdom, newspaperdom, noodledom, noveldom, officialdom, overfreedom, penny-wisdom, popedom, princedom, puppydom, puzzledom, Quakerdom, queendom, queerdom, rascaldom, rebeldom, sachemdom, saintdom, savagedom, Saxondom, scoundreldom, serfdom, sheikdom, sheikhdom, sheriffdom, Slavdom, spinsterdom, squiredom, stardom, subkingdom, swelldom, thanedom, thraldom, thralldom, topsyturvydom, tsardom, underkingdom, unwisdom, villadom, whoredom, wisdom, Yankeedom.

-ferous aluminiferous, amentiferous, antenniferous, argentiferous, auriferous, bacciferous, balsamiferous, bulbiferous, calciferous, carboniferous, celliferous, celluliferous, cheliferous, cobaltiferous, conchiferous, coniferous, coralliferous, corniferous, cruciferous, culmiferous, cupriferous, cupuliferous, diamantiferous, diamondiferous, doloriferous, dorsiferous, ferriferous, flagelliferous, flammiferous, floriferous, foraminiferous, fossiliferous, frondiferous, fructiferous, frugiferous, furciferous, garnetiferous, gemmiferous, glandiferous, glanduliferous, globuliferous, glumiferous, granuliferous, guaniferous, gummiferous, guttiferous, lactiferous, laniferous, laticiferous, lethiferous, luciferous, luminiferous, mammaliferous, mammiferous, manganiferous, manniferous, margaritiferous, melliferous, metalliferous, morbiferous, mortiferous, moschiferous, muciferous, nectariferous, nickeliferous, nubiferous, nuciferous, odoriferous, oleiferous, omniferous, ossiferous, oviferous, ovuliferous, ozoniferous, papilliferous, papuliferous, Permo-Carboniferous, pestiferous, petaliferous, petroliferous, piliferous, platiniferous, plumbiferous, polliniferous, pomiferous, poriferous, proliferous, pyritiferous, quartziferous, reptiliferous, resiniferous, rotiferous, sacchariferous, saliferous, salutiferous, sanguiferous, sebiferous, seminiferous, septiferous, siliciferous, soboliferous, somniferous, soporiferous, spiniferous, spinuliferous, splendiferous, staminiferous, stanniferous, stelliferous, stigmatiferous, stoloniferous, strombuliferous, styliferous, sudoriferous, tentaculiferous, thuriferous, titaniferous, tuberiferous, umbelliferous, umbriferous, unfossiliferous, uriniferous, vitiferous, vociferous, yttriferous, zinciferous, zinkiferous.

-gamy allogamy, apogamy, autogamy, bigamy, chalazogamy, chasmogamy, cleistogamy, clistogamy, cryptogamy, deuterogamy, dichogamy, digamy, endogamy, exogamy, geitonogamy, hercogamy, herkogamy, heterogamy, homogamy, hypergamy, isogamy, misogamy, monogamy, oogamy, pangamy, pantagamy, plasmogamy, plasto-gamy, polygamy, porogamy, siphonogamy, syngamy, trigamy, xenogamy, zoogamy.

-genesis abiogenesis, agamogenesis, anthropogenesis, autogenesis, biogenesis, blastogenesis, carcinogenesis, chondrogenesis, cytogenesis, diagenesis, diplogenesis, dynamogenesis, ectogenesis, electrogenesis, embryogen-esis, epeirogenesis, epigenesis, gametogenesis, gamogenesis, hematogenesis, heterogenesis, histogenesis, homogenesis, hylogenesis, hypogenesis, merogenesis, metagenesis, monogenesis, morphogenesis, mythogenesis, neogenesis, noogenesis, ontogenesis, oogenesis, organogenesis, orogenesis, orthogenesis, osteogenesis, palingenesis, pangenesis, paragenesis, parthenogenesis, pathogenesis, pedogenesis, perigenesis, petrogenesis, phylogenesis, phytogenesis, polygenesis, psychogenesis, pyogenesis, schizogenesis, sperma-togenesis, sporogenesis, syngenesis, thermogenesis, xenogenesis.

-genic aesthesiogenic, allergenic, androgenic, anthropogenic, antigenic, biogenic, blastogenic, carcinogenic, cariogenic, cryogenic, dysgenic, ectogenic, electrogenic, endogenic, epeirogenic, erogenic, erotogenic, eugenic, genic, glycogenic, hallucinogenic, histogenic, hypnogenic, hysterogenic, iatrogenic, lactogenic, lysigenic, mammogenic, mutagenic, myogenic, neurogenic, odontogenic, oestrogenic, oncogenic, ontogenic, orogenic, orthogenic, osteogenic, pathogenic, photogenic, phytogenic, polygenic, psychogenic, pyogenic, pyrogenic, pythogenic, radiogenic, rhizogenic, saprogenic, schizogenic, somatogenic, spermatogenic, telegenic, teratogenic, thermogenic, tumorgenic, tumorigenic, visiogenic, zoogenic, zymogenic.

-gon chiliagon, decagon, dodecagon, endecagon, enneagon, hendecagon, heptagon, hexagon, isogon, nonagon, octagon, pentagon, perigon, polygon, tetragon, trigon.

-gram airgram, anagram, anemogram, angiogram, audiogram, ballistocardiogram, barogram, cablegram, calligram, cardiogram, cartogram, centigram, centimeter-gram, chromatogram, chromogram, chronogram, cryptogram, dactylogram, decagram, decigram, dendrogram, diagram, echogram, electrocardiogram, electroencephalogram, encephalogram, engram, epigram, ergogram, ferrogram, harmonogram, hectogram, hexagram, hierogram, histo-gram, hologram, ideogram, indicator-diagram, isogram, kilogram, lexigram, lipogram, logogram, lymphogram, marconigram, marigram, meteorogram, microgram, monogram, myogram, nanogram, nephogram, neurogram, nomogram, organogram, oscillogram, pangram, paragram, parallelogram, pentagram, phonogram, photogram, phraseogram, pictogram, program, psychogram, pyelogram, radiogram, radiotelegram, röntgenogram, scintigram, seismogram, sialogram, skiagram, sociogram, spectrogram, spectroheliogram, sphenogram, sphymogram, steganogram, stereogram, tachogram, telegram, tephigram, tetragram, thermogram, tomogram, trigram.

-graph Addressograph®;, airgraph, allograph, anemograph, apograph, audiograph, autograph, autoradiograph, ballistocardiograph, bar-graph, barograph, biograph, cardiograph, cathodograph, cerograph, chirograph, choreograph, chromatograph, chromolithograph, chromoxylograph, chronograph, cinematograph, coronagraph, coronograph, cryptograph, cyclograph, cymagraph, cymograph, diagraph, Dictograph®;, digraph, dynamo-graph, eidograph, electrocardiograph, electroencephalograph, electrograph, electromyograph, ellipsograph, encephalograph, epigraph, ergograph, evaporograph, flannelgraph, glyphograph, harmonograph, hectograph, helicograph, heliograph, hierograph, hodograph, holograph, homograph, hydrograph, hyetograph, hyetometrograph, hygrograph, ideograph, idiograph, jellygraph, keraunograph, kinematograph, kinetograph, kymograph, lithograph, logograph, magnetograph, marconigraph, marigraph, meteorograph, micrograph, microphotograph, microseismograph, mimeograph, monograph, myograph, nephograph, nomograph, odograph, odontograph, oleograph, opisthograph, orthograph, oscillograph, pantograph, paragraph, pentagraph, pho-nautograph, phonograph, photograph, photolithograph, photomicrograph, phototelegraph, photozincograph, phraseograph, pictograph, planigraph, plethysmograph, polygraph, pseudograph, psychograph, pyrophotograph, radioautograph, radiograph, radiometeorograph, radiotelegraph, rotograph, seismograph, salenograph, serigraph, shadowgraph, skiagraph, spectrograph, spectroheliograph, sphygmograph, spirograph, steganograph, stenograph, stereograph, Stevengraph, stylograph, syngraph, tachograph, tachygraph,

Telautograph®;, telegraph, telephotograph, thermograph, thermometrograph, tomograph, torsiograph, trigraph, vectograph, vibrograph, xylograph, zincograph.

-graphy aerography, ampelography, angiography, anthropogeography, anthropography, areography, autobiography, autography, autoradiography, autotypography, ballistocardiography, bibliography, biogeography, biography, brachygraphy, cacography, calligraphy, cardiography, cartography, cathodography, ceramography, cerography, chalcography, chartography, chirography, cholangiography, choregraphy, choreography, chorography, chromatography, chromolithography, chromotypography, chromoxylography, chronography, cinematography, cinemicrography, climatography, cometography, cosmography, cryptography, crystallography, dactyliography, dactylography, demography, dermatography, dermography, discography, dittography, doxography, echocardiography, ectypography, electrocardiography, electroencephalography, electrography, electromyography, electrophotography, encephalography, enigmatography, epigraphy, epistolography, ethnography, ferrography, filmography, geography, glossography, glyphography, glyptography, hagiography, haplography, heliography, heresiography, hierography, historiography, holography, horography, hydrography, hyetography, hymnography, hypsography, ichnography, ichthyography, iconography, ideography, lexicography, lexigraphy, lipography, lithography, logography, lymphography, mammography, metallography, microcosmography, micrography, microphotography, mimography, monography, morphography, myography, mythography, nomography, nosography, oceanography, odontography, oleography, opisthography, orchesography, oreography, organography, orography, orthography, osteography, paleogeography, paleography, paleontography, pantography, paroemiography, pasigraphy, pathography, petrography, phonography, photography, photolithography, photomicrography, phototelegraphy, photoxylography, photozincography, physiography, phytogeography, phytography, pictography, polarography, polygraphy, pornography, prosopography, pseudepigraphy, pseudography, psychobiography, psychography, pterylography, pyelography, pyrography, pyrophotography, radiography, radiotelegraphy, reprography, rhyparography, röntgenography, scenography, scintigraphy, seismography, selenography, serigraphy, sialography, snobography, spectrography, sphygmography, steganography, stenography, stereography, stratigraphy, stylography, symbolography, tachygraphy, telautography, telegraphy, telephotography, thalassography, thanatography, thaumatography, thermography, tomography, topography, typography, ultrasonography, uranography, urography, ventriculography, xerography, xeroradiography, xylography, xylopyrography, xylotypography, zincography, zoogeography, zoography.

-graphical autobiographical, bathygraphical, bathyorographical, bibliographical, biobibliographical, biogeographical, biographical, cacographical, calligraphical, cartographical, cerographical, chorographical, cinematographical, climatographical, cosmographical, geographical, glossographical, graphical, hagiographical, hierographical, historiographical, hydrographical, hyetographical, hygrographical, ichnographical, ideographical, lexicographical, lexigraphical, lithographical, logographical, monographical, myographical, oceanographical, oreographical, orographical, orthographical, paleographical, paleontographical, pantographical, paragraphical, pasigraphical, petrographical, photographical, physiographical, prosopographical, pseudepigraphical, psychobiographical, psychographical, pterylographical, seismographical, selenographical, spectrographical, stenographical, stereographical, stratigraphical, tachygraphical, topographical, typographical, xylographical, zincographical, zoogeographical, zoographical.

-hedron chiliahedron, decahedron, dihedron, dodecahedron, enneahedron, hemihedron, hexahedron, holohedron, icosahedron, icositetrahedron, leucitohedron, octahedron, octohedron, pentahedron, polyhedron, pyritohedron, rhombohedron, scalenohedron, tetrahedron, tetrakishexahedron, trapezohedron, triakisoctahedron, trihedron, trisoctahedron.

-hood adulthood, angelhood, apehood, apprenticehood, babyhood, bachelorhood, beadlehood, beasthood, bountihood, boyhood, brotherhood, cathood, childhood, Christhood, companionhood, cousinhood, cubhood, deaconhood, dollhood, drearihood, elfhood, fairyhood, falsehood, fatherhood, flapperhood, fleshhood, gawkihood, gentlehood, gentlemanhood, gianthood, girlhood, godhood, hardihood, high-priesthood, hobbledehoyhood, hoghood, hoydenhood, idlehood, invalidhood, jealoshood, kinghood, kinglihood, knighthood, ladyhood, likelihood, livelihood, lustihood, maidenhood, maidhood, manhood, masterhood, matronhood, misshood, monkhood, motherhood, nationhood, needy-hood, neighborhood, novicehood, nunhood, old-maidhood, orphanhood, pagehood, parenthood, popehood, priesthood, princehood, prophethood, puppyhood, queenhood, sainthood, selfhood, serfhood, sisterhood, spinsterhood, squirehood, statehood, swinehood, tabbyhood, thanehood, thinghood, traitorhood, unlikelihood, virginhood, waiterhood, widowerhood, widowhood, wifehood, wivehood, womanhood, youthhood.

-iac ammoniac, amnesiac, anaphrodisiac, anglomaniac, Anglophobiac, antaphrodisiac, anthomaniac, aphasiac, aphrodisiac, archgenethliac, bacchiac, bibliomaniac, cardiac, celiac, Cluniac, coprolaliac, demoniac, dextrocardiac,

Dionysiac, dipsomaniac, dochmiac, dysthymiac, egomaniac, elegiac, endocardiac, erotomaniac, etheromaniac, Genesiac, genethliac, hebephreniac, heliac, hemophiliac, hypochondriac, iliac, insomniac, intracardiac, Isiac, kleptomaniac, maniac, megalomaniac, meloncholiac, melomaniac, monomaniac, morphinomaniac, mythomaniac, necrophiliac, neurastheniac, nymphomaniac, opsomaniac, orchidomaniac, Pandemoniac, paradisiac, paranoiac, paraphiliac, paroemiac, pedophiliac, pericardiac, phrenesiac, pyromaniac, sacroiliac, scopophiliac, scoriac, simoniac, symposiac, Syriac, theomaniac, theriac, timbromaniac, toxiphobiac, zodiac, zygocardiac.

-iatric chemiatric, chemopsychiatric, geriatric, hippiatric, kinesiatric, pediatric, psychiatric, psychogeriatric.

-iatry chemopsychiatry, geriatry, hippiatry, neuropsychiatry, orthopsychiatry, pediatry, podiatry, psychiatry.

-ician academician, acoustician, aeroelastician, aesthetician, arithmetician, audiometrician, beautician, biometrician, clinician, cosmetician, diagnostician, dialectician, dietician, econometrician, ekistician, electrician, geometrician, geopolitician, geriatrician, informatician, linguistician, logician, logistician, magician, magnetician, mathematician, mechanician, metaphysician, metrician, mortician, musician, obstetrician, optician, pediatrician, patrician, Paulician, phonetician, physician, politician, practician, psychogeriatrician, psychometrician, rhetorician, rubrician, statistician, systematician, tactician, technician, theoretician.

-ics acoustics, acrobatics, aerobatics, aerobics, aerodynamics, aeronautics, aerostatics, aesthetics, agogics, agnostics, ambisonics, apologetics, aquabatics, aquanautics, astrodynamics, astronautics, astrophysics, athletics, atmospherics, autonomics, avionics, axiomatics, ballistics, bioastronautics, biodynamics, bioethics, biomathematics, biomechanics, biometrics, bionics, bionomics, biophysics, biorhythmics, biosystematics, cacogenics, calisthenics, callisthenics, catacoustics, catallactics, cataphonics, catechetics, catoptrics, ceroplastics, chemotherapeutics, chremastics, chromatics, civics, cliometrics, conics, cosmonautics, cosmopolitics, cryogenics, cryonics, cryophysics, cybernetics, cytogenetics, deontics, dermatoglyphics, diacoustics, diagnostics, dialectics, dianetics, didactics, dietetics, dioptrics, dogmatics, dramatics, dynamics, dysgenics, eclectics, econometrics, economics, ecumenics, ekistics, electrodynamics, electrokinetics, electromechanics, electronics, electrostatics, electrotechnics, electrotherapeutics, electrothermics, energetics, entoptics, environics, epigenetics, epistemics, epizootics, ergonomics, ethics, ethnolinguistics, eudaemonics, eudemonics, eugenics, eurhythmics, euthenics, exegetics, floristics, fluidics, forensics, genetics, geodetics, geodynamics, geophysics, geopolitics, geoponics, geostatics, geotectonics, geriatrics, gerontotherapeutics, glyptics, gnomonics, gnotobiotics, graphemics, graphics, gyrostatics, halieutics, haptics, harmonics, hedonics, hermeneutics, hermetics, hippiatrics, histrionics, homiletics, hydraulics, hydrodynamics, hydrokinetics, hydromagnetics, hydromechanics, hydroponics, hydrostatics, hydrotherapeutics, hygienics, hypersonics, hysterics, informatics, irenics, isagogics, isometrics, kinematics, kinesics, kinetics, linguistics, lithochromatics, liturgics, logistics, loxodromics, macrobiotics, macroeconomics, magnetics, magneto-hydrodynamics, magneto-optics, maieutics, mathematics, mechanics, melodics, metalinguistics, metamathematics, metaphysics, metapsychics, meteoritics, microeconomics, microelectronics, microphysics, mnemotechnics, mole-electronics, monostrophics, morphemics, morphophonemics, nautics, nucleonics, numismatics, obstetrics, olympics, onomastics, optics, optoelectronics, orchestics, orthodontics, orthodromics, orthogenics, orthopedics, orthoptics, orthotics, paideutics, pantopragmatics, paralinguistics, party-politics, pataphysics, patristics, pedagogics, pedentics, pediatrics, pedodontics, peptics, periodontics, pharmaceutics, pharmacodynamics, pharmacokinetics, phelloplastics, phonemics, phonetics, phonics, phonocamptics, phonotactics, photics, photochromics, photoelectronics, phototherapeutics, photovoltaics, physics, physiotherapeutics, plastics, pneumatics, pneumodynamics, polemics, politico-economics, politics, power- politics, problematics, prosthetics, prosthodontics, psychics, psychodynamics, psychogeriatrics, psycholinguistics, psychometrics, psychonomics, psychophysics, psychosomatics, psychotherapeutics, pyrotechnics, quadraphonics, quadrophonics, radionics, radiophonics, radiotherapeutics, rhythmics, robotics, semantics, semeiotics, semiotics, Semitics, sferics, significs, sociolinguistics, sonics, sophistics, spherics, sphragistics, statics, stereoptics, strategics, stylistics, subatomics, subtropics, syllabics, symbolics, synectics, systematics, tactics, technics, tectonics, telearchics, thaumaturgics, theatrics, therapeutics, thermionics, thermodynamics, thermotics, toponymics, toreutics, transonics, transsonics, ultrasonics, vitrics, zoiatrics, zootechnics, zymotechnics.

-iform aciform, acinaciform, aciniform, aeriform, alphabetiform, amoebiform, anguiform, anguilliform, antenniform, asbestiform, auriform, aviform, bacciform, bacilliform, biform, bursiform, cactiform, calcariform, calceiform, calyciform, cambiform, campaniform, campodeiform, cancriform, capriform, cauliform, cerebriform, cirriform, claviform, clypeiform, cobriform, cochleariform, coliform, colubriform, conchiform, coniform, coralliform, cordiform, corniform, corolliform, cotyliform, crateiform, cribriform, cristiform, cruciform, cteniform, cubiform, cucumiform, culiciform, cultriform, cumuliform, cuneiform, curviform, cyathiform, cylindriform, cymbiform, cystiform, deiform, dendriform, dentiform, digitiform, dolabriform, elytriform, ensiform, equisetiform, eruciform, falciform, fibriform, filiform, flabelliform, flagelliform, floriform, fringilliform, fungiform, fusiform, gangliform, gasiform, glandiform, granitiform, granuliform, hydatidiform, incisiform, infundibuliform, insectiform, janiform, jelliform, lamelliform, lanciform, lapilliform, larviform, lentiform, limaciform, linguiform, lumbriciform, lyriform, malleiform, mamilliform, mammiform, maniform, medusiform, mitriform, monadiform, moniliform, morbilliform, multiform, mummiform, muriform, mytiliform,, napiform, natiform, naupliiform, nubiform, omniform, oviform, paliform, panduriform, papilliform, patelliform, pelviform, penicilliform, penniform, perciform, phialiform, piliform, pisciform, pisiform, placentiform, planuliform, plexiform, poculiform, proteiform, pulvilliform, pyriform, quadriform, radiciform, raduliform, raniform, reniform, restiform, retiform, sacciform, sagittiform, salpiform, scalariform, scalpelliform, scalpriform, scoleciform, scolopendriform, scutiform, scyphiform, securiform, septiform, serpentiform, spiniform, spongiform, squamiform, stalactiform, stalactitiform, stelliform, stratiform, strigiform, strobiliform, strombuliform, styliform, tauriform, tectiform, telescopiform, thalliform, triform, tuberiform, tubiform, tympaniform, umbraculiform, unciform, unguiform, uniform, vaporiform, variform, vasculiform, vasiform, vermiform, verruciform, versiform, villiform, viperiform, vitriform, vulviform, ypsiliform, zeolitiform.

-ism abnormalism, abolitionism, aboriginalism, absenteeism, absolutism, academicalism, academicism, accidentalism, achromatism, acosmism, acrobatism, acotism, actinism, activism, Adamitism, adiaphorism, adoptianism, Adopttionism, adventurism, aeroembolism, aerotropism, aestheticism, Africanism, ageism, agnosticism, agrarianism, Albigensianism, albinism, albinoism, alcoholism, algorism, alienism, allelomorphism, allotropism, alpinism, altruism, amateurism, Americanism, ametabolism, amoralism, amorism, amorphism, anabaptism, anabolism, anachronism, anagrammatism, anarchism, anastigmatism, androdioecism, andromonoecism, aneurism, Anglicanism, anglicism, Anglo-Catholicism, aniconism, animalism, animatism, animism, annihilationism, antagonism, anthropomorphism, anthropomorphitism, anthropopathism, anthropophuism, anthropopsychism, antichristianism, anticivism, anticlericalism, antidisestablishmentarianism, anti-federalism, anti-Gallicanism, anti-Jacobinism, antinomianism, antiochianism, antiquarianism, anti-Semitism, antisepticism, antisocialism, antitheism, antitrinitarianism, antivaccinationism, antivivisectionism, anythingarianism, apheliotropism, aphorism, apism, aplanatism, apochromatism, apogeotropism, apoliticism, Apollinarianism, apostolicism, apriorism, Arabism, Aramaism, Arcadianism, archaicism, archaism, Arianism, aristocratism, Aristotelianism, Aristotelism, Arminianism, asceticism, asepticism, Asiaticism, aspheterism, asteism, asterism, astigmatism, asynchronism, asystolism, atavism, atheism, athleticism, Atlanticism, atomism, atonalism, atropism, Atticism, attorneyism, Augustinianism, Australianism, authorism, authoritarianism, autism, autochthonism, autoeroticism, autoerotism, automatism, automobilism, automorphism, autotheism, avant-gardism, Averrhoism, Averroism, Baalism, Baathism, Ba'athism, Babbitism, Babeeism, babelism, Babiism, Babism, babuism, bacchanalianism, bachelorism, Baconianism, Bahaism, bantingism, baptism, barbarism, bashawism, bastardism, bathmism, bedlamism, behaviorism, Benthamism, Bergsonism, Berkeleianism, bestialism, betacism, biblicism, bibliophilism, bilateralism, bilingualism, bimetallism, bipedalism, blackguardism, blepharism, bogeyism, bogyism, Bohemianism, bolshevism, Bonapartism, bonism, boobyism, Boswellism, botulism, Bourbonism, bowdlerism, bradyseism, braggartism, Brahmanism, Brahminism, Braidism, Briticism, Britishism, Brownism, bruxism, Buchmanism, Buddhism, bullyism, Burschenism, Byronism, Byzantinism, cabalism, cabbalism, Caesarism, caesaropapism, caffeinism, caffeism, Calvinism, cambism, Camorrism, cannibalism, capitalism, Carbonarism, careerism, Carlism, Carlylism, carnalism, Cartesianism, casualism, catabolism, catastrophism, catechism, catechumenism, Catharism, catheterism, catholicism, causationism, cauterism, cavalierism, Celticism, cenobitism, centenarianism, centralism, centripetalism, centrism, cerebralism, ceremonialism, chaldaism, characterism, charism, charlatanism, chartism, Chasidism, Chassidism, Chaucerism, chauvinism, chemism, chemotropism, chloralism, Christianism, chromaticism, churchism, Ciceronianism, cicisbeism, cinchonism, civisim, classicism, clericalism, cliquism, clubbism, coalitionism, Cobdenism, cocainism, cockneyism, collectivism, collegialism, colloquialism, colonialism, commensalism, commercialism, communalism, communism, compatriotism, comstockism, Comtism, conacreism, conceptualism, concettism, concretism, confessionalism, confrontationism, Confucianism, Congregationalism, conservatism, consortism, constitutionalism, constructionism, constructivism, consubstantialism, consumerism, contact-metamorphism, continentalism, contortionism, contrabandism, conventionalism, conversationism, convictism, copyism, corporatism, corporealism, corybantism, cosmeticism, cosmism, cosmopolitanism, cosmopolitism, cosmotheism, cottierism, Couéism, courtierism, creatianism, creationism, cretinism, cretism, criticism, crotalism, cubism, cultism, curialism, cyclicism, cynicism, czarism, Dadaism, Daltonism, dandyism, Darwinism, deaf-mutism, decimalism, defeatism, deism, demagogism, demagoguism, demoniacism, demonianism, demonism, denominationalism, departmentalism, descriptivism, depotism, deteriorism, determinism, deviationism, devilism, diabolism, diachronism, diageotropism, diaheliotropism, dialecticism, diamagnetism, diaphototropism, diastrophism, diatropism, dichroism, dichromatism, dichromism, diclinism, dicrotism, didacticism, diffusionism, dilettanteism, dilettantism, dimerism, dimorphism, diocism, diorism, diothelism, diphysitism, dirigism, dissenterism, dissolutionism, disyllabism, ditheism, ditheletism, dithelism, dithelitism, divisionism, Docetism, doctrinairism, doctrinarianism, Dogberryism, dogmatism, do-goodism, dolichocephalism, donatism, donnism, do-nothingism, Doricism, Dorism, dowdyism, draconism, dragonism, dramaticism, drudgism, druidism, dualism, dudism, dufferism, dunderheadism, dynamism, dyotheletism, dyothelism, dysphemism, ebionism, ebionitism, echoism, eclecticism, ecumenicalism, ecumenicism, ecumenism, Edwardianism, egalitarianism, egoism, egotheism, egotism, electromagnetism, electromerism, elementalism, elitism, Elizabethanism, embolism, emotionalism, empiricism, enantiomorphism, Encratism, encyclopedism, endemism, Englishism, entrism, environmentalism, eonism, epicism, Epicureanism, epicurism, epiphenomenalism, epiphytism, epipolism, episcopalianism, episcopalism, equalitarianism, equestrianism, Erastianism, eremitism, erethism, ergotism, eroticism, erotism, erythrism, escapism, esotericism, esoterism, Essenism, essentialism, etacism, etherism, ethicism, ethnicism, ethnocentrism, eudemonism, eugenism, euhemerism, eumerism, eunuchism, eunuchoidism, euphemism, euphuism, Eurocommunism, Europeanism, evangelicalism, evangelicism, evangelism, evolutionism, exclusionism, exclusivism, exhibitionism, existentialism, ex-librism, exorcism, exotericism, exoticism, expansionism, experientialism, experimentalism, expressionism, extensionalism, externalism, extremism, Fabianism, factionalism, faddism, fairyism, fakirism, falangism, familism, fanaticism, fantasticism, faradism, fascism, fatalism, Fauvism, favism, favoritism, Febronianism, federalism, femininism, feminism, Fenianism, fetichism, fetishism, feudalism, feuilletonism, fideism, fifth-monarchism, filibusterism, finalism, fissiparism, flagellantism, flunkeyism, fogyism, formalism, fortuitism, Fourierism, fractionalism, Froebelism, functionalism, fundamentalism, fusionism, futurism, gaelicism, Galenism, Gallicanism, gallicism, galvanism, gamotropism, ganderism, gangsterism, Gargantuism, gargarism, gargoylism, Gasconism, Gaullism, generationism, Genevanism, genteelism, gentilism, geocentricism, geomagnetism, geophagism, geotropism, Germanism, giantism, gigantism, Girondism, Gnosticism, Gongorism, gormandism, Gothicism, gradualism, Graecism, grammaticism, Grangerism, Grecism, gregarianism, griffinism, Grobianism, Grundyism, gynandrism, gynandromophism, gynodioecism, gynomonoecism, gypsyism, gyromagnetism, haptotropism, Hasidism, Hassidism, heathenism, Hebraicism, Hebrewism, hectorism, hedonism, Hegelianism, hegemonism, heliotropism, Hellenism, helotism, hemihedrism, hemimorphism, henotheism, hermaphroditism, heroism, hetaerism, hetairism, heterochronism, heteroecism, heteromorphism, heterostylism, heterothallism, heurism, Hibernianism, Hibernicism, hidalgoism, hierarchism, highbrowism, High-Churchism, Hildebrandism, Hinduism, Hippocratism, hispanicism, historicism, historism, histrionicism, histrionism, Hitlerism, Hobbesianism, Hobbianism, Hobbism, hobbledehoyism, hobbyism, hobgoblinism, hoboism, holism, holohedrism, holometabolism, holophytism, homeomorphism, homoeroticism, homoerotism, homomorphism, homothallism, hooliganism, hoydenism, humanism, humanitarianism, Humism, humoralism, hybridism, hydrargyrism, hydrotropism, hylicism, hylism, hylomorphism, hylopathism, hylotheism, hylozoism, hyperadrenalism, hyperbolism, hypercriticism, hyperthyroidism, hyphenism, hypnotism, hypochondriacism, hypocorism, hypognathism, hypothyroidism, Ibsenism, iconomaticism, iconophilism, idealism, idiotism, idolism, illuminism, illusionism, imagism, immanentism, immaterialism, immediatism, immersionism, immobilism, immoralism, imperialism, impossibilism, impressionism, incendiarism, incivism, incorporealism, indeterminism, indifferentism, individualism, industrialism, infallibilism, infantilism, inflationism, Infralapsarianism, inquilinism, inspirationism, institutionalism, instrumentalism, insularism, insurrectionism, intellectualism, interactionism, internationalism, interventionism, intimism, intransigentism, intuitionalism, intuitionism, intuitivism, invalidism, iodism, Ionism, iotacism, irenicism, Irishism, irrationalism, irredentism, Irvingism, Islamism, ism, Ismailism, isochronism, isodimorphism, isolationism, isomerism, isomorphism, isotropism, itacism, Italianism, italicism, Jacobinism, Jacobitism, Jainism, Jansenism, Jesuitism, jingoism, jockeyism, Johnsonianism, Johnsonism, journalism, Judaism, junkerism, kaiserism, Kantianism, Kantism, katabolism, Kelticism, Keynesianism, klephtism, know-nothingism, Krishnaism, labdacism, labialism, laborism, laconicism, laconism, ladyism, Lamaism, Lamarckianism, Lamarckism, lambdacism, landlordism, Laodiceanism, larrikinism, lathyrism, Latinism, latitudinarianism, laxism, leftism, legalism, leggism, Leibnitzianism, Leibnizianism, Leninism, lesbianism, liberalism, liberationism, libertarianism, libertinism, lichenism, lionism, lipogrammatism, Listerism, literalism, literaryism, localism, Lollardism, Londonism, Low- Churchism, Luddism, luminarism, Lutheranism, Lutherism, lyricism, lyrism, Lysenkoism, macarism, Machiavellianism, Machiavellism, Magianism, Magism, magnetism, Magyarism, Mahdiism, Mahdism, maidism, malapropism, Malthusianism, mammonism, Manichaeism, Manicheanism, Manicheism, mannerism, Maoism, Marcionitism, Marinism, martialism, martinetism, Marxianism, Marxism, masochism, materialism, mathematicism, matriarchalism, maudlinism, Mazdaism, Mazdeism, McCarthyism, mechanism, medievalism, Medism, melanism, meliorism, memoirism, Mendelism, mentalism, mephitism, mercantilism, mercenarism, mercurialism, merism, merycism, mescalism, mesmerism, mesocephalism, mesomerism, Messianism, metabolism, metachronism, metamerism, metamorphism, metasomatism, metempiricism, meteorism, methodism, metopism, Micawberism, Michurinism, micro-organism, microseism, militarism, millenarianism, millenarism, millennianism, millenniarism, Miltonism, minimalism, minimism, misoneism, Mithraicism, Mithraism, mithridatism, modalism, moderatism, modernism, Mohammedanism, Mohammedism, Molinism, monachism, monadism, monarchianism, monarchism, monasticism, monergism, monetarism, mongolism, mongrelism, monism, monkeyism, monochromatism, monoecism, monogenism, monolingualism, monometallism, monophysitism, monorchism, monosyllabism, monotheism, monotheletism, monothelism, monothelitism, Monroeism, Montanism, moralism, Moravianism, Morisonianism, Mormonism, morphinism, mosaicism, Mosaism, Moslemism, mountebankism, multiracialism, Munichism, municipalism, Muslimism, mutism, mutualism, myalism, mysticism, mythicism, mythism, namby- pambyism, nanism, Napoleonism, narcissism, narcotism, nationalism, nativism, naturalism, naturism, navalism, Nazaritism, Naziism, Nazism, necessarianism, necessitarianism, necrophilism, negativism, negroism, negrophilism, neoclassicism, neocolonialism, Neo-Darwinism, Neofascism, Neohellenism, Neo- Impressionism, Neo-Kantianism, Neo-Lamarckism, neologism, Neo- Malthusianism, neo-Nazism, neonomianism, neopaganism, neoplasticism, Neo-Plasticism, Neoplatonism, Neopythagoreanism, neoterism, neovitalism, nephalism, Nestorianism, neuroticism, neutralism, newspaperism, nicotinism, Nietzscheanism, nihilism, noctambulism, Noetianism, nomadism, nominalism, nomism, northernism, notaphilism, nothingarianism, nothingism, Novatianism, novelism, nudism, nyctitropism, obeahism, obeism, obiism, objectivism, obscurantism, obsoletism, Occamism, occasionalism, Occidentalism, occultism, Ockhamism, odism, odylism, officialism, old-maidism, onanism, onirocriticism, Ophism, Ophitism, opportunism, optimism, Orangeism, Orangism, organicism, organism, Orientalism, Origenism, Orleanism, orphanism, Orphism, orthognathism, orthotropism, ostracism, ostrichism, Owenism, pacificism, pacifism, Paddyism, paganism, paleomagnetism, palladianism, paludism, panaesthetism, Pan-Africanism, Pan-Americanism, Pan-Arabian, panchromatism, pancosmism, panderism, panegoism, Pan-Germanism, Panhellenism, panislamism, panlogism, panpsychism, pansexualism, Pan-Slavism, pansophism, panspermatism, panspermism, Pantagruelism, pantheism, papalism, papism, parabaptism, parachronism, paragnathism, paraheliotropism, parallelism, paralogism, paramagnetism, paramorphism, parapsychism, parasitism, Parkinsonism, parliamentarism, Parnassianism, Parnellism, parochialism, Parseeism, Parsiism, Parsism, partialism, particularism, partyism, passivism, pasteurism, pastoralism, paternalism, patrialism, patriarchalism, patriarchism, patriotism, Patripassianism, patristicism, Paulinism, pauperism, pedagogism, pedagoguism, pedanticism, pedantism, pedestrianism, pedobaptism, pedomorphism, Pelagianism, pelmanism, pelorism, pennalism, penny- a-linerism, pentadactylism, pentamerism, pentaprism, peonism, perfectibilism, perfectionism, peripateticism, perpetualism, Persism, personalism, perspectivism, pessmism, petalism, Petrarchianism, Petrarchism, Petrinism, phagocytism, phalansterianism, phalansterism, phallicism, phallism, pharisaism, phariseeism, pheism, phenakism, phenomenalism, phenomenism, philhellenism, philistinism, philosophism, phobism, phoneticism, phonetism, phosphorism, photism, photochromism, photoperiodism, phototropism, physicalism, physicism, physitheism, pianism, pietism, piezomagnetism, Pindarism, Pittism, plagiarism, plagiotropism, Platonicism, Platonism, plebeianism, pleiotropism, pleochroism, pleomorphism, plumbism, pluralism, Plutonism, Plymouthism, pococuranteism, pococurantism, poeticism, pointillism, polonism, polychroism, polycrotism, polydactylism, polygenism, polymastism, polymerism, polymorphism, polynomialism, polysyllabicism, polysyllabism, polysyllogism, polysyntheticism, polysynthetism, polytheism, Pooterism, populism, porism, Porphyrogenitism, positivism, possibilism, Post-Impressionism, post-millennialism, Poujadism, Powellism, practicalism, pragmatism, precisianism, predestinarianism, predeterminism, preferentialism, preformationism, prelatism, premillenarianism, premillennialism, Pre-Raphaelism, Pre- Raphaelitism, Presbyterianism, presentationism, preternaturalism, prettyism, priapism, priggism, primitivism, primordialism, probabiliorism, probablism, prochronism, professionalism, prognathism, progressionism, progressism, progressivism, prohibitionism, proletarianism, propagandism, prophetism, prosaicism, prosaism, proselytism, prostatism, prosyllogism, protectionism, Protestantism, proverbialism, provincialism, prudentialism, Prussianism, psellism, psephism, pseudo-archaism, pseudoclassicism, pseudomorphism, psilanthropism, psychism, psychologism, psychopannychism, psychoticism, ptyalism, puerilism, pugilism, puppyism, purism, puritanism, Puseyism, pyrrhonism, Pythagoreanism, Pythagorism, Quakerism, quattrocentism, quietism, quixotism, rabbinism, Rabaelaisianism, racemism, Rachmanism, racialism, racism, radicalism, Ramism, ranterism, rascalism, rationalism, reactionarism, realism, rebaptism, Rebeccaism, Rechabitism, recidivism, red-tapism, reductionism, reformism, regalism, regionalism, reincarnationism, relationism, relativism, religionism, Rembrandtism, representationalism, representationism, republicanism, restitutionism, restorationism, resurrectionism, reunionism, revanchism, revisionism, revivalism, revolutionism, rheotropism, rheumatism, rhopalism, rhotacism, Ribbonism, rigorism, ritualism, Romanism, romanticism, Rosicrucianism, Rosminianism, Rotarianism, routinism, rowdyism, royalism, ruffianism, ruralism, Russianism, Russophilism, Sabaism, Sabbatarianism, sabbatism, Sabellianism, Sabianism, sacerdotalism, sacramentalism, sacramentarianism, Sadduceeism, Sadducism, sadism, sado-masochism, saintism, Saint- Simonianism, Saint-Simonism, Saivism, Saktism, salvationism, Samaritanism, sanitarianism, sansculottism, sapphism, saprophytism, Saracenism, satanism, saturnism, Saxonism, schematism, scholasticism, scientism, sciolism, Scotism, Scotticism, scoundrelism, scribism, scripturalism, scripturism, secessionism, sectarianism, sectionalism, secularism, self- criticism, self-hypnotism, selfism, semi-Arianism, semi- barbarism, Semi-Pelagianism, Semitism, sensationalism, sensationism, sensism, sensualism, sensuism, sentimentalism, separatism, serialism, servilism, servo-mechanism, sesquipedalianism, sexism, sexualism, Shaivism, shakerism, Shaktism, shamanism, shamateurism, Shiism, Shintoism, Shivaism, shunamitism, sigmatism, Sikhism, simplism, sinapism, sinecurism, singularism, Sinicism, Sinophilism, Sivaism, skepticism, Slavism, snobbism, socialism, Socinianism, sociologism, Sofism, solarism, solecism, sol-faism, solidarism, solidism, solifidianism, solipsism, somatism, somnambulism, somniloquism, sophism, southernism, sovietism, specialism, speciesism, Spencerianism, Spinozism, spiritism, spiritualism, spoonerism, spread-eagleism, Stahlianism, Stahlism, Stakhanovism, Stalinism, stand-pattism, statism, stercoranism, stereoisomerism, stereotropism, stibialism, stigmatism, stoicism, strabism, structuralism, strychninism, strychnism, Stundism, subjectivism, sublapsarianism, subordinationism, substantialism, suburbanism, suffragism, Sufiism, Sufism, suggestionism, supernationalism, supernaturalism, superrealism, Supralapsarianism, supremacism, suprematism, surrealism, sutteeism, Swadeshism, swarajism, Swedenborgianism, swingism, sybaritism, sybotism, syllabism, syllogism, symbolism, symphilism, synaposematism, synchronism, syncretism, syndactylism, syndicalism, synecdochism, synergism, synoecism, syntheticism, Syriarcism, Syrianism, systematism, tachism, tactism, Tammanyism, tantalism, Tantrism, Taoism, tarantism, Tartuffism, Tartufism, tautochronism, tautologism, tautomerism, teetotalism, teleologism, tenebrism, teratism, terminism, territorialism, terrorism, tetramerism, tetratheism, Teutonicism, Teutonism, textualism, thanatism, thaumaturgism, theanthropism, theatricalism, theatricism, theism, theomorphism, Theopaschitism, theophilanthropism, theosophism, therianthropism, theriomorphism, thermotropism, thigmotropism, Thomism, thrombo- embolism, thuggism, tigerism, Timonism, Titanism, Titoism, toadyism, tokenism, Toryism, totalitarianism, totemism, tourism, tractarianism, trade-unionism, traditionalism, Traducianism, traitorism, transcendentalism, transformism, transmigrationism, transsexualism, tranvestism, tranvestitism, traumatism, trialism, tribadism, tribalism, trichroism, trichromatism, tricrotism, triliteralism, trimorphism, Trinitarianism, trinomialism, tripersonalism, tritheism, triticism, trituberculism, trivialism, troglodytism, troilism, trophotropism, tropism, Trotskyism, truism, tsarism, tuism, Turcophilism, tutiorism, tutorism, tychism, ultra-Conservatism, ultraism, ultramontanism, undenominationalism, unicameralism, unidealism, uniformitarianism, unilateralism, unionism, unitarianism, unversalism, unrealism, unsectarianism, unsocialism, untuism, uranism, utilitarianism, utopianism, utopism, Utraquism, vagabondism, Valentinianism, valetudinarianism, vampirism, vandalism, Vansittartism, Vaticanism, Vedism, veganism, vegetarianism, ventriloquism, verbalism, verism, vernacularism, Victorianism, vigilantism, vikingism, virilism, virtualism, vitalism, viviparism, vocalism, vocationalism, volcanism, Voltaireanism, Voltairianism, Voltairism, voltaism, voltinism, voluntarism, voluntaryism, voodooism, vorticism, voyeurism, vulcanism, vulgarism, vulpinism, vulturism, Wagnerianism, Wagnerism, Wahabiism, Wahabism, welfarism, werewolfism, Wertherism, werwolfism, Wesleyanism, westernism, Whiggism, wholism, witticism, Wodenism, Wolfianism, xanthochroism, Yankeeism, yogism, zanyism, Zarathustrianism, Zarathustrism, zealotism, Zionism, Zoilism, zoism, Zolaism, zombiism, zoomagnetism, zoomorphism, zoophilism, zootheism, Zoroastrianism, Zwinglianism, zygodactylism, zygomorphism.

-itis adenitis, antiaditis, aortitis, appendicitis, arteritis, arthritis, balanitis, blepharitis, bronchitis, bursitis, carditis, cellulitis, cephalitis, ceratitis, cerebritis, cholecystitis, colitis, conchitis, conjunctivitis, crystallitis, cystitis, dermatitis, diaphragmatitis, diphtheritis, diverticulitis, duodenitis, encephalitis, endocarditis, endometritis, enteritis, fibrositis, gastritis, gastroenteritis, gingivitis, glossitis, hamarthritis, hepatitis, hysteritis, ileitis, iritis, keratitis, labyrinthitis, laminitis, laryngitis, lymphangitis, mastitis, mastoiditis, meningitis, metritis, myelitis, myocarditis, myositis, myringitis, nephritis, neuritis, onychitis, oophoritis, ophthalmitis, orchitis, osteitis, osteo-arthritis, osteomyelitis, otitis, ovaritis, panarthritis, pancreatitis, panophthalmitis, papillitis, parotiditis, parotitis, pericarditis, perigastritis, perihepatitis, perinephritis, perineuritis, periostitis, peritonitis, perityphlitis, pharyngitis, phlebitis, phrenitis, pleuritis, pneumonitis, poliomyelitis, polyneuritis, proctitis, prostatitis, pyelitis, pyelonephritis, rachitis, rectitis, retinitis, rhachitis, rhinitis, rhinopharyngitis, salpingitis, scleritis, sclerotitis, sinuitis, splenitis, spondylitis, staphylitis, stomatitis, strumitis, synovitis, syringitis, thrombo-phlebitis, thyroiditis, tonsilitis, tonsillitis, tracheitis, trachitis, tympanitis, typhlitis, ulitis, ureteritis, urethritis, uteritis, uveitis, uvulitis, vaginitis, valvulitis, vulvitis.

-latrous bibliolatrous, heliolatrous, ichthyolatrous, idolatrous, litholatrous, Mariolatrous, Maryolatrous, monolatrous, ophiolatrous, zoolatrous.

-latry angelolatry, anthropolatry, astrolatry, autolatry, bardolatry, bibliolatry, Christolatry, cosmolatry, demonolatry, dendrolatry, ecclesiolatry, epeolatry, geolatry, hagiolatry, heliolatry, hierolatry, ichthyolatry, iconolatry, idolatry, litholatry, lordolatry, Mariolatry, Maryolatry, monolatry, necrolatry, ophiolatry, physiolatry, plutolatry, pylolatry, symbololatry, thaumatolatry, theriolatry, zoolatry.

-logical aerobiological, aerological, aetiological, agrobiological, agrological, agrostological, algological, alogical, amphibological, analogical, anthropological, arachnological, archaeological, astrological, atheological, audiological, autecological, axiological, bacteriological, batological, battological, biological, bryological, campanological, carcinological, cartological, chorological, Christological, chronological, climatological, codicological, conchological, cosmological, craniological, cryobiological, cryptological, cytological, demonological, dendrological, deontological, dermatological, dysteleological, ecclesiological, ecological, Egyptological, electrophysiological, embryological, enological, entomological, epidemiological, epistemological, eschatological, ethnological, ethological, etymological, futurological, gastrological, gemmological, gemological, genealogical, genethlialogical, geochronological, geological, geomorphological, gerontological, glaciological, glossological, gnotobiological, graphological, gynecological, hagiological, helminthological, hepaticological, herpetological, histological, histopathological, homological, horological, hydrobiological, hydrological, ichthyological, ideological, illogical, immunological, laryngological, limnological, lithological, logical, malacological, mammalogical, martyrological, metapsychological, meteorological, micrological, mineralogical, monological, morphological, musicological, mycological, myological, myrmecological, mythological, necrological, neological, nephological, nephrological, neurological, nomological, nosological, nostological, oceanological, odontological, ontological, ophiological, ophthalmological, oreological, ornithological, orological, osteological, paleontological, paleozoological, palynological, parapsychological, pathological, pedological, penological, pestological, petrological, phenological, phenomenological, philological, phonological, phraseological, phrenological, phycological, physiological, phytological, phytopathological, pneumatological, pomological, posological, potamological, protozoological, psephological, psychobiological, psychological, radiological, reflexological, rheumatological, rhinological, scatological, sedimentological, seismological, selenological, serological, Sinological, sociobiological, sociological, somatological, soteriological, Sovietological, spectrological, speleological, stoechiological, stoicheiological, stoichiological, synecological, tautological, technological, teleological, teratological, terminological, theological, topological, toxicological, traumatological, trichological, tropological, typological, unlogical, untheological, urological, virological, volcanological, vulcanological, zoological, zoophytological, zymological.

-logous analogous, antilogous, dendrologous, heterologous, homologous, isologous, tautologous.

-logue apologue, collogue, decalogue, dialogue, duologue, eclogue, epilogue, grammalogue, homologue, idealogue, ideologue, isologue, monologue, philologue, prologue, Sinologue, theologue, travelogue, trialogue.

-logy acarology, aerobiology, aerolithology, aerology, aetiology, agriology, agrobiology, agrology, agrostology, algology, amphibology, anesthesiology, analogy, andrology, anemology, angelology, anthology, anthropobiology, anthropology, antilogy, apology, arachnology, archaeology, archology, aristology, Assyriology, astrogeology, astrology, atheology, atmology, audiology, autecology, autology, axiology, bacteriology, balneology, batology, battology, bibliology, bioecology, biology, biotechnology, brachylogy, bryology, bumpology, cacology, caliology, campanology, carcinology, cardiology, carphology, cartology, cetology, cheirology, chirology, choreology, chorology, Christology, chronobiology, chronology, cine-biology, climatology, codicology, cometology, conchology, coprology, cosmetology, cosmology, craniology, criminology, cryobiology, cryptology, cytology, dactyliology, dactylology, deltiology, demology, demonology, dendrochronology, dendrology, deontology, dermatology, diabology, diabolology, dialectology, diplomatology, dittology, docimology, dogmatology, dosiology, dosology, doxology, dyslogy, dysteleology, ecclesiology, eccrinology, ecology, edaphology, Egyptology, electrobiology, electrology, electrophysiology, electrotechnology, elogy, embyology, emmenology, endemiology, endocrinology, enology, entomology, enzymology, epidemiology, epistemology, escapology, eschatology, ethnology, ethnomusicology, ethology, Etruscology, etymology, euchology, eulogy, exobiology, festilogy, festology, folk-etymology, futurology, gastroenterology, gastrology, gemmology, gemology, genealogy, genethlialogy, geochronology, geology, geomorphology, gerontology, gigantology, glaciology, glossology, glottology, gnomonology, gnoseology, gnosiology, gnotobiology, graphology, gynecology, hematology, hagiology, hamartiology, haplology, heliology, helminthology, heorology, hepaticology, hepatology, heresiology, herpetology, heterology, hierology, hippology, histiology, histology, histopathology, historiology, homology, hoplology, horology, hydrobiology, hydrogeology, hydrology, hydrometeorology, hyetology, hygrology, hymnology, hypnology, ichnology, ichthyology, iconology, ideology, immunology, insectology, irenology, kidology, kinesiology, koniology, Kremlinology, laryngology, lepidopterology, lexicology, lichenology, limnology, lithology, liturgiology, macrology, malacology, malariology, mammalogy, Mariology, martyrology, Maryology, Mayology, menology, metapsychology, meteorology, methodology, microbiology, microclimatology, micrology, micro- meteorology, microtechnology, mineralogy, misology, monadology, monology, morphology, muscology, museology, musicology, mycetology, mycology, myology, myrmecology, mythology, necrology, nematology, neology, nephology, nephrology, neurobiology, neurohypnology, neurology, neuropathology, neurophysiology, neuroradiology, neurypnology, nomology, noology, nosology, nostology, numerology, numisatology, oceanology, odontology, olfactology, oncology, onirology, ontology, oology, ophiology, ophthalmology, optology, orchidology, oreology, ornithology, orology, orthopterology, oryctology, osteology, otolaryngology, otology, otorhinolaryngology, ourology, paleanthropology, paleethnology, paleichthyology, paleoclimatology, paleolimnology, paleontology, paleopelology, paleophytology, paleozoology, palillogy, palynology, pantheology, papyrology, paradoxology, paralogy, parapsychology, parasitology, paroemiology, pathology, patrology, pedology, pelology, penology, periodontology, perissology, pestology, petrology, phenology, pharmacology, pharyngology, phenology, phenomenology, philology, phonology, photobiology, photogeology, phraseology, phrenology, phycology, physiology, phytology, phytopathology, planetology, plutology, pneumatology, prodology, pomology, ponerology, posology, potamology, primatology, protistology, protozoology, psephology, pseudology, psychobiology, psychology, psychopathology, psychophysiology, pteridology, pyretology, pyroballogy, radiobiology, radiology, reflexology, rheology, rheumatology, rhinology, röntgenology, sacrology, satanology, scatology, Scientology, sedimentology, seismology, selenology, selenomorphology, semasiology, semeiology, semiology, serology, sexology, sindonology, Sinology, sitiology, sitology, skatology, sociobiology, sociology, somatology, soteriology, spectrology, speleology, sphagnology, sphygmology, spongology, stichology, stoechiology, stoichiology, stomatology, storiology, symbology, symbolology, symptomatology, synchronology, synecology, syphilology, systematology, tautology, technology, teleology, teratology, terminology, terotechnology, tetralogy, thanatology, theology, thermology, therology, thremmatology, timbrology, tocology, tokology, topology, toxicology, traumatology, tribology, trichology, trilogy, trophology, tropology, typhlology, typology, ufology, uranology, urbanology, urinology, urology, venereology, vexillology, victimology, vinology, virology, volcanology, vulcanology, xylology, zoopathology, zoophytology, zoopsychology, zymology.

-lysis analysis, atmolysis, autocatalysis, autolysis, bacteriolysis, catalysis, cryptanalysis, cytolysis, dialysis, electroanalysis, electrolysis, hematolysis, hemodialysis, hemolysis, histolysis, hydrolysis, hypno-analysis, leucocytolysis, microanalysis, nacro-analysis, neurolysis, paralysis, photolysis, plasmolysis, pneumatolysis, proteolysis, psephoanalysis, psychoanalysis, pyrolysis, radiolysis, thermolysis, uranalysis, urinalysis, zincolysis, zymolysis.

-lytic analytic, anxiolytic, autocatalytic, autolytic, bacteriolytic, catalytic, dialytic, electrolytic, hemolytic, histolytic, hydrolytic, paralytic, photolytic, plasmolytic, pneumatolytic, proteolytic, psychoanalytic, pyrolytic, sympatholytic, tachylytic, thermolytic, unanalytic.

-mania acronymania, anglomania, anthomania, balletomania, bibliomania, Celtomania, demonomania, dipsomania, egomania, enomania, erotomania, etheromania, francomania, gallomania, hydromania, hypomania, hysteromania, Keltomania, kleptomania, mania, megalomania, melomania, methomania, metromania, monomania, morphinomania, mythomania, nostomania, nymphomania, opsomania, orchidomania, petalomania, phyllomania, potichomania, pteridomania, pyromania, squandermania, theatromania, theomania, timbromania, toxicomania, tulipomania, typomania, xenomania.

-mancy aeromancy, axinomancy, belomancy, bibliomancy, botanomancy, capnomancy, cartomancy, ceromancy, chiromancy, cleromancy, coscinomancy, crithomancy, crystallomancy, dactyliomancy, enomancy, gastromancy, geomancy, gyromancy, hieromancy, hydromancy, lampadomancy, lithomancy, myomancy, necromancy, nigromancy, omphalomancy, oniromancy, onychomancy, ornithomancy, pyromancy, rhabdomancy, scapulimancy, spodomancy, tephromancy, theomancy, zoomancy.

-mantic chiromantic, geomantic, hydromantic, myomantic, necromantic, ornithomantic, pyromantic, scapulimantic, spodomantic, theomantic, zoomantic.

-mathic chrestomathic, philomathic, polymathic.

-mathy chrestomathy, opsimathy, philomathy, polymathy.

-meter absorptiometer, accelerometer, acidimeter, actinometer, aerometer, alcoholometer, alkalimeter, altimeter, ammeter, anemometer, areometer, arithmometer, atmometer, audiometer, auxanometer, auxometer, barometer, bathometer, bathymeter, bolometer, bomb-calorimeter, calorimeter, cathetometer, centimeter, chlorimeter, chlorometer, chronometer, clinometer, colorimeter, Comptometer®;, coulombmeter, coulometer, craniometer, cryometer, cyanometer, cyclometer, decelerometer, declinometer, dendrometer, densimeter, densitometer,

diagometer, diameter, diaphanometer, diffractometer, dimeter, dose-meter, dosimeter, drosometer, dynamometer, effusiometer, electrodynamometer, electrometer, endosmometer, enometer, ergometer, eriometer, evaporimeter, extensimeter, extensometer, fathometer, flowmeter, fluorimeter, fluorometer, focimeter, galactometer, galvanometer, gas-meter, gasometer, geometer, geothermometer, goniometer, gradiometer, gravimeter, harmonometer, heliometer, heptameter, hexameter, hodometer, hydrometer, hyetometer, hygrometer, hypsometer, iconometer, inclinometer, interferometer, isoperimeter, katathermometer, konimeter, kryometer, lactometer, luxmeter, lysimeter, machmeter, magnetometer, manometer, mekometer, meter, micrometer, microseismometer, mileometer, milometer, monometer, nephelometer, Nilometer, nitrometer, octameter, odometer, ohmmeter, ombrometer, oncometer, ophthalmometer, opisometer, opsiometer, optometer, osmometer, oximeter, pachymeter, parameter, passimeter, pedometer, pelvimeter, pentameter, perimeter, permeameter, phonmeter, phonometer, photometer, piezometer, planimeter, planometer, plessimeter, pleximeter, pluviometer, pneumatometer, polarimeter, potentiometer, potometer, psychometer, psychrometer, pulsimeter, pulsometer, pycnometer, pyknometer, pyrheliometer, pyrometer, quantometer, radiogoniometer, radiometer, radiotelemeter, refractometer, rheometer, rhythmometer, saccharimeter, saccharometer, salimeter, salinometer, scintillometer, sclerometer, seismometer, semi- diameter, semiperimeter, sensitometer, slot-meter, solarimeter, spectrophotometer, speedometer, spherometer, sphygmomanometer, sphygmometer, stactometer, stalagometer, stereometer, strabismometer, strabometer, swingometer, sympiesometer, tacheometer, tachometer, tachymeter, taseometer, tasimeter, taximeter, telemeter, tellurometer, tetrameter, thermometer, Tintometer®;, tonometer, torque-meter, tribometer, trigonometer, trimeter, trocheameter, trochometer, tromometer, udometer, urinometer, vaporimeter, variometer, viameter, vibrometer, viscometer, viscosimeter, voltameter, voltmeter, volumenometer, volumeter, volumometer, water-barometer, water- meter, water-thermometer, wattmeter, wavemeter, weathermeter, xylometer, zymometer, zymosimeter.
- **-metry** acidimetry, aerometry, alcoholometry, alkalimetry, anemometry, anthropometry, areometry, asymmetry, barometry, bathymetry, biometry, bolometry, calorimetry, chlorimetry, chlorometry, chronometry, clinometry, colorimetry, coulometry, craniometry, densimetry, densitometry, dissymmetry, dosimetry, dynamometry, electrometry, galvanometry, gasometry, geometry, goniometry, gravimetry, hodometry, horometry, hydrometry, hygometry, hypsometry, iconometry, interferometry, isometry, isoperimetry, micrometry, microseismometry, nephelometry, noometry, odometry, ophthalometry, optometry, pelvimetry, perimetry, photometry, planimetry, plessimetry, pleximetry, polarimetry, pseudosymmetry, psychometry, psychrometry, pyrometry, saccharimetry, seismometry, sociometry, spectrometry, spectrophotometry, spirometry, stalagmometry, stereometry, stichometry, stoechiometry, stoichiometry, symmetry, tacheometry, tachometry, tachymetry, telemetry, tensiometry, thermometry, trigonometry, unsymmetry, uranometry, viscometry, viscosimetry, zoometry.
- **-monger** halladmonger, barber-monger, borough-monger, carpetmonger, cheese-monger, costardmonger, costermonger, fellmonger, fishmonger, flesh-monger, gossip-monger, ironmonger, lawmonger, love-monger, maxim-monger, meal-monger, miracle- monger, mystery-monger, newsmonger, panic-monger, peace-monger, pearmonger, peltmonger, phrasemonger, place-monger, prayer- monger, relic-monger, scandalmonger, scaremonger, sensation- monger, species-monger, starmonger, state-monger, system-monger, verse-monger, warmonger, whoremonger, wit-monger, wonder-monger.
- **-morphic** actinomorphic, allelomorphic, allotriomorphic, anamorphic, anthropomorphic, automorphic, biomorphic, dimorphic, ectomorphic, enantiomorphic, endomorphic, ergatomorphic, gynandromorphic, hemimorphic, heteromorphic, homeomorphic, homomorphic, hylomorphic, idiomorphic, isodimorphic, isomorphic, lagomorphic, mesomorphic, metamorphic, monomorphic, morphic, ophiomorphic, ornithomorphic, paramorphic, pedomorphic, perimorphic, pleomorphic, polymorphic, protomorphic, pseudomorphic, tetramorphic, theomorphic, theriomorphic, trimorphic, xenomorphic, xeromorphic, zoomorphic, zygomorphic.
- **-morphous** amorphous, anamorphous, anthropomorphous, dimorphous, enantiomorphous, gynandromorphous, heteromorphous, homeomorphous, homomorphous, isodimorphous, isomorphous, lagomorphous, mesomorphous, monomorphous, ophiomorphous, perimorphous, pleomorphous, polymorphous, pseudomorphous, rhizomorphous, tauromorphous, theriomorphous, trimorphous, xeromorphous, zygomorphous.
- **-onym** acronym, anonym, antonym, autonym, cryptonym, eponym, exonym, heteronym, homonym, metonym, paronym, polyonym, pseudonym, synonym, tautonym, toponym, trionym.
- **-onymic** acronymic, Hieronymic, homonymic, matronymic, metonymic, metronymic, patronymic, polyonymic, synonymic, toponymic.
- **-osis** abiosis, acidosis, actinobacillosis, actinomycosis, aerobiosis, aeroneurosis, alkalosis, amaurosis, amitosis, anabiosis, anadiplosis, anamorphosis, anaplerosis, anastomosis, anchylosis, anerobiosis, ankylosis, anthracosis,

anthropomorphosis, antibiosis, apodosis, aponeurosis, apotheosis, arteriosclerosis, arthrosis, asbestosis, aspergillosis, ateleiosis, atherosclerosis, athetosis, autohypnosis, avitaminosis, bacteriosis, bagassosis, bilharziosis, biocoenosis, bromhidrosis, bromidrosis, brucellosis, byssinosis, carcinomatosis, carcinosis, chlorosis, cirrhosis, coccidiosis, cyanosis, cyclosis, dermatosis, diarthrosis, diorthosis, diverticulosis, dulosis, ecchymosis, enantiosis, enarthrosis, endometriosis, endosmosis, enosis, enteroptosis, epanadiplosis, epanorthosis, exosmosis, exostosis, fibrosis, fluorosis, furunculosis, gliomatosis, gnotobiosis, gomphosis, gummosis, halitosis, hallucinosis, heliosis, hematosis, heterosis, hidrosis, homeosis, homomorphosis, homozygosis, hydronephrosis, hyperhidrosis, hyperidrosis, hyperinosis, hypersacosis, hypervitaminosis, hypinosis, hypnosis, hypotyposis, ichthyosis, kenosis, keratosis, ketosis, kurtosis, kyllosis, kyphosis, leishmaniosis, leptospirosis, leucocytosis, limosis, lipomatosis, lordosis, madarosis, marmarosis, meiosis, melanosis, metachrosis, metamorphosis, metempsychosis, miosis, mitosis, molybdosis, mononucleosis, monosis, morphosis, mucoviscidosis, mycosis, mycotoxicosis, myosis, myxomatosis, narcohypnosis, narcosis, necrobiosis, necrosis, nephroptosis, nephrosis, neurosis, onychocryptosis, ornithosis, osmidrosis, osmosis, osteoarthrosis, osteoporosis, otosclerosis, parabiosis, paraphimosis, parapsychosis, parasitosis, pedamorphosis, pediculosis, phagocytosis, phimosis, pholidosis, phytosis, pneumoconiosis, pneumokoniosis, pneumonokoniosis, pneumonoultramicroscopicsilicovolcanoconiosis, pollenosis, polyposis, porosis, proptosis, psilosis, psittacosis, psychoneurosis, psychosis, pterylosis, ptilosis, ptosis, pyrosis, resinosis, salmonellosis, sarcoidosis, sarcomatosis, sclerosis, scoliosis, self-hypnosis, siderosis, silicosis, sorosis, spirillosis, spirochetosis, steatosis, stegnosis, stenosis, strongylosis, sycosis, symbiosis, symptosis, synarthrosis, synchrondrosis, syndesmosis, synociosis, synostosis, syntenosis, syssarcosis, thanatosis, theriomorphosis, thrombosis, thylosis, thyrotoxicosis, torulosis, toxoplasmosis, trichinosis, trichophytosis, trichosis, trophobiosis, trophoneurosis, tuberculosis, tylosis, ulosis, urosis, virosis, visceroptosis, xerosis, zoonosis, zygosis, zymosis.

-path allopath, homeopath, kinesipath, naturopath, neuropath, osteopath, psychopath, sociopath, telepath.

-pathic allopathic, anthropopathic, antipathic, empathic, homoeopathic, hydropathic, idiopathic, kinesipathic, naturopathic, neuropathic, osteopathic, protopathic, psychopathic, sociopathic, telepathic.

-pathy allopathy, anthropopathy, antipathy, apathy, cardiomyopathy, dyspathy, empathy, enantiopathy, homeopathy, hydropathy, idiopathy, kinesipathy, myocardiopathy, naturopathy, neuropathy, nostopathy, osteopathy, psychopathy, sociopathy, sympathy, telepathy, theopathy, zoopathy.

-phage bacteriophage, macrophage, ostreophage, xylophage.

-phagous anthropophagous, autophagous, carpophagous, coprophagous, creophagous, endophagous, entomophagous, exophagous, geophagous, hippophagous, hylophagous, ichthyophagous, lithophagous, mallophagous, meliphagous, monophagous, myrmecophagous, necrophagous, omophagous ophiophagous, ostreophagous, pantophagous, phyllophagous, phytophagous, polyphagous, rhizophagous, saprophagous, sarcophagous, scatophagous, theophagous, toxicophagous, toxiphagous, xylophagous, zoophagous.

-phagy anthropophagy, autophagy, coprophagy, dysphagy, endophagy, entomophagy, exophagy, hippophagy, ichthyophagy, monophagy, mycophagy, omophagy, ostreophagy, pantophagy, polyphagy, sacrophagy, scatophagy, theophagy, xerophagy.

-phile ailurophile, arctophile, audiophile, bibliophile, cartophile, discophile, enophile, francophile, gallophile, Germanophile, gerontophile, halophile, hippophile, homophile, iodophile, lyophile, myrmecophile, necrophile, negrophile, ombrophile, pedophile, psammophile, Russophile, scripophile, Sinophile, Slavophile, spermophile, thermophile, Turcophile, xenophile, zoophile.

-philia ailurophilia, anglophilia, canophilia, coprophilia, ephebophilia, Germanophilia, gerontophilia, hemophilia, necrophilia, paraphilia, pedophilia, scopophilia, scoptophilia, zoophilia.

-philist bibliophilist, canophilist, cartophilist, Dantophilist, enophilist, iconophilist, negrophilist, notaphilist, ophiophilist, pteridophilist, Russophilist, scripophilist, stegophilist, timbrophilist, zoophilist.

-phily acarophily, anemophily, bibliophily, cartophily, enophily, entomophily, halophily, hydrophily, myrmecophily, necrophily, notaphily, ornithophily, photophily, scripophily, Sinophily, symphily, timbrophily, toxophily, xerophily.

-phobe ailurophobe, anglophobe, francophobe, gallophobe, Germanophobe, hippophobe, hygrophobe, lyophobe, negrophobe, ombrophobe, photophobe, Russophobe, Slavophobe, Turcophobe, xenophobe.

-phobia acrophobia, aerophobia, agoraphobia, ailurophobia, algophobia, anglophobia, astraphobia, astrapophobia, bathophobia, bibliophobia, canophobia, claustrophobia, cynophobia, dromophobia, ecophobia, ergophobia, gallophobia, hydrophobia, hypsophobia, monophobia, mysophobia, necrophobia, negrophobia, neophobia, nosophobia, nyctophobia, ochlophobia, panophobia, pantophobia, pathophobia, phonophobia, photophobia, Russophobia, satanophobia, scopophobia, sitiophobia, sitophobia, symmetrophobia, syphilophobia, taphephobia, taphophobia, thanatophobia, theophobia, toxicophobia, toxiphobia, triskaidecaphobia, triskaidekaphobia, xenophobia, zoophobia.

-phobic aerophobic, agoraphobic, anglophobic, claustrophobic, heliophobic, hydrophobic, lyophobic, monophobic, phobic, photophobic.

-phone aerophone, allophone, anglophone, Ansaphone®;, audiphone, chordophone, detectophone, diaphone, dictaphone, diphone, earphone, Entryphone®;, francophone, geophone, gramophone, harmoniphone, headphone, heckelphone, homophone, hydrophone, idiophone, interphone, kaleidophone, megaphone, metallophone, microphone, monotelephone, optophone, phone, photophone, Picturephone®;, polyphone, pyrophone, radiogramophone, radiophone, radiotelephone, sarrusophone, saxophone, sousaphone, speakerphone, sphygmophone, stentorphone, telephone, theatrophone, triphone, vibraphone, videophone, videotelephone, viewphone, zylophone.

-phonic acrophonic, allophonic, anglophonic, antiphonic, aphonic, cacophonic, cataphonic, chordophonic, dodecaphonic, dysphonic, euphonic, gramophonic, homophonic, microphonic, monophonic, paraphonic, photophonic, quadraphonic, quadrophonic, radiophonic, stentorophonic, stereophonic, symphonic, telephonic, xylophonic.

-phony acrophony, antiphony, aphony, autophony, cacophony, colophony, dodecaphony, euphony, gramophony, homophony, laryngophony, monophony, photophony, polyphony, quadraphony, quadrophony, radiophony, radiotelephony, stereophony, symphony, tautophony, telephony.

-phorous discophorous, Eriophorous, galactophorous, hypophosphorous, mastigophorous, necrophorous, odontophorous, phosphorous, pyrophorous, rhynchophorous, sporophorous.

-phyte aerophyte, bryophyte, cormophyte, dermatophyte, ectophyte, endophyte, entophyte, epiphyte, gametophyte, geophyte, halophyte, heliophyte, heliosciophyte, holophyte, hydrophyte, hygrophyte, hylophyte, lithophyte, mesophyte, microphyte, neophyte, oophyte, osteophyte, phanerophyte, phreatophyte, protophyte, psammophyte, pteridophyte, saprophyte, schizophyte, spermaphyte, spermatophyte, spermophyte, sporophyte, thallophyte, tropophyte, xerophyte, zoophyte, zygophyte.

-saurus Allosaurus, Ankylosaurus, Apatosaurus, Atlantosaurus, brachiosaurus, brontosaurus, Ceteosaurus, Dolichosaurus, Ichthyosaurus, megalosaurus, Plesiosaurus, Stegosaurus, Teleosaurus, Titanosaurus, tyrannosaurus.

-scope aethrioscope, auriscope, baroscope, bathyscope, benthoscope, bioscope, bronchoscope, chromoscope, chronoscope, colposcope, cryoscope, cystoscope, dichrooscope, dichroscope, dipleidoscope, ebullioscope, electroscope, endoscope, engiscope, engyscope, epidiascope, episcope, fluoroscope, galvanoscope, gastroscope, gyroscope, hagioscope, helioscope, hodoscope, horoscope, hydroscope, hygroscope, iconoscope, iriscope, kaleidoscope, kinetoscope, koniscope, lactoscope, laparoscope, laryngoscope, lychnoscope, megascope, microscope, mutoscope, myringoscope, myrioscope, nephoscope, opeidoscope, ophthalmoscope, oscilloscope, otoscope, pantoscope, periscope, pharyngoscope, phenakistoscope, phonendoscope, polariscope, poroscope, praxinoscope, proctoscope, pseudoscope, pyroscope, radarscope, radioscope, rhinoscope, scintilloscope, scope, seismoscope, sigmoidoscope, somascope, spectrohelioscope, spectroscope, sphygmoscope, splintariscope, statoscope, stereofluoroscope, stereoscope, stethoscope, stroboscope, tachistoscope, teinoscope, telescope, thermoscope, triniscope, ultramicroscope, vectorscope, Vertoscope®;, vitascope.

-scopic autoscopic, bronchoscopic, cryoscopic, deuteroscopic, dichroscopic, ebullioscopic, electroscopic, endoscopic, gyroscopic, hagioscopic, helioscopic, horoscopic, hygroscopic, kaleidoscopic, laryngoscopic, macroscopic, megascopic, metoscopic, microscopic, necroscopic, ophthalmoscopic, orthoscopic, pantoscopic, periscopic, poroscopic, rhinoscopic, seismoscopic, spectroscopic, stethoscopic, stroboscopic, submicroscopic, tachistoscopic, telescopic, thermoscopic, ultramicroscopic, zooscopic.

-scopy autoscopy, bronchoscopy, colposcopy, cranioscopy, cryoscopy, cystoscopy, dactyloscopy, deuteroscopy, ebullioscopy, endoscopy, episcopy, fluoroscopy, hepatoscopy, hieroscopy, horoscopy, laparoscopy, laryngoscopy, metoposcopy, microscopy, necroscopy, omoplatoscopy, oniroscopy, ophthalmoscopy, ornithoscopy, ouroscopy, pharyngoscopy, poroscopy, proctoscopy, radioscopy, retinoscopy, rhinoscopy, röntgenoscopy, skiascopy, spectroscopy, stereoscopy, stethoscopy, telescopy, tracheoscopy, ultramicroscopy, urinoscopy, uroscopy, zooscopy.

-ship abbotship, accountantship, acquaintanceship, administratorship, admiralship, advisership, aedileship, airmanship, aldermanship, amateurship, ambassadorship, apostleship, apprenticeship, archonship, assessorship, associateship, attorneyship, auditorship, augurship, authorship, bachelorship, bailieship, baillieship, bardship, barristership, bashawship, batmanship, beadleship, bedellship, bedelship, benchership, bondmanship, brinkmanship, bursarship, bushmanship, butlership, cadetship, Caesarship, candidateship, captainship, cardinalship, catechumenship, censorship, chairmanship, chamberlainship, championship, chancellorship, chaplainship, chelaship, chiefship, chieftainship, citizenship, clanship, clerkship, clientship, clownship, coadjutorship, colleagueship, collectorship, colonelship, commandantship, commandership, commissaryship, commissionership, committeeship, companionship, compotationship, comradeship, conductorship, confessorship, connoisseurship, conservatorship, constableship, consulship, controllership, copartnership, co-rivalship, corporalship, counsellorship, countship, courtship, cousinship, cowardship, craftmanship, craftsmanship, creatorship, creatureship, curateship, curatorship, custodianship, deaconship, dealership, deanship, demyship, denizenship, devilship, dictatorship, directorship, discipleship, disfellowship, doctorship, dogeship, dogship, dollarship, donship, draftsmanship, dukeship, editorship, eldership, electorship, emperorship, endship, ensignship, entrepreneurship, envoyship, executorship, factorship, fathership, fellowship, foxship, freshmanship, friendship, gamesmanship, generalship, gentlemanship, giantship, gladiatorship, goddess-ship, godship, good-fellowship, governor- generalship, governorship, grandeeship, guardianship, guideship, hardship, headship, hectorship, heirship, heraldship, heroship, hership, hetmanship, horsemanship, hostess-ship, housewifeship, huntsmanship, inspectorship, interpretership, interrelationship, janitorship, jockeyship, judgeship, justiceship, kaisership, keepership, kindredship, kingship, kinship, knaveship, ladyship, lairdship, land-ownership, laureateship, leadership, lectorship, lectureship, legateship, legislatorship, librarianship, lieutenant-commandership, lieutenant-generalship, lieutenant- governorship, lieutenantship, lifemanship, logship, lordship, ludship, mageship, major-generalship, majorship, managership, marshalship, mastership, matronship, mayorship, mediatorship, membership, Messiahship, milk-kinship, minorship, mistress-ship, moderatorship, monitorship, multi-ownership, musicianship, noviceship, nunship, oarsmanship, one-upmanship, overlordship, ownership, partisanship, partnership, pastorship, patroonship, peatship, pendragonship, penmanship, physicianship, poetship, popeship, possessorship, postmastership, praetorship, preachership, precentorship, perfectship, prelateship, premiership, prenticeship, presbytership, presidentship, pretendership, priestship, primateship, primogenitureship, principalship, priorship, probationership, proconsulship, proctorship, procuratorship, professorship, progenitorship, prolocutorship, prophetship, proprietorship, prosectorship, protectorship, provostship, pursership, quaestorship, queenship, rajahship, rajaship, rangership, readership, recordership, rectorship, regentship, registrarship, relationship, residentiaryship, residentship, retainership, rivalship, rogueship, rulership, sachemship, saintship, salesmanship, scholarship, school-friendship, schoolmastership, scrivenership, seamanship, secretaryship, seigniorship, sempstress-ship, senatorship, seneschalship, serfship, sergeantship, serjeantship, servantship, servitorship, sextonship, sheriffship, showmanship, sibship, sizarship, soldiership, solicitorship, sonship, speakership, spectatorship, spinstership, sponsorship, sportsmanship, squireship, statesmanship, stewardship, studentship, subahship, subdeaconship, subeditorship, subinspectorship, subjectship, successorship, suffraganship, sultanship, superintendentship, superiorship, supervisorship, suretyship, surgeonship, surrogateship, surveyorship, survivorship, swordsmanship, teachership, tellership, tenantship, thaneship, thwartship, tide-waitership, township, traineeship, traitorship, treasurership, treeship, tribuneship, truantship, trusteeship, tutorship, twinship, umpireship, uncleship, under- clerkship, undergraduateship, under-secretaryship, unfriendship, ushership, vaivodeship, vergership, vicarship, vice-chairmanship, vice-chancellorship, vice-consulship, viceroyship, virtuosoship, viscountship, viziership, vizirship, voivodeship, waivodeship, wardenship, wardship, watermanship, Whigship, workmanship, worship, wranglership, writership, yachtsmanship.

-sophy anthroposophy, gastrosophy, gymnosophy, pansophy, philosophy, sciosophy, theosophy.

-stat aerostat, antistat, appestat, bacteriostat, barostat, celostat, chemostat, coccidiostat, cryostat, gyrostat, heliostat, hemostat, humidistat, hydrostat, hygrostat, klinostat, pyrostat, rheostat, siderostat, thermostat.

-therapy actinotherapy, balneotherapy, chemotherapy, cryotherapy, curietherapy, electrotherapy, heliotherapy, hydrotherapy, hypnotherapy, immunotherapy, kinesitherapy, musicotherapy, narcotherapy, opotherapy, organotherapy, pelotherapy, phototherapy, physiotherapy, psychotherapy, pyretotherapy, radiotherapy, röntgenotherapy, serotherapy, serum- therapy, zootherapy.

-tomy adenectomy, adenoidectomy, anatomy, anthropotomy, appendectomy, appendicectomy, arteriotomy, autotomy, cephalotomy, cholecystectomy, cholecystotomy, colotomy, cordotomy, craniectomy, craniotomy, cystotomy, dichotomy, duodenectomy, embryotomy, encephalotomy, enterectomy, enterotomy, gastrectomy, gastrotomy, gingivectomy, glossectomy, hepatectomy, herniotomy, hysterectomy, hysterotomy, iridectomy, iridotomy, laparotomy, laryngectomy, laryngotomy, leucotomy, lipectomy, lithotomy, lobectomy, lobotomy, lumpectomy, mastectomy, microtomy, myringotomy, necrotomy, nephrectomy, nephrotomy, neurectomy, neuroanatomy, neurotomy, oophorectomy, orchidectomy, orchiectomy, osteotomy, ovariotomy, pharyngotomy, phlebotomy, phytotomy, pleurotomy, pneumonectomy, pogonotomy, prostatectomy, rhytidectomy, salpingectomy, sclerotomy, splenectomy, stapedectomy, stereotomy, strabotomy, sympathectomy, symphyseotomy, symphsiotomy, syringotomy, tenotomy, tetrachotomy, thymectomy, tonsillectomy, tonsillotomy, topectomy, tracheotomy, trichotomy, tubectomy, ultramicrotomy, uterectomy, uterotomy, varicotomy, vasectomy, zootomy.

-urgy chemurgy, dramaturgy, electrometallurgy, hierurgy, hydrometallurgy, liturgy, metallurgy, micrurgy, theurgy, zymurgy.

-vorous apivorous, baccivorous, carnivorous, fructivorous, frugivorous, graminivorous, granivorous, herbivorous, insectivorous, lignivorous, mellivorous, myristicivorous, nucivorous, omnivorous, ossivorous, piscivorous, radicivorous, ranivorous, sanguinivorous, sanguivorous, vermivorous.

Classified Word-lists

air and space vehicles aerobus, airdrome, aerodyne, aerohydroplane, airplane, aerostat, air-ambulance, air-bus, airship, all-wing airplane, amphibian, autogiro, balloon, biplane, blimp, bomber, cable-car, camel, canard, chopper, comsat, convertiplane, crate, delta-wing, dirigible, dive bomber, fan-jet, fighter, fire-balloon, flying boat, flying saucer, flying wing, glider, gondola, gyrocopter, gyroplane, helibus, helicopter, hoverbus, hovercar, hovercraft, hovertrain, hydro- airplane, hydrofoil, hydroplane, intercepter, jet, jetliner, jetplane, lem, mictolight, module, monoplane, multiplane, plane, rocket, rocket-plane, runabout, sailplane, satellite, seaplane, space platform, space probe, space shuttle, spacecraft, spaceship, spitfire, sputnik, steprocket, stol, strato-cruiser, stratotanker, swingtail cargo aircraft, swing-wing, tanker, taube, téléférique, tow-plane, tractor, triplane, troop-carrier, tube, tug, turbojet, twoseater, UFO, warplane, zeppelin.

alphabets and writing systems Chalcidian alphabet, cuneiform, Cyrillic, devanagari, estrang(h)elo, finger-alphabet, futhark, Glagol, Glossic, Greek, Gurmukhi, hieroglyphs, hiragana, ideograph, kana, katakana, Kuffic, linear A, linear B, logograph, nagari, naskhi, og(h)am, pictograph, Roman, runic, syllabary.

anatomical abductor, acromion, adductor, alvine, ancon, astragalus, atlas, aural, auricular, axilla, biceps, blade-bone, bone, brachial, bregma, buccal, calcaneum, calcaneus, capitate, cardiac, carpal, carpus, cartilage, cephalic, cerebral, cholecyst, clavicle, coccyx, celiac, collar-bone, concha, coracoid, crural, cuboid, cuneiform, deltoid, dental, derm, derma, dermal, dermic, diaphragm, diencephalon, digital, diploe, diverticulum, dorsal, dorsolum-bar, dorsum, duodenal, duodenum, dura mater, earlap, elbow, enarthrosis, encephalic, encephalon, endocardiac, endocardial, endocardium, endocrinal, endocrine, epencephalic, epencephalon, epidermal, epidermic, epidermis, epididymis epigastric, epigastrium, epiglottic, epiglottis, epithelium, eponychium, erythrocyte, esophagus, ethmoid, extensor, Fallopian tubes, false rib, femur, fenestra ovalis, fenestra rotunda, fibula, flexor, floating rib, fontanel(le), fonticulus, foramen magnum, forearm, forebrain, forefinger, foreskin, fourchette, frenum, frontal, funiculus, funny bone, gastric, gastrocnemius, gena, genal, genial, genitalia, genu, gingival, glabella, glabellar, gladiolus, glossa, glossal, glottal, glottic, glottis, gluteus, gnathal, gnathic, gonion, gracilis, gremial, gristle, groin, gula, gular, gullet, guttural, hallux, ham, hamate, hamstring, helix, hemal, hematic, hepatic, hind-brain, hindhead, hip-bone, hip-girdle, hock, huckle-bone, humeral, humerus, hyoid, hypogastrium, hypothalamus, iliac, ilium, incus, inguinal, innominate, innominate bone, intercostal, ischium, jugular, labial, lachrymal, lacrimal, leucocyte, ligament, lumbar, lumbrical, lunate, luz, malar, malleolus, malleus, mamillar(y), mammary, mandible, mandibu-lar, manubrium, marriage-bone, mastoid, maxilla, maxillary, membral, mental, merrythought, metacarpal, metatarsal, mons veneris, mount of Venus, muscle, nasal, nates, navicular, neural, obturators, occipital, occiput, occlusal, occlusion, occlusor, ocular, odontic, omentum, omohyoid, omoplate, optical, orbicularis, orbit(a), origin, os innominatum, oscheal, oscular, ossicle, otic, otolith, palatal, palatine, palpebral, parasphenoid, parietal, paroccipital, parotid, patela, patellar, pecten, pectoral, pedal, pelvic girdle, pelvis, periotic, perone, phalanges, pisiform, plantar, popliteal, poplitic, prefrontal, premaxilla, premaxillary, pronator, prootic, prosencephalon, psoas, pubis, pudenda, pulmonary, quadriceps, radius, renal, rhomboid, rib, rictal, sacrocostal, sacrum, sartorius, scaphoid, scapula, sesamoid, shoulder-blade, shoulder-bone, skull, soleus, spade-bone, sphenoid, spine, splinter-bone, stapes, sternum, stirrup-bone, supinator, sural, talus, tarsal, temporal, tendon, thigh-bone, tibia, trapezium, trapezius, trapezoid, triceps, triquetral, turbinal, tympanic, ulna, umbilicus, unguis, urachus, uterus, uvula, vagus, vas deferens, velum, vermis, vertebra, vertebrae, vertex, vesica, voice-box, vomer, vulva, windpipe, wisdom tooth, womb, wrist, xiphisternum, xiphoid, zygapophysis, zygoma, zygomatic.

architecture and building abacus, abutment, acrolith, acroter, acroterial, acroterion, acroterium, alcove, annulet, anta, antefix, areostyle, architrave, ashlar, ashler, astragal, baguette, bandelet, banderol(e), barge-board, barge-couple, barge-stones, battlement, bellcote, bema, bratticing, canephor, canton, cartouche, caryatid, Catherine-wheel, cavetto, centering, cinque-foil, concha, corbeil, corbel, corner-stone, corona, cradling, crenel, crocket, crossette, cruck, cul-de-four, dado, decorated, demi-bastion, demi-lune, dentil, diaconicon, diaper, diastyle, diglyph, dimension work, dinette, dipteros, distyle, ditriglyph, dodecastyle, dog-leg(ged), dogtooth, dome, domed, domical, donjon, Doric, dormer, double-glazing, doucine, drawbridge, drawing-room, dreamhole, dressing, drip, dripstone, dromic, dromos, drum, dry-stone, duplex, Early English, eaves, echinus, egg-and-anchor, egg-and-dart, egg-and-tongue, egg-box, el, elevation, Elizabethan, embattlement, embrasure, emplection, encarpus, engage, engaged, engrail, enneastyle, entresol, epaule, epaulement, epistyle, eustyle, exedra, extrados, eye-catcher, façade, fan tracery, fan vaulting, fanlight, fascia, fastigium, feathering, fenestella, fenestra, fenestral, fenestration, festoon, fillet, finial, flamboyant, flèche, Flemish bond, fletton, fleuron, foliation, fornicate, fortalice, French sash/window, frieze, fronton, furring, fusarol(e), fust, gable, gablet, galilee, gambrel roof, gargoyle, gatehouse, glacis, glyph, gopura(m), gorgerin, Gothic, gradin(e), griff(e), groin, groundplan, groundsel, guilloche, gutta, hagioscope, half- timbered, hammer-beam, hammer-brace, hance, hanging buttress, harling, haunch, haute époque, headstone, heart, helix, herringbone, hexastyle, hip, hip-knob, holderbat, hood-mold(ing), hypostyle, imbrex, imbricate, imbrication, imperial, impost, impostume, intercolumniation, intrados, jamb, javelin, jerkinhead, knosp, lierne, linen-fold, linen-scroll, lintel, mansard(-roof), mascaron, merlon, metope, modillion, monostyle, mullion, muntin(g), mutule, Norman, oeil-de-boeuf, ogee, opisthodomos, oriel, out-wall, ovolo, ox-eye, pagoda, pantile, pargret, patera, paternoster, patten, pediment, pilaster, pineapple, pinnacle, plafond, platband, plateresque, plinth, poppy-head, predella, propylaeum, propylon, prostyle, pylon, quatrefeuille, quatrefoil, queen-post, quirk, rear-arch, reglet, regula, rere-arch, retrochoir, reredos, revet, rocaille, rococo, Romanesque, rood-loft, rood-screen, rood-steeple, rood tower, roof, roof-tree, rosace, rose, rosette, rotunda, roughcast, sacristy, skew-back, socle, soffit, solidum, spandrel, strap- work, stria, string-course, subbasal, surbase, swag, systyle, tabernacle-work, table, telamon, terrazzo, tierceron, tondino, toroid, torsel, torus, trabeation, tracery, triforium, trumeau, tympanum, vault, vaultage, vaulted, vaulting, Venetian mosaic, vermiculate(d), vice, vitrail, vitrailled, Vitruvian, volute, voussoir, wainscot, wall-plate, water-joint, water-table, weathering, xystus.

art abstract, abstraction, action painting, anaglyph, anastasis, anastatic, anthemion, aquarelle, bas relief, Bauhaus, camaieu, cire perdue, dadaism, decal, decoupage, Der Blaue Reiter, diaglyph, Die Brücke, diptych, dry-point, duotone, écorché, enamel, encaustic, engraving, etch, etchant, faience, fashion-plate, Fauve, Fauvism, fête champêtre, figurine, filigree, flambé, flannelgraph, Flemish, flesh-tint, Florentine, free-hand, fresco, fret, frit, futurism, futurist, gadroon, genre, gesso, glyptics, glyptography, Gobelin, gouache, graphic, graphics, graphium, graticulation, gravure, grecque, grisaille, gumption, hachure, hatch, hatching, haut relief, herm(a), historiated, hound's-tooth, intaglio, linocut, literalism, litho, lithochromatic(s), lithchromy, lithograph, lithoprint, lost wax, mandorla, meander, monotint, monotype, morbidezza, Parian, paysage, phylactery, pietra-dura, piqué, pochoir, pompier, putto, quattrocento, relievo, repoussage, repoussé, reserved, retroussage, rilievo, sculp(t), scumble, sea-piece, seascape, secco, serigraph, statuary, stipple, stylus, surrealism, symbolism, tachism(e), tempera, tenebrism, tessellated, tessera, tondo, trecento, triptych, ukiyo-e, velatura, Venetian mosaic, Venetian red, verditer, verism, vermiculate(d), versal, vitrail, vitraillist, vitrifacture, vitrine, vitro-di-trina, volute, vorticism, woodblock, wood- carving, woodcut, wood-engraving, xoanon, zoomorphic.

canonical hours compline, lauds, matins, none, orthros, prime, sext, terce, undern, vespers.

cattle breeds Africander, Alderney, Angus, Ankole, Ayrshire, Blonde d'Aquitaine, Brahman, Brown Swiss, cattabu, cattalo, Charol(l)ais, Chillingham, Devon, dexter, Durham, Friesian, Galloway, Guernsey, Hereford, Highland, Holstein, Jersey, Latvian, Limousin, Luing, Red Poll, Romagnola, Santa Gertrudis, short-horn, Simmenthaler, Teeswater, Ukrainian, Welsh Black.

cheeses Amsterdam, Bel Paese, Blarney, Bleu d'Auvergne, Blue Vinny, Boursin, Brie, Caboc, Caerphilly, Camembert, Carré, Cheddar, Cheshire, Chevrotin, Colwick, Coulommiers, Crowdie, Danish blue, Derby, Dolcelatte, Dorset Blue, double Gloucester, Dunlop, Edam, Emmental, Emment(h)al(er), Esrom, ewe-cheese, Feta, Fynbo, Gammelost, G(j)etost, Gloucester, Gorgonzola, Gouda, Grana, Grevé, Gruyère, Handkäse, Havarti, Herrgårdsost, Herve, Huntsman, Hushållsost, Islay, Jarlsberg, Killarney, Kryddost, Lancashire, Leicester, Limburg(er), Lymeswold, mouse-trap, mozzarella, Munster, Mysost, Neufchâtel, Parmesan, Petit Suisse, pipo creme, Pont-l'Éveque, Port(-du-)Salut, Prästost, Provolone, Pultost, Raclette, Red Windsor, Reggiano, ricotta, Romadur, Roquefort, sage Derby, Saint-Paulin, Samsø, sapsago, Stilton, stracchino, Tilsit(er), Vacherin, Wensleydale, Wexford.

chemical elements Actinium, Aluminum, Americium, Antimony, Argon, Arsenic, Astatine, Barium, Berkelium, Beryllium, Bismuth, Boron, Bromine, Cadmium, Calcium, Californium, Carbon, Cerium, Cesium, Chlorine, Chromium, Cobalt, Copper, Curium, Dysprosium, Einsteinium, Erbium, Europium, Fermium, Fluorine, Francium, Gadolinium, Gallium, Germanium, Gold, Hafnium, Hahnium, Helium, Holmium, Hydrogen, Indium, Iodine, Iridium, Iron, Krypton, Lanthanum, Lawrencium, Lead, Lithium, Lutetium, Magnesium, Manganese, Mendelevium, Mercury, Molybdenum, Neodymium, Neon, Neptunium, Nickel, Niobium, Nitrogen, Nobelium, Osmium, Oxygen, Palladium, Phosphorus, Platinum, Plutonium, Polonium, Potassium, Praseodymium, Promethium, Protoactinium, Radium, Radon, Rhenium, Rhodium, Rubidium, Ruthenium, Rutherfordium,

Samarium, Scandium, Selenium, Silicon, Silver, Sodium, Strontium, Sulfur, Tantalum, Technetium, Tellurium, Terbium, Thallium, Thorium, Thulium, Tin, Titanium, Tungsten, Uranium, Vanadium, Xenon, Ytterbium, Yttrium, Zinc, Zirconium.

cloths, fabrics abaca, abb, alamonde, alepine, alpaca, American cloth, angora, armozine, armure, arrasene, astrakhan, atlas, baft, bagging, Balbriggan, baldachin, balzarine, barathea, barege, barracan, batiste, batting, bayadère, bearskin, beaver, beige, bengaline, Binca®;, blanket, blanketing, blonde(e)- lace, bobbinet, bobbin-lace, bombasine, bone-lace, botany, bouclé, bolting cloth, box-cloth, broadcloth, brocade, brocatel(le), broché, Brussels lace, buckram, buckskin, budge, buff, bunting, Burberry, burlap, burnet, burrel, butter-cloth, butter-muslin, byssus, caddis, calamanco, calico, cambric, cameline, camlet, candlewick, canvas, carmelite, carpeting, casement-cloth, cashmere, cassimere, catgut, (cavalry) twill, challis, chamois, chantilly (lace), charmeuse, cheesecloth, damask, damassin, delaine, denim, devil's dust, dhoti, d(h)urrie, diamanté, diaper, dimity, doe-skin, doily, domett, dornick, dowlas, drab, drabbet, drap-de-Berry, dreadnought, drill, droguet, drugget, duchesse lace, duck, duffel, dungaree, dupion, durant, Dutch carpet, ecru, éolienne, façonné, faille, far(r)andine, fearnought, felt, ferret, filet, flannel, flannelette, foulard, foulé, frieze, frocking, fustian, gaberdine, galatea, galloon, gambroon, gauze, genappe, georgette, gingham, Gobelini(s), gold-cloth, gold-lace, grass cloth, grenadine, grogram, grosgrain, guipure, gunny, gurrah, habit- cloth, haircloth, harn, Hessian, hodden, holland, homespun, Honiton, hopsack, horsehair, huckaback, humhum, jaconet, Jaeger®;, jamdani, jean, jeanette, jersey, kalamkari, karakul, kente cloth, kersey, kerseymere, khader, khaki, kid, kidskin, kilt, kincob, kip-skin, lamé, lampas, lawn, leather, leather- cloth, leatherette, leghorn, leno, levant, linen, linsey, linsey- woolsey, llama, lockram, loden, longcloth, lovat, Lurex®;, luster, lustring, lutestring, mac(k)intosh, madras, mantling, marcella, marocain, maroquin, marquisette, mazarine, Mechlin, medley, melton, merino, Mexican, mignonette, mohair, moire, moleskin, monk's cloth, moreen, morocco, mourning-stuff, mousseline, mousseline-de-laine, mousseline-de-soie, Moygashel®;, mull, mulmul(l), mungo, musk-rat, muslin, muslinet, musquash, nacarat, nainsook, nankeen, ninon, nitro- silk, nun's-veiling, nylon, oilcloth, organdie, organza, organzine, orleans, osnaburg, orris, ottoman, overcoating, paduasoy, paisley, panne, paper-cloth, paper-muslin, par(r)amatta, peau-de-soie, penistone, percale, percaline, perse, petersham, piña-cloth, pin-stripe, piqué, plaid, plush, point- lace, polycotton, poplin, poplinette, prunella, purple, quilting, rabanna, ratine(ratteen), raven('s)-duck, rep (repp), roan, russel, russel-cord, russet, sackcloth, sacking, sagathy, sail- cloth, samite, sarsenet, satara, sateen, satin, satinette, satin-sheeting, saxony, say, scarlet, schappe, scrim, seersucker, sendal, serge, shagreen, shalloon, shammy(-leather), shantung, sharkskin, sheepskin, Shetland wool, shoddy, Sicilian, sicilienne, silesia, silk, slipper satin, soneri, split, sponge- cloth, spun silk, stammel, strouding, suede, suedette, suiting, surah, surat, swansdown, swan-skin, tabaret, tabbinet, tabby, taffeta, tamin(e), tamise, tammy, tarlatan, tarpaulin, tartan, tat, Tattersall (check), T-cloth, tentage, tent-cloth, terry, Terylene®;, thibet, thickset, thrown-silk, thunder-and- lightning, ticken, tick(ing), tiffany, toile, toilinet(te), torchon lace, toweling, tram, tricot, troll(e)y, tulle, tusser(- silk), tweed, union, Valenciennes, veiling, Velcro®;, velour(s), veloutine, velveret, velvet, velveteen, velveting, vicuña, voile, wadmal, waistcoating, watchet, waterwork, waxcloth, webbing, whipcord, wigan, wild silk, wincey, winceyette, wire gauze, woolsey, worcester, worsted, zanella, zephyr.

coins, currencies agora, antoninianus, as, asper, aureus, baht, balboa, bawbee, bekah, belga, bezant, bit, bod(d)le, bolivar, boliviano, bonnet-piece, broad(piece), buck, cardecu(e), Carolus, cash, cent, centavo, centime, chiao, colon, conto, cordoba, couter, crown, crusado, cruzeiro, dam, daric, deaner, décime, denarius, denier, Deutschmark, didrachm(a), dime, dinar, dirham, doit, dollar, double, doubloon, drachma, ducat, dupondius, duro, eagle, écu, eighteen-penny piece, escudo, farthing, fen, fifty-pence piece, fifty-penny piece, five-pence piece, five-penny piece, florin, forint, franc, geordie, gerah, gourde, groat, groschen, guinea, gulden, haler, half-crown, half- dollar, halfpenny, half-sovereign, heller, jacobus, jane, jitney, joe, joey, jo(h)annes, kina, knife-money, koban(g), kopeck, koruna, kreutzer, krona, krone, Krugerrand, kwacha, kyat, lek, lepton, leu, lev, lion, lira, litre, livre, louis, louis-d'or, mag, maik, make, manch, mancus, maravedi, mark, mawpus, merk, mil, millième, millime, milreis, mina, mite, mna, mohur, moidore, mopus, naira, napoleon, (naya) paisa, (new) cedi, ngwee, nickel, obang, obol, obolus, öre, øre, Paduan, pagoda, paolo, para, patrick, paul, peseta, pesewa, peso, pfennig, piastre, picayune, pice, piece of eight, pine-tree money, pistareen, pistole, pistolet, plack, portague, portcullis, pound, punt, qintar, quetzal, quid, rag, rand, real, red, red cent, reichsmark, reis, rial, rider, riel, ringgit, rix-dollar, riyal, rose-noble, r(o)uble, royal, ruddock, ruddy, rupee, rupiah, ryal, saw-buck, sceat(t), schilling, scudo, semis, semuncia, sen, sequin, sesterce, sestertium, sextans, shekel, shilling, silverling, sixpence, skilling, smacker, sol, soldo, solidus, sou, sovereign, spade-guinea, spur-royal, stater, sterling, stiver, sucre, sword- dollar, sycee, tael, taka, talent, tanner, tenner, tenpence, ten- pence piece, ten-penny piece, tester(n), testo(o)n, testril(l), tetradrachm, thaler, thick'un, thin'un, three-farthings, three-halfpence, threepence, three-penny bit/piece, tical, tick(e)y, tizzy, toman, turner, twenty-pence piece, twenty-penny piece, two bits, twopence, two-pence piece, two-penny piece, unicorn, ure, vellon, wakiki, wampum, won, xerafin, yen, yuan, zack, zecchino, zimbi, zloty, zuz, zwanziger.

collective nouns building of rooks, cast of hawks, cete of badgers, charm of goldfinches, chattering of choughs, clamor of rooks, clowder of cats, covert of coots, covey of partridges, down of hares, drift of swine, drove of cattle, dule of doves, exaltation of larks, fall of woodcock, fesnyng of ferrets, gaggle of geese, gam of whales, gang of elks, grist of bees, husk of hares, kindle of kittens, leap of leopards, leash of bucks, murder of crows, murmuration of starlings, muster of peacocks, mute of hounds, nide of pheasants, pace of asses, pod of seals, pride of lions, school of porpoises, siege (or sedge) of bitterns, skein of geese, skulk of foxes, sloth of bears, sounder of boars, spring of teals, stud of mares, team of ducks, tok of capercailzies, troop of kangaroos, walk of snipe, watch of nightingales.

collectors, enthusiasts abolitionist, ailurophile, antiquary, antivaccinationist, antivivisectionist, arachnologist, arctophile, audiophil(e), balletomane, bibliolatrist, bibliomane, bibliopegist, bibliophagist, bibliophile, bibliophilist, bicameralist, campanologist, canophilist, cartophile, cartophilist, cheirographist, coleopterist, conservationist, cynophilist, Dantophilist, deltiologist, discophile, dog-fancier, ecclesiologist, egger, enophile, enophilist, entomologist, environmentalist, ephemerist, epicure, ex-librist, feminist, Francophile, Gallophile, gastronome, gemmologist, Germanophil(e), gourmet, herpetologist, hippophile, homoeopathist, iconophilist, incunabulist, Kremlinologist, lepidopterist, medallist, miscegenationist, monarchist, myrmecologist, negrophile, negrophilist, notaphilist, numismatist, ophiophilist, orchidomaniac, ornithologist, orthoepist, orthographist, ostreiculturist, pangrammatist, Panhellenist, panislamist, Pan- Slavist, paragrammatist, paroemographer, perfectionist, philanthrope, philatelist, philhellene, phillumenist, philogynist, philologist, philologue, prohibitionist, pteridophilist, reincarnationist, Russophile, Russophilist, scripophile, scripophilist, sericulturist, Sinophile, Slavophile, speleologist, steganographist, stegophilist, supernaturalist, tege(s)tologist, timbrologist, timbromaniac, timbrophilist, tulipomane, tulipomaniac, Turcophile, ufologist, ultramontanist, vexillologist, virtuoso, vulcanologist, xenophile, zoophile, zoophilist.

colors anthochlore, anthocyan(in), anthoxanthin, aquamarine, argent, aurora, avocado, badious, Berlin blue, beryl, biscuit, black, blae, blood-red, blue, bottle-green, brick-red, buff, canary, caramel, carmine, carnation, celadon, celeste, cerise, cerulean, cervine, cesious, champagne, charcoal, cobalt- blue, coral, cyan, dove, drab, dun, Dutch pink, dwale, eau de Nil, ebony, emerald, fawn, feldgrau, ferrugin(e)ous, filemot, flame, flavescent, flaxen, flesh-color, fulvous, fuscous, ginger, glaucous, gold, golden, gray, green, greige (grège), gridelin, griseous, grizzle(d), gules, guly, hoar, horse-flesh, hyacinth, hyacinthine, ianthine, icterine, icteritious, incarnadine, indigo, isabel, isabella, isabelline, jacinth, khaki, lake, lateritious, lemon, lilac, lovat, lurid, luteolous, luteous, lutescent, magenta, mahogany, maize, mandarin(e), maroon, mauve, mazarine, miniate, minium, modena, morel, mouse-color(ed), mous(e)y, mulberry, murrey, nacarat, Naples-yellow, nattier blue, Nile green, nut-brown, ochroleucous, off-white, orange, oxblood, Oxford blue, palatinate, pansy, peach, peach-bloom, peacock, peacock-blue, perse, philomot, piceous, pink, plum, plumbeous, pompadour, ponceau, pongee, porphyry, porraceous, puce, purple, purpure, pyrrhous, red, reseda, roan, rose, rose-colored, rose- pink, rose-red, rosy, rubicund, rubied, rubiginous, rubincous, rubious, ruby, ruby-red, ruddy, rufescent, rufous, russet, rust- colored, rusty, sable, saffron, sage, salmon, sand, sapphire, saxe blue, scarlet, sepia, siena, silver, sky, slate, smalt, straw, tan, taupe, tawny, tenné, Titian, tomato, tusser, Tyrian, ultramarine, vermeil, vermilion, vinous, violet, virescent, vitellary, vitreous, watchet, white, wine, xanthic, xanthous, yellow.

confections, dishes, foods angels-on-horseback, battalia pie, bir(i)yani, blanquette, Bombay duck, borsch(t), bouillabaisse, bubble-and-squeak, bummalo, burgoo, cannelloni, carbon(n)ade, cassoulet, cecils, charlotte russe, chilli con carné, chocolate vermicelli, chop-suey, chowder, chow-mein, cockaleekie, colcannon, consommé, Danish pastry, dariole, devil, devil's food cake, devils-on-horseback, Devonshire cream, diet-bread, dika-bread, dimsum, dough-boy, doughnut, dragée, drammock, duff, dumpling, dunderfunk, Eccles cake, éclair, Edinburgh rock, egg custard, enchilada, eryngo, escalope, escargot, faggot, fancy-bread, farle, fedelini, felafel, fettuc(c)ine, fishball, fishcake, fishfinger, flan, flapjack, floater, flummery, foie gras, fondant, fondue, forcemeat, fortune cookie, fraise, frankfurter, French bread, French dressing, French fry, French stick, French toast, fricandeau, fricassee, friedcake, fritter, fritto misto, friture, froise, fruit cocktail, fruit salad, fruitcake, frumenty, fu yung, fudge, fumado, galantine, game chips, garam masala, Garibaldi biscuit, gateau, gazpacho, gefilte fish, Genoa cake, ghee, ginger nut, gingerbread, gingersnap, gnocchi, gofer, goulash, graham bread, graham crackers, grits, gruel, guacamole, gumdrop, gundy, haberdine, haggis, halva(h), hamburger, hard sauce, hardbake, hardtack, hoe-cake, hominy, hoosh, hot dog, hot-cross-bun, hotpot, howtowdie, humbug, hummus, hundreds-and-thousands, hyson, jemmy, kedgeree, lardy-cake, laverbread, matelote, millefeuille(s), minestrone, mous(s)aka, na(a)n, navarin, olla- podrida, opsonium, paella, panada, pastrami, pavlova, pem(m)ican, pettitoes, pilaff, pilau, pinole, pirozhki, pizza, plowman's lunch, plum-duff, plum-porridge, plum-pudding, poi, polenta, polony, popover, pop(p)adum, porterhouse(-steak), pot-au-feu, prairie-oyster, profiterole, prosciutto, pumpernickel, queen of puddings, queen's pudding, quenelle, quiche, ragout, ramekin, ratatouille, ravioli, remoulade, risotto, roly-poly pudding, Sachertorte, salmagundi, salmi(s), saltimbocca, sauce hollandaise, sauerkraut, scampi, schnitzel, sch(t)chi, Scotch woodcock, shepherd's pie, smørbrød, smörgåsbord, soufflé, spaghetti (alla) bolognese, spotted dick, spring roll, stovies, stroganoff, succotash, sukiyaki, summer pudding, sundae, sup(p)awn, sushi, syllabub, Tabasco®;, tablet, taco, tamal(e), tandoori, tapioca, taramasalata, tempura, timbale, toad-in-the- hole, torte, tortellini, tortilla, trifle, tsamba, turtle-soup, tutti-frutti, tzimmes, velouté sauce, vermicelli, vichyssoise, vienna loaf, vienna steak, vindaloo, vol-au-vent, wafer, waffle, warden pie, wastel-bread, water-biscuit, water-gruel, welsh rabbit (rarebit), white sauce, white-pot, white-pudding, Wiener schnitzel, Wimpy®;, wine-biscuit, wonder, Worcestershire sauce, wurst, yoghurt, Yorkshire pudding, zabaglione, Zwieback.

dances allemande, beguine, belly-dance, bergamask, black bottom, bolero, bossanova, bourree, branle, breakdown, bunny-hug, cachucha, cakewalk, canary, cancan, carioca, carmagnole, carol, cha-cha, chaconne, Charleston, cinque-pace, Circassian, circle, clogdance, conga, coranto, corroboree, cotill(i)on, country- dance, courant, cracovienne, csárdás (czardas), dos-à-dos (dosi- do) dump, écossaise, egg-dance, fading, fado, fandango, farruca, figure-dance, flamenco, fling, flip-flap(-flop), forlana, fox- trot, galliard, gallopade, galop, gavotte, gigue, gopak, habanera, haka, halling, haymaker, hey (hay), hey-de-guy, Highland fling, hoedown, hoolachan, hula-hula, jig, jitterbug, jive, jota, juba, kolo, lancers, loure, malagueña, mambo, matachin, maxixe, mazurka, minuet, Moresco, morris-dance, musette, onestep, Paduan, paso doble, passacaglia, passepied, passy-measure, Paul Jones, pavan(e), petronella, planxty, polacca, polka, polo, polonaise, poule, poussette, quadrille, quickstep, redowa, reel, r(h)umba, rigadoon, ring-dance, romaika, roundel, roundelay, roundle, rumba, saltarello, samba, sand-dance, saraband, schottische, sequidilla, shimmy(-shake), siciliano, spring, square-dance, stomp, strathspey, sword-dance, tamborin, tango, tap-dance, tarantella, the twist, toe-dance, tripudium, turkey-trot, two-step, Tyrolienne, valeta, valse, varsovienne, volta, waltz, war dance, zapateado, ziganka.

dog-breeds affenpinscher, badger-dog, basenji, basset(- hound), Bedlington (terrier), Blenheim spaniel, boar-hound, Border terrier, borzoi, Boston terrier, Briard, Brussels griffon, bull mastiff, bulldog, bull-terrier, cairn terrier, Cavalier King Charles spaniel, chihuahua, chow, clumber spaniel, coach-dog, cocker spaniel, collie, corgi, dachshund, Dalmatian, Dandie Dinmont, Dane, deerhound, dhole, dingo, Doberman(n) pinscher, elkhound, Eskimo dog, foxhound, fox-terrier, German police dog, German Shepherd dog, Great Dane, greyhound, griffon, harlequin, (Irish) water-spaniel, Jack Russell, keeshond, King Charles spaniel, Labrador, laika, lhasa apso, lurcher, lyam-hound, malemute, Maltese, mastiff, peke, Pekin(g)ese, pinscher, pointer, Pomeranian, poodle, pug, pug-dog, retriever, Rottweiler, saluki, Samoyed(e), sausage-dog, schipperke, schnauzer, Scotch-terrier, Sealyham, setter, sheltie, Shetland sheepdog, shih tzu, shough, Skye (terrier), spaniel, Spartan, spitz, St Bernard, staghound, Sussex spaniel, talbot, teckel, terrier, vizsla, volpino, warragal, water-dog, Weimaraner, whippet, wire-hair(ed terrier), wolf-dog, wolf-hound, Yorkshire terrier, zorro.

drinks, alcoholic absinth(e), aguardiente, akvavit, amontillado, anisette, apple-jack, aqua-mirabilis, aquavit, aqua-vitae, arak, Armagnac, arrack, audit ale, ava, bacharach, badminton, barley-bree, Beaujolais, Beaune, Benedic-tine, bingo, bishop, black velvet, bloody Mary, blue ruin, bourbon, brandy- pawnee, bride-ale, Bristol-milk, bucellas, bumbo, burgundy, Calvados, Campari, canary, catawba, Chablis, chain-lightning, Chambertin, Cham-pagne, Chartreuse, cherry brandy, cherry-bounce, Chianti, chicha, cider, claret, claret-cup, cobbler, cobbler's punch, Cognac, Cointreau®;, cold-without, Constantia, cool- tankard, cooper, cordial, corn-brandy, daiquiri, demerara, dog's nose, dop, eau de vie, eau des creoles, egg-flap, eggnog, enamel, enzian, fine, fino, four-ale, geneva, genevrette, geropiga, gimlet, gin, gin and it, gin-fizz, ginger wine, ginsling, glogg, gooseberry wine, grappa, Graves, grog, haoma, heavy wet, herb-beer, hermitage, hippocras, hock, hollands, hoo(t)ch, it, Johannisberger, John Barleycorn, John Collins, kaoliang, kava, kefir, kirsch, kirschwasser, k(o)umiss, kümmel, kvass, London particular, manzanilla, maraschino, marc brandy, Marcobrunner, Marsala, Martini®;, Médoc, metheglin, mirabelle, mobbie, Moselle, mountain, mountain dew, muscat, muscatel, negus, Nipa, noyau, Old Tom, oloroso, olykoek, Orvieto, ouzo, pastis, peach-brandy, Pernod®;, perry, persico(t), Peter-see-me, pils(e)ner, plottie, pombe, port, pot(h)een, pousse-café, pulque, punch, purl, quetsch, ratafia, resinata, retsina, Rhine-wine, Riesling, Rioja, rosé, Rudesheimer, Rüdesheimer, rum, rumbo, rumfustian, rum-punch, rum-shrub, rye, rye-whisky, sack, sack- posset, sake, samshoo, sangaree, sangria, Sauterne(s), schiedam, schnapps, Scotch, shandy, sherry, sherry-cobbler, shrub, sidecar, Sillery, sling, slivovitz, sloe-gin, small beer, small-ale, sour, spruce-beer, St Julien, Steinberger, stengah, stinger, stingo, swipes, swizzle, tafia, Tarragona, tent, tequil(l)a, tipper, toddy, Tokay, Tom Collins, Tom-and-Jerry, twankay, twopenny, usquebaugh, vermouth, vin blanc, vin ordinaire, vin rosé, vinho verde, vodka, wassail, water-brose, whisk(e)y, whisky toddy, white wine, white-ale, Xeres, zythum.

French Revolutionary calendar Brumaire, Floréal, Frimaire, Fructidor, Germinal, Messidor, Nivôse, Pluviôse, Prairiel, Thermidor, Vendémiaire, Ventôse.

furniture, furnishings andiron, banquette, basket-chair, basketwork, bergama, bergamot, bolster, bonheur-du-jour, box-bed, bracket clock, brise-soleil, buffet, buhl, bureau, cabriolet, camp-bed, canterbury, chair-bed, chaise-longue, chesterfield, cheval-glass, chiffonier, coaster, commode, continental quilt, credence (table/shelf), credenza, davenport, day-bed, desk, dinner-table, dinner-wagon, divan, dos-à-dos, drape, drawer, drawing-table, draw-leaf table, dresser, dressing-table, dumb- waiter, easy-chair, elbow-chair, electrolier, encoignure, escritoire, étagere, faldstool, fauteuil, fender, fender-stool, festoon-blind, fire-dog, fireguard, firescreen, four-poster, gasalier, girandole, girnel, guéridon, hallstand, hassock, hearth-rug, highboy, high-chair, hip-bath, humpty, jardinière, lectern, looking-glass, lounge, lounger, love-seat, lowboy, lug- chair, mirror, mobile, ottoman, overmantel, pelmet, pembroke (table), picture rail, piecrust table, pier-glass, pier-table, plaque, plenishings, pouf(fe), prie-dieu, pulpit, pulvinar, radiator, rocking chair, sag-bag, scatter rug/cushion, sconce, secretaire, settee, settle, settle-bed, sideboard, sidetable, sofa, sofa-bed, sofa-table, squab, standard lamp, studio couch, swivel-chair, table, tallboy, tapestry, tatami, teapoy, tea- service, tea-set, tea-table, tea-tray, tea-trolley, tent-bed, tête-à-tête, toilet-table, toilet(te), torchère, tridarn, tringle, umbrella-stand, Vanitory®;, vanity unit, vargueño, veilleuse, vis-à-vis, vitrine, wall-unit, wardrobe, washhand- stand, wash-stand, water bed, Welsh dresser, whatnot, writing- desk, writing-table.

garments, vestments aba, abaya, abba, abolla, achkan, acton, Afghan, alb, alpargata, amice, anorak, antigropelo(e)s, babouche, babushka, balaclava, Balbriggan, balibuntal, balmoral, bandan(n)a, bania(n), barret, basher, bashlyk, basinet, basque, basquine, bathing-costume, bauchle, beanie, bearskin, beaver, bed-jacket, bedsocks, beetle-crushers, belcher, benjamin, Bermuda shorts, Bermudas, bertha, bikini, billycock, biretta, blanket, blouson, blucher, boa, boater, bobbysock, bodice, body stocking, bolero, bomber jacket, bongrace, bonnet, bonnet-rouge, boob-tube, bootee, bottine, box-coat, bow-tie, bra, brassière, breeches, breeks, breton, broad-brim, brogue(s), buckskins, buff, buffalo- robe, buff-coat, buff-jerkin, bumfreezer, Burberry, burdash, burk(h)a, burnous(e), busby, bush jacket, bush shirt, buskin, bustle, bustle, bycoket, caftan, cagoul(e), calamanco, calash, calceamentum, calotte, calyptra, camiknickers, camise, camisole, capa, cape, capel(l)ine, capote, capuche, capuchin, carcanet, car-coat, cardigan, cardinal, carmagnole, cashmere, casque, cassock, casuals, catsuit, caul, cere-cloth, cerement, chadar, chaparajos, chapeau, chapeau-bras, chaperone, chapka, chaplet, chaps, chasuble, collar of esses, corset, corslet, cummerbund, dalmahoy, Dalmatic, décolletage, derby, diadem, diaper, dick(e)y, dinner-gown, dinner-jacket, dirndl, dishabille, dittos, divided skirt, djellaba(h), djibbah, dog-collar, Dolly Varden, dolman, donkey jacket, doublet, drainpipes, drapesuit, drawers, dreadnought, dress uniform, dress-coat, dress-improver, dressing- gown, dressing-jacket, dressing-sack, dress-shirt, dress-suit, dress-tie, duffel coat, dungarees, earmuffs, encolpion, epaulet(te), ephod, epitrachelion, espadrille, Eton collar, Eton jacket, Etons, evening dress, evening-dress, exomis, faldetta, falling band, fannel(l), fanon, farthingale, fascinator, fatigues, fedora, ferronnière, fez, fibula, fichu, filibeg, fillet, finnesko, flat-cap, flip-flop, fob, fontange, fore-and- after, fraise, French knickers, frock, frock-coat, frog, frontlet, fustanella, gaberdine, gaiter, galligaskins, galoshes, gamash, gambeson, garibaldi, gauchos, gay deceivers, gee-string (G-string), geneva bands, geta, gibus, gi(e), gilet, girandole, gizz, grego, gremial, g-suit, guernsey, gumboot, gum(shoe), habergeon, hacqueton, haik, hair-net, hair-piece, half-boot, hat, hatband, hatpin, hattock, hauberk, havelock, headcloth, head- hugger, headsquare, himation, hip-huggers, hipsters, hogger, Homburg, hood, hotpants, housecoat, hug-me-tight, humeral veil, hummel, hunting cap, ihram, indescribables, jabot, jacket, Jap- silk, jeans, jersey, jiz, jubbah (djibbah), jumper, jump-suit, jupon, kabaya, kaffiyeh, kaftan, kagoul, kalpak, kalyptra, kamees, kanzu, kell, kerchief, k(h)anga, k(h)urta, Kilmarnock, Kilmarnock cowl, kimono, kirtle, kiss-me, kiss-me-quick, knickerbockers, knickers, lammy, lava-lava, lederhosen, leggings, leghorn, leg-warmers, leotard, Levis®;, liberty bodice, lingerie, loden, lounger, lounge-suit, lungi, mac(k), mackinaw, mac(k)intosh, madras, manta, manteau, mantilla, mantle, mantlet, manto, matinee, matinee jacket/coat, maud, mazarine, mazarine hood, middy (blouse), mink, miter, mitt, mitten, mob, mob-cap, mode, modius, mohair, moleskins, monkey-jacket, monteith, montero, montero-cap, morning-dress, morning-gown, mortar-board, Mother Hubbard, mourning-cloak, mousquetaire, moz(z)etta, muff, muffin-cap, muffler, mutch, muu-muu, netherstock, newmarket, nightingale, Nithsdale, Norfolk jacket, nubia, obi, omophorion, orarion, orarium, overcoat, overgarment, Oxonian, paduasoy, paenula, pagri, paletot, pall, palla, pallium, paludament, pantable, pantalets, pantaloons, panties, pantihose, pantof(f)le, panton, pantoufle, pants, pants suit, pea-coat, pea-jacket, pearlies, pectoral, pedal-pushers, pelerine, pelisse, pencil skirt, penitentials, peplos, peplum, petasos, petersham, petticoat, petticoat, petticoat-breeches, ph(a)elonion, Phrygian cap, picture-hat, pierrot, pilch, pileus, pill-box, pinafore, pinafore-dress, pinafore-skirt, pinner, pixie-hood, plaid, plimsoll, plus-fours, plushes, pneumonia-blouse, poke-bonnet, polonaise, polo-neck, poncho, pontificals, pos(h)teen, powdering- gown, pressure-helmet, pressure-suit, pressure-waistcoat, princess(e), pumps, puttee, rabato, raglan, raincoat, rami(e), Ramil(l)ie(s), ra-ra skirt, rat-catcher, rational, rationals, rebater, rebato, redingote, reefer, reefing-jacket, riding- breeches, riding-cloak, riding-clothes, riding-coat, riding- glove, riding-habit, riding-hood, riding-robe, riding-skirt, riding-suit, robe, robe-de-chambre, rochet, roll-neck sweater, roll-on, rompers, romper-suit, roquelaure, ruff, rug-gown, sabot, sack, sack-coat, safari jacket, safari suit, sagum, sailor-hat, sakkos, salopette, samfoo, sanbenito, sandal, sarafan, sari, sarong, sash, sayon, scapular, scarf, scarpetto, schema, scotch bonnet, screen, sea-boots, sealskin, semmit, separates, shako, shaps, shauchle, shawl, shawl-waistcoat, shift, shirt, shirt dress, shirtwaist, shirtwaister, shoe, shooting-jacket, short-clothes, short-coats, shortgown, shorts, shovel-hat, silk-hat, silly-how, singlet, siren suit, skeleton suit, skin-tights, skirt, skullcap, slacks, slicker, sling-back, slip, slip-over, slipper(s), slipslop, sloppy Joe, slop(s), slouch(-hat), small- clothes, smalls, smicket, smock, smock-frock, smoking cap, smoking jacket, sneaker(s), snood, snow-boots, snow-shoe(s), sock, sola(r) topi/helmet, solitaire, solleret, sombrero, sontag, soubise, soutane, sou'-wester, space-suit, spat, spattee, spatterdash, spencer, sphendone, sponge-bags, sporran, sports jacket, sports shirt, start-up, stays, steenkirk, steeple-crown, steeple-hat, stephane, step-in, Stetson, sticharion, stock, stockinet(te), stockingette, stocking(s), stola, stole, stomacher, stovepipe (hat), strait-jacket, strait-waistcoat, straw (hat), string vest, string-tie, strip, stuff-gown, subfusc, subucula, succinctorium, sun-bonnet, sundown, sun-dress, sunhat, sunsuit, superhumeral, surcingle, surcoat, surplice, surtout, suspender-belt, suspenders, swaddling-band/cloth/clothes, swagger-coat, swallow-tail, sweat band, sweat suit, sweater, sweat-shirt, swimming costume, swimsuit, swimwear, sword-belt, tabard, taglioni, tail-coat, tails, taj, talar, talaria, tall hat, tallith, talma, tam, Tam O'Shanter, tammy, tanga, tank top, tarboosh, tarpaulin, tasse, tawdry-lace, tea-gown, Teddy suit, tee-shirt, ten-gallon hat, terai, thrum-cap, tiar(a), tie, tights, tile(-hat), tippet, toga, tonnag, top-boots, topcoat, topee, topi, topper, tops, toque, toreador pants, tournure, tower, toy, tozie, track shoe, track suit, trenchard, trench- coat, trencher-cap, trews, tricorn(e), trilby, trollopee, trot- cozy, trouser suit, trousers, trouse(s), trunk-breeches, trunk- hose, trunks, truss(es), trusty, T-shirt, tube-skirt, tunic, tunicle, tuque, turban, turtle-neck, twin-set, ugly, ulster, ulsterette, undercoat, underpants, undershorts, undervest, upper-stock, Vandyke (collar), vareuse, veil, veld(-)schoen, vest, victorine, visite, vitta, volet, waistcloth, waistcoat, wam(p)us, war bonnet, warm, watch cap, watch chain, Watteau bodice, weeper, wellie, wellington, wet-suit, whisk, white tie, wide-awake, wig, wimple, windcheater, windjammer, wing collar, winkle-pickers, woggle, wrap, wraparound, wrapover, wrapper, wrap-rascal, wristlet, wylie-coat, yarmulka, yashmak, Y- fronts, zamarra, zoot suit, zoster, zucchetto.

heraldry abatement, addorsed, affrontee, Albany Herald, allusive, annulet, armorist, assurgent, augmentation, baton- sinister, bendlet, bend-sinister, bendwise, bendy, bezant, bicorporate, billet, bordure, botoné, brisure, caboched, cabré, cadency, canting, canton, catherine-wheel, champ, chequy, chevron, chevrony, chief, coupé, debased, debruised, declinant, delf, device, dexter, difference, dimidiate, dismembered, displayed, dormant, double, doubling, dragonné, dwale, eightfoil, embattled, emblaze, emblazon, emblazoner, emblazonment, emblazonry, enarched, enarmed, engouled, engrail, engrailed, engrailment, enveloped, escrol(l), escutcheon, extendant, fess(e), fesse-point, fetterlock, field, fimbriate, fitché(e), flanch, flanched, flotant, fracted, fret, fructed, fur, fusil, gale, gamb, garb(e), gemel, gerbe, golp(e), gorged, grieced, g(u)ardant, gules, gyron, gyronny, hatchment, haurient, herisson, honor-point, impale, impalement, increscent, inescutcheon, interfretted, invected, jessant, langued, lioncel, lis, lozenge, lozengy, manche, mantling, martlet, mascle, mascled, masculy, moline, morné, morned, mounted, mullet, naiant, naissant, nombril, nowed, nowy, opinicus, or, orle, palewise, pall, passant, patonce, patté(e), pean, percussant, pheon, pile, point, pommelé, pommeled, pommetty, portate, portcullis, posé, potencé, potent, primrose, quarter, quartering, quarterly, queue, ragged staff, raguled, raguly, rampant, raping, rebate, regardant, respect, respectant, roundel, rustre, saltire, sans nombre, satyral, scarp, segreant, sej(e)ant, semé(e), square-pierced, statant, tenné, trangle, tressure, trippant, umbrated, undee, undifferenced, unguled, urinant, vair, vairé, verdoy, vert, voided, vol, volant, vorant, vuln, vulned, waved, weel, wivern, woodwose (wood-house).

herbs, spices amaracus, basil thyme, caraway seeds, cardamom, cassia, cayenne, chervil, chilli, chive, cinnamon, cloves, coriander, cum(m)in, dill, dittany, endive, eyebright, fennel, fenugreek, finoc(c)hio, galega, garlic, gentian, ginger, groundsel, hellebore, henbane, horehound, horseradish, Hyoscyamus, hyssop, isatis, juniper, lemon thyme, licorice, lovage, lungwort, mace, marjoram, mint, motherwort, mustard, myrrh, nutmeg, oregano, orpine, paprika, parsley, peppermint, purslane, rampion, rape, rosemary, rue, saffron, sage, savory, stacte, tarragon, thyme, turmeric, vanilla, verbena, watercress, wintergreen, wormwood, woundwort, yerba.

jewels, gems agate, amber, amethyst, aquamarine, asteria, balas ruby, baroque, beryl, bloodstone, brilliant, cairngorm, cameo, carbuncle, chalcedony, chrysolite, coral, cornelian, crystal, diamond, draconites, emerald, fire-opal, garnet, girasol(e), grossular(ite), heliodor, hyacinth, hyalite, hydrophane, intaglio, jacinth, jade, jango(o)n, jasper, jet, lapis lazuli, ligure, marcasite, marquise, Mocha stone, moonstone, morganite, mother-of-pearl, nacre, olivet, olivine, onyx, opal, oriental amethyst, paragon, pearl, peridot(e), pyreneite, pyrope, Rhinestone, rhodolite, rose, rose-cut, rose- diamond, ruby, sapphire, sard, sardine, sardonyx, smaragd, topaz, tourmaline, turquoise, water-sapphire, wood-opal, yu, yu-stone, zircon.

Jewish calendar Ab, Abib, Adar, Adar Sheni, Elul, Hes(h)van, Iy(y)ar, Kislev, Nisan, S(h)ebat, Sivan, Tammuz, Tebet(h), Tis(h)ri, Veadar.

languages Aeolic, Afghan, Afrikaans, Akkadian, Albanian, Alemannic, Algonki(a)n, Altaic, Ameslan, Amharic, Anatolian, Anglo-Saxon, Arabic, Aramaic, Armenian, Armoric, Aryan, Assyrian, Attic, Austric, Austroasiatic, Austronesian, Avestan, Bahasa Indonesia, Balinese, Baltoslav(on)ic, Baluch(i), Bantu, Basque, Basuto, Bengali, Berber, Bohemian, bohunk, Breton, Brezonek, British, Brythonic, Bulgarian, Bulgaric, Burmese, B(y)elorussian, Cajun, Carib, Catalan, Celtic, Chaldaic, Cherokee, Chinese, Choctaw, Circassian, Cornish, creole, Croat(ian), Cushitic, Czech, Danish, Dardic, Doric, Dravidian, Dutch, Early English, English, Erse, Eskimo, Esperanto, Est(h)onian, Ethiopic, Etruscan, Euskarian, Fanti, Farsi, Finnish, Finno-Ugric(-Ugrian), Flemish, Franglais, French, Frisian, Gadhelic (Goidelic), Gaelic, Gaulish, Geëz (Giz), Gentoo, Georgian, German, Germanic, Greek, Guarani, Gujarat(h)i, Gullah, Hausa, Hawaiian, Hebrew, Hellenic, Herero, High German, Hindi, Hindustani, Hittite, Hottentot, Hungarian, Icelandic, Idiom Neutral, Ido, I(g)bo, Indian, Indic, Indo-European, Indo-Germanic, In(n)uit, Interlingua, Ionic, Iranian, Iraqi, Irish, Iroquoian, Italian, Italic, Japanese, Kalmuck, Kanarese, Kannada, Karen, Kennick, Khmer, Koine, Kolarian, Kuo-yü, Kurdish, Ladin, Ladino, Lallans, Landsmaal, Langue d'oc, Langue d'oil, Langue d'oui, Laplandish, Lapp, Lappish, Latin, Latvian, Lettic, Lettish, lingua franca, lingua geral, Lithuanian, Low German, Magyar, Malagasy, Malay, Malayala(a)m, Maltese, Manchu, Mandaean, Mandarin, Mandingo, Manx, Maori, Marathi, Median, Melanesian, Mexican, Micmac, Middle English, Moeso-gothic, Mohawk, Mohican, Mon, Mongolian, Munda, Nahuati, Neo, Newspeak, Norwegian, Novial, Nynorsk, Old English, Old Norse, Oriya, Oscan, Ostyak, Pali, Pawnee, Pehlevi, Pekin(g)ese, Pennsylvania Dutch, Persian, Persic, Phoenician, Pictish, pig Latin, Pilipino, Platt-Deutsch, Polabian, Polish, Portuguese, Prakrit, Provençal, Provinçal, Prussian, Punic, Punjabi, Pushtu, Quechua, Rabbinic, Rhaetic, Rhaeto-Romance, Rhaeto-Romanic, Rock English, rogues' Latin, Romaic, Romance, Romanes, Romanic, Roman(n)y, Romans(c)h, Rumanian, Russian, Russniak, Ruthenian, Sakai, Samnite, Samoyed(e), Sanskrit, Saxon, Scots, Scythian, Semitic, Serb(ian), Serbo-Croat(ian), Shan, Shona, Siamese, Sinhalese, Siouan, Slavonic, Slovak, Slovenian, Somali, Sorbian, Sorbish, Spanish, Sudanic, Sumerian, Suomi, Swahili, Swedish, Swiss, Syriac, Taal, Tagálog, Taino, Tamil, Tataric, Telugu, Teutonic, Thai, Tibetan, Tocharian, Tswana, Tuareg, Tungus(ian), Tupi, Turki, Turkish, Twi, Ugrian, Ugro-finnic, Ukrainian, Umbrian, Uralic, Urdu, Uzbeg, Vaudois, Vietnamese, Volapük, Volga-Baltic, Volscian, Welsh, Wendic, Wendish, West-Saxon, Wolof, Xhosa, Yakut, Yiddish, Yoruba, Zulu.

legal abate, abatement, absolvitor, abstract of title, acceptilation, accession, accessory, accessory after the fact, accessory before the fact, Acts of Adjournal, (ad)avizandum, adeem, adhere, adjudication, adminicle, administrator, afforce, alienee, alienor, allenarly, allodial, amicus curiae, amove, appointer, apprize, apprizer, assumpsit, attorn, back-bond, bairn's-part, capias, certiorari, chaud-mellé, cognosce, cognovit, compear, compulsitor, copyhold, cross-examine, decree absolute, decree nisi, decreet, decretals, decretist, dedimus, deed, deed of accession, defalcate, defeasance, defeasanced, defeasible, defendant, defender, deforce, deforcement, deforciant, delapidation, delate, delation, delator, delict, demurrer, deodand, detainer, detinue, devastavit, devest, diet, dimissory, disapply, disbar, disbench, discovert, discoverture, disentail, disgavel, disinherison, dispone, disponee, disposition, disseise, disseisin, disseisor, distinguish, distrain, distrainee, distrainer, distrainment, distrainor, distraint, distress, distringas, dittay, dole, donatary, droit, droit du Seigneur, duplicand, duply, dying declaration, easement, ejectment, embracer, embracery, emendals, emphyteusis, en ventre sa mère, enfeoff, enfeoffment, enjoin, enlevé, enlevement, entry, eric, escheat, escrow (escroll), escuage, esnecy, esrepe, essoin, estate, estop, estoppel, estover, estray, estreat, estrepement, examination, excamb, excambion, excambium, executry, exemplify, expromission, extend, extent, extinguishment, extract, extradition, facile, facility, factorize, faldage, felo de se, felony, feme, feme covert, feme sole, feoff, feoffee, feoffer (feoffor), feoffment, feu, feuar, fief, filacer, fire-bote, fiscal, folio, force and fear, force majeure, foreclose, foreclosure, forinsec, forisfamiliate, forjudge, frankalmoign, french-bench, frontager, fugitation, fungibles, garnishee, garnisheement, garnisher, gavelkind, gavelman, granter (grantor), grassum, hamesucken, hedge-bote, hide, homologation, horning, house-bote, hypothec, hypothecary, hypothecate, hypothecation, improbation, indenture, indict, indictee, indictment, induciae, infangthief, infeft, inquirendo, institorial, insucken, interlocutor, interplead, interpleader, interpose, irrepleviable, irreplevisable, ish, John Doe and Richard Roe, joinder, jointure, jus primae noctis, laches, law-agent, law-burrows, legitim, lenocinium, letters of administration, lien, life-rent, malfeasance, mens rea, mesne, messuage, misdemeanant, misfeasance, misfeasor, misprison, mittimus, mora, mortmain, multiplepoinding, nolle prosequi, nolo contendere, non-access, nonage, non-compearance, non-entry, nonsuit, non-user, notour, novalia, noverint, novodamus, noxal, obligant, obligation, obligor, obreption, onus probandi, ouster, outfangthief, overt act, owelty, oyer, pactum nudum, Pandect, panel, pernancy, personalty, pickery, plaint, plaintiff, porteous roll, portioner, practic, prima facie, privy, prorogate, pupil, quadruply, realty, recaption, recusation, reddendo, relator, relaxation, remise, replevin, replevy, repone, reprobator, res gestae, retour, retroact, retroactive, reverser, right of drip, rout, scutage, stillicide, supersedeas, supplicavit, surrebut, surrebuttal, surrebutter, surrejoin, surrejoinder, terminer, tolt, tort, tortfeasor, tortious, udal, udaller, ultimus haeres, unlaw, uses, usucapient, usucapion (usucaption), usucapt, usucaptible, usufruct, usufructuary, ultimogeniture, vacatur, venire (facias), venter, venue, vert, vest, vested, visne, voidable, voir dire, volunteer, wage, waive, waste, watch, watching brief, water- privilege, wit.

minerals adularia, aegirine, aegirite, alabandine, almandine, alum-shale, alum-slate, alum-stone, alunite, amazonite, amazon-stone, amianthus, amphibole, analcime, anatase, andesine, argil, arkose, asbestos, asparagus-stone, asphalt(um), aventurine, baetyl, balas, Barbados earth, barilla, baryta, barytes, basalt, Bath stone, bath-brick, bezoar, bitter-earth, bitter-spar, bitumen, blackjack, blacklead, blaes, blende, bloodstone, blue ground, blue John, blue vitriol, bluestone, Bologna phosphorous, borane, borax, borazon, boride, bornite, boulder-clay, breccia, Bristol-brick, Bristol-diamond, brown spar, brownstone, buhrstone, cacholong, caen-stone, cairngorm, calamine, calc-sinter, calcspar, calc-tuff, caliche, calp, Carborundum®;, cat's-eye, cat-silver, cauk, celestine, cement-stone, ceruse, chalcedony, chalcedonyx, chalk, chert, Chile saltpeter, china clay, china stone, chrome-alum, chrome- spinel, chrysoberyl, chrysocolla, chrysoprase, chrysotile, cinnabar, cinnamon-stone, cipollino, corundum, cryolite, cymophane, dacite, dendrite, Derbyshire spar, diabase, diallage, dialogite, diaspore, diatomite, dice-coal, diopside, dioptase, diorite, dogger, dogtooth-spar, dolerite, dolomite, dopplerite, dropstone, dunite, dyscrasite, dysodyle, eagle-stone, earthflax, earthwax, eclogite, electric calamine, elvan, emery, encrinite, enhydrite, enhydros, epidiorite, epidosite, epidote, epistilbite, epsomite, erinite, erubescite, erythrite, euclase, eucrite, eudialyte, eutaxite, euxenite, fahlerz, fahlore, fakes, fayalite, fel(d)spar, felsite, felstone, flint, fluorite, fluorspar, franklinite, French chalk, fuchsite, fulgurite, fuller's earth, gabbro, gadolinite, gahnite, galena, galenite, gangue, gan(n)ister, garnet-rock, gibbsite, glance, glauberite, glauconite, glimmer, gmelinite, gneiss, goldstone, goslarite, gossan, göthite, granite, granitite, granodiorite, granophyre, granulite, graphic granite, graphite, green earth, greenockite, greensand, greenstone, greisen, greywacke, gummite, gypsum, hälleflinta, halloysite, harmotome, hatchettite, haüyne, heavy spar, hedyphane, hematite, hemimorphite, hepatite, hercynite, (h)essonite, heulandite, hiddenite, honey-stone, hornblende, hornfels, hornstone, horseflesh ore, humite, hyacinth, hyalophane, hypersthene, ice-spar, ice-stone, idocrase, ironstone, jacinth, keratophyre, kermes, kermesite, kieselguhr, kunkur, kupferschiefer, lamprophyre, lapis lazuli, lepidomelane, limestone, lithomarge, marlstone, meerschaum, mellite, mica, microlite, microlith, mispickel, morion, moss-agate, mundic, nail-head-spar, needle-tin, nepheline, nickel-bloom, nickel- ocher, Norway saltpeter, nosean, noselite, obsidian, omphacite, onyx, onyx-marble, orthoclase, orthophyre, ottrelite, ozokerite, peacock-ore, pencil-ore, pencil-stone, peperino, periclase, pericline, petuntse, pipeclay, pipestone, plagioclose, pleonaste, porphyry, potstone, prase, protogine, pyrites, quartz, realgar, rock-oil, rubicelle, ruby-spinel, rutile, saltpeter, sandstone, sanidine, sapphire, sapphire-quartz, sapphirine, sard, sardonyx, satin-spar, satinstone, scaglia, schalstein, schiller-spar, schist, schorl, serpentine, serpentine(-rock), shale, shell- limestone, shell-marl, silica, silver-glance, sinter, slate, soapstone, spar, speiss-cobalt, spelter, sphene, spiegeleisen, spinel, spinel-ruby, spodumene, stinkstone, sunstone, surturbrand, swinestone, sylvine, tabular spar, tachylite, talc, talc-schist, terne, terpene, terpineol, terra alba, terracotta, terra-japonica, terramara, terrarossa, terra-sigillata, terts, thulia, tiger(s)-eye, till, tin-stone, toad-stone, tombac, touchstone, tourmaline, trass, travertin(e), tripoli, troutstone, tufa, tuff, Turkey hone, Turkey stone, turquoise, tutty, uinta(h)ite, umber, Uralian emerald, uralite, uraninite, uranite, uvarovite, vanadinite, variolite, variscite, veinstone, veinstuff, Venice talc, verd-antique, vesuvianite, vitrain, vivianite, vulpinite, wacke, wad(d), wallsend, wavellite, Wernerite, whet-slate, whewellite, whinstone, white pyrites, willemite, witherite, wolfram, wollastonite, wood-coal, wulfenite, wurtzite, zaratite, zarnich, zeolite, zeuxite, zinkenite, zircon, zoisite, zorgite.

musical instruments aeolian harp, aerophone, alpenhorn, alphorn, althorn, alto, Amati, American organ, apollonicon, archlute, arpeggione, atabal, autoharp, balalaika, bandore, banjulele, baryton(e), bass clarinet, bass drum, bass fiddle, bass horn, bass tuba, bass viol, basset horn, bazooka, bombard, bombardon, bongo (drum), bouzouki, buccina, bugle, buglet, bull fiddle, calliope, castanets, celeste, cello, cembalo, chair- organ, chalumeau, chamber organ, chikara, Chinese pavilion, chitarrone, chordophone, cinema-organ, cithara, cither(n), citole, cittern, clarichord, clarinet, clarion, clarsach, clave, clavichord, crwth, cymbal, cymbalo, decachord, dichord, didgeridoo, digitorium, double bass, drum, dulcimer, Dulcitone®;, dumb-piano, echo, electric guitar, electric organ, euphonium, fagotto, fife, fipple-flute, flageolet, flügel, flügelhorn, flute, flûte-à-bec, flutina, French horn, gamelan, German flute, gimbard, gittern, glass harmonica, glockenspiel, grand piano, gu, guitar, gusla, Hammerklavier, hand-horn, hand- organ, harmonica, harmonicon, harmoniphone, harmonium, harp, harpsichord, hautboy, heckelphone, heptachord, horn, hornpipe, humstrum, hunting-horn, hurdy-gurdy, idiophone, jingling Johnny, kazoo, kent-bugle, keyboard(s), keybugle, klavier, koto, krummhorn, Kuh-horn, langsp(i)el, lituus, lur(e), lyraviol, lyre, mandola, mandolin(e), mandora, maraca, marimba, marine trumpet, melodeon, metallophone, mirliton, monochord, Moog synthesizer, mouth-harp, mouth-organ, musette, musical glasses, naker, nose- flute, nun's-fiddle, oboe, oboe d'amore, oboe di caccia, ocarina, octachord, octave-flute, ophicleide, organ-harmonium, orpharion, orpheorion, pandora, panharmonicon, Pan-pipes, Pan's pipes, pantaleon, pianette, pianino, piano, piano- accordion, pianoforte, Pianola®;, piano-organ, piffero, pipe, pipeless organ, pipe-organ, player piano, polyphon(e), posaune, psaltery, pyrophone, quint(e), racket(t), rebec(k), regal, rote, sackbut, salpinx, sambuca, sancho, sang, santir, sarangi, sarrusophone, sausage-bassoon, saxhorn, saxophone, seraphine, serinette, serpent, s(h)amisen, shawm, side-drum, sitar, small- pipes, sourdeline, sousaphone, spinet(te), squeeze-box, squiffer, steel drum, sticcado, stock-and-horn, strad, Stradivari(us), string bass, sultana, symphonion, symphony, synthesizer, syrinx, tabla, tabor, tabo(u)rin, tabret, tambour, tamboura, tambourine, tam-tam, testudo, tetrachord, theater organ, theorbo, timbal, timbrel, timpano, tin whistle, traps, triangle, trichord, tromba marina, trombone, trump, trumpet, trumpet marine, tuba, tubular bells, tympan, uillean pipes, ukulele, vibraharp, vibraphone, vielle, vihuela, vina, viol, viola, viola da braccio, (viola da) gamba, viola da gamba, viola da spalla, viola d'amore, violin, violoncello, violone, virginal(s), vocalion, waldflute, waldhorn, Welsh harp, xylophone, zambomba, zampogna, zanze, zel, zinke, zither, zufolo.

parliaments Althing (Iceland), Congress (USA), Cortes (Spain, Portugal), Dáil (Ireland), d(o)uma (Russia), ecclesia (Athens), Folketing (Denmark), House of Commons (UK), House of Keys (Isle of Man), House of Lords (UK), Knesset (Israel), Lagt(h)ing (Norway), Lagting (Norway), Landst(h)ing (Denmark), Landtag (Germany), Lok Sabha (India), Majlis (Iran), Odelst(h)ing (Norway), Oireachtas (Ireland), Parliament (UK), Pnyx (Athens), Porte (Turkey), Rajya Sabha (India), Reichsrat(h) (Austria), Reichstag (Germany), Rigsdag (Denmark), Riksdag (Sweden), Seanad (Ireland), Senate (Rome, USA, etc.), Skupshtina (Yugoslavia), Sobranje (Bulgaria), Stort(h)ing (Norway), Tynwald (Isle of Man), witenagemot (England).

prosody Alcaic, alexandrine, amphibrach, amphibrachic, amphimacer, Anacreontic, anacrusis, anacrustic, anapaest, anapaestic, antibacchius, antispast, antispastic, antistrophe, Archilochian, arsis, Asclepiad, asynartete, atonic, bacchius, catalectic, choliamb, choree, choriamb, cinquain, cretic, dactyl, decastich, decasyllabic, decasyllable, dipody, dispondaic, dispondee, distich, disyllable, ditrochean, ditrochee, dizain, dochmiac, dochmius, dodecasyllabic, dodecasyllable, dolichurus, duan, ectasis, ecthlipsis, elide, elision, enjamb(e)ment, envoy, epic, epirrhema, epistrophe, epitrite, epode, epopee, epopoeia, epos, epyllion, extrametrical, eye-rhyme, false quantity, feminine caesura, feminine ending, feminine rhyme, fifteener, free verse, galliambic, g(h)azal, glyconic, gradus, haiku, head- rhyme, hendecasyllabic, hendecasyllable, hephthemimer, heptameter, heptapody, heptasyllabic, heterostrophic, heterostrophy, hexameter, hexametric(al), hexapody, hexastich, Hudibrastic, huitain, hypercatalectic, hypercatalexis, hypermetrical, iamb, iambus, ictus, Ionic, irrational, kyrielle, laisse, Leonine, limerick, limma, linked verse, logaoedic, long- measure, macaronic(s), masculine ending, masculine rhyme, meliboean, miurus, monometer, monorhyme, monostich, monostrophic, mora, outride, oxytone, pantoum, pentameter, pentastich, penthemimer, Pherecratean, Pherecratic, Pindaric, poulters' measure, proceleusmatic, pyrrhic, Pythian, quatorzain, quatrain, reported verses, rhopalic, rhyme-royal, rich rhyme, riding-rhyme, rime riche, rime suffisante, rondeau, rondel, rove-over, rubaiyat, run-on, Sapphics, scazon, semeion, senarius, septenarius, sestina, spondee, strophe, synaphe(i)a, tetrameter, tetrapody, tetrasemic, tetrastich, thesis, tirade, tribrach, trimeter, tripody, triseme, trochee, villanelle, virelay.

ranks in armed forces able seaman, acting sub-lieutenant, admiral, admiral of the fleet, air chief marshal, air commandant, air commodore, air vice marshal, aircraftsman, air-marshal, brigadier, captain, chief officer, chief petty officer, chief technician, colonel, commandant, commander, commodore, corporal, field marshal, first officer, fleet chief petty officer, flight lieutenant, flight officer, flight sergeant, flying officer, general, group captain, group officer, junior seaman, junior technician, lance-corporal, lance-jack, lancesergeant, leading aircraftsman, leading seaman, lieutenant, lieutenant-colonel, lieutenant-commander, lieutenant-general, major, major-general, marshal, marshal of the Royal Air Force, master-at-arms, midshipman, ordinary seaman, petty officer, pilot officer, post- captain, private, purser, quartermaster, quartermaster-general, quartermaster-sergeant, quartermistress, rear-admiral, risaldar, ritt-master, second lieutenant, second officer, senior aircraftsman, sergeant, sergeant-major, squadron leader, squadron officer, staff sergeant, sub-lieutenant, superintendent, third officer, vice admiral, warrant officer, wing commander, wing officer.

rhetoric abscission, alliteration, amoebaean, anacoluthia, anacoluthon, anadiplosis, anaphora, anaphoric, anastrophe, antimetabole, antimetathesis, antiphrasis, antiphrastic(al), antithesis, antithetic(al), antonomasia, aporia, asteism, asyndeton, auxesis, catachresis, chiasmus, climax, diallage, diegesis, dissimile, double entendre, dramatic irony, dysphemism, ecbole, echoic, ecphonesis, ellipsis, enallage, enantiosis, enumeration, epanadiplosis, epanalepsis, epanaphora, epanodos, epanorthosis, epexegesis, epiphonema, epizeuxis, erotema, erotetic, figure, flower, head-rhyme, hendiadys, holophrase, hypallage, hyperbaton, hyperbole, hypobole, hypostrophe, hypotyposis, hysteron-proteron, increment, irony, litotes, meiosis, metalepsis, metaphor, metonym, metonymy, mixed metaphor, onomatopoeia, oxymoron, parabole, paral(e)ipsis, parenthesis, prolepsis, simile, syllepsis, symploce, synchoresis, synchysis, synedoche, synoeciosis, trope, vicious circle, zeugma.

titles of rulers abuna, adelantado, ag(h)a, alderman, amir, amman, amtman, ard-ri(gh), atabeg, atabek, ataman, atheling, ayatollah, Ban, beglerbeg, begum, bey, boyar, burgrave, caboceer, cacique, caliph, caudillo, Cid, Dan, Dauphin, Dauphine, Dauphiness, dey, diadochus, doge, duce, duke, ealdorman, elector, emir, emperor, empress, ethnarch, exarch, gospodar, Graf, Gräfin, grave, Great Mogul, harmost, heptarch, hospodar, huzoor, imperator, Inca, infanta, infante, jarl, kaid, kaiser, kalif, khan, khedive, king, kinglet, kingling, landgrave, landgravine, maharaja(h), maharani, mandarin, marchesa, marchese, marchioness, margrave, margravine, marquess, marquis, marquise, mikado, Mirza, Monseigneur, monsieur, Monsignor, Monsignore, mormaor, mpret, nabob, naik, nawab, nizam, nomarch, omrah, padishah, palatine, palsgrave, pasha, pendragon, pentarch, pharaoh, prince, prince- bishop, prince-imperial, princess, raja(h), rajpramukh, rana, rani, Rhinegrave, Rhinegravine, sachem, sagamore, satrap, shah, sheik(h), sherif, shogun, sirdar, sovereign, stad(t)holder, starosta, suba(h)dar, sultan, suzerain, taoiseach, theocrat, toiseach, toparch, tsar, tuchun, voivode, waldgrave.

tools about-sledge, aiguille, auger, auger-bit, awl, boaster, bodkin, bolster, bradawl, broach, bucksaw, burin, burr, buzz-saw, card, caschrom, caulking-iron, celt, center-bit, chaser, chisel, chopper, clamp, cleaver, cold-chisel, cradle- scythe, crosscut-saw, crown-saw, diamond-drill, dibble, dividers, dolly, drawing-knife, draw-knife, drill, drove, els(h)in, extirpator, fillister, float, forceps, forfex, fork, fraise, frame-saw, fretsaw, gad, gang-saw, gavelock, gimlet, gouge, grapnel, grapple, graver, gurlet, hacksaw, hammer, handsaw, hawk, hay fork, hay knife, helve-hammer, hod, hoe, holing-axe, jackhammer, jack-plane, jointer, laster, level, leveling rod, leveling staff, loy, mace, madge, maker, mall, mallet, mattock, maul, monkey, moon-knife, mortar, muller, oliver, oustiti, pachymeter, pad-saw, palstave, panel saw, panga, paper-cutter, paper-knife, pattle, pecker, peel, pestle, pick, pickaxe, pincers, pinch, pinking-shears, piolet, pitchfork, plane, planer, plessor, plexor, pliers, plow, plugger, plumb, plumb-line, plumb- rule, plummet, pocket-knife, pointel, pricker, priest, priming- iron, priming-wire, probang, probe, probing-scissors, prod, prog, pruning-bill, pruning-hook, pruning-knife, pruning-shears, prunt, punch, puncheon, punty, quadrant, quannet, rabble, rake, raspatory, reed-knife, repositor, retractor, ricker, rickstick, riddle, riffle, ripper, ripping-saw, ripple, rip-saw, risp, router, rule, ruler, sash-tool, saw, sax, scalpel, scauper, scissors, scoop, scooper, scorper, scraper, screwdriver, screwjack, screw-wrench, scribe(r), scutch(er), scythe, seam-set, serving-mallet, shave, shears, shovel, sickle, slane, slate-axe, slater, slicker, smoother, snap, snarling-iron, snarling-rod, snips, soldering-bolt, soldering-iron, spade, spanner, spider, spokeshave, spud, squeegee, stadda, stake, stapler, stapling- machine, steel, stithy, stone-hammer, stretching-iron, strickle, strigil, stubble-rake, style, stylet, swage, swingle(-hand), switch, tedder, tenon-saw, threshel, thresher, thrust-hoe, tint- tool, tongs, trepan, trowel, T-square, turfing-iron, turf-spade, turning-saw, tweezers, twist drill, upright, van, vice, vulsella, waster, whip-saw, widener, wimble, wood-shears, wortle, xyster, Y-level.

units of measurement acre, ampere, angstrom, anker, ardeb, are, arpent, arroba, arshin, as, bar, barleycorn, barn, barrel, bath, baud, becquerel, bel, bigha, bit, board-foot, boll, bolt, braccio, bushel, butt, cab, cable, calorie, candela, candle, candy, carat, catty, cell, cental, centner, chain, chalder, chaldron, chenix, chopin, chronon, clove, co(o)mb, cor, cord, coss, coulumb, cran, crith, cubit, cumec, curie, cusec, cyathus, daraf, Debye (unit), degree, demy, dessiatine, digit, dirham, dra(ch)m, dyne, ell, em, en, epha(h), erg, farad, faraday, fathom, fermium, firkin, firlot, foot, fother, fou, furlong, gal, gallon, gerah, gilbert, gill, grain, gram, hectare, henry, hertz, hin, hogshead, homer, hoppus foot, hundredweight, inch, joule, kaneh, kantar, kelvin, k(h)at, kilderkin, kin, knot, league, leaguer, li, liang, liard, ligne, link, lippy, lire lisp(o)und, liter, log, lux, maneh, maund, meter, mho, micrometer, micron, mile, mil(l), mina, minim, minute, mna, modius, mole, morgen, muid, mutchkin, nail, neper, nepit, newton, nit (information), nit (luminance), noggin, obol, oersted, ohm, oke, omer, ounce, oxgang, parasang, pascal, peck, perch, picul, pin, pint, pipe, poise, pole, pood, pound, poundal, quart, quarter, quartern, quintal, quire, radian, ream, rem, rod, rood, rote, rotolo, run(d)let, rutherford, sabin, s(a)eculum, sazhen, scruple, second, seer, semuncia, shekel, shippound, siemens, sievert, sone, span, square, stadium, steradian, stere, stilb, stoke(s), stone, tael, talent, tare, tesla, therm, tical, tierce, tod, toise, tola, ton, tonne, tonneau, tor, truss, tun, vara, verst, virgate, volt, watt, weber, wey, yard, yardland, yojan.

vehicles aerotrain, air-car, amtrack, araba, arba, aroba, automobile, barouche, Bath chair, berlin(e), bicycle, biga, bobsled, bobsleigh, bogie, boneshaker, brake, britzka, brougham, bubble-car, buckboard, buckcart, buck-wagon, buggy, bus, cab, caboose, cabriolet, caisson, calash, camper, caravan, caravanette, caroche, car(r)iole, carry-all, catafalque, chair, chaise, chaise-cart, chapel cart, charabanc, chariot, clarence, coach, convertible, conveyance, cycle, dandy-cart, dandy-horse, dennet, désobligeante, dhooly, diesel, diligence, dilly, Dodgem(s)®;, dog-cart, dogcart, dolly, doolie, dormitory-car, drag, dray, dros(h)ky, duck, ekka, fiacre, fly, fork-lift truck, four-in-hand, gharri, gig, glass-coach, go-kart, Green Goddess, gyrocar, gyrodyne, hack, hackery, hackney-carriage/coach, hatchback, herdic, honey-cart, honey-wagon, hurley-hacket, ice- yacht, inside-car, jeep, jingle, jinricksha(w), jitney, juggernaut, kago, kajawah, kart, kibitka, landau, landaulet(te), limousine, litter, lorry, mail-cart, minibus, monorail, motor caravan, motor-bicycle, motor-bike, motor-bus, motor-car, motor- coach, motor-cycle, motor-lorry, motor-scooter, norimon, omnibus, outside-car, palanquin (palankeen), palki, pantechnicon, pedal cycle, pedicab, people mover, phaeton, pick-up, pill-box, pincers, post-chaise, prairie schooner, pulka, quadriga, rail-bus, rail-car, rail-motor, ricksha(w), roadster, rockaway, runabout, safety bicycle, saloon-car, saloon-carriage, scooter, sedan, sedan-chair, shandry(dan), shooting-brake, sidecar, single-decker, skateboard, ski-bob, sled, sledge, sleeper, sleeping-car, sleeping-carriage, sleeping-coach, sleigh, slip- carriage, slip-coach, slipe, snowmobile, snowplow, sociable, solo, speedster, spider, spring-carriage, spring-cart, squad car, stage-coach, stage-wagon, stanhope, station-wagon, steam-car, steam-carriage, steamer, steam-roller, stillage, stone boat, straddle carrier, street-car, sulky, surrey, tally-ho, tandem, tank, tank-car, tank-engine, tanker, tank-wagon, tarantas(s), tartana, tax(ed)-cart, taxi, taxicab, T-cart, telega, telpher, tender, thoroughbrace, through-train, tilbury, tim-whisk(e)y, tin Lizzie, tip, tip-cart, tipper, toboggan, tonga, tourer, touring- car, tractor, trailer, train, tram, tramway-car, transporter, transport-rider, trap, tricar, tricycle, trike, triplet, trishaw, troika, trolley, trolley-bus, trolley-car, troop-carrier, truck, tube, tumble-car(t), tumbrel, turbocar, two-decker, twoseater, two-wheeler, velocipede, vettura, victoria, village cart, vis-à- vis, volante, wagon, wagonette, wagon-lit, wain, water-cart, water-wagon, weasel, wheelbarrow, wheel-chair, whisk(e)y, Whitechapel cart.

vessels, ships argosy, barca, barque, barquentine, bateau, bawley, Berthon-boat, bilander, billyboy, bireme, birlinn, boat, bomb-ketch, bomb-vessel, brig, brigantine, Bucentaur, budgerow, bum-boat, buss, butty, cabin cruiser, caique, canal-boat, canoe, caravel, Carley float, carrack, casco, cat, catamaran, catboat, clipper, coaster, cob(b)le, cockboat, cockleshell, cog, collier, commodore, coracle, corocore, corvette, cot, crare, crayer, currach, cutter, dandy, deep-sinker, destroyer, d(h)ow, dinghy, diving-bell, dogger, drake, dreadnought, dredger, drog(h)er, dromond, dugout, East-Indiaman, E-boat, faltboat, felucca, flatboat, floating battery, flyboat, flying bridge, fore-and- after, frigate, frigatoon, funny, gabbart, galleass, galleon, galley, gal(l)iot, gallivat, gay-you, geordie, gondola, grab, hatch-boat, herringer, hooker, hovercraft, hoy, hydrofoil, hydroplane, hydrovane, ice-boat, Indiaman, iron-clad, jigger, jollyboat, junk, kayak, ketch, koff, laker, landing-craft, lapstreak, launch, liberty-ship, lighter, line-of-battle-ship, liner, long-boat, longship, lorcha, lugger, lymphad, mackinaw, masoolah, merchantman, mistico, monitor, monkey-boat, monohull, monoxylon, montaria, motor-boat, motor-launch, motor-ship, motoscafo, mud-boat, mudscow, multihull, nacelle, nuggar, outrigger, packet, packet-boat, packet-ship, pair-oar, patamar, pedalo, penteconter, periagua, peter-boat, pink, pinkie, pinky, pinnace, piragua, pirogue, pleasure-boat, pocket battleship, polacca, polacre, pontoon, powerboat, praam, pra(h)u, pram, privateer, puffer, pulwar, punt, puteli, quadrireme, quinquereme, randan, razee, river-boat, river-craft, row-barge, row-boat, rowing-boat, saic, sail-boat, sailing-boat, sailing-ship, salmon- coble, sampan, schooner, schuit, scooter, scow, scull, sculler, sea-boat, seaplane-carrier, settee, shallop, ship, ship-of-the- line, shore-boat, show-boat, skiff, sloop, sloop-of-war, smack, smuggler, snow, speed-boat, speedster, square rigger, steamboat, steamer, steam-launch, steam-packet, steamship, steam-tug, steam- vessel, steam-yacht, stern-wheeler, stew-can, sub, submarine, super-Dreadnought, supertanker, surface-craft, surf-board, surf- boat, surf-canoe, surfing-board, swamp boat, tanker, tartane(e), tender, tern, three-decker, three-master, tilt-boat, torpedo- boat, torpedo-boat destroyer, track-boat, tracker, trader, train ferry, tramp, transport-ship, trawler, trek-schuit, triaconter, trimaran, trireme, troop-carrier, trooper, troop-ship, tub, tug, tug-boat, turbine-steamer, turret-ship, two-decker, two-master, U-boat, umiak, vaporetto, vedette(-boat), vessel, wager-boat, warship, water-bus, well-boat, well-smack, whaleboat, whaler, wherry, whiff, windjammer, xebec, yacht, yawl, zabra.

weapons, armor A-bomb, ack-ack, aerodart, ailette, air rifle, amusette, an(e)lace, arbalest, arblast, Archibald, Archie, arcubalist, armet, arquebus(e), baldric(k), ballista, ballistic missile, bandolier, Bangalore torpedo, basilisk, baton gun, bazooka, beaver, bill, Biscayan, blackjack, blowgun, blowpipe, bludgeon, blunderbuss, boarding-pike, bodkin, Bofors gun, bolas, bomb, bombard, boomerang, bowie knife, brassard, breastplate, breech-loader, Bren(gun), bricole, brigandine, broadsword, brown Bess, brown bill, buckler, buckshot, bulldog, bullet, bundook, burganet, byrnie, caltrop, cannon, carbine, carronade, casque, cataphract, catapult, chain-armor, chain-mail, chamfrain, Chassepot, chausses, cheval-de-frise, chokebore, claymore, cluster-bomb, coal-box, co(e)horn, Colt, Congreve, corium, dag, dagger, dah, Damascus blade, Damascus sword, demi-cannon, demi- culverin, demi-lance, depth-bomb, depth-charge, dirk, dragoon, elephant gun, épée, escopette, Exocet®;, express rifle, falchion, falconet, field gun, fire-arm, fire-arrow, firebomb, firelock, firepot, fission bomb, flail, flame-thrower, flick- knife, flintlock, foil, fougade, fougasse, four-pounder, fusee, fusil, Garand rifle, gatling-gun, gavelock, genouillère, gisarme, gladius, gorget, grapeshot, greave, Greek fire, grenade, gun, habergeon, hackbut, hacqueton, hailshot, halberd, half-pike, hand-grenade, hand-gun, han(d)jar, handstaff, harquebus, hauberk, H-bomb, heaume, helm, helmet, hielaman, howitzer, jack, jamb(e), jazerant, jesserant, Jethart staff, kris, lamboys, lame, lance, Lochaber-axe, Long Tom, machete, machine-gun, mangonel, martel, Martini(-Henry), matchlock, Mauser, Maxim(-gun), mesail, Mills bomb, Mills grenade, mine, mine-thrower, mini-rocket launcher, minnie, mitrailleur, mitrailleuse, morgenstern, morglay, morning- star, mor(r)ion, mortar, musket, musketoon, nulla-nulla, oerlikon, panga, partisan, pauldron, pavis(e), peasecod-cuirass, pederero, pelican, pelta, perrier, petrary, petronel, pickelhaube, pike, pilum, pistol, pistolet, placket, plastron, plate-armor, pocket-pistol, poitrel, pole-ax(e), poleyn, pompom, poniard, potgun, quarter-staff, queen's-arm, rapier, rerebrace, rest, revolver, rifle, rifle-grenade, sabaton, saber, saker, sallet, saloon-pistol, saloon-rifle, sap, sarbacane, schiavone, schläger, scimitar, scorpion, scutum, serpentine, sharp, shell, shield, shillela(g)h, shortsword, shotgun, shrapnel, siege-artillery, siege-gun, siege-piece, singlestick, six-gun, six-shooter, skean(dhu), sling, slung-shot, small-arm, small-sword, smoke-ball, smoke-bomb, snickersnee, spadroon, sparth(e), spear, spear gun, splint-armor, spontoon, spring-gun, squid, steel, sten gun, Sterling, stern-chaser, stiletto, stone axe, stone-bow, stylet, submachine-gun, sumpit(an), switch-blade (knife), swivel-gun, sword, sword bayonet, sword-cane, sword-stick, tace, targe, target, taslet, tasse, tasset, testudo, three-pounder, threshel, throw-stick, time-bomb, toc emma, toggle-iron, tomahawk, tomboc, tommy-gun, tormentum, torpedo, tortoise, trecento, trench-mortar, trident, truncheon, tuille, tuillette, tulwar, turret-gun, twibill, vambrace, vamplate, V- bomb, visor, vou(l)ge, war-wolf, waster, water-cannon, water- pistol, Welsh hook, white-arm, Winchester (rifle), wind-gun, wo(o)mera(ng), yatag(h)an, zumbooruk.

wine-bottle sizes baby, balthasar, jeroboam, magnum, Methuselah, nebuchadnezzar, nip, rehoboam, Salmanazar.

zodiac signs Aquarius, Aries, Cancer, Capricorn, Gemini, Leo, Libra, Pisces, Sagittarius, Scorpio, Taurus, Virgo.